America
and
Its People

Brief Contents

$\mathcal{D}$etailed Contents

3   Provincial America in Upheaval, 1660–1760   72

4   Breaking the Bonds of Empire, 1760–1775   110

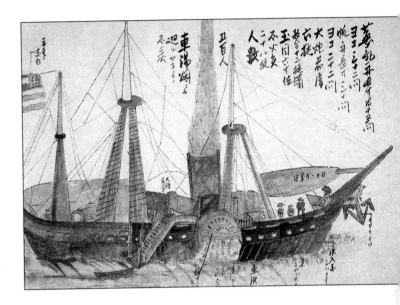

25   The Age of Roosevelt   824

26   The End of Isolation: America Faces the World, 1920–1945   860

Maps

Tables and Figures

Preface

The survey textbook in U.S. history is an essential learning instrument. It must do much more than present a chronological rendering of names, dates, and facts. It must gain the attention of students and engage them, and it must challenge students intellectually. It must not deal in caricature but show real people confronting real problems, complete with their triumphs and failures. It must offer historical perspectives on the lives of diverse groups of peoples as well as on the tumultuous affairs of nations. It must increase the tolerance of students for differing interpretations of formative historical change. As such, it must encourage thinking in historical perspective while seeking to enhance such fundamental skills as the recognition of key issues and the solving of difficult problems. The U.S. survey history text, in sum, must function as a work of synthesis that will assist course instructors in making history interesting and meaningful for students.

This is not an easy set of assignments for any textbook. In our increasingly technocratic culture, students have been repeatedly advised to concentrate their academic energies in courses that will ensure them steady incomes as workers in society. An exciting, intelligently conceived history textbook, we are convinced, can help course instructors challenge this mentality by demonstrating that history functions as a central laboratory for learning about life and for acquiring knowledge and skills essential for successful living.

As instructors actively involved in teaching U.S. survey history, we began the development of *America and Its People* with these thoughts in mind. The most compelling works of history, we concluded, focus on people, both the great and the ordinary. They establish the importance of time, place, and circumstance in comprehending the varieties of human endeavor. They do not smooth over but highlight the dramatic conflict among individuals and groups that has so often produced meaningful historical change. They frame their themes rigorously, and they tell their story with a strong narrative pulse. The most effective works of history, we believe, encourage readers to comprehend their own times and themselves more clearly in the light of what has come before them. In this sense, studying the past provides broadened perspective, if not greater tolerance and understanding about the human condition, not only about the past but also for the formulation of present and future realities.

In writing *America and Its People* we have followed these guidelines. We have sought to impart to today's generation of college students our enthusiasm for the value of historical inquiry and our sense of which fundamentals a well-educated person needs to know about the American experience. In our opinion, the story of the United States—of colonization, Indian removal, the Revolution, slavery, social reform, the Civil War, global expansion, the Great Depression and New Deal, and the more recent civil rights and women's liberation movements—is best told by focusing on the dilemmas and struggles faced by passing generations of Americans. Thus our "people-centered" approach encourages students to grasp and evaluate the difficult choices human beings have made in molding the texture of life in the modern United States.

Besides structuring the book's contents to encourage student involvement, we have worked to keep the needs of history faculty members very much in mind. The text's structure conforms to the course outlines used by most history instructors. *America and Its People* also places a premium on chronological flow, an essential organizational element for college students grappling with the complexities of U.S. history. It also provides a clear narrative rendering of essential political, diplomatic, cultural, social, intellectual, and military history and concisely identifies major historical concepts and themes.

Finally, we have taken great care to present a text offering both breadth and balance. We have found that the often-expressed dichotomies between political and diplomatic history and social and cultural history disappear when history is people-centered from its inception. Materials on ethnicity, gender, and race belong at the core of the historical narrative, not as adjunct information, and we have attempted to include the important findings and insights of both traditional and newer historical subjects. It is our hope that we have achieved a sensitive and compelling presentation.

FEATURES

The book's structure is organized to heighten and sustain student interest. To borrow a phrase associated with computers, we have aimed at the production of a "user-friendly" text. Each chapter begins with an **outline of contents** and a carefully selected **anecdote** or **incident** that frames the chapter's themes while drawing students into the material. A chronological and topical narrative follows, building toward a **chapter conclusion** highlighting and reinforcing essential points. In addition, each chapter contains a **chronology of key events**; a **bibliography of suggested readings**; and a **special feature essay** designed to offer students an in-depth look at a significant topic in one of the following people-oriented categories that illustrate change over time: Aspects of Family Life, Sports and Leisure, The American Mosaic, Medicine, The Human Toll of Combat, and Perspectives on Lawbreaking. For this new edition we have developed two important new special feature categories: **America and the World** and **Primary Source Essays**.

Other features of the text include an extensive **full-color map**, **photo**, and **figure art program** including four full-page battlefield picture maps with accompanying essays; a **multidimensional timeline** at the front of the book that is replete with high interest items; and valuable tables, charts, graphs, and maps in the **Appendix**.

NEW TO THIS EDITION

As authors we are grateful for the extremely positive reception accorded the first edition of *America and*

Its People. As with all books, however, there is always room for improvement, and we have worked very hard to make our text even more balanced in this new edition. One objective was to clarify numerous small points along the way. A second was to update our interpretations according to the latest findings in particular subfields. A third was to enhance coverage of political, diplomatic, and intellectual history. Users will find that we have taken Chapter 7, formerly entitled "Shaping the New Nation, 1789–1815," and expanded it into two chapters: Chapter 7, "Shaping the New Nation, 1789–1800," and Chapter 8, "The Jeffersonians in Power, 1800–1815." This expansion has allowed us to deepen and enrich our narrative of key political and diplomatic events in the young American republic from Washington's presidential administration through the War of 1812.

We have also included new materials on key intellectual trends, such as the flowering of a distinct American literature in antebellum America (Chapter 11), and major developments in science and technology (Chapter 9). With respect to diplomatic and intellectual history, we direct attention to the two new categories of special feature essays, which provide supplementary coverage of pivotal subjects ranging from America's first encounters with Japan to Benjamin Franklin's impressions of George Whitefield as presented in Franklin's *Autobiography*.

Still another objective in this revision was to enhance the chronological flow of our presentation. A number of reviewers suggested that we move the chapter focusing on urbanization and city culture to follow directly the chapter on immigration. Thus the sequence of chapters covering the late nineteenth century is as follows: Chapter 18, "Immigrants and Workers in Industrial America"; Chapter 19, "The Rise of an Urban Society and City People"; Chapter 20, "Imperial America, 1870–1900"; and Chapter 21, "End of the Century Crisis." In addition, in Volume II, we have increased the coverage of Native Americans (Chapter 18), added new material in the Vietnam War (Chapter 29), and refocused the last chapter (Chapter 31) to deal with the economic conditions of the late 1980s and early 1990s and to cover in detail the changes in the United States and the world. The collapse of the Soviet Union and the dramatic conclusion of the Cold War both receive extended discussion.

Finally, we have written new opening vignettes for several of the chapters in order to focus more directly on the chapter's themes. Chapter 7, for example, now begins with a discussion of the United States' first census in 1790; the opening vignette in Chapter 18 deals with Chinese immigrants and the building of the transcontinental railroad; and Chapter 30 opens with a discussion of consumer advocate Ralph Nader. Chapters 4, 8, 11, and 31 also feature new opening vignettes.

ACKNOWLEDGMENTS

Any textbook project is very much a team effort. We would like to thank the many individuals who have worked with us on this project, beginning with the talented historians who have served as reviewers and whose valuable critiques greatly strengthened the final product: Joe S. Anderson, Azusa Pacific University; Larry Balsamo, Western Illinois University; Lois W. Banner, University of Southern California; Robert A. Becker, Louisiana State University; Delmar L. Beene, Glendale Community College; Nancy Bowen, Del Mar College; Blanche Brick, Blinn College; Larry Burke, Dodge City Community Junior College; Frank L. Byrne, Kent State University; Colin G. Calloway, University of Wyoming; Albert Camarillo, Stanford University; Clayborne Carson, Stanford University; Jay Caughtry, University of Nevada at Las Vegas; Raymond W. Champagne, Jr., University of Scranton; John P. Crevelli, Santa Rosa Junior College; Shannon J. Doyle, University of Houston; David Glassberg, University of Massachusetts; James P. Gormly, Washington and Jefferson College; Elliott Gorn, Miami University; Neil Hamilton, Brevard Community College; Nancy Hewitt, Duke University; Alphine W. Jefferson, Southern Methodist University; David R. Johnson, University of Texas at San Antonio; Ellen K. Johnson, Northern Virginia Community College; George W. Knepper, University of Akron; Steven F. Lawson, University of South Florida; Barbara LeUnes, Blinn College; James McCaffrey, University of Houston, Downtown; James McMillan, Arizona State University; Myron Marty, Drake University; Otis Miller, Belleville Area College; William Howard Moore, University of Wyoming; Peter Myers, Palo Alto College; Roger L. Nichols, University of Arizona; Michael Perman, University of Illinois at Chicago; Paula

Petrik, University of Maine; Robert Pierce, Foothill College; George Rable, Anderson College; Max Reichard, Delgado Community College; Leonard R. Riforgiato, Pennsylvania State University, Shenango Valley Campus; Marilyn Rinehart, North Harris County College; John Ray Skates, University of Southern Mississippi; Sheila Skemp, University of Mississippi; Kathryn Kish Sklar, SUNY at Binghamton; James Strandberg, University of Wisconsin—Stout; Robert Striplin, American River College; J. K. Sweeney, South Dakota State University; Alan Taylor, Boston University; Phillip Vaughn, Rose State College; Peter H. Wang, Cabrillo Community College; Valdenia Winn, Kansas City Kansas Community College; Bill Worley, Sterling College; and Eli Zaretsky, University of Missouri.

The dedicated staff at HarperCollins provided us with great support and expert guidance. From the beginning, Bruce Borland has been a very special friend to this project. We also wish to thank Barbara Chernow, Betty Slack, Shuli Traub, Dorothy Bungert, Leslie Coopersmith, and Willie Lane. To all of them, we offer our sincere gratitude and appreciation.

Each author received invaluable help from friends, colleagues, and family. James Kirby Martin thanks Larry E. Cable, Don R. Gerlach, Joseph T. Glatthaar, Karen Guenther, David M. Oshinsky, Jeffrey T. Sammons, Hal T. Shelton, and Karen Martin, whose talents as an editor and critic are too often overlooked. Randy Roberts thanks Terry Bilhartz and Joan Randall, and especially James S. Olson and Suzy Roberts. Steven Mintz thanks Susan Kellogg for her encouragement, support, and counsel. Linda O. McMurry thanks Joseph P. Hobbs, John David Smith, Richard McMurry, and William C. Harris. James H. Jones thanks James S. Olson, Terry Rugeley, Laura B Auwers, and especially Linda S. Auwers, who contributed both ideas and criticisms. All of the authors thank Gerard F. McCauley, whose infectious enthusiasm for this project has never wavered. And above all else, we wish to thank our students to whom we have dedicated this book.

SUPPLEMENTS

A comprehensive and up-to-date supplements package accompanies *America and Its People*.

For Instructors

AMERICA THROUGH THE EYES OF ITS PEOPLE: A COLLECTION OF PRIMARY SOURCES

Prepared by Carol Brown, of Houston Community College, this one-volume collection of primary documents portraying the rich and varied tapestry of American life contains documents of Native Americans, women, African-Americans, Hispanics, and others who helped to shape the course of U. S. history. Designed to be duplicated by instructors for student use, the documents have accompanying student exercises.

"THIS IS AMERICA" IMMIGRATION VIDEO

Produced by the Museum of Immigration, these two 20-minute videos tell the story of immigrant America and the personal stories and accomplishments of immigrants. By showing how the richness of our culture is due to the contributions of millions of immigrant Americans, the videos make the point that America's strength lies in the ethnically and culturally diverse backgrounds of its citizens.

INSTRUCTOR'S RESOURCE MANUAL

This extensive resource by Mark Newman of the University of Illinois, Chicago, begins with essays on teaching history through maps, film, and primary sources. Each chapter contains a synopsis, sample discussion questions, lecture supplements called "Connections and Extensions," and instructional flowcharts. The manual includes a special reproducible set of map exercises by James Conrad of Nichols College, designed to teach basic geographic literacy.

DISCOVERING AMERICAN HISTORY THROUGH MAPS AND VIEWS

Created by Gerald Danzer, University of Illinois, Chicago, the recipient of the AHA's 1989 James Harvey Robinson Award for his work in the development of map transparencies, this set of 140 four-color acetates is a unique instructional tool. It contains an introduction on teaching history through maps and a detailed commentary on each transparency. The collection includes cartographic and pictorial maps, views and photos, urban plans, building diagrams, and works of art.

VIDEO LECTURE LAUNCHERS

Each 2 to 5 minutes in duration, these lecture launchers cover key issues in American history, from 1877 to the present. The launchers are accompanied by an Instructor's Manual.

VISUAL ARCHIVES OF AMERICAN HISTORY

This video laser disc provides over 500 photos, and 29 minutes of film clips of major events in American history. Each photo or film clip may be instantly accessed, making this collection ideal for classroom use.

TEXT MAP TRANSPARENCIES

A set of 30 four-color transparencies from the maps in the text.

TEST BANK

Created by Ken Weatherbie of Del Mar College, this test bank features approximately 45 multiple-choice, 10 essay, and 5 map items per chapter. Multiple-choice items are referenced by topic, text page number, and type (factual or interpretive).

TESTMASTER COMPUTERIZED TESTING SYSTEM

This flexible, easy-to-master computer test bank includes all the test items in the printed Test Bank. The TestMaster software allows you to edit existing questions and add your own items. Tests can be printed in several different formats and can include figures such as graphs and tables. Available for IBM and Macintosh computers.

GRADES

A grade-keeping and classroom management software program that maintains data for up to 200 students.

For Students

LEARNING TO THINK CRITICALLY: FILMS AND MYTHS ABOUT AMERICAN HISTORY

Randy Roberts and Robert May of Purdue University use well-known films such as *Gone with the Wind* and *Casablanca* to explore some common myths about America and its past. Many widely held assumptions about our country's past come from or are perpetuated by popular films. Which are true? Which are patently not true? And how does a student of history approach documents, sources, and textbooks with a critical and discerning eye? This short handbook subjects some popular beliefs to historical scrutiny to help students develop a method of inquiry for approaching the subject of history in general.

STUDY GUIDE AND PRACTICE TESTS

Each chapter of this study guide, by Ken Chiaro of Pima Community College, contains a student introduction, reading comprehension and geography exercises, true-false, completion, and multiple-choice "Practice Tests."

SUPERSHELL COMPUTERIZED TUTORIAL

This interactive program for IBM computers helps students learn the major facts and concepts through drill and practice exercises and diagnostic feedback. SuperShell provides immediate correct answers and the text page number on which the material is discussed. Missed questions appear with greater frequency; a running score of the student's performance is maintained on the screen throughout the session.

MAPPING AMERICAN HISTORY: STUDENT ACTIVITIES

Written by Gerald Danzer of the University of Illinois, Chicago, this free map workbook for students features exercises designed to teach students to interpret and analyze cartographic materials as historical documents. The instructor is entitled to a free copy of the workbook for each copy of the text purchased from HarperCollins.

TIMELINK COMPUTER ATLAS OF AMERICAN HISTORY

This atlas, compiled by William Hamblin of Brigham Young University, is an introductory software tutorial and textbook companion. This Macintosh program presents the historical geography of continental United States from colonial times to the settling of the West and the admission of the last continental state in 1912. The program covers territories in different time periods, provides quizzes, and includes a special Civil War module.

The Authors

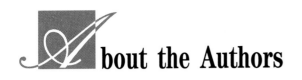

About the Authors

JAMES KIRBY MARTIN is a member of the Department of History at the University of Houston. A graduate of Hiram College in Ohio, he earned his Ph.D. degree at the University of Wisconsin in 1969, specializing in Early American history. His interests also include American social and military history. Among his publications are *Men in Rebellion* (1973), *In the Course of Human Events* (1979), *A Respectable Army* (1982), and *Drinking in America: A History*, rev. ed. (1987), the latter two volumes in collaboration with Mark E. Lender. Martin serves as general editor of the *American Social Experience* series, New York University Press. He recently was a senior fellow at the Philadelphia Center for Early American Studies, University of Pennsylvania, as well as scholar-in-residence at the David Library of the American Revolution, Washington Crossing, Pennsylvania. He is completing a biography of Benedict Arnold.

RANDY ROBERTS earned his Ph.D degree in 1978 from Louisiana State University. His areas of specialization include modern U.S. history and the history of American popular culture and sports. He is a member of the Department of History at Purdue University, where he recently won the Murphy Award for outstanding undergraduate teaching. His publications include *Jack Dempsey: The Manassa Mauler* (1979), *Papa Jack: Jack Johnson and the Era of White Hopes* (1983), and, in collaboration with James S. Olson, *Playing for Keeps: Sports and American Society, 1945 to the Present* (1989) and *Where the Domino Fell: America and Vietnam, 1945–1990* (1991). Roberts serves as co-editor of the *Studies in Sports and Society* series, University of Illinois Press, and is on the editorial board of the *Journal of Sports History*. His current research and writing interests include a biographical investigation of Hollywood actor John Wayne.

STEVEN MINTZ graduated from Oberlin College in Ohio before earning his Ph.D. degree at Yale University in 1979. His special interests include American social history with particular reference to families, women, children, and communities. Mintz is a member of the Department of History at the University of Houston. From 1989 to 1990 he was a visiting scholar at Harvard University's Center for European Studies, and has served as a consultant to the Smithsonian Institution's National Museum of American History. His books include *A Prison of Expectations: The Family in Victorian Culture* (1983), and, in collaboration with Susan Kellogg, *Domestic Revolutions: A Social History of American Family Life* (1988). Mintz is an editor of the *American Social Experience* series, New York University Press, and is completing a book on pre-Civil War American reform.

LINDA O. McMURRY is a member of the Department of History at North Carolina State University. She completed her undergraduate studies at Auburn University, where she also earned her Ph.D. degree in 1976. Her fields of specialization include nineteenth- and twentieth-century U.S. history with an emphasis on the African-American experience and the New South. A recipient of a Rockefeller Foundation Humanities fellowship, she has written *George Washington Carver: Scientist and Symbol* (1981), and *Recorder of the Black Experience: A Biography of Monroe Nathan Work* (1985). McMurry has been active as a consultant to public television stations and museums on topics relating to black history, and is currently completing a study of biracial organizations in the South from the Reconstruction era to World War II.

JAMES H. JONES earned his Ph.D. degree at Indiana University in 1972. His areas of specialization include modern U.S. history, the history of medical ethics and medicine, and the history of sexual behavior. A member of the Department of History at the University of Houston, Jones has been a senior fellow of the National Endowment for the Humanities, a Kennedy fellow at Harvard University, a senior research fellow at the Kennedy Institute of Ethics, Georgetown University, and a Rockefeller fellow at the University of Texas Medical Branch, Galveston. His published writings include *Bad Blood: The Tuskegee Syphilis Experiment* (1981), and he is currently finishing a book on Alfred C. Kinsey and the emergence of scientific research dealing with human sexual behavior.

COMPARATIVE CHRONOLOGIES

POLITICAL/DIPLOMATIC	SOCIAL/ECONOMIC	CULTURAL
30,000 B.C. – 1450		
300–900 Mayan civilization flourishes in present-day Mexico and Guatemala. **c.900** Toltecs rise to power in the Valley of Mexico and later conquer the Maya. **c.1000** Vikings led by Leif Ericson reach Labrador and Newfoundland. **1095** European Christians launch the Crusades to capture the Holy Lands from Muslims. **c.1100** Inca civilization emerges in what is now Peru.	**30,000–20,000 B.C.** First people arrive in North America from Asia across what is now the Bering Strait. **8000–5000 B.C.** Central American Indians begin to practice agriculture.	**1271** Marco Polo begins a 20-year journey to China. **1347–1353** "Black Death" kills one-third of Europe's population. **1420s** Prince Henry of Portugal sends out mariners to explore Africa's western coast. **c.1450** Johannes Gutenberg, a German printer, develops movable type, the basis of modern printing.
1450–1550		
1494 Treaty of Tordesillas divides the New World between Portugal and Spain. **1497–1498** John Cabot's voyages to Newfoundland and Cape Breton Island lay the basis of English claims to North America. **1519** Hernando Cortés and 600 Spanish conquistadores begin the conquest of the Aztec empire. **1531** Francisco Pizarro and 180 Spanish soldiers start the conquest the Inca empire.	**1492** Columbus makes the first of his voyages to the Americas. **1496** Columbus introduces cattle, sugarcane, and wheat to the West Indies. **1501** Spain authorizes the first shipment of African slaves to the Caribbean. **1507** The New World is named America after Florentine navigator Amerigo Vespucci. **1508** First sugar mill is built in the West Indies. **1517** Coffee is introduced in Europe. **1542** Spain outlaws the *encomienda* system and the enslavement of Indians.	**1517** Martin Luther's public protest against the sale of indulgences (pardons of punishment in purgatory) marks the beginning of the Protestant Reformation. **1518** Bartolomé de Las Casas proposes that Spain replace Indian laborers with African slaves. **1527** Henry VIII of England begins to sever ties with the Roman Catholic church. **1539** First printing press in the New World is established in Mexico City.
1550–1650		
1607 English adventurers establish first permanent English settlement at Jamestown in Virginia. **1608** Samuel de Champlain claims Quebec for France. **1610** Spanish found Santa Fe, New Mexico. **1619** First representative assembly in English North America meets in Jamestown. **1620** Pilgrims arrive at Cape Cod on the *Mayflower* and establish a colony at Plymouth.	**1553** Europeans learn about the potato. **1576** Some 40,000 slaves brought to Latin America. **1585–1587** Sir Walter Raleigh sponsors England's first North American settlements at Roanoke Island, along the coast of present-day North Carolina. **1616** Chicken pox wipes out most New England Indians. **1617** England begins transporting criminals to Virginia as punishment.	**1584** Richard Hakluyt's *Discourse of Western Planting* encourages English exploration, conquest, and colonization. **1613** Pocahontas becomes the first Indian in Virginia to convert to Christianity. **1636** Harvard College founded. **1637–1638** Anne Hutchinson convicted of heresy in Massachusetts and flees to Rhode Island. **1640** The first book is published in the colonies, the *Bay Psalm Book*.

POLITICAL/DIPLOMATIC	SOCIAL/ECONOMIC	CULTURAL
		1550–1650
1624 New York is settled by the Dutch and named New Netherland. **1630** The Puritans establish Massachusetts Bay Colony. **1632** Maryland, the first proprietary colony, is established as a refuge for Roman Catholics. **1638** Delaware is settled by Swedes and is named New Sweden. **1649** Charles I of England beheaded.	**1619** Cargoes of Englishwomen begin to arrive in Virginia. **1619** A Dutch ship brings the first Africans to Virginia. **1624** Cattle are introduced into New England. **1630** Colonial population totals about 5700.	**1647** Massachusetts Bay Colony adopts the first public school law in the colonies. **1649** Maryland's Act of Toleration affirms religious freedom for all Christians in the colony.
		1650–1750
1660, 1663 Parliament passes Navigation Acts to ensure that the colonies trade exclusively with England. **1664** Dutch settlers in New Netherlands surrender to the English, who rename the colony New York. **1676** Bacon's Rebellion in Virginia. **1681–1682** William Penn founds Pennsylvania as a "holy experiment" in which diverse groups can live together in harmony. **1688–1689** The English drive James II from the throne in the Glorious Revolution and replace him with William and Mary. **1733** Georgia founded as a haven for debtors and a buffer against Spanish Florida.	**1670** Colonial population totals about 114,500, including 4535 slaves. **1673** Regular mail service between Boston and New York begins. **1699** Parliament outlaws the export of woolen products from the colonies. **1714** Tea is introduced in the colonies. **1739** Stono slave uprising occurs in South Carolina. **1749** Benjamin Franklin invents the lightning rod.	**1650** Anne Bradstreet, New England's first poet, publishes *The Tenth Muse*. **1692** Witchcraft scare in Salem, Massachusetts, results in the execution of 20 men and women. **1731** Benjamin Franklin founds first circulating library in Philadelphia. **1732** Benjamin Franklin begins publishing *Poor Richard's Almanac*. **1735** John Peter Zenger acquitted on charge of seditious libel on ground that truth can be no libel. **1739** George Whitefield begins preaching tours, turning local revivals into the Great Awakening.
		1750
1750 Parliament passes the Iron Act, which prohibits colonists from expanding the production of finished iron or steel products. **1754** Albany Congress draws up a plan to unite the 13 colonies under a single government. **1754–1763** French and Indian War. **1759** British forces under General James Wolfe conquer Quebec.	**1750** The flatboat and the Conestoga wagon appear in Pennsylvania. **1756** Stagecoach line is established between New York and Philadelphia.	**1755** A British army surgeon, Dr. Richard Schuckburg, composes *Yankee Doodle* during the French and Indian war. **1756** Wolfgang Amadeus Mozart born in Salzburg, Austria.

POLITICAL/DIPLOMATIC	SOCIAL/ECONOMIC	CULTURAL

1760

POLITICAL/DIPLOMATIC	SOCIAL/ECONOMIC	CULTURAL
1760 George III becomes king of England. **1763** Pontiac leads an unsuccessful Indian rebellion on the western frontier. **1763** The Proclamation of 1763 forbids white settlement west of the Appalachian Mountains. **1764** The Sugar Act levies new duties on coffee, indigo, sugar, and wine. **1764** Currency Act prohibits colonial governments from issuing paper money and requires all taxes and debts to British merchants to be paid in British currency. **1765** Quartering Act requires colonists to provide barracks, candles, bedding, and beverages to soldiers stationed in their area. **1765** Stamp Act, which requires stamps to be affixed to all legal documents, almanacs, newspapers, pamphlets, and playing cards, among other items, provokes popular protests. **1766** Parliament repeals the Stamp Act, but asserts its authority to tax the colonists in the Declaratory Act. **1767** Townshend Duties Act imposes taxes on imported glass, lead, paint, paper, and tea to defray the cost of colonial administration.	**1760** Colonial population numbers about 1.6 million, including 325,000 slaves. **1763** English surveyors Charles Mason and Jeremiah Dixon set the boundary between Pennsylvania and Maryland—the Mason-Dixon line. **1765** The first medical school in the colonies is established in Philadelphia. **1766** Mastodon bones are discovered along the Ohio River. **1767** Daniel Boone undertakes his first exploration west of the Appalachian Mountains.	**1759** Touro Synagogue in Newport, Rhode Island, is designed. It is the first synagogue in the 13 colonies. **1761** *The Complete Housewife*, a cookbook, is published in New York City. **1766** Robert Rogers writes the first play on a Native American subject, *Ponteach, or the Savages of America*.

1770

POLITICAL/DIPLOMATIC	SOCIAL/ECONOMIC	CULTURAL
1770 The Boston Massacre leaves five colonists dead and others wounded. **1770** Townshend Duties are repealed, except the tax on tea. **1772** Parliament declares that the crown will pay the salaries of royal governors and colonial judges. **1773** Tea Act allows the East India Company to sell tea directly to American retailers. **1773** Boston Tea Party occurs when a band of "Indians" boards three British vessels and dumps 342 chests of tea into Boston Harbor. **1774** The Coercive Acts close the port of Boston; modify the Massachusetts charter; provide for trials outside colonies when royal officials are accused of serious crimes; and call for billeting of troops in unoccupied private homes.	**1770** Colonial population is about 2.2 million. **1773** Harvard College announces that it will no longer rank students in order of social prominence. **1774** Mother Ann Lee, founder of the Shakers in America, lands in New York City.	**1771** Historical painter Benjamin West renders *Death of Wolfe* and *Penn's Treaty with the Indians*. **1773** Phillis Wheatley, the slave of a Boston merchant, publishes *Poems on Various Subjects*. **1776** Thomas Paine publishes *Common Sense*, urging immediate separation from England.

POLITICAL/DIPLOMATIC	SOCIAL/ECONOMIC	CULTURAL
		1770
1775 The shot "heard 'round the world"—the first military clashes between British troops and patriots take place at Lexington and Concord. **1775** George III issues declarations that a state of rebellion exists in the colonies. **1776** Continental Congress adopts the Declaration of Independence. **1778** Benjamin Franklin negotiates an American alliance with France.		
		1780
1781 Lord Cornwallis surrenders to George Washington at Yorktown. **1781** The states approve the nation's first constitution, the Articles of Confederation. **1783** The Treaty of Paris is signed, ending the American Revolution. **1787** Congress passes the Northwest Ordinance, forever barring slavery north of the Ohio River. **1787** Constitutional convention convenes in Philadelphia. **1788** Constitution is ratified. **1789** Electoral College names George Washington the first president.	**1780** U.S. population is about 2,780,400. **1783** Benjamin Franklin invents bifocals. **1784** The *Empress of China* inaugurates sea trade with China. **1786** Western Massachusetts farmers, led by Daniel Shays, close county courthouses to protest low farm prices and high state taxes. **1787** Levi Hutchins, a Concord, New Hampshire, clockmaker invents the alarm clock.	**1782** J. Hector St. John de Crèvecoeur publishes *Letters from an American Farmer*. **1786** Virginia legislature enacts separation of church and state. **1786** Charles Willson Peale opens the first art gallery in Philadelphia. **1789** William Hill Brown's *The Power of Sympathy* is the first novel published in the United States.
		1790
1790 Congress adopts Hamilton's proposal to fund the national debt at full value and to assume state debts from the revolutionary war. **1791** Bank of the United States established. **1791** The Bill of Rights becomes part of the Constitution. **1794** General Anthony Wayne defeats an Indian alliance at the Battle of Fallen Timbers, opening Ohio to white settlement. **1796** Washington issues a Farewell Address, warning against political factionalism and foreign entanglements. **1798** Congress adopts the Alien and Sedition acts. **1798–1799** Kentucky and Virginia resolutions declare the Alien and Sedition acts unconstitutional.	**1790** U.S. population is 3,929,214. **1790** Samuel Slater opens the first textile factory in the United States. **1793** Eli Whitney invents the cotton gin. **1794–1795** The Whiskey Rebellion, protesting the federal excise tax on whiskey, is put down.	**1793** Louis XVI of France sent to the guillotine. **1794** Thomas Paine publishes *The Age of Reason*. **1798** Charles Brockden Brown publishes *Wieland*.

POLITICAL/DIPLOMATIC	SOCIAL/ECONOMIC	CULTURAL

1800

1801 House of Representatives selects Thomas Jefferson as third president.

1801 Jefferson sends eight ships to enforce a blockade of Tripoli.

1803 Thomas Jefferson purchases Louisiana Territory from Napoleon for $15 million or 4 cents an acre.

1803 *Marbury* v. *Madison* upholds the principle of judicial review.

1804 Vice president Aaron Burr kills Alexander Hamilton in a duel.

1807 Jefferson imposes a trade embargo in order to pressure Britain and France to respect American rights.

1807 Congress votes to prohibit the African slave trade.

1809 Embargo Act repealed.

1809 Non-Intercourse Act prohibits trade with Britain and France.

1800 U.S. population is 5,308,483, including 896,849 slaves.

1800 John Chapman, better known as Johnny Appleseed, passes out religious tracts and apple seeds throughout the Ohio Valley.

1804 Lewis and Clark expedition sets out from St. Louis to explore the Louisiana Purchase.

1807 Seth Thomas and Eli Terry begin to manufacture clocks out of interchangeable parts.

1807 Robert Fulton proves the practicality of the steamboat by sailing the *Clermont* from New York City to Albany in 32 hours.

1800 Mason Locke Weems publishes his *Life of Washington*, the source of the legend about Washington chopping down the cherry tree.

1806 Noah Webster's *Compendious Dictionary of the English Language* is published.

1810

1812 Congress declares war against Britain.

1813–1814 Creek War.

1814 United States and Britain sign Treaty of Ghent, which ends the War of 1812.

1816 Second Bank of the United States chartered.

1818 United States and Britain agree to joint occupation of Oregon.

1819 Spain cedes Florida to the United States.

1819 "A Firebell in the Night." A crisis over slavery erupts after Missouri applies for admission to the Union as a slave state.

1810 U.S. population is 7,239,881.

1814 The first totally mechanized factory producing cotton cloth from raw cotton opens in Waltham, Massachusetts.

1817 American Colonization Society is founded to colonize free blacks in Africa.

1819 Panic of 1819.

1819 An asylum for the deaf, dumb, and blind opens in Hartford, Connecticut, inaugurating a new era of humanitarian concern for the handicapped.

1819 The *Savannah* becomes the first steamship to cross the Atlantic.

1819 *Dartmouth* v. *Woodward* upholds the sanctity of contracts. *McCulloch* v. *Maryland* upholds the constitutionality of the second Bank of the United States.

1814 Francis Scott Key writes the lyrics to "The Star-Spangled Banner" during the British assault on Fort McHenry, Maryland.

1818 Washington Irving publishes *Rip Van Winkle*.

1819 William Ellery Channing helps found American Unitarianism.

POLITICAL/DIPLOMATIC	SOCIAL/ECONOMIC	CULTURAL
		1820
1820 Missouri Compromise prohibits slavery in the northern half of the Louisiana Purchase; Missouri enters the union as a slave state and Maine as a free state.	**1820** U.S. population is 9,638,453.	**1821** Emma Willard founds the Troy Female Seminary, one of the first academies to offer women a higher education.
1821 Mexico declares independence from Spain.	**1820** Land Act reduces the price of public land to $1.25 per acre.	**1823** John Howard Payne and Henry Bishop compose the song "Home, Sweet Home."
1823 President James Monroe opposes any further European colonization or interference in the Americas, establishing the principle now known as the Monroe Doctrine.	**1822** Stephen F. Austin founds the first American colony in Texas.	**1823** James Fenimore Cooper publishes *The Pioneers*, the first of his Leatherstocking tales.
	1822 Liberia founded as a colony for free blacks.	**1827** James Audubon publishes *Birds of America*, consisting of 435 lifelike paintings of birds.
	1825 Erie Canal opens.	**1829** David Walker issues his militant "Appeal to the Colored Citizens of the World."
	1827 *Freedom's Journal*, the first black newspaper, begins publication in New York City.	
	1828 The *Cherokee Phoenix*, the first Indian newspaper, begins publication.	
	1829 The first U.S. school for the blind opens in Boston.	
		1830
1830 Indian Removal Act provides funds to purchase Indian homelands in exchange for land in present-day Oklahoma and Arkansas.	**1830** U.S. population is 12,866,020.	**1831** Samuel Francis Smith composes the words to the song "America."
1832 Jackson vetoes the bill to recharter the second Bank of the United States.	**1830** Joseph Smith, Jr., founds the Church of Jesus Christ of Latter-Day Saints.	**1834** *A Narrative of the Life of David Crockett* is published.
1832 South Carolina nullifies the federal triff.	**1830** America's first commercially successful steam locomotive, the *Tom Thumb*, loses a race against a horse.	**1836** William Holmes McGuffey publishes his first and second *Reader*.
1836 Texans under Sam Houston defeat the Mexican army at the Battle of San Jacinto.	**1831** William Lloyd Garrison begins publishing the militant abolitionist newspaper *The Liberator*.	**1838** Sarah Grimké publishes *Letters on the Equality of the Sexes and the Condition of Women*, one of the earliest public defenses of sexual equality.
1837 Panic of 1837 begins.	**1831** Oberlin College opens its doors as the nation's first coeducational college. In 1835, it becomes the first American college to admit blacks.	
	1831 Nat Turner's slave insurrection occurs in Southampton County, Virginia.	
	1832 Samuel F. B. Morse invents the telegraph.	
	1835 The Liberty Bell cracks as it tolls the death of Chief Justice John Marshall.	
	1837 Horace Mann becomes Massachusetts's first superintendent of education.	
	1839 Liberty party founded.	
	1839 Charles Goodyear successfully vulcanizes rubber.	

POLITICAL/DIPLOMATIC	SOCIAL/ECONOMIC	CULTURAL

1840

1846 Britain and the United States divide Oregon along the 49th parallel.	**1840** U.S. population is 17,069,453.	**1841** Edgar Allan Poe publishes "Murders in the Rue Morgue," the first modern detective story.
1846 The United States declares war on Mexico.	**1841** The first wagon train arrives in California.	**1843** New word *millionaire* coined to describe Pierre Lorillard, tobacco magnate.
1848 Treaty of Guadalupe Hidalgo ends the Mexican War.	**1842** The Massachusetts Supreme Court upholds workers' right to organize.	**1848** Karl Marx and Friedrich Engels publish the *Communist Manifesto*.
	1845 A potato blight strikes Ireland.	
	1846 Elias Howe patents the first reliable sewing machine.	
	1846 William Morton, a Boston dentist, uses an anesthetic for the first time during a surgical operation.	
	1846–1847 Brigham Young leads the Mormons to the Great Salt Lake Valley.	
	1848 Alexander T. Stewart opens the first department store in New York City.	
	1848 Gold is discovered at Sutter's Mill in California.	
	1848 The first women's rights convention is held in Seneca Falls, New York.	
	1849 Elizabeth Blackwell becomes the first woman physician in the United States.	

1850

1850 Compromise of 1850 is enacted.	**1850** U.S. population is 23,191,876.	**1850** Nathaniel Hawthorne publishes *The Scarlet Letter*.
1854 Abolitionist William Lloyd Garrison publicly burns the U.S. Constitution, calling it an "agreement with hell and a covenant with death."	**1850** U.S. Navy outlaws flogging.	**1851** Herman Melville publishes *Moby Dick*.
1854 Stephen A. Douglas introduces the Kansas-Nebraska Act. Opponents of the act form the new Republican party.	**1851** The Young Men's Christian Association opens its first American chapter in Boston.	**1852** Harriet Beecher Stowe's *Uncle Tom's Cabin* sells a million copies in its first year and a half.
1854 Commodore Matthew Perry negotiates a treaty opening Japan to American trade.	**1857** Elisha Graves Otis installs the first passenger elevator in a New York City department store.	**1854** Henry David Thoreau publishes *Walden*.
1859 John Brown's raid fails at Harpers Ferry.	**1859** Edwin L. Drake drills the first commercial oil well at Titusville, Pennsylvania.	**1855** Walt Whitman publishes *Leaves of Grass*.
		1859 Charles Darwin publishes *Origin of Species*.

POLITICAL/DIPLOMATIC	SOCIAL/ECONOMIC	CULTURAL

POLITICAL/DIPLOMATIC	SOCIAL/ECONOMIC	CULTURAL
1860 Abraham Lincoln is elected sixteenth president.	**1860** U.S. population is 31,443,321.	**1860** Erastus and Irwin Beadle issue the first dime novels, featuring such figures as Daniel Boone and Kit Carson.
1860 South Carolina secedes from the Union.	**1860** The Pony Express begins carrying mail between St. Joseph, Missouri, and Sacramento, California.	**1865** Mark Twain publishes his first story, "The Celebrated Jumping Frog of Calaveras County."
1861 Confederate States of America formed.	**1862** To help raise revenue for the Civil War, the first federal income tax goes into effect.	
1863 President Lincoln signs the Emancipation Proclamation.	**1863** New York City draft riots.	
1865 John Wilkes Booth assassinates President Lincoln at Ford's Theater in Washington, D.C.; Andrew Johnson becomes seventeenth president.	**1865** The Ku Klux Klan is founded in Pulaski, Tennessee.	
1865 Thirteenth Amendment ratified, abolishing slavery.	**1866** The potato chip is invented by a Saratoga, New York, chef.	
1867 Russia sells Alaska to the United States for $7.2 million, or less than 2 cents an acre.	**1866** Cyrus W. Field lays the first permanent trans-Atlantic telegraph cable.	
1868 House of Representatives impeaches Andrew Jackson; he escapes conviction in the Senate by one vote.	**1867** Christopher Latham Sholes and Carlos Glidden invent the first practical typewriter.	
	1869 William Finley Semple of Mount Vernon, Ohio, receives a patent for chewing gum.	
	1869 First transcontinental railroad is completed.	

POLITICAL/DIPLOMATIC	SOCIAL/ECONOMIC	CULTURAL
1870 Senator Hiram R. Revels of Mississippi becomes the first black U.S. senator.	**1870** U.S. population is 39,818,449.	**1871** P. T. Barnum opens his circus, which he calls "The Greatest Show on Earth."
1875 Civil Rights Act forbids racial discrimination in public accommodations and public transportation and guarantees black Americans the right to serve on juries.	**1871** Great Chicago fire claims 300 lives, destroys 17,500 buildings, and leaves 100,000 people homeless.	**1871** James Whistler paints "Arrangement in Gray and Black No. 1," better known as "Whistler's Mother."
1877 Electoral Commission awards disputed electoral votes to Republican Rutherford Hayes, who is inaugurated nineteenth president.	**1873** Comstock Act bans obscene materials, including rubber prophylactics, from the mails.	**1875** Mary Baker Eddy publishes *Science and Health*, the basic text of Christian Science.
1877 Hayes withdraws the last federal troops from the South, ending Reconstruction.	**1875** The first Kentucky Derby.	**1876** Mark Twain publishes *The Adventures of Tom Sawyer*.
1878 Bland-Allison Act requires the U.S. Treasury to buy $2 to $4 million of silver each month in order to inflate the currency.	**1876** Custer's Last Stand.	**1876** Baseball's National League founded.
	1876 Twenty-nine-year-old Alexander Graham Bell patents the telephone.	**1879** Henry George publishes *Progress and Poverty*.
	1876 The nation celebrates its centennial with a $10 million exposition in Philadelphia.	
	1879 Congress votes to allow women to argue cases before the Supreme Court.	
	1879 Thomas Edison, 32, invents the light bulb.	
	1879 Frank W. Woolworth establishes his first successful 5-and-10-cent store in Lancaster, Pennsylvania.	

POLITICAL/DIPLOMATIC	SOCIAL/ECONOMIC	CULTURAL

1880

1881 President James A. Garfield mortally wounded at a Washington train station; Chester Arthur becomes twenty-first president.

1882 Chinese Exclusion Act suspends Chinese immigration for ten years; extended in 1892 and 1902.

1883 Civil Service Act classifies approximately 15,000 federal jobs as civil service positions to be awarded only after a competitive examination.

1883 Supreme Court declares Civil Rights Act of 1875 unconstitutional.

1887 Congress establishes the Interstate Commerce Commission, the first federal regulatory commission, to regulate railroads.

1887 Dawes Allotment Act subdivides all Indian reservations into individual plots of land of 160 to 320 acres and opens "surplus" land to white settlers.

1880 U.S. population is 50,155,783.

1881 Clara Barton founds the American Red Cross.

1883 U.S. railroads adopt four standard time zones.

1886 Supreme Court extends protection of due process to corporations.

1886 The Statue of Liberty is unveiled.

1886 The American Federation of Labor founded in Columbus, Ohio.

1886 Pharmacist James S. Pemberton invents Coca-Cola.

1888 The first incubators are used for premature infants.

1889 The Johnstown flood kills almost 2300 people.

1881 Helen Hunt Jackson publishes *A Century of Dishonor* describing mistreatment of American Indians.

1883 "Buffalo Bill" Cody organizes his first Wild West Show.

1884 Mark Twain publishes *The Adventures of Huckleberry Finn.*

1888 Edward Bellamy publishes *Looking Backward*, describing life in Boston in the year 2000.

1890

1890 Congress passes the Sherman Antitrust Act, forbidding restraints on trade.

1891 Separate Federal Courts of Appeal are created to relieve the Supreme Court's case load.

1896 William McKinley defeats William Jennings Bryan for the presidency.

1897 President Cleveland vetoes a literacy requirement for adult immigrants.

1898 Spanish-American War begins.

1898 United States acquires Guam, the Philippines, and Puerto Rico, and annexes Hawaii.

1899 Emilio Aguinaldo leads a rebellion against the United States to win Philippine independence.

1899 United States annexes Wake Island.

1890 U.S. population is 62,947,714.

1890 The U.S. Bureau of the Census announces that the western frontier is now closed.

1890 Sequoia and Yosemite National parks in California established.

1891 Basketball is invented by Dr. James A. Naismith in Springfield, Massachusetts.

1892 Ellis Island opens as a center to screen immigrants.

1893 Chlorine is first used to treat sewage in Brewster, New York.

1895 *Pollack* v. *Farmers Loan and Trust Company* declares a federal income tax unconstitutional.

1896 *Plessy* v. *Ferguson* decision rules that the principle of "separate but equal" does not deprive blacks of civil rights guaranteed under the Fourteenth Amendment.

1897 A high society ball, costing $370,000, is held at New York's Waldorf Astoria Hotel despite a serious economic depression.

1890 Jacob A. Riis publishes *How the Other Half Lives.*

1896 The first comic strip appears in Joseph Pulitzer's *New York World.*

1896 Billy Sunday begins his career as an evangelist.

1899 Composer Scott Joplin's "Maple Leaf Rag" helps popularize ragtime.

1899 In *The School and Society*, John Dewey outlines his ideas about "progressive education."

POLITICAL/DIPLOMATIC	SOCIAL/ECONOMIC	CULTURAL
		1900
1902 Oregon, South Dakota, and Utah become first states to adopt initiative and recall.	**1900** U.S. population is 75,994,575.	**1900** Theodore Dreiser publishes his first novel, *Sister Carrie*.
1903 Wisconsin becomes the first state to adopt primary elections.	**1900** Great Galveston, Texas, hurricane kills 6000.	**1900** L. Frank Baum publishes *The Wonderful Wizard of Oz*.
1904 Construction of Panama Canal begins.	**1903** The Wright Brothers make the first piloted flight in a powered airplane.	**1903** W. E. B. Du Bois publishes *The Souls of Black Folk*, declaring that "the problem of the twentieth century is the color line."
1907 President Theodore Roosevelt dispatches 16 battleships ("the great white fleet") on an around-the-world cruise.	**1904** The ice-cream cone and iced tea are introduced at the St. Louis World's Fair.	**1903** Edwin S. Porter's *The Great Train Robbery* is the first American film to tell a story.
	1906 The Great San Francisco earthquake leaves 452 people dead and 225,000 homeless.	**1906** Upton Sinclair's *The Jungle* exposes unsanitary conditions in the meat-packing industry.
	1908 Henry Ford introduces the Model T.	
	1908 Jack Johnson becomes the first black heavyweight boxing champion.	
	1909 The National Association for the Advancement of Colored People formed to press for equal rights for black Americans.	
	1909 Explorers Robert E. Peary and Matthew Henson reach the North Pole.	
		1910
1913 Sixteenth Amendment gives Congress the power to levy an income tax.	**1910** U.S. population is 91,972,266.	**1913** The first crossword puzzle appears in a U.S. newspaper.
1914 World War I begins in Europe.	**1911** Female garment workers (145) lose their lives in a fire at New York's Triangle Shirtwaist Company.	**1914** Edgar Rice Burroughs publishes *Tarzan of the Apes*.
1917 United States enters the war.	**1912** The *Titanic* sinks on its maiden voyage, and 1500 of the ship's 2200 passengers drown.	**1915** Margaret Sanger is arrested in New York City for teaching methods of contraception.
1917 Jeannette Rankin becomes first woman elected to Congress.	**1914** President Wilson proclaims the first Mother's Day.	**1918** Post Office confiscates copies of *The Little Review* on grounds of obscenity. It contains a part of James Joyce's *Ulysses*.
	1918 Influenza epidemic claims more than 20 million lives worldwide.	
		1920
1920 Palmer Raids to arrest suspected Communists.	**1920** U.S. population is 105,710,620.	**1920** F. Scott Fitzgerald publishes his first novel, *This Side of Paradise*.
1920 National Prohibition begins.	**1920** A Chicago grand jury indicts eight Chicago "Black Sox" players for throwing the 1919 World Series.	**1921** The first bathing beauty pageant is held in Atlantic City, New Jersey.
1920 Nineteenth Amendment grants women the right to vote.	**1923** Colonel Jacob Schick receives patent for first electric shaver.	**1922** Tomb of Egyptian Pharaoh Tutankhamen ("King Tut") discovered.
1920 The Panama Canal declared officially opened.	**1924** Clarence Birdseye develops the first packaged frozen foods.	**1925** Scopes trial, the celebrated "Monkey Trial," involving the teaching of evolution in public schools, takes place in Tennessee.
1928 Kellogg-Briand Treaty renounces war "as an instrument of national policy."		

POLITICAL/DIPLOMATIC	SOCIAL/ECONOMIC	CULTURAL

1920

| | **1926** National Broadcasting Company becomes the first nationwide radio network.
 1927 Charles Lindbergh completes 33-hour solo flight from New York to Paris.
 1929 Stock market crashes. | **1927** The first talking motion picture, *The Jazz Singer*, starring Al Jolson, opens.
 1928 Walt Disney releases first Mickey Mouse cartoon. |

1930

| **1933** Adolf Hitler is appointed Chancellor of Germany.
 1935 Italy invades Ethiopia.
 1935 Huey Long is assassinated.
 1936 Civil War breaks out in Spain.
 1938 Munich Pact hands over a third of Czechoslovakia to Nazi Germany.
 1939 Soviet Union and Germany sign a nonaggression pact.
 1939 World War II begins following Germany's invasion of Poland. | **1930** U.S. population is 122,775,046.
 1933 Twenty-first Amendment repeals prohibition.
 1934 Public Enemy Number One, John Dillinger, is shot and killed by FBI agents at a Chicago movie theater.
 1935 Wagner Act guarantees workers' right to bargain collectively.
 1936 The last public hanging in the United States takes place in Owenboro, Kentucky.
 1937 Following a 44-day sit-down strike, General motors recognizes the United Automobile Workers.
 1938 Patent issued for nylon. | **1931** CBS inaugurates the first regular schedule of TV broadcasts.
 1935 Charles Darrow, an unemployed engineer, markets a new board game, Monopoly.
 1936 Jesse Owens wins four gold medals at the Berlin Olympics.
 1937 Ther German zeppelin *Hindenberg* bursts into flames at Lakehurst, New Jersey, killing 35 passengers.
 1938 Action Comics #1 presents the Man of Steel, Superman.
 1938 Orson Welles's broadcasts reports of a Martian invasion.
 1939 John Steinbeck publishes *The Grapes of Wrath*. |

1940

| **1941** Japan attacks Pearl Harbor, killing nearly 2000 U.S. soldiers and sailors.
 1942 Nazis begin their "final solution" to the Jewish problem.
 1942 President Franklin D. Roosevelt authorizes internment of 112,000 West Coast Japanese-Americans.
 1944 D-Day.
 1945 V-E Day.
 1945 Atomic bombs dropped on Hiroshima and Nagasaki, Japan.
 1945 V-J Day.
 1946 Winston Churchill declares that "an iron curtain" had descended across Europe.
 1948 State of Israel is proclaimed.
 1949 Mao Ze-dong's Communist forces win China's civil war. | **1940** U.S. population is 131,669,275.
 1942 Physicist Enrico Fermi sets off the first atomic chain reaction.
 1942 Gasoline rationing goes into effect.
 1943 A race riot in Detroit leaves 25 blacks and 9 whites dead.
 1944 GI Bill of Rights provides educational benefits for veterans.
 1945 The transistor is invented.
 1946 ENIAC, the first electronic computer, begins service.
 1947 Air Force Captain Charles Yeager becomes the first pilot to fly faster than the speed of sound.
 1947 Twenty-eight-year-old Jackie Robinson becomes the first black player in major league baseball. | **1948** Alfred Kinsey publishes *Sexual Behavior in the Human Male*, followed five years later by *Sexual Behavior in the Human Female*.
 1948 The first successful long-playing record is developed.
 1949 French fashion designers introduce the bikini bathing suit. |

POLITICAL/DIPLOMATIC	SOCIAL/ECONOMIC	CULTURAL
		1950

1950 North Korean troops cross the 38th parallel, beginning the Korean War.

1950 Senator Joseph McCarthy claims that 205 State Department employees are members of the Communist party.

1951 Ethel and Julius Rosenberg are sentenced to death for atomic espionage.

1954 The French garrison at Dien Bien Phu falls to Vietnamese nationalists led by Ho Chi Minh.

1954 *Brown* v. *Board of Education* decision holds that "separate educational facilities are inherently unequal."

1959 Fidel Castro leads Cuban revolution against the regime of Fulgencio Batista.

1950 U.S. population is 150,697,361.

1952 United States detonates the first hydrogen bomb.

1954 Dr. Jonas Salk develops a vaccine against polio.

1955 The birth control pill is invented.

1955 Black seamstress Rosa Parks refuses to give up her seat on a Montgomery, Alabama, city bus, sparking a year-long bus boycott.

1957 Nine black students enter Central High School in Little Rock, Arkansas under the protection of 1000 army paratroopers.

1957 Soviet Union rockets *Sputnik*, the first artificial satellite, into space.

1958 European Common Market is formed.

1950 Charles Schulz creates the cartoon strip "Peanuts."

1951 J. D. Salinger publishes *Catcher in the Rye*.

1952 Ralph Ellison publishes *The Invisible Man*.

1956 Elvis Presley's first hit, "Heartbreak Hotel," is released.

1957 Jack Kerouac's *On the Road* is published.

1957 Dr. Seuss publishes *The Cat in the Hat*.

1960

1960 U-2 spy plane is shot down over the Soviet Union.

1961 Cuban exiles stage abortive invasion of Cuba at Bay of Pigs.

1961 Cuban missile crisis erupts.

1963 United States and Soviet Union agree to ban nuclear tests in the atmosphere.

1963 President Kennedy is assassinated; Lyndon Johnson becomes thirty-sixth president.

1964 Civil Rights Act bans discrimination in jobs and public facilities.

1965 United States begins regular bombing missions over North Vietnam and sends American ground combat troops into South Vietnam.

1968 Martin Luther King, Jr., and Robert F. Kennedy are assassinated.

1960 U.S. population is 179,323,175.

1960 First civil rights sit-in takes place in Greensboro, North Carolina.

1961 Russian cosmonaut Yuri Gagarin becomes the first human to orbit the earth.

1964 Martin Luther King, Jr., receives the Nobel Peace Prize.

1965 Congress requires cigarette packages and ads to carry health warnings.

1969 Astronaut Neil Armstrong becomes the first person to walk on the moon.

1960 A House subcommittee accuses disk jockeys of accepting "payola" to play certain records on the air.

1961 FCC Chairman Newton Minow describes TV as a "vast wasteland."

1963 Betty Friedan publishes *The Feminine Mystique*, helping launch a new feminist movement.

1967 The musical *Hair* with its nudity brings controversy to the Broadway stage.

1969 Half a million young people attend a four-day rock concert near Woodstock, New York.

POLITICAL/DIPLOMATIC	SOCIAL/ECONOMIC	CULTURAL
1970		
1972 Five burglars are arrested for breaking into Democratic National Headquarters at Washington's Watergate Office Complex.	**1970** U.S. population is 203,235,175.	**1970** Satirical comic strip *Doonesbury* begins appearing in 30 newspapers.
1973 United States ends direct military involvement in Vietnam.	**1971** Twenty-sixth Amendment gives 18-year-olds the right to vote.	**1971** Controversial situation comedy "All in the Family" debuts.
1973 Vice President Spiro Agnew pleads no contest to a charge of income tax evasion and resigns his office.	**1973** Arab oil embargo begins; oil prices quadruple.	**1977** Record television audiences watch the dramatization of Alex Haley's black family history *Roots*.
1974 Richard Nixon becomes the first president to resign from office.	**1977** United States ends a ten-year moratorium on capital punishment.	**1977** The film *Saturday Night Fever* popularizes disco dance music.
1975 Vietnam War ends as Communist troops occupy Saigon.	**1979** The nation's most serious nuclear power accident occurs at Pennsylvania's Three Mile Island nuclear plant.	
1978 Jimmy Carter mediates Egyptian-Israeli peace settlement.	**1979** Oil price climbs from $10 to $20 a barrel.	
1979 Iranian militants seize American hostages.		
1979 Soviet Union invades Afghanistan.		
1980		
1981 Ronald W. Reagan inaugurated as fortieth president; minutes later, Iran releases American hostages after 444 days of captivity.	**1980** U.S. population is 226,545,805.	**1987** *Platoon*, a highly sympathetic account of the plight of U.S. troops in Vietnam, wins the Academy Award for best picture.
1981 Sandra Day O'Connor becomes the first female Supreme Court Justice.	**1981** Doctors diagnose the first cases of AIDS.	**1987** The publication of Allan Bloom's *The Closing of the American Mind* triggers widespread debate about American education.
1984 Democrats make Geraldine Ferraro the first female vice-presidential nominee of a major party.	**1981** President Reagan dismisses 15,000 striking air traffic controllers.	**1987** Baby M case raises moral and ethical issues involved in surrogate parenting.
1985 Mikhail S. Gorbachev becomes leader of the Soviet Union.	**1982–1983** The nation's worst post–World War II recession raises unemployment to 10.2 percent, but reduces inflation and interest rates.	
1985 United States begins secret arms-for-hostages negotiations with Iran.	**1986** Crack, a highly addictive form of cocaine, appears in U.S. cities.	
1986 Profits from Iranian arms sales are diverted to Nicaraguan contras.	**1987** The Dow Jones Industrial Average plummets a record 509 points in a single day.	
1988 George Bush is elected forty-first president.		
1989 Communist regimes collapse in Eastern Europe.		

POLITICAL/DIPLOMATIC	SOCIAL/ECONOMIC	CULTURAL
1990 Iraqi troops invade and occupy Kuwait.	**1990** The two Germanys are reunited after 45 years.	**1990** Soviet President Mikhail S. Gorbachev wins the Nobel Peace Prize for promoting political liberalization in Eastern Europe and ending the Cold War.
1990 Margaret Thatcher steps down as prime minister of Great Britain.	**1991** Confirmation hearings of Clarence Thomas for the Supreme Court focus attention on the issue of sexual harassment.	**1990** Emperor Akihito is enthroned in Japan, the 125th occupant of the Chrysanthemum Throne.
1990 President Bush and Soviet President Mikhail S. Gorbachev sign agreements to cut stockpiles of long-range nuclear arms and eliminate most chemical weapons.	**1992** Riots erupt in Los Angeles following the "not guilty" verdict in the Rodney King case.	
1991 U.S., Western European, and Arab forces eject Iraq from Kuwait by force.	**1992** *Roe* v. *Wade* is upheld, with modifications.	
1991 Attempted coup in the Soviet Union fails.		
1991 Israel and its Arab neighbors begin peace talks.		
1992 Bill Clinton is elected forty-second president.		

America
and
Its People

CHAPTER 1

The Peopling and Unpeopling of America

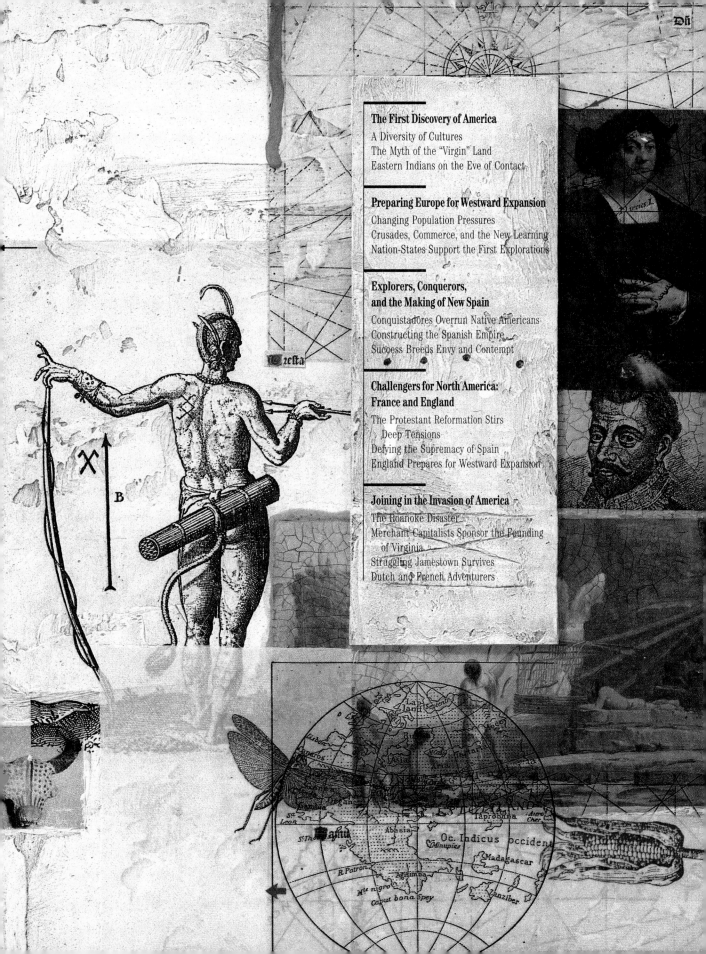

*E*ach Thanksgiving Americans remember Squanto as the valued Indian friend who saved the suffering Pilgrims from starvation. Few know the other ways in which Squanto's life reflected the disastrous collision of human beings occurring in the wake of Christopher Columbus's first voyage of discovery to America in 1492. European explorers believed that they had stumbled upon two empty continents, which they referred to as the "new world." In actuality, the new world was both very old and the home of millions of people. These Native Americans experienced chaos and death when they came into contact with the Europeans. A little more than 100 years after Columbus, at the time of the Pilgrims, Indian population had declined by as much as 90 percent. The tragic story of Squanto and his tribe, the Patuxets of eastern Massachusetts, vividly portrays what happened.

Born about 1590, Squanto acquired the values of his Algonquian-speaking elders before experiencing much contact with adventurers from overseas. Tribal fathers taught him that personal dignity came from respecting the bounties of nature and serving one's clan and village, not from acquiring material possessions. He also learned the importance of physical and mental endurance. To be accepted as an adult, he spent a harrowing winter surviving alone in the wilderness. When he returned the next spring, his Patuxet fathers fed him poisonous herbs for days on end, which he unflinchingly ate—and survived by forced vomiting. Having demonstrated his fortitude, tribal members declared him a man.

Living among 2000 souls in the Patuxet's principal village, located on the very spot where the Pilgrims settled in 1620, Squanto may well have foreseen trouble ahead when fair-skinned Europeans started visiting the region. First there were fishermen; then in 1605 the French explorer, Samuel de Champlain, stopped at Plymouth Bay. More fatefully, Captain John Smith, late of the Virginia colony, passed through in 1614. Smith's party treated the Patuxets with respect, but they viewed the natives as little more than wild beasts, to be exploited if necessary. Before sailing away, Smith ordered one of his lieutenants, Captain Thomas Hunt, to stay behind with a crew of mariners and gather up a rich harvest of fish. After completing his assignment, Hunt lured 20 Indians, among them Squanto, on board his vessel and, without warning, set his course for the slave market in Malaga, Spain.

Somehow Squanto avoided a lifetime of slavery. By 1617 he was in England, where he devoted himself to mastering the English tongue. One of his sponsors, Captain Thomas Dermer, who had been with Smith in 1614, asked Squanto to serve as an interpreter and guide for yet another New England expedition. Anxious to return home, the native readily agreed and sailed back to America in 1619.

When Dermer's party put in at Plymouth Bay, a shocked Squanto discovered that nothing remained of his once-thriving village, except overgrown fields and rotting human bones. As if swept away by some unnamed force, the Patuxets had disappeared from the face of the earth. Trained to hide his emotions, Squanto grieved privately. Soon he learned about a disastrous epidemic. Thousands of Indians had died in the Cape Cod vicinity. They were victims of diseases heretofore unknown in New England, in this case probably chicken pox carried there from Europe by fishermen and explorers. When these microorganisms struck, the native populace, lacking antibodies, had no way of fending them off.

Squanto soon left Dermer's party and went in search of possible survivors. He was living with the Pokanoket Indians when the Pilgrims stepped ashore in December 1620 at the site of his old village. The Pilgrims endured a terrible winter in which half their numbers died. Then in the early spring of 1621 a lone Indian, Samoset, appeared in Plymouth Colony. He spoke halting English and told of another who had actually lived in England. Within a week Squanto arrived and agreed to stay and help the Pilgrims produce the necessities of life.

Squanto taught the Pilgrims how to grow Indian corn (maize), a crop unknown in Europe, and how to catch great quantities of fish. His efforts resulted in an abundance of food, celebrated in the first Thanksgiving feast during the fall of 1621. To future Pilgrim Governor William Bradford, Squanto "was a special instrument sent of God for their good beyond their expectation."

The story does not have a pleasant ending. Contact with the English had changed Squanto, and he adopted some of their practices. In violation of his childhood training, he started to serve himself. As Bradford recorded, Squanto told neighboring Indian tribes that the Pilgrims would make war on them unless they gave him gifts. Further, he would unleash the plague, which the English "kept ... buried in the ground, and could send it among whom they would." By the summer of 1622 Squanto had become a problem for the Pilgrims, who were anxious for peace. Then he fell sick, "bleeding much at the nose," and died within a few days as yet another victim of some European disease.

Squanto is best remembered for the assistance he gave the Pilgrims in providing for the necessities of life, but his own life—and death— illustrate the tensions and problems created by contact between Native American and European cultures.

As demonstrated by Squanto's life, white-Indian contacts did not point toward a fusing of Native American and European customs, values, and ideals. Rather, the westward movement of peoples destroyed Indian societies and replaced them with European-based communities. The history of the Americas (and of the United States) cannot be fully appreciated without understanding why thousands of Europeans crossed the Atlantic Ocean and sought dominance over the American continents. Three groups in particular, the Spanish, French, and English, succeeded in this life-and-death struggle that changed forever the course of human history.

THE FIRST DISCOVERY OF AMERICA

The world was a much colder place 75,000 years ago. A great ice age, known as the Wisconsin glaciation, had begun. Year after year, water being drawn from the oceans formed into mighty ice caps, which in turn spread over vast reaches of land. This process dramatically lowered ocean levels. In the area of the Bering Straits, where today 56 miles of ocean separate Siberia from Alaska, a land bridge emerged. At times this link between Asia and America, *Beringia*, may have been 1000 miles wide. This corridor, most experts believe, provided the pathway used by early humans to enter a new world.

These people, known as Paleo-Indians, were nomads and predators. With stone-tipped spears, they hunted mastodons, woolly mammoths, giant beavers, giant sloths, and bighorn bison, as well as many smaller animals. The mammals led prehistoric men and women to America up to 30,000 or more years ago. For generations, these humans roamed Alaska in small bands, gathering seeds and berries when not hunting the big game or attacking and killing one another.

Eventually, corridors opened through the Rocky Mountains as the ice started to recede. The migratory cycle began again. Humans and animals trekked southward and eastward, reaching the bottom of South America and the east coast of North America by about 8000 B.C. It had been a long journey, covering thousands of miles, and in the process Paleo-Indians had become Native Americans.

A Diversity of Cultures

As these first Americans fanned out over two continents, they improved their weapons by flaking and crafting such hard quartz stones as flint into sharper spear points, which allowed them to slaughter the big game more easily. Also, with the passing of time, the atmosphere began to warm as the ice age came to an end. Mammoths, mastodons, and other giant mammals did not survive the warming climate and needless overkilling.

The first Americans now faced a serious food crisis. Their solution showed ingenuity. Beginning in Central America between roughly 8000 and 5000 B.C., groups of humans started cultivating plant life as an alternate food source. They soon mastered the basics of agriculture. They raked the earth with stone hoes and

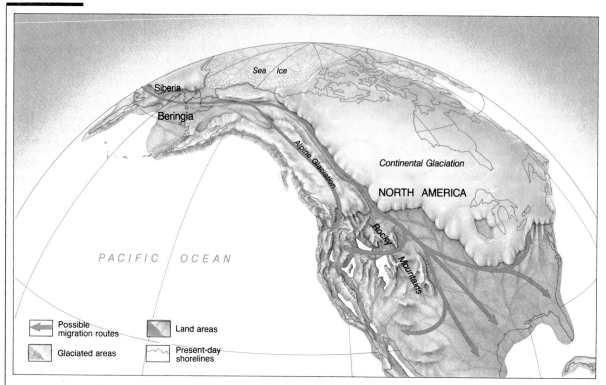

Routes of the First Americans
The Paleo-Indians traveled the land bridge that once linked Asia and America. They then migrated southward and eastward to populate the New World.

planted seeds that produced crops as varied as maize, potatoes, squashes, pumpkins, and tomatoes.

This agricultural revolution profoundly affected Native American life. Those who engaged in farming were no longer as nomadic. They constructed villages and ordered their religious beliefs around such elements of nature as the sun and rain. With dependable food supplies, they had more children, resulting in a population explosion. Work roles became differentiated by gender. Men still hunted and fished for game, but they also prepared the fields for crops. When not caring for children, women did the planting, weeding, and harvesting.

Ultimately out of these agriculturally oriented cultures evolved complex Native American societies, the most sophisticated of which appeared in Central America and the Ohio and Mississippi river valleys. Emerging before A.D. 300, the Mayas of Mexico and Guatemala based their civilization on abundant agricultural production. They also built elaborate cities and temples. Their craft workers produced jewelry of gold and silver, and their merchants developed extensive trading networks. Their intellectuals devised forms of hieroglyphic writing, mathematical systems, and several calendars, one of which was the most accurate in the world at that time.

Although their society was highly stratified with powerful kings and priests ruling over the ordinary citizens, the Mayas did not develop a warrior class. After A.D. 1000 warlike peoples from the north began to conquer their cities. First came the Toltecs, then the Aztecs. The Aztecs called their principal city Tenochtitlán (the site of present-day Mexico City). At its zenith just before the Spanish conquistadores appeared in 1519, Tenochtitlán contained a population of 300,000, making it one of the largest cities in the world at that time. Although imitators of Mayan culture, the Aztecs brutally extracted tribute, both in wealth and lives, from subject tribes. Their priests reveled in human sacrifice, since Huitzilopochtli, the Aztec war god, voraciously craved human hearts. At one temple dedication, Aztec priests sacrificed some 20,000 subject peoples. Not surprisingly, these tribes hated their oppressors. Many later cooperated with the Spanish in destroying the Aztecs.

Other mighty civilizations also emerged, such as the Incas of Peru, who came into prominence after A.D. 1100. Settling in the Andes Mountains, the Incas developed a sophisticated food supply network. They trained all young males as warriors to protect the empire and their kings, whom they thought of as gods and to whom all riches belonged. The Incas were even wealthier than the Aztecs, and they particularly prized gold and silver, which they mined in huge quantities—and which made them a special target for Spanish conquerors.

In North America the Mound Builders (Adena and Hopewell peoples) appeared in the

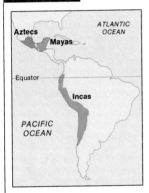

The Aztecs, Mayas, and Incas evolved from simpler agriculturally based groups to become politically and socially complex civilizations.

The Aztecs, Mayas, and Incas

Tlaloc (above), the Aztec rain god, represented fertility and emphasized the importance of water and moisture as a basis for agricultural abundance. The mural at the left depicts the many facets of Mayan civilization. Their culture revolved around agricultural production, elaborate architecture, jewelry making, and complex trade networks.

The Great Serpent Mound, which is in the shape of a snake almost a quarter-mile long, is one of the most lasting legacies of the Adena and Hopewell cultures.

Ohio River valley around 1000 B.C. and lasted until A.D. 700. These natives hunted and gathered food, but they obtained most of their diet from agriculture. They also raised such crops as tobacco for ceremonial functions. Their merchants traded far and wide. Fascinated with death, they built elaborate burial sites, such as the Great Serpent Mound in Ohio. In time they gave way to the Temple Mound Builders (Mississippian peoples), who were even more sedentary and agriculturally minded. They too were great traders, and they constructed large cities, including a huge site near Cahokia, Illinois, where as many as 75,000 people lived amid 85 large temple mounds, the most prominent of which had a base larger than the Great Pyramid of the pharaoh Khufu in Egypt (built around 2600 B.C.).

For unknown reasons the Mississippian culture broke apart before European contact. Remnant groups may have included the Choctaws and Creeks of Mississippi and Alabama, as well as the Natchez Indians. In the rigidly stratified Natchez society the Great Sun was the all-powerful chief, and he ruled over nobles and commoners, the latter bearing the unpleasant name of "stinkards." As with their Mississippian predecessors, when important individuals died, others gave up their lives so that central figures would have company as they passed into eternity. All but exterminated by the French in the 1730s, the Natchez were the last of the Mound Builders in North America.

The Myth of the "Virgin" Land

Beginning with the agricultural revolution, population in the Americas increased rapidly. Estimates vary widely, and one authority has claimed a native populace of up to 120 million persons by the 1490s. Other experts consider this estimate too high, suggesting a figure of 50 to 80 million, with 5 to 8 million inhabitants of North America. Europe's population, by comparison, was roughly 75 million at the time of Columbus, which underscores the mistaken impression among European explorers that America was a "virgin" or "vacant" land.

Over several centuries, moreover, Indian groups developed as many as 2200 different languages, some 550 to 650 of which were in use in Central and North America at the time of Columbian contact. So many languages implied immense cultural diversity. While there were sophisticated civilizations of enormous wealth, most natives belonged to smaller, less complex groups in which families formed into clans—and clans into tribes.

Developing life-styles to fit their environments, native groups varied greatly. Tribes in Oregon and Washington, such as the Chinooks, did some farming, but fishing for salmon was their primary means of subsistence. In the Great Plains region, Indians such as the Arapahos and Pawnees, while wandering less aimlessly than their ancestors, still pursued wild game within more or less fixed hunting zones. Men concentrated on bringing in meat, and women functioned as gatherers of berries and seeds. In the Southwest, Hopi and Zuni tribes relied upon agriculture since edible plant and animal life was scarce in their desert environment. These Indians even practiced irrigation. Perhaps they are best known for their flat-roofed, multitiered villages that the Spanish called *pueblos*.

Eastern Indians on the Eve of Contact

In the East, where English explorers and settlers first made contact with Native Americans, there were dozens of small tribal groups. Southeastern natives, including Cherokees, Chickasaws, Creeks, Choctaws, and Seminoles, were more attuned to agriculture because of lengthy growing seasons. Northeastern tribes, such as the Mahicans and Micmacs, placed more emphasis upon hunting and gathering. This is not to say that southeastern Indians never hunted or that northeastern peoples never planted crops. In each case it was a matter of emphasis.

Eastern Woodland Indians spoke several different languages but held many cultural traits in common. Perhaps linked to memories of the period of overkilling, they treated plant and animal life with respect. Essential to their religious values was the notion of an animate universe. They considered trees, plants, and animals to be spiritually alive (filled with *manitou*). As

such, animals were not inferior to humans. They too organized themselves into nations, and through their "boss spirits," permitted some thinning of their numbers for humans to survive. Boss spirits, however, would never tolerate overkilling. If tribes became gluttonous, animal nations could either leave the region or declare war, causing starvation and death.

Tribal *shamans*, or medicine men, communicated with the boss spirits and prescribed elaborate rules, or taboos, regarding the treatment of plants and animals. Indian parents, having mastered such customs, taught children like Squanto that nature contained the resources of life. Although there was intertribal trading and much gift-giving in pottery, baskets, jewelry, furs, and wampum (conch and clam shells), religious values deterred tribal members from exploiting the landscape for the sake of acquiring great personal wealth.

Eastern Woodland parents introduced their children to many other concepts. There was no

Tribes like the Micmac Indians of eastern Canada were corrupted by the arrival of the Europeans. The Indians began killing animals not only for food but also for fur to supply clothing for markets in Europe. Also, many medicine men lost tribal favor when they failed to combat devastating European diseases.

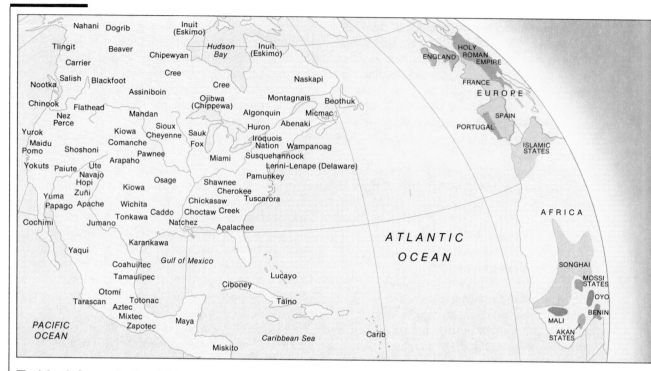

The Atlantic Community, Late 1400s
Indian groups in America and nation-states in Europe made up a triad around the Atlantic Ocean.

individual ownership of land. Tribal boundaries consisted of geographic locales large enough to provide for basic food supplies. Although individual dignity did matter, cooperation with tribal members rather than individual competitiveness was the essential ideal, even in sports. Eastern Woodland tribes enjoyed squaring off with one another in lacrosse matches, archery contests, and foot races. Betting and bragging occurred regularly, as did serious injuries in the heat of competition, but it was all group-oriented. Individuals did not enter events for personal glory, rather to bring accolades to their tribes.

Sports and the refinement of athletic skills also represented useful training for war. Intertribal warfare was sporadic and resulted from any number of factors, such as competition over valued hunting grounds. Skirmishes and the taking of a few lives by roving bands of warriors usually ended the conflict, but not necessarily the ill will, especially among different language groups. Festering tensions and language barriers worked against intertribal cooperation in repelling the Europeans.

Even though males served as warriors, they did not always control tribal decision making. Among the powerful Five Nations of Iroquois (Mohawks, Oneidas, Onondagas, Cayugas, and Senecas) in central New York, tribal organization was matrilineal. Women headed individual family units that in turn formed into clans. Clan leaders were also women, and they decided which males would sit on tribal councils that considered policies regarding diplomacy and war. Women held the power of removal as well, so males had no choice but to respect the authority of female clan heads. Among other Eastern Woodland Indians, women occasionally served as tribal *sachems* (chiefs), much to the shock of Europeans.

When European fishermen and explorers started making contact, there were 500,000 to 800,000 Indians inhabiting the region between the North Atlantic coastline and the Appalachian Mountains. The Europeans, in a pattern that was essentially the same throughout the Americas, were initially curious as well as fearful, but these feelings soon gave way to expressions of contempt. Judging all people by European standards, they regarded the Indians as inferior. Native Americans looked and dressed differently. Their religious conceptions did not conform to European forms of Christianity. The men seemed lazy since women did the bulk of the farming, and there was no consuming drive to acquire personal wealth, leaving the mistaken impression of much "want in a land of plenty," as one historian has summarized European perceptions.

To make matters worse, the natives, like those of Squanto's Patuxet tribe, quickly began to die in huge numbers, which further confirmed European perceptions that Indian peoples were inferior rather than merely different. These native "savages" were blocking the path of a more advanced civilization desirous of expansion, or so Europeans argued. Thus commenced what many historians have come to call the "invasion" of America.

PREPARING EUROPE FOR WESTWARD EXPANSION

Nearly 500 years before Columbus's first westward voyage, Europeans made their first known contacts with North America. Around A.D. 1000, the Vikings (Scandinavians) explored barren regions of the North Atlantic. Eric the Red led an expedition of Vikings to Greenland, and one of his sons, Leif Ericson, continued exploring south and westward, stopping at Baffin Island, Labrador, and Newfoundland (described as *Vinland*). There were some settlement attempts, but they did not survive. The

Vinland
Leif Ericson made contact with North America almost 500 years before Columbus's first westward voyage, but he left no permanent impact.

Viking voyages had no long-term impact because Europe was not yet ripe for westward expansion.

Changing Population Pressures

Most Europeans of the Middle Ages (approximately A.D. 500–1400) lived short, demanding lives. Most tilled the soil as peasants, owing allegiance to manor lords and eking out meager subsistences. Their crops, grown on overworked soil, were not nutritious. Because they rarely ate fruits, they suffered from constipation and rickets among other diseases. These peasants worshiped as Roman Catholics, regularly attending church services that emphasized the importance of preparing for a better life after death. In the meantime the dominant concern was to survive long enough to help the next generation begin the cycle anew.

A variety of factors, including rapid population growth, gradually altered the established rhythms of life in the Middle Ages. Between A.D. 1000 and 1350 Europe's population doubled, reaching over 70 million people. Even with improved methods of agricultural production, a new problem—overcrowding on the land—emerged. Overcrowding represents a condition in which too many individuals try to provide for themselves and their families on fixed supplies of farmland. To ease the pressure, manor lords forced some peasants off the land. These dispossessed persons struggled to avoid starvation. Some joined the growing class of beggars, or they became highway bandits. Others moved into the developing towns where they offered their labor for wages of any kind while seeking to acquire craft skills. Only a handful advanced beyond marginal existences.

By 1350 Europe was bulging at the seams, but the knowledge and technology were not yet in place to move some people to other regions. Then, suddenly, a frightening disaster relieved the pressure. Italian merchant ships trading in Muslim ports in the eastern Mediterranean hauled rats as well as cargoes back to their home ports. These rats carried fleas infested with microbes that caused bubonic plague. The plague, or "Black Death," spread mercilessly through a populace already suffering less virulent maladies related to inadequate diet and unclean personal hygiene. When the plague struck the Italian city of Florence in 1348, for example, between half and two-thirds of the population of 85,000 lost their lives. More generally, between 1347 and 1353 about one-third of all Europeans died in a medical calamity not to be outdone until the plague and other killer diseases started wiping out Native Americans.

The unpeopling of Europe caused by the Black Death temporarily eliminated any compelling need to find and inhabit new territories. In another two centuries rapid population growth, overcrowding, and consequent problems of destitution and starvation were again hovering over the European landscape. By this time other factors would facilitate the westward migration of peoples in search of new beginnings, perhaps even prosperity, for themselves and their posterity.

Crusades, Commerce, and the New Learning

Long before the Black Death, Europeans were gathering knowledge about previously unknown peoples and places. The Crusades, designed to oust the Muslim "infidels" from such Christian holy sites as Jerusalem, broadened their horizons. Sanctioned by the Roman Catholic church and begun in 1095, the Crusades lasted for two centuries. Although European warriors failed to break Muslim sovereignty, they did discover that they could carry on trade with the Orient. They learned of spices that would preserve meats over long winters, fruits that would bring greater balance to diets, silk and velvet clothing, hand-crafted rugs, delicate glassware, and dozens of other commodities that would make European lives more comfortable.

Italian merchants, living in independent city-states such as Venice and Genoa, took the lead in developing the Mediterranean trade. Other European cities mushroomed in size at key trading points when Oriental goods started making their way from Italy into Switzerland, France, and Germany. One benefit of this striking increase in commercial activity was to create work for dislocated peasants. Of even more lasting consequence was the rise of great merchants who devoted themselves to securing scarce commodities—and selling them for handsome profits.

The new wealth displayed by the great merchants promoted a pervasive spirit of material acquisition. The merchants, however, did more than merely reinvest profits in additional trading ventures. They also underwrote a resurgence in learning, known as the *Renaissance*. Beginning in Italy, the Renaissance soon captivated much of Continental Europe. There were new probings in all subjects. Learned individuals rediscovered the writings of such ancient scholars as Ptolemy, who had mapped the Earth, and Eratosthenes, who had estimated the circumference of the planet. By the mid-fifteenth century educated Europeans knew the world was not flat. Indeed, early in 1492, just a few months before Columbus sailed, a German geographer, Martin Behaim, constructed a round globe for all to see.

Enhanced geographical knowledge went hand in hand with developments in naval science. Before the fifteenth century, Europeans risked their lives when they did not sail within sight of land. The Muslims provided knowledge about the astrolabe and sextant and their uses as basic navigational instruments. Contact with

Hans Holbein's *Dance of Death* depicts the horror of the Black Death, which killed nearly one-third of all Europeans between 1347 and 1353.

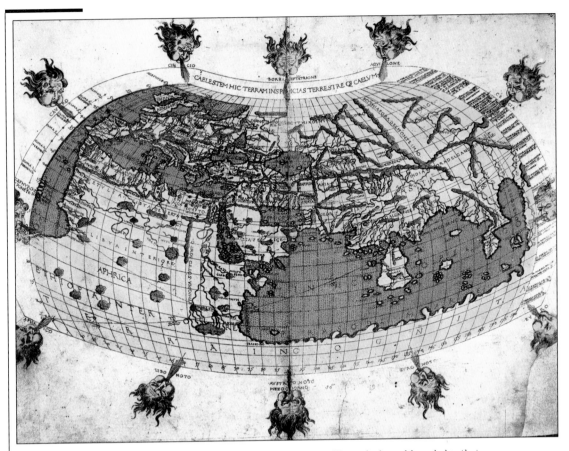

Ptolemy prepared his *Guide to Geography* in the second century A.D. His work showed knowledge that the world was round, but he underestimated the circumference and imagined Asia to be a larger continent than it actually was. Ptolemy's work was widely reprinted in Europe after 1475 as part of the New Learning.

the Arabs also introduced Europeans to more advanced ship and sail designs. Europeans soon abandoned their outmoded square-rigged galleys, which required oarsmen to maneuver them against the wind, in favor of lateen-rigged caravels. These craft were sleeker in design, making them faster. Since their triangular sails could also swivel, the caravels were more mobile. Tacking, or sailing at angles into the wind, was now possible. These breakthroughs heightened prospects for worldwide exploration in the ongoing search for valuable trading commodities.

The adventures of Marco Polo (1254?–1324?) underscored the new learning and exemplified its relationship to commerce and exploration. Late in the thirteenth century, this young Venetian trader traveled throughout the Orient. He recorded his findings and told of unbelievable wealth in Asian kingdoms such as Cathay (China). Around 1450, Johannes Gutenberg, a German printer, perfected movable type, making it possible to reprint limitless copies of manuscripts, heretofore laboriously copied by hand. The first printed edition of Marco Polo's *Journals* appeared in 1477. Merchants and explorers alike, among them Christopher Columbus, read Polo's *Journals*, which spurred them on in the prospect of gaining complete access to Oriental riches.

Nation-States Support the First Explorations

Although there was a new vitality in Europe, it did not pervade all elements of society. Powerful manor lords still controlled the countryside, and they made it difficult for merchants to move goods across their lands, unless traders paid heavy tolls. These nobles also sneered at monarchs wanting to collect taxes. Tapping into peasant manpower, manor lords quite often had stronger armies, leaving royal figures unable to enforce their will. Over time, merchants and monarchs started working together. Using mercantile capital, they formed armies that challenged the nobility.

The process of forming modern nation-states commenced during the fifteenth century. The marriage of Ferdinand of Aragon to Isabella of Castile in 1469 represented the beginnings of national unity in Spain. These joint monarchs hired mercenary soldiers to break the power of defiant nobles. In 1492 they also crushed the Muslims (Moors) inhabiting southern Spain, driving them as well as Jewish inhabitants out of the country. Working closely with the Roman Catholic church, Ferdinand and Isabella used inquisition torture chambers to break the will of others whose loyalty they doubted. By 1500 their subjects no longer owed first allegiance to local manor lords. Whether or not they liked it, they had become full-fledged Spaniards expected to serve their nation with loyalty.

Portugal, France, and England also faced the turbulence of nation-making. John I led the way by consolidating Portugal in the 1380s. Louis XI, known as the "Spider King," was responsible for unifying France in the 1460s at the end of more than 100 years of intermittent but debilitating warfare with England. Two powerful English noble lines, the houses of York and Lancaster, fought endlessly and devastated themselves in the Wars of the Roses (1455–1485). Henry Tudor, who became Henry VII (reigned 1485–1509), arose from the chaos, worked to crush the power of the nobility forever, and initiated a lengthy internal unification process that set the stage for England's westward expansion.

Unification was critical to focusing national efforts on exploration, as demonstrated by Portugal. Secure in his throne, King John I was able to support his son, Prince Henry, called "the Navigator" (1394–1460), in the latter's efforts to learn more about the world. Henry set up a school of navigation at Sagres on the rocky, southwestern coast of Portugal. With official state support, he sent out ships on exploratory missions. When the crews returned, they worked to improve maps, sailing techniques, navigational procedures, and ship designs.

Initially, the emphasis was on learning, but then it shifted to a quest for valuable trade goods as Henry's mariners conquered such islands as the Azores and brought back raw wealth (gold, silver, and ivory) from the west coast of Africa. Trading ties developed with Africans, including the first dealings in black slaves by early modern Europeans. The lure of wealth drove Portuguese ships farther south along the African coast. Bartholomeu Dias made it to the Cape of Good Hope in 1487. Ten years later, Vasco da Gama took a small flotilla around the lower tip of Africa and on to the riches of India.

Besides returning a 400 percent profit, da Gama's expedition led to the development of Portugal's Far Eastern empire. It also proved that the Muslim world, with its heavy trade tolls, could be circumvented in getting European hands on Oriental riches. None of this would have been possible without a unified Portuguese government able to tax the populace and thus sponsor Prince Henry's attempts to probe the boundaries of the unknown.

Ferdinand and Isabella were intensely aware of Portugal's triumphs when a young Genoese mariner, Christopher Columbus (1451–1506), asked them to underwrite his dream of sailing west to reach the Orient. Too consumed with their struggle for internal unification, they refused him, but Columbus persisted. He had already contacted King John II of Portugal, who rebuffed him as "a big talker and boastful." Columbus also turned to France and England but gained no sponsorship. Finally, Queen Isabella reconsidered. She met Columbus's terms, which included 10 percent of all profits from his discoveries, and proclaimed him "Admiral of the Ocean Sea." It was a monumental decision, made possible by Spain's unification.

On August 3, 1492, Columbus and some 90 mariners set sail from Palos, Spain, in the *Niña*, *Pinta*, and *Santa María*. Based on faulty calculations, the admiral estimated Asia to be no more than 4500 miles to the west (the actual distance is closer to 12,000 miles). Some 3000 miles out, his crew became fearful and almost rebelled. They wanted to return home, but he convinced them to keep sailing west. Just two days later, on October 12, they landed on a small island in the Bahamas, which Columbus named San Salvador (holy savior). There they found hospitable natives, the Arawaks, whom Columbus described as "a loving people without covetousness." He called them Indians, a misnomer that stuck, because he believed that he was near Asia (the Indies). Proceeding on, Columbus landed on Cuba, which he thought was Japan, and then on Hispaniola, where he traded for gold-laden native jewelry. In 1493 Columbus and his crew returned home to a hero's welcome and to funding for three more expeditions to America.

EXPLORERS, CONQUERORS, AND THE MAKING OF NEW SPAIN

A fearless explorer, Columbus turned out to be an ineffective administrator and a poor geographer. He ended up in debtors' prison, and to his dying day in 1506 he never admitted to locating a world unknown to Europeans. Geographers named the western continents after another mariner, Amerigo Vespucci, a merchant from Florence who participated in a Portuguese expedition to South America in 1501. In a widely reprinted letter, Vespucci claimed that a new world had been found, and it was his name that caught on.

Columbus's significance lay elsewhere. His 1492 venture garnered enough extractable wealth to excite the Spanish monarchs. They did not care whether Columbus had reached Asia, only that further exploratory voyages might produce unimaginable riches. Because they feared Portuguese interference, Ferdinand and Isabella moved quickly to solidify their interests. They went to Pope Alexander VI, who issued a papal bull, *Inter Caetera*, that divided the unknown world between Portugal and

Columbus first landed on the Bahamian island which he named San Salvador. He described the local natives as peaceful and generous, an image that changed rapidly as conquistadores swept over the native populace in their rush to tap into the riches of the Americas.

Spain. In 1494 they worked out a formal agreement with Portugal in the Treaty of Tordesillas, drawing a line some 1100 miles west of the Cape Verde Islands.

All undiscovered lands to the west of the demarcation line belonged to Spain. Those to the east were Portugal's. Inadvertently, Ferdinand and Isabella had given away the easternmost portion of South America. In 1500 a Portuguese mariner, Pedro Alvares Cabral, laid claim to this territory, which came to be known as Brazil. The Spanish monarchs claimed title to everything else, which of course left nothing for emerging nation-states like France and England.

The Spanish monarchs used their strong army, seasoned by its struggle for unification, as a weapon to conquer the Americas. These *conquistadores* did so with relish. Befitting their crusader's ideology, they agreed to subdue the

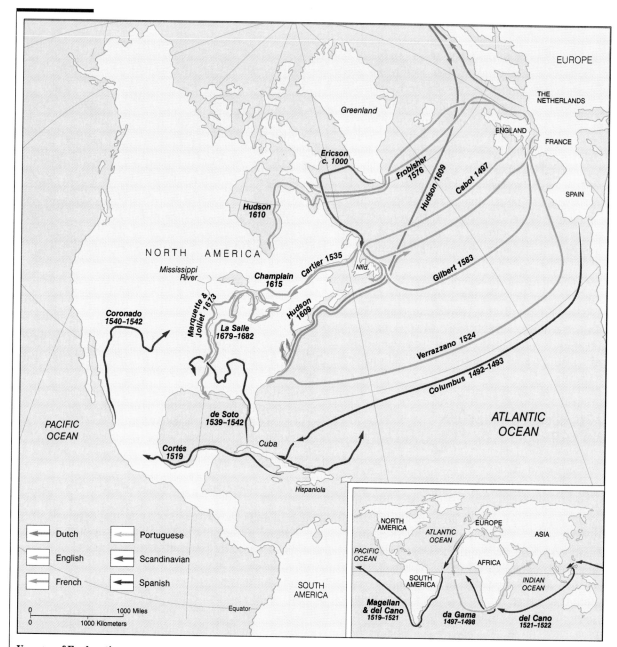

Voyages of Exploration

Except for abortive attempts by Norsemen in the late tenth century, contact between North America and Europe began at the end of the 1400s. In the 1500s settlements were founded by Spain in Mexico and Florida, and in the early 1600s France, England, Sweden, and Holland claimed territory along the Atlantic coast.

natives and, with the support of church leaders, to convert them to Roman Catholicism. Bravery and courage, these warriors believed, would bring distinction to themselves and to their nation. Further, they could gain much personal wealth, even if shared with the Crown. Gold, glory, and the gospel formed a triad of factors motivating the Spanish conquistadores, and their efforts resulted in a far-flung empire known as New Spain.

Conquistadores Overrun Native Americans

Before 1510 the Spanish confined their explorations and settlements to the Caribbean islands. The conquistadores met with Indians, searched diligently for rare metals and spices, and listened to tales of fabulous cities of gold somewhere over the horizon. Most natives remained friendly, but they were hostile in some locales, such as the Lesser Antilles where the cannibalistic Caribs dined on more than one Spanish warrior.

Unwittingly, the conquistadores carried their microbic weapons of retaliation against all Indians—friend and foe alike. Natives on all the islands lacked the antibodies to fend off European diseases. Smallpox, typhoid, diphtheria, the measles, and various plagues and fevers took a rapid toll. In 1492, for example, more than 200,000 Indians inhabited Hispaniola. Just 20 years later, there were fewer than 30,000.

After 1510 the conquistadores moved onto the mainland. Vasco Núñez de Balboa reached Panama in 1513. He organized an exploratory expedition, cut across the isthmus, and became the first European to see the Pacific Ocean, which he dutifully claimed for Spain. The same year Juan Ponce de Léon, governor of Puerto Rico, led a party to Florida in search of gold and a rumored fountain of youth. Although disappointed on both counts, he claimed Florida for Spain.

Then in 1519 Hernando Cortés (1485–1547), a leader of great bravado, mounted his dramatic expedition against the Aztecs. Landing on the Mexican coast with 600 soldiers, his party began a difficult overland march toward Tenochtitlán on the site of modern-day Mexico City. Along the way Cortés won to his side var-

ious tribes subservient to the Aztecs. These natives may have thought him a god. They certainly admired his horses—unknown in America—as well as the armor and weapons of his soldiers. Still, so small an invading force, even if well armed, could never have prevailed over thousands of Aztec warriors, if other factors had not intervened.

Aztec emperor Montezuma II, who feared that Cortés was the old Toltec war god Quetzalcoatl coming back to destroy the Aztecs, tried to keep the Spaniards out of Tenochtitlán. He offered mounds of gold and silver, but this gesture only intensified the conquistadores' greed. They boldly marched into the city and took Montezuma prisoner. The Aztecs finally drove off Cortés's army in 1520, but not before smallpox had broken out. Less than a year later, the Spaniards retook Tenochtitlán and claimed all Aztec wealth and political authority as their prize.

Carried away with success, Cortés's soldiers razed the city and boasted of their great prowess as warriors and the superiority of their weapons and knowledge of warfare. They even claimed that God had willed their victory. But

This Aztec drawing presumably represents Cortés's conquest of Tenochtitlán in 1519–1522.

the germs they brought were the true victors. As a participant wrote, when they reentered the Tenochtitlán, "the streets, squares, houses, and courts were filled with bodies, so that it was almost impossible to pass. Even Cortés was sick from the stench in his nostrils."

It has been estimated that the spread of European germs resulted in 17 major epidemics in the Americas during the sixteenth century—there were 14 in Europe. One of these 17 wreaked havoc among the Aztecs of Tenochtitlán and destroyed their ability to continue effective resistance. As additional epidemics struck, the native population of 20 to 25 million in Mexico declined dramatically—by about 90 percent during the 50 years following the invasion of Cortés's army.

Cortés's stunning victory spurred on many other conquistadores, such as aggressive Francisco Pizarro (1470–1541). With fewer than 200 soldiers, he overwhelmed thousands of Incas in

Peru, seizing the capital city of Cuzco in 1533 after hardly any fighting. Again, diseases stalked wherever Pizarro went. The Incan rulers, paralyzed by fear, provided little leadership in fending off the Spanish and their powerful germ allies. Pizarro showed no mercy; he executed the great chief Atahualpa and proclaimed Spain's sovereignty. By the 1550s the Spanish had conquered much of the rest of South America.

To the north, various expeditions scoured the landscape but found nothing comparable to the wealth of the Aztecs and Incas. Four hundred men under Pánfilo de Narváez began a disastrous adventure in 1528. They landed in Florida and searched the Gulf Coast region before being shipwrecked in Texas. Only four men survived, and one of whom, Cabeza de Vaca, wrote a tract telling of seven great cities laden with gold. Vaca's writings stimulated Hernando de Soto and 600 others, beginning in 1539, to investigate the lower Mississippi River valley. In 1540 another party under Francisco Vásquez de Coronado began exploring parts of New Mexico, Texas, Oklahoma, and Kansas. They were the first Europeans to see the Grand Canyon. During 1542–1543 mariners under João Rodrigues Cabrilho sailed along the California coast as far north as Oregon. None of these groups ever located the fabled cities, but they advanced geographic knowledge of North America while claiming everything they came in contact with for Spain.

Constructing the Spanish Empire

To keep out intruders and to maintain order in New Spain, the Spanish Crown set up two home-based administrative agencies in Madrid. The House of Trade formulated economic policies and provided for annual convoys of galleons, called plate fleets, to haul American booty back to Spain. The Council for the Indies controlled all political matters in what became an autocratic, rigidly managed empire for the exclusive benefit of the parent state.

The Council for the Indies ruled through viceroys that headed four regional areas of administration. Viceroys, in turn, consulted with *audiencias* (appointed councils) on matters of local concern, but there were no popularly

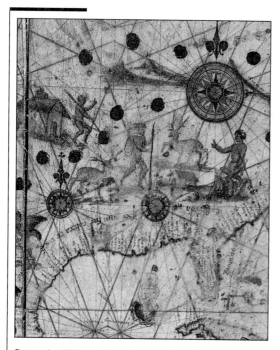

Drawn in 1551, this Spanish map shows that the unknown interior of America was filled with Indians, birds, and deer. More details were filled in as various explorations continued.

based representative assemblies. Normally, only pure-blooded Spaniards could influence decision making—and only if they had ties to councilors or viceroys. Those who questioned their political superiors soon learned there was little tolerance for divergent opinions.

During the sixteenth century about 200,000 Spaniards, a modest number, migrated to the Americas. There was plenty of work at home, and Spain's population was in decline, reflecting the government's constant warfare in Europe. Most migrants were young males looking for adventure and material riches. They did not find much of either, but some became wealthy as manor holders, ranchers, miners, and government officials.

From the very outset, Spanish settlers complained about a shortage of laborers. One solution was the *encomienda* system, initially approved by the Crown to reward conquistadores for outstanding service. Favored warriors and settlers received land titles to Indian villages and the surrounding countryside. As *encomenderos*, or landlords, they agreed to educate the natives under their jurisdiction and to guarantee instruction in the Roman Catholic faith. In return, the landlords gained control of the labor of whole villages of Indians, and they were to receive portions of annual crops and other forms of tribute in recognition of their efforts to "civilize" the native populace.

There were serious problems with the *encomienda* system. Landlords regularly abused the Indians, treating them like slave property. They maimed or put troublemakers to death and bought and sold many others as if they were commodities. There was so much exploitation and death that one Dominican priest, Bartolomé de Las Casas (1474–1566), later a bishop in southern Mexico, repeatedly begged officials in Madrid to stop such barbarities.

In 1542 the Crown settled the issue by outlawing both the *encomienda* system and the enslavement of Indians. This ruling did not change matters that much. Governing officials continued to award pure-blooded Spaniards vast landed estates (*haciendas*), on which Indians lived in a state of peonage, cultivating the soil and sharing their crops with their landlords (*hacendados*).

Since the native populace also kept dying off from contact with European diseases, a second solution to the labor problem was to import Africans. In 1501 the Crown authorized the first shipment of slaves to the Caribbean islands, a small beginning to what became a vast, forced migration of some 10 million human beings to the Americas.

Slavery as it developed in New Spain was harsh. *Hacienda* owners and mine operators wanted only young males who could literally be worked to death, then replaced by new shiploads of Africans. On the other hand, Spanish law and Roman Catholic doctrine restrained some brutality. The Church believed that all souls should be saved, and it recognized marriage as a sacrament, meaning that slaves could wed and aspire to family life. Spanish law even permitted slaves to purchase their freedom. Such allowances were well beyond those made in future English-speaking colonies, and many blacks, particularly those who became artisans and house servants in the cities, did gain their independence.

Also easing slavery's harsh realities was the matter of skin color gradation: The lighter the skin, the greater the privileges. Pure-blooded natives of Spain (*peninsulares*) were at the apex of society. Next came the creoles (*criollos*), or whites born in New Spain. Since so many of the first Spanish migrants were males, they often intermarried with Indians, their children forming the *mestizo* class; or they intermarried with Africans, their children making up the *mulatto* class. The mixture of skin colors in New Spain helped Africans escape some of the racial contempt experienced by blacks in English North America, where there was less skin color variation because of legal restrictions against racial intermarriage.

Success Breeds Envy and Contempt

Still, most slaves and Indians lived in privation at the bottom of society. Many church officials, as suggested by the pleas of Las Casas, worked to ease their burdens. Las Casas himself even went so far as to denounce the enslavement of Africans; but the Crown ignored him, realizing that without slavery there would be fewer shipments of gold, silver, and other valuable commodities back to Spain.

As Spanish authority spread north into areas like New Mexico, Arizona, and California, Franciscan, Dominican, and Jesuit friars opened missions and offered protection to natives who would accept Roman Catholic beliefs. Quite often local Indians simply incorporated Catholic doctrines into their own belief systems. When in the late 1660s and early 1670s a prolonged drought followed by a devastating epidemic ravaged Pueblos living in the upper Rio Grande valley of New Mexico, these natives openly questioned their new Catholic faith—and conquering masters.

Spanish friars and magistrates reacted harshly and imprisoned some of the leading dissidents. The Pueblos eventually rallied around a native spiritual leader named Popé. In 1680 they rose in rebellion and killed or drove some 2500 Spanish inhabitants out of New Mexico. By 1700 persistent Spanish warriors had reconquered the region, maiming and killing hundreds of Pueblos in the process. With their numbers already in rapid decline, the Pueblos never again seriously challenged what seemed like the ever-expanding reach of Spanish authority.

As it took shape, then, the Spanish empire was more brutal than tolerant and contained many sharp contrasts. The construction of European-like cathedrals and founding of great universities could not cover over the terrible price in native lives lost, the endemic poverty of surviving Indian and *mestizo* villagers on *haciendas*, or the brutal treatment of slaves in gold and silver mines. These contrasts reflected the acquisitive beginnings of New Spain, which operated first and foremost as a treasure chest for the monarchs back in Madrid.

The flow of wealth made Spain the most powerful—and envied—nation in Europe during the sixteenth century. Such success also became a source of contempt. When Las Casas, for example, published *A Very Brief Relation of the Destruction of the Indies* (1552), he described the Indians as "patient, meek, and peaceful . . . lambs" whom bloodthirsty conquistadores had "cruelly and inhumanely butchered." Las Casas's listing of atrocities became the basis of the "Black Legend," a tale that other Europeans started employing as a rationale for challenging Spain's New World supremacy. They promised to treat Native Americans more humanely, but in reality their primary motivation was to garner a share of America's riches for themselves.

CHALLENGERS FOR NORTH AMERICA: FRANCE AND ENGLAND

When Henry VII of England realized how successful Columbus had been, he chose to ignore the Treaty of Tordesillas and underwrote another Italian explorer, Giovanni Caboto (John Cabot), to seek Cathay on behalf of the Tudor monarchy. Cabot's was the first exploratory expedition to touch North America since the Viking voyages. He landed on Newfoundland and Cape Breton Island in 1497. A second expedition in 1498 ended in disaster when Cabot was lost at sea. Still, his voyages served as the basis for English claims to North America.

Soon France joined the exploration race. In 1524 King Francis I authorized yet another Italian mariner, Giovanni da Verrazzano, to sail westward. He tracked along the American coast from North Carolina to Maine. Unfortunately, during another voyage in 1528 he died somewhere in the Lesser Antilles where either Spaniards hanged him as an intruder or Caribs dined on his carcass. More important for later French claims, Jacques Cartier mounted three expeditions to the St. Lawrence River area, beginning in 1534. He scouted as far inland as modern-day Quebec and Montreal. Cartier even started a colony in 1541–1542, but there was too much internal turmoil in France to sustain support for trading stations or permanent settlements.

Verrazzano and Cartier were among the first to show interest in finding an all-water route—the "Northwest Passage"—through North America to the Orient. This was a response to the epic voyage of Ferdinand Magellan (1519–1522) under the Spanish flag. Magellan's party circumnavigated the globe by sailing around the southern tip of South America and proved, once and for all, that the world was round and that there was vast ocean space between America and Asia. Searching for the Northwest Passage was a means of avoiding New Spain while gaining access to Oriental wealth, since no one, as yet, had found readily extractable riches in North America. It was also a way of dismissing the worldwide ambitions of Portugal and Spain, particularly after 1529 when these two powers extended the demarcation line down through the Pacific Ocean.

The Protestant Reformation Stirs Deep Tensions

Throughout the sixteenth century, the monarchs of England and France did not directly challenge Spain's supremacy in the Americas. There were too many problems at home, such as those related to religious turmoil. The Protestant Reformation shattered the unity of the Roman Catholic church, convulsed Europe, and provoked bloody wars. At the same time, the Reformation helped stimulate many Europeans, experiencing repression at home because of their newfound beliefs, to think about moving and resettling elsewhere. This proved to be particularly true in the case of England.

The Roman Catholic church was the most powerful institution in medieval Europe. When occasional dissenters emerged, they were invariably burned at the stake, unless they publicly recanted their heretical views. Then in 1517, Martin Luther (1483–1546), an obscure Catholic friar of the Augustinian order and a professor of Scripture at the University of Wittenberg in Germany, tacked "Ninety-Five Theses" on a local church door. Luther was upset with what he thought were a number of unscriptural practices, particularly the selling of "indulgences" in the form of cash payments to the church to make amends for sins. As a form of penance, individuals could purchase indulgences for themselves or for others, such as deceased loved ones to assure quick journeys through purgatory to heaven.

Luther found no biblical basis for indulgences. He could not understand why the church, which he described as "wealthiest of the wealthy," wanted money from hard-pressed peasants to help complete such building projects as St. Peter's Basilica in Rome. He also despised agents who were selling indulgences with various clever sayings, including "As soon as coin in the coffer rings, the soul from purgatory springs." Luther had agonized for years over the ways to earn God's grace, and he had concluded that faith was all that mattered, not ritual or good works. The papacy demanded that Luther recant his heretical notions, but the determined friar refused, knowing full well his penalty would be his excommunication from the church.

Martin Luther's reforms spread quickly among Europeans who were resentful of the Roman Catholic church's power. His reforms resulted in the Protestant Reformation, which caused political and social upheaval throughout Europe.

Luther's ideas caught on quickly. He insisted that people did not need priests to interpret scriptures for them but should be allowed to read the Bible for themselves in developing their own faith in God. Luther thus advocated a "priesthood of all believers" in comprehending the mysteries of Christianity. By doing so, he was attacking the widespread illiteracy of his era. He envisioned an educated populace capable of improving its lot in life. By the 1550s the doctrines of Lutheranism had taken firm hold in parts of Germany and the Scandinavian countries, often in the wake of enormous social turmoil.

Once underway, the Reformation, as the movement that Luther spawned became known, gained rapid momentum. It also took on many forms. In England politics rather than theology dictated the split with Rome. Henry VIII (reigned 1509–1547) prided himself on his devotion to Catholicism. In 1521 he published a *Defense of the Seven Sacraments*, which castigated Luther for arguing in favor of only two sacraments—baptism and communion. The Pope responded by awarding Henry a new title, "Defender of the Faith." At the same time,

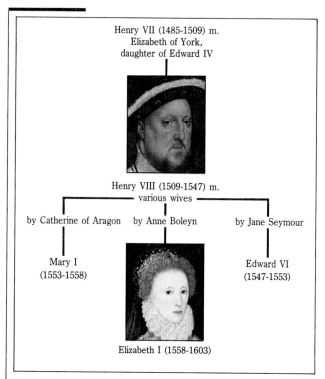

Henry VII (1485-1509) m.
Elizabeth of York,
daughter of Edward IV

Henry VIII (1509-1547) m.
—— various wives ——

by Catherine of Aragon   by Anne Boleyn   by Jane Seymour

Mary I   Edward VI
(1553-1558)   (1547-1553)

Elizabeth I (1558-1603)

Figure 1.1

The Tudor monarchy of England. In England, the Protestant Reformation was rooted in Henry VIII's obsession with securing the Tudor line with a male heir to the throne. When the Pope denied Henry a divorce from his first wife, who had failed to bear a son, Henry severed all ties with Rome. The Tudors reached their height under Elizabeth I, Henry's daughter by his second wife, Anne Boleyn.

Henry worried about not having a male heir. His queen, Catherine of Aragon, daughter of Ferdinand and Isabella, bore him six children; but only one, a daughter named Mary, survived early childhood. Henry still wanted a male heir to assure perpetuation of the Tudor line. In 1527 he asked Pope Clement VII to annul his marriage. When the Pope refused, Henry severed all ties with Rome.

Henry's actions were also spurred by his infatuation with Anne Boleyn, who bore him Elizabeth before being beheaded as an alleged adulteress. Through a series of parliamentary acts, Henry closed monasteries and seized church property. In the 1534 Act of Supremacy he formally repudiated the Pope and declared himself God's regent over England. Henceforth, all subjects would belong to the Anglican (English) Church. The Church of England, unlike the Lutheran church, was similar to its predecessor in doctrine and ritual.

After his death Henry's reformation became a source of internal political chaos. When his daughter Mary I (reigned 1553–1558) came to the throne, she tried to return England to the Roman Catholic faith. Her government persecuted Protestants relentlessly, condemning nearly 300 to fiery deaths at the stake. Her opponents dubbed her "Bloody Mary," and many church leaders fled the land. Some of these "Marian exiles" went to Geneva, Switzerland, to study with John Calvin, whose Biblical ideas formed the basis of the Reformed Protestant tradition.

John Calvin (1509–1564) was a French lawyer who had fled to Switzerland because of his controversial theological ideas. A brilliant and persuasive man, he soon controlled Geneva and ordered life there according to his understanding of scripture. Calvin believed God to be both all-powerful and wrathful. To avoid eternal damnation, it was necessary to gain His grace through a conversion experience denoted by accepting Jesus Christ as one's savior. However, while all had to seek, God had already predestined who would be saved and who would be damned. Since it was difficult to discern God's chosen "saints," Calvin taught that correct moral behavior according to the Bible and outward prosperity—physical and mental as well as material—represented possible signs of divine favor.

The Reformed Protestant tradition is based on the biblical ideas of John Calvin. His followers included many Marian exiles—English Protestants persecuted under the Catholic reign of Mary I. They later returned to England as Puritans, some of whom later settled in North America.

Individuals disenchanted with Catholicism studied Calvin's famous *Institutes of the Christian Religion* (1536). Many, such as the Marian exiles, traveled to Geneva to learn more. Then they returned to their homelands determined to set up godly communities. Their numbers included founders of the German and Dutch Reformed churches, as well as Huguenots who eventually suffered from organized state persecution back in France. John Knox, another disciple of Calvin, established the Presbyterian church in Scotland.

The Marian exiles began reappearing in England after the death of Queen Mary. In time, they developed a large following, many of whom called themselves "Puritans." They wanted to continue Henry's reformation, but now along theological lines. Fiercely dedicated to their beliefs, they had a startling impact on the course of English history, particularly after the reign of Elizabeth I (reigned 1558–1603), when some of them moved to North America and others precipitated a civil war.

Defying the Supremacy of Spain

Spain's success in the Americas in combination with religious disagreements between Catholics and Protestants fostered unending turmoil among sixteenth-century nation-states. Some of the tension related to America, where French, Dutch, and English "sea dogs" attacked Spanish commerce or traded covertly within the empire. Some related to attempted Huguenot, or French Protestant settlements in South Carolina and Florida. Spain, cast as the primary defender of Roman Catholicism, fought back, using wealth extracted from America to pay for military forces capable of protecting its interests.

France, remaining overwhelmingly Roman Catholic, was at first tolerant of the Huguenots. Leaders, however, did encourage Huguenot emigration to America as a way of ridding the realm of these zealous dissenters. During the 1550s the French Crown permitted a party to colonize off the coast of Brazil, but the Portuguese wiped them out. In 1562 another group located in South Carolina, but food shortages destroyed that effort. Yet a third colonization attempt occurred in 1564 when 142 men, women, and children selected northern Florida for their Fort Caroline settlement site.

Spanish officials responded decisively. In 1565 they sent out a small army under Pedro Menéndez de Avilés, who first constructed a Spanish fort at St. Augustine (the beginnings of the oldest European-style city in North America), then turned on the Huguenots. Menéndez's party massacred the Fort Caroline settlers. Just to make sure other outsiders, especially Protestants, understood the danger of locating so close to New Spain, Menéndez ordered his soldiers to hack up the bodies before dumping the remains into a river. The butchery of Menéndez helped curtail sixteenth-century French settlement ventures.

Raids on Spanish treasure ships served as another source of tension. As early as the 1520s French freebooters started attacking Spanish vessels. The most daring of the sea dogs were Englishmen like John Hawkins and Francis Drake. During the 1560s and 1570s Hawkins traded illegally and raided for booty in New Spain. Drake's adventures were even more dramatic. With private financial backing, including funds from Queen Elizabeth, he began a voyage in 1577 that took him around the globe. Drake attacked wherever Spanish ports of call existed before returning home in 1580. Elizabeth gratefully dubbed him a knight, not only for being the first Englishman to circumnavigate the globe but also for securing a 4600 percent profit for investors.

Elizabeth's professions of innocence to the contrary, King Philip II of Spain suspected her of actively supporting the sea dogs, whom he considered piratical scum. Further, he was furious with the English for giving military aid to the Protestant Dutch, who since 1567 had been fighting to free themselves from Spanish rule. Philip so despised Elizabeth that he conspired with her Catholic cousin Mary Stuart, Queen of Scots, to overthrow the English Protestant government. Always wary of plots, Elizabeth had Mary beheaded in 1587, at which point Philip decided to conquer the troublesome English heretics.

Philip and his military advisors pulled together an armada of Spanish vessels. They planned to sail 130 ships, including many hulking galleons, through the English Channel, pick up thousands of Spanish troops fighting the Dutch, and then invade England. The expedition ended in disaster for the Spanish when a host of English ships, most of them smaller but far more maneuverable than the slow-moving galleons, appeared in the channel and offered battle under Drake's command. Then the famous "Protestant Wind" took over and blew the Spanish Armada to bits. The war with Spain did not officially end until 1604, but the destruction of the Armada in 1588 established England's reputation as a naval power. It also demonstrated that little England, heretofore a minor kingdom, could prevail over Europe's most powerful nation, which encouraged some English subjects to press forward in securing territories in North America.

England Prepares for Westward Expansion

Besides the diminished Spanish threat, other factors helped to pave the way for England's westward expansion. None was more important than rapid population growth, which supplied a large pool of potential migrants. During the sixteenth century, England's population doubled in size, reaching 4 million people by the 1590s. Yet opportunities for employment or decent wages lagged behind the population explosion. The phenomenal growth of the woolens industry, for instance, forced peasants from the land as manor lords fenced in their fields to make pastures for sheep. By 1600, there were three times as many sheep as people in England as a result of the "enclosure movement." Meantime, cities such as London exploded in size as displaced persons poured in from the countryside and subsisted as best they could, some by working as day laborers for pitiful wages and others by begging and stealing.

Not only the uprooted peasants faced serious economic difficulties. Everyone confronted the major problem of rapid inflation, a reflection of what has been called the "Price Revolution." Between 1500 and 1600 the cost of goods and services spiraled upward by up to five times. The principal inflationary culprit was an overabundance of precious metal, mostly Spanish silver mined in America (7 million pounds in weight by about 1650) and then pumped into the European economy in exchange for various commodities. The money in circulation expanded more quickly than did the supply of goods or services. As a result, prices jumped dramatically.

In England even farmers owning their own land struggled to make ends meet since the cost of most necessities rose faster than what they received in the marketplace for their agricultural produce. A prolonged decline in real income on top of heavy taxes under the Tudors left many yeoman farmers destitute. In time, the abundant land of America attracted great numbers of England's failing independent farmers and permanently poor (or sturdy beggars).

The presence of so much poverty and suffering became a powerful argument for westward expansion. As the Elizabethan expansionist Richard Hakluyt wrote in his influential *Discourse of Western Planting* (1584), "infinite numbers may be set to work" in America, "to the unburdening of the realm . . . at home." Hakluyt also viewed American settlement as the key to achieving national greatness. Besides putting sturdy beggars and other indigents back to work, colonies could serve as a source of valuable commodities. They would likewise stimulate England's shipbuilding industry. They would help "enlarge the glory of the gospel" by offering the Indians "sincere religion" in the form of instruction from the Church of England. Furthermore, Hakluyt argued, there could never be "humanity, courtesy, and freedom" in America, especially for Native Americans, unless England challenged Spain's tyrannical sway by planting true "liberty" in overseas settlements.

As with other New World colonizers, the English considered their motives to be above reproach on all counts. Certainly Queen Elizabeth recognized the merits of Richard Hakluyt's arguments, especially as they related to building up the power of the realm. On the other hand, she was a tight-fisted Tudor monarch who remained unwilling to plunge vast sums of royal funds into highly speculative New World ventures. She preferred to let her favored courtiers, such as those who were currently subduing Ireland, expend their own capital and energies in searching for riches across the Atlantic Ocean.

JOINING IN THE INVASION OF AMERICA

England's path to America lay through Ireland. Off and on over four centuries there had been sporadic raids on the "wild" Irish, as the English thought of their Gaelic-speaking neighbors. During Elizabeth's reign, these forays became routine. The goal was to establish political control of Ireland. The queen and her court favorites also hoped to set up agricultural colonies because ample food supplies had become a problem at home with the spread of the enclosure movement.

Elizabeth named as governor one of her court favorites, Sir Humphrey Gilbert (1539?–1583), and instructed him to subdue the Irish. Gilbert did so with a vengeance, operating as if the only good Irish subject was one whose head had been cut off. The Irish, a million strong, fought back relentlessly, causing the English "plantations" there to exist precariously as military outposts in an alien environment.

For Elizabethan courtiers, Ireland became a laboratory for learning how to crush one's adversaries. Assumptions of cultural superiority abetted the onslaught. The English conquerors condemned the Irish, who were Roman Catholics, as religious heathens. They faulted them for using the land improperly, since the Irish were not sedentary farmers but people of migratory habits who tilled the soil only when they needed food. England's expansionists held these same attitudes when they began American settlements. This time, though, the Indians would be the wild, unkempt, "savage" peoples in need of subjugation or eradication.

The Roanoke Disaster

Sir Humphrey Gilbert was as intolerant and contemptuous of the Spanish as he was of the Irish. It bothered him that Spain claimed every-thing in America. He dreamed of finding the Northwest Passage to facilitate a flow of Oriental riches back to England, and he was willing to risk his personal fortune in the quest. Gilbert had other visions as well, including the effective occupation of North America and the founding of American colonies. He appealed to Elizabeth for exclusive rights to carry out his plans, and she acceded in 1578.

Sir Humphrey Gilbert's patent for founding the North American colonies established important guidelines for England's westward expansion.

Gilbert's patent represented an important statement with respect to future guidelines for England's westward expansion. On the monarch's authority, he could occupy "heathen and barbarous lands . . . not actually possessed of any Christian prince or people." He would share in profits from extractable wealth, as would the Crown. Even more significant, prospective settlers would be assured the same rights of Englishmen "as if they were born and personally resident" at home. Not guaranteeing fundamental liberties would have inhibited the development of colonies.

Gilbert did not live to see his dreams fulfilled. He disappeared in a North Atlantic storm after searching for the Northwest Passage. In 1584 his half-brother, Sir Walter Raleigh (1552?–1618), requested permission to carry on Gilbert's work. Elizabeth agreed, and Raleigh took quick action. He sent out a reconnoitering party, which explored the North Carolina coast and surveyed Roanoke Island. Then in 1585 he sponsored an expedition of 600 men, many of them veterans of the Irish wars. After some raiding for booty in New Spain, Raleigh's adventurers sailed north and dropped off 107 men under Governor Ralph Lane at the chosen site.

Lane's party found the local Croatian and Roanoke Indians to be friendly. Then diseases struck. "That people," an eyewitness exclaimed,

(Text continues on p. 28)

INDIAN SCALPING AND EUROPEAN WAR DOGS

When Native Americans and Europeans first came into contact, each seemed genuinely curious about the other. Curiosity, however, soon turned to mistrust, and mistrust to a state of unending warfare. Both sides employed "the tactics of remorseless terrorism" in their combat, as one student of early white-Indian relations has written, because both were fighting for control of the landscape—the Indians to retain their ancient tribal homes and the Europeans to inhabit the same.

In their life-and-death struggle, Europeans and Indians drew upon long-accepted styles of waging combat. Neither showed much mercy toward the other. Europeans rationalized their acts of butchery by claiming that they were dealing with "savages" who were at best "inhumanely cruel" and at worst "carnivorous beasts of the forest." Because of language barriers, the thoughts of Native Americans are not known, but they learned to fear

and hate the invaders from across the ocean, and they too fought with a vengeance, although at times with more mercy than Europeans.

Long before the English first made contact, Eastern Woodland Indians regularly engaged in small-scale, intertribal wars. Their weapons included bows and arrows, knives, tomahawks, spears, and clubs. War parties did not attack in battle formations but used the forest as their cover as they ambushed enemies in surprise, guerrilla-like raids. Employing hit-and-run tactics, intertribal combat rarely resulted in much bloodshed, since battles seldom lasted for more than a few minutes before attacking warriors melted back into the forest.

When possible, Indian war parties celebrated their victories by the taking of enemy scalps, which for them were war trophies filled with religious meaning. Native Americans believed that the piece of scalp and hair sliced from an enemy's head

contained the victim's living spirit, which now belonged to the holder of the scalp. To take a scalp, then, was to gain control over that person's spirit (*manitou*). Even if victims survived scalping, which happened on occasion, they were spiritually dead, since they no longer possessed the essence of human life.

Because of their spiritual meaning and power, scalps were treated with great respect. Indians decorated them with jewelry and paint, and warriors kept them on display, even strapping them on their belts as symbols of individual prowess. In other instances warriors gave scalps to families who had lost relatives in battle. Since they contained life, scalps took the place of deceased tribal members.

When Europeans first saw scalps, they did not know what to think. They certainly attached no spiritual significance to them. Frenchman Jacques Cartier, exploring along the St. Lawrence River in 1535, wrote about local Indians who showed him "the skins of five men's heads, stretched on hoops, like parchment." The local chief explained that the scalps were from Micmacs living to "the south, who waged war continually against his people." Just five years later in west Florida, natives killed two Spanish conquistadores exploring with Hernando de Soto. The Indians then "removed" the "head" of one victim, "or rather all around his skull—it is unknown with what skill they removed it with great ease—and carried it off as evidence of their deed."

Europeans quickly concluded that scalping was another barbarous practice of "savage" Native Americans. Also frightening was the way in which Indians conducted combat. They would not stand and fight in "civilized" fashion, holding to linear formations as Europeans did. Rather "they are always running and traversing from one place to another," complained de Soto, making it impossible for musket-wielding Europeans to shoot them down. Worse yet, an expert Indian bowman could easily "discharge three or four arrows" with great accuracy by the time musketeers went through the elaborate steps of preparing their cumbersome weapons for firing. This made combat with Native Americans particularly dangerous because, as de Soto concluded, an Indian bowman "seldom misses what he shoots at."

The Indian style of fighting caused a stream of negative commentary from the first European New World adventurers. Natives did not fight fairly, they wrote, but used "cunning tricks" and "slippery designs" to defeat their adversaries. Rather than engaging in manly combat, they were "as greedy after their prey as a wolf," wanting above all else to mutilate their opponents by taking their scalps. The only

effective way to deal with Indian tactics, reasoned these early adventurers, was to counter them with the most brutal forms of corporal punishment then known—and commonly used—in Europe.

In times of combat the Europeans treated Indians as if they were criminals. This meant that natives, in various combinations, would be hanged, drawn and quartered, disemboweled, and like the "savage" and "wild" Irish, beheaded. Captain Miles Standish, charged with protecting the Pilgrims, killed one troublesome Indian and then carried his head back to Plymouth where he had it publicly displayed. When the Dutch in New Netherland went to war with local natives in the 1640s, they regularly beheaded their opponents and had their "gory heads . . . laid in the streets of New Amsterdam, where the governor's mother kicked them like footballs."

Such wanton cruelty, when measured by modern standards, recently resulted in claims from some students of Native American history that Indians, before making contact with Europeans, did not scalp their enemies. Scalping, they claimed, was modeled on beheading but was a more efficient means of gaining war trophies for highly mobile Indian warriors not wanting to carry the extra weight of human heads.

This line of reasoning, which sought to demonstrate the "barbarous" influence of "civilized" Europeans expanding westward, has been thoroughly refuted. Among other forms of evidence, Indian cultural traditions and the astonishment of explorers who first saw scalps support the conclusion that Europeans learned about scalping from Indians and soon incorporated the practice into their arsenal of punishments.

In at least one area, however, European adventurers reached beyond accepted methods for exacting terror, pain, and death. The Spanish conquistadores used war dogs to maim and kill their victims. The English, who during the sixteenth century reveled in horror stories about Spanish New World barbarities (the so-called "Black Legend"), thought of war dogs as a new low point in human warfare. Yet within a few years of founding their first settlements, the English likewise were training and unleashing war dogs on Native Americans.

Apparently the favored breed was the English Mastiff. These were huge, ugly dogs, weighing up to 150 pounds and naturally protective of their masters. In sixteenth-century England their owners trained them to "bait the bear, to bait the bull and other such like cruel and bloody beasts." The next logical step was to turn these dogs loose on the "heavy beast" in America. In retaliation for Opechancanough's 1622 massacre of Virginians, surviving settlers used dogs, presumably mastiffs, to track down and kill local Indians. War dogs participated in the slaughter of Pequot Indians in Connecticut during the 1630s and would perform similar duty throughout the colonial period.

If prospects of facing the scalping knife filled European New World settlers with horror, war dogs, whether on guard duty or on the attack, represented an "extreme terror to the Indians," as one New England minister wrote in the early eighteenth century. This clergyman wanted yet more dogs "trained up to hunt Indians as they do the bear." He understood the nature of "total war" between whites and Indians in the bloody contest for the Americas, and he wanted to survive.

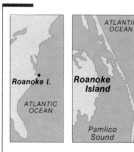

Roanoke Island

The fate of the lost colony of Roanoke Island may never be known. The settlement was too small and underfinanced to survive disease, war, and the Indians.

"began to die very fast, and many in short space." In the spring of 1586 a local chief, Wingina, probably trying to get his tribe away from an illness "so strange that they neither knew what it was, nor how to cure it," moved inland. Ralph Lane went after the natives and ordered an attack, during which one of his men beheaded Wingina in the tradition of dealing with the "wild" Irish. Fortunately for Lane, Sir Francis Drake, fresh from completing a raiding expedition against New Spain, appeared and carried the English party away before the Indians counterattacked.

Raleigh persisted, and he decided to send out families in 1587, with John White, a capable, gentle person, as their governor. White had been on the 1585 expedition. Besides preparing many famous drawings of native life in the Roanoke area, he had spoken out against butchering the Indians. White and the other 114 settlers arrived on Roanoke Island during late July. In mid-August his daughter Elinor gave birth to Virginia Dare, the first English subject born in America. A few days later, White sailed back to England to obtain additional supplies. The outbreak of war with Spain delayed his return, and he did not get back to Roanoke until 1590. Nothing was left, except the word CROATOAN carved on a tree.

What happened to the lost colony will never be known. No European ever saw the settlers again. Local Indians either killed or absorbed them into their tribes. As for Raleigh, he had ruined himself financially, proving that funding overseas ventures lay beyond the means of any one person. All that was left for him was a patent that he turned over to others during the 1590s, a sense that colonizing in America was a hazardous undertaking at best, and a name, Virginia, which Raleigh had offered in thanks to his patron, Elizabeth, the Virgin Queen.

John White captured the life-style of the natives of Roanoke Island in his famous drawings.

Merchant Capitalists Sponsor the Founding of Virginia

A few sixteenth-century English subjects did prosper in the wake of economic dislocation and spiraling inflation. Among these fortunate few were manufacturers of woolen goods and merchants who made all of Europe a marketplace for English cloth. With their profits, these gentlemen of capital gained social respectability. Many purchased landed estates, and some married into England's titled nobility. Now members of the gentry class, they started pooling their capital and sponsoring risky overseas business ventures by investing in *joint-stock* trading companies.

In 1555 the Crown chartered the Muscovy Company, giving that business venture the exclusive right to develop England's trade with Russia. Having a monopoly made the enterprise more attractive to potential stockholders, who could invest according to their personal willingness to take risks. While they hoped to make handsome profits, they could lose no more than they could afford to invest. Meantime, the company would have a large pool of working capital to underwrite its business activities. Queen Elizabeth liked this model of business organization because private capital rather than royal assets would be marshaled to finance England's economic—and eventually political—expansion abroad. The Crown, of course, would share in any profits.

The Muscovy Company was a success, and other joint-stock undertakings followed, such as the East India Company, chartered in 1600 to develop England's Far Eastern interests. Then in 1606 a charter for the Virginia Company received royal approval. Ironically, even though this business enterprise failed its stockholders, company activities produced England's first enduring settlement in North America.

During the 1590s, English courtiers and merchant capitalists did not pick up on Raleigh's failed efforts. The ongoing war with Spain took precedence, and profits came easily from capturing Spanish vessels on the high seas. Once the war ended, influential merchants were anxious to pool their capital, spread the financial risk, and pursue Raleigh's patent. They took their case to the new king, the Stuart monarch James I (reigned 1603–1625), who willingly granted them a generous trading company charter.

Initially, there were two sets of investors in the Virginia Company. The first, a group of London merchants, held Raleigh's patent. They had earned bountiful profits from investing in other joint-stock ventures and were ready to take further risks. Foolishly, they dreamed of heaping piles of gold and silver. More realistically, they

hoped to trade for valuable commodities with the native populace and to plant vineyards and silk-producing mulberry trees. The London merchants had first claim to all land between the Cape Fear River in southern North Carolina and present-day New York City.

In December 1606 they sent out 144 adventurers under Captain Christopher Newport aboard the *Susan Constant*, *Godspeed*, and *Discovery*. The crossing was difficult, and 39 men died. In May 1607 the survivors located on an island some 30 miles up the James River off Chesapeake Bay. They called their settlement, really meant as a trading post, Jamestown.

The second set of investors were from West Country port towns such as Plymouth. In response to bitter complaints over the years about London's dominance of joint-stock ventures, the Virginia Company granted the West Country merchants lands lying between the mouth of the Potomac River and northern Maine. This meant there was an overlapping middle zone that both investor groups could develop, so long as their settlements were at least 100 miles apart.

Conflicting Land Claims

The West Country merchants hoped to reap profits by harvesting America's timber, from fur trading with the natives, and from fishing off the New England coast, which had been going on for over a century. They dispatched a party in 1607, which located at Sagadahoc, Maine, near the mouth of the Kennebec River. These 44 adventurers squabbled incessantly among themselves and did not maintain good relations with the Indians. Those who survived the first winter gave up and returned home in 1608. The Plymouth investors refused to expend more funds, and their patent fell dormant—to be revived at a later date.

As with the Irish invasion, both groups of adventurers came forth in military fashion. They built forts to protect themselves from unfriendly natives and Spanish raiding parties. In its early days, Jamestown functioned as an outpost in another alien environment. The early participants were not settlers. They wanted to get in, gain access to easy forms of wealth, and get out before losing their lives.

Struggling Jamestown Survives

It is amazing that Jamestown lasted at all; Newport's adventurers were miscast for survival in the wilderness. Many were second and third sons of English noblemen. Because of primogeniture and entail (laws that specified that only first-born male heirs could inherit landed estates and family titles), these younger sons had to choose alternate careers. Many became lawyers, clergymen, or high-ranking military officers, but none toiled in the fields, as that was hardly a gentleman's calling. When Jamestown ran short of food, these company adventurers still avoided agricultural work, preferring to search for gold, silver, or the Northwest Passage. Some starved to death as a result.

Besides gentleman-adventurers, other equally ill-prepared individuals, such as valets and footmen, joined the expedition. Their duties extended only to waiting on their aristocratic masters. Then there were goldsmiths and jewelers, plus a collection of ne'er-do-wells who knew no occupation but apparently functioned as soldiers under gentleman officers in dealings with the natives.

The social and economic makeup of these first adventurers suggests that the London investors may have modeled the expedition after the early Spanish conquests—with the idea of forcing the local Indians to become agricultural workers as peons or slaves. As it turned out, the natives supplied food, but even with their assistance, only 38 Englishmen were still alive by the early spring of 1608.

Another problem was the settlement site. Company directors had ordered the adventurers to locate on high ground far enough inland so as to go undetected by the Spanish. Jamestown Island met the second requirement, but it was a low, swampy place lying at a point on the James River where salt and fresh water mingled.

The brackish water was "full of slime and filth," as one observer noted. The water could cause salt poisoning and was also a breeding ground for malaria, typhoid fever, and dysentery.

Several factors saved the Jamestown settlement. The local Indians under Powhatan, an Algonquian-speaking Pamunkey, initially offered sustenance. Powhatan had organized a confederacy of some 30 coastal tribes, numbering 20,000 people, to defend themselves against aggressive interior neighbors. The defensive alliance may also have resulted from a serious population decline because of killer diseases long since introduced into the area by Europeans like those at Roanoke.

Powhatan tried to stay clear of the Jamestown adventurers, but when he was around them, he could not help but notice their large ships, gaudy body armor, and noisy (though less-than-deadly) firearms. He viewed the English as potential allies in warfare with interior tribes, a faulty evaluation but one that kept him from wiping out the weakened adventurers.

At the same time, Company investors in London refused to quit. They kept sending out supplies and adventurers, as many as 800 more young men plus a few women in 1608 and 1609. Upon their arrival, however, many quickly died of such diseases as malaria. Others, so debilitated from illnesses, were unable to work. They became a drain on Jamestown's precarious food supply.

At that time, the dynamic and ruthless local leadership of Captain John Smith (1580?–1631) kept the Jamestown outpost from totally collapsing. Smith, who loved to brag about his far-flung military exploits, had crossed the Atlantic with the original adventurers. Once in Jamestown, he emerged as a virtual dictator. Smith

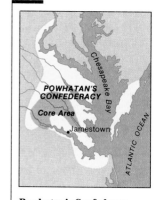

Powhatan's Confederacy
Powhatan's Confederacy, established for defense against aggressive neighbors, consisted of some 30 coastal tribes.

helped save many lives by imposing discipline and forcing everyone—gentleman or servant, sick or well—to adhere to one rule: "He who works not, eats not."

In October 1609 Smith returned to England after suffering severe burns from an accidental explosion of gunpowder. Lacking authoritarian leadership, the adventurers experienced a tragic "starving time" during the winter of 1609–1610. Hundreds died as food supplies, described as "moldy, rotten, full of cobwebs and maggots," gave out. Only about 60 survived by eating everything from rats to snakes, and there was even an alleged instance of cannibalism. One man completely lost his mind; he murdered his wife, then "powdered [salted] her up to eat her, for which he was burned" at the stake.

Smith's presence might not have averted the disaster. Too often, he, like the other early adventurers, had treated the Indians with contempt. Bad relations caused Powhatan to cut off food supplies. For some reason, however, the native chief did not seize the opportunity to wipe out Jamestown. Perhaps still hoping for an alliance, he simply allowed the feeble English to die on their own.

Back in England, Virginia Company stockholders refused to concede defeat. By 1610 they realized that mineral wealth was an illusion but still they sent out more people. One of them, John Rolfe, experimented with local tobacco plants, which produced a harsh-tasting crop. Rolfe, like the company, persisted. He procured some plants from Trinidad in the West Indies and grew a milder, more flavorful leaf. Tobacco soon became Virginia's gold and silver. The colony now had a valuable trading commodity, and settlements quickly spread along the banks of the James River. Englishmen had found an economic reason to stay in the Americas.

Dutch and French Adventurers

In the early 1600s the Spanish contented themselves with drawing wealth from their Caribbean basin empire. They did not challenge various European interlopers seeking to stake North American claims. Ultimately, Dutch settlements in New York were seized by the English, but France's efforts resulted in a Ca-

John Smith, a prime explorer of Virginia, published this map with an accompanying description of the country in 1612.

nadian empire capable of rivaling those of Spain and England.

Once fully liberated from Spanish domination at home, the Dutch grabbed at a portion of North America. In 1609 they sent out an English sea captain, Henry Hudson, to search for the Northwest Passage. He explored Delaware Bay, then the New York waterway that bears his name. Hudson made contact with the Iroquois Indians, probably the Mohawks, and talked of trade in furs. Broad-brimmed beaver hats were the fashion rage in Europe, but fur supplies were giving out. North America could become a new source of pelts, if the natives would cooperate. The Dutch established trading stations on Manhattan Island (later called New Amsterdam) and Albany (Fort Orange) in 1624. The Iroquois did their part in delivering furs, and the colony of New Netherland took hold under the auspices of the Dutch West India Company.

Profits from furs also helped to motivate the French. In 1608 Samuel de Champlain set up an outpost at Quebec on the St. Lawrence River, and he found local Indians ready to trade. Quebec was the base from which New France spread. Yet only after 1663, when the Crown took control of managing the colony, did the

CHRONOLOGY
OF KEY EVENTS

30,000–20,000 B.C. First humans arrive in North America from Asia across what is now the Bering Strait

8000–5000 B.C. Central American Indians begin to practice agriculture

A.D. 300–900 Mayan civilization flourishes in present-day Mexico and Guatemala

c. 900 Toltecs rise to power in the Valley of Mexico and later conquer the Mayas

c. 1000 Vikings led by Leif Ericson reach Labrador and Newfoundland (*Vinland*)

1095 European Christians launch the Crusades to capture the Holy Lands from Muslims

c. 1100 Inca civilization emerges in what is now Peru

1271 Marco Polo begins a 20-year journey to China

1347–1353 "Black Death" kills one-third of Europe's population

1420s Prince Henry the Navigator of Portugal sends mariners to explore Africa's western coast

c. 1450 Johannes Gutenberg, a German printer, develops movable type, the basis of modern printing

1469 Ferdinand and Isabella marry and begin to unify Spain

1492 Columbus makes the first of his voyages of discovery to the Americas

1494 Treaty of Tordesillas divides the known world between Portugal and Spain

1497–1498 John Cabot's voyages to Newfoundland and Cape Breton Island lay the basis for English claims to North America

1501 Spain authorizes the first shipment of African slaves to the Caribbean

1517 Martin Luther's public protests against the sale of indulgences (pardons of punishment in Purgatory) mark the beginning of the Protestant Reformation

1519 Hernando Cortés and 600 Spanish conquistadores begin the conquest of the Aztec empire

1527 Henry VIII of England begins to sever ties with the Roman Catholic church

1531 Francisco Pizarro and 180 Spanish soldiers start the conquest of the Inca empire

1534 Jacques Cartier explores the St. Lawrence River and claims the region for France

1542 Spain outlaws the *encomienda* system and the enslavement of Indians

1585–1587 Sir Walter Raleigh sponsors England's first North American settlements at Roanoke Island in present-day North Carolina

1607 English adventurers establish the first permanent English settlement at Jamestown in present-day Virginia

French population in Canada grow significantly, reaching 10,000 people by the 1680s.

The French Canadians were energetic. Following Champlain's lead, they explored everywhere and claimed everything in sight. They also established harmonious relations with dozens of different Indian tribes. They even joined in native wars as a way of solidifying trading ties. The French, with their small numbers, could not completely impose their cultural values. They did use the natives for their own purposes, but they also showed respect, which paid off handsomely when their many Indian allies willingly fought beside them in a series of imperial wars that beset America beginning in 1689.

CONCLUSION

Except in Canada, the Europeans who explored the Americas and began colonies after 1492 acted as foreign invaders. Although a few were at first curious, they generally viewed the natives as their adversaries, describing them as "worse than those beasts which are of the most wild and savage nature." Judgments of cultural superiority seemed to justify the destruction of Native Americans.

Still, there was a "Columbian exchange" of sorts. The Indians taught the Europeans about tobacco, corn, potatoes, varieties of beans, peanuts, tomatoes, and many other crops then unknown in Europe. In return, Europeans introduced the native populace to wheat, oats, barley, and rice, as well as to grapes for wine and various melons. The Europeans also brought over domesticated animals, including horses, pigs, sheep, goats, and cattle. Horses proved to be important, particularly for Great Plains Indians, who used them in fighting against future generations of white settlers, just as tobacco production in the Chesapeake area had the unintended effect of attracting enough Europeans to end native control of that area.

Perhaps more than anything else, killer diseases served to unbalance the exchange. From the first moments of contact, great civilizations like the Aztecs and more humble groups like Squanto's Patuxets faced devastation. In some cases the Indians who survived, as in New Spain, had to accept the status of peons. Along the Atlantic coastline, survivors were drawn into the European trading network. In exchange for furs, the Indians wanted firearms to kill yet more animals whose pelts could be traded for still more guns and for alcohol to help them forget, even for a moment, what was happening to their way of life in the wake of European westward expansion.

The English would send the most settlers. They left home for various reasons. Some, like the Pilgrims, crossed the Atlantic to avoid further religious persecution. Others, such as the Puritans, sought to build a holy community that would shine as a light upon Europe. Still others, including colonists in the Chesapeake Bay area, desired land for growing tobacco. The latter group wanted laborers to help them raise their crops. Unable to enslave the Indians, they ultimately borrowed from the Spanish model and enslaved Africans. In so doing, they forced blacks to enter their settlements in chains and to become a part of a peopling and unpeopling process that helped to shape the contours of life in colonial America.

SUGGESTIONS FOR FURTHER READING

OVERVIEWS AND SURVEYS

Daniel J. Boorstin, *The Americans: The Colonial Experience* (1958); James A. Henretta and Gregory H. Nobles, *Evolution and Revolution: American Society, 1600–1820* (1987); Alvin M. Josephy, Jr., *The Indian Heritage of America* (1968); Paul R. Lucas, *American Odyssey, 1607–1789* (1984); D. W. Meinig, *The Shaping of America*, Vol. I: *Atlantic America, 1492–1800* (1986); Gary B. Nash, *Red, White, and Black: The Peoples of Early America*, 2d ed. (1982); Jerome R. Reich, *Colonial America*, 2d ed. (1989); Richard C. Simmons, *The American Colonies: From Settlement to Independence* (1976); Clarence L. Ver Steeg, *The Formative Years, 1607–1763* (1964); Wilcomb E. Washburn, *The Indian in America* (1975).

THE FIRST DISCOVERY OF AMERICA

James Axtell, *After Columbus: Essays in the Ethnohistory of Colonial North America* (1988), *The European and the Indian* (1981), and *The Invasion Within: The Contest of Cultures in Colonial North America* (1985); Henry W. Bowden, *American Indians and Christian Missions: Studies in Cultural Conflict* (1981); William Cronon, *Changes in the Land: Indians, Colonists, and the Ecology of New England* (1983); Alfred W. Crosby, *The Columbian Exchange: Biological and Cultural Consequences of 1492* (1972); William N. Denevan, ed., *The Native Population of the Americas in 1492* (1977); Henry F. Dobyns, *Their Number Become Thinned: Native American Population Dynamics in Eastern North America* (1983); Harold E. Driver, *The Indians of North America*, 2d ed. (1969); Brian M. Fagan, *The Great Journey: The Peopling of Ancient America* (1987); John S. Henderson, *The World of the Ancient Maya* (1981); Francis Jennings, *The Invasion of America: Indians, Colonialism, and the Cant of Conquest* (1975), and *The Ambiguous Iroquois Empire* (1984); Alvin M.

Josephy, Jr., ed., *America in 1492* (1992); Yasuhide Kawashima, *Puritan Justice and the Indian* (1986); Shepard Krech, III, ed., *Indians, Animals, and the Fur Trade* (1981); Calvin Martin, *Keepers of the Game: Indian-Animal Relationships and the Fur Trade* (1978), and ed., *The American Indian and the Problem of History* (1987); James H. Merrell, *The Indians' New World: Catawbas and Their Neighbors* (1989); Neal Salisbury, *Manitou and Providence: Indians, Europeans, and New England, 1500–1643* (1982); Bernard Sheehan, *Savagism and Civility: Indians and Englishmen in Colonial Virginia* (1980); Timothy Silver, *A New Face on the Countryside: Indians, Colonists, and Slaves in the South Atlantic Forests, 1500–1800* (1990); Margaret C. Szasz, *Indian Education in the American Colonies, 1607–1783* (1988); Alden T. Vaughan, *The New England Frontier: Puritans and Indians, 1620–1675*, rev. ed. (1979); J. Leitch Wright, Jr., *The Only Land They Knew: American Indians of the Old South* (1981).

PREPARING EUROPE FOR WESTWARD EXPANSION

Paul H. Chapman, *The Norse Discovery of America* (1981); Carlo M. Cipolla, *Guns, Sails, and Empires: Technological Innovation and the Early Phases of European Expansion, 1400–1700* (1965); Alfred W. Crosby, *Ecological Imperialism: The Biological Expansion of Europe, 900–1900* (1986); E. L. Jones, *The European Miracle: Environments, Economics, and Geopolitics in the History of Europe and Asia*, 2d ed. (1987); William H. McNeill, *The Rise of the West* (1970), and *Plagues and Peoples* (1976); Frederick J. Pohl, *The Viking Settlements of North America* (1972); Robert L. Reynolds, *Europe Emerges: Transition Toward an Industrial World-Wide Society, 600–1750* (1961).

EXPLORERS, CONQUERORS, AND THE MAKING OF NEW SPAIN

Charles R. Boxer, *The Portuguese Seaborne Empire* (1969); David Carrasco, *Quetzalcoatl and the Irony of Empire* (1982); Nigel Davies, *The Aztecs* (1973); J. H. Elliott, *Imperial Spain, 1469–1716* (1963), and *The Old World and the New, 1492–1650* (1970); Charles Gibson, *The Aztecs under Spanish Rule* (1964), and *Spain in America* (1966); J. R. Hale, *Renaissance Exploration* (1968); Clarence H. Haring, *The Spanish Empire in America* (1947); James Lockhart and Stuart B. Schwartz, *Early Latin America: Colonial Spanish America and Brazil* (1983); Samuel E. Morison, *The European Discovery of America: The Southern Voyages, A.D. 1492–1616* (1979); J. H. Parry, *The Age of Reconnaissance* (1963), *The Spanish Seaborne Empire* (1966), and *The Discovery of South America* (1979); Daniel Peters, *The Incas* (1991); G. V. Scammell, *The World Encompassed: The First European Maritime Empires* (1981); Tzvetan Todorov, *The Conquest of America* (1984); Nathan Wachtel, *The Vision of the Vanquished* (1977); Silvio Zavala, *New Viewpoints on the Spanish Colonization of America* (1943).

CHALLENGERS FOR NORTH AMERICA: FRANCE AND ENGLAND

Carl Bridenbaugh, *Vexed and Troubled Englishmen, 1590–1642* (1968); Mildred Campbell, *The English Yeoman under Elizabeth and the Early Stuarts* (1942); Owen Chadwick, *The Reformation* (1972); Patrick Collinson, *The Elizabethan Puritan Movement* (1967); G. R. Elton, *England under the Tudors*, 2d ed. (1974); C. H. and Katherine George, *The Protestant Mind of the English Reformation* (1961); Peter Laslett, *The World We Have Lost*, 3d ed. (1984); Samuel E. Morison, *The European Discovery of America: The Northern Voyages, A.D. 500–1600* (1971); Wallace Notestein, *The English People on the Eve of Colonization, 1603–1630* (1954); Steven Ozment, *The Age of Reform, 1250–1550* (1980); Theodore K. Rabb, *Enterprise & Empire: Merchant and Gentry Investment in the Expansion of England, 1575–1630* (1967); Lacey Baldwin Smith, *This Realm of England, 1399–1688*, 3d ed. (1976); Lewis Spitz, *The Protestant Reformation, 1517–1559* (1985); Lawrence Stone, *The Crisis of the Aristocracy, 1558–1641* (1965); Michael Walzer, *The Revolution of the Saints* (1965); Keith Wrightson, *English Society, 1580–1680* (1982).

JOINING IN THE INVASION OF AMERICA

Charles R. Boxer, *The Dutch Seaborne Empire* (1965); Carl Bridenbaugh, *Jamestown, 1544–1699* (1980); Nicholas P. Canny, *The Elizabethan Conquest of Ireland* (1976); Ralph Davis, *The Rise of the Atlantic Economies* (1973); W. J. Eccles, *The Canadian Frontier, 1534–1821*, rev. ed. (1983), and *France in America*, rev. ed. (1990); Paul E. Hoffman, *A New Andalucia and a Way to the Orient: The American Southeast during the Sixteenth Century* (1990); Alice P. Kenney, *Stubborn for Liberty: The Dutch in New York* (1975); Karen O. Kupperman, *Settling with the Indians: English and*

Indian Cultures in America, 1580–1640 (1980), and *Roanoke: The Abandoned Colony* (1984); James Lang, *Conquest and Commerce: Spain and England in the Americas* (1975); David B. Quinn, *The Elizabethans and the Irish* (1966), *North America from Earliest Discovery to First Settlements* (1977), and *Set Fair for Roanoke, 1584–1606* (1985); Helen C. Rountree, *Pocahontas's People* (1990); A. L. Rowse, *The Expansion of Elizabethan England* (1955), and *The Elizabethans and America* (1959); George L. Smith, *Religion and Trade in New Netherland* (1973); Allen W. Trelease, *Indian Affairs in Colonial New York* (1960).

BIOGRAPHIES

Roland H. Bainton, *Here I Stand: Martin Luther* (1950); William J. Bouwsma, *John Calvin* (1988); Carolly Erickson, *The First Elizabeth* (1983); Erik H. Erikson, *Young Man Luther* (1962); Samuel E. Morison, *Samuel de Champlain* (1972), and *Christopher Columbus, Mariner* (1955); T. H. L. Parker, *John Calvin: A Biography* (1975); Andrew Sinclair, *Sir Walter Raleigh and the Age of Discovery* (1984); Alden T. Vaughan, *American Genesis: Captain John Smith and Virginia* (1975); John Noble Wilford, *The Mysterious History of Columbus* (1991).

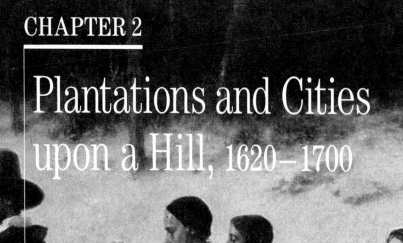

CHAPTER 2

Plantations and Cities upon a Hill, 1620–1700

NOVA BRITANNIA.

OFFERING MOST

Excellent fruites by Planting in
VIRGINIA.

Exciting all such as be well affected
to further the same.

LONDON
Printed for SAMVEL MACHAM, and are to be sold at
his Shop in Pauls Church-yard, at the
Signe of the Bul-head.
1609.

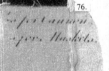

[Disastrous First Winter]

But that which was most sad and lamentable was, that in two or three months' time half of their company died, especially in January and February, being the depth of winter, and wanting houses and other comforts; being infected with the scurvy and other diseases which this long voyage and their inaccommodate condition had brought upon them. So as there died some times two or three of a day in the foresaid time, that of 100 and odd persons, scarce fifty remained. And of these, in the time of most distress, there was but six or seven sound persons who to their great commendations, be it spoken, spared no pains night nor day, but with abundance of toil and hazard of their own health, fetched them wood, made them fires, dressed them meat, made their beds, washed their loathsome clothes, clothed and unclothed them. In a word, did all the homely and necessary offices for them which dainty and queasy stomachs cannot endure to hear named; and all this willingly and cheerfully, without any grudging in the least, showing herein their true love unto their friends and brethren; . . . And yet the Lord so upheld these persons as in this general calamity they were not at all infected either with sickness or lameness. . . .

But I may not here pass by another remarkable passage not to be forgotten. As this calamity fell among the passengers that were to be left here to plant, and were hasted ashore and made to drink water that the seamen might have the more beer, and one in his sickness desiring but a small can of beer, it was answered that if he were their own father he should have none. The disease began to fall amongst them also, so as almost half of their company died before they went away, and many of their officers and lustiest men, as the boatswain, gunner, three quartermasters, the cook and others. At which the Master was something strucken and sent to the sick ashore and told the Governor he should send for beer for them that had need of it, though he drunk water homeward bound. . . .

[A Ban on Celebrating Christmas]

And herewith I shall end this year [1621]. Only I shall remember one passage more, rather of mirth than of weight. On the day called Christmas Day, the Governor called them out to work as was used. But the most of this new company excused themselves and said it went against their consciences to work on that day. So the Governor told them that if they made it matter of conscience, he would spare them till they were better informed; so he led away the rest and left them. But when they came home at noon from their work, he found them in the street at play, openly; some pitching the bar, and some at stool-ball and such like sports. So he went to them and took away their implements and told them that was against his conscience, that they should play and others work. If they made the keeping of it matter of devotion, let them keep their houses; but there should be no gaming or reveling in the streets. Since which time nothing hath been attempted that way, at least openly.

Bradford began writing his history around 1630, first covering the years from the Protestant Reformation through the voyage of the *Mayflower* to New England. As time passed and spare moments allowed, he carried the colony's story down through the year 1646. His major primary source, at least for the years from his initial involvement with the Scrooby congregation through the first years of settlement in America, was his own memory of events in which he was a prominent participant.

No one can say for sure whether Bradford ever intended to publish his history of Plymouth Colony. His straightforward, unadorned writing style, in juxtaposition to the convoluted prose of the more scholarly works of his day, suggests a desire to communicate with general audiences. Bradford himself, however, never made any arrangements for publication, and he willed the manuscript to his heirs, who were not always careful in their treatment of what remains the most readable contemporary history of settlement in seventeenth-century America. During the revolutionary era the manuscript was lost and ended up in England, most likely carried there by a souvenir-hunting British army officer. Published for the first time in 1856 and returned to the United States in 1897, the original manuscript now resides safely in the Massachusetts State House library in Boston.

Even though unpublished until the mid-nineteenth century, Bradford's study was well-known among learned citizens in the Bay Colony. The Rev. Cotton Mather was among those who borrowed the manuscript. He utilized it in writing a section on Plymouth Colony for his magisterial historical tome on early New England, entitled *Magnalia Christi Americana* and first published in London in 1702. Another borrower was Governor Thomas Hutchinson, who employed it in preparing Volume II of his detailed *History of Massachusetts Bay*, initially printed in Boston in 1767.

What certainly appealed to borrowers like Mather (less so Hutchinson) was Bradford's interpretive viewpoint. In each and every event the Pilgrim leader found evidence of the active hand of divine Providence. God was no prime mover but a real, interventionist force in the world. Thus the death of the bothersome sailor and keeping the *Mayflower* afloat, despite the batterings of many storms, all represented proof to Bradford that the Pilgrims were carrying out God's will in migrating westward. By implication, had they not been doing so, God would have ignored the sailor, let the *Mayflower* sink, or even allowed all the Pilgrims to die during their first terrible winter in New England. By permitting a few to avoid serious sickness, however, God once again was encouraging the Pilgrims to persist.

In our own time providential theories of history have few proponents. This does not mean that Bradford should be dismissed. His work stands as a valuable source of information about the Pilgrims and the mentality that brought them to America. In addition, Bradford offers many insights into the social and cultural habits of his era. The plea for beer, most likely made by Bradford himself, suggests the common use of that beverage in the lives of early settlers. Most Europeans drank large amounts of alcohol because water in the Old World was so polluted. It would take some time for the first settlers to realize that American water was not so unhealthy or disgusting to taste. Bradford, likewise, wanted nothing to do with Christmas, which he considered a pagan holiday as opposed to the true birth date of Jesus Christ. This does not mean that the Pilgrims were against all merrymaking. Just as they drank, they enjoyed great celebrations, so long as they were honoring divine Providence for so bountifully blessing them. That is why they held the first Thanksgiving during the fall of 1621. They were thanking God for having sustained them in their quest to worship as they thought best after so many vexing tribulations in coming to America.

Forty-one Pilgrims signed the Mayflower Compact, which provided government in Plymouth Colony, just before arriving in America.

John Calvin's legacy, took Biblical matters seriously. They believed that God's word should order the steps of every person's life. What troubled them most about the Protestant Reformation in England was that it had not gone far enough. They viewed the Church of England as "corrupt" in organization and guided by unscriptural doctrine; they longed for far-reaching institutional change that would rid the Anglican church of its imperfections. When church and state leaders harassed them, they responded in various ways, including the planting of a model utopian society—Massachusetts Bay Colony—in New England.

By the early 1600s the Puritans numbered in the hundreds of thousands. Their emphasis upon reading scripture particularly appealed to literate members of the middle classes and lesser gentry—merchants, skilled craft workers, professionals, and freehold farmers. The Puritans prided themselves on hard work and the pursuit of one's "calling" as a way to glorify the

Almighty. They also searched for signs of having earned God's saving grace, which all Puritans sought through a personal conversion experience. They testified in their prayer groups to these experiences—and hoped that others would agree that they had joined God's "visible saints" on earth. To be a visible saint meant that a person was fit for church membership.

By comparison, the Church of England, as a state-supported church, claimed all citizens, regardless of their spiritual nature, as church members. Besides this problem, the Anglican church, from the Puritan perspective, put too much emphasis on ritual. Its elaborate hierarchy of church officials did not include enough educated ministers who understood the Bible, let alone the need to teach parishioners to seek God's grace; rather, Anglican clergymen were the friends and relatives of the well connected. They were like "Mr. Atkins, curate of Romford, thrice presented for a drunkard," "Mr. Goldringe, parson of Laingdon Hills, . . . convicted of fornication," and "Mr. Cuckson, vicar of Linsell, . . . a pilferer, of scandalous life."

In his youth in Scotland, James Stuart, now King James I, had regular dealings with John Knox and his Presbyterian (Scottish Puritan) followers. He developed a decided distaste for religious dissenters. "I will harry them out of the land," he boldly proclaimed after becoming king of England, "or else do worse." But like Queen Elizabeth before him, James quietly endured the Puritans. He never felt secure enough in his own authority to test his will against their rapidly expanding influence.

During King James's reign, the Puritans moved aggressively to realize their goal. They built a political base from which to demand church reform by winning elections for seats in Parliament. James put up with their protests, but his son, Charles I, confronted the Puritans more boldly. He named William Laud, whom the Puritans considered a Roman Catholic in Anglican garb, as archbishop of the Church of England. Laud was particularly adept at persecuting his opponents. In response, the Puritans pushed a bill through Parliament denouncing "popish" practices in church and state. Finally, Charles used his royal prerogatives to disband Parliament and tried to rule by himself between 1629 and 1640, thus abetting the advent of a bloody civil war.

In the late 1620s the Puritans were not ready for war, but some in their numbers had decided upon an "errand into the wilderness." In 1629 they secured a joint-stock charter for the Massachusetts Bay Company. Investors knew that they were underwriting the peopling of a utopian religious experiment in America. As for King Charles, the prospect of ridding the realm of thousands of Puritans was incentive enough to give royal approval to the Bay Company charter.

Godly Mission to New England

The Puritans organized their venture carefully. They placed their settlement effort under John Winthrop (1588–1649), a prominent lawyer and landholder. In 1630 some 700 Puritans crowded onto 11 ships and joined Winthrop in sailing to Massachusetts. They were the vanguard of what

became the *Great Migration*, or the movement of an estimated 20,000 persons to New England by 1642. These men and women did not cross the Atlantic as indentured servants but as families leaving behind the religious repression and worsening economic conditions of Charles I's England.

More than any other person, John Winthrop worked tirelessly to promote the Puritan errand. Aboard the flagship *Arbella* before landing in Massachusetts Bay, he delivered a sermon entitled "A Model of Christian Charity," in which he asserted: "We must consider that we shall be as a city upon a hill; the eyes of all people are upon us." The Puritan mission was to order human existence in the Bay Colony according to God's word. Such an example, Winthrop and other company leaders hoped, would inspire England and the rest of Europe, thereby causing the full realization of the Protestant Reformation.

John Winthrop led the Puritans to New England, where he served several terms as governor of the Massachusetts Bay Colony.

Curious events back in England facilitated attempts to build a model society in the wilderness. For some reason, perhaps because of a well-placed bribe, the Bay Company charter did not specify a location for stockholder (General Court) meetings. Seizing the opportunity, John Winthrop and others drafted the Cambridge Agreement in August 1629; they decided to carry the charter with them and hold all stockholder meetings in New England—3000 miles from meddlesome king's officials. Of the stockholders who migrated, all were fervent Puritans, which meant that decision making for the colony would be controlled in General Court sessions by a handful of men fully committed to the Puritan mission.

Winthrop and other stockholders, once in Massachusetts, soon faced challenges to their

early Pilgrims, Metacomet felt threatened by the spread of white settlements. In 1671 the Pilgrims hauled him into court on the grounds of plotting against their colony and exacted a statement of submission to English authority. Thoroughly humiliated, Metacomet swore revenge.

The life and death struggle known as King Philip's War began during the summer of 1675 when various Indian tribes joined Metacomet's warriors in raiding towns along the Massachusetts-Connecticut frontier. Taking advantage of the settlers' habits, the natives often struck during Sunday church meetings. By early 1676 all of New England was in chaos. Metacomet's forces even attacked towns within 20 miles of Boston, but there were too many Puritans (around 50,000) and not enough Indians (fewer than 12,000) to annihilate the whites. When a "praying" Indian shot and killed Metacomet, King Philip's War rapidly lost its momentum.

Metacomet's warriors had leveled or done substantial damage to several towns, and around 2000 Puritan settlers died in the war. Roughly twice as many Indians lost their lives in what proved to be a futile effort to drive away the ever-expansive English. Still, King Philip's War was not the Indians' last gasp. In a few years remnant native groups began getting support from the French in Canada and once again started attacking New England's frontier towns.

King Philip's War was bloody, indeed, but surviving in New England was less difficult than surviving in the Chesapeake region, where local Indians had been crushed by the mid-1640s. Although having its precarious moments, life in early New England was far more secure than in the South, as comparative experiences reveal so graphically.

Life and Death, North and South

During the seventeenth century New England's population grew steadily by natural increase. Most of the 25,000 migrants crossed the ocean before the outbreak of England's civil war in the 1640s, yet by the end of the century some 93,000 colonists inhabited New England. In the Chesapeake, by comparison, as many as 100,000 persons attempted settlement, but only about 85,000 were living in Virginia and Maryland in

1700. If it had not been for the constant influx of new migrants, these two colonies might have ceased to exist altogether.

The Chesapeake colonists experienced shorter, less fertile lives than their New England counterparts. In 1640, for example, Chesapeake migrants had no more than a 50 percent chance of surviving their first year in America. Hot, steamy summers fostered repeated outbreaks of malaria and typhoid fever, which along with dysentery and poisoning from brackish drinking water killed thousands. New England's drinking water was safer, although Puritans generally preferred home-brewed beer, and the harsher winter climate helped to kill off deadly germs. As a result, the Puritans enjoyed longer, healthier lives.

In New England 20 percent of all Puritan males who survived infancy lived into their seventies. Even with the hazards of childbirth, Puritan women lived almost as long. In Virginia

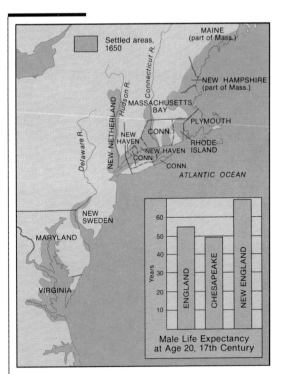

Population Comparison of New England and Chesapeake, Mid-1600s

Disease and brackish water of the Chesapeake resulted in shorter life spans than in New England.

A unique characteristic of Puritan New England was families with living grandparents, as illustrated in this portrait of Abigail Gerrish and her grandmother.

and Maryland men who survived into their early twenties had reached middle age; on the average, they would not live beyond their mid-forties. For women in their early twenties, there was little likelihood of surviving beyond their late thirties. Given an average life expectancy of 50 to 55 years back in England, the Chesapeake region deserved its reputation as a human graveyard. In comparison early New England represented a utopian health environment.

Good health sustained life and meant longer marriages and more children. Men in New England were usually in their mid-twenties when they married, and their wives were only 2 to 3 years younger. Marriages lasted an average of 25 years before one or the other spouse died. Longevity also resulted in large families, averaging seven to eight children per household. In some locales nine out of ten children survived infant diseases and grew to adulthood knowing not only their parents but their grandparents as well. Families with living grandparents were a unique characteristic of Puritan New England,

reflecting life spans more typical of modern America than early modern Europe.

From a demographic perspective, then, New England families were far more stable and secure than those of the Chesapeake. Because Puritans crossed the Atlantic in family units, the ratio of women to men was more evenly balanced than in Virginia or Maryland, where most migrants were not married. Planters seeking laborers for their tobacco fields preferred young males, which skewed the sex ratio against women and retarded the development of family life. Before 1640 only one woman migrated to the Chesapeake for every six men; and as late as 1700, males still outnumbered females by a ratio of more than three to two.

The system of indentured servitude also affected population patterns. Servants could not marry until they had completed their terms. Typically, women were in their mid-twenties before they first wed, which in combination with short adult life expectancies curbed the numbers of children they could bear. Seventeenth-century Chesapeake families averaged only two to three children, and a quarter of them did not survive their first year of life. Marriages lasted an average of seven years before one or the other spouse died. Two-thirds of all surviving children lost one parent by the age of 18, and one-third lost both. Rarely did children know grandparents. Death was as much a daily reality as life for Chesapeake families, at least until the early eighteenth century when disease stopped wreaking such havoc.

Roles for Men, Women, and Children

The early Puritans looked at their mission as a family undertaking, and they referred to families as "little commonwealths." Not only were families to "be fruitful and multiply," but they also served as agencies of education and religious instruction as well as centers of vocational training and social welfare. Families cared for the destitute and elderly; they took in orphans; and they housed servants and apprentices—all under one roof and subject to the authority of the father.

The Puritans carried *patriarchal* values across the Atlantic and planted them in America. New England law, reflecting its English base, subscribed to the doctrine of *coverture*, or subordinating the legal identity of women in their husbands, who were the undisputed heads of households. Unless there were prenuptial agreements, all property brought by women to marriages belonged to their mates. Husbands, who by custom and law directed their families in prayer and scripture reading, were responsible for assuring decency and good order in family life. They also represented their families in all community political, economic, and religious activities.

Wives also had major family responsibilities. "For though the husband be the head of the wife," the Reverend Samuel Willard explained, "yet she is the head of the family." It was the particular calling of mothers to nurture their children in godly living, as well as to perform many other tasks—tending gardens, brewing beer, raising chickens, cooking, spinning, and sewing—when not helping in the planting and harvesting of crops.

Most Puritan marriages functioned in at least outward harmony. If serious problems arose, local churches and courts intervened to end the turmoil. Puritan law, again reflecting English precedent, made divorce quite difficult. The process required the petitioning of assemblies for bills of separation, and the only legal grounds were bigamy, desertion, and adultery. A handful of women, most likely battered or abandoned wives, effected their own divorces by setting up separate residences. On occasion the courts brought unruly husbands under control, for example, a Maine husband who brutally clubbed his wife for refusing to feed the family pig. There were instances when wives defied patriarchalism, including one case involving a Massachusetts woman who faced community censure for beating her husband and even "egging her children to help her, bidding them knock him in the head."

Family friction arose from other sources as well, some of which stemmed from the absolute control that fathers exercised over property and inheritances. If sons wanted to marry and establish separate households, they had to conform to the will of their fathers, who controlled the land. Family patriarchs normally delayed the passing of property until sons had reached their mid-twenties and selected mates accept-

able to parents. Delayed inheritances help to explain why so many New Englanders did not marry until several years after puberty. Since parents also bestowed dowries on daughters as their contributions to new family units, romantic love had less to do with mate selection than parental desires to unite particular family names and estates.

Puritans expected brides and grooms to learn to love one another as they went about their duty of conceiving and raising the next generation of children. In most cases spouses did develop lasting affection for one another, as captured by the gifted Puritan poetess Anne Bradstreet in 1666 when she wrote to her "Dear and loving Husband":

> If ever two were one, then surely we.
> If ever man were lov'd by wife, then thee;
> If ever wife was happy in a man,
> Compare with me the women if you can.

Young adults who openly defied patriarchal authority were rare. Those who did could expect to hear what one angry Bay Colony father told his unwanted son-in-law: "As you married her without my consent, you shall keep her without my help." Also unusual were instances

(Text continues on p. 62)

Many indentured servants risked early deaths in the Chesapeake Bay region in return for the prospect of gaining economic freedom as independent landholders.

CHILDBIRTH IN EARLY AMERICA

When the *Mayflower* left Plymouth, England, September 16, 1620, on its historic voyage to the New World, 3 of its 102 passengers were pregnant. Elizabeth Hopkins and Susanna White were each in their seventh month of pregnancy. Mary Norris Allerton was in her second or third month.

Their pregnancies must have been excruciatingly difficult. After a few days of clear weather, the *Mayflower* ran into "fierce storms" that lasted for six of the voyage's nine-and-a-half weeks. For days on end, passengers were confined to the low spaces between decks, while high winds blew away clothing and supplies and the ship tossed and rolled on the heavy seas.

While the ship was still at sea, Elizabeth Hopkins gave birth to a baby boy named Oceanus after his birthplace. Two weeks later, while the *Mayflower* was anchored off Cape Cod, Susanna White also had a baby boy. He was christened Peregrine, a name that means "pilgrim." Peregrine White would live into his eighties, but Oceanus Hopkins died during the Pilgrims' first winter in Plymouth. In the spring of 1621, Mary Norris Allerton died in childbirth; her baby was stillborn.

Childbirth in colonial America was a difficult and sometimes dangerous experience for women. During the seventeenth and eighteenth centuries, between 1 and 1.5 percent of all births ended in the mother's death—as a result of exhaustion, dehydration, infection, hemorrhage, or convulsions. Since the typical mother gave birth to between five and eight children, her lifetime chances of dying in childbirth ran as high as one in eight. This meant that if a woman had eight female friends, it was likely that one would die in childbirth.

Understandably, many colonial women regarded pregnancy with dread. In their letters, women often referred to childbirth as "the Dreaded apparition," "the greatest of earthly miserys," or "that evel hour I loock forward to with dread." Many, like New England poet Ann Bradstreet, approached childbirth with a fear of impending death. In a poem entitled "Before the Birth of One of Her Children," Bradstreet wrote,

> How soon, my Dear, death may my steps attend,
> How soon't may be thy lot to lose thy friend.

In addition to her anxieties about pregnancy, an expectant mother was filled with apprehensions about the survival of her newborn child. The death of a child in infancy was far more common then than it is today. In the healthiest seventeenth-century communities, 1 infant in 10 died before the age of 5. In less healthy environments, 3 children in 10 died before their fifth birthday. Puritan minister Cotton Mather saw 8 of his 15 children die before reaching the age of 2. "We have our children taken from us," Mather cried out, "the Desire of our Eyes taken away with a stroke."

Given the high risk of birth complications and infant death, it is not surprising to learn that pregnancy was surrounded by superstitions. It was widely believed that if a mother looked upon a "horrible spectre" or was startled by a loud noise her child would be disfigured. If a hare jumped in front of her, her child was in danger of suffering a harelip. There was also fear that if the mother looked at the moon, her child might become a lunatic or sleepwalker. A mother's ungratified longings, it was thought, could cause a miscarriage or leave a mark imprinted on her child's body. At the same time, however, women were expected to continue to perform work until the onset of labor, since hard work supposedly made for an easier labor. Pregnant women regularly spun thread, wove fabric on looms, performed heavy lifting and carrying, milked cows, and slaughtered and salted down meat.

Today, most women give birth in hospitals under close medical supervision. If they wish, women can take anesthetics to relieve labor pangs. During the seventeenth and eighteenth centuries, the process of childbirth was almost wholly different. In colonial America, the typical woman gave birth to her children at home, while female kin and neighbors clustered at her bedside to offer support and encouragement. When the daughter of Samuel Sewall, a Puritan magistrate, gave birth to her first child on the last day of January, 1701, at least eight other women were present at her bedside, including her mother, her mother-in-law, a midwife, a nurse, and at least four other neighbors.

Most women were assisted in childbirth not by a doctor but by a midwife. Most midwives were older women who relied on practical experience in delivering children. One midwife, Martha Ballard, who practiced in Augusta, Maine, delivered 996 babies with only 4 recorded fatalities. Skilled midwives were highly valued. Communities tried to attract experienced midwives by offering a salary or a rent-free house. In addition to assisting in childbirth, midwives helped deliver the offspring of animals, attended the baptisms and burials of infants, and

testified in court in cases of bastardy.

During labor, midwives administered no painkillers, except for alcohol. Pain in childbirth was considered God's punishment for Eve's sin of eating the forbidden fruit in the Garden of Eden. Women were merely advised to "arm themselves with patience" and prayer and to try, during labor, to restrain "those dreadful groans and cries which do so much discourage their friends and relations that are near them."

After delivery, new mothers were often treated to a banquet. At one such event, visitors feasted on "boil'd pork, beef, fowls, very good roast beef, turkey-pye, [and] tarts." Women from well-to-do families were then expected to spend three to four weeks in bed convalescing. Their attendants kept the fireplace burning and wrapped them in a heavy blanket in order to help them sweat out "poisons." Women from poorer families were generally back at work in one or two days.

During the second half of the eighteenth century, customs of childbirth began to change. One early sign of change was the growing insistence among women from well-to-do urban families that their children be delivered by male midwives and doctors. Many upper-class families assumed that in a difficult birth trained physicians would make childbirth safer and less painful. In order to justify their presence, physicians tended to take an active role in the birth process. They were much more likely than midwives to intervene in labor with forceps and drugs.

Another important change was the introduction in 1847 of two drugs—ether and chloroform—to relieve pain in childbirth. By the 1920s, the use of anesthesia in

childbirth was almost universal. The practice of putting women to sleep during labor contributed to a shift from having children at home to having children in hospitals. In 1900, over 90 percent of all births occurred in the mother's home. But by 1940, over half took place in hospitals and by 1950, the figure had reached 90 percent.

The substitution of doctors for midwives and of hospital delivery for home delivery did little in themselves to reduce mortality rates for mothers. It was not until around 1935, when antibiotics and transfusions were introduced, that a sharp reduction in the maternal mortality rate occurred. In 1900, maternal mortality was about 65 times higher than it is today, and not much lower than it had been in the mid-nineteenth century. By World War II, however, death in childbirth had been cut to its present low level.

In recent years, a reaction has occurred against the sterile impersonality of modern hospital delivery. Women today are much more likely than their mothers or grandmothers to want a "natural childbirth." Beginning in the 1960s, a growing number of women elected to bear their children without anesthesia, so that they could be fully conscious during childbirth. Many women also chose to have their husbands or a relative or a friend present during labor and delivery and to bear their children in special "birthing rooms" that provide a homelike environment. In these ways, many contemporary women have sought to recapture the broader support network that characterized childbearing in the colonial past, without sacrificing the tremendous advances that have been made in maternal and infant health.

of illegitimate children, despite the lengthy gap between puberty and marriage. As measured by illegitimate births, premarital sex could not have been that common in early New England, not a surprising finding among people living in closely controlled communities and seeking to honor the Almighty by reforming human society.

The experiences of seventeenth-century Chesapeake colonists were very different. The system of indentured servitude was open to abuse. Free planters ruled as patriarchs but with no sense of nurturing the next generation; rather, they presumed that they were dealing with "lazy, simple people" who "professed idleness and will rather beg than work," as a contemporary noted. The goal was to get as much labor as possible out of servants, since 40 percent died before completing their contracts. Disease was the major killer, but hard-driving planters also contributed to many early deaths.

Servants responded to cruel treatment in various ways. A few committed suicide. Others, like John Punch, ran away. Some killed farm animals, set buildings on fire, or broke tools. Local laws, as drafted by freeholding planters, specified harsh penalties. Besides floggings and brandings, resisting servants faced extensions of service, as one unfortunate man learned after he killed three pigs belonging to his master. The court added six years to his term of service.

Indentured servitude also inhibited family life. Since servants could not marry, the likelihood of illicit sexual activity increased. Quite frequently, women became the unwilling sexual partners of lustful masters or male servants. Margerie Goold, for example, warded off attempted rape by her master in 1663, but another servant, Elizabeth Wild, was less successful. The planter, however, helped her induce an abortion. One-fifth of Maryland's indentured females faced charges of "bastardy," reflecting both a shortage of women and a labor system giving masters much leeway in managing their servants. Finally in 1692, Virginia officials tried to improve the situation by adopting a statute that mandated harsh penalties for "dissolute masters" getting "their maids with child."

Still, the fate of female and male servants was not always abuse or death. Many survived, gained title to land, and enjoyed, however briefly, personal freedom in America. A few women, usually widows, gained influence. Margaret Brent, for example, controlled over 1000 acres in Maryland and even served as the executor of Governor Leonard Calvert's estate in 1647. Brent was daring enough to demand the right to vote, a plea that male legislators dismissed as a subversive attempt to undermine the natural order of human relationships.

Brent's case suggests that high death rates in combination with an unbalanced sex ratio may have, at least temporarily, enhanced the status of some Chesapeake women. English and colonial law recognized the category of *femes sole*, or permitting single, adult women and widows to own and manage property and households for themselves. Chesapeake women who outlived two or three husbands could acquire significant holdings through inheritances and then maintain control by requiring prenuptial contracts from future spouses. Once married, however, any property not so protected fell to new husbands because of *coverture*.

Since widowed mothers could presume that they would outlive new husbands, most prenuptial contracts protected property for children by previous marriages. Indeed, few children grew to adulthood without burying one or both parents, and there were extreme cases like that of Agatha Vause, a Virginia child whose father, two stepfathers, mother, and guardian uncle all died before she was 11 years old.

The fragility of life resulted in complex family genealogies with some households containing children from three or four marriages. In some instances local Orphans' Courts had to take charge because all adult relatives had died. Because parents did not live that long, children quite often received their inheritances by their late teens, much earlier than in New England. This advantage only meant that economic independence, like death, came earlier in life.

COMMERCIAL VALUES AND THE RISE OF CHATTEL SLAVERY

By 1650 there were signs that the Puritan mission was in trouble. From the outset many non-Puritan settlers, including merchants in Boston, had shunned the religious values of the Bay

Colony's founders. By the 1660s, children and grandchildren of the migrating generation displayed less zeal about earning God's grace; they were becoming more like southern settlers in their eagerness to get ahead economically. By 1700, their search for worldly prosperity even brought some New Englanders into the international slave trade.

Declension in New England

Declension, or movement away from the ideals of the Bay Colony's founding fathers, resulted in tensions between settlers adhering to the original mission and those attracted to rising commercial values. When clergymen proposed a major compromise known as the "Half-Way Covenant" in 1662, more secular-minded settlers cheered while traditionalists jeered. The covenant recognized that many children were not preparing for salvation, a necessary condition for full church membership, as their parents had done. The question was how to keep them—and their offspring—aspiring toward a spiritual life. The solution was half-way membership, which permitted the baptism of the children and grandchildren of professing saints. If still in the church, ministers and full members could continue to urge them to focus their lives on seeking God's eternal rewards.

Many communities disdained the Half-Way Covenant because of what it suggested about changing values. As one minister wrote, it was "as if the Lord had no further work for his people to do but every bird to feather his own nest." With the passage of time most accepted the covenant to help preserve some semblance of a godly society in New England.

Spreading commercial values took hold for many reasons, including the natural abundance of the New England environment and an inability to sustain fervency of purpose among American-born offspring who had not personally felt the religious repression of early Stuart England. Also, Puritans back in England, after overthrowing Charles I, generally ignored the model society in America; this left the impression that the errand had been futile, that no one back in Europe really cared.

The transition in values occurred gradually, as shown in various towns where families bought and sold common field strips so that all of their landholdings were in one place. The next step was to build homes on these sites and become "outlivers," certainly a more efficient way to practice agriculture yet also a statement that making one's living was more important than daily participation in village life—with its emphasis on laboring together in God's love.

In Boston and other port towns, such as Salem, merchants gained increasing community stature because of their wealth. By the early eighteenth century, some of them were earning profits by participating in the African slave trade. Their new-found status was symbolized by retinues of household servants or, more properly, slaves taken from Africa.

Clergymen disapproved of these trends. Their sermons took on the tone of "jeremiads," modeled on the prophet Jeremiah who kept urging Israel to return to the path of godliness. In Calvinist fashion, they warned of divine retribution or "afflictions" from the Almighty, and they pointed to events like King Philip's War as proof that Jehovah was punishing New England. In 1679 the ministers met in another synod and listed several problems, everything from working on the sabbath to swearing in public and sleeping during sermons. Human competitiveness and contention, they sadly concluded, were in ascendance. Worse yet, the populace, in its rush to garner worldly riches, showed little concern that Winthrop's "city upon a hill" had become the home of the acquisitive Yankee trader.

Stabilizing Life in the Chesapeake Region

In Maryland and Virginia there were indications by 1675 that life could be something more than brief and unkind. The death rate dropped; more children survived; the sex ratio started to balance out; and life expectancy figures rose. By the early 1700s Chesapeake residents lived well into their fifties. This was comparable to longevity estimates for England but still 10 to 15 years shorter than in New England. These patterns suggested greater family stability, as shown by longer marriages and more children—the average union now produced seven to eight offspring with five to six children surviving into adulthood.

Lavish estates like Westover, built by William Byrd II, illustrate the wealth and dominance of the gentleman-planters in Virginia.

Not only did life become more stable, but an elite group of families, controlling significant property and wealth, had begun to emerge. By 1700 the great tidewater families—the Byrds, Carters, Fitzhughs, Lees, and Randolphs among others—were making their presence felt and had started to dominate social and political affairs in the Chesapeake region. These gentleman-planters aped the life-style of England's rural gentry class. They constructed lavish manor houses from which they ruled over their plantation estates, dispensing hospitality and wisdom as the most important local leaders of their tobacco-producing colony.

Such a person was William Byrd II (1674–1744), who inherited 26,000 fertile acres along the James River in 1705. He built the magnificent Westover plantation, raised a large family, served on the governor's council, and assumed, as he wrote to an English correspondent, that he was "one of the patriarchs" of Virginia society. By the time of his death Byrd had holdings of 180,000 acres, and he owned at least 200 slaves.

Educated in England, Byrd read widely, put together an impressive personal library, and wrote extensively on any subject that interested him. His "secret" diaries describe how he treated others, including his wife, Lucy Parke Byrd. When they argued, Byrd on occasion demonstrated his presumed masculine superiority with sexual bravado. In 1710 "a little quarrel" was "reconciled with a flourish . . . performed on the billiard table." Byrd's behavior was part of his assertive, self-confident manner. He was the master of everything on his magnificent plantation, making him a patriarch of the realm of Virginia.

For every great planter, there were dozens of small farmers who lacked the wealth to obtain land, slaves, and high status in society. Most eked out bare livings, yet they dreamed of the day when they, or their children, might live in the style of a William Byrd. Meanwhile, they deferred to their "betters" among the planter elite, who in turn "treated" them to large quantities of alcohol on election days and expressed gentlemanly concern about the welfare of their families. All of this was part of an ongoing bonding ritual among white inhabitants who, no matter how high or low in status, considered themselves superior to black slaves—whose numbers were now growing rapidly on the bottom rung of Maryland and Virginia society.

The Beginnings of American Slavery

The system of perpetual servitude that shaped the lives of persons of African heritage like John Punch and Emmanuel had an ancient history. However, slavery was dying out in much of Europe by the fifteenth century. Then the Portuguese mariners of Prince Henry started coasting along sub-Saharan Africa, making contact with various cultures and peoples, some of whom were willing to barter in human flesh as well as in gold and ivory. The first Portuguese expeditions represented the small beginnings of a trade that forcibly relocated an estimated 10 million Africans to the Americas during the next 350 years.

Africa had a population of about 50 million at the time of Columbus. There was great geographic diversity with vast deserts, grassy plains, and tropical rain forests. Mighty kingdoms like Ghana had flourished in West Africa but had been overrun by Muslims from the north during the eleventh century, resulting in the empire of Mali and its magnificent trading and learning center, Timbuktu. Farther to the south in Guinea were smaller kingdoms like Benin in which the populace farmed or worked at such crafts as pottery making, weaving, and metalworking. These cultures valued family life and were mostly matrilineal in the organization of kinship networks. They also had well-developed political systems and legal codes.

West African Kingdoms, Late 1400s

European and Portuguese traders in the late 1400s found the West African kingdoms rich with rice, gold, and slaves.

In addition, these kingdoms thrived on elaborate regional trading networks, which the Portuguese and other Europeans, offering guns and various iron products, tapped into easily. As time passed Europeans came to identify certain coastal areas with particular commodities. Upper Guinea contained the rice and grain coasts, and Lower Guinea the ivory, gold, and slave coasts.

Slave decks on many of the ships arriving in America were overcrowded and cramped. As indicated in this picture, slaves became emaciated from inadequate food during the crossing.

Early European traders learned that Africans held slaves—mainly individuals captured in tribal wars—who had the status of family members. The Portuguese found that coastal chiefs were willing to trade for European firearms, which they could use when attacking interior kingdoms. A new objective of this tribal warfare became the capturing of peoples who would then be transported back to the coast and sold into slavery in exchange for yet more European goods.

Once this vicious trading cycle began, there did not seem to be any way to stop it. Decade after decade, thousands of Africans experienced the agony of being shackled in collars and ankle chains, marched in gangs, or *coffles*, to the coast, thrown into *barracoons*, or slave pens, and then packed aboard ships destined for ports of call in the Americas. One slave, Olaudah Equiano, who made the voyage during the eighteenth century, recalled the "loathsome-

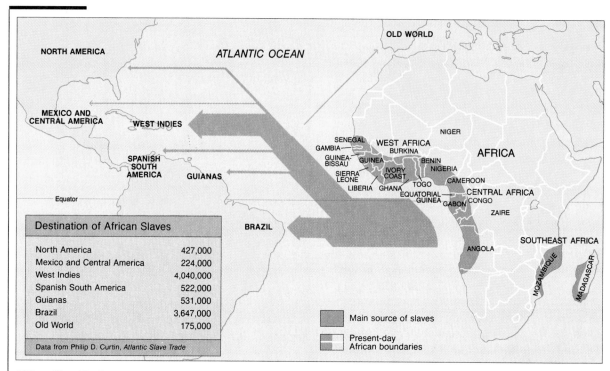

Destination of African Slaves	
North America	427,000
Mexico and Central America	224,000
West Indies	4,040,000
Spanish South America	522,000
Guianas	531,000
Brazil	3,647,000
Old World	175,000

Data from Philip D. Curtin, *Atlantic Slave Trade*

African Slave Trade

The destinations of slaves traded between 1520 and 1810 show the heaviest concentration in Central and South America.

ness of the stench" from overcrowded conditions, which made him "so sick and low" that he neither was "able to eat, nor had . . . the desire to taste anything."

Some Africans resisted by refusing to eat and died, but the Europeans made tools that would break jaws, pry open mouths, and jam food down unwilling throats. Others jumped overboard and drowned, but the Europeans soon placed large nets on the sides of their vessels. About 15 percent of those forced onto slave ships did not survive. For those who did, there was the frightening realization of having lost everything familiar in their lives—and not knowing what might happen next.

During the sixteenth century the Spanish and Portuguese started pouring Africans into their colonies. These slaves were not thought of as family members, rather as disposable beings whose energy was to be used, so long as it lasted, in mining or agricultural operations. High mortality rates among the migrants did not seem to bother their European masters because

more slave ships always appeared on the horizon. As a result, areas such as Brazil and the West Indian sugar islands earned deserved reputations as centers of human exploitation and death.

Shifting to Slavery in Maryland and Virginia

The English North American colonies existed at the outer edge of the African slave trade until the very end of the seventeenth century. In 1650 the population of Virginia approached 15,000 settlers, including only 500 persons of African descent. By comparison, the English sugar colony of Barbados already held 10,000 slaves, a majority of the population. English Barbadians had started to model their economy on that of other Caribbean sugar islands whereas Virginians, with a steady supply of indentured servants, had not yet made the transition to slave labor.

Factors supporting a shift, however, were present by the 1640s, as evidenced in laws discriminating against Africans and court cases involving blacks like John Punch and Emmanuel. During the same decade, a few Chesapeake planters started to invest in Africans. Governor Leonard Calvert of Maryland, for example, asked "John Skinner mariner" to ship him "fourteen negro-men-slaves and three women-slaves." Planters like Calvert were ahead of their time because slaves cost significantly more to purchase than indentured servants. Yet for those who invested, they owned their laborers for their lifetimes and did not have to pay "freedom dues." Further, they soon discovered that Africans, having built up immunities to tropical diseases like malaria and typhoid fever, generally lived longer than white servants. Resistance to such diseases made Africans a better long-term investment, at least for well-capitalized planters.

Then in the 1660s two additional factors encouraged the shift toward slave labor. First, Virginia legislators in 1662 decreed that slavery was an inheritable status, "according to the condition of the mother." The law made yet unborn generations subject to slavery, a powerful incentive for risking an initial investment in human chattels. If slaves kept reproducing, planters would control a never-ending supply of laborers. Second, the supply of new indentured servants began to shrink as economic conditions improved in England. With expanded opportunities for work, poorer citizens were less willing to risk life and limb for a chance at economic independence in America.

Also abetting the shift was the chartering of the Royal African Company in 1672 to develop England's role in the slave trade. Royal African vessels soon made regular visits to Chesapeake Bay; and as the supply of slaves increased, asking prices started to drop—at the very time that the cost of buying indentured servants began to climb. In 1698 the company lost its monopoly, and some New England merchants vigorously entered the slave trade. Yankee merchants now had something in common with Chesapeake planters, besides English roots and language. Both were profiting from the international traffic in human beings.

Population figures explain the rest. In 1670 Virginia contained about 40,000 settlers, which included an estimated 6000 white servants and 2000 black slaves. By 1700 the number of slaves had grown to 16,000, and by 1750 white Virginians owned 120,000 slaves—about 40 percent of the total population. The same general pattern characterized Maryland, where by 1750 there were 40,000 slaves—some 30 percent of the populace. In the Chesapeake area, indentured servitude was by then a moribund institution. White planters, great and small, now measured their wealth and status in terms of plantations and slaves owned and managed.

The World the Slaves Made

Historians once argued that slavery in English North America was harsher than the Spanish-American version. They pointed to the moderating influence of the Roman Catholic church, which mandated legal recognition of slave marriages as a sacramental right, and ancient legal precedents influencing Spanish law, which meant that slaves could earn wages for their labor in off hours and buy their freedom. Although Spanish laws may have been more humane, daily working and living conditions were not. Most slaves destined for Caribbean or South American settlements did not survive long enough to marry or enjoy other legal rights. By contrast, in North America where early

Old Plantation shows that slaves succeeded in creating separate lives for themselves, but in reality they had no legal status. Masters thought of slaves as property.

deaths were not so pervasive among migrants, slaves more easily reconstructed meaningful lives for themselves.

About 10 percent of those Africans coming to the colonies entered port towns in the North like Boston and became domestic servants, craft workers, or in rare cases, farmhands out in the countryside. The rest labored in the South, mostly on small plantations where field work dominated their existence. There was little chance for family life, at least in the early years, because planters purchased an average of three males for every female. In addition, southern law did not recognize slave marriages—in case masters wanted to sell off some of their chattels. Anglican church leaders accepted the situation. In New England, by contrast, the Congregational church insisted that slave marriages be recognized and respected by masters.

Facing a loss of personal freedom and pervasive racism, southern slaves made separate lives for themselves, particularly on larger plantations where their numbers were large enough to form their own communities in the slave quarters. Here they maintained African cultural traditions and developed distinctive forms of music. In South Carolina's sea island region, slaves continued to give their children African names, and they worked out a distinct dialect, known as *Gullah*, to communicate with one another in a unique combination of African and English sounds. In many places, female slaves managed slave quarter life, thus maintaining the matrilineal nature of African kinship ties.

Contrary to white owners' contentions, most slaves did not engage in promiscuous sexual relations. Whenever possible, they selected mates and had large families, even if slave quarter marriages had no standing in law. As a consequence, the ratio of men to women balanced itself out over time, which in turn sped up natural population growth. Large families became a source of slave community pride. Natural increase also undercut the need to continue heavy importations of chattels. As a result, only 5 percent—399,000 persons—of all imported Africans ended up in English North America.

Such comparisons are relative. Nowhere in the Americas did slavery function in an uplifting fashion. Although blacks on large southern plantations carried on traditional cultural practices, they still had to face masters or overseers who might whip them, sell off their children, or maim or kill them if they tried to run away. Always present was the realization that whites considered them to be a subhuman species of property, which left scant room for human dignity in life beyond the slave quarters.

Despite the oppression, Africans did contribute to that life. In South Carolina, for example, many early slave migrants were expert at raising and herding animals, and they helped to make possible a thriving trade in cattle. Others who came from the rice coast region of Africa used their agricultural skills in fostering South Carolina's development as a major producer of rice. These and many other contributions went unrecognized in the rush for profits in the maturing commercial world of the American colonies, except in the ironic sense of creating further demand among white settlers for additional black laborers.

CONCLUSION

Although most blacks adapted to slavery, some remained defiant. They stole food, broke farm tools, or in a few cases poisoned their masters. In rare instances they resorted to rebellion. In September 1739 twenty slaves in the Stono River area of South Carolina rose up, seized some weapons, killed a few whites, and started marching toward Spanish Florida. Within a few days frightened planters rallied together and crushed the Stono uprising by shooting or hanging the rebels.

The South Carolina legislature soon approved a more repressive slave code, which all but restricted the movement of blacks from their home plantations. No legislator gave thought to the other possibility, which was to abandon the institution of slavery. Even though long in development, slavery now supported southern plantation agriculture and the production of such cash crops as tobacco and rice.

Just as the southern colonies had made a fateful shift from servitude to slavery, New Englanders experienced another kind of transition. Slowly but surely, they had forsaken their utopian, religiously oriented errand into the wilderness, and service to mammon had replaced loy-

CHRONOLOGY
OF KEY EVENTS

1608 Pilgrims flee to Holland to avoid religious persecution in England

1617 Virginia begins to export tobacco

1619 The first persons of African descent arrive in Virginia; first representative assembly in English North America meets in Jamestown

1620 Pilgrims arrive at Cape Cod on the *Mayflower* and establish a colony at Plymouth

1622 Opechancanough's Indians fail in an attempt to massacre all English settlers in Virginia; first settlement in New Hampshire

1624 English Crown takes control of Virginia; New York is settled by the Dutch and named New Netherland

1630 Puritans establish the Massachusetts Bay Colony

1632 Maryland becomes the first proprietary colony

1635 Roger Williams is banished from Massachusetts Bay

1636 Harvard College is founded; first permanent English settlements in Connecticut and Rhode Island

1637–1638 Anne Hutchinson is convicted of heresy in Massachusetts and flees to Rhode Island

1640s Legal status of African-Americans deteriorates

1644 Second attempted Indian massacre of Virginia settlers fails

1646 Powhatan's Confederacy accepts English rule

1647 Massachusetts Bay Colony adopts the first public school law in the colonies

1649 Maryland's Act of Toleration affirms religious freedom for all Christians in the colony; Charles I of England is beheaded

1660 Charles II is restored to the English throne

1664 English conquer New Netherland and rename the colony New York

1675–1676 King Philip's (Metacomet's) War inflicts heavy casualties on New Englanders

1681–1682 William Penn founds Pennsylvania as a "holy experiment" in which diverse groups of people can live together harmoniously

1688 Glorious Revolution drives James II from England

1732 Georgia is founded as a haven for debtors and a buffer against Spanish Florida

1739 Stono slave uprising occurs in South Carolina

---

alty to God and community. The religious side would remain, but the fervor of a nobler spiritual mission was in rapid decline by 1700. Material gain was now a quality shared in common by white English colonists in America—North and South.

Prosperity, which had come after so much travail and death, promoted a sense of unlimited opportunity in profiting from the abundance of the American environment. Other realities, however, were also in the making. The colonists had learned that Crown officials now expected them to conform to new laws governing the emerging English empire. Because of these imperial rules, much turmoil lay ahead for the people now inhabiting English North America.

SUGGESTIONS FOR FURTHER READING

OVERVIEWS AND SURVEYS

Sydney E. Ahlstrom, *A Religious History of the American People* (1972); Bernard Bailyn, *Education in the Forming of American Society* (1960); Thomas Bender, *Community and Social Change in America* (1978); Carol R. Berkin, *Within the Conjurer's Circle: Women in Colonial America*

(1974); Rowland Berthoff, *An Unsettled People* (1971); Richard D. Brown, *Modernization: The Transformation of American Life, 1600–1865* (1976); David Brion Davis, *The Problem of Slavery in Western Culture* (1966), and *Slavery and Human Progress* (1984); David Hackett Fischer, *Albion's Seed: Four British Folkways in America* (1989); John Hope Franklin and Alfred A. Moss, Jr., *From Slavery to Freedom*, 6th ed. (1987); Philip Greven, *The Protestant Temperament* (1977); E. Brooks Holifield, *Era of Persuasion: American Thought and Culture, 1521–1680* (1989); Nathan I. Huggins, *Black Odyssey: The Afro-American Ordeal in Slavery* (1977); Steven Mintz and Susan Kellogg, *Domestic Revolutions: A Social History of American Family Life* (1988); Edwin J. Perkins, *The Economy of Colonial America*, 2d ed. (1988); John E. Pomfret and Floyd M. Shumway, *Founding the American Colonies, 1583–1660* (1970); Helena M. Wall, *Fierce Communion: Family and Community in Early America* (1990); Robert V. Wells, *The Population of the British Colonies in America before 1776* (1975).

FROM SETTLEMENTS TO SOCIETIES IN THE SOUTH

Carl Bridenbaugh, *Myths and Realities: Societies of the Colonial South* (1952); Paul G. E. Clemens, *The Atlantic Economy and Colonial Maryland's Eastern Shore* (1980); Converse D. Clowse, *Economic Beginnings of Colonial South Carolina, 1670–1730* (1971); Wesley Frank Craven, *The Southern Colonies in the Seventeenth Century* (1949); David Galenson, *White Servitude in Colonial America* (1981); David W. Jordan, *Foundations of Representative Government in Maryland, 1632–1715* (1987); Aubrey C. Land, et al., eds. *Law, Society, and Politics in Early Maryland* (1977); Richard L. Morton, *Colonial Virginia*, 2 vols. (1960); James R. Perry, *The Formation of a Society on Virginia's Eastern Shore, 1615–1655* (1990); David B. Quinn, ed., *Early Maryland in a Wider World* (1982); M. Eugene Sirmans, *Colonial South Carolina, 1663–1763* (1966); Abbot E. Smith, *Colonists in Bondage: White Servitude and Convict Labor, 1607–1776* (1947); Clarence L. Ver Steeg, *Origins of a Southern Mosaic* (1975).

RELIGIOUS DISSENTERS COLONIZE NEW ENGLAND

David Grayson Allen, *In Engish Ways: The Movement of Societies and the Transferal of English Local Law and Custom to Massachusetts Bay* (1981); Bernard Bailyn, *The New England Merchants in the Seventeenth Century* (1955); Francis J. Bremer, *The Puritan Experiment* (1976); Charles E. Clark, *The Eastern Frontier: The Settlement of Northern New England, 1610–1763* (1970); Charles L. Cohen, *God's Caress: The Psychology of Puritan Religious Experience* (1986); Andrew Delbanco, *The Puritan Ordeal* (1989); Kai T. Erikson, *Wayward Puritans* (1966); Stephen Foster, *The Long Argument: English Puritanism and New England Culture, 1570–1700* (1991), and *Their Solitary Way: The Puritan Social Ethic* (1971); Philip F. Gura, *A Glimpse of Sion's Glory: Puritan Radicalism, 1620–1660* (1984); David D. Hall, *The Faithful Shepherd: A History of the New England Ministry* (1972), and *Worlds of Wonder, Days of Judgment: Popular Religious Belief in Early New England* (1989); James Holstun, *A Rational Millennium: Puritan Utopias* (1987); Sydney V. James, *Colonial Rhode Island* (1975); Mary J. A. Jones, *Congregational Commonwealth: Connecticut, 1636–1662* (1968); Lyle Koehler, *A Search for Power: The "Weaker Sex" in New England* (1980); David Konig, *Law and Society in Puritan Massachusetts, 1629–1692* (1979); George D. Langdon, Jr., *Pilgrim Colony, 1620–1691* (1966); John Frederick Martin, *Profits in the Wilderness: Entrepreneurship and the Founding of New England Towns* (1991); Perry Miller, *Orthodoxy in Massachusetts, 1630–1650* (1933), *The New England Mind: The Seventeenth Century* (1939), and *The New England Mind: From Colony to Province* (1953); Edmund S. Morgan, *Visible Saints: The History of a Puritan Idea* (1963); Robert G. Pope, *The Half-Way Covenant* (1969); Darrett B. Rutman, *American Puritanism: Faith and Practice* (1970); William K. B. Stoever, *A Faire and Easy Way to Heaven: Covenant Theology and Antinomianism* (1988); Harry S. Stout, *The New England Soul: Preaching and Religious Culture* (1986); Laurel Thatcher Ulrich, *Good Wives: Image and Reality in the Lives of Women in Northern New England, 1650–1750* (1982); David E. Van Deventer, *The Emergence of Provincial New Hampshire, 1623–1741* (1976); Robert E. Wall, Jr., *Massachusetts Bay: The Crucial Decade, 1640–1650* (1972).

FAMILIES, INDIVIDUALS, AND COMMUNITIES: SURVIVING IN EARLY AMERICA

Lois Green Carr, et al., eds., *Colonial Chesapeake Society* (1988), and Carr, et al., *Robert Cole's World: Agriculture and Society in Early Maryland* (1991); Wesley Frank Craven, *White, Red, and Black: The Seventeenth-Century Virginian* (1971); John Demos, *A Little Commonwealth: Family Life in Plymouth Colony* (1970); Carville Earle, *The Evolution of a Tidewater Settlement System* (1975); Richard P. Gildrie, *Salem, Massachusetts* (1975);

Philip J. Greven, Jr., *Four Generations: Colonial Andover, Massachusetts* (1970); Stephen Innes, *Labor in a New Land: Economy and Society in Springfield* (1983); Douglas E. Leach, *Flintlock and Tomahawk: King Philip's War* (1958); Judith Walzer Leavitt, *Brought to Bed: Childbearing in America* (1986); Kenneth A. Lockridge, *A New England Town: Dedham, Massachusetts, 1636–1736*, rev. ed. (1985); Paul R. Lucas, *Valley of Discord: Church and Society along the Connecticut River, 1636–1725* (1976); Gloria L. Main, *Tobacco Colony: Life in Early Maryland, 1650–1720* (1982); Sally G. McMillen, *Motherhood in the Old South: Pregnancy, Childbirth, and Infant Rearing* (1990); Edmund S. Morgan, *The Puritan Family*, rev. ed. (1966), and *American Slavery, American Freedom: The Ordeal of Colonial Virginia* (1975); Darrett B. Rutman, *Winthrop's Boston, 1630–1649* (1965), and with Anita H. Rutman, *A Place in Time: Middlesex County, Virginia, 1650–1750*, 2 vols. (1984); Catherine M. Scholten, *Childbearing in American Society* (1985); David E. Stannard, *The Puritan Way of Death* (1977); Thad W. Tate and David L. Ammerman, eds., *The Chesapeake in the Seventeenth Century* (1979); Roger Thompson, *Sex in Middlesex: Popular Mores in a Massachusetts County, 1649–1699* (1986); Robert V. Wells, *Revolutions in Americans' Lives: A Demographic Perspective* (1982).

COMMERCIAL VALUES AND THE RISE OF CHATTEL SLAVERY

Timothy H. Breen and Stephen Innes, *"Myne Owne Ground": Race and Freedom on Virginia's Eastern Shore, 1640–1676* (1980); Jay Coughtry, *The Notorious Triangle: Rhode Island and the Atlantic Slave Trade, 1700–1807* (1981); Basil Davidson, *The African Genius* (1969); Richard S. Dunn, *Sugar and Slaves: The Rise of the Planter Class in the English West Indies, 1624–1713* (1972); Winthrop D. Jordan, *White Over Black, 1550–1812* (1968); Herbert S. Klein, *Slavery in the Americas: Virginia and Cuba* (1967), and *The Middle Passage* (1978); Allan Kulikoff, *Tobacco and Slaves: Southern Cultures in the Chesapeake, 1680–1800* (1986); Daniel C. Littlefield, *Rice and Slaves: Ethnicity and the Slave Trade in Colonial South Carolina* (1981); Edgar J. McManus, *Black Bondage in the North* (1973); Gerald W. Mullin, *Flight and Rebellion: Slave Resistance in Virginia* (1972); Richard Olaniyan, ed., *African History and Culture* (1982); James Rawley, *The Transatlantic Slave Trade* (1981); Daniel Blake Smith, *Inside the Great House: Planter Family Life in Chesapeake Society* (1980); Peter H. Wood, *Black Majority: Negroes in Colonial South Carolina from 1670 through the Stono Rebellion* (1974); Donald R. Wright, *African Americans in the Colonial Era* (1990).

BIOGRAPHIES

Emery Battis, *Saints and Sectaries: Anne Hutchinson and the Antinomian Controversy* (1962); Kenneth A. Lockridge, *The Diary, and Life, of William Byrd II of Virginia, 1674–1744* (1987); Robert Middlekauff, *The Mathers: Three Generations of Puritan Intellectuals* (1971); Edmund S. Morgan, *The Puritan Dilemma: The Story of John Winthrop* (1958), and *Roger Williams: The Church and the State* (1967); Bradford Smith, *Bradford of Plymouth* (1951).

A TOBACCO PLANTATION

FIG. V.

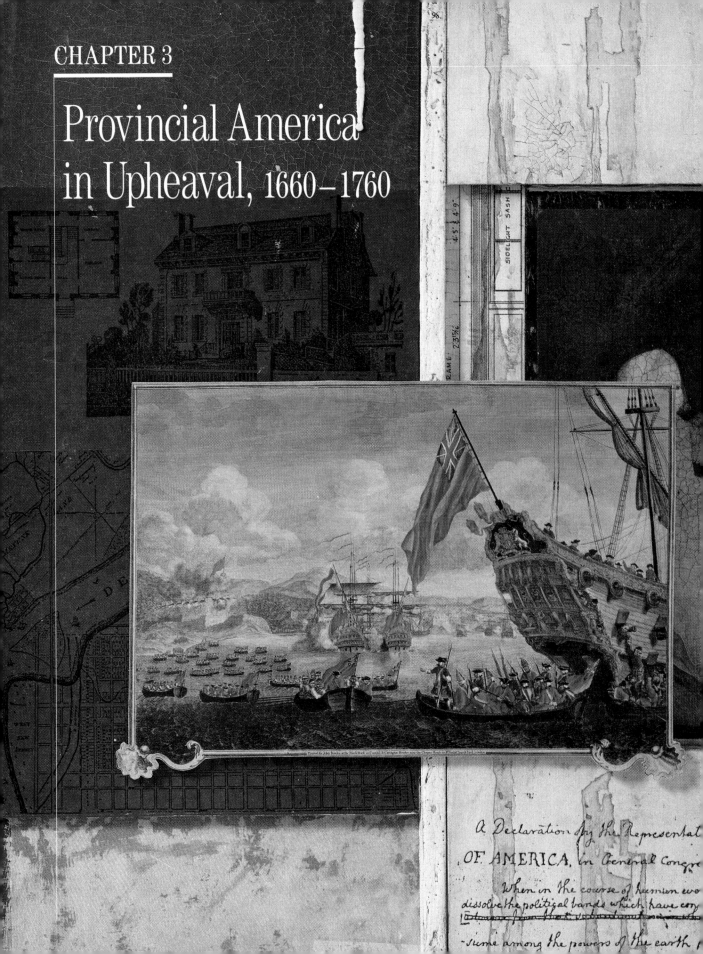

CHAPTER 3

Provincial America in Upheaval, 1660–1760

*H*annah Dustan (1657–1736) and Eliza Lucas (1722–1793) never knew one another. Dustan lived in the town of Haverhill on the Massachusetts frontier, and Lucas spent her adult years in the vicinity of Charleston, South Carolina. Even though of different generations, both were inhabitants of England's developing North American empire. Like so many other colonists, perpetual imperial warfare affected their lives as England, France, and Spain repeatedly battled for supremacy in Europe and America between 1689 and 1763.

During the 1690s, as part of a war involving England and France, frontier New Englanders experienced devastating raids by Indian parties from French Canada. On the morning of March 15, 1697, a band of Abenakis struck Haverhill. Hannah Dustan's husband and seven of her children saved themselves by racing for the community's blockhouse. Hannah, who had just given birth a few days before, was not so fortunate. The Abenakis captured her, as well as her baby and midwife Mary Neff.

After some discussion, the Indians "dashed out the brains of the infant against a tree," as the well-known Puritan minister, the Reverend Cotton Mather, later wrote; but they decided to spare Hannah and Mary along with a few other captives. The plan was to march these residents to the principal Abenaki village in Canada where they would "be stripped and scourged and [made to] run the gauntlet through the whole army of Indians." If they survived, they would be adopted into the tribe, literally to become white Indians.

The Abenakis split up their captives. Two male warriors, three women, and seven children escorted Hannah, Mary, and a young boy named Samuel Lenorson. Hannah, although in a virtual state of shock, maintained her composure as the party walked northward day after day. She prayed fervently, noted Mather, for some means of escape. Just before dawn one morning, she awoke to find all her captors sound asleep. Seizing the moment, she roused Mary and Samuel, handed them hatchets, and told them to crush as many skulls as possible. Suddenly the Indians were dying, and only two, a badly wounded woman and a child, escaped.

Hannah then took a scalping knife and finished the bloody work. When she and the other captives got back to Haverhill, they had ten scalps, for which the Massachusetts General Court awarded them a bounty of £50 in local currency. New Englanders hailed Hannah Dustan as a true heroine—a woman whose courage overcame the French and Indian enemies of England's empire in America.

Cotton Mather spread Dustan's story far and wide, hoping to rekindle the faith of New England's founders. If citizens would just "humble" themselves before God, he argued, the Almighty would stop afflicting society with the horrors of war and provide for the "quick extirpation" of all "bloody and crafty" enemies. Mather's jeremiad, however, had little effect. The war soon ended, and New Englanders devoted themselves more than ever before to acquiring personal wealth.

After a long and full life, Hannah Dustan died in 1736. Two years later, George Lucas, a prosperous Antigua planter who was also an officer in the British army, moved to South Carolina, where he owned three rice plantations. He wanted to get his family away from the Caribbean region, since hostilities were brewing with Spain.

When war did come a year later, Lucas returned to Antigua to resume his military duties. Leaving an ailing wife, he placed his 17-year-old daughter Eliza in charge of his Carolina properties. The responsibility did not faze her; she wrote regularly to her "Dear Papa" for advice, and the plantations prospered. The war, however, disrupted rice trading routes into the West Indies, and planters needed other cash crops to be sold elsewhere. George Lucas was aware of the problem and sent Eliza seeds for indigo plants, the source of a valued deep-blue dye, to see whether indigo could be grown profitably in South Carolina.

With the help of knowledgeable slaves, Eliza conducted successful experiments. In 1744 a major dye broker in England tested her product "against some of the best French" indigo and rated it "in his opinion . . . as good." Just 22 years old, Eliza had pioneered a cash crop that brought additional wealth to Carolina's planters and became a major trading staple of the British empire.

Because of the experiments of young Eliza Lucas, South Carolina became a major center of indigo production in the British empire.

Had Eliza chosen to marry before this time, she could have lost the legal independence to conduct her experiments; but she favored no suitor until she met and wed Charles Pinckney, a widower of great wealth and high social standing. In later life she took pride in the success of her children. Charles Cotesworth Pinckney (b. 1746) was a powerful voice in the Constitutional Convention of 1787, and Thomas Pinckney (b. 1750) represented President Washington during 1795 in negotiating an agreement called Pinckney's Treaty (see p. 227), which resolved western boundary questions with Spain.

A heralded woman of her generation, Eliza Lucas Pinckney died at the end of the revolutionary era, nearly 140 years after the birth of Hannah Dustan. Dustan's life paralleled the years in which England laid the foundations for a mighty empire in America. Between 1660 and 1700, the colonists offered resistance but had to adjust to new imperial laws governing their lives. Then a series of wars with France and Spain that affected both Dustan and Pinckney caused yet more turbulence. Even with so much upheaval, the colonies grew and prospered.

After 1760 provincial Americans were in a position to question their subordinate relationship with Britain. The coming of the American Revolution cannot be appreciated without looking at the development of the English empire in America—and how that experience related to the lives of passing generations of colonists like Hannah Dustan and Eliza Lucas Pinckney.

DESIGNING ENGLAND'S NORTH AMERICAN EMPIRE

During the 1760s Benjamin Franklin tried to explain why relations between England and the colonies had turned sour. He blamed British trade policies designed to control American commerce. "Most of the statutes, or acts, . . . of parliaments, . . . for regulating, directing, or restraining of trade," Franklin declared, "have been . . . political blunders, . . . for private advantage, under pretense of public good." The trade system, he believed, had become both oppressive and corrupt.

Little more than a hundred years before,

the colonists had traded as they pleased. After 1650, however, Oliver Cromwell and then the restored Stuart monarch Charles II (reigned 1660–1685) worked closely with Parliament to design trade policies that exerted greater control over the activities of the American colonists.

To Benefit the Parent State

Certain key ideas underlay the new, more restrictive policies. Most important was the concept of *mercantilism*, a term not invented until the late eighteenth century but one that describes what England's leaders set out to accomplish. Their goal was national greatness and, as one courtier told Charles II, the challenge was to develop "trade and commerce" so that it "draws [a] store of wealth" into England.

Mercantilist thinkers believed the world's supply of wealth was not infinite but fixed in quantity. Any nation that gained wealth automatically did so at the expense of another. In economic dealings, then, the most powerful nations always maintained a favorable balance of trade by exporting a greater value of goods than they imported. To square accounts, hard money in the form of gold and silver would flow into creditor nations. Governments controlling the most precious metals would be the most self-sufficient and could use such wealth to stimulate internal economic development as well as strengthen military forces. This ensured not only national survival but ascendancy over other countries.

Mercantilist theory also demonstrated how colonies could best serve their parent nations. Gold and silver extracted from Central and South America had underwritten Spain's rise to international glory in the sixteenth century. Although such easy wealth did not exist in eastern North America, the colonies could contribute to a favorable trade balance for England by producing such staple crops as tobacco, rice, and sugar, thus ending any need to import these goods from other countries.

The American provinces, in addition, could supply valuable raw materials—for example, timber products. England had plundered its own forests to provide winter fuel and construct

This ship's carpenter was typical of those employed in a booming colonial industry—one-fourth or more of all English-registered vessels were produced in the colonies.

a strong naval fleet, making it necessary to import wood from the Baltic region. Now the colonies could help fill timber demands, again reducing foreign imports while supplying a commodity vital to national security. Great stands of American timber could also be fashioned into fine furniture and sold back to the colonists. Ideally, England's overseas colonies would serve as a source of raw materials and staple crops as well as a marketplace for manufactured goods.

Mercantilist reasoning affirmed the principle that the colonies existed to benefit and strengthen the parent nation. As such, provincial economic and political activities had to be closely managed. To effect these goals, Parliament passed a series of Navigation Acts (1651, 1660, 1663, and 1673), which formed the cornerstone of England's commercial relations with the colonies and the rest of the world. The acts banned foreign merchants and vessels from participating in the colonial trade; proclaimed that certain "enumerated" goods could only be shipped to England or other colonies (the first list included dyewoods, indigo, sugar, and tobacco, with furs, molasses, rice, and wood products such as masts, pitch, and tar being added later); and specified that European goods destined for America had to pass through England.

Through the Navigation System, England became the central trading hub of the empire, which resulted in a great economic boom at home. Before 1660, for example, the Dutch operated the largest merchant fleet in Europe and dominated the colonial tobacco trade. They went to war with England over the first Navigation Act (1651), but this short-lived contest (1652–1654) proved futile. After 1660 key industries like shipbuilding began to prosper as never before. By the late 1690s the English merchant fleet had outdistanced all competitors, including the Dutch, which seemed to bear out mercantilist ideas regarding one nation's strength coming at another's expense.

In the colonies the Navigation Acts had mixed effects. New Englanders, taking advantage of nearby timber supplies, strengthened their economy by heavy involvement in shipbuilding. By the early 1700s Americans were constructing one-fourth or more of all English merchant vessels. In the Chesapeake Bay region, however, the enumeration of tobacco resulted in economic difficulties. By the 1660s planters were producing too much tobacco for consumption in the British Isles alone. Because of the costs of merchandising the crop through England, the price became too high to support large sales in Europe. Consequently, the glut of tobacco in England caused prices to decline, resulting in hard times and much furor among Chesapeake planters.

Seizing Dutch New Netherland

Charles II learned from his father's mistakes. He never claimed divine authority in decision making; and so as not to appear too power hungry, he passed himself off at court as a sensuous, lazy, vulgar man whose major objectives were to attend horse races, tell bawdy jokes, and seduce women. His mistresses, like Nell Gwynn,

became national celebrities and bore him at least 14 illegitimate children. When asked about his lustful ways, he replied, as if mocking the Puritans who had beheaded his father, "God will not damn a man for taking a little unregular pleasure by the way."

Charles often played the foppish fool, but he was an intelligent person with a vision for England's greatness. He began his reign determined "to improve the general traffic and trade of the kingdom," as one courtier observed. Besides urging Parliament to legislate the Navigation System, Charles pursued other plans for enhancing England's imperial power. None was more important than challenging Dutch supremacy over the Hudson and Delaware river valleys.

The precedent for attacking territory claimed by England's imperial rivals came in 1654 when Cromwell launched a fleet with 8000 troops to strike at the heart of New Spain. Cromwell's "Western Design" expedition failed to conquer the primary targets of Puerto Rico, Hispaniola, or the port city of Cartagena (located in modern-day Colombia). The fleet, however, seized the island of Jamaica, which in time became a center for illegal commerce with New Spain, as well as a major slave trade marketing center.

Charles hated everything about Cromwell and proved it by having the Lord Protector's corpse exhumed and hanged in public before a cheering crowd. Still, he borrowed freely from Cromwell's precedents. New Netherland, a colony having the geographic misfortune of lying between New England and the southern colonies, was an obvious target, especially since Dutch sea captains used it as a base for conducting illegal trade with English settlers. To enforce the Navigation Acts, reasoned Charles and his advisors, the Dutch colony had to be conquered.

New Netherland was the handiwork of the Dutch West India Company, a joint-stock venture chartered in 1621. The company soon sent out a governor and employees to the Hudson River area to develop the fur trade with local Indians, particularly the Five Nations of Iroquois inhabiting upper New York west of Fort Orange (Albany).

Iroquois Nations

The Dutch West India Company developed the fur trade primarily with the Five Nations of Iroquois.

At the outset the company showed little interest in settlement, but leaders had to reckon with food shortages. To encourage local agricultural production, the company announced in 1629 that vast landed estates, known as *patroonships*, would be made available to men of wealth who transported at least 50 families to New Netherland. The migrants would become tenant farmers for their masters, or *patroons*, who hoped to live like medieval lords on manorial estates. Since the Dutch home economy was booming, few subjects accepted these less-than-generous terms; and only the patroonship of Rensselaerwyck, surrounding Fort Orange, was much of a success.

The New Netherland colony was also internally weak and unstable. The governors were a sorry lot, typified by Wouter van Twiller (served 1633–1638), a vain, crude man who was pleasant, claimed a contemporary, only "as long as there is any wine." In 1643 his successor, William Kieft, started a war with natives around New Amsterdam (New York City) that devastated the colony's settlers. Facing bankruptcy in 1647, company directors asked Peter Stuyvesant to save the venture. However, Stuyvesant became embroiled in bitter disputes with the settlers, whom he repeatedly infuriated with his highhanded policies.

Still, New Netherland's population pushed toward 8000 by 1660, counting Puritans who had settled on Long Island. New Amsterdam held people from all over Europe, as well as many African slaves. The unpopularity of Stuyvesant, the absence of any voice in government, and the denial of freedom of worship separate from the Dutch Reformed church all undermined feelings of loyalty and favored an English takeover.

In the early days of his monarchy, Charles II strengthened his political base at home by making generous land grants in America, such as rewarding eight loyal court favorites with the Carolinas patent (see p. 44). In 1664 the king gave his brother, James, the Duke of York, title to all Dutch lands in North America, on the obvious condition that they be conquered. James quickly hired Colonel Richard Nicolls to organize a small invasion fleet. When the flotilla appeared before New Amsterdam in August 1664, Governor Stuyvesant failed to rally the populace. With hardly an exchange of shots, New Netherland became the Duke of York's English province of New York.

Proprietary Difficulties in New York and New Jersey

Unlike his older brother, James was an inflexible man. Although hard-working, he was a humorless autocrat. He even treated his mistresses coldly, as if they were "given him by priests for penance," wrote one court wag. Nor was James sensitive to the political trends of his time. He hated Parliament for having executed his father and was intolerant of representative government. As he once explained, popular assemblies of any kind often "prove destructive to, or very often disturb, the peace of the government wherein they are allowed."

James's proprietary charter had no clause mandating an assembly for his colony, and he instructed Colonel Nicolls to make no concessions. As a shrewd administrator, Nicolls got around the problem by granting other rights. In his Articles of Capitulation, he confirmed all inhabitants, including the Dutch, in their land titles. Next he announced the Duke's Laws, which provided for local government and guaranteed basic liberties such as trial by jury and religious toleration, so long as settlers belonged to and supported some church.

The Long Island Puritans, however, kept demanding a representative assembly. They refused to pay local taxes, arguing that they were "enslaved under an arbitrary power." The absence of a popularly based assembly for New York's colonists continued to be a source of friction. Finally, in the early 1680s James conceded the point, and an assembly met for the first time in 1683. Once he became king in 1685, James disallowed further assembly meetings, which was one reason for a local rebellion in 1689 (see p. 85).

To make matters more confusing, James in 1664 turned over all his proprietary lands between the Hudson and Delaware rivers to John, Lord Berkeley, and Sir George Carteret, two court favorites who were also Carolina proprietors. Unfortunately, Colonel Nicolls did not learn of this grant until after he had offered some Puritans land patents in the eastern portion of what became the colony of New Jersey, named after Carteret's childhood home, the Isle of Jersey off the coast of England.

Until the end of the century, questions regarding proprietary ownership of New Jersey plagued the colony's development. Settlement proceeded slowly, with the population moving toward 15,000 by 1700. Most colonists engaged in commercial farming and raised a variety of grain crops, which they marketed through New York City and Philadelphia, the two port towns that would dominate the region. Because of ongoing confusion over land titles, as well as proprietary political authority, the Crown decided in 1702 that New Jersey would henceforth be a royal province.

Planting William Penn's "Holy Experiment"

During the English Civil War of the 1640s a number of radical religious sects—Ranters, Seekers, and Quakers among them—began to appear in England. Each represented a small band of fervent believers determined to recast human society in the mold of a particular religious vision. George Fox founded the Society of Friends, and his followers came to be called "Quakers," because Fox, who went to jail many times, warned one judge to "tremble at the word of the Lord."

The Quakers adhered to many controversial ideas. They believed that all persons had a divine spark, or "inner light," which, when fully nurtured, allowed them to commune directly with God. Like Anne Hutchinson before them, they saw little need for human institutions. They had no ministers and downplayed the importance of the Bible, since they could order their lives according to revelation received directly from God.

In addition, the Quakers held a unique social vision. All humans, they argued, were equal in the sight of God. Thus they wore unadorned black clothing and refused to remove their broad-brimmed hats when social superiors passed by them. Women had full access to leadership positions and could serve as preachers and missionaries. Members of the sect also refused to take legal oaths, which they considered a form of swearing, and they were pacifists, believing that warfare would never solve human problems. In time, Quakers became antislavery advocates, arguing that God did not hold some persons inferior because of skin color.

Early English Quakers were intensely fervent, and during the 1650s and 1660s they sent many witnesses of their faith to America. These individuals, about half of them women, fared poorly in the colonies. Puritan magistrates in

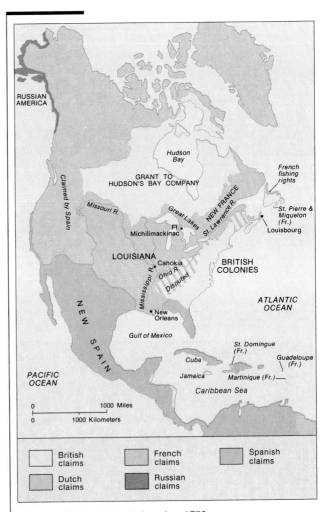

European Claims in North America, 1750

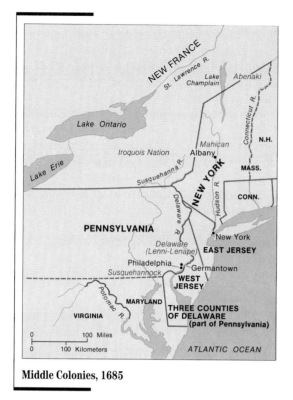

Middle Colonies, 1685

acceded to Penn's request for a proprietary charter in 1681, stating that his purpose was to "enlarge our British empire" and pay off a £16,000 debt long since due the estate of Penn's father. Years later, Penn claimed that Charles's real motivation was "to be rid of" the Quakers "at so cheap a rate" by conveying to him title to "a desert [wilderness] three thousand miles off."

Pennsylvania, meaning Penn's woods, was hardly a desert. It was a bountiful tract, and Penn wanted to make the most of it, both as a sanctuary for oppressed religious groups and as a source of personal income from quitrents. He laid his plans carefully, making large grants to English Quakers, and he drew up a blueprint for a commercial center—Philadelphia, or the City of Brotherly Love. Penn sent agents to Europe in search of settlers, offering generous land packages with low annual quitrents. He also wrote his First Frame of Government (1682), which guaranteed a legislative assembly and full freedom of religion.

Like the Puritans before him, Penn had a utopian vision, in this case captured by the phrase "holy experiment." Unlike the Puritans, Penn wanted to mold a society in which peoples of diverse backgrounds and religious beliefs lived together harmoniously—a bold idea in an era not known for its toleration.

Determined to succeed, Penn sailed to America in 1682, landing first in the area known as the Three Lower Counties, later to become the colony of Delaware. He had purchased this strip of land from the Duke of York to assure an easy exit for commerce flowing out of Philadelphia to Atlantic trade routes. Until 1701, Delaware existed as an appendage of Pennsylvania, but then Penn granted it a separate assembly. Until the Revolution, however, the proprietary governors of Pennsylvania also headed Delaware's government.

Next Penn journeyed upriver to lay out Philadelphia. Some settlers were already present, and during the next few years others migrated not only from England but also from Wales, Scotland, Ireland, Holland, Germany, and Switzerland. Typical were Germans from the Rhineland who followed their religious leader, Francis Daniel Pastorius, and founded Germantown to the north of Philadelphia. From the very outset, Pennsylvania developed along

Massachusetts told them of their "free liberty to keep away from us" and threw them out. Two Quaker males were so persistent in coming back to Boston that officials finally hanged them in 1659, and they gave a third witness, Mary Dyer, a gallows reprieve. Dyer, however, returned the next year, was hanged, and became a martyr to her vision of a more harmonious world.

William Penn (1644–1718) first became a Quaker in the early 1660s while a college student at Oxford. Hoping to cure his son's zealousness, Penn's father, who had received estates in Ireland for his part in leading Cromwell's 1654 expedition against New Spain, sent William on a tour of the Continent. Penn returned in a more worldly frame of mind, but he soon adopted Quaker beliefs again. He was so outspoken that he even spent time in jail, but his father's high standing at court—the elder Penn supported the Stuart restoration—gave Penn access to Charles II.

During the 1670s, George Fox traveled to America, hoping to find a haven for his followers. He also encouraged Penn to use his family connections to obtain a land grant. King Charles

In his treaty with the Indians, William Penn sought to treat Native Americans fairly in negotiating land rights. However, Pennsylvania colonists and Penn's own officials wanted to push the native populace westward as rapidly as possible.

pluralist lines, an early sign of what later characterized the cultural ideal of the United States as a whole.

Penn envisioned a "peaceable kingdom" and sought cordial relations with local Indians. Before leaving England, he wrote to the Delawares, the dominant tribe in the region, explaining that the king of England "hath given me a great province." He asked that "we may always live together as neighbors and friends." True to his word, Penn met with the Delawares and told them that he would not take land from them unless sanctioned by tribal chieftains. What emerged was the "walking purchase" system in which the natives sold land based on the distance that a person could travel on foot in a day. Even though the system was open to abuse, Penn's goal was honest dealing, which had rarely been the case in other colonies.

Completing these and other tasks, Penn returned to England in 1684 to encourage further

settlement. That was no problem. Pennsylvania was very attractive, particularly with dissenter religious groups. By the early 1700s the population exceeded 20,000. Colonists poured through the booming port of Philadelphia and then fanned out into the fertile countryside. There they established family farms, raising livestock and growing abundant grain crops, which they marketed to the West Indies and Europe. The settlers prospered, and Pennsylvania gained a reputation as "one of the best poor man's countries in the world."

Still, not all was perfect in the peaceable kingdom. Religious sects segregated themselves, wanting little to do with one another. To Penn's dismay, life in Philadelphia was more raucous than pious. Drinking establishments and brothels sprang up in large numbers, and endless bickering characterized local politics. Quakers dominated the government but fought endlessly over the prerogatives of power. Penn thought these "brutish, . . . scurvy quarrels" were a "disgrace" to the colony, but his pleas for harmony went unheeded. Equally disturbing from his point of view, settlers refused to pay quitrents "to supply me with bread," yet he kept funding the colony's development.

Hoping to solve such problems, Penn returned in 1699. His presence had a moderating influence—but only so long as he stayed. Before leaving for the last time, he announced a new Charter of Liberties (1701), which placed all legislative authority in an elective assembly, to be checked only by a proprietary governor with the advice of a council of well-to-do local gentlemen. This document served as the basis of Pennsylvania's unicameral government until the Revolution.

Peace, prosperity, pluralism, and religious toleration were the hallmarks of Penn's utopian vision. In his old age, however, he considered the "holy experiment" a failure. He concluded that peaceable kingdoms on earth lay beyond human reach, and having even endured prison for debts contracted on behalf of his colony, Penn died an embittered man in 1718. Still, by seeking a better life for all peoples, he had infused a sense of high social purpose into the American experience.

Characteristic of Quaker farms in Pennsylvania, David Twining's homestead emphasizes harmonious and peaceful relations.

DEFYING THE IMPERIAL WILL: PROVINCIAL CONVULSIONS AND REBELLIONS

Establishing the Middle Colonies was an integral part of England's imperial expansion within the framework of mercantilist thinking. Certainly the Dutch understood this, and they fought two additional wars with England (1664–1667 and 1672–1674), hoping to recoup their losses. In the last war they recaptured New York only to renounce all claims in the peace settlement. After that time, the Dutch focused their activities on other parts of the world, even if some of their mariners continued to trade illegally with the colonists.

Besides standing up to the Dutch, Charles II and his advisors worked to build the emerging empire in other ways. Crown officials crossed the Atlantic to determine whether the colonists were cooperating with the Navigation System. They also sent the first customs officers to America to collect duties on enumerated goods being traded between colonies—and then to foreign ports. Increasingly the Americans felt England's constraining hand, which in some locales helped to bring on violence.

Bacon's Bloody Rebellion in Virginia

With tobacco glutting the market in England, Virginia's economy went into a tailspin during the 1660s. The planters blamed the Navigation Acts, which stopped them from dealing directly with such foreign merchants as the Dutch; and it did not improve the planters' mood when, in 1667, Dutch war vessels captured virtually the whole English merchant fleet hauling the annual crop out of Chesapeake Bay, resulting in nearly the total loss of a year's worth of work.

Besides economic woes, there were other problems. Some Virginians thought that their longtime royal governor, Sir William Berkeley (1606–1677), had become a tyrant. Berkeley handed out patronage jobs to a few favored planters, known as the "Green Spring" faction (named after Berkeley's plantation). Such favors allowed the governor to dominate the assembly and lay heavy taxes at a time when settlers were suffering economically. As a consequence, some planters lost their property, and young males just completing terms of indentured service saw few prospects for ever gaining title to land and achieving economic independence. In 1670 Berkeley and the assembly approved a 50-acre property holding requirement for voting privileges. This action fed suspicions that the governor and his cronies were out to amass all power for themselves.

In 1674 young Nathaniel Bacon (1647–1676) jumped into the simmering pot. From a wealthy English family and educated at Cambridge, he had squandered his inheritance before reaching his mid-twenties. Bacon's despairing father sent him to Virginia with a stipend to start a plantation, hoping that the experience would force his son to grow up. When Bacon arrived, Berkeley greeted him warmly, stating that "gentlemen of your quality come very rarely into this country."

Bacon was ambitious, and he sought acceptance among Berkeley's favored friends, who controlled the lucrative Indian trade. He asked the governor for a trading license, but Berkeley denied the request, feeling that the young man had not yet proven his worth. Incensed by his rejection, Bacon started opposing Berkeley at every turn. He organized other substantial planters—also not favored by Berkeley—into his own "Castle" faction (after his plantation), and he also appealed to Virginia's growing numbers of propertyless poor for support.

Stirrings among Indian tribes made matters worse. Far to the north in New York, the Five Nations of Iroquois had become more aggressive in their quest for furs. They started pushing other tribes southward toward Virginia, and some spilled onto frontier plantations, resulting in a few killings.

Bacon demanded reprisals, but Berkeley urged caution, noting that a war would only add to Virginia's tax burdens. Bacon asked for a military commission, stating that he would organize an army of volunteers. The governor refused, at which point Bacon charged his adversary with being more interested in protecting profits from his Indian trading monopoly than in saving settlers' lives. Bacon pulled together a force of over 1000 men, described as "the scum of the country" by Berkeley's supporters, and indiscriminately started killing local Indians.

In response, Berkeley declared Bacon "the greatest rebel that ever was in Virginia" and sent out militiamen to corral the volunteers, but Bacon's force eluded them. The governor also called a new assembly, which met at Jamestown in June 1676. Among reforms designed to pacify the "mutineers," the burgesses restored voting rights to all adult freemen, even if they did not own property. Events had gone too far, however, and a shooting war broke out. Before the fighting ceased, Bacon's force burned Jamestown to the ground, and Berkeley fled across Chesapeake Bay. What finally precipitated an end to the struggle was Bacon's death from dysentery in October 1676.

When Charles II learned of the uprising, he considered it an affront to royal authority and a threat to his tax revenues on tobacco. The colonists had to be disciplined, so he authorized a flotilla of 11 ships and 1000 troops to cross the Atlantic and restore order. By the time the troops arrived, Berkeley was back in control. Royal advisors with the king's army, however, removed the aging governor from office on the grounds that his policies had helped to stir up trouble. Governors who placed self-interest above the need for stability and order in the empire would no longer be tolerated.

After 1676 the Crown started sending royal governors to Virginia with detailed instructions on managing the colony as an imperial enterprise—at times at the expense of local interests. In response, Virginia's leading gentleman-planters, previously divided into pro- and anti-Berkeley factions, settled their differences in the face of what they saw as threats to local autonomy. They rallied the people to their side, got themselves elected regularly to the House of Burgesses, and worked together to protect the colony's interests.

This fundamental recasting of political lines was an important development. No longer would rising planter elite leaders fight to the death among themselves. They would stand united in defense of local rights and privileges, making it clear that the Crown, if it wanted harmony and stability, had to show at least some respect for the welfare of its colonists.

The Glorious Revolution Spills into America

The king's reactions to Bacon's Rebellion fit a larger pattern of asserting more authority over America. New England, with its independent ways, was an obvious target. Back in the mid-1660s royal commissioners had visited Massachusetts and seen Dutch merchant vessels trading openly in Boston harbor in violation of the Navigation Acts. Puritan leaders were surly about the matter, stating that "the laws of England . . . do not reach [to] America." Once home, the angry commissioners urged the Crown to take over the colony, but nothing happened—at least not for a few years.

Then in 1675 King Charles, seeking more effective control over the colonies, designated certain Privy Council members to serve as the Lords of Trade and Plantations. The lords, in turn, sent agents and customs officials to America. The most notorious was Edward Randolph, a grim, dedicated bureaucrat who never met a Puritan he liked. Soon he was bombarding the Lords of Trade with negative reports. In response to Randolph's accusations the lords began legal proceedings and got the Bay Colony charter revoked in 1684.

Randolph, however, was not solely responsible for voiding the charter. The lords had developed plans for setting up two or three large administrative territories in North America. New England made a natural unit, based on geographic cohesion and forms of economic production. King Charles thought the scheme too radical, but when James became king in 1685, the lords gained permission to set up the Dominion of New England, which stretched from Nova Scotia to the Delaware River.

James II liked the Dominion concept not only because it favored the Church of England but also because it centralized political power in the hands of a governor and a large advisory council made up of Crown appointees. As a result, local representative assemblies would cease to exist. James gladly wrote the New

Yorkers and informed them that they would be under the authority of the Dominion. As for Connecticut and Rhode Island, the lords were already trying to void their charters in court.

From the outset the Dominion was a bad idea, perhaps made worse by naming as governor Sir Edmund Andros (1637–1714), a man of aristocratic bearing with impressive military credentials. Among his councilors was the despised Edward Randolph. Images of political tyranny floated through Puritan minds when Andros debarked in Boston in late 1686 and demanded that a building be found for holding Anglican church services. It all smacked of garrison government in which the highest ranking military officer had complete authority, with no popular checks whatsoever.

Andros expected the Puritans to conform to the imperial will. He announced plans to rewrite all land deeds, none of which the General Court had awarded in the king's name and, then, to impose quitrents, which New Englanders had never paid. He announced import taxes to underwrite the expenses of his government, and he started prosecuting violators of the Navigation Acts.

Meanwhile, in England, James II had created an uproar by pushing royal authority too far. In defiance of England's Protestant tradition, he flaunted his Roman Catholic beliefs in public and declared that his newborn son, now next in line for the throne, would be raised a Roman Catholic. The thought of yet more turbulence over religious beliefs was too much for influential English leaders to bear. In December 1688 they drove James from the realm and offered the throne to his Protestant daughter, Mary, and her husband, the Dutch prince, William of Orange, as joint monarchs. As part of the Glorious Revolution, Parliament also placed strict limitations on royal prerogatives by adopting the Declaration of Rights (1689), which at long last assured Parliament an equal, if not dominant, voice in Britain's political affairs.

When news of the Glorious Revolution reached Boston, local Puritan leaders went into action, urged on by wild rumors that James, who had fled to France, was conspiring with Andros, French Canadians, and Indians to seize New England and turn it into a bastion of Roman Catholicism. Denouncing Andros and his followers as "bloody devotees of Rome," they seized the governor on April 18, 1689, threw him in jail, and then shipped him back to England. They did so, they insisted, to end Andros's arbitrary rule, and they asked William and Mary to restore their original corporate charter.

The coup in Massachusetts helped spark a rebellion in New York, where a volatile mix of ethnic and class tensions resulted in a violent upheaval. Francis Nicholson served in New York City as the Dominion's lieutenant governor. Wealthy Dutch and English landholders and merchants cooperated with his rule, which bred resentment among poorer Dutch and English settlers, such as the Puritans on Long Island. Jacob Leisler, a combative local merchant of German origin, also hated the favored families. They had snubbed him socially, despite his marriage to a wealthy Dutch widow. Even worse from his point of view, they cared little about securing popular political rights.

When reports of the rumored "popish" plot and the Massachusetts coup reached New York, Leisler exhorted the anti-Nicholson settlers to rise up and defend themselves. He organized 500 of them into a military force, and on May 31 they captured Fort James guarding New York harbor. Within a few days, Nicholson fled to England amid cries that all Dominion "popish dogs and devils" must be jailed. Leisler then set up an interim government and waited for advice from England, hoping that the new monarchs would make a permanent grant of a popularly based assembly. In addition, Leisler allowed mobs to harass and rob wealthy families.

The third colony jolted by a revolt in 1689 was Maryland, where quarrels between Roman Catholics and Protestants remained a perpetual source of tension. The proprietary governor, William Joseph, tried to contain the popish conspiracy rumors, but John Coode, a nervous local planter, organized the Protestant Association to defend Marylanders from the impending slaughter. Rumormongers soon were whispering that the Catholic proprietor and his local governor were in on the plot. That was all Coode needed. He led 250 followers to St. Mary's, where in July 1689 they removed Joseph from office, called their own assembly, and then sent representatives to England to plead for royal government.

In a chain reaction, three uprisings had oc-curred in the American colonies during a span of four months. Although each had its own local character, the common issue, besides the rumored Catholic conspiracy, was the question of how extensive colonial rights would be in the face of tightening imperial administration. All the colonists could do now was wait to hear from the new monarchs—and hope for the best.

New England's Witchcraft Hysteria

William and Mary, at first, had little time to deal with the provincial rebellions. Warfare had broken out in Europe (the War of the League of Augsburg, 1689–1697). Spilling over into America, the contest caused havoc in the lives of frontier settlers like Hannah Dustan. French and Indian raiding parties made orphans of many children, including a few who ended up in Salem Village (now Danvers), Massachusetts, the center of the 1692 witchcraft episode.

Puritans, like most Europeans and colonists elsewhere, believed in witchcraft. They thought that the devil could materialize in various shapes and forms, damaging lives at will. Satan's agents included witches and wizards, women and men possessed by his evil spirits. Eighty-one New Englanders had faced accusations of practicing witchcraft before 1692, 16 of whom were put to death. These numbers were insignificant in comparison to accused witches hunted down and executed in Europe.

Reasons abound for the outbreak of the witchcraft hysteria. By the early 1690s New Englanders had lost their charter, lived under the Dominion, rebelled against Edmund Andros, and engaged in war with the hated French. These unsettled conditions may have made the populace overly suspicious and anxious about evil influences in their midst.

In addition, special tensions affected the Salem area. Salem Town, the port, was caught up in New England's commercial life while outlying settlers around Salem Village remained quite traditional in seeking God's grace before material wealth. Resentment by the villagers was growing, described even before 1690 as "uncharitable expressions and uncomely reflections tossed to and fro."

These tensions came out in the pattern of accusations when in early 1692 a few adolescent

As the witchcraft trials proceeded, many young girls became more strident in their accusations. They fell into fits and shouted that the accused had cast evil spells over them.

girls, among them some of the war orphans from Maine, started having their "fits." Anxious about their own lives, the girls had asked Tituba, a local slave woman from the West Indies, to tell them their fortunes. She did so. Soon thereafter the girls started acting hysterically, observers claimed, as if possessed by Satan's demons. When asked to name possible witches, the girls did not stop with Tituba.

Before the hysteria ended, the "afflicted" girls made hundreds of accusations before a special court appointed to root the devil out of Massachusetts. With increasing frequency they pointed to prosperous citizens like those of Salem Town. The penalty for practicing witchcraft was death. Some 50 defendants, among them Tituba, saved themselves by admitting their guilt; but 20 men and women were executed (19 by hanging and 1 by the crushing weight of stones) after steadfastly refusing to admit that they had practiced witchcraft.

By the end of the year the craze was over, probably because too many citizens of rank and influence, including the wife of the new royal governor, Sir William Phips, had been accused of doing the devil's work. In time, most participants in the Salem witchcraft trials admitted to being deluded. Although their victims could not be brought back to life, the episode, more dramatic than consequential in its long-term significance, stood as a cautionary reminder in the colonies about the dangers of mass hysteria at a time when Europeans were still actively ferreting out and prosecuting alleged witches. The incident also helped sustain New England's transition to a commercial society by making traditional folk beliefs—and those who espoused them—appear foolish.

Settling Anglo-American Differences

In 1691 William and Mary began to address colonial issues. As constitutional monarchs, they were not afraid of popularly based assemblies. In the case of Massachusetts they approved a royal charter that gave the Crown the authority to name royal governors and stated that all male property holders, not just church members, had the right to vote. On the other hand, the monarchs did not tamper with the established Congregational church, thereby reassuring old-line Puritans that conforming to the Church of England was not necessary so long as Bay Colony residents supported England's imperial aspirations.

New York also gained permanent status as a royal colony in 1691, complete with a local representative assembly. Henry Sloughter, the governor, delivered the news; but Jacob Leisler hesitated to step aside, fearing that Sloughter might be an agent of King James. Leisler's obstinacy led to his arrest and hasty trial for treason. His enemies gave all the testimony that the court needed to sentence him to a ghastly death by hanging, disemboweling, drawing and quartering and, if that were not enough, decapitation. It was little solace to Leisler's followers that Parliament, in reviewing the evidence, later declared him innocent of treason.

In Maryland's case the Calverts lost political control in 1692 in favor of royal government, although they still held title to the land and could collect quitrents. Shortly thereafter, a Protestant assembly banned Roman Catholics from political office. Not until 1715 did the Calverts regain political control. By then the proprietary family had converted to Anglicanism and was no longer a threat to Protestant sensibilities.

The transformation revealed a movement toward the royal model of government in which the colonies established legislative assemblies to express and defend their local concerns. Crown-appointed governors, in turn, pledged themselves to enforce the Navigation Acts and other imperial laws. So long as the colonists cooperated, they would not face autocratic forms of government. Nor would the Crown permit the kind of loose freedom of early colonial days, because in gaining basic rights, the Americans also accepted responsibility for conducting their daily affairs within the imperial framework. The Glorious Revolution and its reverberations in America had made this compromise possible.

Maintaining the delicate balance between imperial intrusiveness and local autonomy was the major challenge of the eighteenth century. Until the 1760s both sides tried to make the

compromise work. The Crown demonstrated its resolve through the Navigation Act of 1696, which set up the Board of Trade and Plantations as a permanent administrative agency to advise England's leaders on colonial issues. This act also mandated the establishment of vice-admiralty courts in America to punish smugglers and others who violated the rules of trade. The Board of Trade operated to promote efficiency, not officiousness; yet colonists who cheated and got caught faced stiff penalties from vice-admiralty court judges.

The Board of Trade generally acted with discretion, even in recommending a few acts to restrain colonial manufacturers competing with home industries. Parliament in 1699 adopted legislation (the Woolen Act) that outlawed any exportation of woolen products from America or from one colony to another. The intent was to get the colonists to buy finished woolens from manufacturers in England rather than develop their own industry. In 1732 there was similar restrictive legislation (the Hat Act) concerning the production of beaver and felt hats. Then in

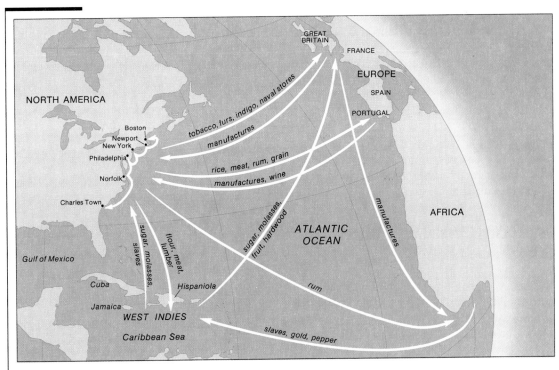

Colonial Trade Routes, 1750

1750 Parliament passed the Iron Act, which forbade the colonists from building new facilities or expanding old ones for the manufacture of finished iron or steel products. On the other hand, the act encouraged them to keep preparing raw iron for final processing in England. As a whole, these acts had few adverse effects on the provincial economy. They simply reinforced fundamental mercantile notions regarding colonies as sources of raw materials and as markets for finished goods.

Occasionally, imperial administrators went too far, such as with the Molasses Act of 1733. In support of a thriving rum industry based mostly in New England, colonial merchants roamed the Caribbean for molasses, which cost less on French and Dutch West Indian islands. To placate British West Indian planters, Parliament tried to redirect the trade with a heavy duty (6 pence per gallon) on foreign molasses brought into the colonies. Enforcing the trade duty could have ruined the North American rum industry, but customs officers wisely ignored collecting the duty, a sensible solution to a potentially inflammatory issue.

As the eighteenth century progressed, imperial officials tried not to be overbearing. In certain instances they actually stimulated provincial economic activity by offering large cash bounties for growing such export commodities as indigo; it seems that Eliza Lucas's efforts had the potential to challenge France's dominant position in the production of that valued dye. Caught up as the empire was in warfare with France and Spain, home leaders did not want to tamper with a system that, by and large, worked. The colonists, for their part, gladly accepted what many have referred to as the "era of salutary neglect."

MATURING COLONIAL SOCIETIES IN UNSETTLED TIMES

Besides the maintenance of stable relations with the parent state, other factors stimulated the maturing of the American provinces after 1700. Certainly the expanding population base, which saw a near doubling of numbers nearly every 20 years, strengthened the colonies, as did the pattern of widespread economic prosperity, even if not shared evenly among the populace. In times of internal social turmoil, such as during the religious upheaval known as the Great Awakening (see pp. 96–102), the colonists disagreed heatedly among themselves but did not lose sight of their joint need to keep building their communities. Finally, participating in a series of imperial wars, in which the colonists made valuable contributions to Britain's military triumphs, instilled a vital sense of self-confidence. By the 1760s provincial Americans took pride in what they had accomplished as subjects inhabiting the British empire in North America.

An Exploding Population Base

Between 1700 and 1760 the colonial population mushroomed from 250,000 to 1.6 million persons—and to 2.5 million by 1775. "People multiply faster here than in Europe," noted one foreign visitor at midcentury. "As soon as a person is old enough he may marry without any fear of poverty," he claimed, because "a newly married man can, without difficulty, get a spot of ground where he may comfortably subsist with his wife and children."

Natural population increase, predicated upon abundant land, early marriages, and high fertility rates, was only one source of the population explosion. Equally significant was the

TABLE 3.1

Colonial Population Growth, 1660–1760

Year	White	Black	Total
1660	70,200	2900	73,100*
1680	138,100	7000	145,100
1700	223,100	27,800	250,900
1720	397,300	68,900	466,200
1740	755,500	150,000	905,500
1760	1,267,800	325,800	1,593,600
1780	2,111,100	566,700	2,677,800

Note: All estimates rounded to the nearest hundred.
*Includes the population of New Netherland.
From *The American Colonies: From Settlement to Independence* by R.C. Simmons. Copyright © 1976 by R.C. Simmons. Reprinted by permission of Harold Matson, Inc.

introduction of non-English peoples. Between 1700 and 1775, for example, the British North American slave trade reached its peak, resulting in the involuntary entry of an estimated 250,000 Africans into the colonies. The black population grew from 28,000 in 1700 to over 500,000 in 1775, with most living as chattel slaves in the South. At least 40 to 50 percent of the African-American population increase was attributable to the booming slave trade.

Among European groups, the Scots-Irish and Germans were predominant, although a smattering of French Huguenot, Swiss, Scottish, Irish, and Jewish migrants joined the westward stream. The Scots-Irish had endured many privations. Originally Presbyterian lowlanders from Scotland, they had migrated to Ulster (northern Ireland) in the seventeenth century at the invitation of the Crown. Once there, they harassed the Catholic Irish with a vengeance, only to face discrimination themselves when a new Parliamentary law, the Test Act of 1704, stripped non-Anglicans of political rights. During the next several years they also endured crop failures and huge rent increases from their English landlords.

In a series of waves between 1725 and 1775 over 100,000 Scots-Irish descended upon North America, lured by reports of "a rich, fine soil before them, laying as loose . . . as the best bed in the garden." Philadelphia was their main port of entry, and they moved out into the backcountry where they squatted on open land and earned reputations as bloodthirsty Indian fighters. In time, the Scots-Irish took the Great Wagon Road through the Shenandoah Valley and started filling in the southern backcountry.

Even before the first Scots-Irish wave, Germans from the area of the upper Rhine River began streaming into the Middle Colonies. Some, like Amish, Moravian, and Mennonite sectarians, were fleeing religious persecution; others were escaping crushing economic circumstances caused by overpopulation, crop failures, and heavy local taxes. So many Germans came through Philadelphia that Benjamin Franklin questioned whether "Pennsylvania, founded by the English, [will] become a colony of aliens, who will shortly be so numerous as to Germanize us, instead of our Anglifying them," since they "will never adopt our language or

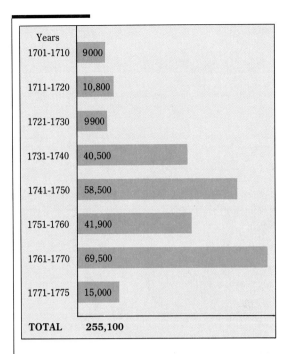

Figure 3.1
Slave importation estimates, 1701–1775. From *The American Colonies: From Settlement to Independence,* by R. C. Simmons. Copyright © 1976 by R. C. Simmons. Reprinted by permission of Harold Matson Company, Inc.

customs any more than they can acquire our complexion?" Franklin's fears could not stop the German migrants, whose population exceeded 100,000 by 1775.

Many destitute Germans crossed the Atlantic as "redemptioners." This system was similar to indentured servitude, except that families migrated together and shippers promised heads of households a few days' time, upon arrival in America, to find some person or group to pay for the family's passage in return for a set number of years of labor (usually three to six years per family member). If they failed, then ship captains held auctions at market with the expectation of making tidy profits. The redemptioner system was full of abuses, such as packing passengers on vessels like cattle and serving them worm-infested food. Hundreds died before seeing America. For those who survived, the dream of prospering someday as free colonists remained viable.

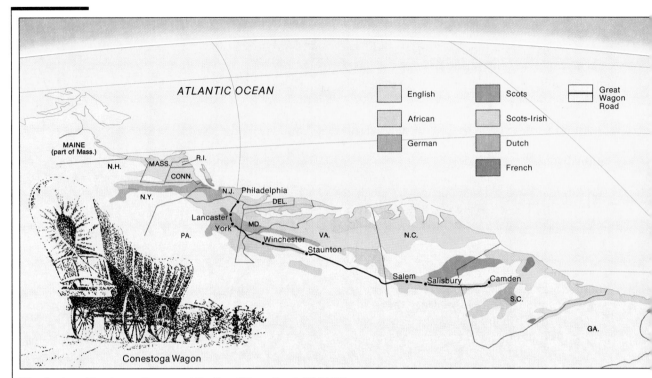

Distribution of Immigrant Groups and the Great Wagon Road, Mid-1700s
The Conestoga wagon was important to the settlement of and movement in the colonies.

One reason for such optimism was that more settlers were enjoying longer life spans, as reflected in higher birth- and lower deathrates. Estimates indicate that post-1700 Americans were dying at an average of 20 to 25 per 1000 annually, but births numbered 45 to 50 per 1000 settlers. The rates in England between 1700 and 1750, by comparison, were 34 births per 1000 for every 33 deaths.

Longer lives reflected better health and agricultural abundance. Colonists had plentiful supplies of food. Nutritious diets led to improved overall health, making it easier for Americans to fight virulent diseases. Even the poorest people, claimed a New England doctor, had regular meals of "salt pork and beans, with bread of Indian corn meal," as well as ample quantities of home-brewed beer and distilled spirits. In the same period, food supplies in Europe were dangerously low. Thousands of western Europeans starved to death between 1740 and 1743 because of widespread crop failures.

The "Europeanizing" of America

Compared to Europe, America was a land of boundless prosperity. To be sure, however, there were wide disparities in wealth, rank, and privilege, which the colonists accepted as part of the natural order of life. They did so because of the pervasive influence of European values, such as the need for hierarchy and deference in social and political relations. The eighteenth century was still an era in which individuals believed in three distinct social orders—the monarchy, the aristocracy, and the "democracy" of common citizens. All persons had an identifiable place in society, fixed at birth; and to try to improve one's lot was to risk instability in the established rhythms of the universe.

These notions, dating back to Aristotle and other ancient thinkers, served as justifications for the highly stratified world of early modern Europe, featuring monarchical families like the Tudors and Stuarts and bloodline aristocrats

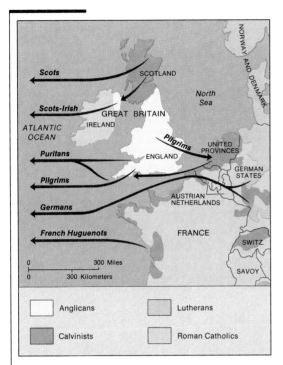

Western European Migration

Western Europeans, escaping religious persecution and dwindling food supplies, migrated in great numbers to North America.

tocratic life-styles. Wealthy southern gentlemen utilized gangs of slaves to produce the staple crops that generated the income to construct lavish manor houses with elaborate formal gardens. Northern merchants built residences of Georgian design and filled them with fashionable Heppelwhite or Chippendale furniture. Together, they thought of themselves as the "better sort," and they expected the "lower sort" (also described as the "common herd" or "rabble") to defer to their judgment in social and political decision making.

One characteristic, then, of the "Europeanizing" of colonial society was growing economic stratification, with extremes of wealth and poverty becoming more visible. In Chester County, Pennsylvania, where commercial farming was predominant, the wealthiest 10 percent of the people owned 24 percent of the taxable property in the 1690s, which jumped to 34 percent by 1760. Their gain came at the expense of the bottom 30 percent, who held 17 percent in the 1690s but only 6 percent in 1760. The pattern

(Text continues on p. 94)

who passed hereditary titles from one generation to the next. Among those threatening Europe's established social order were ambitious commoners who had acquired great wealth through commerce. They too craved public recognition and high status, and they tried to earn a place for themselves at the top of the social pyramid by copying the manners and customs of those born into privileged social stations.

The same could be said for wealthy elite families that had emerged in America by the early eighteenth century. In Virginia names like Byrd, Carter, and Lee were of the first rank; the Pinckneys and Rutledges dominated South Carolina; in New York the Livingstons and Schuylers were among the favored with great estates along the Hudson River, modeled after Dutch patroonships; and in Massachusetts those of major consequence included merchant families like the Hutchinsons and Olivers.

Elite families set themselves apart from the rest of colonial society by imitating English aris-

A room from the Samuel Powel house in Philadelphia depicts the gracious life-style of wealthy urban merchants.

COLONIAL PASTIMES

For much of the past 300 years, Puritans have been the subject of considerable bad press. Novelists and historians have pictured them as dour, sour individuals, dressed in black with faces cast in a permanently disapproving expression. H. L. Mencken, the twentieth-century opponent of what he saw as the Puritan legacy in America, defined Puritanism as "the haunting fear that some one, some where, may be happy." Thomas Babington Macaulay, the nineteenth-century English writer, perhaps best set the tone for Mencken. "The Puritan," Macaulay noted, "hated bear-baiting, not because it gave pain to the

bear, but because it gave pleasure to the spectators."

Is there any truth to such broad-brushed stereotyping? What was the Puritans' attitude toward games, sports, and amusements? And how did their attitudes differ from southern Americans? The answers to such questions indicate the differences between Americans North and South.

Commenting on Puritan religious leaders Increase and Cotton Mather, one historian observed, "Though father and son walked the streets of Boston at noonday, they were only twilight figures, communing with ghosts, building with shadows."

Certainly, as the quote suggests, the Puritan clergy were sober figures. They looked askance at frivolous behavior. Into this category they lumped sports, games, and amusements played for the pure joy of play. In 1647 the Massachusetts Bay Colony outlawed shuffleboard. A ban against bowling followed in 1650. Football and other sports were similarly treated.

Puritan leaders were opposed to any Sabbath amusements. Sunday was a day for worship—not work, and certainly not play. Remaining true to the teachings of the Prophet Isaiah, Cotton Mather condemned those who tried to justify Sabbath sports: "Never did anything sound more sorrowfully or odious since the day the World was first bless'd with such a day." Those who broke the Sabbath were punished. They were denied food, publicly whipped, or placed in stocks.

Nor did Puritans condone pit sports which matched animal against animal. Before the eighteenth century, pit sports (or blood sports) were popular and commonplace in Europe and the American South. People would travel long distances to watch dogs fight bulls, bears, badgers, or other dogs. Cockfighting was equally popular. Were these spectators cruel? Perhaps not. The "bloodied animals," noted a historian of humanitarianism, "were probably not victims of cruelty. Cruelty implies a desire to inflict pain and thus presupposes an empathic appreciation of the suffering of the object of cruelty. Empathy, however, seems not to have been a highly developed trait in premodern Europe."

Unlike Europeans and southerners, Puritans condemned such activity. They did emphasize with the animals. "What Christen [sic] heart," wrote Puritan Philip Stubbes, "can take pleasure to see one poor beast to rent, teare, and kill another, and all for his foolish pleasure?"

Although Puritans outlawed pit sports and insisted on the strict observance of the Sabbath, they did not oppose all sports and games. They supported such activities as walking, archery, running, wrestling, fencing, hunting, fishing, and hawking—as long as they were engaged in at a proper time and in a proper manner. Moderate recreation devoid of gambling, drunkenness, idleness, and frivolousness could refresh the body and spirit and thus serve the greater glory of God. This last point was the most important for the Puritans. Recreations had to help men and women better serve God; they were never to be ends in themselves.

Different attitudes toward sports and games emerged in the southern colonies. Almost from the time of settlement, southerners exhibited an interest—oftentimes bordering on a passion—for various sports. They were particularly attracted to sports that involved opportunities for betting and demonstrations of physical prowess.

Cockfights attracted southerners from every class. The matches were advertised in newspapers and eagerly anticipated; and at important events thousands of dollars in bets would change hands. For northern observers the entire affair attracted only scorn and disgust. Elkanah Watson, who traveled to the South in the mid-1800s, was upset to see "men of character and intelligence giving their countenance to an amusement so frivolous and scandalous, so abhorrent to every feeling of humanity, and so injurious in its moral influence."

Horse racing even surpassed cockfighting as a favorite southern pastime. Wealthy southerners liked to trace their ancestry to the English aristocracy, and they viewed horse racing and horse breeding as aristocratic occupations. In fact, by the eighteenth century the ownership of horses had taken on a cultural significance. As one student of the subject explained, "By the turn of the century possession of . . . these animals had become a social necessity. Without a horse, a planter felt despised, an object of ridicule. Owning even a slow footed saddle horse made the common planter more of a man in his own eyes as well as those of his neighbors."

Horse races matched owner against owner, planter against planter, in contests where large sums of money and sense of personal worth often rode on the outcome. In most races planters rode their own horses, making the outcome even more important. Intensely competitive men, planters sometimes cheated to win, and many races ended in legal courts rather than on the racetrack.

If planters willingly battled each other on the racetrack, they did not ride against their social inferiors. When James Bullocke, a tailor, challenged Mr. Mathew Slader to a race in 1674, the county court informed the tailor that it was "contrary to Law for a Labourer to make a race being a Sport for Gentlemen." For his efforts, the court fined Bullocke 200 pounds of tobacco and cask. Although laborers and slaves watched the contests, and even bet among each other, they did not mix socially with the gentry.

Unlike the Puritans who believed sports should serve God, southerners participated in sports as an outlet for their very secular materialistic, individualistic, and competitive urges. But neither North nor South had a modern concept of sports. Colonial Americans seldom kept records, respected equality of competition, established sports bureaucracies, standardized rules, or quantified results—all hallmarks of modern sports. Yet each section engaged in leisure activities that reflected their social and religious outlooks.

was even more striking in urban areas like Boston and Philadelphia. By 1760 the top 10 percent controlled over 60 percent of the available wealth; the bottom 30 percent owned less than 2 percent.

Nevertheless there was a large middle class, and it was still possible to get ahead in provincial America. Over 90 percent of the colonists lived in the countryside and made their livings from some form of agricultural production. By European standards, the ownership of property was widespread, yet there were also many instances of extreme poverty. Some of the worst cases were among urban dwellers, many of whom eked out the barest of livelihoods as unskilled day laborers or merchant seamen. These individuals at least enjoyed some personal freedom, which placed them above black slaves, who formed 20 percent of the population but enjoyed none of its prosperity or political rights.

With colonial wealth concentrated in fewer and fewer hands, a second "Europeanizing" trend was toward the hardening of class lines. Elite families increasingly intermarried among themselves, and they spoke openly of an assumed right to serve as political stewards for the people. As one Virginia gentleman proclaimed in the 1760s, "men of *birth and fortune*, in every government that is free, should be invested with power, and enjoy higher honors than the people. If it were otherwise, their privileges would be less, and they would not enjoy an equal degree of liberty with the people."

Here was a classic statement of "deferential" thinking. Although widespread property holding allowed great numbers of free white males to vote, they most often chose among members of the elite to represent them in elective offices, particularly in colonial assemblies. Once elected, these stewards did constant battle with Crown-appointed governors and councilors in upper houses over the prerogatives of decision making. In colony after colony during the eighteenth century, elite leaders chipped away at royal authority, arguing that the assemblies were "little parliaments" with the same legislative rights in their respective territorial spheres as Parliament had over all British subjects.

More often than not, governors had only feeble backing from the home government and lost these disputes. As a result, the provincial assemblies gained many prerogatives, including the right to initiate all money and taxation bills. Because governors depended on the assemblies for their salaries, they often approved local legislation not in the best interests of the Crown in exchange for bills appropriating their annual salaries. By the 1760s the colonial assemblies had thus emerged as powerful agencies of government.

As self-conscious, assertive elite leaders, colonial gentlemen also read widely and kept themselves informed about European political activities. They were particularly attracted to the writings of a band of "radical" whig pamphleteers in England who repeatedly warned of ministerial officials who would use every corrupting device to grab all power and authority as potential tyrants at home. The radical whigs spoke of the delicate fabric of liberty; and provincial leaders, viewing themselves as the protectors of American rights, were increasingly on guard, in case the Crown became too oppressive, as it had been during the 1680s in demanding conformity to the imperial will.

Since gentlemen of birth and fortune lived each day knowing that home government leaders viewed them as second-class citizens, they took challenges to their local autonomy seriously. At least some in their number were ready to mobilize and lead the populace in resisting any new wave of perceived imperial tyranny, should a time ever come when the parent state attempted to return to arbitrary government.

Intellectual and Religious Awakening

Besides politics, colonial leaders were fascinated by Europe's dawning Age of Reason, also called the *Enlightenment*. The approach to learning was secular, based on scientific inquiry and the systematic collection of information. A major goal was to unlock the physical laws of nature, as the great English physicist Sir Isaac Newton (1642–1727), often considered the father of the Enlightenment, had done in explaining mathematically how the force of gravity held the universe together (*Principia Mathematica*, 1687).

Europe's leading intellectuals, likewise heavily influenced by English political thinker John Locke (1632–1704), tried to identify laws governing human behavior. In his *Essay Concerning Human Understanding* (1690), Locke described the human mind as a blank sheet (*tabula rasa*) at birth waiting to be influenced by the experiences of life. If people followed the insights of reason, social and political ills could somehow be reduced or eliminated from society, and each person, as well as humanity as a whole, could advance toward greater harmony and perfection.

The key watchword of the Enlightenment was *rationalism*, meaning a firm trust in the ability of the human mind to solve earthly problems—and much less faith in the centrality of God as an active, judgmental force in the universe. Whereas John Winthrop believed that earthquakes were signs of God's wrath, his great-great-grandson, John Winthrop IV, who became the Hollis Professor of Mathematics and Natural Philosophy at Harvard College in the mid-1730s, argued that movements in the earth's surface had natural causes, which he explained in scientific terms.

Like their counterparts in Europe, learned colonists pursued all forms of knowledge. Naturalists John Bartram of Pennsylvania and Dr. Alexander Garden of Charleston, South Carolina, were among those who systematically collected and classified American plants. The wealthy merchant James Logan of Philadelphia was not only a skilled mathematician but conducted experiments in botany that revealed how pollen functioned as a fertilizing agent in corn.

Benjamin Franklin (1706–1790) became the best known provincial student of science. After moving from Boston to Philadelphia in the early 1720s, he formed the Junto, a club for individuals interested in exploring useful knowledge. In 1743 he helped found the American Philosophical Society, devoted to supporting the compilation of scientific knowledge that would help "multiply the conveniences and pleasures of life." Flying his famous kite, Franklin himself performed experiments with lightning, seeking to reveal the mysteries of electrical energy. After publishing his *Experiments*

Benjamin Franklin typified colonial men of science and the Enlightenment in his search to unlock the mysterious laws of the universe. A man of many accomplishments, Franklin was a politician, statesman, philosopher, and newspaperman.

and Observations on Electricity (1751), Franklin's fame spread throughout the western world; but he derived just as much pleasure from inventing the lightning rod (1752), which he first developed to protect his own home from the destructive energy contained in flashes of lightning.

Franklin was very much a man of secular learning. Yet even clergymen, such as Boston's Cotton Mather, dabbled in science but without forsaking strongly held religious convictions. During a terrible New England smallpox epidemic in 1720 and 1721, Mather was outspokenly in favor of inoculation, which involved purposely inducing slight infections. Many thought that inoculations would only spread the disease, but Mather proved its preventive effects by collecting statistics. Whereas 15 percent of uninoculated smallpox victims did not survive, just 3 percent died from inoculations.

Mather conducted his experiment in the face of strong public opposition. Even local physicians railed against him, and one irate citizen threw a rock through the window of the clergyman's home with the message: "Mather, you dog; damn you: I'll enoculate you with this, with a pox to you." Years would pass before most provincial Americans accepted inoculation as a sensible medical procedure for controlling this terrible disease.

Unlike Mather, many ministers viewed Enlightenment rationalism with great suspicion. It seemed to undermine orthodox religious values by reducing God to a prime mover who had set the universe in motion only to leave humans to chart their own destiny. (This system of thought was known as Deism.) Others worried about the loss of religious faith emphasizing the need for repentance, conversion, and God's saving grace. They felt that the populace, rushing to achieve material prosperity, had become too complacent, as if affluence and good works would guarantee eternal salvation. For some clergymen, then, the time was at hand for placing a renewed emphasis on vital religious faith.

During the 1720s and 1730s in Europe and America, some ministers started holding revivals. They did so in the face of declining popular interest in formal religion, as expressed by dwindling church attendance in many locales. The first colonial outpouring of rejuvenated faith occurred during the mid-1720s in New Jersey and eastern Pennsylvania, where the determined Dutch Reformed minister, Theodorus Frelinghuysen, and his Presbyterian counterpart, Gilbert Tennent, attacked what the latter called the "presumptuous security" of his parishioners. Through impassioned sermons delivered from their hearts, these two ministers exhorted great numbers of people to seek after God's saving grace. Theirs was the first in a succession of revival harvests known collectively as the Great Awakening.

The next harvest came in New England. With each passing year fewer descendants of the Puritans seemed interested in seeking God's grace and gaining full church membership. Attempting to reverse matters in the early eighteenth century, the longtime Congregational minister, Solomon Stoddard (1643–1729) of

Jonathan Edwards (1703–1758) entered Yale before he was 13 years old, graduated in 1720, and was licensed to preach at the age of 19. In "Sinners in the Hands of an Angry God," he admonished his listeners to acknowledge their own sinfulness and thus take the necessary first step toward spiritual reawakening.

Northampton, Massachusetts, threw open the doors of his church and encouraged everyone in his community to join in communion services—the hallmark of full church membership. Stoddard's openness worked, and he temporarily reversed the slide.

Then in 1734 Jonathan Edwards (1703–1758), who had succeeded Stoddard, his grandfather, in the Northampton pulpit, initiated a series of revival meetings aimed at the youth of the community. Edwards was a learned student of the Enlightenment who argued that experiencing God's grace was essential to the comprehension of the universe and its laws. Like his grandfather before him, he joyously preached about the need for salvation, soon noting that the inhabitants of Northampton, both young and old, were now "so full of love" with "remarkable tokens of God's presence in almost every home."

In 1741 Edwards delivered his best known sermon, "Sinners in the Hands of an Angry God." Preaching with great fervency, he reminded each person present of the "manifold . . . abominations of your life," vividly picturing how each was "wallowing in sensual filthiness, as swine in mire." He also dangled his audience over "the abyss of *hell*" as a graphic reminder to place God at the center of human existence. Appealing to the senses more than to rational inquiry, Edwards felt, was the surest way to uplift individual lives, win souls for God, and improve society as a whole.

Such local revivals did not become broad and general until after the dynamic English preacher, George Whitefield (1714–1770), arrived in America. Whitefield was a disciple of John Wesley, the founder of the revival-oriented Methodist movement in England. Possessing a booming, melodious voice and charismatic presence, he preached with great simplicity, always stressing the essentials of God's "free gift" of grace for those seeking conversion. Even Benjamin Franklin, a confirmed skeptic, felt moved when Whitefield appeared in Philadelphia. He went to the meeting determined to give no money; but in the end, as Franklin confessed, "I emptied my pocket wholly into the collector's dish, gold and all."

Whitefield, known as the "grand itinerant," made seven preaching tours to the colonies, traveled thousands of miles, delivered hundreds of sermons, and spoke to gatherings as large as 30,000. Perhaps his most dramatic tour was to New England in the autumn of 1740. Everywhere he went citizens greeted him enthusiastically with every horse striving "with all his might to carry his rider to hear news from heaven for the saving of souls." In Boston over 20,000 heard him preach in a three-day period. Concluding his tour in less than a month, Whitefield left behind churches full of congregants anxious to experience conversion and bask in the glow of fellowship with God.

Concerned with reviving vital religion, the Awakening soon became a source of great contention, splitting America's religious community into "new" and "old" light camps. When in 1740 Gilbert Tennent preached his widely read sermon, "The Danger of an Unconverted Ministry," he expressed the feeling of many revivalists in advising their flocks of believers to shun clergymen who, while well educated in formal theology, showed no visible signs of having gained God's saving grace. Thousands paid attention, and they started breaking away from congregations where ministers were suspect.

In response, Old Light clergymen, who at first rejoiced about having so many people return to the fold, began denouncing the Awakening as a fraudulent hoax being perpetrated by unlettered fools of no theological training. In New England traditional ministers of the established Congregational church got their legislative assemblies to adopt anti-itinerancy laws, which barred traveling evangelists like Whitefield and Tennent from preaching in their communities. The contention between Old Lights and New Lights became so heated in many New England towns that friends and neighbors, when not arguing, stopped speaking.

All of the turmoil had significant long-term repercussions. Those feeling a new relationship with God were less willing to submit to established authority and more determined to speak out on behalf of basic liberties. Typical were colonists in New England who had started calling themselves Baptists. Under the persistent leadership of Isaac Backus they demanded the right to separate completely from the established Congregational church, to which all citizens owed taxes, and the right to support their own ministers and churches. Theirs would be a long and hard-fought campaign for an end to state-supported religion.

The liberty to worship and support whatever church one pleased was a central outcome of the Awakening movement, as was a concern with the proper training of clergymen. Prior to the 1740s, there were only three colonial colleges, Harvard (1636), William and Mary (1693), and Yale (1701). In demanding toleration for diverse ideas, Presbyterian revivalists set up the College of New Jersey (1747, later Princeton), to train New Light clergymen; Baptists founded the College of Rhode Island (1764, later Brown); and the Dutch Reformed established Queen's College (1766, later Rutgers). In 1769 a New Light Congregational minister, Eleazar Wheelock, received a charter for Dartmouth College to carry the new birth message to Native Americans. Of the remaining colonial institutions, only King's College (1757, later Columbia), founded by Anglicans, and the College of Philadelphia (1755, later the University of Pennsylvania) had no particular interest in training New Light clergymen; but in recognizing growing religious pluralism, these two colleges regularly admitted students on a nonsectarian basis.

As the Great Awakening spread into the South, it had a variety of lasting effects. During the late 1740s and 1750s the Reverend Samuel Davies inspired the emergence of Presbyterian congregations in Virginia, thereby calling into question the authority of the established Anglican church. By the mid-1750s swelling numbers of Baptists were displaying anything but a deferential regard for the mores of Virginia's planter elite. They started demanding, for example, the "entire banishment of *dancing*, *gaming*, and sabbath-day diversions."

Sometimes those in authority reacted viciously. A Virginia sheriff "violently jerked" a Baptist speaker off a platform and "beat his head against the ground" before administering "twenty lashes with his horse whip." The victim responded by returning to the stage and preaching even more vigorously "with a great deal of liberty." Persistence in the face of official hostility even led Awakening preachers to spread the gospel among the expanding slave population of the Chesapeake Bay region. The Awakening stimulated Protestant forms of worship among blacks, who did not forsake their African religious traditions but blended them with Christian faith in a savior who offered eternal life through God's saving grace as well as hope for triumphing over oppression in their search for human freedom.

As the Great Awakening spread through the British North American provinces, then, its proponents questioned established authority at every turn and provoked movement toward a clearer definition of fundamental human rights as well as toleration of divergent ideas. The Awakening also served to direct the colonists toward the day when Americans would naturally accept religious pluralism, as expressed in the dramatic rise of such non-state-supported denominational groups as the Baptists and Presbyterians. Greater toleration of dissenters and diverse religious ideas were hallmark legacies of the Awakening.

None of this came easily, and some of it, especially the emphasis on the search for personal liberty and freedom of conscience, along

The College of New Jersey (1747, later Princeton University) was established by Presbyterian revivalists to train New Light clergymen.

(Text continues on p. 102)

PRIMARY SOURCE ESSAY

GEORGE WHITEFIELD IN BENJAMIN FRANKLIN'S *AUTOBIOGRAPHY*

Benjamin Franklin struggled as a lad to make something of himself. He was the youngest son of Josiah Franklin, who had 17 children by two wives. In the early 1680s the devout Josiah had migrated from England to Puritan Boston, where he labored day and night as a candle and soap maker to provide a very modest living for his ever-growing family. He wanted Benjamin, his tenth son (he called him "the tithe of his sons"), to become a minister. Josiah taught young Ben to read and sent him to the Boston Grammar School. When he could no longer afford his son's education, Josiah put him to work making soap and candles. Two years later he apprenticed him to James, one of Ben's half-brothers who had become a printer in Boston.

Continual arguments with James led to Franklin's legendary flight to Philadelphia in 1723. Only 17 years old and lacking money, Franklin would skillfully employ his many talents to earn fame and a respectable fortune as a printer, author, inventor, scientist, politician, and dip-

Though Whitefield failed to convert Franklin, the evangelist's eloquence moved Franklin to make a generous contribution to the preacher's collection.

Franklin was one of the trustees of the Old Academy in Philadelphia, the first building in the country designated specifically for the use of itinerant preachers. The Academy was the first building of what later became the University of Pennsylvania.

lomat. While doing so he often thought about his Boston childhood. Franklin had long since rejected his father's Calvinist creed with its emphasis on eternal damnation for those who did not earn God's grace through a "new birth" experience. He favored more worldly tenets based on "one God who made all things" and who "will certainly reward virtue and punish vice either here or hereafter."

At the same time Franklin always remained curious about those who subscribed to his father's form of faith. George Whitefield, the grand itinerant of the Great Awakening, particularly intrigued him. The two became good friends during the evangelist's first visit to Philadelphia in late 1739. Late in life Franklin wrote passages in his classic *Autobiography* about Whitefield's effectiveness as a minister, the calling Josiah Franklin had once thought best for his tenth son.

The title page from the first publication of Benjamin Franklin's *Autobiography*, originally titled the *Memoirs of the Life and Writings of Benjamin Franklin, LL.D.*

In 1739 arriv'd among us from England the Rev. Mr Whitefiel[d], who had made himself remarkable there as an itinerant Preacher. He was at first permitted to preach in some of our Churches; but the Clergy taking a Dislike to him, soon refus'd him their Pulpits and he was oblig'd to preach in the Fields. The Multitudes of all Sects and Denominations that attended his Sermons were enormous, and it was a matter of Speculation to me who was one of the Number, to observe the extraordinary Influence of his Oratory on his Hearers, and how much they admir'd & respected him, notwithstanding his common Abuse of them, by assuring them they were naturally *half Beasts and half Devils.* It was wonderful to see the Change soon made in the Manners of our Inhabitants; from being thoughtless or indifferent about Religion, it seem'd as if all the World were growing Religious; . . . Mr Whitefield, in leaving us, went preaching all the Way thro' the Colonies to Georgia. The Settlement of that Province had lately been begun; but instead of being made with hardy indus-

trious Husbandmen accustomed to Labour, the only People fit for such an Enterprise, it was with Families of broken Shopkeepers and other insolvent Debtors, many of indolent & idle habits, taken out of the Goals, who being set down in the Woods, unqualified for clearing Land, & unable to endure the Hardships of a new Settlement, perished in Numbers, leaving many helpless Children unprovided for. The Sight of their miserable Situation inspired the benevolent Heart of Mr Whitefield with the Idea of building an Orphan House there, in which they might be supported and educated. Returning northward he preach'd up this Charity, & made large Collections; . . .

Some of Mr Whitfield's Enemies affected to suppose that he would apply these Collections to his own private Emolument; but I, who was intimately acquainted with him, (being employ'd in printing his Sermons and Journals, &c.) never had the least Suspicion of his Integrity, but am to this day decidedly of Opinion that he was in all his Conduct, a perfectly *honest Man.* And methinks my Testimony in his Favour ought to have the more Weight, as we had no religious Connection. He us'd indeed sometimes to pray for my Conversion, but never had the Satisfaction of believing that his Prayers were heard. Ours was a mere civil Friendship, sincere on both Sides, and lasted to his Death.

The following Instance will show something of the Terms on which we stood. Upon one of his Arrivals from England at Boston, he wrote to me that he should come soon to Philadelphia, but knew not where he could lodge when there, as he understood his old kind Host Mr Benezet was remov'd to Germantown. My Answer was; You know my House, if you can make shift with its scanty Accommodations you will be most heartily welcome. He reply'd, that if I made that kind Offer for Christ's sake, I should not miss of a Reward. And I return'd, *Don't let me be mistaken; it was not for Christ's sake, but for your sake.* One of our common Acquaintance jocosely remark'd, that knowing it to be the Custom of the Saints, when they receiv'd any favour, to shift the Burthen of the Obligation from off their own Shoulders, and place it in Heaven, I had contriv'd to fix it on Earth. . . .

He had a loud and clear Voice, and articulated his

Words & Sentences so perfectly that he might be heard and understood at a great Distance, especially as his Auditories, however numerous, observ'd the most exact Silence. He preach'd one evening from the Top of the Court House Steps, which are in the Middle of Market Street, and on the West Side of Second Street which crosses it at right angles. Both Streets were fill'd with his Hearers to a considerable Distance. . . . I had the Curiosity to learn how far he could be heard. . . . Imagining then a Semi-Circle, of which my Distance should be the Radius, and that it were fill'd with Auditors, to each of whom I allow'd two square feet, I computed that he might well be heard by more than Thirty-Thousand. This reconcil'd me to the Newspaper Accounts of his having preach'd to 25000 People in the Fields, and to the antient Histories of Generals haranguing whole Armies, of which I had sometimes doubted.

By hearing him often I came to distinguish easily between Sermons newly compos'd, & those which he had often preach'd in the Course of his Travels. His Delivery of the latter was so improv'd by frequent Repetitions, that every Accent, every Emphasis, every Modulation of Voice, was so perfectly well turn'd and well plac'd, that without being interested in the Subject, one could not help being pleas'd with the Discourse, a Pleasure of much the same kind with that receiv'd from an excellent Piece of Musick. This is an Advantage itinerant Preachers have over those who are stationary: as the latter cannot well improve their Delivery of a Sermon by so many Rehearsals. . . .

In 1771 Benjamin Franklin was residing in London where he was acting as a political agent for Pennsylvania and other colonies before the British government. During the summer he accepted an invitation to spend some days of leisure near Twyford at the country home of Jonathan Shipley, the Anglican bishop of St. Asaph. Away from the hustle and bustle of London, Franklin, now 65 years old, decided to enjoy "a little scribbling in the garden study." He started writing a narrative about himself for his son William, who had recently become the royal governor of New Jersey. In the form of a letter Franklin hoped to impart to William "the Circumstances of *my* Life, many of which you are yet unacquainted with." Thus he began his *Autobiography*, now considered a great classic of American literature.

Writing for nearly two weeks, Franklin produced the first of four parts of what he called "my Memoirs." The immediate press of political activities and then the American Revolution prevented him from returning to this project until 1784. Franklin composed the second segment in Passy, a suburb of Paris, while still serving as the new American republic's ambassador to France. He lacked his earlier enthusiasm, however, because he and William had stopped communicating—William had remained loyal to the British Crown. Franklin completed the third portion nearly a year after his participation in the Constitutional Convention of 1787, and he added yet more lines shortly before his death in 1790. Because of his lack of persistence Franklin only covered the first 50 years of his life.

Having compiled his own story, Franklin was not sure whether it was an appropriate work for publication. In late 1789 he sent copies to acquaintances in France and England for their advice. As a memorial to him, these copies became the basis of the first editions in French, German, Swedish, and English. His grandson, William Temple Franklin, published the first American edition in 1818. Since the word "autobiography," defined as a life of oneself, had not yet been coined from its Greek roots, these early editions bore the title of memoirs. In time the volume came to be known as Franklin's *Autobiography*, almost as a tribute to the literary form of self-inquiry that this inventive man of letters helped pioneer.

Part of the strength and charm of the *Autobiography* comes from Franklin's capacity to connect his own life story with other leading figures, among them George Whitefield. Although Franklin did not agree with Whitefield's new birth theology, he respected the young itinerant's sincerity and capacity to move the hearts of large crowds of listeners. He thought many of Whitefield's critics, particularly "old light" clergymen, were needlessly harsh in their evaluations. Franklin disagreed with those who viewed the itinerant as a fraudulent preacher who was just out to filch money from gullible people rather than support his preaching tours and orphanage project in Georgia.

To Franklin, the rationalist, Whitefield, who was America's first traveling evangelist, was a man of high purpose. At the same time, Whitefield brought out Franklin's curiosity. As a practical scientist, he could not stop himself from measuring how large an outdoor audience could actually hear one of Whitefield's sermons. That Franklin was making calculations, rather than listening to Whitefield's words, may well suggest why Josiah Franklin's son was better suited for other callings than that of the ministry.

with the questioning of established authority, may have unwittingly served to predispose many colonists to the political rebellion against Great Britain that lay in the not too distant future. Historians have divided opinions on this matter, but most would agree that the Awakening demonstrated that American communities showed considerable strength in weathering so much divisiveness. The provinces had indeed grown up and matured during the previous 100-year period, even if the British Crown failed to appreciate the new-found self-confidence of its North American colonists.

International Wars Beset America

Successful participation in a series of wars involving Britain and its two North American rivals, France and Spain, also contributed to America's growing self-confidence. During the seventeenth century Spain maintained its grip

René-Robert Cavelier, Sieur de La Salle, claimed the whole of the Mississippi Valley for France. He inspired other French leaders with his dream of an empire encircling the British North American colonies.

on Florida as well as the Gulf coast. French Canadians, operating from bases in Montreal and Quebec, explored throughout the Great Lakes region and then down into the Mississippi Valley. In 1682 an expedition headed by René-Robert Cavelier, Sieur de La Salle, reached the mouth of the Mississippi River. La Salle, who dreamed of a mighty French empire west of the Appalachian Mountains, claimed the whole region for his monarch, Louis XIV.

La Salle's grand vision was ahead of its time. In 1699 the French located their first settlement in the Louisiana country at Biloxi, Mississippi. A second small community soon took shape on Mobile Bay (present-day Mobile, Alabama). Then in 1718 Jean Baptiste le Moyne, Sieur de Bienville, founded New Orleans, which became the French capital in the region. None of these posts contained a significant population, and they survived on the basis of the development of trading ties with local Indians.

One reason for the lack of significant population growth was that the French monarchy, consumed by European affairs, did not actively encourage settlement in New France. As late as 1760, no more than 75,000 French subjects lived in all of Canada and the Mississippi Valley. Some were farmers or fisherman, and most others were fur traders, known as *coureurs de bois*. On the whole, they treated Native Americans with respect, and because the French population was so small, the Indians did not worry about losing ancient tribal lands. Sound relations with the Indians certainly paid off, especially after European warfare spilled over into America. The advantage of having thousands of potential allies willing to join in combat against British settlers made the French Canadians a very dangerous enemy, as events proved during the imperial wars between 1689 and 1763.

Each of the four wars had a European as well as an American name. The first, the War of the League of Augsburg (1689–1697), known in the colonies as King William's War, was a limited conflict with no major battles in America. What made this war so frightening were bloody border clashes involving Indians and colonists—typical was the attack on Hannah Dustan's Haverhill—which resulted in some 650 deaths among the English colonists. The Treaty of Ryswick, which ended the contest, did not upset the balance of international power because there were no major exchanges of territory.

Five years later the next war erupted after Louis XIV succeeded in placing his grandson Philip of Anjou on the Spanish throne. Other nations feared that Louis intended to run Spain himself, a threat to the established balance of power among European countries. What ensued was the War of the Spanish Succession (1702–1713), which the colonists called Queen Anne's War—named after the new English monarch Anne (reigned 1702–1714), another Protestant daughter of James II. This time, the Anglo-Americans found themselves dueling with Spain as well as France. The French and their native allies launched forays against frontier communities in Maine and Massachusetts. In 1702 South Carolinians attacked the Spanish town of St. Augustine, Florida, only to have to stave off a strong counterassault against Charleston four years later. In terms of casualties the war was not particularly bloody for the English colonists, who lost fewer than 500 people over an 11-year period.

The Treaty of Utrecht, which ended the conflict, was a virtual declaration of Britain's growing imperial might. The British realized major territorial gains, including Hudson Bay, Newfoundland, and Nova Scotia in Canada. In addition, they secured from Spain the strategically vital Rock of Gibraltar, guarding the entrance to the Mediterranean Sea, as well as the *Asiento*—a trading pact allowing the English to sell 4800 slaves annually in New Spain.

The scope of Britain's triumph, coming at the expense of its two major European rivals, deterred additional warfare for 26 years, but further conflict seemed inevitable. In 1721 the Board of Trade urged the "enlarging and extending of the British settlements" in North America as "the most effectual means to prevent the growing power . . . of the French in those parts." Ten years later, board members called for the creation of a military colony in the buffer zone between South Carolina and Florida, and they talked of sending over convicted felons and other desperate persons to act as soldier/settlers.

General James Oglethorpe (1696–1785), a wealthy member of Parliament known for his "strong benevolence of soul," heard of these dis-

TABLE 3.2

The Imperial Wars, 1689–1763

European Name	American Name	Dates	Peace Treaty
War of the League of Augsburg	King William's War	1689–1697	Ryswick
War of the Spanish Succession	Queen Anne's War	1702–1713	Utrecht
War of Jenkins's Ear		1739–1748	
War of the Austrian Succession	King George's War	1744–1748	Aix-la-Chapelle
Seven Years' War	French and Indian War*	1756–1763	Paris

*This term came into vogue when nineteenth-century historians first employed the phrase "French and Indian War." The colonists most often referred to this contest as "the war."

cussions and pursued the idea. A true philanthropist as well as imperialist, he hoped to roll back Spanish influence in America while improving the lot of England's downcast poor, especially imprisoned debtors. In 1732 King George II (reigned 1727–1760) issued a charter for Georgia, granting 21 trustees all the land between the Savannah and Altamaha rivers for 21 years to develop the region, after which the colony would revert to the Crown and function under royal authority.

Oglethorpe played on anti-Spanish sentiment, and large monetary donations poured in to underwrite the first settlements. Colonists were hard to find, largely because of the rules devised by Oglethorpe and the other trustees. To assure good order, they outlawed liquor. To promote personal industry and hard work as well as spread out settlements in an effective defensive line, they limited individual grants to 500 acres, and they banned slavery. To guard against breaches in the settlement line, property could only be passed from father to son. If there were no male heirs, it then reverted to the trustees.

Those who did migrate to Georgia complained endlessly. Some wanted slaves; others, referring to Oglethorpe as "our perpetual dictator," called for a popular assembly; and they all demanded alcohol. As a social experiment to uplift the poor, the colony failed. The trustees acknowledged this failure by turning Georgia back over to the Crown in 1752, a year ahead of schedule. By that time, they had already conceded on the issues of slavery and strong drink. Thereafter, Georgia looked more and more like South Carolina, with large rice and indigo plantations underpinning the local economy. By 1770, the colony's populace was pushing toward 25,000, nearly half of whom were slaves.

The founding of Georgia angered the Spanish, as did England's cheating on the *Asiento* agreement, especially in relation to a clause that permitted just one English vessel a year to sell goods off the coast of Panama. The one turned into shiploads, involving reputed smugglers like Captain Robert Jenkins, whom the Spanish caught in 1731. As a warning to others, his captors cut off his ear. Seven years later Jenkins appeared before Parliament and held high the severed remains of his ear as an affirmation of Spanish barbarity. When asked to describe his feelings when facing mutilation, he boldly replied: "I commended my soul to God, and my cause to my country!"

The testimony of Jenkins was part of a campaign by powerful merchants in England to provoke anti-Spanish sentiment, with the hope of using cries for war to gain more trading rights in New Spain. In 1739 the War of Jenkins's Ear resulted. Then a dispute among rival European claimants over who belonged on the Austrian throne—male aspirants were upset by the rightful accession of Queen Maria Theresa—brought England and France to formal blows in the War of the Austrian Succession, which in its American phase the colonists called King George's War (1744–1748).

Prior to French involvement, this international conflict saw James Oglethorpe mount an unsuccessful expedition against Florida in 1740. In 1741 a combined British-colonial force tried to capture the major Spanish port of Cartagena (located in modern-day Colombia). It was a disaster, with three-fourths of the 3000 American troops dying from disease. Then in June 1745 a New England army achieved a brilliant success against the French. After a prolonged siege some 4000 colonists under the command of William Pepperrell, a well-to-do merchant from Kittery, Maine, captured the mighty fortress of Louisbourg, the so-called "Gibraltar of the New World" guarding the entrance to the St. Lawrence River. Here was a remarkable American victory, since the British only offered limited naval assistance.

The war cost as many as 5000 Anglo-American lives, but the victory at Louisbourg represented the fruit of that sacrifice. Then in 1748 Britain signed the Treaty of Aix-la-Chapelle, which ended the war. The peace settlement returned Louisbourg to the French in exchange for Madras, India, which the French had captured. The king's negotiators reasoned that Madras was of much greater value as a center for imperial trade—and expansion—in the Orient than a huge, non-income-producing fortress in the American wilderness. The colonists were furious about this action, but they were powerless to do anything except complain among themselves about their subordinate—and unappreciated—status in the empire.

In 1745 William Pepperrell led 90 vessels and 4000 soldiers in an attack to capture the French fortress at Louisbourg. Forty days later the siege ended and the New England army won control.

Showdown: The Great War for the Empire

The Treaty of Aix-la-Chapelle really settled nothing. The three combatants were on a show-down course, and this time warfare would result from conflicting interests in America. In 1748 fur traders from Pennsylvania and Virginia began establishing contacts with natives in the Ohio River valley. The French, who had controlled the fur trade in that region, responded by warning all tribes to stop trading with the land-hungry English who, as one French envoy stated, "are much less anxious to take away your peltries than to become masters of your lands."

This observation was essentially correct. With the boom in colonial population, leading planters in Virginia were among those casting a covetous eye on the development of the Ohio Valley. With the backing of London merchants one group formed the Ohio Company in 1747 and two years later secured a grant of 200,000 acres from the Crown. Should the company settle 200 families in the valley within seven years, then its investors would receive a patent to an additional 300,000 acres.

Determined to secure the region against encroaching Anglo-American traders and land speculators, the French in the early 1750s started constructing a chain of forts in a line running southward from Lake Erie in western Pennsylvania. They decided to locate their principal fortress—and trading station—at a strategic site (the location of modern-day Pittsburgh) where the Monongahela and Allegheny rivers join to form the Ohio River.

By 1753 the British ministry knew of these plans and ordered colonial governors to challenge the French advance and "repel force by force" if necessary. Virginia's Governor Robert Dinwiddie, who happened to be an investor in the Ohio Company, acted quickly. He sent a young major of militia, 21-year-old George Washington, whose older half-brother Lawrence was also an Ohio Company investor, to northwestern Pennsylvania with a message to get out. Politely, the French declined.

In the spring of 1754 Washington led 200 Virginia soldiers toward the forks of the Ohio River and learned that the French were already there constructing Fort Duquesne. Foolishly, he

This woodcut, displayed in the *Pennsylvania Gazette*, failed to overcome long-standing jealousies that thwarted attempts at intercolonial cooperation.

skirmished with a French party, killing 10 and capturing 21. Washington then hastily retreated and constructed Fort Necessity, but a superior French and Indian force attacked on July 3. Facing extermination, Washington surrendered and signed articles of capitulation on July 4, 1754, which permitted him to lead his troops back to Virginia as prisoners of war. Out of these circumstances erupted a world war that cost France the whole of its North American empire.

At the very time (June 1754) that Washington was preparing to defend Fort Necessity, delegates from seven colonies had gathered in Albany, New York, to plan for their defense in case of war and to secure active support from the powerful Iroquois Confederacy. The Indian chiefs readily accepted 30 wagons loaded with gifts but did not promise to turn their warriors loose on the French. So as not to get caught on the losing side and face eviction from their ancient tribal lands in New York, the Iroquois assumed a posture of neutrality, waiting to see which side was winning the war. Some Senecas did fight for the French; but when the tide shifted in favor of the English after 1758, the Iroquois helped crush the French.

In other major business at the conference, delegates Benjamin Franklin and Thomas Hutchinson proposed an intercolonial plan of government, known as the Albany Plan of Union. The idea was to have a "grand council" made up of representatives from each colony

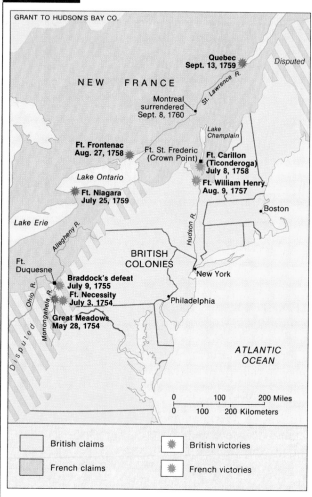

Significant Battles of the French and Indian War, 1756–1763

who would work with a "president general" appointed by the Crown to plan for defense and even to tax the provinces on an equitable basis in keeping the North American colonies secure from external enemies. The Plan of Union stirred little interest at the time, since the assemblies were not anxious to share their prerogatives, especially the power of taxation, with anyone. The plan's significance lay in its attempt to effect intercolonial cooperation against a common enemy—an important precedent in later years. Meantime, as Franklin stated, "everyone cries, union is necessary, but when they come to the . . . form of the union, their weak noodles are perfectly distracted."

Home government officials ignored the Albany Plan of Union, but the Fort Necessity debacle resulted in a fateful decision to send Major General Edward Braddock, an unimaginative 60-year-old officer who had never commanded troops in battle, to Virginia. Braddock arrived in February 1755 with two regiments of redcoats and orders to raise additional troops among the Americans. He eventually got his army of 3000 moving—Washington came along as a volunteer officer—toward Fort Duquesne. On July 9, about eight miles from the French fort, a much smaller French and Indian force, attacking from all sides, nearly destroyed the British column, leaving two-thirds of Braddock's soldiers dead or wounded. Washington, appalled by one of the worst defeats in British military history, spoke of being "most scandalously beaten by a trifling body of men." Braddock himself sustained mortal wounds; but before he died, he stated wryly: "We shall better know how to deal with them another time."

Braddock's defeat was an international embarrassment, yet King George II and his advisors hesitated to plunge into full-scale war. They knew the financial burden would be immense. Finally, a formal declaration of war did come in May 1756. The Seven Years' War (1756–1763), later referred to in America as the French and Indian War, more accurately should be called "the great war for the empire." Certainly William Pitt (1708–1778), the king's new chief minister, viewed America as the place "where England and Europe are to be fought for." Not a modest man, Pitt stated categorically that he alone could "save England and no one else can."

Pitt's strategic plan was simple enough. He let King Frederick the Great of Prussia, Britain's ally, bear the brunt of warfare in Europe, and he placed the bulk of England's military resources in America with the intent of strangling New France. He also advanced a young group of dynamic officers, such as General James Wolfe, over the heads of less capable men. It all paid off in a series of carefully orchestrated military advances that saw Quebec fall in September 1759 to the forces of General Wolfe. Then in September 1760 with hardly an exchange of musket fire, Montreal surrendered to the army of General Jeffrey Amherst.

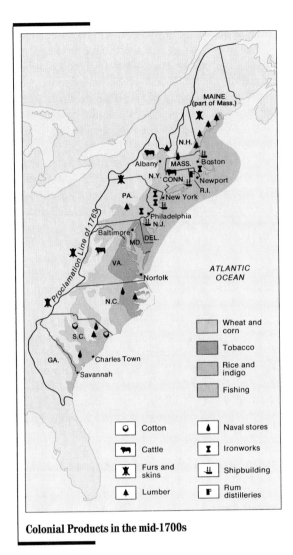

Colonial Products in the mid-1700s

"LIBERTY, PROPERTY, AND NO STAMPS"

Certainly the colonists were not plotting independence in 1763. They were proud to be citizens of the far-flung British empire, stretching as it did from India in the East across the globe to some 30 American colonies in the West, including such Caribbean islands as Barbados and Jamaica. With the elimination of French authority in North America, the mainland colonists were also experiencing a buoyant new sensation of freedom. Paradoxically, the reinvigorated imperial program came at the very point in time when the colonists, feeling great pride but needing much less government protection from across the ocean, hoped for a continuation if not expansion of the local autonomy to which they had become accustomed. Psychologically, they were ready for anything but new imperial constraints on their lives.

Emerging Patterns of Resistance

As the Grenville program took shape, the colonists evidenced various emotions. Dismay gave way to disappointment and anger. Initial reactions involved petitioning King and Parliament for a redress of grievances. By the summer of 1765 colonial protest took an extralegal turn as Americans resorted to such tactics of resistance as crowd intimidation and violence, economic boycott, and outright defiance of imperial law. The colonists no longer liked to think of themselves as Britain's children. Through their tactics of resistance they were asking to be treated more like adults. Very few British officials seemed to understand this message, which in time resulted in the full rupture of British-American relations.

The first words of protest were quite mild, expressed in a flurry of petitions and pamphlets that laid out an American position with respect to essential political rights. In reaction to the Sugar Act of 1764, the New York Assembly complained about "all impositions" by Parliament, "whether they be internal taxes, or duties paid, for what we consume." Stephen Hopkins of Rhode Island was more specific in his widely read pamphlet, *The Rights of Colonies Exam-*

A few members of Parliament comprehended the inherent value of the provinces and did not think of the colonists as overindulged children. Colonel Isaac Barré, who had served under General James Wolfe at Quebec, was one such person. "They grew by your neglect of them," he stated sharply during the Stamp Act debates in Parliament. Now, the tightening imperial grip would cause "the blood of those *sons of liberty* to recoil within them. . . . And remember I this day told you so, that same spirit of freedom which actuated that people at first, will accompany them still." Barré's words were prophetic. The Stamp Act would not fare very well with the Americans.

The Stamp Act, which required Americans to purchase stamps for everything from playing cards to marriage licenses, provoked intense colonial protest. Many expressed their outrage by using a skull and crossbones to mark the spot where the stamp was to be embossed, as shown here in the October 31, 1765, issue of the *Pennsylvania Journal and Weekly Advertiser.*

ined, published in December 1764, when he stated that "British subjects are governed only agreeable to laws to which [they] themselves have [in] some way consented." Hopkins then warned his fellow citizens: "Those who are governed at the will . . . of others, and whose property may be taken from them by taxes, or otherwise, without their own consent, and against their will, are in the miserable condition of slaves." Hopkins's line represented what so many others were thinking and may be captured in the phrase "no taxation without representation." Here was the essential constitutional argument against Parliamentary taxation.

In many ways protest by pamphlet and petition was so mild in tone during 1764 (only eight provincial assemblies bothered to send petitions to Parliament protesting the Sugar Act) that it encouraged George Grenville to pursue more comprehensive taxation plans. The intensity of American ill feeling in reaction to the Stamp Act thus shocked the home government.

First news of the Stamp Act arrived in the provinces during April 1765, which left ample time to organize effective resistance before November 1. Colonial protest soon became very turbulent, with Samuel Adams's Boston taking the lead in stirring up resistance. In Massachusetts, as in many other provinces, there were a small number of royal officials favored by the parent nation's patronage. This group held the most prominent offices in colonial government, and they were known as the "royalist" or "court" political faction. Besides Lieutenant Governor and Chief Justice Thomas Hutchinson, other leading members of the royalist faction were Governor Francis Bernard, Secretary and Councilor Andrew Oliver, and Associate Justice and Councilor Peter Oliver (Andrew's younger brother). Hutchinson and the Oliver brothers were natives of New England and had all graduated from Harvard College. They were interrelated by marriage, and they were among the wealthiest citizens in America.

Even though these gentlemen were at the apex of provincial society, their opponents in the "popular" or "country" faction did not defer to them. Besides Samuel Adams, another local leader, the brilliant lawyer James Otis, Jr., viewed the likes of Hutchinson and the Oliver brothers with contempt. In 1760 when Bernard became governor and appointed Hutchinson to the chief justiceship, he ignored the claims of assembly speaker James Otis, Sr., who had been

Thomas Hutchinson was a key leader of the royalist political faction in Massachusetts.

promised this post by an earlier governor. Enraged by Bernard's slight to his father, Otis stated that he would "kindle such a fire in the province as shall singe the governor, though I myself perish in the flames."

Otis was soon speaking out on behalf of American rights and against royal appointees charged with enforcing imperial laws in Massachusetts. Before the end of 1760, for instance, customs collectors in the Bay Colony had started using blanket search warrants, known as *writs of assistance*, to catch suspected smugglers, particularly those rumored to be trading with the enemy. The writs did not require any form of prior evidence to justify searches; as such, many respected attorneys in England questioned their legality, since they violated the fundamentals of due process in cases of search and seizure.

In 1761 on behalf of merchants in Boston, some number of whom were likely smugglers, Otis argued against the writs in a well-publicized case before the Massachusetts superior court. Chief Justice Thomas Hutchinson ruled in favor of the writs, politely explaining how they were also then in use in England. In turn, Otis declared that the power of King and Parliament had defined boundaries, implying that only tyrants would uphold the use of writs.

Otis and the merchants may have lost, but they had put Hutchinson in an embarrassing position. They portrayed him as a person blinded to the protection of fundamental legal rights because of his insatiable lust for offices and power. In this sense Otis had won the case, but unfortunately for him he would eventually lose his personal mental stability. As a result, after the mid-1760s Samuel Adams would assume overall leadership of the popular rights faction in Massachusetts politics.

Adams won his first term to the Assembly in 1765 as a representative from Boston. For him personally the emerging Stamp Act crisis represented an opportunity to launch a simultaneous attack on unacceptable imperial policies and old political adversaries. The twin assault unfolded in August 1765 shortly after citizens learned that none other than Andrew Oliver was the Bay Colony's proposed Stamp Act distributor.

Protest Takes a Violent Turn

Samuel Adams did not participate directly in crowd actions. Nor did the informal popular rights governing body, known as the Loyal Nine. (Adams and Otis were not members of this group but were the principal guides in directing the politics of defiance.) The Loyal Nine communicated specific protest plans to men like Ebenezer Mackintosh, a shoemaker living in the South End of town, and Henry Swift, a cobbler from the North End. Prior to 1765 these two craft workers were leaders of "leather apron" gangs (workers' associations) from their respective districts. The North End and South End gangs, as the "better sort" of citizens called them, were in reality fraternal organizations providing fellowship for artisans, apprentices, and common day laborers.

Each year these leather apron workers looked forward to November 5, known as Pope's Day. This referred to an alleged plot in 1605 by Guy Fawkes, a Roman Catholic, to blow up Parliament. November 5 was an established anti-Catholic holiday during which leaders like Swift and Mackintosh headed parades of North and South End workers marching through the streets, holding high crude effigies of the devil and the pope. These working people not only vented their anti-Catholic feelings and their fears of Satanic influences as they marched, but they also prepared for the annual fistfight between North Enders and South Enders, which traditionally took place after the two groups had converged on the center of Boston. The fighting was so vicious in 1764 that at least one person died.

During the summer of 1765 Samuel Adams and the Loyal Nine convinced the North and South End associators to stop fighting among themselves and to unite in defense of essential political liberties. This juncture proved a critical step in ending any attempted implementation of the Stamp Act in Massachusetts.

On the morning of August 14, 1765, the local populace awoke to find an effigy of Peter Oliver (and a boot, representing Lord Bute, Grenville's predecessor) hanging in an elm tree—later called the Liberty Tree—in the South End of Boston. An appalled Governor
(Text continues on p. 124)

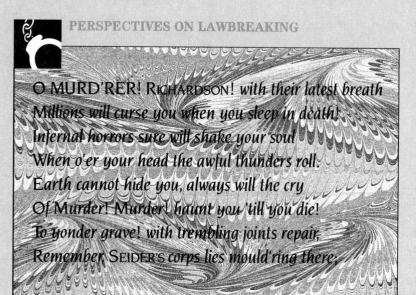

O MURD'RER! RICHARDSON! with their latest breath
Millions will curse you when you sleep in death!
Infernal horrors sure will shake your soul
When o'er your head the awful thunders roll.
Earth cannot hide you, always will the cry
Of Murder! Murder! haunt you 'till you die!
To yonder grave! with trembling joints repair,
Remember SEIDER's corps lies mould'ring there;

THOSE HATED CUSTOMS INFORMERS

Benedict Arnold, who later became famous for turning against the American cause of liberty, was a prospering merchant in New Haven, Connecticut, prior to the Revolution. One of Arnold's trading vessels returned from the West Indies during January 1766 and managed to unload its cargo of rum and molasses without paying the required trade duties. Like hundreds of other colonial merchants, Arnold thought nothing of evading imperial customs collectors in American port towns. The economy was depressed, and many merchants were struggling to avoid bankruptcy. In addition, many argued that not paying duties at a time when the colonists were demanding repeal of the Stamp Act was a justifiable form of protest against the willfulness of the home government.

In attempting to stop colonial smuggling, British customs officers were in regular contact with informers, or local inhabitants who listened for rumors in the streets and secretly provided evidence about merchants evading the law. Informers expected cash payments for their services, and if vice-admiralty courts ruled against an offending merchant, informers sometimes shared in profits gained from the sale of confiscated cargoes. To be an informer could be lucrative, but it also assured the wrath of local citizens, should colonists caught smuggling find out who had broken the unwritten law of noncooperation with customs collectors.

Peter Boles was a seaman working for Benedict Arnold who had helped to unload the smuggled cargo. Late in January he approached Arnold and asked for extra wages, implying that the money would help keep him quiet. Arnold responded tersely that he did not hand out bribes. Boles went straight to the New Haven customs office. The chief collector was not there, so the informer announced his intention to return later with important information.

When Arnold learned of Boles's action, he sought out the mariner, "gave him a little chastisement," and told him to get out of New Haven. Boles agreed to leave, but two days later he was still in town. Arnold, now backed by a number of seamen, confronted Boles at a local tavern and forced him to sign a prepared confession. "Being instigated by the devil," Boles admitted, under some duress, that "I justly deserve a halter for my malicious and cruel intentions." He also promised "never to enter the same [town] again."

Four hours later, at 11 P.M., Boles was still tippling at the tavern. This time Arnold returned with yet more followers. The party grabbed Boles and dragged the informer to the town's whipping post, where he "received forty lashes with a small cord, and was conducted out of town." Peter Boles was not heard from again.

More law-abiding community leaders were outraged when they heard about Boles's punishment. They had Arnold and a few members of his crowd arrested for disturbing the peace, which ultimately cost each a small fine. In response, Arnold organized a demonstration and parade. Dozens of citizens participated in this evening spectacle, which saw effigies of the local magistrates who had issued the arrest warrants carried through the streets on pretended gallows and then consumed in a huge bonfire. As Arnold wrote later, these magistrates had acted as if they wanted to "vindicate, protect, and caress an informer," rather than stand up for American rights when colonial trade "is nearly ruined by the . . . detestable Stamp and other oppressive acts." Vigilante justice for "infamous informers" like Boles, Arnold maintained, was an effective way to loosen the stranglehold of imperial restrictions on provincial commerce and, at the same time, defend basic rights.

The whipping and banishment of Boles were relatively mild punishments. Angry crowds often covered informers with tar and feathers before strapping them onto wooden rails and "riding" them out of town. In some cases, such as that of Ebenezer Richardson of Boston, informers nearly lost their lives. A combative person and occasional employee of the customs office, Richardson provided damaging information about a prominent local merchant in 1766, for which this informer was "frequently abused by the people." Then in early 1770 Richardson gained the community's wrath by defying citizens enforcing Boston's nonimportation agreement protesting the Townshend Duties. Events got out of hand, and he became known as the greatest "monster of the times."

Since August 1768 when Bostonians accepted Samuel Adams's call for nonimportation, an informal group known as "the Body" managed the harassment of violators. Merchants who kept importing British goods endured much abuse as "importers." Roving bands of citizens struck at night, breaking windows and defacing their property, which included coating walls with a combination of mud and feces known as "Hillsborough treat." During the day, crowds moved from location to location, posting large wooden hands pointing toward the shops of offending merchants. As customers came and went, they received verbal abuse while dodging flying handfuls of Hillsborough treat.

On February 22 a crowd visited such a shop in Boston's North End, unfortunately across the street from Richardson's residence. The ever belligerent informer suddenly appeared and, in the face of verbal taunts and flying debris, tried to remove the hand. Soon he retreated to his house with the crowd, including a large number of boys, following close behind. "Come out, you damn son of a bitch," they shouted, and they started to break the windows. Inside Richardson and another man loaded their muskets. When the crowd threatened to enter the house, the informer first warned his assailants and then fired. He severely wounded an 11-year-old boy, Christopher Seider, who died several hours later. Only the intervention of well-known patriot gentlemen saved Richardson from being lynched.

Samuel Adams and other popular leaders in Boston took full advantage of this ugly incident. They planned an elaborate funeral during which some 2500 mourners solemnly marched in front and back of Seider's coffin from Liberty Tree to the burial ground. Hundreds more lined the streets as the procession passed by. Popular rights advocate John Adams considered young Seider a martyr to the cause of liberty. Lieutenant Governor Thomas Hutchinson was less charitable. His political adversaries, had they had the power to restore Seider's life, "would not have done it, but would have chosen the grand funeral," he declared.

Christopher Seider's death and emotional funeral were signs of the tension filling the streets of Boston over such imperial policies as the Townshend Duties. That British redcoats were present to help enforce imperial law and keep the populace under control only made matters worse. In the week following Seider's funeral, there was a dramatic increase in incidents of troop baiting, including the fight at John Gray's ropemaking establishment, all of which culminated in the Boston Massacre.

As for Ebenezer Richardson, he soon stood trial on the charge of willfully murdering Seider. His argument was self-defense. His wife and two daughters were in the house and had been struck by eggs, stones, and various forms of Hillsborough treat. The Superior Court judges realized that manslaughter was the proper charge, not "damn him—hang him—murder no manslaughter," the phrase enraged Bostonians shouted as the jurors left the courtroom to deliberate.

The jury did return a verdict of guilty of murder; however, the court, headed by Thomas Hutchinson, initiated a series of legal maneuvers that in 1772 secured Richardson's freedom by king's pardon. Now an outcast, Boston's most notorious informer tried to find work, only to be reviled and sent on his way. Finally, he secured employment with the customs office in Philadelphia, but more than once he disappeared to avoid a coat of tar and feathers because everywhere colonists knew him as the "execrable villain, . . . as yet unhanged" customs informer who had shot down young Christopher Seider.

Bernard demanded that the figures be removed; but no one touched them, knowing that they were under the protection of the associators—in time called the Sons of Liberty. That evening a crowd numbering in the thousands gathered around the tree to watch Ebenezer Mackintosh, who soon gained the title "Captain General of Liberty Tree," solemnly remove the effigies and exhort everyone present to join in a march through the streets. Holding the effigies high on a staff, Mackintosh and Swift led what was an orderly procession. As they marched, the people shouted: "Liberty, Property, and No Stamps."

The crowd worked its way to the local dockyards, where the Sons of Liberty ripped apart a building recently constructed by Andrew Oliver. Rumor had it that Oliver intended to store his quota of stamped paper there. Next, the crowd moved toward Oliver's stately home. Some of the Sons of Liberty tore up the fence, ransacked

Crowds protesting imperial policies, in this case burning stamped documents and newspapers, were normally made up of ordinary citizens, particularly the working poor.

the first floor (the Oliver family had fled), and imbibed from the well-stocked wine cellar. Others gathered on a hill behind the Oliver residence. Materials from Oliver's building as well as his wooden fence provided kindling for a huge bonfire that ultimately consumed the effigies as the working men and women of Boston cheered. By midnight this crucial crowd action was over.

Early the next morning, as Thomas Hutchinson later wrote, the thoroughly intimidated Oliver "despairing of protection, and finding his family in terror and distress, . . . came to the sudden resolution to resign his office before another night." Mackintosh's crowd, rather than Crown officials, now were in control of Boston. After this action of August 14, moreover, no one thought at all about taking Oliver's Stamp distributorship. Intimidating threats and selective property destruction had preserved the interests of the community over those of the Crown.

Had Boston's Sons of Liberty and their leaders been solely concerned with rendering the Stamp Act unenforceable, they would have ceased their rioting after Oliver's resignation; however, they had other accounts to settle. A misleading rumor began to circulate through the streets claiming that Thomas Hutchinson was very much in favor of the Stamp Act, indeed had even helped to write the tax plan. As a result, the Sons of Liberty came out again on the evening of August 26. After visiting a few others, the crowd descended upon Hutchinson's palatial home, one of the most magnificent in the province. They ripped it apart. As the lieutenant governor later described the scene, "they continued their possession until daylight; destroyed, carried away, or cast into the street, everything that was in the house; demolished every part of it, except for walls, as lay in their power."

Who started the rumor remains a moot point, but Hutchinson's political enemies were well known. Further, some Bostonians may have vented their frustrations with the depressed local economy by ransacking the property of a well-placed person with imperial connections who was prospering during difficult times. Whatever the explanation, royal authority in the Bay Colony had suffered another serious blow. The mere threat of crowd violence gave Samuel Adams and his popular rights faction a powerful weapon that Hutchinson and other royalist officials never overcame.

Resistance Spreads Across the Landscape

By rendering the office of stamp distributor powerless, Boston had established a model for resistance. Colonists elsewhere were quick to act. Before the end of the month Augustus Johnston, Rhode Island's distributor-designate, had been cowed into submission. In September Maryland's distributor, Zachariah Hood, not only resigned but fled the province after a crowd destroyed his home. Jared Ingersoll was the victim in Connecticut. While on the road to Hartford, the local Sons of Liberty surrounded him and demanded his resignation. They then rode with him to Hartford where the staid Ingersoll renounced the office in public, threw his periwig in the air, and cheered for liberty—to the delight of a menacing crowd. By November 1 there was virtually no one foolish or bold enough to distribute stamps in America. Only Georgians experienced a short-lived implementation of the despised tax.

While the colonists employed intimidation and violence, they also petitioned King and Parliament. Assembly after assembly prepared remonstrances stating that taxation without representation was a fundamental violation of the rights of Englishmen. Patrick Henry, a young and aggressive backcountry Virginia lawyer, had a profound influence on these official petitions. Henry first appeared in the Virginia House of Burgesses (lower house of the Assembly) in mid-May 1765. The session, meeting in Williamsburg, was coming to a close. Only a handful of burgesses were still present when Henry proposed a series of resolutions. They endorsed the first four, which reiterated the no taxation without representation theme, but they rejected the fifth as too categorical a denial of Parliament's authority. Henry did not bother to present his remaining two resolutions.

Some newspapers in other provinces reprinted all seven of Henry's resolutions. The fifth stated that the Virginia Assembly held "the only exclusive right and power to lay taxes and

Patrick Henry first entered the Virginia House of Burgesses in May 1765 and presented a series of resolutions denouncing the Stamp Act.

impositions upon the inhabitants of this colony." The sixth asserted that Virginians were "not bound to yield obedience to any law" not approved by their Assembly. The seventh indicated that anyone thinking otherwise would "be deemed an enemy by His Majesty's colony."

These three resolutions read as if the Virginia burgesses had denied King and Parliament all legislative authority over the American provinces. They seemed to be advocating some form of dual sovereignty in which the American assemblies held final authority over legislative matters in America—comparable in scope to Parliament's authority over the British Isles. This was a radical concept, in fact too radical for the Virginia burgesses. Yet the reprinting of all seven of the Virginia Resolutions, as they came to be known, encouraged other assemblies to prepare strongly worded petitions during the summer and fall of 1765.

An important example of intercolonial unity, also bearing on the petitioning process, was the Stamp Act Congress, held in New York City during October 1765. At the urging of James Otis, Jr., the Massachusetts General Court sent letters to the other provincial assemblies and called for an intercolonial congress to draft a full statement of grievances. Nine colonies responded, and 27 delegates appeared.

Generally speaking, cautious gentlemen of the upper ranks dominated the Stamp Act Congress. Their "declarations" on behalf of American rights had a far more conciliatory tone than the Virginia Resolutions. The delegates attested to "all due subordination to that august body, the Parliament of Great Britain." Since it was not feasible for Americans "from their local circumstances" to be represented in Parliament, the only way to protect "all the inherent rights and liberties" of the colonists was for Parliament to relinquish its right of taxation, more or less on a permanent basis, to the provincial assemblies. With these words the Stamp Act Congress disbanded, having shown that leaders from different colonies could meet together and agree on common principles. The congress also suggested that unified intercolonial resistance might be possible, should events ever make that necessary.

Another, more telling blow to the Stamp Act was an intercolonial economic boycott. Merchants in New York City were the first to act. On October 31 they pledged not to order "goods or merchandise of any nature, kind, or quality whatsoever, usually imported from Great Britain, . . . unless the Stamp Act be repealed." Within a month merchants in the other principal port towns, including Boston and Philadelphia, drafted similar agreements. A trade boycott of British goods, particularly with the remnants of economic depression still plaguing the empire, was bound to win support for repeal among merchants and manufacturers in Britain.

On November 1, 1765, commerce in the colonies came to a halt. Trading vessels remained in ports because no stamped clearance papers could be obtained. Courts ceased functioning, since so many legal documents required stamps. Newspapers stopped publication, at least temporarily. For all of their bravado the

Americans really did not want to defy the law. As November gave way to December, however, popular leaders began to apply various forms of pressure on more timid citizens. By the beginning of 1766 colonial business and legal activity started returning to normal, and newspaper editors commenced printing again—all in open defiance of the Stamp Act.

George Grenville thus had grossly miscalculated. Not willing to be treated as errant children, the colonists, in defending their liberties, sent petitions to Parliament, intimidated and harassed royal officials, destroyed property, cut off the importation of British goods and, finally, openly defied the law. Americans hoped for a return to the old days of salutary neglect, but they also wondered whether the king's ministers would understand and back down in the face of such determined resistance.

Parliament Retreats

Instability in the British cabinet, as much as American protest, helped to bring about repeal of the Stamp Act. George III had never liked Grenville. In July 1765 the king asked him to step aside in favor of the Marquis of Rockingham, who was more sympathetic toward the Americans. Rockingham's political coalition was brittle, and his term as chief minister lasted just long enough to bring about repeal.

Looking for political allies, Rockingham took advantage of pressure from English traders and manufacturers who were extremely worried about the American boycott. He also linked arms with William Pitt, England's most influential politician. Pitt was eloquent in the repeal debates before Parliament. He exhorted his fellow M.P.s to recognize the colonists as "subjects of this kingdom equally entitled . . . to all the natural rights of mankind and peculiar privileges of Englishmen." The M.P.s listened and in March 1766 repealed the Stamp Act.

Home government leaders had by no means accepted colonial arguments. They insisted upon a face-saving statement designed to make it clear that King and Parliament were the supreme legislative voices of empire. In conjunction with rescinding the Stamp Act, the M.P.s approved the Declaratory Act, which specifi-

This mournful group of government members carries the dead Stamp Act to its grave after its repeal in 1766.

cally denied the claims of American assemblies to "the sole and exclusive right of imposing duties and taxes . . . in the colonies." The Declaratory Act forcefully asserted that Parliament had "full power and authority to make laws and statutes . . . , *in all cases whatsoever*." Having repealed the Stamp Act for the sake of imperial harmony, Parliament still had the right to tax all British subjects anytime it chose. The M.P.s had stated their position—and in terms irreconcilable with the stance taken by the Americans.

A SECOND CRISIS: THE TOWNSHEND DUTIES

What was needed in 1766 was an extended cooling-off period, but that was not to happen. The Rockingham ministry, which would have been willing to leave the colonists alone, collapsed. King George III called for a new cabinet in the summer of 1766. He wanted William Pitt to be in charge of the government. In poor health, Pitt agreed to organize a ministry in return for peerage status as the Earl of Chatham. No longer "the Great Commoner," Pitt retired to the House of Lords, letting others provide for legislation in the House of Commons. One man in particular, Chancellor of the Exchequer Charles Townshend (1725–1767), sometimes called "Champagne Charlie" because of his penchant for that bubbly drink, rushed forward to fill the void in leadership. To the amazement of many, Townshend proclaimed that he knew how to tax the colonists. The result was the ill-advised Townshend Duties of 1767, which renewed tension between Britain and America.

Formulating a New Taxation Scheme

Benjamin Franklin, who was in England serving as an agent for various colonies, inadvertently helped to formulate Townshend's plan. In a lengthy interview before Parliament during the repeal debates, Franklin, who was out of touch with American sentiment, stated emphatically that the colonists only objected to *direct* or "internal" taxes, such as those embodied in the Stamp Act. They did not object, he claimed, to *indirect* or "external" taxes, which may be defined as duties placed on trade goods for the purpose of gaining imperial revenue. Pointing out that Franklin was the most respected colonist of the era, Charles Townshend seized upon this distinction and came up with his ill-advised taxation scheme.

Townshend believed that the Americans had to be taxed, if for no other reason than to prove the complete, indivisible sovereignty of King and Parliament. In June 1767 Parliament agreed with him by authorizing the Townshend Duties, which were nothing more than import duties on a short list of trade items: British-manufactured glass, paper and lead products, painters' colors, and a three-pence-a-pound duty on tea. Townshend proclaimed that his plan would net the Crown £35,000 to £40,000 per year. In time, once the colonists got used to the idea, the list of taxable products could be lengthened. Meantime, the revenue would defray the costs of royal governments in America.

At first, it appeared that Townshend knew what he was doing. The plan was subtle and generated very little colonial opposition. Except for tea, the duties were on luxury items, rarely used by the majority of colonists. The tea tax could be evaded by opening illicit trading connections with Dutch tea merchants—and Americans were still quite adept at the art of smuggling.

Mustering Further American Resistance

Late in the year John Dickinson, a landholder and lawyer residing in the area of Philadelphia, began publishing a series of newspaper essays, later printed as a pamphlet entitled *Letters from a Farmer in Pennsylvania*. Dickinson assailed Townshend's logic. Americans, he pointed out, had not distinguished between internal and external taxes. Certainly they had long accepted duties designed "to regulate

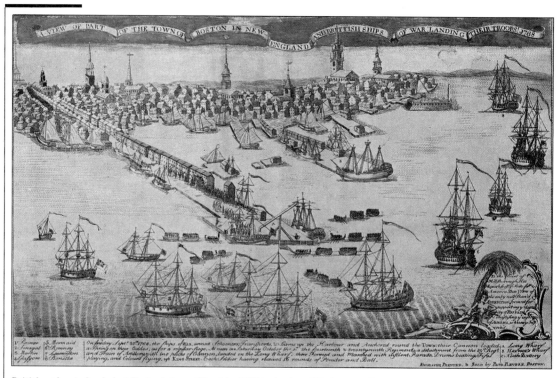

British redcoats landed at Boston's Long Wharf in 1768 to try to settle increased unrest among the colonists in that port town.

trade" and facilitate the flow of imperial commerce. They now faced trade duties "for the single purpose" of raising revenue. Taxes disguised as trade duties, warned a most suspicious Dickinson, were "a most dangerous innovation" with the potential for turning the colonists into "abject slaves." Yet Dickinson, a man of considerable wealth who feared the destructive potential of violent crowds, urged caution in resistance; he called for the colonial assemblies merely to petition Parliament, hoping the M.P.s would listen to reason.

In February 1768 the Massachusetts General Court, at the prompting of Samuel Adams, sent a Circular Letter to the other assemblies with arguments predicated upon Dickinson's widely reprinted pamphlet. Mild in tone, the Circular Letter reiterated Dickinson's call for petitions. If the British ministry had ignored the Massachusetts document, nothing of consequence might have happened. However, Wills Hill, Lord Hillsborough (1718–1793), who had recently taken the new cabinet post of Secretary for American Affairs, overreacted and provoked needless conflict.

Hillsborough believed that the Circular Letter was insubordinate. He quickly fired off orders to Governor Bernard to confront the General Court and demand an apology. If the delegates refused (they did overwhelmingly), Bernard was to dissolve the assembly and call for new elections. In addition, Hillsborough sent his own circular letter to the other colonial governors, insisting that they not allow their assemblies "to receive or give any countenance to this seditious paper" from Massachusetts. If they did, such assemblies were also to be dissolved. The result of Hillsborough's actions actually strengthened the colonists' resolve when new elections swelled the ranks of delegates firmly committed to standing up to any form of Parliamentary taxation.

Just as the Massachusetts Circular Letter infuriated Hillsborough, so did the rough treatment experienced by royal customs officials, particularly in Boston where the Crown had recently located a new five-man Board of Customs Commissioners. When members of the board, which was to coordinate all customs collections in America, arrived at the end of 1767, jeering crowds greeted them at the docks. The com-

missioners found it virtually impossible to walk the streets or carry out their official duties without harassment.

More serious trouble erupted in June 1768 when a crowd attacked local customs collectors who had seized John Hancock's sloop *Liberty* on charges of smuggling in a cargo of Madeira wine. (Hancock was notorious for illegal trading.) The new commissioners fled to Fort Castle William in Boston harbor for personal safety. Even before the *Liberty* riots, they had sent reports to Hillsborough about the unruly behavior of Bostonians, and they had asked for military protection.

In the wake of the August 1765 Stamp Act riots, members of the royalist political faction had likewise talked in private about calling for military support. Governor Bernard demurred, thinking that the presence of redcoats might provoke even greater turmoil in the streets. Hillsborough, in turn, was not going to tolerate such abusive behavior from the Bostonians, even in the absence of a formal gubernatorial request for troops. Just before the *Liberty* riots took place, the American secretary issued orders for four regiments of redcoats to proceed to Boston. The troops were "to give every legal assistance to the civil magistrate in the preser-

---

TABLE 4.1

Estimated Population of Colonial Port Towns Compared to London, England (1775)

London, the capital of the British empire, had an enormous population base by the standards of the largest cities in the colonies. The king's ministers were aware of this striking discrepancy, and they regarded American port towns like Boston as minor trading outposts in which a few well-trained redcoats could easily restore order among protesting colonists. Lord Hillsborough certainly believed so, but events proved him wrong.

London	700,000
Philadelphia	28,000
New York City	23,000
Boston	16,000
Charleston	12,000
Newport	11,000
Baltimore	10,000

vation of the public peace; and to the officers of the revenue in the execution of the laws of trade and revenue."

When the first redcoats arrived in the fall of 1768 without serious incident, members of the royalist political faction breathed more easily and went about their duties with new courage. It looked as if crowd rule, civil anarchy, and open harassment were tactics of the past. Samuel Adams and the popular rights faction, however, kept demanding more resistance. On August 1, 1768, they convinced an enthusiastic town meeting to accept a nonimportation boycott of British goods. New Yorkers signed a similar document a few days later. Philadelphians refused at first to go along with their two northern neighbors, bowing to the pressure of influential merchants. They hoped that a petition from the Pennsylvania Assembly would change Parliament's mind. Somewhat reluctantly, they finally joined the trade boycott in February 1769. Pressure from South Carolina's popular leader, Christopher Gadsden, backed by threats of crowd action, forced the merchants of Charleston into line during August 1769. It had taken a year, but now all the major port towns had endorsed yet another trade boycott in defense of political liberties.

The colonists did more than boycott. In some of the port towns there was talk about producing their own manufactured goods, such as woolen cloth, in direct defiance of imperial restrictions. With the boycott in full force wealthier citizens could no longer get the most fashionable fabrics from London, and popular leaders encouraged them to join poorer colonists in wearing homespun cloth—a sign of personal sacrifice for the cause. Some leaders urged all "genteel ladies" to master the skills of spinning and weaving. The *Boston Gazette* asked "Daughters of Liberty" everywhere to:

> First then throw aside your high top knots of
>   pride
> Wear none but your own country linen
> Of economy boast. Let your pride be the most
> To show clothes of your make and spinning.

Upper-class women, by and large, were not persuaded. They did not like the itchy feeling of homespun, and they considered spinning and weaving to be beneath their station in society. For poorer women, particularly those in the port towns, the trade boycott generated opportunities for piecemeal work in the production of homespun cloth. This meant some extra income, but there was virtually no long-term effect in improving the lot of the poor in America. Homespun was abundant, and the market price remained quite low. While wealthier women itched, complained, and worried about losing their status, poorer women were virtually donating their labor to the defense of American rights. For them the term "sacrifice" held a special meaning.

A "Bloody Massacre" in Boston

The citizens of Boston deeply resented the redcoats in their midst. When the king's troops had first disembarked in October 1768, a concerned local minister proclaimed: "Good God! What can be worse to a people who have tasted the sweets of liberty! Things have come to an unhappy crisis, . . . and the moment there is any bloodshed all affection will cease."

Besides symbolizing political tyranny, the redcoats also competed for scarce jobs because, when not on duty, their officers allowed them to work for extra wages on a piecemeal basis. As a result, the troops made hard economic times even harder for common day laborers, semiskilled workers, and other poorer Bostonians already suffering from the prolonged economic depression besetting their community.

Throughout 1769 troop baiting by Boston's working men and women had resulted in fistfights and bloodied faces. Bad feelings continued to mount as winter snows covered the ground. Then on March 2, 1770, an ugly confrontation took place. A young, off-duty soldier, Patrick Walker, entered John Gray's ropemaking establishment and asked for work. Seizing the opportunity to be insulting, one of Gray's workers snorted: "Well, then go and clean my shithouse." Taken aback, the soldier snapped in response: "Empty it yourself." Upset and angry, Walker fled amid taunts and threats from other laborers.

Walker told his story to comrades like Mathew Kilroy and William Warren in the 29th regiment. He convinced several of them to join him in teaching these workers a lesson. The soldiers soon appeared at Gray's, and a general brawl ensued before Gray's workers drove off the redcoats. This nasty fight would have been lost to history had it not been an important precursor of the so-called Boston Massacre three days later.

Monday, March 5, was bitterly cold, but heated emotions among workers and soldiers could have melted the deep piles of snow in the streets. A number of isolated fights had occurred over the weekend, and an eerie calm pervaded on Monday because Boston's working people had decided to challenge the redcoats' continued presence in their community. Toward evening small parties of day laborers, apprentices, and merchant seamen began milling about in the streets. Slowly, but without an appearance of overall direction, these groups moved toward King Street, the site of the Customs House. Here a small detachment of soldiers from the 29th regiment, including Privates Kilroy and Warren, were on guard duty.

As the crowd grew, it began to press in upon the troops. Suddenly, angry citizens began pelting the soldiers with mud, snowballs, rocks—indeed anything that could be thrown. Captain Thomas Preston tried to steady his detachment, but one of his soldiers, fearing for his life, panicked. He leveled his musket and a shot rang out. Ignoring Preston's orders to stop, other soldiers also fired their weapons. Before the shooting ceased, a number of civilians lay wounded and dying.

All told, five colonists lost their lives, including Samuel Gray, a relative of John Gray and a participant in the March 2 brawl; seventeen-year-old Samuel Maverick, brother-in-law of shoemaker Ebenezer Mackintosh; and Crispus Attucks, an unemployed mulatto merchant seaman. Bostonians would soon hail these men as martyred heroes in the struggle to defend American liberties.

Captain Preston and his troops faced trials for murder. The court found all but two of the redcoats innocent on the grounds of having been forced into a life-threatening situation by an enraged crowd of citizens. The court declared Private Kilroy and another soldier guilty

Effective propaganda, such as Paul Revere's engravings of the Boston Massacre, helped increase outrage over the event. Here, the British soldiers appear to be firing without provocation into an innocent-looking crowd of citizens.

of manslaughter. By pleading benefit of clergy these two men had their thumbs seared with a hot branding iron before regaining their freedom.

Long before these verdicts, royal officials removed the hated redcoats from Boston. In this important sense the working citizens of Boston had won at the cost of five lives. They had freed their community of British regulars and unwanted economic competition. Just as important, the Boston Massacre caused colonists everywhere to ask just how far King and Parliament would go to sustain their policies. With lives now lost, Americans were more wary of imperial decisions that might ultimately threaten them with some detestable form of political tyranny. As such the legacy of the Boston Massacre was even greater mistrust of the intentions of the home government.

Parliament Backs Down Again

The colonists' trade boycott seriously hurt merchants and manufacturers in the British Isles. By the beginning of 1770 the Townshend program had netted only about £20,000 in revenue, a paltry sum when compared to the loss in American trade, estimated to be as high as £7 million. Once again, the colonists had found the means to force Parliament to reevaluate its position.

It may have been fortunate for Charles Townshend that he died unexpectedly in September 1767. He did not have to listen to the abuse that his infamous duties took before Parliament in early 1770. By that time the Pitt ministry had collapsed. In January 1770 George III asked amiable Lord Frederick North (1732–1792) to form a new cabinet and give some direction to drifting governmental affairs.

North, listening to the wrath of powerful merchants and manufacturers in the British Isles, moved quickly to settle differences with America. He went before Parliament on March 5, 1770 (ironically the same day as the Boston Massacre), and called for repeal of the Townshend Duties, except for the tax on tea, which was to stand as a face-saving, symbolic reminder of Parliament's right to tax and legislate for the Americans in all cases whatsoever. As with the Stamp Act confrontation, the colonial trade boycott of 1768–1770 most certainly had a telling effect. King and Parliament had backed off again, but it was going to be their last retreat.

THE RUPTURING OF IMPERIAL RELATIONS

Lord North was a sensible leader who wanted to avoid taxation schemes and other forms of legislation that could provoke more trouble. He knew that imperial relations had been strained almost to a breaking point by too many restrictive policies thrown at the colonists in too short a time after so many years of salutary neglect. North carefully avoided challenging the Americans between 1770 and 1773. In turn, the colonial resistance movement clearly waned. For a brief period, then, there were no new issues to stir further conflict—only old problems needing resolution.

When Parliament stepped away from the Townshend Duties, most colonists wanted to discontinue the boycott and return to normal trade relations, despite the irritating tax on tea. They knew that the duty could be avoided by the continued smuggling of Dutch tea. Slowly, economic relations with Britain improved, and his Majesty's subjects in England and America enjoyed a brief period of mutually supportive economic prosperity.

The Necessity of Vigilance

Political relations were not so resilient. Many colonists had become very suspicious of the intentions of home government officials. Provincial leaders tried to explain what had happened since 1763 by drawing on the thoughts of England's "radical" whig opposition writers of the early eighteenth century. Men such as John Trenchard and Thomas Gordon, who had penned an extended series of essays known as *Cato's Letters* (1720–1723), had repeatedly warned about corruption in government caused by high ministerial officials lusting after power. If not somehow checked, citizens like the colonists would find themselves stripped of all liberties and living in a state of tyranny (often described as "political slavery").

What took firm hold during the 1760s was an American worldview, or ideology, that saw liberties under attack by such grasping, power-hungry leaders as George Grenville and Charles Townshend in England and their royalist puppets in America, personified by such officials as Thomas Hutchinson and Andrew Oliver. In attempting to explain what had happened, the evidence of a conspiracy seemed overwhelming. There were his Majesty's regular troops along the frontier and in Boston, and there were ships of the Royal Navy patrolling in American waters, all during peacetime. The colonists had been cut off from frontier lands, and perhaps worst of all, there had been three willful attempts to tax them, literally to deprive them of property without any voice in the matter.

As never before, great numbers of colonists doubted the goodwill of the home government.

Even if Lord North was behaving himself and keeping Parliament in check, many suspected that ministerial inaction was only a ploy, nothing more than a trick designed to lull Americans into a false sense of security while conspiring royal officials devised new and even more insidious plans to strip away all political rights.

Popular leaders exhorted the citizenry to be vigilant at all times. They employed various devices to ensure that the defense of liberties was not forgotten. In Boston, for example, Samuel Adams and his political lieutenants declared March 5 to be an annual commemorative holiday to honor the five fallen martyrs of the Massacre. Each year there was a large public meeting and grand oration to stir memories and to remind the populace of the possible dangers of a new ministerial assault.

At the 1772 observance, Dr. Joseph Warren, a committed radical and close associate of Samuel Adams, delivered an impassioned speech. He vividly recalled *"that dreadful night . . . when our streets were stained with the blood of our brethren; . . . and our eyes were* tormented with the sight of the mangled bodies of the dead." Then Warren turned to future prospects, reminding the hundreds in attendance that it might happen again—and in much more destructive terms. Warren's "imagination" conjured up "our houses wrapped in flames, our children subjected to the barbarous caprice of a raging soldiery; our beauteous virgins exposed to all the insolence of unbridled passion." The message of constant vigilance to preserve liberties could not be missed.

Local confrontations also kept emotions stirred up. One such incident occurred in June 1772 and involved a Royal Naval vessel, the *Gaspée*, that regularly patrolled for smugglers in the waters of Rhode Island. The ship's crew and its captain, William Dudingston, were particularly efficient. Finally, Rhode Islanders had endured enough. One day they sent out a sloop that purposely flaunted itself before the *Gaspée*. Suspecting illicit trading activity, Dudingston gave chase but ran aground as the smaller vessel swept close to shore. That evening, a crowd, disguised as Indians, descended upon the stranded

Tension increased between Great Britain and America when Rhode Islanders burned the *Gaspée*, a Royal Naval vessel that patrolled the area for smugglers.

ship and burned it. One Indian delivered the supreme insult by firing a load of buckshot into Dudingston's buttocks.

Crown officials were furious about the *Gaspée*'s destruction. They set up a royal commission of inquiry but never obtained any useful information concerning the perpetrators of this crowd action. Curiously, popular leaders, ignoring the reasons why the *Gaspée* was in American waters in the first place, set up a hue and cry about the royal commission. They were fearful that its intent was to send suspects to England for trial. As a result, several provincial assemblies established committees of correspondence to communicate with each other, should home government leaders appear to threaten liberties of any kind, in this case trials of citizens outside districts where alleged crimes had been committed. These committees were soon writing back and forth regarding serious problems over tea.

The Tea Crisis of 1773

The final assault on American rights, as the colonists perceived matters, grew out of a rather inconspicuous piece of legislation known as the Tea Act of 1773. When Lord North proposed this bill, he had no idea that it would precipitate a disastrous sequence of events; in fact, he was hardly even thinking about the American provinces. His prime concern was the East India Company, a joint-stock trading venture that dated back to the early seventeenth century whose officials ruled over British interests in India.

Having prospered for years, the company was in desperate economic straits in the early 1770s. One reason was that the recent colonial boycott had cost the company its place in the American tea market. With tea warehouses bulging, company directors sought marketing concessions from Parliament in 1773 (they also requested a £1.5 million loan to refinance company operations). They asked to have the authority to ship tea directly from India to America. As matters then stood, company tea had to be sent through England, adding significantly to the final market price. In May 1773 King and Parliament acceded to these various requests

and, in turn, forced the company to give up some of its political authority in India.

To reduce costs further, the company proceeded to name its own tea agents in the major American ports. They were to function as local distributors for 6 percent commissions. The net effect of these changes was to make company tea much more competitive with, if not cheaper than, smuggled Dutch blends—a fact that pleased Lord North very much.

North was even more pleased to have found a way, he thought, to get the Americans to accept the tea tax—and symbolically, at least, recognize Parliament's sovereignty. How could they refuse cheaper tea, even with the Townshend duty added to the price? North could not imagine that the colonists would stand on principle and keep purchasing more expensive Dutch tea just to avoid the three-pence-a-pound trade duty. The chief minister should have listened to the M.P. who warned him during the debates on the Tea Act that "if we don't take off the duty they won't take the tea."

In September 1773 the company dipped into its warehouses and readied its first American consignment of 600,000 pounds of tea worth £60,000. Vigilant Americans were waiting. Conditioned by years of warding off undesirable imperial legislation, they were looking for signs of further conspiratorial acts. A small economic saving meant nothing in the face of what appeared to be another, more insidious plot to reduce the colonists to a state of political slavery. Although such a worldview may seem far-fetched today, popular leaders and the general populace were thinking in confrontational terms. East India Company tea had to be resisted.

Once again, the port city of Boston became the focal point of significant protest. In early November a crowd took to the streets and tried to intimidate the tea agents (among them Thomas and Elisha Hutchinson, sons of Thomas who was now the royal governor) into resigning. The merchant agents, who had not received official commissions as yet, refused to submit; the crowd did not press the matter, waiting for a more timely moment to force resignations.

On November 28 the first tea ship, the *Dartmouth*, docked in Boston. The local customs collectors fled to Fort Castle William, and the local committee of correspondence, headed by Samuel Adams and his associates, put guards on the *Dartmouth* and two other tea ships entering the port within the next few days. The popular rights faction repeatedly insisted that the three tea ships be sent back to England. But Governor Thomas Hutchinson refused. Instead, he called upon Royal Naval vessels in the vicinity to block off the port's entrance.

No person in Massachusetts had taken more of a political drubbing from Samuel Adams and his popular party following. This native-son royal governor could be fair-minded but also stubborn, and this time Hutchinson decided that a showdown was necessary. The popular rights group had gotten its way by threats and intimidation for far too long. After all, the crowd had backed off in early November, and the governor mistakenly viewed this as a sign of popular indifference about the tea issue.

According to imperial law, unclaimed cargo had to be unloaded after 20 days in port and sold at public auction. Since the tea ships could not escape the harbor, Hutchinson fully expected to have them unloaded after the 20-day waiting period. Once the tea had been sold, the Townshend duty would be paid from the revenues obtained, and the governor would have upheld the law of King and Parliament. Hutchinson's plan to stand firm on behalf of imperial authority—and against his troublesome, long-time enemies—failed to work.

The waiting period for the *Dartmouth* was over on December 16. That day a mass meeting of local citizens took place at Old South Church. The Adams faction made one last attempt to communicate the gravity of the situation to Hutchinson. They sent a messenger to him with a very clear message—remove the tea ships or else. Hutchinson refused again. Late in the day, Adams appeared before the huge gathering and reportedly shouted: "This meeting can do no more to save the country." The moment for crowd action had been proclaimed. Several dozen artisans, apprentices, and day laborers, led by Ebenezer Mackintosh, went to the docks disguised as Indians. They jumped onto the tea ships and dumped 342 chests of tea valued at £10,000 into the harbor. It took nearly three hours to complete the work of the Boston Tea Party.

Tea confrontations occurred later in other ports, but none so destructively as in Boston. Philadelphians used the threat of tar and feathers to convince local officials to send back the first tea ships to arrive there. The governor of South Carolina outmaneuvered the local populace and managed to get the tea landed, but the company product lay rotting in a warehouse and was never sold. New Yorkers had to wait until the spring of 1774 for tea ships to appear in their port. They jeered loudly at the docks, and an intelligent sea captain raised anchor and fled for the high seas. Once again, then, the Bostonians stood out for their bold defiance of imperial law.

Parliament Adopts the Coercive Acts

The Boston Tea Party shocked Lord North and other British officials. North decided that the "rebellious" Bostonians simply had to be taught a lesson, and Parliament adopted a series of legislative bills, collectively known as the *Coercive Acts*. Although the home government aimed these laws against Massachusetts, the Coercive Acts held implications for colonists elsewhere who believed that the tyrannical parent nation was only using the Tea Party as a pretext for the final destruction of American liberties.

King George III signed the first act, known as the Boston Port Bill, into law at the end of March 1774. This act closed the port of Boston, making trade illegal until such time as local citizens paid for the tea. In May Parliament passed the Massachusetts Government Act and the Administration of Justice Act. The first suspended the colony's royal charter (which dated to 1691), vastly expanded the powers of the royal governor, abolished the elective council (upper house of the General Court), and replaced that body with appointed councilors of the Crown's choosing. Town meetings could only be held with the governor's permission, except for annual spring election gatherings.

As matters turned out, Governor Hutchinson never exercised this vastly expanded authority. Dismayed by the Tea Party, he asked for a leave of absence and went to England. The

Crown replaced him with General Thomas Gage, Britain's North American military commander, who held the governorship until the final disruption of royal government in the Bay Colony.

The Administration of Justice Act provided greater protection for customs collectors and other imperial officials in Massachusetts. If they injured or killed anyone while carrying out their duties, the governor had the right to move trials to some other colony or to England. The assumption was that local juries were too biased to render fair judgments.

Finally, in early June 1774 Parliament sanctioned the fourth coercive bill, which was an amendment to the Quartering Act of 1765. The earlier law had outlined procedures relating to the provision of housing for redcoats and had specifically excluded the use of private dwellings of any kind. The 1774 amendment gave General Gage the power to billet his troops anywhere, including unoccupied private homes, so long as the army paid fair rental rates. Parliament passed this law because Gage was bringing several hundred troops to Boston with him.

Quebec Act of 1774

By making the Ohio River the new southwest boundary of Quebec, the Quebec Act cut into land the colonists wanted for expansion.

The Quebec Act, approved in June 1774, was seen by the colonists as another piece of coercive legislation. Actually, this bill mainly concerned itself with the territorial administration of Canada by providing for a royal governor and a large appointed advisory council, but no popularly elected assembly. Roman Catholicism was to remain the established religion for the French-speaking populace. In addition, the Ohio River was to become the new southwestern boundary of Quebec.

Ever vigilant colonial leaders viewed the Quebec Act as confirming all the worst tendencies of imperial legislation over the past decade.

Parliament had denied local representative government; it had ratified the establishment of a branch of the Christian faith that was repugnant to militantly Protestant Americans, especially New Englanders; and it had wiped out the claims of various colonial governments to millions of acres of western land, in this case all of the Ohio country. The latter decision particularly infuriated well-placed provincial land speculators, among them Benjamin Franklin and George Washington, who had fixed upon this region for future development and population expansion. The Quebec Act, thousands of Americans concluded, smacked of abject political slavery.

Even without the Quebec Act, Lord North had made a tactical error by encouraging Parliament to pass so much legislation. The port bill punishing Boston was one thing; some Americans felt that the Bostonians had gone too far and deserved some chastisement. The sum total of the Coercive Acts, however, caused widespread concern because they seemed to violate the sanctity of local political institutions, to distort normal judicial procedures, and to favor military over civil authority. For most colonists the acts resulted in feelings of solidarity with (rather than separateness from) the Bostonians, which was critical to mounting yet higher levels of unified resistance.

Hurling Back the Challenge: The First Continental Congress

News of the full array of Coercive Acts provoked an outburst of intercolonial activity, the most important expression of which was the calling of the First Continental Congress. This body assembled in Philadelphia on September 5, 1774, and gentlemen of all political persuasions were there (Georgia was the only colony not represented). Among the more radical delegates were Samuel Adams and his younger cousin John, as well as Patrick Henry. George Washington was present, mostly silent in debates but firmly committed to protecting fundamental rights. More conservative delegates were also in attendance, such as Joseph Galloway of Pennsylvania and John Jay of New York. The central question facing all the delegates was how belligerent the Congress should be. The more cau-

As the largest American city and a central geographic point, Philadelphia was a logical choice for the delegates of the First Continental Congress to gather in 1774.

tious delegates wanted to find some means to settle differences with Britain, but the radicals believed that well-organized resistance could get King and Parliament to back down yet a third time.

Political maneuvering for dominance of the Congress began even before the sessions got under way. More conservative delegates favored meeting in the Pennsylvania State House, a building symbolizing ties with British rule. The radicals argued in favor of Carpenter's Hall, a gathering place for Philadelphia's laborers. The latter building was chosen. The delegates thus seemed to identify with the people and their desire to preserve political liberties rather than with the suspect hand of British authority. Then the radicals insisted upon naming Charles Thomson, a popular leader in Philadelphia, secretary for the Congress. He gained the post and was able to manipulate the minutes so that the actions of the radicals dominated the official record.

These signs foreshadowed what was to come. Accounts of the work of the First Continental Congress make clear that Samuel Adams,

Patrick Henry, and others of their more radical persuasion dominated the proceedings. Although they went along with the preparation of an elaborate petition to Parliament, known as the "The Declaration of Colonial Rights and Grievances," these experienced molders of the colonial protest movement demanded much more. They drew upon the old weapons of resistance that had caused Parliament to retreat before, and they added a new cudgel. Just in case they could not convince King and Parliament to repeal the Coercive Acts, they argued that Americans should begin to prepare for war.

To assure that Congress moved in the right direction, Samuel Adams and his political allies back in Massachusetts had done some careful planning. Their efforts came to light on September 9, 1774, when a convention of citizens in Suffolk County (Boston and environs) adopted a series of resolutions written by Dr. Joseph Warren. Once approved, Paul Revere, talented silversmith and active member of Adams's popular rights faction, mounted his horse and rode hard for Philadelphia. Revere arrived in mid-September and laid the Suffolk Resolves before

Congress. Not only did these statements strongly profess American rights, but they also called for a complete economic boycott and the rigorous training of local militia companies, just in case it became necessary to defend lives, liberty, and property against the redcoats of Thomas Gage.

Congress approved the Suffolk Resolves—and with them the initial step in organization for possible military confrontation. The delegates also committed themselves to a plan of economic boycott, which came to be called the Continental Association. The association represented a comprehensive plan calling for the nonimportation and nonconsumption of British goods, to be phased in over the next few months, as well as nonexportation of colonial products if Parliament did not retreat within a year.

The association also called upon every American community to establish a local committee of observation and inspection charged with having all citizens subscribe to the boycott. In reality, the association was a loyalty test. Citizens who refused to sign were about to become outcasts from the cause of liberty. The term of derision applied to them was *tory*; however, they thought of themselves as *loyalists*—maintaining their allegiance to the Crown.

The only conciliationist countercharge of any consequence during the first Congress came from Joseph Galloway, a wealthy Philadelphia lawyer who had long served as Pennsylvania's speaker of the house. Galloway desperately wanted to maintain imperial ties because he feared what the "common sort" of citizens might do if that attachment was irrevocably severed. He could imagine nothing but rioting, dissipation, and the confiscation of the property of economically successful colonists. For him, the continuation of any kind of political and social order in America depended on the stabilizing influence of British rule.

Galloway drew on the Albany Plan of Union of 1754 (see p. 105) and proposed a central government based in America that would be superior to the provincial assemblies. As with the Albany plan, there would be a "grand council" to be elected by colonial assemblymen and a "president general" to be appointed by the Crown. Grand council legislation would have to

gain Parliament's approval; at the same time imperial acts from King and Parliament would have to earn the assent of the grand council and president.

Galloway's Plan of Union, as this blueprint came to be known, represented a structural alternative allowing Americans a greater voice in imperial decision making affecting the colonies, and it foreshadowed the future commonwealth organization of the British empire. But the more radical delegates called the proposal impractical and belittled it as an idea that would divert everyone from the task of the moment, which was to get Parliament to rescind the Coercive Acts. In a close vote the delegates remanded Galloway's plan to a committee, where it lay dormant for lack of majority support.

Later, at the urging of the radicals, Secretary Thomson expunged all references to Galloway's plan from the official minutes of Congress on the grounds of displaying American unity to King and Parliament. As for Galloway, he faced growing harassment as a loyalist in the months ahead and eventually fled to the British army for protection.

When the First Continental Congress ended its deliberations in late October 1774, its program was one of continued defiance, certainly not conciliation or submission. The delegates understood the course they had chosen. One of their last acts was to call for the Second Continental Congress, to convene in Philadelphia on May 10, 1775, "unless the redress of grievances, which we have desired, be obtained before that time."

As the fall of 1774 gave way to another cold winter, Americans awaited the verdict of King and Parliament. Would the Coercive Acts be withdrawn, or would there be further steps pointing toward war? Local committees of observation and inspection were busily at work encouraging—and in some cases coercing—the populace to boycott British goods. Local militia companies were vigorously training. Even as they prepared for war, colonists everywhere waited anxiously for the reaction of King George III, Lord North, and Parliament. They would soon learn that Britain's leaders had dismissed the work of the First Continental Congress, having concluded that the parent nation could not retreat a third time.

CHRONOLOGY
OF KEY EVENTS

1760 George III becomes king of England

1763 Treaty of Paris ends the Seven Years' War; Pontiac leads an unsuccessful Indian rebellion on the western frontier; Orders in Council station Royal Naval vessels in American waters to run down smugglers; Proclamation of 1763 forbids white settlement west of the Appalachian Mountains

1764 Sugar Act levies new trade duties on coffee, indigo, sugar, and wine; Currency Act prohibits colonial governments from issuing paper money and requires all taxes and debts to British merchants to be paid in British currency

1765 Quartering Act directs colonists to provide barracks, candles, bedding, and beverages to soldiers stationed in their area; Stamp Act, which requires stamps to be affixed to all legal documents, almanacs, newspapers, pamphlets, and playing cards, among other items, provokes popular protests; representatives from nine colonies deny that Parliament has the right to tax the colonists at the Stamp Act Congress in New York

1766 Parliament repeals the Stamp Act, but asserts its authority to tax the colonies in the Declaratory Act

1767 Townsend Duties Act imposes taxes on imported glass, lead, paint, paper, and tea to defray the cost of colonial administration

1768 British troops sent to Boston; colonists begin to mount a trade boycott of British goods to protest the Townshend Duties

1770 Boston Massacre leaves five colonists dead and others wounded

1772 British naval vessel *Gaspée* is burned in Rhode Island

1773 Tea Act allows the East India Company to sell tea directly to American retailers; Boston Tea Party occurs when a band of "Indians" boards three British vessels and dumps 342 chests of tea into Boston Harbor

1774 Coercive Acts close the port of Boston, modify the Massachusetts charter, provide for trials outside colonies when royal officials are accused of serious crimes, and call for billeting of troops in unoccupied private homes; Quebec Act expands the boundaries of Quebec to the Mississippi and Ohio rivers; First Continental Congress, meeting in Philadelphia, protests oppressive Parliamentary legislation, votes to boycott trade with Britain, and defeats the Galloway Plan of Union

CONCLUSION

In September 1774 Lord North observed: "The die is now cast, the colonies must either submit or triumph." The once harmonious relations between Britain and America had become increasingly discordant between 1763 and the end of 1774. The colonists refused to accept undesirable imperial acts, and they successfully resisted such taxation plans as the Stamp Act and the Townshend Duties. In the process they came to believe firmly that ministerial leaders in England were engaging in a deep-seated plot to deprive them of their fundamental liberties. When something as inconsequential as the Townshend duty on tea precipitated yet another crisis in 1773, neither side was willing to disengage. By early 1775 both had decided to show their resolve.

A small incident that well illustrates the deteriorating situation occurred in Boston during March 1774. At the state funeral of Andrew Oliver, the Bay Colony's most recent lieutenant governor and former stamp distributor-designate, a large gathering of ordinary citizens came out to watch the solemn procession. As Oliver's coffin was slowly lowered into the ground, these Bostonians, many of them veterans of the American resistance movement, suddenly burst into loud cheers.

Such an open expression of bad will epitomized the acute strain in British-American relations. It was almost as if the cheers were for the burial of imperial authority in America. Certainly these colonists demonstrated contempt, not pride, in their British citizenship that day. Such striking changes in attitudes, over just a few years, pointed toward the fateful clash of arms known as the War for American Independence.

SUGGESTIONS FOR FURTHER READING

OVERVIEWS AND SURVEYS

Richard Maxwell Brown, *Strain of Violence: Historical Studies of American Violence and Vigilantism* (1975); Robert M. Calhoon, *Revolutionary America: An Interpretive Overview* (1976); Marc Egnal, *A Mighty Empire: The Origins of the Revolution* (1988); Lawrence Henry Gipson, *The Coming of the Revolution, 1763–1775* (1954); Merrill Jensen, *The Founding of a Nation, 1763–1776* (1968); Stephen G. Kurtz and James H. Hutson, eds., *Essays on the American Revolution* (1973); James Kirby Martin, *In the Course of Human Events: An Interpretive Exploration of the Revolution* (1979); Robert Middlekauff, *The Glorious Cause, 1763–1789* (1982); Edmund S. Morgan, *The Birth of the Republic, 1763–89*, rev. ed. (1977); Robert E. Shalhope, *The Roots of Democracy: American Thought and Culture, 1760–1800* (1990); Neil R. Stout, *The Perfect Crisis: The Beginning of the Revolutionary War* (1976); Gordon S. Wood, *The Radicalism of the American Revolution* (1992); Esmond Wright, *Fabric of Freedom, 1763–1800*, rev. ed. (1978).

PROVOKING AN IMPERIAL CRISIS

Thomas C. Barrow, *Trade and Empire: The British Customs Service in America, 1660–1775* (1967); Robert A. Becker, *Revolution, Reform, and the Politics of American Taxation, 1763–1783* (1980); Colin Bonwick, *English Radicals and the American Revolution* (1977); John Brewer, *Party Ideology and Popular Politics at the Accession of George III* (1976); John L. Bullion, *A Great and Necessary Measure: George Grenville and the Genesis of the*

Stamp Act, 1763–1765* (1982); Ian R. Christie, *Crisis of Empire, 1754–1783* (1966), and with Benjamin W. Labaree, *Empire or Independence, 1760–1776* (1976); John Derry, *English Politics and the American Revolution* (1976); Joseph A. Ernst, *Money and Politics in America, 1755–1775* (1973); Michael Kammen, *A Rope of Sand: Colonial Agents, British Politics, and the Revolution* (1968); Lewis B. Namier, *England in the Age of the American Revolution*, rev. ed. (1961), and *The Structure of Politics at the Accession of George III*, rev. ed. (1957); Howard H. Peckham, *Pontiac and the Indian Uprising* (1947); Francis Philbrick, *The Rise of the West, 1754–1830* (1965); John Shy, *Toward Lexington: The Role of the British Army in the Coming of the Revolution* (1965); Jack M. Sosin, *Whitehall and the Wilderness: The Middle West in British Colonial Policy, 1760–1775* (1961), and *The Revolutionary Frontier, 1763–1783* (1967); Neil R. Stout, *The Royal Navy in America, 1760–1775* (1973); Robert W. Tucker and David C. Hendrickson, *The Fall of the First British Empire* (1982); Carl Ubbelohde, *The Vice-Admiralty Courts and the American Revolution* (1960); Franklin B. Wickwire, *British Subministers and Colonial America, 1763–1783* (1966).

"LIBERTY, PROPERTY, AND NO STAMPS" and A SECOND CRISIS: THE TOWNSHEND DUTIES

Paul Gilje, *Road to Mobocracy: Popular Disorder in New York City, 1763–1834* (1987); Dirk Hoerder, *Crowd Action in Revolutionary Massachusetts, 1765–1780* (1977); Pauline R. Maier, *From Resistance to Revolution: Colonial Radicals and the Development of Opposition to Britain, 1765–1776* (1972), and *The Old Revolutionaries: Political Lives in the Age of Samuel Adams* (1980); Edmund S. and Helen M. Morgan, *The Stamp Act Crisis*, rev. ed. (1962); Gary B. Nash, *The Urban Crucible: Social Change, Political Consciousness, and the Origins of the Revolution* (1979); Charles S. Olton, *Artisans for Independence: Philadelphia Mechanics and the Revolution* (1975); Peter Shaw, *The Character of John Adams* (1976), and *American Patriots and the Rituals of Revolution* (1981); Peter D. G. Thomas, *British Politics and the Stamp Act Crisis* (1975), and *The Townshend Duties Crisis: The Second Phase of the Revolution, 1767–1773* (1987); John W. Tyler, *Smugglers and Patriots: Boston Merchants and the Advent of the Revolution* (1986); John J. Waters, Jr., *The Otis Family in Provincial and Revolutionary Massachusetts* (1968); Hiller B. Zobel, *The Boston Massacre* (1970).

THE RUPTURING OF IMPERIAL RELATIONS

David Ammerman, *In the Common Cause: American Response to the Coercive Acts of 1774* (1974); Bernard Bailyn, *The Ideological Origins of the American Revolution* (1967), and *The Origins of American Politics* (1968); Richard R. Beeman, *The Evolution of the Southern Backcountry: A Case Study of Lunenburg County, Virginia, 1746–1832* (1984); Ruth H. Bloch, *Visionary Republic: Millennial Themes in American Thought, 1756–1800* (1985); Richard D. Brown, *Revolutionary Politics in Massachusetts: The Boston Committee of Correspondence, 1772–1774* (1970); Edwin G. Burrows and Michael Wallace, "The Ideology and Psychology of National Liberation," *Perspectives in American History*, 6 (1972), pp. 167–306; Richard L. Bushman, *King and People in Provincial Massachusetts* (1985); H. Trevor Colbourn, *The Lamp of Experience: Whig History and the Intellectual Origins of the Revolution* (1965); Jere R. Daniell, *Experiment in Republicanism: New Hampshire Politics and the Revolution, 1741–1794* (1970); Bernard Donoughue, *British Politics and the American Revolution: The Path to War, 1773–1775* (1964); A. Roger Ekirch, *"Poor Carolina": Politics and Society in North Carolina, 1729–1776* (1981); Jay Fliegelman, *Prodigals and Pilgrims: The American Revolution Against Patriarchal Authority, 1750–1800* (1982); Larry R. Gerlach, *Prologue to Independence: New Jersey in the Coming of the Revolution* (1976); Ronald Hoffman, *A Spirit of Dissension: Economics, Politics, and the Revolution in Maryland* (1973); Benjamin W. Labaree, *The Boston Tea Party* (1964); David S. Lovejoy, *Rhode Island Politics and the Revolution, 1760–1776* (1958); Stephen E. Lucas, *Portents of Rebellion: Rhetoric and Revolution in Philadelphia, 1765–1776* (1976); Bernard Mason, *The Road to Independence: The Revolutionary Movement in New York, 1773–1777* (1966); John A. Neuenschwander, *The Middle Colonies and the Coming of the American Revolution* (1973); Gregory H. Nobles, *Divisions Throughout the Whole: Politics and Society in Hampshire County, Massachusetts, 1740–1775* (1983); J. G. A. Pocock, *The Machiavellian Moment: Florentine Political Thought and the Atlantic Republican Tradition* (1975); Caroline Robbins, *The Eighteenth-Century Commonwealthman* (1959); Clinton Rossiter, *Seedtime of the Republic: The Origin of the American Tradition of Political Liberty* (1953); Richard A. Ryerson, *The Revolution Is Now Begun: The Radical Committees of Philadelphia, 1765–1776* (1978); David Curtis Skaggs, *Roots of Maryland Democracy, 1753–1776* (1973); Alan Taylor, *Liberty Men and Great Proprietors: The Maine Frontier, 1760–1820* (1990).

BIOGRAPHIES

Bernard Bailyn, *The Ordeal of Thomas Hutchinson* (1974); Richard R. Beeman, *Patrick Henry* (1974); John Brooke, *King George III* (1972); John H. Cary, *Joseph Warren* (1961); John Ferling, *The First of Men: George Washington* (1988), and *John Adams* (1992); William M. Fowler, Jr., *The Baron of Beacon Hill: John Hancock* (1979); Don R. Gerlach, *Philip Schuyler and the Revolution in New York, 1733–1777* (1964); E. Stanly Godbold, Jr., and Robert W. Woody, *Christopher Gadsden* (1982); James L. McKelvey, *George III and Lord Bute* (1973); John C. Miller, *Sam Adams: Pioneer in Propaganda* (1936); Lewis B. Namier and John Brooke, *Charles Townshend* (1964); Sheila Skemp, *William Franklin: Son of a Patriot, Servant of a King* (1990); Peter D. G. Thomas, *Lord North* (1976).

CHAPTER 5

The Times That Tried Many Souls, 1775–1783

76.

FIG. V.

Joseph Plumb Martin was a dedicated patriot soldier, one of 11,000 men and women who formed the backbone of General George Washington's Continental forces. When that army entered its Valley Forge winter campsite in December 1777, Martin recorded despondently that the soldiers' trail could "be tracked by their blood upon the rough frozen ground." The Continentals were "now in a truly forlorn condition,—no clothing, no provisions, and as disheartened as need be." They had fought hard against British regulars and Hessians that summer and autumn but had not prevented the forces of General Sir William Howe from taking Philadelphia, the rebel capital. Washington had chosen Valley Forge as a winter encampment because, as a hilly area, it represented an easily defensible position some 20 miles northwest of Philadelphia, should Howe's soldiers venture forth from their far more comfortable quarters.

General Washington himself was very worried about the conditions facing his troops. If something was not done, and soon, the commander in chief stated, "this army must inevitably . . . starve, dissolve, or disperse." Private Martin thought the same: "Had there fallen deep snows (and it was the time of year to expect them) or even heavy and long rainstorms, the whole army must inevitably have perished." The weather was bitterly cold, but the Continentals, using what energy they had left, constructed "little shanties that are scarcely gayer than dungeon cells," as the Marquis de Lafayette described their housing.

Making matters more difficult was the lack of food and clothing. Martin claimed that, upon first entering Valley Forge, he went a full day and two nights without anything to eat, "save half a small pumpkin, which I cooked by placing it upon a rock, the skin side uppermost, and making fire upon it." His comrades fared no better. Within two days of moving into Valley Forge, a common grumble could be heard everywhere: "No Meat! No Meat!" By the first of January the words had become more ominous: "No bread, no soldier!"

Thus began a tragic winter of desperation for Washington's Continentals. Some 2500 soldiers, or nearly one-fourth of the troops, perished before the army broke camp in June 1778.

They died from exposure to the elements, malnutrition, and such virulent diseases as typhus and smallpox. It was not uncommon for soldiers to languish for days in their rudely constructed huts because they were too weak to drill or to go on food hunting expeditions. Sometimes for lack of straw and blankets, they simply froze to death in their beds. To add to the woes of the camp, more than 500 of the army's horses starved to death that winter. It was impossible to bury their carcasses in the frozen ground, which only magnified the deplorable sanitation conditions and the consequent spread of disease.

Under such forsaken circumstances, hundreds of soldiers deserted. If Washington had not let his troops leave camp to requisition food in the countryside or if there had not been an unusually early shad run in the Schuylkill River, which flowed behind the encampment, the army might well have perished.

The extreme suffering at Valley Forge has usually been attributed to the severe weather and a complete breakdown of the army's supply system. In fact, weather conditions were no worse than in other years. (The most miserable winter encampment in terms of frigid temperatures and deep piles of snow came two years later when the Continentals settled into Jockey Hollow near Morristown, New Jersey.) Certainly a major reason for the deprivation at Valley Forge was widespread indifference toward an army made up of the poor, the expendable, and the unfree in American society.

Joseph Plumb Martin clearly thought this was the case. He was a young man from Connecticut, without material resources, who had first enlisted during 1776 at the very peak of patriot enthusiasm for the war—sometimes called the *rage militaire*. He soon learned that there were few glories in soldiering. Camp life was both dull and dangerous, given the many killer diseases that ravaged armies of the era, and battle was a frightening experience. Before 1776 was over, Martin had faced the hurtling musket balls and bloodied bayonets of British soldiers in the Continental army's vain attempt to defend New York City and vicinity. He did not renew his enlistment and returned to Connecticut.

For a poor, landless person, economic pros-

George Washington led a bedraggled, half-starved army of 11,000 men and women into Valley Forge in December 1777.

pects at home were not much better than serving for promises of regular pay in the Continental army. In 1777 Martin stepped forth again and agreed to enlist as a substitute for some local gentlemen being threatened by an attempted draft. For a specified sum of money ("I forgot the sum"), he became their substitute. As Martin later wrote, "they were now freed from further trouble, at least for the present, and I had become the scapegoat for them."

The experiences of Martin typified those of so many others who performed long-term Continental service on behalf of the cause of liberty. After an initial rush to arms in defiance of British authority in 1775, the harsh realities of military life and pitched battles dampened patriot enthusiasm to the point that by December 1776 the Continental army all but ceased to exist. Washington's major task became that of securing enough troop strength and material support to shape an army capable of standing up time after time to British forces.

The commander-in-chief found his long-term soldiers among the poor and deprived groups of revolutionary America. In addition, major European nations like France, Spain, and Holland also came to the rescue with additional troops, supplies, and vital financial support. Working together, even in the face of so much popular indifference, these allies-in-arms outlasted the mighty land and sea forces of Great Britain, making possible a generous peace settlement in 1783 that guaranteed independence for the group of former British colonies that now called themselves the 13 United States.

RECONCILIATION OR INDEPENDENCE

Crown officials in England gave scant attention to the acts of the First Continental Congress because they believed that the time had come to teach the American provincials a military lesson. George III explained why. The colonists, he asserted, "have boldly thrown off the mask and avowed nothing less than a total independence of the British legislature will satisfy them." This was an inaccurate perception, but it lay behind the decision to turn the most powerful military machine in the western world, based on its record in recent wars, against the troublemakers in America and to crush resistance to British authority once and for all.

The Shooting War Starts

During the winter of 1774–1775 the king's ministers prepared for what they thought would be nothing more than a brief demonstration of military force. General Gage received "secret" orders to employ the redcoats under his command "to arrest and imprison the principal actors and abettors" of rebellion; however, if the likes of Samuel Adams, John Hancock, and Joseph Warren could not be captured, then Gage was to challenge in any way he deemed appropriate "this rude [American] *rabble* without plan, without concert, and without conduct . . . unprepared to encounter with a regular force." Above all else, Gage was to strike hard with a decisive blow.

In a series of related showdown decisions, King and Parliament authorized funds for a larger force of regular troops in America and named three high ranking generals—William Howe, Henry Clinton, and "Gentleman Johnny" Burgoyne—to sail to Boston and join Gage. They also declared Massachusetts to be in a state of rebellion, which permitted redcoats to shoot down suspected rebels on sight, should that be necessary to quell opposition. Eventually this act would be applied to all 13 provinces.

General Gage received the ministry's secret orders in mid-April 1775. Being on the scene, he was not quite as convinced as his superiors about American martial weakness. Gage had repeatedly urged caution in his reports to home officials, but now there was no choice; he had to act. Because the rebel leaders had already gotten word of the orders and fled to the countryside, Gage decided upon a reconnaissance in force mission. He would send a column of regulars to Concord, a town some 20 miles northwest of Boston that also served as a storage point for patriot gunpowder and related military supplies. Once there, the troops were to seize or destroy as much weaponry and ammunition

This painting, created from an eyewitness sketch, shows British troops marching into Concord to destroy patriot stores of gunpowder and military supplies.

who were running out of ammunition. It was the bloodiest engagement of the whole war. The British suffered 1054 casualties—40 percent of the redcoats engaged. American casualties amounted to 411, or 30 percent. Among those slain was Samuel Adams's close political associate, Dr. Joseph Warren, mourned by patriots everywhere.

The realization that patriot soldiers had been driven from the field undermined the euphoria that followed the rout of the redcoats at Lexington and Concord. Still, the British gained little advantage because they had failed to pursue the fleeing rebels. They remained trapped in Boston, surrounded by thousands of armed and angry colonists. Henry Clinton summarized it best when he called Bunker Hill "a dear bought victory," adding dryly that "another such would have ruined us."

Lord Dunmore's Proclamation of Emancipation

New England and Canada did not long remain the only theaters of war. Before the end of 1775 fighting erupted in the South. In Virginia the protagonist was John Murray, Lord Dunmore, who was the last royal governor of the Old Dominion. In May 1774 Dunmore had dissolved the Assembly because the burgesses had called for a day of fasting and prayer in support of the Bostonians. Incensed at Dunmore's arbitrary action, Virginia's gentleman-planters started meeting in provincial conventions, acting as if royal authority no longer existed.

Dunmore resented such impudence. In June 1775 he fled Williamsburg and announced that British subjects still loyal to the Crown should join him in bringing the planter elite to its senses. Very few citizens came forward. By autumn Dunmore, who used a naval vessel in Chesapeake Bay as his headquarters, had concluded that planter resistance could only be broken by turning Virginia's slaves against their masters. On November 7, 1775, he issued an emancipation proclamation. It read in part: "And I do hereby further declare all indentured servants, Negroes, or others . . . free, that are able and willing to bear arms."

Dunmore hoped that Virginia's slaves would break their chains and join with him in teaching their former masters that talk of liberty was a two-edged sword. The plan backfired. Irate planters suppressed copies of the proclamation and spread the rumor of a royal hoax designed to lure blacks into Dunmore's camp so that he could sell them to the owners of West Indian sugar plantations, where inhuman working conditions and very high mortality rates prevailed. Despite this, as many as 2000 slaves did take their chances and escaped to the royal standard.

Those blacks who first fled became a part of Dunmore's "Ethiopian" regiment, which made the mistake of engaging Virginia militiamen in a battle at Great Bridge in December 1775. Having had no time for even the fundamentals of military training, the regiment took a drubbing. This battle ended any semblance of royal authority in Virginia. Dunmore and his following soon retreated to a flotilla of vessels in Chesapeake Bay. During the next few months the numbers of royalist adherents kept growing, but then smallpox struck, killing hundreds of people. In the summer of 1776 Dunmore sailed away, leaving behind a planter class that closely guarded its human property while demanding independence from those in Britain whom it denounced as tyrants.

Resolving the Independence Question

Lord Dunmore's experiences highlighted the collapse of British political authority. Beginning in the summer of 1775, colony after colony witnessed an end to royal government. To fill the void, the patriots elected ad hoc provincial congresses. These bodies functioned as substitute legislatures and dealt with pressing local issues. They also took particular interest in suppressing suspected loyalists.

During that same summer Massachusetts moved one step further by asking the Continental Congress for permission to establish a more enduring government based on a written constitution. After ousting its royal governor New Hampshire followed suit. These requests forced Congress to act. The delegates did so in early November, stating that Massachusetts, New Hampshire, and any others might adopt "such a form of government, as . . . will best produce the happiness of the people," yet only if written

(Text continues on p. 154)

THE BATTLE OF BUNKER HILL

Early on Friday evening, June 16, 1775, rebel military leaders held an urgent meeting in Cambridge, Massachusetts. Intelligence had just reached them that redcoats under Lieutenant General Thomas Gage would soon attempt to break out of Boston. The British plan was to cross the body of water south of Boston, take Dorchester Heights, then sweep north through Cambridge, the patriot army command base, and send the rebels, now numbering well over 10,000 volunteers, reeling back into the countryside. The target date for this operation was Sunday, June 18.

The assembled rebel officers decided to divert the British from their plans by moving patriot lines yet closer to Boston. They gave orders to Colonel William Prescott to fortify Bunker Hill on Charlestown

peninsula, just to the north of Boston. The rebels would now control terrain from which they could cannonade British vessels in the harbor and even the city, if necessary. Should the British attempt to dislodge the rebels, they would have to storm up a hill rising 130 feet above sea level into withering patriot fire.

Before midnight on the 16th, Prescott, leading more than 1000 troops, reached Bunker Hill. At this point he called together the other officers, including Colonel Richard Gridley, an experienced military engineer, to discuss the placement of earthworks. As they studied the terrain around them, they could see another hill some 600 yards closer to Boston, which rose sharply to 75 feet above sea level. Gridley recommended a line of trenches and a redoubt on that site. Bunker Hill,

the group concluded, should serve as a secondary line of defense.

Moving forward as quietly as possible, the Americans dug in rapidly on Breed's Hill, knowing that daylight would expose their activity. At dawn on Saturday, June 17, sailors on board a British war vessel in the harbor spied the new rebel position and opened up with artillery fire. The cannonade awoke everyone in the vicinity, including General Gage, who soon met in a council of war with three other generals—William Howe, Henry Clinton, and John Burgoyne—all of whom had recently arrived in Boston.

General Gage, despite his superior rank as commander of British military forces in North America, deferred to the three major generals in his presence. Since Gage had repeatedly urged caution in handling the rebels, many home leaders had started asking whether he was too timid for the task at hand. The appearance of Howe, Clinton, and Burgoyne, he knew, was hardly a vote of confidence.

During the imperial wars, British military officers had repeatedly characterized the colonists as faint-hearted fighters. Reflecting this attitude, the three generals could not fathom how Gage had gotten his troops trapped in Boston by untrained, disorganized, and ill-disciplined rebels. The generals, not surprisingly, demanded an immediate offensive against Prescott's troops. They hoped for so crushing a victory that rebel resistance would disintegrate completely.

Then they debated tactics. Henry Clinton wanted to seize control of the narrow neck of land behind Bunker Hill connecting Charlestown peninsula to the mainland. That maneuver would trap Prescott's force, which then could be defeated and captured in detail. Howe and Burgoyne favored a direct frontal assault. The rebels would wither and run, they argued, in the face of concentrated, disciplined British arms. Gage reluctantly agreed to a frontal assault. He hoped that the other generals were right, that the Americans would flee rather than fight, but deep inside he expected heavy casualties.

British regulars were very well trained soldiers. They would rather stand up to furious enemy fire than to the wrath of their officers and the brutal military penalties for insubordination of any kind. Insolence toward an officer or attempted desertion resulted in punishments of up to 1000 lashes well laid on, which few persons could survive.

New soldiers received rigorous training in the basics of combat. When deployed in front of the enemy, they moved easily from column formations into three battle lines. After troops in the first line fired their smoothbore muskets, affectionately known as the "Brown Bess," they reloaded as their comrades in the next two lines stepped in front of them and fired their muskets in turn.

Smoothbore muskets were inaccurate weapons with an effective range of less than 80 yards. Experienced soldiers going through the steps of ramming powder and ball down the barrel could rarely get off more than two shots a minute. Thus most battle casualties came from bayonet wounds when competing armies, once having fired three or four rounds at very close range, charged forward and engaged in hand-to-hand combat. The bayonet, fastened to the end of the musket, was the major killing weapon of

eighteenth-century European-style warfare, and the proficient soldier more often stabbed than shot his opponent to death.

Knowing all of this, General Howe, whom Gage placed in charge of the assault, envisioned an overwhelming victory over a motley band of rebels. By 3 P.M., more than 2000 redcoats had been ferried across the bay and were ready to advance. Howe sent forward troops on his left under General Robert Pigot directly at Breed's Hill to divert the Americans. In turn, he led his column along the shore to break through a patriot line behind a rail fence. He expected to sweep these defenders aside in a classic flanking maneuver, then swing sharply to the left and cut Prescott's soldiers off from retreat as they dueled with Pigot's redcoats on their front. Bayonets would finish the assignment.

Galling rebel fire ruined the first British assault. The patriots held off shooting until the last possible moment, then unleashed a furious series of blasts. The redcoats staggered and fell back. Wrote one British officer with Howe, we "were served up in companies against the grass fence, without being able to penetrate.... Most of our grenadiers and light infantry, in presenting themselves, lost three-fourths, and many nine-tenths, of their men." Far to the left Pigot's soldiers also ran back from the blistering volleys of musket fire being laid down by Prescott's defenders.

Retreating on all fronts, the British regrouped and then tried to execute Howe's plan a second time. "It was surprising," wrote an observer, to watch the redcoats "step over ... dead bodies, as though they had been logs of wood." Once again, exclaimed one British officer, "an

incessant stream of fire" forced them back. From his vantage point in Boston, General Burgoyne described what was happening as "a complication of horror ... more dreadfully terrible" than anything he had ever seen. He wondered whether "defeat" would bring on "a final loss to the British empire in America."

At this critical juncture, Howe, reinforced by 400 fresh troops, decided to throw everything against the redoubt, where, unknown to him, Prescott's troops were running out of ammunition. Now the British, with regimental pride at stake, shouted "push on, push on." Within minutes they overran the Americans, most of whom lacked bayonets to defend themselves. Prescott's coolness under heavy fire resulted in an orderly retreat, but most of the rebel casualties occurred among defenders who did not evacuate in time. Included among them was Samuel Adams's valued political associate, Dr. Joseph Warren, already wounded but who died from bayonet wounds inflicted by an enraged redcoat who apparently recognized him and cried out that agitators like Warren were responsible for such horrible carnage.

The misnamed Battle of Bunker Hill was over within little more than an hour. Most of the patriots did escape, having no way of knowing that they had participated in the bloodiest fight of the Revolutionary War. The figure of 1465 combined casualties shocked everyone in what General Clinton called "a dear bought victory." The British had really gained nothing of consequence, since the American patriots still controlled the countryside surrounding Boston and Charlestown peninsula.

constitutions specified that these governments would exist until "the present dispute between Great Britain and the colonies" came to an end. The moderates realized that new state governments, as much if not more than a separate army, had the appearance of de facto independence. They did everything they could to prevent a total rejection of British political authority in America.

John Dickinson led the campaign in Congress to suppress discussion of a declaration of independence. In early November 1775 he got the Pennsylvania Assembly to instruct its congressional delegates to "dissent from, and utterly reject, any propositions . . . that may cause or lead to a separation from our mother country." New York, Delaware, Maryland, and South Carolina soon followed suit. Thus there was to be no resolution of the independence question before 1776.

Events outside of Congress were about to overwhelm the moderates. In January 1776 Thomas Paine, a recent migrant from England who had once been a corsetmaker's apprentice, published a pamphlet entitled *Common Sense*. It became an instant best-seller, running through 25 editions and 120,000 copies over the next three months. *Common Sense* electrified the populace with its dynamic, forceful language. It communicated a sense of urgency about moving toward independence, and it attacked congressional moderates for not being bold enough to break with the past.

Paine likewise denounced the British monarchy. He wrote: "The folly of hereditary right in Kings, is that nature disapproves it . . . by giving mankind *an ass for a lion.*" He encouraged Americans to adopt republican forms of government, since "every spot of the old world is overrun with oppression." The fate of all humans everywhere, he concluded, hung in the balance. *Common Sense* put severe pressure on the moderates, but they held on doggedly, hoping against hope that Great Britain would turn from its belligerent course and begin serious negotiations with Congress.

At the end of February 1776 another significant incident took place in the form of a short, bloody battle between loyalists and patriot militia at Moore's Creek Bridge in North Carolina. This engagement resulted in more than a rout of local tories. Now facing a shooting war, North Carolina's provincial congress reversed orders to its congressional delegates and allowed them to discuss independence and vote on a plan of national government. Soon thereafter the Virginians, furious about Lord Dunmore's activities, issued similar instructions. Then leaders in Rhode Island, impatient with everyone else, boldly declared their own independence in early May. The moderates were rapidly losing their ability to block resolution of the independence question.

On June 7, 1776, Richard Henry Lee, speaking on behalf of the Virginia provincial convention, presented formal resolutions to Congress. Lee urged "that these United Colonies are, and of right ought to be, free and independent states, . . . and that all political connection between them and the State of Great Britain is, and ought to be, totally dissolved." The resolutions also called for the creation of a national government and the formation of alliances with foreign nations in support of the war effort.

Within a few days Congress established two committees, one headed by John Dickinson to produce a plan of central government and another to prepare a statement on independence. Thomas Jefferson (1743–1826), a tall, young, red-haired Virginian, agreed to write a draft text on independence, which the committee laid be-

COMMON SENSE;

ADDRESSED TO THE

INHABITANTS

O F

A M E R I C A,

On the following interesting

S U B J E C T S.

I. Of the Origin and Design of Government in general, with concise Remarks on the English Constitution.
II. Of Monarchy and Hereditary Succession.
III. Thoughts on the present State of American Affairs.
IV. Of the present Ability of America, with some miscellaneous Reflections.

Man knows no Master save creating HEAVEN,
Or those whom choice and common good ordain.
THOMSON.

PHILADELPHIA;
Printed, and Sold, by R. BELL, in Third-Street.
MDCCLXXVI.

Thomas Paine's *Common Sense*, first published in January 1776, urged the colonists toward independence and a bold new world of political freedom.

The Declaration of Independence came before Congress for debate on July 1, 1776, and was pronounced publicly on July 4.

fore Congress on Friday, June 28. John Adams was expecting "the greatest debate of all" on Monday, July 1. In the session that day John Dickinson spoke forcefully against a formal severance of ties with Great Britain. He argued that Americans could not endure against superior British arms, especially "when we are in so wretched a state of preparation" for war. Nor did he think that significant foreign aid from France and other nations would be readily forthcoming. Moving forward with independence, he concluded, would be like reading "a little more in the Doomsday Book of America."

The delegates listened politely, but Dickinson was no longer in step with the mood of Congress. At the end of the day they voted on Lee's resolutions, and 9 state delegations gave their assent. Political maneuvering produced what could be described as a unanimous vote the next day when 12 states voted affirmatively. New York's delegates had not yet received instructions from leaders back home, so they ab-

stained, even though they were now personally in favor of independence. By so overwhelming a ratification of Lee's resolutions, Congress thus technically declared independence on Tuesday, July 2.

Congress next turned to the consideration of Jefferson's draft, which one delegate in a classic understatement called "a pretty good one." He hoped that the text would "not be spoiled by canvassing in Congress." The delegates made only a few changes. They deleted a controversial statement blaming the slave trade on the king as well as words repudiating friendship with the British people. By Thursday evening, July 4, 1776, everything was in place, and Congress quickly adopted Jefferson's document, a masterful explanation of the reasons why the colonists were seeking independence.

The Declaration of Independence proclaimed to the world that Americans had been terribly mistreated by the parent nation. Indeed, much of the text represents a summary list of grievances, ranging from misuse of a standing army of redcoats in the colonies and the abuse of the rightful powers of popularly elected colonial assemblies to the ultimate crime, starting an unjustified war against loyal subjects. The Declaration blamed George III for the pattern of tyranny. He had failed to control his ministers, thereby abandoning his role as a true servant of the people.

The Declaration likewise offered its readers much more than a succinct interpretation of issues and events culminating in civil war. Thomas Jefferson believed that if the American Revolution was to succeed, it must be predicated on a clear and noble purpose. Since "all men are created equal" and have "certain unalienable rights," which Jefferson defined as "life, liberty, and the pursuit of happiness," Americans needed to dedicate themselves to the establishment of a whole new set of political relationships guaranteeing all citizens fundamental liberties. The great task facing the revolutionary generation would be to institute republican forms of government, based on the rule of law and human reason. Governments had "to effect" the "safety and happiness" of all citizens in the name of human decency, and all citizens would be obligated to work for the greater good of the whole community.

Through Jefferson's words, the patriots of 1776 committed themselves to uplifting humanity in a world overrun by greed and petty human ambition. None of these ideals was going to be realized, however, unless the means could be found to defeat the huge British military force arriving in America at the very time that Congress was debating and approving the Declaration of Independence.

WITHOUT VISIBLE ALLIES: THE WAR IN THE NORTH

British officials had made a great blunder in 1775. Thinking of the colonists as "a set of upstart vagabonds, the dregs and scorn of the human species," they had woefully underestimated their opponent. Lexington and Concord drove home this reality. Although cabinet leaders and generals continued to presume their superiority, they became far more serious about planning for the war. It was now clear that snuffing out the rebellion was a complex military assignment, given the sheer geographic size of the colonies and the absence of a strategically vital center, such as a national capital, which, if captured, would end the war. It was also clear that the use of an invading army was not the easiest way to regain the political allegiance of a people no longer placing such high value on being British subjects.

Britain's Massive Military Buildup

Directing the imperial war effort were King George, Lord North, and Lord George Germain (1716–1785), who became the American Secretary in 1775. Germain, who had once been court-martialed on charges of cowardice in battle and thrown out of the British army, was a surprisingly effective administrator and adept at working within England's complicated and inefficient military bureaucracy. His skills became evident in planning for the campaign of 1776—the largest land and sea offensive executed by any western nation until the Allied invasion of North Africa in 1942.

Step by step, Germain pulled the elements together. Of utmost importance was overall campaign strategy. It involved concentrating as many troops as possible on the port of New York City, where great numbers of loyalists lived, then subduing the surrounding countryside as a food and supply base. Loyalists would be used to reinstitute royal government, and the king's forces would engage and destroy the rebel army. Germain believed that the American will to resist had to be shattered, and he hoped that it would take only one campaign season. The longer the rebels lasted, he argued, the greater would be their prospects for success.

Next came the matter of assembling the military forces. It was not the practice in Britain, or anywhere in Europe for that matter, to draw upon all able-bodied, adult males. By and large the middle classes were exempt from service because they were considered productive members of society. This meant that the rank and file would come from two sources. First, there were poorer, less productive citizens in the British Isles who would be recruited or dragooned into service. Since life in European armies was often brutal, it was not always possible to convince or coerce even the most destitute of subjects to sign enlistment papers.

To ensure adequate troop strength, George III and his advisors turned to a second source, the principalities of Germany. Before the end of the war, six German states procured 30,000 soldiers. Some 17,000 came from Hesse-Cassel, where the local head of state forced many of his subjects into service. In return, he received direct cash payments from the British Crown for each soldier that he supplied. Hessians and downtrodden Britons, including many Irish subjects, thus made up the king's army.

Certainly as significant a matter as troop recruitment was military leadership. Home gov-

ernment leaders viewed General Gage as too timid and too respectful of Americans. The king recalled Gage in October 1775, naming William Howe (1729–1814) to replace him as overall commander-in-chief. William's brother Richard, Admiral Lord Howe (1726–1799), took charge of the naval flotilla that would carry thousands of troops to America.

Lord Germain expected the Howe brothers to use their combined land-naval forces to smash and bayonet the rebels into submission; but they did not turn out to be hard-hitting military commanders. Politically, they identified with whig leaders in England who believed that the Americans had some legitimate grievances. They intended to move in careful steps, using

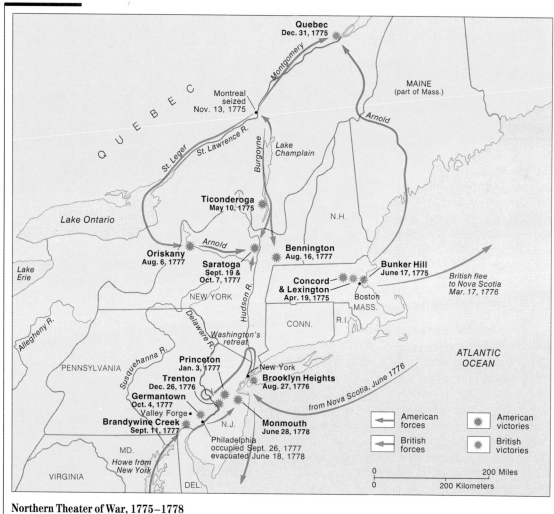

Northern Theater of War, 1775–1778

While Washington's officers urged that New York be burned to keep the enemy from using it as a base, Congress vetoed the proposal. However, a fire broke out in the city on September 20, 1776, and each side accused the other of starting it.

the presence of so many well-trained regulars to persuade Americans to sign loyalty oaths and renounce the rebellion. In failing to achieve the strategic goal of wiping out patriot resistance in only one campaign season, the less than daunt-less Howe brothers helped save the patriot cause from early extinction.

The Campaign for New York

Not yet aware of the scale of British mobiliza-tion, New Englanders cheered loudly in mid-March 1776 when General Howe took redcoats and loyalists in tow and fled by sea to Halifax, Nova Scotia. British control of Boston had be-come untenable because General Washington placed the cannons captured at Ticonderoga on Dorchester Heights overlooking the city. Howe's choice was to retreat or be bombarded into sub-mission. Washington, however, did not relax. For months he had predicted that the British would strike at New York City. He was abso-lutely right.

The king's army soon converged on Staten Island, across the bay from Manhattan. William Howe, sailing from Halifax, arrived with 10,000 soldiers at the end of June. During July, even as Americans excitedly read their Declaration of Independence, more and more British troops appeared, another 20,000 by mid-August. They came in some 400 transports escorted by 70 na-val vessels and 13,000 sailors under Admiral Lord Howe's supervision. All told, the Howe brothers had some 43,000 well-supplied, well-trained, and well-armed combatants. By com-parison, George Washington had 28,000 troops on his muster rolls, but only 19,000 were present and fit for duty. To make matters worse, the bulk of the rebel army lacked good weapons or supplies and was deficient in training and discipline.

The decision to defend New York, which the Continental Congress insisted upon and to which Washington acceded, was one of the great rebel blunders of the war. Completely out-numbered, the American commander unwisely divided his soldiers between Manhattan and Brooklyn Heights, separated by the East River. The Howe brothers responded on August 22 by landing troops at Gravesend, Long Island, thereby putting them in an excellent position to trap Washington's force in Brooklyn. For some inexplicable reason, however, Lord Howe chose not to move his naval vessels into the East River, which would have sealed off Washington's escape route. The rebels took a severe beating from the redcoats and Hessians, but they escaped back across the East River. Washington had been lucky, and he clearly learned from his error. Never again did he place his troops in so potentially disastrous a position.

The Howe brothers moved along indecisively through the rest of the campaign season. Every time they had the advantage, they failed to destroy the rebel army. They drove Washington's forces northward out of Manhattan, then wheeled about and captured some 2000 rebels defending Fort Washington (November 16, 1776), located high on a bluff overlooking the Hudson River. Two days later a British column under Charles, Lord Cornwallis (1738–1805) crossed the Hudson and nearly caught another sizable patriot contingent at Fort Lee in New Jersey, across from Fort Washington. One of Washington's most talented field commanders, Nathanael Greene of Rhode Island, managed to extricate his force just in time.

Washington had already moved into New Jersey. He took charge and ordered a retreat, hoping that he could get his soldiers across the Delaware River and into Pennsylvania before the onrushing Cornwallis, who was far more aggressive than the Howes, caught up with the dispirited rebel band. By early December what remained of Washington's army had made it into Pennsylvania.

Saving the Cause at Trenton

As the half-starving, battle-wearied patriot troops fled, hundreds of them also deserted. They had learned that British muskets and bayonets could maim and kill. Others, ravaged by disease or wounded in battle, were left behind along the way with the hope of receiving decent treatment from their pursuers. The American army was all but extinct. As Washington wrote in mid-December, "I think the game is pretty near up. . . . No man, I believe, ever had a greater choice of difficulties and less means to extricate himself from them." Having virtually destroyed his prey, William Howe ordered his troops into winter camps and returned to New York City. He ignored his charge to end the rebellion in one campaign season, fully satisfied that mopping up operations could be easily conducted in the spring of 1777.

At this juncture George Washington established his credentials as an innovative commander. He assessed his desperate position and decided upon a bold counterstroke. The success of this maneuver might save his army; defeat would surely ruin it. With muster rolls showing only 6000 troops, he divided his soldiers into three groups and tried to recross the icy Delaware River on Christmas evening. Their targets were British outposts in New Jersey. Of the three contingents, only Washington's near-frozen band of 2400 soldiers accomplished this daring maneuver.

At dawn they reached Trenton, where Colonel Johann Rall's unsuspecting Hessians were still groggy with liquor from their Christmas celebration. The engagement was over in a moment. Four hundred enemy troops escaped, but the Continentals captured almost 1000 Hessians. Within another few days the elated Americans again outdueled British units at Princeton. Stunned by this flurry of rebel activity, Howe redeployed his New Jersey outposts in a semicircle much closer to New York.

Washington had done much more than just regain lost ground. He had saved the Continental army from virtual extinction. Never again during the war would the British come so close to total victory—and all because of a failure to annihilate Washington's shattered forces when the opportunity was there. William Howe never seemed to understand this mistake. He relaxed in his winter quarters in New York and gloried in the knighthood awarded him for his victory at Brooklyn Heights.

Also of importance was Howe's decision to pull in his outposts. As the British army had marched across New Jersey, it lured thousands of neutrals and loyalists under its banner. These individuals had signed loyalty oaths, thus identifying themselves publicly as enemies of the

Revolution. As the British army drew back toward New York, it left the tories exposed to the fury of local patriots, who had anything but warm feelings for neighbors whose true allegiance had been revealed.

Time and again throughout the war, British military commanders committed the error of not sustaining support for the king's friends in America. They rarely took advantage of the reservoir of loyal subjects, an estimated 20 percent of the populace, who stood ready to fight the rebels and to do anything else within reason to assure a continuation of British rule. Before the war was over an estimated 50,000 loyalists formed into nearly 70 regiments with the idea of helping the British army regain control in America. British commanders by and large used this valuable source of troop strength ineffectively. They did not really trust loyalists or respect their fighting prowess. The official attitude seemed to be that loyalists were just colonists, a part of the "rude" American rabble. Such presumed superiority represented a major blindspot, when an essential military task involved regaining the allegiance of enough citizens to effect a complete revival of imperial political authority in America.

On the rebel side, the Trenton and Princeton victories did not result in a revived outpouring of popular support for Washington's army. When the Continentals had been in flight across New Jersey, Thomas Paine stepped forth with his first *Crisis* paper. He begged the populace to rally at this moment of deep despair. "These are the times that try men's souls," Paine stated forcefully. "The summer soldier and the sunshine patriot will, in this crisis, shrink from the service of his country; but he that stands it now, deserves the love and thanks of man and woman." Many read Paine's words, but the massive British campaign effort of 1776 had snuffed out the *rage militaire*.

The Real Continentals

One of the greatest problems facing Washington and the Continental Congress after 1776 was sustaining the rebel army's troop strength. In May 1777 the commander-in-chief only had 10,000 soldiers, of which 7363 were present and

Diversity of dress among American soldiers was common, but more common was the fact that few soldiers ever had the prescribed clothing.

fit for duty. This number increased substantially during the summer and fall, although only an estimated 11,000 Continentals entered Valley Forge. For the remainder of the war Washington's core of regulars rarely was more sizable. At times, as few as 5000 soldiers stood with him.

Certainly after his experiences in 1776, Washington understood that he must maintain "a respectable army" in the field and wear down the enemy, hoping ultimately to break Britain's will to continue the fight. He needed troops who would commit themselves to long-term service (three years or the duration), would submit to rigorous training and discipline, and would accept privation in the field. These were hardly glamorous prospects, especially when service often entailed death or permanent dismemberment. Still, Washington, Congress, and the states could promise cash bounties for enlisting, as well as regular pay, decent clothing, adequate food, and even land at war's end. For people who had nothing to lose, long-term service in the Continental army was at least worth considering.

After 1776 the rank and file of the Continental army came to be made up of economically hard pressed and unfree citizens. Private Joseph Plumb Martin was probably better off than most who enlisted—or were forced into service. The bulk of Washington's long-term Continentals were young (ranging in age from their early teens to mid-twenties), landless, unskilled, poverty-stricken males whose families were likewise quite poor. Also well represented were indentured servants and slaves who stood as substitutes for their masters in return for guarantees of personal freedom at the war's end.

In 1777 Massachusetts became the first state to authorize the enlistment of blacks— both slaves and freemen. Rhode Island soon followed suit by raising two black regiments. Southern states were far more reluctant to allow slaves to substitute for their masters. Maryland and Virginia ultimately did so, which caused one patriot general to query why so many "sons of freedom" seemed so anxious "to trust their all to be defended by slaves." Add to these groups captured British soldiers and deserters, particularly Hessians and Irishmen, as well as tories and criminals who were

The title page of a first edition of a history of black fighters.

often given a choice between military service or the gallows, and a composite portrait of the real Continental army begins to emerge.

Eighteenth-century armies also accepted women in the ranks. Like their male counterparts, they were invariably living on the margins of society. These women "on the ration" (more literally half rations) must be differentiated from so-called camp followers— those who marched along with their husbands or were prostitutes. Women in service performed various functions, ranging from caring for the sick and wounded, cooking, and

Deborah Sampson served in the army under the name of Timothy Thayer.

mending clothes to scavenging battlefields for clothing and equipment and burying the dead. On occasion they became directly involved in combat. Such a person was hard-drinking Margaret "Dirty Kate" Corbin. Her husband, a cannoneer, was shot dead when British forces attacked and captured Fort Washington in November 1776. Kate Corbin stepped forth, took his place, and helped fire the artillery piece until she also sustained a serious wound, from which she eventually recovered. The British army allowed 1 woman in the ranks for every 10 men; the Continental ratio was closer to 1 in 15.

Whether male or female, a unifying characteristic of Washington's post-1776 Continentals was poverty and, in many cases, lack of personal freedom. In their social profile, they looked very much like their counterparts in the British army. And as a group, they repeatedly risked their lives in return for promises: food, clothing, pay, and even land on which to make a decent living after the war. Their dreams of future prosperity depended upon the success of the rebellion, and that is one reason why they willingly endured, even though the far more prosperous civilian populace ignored their privation at such encampments as Valley Forge.

RESCUING THE PATRIOTS: TOWARD GLOBAL CONFLICT

The struggles of the American rebels did not go unobserved in European diplomatic circles. France and Spain, in particular, hoped that the rebellion would succeed. Their concerns, however, were not wholly altruistic. Territorial losses sustained during the Seven Years' War had swung the European balance of power decisively in Britain's favor. From the perspective of the Duc de Choiseul, France's foreign minister, post-1763 disagreements between Britain and America represented an opportunity to deflate the puffed-up British lion. Losing the colonies would weaken Britain immeasurably. France, concluded Choiseul, could only benefit by Americans gaining their independence.

Neither Choiseul nor his protégé, the Comte de Vergennes, who became France's foreign minister in 1774, were beacons of the Age of Enlightenment. They supported monarchism, not republicanism, and they had little interest in fostering political liberties. As hardened and cynical diplomatic veterans, they hoped to take advantage of this new set of circumstances. If they could shape events properly, they would advance France's future while exacting revenge on an old and despised enemy.

France Offers Covert Assistance

Before 1775, the French sent spies to America to report on events, and when possible to help stir up ill-will toward Britain. Once the war started, Vergennes adopted the shrewd posture of providing secret assistance to the rebels while maintaining a public stance of disinterested neutrality. He did not want France to get caught between the colonies and England, should the Americans falter on the battlefield or suddenly reconcile differences. If the rebels demonstrated their long-term resolve and proved worthy in combat, then France would enter the war and help crush the British.

Vergennes was a master manipulator in the court of Louis XVI. In 1775 one of his diplomatic agents, the courtier Pierre-Augustin Caron de Beaumarchais (1732–1799), perhaps best known for writing librettos for the *Marriage of Figaro* and the *Barber of Seville*, made contacts with prominent Americans in London. Beaumarchais reported back to Vergennes, and the two of them eventually agreed on the formation of a private trading company, Roderigue Hortalez & Cie., the sole purpose of which was to funnel war matériel (initially paid for by loans from the French and Spanish governments) to the patriots.

Meanwhile, the Continental Congress had selected one of its members, Connecticut merchant Silas Deane, to travel to Europe in search of loans and war goods. In July 1776 Deane made his first contact with Beaumarchais, who informed him that the structure was in place to provide covert aid in the form of war matériel to the rebels. A delighted Deane soon was working with Beaumarchais and others in obtaining supplies.

Although some of the merchandise was shoddy, much of it was invaluable to the patriot cause. Shipments made in 1777, for example, mostly went to the Continental army's Northern Department in upstate New York where weapons, powder, tents, clothing, and shoes were in desperately short supply. French goods sustained the patriot army that defeated John Burgoyne's British army at Saratoga. Secret French aid, which came in the form of cash subsidies and loans, strengthened the rebel cause immeasurably, thus helping the patriots to endure long enough until Vergennes and the French government came out publicly against Great Britain.

In September 1776 Congress designated two additional commissioners to join Deane in France. They were Benjamin Franklin and Arthur Lee, Richard Henry's irascible younger brother who had lived for many years in England and had met with Beaumarchais in 1775. Franklin, well-known before his arrival in Paris (he had been admitted to the French Academy of Sciences during 1772 in recognition of his electrical experiments), dominated the American delegation, whose assignment was to seek diplomatic recognition and a formal alliance. The aging Philadelphian became a popular celebrity. With his simple dress, witty personality, worldly charm, and shrewd mind, he embodied the ideals of republicanism. Painted likenesses of him appeared everywhere, even one place that Franklin did not find very flattering—inside chamber pots.

It was not just the Philadelphian's personal charm and skillfulness as a diplomat that resulted in an alliance. Dating back to 1775, Vergennes had worked to support the Americans while appearing neutral. He did so to avoid serious problems with the British, who kept trying to catch the French in the act of assisting the Americans. In public gatherings Vergennes usually treated the three commissioners with virtual disdain, but in private he had primed the government of Louis XVI (reigned 1774–1793) to enter the war, once conditions in America were right. Britain's military failures during 1777 were critical to prompting formal French intervention.

The British Seize Philadelphia

Sir William Howe had ideas of his own regarding how to conduct the war in America. He may have been a good tactician in battle, but he had little appreciation of strategy, which Lord George Germain kept attempting to explain to him. The home government's plan for 1777 was to send an army under Burgoyne south from Canada through the Lake Champlain corridor. In turn, Howe was to move troops up the Hudson River, eventually linking with Burgoyne at Albany. Called the Hudson Highlands strategy, the goal was to cut off New England from the rest of the colonies before sweeping eastward in reconquering the very region that had been the seedbed of rebellion.

Sir William favored going after and destroying the main Continental army. During May and June 1777 he tried to lure Washington into a major battle, but the American commander refused the bait and held to a very defensible position in New Jersey's Watchung Mountains. At this juncture Howe made a decision that may have cost Britain the war. All but abandoning the primary campaign goal of joining up with Burgoyne, he resolved to seize Philadelphia,

(Text continues on p. 166)

Washington's plan for the Battle of Germantown was too complex, and American columns, attacking from different directions, became confused and started firing at one another.

AMERICA AND THE WORLD
AMERICA'S FIRST TENTATIVE DIPLOMATIC STEPS

The Treaty of Alliance between France and the United States was written in both French and English (the first and last pages of the document are shown here). The signatories were Conrad Alexandre Gérard, France's minister to the United States, and the three American delegates to France, Benjamin Franklin, Silas Deane, and Arthur Lee.

Delegates to the Second Continental Congress, which first met in Philadelphia during May 1775, certainly had no standing as representatives of a legitimate nation. They made up a body that one delegate would later call "this stranger in the states of the world." Even worse from the point of view of gaining foreign sympathy or support, the majority of delegates were not yet committed to independence as a new nation separate from Great Britain. The primary goal was to resolve political differences with the parent nation of England.

The posture of seeking reconciliation rather than independence placed the Continental Congress in an awkward diplomatic position. In mid-June, for example, the delegates assumed responsibility for an army, but Congress lacked the material resources—arms, ammunition, food, clothing, and provisions—to support that Continental force. The delegates had to locate sources for desperately needed war goods as well as loans and cash subsidies to pay for these supplies. Nations such as France and Spain, Britain's traditional enemies, beckoned as possibilities. The diplomatic challenge was how to communicate with and perhaps even obtain material aid from these governments while still attempting to settle differences with England.

There certainly was no incentive for France, Spain, or other foreign powers to provide assistance so long as the American rebels were only fighting to guarantee their liberties without forsaking the British empire. Leaders such as Samuel and John Adams and other New England delegates, who were now advocating independence with the war spreading in their region, appreciated this point. They also understood that making diplomatic overtures to such powers as France would represent a major step toward de facto independence. So did more moderate delegates, among them Pennsylvania's John Dickinson, who had emerged as the leader of the majority in Congress favoring reconciliation. Approaching Britain's national rivals, Dickinson realized, had as much potential for damaging any hoped-for political settlement with the parent nation as did fighting against the king's regular troops at Lexington, Concord, Ticonderoga, and Bunker Hill.

Despite the hopes of the moderate delegates, conditions favoring reconciliation kept deteriorating. One piece of evidence was the declaration by George III on August 23, 1775, that all 13 colonies were to be treated as if in a state of rebellion. The king and his advisors had mistakenly come to believe in a deep-seated colonial plot to secure independence. The king's proclamation, which labeled every colonist a potential traitor, was sure evidence that Lord North's ministry would be emphasizing a military as opposed to a negotiated resolution of political differences.

In response to the king's pronouncement, delegates like John Adams and Benjamin Franklin, now almost 70 years old, urged their congressional colleagues to begin communicating with other nations regarding material support—before it was too late. Dickinson and other moderates resisted, until a compromise was struck. Congress established a standing Committee of Secret Correspondence on November 29, 1775, "for the sole purpose of corresponding with our friends in Great Britain, Ireland, and other parts of the world," but membership would be dominated by more moderate delegates such as Dickinson. This committee, the first agency charged with guiding American foreign policy, also counted among its members Benjamin Franklin, who gladly wrote letters to friends in foreign nations with hints about embracing—and supporting—the rebel cause.

The Committee of Secret Correspondence hardly had time to plan its activities before a young French aristocrat, Achard de Bonvouloir, appeared in Philadelphia. Acting as a private citizen, Bonvouloir was actually an agent of the Comte de Vergennes, the foreign minister of France. In meetings with Bonvouloir committee members asked whether the French government might support the rebel cause, especially with arms and related war goods. Bonvouloir, who kept maintaining the fiction of only representing himself, repeatedly spoke of likely French interest in backing the Americans.

Vergennes, indeed, was very favorably disposed, or he would not have sent Bonvouloir to America in the first place. The French minister saw in the brewing Anglo-American conflict an opportunity to chasten an ancient foe, one which had so recently cost the French their imperial holdings in North America. Thus it delighted Vergennes when he received exaggerated reports from Bonvouloir about thousands of "well clothed, well paid, and well commanded" rebel troops who were eager to fight and who only lacked good military engineers and adequate war supplies.

While persistently maintaining a posture of complete French neutrality, Vergennes set in motion during the spring of 1776 his plan for secretly aiding the Americans. He likewise began working to get Spain to assist the rebels, and he supported building up the French navy so that his nation could enter the war at a propitious moment and help defeat the British. He did so based on his firm belief, as he wrote privately, "that Providence had marked out this moment for the humiliation of England."

Because Britain had longstanding national enemies, then, the Committee of Secret Correspondence did not have to do very much to get the upstart Americans launched into the world of international diplomacy. Along with another secret committee seeking arms purchases, the committee sent the first American diplomatic repre-

sentative, merchant and former congressional delegate Silas Deane of Connecticut, abroad in the spring of 1776. When Deane, who like Bonvouloir acted as if he were a private citizen, reached Paris, he was delighted to find that Vergennes already had a mechanism in place for delivering cash subsidies, loans, and war goods.

By the end of 1776 the American diplomatic delegation to France consisted of Benjamin Franklin and Arthur Lee of Virginia as well as Deane. These rebel emissaries could now operate in the open, since Congress had finally renounced reconciliation in favor of independence. In fact, even as the delegates addressed the independence question back in June, they also named a committee to construct a model treaty plan to serve as a guide in forming alliances with foreign powers. John Adams took the lead in drafting the model treaty, a document approved by Congress in September. Known as the "Plan of 1776," the general idea was to lure France (and if possible Spain) into a formal recognition of American independence in return for favorable trading privileges.

In February 1778 the model plan became the basis of the Treaty of Amity and Commerce with France. For Vergennes the prospect of conducting—perhaps even dominating—international trade with the Americans was another way of weakening the British by helping to destroy their heretofore monopolistic control of commerce with the former colonists. Still, trading concessions were really not enough to entice the French into an alliance. What Vergennes and Louis XVI really wanted was the opportunity to strike devastating military blows at the British; they knew that the Treaty of Amity and Commerce would likely provoke England into an act of war with France, so they insisted upon a second agreement, the more entangling Treaty of Alliance by which the young United States and France would stand as "good and faithful" allies in the event of such hostilities.

Without critical French—and eventually Spanish and Dutch—support, the Americans might never have had the wherewithal to win their own War for Independence. That the patriot cause did succeed was directly related to the first small diplomatic steps taken by the Committee of Secret Correspondence of the Second Continental Congress. This committee both played its part well and served in turn as the seedling of the modern American State Department. In 1777 it became the Committee for Foreign Affairs, to be superseded in 1781 by a secretary for foreign affairs and in 1790 by a secretary of state, the first of whom was Thomas Jefferson, the author of the Declaration of Independence.

hoping at the same time to catch and crush Washington's Continentals as they moved into eastern Pennsylvania to protect the rebel capital. Howe loaded 15,000 soldiers onto vessels in New York harbor—he left behind a reserve force under General Sir Henry Clinton—and sailed out to sea in the middle of the campaign season.

Howe's flotilla came up through Chesapeake Bay in August, landing at Head of Elk in Maryland. On September 11 the British mauled the Continentals at Brandywine Creek, southwest of Philadelphia; but the engagement did not destroy the rebel army. Within another two weeks Sir William proudly led his troops into Philadelphia; yet except for the establishment of comfortable winters quarters, the British commander had accomplished nothing of consequence. The Continental Congress had already moved westward to York, Pennsylvania. Howe's presence cheered local loyalists (they did not know they were to be abandoned in the spring of 1778), and all British proponents felt relief when Washington's attack on British troops at Germantown on October 4 failed. Then the realization began to dawn that chasing after the main rebel army and seizing the enemy's capital had been a hollow quest—and had cost the British dearly.

Capturing Burgoyne's Army at Saratoga

The 1777 British descent from Canada had been planned carefully, at least on paper. One of its many aspects involved the use of Indian allies as auxiliary troops. When the war broke out, both sides asked the tribes of the North, particularly the powerful Six Nations of Iroquois, to remain neutral in what the Continental Congress called a "family quarrel." Soon trying to gain every possible advantage, the combatants could not long resist tapping into Indian manpower. Guy Johnson, Britain's Superintendent of Indian Affairs in the northern colonies, invited various tribes to fight under the king's banner. Similarly, American commissioners requested direct assistance. The British had the advantage of more supplies, especially arms and gunpowder. In addition, they had the better ar-

gument, since colonial settlers were the obvious culprits in seizing tribal lands, whereas British officials had tried to stop these encroachments by insisting that territory west of the Appalachians was a permanent Indian reserve.

The army of General John Burgoyne (1722–1792), strengthened by hundreds of Indians now on the warpath, moved southward out of Canada in mid-June. The main column of nearly 8000 pushed into Lake Champlain and drove the rebels from Fort Ticonderoga in early July. A second column of 1700 under Colonel Barry St. Leger proceeded up the St. Lawrence River and into Lake Ontario, before sweeping south toward Fort Schuyler (formerly Fort Stanwix) at the western end of the Mohawk Valley. St. Leger's troops were to act as a diversionary force. Soon they had 750 desperate rebel defenders of Fort Schuyler under siege. Seemingly nothing could stop these two columns, which were to converge again in Albany.

After seizing Ticonderoga, Burgoyne became more tentative about his southward movement. Like William Howe in 1776, he did not take his opponent seriously enough. Under the leadership of General Philip Schuyler, the Continental army's Northern Department had started to rally. The rebels blocked Burgoyne's path by cutting down trees, ripping up bridges, and moving boulders into fording points on streams. Soon the British advance had been slowed to less than a mile a day. Then Congress replaced Schuyler—New Englanders did not like him because of his supposed aristocratic airs—with General Horatio Gates.

Word of Gates's elevation was a factor in getting New England militiamen to come out and support the Continentals. Another was Burgoyne's lack of control of his Indians. A few of them murdered and scalped a young woman, Jane McCrea, who was betrothed to one of his loyalist officers. Burgoyne refused to punish the culprits, fearing he might drive off all of his Indian allies. In so doing he conveyed a message of barbarism that impelled hundreds more militiamen, determined to save their families from scalping knives, to take gun in hand.

In addition, St. Leger's diversionary force ran into trouble. Militiamen in the Mohawk Valley under General Nicholas Herkimer, in alliance with Oneidas and Tuscaroras of the Six Nations, tried to break through to Fort Schuyler. On August 6, 1777, they clashed with St. Leger's loyalists and Indians, among them Mohawks, Cayugas, and Senecas also of the Six Nations, at the Battle of Oriskany. Herkimer and nearly half of his column were killed or wounded that day, one of the bloodiest of the war.

Oriskany was the beginning of the end for the once mighty Iroquois nation, whose tribes were now hopelessly divided and consuming each other in combat. When war chieftain Joseph Brant (Thayendanegea) of the Mohawks led numerous bloody frontier raids for the British, a Continental army expedition under General John Sullivan marched into central New York during 1779 and destroyed every Iroquois village it came upon. After the war was over, the more aggressive Iroquois migrated north to Canada or west into the Ohio country, where they fought to keep out white frontiersmen; others, less militant, moved quietly onto reservations in western New York.

St. Leger's victory was temporary. Continentals under Benedict Arnold rushed west and drove off St. Leger without a second major fight. Arnold sent a dim-witted local loyalist into St. Leger's camp with fabricated news of thousands of rebel soldiers moving rapidly toward Fort Schuyler. The Indians, satiated with the bloodshed at Oriskany, quickly broke camp and fled, leaving the British colonel no alternative but to retreat back into Canada.

Burgoyne had now lost his diversionary force. He suffered yet another major setback on August 16 when New Hampshire militiamen under General John Stark overwhelmed some 900 Hessians who were out raiding for supplies near Bennington in the Vermont territory. With little prospect of relief from New York City, Burgoyne's army was now all but entrapped some 30 miles north of Albany along the Hudson River. In two desperate battles (September 19 and October 7) the British force tried to find a way around the well-entrenched rebels, but the brilliant field generalship of Benedict Arnold inspired the Americans to victory. It was all over for Burgoyne, and at Saratoga he surrendered

Joseph Brant (Thayendanegea), a Mohawk war chieftain, believed the Iroquois could not remain neutral and that their only chance was to side with the British.

what remained of his army—some 5000 soldiers—to General Gates on October 17, 1777.

According to one British soldier on the Saratoga surrender field, "we marched out, . . . with drums beating and the honors of war, but the drums seemed to have lost their former inspiring sounds, . . . as if almost ashamed to be heard on such an occasion." Losing an army at Saratoga was an unnecessary disaster for Britain, caused primarily by William Howe's unwillingness to work in concert with Burgoyne and follow through on the Hudson Highlands strategy. The victory was a major triumph for the Americans. It convinced Vergennes that it was now safe for France to commit to the rebel cause publicly.

On February 6, 1778, the French government signed two treaties with the American commissioners. The Treaty of Amity and Commerce recognized American independence and encouraged the development of trading ties. The Treaty of Alliance established a military pact between the two allies should hostilities break out between France and Britain. On

March 20 Louis XVI formally greeted the American commissioners at court and announced that the new nation had gained France's diplomatic recognition. In June 1778 a naval battle in the English Channel between British and French warships resulted in formal declarations of war by both powers. The drum beat for British rule over the 13 states had taken on the cadence of a death march.

THE WORLD TURNED UPSIDE DOWN

When George Washington learned about the French alliance, he declared a holiday for "rejoicing throughout the whole army." On that spring day in early May 1778, the Continentals at Valley Forge enjoyed themselves immensely. There was much to celebrate. They had survived the winter, and they had also benefited from the rigorous field training of colorful Baron Friedrich von Steuben, a pretended Prussian nobleman who had volunteered to teach the soldiery how to fight in a more disciplined fashion. Equally important was the announcement of open, direct aid from France, which would include land troops and naval reinforcements. Having the support of a major European ally certainly enhanced prospects for actually beating the British. Washington, so elated by this turn in events, winked at the issuance of "more than the common quantity of liquor" to his soldiers, which he knew would result in "some little drunkenness among them."

Revamping British Strategy

The alliance with France changed the fundamental character of the War for Independence. British officials realized that they were no longer just contending with upstart rebels in America. They were getting themselves ensnared in a world war. France, with its well-trained army and highly mobile navy, had the ability to strike British territories anytime and anywhere it chose. The French, in fact, started to put together a powerful land-naval expedition with the objective of invading England, although bad weather and poor organization in the French high command undercut this effort.

While renouncing any desire to retake Canada, the French did have designs on the valuable British sugar islands in the Caribbean. They built up troop strength in the French West Indies and soon had a four-to-one advantage.

The British military problem became even more complex in 1779 when Spain joined the war but only after signing a secret agreement with France—the Convention of Aranjuez—stipulating that Louis XVI's military forces would not stop fighting until the Spanish regained the Rock of Gibraltar (lost to the British at the end of the War of the Spanish Succession, see p. 103). Then in late 1780 the British declared war on the Netherlands, partly so they could capture the Dutch Caribbean island of St. Eustatius, which served as a major source of war supplies for the American patriots.

The dawning reality of world war threatened the British empire with major territorial losses across the globe. One result was a redesigned war plan—the Southern strategy—for reconquering the rebellious American provinces. The piecemeal adoption of this plan began during the spring of 1778. The assumption was that his Majesty's troops could no longer be massed against the American rebels; instead, they would have to be dispersed to threatened points, such as islands in the West Indies, and later Gibraltar.

The first step came in May 1778 when General Sir Henry Clinton (1738?–1795), who had taken over as North American commander from a discredited William Howe, received orders to evacuate Philadelphia. In June Clinton's troops retreated to New York City, narrowly averting a disastrous defeat by Washington's pursuing Continentals at Monmouth Court House (June 28) in central New Jersey. Clinton was to hang on as best he could at the main British base, but he would have to accept a reduction in forces for campaigning elsewhere. The process of dispersal began during the autumn of 1778. Sir Henry avoided major battles with Washington's army in the North while he implemented the Southern strategy.

Lord George Germain and other Crown officials mistakenly assumed that, in the South, loyalists existed in far greater numbers than they did. In what was a slight modification of

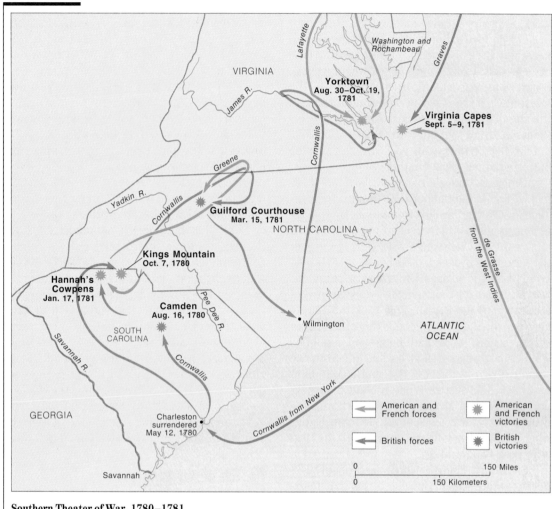

Southern Theater of War, 1780–1781

the Hudson Highlands strategy, the idea was to employ the king's friends, primarily as substitutes for depleted British forces, in partisan (guerrilla) warfare. Bands of armed loyalists would operate in conjunction with a main red-coat army to subdue all rebels, beginning in Georgia and then moving in carefully planned steps northward. When any previously rebel-dominated region had been fully secured, royal government would be reintroduced. Ultimately through attrition, the whole South would be brought back into the British fold, opening the way for eventual subjugation of the North. The Southern strategy required patience as well as careful nurturing of loyalist sentiment. Both

seemed very possible when a detachment of 3500 redcoats sailed south from New York in November 1778 and quickly reconquered Georgia.

Until the French alliance the South was a secondary theater of war, although there had been sporadic fighting between loyalists and rebel militia. White-Indian relations were bloodier. As in the North, both sides maneuvered for the favor of the most powerful Indian nations, the Cherokees, Creeks, Choctaws, and Chickasaws. These four nations had 10,000 warriors among them, compared to an estimated 2000 among all the northern Iroquois.

John Stuart, Britain's Superintendent of Indian Affairs in the southern colonies, had a network of agents working among the tribes. Late in 1775 he focused on winning over the Cherokees and Creeks, who had the most warriors, urging them to fight in concert with loyalists. Stuart was particularly successful with the Overhill Cherokees led by Dragging Canoe. In the summer of 1776 they attacked frontier settlements from Virginia to South Carolina, butchering settlers who had unwisely moved onto traditional tribal hunting grounds.

Dragging Canoe's raids had two major effects. First, in September 1776 hundreds of Virginia and North Carolina frontiersmen came together as militia and wreaked mayhem on the most easterly Cherokee towns. During October the Virginians proceeded farther west to the Overhill Cherokee villages. Dragging Canoe and his warriors retreated, agreeing to forswear further assistance to the British. This took the Cherokees out of the war. Second, the other major tribes, seeing what had happened, snubbed John Stuart's agents and backed off from the "family quarrel." By 1777 the southern Indians had been neutralized. While a band of Creeks under Alexander McGillivray did work with the British after their invasion of Georgia, Native Americans did not figure prominently in Britain's post-1778 strategy.

Sir Henry Clinton, who was probably less decisive than William Howe, took his time in expanding on the redcoats' success in Georgia. Finally in late 1779 he sailed with 7600 troops toward his target—Charleston, South Carolina. There General Benjamin Lincoln, with just 3000 Continental regulars and a smattering of militia, found himself completely outnumbered and trapped when part of Clinton's force moved inland and cut off escape routes. Facing prospects of extermination, Lincoln surrendered without much of a fight on May 12, 1780. This was the only occasion during the entire war when the British captured an American army.

Clinton's victory at Charleston was a second major advance in the Southern strategy. The British commander sailed back to New York in high spirits, leaving behind Lord Cornwallis to secure all of South Carolina. Clinton had ordered Cornwallis to move forward with care, making sure that loyalist partisans always had firm control of territory behind his advancing army. Ironically, Cornwallis was one of the few aggressive British generals in America. His desire to rush forward and get on with the fight helped undermine the Southern strategy.

At first, Cornwallis's boldness reaped dividends. After learning about the fall of Charleston, the Continental Congress ordered Horatio Gates, now known as the "hero of Saratoga," to proceed south, pull together a new army, and check Cornwallis. Gates botched the job completely. He gathered troops, mostly raw militiamen, in Virginia and North Carolina, then hastily rushed his soldiers into the British lair.

Early on the morning of August 16, 1780, Cornwallis's force intercepted Gates's column near Camden, South Carolina. Not only did the American troops lack training, but bad provisions had made them ill. The evening before the Battle of Camden they had supped on "a hasty meal of quick baked bread and fresh beef, with a dessert of molasses, mixed with mush or dumplings," which, according to one of Gates's officers, "operated so cathartically as to disorder many of the men" just before the engagement. Cornwallis's army devastated the rebels in yet another crushing American defeat in the South.

The Tide of War Turns at Last

During 1780 everything seemed to go wrong for the patriot cause. Besides major setbacks in the South, officers and soldiers directly under Washington's command were increasingly restive about long overdue wages and inadequate supplies. In July 1780 the officers threatened mass resignations unless Congress did something—and speedily. In September a frustrated Benedict Arnold switched his allegiance back to the British. By the end of the year Continental army troop strength fell below 6000. Then, as the new year dawned, Washington faced successive mutinies among his hardened veterans in the Pennsylvania and New Jersey lines. The Continental army seemed to be disintegrating, so much so that the commander-in-chief put aside plans for a possible strike against New York City. Even though French troops under the Comte de Rochambeau were now in the vicinity, his own Continental numbers were too few to pursue such an elaborate venture.

Quite simply, it looked as if the British were winning the endurance contest of wills. As one despondent Continental officer wrote: "It really gives me great pain to think of our public affairs; where is the public spirit of the year 1775? Where are those flaming *patriots* who were ready to sacrifice their lives, their fortunes, their all, for the public?" At no time during the war, except for those dark days just before Washington's counterstrike at Trenton, had the rebel cause appeared more forlorn.

What could not be seen was that British successes in the South moved the redcoats toward a far greater failure. Encouraged by its victories, General Cornwallis's army overreached itself. After Camden, Cornwallis started pushing toward North Carolina. His left wing under Major Patrick Ferguson, whose soldiers were mostly loyalists, was soon under the eye of growing numbers of "over-the-mountain" frontiersmen. They were grimly determined to protect their homesteads and families from Ferguson's loyalists, who repeatedly shot down or hanged patriots who fell in their path. Feeling their presence, Ferguson began retreating. When he spied Kings Mountain rising up from the rolling Piedmont landscape of northern South Carolina, he calculated that he and his 1100 followers could withstand any assault from atop the promontory. On October 7, 1780, the over-the-mountain force attacked from all sides. Ferguson fell mortally wounded; the rest of his column was killed, wounded, or captured; and the frontiersmen hanged nine of Ferguson's loy-

Rebel resistance was kept alive by guerrilla leaders like Francis Marion. Here he leads his troops across the Pee Dee River to attack the British in South Carolina.

With combined Franco-American forces, General Washington put Yorktown under siege and entrapped General Cornwallis's army.

alists as a warning to others who might fight for the king.

The Battle of Kings Mountain destroyed the left wing of Cornwallis's army. Compounding the damage, the main British force had not tightly secured South Carolina. Whenever Cornwallis moved his troops to a new locale, rebel guerrilla bands under such leaders as "Swamp Fox" Francis Marion emerged from their hiding places and wreaked vengeance on tories who had aided the British force or threatened rebels. Once again, the British had not effectively protected citizens favorably disposed toward them, which in combination with the debacle at Kings Mountain cut deeply into the reservoir of loyalist support available to Cornwallis.

Despite these reverses, the British general seemed unconcerned. Like his fellow officers,

Cornwallis held Americans in contempt, believing that it was only a matter of time until superior British arms would destroy the rebels. However, Cornwallis did not bargain on facing the likes of General Nathanael Greene (1742–1786), whom George Washington insisted should replace Gates as the Southern Department commander. Greene arrived in North Carolina during December 1780. Not surprisingly, there were very few troops available for duty and, as Greene stated despondently, the "appearance" of those in camp "was wretched beyond description."

Greene was a military genius. Violating the military maxim of concentrating troop strength as much as possible, he decided to divide his soldiers into three groups, one of which would work with partisan rebel bands. The idea was to let Cornwallis chase after the other two columns of just over 1000 each, until the redcoats were worn out. At that point Greene and his contingent would fight.

Cornwallis took the bait. He went after Greene and sent a detached force after the other rebel column headed by shrewd, capable General Daniel Morgan of Virginia. Morgan's troops lured the onrushing British into a trap at Hannah's Cowpens in western South Carolina on January 17, 1781. Only 140 of the some 1100 British soldiers escaped being killed, captured, or wounded. Meanwhile, Cornwallis relentlessly pursued Greene, who kept retreating before him. Finally, on March 15, 1781, the rebels squared off for battle at Guilford Courthouse in central North Carolina. The combatants fought throughout the afternoon, when the Americans abandoned the field. Greene's force had inflicted 506 casualties, as compared to 264 of their own. Cornwallis had gained a technical victory, but his troops were exhausted from Greene's game of "fox and hare," and the rebels were still very much in the field.

Franco-American Triumph at Yorktown

Cornwallis retreated to the seacoast to rest his army, then decided to take over British raiding operations in Virginia, which had begun in January 1781 under turncoat Benedict Arnold. In storming northward, Cornwallis totally abandoned the Southern strategy. Nathanael Greene was now free to reassert full patriot authority in the states south of Virginia.

Back in New York, Sir Henry Clinton fumed. He wanted to discipline his subordinate but lacked the courage. Instead, he sent Cornwallis orders in July to establish a defensive base and to refrain from conducting any offensive operations. His army was to function only as a garrison force, until such time as Clinton issued further orders. A most reluctant Cornwallis selected Yorktown, with easy access to Chesapeake Bay.

At this juncture everything fell into place for the Americans. George Washington learned from General Rochambeau that a French naval fleet would be making its way north from the West Indies. If that fleet could seal off the entrance to the Bay and Washington could surround Cornwallis's army on land, a major victory was in the making.

The rebel commander seized the opportunity. In concert with Rochambeau, he started marching soldiers south, leaving only enough troops behind to keep Clinton tied down and wondering whether a combined Franco-American assault force might strike at New York City. In early September the French fleet, after dueling with British warships, took control of Chesapeake Bay. As the month came to a close, some 7800 French troops and 9000 Continentals and militiamen surrounded the British army of 8500 at Yorktown. Cornwallis wrote Clinton: "If you cannot relieve me very soon you must expect to hear the worst." His army was trapped, and he knew it.

Using traditional siege tactics, Washington and Rochambeau squeezed Cornwallis into submission. It did not take long. On October 17 a lone British drummer marched toward the Franco-American lines with a white flag showing. Two days later, on a bright, sunny autumn afternoon, the army of Charles, Lord Cornwallis, marched out from its lines in solemn procession and laid down its arms. As these troops did so, their musicians played an appropriate song, "The World Turned Upside Down." The surrender at Yorktown was an emotional scene. A second British army had been captured in America, and the question now was whether Great Britain still had the resolve to continue the war.

A Most Generous Peace Settlement

It was not the great Franco-American victory at Yorktown alone that brought the British to the peace table. It was the accumulated total of wounds being inflicted by the Americans and their European allies, with Yorktown being the most damaging, that forced the home ministers into peace negotiations.

As early as 1778 Britain had felt the effects of world war. Daring seaman John Paul Jones (1747–1792), known as the "father of the American navy," had conducted raids along the English and Scottish coasts during that year. In

CHRONOLOGY
OF KEY EVENTS

1775 The shot "heard 'round the world"—the first military clashes between British troops and colonists take place at Lexington and Concord; Second Continental Congress meets in Philadelphia; fighting breaks out in New York, Massachusetts, and Canada; Continental army forms under the command of George Washington

1776 Thomas Paine publishes *Common Sense*; Continental Congress adopts the Declaration of Independence; British rout rebel soldiers in vicinity of New York City; Virginia and North Carolina frontiersmen neutralize southern Indians; American forces defeat British units at Trenton

1777 Continental army begins enlisting free blacks; British forces seize Philadelphia after defeating Washington's troops at Brandywine Creek in Pennsylvania; American forces capture General Burgoyne's army at Saratoga

1778 America forms an alliance with France; John Paul Jones raids along the British coastline; British troops invade the Deep South and conquer Savannah, Georgia

1779 Spain joins the war against Britain

1780 British forces defeat American armies at Charleston and Camden, South Carolina, but lose at Kings Mountain; Benedict Arnold offers to exchange West Point in return for a commission in the British army; the Dutch enter the war against Britain

1781 American forces defeat British soldiers at Hannah's Cowpens in western South Carolina and fight to a draw at Guilford Courthouse in central North Carolina; British surrender to combined Franco-American forces at Yorktown, Virginia

1783 Treaty of Paris ends the War for American Independence

1779, while sailing in the North Sea, Jones lost his own vessel, the *Bon Homme Richard*, but captured the British war frigate *Serapis* in a dramatic naval engagement, all within sight of England.

By 1781 French and Spanish warships were attacking British vessels at will in the English Channel, and French warships threatened British possessions in the West Indies. France and Spain were about to launch a major expedition against Gibraltar. In the spring of 1781 a Spanish force under Bernardo de Gálvez captured a sizable British garrison at Pensacola, Florida, and the British soon experienced setbacks as far away as India. The allies had demonstrated that they could carry the war anywhere, even to the shores of England, suggesting the prospect of disastrous consequences for the powerful British empire.

Keenly aware of these many threats, Lord North received the news of Yorktown "as he would have taken a [musket] ball in the breast." In March 1782 North's ministry collapsed, and a new cabinet opened negotiations with designated American peace commissioners—Benjamin Franklin, John Adams, and John Jay—in France. On November 30, 1782, the representatives agreed to preliminary peace terms, pending final ratification by both governments. The other belligerents also started coming to terms, largely because the naval war had turned against France and Spain and British troops had saved Gibraltar. All parties signed the final peace accords at Paris on September 3, 1783.

The major European powers now recognized the 13 rebellious colonies as a separate nation, capable of carving out their own existence in the western world. Further, the peace accords established the Mississippi River as the western boundary line of the new nation and 31 degrees of north latitude as the southern boundary. Britain returned the lands south of this line, constituting Florida, to Spain.

Although the American commissioners failed to gain Canada, which they tried to get, they had obtained title to the vast reserve of Indian territory lying between the Appalachian Mountains and the Mississippi River. The treaty was silent about the rights of Indians, whose interests the British ignored, despite repeated promises during the war to protect the lands of Native Americans who joined the king's cause. All told, effective bargaining by the American peace commissioners gave the former colonists a huge geographic base on which to build their new republic.

The peace settlement also contained other significant provisions. Britain recognized American fishing rights off the coast of eastern Canada, thus sustaining a major New England industry. The British promised not to carry away slaves when evacuating their troops (which they did anyway). At the same time, they demanded that prewar debts be paid in full to British merchants (few actually were) and insisted upon the complete restoration of the rights and property of loyalists. The American commissioners agreed to have Congress make such a recommendation to the states (which they generally ignored). The peace treaty, then, both established American independence and laid the groundwork for future conflict.

CONCLUSION

The Americans came out remarkably well in 1783. They emerged victorious not only in war but at the peace table as well. The young republic had endured over its parent nation, Great Britain and, with invaluable assistance from foreign allies, particularly France, had earned its freedom from European monarchism and imperialism. On the other hand, it was far from certain whether the United States could sustain its independence or have much of a future as a nation, given the many internal problems facing the 13 sovereign states.

One group that did not cheer heartily at the prospect of peace were the officers and soldiers of the Continental army. They had made great personal sacrifices and had every reason to be proud of their accomplishments; however, they deeply resented the lack of civilian support that had plagued them throughout the long conflict. Even in leaving the service, wrote Private Joseph Plumb Martin, they were "turned adrift like old worn-out horses" without just financial compensation for their services. Still, they had the personal satisfaction of knowing that their pain and suffering had sustained the vision of a bright and glorious future for the infant United States, but only if revolutionary Americans resolved their own political differences—especially those relating to the implanting of republican ideals in institutions of government.

SUGGESTIONS FOR FURTHER READING

OVERVIEWS AND SURVEYS

John R. Alden, *The American Revolution, 1775–1783* (1954); Lawrence D. Cress, *Citizens in Arms: The Army and the Militia in American Society to the War of 1812* (1982); R. Ernest Dupuy, et al., *The American Revolution: A Global War* (1977); John Ferling, ed., *The World Turned Upside Down: The American Victory in the War of Independence* (1988); Don Higginbotham, *The War of American Independence, 1763–1789* (1971), and ed., *Reconsiderations on the Revolutionary War* (1978); Ronald Hoffman and Peter J. Albert, eds., *Arms and Independence: The Military Character of the American Revolution* (1984); Piers Mackesy, *The War for America, 1775–1783* (1964); James Kirby Martin and Mark Edward Lender, *A Respectable Army: The Military Origins of the Republic, 1763–1789* (1982); Dave R. Palmer, *The Way of the Fox: American Strategy in the War for America, 1775–1783* (1975); Eric Robson, *The American Revolution in Its Political and Military Aspects, 1763–1783* (1955); Charles Royster, *A Revolutionary People at War: The Continental Army and American Character, 1775–1783* (1979); John Shy, *A People Numerous and Armed: Reflections on the Military Struggle for American Independence,* rev. ed. (1990); Reginald C. Stuart, *War and American Thought: From the Revolution to the Monroe Doctrine* (1982); Robert K. Wright, Jr., *The Continental Army* (1984).

RECONCILIATION OR INDEPENDENCE

Joseph L. Davis, *Sectionalism in American Politics, 1774–1787* (1977); H. James Henderson, *Party Politics in the Continental Congress* (1974); Merrill Jensen, *The Articles of Confederation: An Interpretation of the Social-Constitutional History of the American Revolution, 1774–1781* (1940); Jackson Turner Main, *The Sovereign States, 1775–1783* (1973); Jerrilyn Greene Marston, *King and Congress: The Transfer of Political Legitimacy, 1774–1776* (1987); Jack N. Rakove, *The Beginnings of National Politics: An Interpretive History of the Continental Congress* (1979).

WITHOUT VISIBLE ALLIES: THE WAR IN THE NORTH

Rodney Atwood, *The Hessians* (1980); George A. Billias, ed., *George Washington's Generals* (1964), and ed., *George Washington's Opponents* (1969); Richard Buel, Jr., *Dear Liberty: Connecticut's Mobilization for the Revolutionary War* (1980); John C. Dann, ed., *The Revolution Remembered: Eyewitness Accounts of the War for Independence* (1980); Linda Grant DePauw, "Women in Combat: The Revolutionary War Experience," *Armed Forces and Society*, 7 (1981), pp. 209–226; Sylvia R. Frey, *The British Soldier in America* (1981); Barbara Graymont, *The Iroquois in the American Revolution* (1972); Robert A. Gross, *The Minutemen and Their World* (1976); Robert McConnell Hatch, *Thrust for Canada: The American Attempt on Quebec in 1775–1776* (1979); Richard M. Ketchum, *The Winter Soldiers* (1973); Joseph Plumb Martin, *Private Yankee Doodle: Being a Narrative . . . of a Revolutionary Soldier*, ed. George F. Scheer (1962); John S. Pancake, *1777: The Year of the Hangman* (1977); Gary Alexander Puckrein, *The Black Regiment in the American Revolution* (1978); Jonathan Gregory Rossie, *The Politics of Command in the American Revolution* (1975); Steven Rosswurm, *Arms, Country, and Class: The Philadelphia Militia and "Lower Sort" during the Revolution, 1775–1783* (1987); Paul H. Smith, *Loyalists and Redcoats: A Study in British Revolutionary Policy* (1964).

RESCUING THE PATRIOTS: TOWARD GLOBAL CONFLICT

Samuel F. Bemis, *The Diplomacy of the American Revolution*, rev. ed. (1957); Light Townsend Cummins, *Spanish Observers and the American Revolution, 1775–1783* (1992); Jonathan R. Dull, *A Diplomatic History of the American Revolution* (1985); Ronald Hoffman and Peter J. Albert, eds., *Diplomacy and Revolution: The Franco-American Alliance of 1778* (1981); Reginald Horsman, *The Diplomacy of the New Republic, 1776–1815* (1985); James H. Hutson, *John Adams and the Diplomacy of the American Revolution* (1980); Lawrence S. Kaplan, ed., *The American Revolution and "A Candid World"* (1977); Richard B. Morris, *The Peacemakers: The Great Powers and American Independence* (1965); Charles R. Ritcheson, *British Politics and the American Revolution* (1954); H. M. Scott, *British Foreign Policy in the Age of the American Revolution* (1991); William C. Stinchcombe, *The American Revolution and the French Alliance* (1969); Gerald Stourzh, *Benjamin Franklin and American Foreign Policy*, 2d ed. (1969); Richard W. Van Alstyne, *Empire and Independence: The International History of the American Revolution* (1965); Paul A. Varg, *Foreign Policies of the Founding Fathers* (1963).

THE WORLD TURNED UPSIDE DOWN

R. Arthur Bowler, *Logistics and the Failure of the British Army in America, 1775–1783* (1975); E. Wayne Carp, *To Starve the Army at Pleasure: Continental Army Administration and American Political Culture, 1775–1783* (1984); Jeffrey J. Crow and Larry E. Tise, eds., *The Southern Experience in the American Revolution* (1978); John Morgan Dederer, *Making Bricks Without Straw: Nathanael Greene's Southern Campaign and Mao Tse-Tung's Mobile War* (1983); Jonathan R. Dull, *The French Navy and American Independence, 1774–1787* (1975); William M. Fowler, Jr., *Rebels under Sail: The American Navy During the Revolution* (1976); W. Robert Higgins, ed., *The Revolutionary War in the South* (1979); Ronald Hoffman, Thad W. Tate, and Peter J. Albert, eds., *An Uncivil War: The Southern Backcountry During the American Revolution* (1985); Lee Kennett, *The French Forces in America, 1780–1783* (1977); Henry Lumpkin, *From Savannah to Yorktown* (1981); George S. McCowen, Jr., *The British Occupation of Charleston, 1780–82* (1972); James H. O'Donnell, III, *Southern Indians in the American Revolution* (1973); John S. Pancake, *This Destructive War: The British Campaign in the Carolinas, 1780–1782* (1985); John E. Selby, *The Revolution in Virginia, 1775–1783* (1988); David Syrett, *Shipping and the American War, 1775–83: A Study of British Transport Organization* (1970); John A. Tilley, *The British Navy and the American Revolution* (1987); Russell F. Weigley, *The Partisan War: The South Carolina Campaign of 1780–1782* (1970).

BIOGRAPHIES

Edward J. Cashin, *The King's Ranger: Thomas Brown and the Revolution on the Southern Frontier* (1989); Marcus Cunliffe, *George Washington: Man and Monument*, rev. ed. (1982); Don R. Gerlach, *Proud Patriot: Philip Schuyler and the War of Independence, 1775–1783* (1987); Louis R. Gottschalk, *Lafayette Joins the American Army* (1937); Ira D. Gruber, *The Howe Brothers and the American Revolution* (1972); Richard J. Hargrove, Jr., *General John Burgoyne* (1983); Don Higginbotham, *Daniel Morgan* (1961), and *George Washington and the American Military Tradition* (1985); Max M. Mintz, *The Generals of Saratoga: John Burgoyne and Horatio Gates* (1990); Samuel E. Morison, *John Paul Jones* (1959); Orville T. Murphy, *Charles Gravier, Comte de Vergennes* (1982); Paul David Nelson, *General Horatio Gates* (1976), and *Anthony Wayne: Soldier of the Early Republic* (1985); Louis W. Potts, *Arthur Lee: A Virtuous Revolutionary* (1981); Hugh F. Rankin, *Francis Marion: The Swamp Fox* (1973); Willard M. Wallace, *Traitorous Hero: Benedict Arnold* (1954); Franklin B. and Mary Wickwire, *Cornwallis: The American Adventure* (1970); William B. Willcox, *Portrait of a General: Sir Henry Clinton in the War of Independence* (1964).

A TOBACCO PLANTATION

FIG. II.

TO BE SOLD,
On Thursday the third Day
of August next,
A CARGO
OF
NINETY-FOUR
PRIME, HEALTHY
NEGROES,
CONSISTING OF
Thirty-nine MEN, Fifteen Boys,
Twenty-four WOMEN, and
Sixteen GIRLS.
JUST ARRIVED,
In the Brigantine DEMBIA, *Fran-
cis Bare*, Master, from SIERRA
LEON, by
DAVID & JOHN DEAS.

94.

DELAW

ONE SHILLING AND FOURPENCE
ONE SIXTH OF A DOLLAR. N.
THIS BILL shall pass current
in all Payments in this Colony,
for One Shilling and Four Pence,
(being equal to One Sixth of a Spanish Mill'd Dollar) or the Value
thereof in Gold or Silver, according
to the Resolution of the Provincial
Congress of New-York, on the 5th
Day of March, 1776.

CHAPTER 6

Securing the Republic and Its Ideals, 1776–1789

DESCRIPTION OF A SLAVE SHIP.

Stove Room   Stove Room

FIG. IV.

FIG. VII.

PLATE 33

A Declaration by the Representatives of the UNITED STATES

F AMERICA, in General Congress assembled.

When in the course of human events it becomes necessary for one people to
dissolve the political bands which have connected them with another, and to

Nancy Shippen was a product of Philadelphia's best lineage. Although she was born in 1763, the political turmoil leading to rebellion did not affect her early life. As a privileged daughter in an upper-class family, it was her duty to blossom into a charming woman, admired for her beauty and social graces, rather than develop her intellect. Her education consisted of the refinement of skills that would please and entertain—dancing, cultivating her voice, playing musical instruments, painting on delicate china, and producing pieces of decorative needlework.

Had Nancy shown any interest in politics, an exclusively masculine preserve, she would have shocked everyone, including her father, William Shippen. Shippen was a noted local physician who espoused independence in 1776. That was his prerogative as paterfamilias; where he led, according to the customs of the time, his family followed. Indeed, he was a proud father in 1777 when, at his urging, Nancy displayed her patriotic virtue by sewing shirt ruffles for General Washington.

Three hundred miles away in Boston, another woman by the name of Phillis Wheatley was also reckoning with the American Revolution. Her life had been very different from Nancy's. Born on Africa's West Coast around 1753, she had been snatched from her parents by slave catchers. At the Boston slave market, Mrs. Susannah Wheatley, looking for a young female slave to train in domestic service, noticed her. In Phillis the Wheatley family got much more; their new slave yearned to express her thoughts and feelings through poetry.

Conventional wisdom dictated that slaves should not be educated. Exposure to reading and writing might make them resentful, perhaps even rebellious. Sensing Phillis's talents, the Wheatley family defied convention. She mastered English and Latin, even preparing translations of ancient writings. By 1770 some of her poems had been published, followed in 1773 by a collection entitled *Poems on Various Subjects, Religious and Moral*. In one verse addressed to Lord Dartmouth, Britain's secretary for American affairs, she queried:

I young in life, by seeming cruel fate
Was snatch'd from Afric's fancy'd seat:

Such was my case. And can I then but pray
Others may never feel tyrannic sway?

Experiencing the tyranny of slavery influenced Phillis's feelings about the presence of redcoats in Boston. Late in 1775 she sent a flattering poem to George Washington. He responded gratefully and called her words "striking proof of your great poetical talents."

Little as Phillis Wheatley and Nancy Shippen had in common, they lived during an era in which men thought of all women, regardless of their rank in society, as second-class human beings. In the case of Phillis she carried the additional burden of being black in an openly racist society. Like other women in revolutionary America, they could only hope that the ideals of human liberty might someday apply to them.

For Nancy Shippen there were two male tyrants in her life. The first was her father William, who in 1781 forced her into marriage with Henry Beekman Livingston, a son of one of New York's most powerful and wealthy families. The man she truly loved had only "honorable expectations" of a respectable income. So her father insisted that she wed Livingston. The rejected suitor wanted to know "for what reason in this *free* country a lady ... must be married in a hurry and given up to a man whom she dislikes." None of the Shippens responded. In truth, the answer was that Nancy legally belonged to her father until she became the property of the second tyrant in her life—her husband Henry.

The marriage was a disaster, most likely because Henry was a known philanderer. Nancy eventually took her baby daughter and moved back to her family. She wanted full custody of the child, who by law was the property of her husband. Henry made it clear that he would never give up his legal rights to his daughter, should Nancy embarrass him in public by seeking a bill of divorcement. Even if she had defied him, divorce bills were very hard to get because they involved proving adultery or desertion.

To keep actual custody of her daughter, Nancy accepted her entrapment. Several years later Henry relented and arranged for a divorce, but by that time Nancy's spirit was broken. This former belle of Philadelphia society lived on unhappily in hermit-like fashion until her death in 1841. Having been so favored at birth, her adult

Although they were from diverse cultures, Phillis Wheatley and Nancy Shippen were considered second-class citizens because they were women.

years were a personal tragedy, primarily because of her legal dependence on the will of men.

Phillis Wheatley, by comparison, enjoyed some personal freedom before her untimely death in 1784. Mr. and Mrs. Wheatley died during the war period, and their will provided for Phillis's emancipation. She married John Peters, a free black man, and bore him three children. But John Peters was poor, and there was scant time for poetry. It was very difficult for free blacks to get decent jobs, and Phillis struggled each day to help her family avoid destitution. She lived long enough to see slavery being challenged in the North; but she died knowing that African-Americans, even when free, invariably faced discrimination based on race, forcing families like hers to exist on the margins of Revolutionary society.

The experiences of Phillis Wheatley and Nancy Shippen raise basic questions about the character of the Revolution. Did the cause of liberty really change the lives of Americans? If it was truly a movement to end tyranny, secure human rights, and ensure equality of opportu-

nity, then why did individuals like Wheatley and Shippen benefit so little? A major reason was that white, adult males of property and community standing put greater emphasis on setting up an independent nation between 1776 and 1789 than on securing human rights. Still, the ideology of liberty could not be denied. Primarily, the revolutionary era saw the creation of a new nation and the articulation of fundamental ideals regarding human freedom and dignity—ideals that shaped the course of American historical development.

ESTABLISHING NEW REPUBLICAN GOVERNMENTS

Winning the war and working out a favorable peace settlement represented two of three crucial elements that made for a successful rebellion. The third factor centered on the formation of stable governments, certainly a challenging assignment because it involved the careful definition of how governments should function to support life, liberty, and property (or happiness, as Jefferson framed the triad). Everyone agreed that a monarchical system, indeed any form capable of producing political tyranny, was unacceptable. A second point of consensus was that governments should be republican in character. Sovereignty, or ultimate political authority, previously residing with King and Parliament, should be vested in the people. After all, political institutions presumably existed to serve them. As such, citizens should be governed by laws, not by power-hungry officials, and laws should be the product of collective deliberations of representatives elected by the citizenry.

Defining the core ideals of republicanism—popular sovereignty, rule by law, and legislation by elected representatives—was not a source of disagreement. Yet revolutionary leaders argued passionately about the organization and powers of new governments, both state and national, as well as the extent to which basic political rights should be put into practice. At the heart of the argument was the concept of *public virtue*: whether citizens were capable of subordinating their self-interest to the greater good of the whole community. Although some leaders answered in the affirmative, others did not. Their trust or distrust of the people directly affected how far they were willing to go in implementing republican ideals.

TABLE 6.1

Personal Wealth and Occupations of Approximately 900 Representatives Elected to Prewar and Postwar Assemblies (Expressed in Percentages)

	New Hampshire, New York, and New Jersey		Maryland, Virginia, and South Carolina	
	Prewar	*Postwar*	*Prewar*	*Postwar*
Property holdings				
Over £5000	36%	12%	52%	28%
£2000–£5000	47	26	36	42
Under £2000	17	62	12	30
Occupations				
Merchants and lawyers	43%	18%	23%	17%
Farmers*	23	55	12	26

*Plantation owners with slaves are not included with farmers.
Derived from Jackson T. Main, "Government by the People: The American Revolution and the Democratization of the Legislatures," *William and Mary Quarterly*, 3d ser., 23 (1966), 45.

TABLE 6.2

Family and Personal Wealth of Approximately 450 Executive Officials* in Late Colonial and Early Revolutionary Governments (Expressed in Percentages)

	Family Wealth†		*Personal Wealth*	
	1774	*1777*	*1774*	*1777*
Over £5000	40%	26%	65%	37%
£2000–£5000	34	33	29	52
Under £2000	26	41	6	11

*Officeholders included are governors, lieutenant governors, secretaries, treasurers, members of upper houses of assemblies (councilors before the Revolution), attorneys general, chief judges, and associate judges of the highest provincial and state courts.
†Refers to the wealth of parents. A higher percentage of late colonial leaders (74 percent) than early revolutionary leaders (59 percent) came from upper-class and upper-middle-class families.
Derived from James Kirby Martin, *Men in Rebellion: Higher Governmental Leaders and the Coming of the American Revolution* (New Brunswick, N.J.: Rutgers University Press, 1973).

Leaders who believed that citizens could govern themselves and not abuse public privileges for private advantage were in the vanguard of political thinking in the western world. As such, they may be called radicals. They were willing to establish "the most democratical forms" of government, as Samuel Adams so aptly capsulized their thinking.

More cautious, elitist revolutionary leaders feared what the masses might do without the restraining hand of central political authority. As one of them wrote: "No one loves liberty more than I do, but of all tyranny I most dread that of the multitude." These leaders remained attached to traditional notions of hierarchy and deference in social and political relationships. They still thought that the "better sort" of citizens—men of education, wealth, and proven ability, whom they now defined as "natural aristocrats"—should be the stewards who guided the people. For such leaders the success of the Revolution depended on a transfer of power from the despoilers of liberty in Britain to "enlightened" gentlemen like themselves in America. As a precaution against a citizenry abusing its liberty, they wanted a strong central government to replace King and Parliament, a govern-

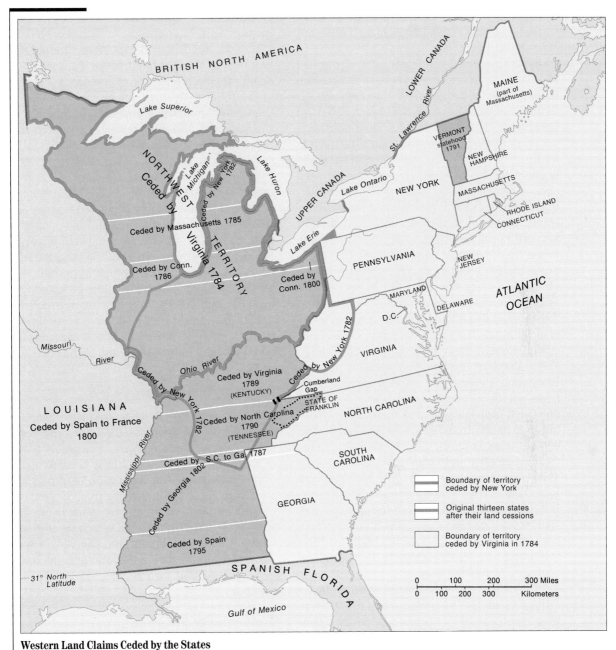

Western Land Claims Ceded by the States
The battle over conflicting state claims to western lands was a major issue facing the Continental Congress.

foreign powers, and guarding against domestic insurrections.

Over time, those who advocated a strong central government formed an informal political bloc, since known as the *nationalists*. With each passing year the nationalists became more and more frustrated by the Confederation. Finally, in 1787 they overwhelmed their opposi-

tion by pressing for and getting a new plan of national government.

Struggle to Ratify the Articles

Given the wartime need for national unity in the face of a common enemy, Congress asked each state to approve the Articles of Confederation quickly. Overcoming much indifference, 12 states had finally ratified by January 1779—but Maryland still held out.

The propertied gentlemen who controlled Maryland's revolutionary government objected to one specific provision in the Articles. Although Dickinson's draft had designated all lands west of the Appalachian Mountains as a *national domain,* belonging to all of the people for future settlement, the final version left these lands in the hands of states having sea-to-sea clauses in their colonial charters. This was a logical extension of the principle of state sovereignty. Maryland, having a fixed western boundary, had no such western claim. Nor did Rhode Island, New Jersey, Pennsylvania, or Delaware.

Maryland's leaders simply refused to be cut off from western development. In public they talked in terms of high principle. Citizens from "landless" states should have as much right to resettle in the West as inhabitants of "landed" states. Equal access was not the only issue. Many Maryland leaders had invested in pre-Revolution land companies trying to gain title to large parcels of western territory. They had done so by appealing to the Crown and by making purchases from individual Indians, who without tribal approval often "sold" rights in return for alcohol and other "gifts." Wanting to avoid costly frontier warfare, the Crown had promulgated the Proclamation of 1763 (see p. 116) and thereafter refused to recognize any such titles. After independence there was new hope for these land speculators, but only if the Continental Congress rather than some of the states controlled the West.

The Maryland Assembly adamantly refused ratification unless the landed states turned over their charter titles to Congress. Virginia, which had the largest claim, including the vast region north of the Ohio River that came to be known as the "Old Northwest," faced the most pressure. Forsaking local land speculators for the national interest, the Virginia Assembly broke the deadlock in January 1781 by agreeing to cede its claims to Congress.

If self-interest had not been involved, ratification would have followed quickly; however, greedy Maryland leaders still held out. They pronounced Virginia's grant unacceptable because of a condition not permitting Congress to award lands on the basis of Indian deeds. Fortunately for the republic, the war intervened. In 1781, with the British raiding in the Chesapeake Bay region, Marylanders became quite anxious about their defense. Congressional leaders urged ratification in exchange for promises of Continental military support. All but cornered, the Maryland Assembly reluctantly gave in and approved the Articles of Confederation.

March 1, 1781, the day formal ratification ceremonies finally took place, elicited only muted celebrations. Some cheered "the union," at long last "indissolubly cemented," as an optimist wrote. Certainly, too, the prospect of a national domain for a rapidly expanding population pleased many citizens. The nationalists, on the other hand, believed that Maryland's behavior showed how self-interest could be masked as public virtue. With so many problems needing solutions, they wondered how long the republic could endure when any sovereign state had the ability to thwart the will of the other 12.

Contention over Financing the War

From the very first financial problems plagued the new central government. Under the Articles, Congress had no power of taxation; it repeatedly asked the states to pay a fair proportion of war costs. The states, also hard pressed for funds, rarely sent in more than 50 percent of their requisitions. Meantime, soldiers like Joseph Plumb Martin endured shortages of food, clothing, camp equipment, and pay. As a result, with each passing month the army grew increasingly angry about its role as a creditor to the republic.

The lack of tax revenues forced Congress to resort to various expedient measures to meet war costs. Between 1775 and 1780 it issued some $220 million in paper money. Lacking any financial backing, these "Continentals" became so worthless by 1779 that irate army officers complained how "four months' pay of a private [soldier] will not procure his wretched wife and children a single bushel of wheat." In addition, Congress, largely to get military supplies, issued interest-bearing certificates of indebtedness. Without any means to pay interest, these notes, which also circulated as money, rapidly lost value. In 1780 there was an attempt to refinance

Continental dollars at a 40 to 1 ratio, but the plan failed. If it had not been for grants and loans from allies like France and the Netherlands (Spain offered little direct financial support), the war effort might well have floundered.

Deeply disturbed by these conditions, many nationalists in the Continental Congress acted forcefully to institute financial reform. Their leader was the wealthy Philadelphia merchant, Robert Morris (1734–1806), sometimes called the "financier of the Revolution," who became Congress' Superintendent of Finance in 1781. His assistant superintendent, Gouverneur Morris (no relation), a wealthy New Yorker then practicing law in Philadelphia, was also critical to shaping the events that lay ahead, as were Alexander Hamilton of New York and James Madison of Virginia. Hamilton summarized their feelings this way: "The Confederation . . . gives the power of the purse too entirely to the state legislatures. . . . That power, which holds the purse strings absolutely, must rule."

At the urging of the nationalists, congressional delegates approved the Impost Plan of 1781. It called for import duties of 5 percent on all foreign trade goods entering the United States, the revenues to belong to Congress. These funds could be used to pay the army, to back a stable national currency, and, ultimately, to meet foreign loan obligations. Because the Plan involved giving Congress taxation authority, the delegates recommended it in the form of an amendment to the Articles. Amendments required the approval of all 13 states.

Reluctant as they were to share taxation powers with the central government, many state leaders agreed with Robert Morris, who had warned: "The political existence of America depends on the accomplishment of this [Impost] plan." By the fall of 1782 12 states had ratified. Only Rhode Island hesitated, reasoning that, with little land to tax, its own war debt could be most easily funded through state import duties. If there had to be a choice, state interests came first. The Assembly voted against ratification. Once again local interests had prevailed; one state had blocked the will of the other 12.

In this crucial matter the nationalists had allies. Most prominent were disgruntled officers in the Continental army. Rarely had the soldiers

Robert Morris and Gouverneur Morris were key figures in the institution of financial reform.

been paid, and in 1780 the officers had exacted from Congress a promise of half-pay postwar pensions as their price for staying in the service. Without a fixed source of revenue, Congress lacked the ability to meet these obligations.

After a group of high-ranking officers learned about Rhode Island's decision, they sent a menacing petition to Congress in December 1782. It stated: "We have borne all that men can bear—our property is expended—our private resources are at an end." With no likelihood of pensions being funded, they insisted upon five years of full pay when mustering out of the service. Even with British troops still on American soil, the angry officers warned Congress: "Any further experiments on their patience may have fatal effects."

Threatened Military Coup: The Newburgh Conspiracy

For years Continental officers and soldiers alike had been complaining about the ungenerous treatment they received from revolutionary leaders and civilians. Convinced that the general populace had lived well at home while the army endured privation, sickness, and death in the field, they spoke with impassioned feelings about the absence of citizen virtue. As one officer bluntly wrote: "I hate my countrymen." Personal sacrifice for the good of the whole community, it seemed to the Continentals, had been exacted only from those with the fortitude to fulfill the obligation of long-term military service.

After the British surrender at Yorktown, Washington moved 11,000 troops north to Newburgh, New York. From this campsite on the Hudson River, the Continental army waited for peace terms and kept its eye on British forces in New York City. As peace negotiations dragged on during 1782, officers and soldiers worried about being demobilized without back pay and promised pensions. When Rhode Island refused to ratify the Impost Plan, their worst fears seemed to be realized.

Curiously, when the congressional nationalists received the officers' hotly worded petition, they were more pleased than alarmed. They soon devised a scheme to use these threats to extort taxation authority from the states. If need be, they would encourage the army to go back into the field and threaten the civilian populace with a military uprising. The danger, of course, was that the army might get out of control, seize the reins of government, and push the Revolution toward some form of military dictatorship.

Making no headway with the states, which refused to be bullied, the nationalists turned to George Washington in February 1783. As his former military aide, Alexander Hamilton (1757?–1804), wrote to him, the critical issue was "the establishment of general funds. . . . In this the influence of the army, properly directed, may cooperate." Washington refused any help; perhaps better than anyone in revolutionary America, he understood that military power had to remain subordinate to civilian authority, or the republic would never be free. At this juncture, Robert Morris and other congressional nationalists began "conspiring" with General Horatio Gates, second in command at Newburgh, who had often dreamed of replacing Washington at the head of the Continental army.

Gates made his move in early March. He au-thorized two Newburgh Addresses, both prepared by members of his staff. The addresses warned the officers to "suspect the man [Washington] who would advise to more moderation and forbearance." If peace comes, let nothing separate you "from your arms but death," or at least not until the army had realized financial justice. The first address instructed the officers to attend a meeting to vent grievances—and take action. Dismayed, Washington called this proposal "disorderly," but he nevertheless approved a meeting for March 15. He would not attend, he stated, but would let Gates chair the gathering.

Despite his promise, Washington appeared at this showdown meeting. He pleaded with the officers to temper their rage and not go back into the field. That would destroy everything the army had accomplished during eight long years of war. The officers appeared unmoved. Then preparing to read a letter, Washington reached into his pocket, pulled out spectacles, and put them on. The officers, never having seen him wear eyeglasses before, started to murmur. Sensing a mood shift, the commander calmly stated: "Gentlemen, you must pardon me. I have grown gray in your service and now find myself growing blind." These heartfelt words caught the angry officers off guard. They recalled that they, as exemplars of truly virtuous citizenship, likewise had offered their lives for a cause larger than any of them. Many openly wept, even as the threat of a possible mutiny, or worse, a military coup directed against the states and the people, suddenly came to an end.

Washington promised that he would do everything in his power to secure "complete and ample justice" for the army. He did send a circular letter to the states imploring them to give more power to Congress. He warned them that "the Union could not be of a long duration" with a central government lacking in the capacity "to regulate and govern the general concerns of the Confederated republic." The states ignored Washington's plea for a strengthened national government.

Even though British troops were still in New York City, Washington also started "furloughing" soldiers, so that further troublesome incidents would not occur. After leaving the army one angry group of Pennsylvania Continentals marched on Philadelphia in June 1783. They surrounded Independence Hall (the Pennsylvania State House) where Congress held its sessions. In threatening fashion these veterans refused to leave until they received back pay. The frightened delegates asked the Pennsylvania government for protection with local militia troops, but state officials turned down their request. Amid the taunts and jeers of the angry soldiers, the delegates finally abandoned Independence Hall. They never came back.

Thoroughly humiliated by armed soldiers and a state government that would not defend them, the delegates first moved to Princeton, New Jersey, then to Annapolis, Maryland, and finally to New York City. One newspaper, in mocking the central government, spoke of "the itinerant genius of Congress," a body that would "float along from one end of the continent to the other" as would a hot-air balloon.

Many citizens did not seem to care much one way or the other, since Congress was so lacking in authority. Nationalist leaders, on the other hand, kept trying to redress the balance of power between the impotent central government and the sovereign states. They drafted the Impost Plan of 1783, but this one, too, failed to secure unanimous state ratification. The plan was still languishing in late 1786, but by that time the nationalists were pursuing other avenues of change.

Drifting Toward Disunion

Despite the Paris peace settlement and the final removal of British troops, most citizens engaged in another battle beginning in late 1783—this one against a hard-hitting economic depression. It had many sources. Planters in the South had lost 60,000 slaves, many of whom the British had carried off. In addition, crop yields for 1784 and 1785 were small, largely because of bad weather. Farmers in New England reeled from the effects of new British trade regulations—in essence turning the Navigation system against the independent Americans. The Orders in Council of 1783 prohibited the sale of many American agricultural products in the British West Indies, formerly a key market for New England goods, and required many commodi-

ties to be conveyed to and from the islands in British vessels. The orders represented a serious blow to New England's agricultural, shipping, and shipbuilding trades.

Making matters even worse, merchants in all the states rushed to reestablish old trading connections with their British counterparts. Overly optimistic, they purchased far too many trade goods on easy credit terms, only to discover they could not sell these commodities to citizens feeling the effects of the postwar depression. Many of these merchants faced total economic ruin by 1785.

The central government could do little. It did send John Adams to Britain in 1785 as the first minister from the United States. Adams, however, made no headway in getting British officials to back off from the Orders in Council. He dejectedly reported to Congress that "they rely upon our disunion" to avoid negotiations.

To add to these economic woes, significant postwar trading ties did not develop with France. In fact, American exports to France far exceeded the value of imports (by roughly $2 million a year during the 1780s). The same held true with the Dutch. Even though some venturesome merchants sent a trading vessel—the *Empress of China*—to the Far East in 1784, all the new activity was insignificant in comparison to the renewed American dependency on British manufactured goods. The former colonists stayed glued to the old imperial trading network; it would be years before they would gain full economic independence.

Some merchants, primarily from the Middle Atlantic states, were anxious to break free of Britain's economic hold. An opportunity presented itself in 1784

Named in 1784 as secretary for foreign affairs, John Jay was unsuccessful in his efforts to negotiate a treaty with Spain.

after Congress named John Jay (1745–1829), one of the Paris peace commissioners, to be its secretary for foreign affairs. Jay soon started negotiations with Don Diego de Gardoqui,

Spain's first minister to the United States. Gardoqui talked about his government's concern that Americans, now streaming into the trans-Appalachian west, would in time covet Spanish territory beyond the Mississippi River. To stem the tide, Gardoqui informed Congress that Spain would not allow the Mississippi to serve as an outlet for western agricultural goods. Attempting to assuage possible bad feelings, Gardoqui offered an advantageous commercial treaty.

Jay and a number of powerful merchants from the Middle Atlantic states saw merit in the Spanish proposal. They viewed a developing west—settlements were sprouting in Kentucky and Tennessee—as a potential threat to eastern economic dominance. Meanwhile, Gardoqui had Spanish agents circulating through the west. They encouraged American settlers to become Spanish subjects in return for trade access to the Mississippi River. Gardoqui's idea was to build a wall of settlers in the trans-Appalachian west to protect Spanish holdings beyond the Mississippi. Basically his agents did little more than stir up resentment, both toward Spain and eastern leaders like Jay, who appeared to be selling out western interests for a commercial treaty of undetermined value.

When Jay reported on his discussions to Congress in the summer of 1786, tempers flared. The southern states voted as a bloc against any such treaty, which ended the Jay-Gardoqui negotiations. But southerners and westerners still suspected that Jay and his eastern merchant allies would not hesitate to abandon them altogether for petty commercial gains. Some leaders in Congress, as one delegate explained, started speaking "lightly of a separation and dissolution of the Confederation." Such talk helped galvanize the nationalists into dramatic action, as did a rebellion that now convulsed Massachusetts.

Shays's Rebellion convinced many citizens throughout the republic that a strong national government was needed, if for no other reason than to control domestic insurrections.

Daniel Shays's Rebellion

Postwar economic conditions were so bad in several states that citizens began demanding tax relief from their governments. In western Massachusetts desperate farmers complained about huge property tax increases by the state government to pay off the state's war debt. Taxes on land rose by more than 60 percent in the period 1783–1786, exactly when a depressed postwar economy meant that farmers were getting little income from the sale of excess agricultural goods.

Local courts, in the absence of tax payments, started to seize the property of men like Daniel Shays (1747?–1825), a revolutionary war veteran. Some lost their freehold farms—in certain cases the courts remanded delinquent taxpayers to debtors' prison. Viewing their plight in terms of tyranny, the farmers of western Massachusetts believed that they had the right to break the chains of political oppression, just as they had done in resisting British rule a few years before. This time, however, the enemy was their own state government.

The Shaysites, as they came to be known, tried to resist in orderly fashion. They first met in impromptu conventions and sent petitions to the state assembly. Getting no relief, they turned to more confrontational means of resistance. In late August 1786 an estimated 1000 farmers poured into Northampton and shut down the county court. This crowd action represented the first of many such closures. By popular mandate citizens would no longer permit judges to seize property or condemn people to debtors' prison as the penalty for not paying taxes.

State leaders in Boston started to panic, fearing the "rebels" would soon descend upon them. Desperately, they conducted an emotional public appeal for funds. Frightened Bostonians opened their purses. They subscribed $5000 to pay for an eastern Massachusetts army headed by former Continental general Benjamin Lincoln. Lincoln's assignment was to march his army into western parts of the state and subdue the Shaysites.

The insurrection soon fizzled. Lacking weapons and suffering in bitter cold weather, Daniel Shays and his followers were desperate.

On January 25, 1787, they attacked the federal arsenal at Springfield. A few well-placed cannon shots, which resulted in 24 Shaysite casualties (including 4 killed), drove them off. In early February the eastern Massachusetts army, after pursuing the western rebels through a driving snowstorm, fell upon Shays's followers at Petersham. Lincoln's force quickly routed the farmers, who lacked guns to defend themselves. The Petersham engagement, along with tax relief from the assembly and amnesty for the leaders of the rebellion, ended the uprising.

Shays's Rebellion, however, held broader significance. The confrontation further coalesced the nationalists. Wrote George Washington: "Good God! . . . There are combustibles in every state, which a spark might set fire to." Only a national government of "energy" could save the republic from sinking "into the lowest state of humiliation and contempt." The nationalists thus intensified their campaign for a new constitutional settlement, one designed to bring the self-serving sovereign states and the people under control.

HUMAN RIGHTS AND SOCIAL CHANGE

The years between 1776 and 1787 were not just a time of mounting political confrontation between nationalists and localists. The period also witnessed the establishment of many fundamental human rights. When Thomas Jefferson penned his famous words, "all men are created equal," he informed George III that kings were not superior to the people by some assumed right of birth. Jefferson went on to say that all human beings had "certain unalienable rights," or rights literally beyond governmental control. Republican governments had the responsibility to respect and guarantee these rights, including "life, liberty, and the pursuit of happiness" for all citizens.

At the same time Americans had waged civil war against Britain to preserve property rights. Tyrannical governments, for example, threatened property through taxation without representation. In trying to protect property rights while expanding human rights, revolutionary leaders learned that the two could clash. They found it much easier to guarantee human rights when property rights, such as those relating to the ownership of slaves, were not also at stake. Thus there were some striking contradictions in efforts to enshrine greater freedom for all inhabitants in revolutionary America.

In Pursuit of Religious Freedom

Since the days of the Great Awakening, dissenter religious groups had expressed opposition to established churches in the colonies. The Baptists were particularly outspoken. They wanted official toleration and an end to taxes used exclusively for state-supported churches. A major breakthrough came in 1776, thanks to George Washington's close friend George Mason, who wrote the Virginia Declaration of Rights, a document appended to the new state constitution. It guaranteed all citizens equal entitlement "to the free exercise of religion, according to the dictates of conscience." This statement provided for official toleration of dissenter sects but did not halt taxes going exclusively to the established Anglican church.

Three years later, Thomas Jefferson, with the support of Baptists from the backcountry, took up the cause. Jefferson presented legislation calling for the complete separation of church and state. On and off for seven years, the Virginia Assembly debated this bill. In 1786 the will of those who argued for complete freedom of conscience, including the right to believe nothing and support no church, prevailed. In later years Jefferson would be labeled an atheist for his part in guaranteeing religious freedom. For him the Virginia Statute of Religious Freedom was just as significant as the Declaration of Independence, and he had these sentiments engraved on his tombstone.

Disestablishment quickly followed in other states, particularly in the South where the Anglican church (soon to become the Protestant Episcopal Church of America) had been dominant. In New England, only Rhode Islanders, following in the tradition of Roger Williams, had enjoyed full latitude in worship. With the Revolution the cause of religious freedom started to move forward in other New England states. Lawmakers began letting citizens decide which local church to support with their tax monies.

This development represented a partial victory for individuals who preferred worshipping as Baptists or Presbyterians. These and other dissenters still had to accept Congregationalism as the established state church, continuing a pattern of official favoritism dating back to Puritan times. Complete separation of church and state, including the right not to support any church or to deny all religious creeds, did not occur in New England until the early nineteenth century.

Freedom of religion was one among a number of fundamental rights to make headway during the revolutionary era. Several of the states adopted bills of rights similar to Virginia's, guaranteeing freedom of speech, assembly, and the press, as well as trials by jury. Other states started revising their legal codes, making penalties for crimes less harsh. There was a sense that criminals could become useful citizens, which eventually resulted in prisons oriented more toward rehabilitation. Fewer crimes would now carry the death penalty. In Virginia, Thomas Jefferson revised the state legal code. His work put an end to such feudal practices as primogeniture and entail (passing and committing property only to eldest sons through the generations). Running through all these acts was the republican assumption that citizens should have the opportunity to lead productive lives, uninhibited by laws violating personal conscience or denying the opportunity to acquire property.

The Propertyless Poor and the West

For many revolutionary Americans gaining property remained only a dream. At least 20 percent of the population lived at the poverty level or below, eking out precarious existences as unskilled laborers. Indeed, wealth was more unevenly distributed in 1800 than it had been in 1750. For poor Americans, then, there were many missed opportunities, unless one counts the striking increase in almshouses and other relief organizations, evidence in itself that poverty was spreading, especially in the cities.

One missed opportunity related to the property of an estimated 500,000 loyalists, of whom one-fifth fled permanently to such places as England, Canada, the Bahamas, and various West Indian islands. State governments seized their land and other forms of property, worth millions, which could have been redistributed to poorer citizens. Instead, the states quickly sold off confiscated property to the highest bidders as a source of wartime revenues. This practice favored men of wealth with investment capital and worked against any substantial redistribution of property.

Another opportunity lay with the enormous trans-Appalachian frontier awaiting development. Washington's Continental soldiers, who ranked among the poorest members of revolutionary society, had been promised western lands for long-term service. When they mustered out in 1783, they received land warrant certificates. In order to survive, most veterans soon exchanged these paper certificates for the bare necessities of life. As a result, very few were ever able to begin anew in the Ohio country, once military tracts had been set aside and surveyed.

Still, western lands remained a source of hope for economically downtrodden soldiers and civilians alike. In 1775 explorer Daniel Boone blazed open the "Wilderness Road" to Kentucky. Others, like rugged Simon Kenton, scouted down the Ohio River from Pittsburgh. Where these frontiersmen went, thousands of land-hungry easterners soon followed. By 1790 Kentucky contained a population of 74,000, and Tennessee held 36,000. These settlers paid

TABLE 6.3

Rising Rates of Poor Relief in Revolutionary America*

	Boston		
Years	Population	Average Annual Expenditure (£)	Expenditure per 1000 People (£)
1731–1740	15,850	498	31
1751–1760	15,660	1,204	77
1761–1770	15,520	1,909	123
1771–1775	15,550	2,478	158

	New York City		
Years	Population	Average Annual Expenditure (£)	Expenditure per 1000 People (£)
1731–1740	10,100	351	21
1751–1760	13,200	667	39
1761–1770	18,100	1,667	92
1771–1775	22,600	2,778	123

	Philadelphia		
Years	Population	Average Annual Expenditure (£)	Expenditure per 1000 People (£)
1731–1740	8,800	471	49
1751–1760	15,700	1,083	67
1761–1770	22,100	2,842	129
1771–1775	27,900	3,785	136

*Poverty was a spreading problem in eighteenth-century America, particularly in the major port towns. With each passing decade, citizens paid more in taxes to provide poor relief for growing numbers of poor persons. The pattern continued into and beyond the revolutionary period.
Derived from Gary B. Nash, *The Urban Crucible: Social Change, Political Consciousness, and the Origins of the American Revolution* (Cambridge, Mass.: Harvard University Press, 1979), p. 402.

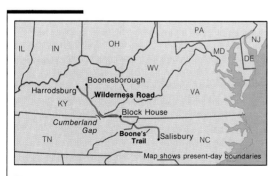

Wilderness Road

One of the most famous frontiersmen of his day, Daniel Boone blazed the Wilderness Road to Kentucky in 1775.

dearly for their invasion of Indian lands. The Shawnees, Cherokees, and Chickasaws fought back in innumerable bloody clashes. The white death toll reached 1500. Besides losing ancient tribal lands, Indian casualties were also considerable.

White settlements in Kentucky and Tennessee created pressures to open territory north of the Ohio River. After ceding the Old

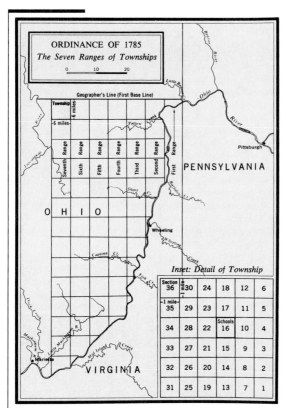

The first survey of national lands was directed by Thomas Hutchins, a native of New Jersey.

the region. Townships of 6 miles square were to be laid out in grid-like fashion—townships to contain 36 sections of 640 acres each with proceeds from the sale of the sixteenth section to be used to finance public education. The Northwest Ordinance of 1787 refined governmental arrangements, gave a bill of rights to prospective settlers, and proclaimed slavery forever banned north of the Ohio River—a prohibition that Thomas Jefferson had wanted but failed to get included in the 1784 Ordinance. In providing for orderly development and eventual statehood, the land ordinances may well have been the most significant legislation of the Confederation-period Congress.

The ordinances were not fully enlightened. Congress, in its desperate search for revenue, viewed the Old Northwest as a source of long-term income. The smallest purchase individual settlers could make was 640 acres, priced at $1.00 per acre, and there were to be no purchases on credit. Families of modest means, let alone poorer ones, could not meet such terms. As a result, Congress dealt mainly with well-to-do land speculators—and even extended them deeds to millions of acres on credit! All of these actions cut off the poorest citizens from the West, unless they were willing to squat on uninhabited land until driven off. And that is what many did to survive economically.

Northwest to the United States in 1783, however, the British did not abandon their military posts there. To maintain the lucrative fur trade with the Indians, they bolstered the Miamis, Shawnees, Delawares, and remnant groups of the Iroquois nation with a steady supply of firearms. Whites foolish enough to venture north of the Ohio River rarely survived, and the region remained closed to large numbers of westward-moving settlers well into the 1790s.

Despite the British and Indians, Congress was eager to open the Ohio country. With this goal in mind the delegates approved three land ordinances. The 1784 Ordinance provided for territorial government and guaranteed settlers that they would not remain in permanent colonial status. When enough people (later specified at 60,000) had moved in, a constitution could be written, state boundaries set, and admission to the union as a full partner would follow. The 1785 Ordinance called for orderly surveying of

Women Appeal for Fundamental Liberties

Like the poor, women experienced little success in improving their lot during the revolutionary era. Among their advocates was Abigail Adams (1744–1818). In the spring of 1776 she wrote her husband John, then in Philadelphia arguing for independence, and admonished him to "remember the ladies, and be more generous and favorable to them than

In her letters to her husband John, Abigail Adams was an early advocate of women's rights.

McDonald, *We the People: The Economic Origins of the Constitution* (1958), and *Novus Ordo Seclorum: The Intellectual Origins of the Constitution* (1985); Edmund S. Morgan, *Inventing The People: The Rise of Popular Sovereignty in England and America* (1988); Clinton Rossiter, *1787: The Grand Convention* (1966); Robert A. Rutland, *The Ordeal of the Constitution: The Antifederalists and the Ratification Struggle of 1787–88* (1966); Garry Wills, *Explaining America: The Federalist* (1981).

BIOGRAPHIES

George A. Billias, *Elbridge Gerry* (1976); Fawn Brodie, *Thomas Jefferson: An Intimate History* (1974); Roger J. Champagne, *Alexander McDougall* (1975); Christopher Collier, *Roger Sherman's Connecticut: Yankee Politics and the Revolution* (1971); Jacob E. Cooke, *Alexander Hamilton* (1982); Eric Foner, *Tom Paine and Revolutionary America* (1976); Ralph Ketcham, *James Madison* (1971); Elizabeth P. McCaughey, *From Loyalist to Founding Father: William Samuel Johnson* (1980); Merrill D. Peterson, *Thomas Jefferson and the New Nation* (1970); Jack N. Rakove, *James Madison and the Creation of the American Republic* (1990); C. Edward Skeen, *John Armstrong, Jr., 1758–1843* (1981); Laurel Thatcher Ulrich, *A Midwife's Tale: The Life of Martha Ballard, 1785–1812* (1990); Clarence L. Ver Steeg, *Robert Morris: Revolutionary Financier* (1954); Lynne Withey, *Dearest Friend: A Life of Abigail Adams* (1981).

CHAPTER 7

Shaping the New Nation, 1789–1800

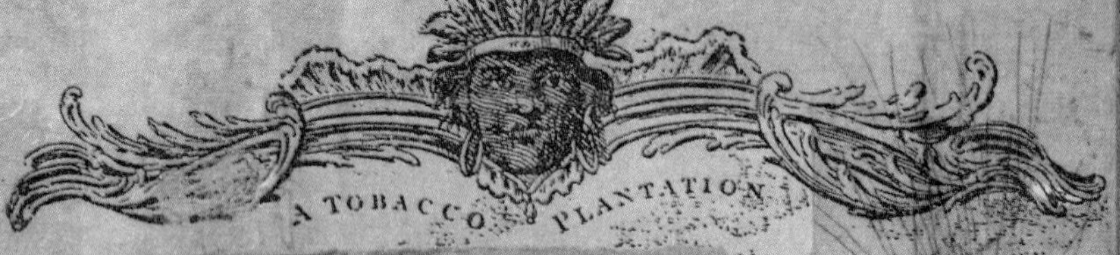
A TOBACCO PLANTATION

FIG. II.

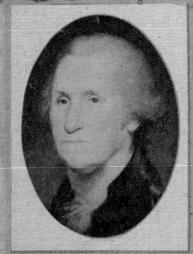

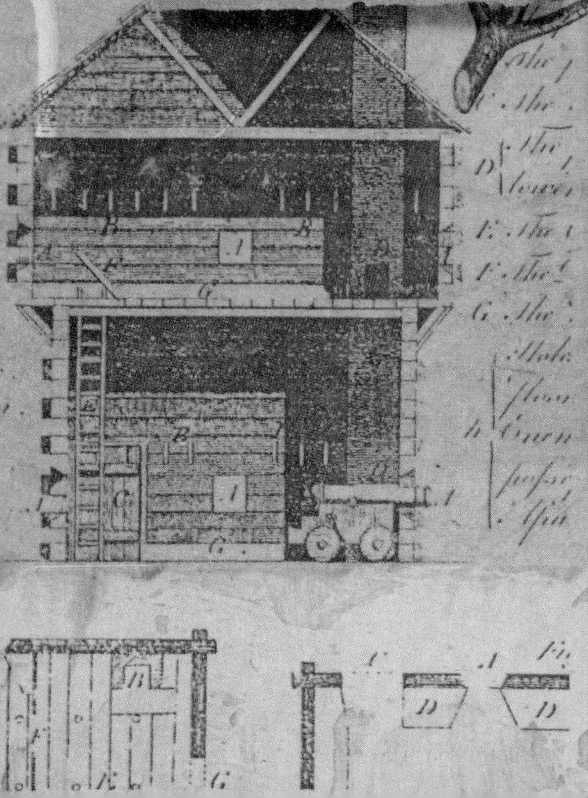

FIG. V.

Putting the New National Government into Operation

- Setting Up a New Government
- Defining the Presidency
- Setting Up a Cabinet
- Alexander Hamilton's Financial Program

The Birth of Political Parties

- World Events and Political Polarization
- 1793 and 1794: Years of Crisis
- Washington Decides to Retire

A New President and New Challenges

- The Presidency of John Adams
- A New National Capital
- The Quasi-War with France

The Revolution of 1800

Early in August 1790, David Howe, an assistant federal marshal, began the difficult task of counting all the people who lived in Hancock County, Maine (then part of Massachusetts). One of 650 federal census takers, charged with making "a just and perfect enumeration and description of all persons" in the United States, he began by writing down his own name followed by his wife's and child's. He then listed the names of all the other people who lived in his hometown of Penobscot and proceeded to crisscross the Maine coast, recording the names of 9549 residents. In March 1791, he submitted his findings: 2436 free white males, 16 years and older; 2531 free white males under the age of 16; 4544 free white females; and 38 "other free persons" (including Peter Williams, "a black," and his wife and child).

Taking the nation's first census was an extraordinarily difficult challenge. The nation's sheer physical size—stretching across 867,980 square miles—made it impossible to conduct an accurate count. Many people refused to speak to census takers; some because they feared that this was a step toward enactment of new taxes, others because they felt that the Bible prohibited census taking. To make matters worse, census takers were abysmally paid, receiving just $1 for every 150 rural residents and $1 for every 300 city dwellers counted. Indeed, the pay was so low that one judge found it difficult to find "any person whatever" to take the census.

The United States was the first nation in history to institute a periodic national census. Since 1790, the country has tried to count each man, woman, and child every ten years. The first census asked just six simple questions, yet when supplemented with other statistical information, it provides a treasure chest of information about the social and economic life of the American people.

What was the United States like in 1790? According to the first census, the United States contained just 3,929,214 people, about half living in the northern states, half in the South. At first glance, the population seems quite small (it was only about a quarter the size of England's and a sixth the size of France's). But it was growing extraordinarily rapidly. Just 1.17 million in 1750, the population would pass 5 million by 1800.

The 1790 census reveals a nation still overwhelmingly rural in character. In a population of nearly 4 million people, just 202,000 lived in the 24 towns or cities that had at least 2500 inhabitants; only 2 cities had more than 25,000 people. Yet the urban population, while small, was growing extremely rapidly, especially in the West, where frontier towns like Louisville started to sprout.

In 1790, most Americans still lived on the Atlantic coast. The center of the nation's population was located on Maryland's eastern shore, a few miles from the ocean. Nevertheless, the West was the most rapidly growing part of the nation. During the 1790s, the population of Kentucky and Tennessee increased nearly 300 percent, and by 1800, Kentucky had more people than 5 of the original 13 states.

What else does the first census reveal about the American people? For one thing, it reveals an extraordinarily youthful population, with half the people under the age of 16. And it also reveals an exceptionally diverse population. Three-fifths of the white population was English in ancestry and another fifth was Scottish or Irish. The remainder was of German, Dutch, French, Swedish, or other background. A fifth of the entire population was African-American.

What else do we know about America in 1790? Records indicate that the American economy was still quite undeveloped. There were fewer than 100 newspapers in the entire country; 3 banks (with total capital of less than $5 million); 3 insurance companies; and 75 post offices. And yet the United States was perched on the edge of an extraordinary decade of growth.

Over the next ten years, the society made tremendous economic advances. During the 1790s, states chartered 295 corporations, banks, and transportation companies, compared to just 33 during the 1780s. The number of newspapers climbed from 100 in 1790 to 200 a decade later; the number of banks rose from 3 to 29 (while their capital rose sixfold); the number of insurance companies multiplied from 3 to 33; the number of post offices increased from just 75 to 903; exports climbed from $29 million to $107 million; cotton production rose from 3000 bales to 73,000 bales. The number of patents issued increased from just 3 in 1790 to 44 in 1800.

During the 1790s, the foundations of future economic growth were laid. In 1791, an English immigrant named Samuel Slater introduced the factory system into the United States in Pawtucket, Rhode Island. Altogether, 11 mechanized mills were built in the country during the 1790s. Other factories produced iron, brass, paper, glass, firearms, nails, umbrellas, and hats. The first blast furnace west of the Allegheny mountains opened in 1790, and that same year a Connecticut Yankee named John Fitch started the first commercial steamship service, connecting Philadelphia with Trenton, New Jersey.

In 1800, as in 1790, the United States remained a nation of farms, plantations, and small towns, of yeomen, slaves, and artisans. Nevertheless, the nation was undergoing far-reaching social and economic transformations. Improvements in education and culture were particularly striking. During the 1790s, 266 circulating libraries opened in the United States (there were only 2 public libraries back in 1700); New Hampshire and Kentucky founded new medical schools; literary, historical, and philosophic societies, like the Massachusetts Historical Society organized in 1791, multiplied. Between 1783 and 1800, Americans founded 17 new colleges and a large number of female academies.

For the young United States, the last years of the eighteenth century were a period of rapid demographic and economic growth. They were also years of crucial political developments. During this period the United States adopted a bill of rights protecting individual liberties, enacted a financial program securing the nation's credit, and created its first political parties. It was during this dramatic era that the United States established a strong and vigorous national government.

PUTTING THE NEW NATIONAL GOVERNMENT INTO OPERATION

The United States was the first modern nation to achieve independence through a successful revolution against colonial rule. Its example was

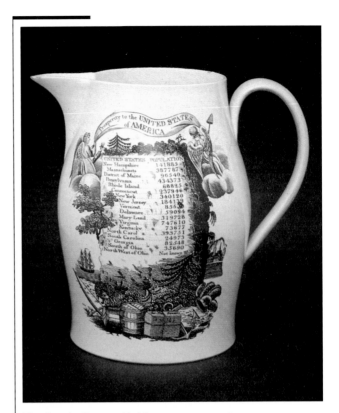

The Constitution provided for a census every ten years. The first census, conducted in 1790, estimated the population of the United States at 3.9 million people. This jug, made in England after the 1790 census, shows the figures gathered in that census.

followed in the nineteenth century by the Spanish colonies of Central and South America and in the twentieth century by the Belgian, British, Dutch, French, and Portuguese colonies of Africa and Asia. Although many colonies in the nineteenth and twentieth centuries followed the example of the United States in winning independence through revolution, few were as successful in subsequently developing politically and economically.

Even the United States, however, faced serious problems in its first decade under the Constitution. One major problem was to consolidate support among the American people. Two states, North Carolina and Rhode Island, continued to support the Articles of Confederation. Citizens of Vermont threatened to join Canada.

The new nation also faced severe economic and foreign policy problems. A huge debt remained from the Revolutionary War, and paper money issued during the war was virtually worthless. Along with these pressing economic problems were foreign threats to the new nation's independence. In violation of the peace treaty of 1783 ending the Revolutionary War, Britain continued to occupy forts in the Old Northwest and Spain refused to recognize the new nation's southern and western boundaries.

In 1790, economic problems, domestic political conflict, and foreign policy issues challenged the new nation in its efforts to establish a stable republic.

Setting Up a New Government

During the 1790s, the young republic confronted many of the same problems faced by the newly independent nations of Africa and Asia. Like other new nations born in anticolonial revolutions, the United States lacked revenue and organizational structure.

The first task facing American leaders was to establish the machinery of government. The new United States government consisted of nothing more than 75 post offices, a large debt, a small number of unpaid clerks, and an army of just 46 officers and 672 soldiers. There was no federal court system, no navy, and no system for collecting taxes.

It fell to Congress to take the initial steps toward putting the new national government into operation. The House of Representatives, under the leadership of James Madison, took the lead. To raise revenue, it passed a tariff on imported goods and an excise tax on liquor. To encourage American shipping, it imposed duties on foreign vessels. To provide a structure for the executive branch of government, it created departments of State, Treasury, and War. In addition, Congress adopted the Judiciary Act of 1789, which organized a federal judiciary. The federal judicial system consisted of a Supreme Court (as established by the Constitution) with six justices, a district court in each state, and three appeals courts, each comprised of two Supreme Court justices sitting with a district judge.

In its first session, Congress organized a federal judicial system as part of the new national government. This depiction of an early courthouse was drawn in 1804 by Lewis Miller.

To strengthen popular support for the new government, Congress also approved a Bill of Rights for the Constitution, sending the amendments to the states for ratification. Congress considered 210 amendments to the Constitution proposed by state ratifying conventions, including proposals to restrict the federal government's power to tax, to prohibit a standing army in peacetime, and to curtail the power of the federal courts. The House approved 17 of these, the Senate agreed to 12. The states subsequently ratified 10 amendments.

These first ten amendments guaranteed the rights of free press, free speech, and religion; the right to peaceful assembly; and the right to petition government. The Bill of Rights also ensured that the national government could not infringe on the right to trial by jury. In an effort to reassure Antifederalists that the powers of the new government were limited, the tenth amendment "reserved to the States respectively, or to the people" all powers not specified in the Constitution.

Defining the Presidency

The Constitution provided only a broad outline of the office and powers of the president. Important issues that would profoundly affect future generations of Americans remained unsettled. The Senate spent three weeks simply debating what to call the president. A committee proposed calling him "His Highness the President of the United States and Protector of their Liberties." James Madison saw no need for such an ostentatious title and persuaded a majority of Congress to address the chief executive simply as "President of the United States."

It would be up to George Washington, as the first president, to define the office. He fully realized the importance of the task before him. "I walk on untrodden ground," he observed. "There is scarcely any part of my conduct that may not hereafter be drawn into precedent."

Washington's first concern was to establish respect for the presidency. As such, he tried to comport himself with dignity and invest his office with formality and authority. He was available to public visitors only two afternoons a week, an hour at a time. Once a week he held a levee, at which he would formally meet visitors, bow to them, but shake no hands. He traveled in an elegant coach pulled by six horses and paraded on a white steed, sitting upon a leopard-skin saddlecloth. He resided in the "grandest" mansion in New York City.

As the first president, Washington was responsible for organizing the executive branch and establishing many precedents regarding the president's relationship with the other branches of government. It was unclear, for example, whether the president was to personally run the executive branch or, instead, act like a constitutional monarch and delegate responsibility to the vice president and executive officers, called the "cabinet." Washington favored a strong and active role for the president. Instead of governing through his vice president and secretaries, along the lines of the British government, he modeled the executive branch along the lines of a general's staff. Washington consulted his cabinet officers and listened to them carefully, but he made the final decisions, just as he had done while serving as commander-in-chief.

The relationship between the executive and legislative branches was also uncertain. Should a president, like Britain's prime minister, personally appear before Congress to defend administration policies? Should the Senate have sole power to dismiss executive officials? The answers to such questions were not clear. In many state constitutions the executive branch was subservient to the legislative branch. Washington decided that there should be a clear line of demarcation between the executive and legislative branches of government. He envisioned an independent executive with administrative responsibility for conducting the business of the federal government. Washington insisted that the president could dismiss presidential appointees without the Senate's permission. A bitterly divided Senate approved this principle by a single vote.

At first, Washington tried to follow the literal words of the Constitution, which stated that the president should negotiate treaties with the advice and consent of the Senate. He appeared before the Senate in person to discuss a pending Indian treaty. The senators, however, refused to provide immediate answers and referred the matter to a committee. "This defeats every purpose of my coming here," Washington declared. In the future he negotiated treaties first and then sent them to the Senate for ratification.

Setting Up a Cabinet

The most difficult task that the president faced was deciding whom to nominate for public office. When he took office, the president and the vice president were the only members of the executive branch of the new government. Washington was besieged by office seekers, and facing them was a "delicate," "unpleasing" job.

As secretary of war, Washington nominated Henry Knox, an old military comrade, who had held a similar position under the Articles of Confederation. As postmaster general, he named Samuel Osgood of Massachusetts, who carried out his tasks in a single room with the help of two clerks. As attorney general, he tapped fellow Virginian Edmund Randolph, who had introduced the Virginia plan at the Constitutional Convention. As secretary of state, he originally planned to name John Jay, the head of foreign affairs under the Articles of Confederation. But when Jay declared his preference for serving as chief justice of the Supreme Court, Washington agreed. He nominated a fellow Virginian, Thomas Jefferson, to the State Department.

Washington considered the secretary of the treasury the most important post in his administration. The Confederation government failed largely because it was unable to collect revenue, pay off its debts, or attract foreign credit. He named his former aide-de-camp, the 34-year-old Alexander Hamilton, to head the Treasury Department.

By the fall of 1790, Washington had filled nearly 125 government offices, ranging from appointments to the Supreme Court to local post offices. One of his nominees—a naval officer for the port of Savannah—was rejected, after Georgia's two senators objected. This action established the principle of "senatorial courtesy"—that local appointments would be made in consultation with each state's two senators.

George Washington's first cabinet consisted of Secretary of War Henry Knox, Secretary of the Treasury Alexander Hamilton, Secretary of State Thomas Jefferson, and Attorney General Edmund Randolph.

Alexander Hamilton's Financial Program

The most pressing problems facing the new government were economic. As a result of the Revolution, the federal government had acquired a huge debt: $54 million including interest. The states owed another $25 million. Paper money issued under the Continental Congresses and the Articles of Confederation was worthless. Foreign credit was unavailable.

Ten days after Alexander Hamilton became treasury secretary, Congress asked him to report on ways to solve the nation's financial problems. Hamilton, a man of strong political convictions, immediately realized that he had an opportunity to create a financial program that would embody his political principles.

Hamilton believed that the nation's stability depended on an alliance between the government and citizens of wealth and influence. No society could succeed, he maintained, "which did not unite the interest and credit of rich individuals with those of the state." Unlike Thomas Jefferson, Hamilton doubted the capacity of common people to govern themselves. "All

communities," he maintained, "divide themselves into the few and the many. The first are rich and well-born, the other the mass of the people. . . . The people are turbulent and changing; they seldom judge or determine right." He expressed open contempt for ordinary citizens; he once declared, "Your people is a beast."

To keep the masses in check, Hamilton favored a strong national government. Born in the British West Indies of an illegitimate union in 1755, Hamilton never developed the intense loyalty to a state that was common among many Americans of the time. A staunch nationalist, he wanted to create a unified nation and a powerful federal government. During the Constitutional Convention, Hamilton had proposed to extinguish the states or reduce them to a smaller scale, and he remained an advocate of a powerful national government. His ideal was the Britain of George III: "I have no scruple in declaring . . . that the British government is the best in the world, and I doubt much whether anything short of it will do in America."

As a nationalist who admired economic and political elites, Hamilton intended to use government fiscal policies to strengthen federal power at the expense of the states and "make it in the immediate interest of the moneyed men to co-operate with government in its support."

Although Americans today may find his antidemocratic sentiments unpalatable, Hamilton was a man of initiative and daring who created the foundations of a strong and vigorous economy. As Daniel Webster would later say of him: "He smote the rock of the national resources and abundant streams of revenue gushed forth; he touched the dead corpse of Public Credit, and it sprang upon its feet."

Restoring Public Credit

The paramount problem facing Hamilton was the huge national debt. In 1790, the national debt totaled about $79 million. The federal treasury was so poor that the United States was unable to pay the interest on French and Dutch loans, the ransoms of American sailors held by North African pirates, or even its diplomatic staff abroad.

Hamilton argued that it was vital for the nation to fund these debts in order to establish the credit of the federal government. "States, like individuals, who observe their engagements are respected and trusted," he wrote. As a step toward restoring the nation's credit, Hamilton proposed in his "Report on the Public Credit" (1790) that the government assume the entire indebtedness—principle and interest—of the federal government and the states. His plan was to retire the old depreciated obligations by borrowing new money at a lower interest rate.

Hamilton's proposal to fund the national debt and assume all state debts ignited a firestorm of controversy. States like Maryland, Pennsylvania, North Carolina, and Virginia, which had already paid off their war debts, opposed assumption of state debts. They saw no reason why they should be taxed by the federal government to pay off the debts of states like Massachusetts and South Carolina. Many southern states claimed that the proposal benefited northern interests at the expense of the South, since four-fifths of the debt was owed to northern merchants and creditors.

The greatest objection to Hamilton's scheme was that it would provide unconscionable profits to speculators who had bought bonds from Revolutionary War veterans and small merchants for as little as 10 or 15 cents on the dollar. Many of these financial speculators were associates of Hamilton or members of Congress who knew that Hamilton's report would recommend full payment of the debt.

James Madison offered an alternative to Hamilton's plan. He recommended that speculators receive no more than 50 cents on the dollar and that, in the interest of fairness, the federal government pay the other 50 cents on the dollar to the original holders of the debt.

Hamilton rejected Madison's proposal. At the time speculators purchased these bonds they were almost worthless. The sellers were glad to recoup at least part of their investment, and the purchasers had no reason to anticipate a change in political climate that would result in high profits. It was, for the purchasers, a gamble on the nation's future. As a result, Hamilton saw nothing improper about paying profits to individuals who had acquired certificates of indebtedness from revolutionary soldiers and other patriots at a fraction of their face value. He was convinced that the nation's future prosperity depended on concentrating capital in the hands of men who would invest it in commerce and manufacturing.

For six months Congress remained deadlocked, soundly defeating Madison's plan and then narrowly rejecting Hamilton's funding scheme. As the debate raged, sectional animosities mounted. Several New England congressmen threatened secession. Senator Richard Henry Lee of Virginia responded by declaring that he preferred disunion "to the rule of a fixed insolent northern majority." The nation's future seemed in jeopardy until a compromise orchestrated by James Madison and Thomas Jefferson secured passage of Hamilton's plan. In exchange for southern votes in Congress, Hamilton promised his support for locating the future national capital on the banks of the Potomac River, the border between two southern states, Virginia and Maryland.

Hamilton's debt program was a remarkable success. Funding and assumption of the debt created pools of capital for business investment and firmly established the credit of the United States abroad. By demonstrating Americans' willingness to repay their debts, he made America a good credit risk attractive to foreign investors. European investment capital started pouring into the new nation in large amounts.

The Bank of the United States

Hamilton's next objective was to create a Bank of the United States, modeled after the Bank of England, to issue currency, collect taxes, hold government funds, regulate the nation's financial system, and make loans to the government and private borrowers. This proposal, like his debt scheme, unleashed a storm of protest.

One criticism directed against the bank was that it threatened to undermine the nation's republican values. Banks—and the paper money they issued—would simply encourage speculation, stock-jobbing, paper shuffling, and corruption. The bank was also opposed on constitutional grounds. Adopting a position known as "strict constructionism," Thomas Jefferson and

James Madison charged that a national bank was unconstitutional since the Constitution did not specifically give Congress the power to create a bank. Other grounds for criticism were that the bank would subject America to foreign influences (because foreigners would have to purchase a high percentage of the bank's stock) and give a propertied elite disproportionate influence over the nation's fiscal policies (since private investors would control the bank's board of directors). Worse yet, the bank would increase the public debt, which, in turn, would add to the nation's tax burden. Under Hamilton's plan, the bank would raise capital by selling stock to private investors. Investors could pay for up to three-quarters of the bank stock they purchased with government bonds of indebtedness. The burden of financing the bank, therefore, would ultimately rest on the public treasury.

Hamilton responded to the charge that a bank was unconstitutional by formulating the doctrine of "implied powers." He argued that

The National Bank of the United States, which opened in Philadelphia in 1791, was a key part of Alexander Hamilton's economic plan for a strong central government.

Congress did have the power to create a bank since the Constitution granted the federal government authority to do anything "necessary and proper" to carry out its constitutional functions (in this case its fiscal duties). This represented the first attempt to defend a "loose" interpretation of the Constitution. Hamilton also defended his bank plan on another ground. He asserted that his plan would transform the public debt into a public good by using it to expand credit, finance business expansion, and provide a much needed pool of capital.

In 1791, Congress passed a bill creating a national bank for a term of 20 years, leaving the question of the bank's constitutionality up to President Washington. After listening to Madison, Jefferson, and Hamilton, the president reluctantly decided to sign the measure out of a conviction that a bank was necessary for the nation's financial well-being.

The first Bank of the United States, like Hamilton's debt plan, was a great success. It helped regulate the currency of private banks. It provided a reserve of capital on which the government and private investors drew. It helped attract foreign investment to the credit-short new nation. In 1811, however, the jealousy of private commercial banks convinced Congress to allow the bank, which was chartered for a maximum of 20 years, to expire.

Stimulating American Industry

The final step in Hamilton's economic program was a proposal to aid the nation's infant industries. In his *Report on Manufactures* (1791), Hamilton argued that the nation's long-term interests "will be advanced, rather than injured, by the due encouragement of manufactures." Through high tariffs designed to protect American industry from foreign competition, government bounties and subsidies, and internal improvements of transportation, he hoped to break Britain's manufacturing hold on America.

Opposition to Hamilton's proposal came from many quarters. Many Americans feared that the proposal would excessively cut federal revenues by discouraging imports. Shippers worried that the plan would reduce foreign trade. Farmers feared the proposal would lead foreign countries to impose retaliatory tariffs on agricultural products, thereby raising the price of manufactured goods. Many southerners regarded the plan as a brazen attempt to promote northern industry and commerce at the South's expense, since it provided no assistance to agriculture.

The most eloquent opposition came from Thomas Jefferson, who believed that the growth of manufacturing threatened the values of an agrarian way of life. Hamilton's industrial vision of America's future directly challenged Jefferson's ideal of a nation of freehold farmers, tilling the fields, communing with nature, and maintaining personal freedom by virtue of land ownership. Manufacturing, Jefferson believed, should be left to Europe, since it bred cities, which were cesspools of human corruption. Like slaves, factory workers would be manipulated by their masters, who not only would deny them satisfying lives but also would make it impossible for them to think and act as independent citizens.

Although Congress did provide limited assistance to a number of depressed industries, notably fisheries, it rejected most of Hamilton's proposals to aid industry. Nevertheless, the debate over Hamilton's plan carried fateful consequences for the future. Fundamental disagreements had arisen between Hamiltonians and Jeffersonians over the federal government's role, constitutional interpretation, and distinct visions of how the republic should develop. How could the country resolve these fundamental differences? How could Americans represent their views? The answer to these questions lay in the creation of modern political parties—parties the writers of the Constitution neither wanted nor planned for.

THE BIRTH OF POLITICAL PARTIES

When George Washington assembled his first cabinet, there were no national political parties in the United States. In selecting cabinet members, he paid no attention to partisan labels and simply chose the individuals he believed were best qualified to run the new nation. Similarly, the new Congress had no party divisions. In all the states except Pennsylvania, politics was not waged between parties, but, rather, between impermanent factions built around leading fam-

(Text continues on p. 222)

YELLOW FEVER IN PHILADELPHIA: PILLS AND POLITICS

Death stalked the streets of Philadelphia in 1793 in the form of a yellow fever epidemic. The first case appeared in August, and by the time the epidemic disappeared in November, yellow fever had killed 10 percent of the city's population, while another 45 percent had fled in terror. At the height of the epidemic, Philadelphia was a city under siege; with city services interrupted; communications impaired; the port closed; the economy in shambles; and people locked in their homes, afraid to venture beyond their doorsteps. To make matters worse, the city's leaders—unable to reach agreement on what caused the disease or what should be done to combat it—attacked each other in endless debates. The result was that Philadelphia, America's premiere city, all but shut down.

Philadelphia's plight is not hard to explain, for yellow fever is a pulverizing, terrifying disease. Caused by a virus, the disease is spread by the female mosquito. Yellow fever's early symptoms are nearly identical to those of malaria; the victim feels flush and then develops chills, followed by a sizzling fever, accompanied by a severe headache or backache. The fever lasts for two or three days, and then the patient usually enjoys a remission.

Mild cases of yellow fever stop here. For the less fortunate, however, remission soon gives way to jaundice (hence "yellow" fever), and the victim starts to hallucinate. Massive internal hemorrhaging follows, and the patient starts vomiting huge quantities of black blood. Next, the victim goes into a coma. A lucky few emerge from the coma to escape death, but the vast majority die from internal bleeding.

If any American city seemed well equipped to handle a medical crisis, it was Philadelphia. It was the nation's leading center of medicine, home to the prestigious College of Physicians, America's first medical school (1765), and to America's most famous physician, Dr. Benjamin Rush, a founder of the Pennsylvania Society for Promoting the

Abolition of Slavery and a signer of the Declaration of Independence. The City of Brotherly Love could also point with pride to Franklin's Pennsylvania Hospital (1752), the first hospital in America and a model facility for the worthy poor.

Yet for all of its luster, Philadelphia's medical community was no match for yellow fever. The basic problem was that doctors in 1793 could not agree on what caused the disease, how it spread, or how to treat it. Many physicians, including Dr. Rush, cited local factors. They blamed the disease on the decaying vegetation and rotting filth that littered Philadelphia's streets and docks, producing an atmospheric "miasma" that was carried by the wind, infecting anyone who breathed its noxious fumes. Rejecting local causes, other physicians argued that yellow fever was a contagious disease. It had been imported to Philadelphia, they insisted, by the 2000 French refugees who had fled the revolution (and a yellow fever epidemic!) in Haiti to seek political asylum in the United States.

Physicians in 1793 had no way of settling the dispute. Those who blamed the epidemic on dirty streets sounded just as believable as those who pointed an accusing finger at sickly foreigners. What made the controversy truly remarkable, however, was the extent to which it became embroiled in politics, for what began as a purely medical debate quickly degenerated into a raging political battle.

With very few exceptions, the doctors who insisted that yellow fever was contagious were Federalists, while the anticontagionists were almost all Jeffersonian Republicans. Taught by the French Revolution to be wary of free-thinking political ideas, Federalist doctors regarded

yellow fever as just another unwanted French import. Ablaze with pro-French sympathies, anticontagionist Republicans saw the French refugees as honored friends who brought virtue rather than death. The source of the epidemic, they insisted, lay with unvirtuous filth at their doorsteps.

Partisan leaders tried desperately to bend this medical debate to their political advantage. To Federalists, the doctrine of importation demanded that the United States protect itself from the French menace. Therefore, trade with French West Indian islands should be suspended; French refugees who had gained entry to the United States should be quarantined and future refugees excluded. Republicans, by contrast, denounced these demands as a federal plot to ruin profitable trade with the West Indies and to infect Americans with a new disease—hatred of all things French. Nor was their concern unfounded, for public hysteria was definitely building. At one point, amid persistent rumors that the French had poisoned the public drinking wells in preparation for a full-scale invasion, Philadelphians threatened violence against the innocent refugees.

At the height of the turmoil, politics even influenced how physicians treated the victims of yellow fever. At the beginning of the epidemic, doctors were pretty evenly divided, without regard to politics, into two schools. One prescribed stimulants—quinine bark, wine, and cold baths; while the other recommended bleeding—drawing off huge quantities of the patient's blood. (Dr. Rush had long been an advocate of the bleeding treatment. He recommended removing about four-fifths of the patient's blood

supply, more than enough to kill all but the unkillable!)

Alexander Hamilton was personally responsible for converting this medical squabbling into a political issue. After managing to survive an attack of yellow fever, he published a ringing testimonial to the life-saving properties of the bark and wine cure. The treatment had been prescribed, he declared, by Dr. Edward Stevens of Philadelphia, a longtime friend of Hamilton. Dr. Stevens was the only physician in the City of Brotherly Love who was a publicly confessed Federalist.

A few days after his testimonial appeared, Hamilton published a second article in which he ridiculed Dr. Rush's "new treatment." Hamilton's attack was immediately echoed by Federalist editors across the country, and in the wake of their articles, the public came to regard "bark" as the Federalist cure and "bleeding" as the Republican cure.

The controversy over yellow fever raged until the epidemic ended in the fall. Philadelphia's struggle against yellow fever was one of the many times that Americans would infuse their discussions of health problems with nonmedical concerns. In future epidemics, notions of class, race, individual virtue, and even gender would color public discussions of health, just as surely as politics enlivened the medical debate over yellow fever in Philadelphia in 1793 when the republic was young.

ilies, political managers, ethnic groups, or such interest groups as debtors and creditors.

By the time Washington retired from the presidency in 1797, the nature of the American political system had radically changed. The first president devoted part of his "Farewell Address" to denouncing "the baneful effects of the Spirit of Party," which had come to dominate American politics. Local and state factions had given way to two competing national parties, known as the Federalists and the Republicans. They nominated political candidates, managed electoral campaigns, and represented distinctive outlooks or ideologies. By 1796, the United States had produced its first modern party system. These political parties breathed new life into the concept of popular sovereignty, by making the people the ultimate arbiters in American political life.

The process of party formation did not take place smoothly. The framers of the Constitution had not prepared their plan of government with political parties in mind. They associated parties with the political factions and interest groups that dominated the British government and hoped that in the United States the "better sort of citizens," rising above popular self-interest, would debate key issues and reach a harmonious consensus regarding how best to legislate for the nation's future. Thomas Jefferson reflected widespread sentiments when he declared in 1789, "If I could not go to heaven but with a party, I would not go there at all."

Yet despite a belief that parties were evil and posed a threat to enlightened government, political factions gradually coalesced into political parties during Washington's first administration. To build support for his proposals to create a strong federal government committed to fostering an industrial economy, Alexander Hamilton relied on government patronage. As treasury secretary, Hamilton took over military procurement from the War Department and used army supply contracts to build support for his program. Government office was also used to establish a political base of support. Of 2000 federal officeholders appointed between 1789 and 1801, two-thirds were Federalist party activists, who used positions as postmasters, tax collectors, judges, and customs house officials to favor the interests of the Federalists. Hamilton also secured John Fenno to publish the *Gazette of the United States* to "endear the General government to the people," and assisted the paper with Treasury printing contracts. By 1794, Hamilton's faction and its opponents had evolved into the first national political parties in history capable of nominating candidates, coordinating votes in Congress, staging public meetings, organizing petition campaigns, and disseminating propaganda.

Hamilton's opponents struck back. On the grounds that Hamilton's fiscal plans threatened his vision of the republic, James Madison organized congressional opposition and retained the poet Philip Freneau to edit a newspaper, the *National Gazette*, as an instrument to warn the populace about Hamilton's designs. Madison and his ally Thomas Jefferson saw in Hamilton's program an effort to establish the kind of corrupt patronage society that existed in Britain, with a huge public debt, a standing army, high taxes, and government-subsidized monopolies. Hamilton's aim, declared Jefferson, was to assimilate "the American government to the form and spirit of the British monarchy."

To generate party identity among the people, the Republicans worked closely with a series of local voluntary associations. The Tammany Society of New York, originally a fraternal and charitable brotherhood with arcane Indian rites, campaigned for Republican candidates in New York City. As early as 1794, 35 Democratic-Republican societies, which had sprouted up from Maine to Georgia in support of the French Revolution, threw their support behind Republican programs and candidates.

World Events and Political Polarization

World events intensified partisan divisions. On July 14, 1789, 20,000 French men and women stormed the Bastille, a hated royal fortress, marking the beginning of the French Revolution. For three years France experimented with a constitutional monarchy. Then in 1792, the revolution took a violent turn. In August, Austrian and Prussian troops invaded France to put an end to the revolution. French revolutionaries responded by officially deposing King Louis XVI and placing him on trial. He was found guilty and, in January 1793, beheaded. France declared itself a republic and launched a reign of terror against counterrevolutionary elements in the population. Three hundred thousand suspects were arrested; 17,000 were executed. A general war erupted in Europe pitting revolutionary France against a coalition of European monarchies, led by Britain. With two brief interruptions, this war would last 23 years.

Many Americans reacted enthusiastically to the overthrow of the French king and the creation of a French republic. The French people appeared to have joined America in a historic struggle against royal absolutism and aristocratic privilege. In imitation of the French revolutionaries, some Americans began to address each other as "citizen" and to wear liberty caps. Thomas Jefferson expressed the attitude of staunch defenders of the French Revolution when he said that he was willing to see "half the earth desolated" if this were necessary to secure human liberty and freedom.

More cautious gentlemen expressed horror at the cataclysm sweeping France. The French Revolution, they feared, was not merely a rebellion against royal authority, but a mass assault against property and Christianity. Conservatives urged President Washington to support England in its war against France. "Gallomen" asked him to support France.

Washington believed that involvement in the European war would weaken the new nation before it had firmly established its own independence. He proposed to keep the country "free from political connections with every other country, to see them independent of all, and under the influence of none." The president, however, faced a problem. During the War for American Independence, the United States had signed an alliance with France (see pp. 167–168). Washington asked his cabinet whether the alliance was still in force. Jefferson argued the alliance was still valid, since the treaties were made with the people of a nation and any people have the right to alter their form of government without forfeiting claims upon other nations. Hamilton said that it was not because the alliance had been made with the deposed government of King Louis XVI.

Washington agreed with Jefferson that treaty obligations must be met. Yet while he continued to make payments on America's war debt to France, he refused to commit the United States to support the French Republic. On April 22, 1793, he issued a proclamation of neutrality, stating that the "conduct" of the United States would be "friendly and impartial toward the belligerent powers."

1793 and 1794: Years of Crisis

During 1793 and 1794 a series of explosive new controversies further divided the followers of Hamilton and Jefferson. Washington's administration confronted a French effort to entangle America in its war with England, armed rebellion in western Pennsylvania, Indian uprisings, and the threat of war with Britain. These controversies intensified party spirit and promoted an increase in voting along party lines in Congress.

Citizen Genêt Affair

In April 1793, "Citizen" Edmond Charles Genêt, minister of the French Republic, disembarked at Charleston, South Carolina. His mission was to persuade American citizens to join in France's "war of all peoples against all kings." As he proceeded up the coast, the French minister passed out military commissions and privateering letters authorizing Americans to attack British commercial vessels. He purchased armed vessels to attack British shipping. He set up courts to condemn British ships captured by Americans. He even persuaded a group of western frontiersmen to attack Spanish New Orleans. Wherever he traveled, crowds gathered and cheered.

Washington was not impressed. He did not think Genêt had any right to involve American citizens in European disputes. Although he accorded the French minister formal diplomatic recognition, he demanded that France recall him. Jefferson, who had once been friendly with Genêt, agreed, describing the Frenchman as "hot headed, all imagination, no judgment."

Genêt quickly faded from the scene (in fact he became the first foreigner to be granted po-

President Washington is reviewing the troops at Fort Cumberland, Maryland. These troops formed part of the force of 15,000 militiamen Washington assembled to disperse the Whiskey Rebellion in western Pennsylvania, a protest against the whiskey excise tax.

litical asylum in the United States because his political faction was overturned by one yet more radical). His brief flurry did have an important effect—it intensified party feeling. Citizens, in states from Vermont to South Carolina, organized Democratic-Republican clubs to celebrate the triumphs of the French Revolution. Hamilton suspected that these societies really existed to stir up grass-roots opposition to the Washington administration. Jefferson hotly denied these accusations, but the practical consequence was to further divide followers of Hamilton and Jefferson.

Whiskey Rebellion

Political polarization was further intensified by the outbreak of popular protests in western Pennsylvania against Hamilton's financial program. To help fund the nation's war debt, Congress in 1791 passed Hamilton's proposal for a whiskey excise tax. Frontier farmers objected to the tax on whiskey as unfair. On the frontier, because of high transportation costs, the only practical way to sell surplus corn was to distill it into whiskey. Thus, frontier farmers regarded a tax on whiskey in the same way as American colonists had regarded Britain's stamp tax.

By 1794, western Pennsylvanians had had enough. Like the Shaysites of 1786, they rose up in defense of their property and the fundamental right to earn a decent living unfettered by oppressive taxes. Tax collectors were met with muskets and tarred and feathered. Frontiersmen organized a march on Pittsburgh, and 7000 westerners participated in this demonstration of unity. With that, the whiskey "rebels" dispersed, having shown that they could stop collection of the tax.

Before the march on Pittsburgh took place, Washington ordered Pennsylvania and surrounding states to send 15,000 militiamen to Harrisburg, where, dressed in full military regalia, he greeted them. Washington agreed to send troops to create a precedent for the federal government's authority. He ordered the troops to disperse the rebels, but by the time the army crossed the mountains, the uprising was over. The army did round up a few leaders, but the president later pardoned the two men convicted of treason. The new government had proved to the nation that it would enforce laws enacted by Congress.

Thomas Jefferson, who had resigned as secretary of state in 1793, viewed the Whiskey Rebellion from quite a different perspective. He saw the fiendish hand of Hamilton in putting down what he called a rebellion that "could never be found." Hamilton had "pronounced and proclaimed and armed against" the people for the sheer pleasure of suppressing liberties. And further, Jefferson claimed, Hamilton had done so because westerners no longer supported Washington's administration. He had used the army to stifle legitimate opposition to unfair government policies.

The Continuing Threat from Britain

The year 1794—the year of the Whiskey Rebellion—also brought a crisis in America's relations with Britain. For a decade, Britain had refused to evacuate forts in the Old Northwest as promised in the treaty ending the Revolution. Control of those forts impeded white settlement of the Great Lakes region and allowed the British to monopolize the fur trade. Frontiersmen believed that British officials at those posts sold firearms to the Indians and incited uprisings against white settlers. American resentment grew when the British governor-general of Canada told a delegation of western Indians that Britain would soon join them in a war against the United States. War appeared imminent when British warships stopped 300 American ships carrying food supplies to France and to France's overseas possessions, seized their cargoes, and forced seamen suspected of deserting from British ships into the British navy.

Washington acted decisively to end the crisis. He first moved to end the Indian threat. He called upon Anthony Wayne, an outstanding

Revolutionary War general, to clear the Ohio country of Indians. On August 20, 1794, Wayne's soldiers overwhelmed the resisting Indians at the Battle of Fallen Timbers in northwestern Ohio, after destroying every Indian village on the way to the battle. During the summer of 1795, Wayne met with representatives of the Miami Confederacy and negotiated the Treaty of Greenville. Under this agreement, Native Americans ceded much of the present state of

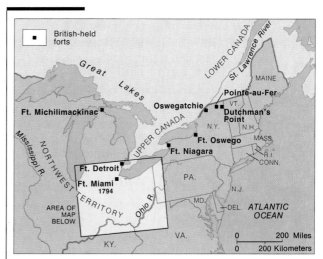

British Posts and Indian Battles

Because Americans still felt threatened by the continuing British refusal to evacuate forts and by Indian uprisings in the Northwest, John Jay, the first chief justice of the United States, was sent to negotiate a treaty with Great Britain.

Ohio in return for cash, presents, and a promise that the federal government would treat the Indian nations fairly in land dealings.

The president next sent Chief Justice John Jay to London to seek a negotiated settlement with the British. The United States's strongest bargaining chip was a threat to join an alliance of European trading nations to resist British trade restrictions. Alexander Hamilton may have undercut Jay by secretly informing the British minister that the United States would not join the alliance.

Jay secured the best agreement he could and achieved two American aims. Armed with the knowledge of Wayne's victory at Fallen Timbers, he persuaded Britain to evacuate its forts on American soil. Jay also got the British negotiators to agree to cease harassing American shipping (provided the ships did not carry contraband to Britain's enemies). Britain additionally agreed to pay damages for the ships it had seized and to permit the United States to trade with India and to carry on restricted trade with the British West Indies. But Jay failed to win concessions on a host of other American grievances. The treaty said nothing at all about British incitement of the Indians, British searching of American ships for escaping deserters, or compensation for slaves carried off by the British army during the Revolution.

As a result of the debate over Jay's Treaty, the first party system fully emerged. Publication of the terms of the treaty unleashed a storm of protest from the emerging Jeffersonian Republicans. Republican newspapers and pamphlets denounced the treaty as craven submission to British imperial power and as a sop to wealthy commercial, shipping, and trading interests. Southerners were particularly vocal in their disapproval because the treaty required them to repay prerevolutionary debts owed to British merchants, while northern shipping interests collected damages for ships and cargoes that had been seized. Republicans in Philadelphia carried an effigy of the chief justice through the streets, guillotined it, and blew it up with gunpowder. In the same city, a crowd broke windows at the British embassy, and in New York a mob pelted Alexander Hamilton with stones. In Boston, graffiti appeared on a wall: "Damn John Jay! Damn everyone who won't damn John Jay!!

Angry Republicans denounced John Jay's treaty as submission to British power and hanged his effigy in Charleston, South Carolina.

Damn everyone that won't put lights in his windows and sit up all night damning John Jay!!!" Washington declared that public unrest was greater "than it has been at any period since the Revolution."

Washington called a special session of the Senate to study the treaty. By exactly the two-thirds majority required by the Constitution, the Federalist-controlled Senate approved the treaty, with the exception of a single section restricting American trade with the British West Indies.

Undecided whether to sign the treaty, Washington learned that the British had captured French diplomatic messages that indicated that Secretary of State Edmund Randolph had divulged state secrets to the French. At a cabinet meeting, Washington forced Randolph to read the dispatches and provide an explanation of his conduct. The embarrassed Randolph denied any guilt, but resigned. Washington, fearful that the French government was trying to transform the United States into a French satellite, signed the treaty.

Washington never anticipated the wave of

outrage that greeted his decision. Republicans accused him of forming an Anglo-American alliance, and they made his last years in office miserable by attacking him for conducting himself like a "tyrant." Benjamin Franklin's grandson called the president a dictator: "If ever a nation was debauched by a man, the American Nation has been debauched by Washington . . . . If ever a nation has been deceived by a man, the American Nation has been deceived by Washington." It was even suggested that he should be impeached because he had overdrawn his $25,000 salary. Privately, Washington complained that he was being compared to the Roman emperor "Nero" and to a "common pickpocket."

Republicans sought to kill the treaty in the House of Representatives by refusing to appropriate the funds necessary to carry out the treaty's terms unless the president submitted all documents relating to the treaty negotiations. Washington refused to comply with the House's request for information, thereby establishing the principle of executive privilege. This precedent gives the chief executive authority to withhold information from Congress on grounds of national security. In the end, fear that rejection of the Jay Treaty would result in disunion or war convinced the House to approve the needed appropriations.

Washington's popularity returned within a few months when he was able to announce that a treaty had been negotiated with Spain opening up the Mississippi River to American trade. Spain, fearing joint British and American action against her American colonies, recognized the Mississippi River as the new nation's western boundary and the 31st parallel (the northern border of Florida) as America's southern boundary. Pinckney's Treaty (1795)—also known as the Treaty of San Lorenzo—also granted Americans the right to navigate the Mississippi River as well as the right to export goods, duty free, through New Orleans, which was still a Spanish city.

Washington Decides to Retire

President Washington was now in a position to retire gracefully. He had avoided war, crushed the Indians, pushed the British out of western forts, established trade with selected parts of Asia, and opened the Northwest Territory to settlement. He had even reached agreement with North African pirates to release American prisoners and let American ships alone.

In a farewell address, published in a Philadelphia newspaper in September 1796, Washington announced his retirement and offered his countrymen "the disinterested warnings of a parting friend." He warned his countrymen against the growth of partisan divisions. In foreign affairs, he warned against long-term alliances. Declaring the "primary interests" of America and Europe to be fundamentally different, he argued that "it is our true policy to steer clear of permanent alliance with any portion of the foreign world."

A NEW PRESIDENT AND NEW CHALLENGES

Washington's decision to retire set the stage for one of the most critical presidential elections in American history. The election of 1796 was the first in which voters could choose between competing political parties; it was also the first election in which candidates were nominated for the vice presidency. It was a critical test of whether the nation could transfer power through a contested election.

The Federalists chose John Adams, the first vice president, as their presidential candidate, and the Republicans selected Thomas Jefferson. In an effort to attract southern support, the Federalists named Thomas Pinckney of South Carolina as Adams's running mate. The Republicans, hopeful of attracting votes in New York and New England, chose Aaron Burr of New York as their vice presidential nominee.

John Adams was elected the second president of the United States by only three electoral votes. During his presidency, he strengthened the military and averted war with France.

Both parties turned directly to the people for support, rallying supporters through the use of posters, handbills, and mass rallies. Republicans portrayed their candidate as "a firm Republican" while they depicted his opponent as "the champion of rank, titles, and hereditary distinctions." Federalists countered by condemning Jefferson as the leader of a "French faction" intent on undermining religion and morality.

For the first time in American history, the mass of people became directly involved in a presidential election—a development illustrated by an incident that took place in New York City in early November 1795. A prominent Federalist alderman ordered two Irish boatmen to take him across the East River from Brooklyn to Manhattan. When the boatmen refused, the alderman had the "impudent rascals" arrested, locked in a local jail, and tried without a jury and without being allowed to testify in their own behalf. They were found guilty of "insulting a magistrate" and sentenced to two months of hard labor.

Jeffersonians quickly seized upon this incident as a way of generating support among the laboring classes in the election of 1796. New York Republicans demanded that the state legislature remove the alderman from office for oppressing the "innocent poor." When the legislature refused to act, a Republican attorney named William Keteltas attacked the Federalist-controlled legislature for "the most flagrant abuse of rights." The legislature found the Republican attorney guilty of contempt and jailed him for more than a month when he refused to apologize. To protest the legislature's actions, the Republican party assembled the largest crowd that had ever gathered in New York City—2000 people. When Keteltas was finally released from prison, another large Republican crowd that included many poor craftsmen drove him through the city's streets in a carriage decorated with a French and an American flag, a picture of a man being whipped, and a banner stating ironically: "What you rascal, insult your superiors." Such events dramatized the differences between the two parties and actively involved large numbers of people in the election.

In the popular voting, Federalists drew support from New England; commercial, shipping, manufacturing, and banking interests; Congregational and Episcopalian clergy; professionals; and farmers who produced for markets. Republicans attracted votes from the South and from smaller planters; backcountry Baptists, Methodists, and Roman Catholics; small merchants, tradesmen, and craftsmen; and subsistence farmers.

John Adams won the election, despite backstage maneuvering by Alexander Hamilton against him. Hamilton disliked Adams (he declared that Adams had "disgusting egotism" and an "ungovernable indiscretion of . . . temper") and wanted a president with whom he was more compatible. He developed a complicated scheme to elect Thomas Pinckney, the Federalist candidate for vice president. Under the electoral system originally set up by the Constitution, each presidential elector was allowed to vote twice, with the candidate who received the most votes becoming president, while the candidate who came in second was elected vice president. According to Hamilton's plan, southern electors would drop Adams's name from their ballots, while still voting for Pinckney. Thus Pinckney would receive more votes than Adams and be elected president. When New Englanders learned of this plan, they dropped Pinckney from their ballots, ensuring that Adams won the election. When the final votes were tallied, Adams received 71 votes, only 3 more than Jefferson. As a result, Jefferson became vice president.

The Presidency of John Adams

The new president was a 61-year-old Harvard-educated lawyer who had been an early leader in the struggle for independence. As a delegate to the First and Second Continental Congress, Adams had nominated George Washington to command the Continental Army and served on the five-member committee that drafted the Declaration of Independence. Between 1778 and 1788, he represented the United States as a diplomat in France, Holland, and Britain and helped negotiate the Treaty of Paris ending the Revolution. Short, bald, overweight, and vain (he was known, behind his back, as "His Ro-

Abigail Adams supervises the work of a maidservant hanging laundry in the East Room of the White House.

tundity"), Adams found the vice presidency extremely frustrating. He complained to his wife Abigail: "My country has contrived for me the most insignificant office that ever the invention of man contrived or his imagination conceived."

His presidency also proved frustrating. He had failed to win a decisive electoral mandate and was saddled with the opposition leader as his vice president. He faced intense opposition within his own party and continuing problems from France throughout his four years in office. He avoided outright war with France, but he destroyed his political career. He suggested for his epitaph: "Here lies John Adams, who took upon himself the responsibility of the peace with France, in the year 1800."

A New National Capital

John Adams was the first president to live in what would later be called the White House. In 1800 the national capital moved to Washington, D.C., from Philadelphia (in 1790, it had moved to Philadelphia from New York). When Adams moved into the unfinished executive mansion,

just 6 of the structure's 30 rooms were plastered; the main staircases were not installed for another four years. The mansion's grounds were cluttered with workers' shanties, privies, and stagnant pools of water. The president's wife, Abigail, hung laundry to dry in the East Room.

The nation's Capitol was also uncompleted. Construction of the building's central portion had not even begun. All that stood were the House and Senate wings connected by a covered boardwalk.

The city of Washington consisted of a brewery, a half-finished hotel, an abandoned canal, an empty warehouse and wharf, and 372 "habitable" dwellings, "most of them small miserable huts." Cows and hogs ran freely in the capital's streets, and snakes frequented the city's many bogs and marshes. A bridge, supported by an arch of 13 stones—symbolizing the first 13 states—had collapsed. The entire population consisted of 500 families and some 300 members of government. A vistor saw "no fences, gardens, nor the least appearance of business." Lacking any diversions or sources of entertainment, members of Congress referred to themselves as "monks in a monastery."

The Quasi-War with France

A decade after the Constitution was written, the United States faced its most serious international crisis: an undeclared naval war with France. In the Jay Treaty, France perceived an American tilt toward Britain, especially in the provision permitting the British to seize French goods from American ships in exchange for financial compensation. France retaliated by launching an aggressive campaign against American shipping, particularly in the West Indies, capturing hundreds of vessels flying the United States flag.

Adams attempted to negotiate with France, but the French government refused to receive the American envoy and suspended commercial relations. Adams then called Congress into special session. Determined not to permit the United States to be "humiliated under a colonial spirit of fear and a sense of inferiority," he recommended that Congress arm American merchant ships, purchase new naval vessels, fortify harbors, and expand the artillery and cavalry.

To pay for the increased defense spending, Adams asked Congress to enact a land tax, a tax on houses (popularly known as the "window tax"), a stamp tax, and a tax on slaves. Finally, the president told Congress that the best way for the country to protect its neutral rights was to threaten to join with other neutral states in a defensive naval alliance. By a single vote, a bitterly divided House of Representatives authorized the president to arm American merchant ships, but it postponed consideration of the other defense measures.

Adams then sent three commissioners to France to try to negotiate a settlement. Charles Maurice de Talleyrand, the French foreign minister, continually postponed official negotiations. In the meantime, three emissaries of the French minister (known later simply as X, Y, and Z) said that the only way the Americans could see the minister was to pay a bribe of $250,000 and provide a $10 million loan. "It is expected that you will offer money," an agent of the French government told them. "What is your answer?" "It is no; no; no," one of the American negotiators said. "Not a sixpence!"

Word of this incident, known as the XYZ affair, aroused a popular demand for war. The popular slogan was "millions for defense, but not one cent for tribute." The Federalist-controlled Congress authorized a standing army of 20,000 troops, a 30,000 man reserve army, and created the nation's first navy department. It also unilaterally abrogated America's 1778 treaty with France.

Adams named George Washington commanding general of the United States army, and, at Washington's insistence, designated Alexander Hamilton second in command. During the winter of 1798, 14 American warships backed by some 200 armed merchant ships captured some 80 French vessels and forced French warships out of American waters and back to bases in the West Indies. But the president refused to ask Congress for an official declaration of war. This is why this conflict is known as the quasi-war.

Despite intense pressure to declare war against France or to seize territory belonging to France's ally Spain, President Adams succeeded in averting full-scale war and achieving a peaceful settlement. Early in 1799, with the backing of moderate Federalists and Republicans, Adams proposed reestablishing diplomatic relations with France. When more extreme Federalists refused to go along with the plan, Adams threatened to resign and leave the presidency in the hands of Vice President Jefferson.

In 1800, after seven months of wearisome negotiations, negotiators worked out an agreement known as the Convention of 1800. The agreement freed the United States from its alliance with France; in exchange, America forgave $20 million in damages caused by the illegal seizure of American merchant ships during the 1790s.

Adams kept the peace, but at the cost of a second term as president. The more extreme Federalists reacted furiously to the negotiated settlement. Hamilton vowed to destroy Adams: "If we must have an enemy at the head of Government, let it be one whom we can oppose, and for whom we are not responsible."

The Alien and Sedition Acts

During the quasi-war, the Federalist-controlled Congress attempted to suppress political opposition and stamp out sympathy for revolutionary France by enacting four laws in 1798 known as the Alien and Sedition acts. The first law, the Naturalization Act, lengthened the period necessary before immigrants could receive citizenship from 5 to 14 years. The second law was the Alien Act, which gave the president the power to imprison or deport any foreigner believed to be dangerous to the United States. The next law, the Alien Enemies Act, allowed the president to deport enemy aliens in time of war. And finally, the Sedition Act made it a crime to attack the government with "false, scandalous, or malicious" statements or writings. Adams, bitterly unhappy with the "spirit of falsehood and malignity" that threatened to undermine loyalty to the government, signed the measures.

The Alien acts were so broadly written that hundreds of foreign refugees—French intellectuals, Irish nationalists, and English radicals—fled to Europe fearing detention. But it was the Sedition Act that produced the greatest fear within the Republican opposition. Federalist prosecutors and judges used the Sedition Act to attack leading Republican newspapers, securing indictments against 25 people, mainly Republican editors and printers. Ten people were eventually convicted, one a Republican Representative from Vermont.

One of the most notorious uses of the law to suppress dissent took place in July 1798. Luther Baldwin, the pilot of a garbage scow, was arrested in a Newark, New Jersey, tavern for criminal sedition. While cannons roared through Newark's streets to celebrate a presidential visit to the city, Baldwin was overheard saying "that he did not care if they fired through [the president's] arse." For his drunken remark, Baldwin was arrested, locked up for two months, and fined.

Republicans accused the Federalists of conspiring to subvert fundamental liberties. In Virginia, the state legislature adopted a resolution written by James Madison that advanced the idea that states have the right to determine the constitutionality of federal law, and pronounced the Alien and Sedition acts unconstitutional. Kentucky's state legislature went even further, adopting a resolution written by Thomas Jefferson that declared the Alien and Sedition acts "void and of no force." The Kentucky resolution raised an issue that would grow increasingly important in American politics in the years before the Civil War: Did states have the power to declare acts of Congress null and void? In 1799, however, no other states were willing to go as far as Kentucky and Virginia.

With the Union in danger, violence erupted. In the spring of 1799, resentment against the window tax provoked German settlers in eastern Pennsylvania to defy federal tax collectors. President Adams called out federal troops to suppress the so-called Fries Rebellion. The

In the early days of the Republic, political dissent sometimes escalated into physical violence. This fight between Republican Matthew Lyon and Federalist Roger Griswold took place on the floor of Congress on February 15, 1798. Lyon was later arrested for violating the Sedition Act by publishing a letter attacking the government in his newspaper.

leader of the rebellion, an auctioneer named John Fries, was captured, convicted of treason, and sentenced to be hanged. Adams followed Washington's example in the Whiskey Rebellion and pardoned Fries, but Republicans feared that the Federalists were prepared to use the nation's army to suppress dissent.

THE REVOLUTION OF 1800

In 1800, the young republic faced another critical test: Could national leadership pass peacefully from one political party to another? Once again, the nation had a choice between John Adams and Thomas Jefferson. But this election was more than a contest between two men; it was also a real party contest for control of the national government. Deep substantive and ideological issues divided the two parties and partisan feelings ran deep. Federalists feared that Jefferson would reverse all the accomplishments of the preceding 12 years. A Republican president, they thought, would overthrow the Constitution by returning power to the states, dismantling the army and navy, and overturning Hamilton's financial system.

The Republicans charged that the Federalists, by creating a large standing army, imposing heavy taxes, and using federal troops and the federal courts to suppress dissent, had shown contempt for the liberties of the American people. They worried that the Federalists' ultimate goal was to centralize power in the national government and involve the United States in the European war on the side of Britain.

The contest was one of the most vigorous in American history and emotions ran high. Jefferson's Federalist opponents called him an "atheist in religion, and a fanatic in politics." They claimed he was a drunkard, an enemy of religion, and the father of numerous mulatto children. Timothy Dwight, the president of Yale, predicted that a Jefferson administration would see "our wives and daughters the victims of legal prostitution; soberly dishonored; speciously polluted." The Federalist *Connecticut Courant* warned that "there is scarcely a possibility that we shall escape a Civil War. Murder, robbery,

rape, adultery, and incest will be openly taught and practiced."

Jefferson's supporters responded by charging that President Adams was a warmonger, a spendthrift, and a monarchist who longed to reunite Britain with its former colonies. Republicans even claimed that the president had sent General Thomas Pinckney to England to procure four mistresses, two for himself and two for Adams. Adams's response: "I do declare if this be true, General Pinckney has kept them all for himself and cheated me out of my two."

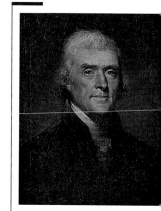

Thomas Jefferson described his election as president in 1800 as a "revolution." His goal was to reverse the centralizing policies of the Federalists.

The election was extremely close. The Federalists won all of New England's electoral votes, while the Republicans dominated the South and West. The final outcome hinged on the results in New York. Rural New York supported the Federalists, and Republican fortunes therefore depended on the voting in New York City. There, Jefferson's running mate, Aaron Burr, had created the most successful political organization the country had yet seen. Burr organized rallies, established ward committees, and promoted loyal supporters for public office. Burr's efforts paid off; Republicans won a majority in New York's legislature, which gave the state's 12 electoral votes to Jefferson and Burr. Declared one Republican: The election "has been conducted . . . in so miraculous a manner that I cannot account for it but from the inter-

TABLE 7.1		
Election of 1800		
Candidate	*Party*	*Electoral Vote*
Jefferson	Republican	73
J. Adams	Federalist	65

CHRONOLOGY
OF KEY EVENTS

1789 First session of Congress meets; Electoral College names George Washington the first president; Washington selects the first cabinet; Federal Judiciary Act establishes federal court system; French Revolution begins

1790 Congress adopts Hamilton's proposal to fund the national debt at full value and to assume all state debts from the Revolutionary War

1791 Bank of the United States is established; Congress adopts an excise tax on distilled liquors; the Bill of Rights becomes part of the Constitution

1793 King Louis XVI of France is beheaded and war breaks out in Europe; Washington issues the Proclamation of Neutrality; Citizen Genêt affair

1794 Jay's Treaty with Britain; Whiskey Rebellion in western Pennsylvania; General Anthony Wayne defeats an Indian alliance at the Battle of Fallen Timbers in Ohio

1795 Treaty of Greenville opens Ohio to white settlement; Pinckney's Treaty is negotiated with Spain

1796 Washington issues Farewell Address warning against political factionalism and foreign entanglements

1797 John Adams is inaugurated as second president

1798 Adams reports XYZ Affair to Congress; undeclared naval war with France begins; Alien and Sedition acts give the president the power to imprison or deport dangerous foreigners and make it a crime to attack the government with "malicious" statements or writings; Virginia and Kentucky resolutions, drawn up by Jefferson and Madison, declare the Alien and Sedition acts unconstitutional

1800 Washington, D.C., replaces Philadelphia as the nation's capital; Convention of 1800 supplants treaties of 1778 with France

1801 House of Representatives elects Thomas Jefferson as third president

---

vention of a Supreme Power and our friend Burr the agent."

Jefferson appeared to have won by a margin of eight electoral votes. But a complication soon arose. Because each Republican elector had cast one ballot for Jefferson and one for Burr, the two men received exactly the same number of electoral votes.

Under the Constitution, the election was now thrown into the Federalist-controlled House of Representatives. Instead of emphatically declaring that he would not accept the presidency, Burr refused to say anything, spending the crucial weeks between early December, when the tie became known, and mid-

February, when the issue was finally resolved, in Albany, New York. So the Federalists faced a choice. They could help elect Jefferson—whom they had called "a brandy-soaked defamer of churches," "a contemptible hypocrite"—or they could throw their support to Burr—considered by Federalists to be "a profligate," "a voluptuary." Hamilton disliked Jefferson, but he believed he was a far more honorable man than Burr, whose "public principles have no other spring or aim than his own aggrandizement." Most other Federalists supported the New Yorker.

As the stalemate persisted, Virginia and Pennsylvania mobilized their state militias. Recognizing "the certainty that a legislative usurpation would be resisted by arms," as Jefferson noted, the Federalists finally backed down. On February 17, 1801, after six days of balloting and 36 ballots, the House of Representatives finally elected Thomas Jefferson the third president of the United States. And as a result of the election, Congress adopted the Twelfth Amendment to the Constitution, which gives each elector in the Electoral College one vote for president and one for vice president.

CONCLUSION

Between two and three in the morning, December 13, 1799, George Washington woke his wife, complaining of severe pains. Martha Washington called for an overseer, who inserted a lancet in the former president's arm and drew blood. Over the course of that day and the next, doctors arrived and attempted to ease General Washington's pain by applying blisters, administering purges, and additional bloodletting—altogether removing perhaps four pints of Washington's blood. Medical historians generally agree that Washington needed a tracheotomy (a surgical operation into the air passages), but this was too new a technique to be risked on the former president, who died on December 14.

During the early weeks of 1800, every city in the United States commemorated the death of the former leader. In Philadelphia, an empty coffin, a riderless horse, and a funeral cortege moved through the city streets. In Boston, business was suspended, cannons roared, bells pealed, and 6000 people—a fifth of the city's population—stood in the streets to express their last respects for the fallen general. In Washington, Richard Henry Lee delivered the most famous eulogy: "First in war, first in peace, and first in the hearts of his countrymen."

In 1789, it was an open question whether the Constitution was a workable plan of government. It was still unclear whether the new nation could establish a strong and vigorous national government or win the respect of foreign nations. For a decade, the new nation battled threats to its existence. It faced bitter party conflict, threats of secession, and foreign interference with American shipping and commerce.

By any standard, the new nation's achievements were impressive. During the first decade under the Constitution, the country adopted a bill of rights, protecting the rights of the individual against the power of the central and state governments; enacted a financial program that secured the government's credit and stimulated the economy; and created the first political parties that directly involved the enfranchised segment of the population in national politics. In the face of intense partisan conflict, the United States became the first nation to peacefully transfer political power from one party to another as a result of an election. A nation, strong and viable, had emerged from its baptism by fire.

SUGGESTIONS FOR FURTHER READING

OVERVIEWS AND SURVEYS

Jacob E. Cooke, "The Federalist Age: A Reappraisal," in George A. Billias and Gerald N. Grob, eds., *American History: Retrospect and Prospect* (1971); John R. Howe, *From the Revolution Through the Age of Jackson* (1973); Seymour M. Lipset, *The First New Nation: The United States in Perspective* (1963); John C. Miller, *The Federalist Era, 1789–1801* (1960); Robert E. Shalhope, *The Roots of Democracy: American Thought and Culture, 1760–1800* (1990).

PUTTING THE NEW NATIONAL GOVERNMENT INTO OPERATION

Margo J. Anderson, *The American Census: A Social History* (1988); Richard R. Beeman, *The Old Dominion and the New Nation, 1788–1801* (1972); Thomas E. Cronin, ed., *Inventing the American Presidency* (1989); Noble Cunningham, Jr., *The United States in 1800: Henry Adams Revisited* (1988); Richard H. Kohn, *Eagle and Sword: The Federalists and the Creation of the Military Establishment in America, 1783–1802* (1975); Forrest McDonald, *The Presidency of George Washington* (1974); Carl Prince, *The Federalists and the Origins of the U.S. Civil Service* (1977); Robert A. Rutland, *The Birth of the Bill of Rights, 1776–1791* (1955); Barry Schwartz, *George Washington: The Making of an American Symbol* (1987); Bernard Schwartz, *The Great Rights of Mankind: A History of the American Bill of Rights* (1977); Gerald Stourzh, *Alexander Hamilton and the Idea of Republican Government* (1970); Leonard D. White, *The Federalists: A Study in Administrative History* (1948).

THE BIRTH OF POLITICAL PARTIES

Harry Ammon, *The Genet Mission* (1973); Joyce Appleby, *Capitalism and a New Social Order: The Republican Vision of the 1790s* (1984); James M. Banner, *To the Hartford Convention: The Federalists and the Origins of Party Politics in Massachusetts, 1789–1815* (1970); Lance Banning, *The Jeffersonian Persuasion* (1978); Richard Beeman, *The Old Dominion and the New Nation, 1788–1801* (1972); Samuel Flagg Bemis, *Jay's Treaty* (1923), and *Pinckney's Treaty* (1926); Steven R. Boyd, ed., *The Whiskey Rebellion* (1985); Richard Buel, Jr., *Securing the Revolution: Ideology in American Politics, 1789–1815* (1972); William N. Chambers, *Political Parties in a New Nation* (1963); Joseph Charles, *The Origins of the American Party System* (1956); Jerald A. Combs, *The Jay Treaty* (1970); Noble E. Cunningham, Jr., *The Jeffersonian Republicans: The Formation of Party Organization, 1789–1801* (1957); David Brion Davis, *Revolutions: Reflections on American Equality and Foreign Liberations* (1990); Alexander De Conde, *Entangling Alliance: Politics and Diplomacy under George Washington* (1958); Felix Gilbert, *To the Farewell Address* (1961); Paul Goodman, *The Democratic-Republicans of Massachusetts* (1964); Sanford W. Higginbotham, *The Keystone in the Democratic Arch: Pennsylvania Politics, 1800–1816* (1952); John F. Hoadley, *Origins of American Political Parties, 1789–1803* (1986); Richard Hofstadter, *The Idea of a Party System: The Rise of Legitimate Opposition in the United States, 1780–1840* (1969); Lawrence S. Kaplan, *Jefferson and France: An Essay on Politics and Political Ideas* (1967); Eugene P. Link, *Democratic-Republican Societies, 1790–1800* (1942); Gilbert L. Lycan, *Alexander Hamilton and American Foreign Policy: A Design for Greatness* (1970); Carl E. Prince, *New Jersey's Jeffersonian Republicans* (1967); Norman Risjord, *Chesapeake Politics, 1781–1800* (1978); Arthur M. Schlesinger, Jr., ed., *History of United States Political Parties, Volume I: 1798–1860: From Factions to Parties* (1973); Bernard Schwartz, *The Great Rights of Mankind: A History of the American Bill of Rights* (1977); Louis M. Sears, *George Washington and the French Revolution* (1960); Thomas P. Slaughter, *The Whiskey Rebellion* (1986); James Morton Smith, *Freedom's Fetters: The Alien and Sedition Laws and American Civil Liberties* (1956); Paul A. Varg, *Foreign Policies of the Founding Fathers* (1963); Patricia Watlington, *The Partisan Spirit* (1972); Alfred F. Young, *The Democratic Republicans of New York* (1967); John Zvesper, *Political Philosophy and Rhetoric: A Study of the Origins of American Party Politics* (1977).

A NEW PRESIDENT AND NEW CHALLENGES

Ralph Adams Brown, *The Presidency of John Adams* (1975); Manning J. Dauer, *The Adams Federalists* (1953); Alexander De Conde, *The Quasi-War: Politics and Diplomacy of the Undeclared War with France, 1797–1801* (1966); John R. Howe, *The Changing Political Thought of John Adams* (1966); Lawrence S. Kaplan, *Colonies into Nation: American Diplomacy, 1763–1801* (1972); Stephen G. Kurtz, *The Presidency of John Adams: The Collapse of Federalism, 1795–1800* (1957); Leonard W. Levy, *Legacy of Suppression: Freedom of Speech and Press in Early American History* (1960); John C. Miller, *Crisis in Freedom: The Alien and Sedition Acts* (1951); John R. Nelson, *Liberty and Property: Political Economy and Policymaking in the New Nation* (1987); Bradford Perkins, *The First Rapprochement: England and the United States, 1795–1805* (1955); Peter Shaw, *The Character of John Adams* (1976); William Stinchcombe, *The XYZ Affair* (1980).

THE REVOLUTION OF 1800

David Hackett Fischer, *The Revolution of American Conservatism: The Federalist Party in the Era of Jeffersonian Democracy* (1965); Robert M. Johnstone, Jr., *Jefferson and the Presidency: Leadership in the Young Republic* (1978); Linda K. Kerber, *Federalists in Dissent* (1970); A. M. Schlesinger, Jr., and Fred L. Israel, eds., *History of American Presidential Elections, 1789–1968* (1971); Daniel Sisson, *The American Revolution of 1800* (1974).

BIOGRAPHIES

Charles Akers, *Abigail Adams: An American Woman* (1980); Irving Brant, *James Madison*, 6 vols. (1941–1961); Fawn M. Brodie, *Thomas Jefferson: An Intimate History* (1974); Jacob Ernest Cooke, *Alexander Hamilton* (1982); Marcus Cunliffe, *George Washington: Man and Monument* (1958); Noble E. Cunningham, Jr., *In Pursuit of Reason: The Life of Thomas Jefferson* (1987); James Thomas Flexner, *George Washington*, 4 vols. (1965–1972); Douglas Southall Freeman, *George Washington: A Biography*, 7 vols. (1948–1957); Ralph Ketcham, *James Madison* (1971); Phyllis Lee Levin, *Abigail Adams* (1987); Milton Lomask, *Aaron Burr*, 2 vols. (1979–1982); Dumas Malone, *Jefferson and His Time*, 6 vols. (1948–1981); John C. Miller, *Alexander Hamilton* (1959); Broadus Mitchell, *Alexander Hamilton*, 2 vols. (1957–1962); Merrill Peterson, *The Jefferson Image in the American Mind* (1960), and *Thomas Jefferson and the New Nation* (1970); Lynne Withey, *Dearest Friend: A Life of Abigail Adams* (1981).

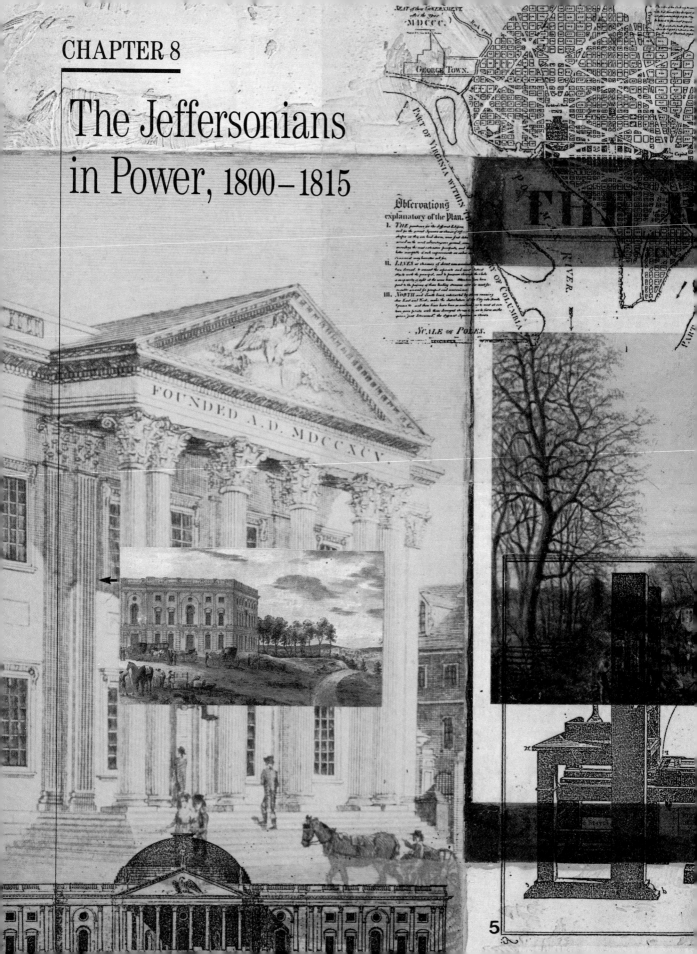

The Jeffersonians in Power, 1800–1815

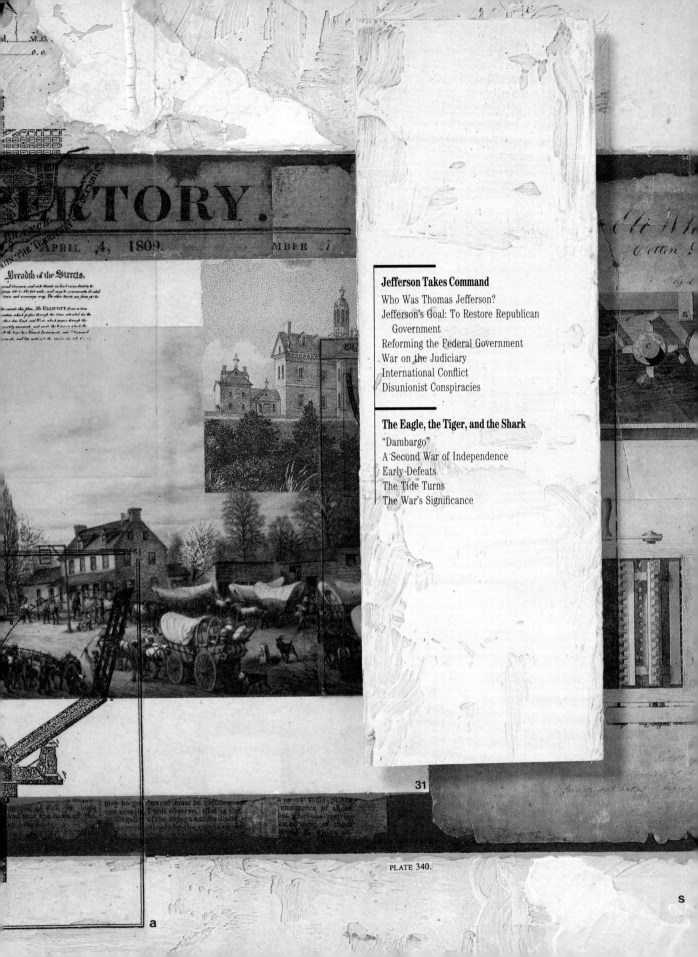

31

PLATE 340.

a

S

On the morning of June 18, 1804, a visitor handed a package to the former treasury secretary Alexander Hamilton. Inside was a newspaper clipping and a terse three-sentence letter. The clipping said that Hamilton had called Vice President Aaron Burr "a dangerous man, and one who ought not to be trusted with the reins of government." It went on to say that Hamilton had "expressed" a "still more despicable opinion" of Burr—apparently a bitter personal attack on Burr's public and private morality, not merely a political criticism. The letter, signed by Burr, demanded a "prompt and unqualified" denial or an immediate apology.

Hamilton and Burr had sparred verbally for decades. Hamilton regarded Burr as an unscrupulous man and considered him partly responsible for a duel in 1801 that had left his son Philip dead. Burr, in turn, blamed Hamilton for his defeat in the race for governor of New York earlier in the year. When, after three weeks, Hamilton had failed to respond to his letter satisfactorily, Burr insisted that they settle the dispute according to the code of honor.

Shortly after 7 o'clock on the morning of July 11, 1804, Burr and Hamilton met on the wooded heights of Weehawken, New Jersey, a customary dueling ground directly across the Hudson River from New York. It was the exact spot where Hamilton's eldest son Philip had died.

Hamilton's second handed Burr one of two pistols equipped with hair-spring triggers. After he and Burr took their positions ten paces apart, Hamilton raised his pistol on the command to "Present!" and fired. His shot struck a tree a few feet to Burr's side. Then Burr fired. His shot struck Hamilton in the right side and passed through his liver. Gravely wounded, Hamilton was taken back to New York City, where he survived in intense pain for 36 hours. About 2 o'clock in the afternoon of July 12, he died.

The popular view was that Hamilton had intentionally fired to one side, while Burr had slain the Federalist leader in an act of cold-blooded murder. A popular poem conveyed the conventional wisdom:

In 1800, Burr ran as Jefferson's vice-presidential candidate. Burr's effective campaigning tactics and efficient political machine in New York helped bring victory to the Republican party.

Oh Burr, oh Burr, what hast thou done,
Thou has shooted dead great Hamilton!
You hid behind a bunch of thistle,
And shooted him dead with a great hoss pistol!

In fact, historians do not know whether Burr was guilty of willful murder. Burr had no way of knowing whether Hamilton had purposely missed. Hamilton, after all, had accepted the challenge, raised his pistol, and fired. According to the code of honor, if Burr missed on his first try, Hamilton would have a second chance to shoot.

The states of New York and New Jersey wanted to try Burr for murder; New Jersey actually indicted him. The vice president fled through New Jersey by foot and wagon to Philadelphia, then took refuge in Georgia and South Carolina, until the indictments were quashed and he could finish his term in office.

The Jeffersonian era—the period stretching from 1800 to 1815—was rife with conflict, partisan passion, and larger-than-life personalities. On the domestic front, a new political party, the Republicans, came to office for the first time and a former vice president was charged with treason against his country. The era was also marked by foreign policy chal-

Alexander Hamilton and Aaron Burr were long-time political rivals. In 1804, Hamilton worked to defeat Burr for the governorship of New York. After the election, Burr challenged Hamilton to a duel. The specific reason for the challenge is still unknown. The two men met in New Jersey and Hamilton was killed.

lenges. Pirates, operating from bases on the coast of North Africa, harassed American shipping and enslaved American sailors. Britain and France interfered with American shipping. Finally, the United States once again waged war with Britain, the world's strongest power. These developments raised profound questions: Could the country peacefully transfer political power from one party to another? Could the country preserve political stability? And most importantly of all, could the nation preserve its neutral rights and national honor in the face of grave threats from Britain and France?

JEFFERSON TAKES COMMAND

Thomas Jefferson's goal as president was to restore the principles of the American Revolution. In his view a decade of Federalist party rule had threatened republican government. Not only had the Federalists levied oppressive taxes, stretched the provisions of the Constitution, and established a bastion of wealth and special privilege in the creation of a national bank, they also had subverted civil liberties and expanded the powers of the central government at the expense of the states. A new revolution was necessary, "as real a revolution in the principles of our government as that of 1776 was in its form." What was needed was a return to basic republican principles.

Jefferson told a story that illustrated the fundamental difference between Federalists and Republicans—their conflicting views of the people. Shortly after George Washington was elected president, Jefferson discussed political theory with Treasury Secretary Alexander Hamilton and Vice President John Adams. Jefferson had expressed his faith in popular government. Adams disagreed, asserting that monarchy was preferable to democracy. Adams said that if the British government was purged of corruption, it would be the best political system ever created. Hamilton rejected both Adams's and Jefferson's views and said that the British government was ideal as it stood.

Beginning with his very first day in office, Jefferson sought to demonstrate his administration's commitment to republican principles. At noon, March 4, 1801, Jefferson, clad in clothes

Republicans celebrated Thomas Jefferson's victory in the election of 1800 with a flag inscribed: "T. Jefferson President . . . John Adams no more."

of plain cloth, walked from a nearby boarding house to the new United States Capitol in Washington. Without ceremony, he entered the Senate chamber, and took the presidential oath of office. Then, in a weak voice, he delivered his inaugural address—a classic statement of republican principles.

His first concern was to urge conciliation and to allay fear that he planned a Republican reign of terror. "We are all Republicans," he said, "we are all Federalists." Echoing George Washington's Farewell Address, he asked his listeners to set aside partisan and sectional differences and remember that "every difference of opinion is not a difference of principle." Only a proper respect for principles of majority rule and minority rights, he declared, would allow the new nation to thrive.

In the remainder of his address he laid out the principles that would guide his presidency: a frugal, limited government; reduction of the public debt; respect for states' rights; encouragement of agriculture; and a limited role for government in peoples' lives. He committed his administration to repealing oppressive taxes, slashing government expenses, cutting military expenditures, and paying off the public debt.

Who Was Thomas Jefferson?

In 1962, President John F. Kennedy hosted a White House dinner for America's Nobel Laureates. He told the assemblage that this was "probably the greatest concentration of talent and genius in this house except perhaps for those times when Thomas Jefferson ate alone."

Thomas Jefferson, the nation's third president, was a man of many talents and accomplishments. He began his career as a lawyer, served in the Virginia House of Delegates and subsequently became governor of Virginia, ambassador to France, secretary of state, vice president, and president. But when he wrote the epitaph that appears over his grave, he mentioned none of these public offices. He simply stated that he was the author of the Declaration of Independence and the Statute of Virginia for Religious Freedom and the father of the University of Virginia.

An architect, inventor, philosopher, planter, and scientist, Jefferson was convinced that the yeoman farmer, who labored in the earth, provided the backbone of democracy. A stalwart defender of political freedom, equality, religious freedom, and intellectual freedom, he took as his inspiration the motto on his family crest: "Resistance to tyrants is obedience to God." A child of the Enlightenment, he popularized the idea that a democratic republic required an enlightened and educated citizenry and that government had a duty to assist in the education of a meritocracy based on talent and ability.

Jefferson was an extremely complex man, and his life was filled with apparent inconsistencies. An idealist who repeatedly denounced slavery as a curse and expressed his willingness to support any feasible plan to eradicate the institution, the "Apostle of Liberty" owned 200 slaves when he wrote the Declaration of Independence and freed only 5 slaves at the time of his death. A vigorous opponent of all forms of human tyranny and staunch defender of human equality, he adopted a patronizing attitude toward women, declaring that their proper role was to "soothe and calm the minds of their husbands." "The tender breasts of ladies," he said, "were not formed for political convulsion."

Yet Jefferson remains this country's most eloquent exponent of democratic principles. Abraham Lincoln said that his words will always "be a rebuke and stumbling block to . . . tyranny and oppression."

Jefferson's Goal: To Restore Republican Government

As president, Jefferson strove to return the nation to republican values. Through his personal conduct and public policies he sought to return the country to the principles of democratic simplicity, economy, and limited government.

Jefferson associated formality with aristocracy and informality with republicanism, and, as president, he took a number of steps designed to rid the White House of "monarchist" customs. He introduced the custom of having guests shake hands instead of bowing stiffly, a custom observed by presidents Washington and Adams. He also placed dinner guests at a round table, so that no individual would have to sit in a more important place than any other. In an effort to discourage a "cult of personality," he refused to sanction public celebrations of his birthday declaring, "The only birthday I ever commemorate is that of our Independence, the Fourth of July." As another symbol of republican simplicity, he

One of Thomas Jefferson's inventions was this polygraph machine, which made copies of Jefferson's letters as he wrote them.

kept a 1235-pound cheese, a gift from the people of West Chester, Massachusetts, in the East Room of the White House and invited visitors to eat some of it. To further dramatize his disdain for pomp and pageantry, he received the British minister in his dressing gown and slippers.

Jefferson repudiated certain "monarchical practices" that had marked the Washington and Adams presidencies. He refused to ride an elegant coach or host elegant dinner parties and balls. Instead, he invited small groups of senators and representatives to dinner and wore clothes made of homespun cloth. He believed that presidents should not try to impose their will on Congress, and consequently he refused to openly initiate legislation or to veto congressional bills on policy grounds. Convinced that presidents Washington and Adams had acted like British monarchs by personally appearing before Congress and requesting legislation, Jefferson simply sent Congress written messages. It would not be until the presidency of Woodrow Wilson that another president would publicly address Congress and call for legislation.

Jefferson's commitment to republican simplicity was matched by his stress on economy in government. His ideal was "a wise and frugal Government, which shall . . . leave [Americans] free to regulate their own pursuits of industry and improvement." He slashed army and navy expenditures, cut the budget, eliminated taxes on whiskey, houses, and slaves, and fired all federal tax collectors. He reduced the army to 3000 soldiers and 172 officers, the navy to 6 frigates, and foreign embassies to 3—in Britain, France, and Spain.

His budget cuts allowed him to cut the federal debt by a third, despite the elimination of all internal taxes. In seven years the federal debt fell from $83 million to $50 million.

Jefferson did not conceive of government in entirely negative terms. Convinced that ownership of land and honest labor in the earth were the firmest bases of political stability, Jefferson convinced Congress to cut the price of public lands and to extend credit to purchasers in order to encourage landownership and rapid western settlement A firm believer in the idea that America should be the "asylum" for "oppressed humanity," he persuaded Congress to reduce the residence requirement for citizenship from 14 to 5 years. In the interest of protecting civil liberties, he allowed the Sedition Act to expire in 1801, freed all people imprisoned under the act, and refunded their fines. And finally, to ensure that the public would know the names and number of all government officials, Jefferson ordered publication of a register of all federal employees.

In one area Jefferson felt his hands were tied. He considered the Bank of the United States "the most deadly" institution to republican government. But Hamilton's bank had been legally chartered for 20 years and Jefferson's secretary of the treasury, Albert Gallatin, said that the bank was needed to provide credit for the nation's growing economy. So Jefferson allowed the bank to continue to operate, but he weakened its influence by distributing the federal government's deposits among 21 state banks. "What is practicable," Jefferson commented, "must often control pure theory."

Contemporaries were astonished by the sight of a president who had renounced all the practical tools of government: an army, a navy, and taxes. Jefferson's actions promised, said a British observer, "a sort of Millennium in government." Jefferson's goal was, indeed, to create a new kind of government, a republican government wholly unlike the centralized, corrupt, patronage-ridden one against which Americans had rebelled in 1776.

Reforming the Federal Government

Jefferson thought that one of the major obstacles to restoring republican government was the 3000 Federalist officeholders. Of the first 600 political appointees named to federal office by presidents Washington and Adams, all but 6 were Federalists. During his last weeks in office, President Adams had rubbed this fact in Jefferson's face. After learning of his defeat, Adams appointed Federalists to every vacant government position. The most dramatic postelection appointment was naming John Marshall, a Federalist, chief justice of the Supreme Court.

Jefferson was committed in principle to the idea that government office should be filled on the basis of merit, not political connections.

Only government officeholders guilty of malfeasance or incompetence should be fired. Nothing more should be asked of government officials, he felt, than that they be honest, able, and loyal to the Constitution. Jefferson wholly rejected the idea that a victorious political party had a right to fill public offices with loyal party supporters.

Although many Republicans felt that Federalists should be replaced by loyal Republicans, Jefferson declared that he would remove only "midnight" appointees who had been named to office by President Adams after he learned of his electoral defeat. Nevertheless, Jefferson fired relatively few Federalists. During his first two years in office, he replaced just one-third of all government officials.

War on the Judiciary

When Thomas Jefferson took office, not a single Republican served as a federal judge. In Jefferson's view, the Federalists had prostituted the federal judiciary into a branch of their political party and intended to use the courts to frustrate Republican plans. "From that battery," said Jefferson, "all the works of republicanism are to be beaten down and erased."

The first major political battle of Jefferson's presidency involved his effort to weaken Federalist control of the federal judiciary. The Republican party decided to wage war on the courts, and "sink Federalism into an abyss from which there shall be no resurrection for it."

The specific issue that provoked Republican anger was the Judiciary Act of 1801, which was passed by the lame-duck Federalist-dominated Congress five days before Adams's term expired. The law created 16 new federal judgeships—along with nearly 200 marshals, attorneys, bailiffs, and messengers. President Adams had filled all the newly created positions with Federalists. Even more damaging, from a Republican perspective, the act strengthened the power of the central government by extending the jurisdiction of the federal courts over such issues as bankruptcy and land disputes, which were previously the exclusive domain of state courts. Finally, the act reduced the number of Supreme Court justices effective with the next

vacancy, delaying Jefferson's opportunity to name a new Supreme Court justice.

Jefferson's supporters in Congress demanded repeal of the Judiciary Act, but Federalists declared that the act could not be revoked, since the Constitution provided that federal judges could only be removed by impeachment. Republicans replied that since the Constitution gave Congress the right to create federal courts and to determine their jurisdiction, it also gave Congress the power to eliminate judgeships as well. The repeal passed, but just barely. In the Senate, Vice President Aaron Burr cast the deciding vote for repeal, and the House of Representatives went along by a margin of 27 votes.

While Congress debated repeal of the Judiciary Act of 1801, another skirmish erupted in the war over the federal courts. One of Adams's "midnight appointments" to a judgeship was William Marbury, a loyal Federalist. Although approved by the Senate, Marbury never received his letter of appointment from Adams. When Jefferson became president, Marbury demanded that the new secretary of state, James Madison, issue the commission. Madison refused and Marbury sued, claiming that under section 13 of the Judiciary Act of 1789, the Supreme Court had the power to issue a court order that would compel Madison to give him his judgeship.

The case threatened to provoke a direct confrontation between the judiciary on the one hand and the executive and legislative branches of the federal government on the other. If the Supreme Court ordered Madison to give Marbury his judgeship, the secretary of state was likely to ignore the Court, and Jeffersonians in Congress might try to limit the high court's power. This is precisely what had happened in 1793 when the Supreme Court had ruled that a state might be sued in federal court by nonresidents. Congress had retaliated by initiating the Eleventh Amendment, which restricted such suits.

John Marshall, the new chief justice of the Supreme Court, was well aware of the court's predicament. When Marshall became the nation's fourth chief justice in 1801, the Supreme Court lacked prestige and public respect. Pres-

John Marshall, the fourth chief justice of the United States, expanded the Court's power in *Marbury* v. *Madison* by establishing the right of judicial review. He thus gave the federal courts the power to determine the constitutionality of federal laws and congressional acts.

idents found it difficult to find willing candidates to serve as justices. The Court was considered so insignificant that it held its sessions in a clerk's office in the basement of the Capitol and only met six weeks a year.

In his opinion in *Marbury* v. *Madison*, the chief justice ingeniously expanded the court's power without directly provoking the Jeffersonians. Marshall conceded that Marbury had a right to his appointment but ruled the Court had no authority to order the secretary of state to act, since the section of the Judiciary Act that gave the Court the power to issue an order was unconstitutional. "A law repugnant to the constitution is void," Marshall declared. "It is emphatically the province and duty of the judicial department to say what the law is." For the first time, the Supreme Court had declared an act of Congress unconstitutional.

Marbury v. *Madison* was a landmark in American constitutional history. The decision firmly established the power of the federal courts to review the constitutionality of federal laws and to invalidate acts of Congress when they are determined to conflict with the Constitution. This power, known as *judicial review*, provides the basis for the important place that the Supreme Court occupies in American life today. Ironically, the Marshall Court never declared another federal law unconstitutional. In fact, the Supreme Court did not invalidate another act of Congress for half a century. Chief Justice Marshall recognized that the judiciary was the weakest of the three branches of government, and in the future the high court refrained from rulings in advance of national sentiment.

Marshall's decision in *Marbury* v. *Madison* intensified Republican party distrust of the courts. Jefferson complained that Marshall's opinion threatened to "make the judiciary a despotic branch" and to turn the Constitution into "a mere thing of wax" that the Court could shape any way it pleased.

Republicans then tried to use the impeachment process to rid the federal courts of judges they considered unfit or overly partisan. "We shall see who is master of the ship," declared one Jeffersonian. "Whether men appointed for life or the immediate representatives of the people . . . are to give laws to the community." In Jefferson's eyes, impeachment was the only effective way to make the federal courts responsive to the public will. Federalists responded by accusing the administration of endangering the independence of the federal judiciary.

In February 1803, three weeks before the Court handed down its decision in *Marbury* v. *Madison*, congressional Republicans launched impeachment proceedings against Federal District Judge John Pickering of New Hampshire. An alcoholic, who may have been insane, Pickering was convicted and removed from office.

On the day of Pickering's conviction, the House voted to impeach Supreme Court Justice Samuel Chase, a staunch Federalist and a signer of the Declaration of Independence. After the repeal of the Judiciary Act of 1801, Justice Chase asserted that the doctrine of equal rights had brought "mischief upon us" and declared that "mobocracy" had undermined the Constitution. From the bench, he had openly denounced equal rights and universal suffrage and accused the Jeffersonians of atheism and being power hungry. Undoubtedly, Chase was guilty of unrestrained partisanship and injudicious statements. An irate President Jefferson called for Chase's impeachment. "Ought this seditious and official attack on the principles of the Constitution . . . to go unpunished?" he asked Republicans in Congress.

Chase was put on trial for holding opinions "hurtful to the welfare of the country" and endangering the liberties of the American people. But the real issue was whether Chase had committed an impeachable offense, since the Constitution specified that a judge could only be removed from office for "treason, bribery, or other high crimes" and not for partisanship or judicial misconduct.

In a historic decision that helped to guarantee the independence of the judiciary, the Senate voted to acquit Chase. Although a majority of the Senate found Chase guilty, seven Republicans broke ranks and denied Jefferson the two-thirds majority needed for a conviction. "Impeachment is a farce which will not be tried again," Jefferson commented.

Chase's acquittal had momentous consequences for the future. If the Jeffersonians had succeeded in removing Chase, they would probably have removed other Federalist judges from the federal bench. However, since Chase's acquittal, no further attempts have ever been made to remove federal judges solely on the grounds of partisanship or to reshape the federal courts through impeachment. Despite the Republicans' active hostility toward an independent judiciary, the Supreme Court successfully established the principles of judicial supremacy and judicial review. The federal courts had emerged as a vigorous third branch of government.

International Conflict

In his inaugural address, Thomas Jefferson declared that his fondest wish was for peace. "Peace is my passion," he repeatedly insisted. As president, however, Jefferson was unable to realize his wish. Like Washington and Adams before him, Jefferson faced the difficult task of preserving American independence and neutrality in a world torn by war and revolution.

The Barbary Pirates

Jefferson's first major foreign policy crisis came from the "Barbary pirates" who preyed on American shipping off the coast of North Africa. The conflict began in 1785, when Algerian pirates boarded an American merchant schooner sailing off the coast of Portugal, took its 21-member crew to Algeria, and enslaved them for 12 years. After 8 years, 100 more American hostages seized from American ships joined the captives. Finally, in 1795, Congress approved a

$1 million ransom for release of the hostages; it was 2 more years before the captured Americans were released. By 1800, one-fifth of all federal revenues were being paid to the North African states as tribute. (For more information about American policy toward the so-called Barbary pirates, see pp. 258–259).

Early in Jefferson's first term, he refused to pay additional tribute demanded by the North African states. Determined to end the humiliating demands for tribute, he sent warships to the Mediterranean to enforce a blockade of Tripoli. The result was a protracted conflict with Tripoli, which lasted until 1805. The key event occurred after an American ship, the *Philadelphia*, was captured and its crew imprisoned. On the night of February 16, 1804, Lieutenant Stephen Decatur slipped into Tripoli harbor, boarded the captured ship, and set it afire. A year later, a small force of American marines marched 520 miles across the desert from Egypt and attacked and captured the Tripolitan city of Derna. Tripoli agreed to make peace, though the United States continued to pay tribute to other Barbary states until 1816. The phrase "To the shores of Tripoli" in the Marine Corps hymn refers to this military conflict.

Barbary States

Thomas Jefferson's first foreign policy crisis occurred when he refused to pay tribute to the Barbary States for the release of hostages captured by Algerian pirates. Instead, he sent eight ships to enforce a blockade of Tripoli.

The Louisiana Purchase

At the same time that conflict raged with the Barbary pirates, a more serious crisis loomed on the Mississippi River. In 1795, Spain granted western farmers the right to ship their produce down the Mississippi River to New Orleans, where their cargoes of corn, whiskey, and pork were loaded aboard ships bound for the east coast and foreign ports. In 1800, Spain secretly ceded the Louisiana territory to France, and closed the port of New Orleans to American farmers. Westerners, left without a port from which to export their goods, exploded with anger. Many demanded war.

The prospect of French control of the Mississippi alarmed Jefferson. Spain had held only a weak and tenuous grip on the Mississippi, but France was a much stronger power. Jefferson feared the establishment of a French colonial empire in North America blocking American expansion. The transfer of Louisiana from Spain, stated Jefferson, "reverses all the political relations of the United States. . . . The day France takes possession of New Orleans . . . we must marry ourselves to the British fleet and nation." The United States appeared to have only two options: diplomacy or war.

The president sent James Monroe to join Robert Livingston, the American minister to France, with instructions to purchase New Orleans and as much of the Gulf Coast as they could for $2 million. If these proposals failed, Jefferson instructed Monroe to begin talks with Britain to form a military alliance against France.

Circumstances played into American hands when France failed to suppress a slave rebellion in Haiti. One hundred thousand slaves, inspired by the French Revolution, had revolted, destroying 1200 coffee and 200 sugar plantations. In 1800, France sent troops to crush the insurrection and reconquer Haiti. First, they met a determined resistance led by a former slave named Toussaint L'Ouverture. Then, they were wiped out by mosquitoes carrying yellow fever. "Damn sugar, damn coffee, damn colonies," declared Napoleon. Without Haiti, which he regarded as the centerpiece of an American empire, Napoleon had little interest in keeping Louisiana.

Two days after Monroe's arrival, the French finance minister unexpectedly announced that France was willing to sell not just New Orleans but all of Louisiana Province, a territory extending from Canada to the Gulf of Mexico and westward as far as the Rocky Mountains. The American negotiators agreed on a price of $15 million, or about 4 cents an acre.

Since the Constitution did not give the president specific authorization to purchase land, Jefferson considered asking for a constitutional amendment empowering the government to acquire territory. In Congress, Federalists bitterly denounced the purchase. They noted that it would take a stack of silver dollars 12 miles high to pay for Louisiana. Jefferson himself said that the purchase made a "blank paper of the Constitution." In the end Jefferson, fearing that Napoleon might change his mind, simply sent the agreement to the Senate, which ratified it. "The less said about any constitutional difficulty, the better," he stated. In a single stroke, Jefferson had doubled the size of the country.

To gather information about the geography, natural resources, wildlife, and peoples of Louisiana, President Jefferson dispatched an expedition led by his private secretary Meriwether Lewis and William Clark, a Virginia-born military officer. For 2 years Lewis and Clark led some 30 soldiers and 10 civilians up the Missouri River

The American flag was raised over New Orleans in 1803 after the Louisiana Purchase.

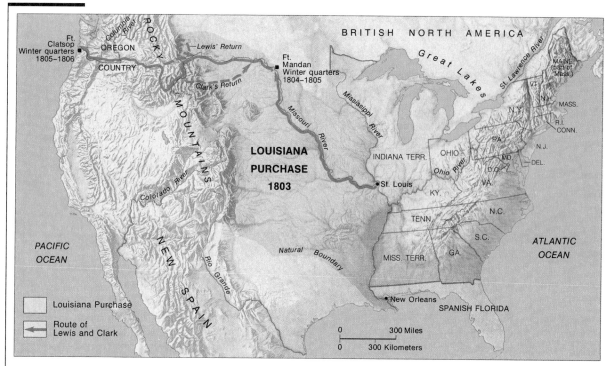

The Louisiana Purchase and Route of Lewis and Clark
No one realized how much territory Jefferson had acquired through the Louisiana Purchase until Lewis and Clark explored the far West.

as far as present-day central North Dakota and then west to the Pacific. (For more information on the Lewis and Clark expedition, see p. 403).

Disunionist Conspiracies

The acquisition of Louisiana terrified many Federalists, who knew that the creation of new western states would further dilute their political influence. "Adopt this Western World into the Union," warned one Federalist, "and you destroy at once the weight and importance of the Eastern States." In the winter of 1803–1804, a group of Federalist congressmen devised a plan for "a new confederacy, exempt from the corrupt and corrupting influence and oppression of the aristocratic Democrats of the South." This "Northern Confederacy," which would consist of New Jersey, New York, New England, and Canada, was to be established with the support of Britain.

Alexander Hamilton repudiated this scheme, and the conspirators turned to Vice

President Aaron Burr. In return for Federalist support in his campaign for the governorship of New York, Burr was to swing New York into the Northern Confederacy. Burr carried New York City, largely with Federalist votes, but was badly beaten upstate, in part because of Hamilton's opposition. Incensed and irate, Burr challenged Hamilton to the duel described at the beginning of this chapter.

Because of the duel Burr was now a ruined politician and a fugitive from the law. The Republican party stripped away his control over political patronage in New York. In debt, on the edge of bankruptcy, his fortunes at their lowest point, the desperate Burr became involved in a conspiracy for which he would be put on trial for treason.

During the spring of 1805, Burr traveled to the West, where he and an old friend, James Wilkinson, commander of United States forces in the Southwest and military governor of Louisiana, hatched an adventurous scheme. It is still uncertain what the conspirators' goal was, since

Burr, in his efforts to attract support, told different stories to different people. Spain's minister believed that Burr planned to set up an independent nation in the Mississippi Valley. Others reported that he planned to seize Spanish territory in what is now Texas, California, and New Mexico. The British minister was told that for $500,000 and British naval support, Burr would separate the states and territories west of the Appalachians from the rest of the Union and create an empire with himself as its head.

In the fall of 1806, Burr and some 60 schemers traveled down the Ohio River toward New Orleans to assess possibilities and perhaps to incite disgruntled French settlers to revolt. Wilkinson, recognizing that the scheme was doomed to failure, decided to betray Burr. He wrote a letter to Jefferson describing a "deep, dark, wicked, and widespread conspiracy, . . . to seize on New Orleans, revolutionize the territory, and carry an expedition against Mexico."

After hearing of his betrayal, Burr fled. The government offered a $2000 reward, and the 51-year-old Burr was finally apprehended in the Mississippi Territory. He was then taken to the Richmond, Virginia, circuit court, where, in 1807, he was tried for treason. Supreme Court Chief Justice John Marshall presided over a bitter trial. (Until 1891, Supreme Court justices heard cases in the federal circuit courts.)

Jefferson, convinced that Burr was a dangerous man, wanted a conviction regardless of the evidence. Chief Justice Marshall was equally eager to discredit Jefferson. Ultimately, Burr was acquitted. After a brief deliberation, the jury declared, "We . . . say that Aaron Burr is not proved to be guilty . . . by any evidence submitted to us." The reason for the acquittal was the Constitution's very strict definition of treason as "levying war against the United States" or "giving . . . aid and comfort" to the nation's enemies. In addition, each overt act of treason had to be attested to by two witnesses. The prosecution was unable to meet this strict standard, and as a result of Burr's acquittal, few future cases of treason have ever been tried in the United States.

Was Burr guilty of conspiring to destabilize the United States and separate the West by force? Probably not. The prosecution's case was extremely weak. It rested largely on the unreliable testimony of co-conspirator James Wilkinson, who was a spy in the pay of Spain while also a U.S. army commander and governor of Louisiana. What, then, was the purpose of Burr's mysterious scheming? It appears likely that the former vice president was planning a filibuster expedition—an unauthorized military attack—on Mexico, which was then controlled by Spain. The dream of creating a western republic in Mexico, Florida, or Louisiana appealed to many early nineteenth-century Americans—especially to many westerners who feared that a European power might seize Spain's New World colonies unless America launched a preemptive strike. Alexander Hamilton himself, back in 1798, had proposed a plan to conquer Louisiana and the Floridas. To the end of his life, Burr denied that he had plotted treason against the United States. Asked by one of his closest friends whether he had sought to separate the West from the rest of the nation, Burr responded with an emphatic "No!" "I would as soon have thought of taking possession of the moon and informing my friends that I intended to divide it among them."

THE EAGLE, THE TIGER, AND THE SHARK

In 1804, Jefferson was easily reelected, carrying every state except Connecticut and Delaware. He received 162 electoral votes to only 14 for his Federalist opponent, Charles C. Pinckney. Although his second term began, he later wrote, "without a cloud on the horizon," storm clouds soon gathered as a result of renewed war in Europe. Jefferson faced the difficult challenge of keeping the United States out of the European war, while defending the nation's rights as a neutral.

In May 1803, just two weeks after Napoleon sold Louisiana to the United States, France declared war on Britain. For the next 12 years, war engulfed Europe. In 1805 France defeated the armies of Austria and Russia at Austerlitz thereby winning control of much of the European continent. Napoleon then massed his troops and assembled a fleet of flat boats for an invasion of England. The invading force was to

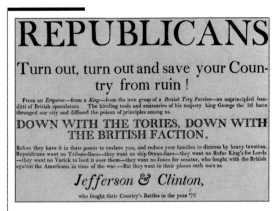

In the election of 1804, Thomas Jefferson dropped Aaron Burr from the Republican ticket and replaced him with another New Yorker, George Clinton.

be protected by the French navy, but, at the battle of Trafalgar off the Spanish coast, the British fleet under Admiral Horatio Nelson sank 18 French and Spanish ships and captured 14,000 men. Napoleon's hopes of invading England ended. Britain was now master of the seas; but France remained supreme on the land.

American merchants and shipowners profited immensely from the European war. They lined their pockets, said John Adams, while Europeans slit each others' throats. But American trade soon brought the country into the conflict.

Britain and France were determined to starve each other by restricting international trade. To stop British exports and destroy British industry, France instituted the "Continental System," which closed European ports to British goods and ordered the seizure of any neutral vessel that carried British goods or stopped in a British port. Britain retaliated in 1807 by issuing Orders in Council, which required all neutral ships to land at a British port to obtain a trading license and pay a tariff. Britain threatened to seize any ship that failed to obey the Orders in Council. United States shipping was caught in the crossfire. By 1807, France had seized 500 ships and Britain nearly 1000.

The most outrageous violation of America's neutral rights was the British practice of impressment. The British navy desperately needed sailors. Unable to procure sufficient vol-

unteers, the British navy resorted to seizing—impressing—men on streets, in taverns, and on British merchant ships. When these efforts failed to muster sufficient men, the British began to stop foreign ships and remove seamen alleged to be British subjects. By 1811, nearly 10,000 American sailors had been forced into the British navy, although an undetermined number were actually deserters from British ships who made more money sailing on U.S. ships.

Outrage over impressment reached a fever pitch in 1807 when the British man-of-war *Leopard* fired three broadsides at the American naval frigate *Chesapeake*, which had refused to allow British officers to search the American ship for Royal Navy deserters. The blasts killed 3 American sailors and wounded 18 more. British authorities then boarded the American ship and removed 4 sailors, only 1 of whom was really a British subject.

Americans were infuriated. The country clamored for war. Even Federalists joined in the anti-British outcry. Said one: "Without substantial reparation for the crying offense against our honor, rights and independence, we must go to war." "Never, since the battle of Lexington," observed Jefferson, "have I seen this country in such a state of exasperation."

"Dambargo"

In a desperate attempt to stave off war, for which it was ill-prepared, and win respect for America's neutral rights, the United States imposed an embargo on foreign trade. Convinced that American trade was vital to European industry, Jefferson persuaded Congress in late 1807 to adopt a policy of "peaceable coercion": a ban on all foreign shipping and exports.

Jefferson regarded the embargo as an idealistic experiment—a moral alternative to war. Jefferson was not a doctrinaire pacifist, but he had long advocated economic coercion as an instrument of diplomacy. Now he had a chance to put his ideas into practice.

The embargo was an unpopular and costly failure. It hurt the American economy far more than the British or French, breathed new life into the Federalist party, and resulted in widespread smuggling. Exports fell from $108 million in 1807 to just $22 million in 1808. Without the European export market, warehouses were crammed with huge stockpiles of unsold grain and cotton. Farm prices fell sharply. Shippers also suffered. Without the lucrative wartime trade, harbors filled with idle ships and nearly 30,000 sailors found themselves jobless. The embargo resuscitated the Federalist party, which regained power in several New England states and made substantial gains in the Congressional elections of 1808. "Would to God," said one American, "that the embargo had done as little evil to ourselves as it has done to foreign nations!"

Jefferson believed that Americans would cooperate with the embargo out of a sense of patriotism. Instead, evasions of the embargo were widespread, and smuggling flourished, particularly through Canada. To enforce the embargo, Jefferson took steps that infringed on his most cherished principles: individual liberties and opposition to a strong central government. He mobilized the army and navy to enforce the blockade, and in April, 1808, he declared the Lake Champlain region of New York, along the Canadian border, in a state of insurrection.

Pressure to abandon the embargo mounted. Boston seamen draped their ships in mourning. Flags in the Beverly, Massachusetts, harbor flew at half mast. Early in 1809, just 3 days before Jefferson left office, Congress yielded to the pressure and repealed the embargo. In effect for 15 months, the embargo exacted no political concessions from either France or Britain. But it had produced economic hardship, evasion of the law, and political dissension at home. Upset by the failure of his policies, the 65-year-old Jefferson looked forward to his retirement: "Never did a prisoner, released from his chains, feel such relief as I shall on shaking off the shackles of power."

The problem of American neutrality now fell to Jefferson's hand-picked successor, James Madison. "The Father of the Constitution" was small in stature and frail in health. A quiet, and scholarly man, who secretly suffered from epilepsy, Madison brought a keen intellect and a wealth of experience to the presidency. At the Constitutional Convention, he had played a leading role in formulating the principles of federalism and separation of powers that underlie the American system of government. As a member of Congress, he had sponsored the Bill of Rights and founded the Republican party. As Jefferson's secretary of state, he had kept the United States out of the Napoleonic wars. And now as president, Madison, like Jefferson before him, was committed to using economic coercion to force Britain and France to respect America's neutral rights.

In 1809, Congress replaced the failed embargo with the Non-Intercourse Act, which reopened trade with all nations except Britain and France. At first, the Non-Intercourse Act seemed to work. The British government opened negotiations with the United States. After reaching a favorable agreement with a friendly British minister, the United States reopened trade with Britain. Subsequently, however, the British government repudiated the agreement, claiming the minister had exceeded his instructions. Again, British trade was prohibited.

In 1810, Congress replaced the Non-Intercourse Act with a new measure, Macon's Bill No. 2. This policy reopened trade with France and Britain. It stated, however, that if either Britain or France agreed to respect America's neutral rights, the United States would immediately stop trade with the other nation. Napoleon seized on this new policy in an effort to entangle the United States in his war with Britain. In the summer of 1810, he announced repeal of all French restrictions on American trade. Even though France continued to seize American ships and cargoes, President Madison snapped at the bait. In early 1811, he cut off trade with Britain and recalled the American minister.

For 19 months, the British went without American trade, but gradually economic coercion worked. In May 1812, food shortages, mounting unemployment, and increasing inventories of unsold manufactured goods led British Prime Minister Spencer Perceval to end his country's trade restrictions (though not the British navy's policy of impressment). Unfortunately, Perceval was assassinated before he actually revoked the restrictions. When the restrictions were finally suspended on June 16, it was too late. President Madison had asked Congress for a declaration of war on June 1. A divided House and Senate concurred. The House voted to declare war on Britain by a vote of 79 to 49; the Senate by a vote of 19 to 13.

A Second War of Independence

Why did the United States declare war on Britain in 1812? Resentment at British interference with American rights on the high seas was certainly the most loudly voiced grievance. "Free Trade and Sailors' Rights" was a popular battlecry. British trade restrictions, impressment of thousands of American seamen, and British blockades humiliated the country and undercut America's national honor and neutral rights.

But if British harassment of American shipping was the primary motivation for war, why then did the prowar majority in Congress come largely from the South, the West, and the frontier, and not from northeastern shipowners and sailors? The vote to declare war on Britain divided along sharp regional lines. Representatives from western, southern, and frontier states voted 65 to 15 for war, while representatives from New England, New York, and New Jersey, states with strong shipping interests, voted 34 to 14 against war.

Northeastern Federalists and a handful of Republicans from coastal regions of the South regarded war with Britain as a grave mistake. The United States, they insisted, could not hope to successfully challenge British supremacy on the seas and the government could not finance a war without bankrupting the country. Above all, a war carried serious international implications, placing the United States clearly on the side of Napoleon in his struggle with Britain. John Randolph, a Republican, pleaded that the United States not enlist "under the banner of the tyrant."

Southerners and westerners, in contrast, were eager to avenge British insults against American honor and British actions that mocked American sovereignty on land and sea. Many southerners and westerners blamed British trade policies for depressing agricultural prices and producing an economic depression.

War with Britain also offered another incentive: the possibility of clearing western lands of Indians by removing the Indians' strongest ally—the British. And finally, many westerners and southerners had their eye on expansion, viewing war as an opportunity to add Canada and Spanish-held Florida to the United States.

Weary of Jefferson and Madison's patient and pacifistic policy of economic coercion, voters swept 63 out of 142 representatives out of Congress in 1810 and replaced them with young Republicans that Federalists dubbed "War Hawks." These second-generation Republicans avidly supported national expansion and national honor. These young Republicans elected Henry Clay, a representative from frontier Kentucky, Speaker of the House on his very first day in Congress. Clay then assigned other young Republicans, such as John C. Calhoun, a freshman representative from South Carolina, to key House committees.

Having grown up on tales of heroism during the American Revolution, second-generation Republicans were eager to prove their manhood in a "second war of independence." Even Thomas Jefferson came to share their eagerness. War, said the former president, would be "the second weaning from British principles, British attachments, British manners and manufactures." Staunchly nationalist and rabidly anti-British, eager for territorial expansion and economic growth, the young Republicans regarded the Napoleonic Wars in Europe as an unparalleled opportunity to defend national honor, assert American interests, and conquer Canada and Florida.

Further contributing to their prowar fervor was the belief that the British incited frontier Indian attacks. Anti-British feeling soared in November 1811, when General William Henry Harrison precipitated a fight with an Indian alliance led by the Shawnee Prophet, Tenskwatawa, at Tippecanoe Creek in Indiana. More than 60 American soldiers were killed and 100 were wounded. Since British guns were found on the battlefield, young Republicans concluded that the British were responsible for the incident.

Although Congress voted strongly in favor of war, the country entered the conflict deeply divided. In the presidential election of 1812, Ma-

On August 24, 1814, British troops avenged an American attack on York, Ontario, by marching into Washington, D.C., and setting fire to the Capitol and the White House.

States. The British planned to invade the United States at three points: upstate New York across the Niagara River and Lake Champlain, the Chesapeake Bay, and New Orleans. The London *Times* accurately reflected the confident English mood: "Oh, may no false liberality, no mistaken lenity, no weak and cowardly policy interpose to save the United States from the blow! Strike! Chastise the savages, for such they are. . . . Our demands may be couched in a single word—Submission!"

At Niagara, however, a small American army stopped the British advance in hard-fought battles at Chippewa and Lundy's Lane. Then, at Plattsburgh Bay on Lake Champlain, American naval forces commanded by Thomas Macdonough placed British supply lines in jeopardy, forcing 11,000 British troops to retreat into Canada. Outnumbered more than three to one, American forces had halted Britain's invasion from the north.

In a second attempt to invade the United States, Britain landed 4000 soldiers on the Chesapeake Bay coast. But no one knew if the British planned to march first on Baltimore or on Washington, D.C. The answer was Washington, where untrained soldiers lacking uniforms and standard equipment were protecting the capital. The result was utter chaos. While President Madison was inspecting the troops and offering encouragement, he narrowly escaped capture by British forces.

On August 24, 1814, the British humiliated the nation by capturing and burning Washington, D.C. President Madison and his wife Dolley were forced to flee the capital—carrying with them many of the nation's treasures, including the Declaration of Independence and Gilbert Stuart's portrait of George Washington. For 72 hours, the president was forced to hide in the Virginia and Maryland countryside. The British arrived so soon after the president fled that the officers dined on a White House meal that had been prepared for the Madisons and 40 invited guests.

Britain's next objective was Baltimore. To reach the city, British warships had to pass the guns of Fort McHenry, which was manned by 1000 American soldiers. Waving atop the fort was the largest garrison flag ever designed—30 feet by 42 feet. On September 13, 1814, British warships began a 25-hour bombardment of Fort McHenry. British vessels anchored two miles off shore—close enough so that their guns could hit the fort, but too far for American shells to reach them.

All through the night British cannons bombarded Fort McHenry, firing between 1500 and 1800 cannon balls at the fort. In the light of the "rockets' red glare, the bombs bursting in air," Francis Scott Key, a young lawyer detained on a British ship, saw the American flag waving over the fort. At dawn on September 14, he saw the flag still waving. The Americans had repulsed the British attack, with only 4 soldiers killed and 24 wounded. Key was so moved by the American victory that he wrote a poem entitled "The Star-Spangled Banner" on the back of an old envelope. Soon, the words of the poem were sung to an old English tune, "To Anacreon in Heaven." The song was destined to become the young nation's national anthem.

The country still faced grave threats in the South. In 1813, the Creek Indians, encouraged by the British, had attacked American settlements in what are now Alabama and Mississippi. Frontiersmen from Georgia, Mississippi, and Tennessee, led by Major General Andrew Jackson, retaliated and succeeded in defeating the Creeks in March 1814, at the battle of Horseshoe Bend in Alabama. When the Creek War ended, Jackson proceeded to cut British supply lines in the South. He knew that Spain, supposedly neutral, had allowed Britain to use the Florida port of Pensacola as a base of operations for a planned invasion of New Orleans. In a week, Jackson marched from Mobile, Alabama, to Pensacola and seized the city, forcing the British to delay their invasion.

But, on January 8, 1815, the British fleet and a battle-tested 10,000-man army finally attacked New Orleans in an attempt to seize control of the mouth of the Mississippi River. To defend the city, Jackson assembled a ragtag army, including French pirates, Choctaw Indians, western militia, and freed slaves. Although British forces outnumbered Americans by more than 2 to 1, American artillery and sharpshooters stopped the invasion. American losses totaled only 8 dead and 13 wounded, while British casualties were 2036, including their commanding officer. Almost 400 British soldiers were killed. Ironically, Jackson's astonishing victory at the battle of New Orleans took place two weeks after the signing of the peace treaty ending the War of 1812.

These negotiations had commenced in Ghent, Belgium, in August 1814. Having just defeated Napoleon in Europe, Britain was eager to punish its one remaining enemy—the United States. Therefore, British negotiators demanded retention of British forts on United States soil, cessions of territory in Maine and New York, and an independent state for Britain's Indian allies in the American Northwest. American negotiators, who had been told to accept no treaty that did not explicitly end Britain's impressment policy, rejected these demands. But when the negotiations dragged on, the Americans decided to ask Britain for a return to the conditions that existed before the war. Britain, now convinced that the American war was so difficult and costly that nothing would be gained from further fighting, accepted the American proposal. On December 24, 1814, a peace treaty was signed. None of the issues over which Americans had fought the war—impressment, naval blockades, or the British Orders in Council—were mentioned in the peace treaty.

The War's Significance

Although often treated as unimportant, a minor footnote to the bloody European war between France and Britain, the War of 1812 was crucial

JEFFERSON TAKES COMMAND

Henry Adams, *History of the United States During the Administrations of Thomas Jefferson [and] of James Madison*, 9 vols., (1889–1891); James H. Broussard, *The Southern Federalists, 1800–1816* (1978); Robert Lowry Clinton, *Marbury v. Madison and Judicial Review* (1989); Edward S. Corwin, *The "Higher Law" Background of American Constitutional Law* (1929); Noble E. Cunningham, Jr., *The Jeffersonian Republicans in Power: Party Operations, 1801–1809* (1963), and *The Process of Government under Jefferson* (1978); Alexander De Conde, *The Affair of Louisiana* (1976); D. O. Dewey, *Marshall Versus Jefferson: The Political Background of Marbury v. Madison* (1970); Richard E. Ellis, *The Jeffersonian Crisis: Courts and Politics in the Young Republic* (1971); David Hackett Fischer, *The Revolution of American Conservatism: The Federalist Party in the Era of Jeffersonian Democracy* (1965); Charles G. Haines, *The American Doctrine of Judicial Supremacy*, 2d ed. (1932); George Lee Haskins and Herbert A. Johnson, *History of the Supreme Court of the United States, vol. 2, Foundations of Power: John Marshall, 1801–15* (1981); C. William Hill, *The Political Theory of John Taylor* (1977); Ray W. Irwin, *Diplomatic Relations of the United States with the Barbary Powers* (1931); Robert M. Johnstone, Jr., *Jefferson and the Presidency: Leadership in the Young Republic* (1978); Linda K. Kerber, *Federalists in Dissent* (1970); Ralph Ketcham, *Presidents above Party: The First American Presidency, 1789–1829* (1984); Shaw Livermore, *The Twilight of Federalism* (1962); Drew McCoy, *The Elusive Republic: Political Economy in Jeffersonian America* (1980); Forrest McDonald, *The Presidency of Thomas Jefferson* (1976); R. Kent Newmyer, *The Supreme Court under Marshall and Taney* (1968); Howard B. Rock, *Artisans of the New Republic: The Tradesmen of New York City in the Age of Jefferson* (1979); Robert E. Shalhope, *John Taylor of Caroline: Pastoral Republican* (1980); Daniel Sisson, *The American Revolution of 1800* (1974); Marshall Smelser, *The Democratic Republic, 1801–1815* (1968); Charles G. Steffen, *The Mechanics of Baltimore: Workers and Politics in the Age of Revolution* (1984); Shannon C. Stimson, *The American Revolution in the Law: Anglo-American Jurisprudence Before John Marshall* (1990); Robert W. Tucker and David C. Hendrickson, *Empire of Liberty: The Statecraft of Thomas Jefferson* (1990); Leonard D. White, *The Jeffersonians: A Study in Administrative History, 1801–1829* (1951); James S. Young, *The Washington Community, 1800–1828* (1966).

THE EAGLE, THE TIGER, AND THE SHARK

James Banner, *To the Hartford Convention* (1970); Samuel Flagg Bemis, *John Quincy Adams and the Foundations of American Foreign Policy* (1949); Roger H. Brown, *The Republic in Peril: 1812* (1964); Gregory Dowd, *A Spirited Resistance: The North American Indian Struggle for Unity* (1991); H. S. Halbert and T. H. Ball, *The Creek War of 1813 and 1814* (1969); Regionald Horsman, *The Causes of the War of 1812* (1962); Drew R. McCoy, *The Last of the Fathers: James Madison and the Republican Legacy* (1989); Bradford Perkins, *Castlereagh and Adams: England and the United States, 1812–1823* (1964), and *Prologue to War: England and the United States, 1805–1812* (1961); Robert A. Rutland, *Madison's Alternatives: The Jeffersonian Republicans and the Coming of War* (1975), and *The Presidency of James Madison* (1990); Burton Spivak, *Jefferson's English Crisis: Commerce, Embargo, and the Republican Revolution* (1979); J. C. A. Stagg, *Mr. Madison's War: Politics, Diplomacy, and Warfare in the Early American Republic, 1783–1830* (1983).

BIOGRAPHIES

Leonard Baker, *John Marshall: A Life in Law* (1974); Alexander Balinky, *Albert Gallatin: Fiscal Theories and Policies* (1958); Irving Brant, *James Madison*, 6 vols. (1941–1961); Fawn M. Brodie, *Thomas Jefferson: An Intimate History* (1974); Noble E. Cunningham, Jr., *In Pursuit of Reason: The Life of Thomas Jefferson* (1987); R. David Edmunds, *Shawnee Prophet* (1983), and *Tecumseh and the Quest for Indian Leadership* (1984); Ralph Ketcham, *James Madison* (1971); Milton Lomask, *Aaron Burr*, 2 vols. (1979–1982); Dumas Malone, *Jefferson and His Time*, 6 vols. (1948–1981); Drew R. McCoy, *The Last of the Fathers: James Madison and the Republican Legacy* (1989); John C. Miller, *Alexander Hamilton* (1959); Broadus Mitchell, *Alexander Hamilton*, 2 vols. (1957–1963); Merrill Peterson, *The Jefferson Image in the American Mind* (1960); M. Peterson, *Thomas Jefferson and the New Nation* (1970); Robert Allen Rutland, *James Madison* (1987); Ernest Spaulding, *His Excellency George Clinton* (1938); Raymond Walters, Jr., *Albert Gallatin: Jeffersonian Financier and Diplomat* (1957).

CHAPTER 9

Nationalism, Economic Growth, and the Roots of Sectional Conflict, 1815–1824

PLATE 333.

When was a little

As the year 1810 began, Francis Cabot Lowell, a 36-year-old Boston importer, was bitterly discouraged. His health was failing and, as a result of war between Britain and France and the U.S. policy of discouraging trade by embargo and other legislation, his importing business was in ruins. Uncertain about which way to turn, he decided to travel abroad. While overseas, he discovered his life's calling. In Britain, he marveled at textile factories at Manchester. Although it was illegal to export textile machinery or plans, Lowell carefully studied the power looms and secretly made sketches of the designs.

Upon his return to Boston in 1813, Lowell constructed textile machinery superior to any he had seen in England. The next year, in Waltham, Massachusetts, he and two associates spent a half million dollars to build the world's first factory able to convert raw cotton into cloth by power machinery under one roof.

To staff his new textile mill, Lowell chose a labor force different from that found in any previous factory. Determined to avoid the misery of England's textile mills, Lowell recruited his labor force not from the families of the poor or from young children but from among the virtuous daughters of New England farmers, who agreed to work in Lowell's mill for two or three years as a way of earning a dowry or an independent income. Because spinning and weaving had long been performed by women in the home, and because young women were willing to work for half or a third the wages of young men, they seemed to offer a perfect solution to the factory's labor needs.

To break down the prejudice against factory work as degrading and immoral, the company announced that it would employ only women of good moral character. It threatened to fire any employee guilty of smoking, drinking, lying, swearing, or any other immoral conduct. To keep a close watch over employees' moral character, the company required employees to attend church and provided boarding houses where mill girls lived under the careful supervision of housekeepers of impeccable character. Within a few years, the new factory was overwhelmed with job applicants and was "more puzzled to get rid of hands than to employ them."

The opening of the Boston Manufacturing Company's textile mill in 1814 marked a symbolic beginning to a new era in the nation's history. For the Western world, the conclusion of the Napoleonic Wars ended a period of global war and revolution, and began a new period of nationalism and economic growth. For Americans, the end to the War of 1812 unleashed a surge of nationalism, dramatic urban and industrial growth, and rapid expansion to the West.

As a result of the War of 1812 and Andrew Jackson's smashing victory at the Battle of New Orleans, American national pride and unity were restored. In the aftermath of the war, patriotic fervor swept aside bitter political and sectional divisions. Intense nationalism was apparent in the adoption of programs to promote national economic growth, a series of Supreme Court decisions establishing the supremacy of the federal government and expanding the powers of Congress, and the proud assertion of American interest and power in foreign policy.

Explosive economic growth was another characteristic of the period after the War of 1812. The United States underwent a dramatic economic transformation symbolized by im-

The new textile mills offered a source of income to daughters of New England farmers.

Lowell, Massachusetts, along the Merrimack River, was one of the first American mill towns.

provements in transportation, rapid urban growth, improvements in farming, and many technological innovations.

Paradoxically, it was during these years of nationalism and growth, known to contemporaries as "the Era of Good Feelings," that sectional and political conflicts were exacerbated. Westward expansion, the rapid growth of industry in the North, and the strengthening of the federal government created problems that dominated American political life for the next 40 years.

THE GROWTH OF AMERICAN NATIONALISM

Early in the summer of 1817, as a conciliatory gesture toward the Federalists who had opposed the War of 1812, James Monroe, the nation's fifth president, embarked on a goodwill tour through the Northeast and Midwest. Everywhere Monroe went, citizens greeted him warmly, holding parades and banquets in his honor. In Federalist Boston, a crowd of 40,000 welcomed the Republican president. John Quincy Adams expressed amazement at the acclaim with which the president was greeted: "Party spirit has indeed subsided throughout the Union to a degree that I should have thought scarcely possible." A Federalist newspaper, reflecting on the end of party warfare and the renewal of national unity, called the times the "Era of Good Feelings."

The phrase "the era of good feelings" describes the period of James Monroe's presidency, which, at least in its early years, was marked by a relative absence of political strife and opposition. With the collapse of the Federalist party, the Jeffersonian Republicans dominated national politics. Reflecting a new spirit of political unity, the Republicans adopted many of the nationalistic policies of their former opponents, establishing a second national bank, a protective tariff, and improvements in transportation.

The spirit of nationalism was also apparent in a series of landmark Supreme Court decisions that established national supremacy over the states and in a series of foreign policy triumphs that extended the nation's boundaries and protected its shipping and commerce. The new spirit of national political unity reached its climax in the presidential election of 1820. When Monroe ran for reelection, he won the electoral vote 231 to 1.

To the American people, James Monroe was the popular symbol of the Era of Good Feelings.

His life embodied much of the history of the young republic. He had joined the revolutionary army in 1776 and had spent the terrible winter of 1777–1778 at Valley Forge. He had been a member of the Confederation Congress and served as minister to both France and Great Britain. During the War of 1812, he had performed double duty as secretary of state and secretary of war. With the Federalist party in a state of collapse, he had been easily elected president, carrying all but three states.

His physical appearance reminded Americans of an earlier era. A dignified and formal man, nearly 6 feet in height, Monroe was the last president to don the fashions of the eighteenth century. He wore his hair in a powdered wig tied in a queue and dressed himself in a cocked hat, a black broadcloth tailcoat, knee breeches, long white stockings, and buckled shoes.

His political values, too, were those of an earlier day. Like George Washington, Monroe worked to eliminate party and sectional rivalries by his attitudes and behavior. He hoped for a country without political parties, governed by leaders chosen on their merits. Anxious to unite all sections of the country, he tried to appoint a representative of each section to his cabinet and named John Quincy Adams, a former Federalist and son of a Federalist president, as secretary of state. A new era of national unity appeared to have dawned.

Neo-Hamiltonianism

Traditionally, the Republican party stood for limited government, states' rights, and a strict interpretation of the Constitution. By 1815, however, the party had adopted former Federalist positions on a national bank, protective tariffs, a standing army, and national roads.

In a series of policy recommendations to Congress at the end of the War of 1812, President Madison revealed the extent to which Republicans had adopted Federalist policies. He had called for a program of national economic development directed by the central government. He advocated creation of a second Bank of the United States to produce a stable currency, a protective tariff to encourage industry, a program of internal improvements to facilitate transportation, and a permanent 20,000-man

army. In subsequent messages, he recommended an extensive system of roads and canals, new military academies, and establishment of a national university in Washington.

Old-style Republicans, who clung to the Jeffersonian ideal of limited government, dismissed Madison's proposals as nothing but "old Federalism, vamped up into something bearing the superficial appearance of Republicanism." But Madison's nationalistic program found enthusiastic support among the new generation of political leaders. Convinced that inadequate roads, the lack of a national bank, and dependence on foreign imports had nearly resulted in a British victory in the war, these young leaders were eager to use the federal government to promote national economic development.

Henry Clay, John C. Calhoun, and Daniel Webster were the preeminent leaders of the second generation of American political life— the period stretching from the War of 1812 to almost the eve of the Civil War. All shared similar backgrounds. Each was born on a poor or modest farm. Each became a lawyer. Each arrived in Washington, D.C., around the beginning of the War of 1812 and became the preeminent spokesman of his region—Clay of the West, Calhoun of the South, Webster of the North. Each possessed extraordinary oratorical talent. Each served in the cabinet as secretary of state or secretary of war. They died within a few months of each other in the early 1850s.

The leader of this group of younger politicians was Henry Clay, a Republican from Kentucky. Named Speaker on his very first day in the House of Representatives in 1811, Clay was one of the "War Hawks" who had urged President Madison to wage war against Britain. After the war, Clay became one of the strongest proponents of an active federal role in national economic development. He used his position as Speaker of the House to advance an economic program that he later called the "American System." According to this plan, the federal government would erect a high protective tariff to keep out foreign goods, stimulate the growth of industry, and create a large urban market for western and southern farmers. Revenue from the tariff, in turn, would be used to finance internal improvements of roads and canals to stimulate the growth of the South and West.

Another leader of postwar nationalism was John C. Calhoun, a Republican from South Carolina. Calhoun, like Clay, entered Congress in 1811, and later served with distinction as secretary of war under Monroe and as vice president under both John Quincy Adams and Andrew Jackson. Later, Calhoun became the nation's leading exponent of states' rights, but at this point he seemed to John Quincy Adams, "above all sectional and factious prejudices more than any other statesman of this Union with whom I have ever acted."

The other dominant political figure of the era was Daniel Webster. First elected to Congress in 1812, Webster would serve not only as a representative and senator but also as secretary of state. Nicknamed "Black Dan" for his dark hair and eyebrows, and "the Godlike Daniel" for his magnificent speaking style, Webster argued 168 cases before the Supreme Court. When he entered Congress as a Massachusetts Federalist, he opposed the War of 1812, the creation of a second national bank, and a protectionist tariff. But, later in his career, after industrial interests supplanted shipping and importing interests in the Northeast, Webster became a staunch defender of the national bank and a high tariff, and perhaps the nation's strongest exponent of nationalism and strongest critic of states' rights. He would insist that the United States was not only a union of states but a union of people. His words—that the United States was a "people's government, made for the people, by the people, and answerable to the people"—would later be seized on by Abraham Lincoln.

Strengthening American Finances

The severe financial problems created by the War of 1812 led to a wave of support for the creation of a second national bank. The demise of the first Bank of the United States just before the war had left the nation ill-equipped to deal with the war's financial demands. To finance the war effort, the government borrowed from private banks at high interest rates. As demand for credit rose, the private banks issued bank notes greatly exceeding the amount of gold or silver that they held. One Rhode Island bank issued $580,000 in notes backed up by only $86.48 in

Eager to use the federal government to promote economic development, young politicians like Henry Clay of Kentucky (left) and John C. Calhoun of South Carolina (right) supported a protective tariff to stimulate industry, a national bank to promote economic growth, and federally funded aid for transportation.

gold and silver. The result was high inflation. Prices jumped 40 percent in just two years.

To make matters worse, the United States government was unable to redeem millions of dollars deposited in private banks. In 1814, after the British burned the nation's capital, many banks outside of New England stopped redeeming their notes in gold or silver. Soldiers, army contractors, and government securities holders went unpaid, and the Treasury temporarily went bankrupt. After the war was over, many banks still refused to resume payments in gold or silver.

Supporters of a second national bank argued that it would provide a safe place to deposit government funds and a convenient mechanism for transferring money between states. Supporters also claimed that a national bank would promote monetary stability by regulating private banks. A national bank would strengthen the banking system by refusing to accept the notes issued by overspeculative private banks and ensuring that bank notes were readily exchangeable for gold or silver. Opposition to a national bank came largely from private banking interests and traditional Jeffersonians, who considered a national bank to be unconstitutional and a threat to republican government.

In 1816, Congress voted by a narrow margin to charter a second Bank of the United States for 20 years and give it the privilege of holding government funds without paying interest for their use. In return, it required the bank to pay a bonus of $1.5 million to the federal government and let the president name 5 of the bank's 25 directors.

Protecting American Industry

The War of 1812 provided tremendous stimulus to American manufacturing. It encouraged American manufacturers to produce goods previously imported from overseas. By 1816, 100,000 factory workers, two-thirds of them women and children, produced more than $40 million worth of manufactured goods a year. Capital investment in textile manufacturing, sugar refining, and other industries totaled $100 million.

Following the war, however, cheap British imports flooded the nation, threatening to undermine local industries. In 1815, $83 million worth of British goods reached American shores; the next year imports climbed to $155 million. In Parliament, a British minister defended the practice of dumping goods at prices below their actual cost on grounds that outraged Americans. "It is well worth while," the minister declared, "to incur a loss upon the first exportation, in order, by a glut, to stifle in the cradle those rising manufactures in the United States which the war had forced into existence." So severe was the perceived threat to the nation's economic independence that Thomas Jefferson, who had once denounced manufacturing as a menace to the nation's republican values, spoke out in favor of protecting manufacturing industries: "We must now place the manufacturer by the side of the agriculturalist."

Congress responded to the flood of imports by continuing a tariff to protect America's infant industries from low-cost competition. Shipping and farming interests opposed the tariff on the grounds that it would make foreign goods more expensive to buy and would provoke foreign re-

taliation. John Randolph of Virginia argued that a tariff was discriminatory because it benefited certain privileged business interests at the expense of consumers. He asked rhetorically, "On whom bears the duty on coarse woollens and linens, and blankets, upon salt and all the necessities of life?" His answer: "On poor men and slaveholders."

Proponents of the tariff prevailed, continuing protective duties set during the War of 1812. With import duties ranging from 15 to 30 percent on cotton, textiles, leather, paper, pig iron, wool, and other goods, the tariff promised to protect America's growing industries from foreign competition.

Conquering Space

Prior to 1812, westward expansion had proceeded slowly. Most Americans were nestled along the Atlantic coastline. More than two-thirds of the new nation's population still lived within 50 miles of the Atlantic seaboard, and the center of population rested within 18 miles of Baltimore. Only two roads cut across the Allegheny Mountains, and no more than half a million pioneers had moved as far west as Kentucky, Tennessee, Ohio, or the western portion of Pennsylvania. Cincinnati was a town of 15,000 people; Buffalo and Rochester, New York, did not yet exist. Kickapoo, Miami, Wyandot, and other Indian tribes populated the areas that would become the states of Illinois, Indiana, Michigan, and Wisconsin, while the Cherokee, Chickasaw, Choctaw, and Creek Indians considered the future states of Alabama, Mississippi, and western Georgia their territory.

Between 1803, when Ohio was admitted to the Union, and the beginning of the War of 1812, not a single new state was carved out of the west. Thomas Jefferson estimated in 1803 that it would be a thousand years before settlers occupied the region east of the Mississippi.

The end of the War of 1812 unleashed a rush of pioneers to Indiana, Illinois, Ohio, northern Georgia, western North Carolina, Alabama, Mississippi, Louisiana, and Tennessee. Congress quickly admitted five states to the Union: Louisiana in 1812, Indiana in 1816, Mississippi in 1817, Illinois in 1818, and Alabama in 1819. Pioneers demanded cheaper land and clamored

The Conestoga wagon carried people and goods in the rush of westward expansion. Settlers moved west and north along the Ohio and Mississippi rivers before moving to open farmlands further inland.

for better transportation to move goods to Eastern markets.

Farmers demanded that Congress revise legislation to make it easier to obtain land. Originally, Congress viewed federal lands as a source of revenue, and public land policies reflected that view. Under a policy adopted in 1785 and reaffirmed in 1796, the federal government only sold land in blocks of at least 640 acres. In practice, this policy tended to retard land sales and concentrate land ownership in the hands of a few large land companies and wealthy land speculators. The Land Act of 1800 made land available in 320-acre lots and made credit available for the purchase of land. In 1820, Congress sought to make it easier for farmers to purchase homesteads in the West by selling land in small lots suitable for operation by a family. Congress reduced the minimum allotment offered for sale

from 320 to 80 acres. The minimum price per acre fell from $2 to $1.25. In 1796, a pioneer farmer purchasing a western farm from a federal land office had to buy 640 acres costing $1280. In 1820, a farmer could purchase 80 acres for just $100. The second Bank of the United States encouraged land purchases by liberally extending credit. The result was a boom in land sales. For a decade, the government sold approximately a million acres of land annually.

Westward expansion also created a demand to expand and improve the nation's roads and canals. In 1808, Albert Gallatin, Thomas Jefferson's Treasury secretary, proposed a $20 million program of canal and road construction. As a result of state and sectional jealousies and charges that federal aid to transportation was unconstitutional, the federal government funded only a single turnpike, the National Road, at this time stretching from Cumberland, Maryland, to Wheeling, Virginia (later West Virginia), but much later extending westward from Baltimore through Ohio and Indiana to Vandalia, Illinois.

In 1816, John C. Calhoun introduced a new proposal for federal aid for road and canal construction. Failure to link the nation together with an adequate system of transportation would, Calhoun warned, lead "to the greatest of calamities—disunion." "Let us," he exclaimed, "bind the republic together with a perfect system of roads and canals. Let us conquer space." Narrowly, Calhoun's proposal passed. But on the day before he left office, Madison vetoed the bill on constitutional grounds.

Despite this setback, Congress did adopt major parts of the nationalist neo-Hamiltonian economic program. It had established a second Bank of the United States to provide a stable means of issuing money and a safe depository for federal funds. It had enacted a tariff to raise duties on foreign imports and guard American industries from low-cost competition. It had also instituted a new public land policy to encourage western settlement. In short, Congress had translated the spirit of national pride and unity that the nation felt after the War of 1812 into a legislative program that placed the national interest above narrow sectional interests.

Judicial Nationalism

The decisions of the Supreme Court also reflected the nationalism of the postwar period. With John Marshall as chief justice, the Supreme Court greatly expanded its powers, prestige, and independence. When Marshall took office, in the last days of John Adams's administration in 1801, the Court met in the basement of the Capitol and was rarely in session for more than six weeks a year. Since its creation in 1789, the Court had only decided 100 cases.

In a series of critical decisions, the Supreme Court, under Chief Justice Marshall, greatly expanded its authority. As previously noted (pp. 242–243), *Marbury* v. *Madison* (1803) established the Supreme Court as the final arbiter of the Constitution and its power to declare acts of Congress unconstitutional. *Fletcher* v. *Peck*

John Marshall established many basic principles of constitutional law in the 34 years he served as chief justice of the United States. Marshall and the six other members of the Supreme Court appear on the podium in this 1822 painting of the House of Representatives by Samuel F. B. Morse.

(1810) declared the Court's power to void state laws. *Martin* v. *Hunter's Lessee* (1816) gave the Court the power to review decisions by state courts.

After the War of 1812, Marshall wrote a series of decisions that further strengthened the powers of the national government. *McCulloch* v. *Maryland* (1819) established the constitutionality of the second Bank of the United States and denied to states the right to exert independent checks on federal authority. The case involved a direct attack on the second Bank of the United States by the state of Maryland, which had placed a tax on the bank notes of all banks not chartered by the state, including the Baltimore branch of the national bank. In his decision, Marshall dealt with two fundamental questions. The first was whether the federal government had the power to incorporate a bank. The answer to this question, the Court ruled, was yes because the Constitution granted Congress implied powers to do whatever was "necessary and proper" to carry out its constitutional powers—in this case, the power to manage a currency. In a classic statement of "broad" or "loose" construction of the Constitution, Marshall said, "Let the end be legitimate, let it be within the scope of the Constitution, and all means which are appropriate, which are plainly adapted to that end, which are not prohibited, but consistent with the letter and spirit of the Constitution, are constitutional."

The second question raised in *McCullouch* v. *Maryland* was whether a state had the power to tax a branch of the Bank of the United States. In answer to this question, the Court said no. The Constitution, the Court asserted, created a new government with sovereign power over the states. "The power to tax involves the power to destroy," the Court declared, and the states do not have the right to exert an independent check on the authority of the federal government.

Economic competition and development were encouraged through *Dartmouth* v. *Woodward* (1819) and *Gibbons* v. *Ogden* (1824). The first encouraged business growth by denying states the right to alter or impair contracts unilaterally. The case involved the efforts of the New Hampshire legislature to alter the charter of Dartmouth College, which had been granted by George III in 1769. The Court held that a charter was a valid contract protected by the Constitution and that states do not have the power to alter contracts unilaterally.

Five years later, in *Gibbons* v. *Ogden*, the Court broadened federal power over interstate commerce. The Court overturned a New York law that had awarded a monopoly over steamboat traffic on the Hudson River, ruling that the Constitution had specifically given Congress the power to regulate commerce.

Under John Marshall, the Supreme Court established a distribution of constitutional powers that the country still follows. The Supreme Court became the final arbiter of the constitutionality of federal and state laws, and the federal government exercised sovereign power over the states. As a result of these decisions, it would become increasingly difficult in the future to argue that the union was a creation of the states, that states could exert an independent check on federal government authority, or that Congress's powers were limited to those specifically conferred by the Constitution.

Defending American Interests in Foreign Affairs

The War of 1812 stirred a new nationalistic spirit in foreign affairs. In 1815, this spirit resulted in a decision to end the raids by the Barbary pirates on American commercial shipping in the Mediterranean. For 17 years the United States had paid tribute to the ruler of Algiers (for more on the so-called Barbary pirates, see pp. 258–259). Taking advantage of the War of 1812, the Algerian leader had declared the United States owed him another $27,000, dismissed the American ambassador, seized American ships, and once again enslaved American citizens. Congress responded in March 1815, by sending Captain Stephen Decatur and a fleet of ten ships into the Mediterranean, where they captured two Algerian gunboats, towed the ships into Algiers harbor, and threatened to bombard the city. As a result, all the North African states agreed to treaties releasing American prisoners without ransom, ending all demands for American tribute, guaranteeing that American commerce would not be interfered with, and providing compensation for American vessels that had been seized.

After successfully defending American interests in North Africa, Monroe acted to settle old grievances with the British. Britain and the United States had left a host of issues unresolved in the peace treaty ending the War of 1812, including disputes over boundaries, trading and fishing rights, and rival claims to the Oregon region. The two governments moved quickly to settle these issues. The Rush-Bagot Agreement, signed with Great Britain in 1817, removed most military ships from the Great Lakes. In 1818, Britain granted American fishermen the right to fish in eastern Canadian waters, agreed to the 49th parallel as the boundary between the United States and Canada from Minnesota to the Rocky Mountains, and consented to joint occupation of the Oregon region.

But, the critical foreign policy issue facing the United States after the War of 1812 was the fate of Spain's New World empire. In 1808, Napoleon deposed the Spanish king, and Spain's New World colonies took advantage of the situation to fight for their independence. These revolutions, lasting from 1810 to 1821, aroused

In a daring naval raid on Tripoli, Stephen Decatur led a small force onto a Tripolitan gunboat, shot the captain, and burned the vessel.

enormous sympathy in the United States. But this unrest also raised American fears of European intervention in the New World. Austria, France, Prussia, and Russia had agreed to "put an end to the system of representative government, in whatever country it may exist in Europe," and they subdued uprisings in Italy in 1820 and Spain in 1822. Americans feared that these powers might seek to put down revolutionary movements and restore monarchical order in Spain's New World.

Monroe's initial objective was to secure the nation's southern and southwestern borders. A source of particular concern was Florida, which was still under Spanish control. Pirates, fugitive slaves, and Native Americans used Florida as a sanctuary and as a jumping off point for raids on settlements in Georgia. In December 1817, to end these incursions, Monroe authorized General Andrew Jackson to lead a punitive expedition against the Seminole Indians in Florida.

Jackson attacked the Seminoles, destroyed their villages, and overthrew the Spanish governor. He also courtmartialed and executed two British citizens whom he accused of inciting the Seminoles to commit atrocities against Americans.

Jackson's actions provoked a furor in Washington. Spain protested Jackson's acts and demanded that he be punished. Secretary of War John C. Calhoun and other members of Monroe's cabinet urged the president to reprimand Jackson for acting without specific authorization. In Congress, Henry Clay called for Jackson's censure. Secretary of State Adams, however, saw in Jackson's actions an opportunity to wrest Florida from Spain.

Instead of apologizing for Jackson's conduct, Adams declared that the Florida raid was a legitimate act of self-defense justified by a 1795 treaty in which Spain had promised to check hostile incursions into American terri-

came clear after 1830 that railroads were destined to become the nation's chief means of moving freight. During the 1830s, construction companies laid down 3328 miles of track, roughly equal to all the miles of canals in the country. With an average speed of 10 miles an hour, railroads were faster than stagecoaches, canalboats, and steamboats, and, unlike watergoing vessels, could travel in any season.

The transportation revolution sharply reduced the cost of shipping goods to market and stimulated agriculture and industry. New roads, canals, and railroads speeded the pace of commerce and strengthened ties between the East and West.

Speeding Communications

Poor communications had also impeded development. During the 1790s, it took 3 weeks for a letter to travel from New York to Cincinnati or Detroit and 4 weeks to arrive in New Orleans. In 1799 it took 1 week for news of George Washington's death to reach New York City from Virginia. A decade and a half later, it still took 49 days for word of the peace treaty ending the War of 1812 to reach New York from London.

By the early 1830s, a decade before Samuel F.B. Morse invented the telegraph, the transmission of information had improved considerably as a result of improved roads and faster sailing ships. In 1831 it took just 15.5 hours for the text of Andrew Jackson's State of the Union address to travel from Washington to New York—eight times faster than in 1799. By 1841 a letter traveled between New York and New Orleans in 9 days and between New York and Cincinnati in 5 days—three times faster than in 1815.

The volume of information transmitted also increased considerably. In 1790 the United States had just 92 newspapers, with a total annual circulation of less than 4 million. By 1820 the number of papers published had jumped to 512, with an annual circulation of 50 million; by 1835 there were 1258 newspapers in the United States with a circulation of over 90 million. When Alexis de Tocqueville, a French observer, visited the United States in 1831, he was shocked at the amount of information available even in frontier regions: "I do not think that in the most enlightened rural districts of France there is an intellectual movement either so rapid or on such a scale as in this wilderness."

Transforming American Law

The growth of an industrial economy in the United States required a shift in American law. At the beginning of the nineteenth century, American law was rooted in concepts that reflected the values of a slowly changing, agricultural society. The law presumed that goods and services had a just price, independent of supply and demand. Courts forbade many forms of competition and innovation in the name of a stable society. Courts and judges legally protected monopolies and prevented lenders from charging "usurous" rates of interest. The law allowed property owners to sue for damages if a mill was built upstream and it flooded their land or impeded their water supply. After 1815, however, the American legal system favored economic growth, profit, and entrepreneurial enterprise. Courts increasingly viewed risk and profit as beneficial.

In the 1810s and 1820s American law shifted from a premarket to a market economy perspective. By the 1820s, courts, particularly in the Northeast, had begun to abandon many traditional legal doctrines that stood in the way of a competitive market economy. Courts dropped older doctrines that assumed that goods and services had an objective price, independent of supply and demand. Courts rejected many usury laws, which limited interest rates, and struck down legal rules that prevented tenants from making alterations on a piece of land, including the addition of a building or clearing of trees. Courts increasingly held that only the market could determine interest rates or prices or the equity of a contract.

To promote rapid economic growth, courts and state legislatures gave new powers and privileges to private firms. Companies building roads, bridges, canals, and other public works were given the power to appropriate land; private firms were allowed to avoid legal penalties for fires, floods, or noise they caused on the grounds that the companies served a public purpose. Courts also reduced the liability of companies for injuries to their own employees, ruling that an injured party had to prove negligence or carelessness on the part of an employer in order to collect damages. The legal barriers to economic expansion had been struck down.

Resistance to Technological Innovation

At the beginning of the nineteenth century, a lack of skilled mechanics, an inadequate system of higher education, and widespread resistance to technological innovation also hampered economic progress. The United States lagged far behind Europe in the practical application of science and technology. There was probably just one steam engine in regular operation in the United States in 1800, one hundred years after simple engines had first been used in Europe. Ten years after the first cotton mill opened in the United States in 1791, only eight cotton mills operated in the country. Inventors, like Oliver Evans, designer of an early locomotive, and John Fitch, creator of the first American steamboat, failed because they were unable to finance their projects or persuade the public to use their inventions.

The lack of skilled mechanics presented a particularly severe barrier to innovation. In 1805, when Robert Fulton wanted to build a torpedo, he could find only one mechanic in New York who could follow his plans, a Frenchman who spoke virtually no English. Two years later, when he needed an engine to propel the *Clermont* up the Hudson River, he had to import a steam engine from England, since American craftsmen could not construct such a complicated machine.

The inadequate state of higher education also slowed technological innovation. At the beginning of the nineteenth century, Harvard, the nation's most famous college, graduated just 39 men a year, no more than it had graduated in 1720. Harvard's entire undergraduate faculty consisted of the college president, a professor of theology, a professor of mathematics, a professor of Hebrew, and four tutors. All the nation's libraries put together contained barely 50,000 volumes. Noah Webster, author of the

nation's first dictionary, admitted grudgingly: "Our learning is superficial in shameful degree . . . our colleges are disgracefully destitute of books and philosophical apparatus."

Even in educated circles, resistance to technological change was widespread—despite the well-known and widely publicized experiments of Benjamin Franklin and Thomas Jefferson. At the end of the eighteenth century, Jedidiah Morse, a graduate of Yale College and pastor of a church near Boston, gave pointed expression to the widespread hostility toward change. "Let us guard against the insidious encroachments of innovation," he wrote, "the evil and beguiling spirit which is now stalking to and fro through the earth, seeking how he may destroy."

By the 1820s, however, the United States had largely overcome resistance to technological innovation. When Friedrich List, a German traveler, visited the United States in the 1820s, he was astonished by the amount of public interest in technology. "Everything new is quickly introduced here," List wrote. "There is no clinging to old ways; the moment an American hears the word 'invention' he pricks up his ears."

How had Americans overcome resistance to technological innovation? The answer lies in the efforts of literally hundreds of inventors, tinkerers, and amateur scientists, who transformed European ideas into practical technologies. Their inventions inspired in Americans a boundless faith in technology.

Early American technology was pioneered largely by self-taught amateurs, whose zeal and self-assurance led them to create inventions that trained European scientists did not attempt. As early as the 1720s, it was known that electricity could be conducted along a wire to convey messages, but it was not until 1844 that an American artist and inventor named Samuel F. B. Morse demonstrated the practicality of the telegraph and devised a workable code for sending messages. A Frenchman built the first working steamship in 1783, but it was 24 years later that Robert Fulton, an American, produced the first commercially successful steamship. Eighteenth-century Europeans knew that ether would induce unconsciousness, but it was not until 1842 that a Georgia surgeon named Crawford Long used ether as an anesthetic. The first real steam engine was invented by an Englishman in 1699, but it was an American named Oliver Evans who in 1805 produced a light and powerful steam engine with high-pressure cylinders.

During the mid-eighteenth century, an Englishman had devised plans for a submarine, but in 1776, an American, David Bushnell, built the first workable submarine—a one-man, hand-crank powered vessel called the *Turtle*, which attempted to fasten an explosive charge on the hull of the British ship the *Eagle*. Mechanical clocks could be found in the late middle ages, but it was an American, Eli Terry, who found a way to mass produce wooden clocks around 1800.

Early Industrialization

In the 1820s and 1830s, America became the world's leader in adopting mechanization, standardization, and mass production. Manufacturers began to adopt labor-saving machinery that allowed workers to produce more goods at lower costs. So impressed were foreigners with these methods of manufacture that they called them the "American system of production."

The single most important figure in the development of the American system was Eli Whitney, the inventor of the cotton gin. In 1798, Whitney persuaded the U.S. government to award him a contract for 10,000 muskets to be delivered within two years. At the time Whitney made his offer, the federal arsenal at Springfield, Massachusetts, was capable of producing only 245 muskets in two years. Since Whitney had no factory and no experience making guns, his offer seemed preposterous.

Whitney proposed manufacturing muskets according to a "new principle," which would enable an unskilled worker to produce muskets faster than those made by a gunsmith. Until then, rifles had been manufactured by skilled artisans, who made individual parts by hand and then carefully fitted the pieces together. Whitney's idea was to develop precision machinery to make parts that would be interchangeable from one gun to another. For months, Whitney struggled to develop drill presses, lathes, cut-ters, and grinders that would allow a worker with little manual skill to manufacture identical gun parts. The first year he produced 500 muskets.

In 1801, in order to get an extension on his contract, Whitney demonstrated his new system of interchangeable parts to President John Adams and Vice President Thomas Jefferson. He disassembled ten muskets and put ten new muskets together out of the individual pieces. His system was a success. (In fact, the muskets used in the demonstration were not assembly line models, they had been carefully hand-fitted beforehand).

Other industries soon adopted the "American system of manufacturing." As early as 1800 manufacturers of wooden clocks began to use interchangeable parts. Makers of sewing machines used mass production techniques as early as 1846, and the next year, manufacturers mechanized the production of farm machinery.

Innovation was not confined to manufacturing. During the years following the War of 1812, American agriculture underwent a transformation nearly as profound and far-reaching as the revolution taking place in industry.

During the eighteenth century, most farm families were largely self-sufficient. They raised their own food, made their own clothes and shoes, and built their own furniture. Cut off from markets by the high cost of transportation,

With Eli Whitney's cotton gin, the amount of cotton fiber that a slave could separate from seed each day increased from 1 pound to 50 pounds.

farmers sold only a few items, like whiskey, corn, and hogs, in exchange for such necessities as salt and iron goods. Farming methods were primitive. With the exception of plowing and furrowing, most farmwork was performed by hand. European travelers deplored the backwardness of American farmers, their ignorance of the principles of scientific farming, their lack of labor-saving machinery, and their wastefulness of natural resources. Few farmers applied manure to their fields as fertilizer or practiced crop rotation. As a result, soil erosion and soil exhaustion were commonplace. Commented one observer: "Agriculture in the South does not consist so much in cultivating land as in killing it."

But beginning in the last decade of the eighteenth century, agriculture underwent profound changes. Some farmers began to grow larger crop surpluses and to specialize in cash crops. A growing demand for cotton for England's textile mills led to the introduction of long-staple cotton from the West Indies into the islands and lowlands of Georgia and South Carolina. Eli Whitney's invention of the cotton gin in 1793—which permitted an individual to clean 50 pounds of short-staple cotton in a single day, 50 times more than could be cleaned by hand—made it practical to produce short-staple cotton in the South (which was much more difficult to clean and process than long-staple cotton). Other cash crops raised by southern farmers included rice, sugar, flax for linen, and hemp for rope fibers. In the Northeast, the growth of mill towns and urban centers created a growing demand for hogs, cattle, sheep, corn, wheat, wool, butter, milk, cheese, fruit, vegetables, and hay to feed horses.

As production for the market increased, farmers began to demand improved farm technology. In 1793 Charles Newbold, a New Jersey farmer, spent his entire fortune of $30,000 developing an efficient cast-iron plow. Farmers refused to use it, fearing that iron would poison the soil and cause weeds to grow. Twenty years later, a Scipio, New York, farmer named Jethro Wood patented an improved iron plow made out of interchangeable parts. Unlike wooden plows, which required two men and four oxen to plow an acre in a day, Wood's cast-iron plow allowed

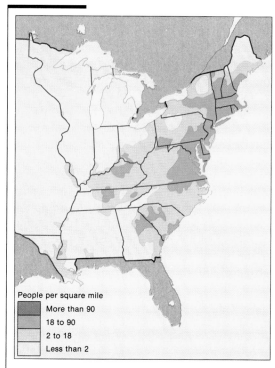

People per square mile
- More than 90
- 18 to 90
- 2 to 18
- Less than 2

1810 Population Density

one man and one yoke of oxen to plow the same area. Demand was so great that manufacturers infringed on Wood's patents and produced thousands of copies of this new plow yearly.

A shortage of farm labor encouraged many farmers to adopt labor-saving machinery. Prior to the introduction in 1803 of the cradle scythe—a rake used to cut and gather up grain and deposit it in even piles—a farmer could not harvest more than half an acre a day. The horse rake—a device introduced in 1820 to mow hay—allowed a single farmer to perform the work of eight to ten men. The invention in 1836 of a mechanical thresher, used to separate the wheat from the chaff, helped to cut in half the man-hours required to produce an acre of wheat.

By 1830 the roots of America's future industrial growth had been firmly planted. Back in 1807, the nation had just 15 or 20 cotton mills, containing approximately 8000 spindles. By 1831 the number of spindles in use totaled nearly a million and a quarter. By 1830 Pitts-

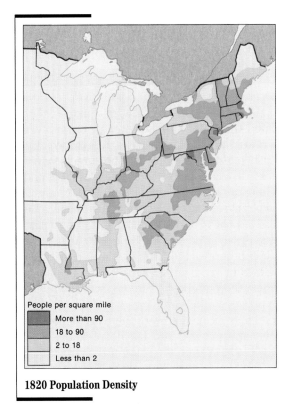

1820 Population Density

People per square mile
- More than 90
- 18 to 90
- 2 to 18
- Less than 2

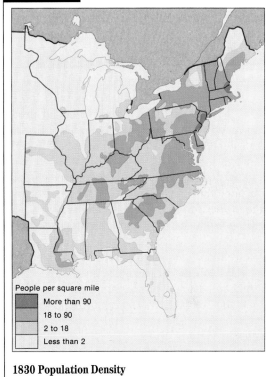

1830 Population Density

People per square mile
- More than 90
- 18 to 90
- 2 to 18
- Less than 2

burgh produced 100 steam engines a year; Cincinnati, 150. Factory production had made household manufacture of shoes, clothing, textiles, and farm implements obsolete. The United States was well on its way to becoming one of the world's leading manufacturing nations.

The Growth of Cities

At the beginning of the nineteenth century, the United States was a nation of farms and rural villages. The nation's four largest cities together contained only 180,000 persons and were the country's only cities with more than 10,000 inhabitants. Boston, which in 1800 contained just 25,000 inhabitants, looked much as it had prior to the Revolution. Its streets, still paved with cobblestones, were unlighted at night. Older gentlemen could still be seen dressed in three-cornered hats, knee-breeches, white-topped boots, ruffled shirts, and powdered wigs. New York was so small that Wall Street was considered to be uptown and Broadway was a country

drive. New York's entire police force, which only patrolled the city at night, consisted of 2 captains, 2 deputies, and 72 assistants.

During the 1820s and 1830s, the nation's cities grew at an extraordinary rate. The urban population increased sixty percent a decade, five times as fast as that of the country as a whole. In 1810, New York City's population was less than 100,000. Two decades later it was more than 200,000. Western cities grew particularly fast. Between 1810 and 1830, Pittsburgh's population climbed from 4768 to 15,369; and Louisville from 1357 to 10,341.

The chief cause of the increase was the migration of sons and daughters away from farms and villages. The growth of commerce drew thousands of farm children to the cities to work as bookkeepers, clerks, and salespeople. The expansion of factories demanded thousands of laborers, mechanics, teamsters, and operatives. The need of rural areas for services available only in urban centers also promoted the growth of cities. Farmers needed their grain milled and their livestock butchered. In response, a grain processing and meat-packing industry sprouted up in "Porkopolis," Cincinnati. Manufacturers in Lexington produced hemp sacks and ropes for Kentucky farmers, and Louisville businesses cured and marketed tobacco.

Pittsburgh's growth illustrates these processes at work. Frontier farmers needed products made of iron, such as nails, horseshoes, and farm implements. Pittsburgh lay near western Pennsylvania's coal fields. Because it was cheaper to bring the iron ore to the coal supply for smelting than to transport the coal to the side of the iron mine, Pittsburgh became a major iron producer. Iron foundries and blacksmith shops proliferated. So did glass factories, which required large amounts of fuel to provide heat for glassblowing. As early as the 1820s, Pittsburgh had three newspapers, nine churches, three theaters, a piano maker, five glass factories, three textile mills, and a steam engine factory.

As urban areas grew many problems were exacerbated, including the absence of clean drinking water, the pressing need for cheap public transportation, and most importantly, poor sanitation. Sanitation problems led to heavy urban mortality rates and frequent typhoid, dysentery, typhus, cholera, and yellow fever epidemics.

Most city dwellers used outdoor privies, which emptied into vaults and cesspools that sometimes leaked into the soil and contaminated the water supply. Kitchen wastes were thrown into ditches; refuse was thrown into trash piles by the side of the streets. Every horse in a city deposited as much as 20 pounds of manure and urine on the streets each day. To help remove the garbage and refuse, many cities allowed packs of dogs, goats, and pigs to scavenge freely. The editor of one New York newspaper described the filth that plagued that city's streets in vivid terms: "The offal and filth, of which there are loads thrown from the houses in defiance of an ordinance which is never enforced, is scraped up with the usual deposits of mud and manure into big heaps and left for weeks together on the sides of the streets."

Following the War of 1812, steps were taken to promote a more comfortable life in the cities, but unfortunately many of the improvements could be enjoyed only by the well-to-do.

This painting, dated 1832–1834, by Russell Smith depicts a saltworks, one of the leading industrial enterprises of the early nineteenth century.

Broadway, New York, c. 1834. By the 1830s numerous street trades were operating on Broadway, which had evolved into an urban thoroughfare traversed by a variety of vehicles, including the urban stagecoach.

About 1815 primitive toilets, called water closets, began to appear in the homes of richer families. Around the same time, coal-burning iron ranges began to replace open fireplaces for cooking, and houses were heated during the winter by iron stoves. To provide light after darkness fell, Boston in 1822 introduced the first gas-fueled street lights, and individual households relied on new kinds of lamps burning whale oil or turpentine. The first urban stagecoach service (the forerunner of the public bus system) appeared in New York City in 1828. Then in the 1830s, the first full-time professional police forces in the United States were formed.

Although elite urbanites were beginning to enjoy some amenities, many of the cities' poorest inhabitants lived in slums. Slums appeared on New York's lower east side as early as 1815. By the 1840s, more than 18,000 men, women, and children were crowded into damp, unlighted, ill-ventilated cellars with 6 to 20 persons living in a single room. In 1849, Boston's Committee on Internal Health reported that men, women, and children lived "huddled together like brutes without regard to sex, age or a sense of decency, grown men and women sleeping together in the same apartment, and sometimes wife, brothers and sisters in the same bed." Despite growing public awareness of the problems of slums and urban poverty, conditions remained unchanged for several generations.

THE GROWTH OF POLITICAL FACTIONALISM AND SECTIONALISM

The Era of Good Feelings began with a burst of nationalistic fervor. The economic program adopted by Congress, including a national bank and a protective tariff, reflected the growing feeling of national unity. The Supreme Court promoted the spirit of nationalism by establishing the principle of federal supremacy. Industrialization and improvements in transportation

(Text continues on p. 286)

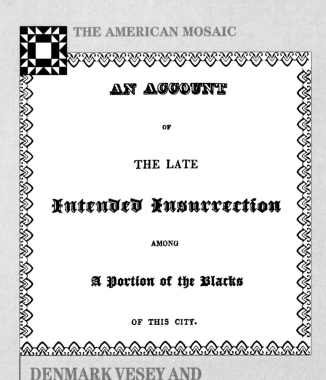

AN ACCOUNT

OF

THE LATE

Intended Insurrection

AMONG

A Portion of the Blacks

OF THIS CITY.

DENMARK VESEY AND THE SLAVE CONSPIRACY OF 1822

"Do not open your lips! Die silent, as you shall see me do." Speaking from the gallows, Peter Poyas soon met his death with stoic dignity— as did five others on the second day of July in 1822. Among the five was Denmark Vesey, whose quiet composure at death reflected the steely courage with which he had led blacks in and around Charleston, South Carolina, in plotting insurrection. As their trials revealed, for over a year Vesey and his lieutenants had planned, recruited, and hoarded the provisions for the fight. Only betrayal by a few slaves had prevented what could well have become the bloodiest slave revolt in America's history.

Many whites were surprised at the revelation of Vesey's leadership. In their eyes he seemed to have few grievances. Born in the late 1760s in either Africa or the Caribbean, he served as a slave to Captain Joseph Vesey, a Bermuda slave trader who settled in Charleston in 1783 as a slave broker and ship merchandiser. In 1800 Denmark Vesey won $1500 in the East Bay Lottery. He then purchased his freedom for $600 and opened a carpentry shop; by 1817 he had amassed savings of several thousand dollars. He was literate and well traveled. He had once been offered the opportunity to return to Africa as a free man and rejected it. "What did he have to be upset about?" many whites must have asked. Well, for one thing, his wife and several of his children were still in bondage.

He also deeply resented white interference in the lives of free blacks as well as slaves.

Vesey was a proud man and frequently rebuked friends who acquiesced to such traditional displays of deference as bowing to whites on the street. One remembered Vesey telling him "all men were born equal, and that he was surprised that anyone would degrade himself by such conduct; that he would never cringe to whites, nor ought any who had the feelings of a man."

As in cities throughout the nation, blacks in Charleston were meeting oppression by forging their own institutions and creating self-affirming communities. A key part of this process was religious independence. At the close of the War of 1812 black Methodists in Charleston outnumbered white ones ten to one. After an unsuccessful attempt by blacks to control their destinies within the white church, Morris Brown went to Philadelphia and was ordained by the African Methodist Episcopal church. In 1818, following a dispute over a burial ground, more than three-fourths of the 6000 black Methodists of Charleston withdrew from the white-led churches. Morris Brown was appointed bishop, and the African Church of Charleston was established.

White authorities quickly saw the danger of such independent churches as possible seedbeds of radicalism. Thus they harassed church meetings and jailed church leaders. Beginning in 1820 legislation was passed to reduce the free black population of South Carolina. Finally in 1821 the city of Charleston closed the Hampstead Church, which had been the leader of the independent church movement—and which included Denmark Vesey among its members. That closing became the spark that ignited Vesey to action. He began holding meetings, often in his own home, with other members of the congregation, such as Rolla Bennett, "Gullah Jack" Pritchard, Monday Gell, and Ned and Peter Poyas. They became the nucleus of what came to be called the Vesey Conspiracy.

Later testimony indicates that Vesey was well aware of several recent events that convinced him that the tide of history was changing. Foremost was the successful slave rebellion in Haiti that began in 1791. Vesey "was in the habit of reading to me all the passages in the newspapers that related to St. Domingo, and apparently every pamphlet he could lay his hands on that had any connection with slavery," one rebel testified. Vesey was also knowledgeable about the Missouri debates; the same rebel reported, "He one day brought me a speech which he told me had been delivered in congress by a Mr. [Rufus] King on the subject of slavery; he told me this Mr. King was the black man's friend, that he, Mr. King, had declared . . . that slavery was a great disgrace to the country."

Vesey used religion as a potent force to spur blacks to join him in armed rebellion. At almost every meeting he "read to us from the Bible, how the children of Israel were delivered out of Egypt from bondage." He also frequently used the passage: "Behold the day of the Lord cometh, and thy spoil shall be divided in the midst of thee. For I shall gather all nations against Jeruselem to battle; and the city shall be taken." In addition, "Gullah Jack," born in Africa, was known

as a powerful conjurer, and many were convinced his power could protect them from harm.

There was a distinctly Pan-African cast to the conspiracy. A number of the leaders had lived in either Africa or the Caribbean. One of them, Monday Gell, had apparently corresponded with the president of Haiti. Charleston blacks were told that "Santo Domingo and Africa will assist us to get our liberty, if we will only make the motion first." The motion they planned was bold indeed. They were to attack the city at seven different points, capture weapons at the arsenal, set fire to the city, and kill all whites they encountered.

The plan was bold but not rashly undertaken. They prepared for a deadline in the second week of July 1822. Large numbers were needed and available. Blacks outnumbered whites ten to one in the area surrounding Charleston, and recruiting extended to plantations as far away as 80 miles. The big problem was a shortage of arms until the arsenal was taken. So blacksmiths began making bayonets and spikes. Anything that could be used as a weapon was hoarded, along with gun powder. Draymen, caters, and butchers were recruited to supply horses. Hundreds of blacks from all classes and occupations were contacted, but the nucleus remained skilled artisans, free and slave, from Charleston.

The dangers of advance planning and a widespread network were leaks and betrayal. For months luck held, but in late May 1822 a slave reported an attempt to recruit him to the insurrection. As authorities began to investigate, the betrayals escalated, and the authorities deployed military force to quash the

rebellion before it had a chance to get started. Ten slaves were arrested on June 17–18, and the court began hearings. On June 22 Vesey was captured and stood trial the next day, while "Gullah Jack," the only major leader still free, tried to continue the revolt. Three days after the July 2 executions "Gullah Jack" was arrested. By August 9 more than 30 blacks had been hanged and many more deported.

White retaliation was swift and sure. So was white hysteria. The executions were public, and blacks were forbidden to dress in black or wear black crepe to mourn the dead. Examples were also made of the informers, who were freed and granted life-time annuities. Finally, whites responded to Vesey's conspiracy with further antiblack legislation.

On the surface little good came from Denmark Vesey's bold plan. Its chances of success were meager at best. During Vesey's sentencing, the presiding magistrate told him, "It is difficult to imagine what *infatuation* could have prompted you to attempt an enterprise so wild and visionary. You were a free man; were comparatively wealthy; and enjoyed every comfort, compatible with your situation. You had therefore, much to risk and little to gain. From your age and experience you *ought* to have known, that success was impracticable." Nevertheless Vesey took his indomitable stand. While recruiting for the Union army, the great black abolitionist Frederick Douglass called upon blacks "to remember Denmark Vesey."

also added to the sense of national unity by contributing to the nation's economic strength and independence and by linking the West and the East together.

But this same period also witnessed the emergence of growing factional divisions in politics, including a deepening sectional split between the North and South. A severe economic depression between 1819 and 1822 provoked bitter division over questions of banking and tariffs. Geographic expansion exposed latent tensions over the morality of slavery and the balance of economic power. It was during the Era of Good Feelings that the political issues arose that would dominate American politics for the next 40 years.

The Panic of 1819

In 1819 a financial panic swept across the country. The growth in trade that followed the War of 1812 came to an abrupt halt. Unemployment mounted, banks failed, mortgages were foreclosed, and agricultural prices fell by half. Investment in western lands collapsed.

The panic was frightening in its scope and impact. In New York State, property values fell from $315 million in 1818 to $256 million in 1820. In Richmond, property values fell by half. In Pennsylvania, land values plunged from $150 an acre in 1815 to $35 in 1819. In Philadelphia, 1808 individuals were committed to debtors' prison. In Boston, the figure was 3500.

For the first time in American history, the problem of urban poverty commanded public attention. In New York in 1819, the Society for the Prevention of Pauperism counted 8000 paupers out of a population of 120,000. The next year, the figure climbed to 13,000. Fifty thousand people were unemployed or irregularly employed in New York, Philadelphia, and Baltimore, and one foreign observer estimated that half a million people were jobless nationwide. To address the problem of destitution, newspapers appealed for old clothes and shoes for the poor, and churches and municipal governments distributed soup. Baltimore set up 12 soup kitchens in 1820 to give food to the poor.

The downswing spread like a plague across the country. In Cincinnati, bankruptcy sales occurred almost daily. In Lexington, Kentucky,

factories worth half a million dollars were idle. Matthew Carey, a Philadelphia economist, estimated that 3 million people, one-third of the nation's population, were adversely affected by the panic. In 1820, John C. Calhoun commented: "There has been within these two years an immense revolution of fortunes in every part of the Union; enormous numbers of persons utterly ruined; multitudes in deep distress."

The panic had several causes, including a dramatic decline in cotton prices, a contraction of credit by the Bank of the United States designed to curb inflation, an 1817 congressional order requiring hard-currency payments for land purchases, and the closing of many factories due to foreign competition.

The panic unleashed a storm of popular protest. Many debtors agitated for "stay laws" to provide relief from debts as well as the abolition of debtors' prisons. Manufacturing interests called for increased protection from foreign imports, but a growing number of southerners believed that high protective tariffs, which raised the cost of imported goods and reduced the flow of international trade, were the root of their troubles. Many people clamored for a reduction in the cost of government and pressed for sharp reductions in federal and state budgets. Others, particularly in the South and West, blamed the panic on the nation's banks and particularly the tight-money policies of the Bank of the United States.

By 1823 the panic was over. But it left a lasting imprint on American politics. The panic led to demands for the democratization of state constitutions, an end to restrictions on voting and officeholding, and heightened hostility toward banks and other "privileged" corporations and monopolies. The panic also exacerbated tensions within the Republican party and aggravated sectional tensions as northerners pressed for higher tariffs while southerners abandoned their support of nationalistic economic programs.

The Missouri Crisis

In the midst of the panic, a crisis over slavery erupted with stunning suddenness. It was, Thomas Jefferson wrote, like "a firebell in the night." The crisis was ignited by the application of Missouri for statehood, and it involved the status of slavery west of the Mississippi River.

East of the Mississippi, the Mason-Dixon line and the Ohio River formed a boundary between the North and South. States south of this line were slave states; states north of this line had either abolished slavery or adopted gradual emancipation policies. West of the Mississippi, however, no clear line demarcated the boundary between free and slave territory.

Representative James Tallmadge, a New York Republican, provoked the crisis in February 1819 by introducing an amendment to restrict slavery in Missouri as a condition of statehood. The amendment prohibited the further introduction of slaves into Missouri and provided for emancipation of all children of slaves at the age of 25. Voting along ominously sectional lines, the House approved the Tallmadge Amendment. But, the amendment was defeated in the Senate, where Senators from the South received support from northern allies.

Southern and northern politicians alike responded with fury. Southerners condemned the Tallmadge proposal. John Randolph declared that "God has given us Missouri and the devil shall not take it from us." Southern leaders denounced Tallmadge's amendment as part of a northeastern plot to dominate the government. They declared the United States to be a union of equals, claiming that Congress had no power to place special restrictions upon a state. Talk of disunion and civil war was rife. Senator Freeman Walker of Georgia envisioned "civil war . . . a brother's sword crimsoned with a brother's blood."

Northern politicians responded with equal vehemence. Said Representative Tallmadge, "If blood is necessary to extinguish any fire which I have assisted to kindle, I can assure you gentlemen, while I regret the necessity, I shall not forbear to contribute my mite." Northern leaders argued that national policy, enshrined in the Northwest Ordinance, committed the government to halt the expansion of the institution of slavery. They warned that the extension of slavery into the West would inevitably increase the pressures to reopen the African slave trade.

This was not the first congressional crisis over slavery. In 1790, a bitter dispute had arisen over whether Congress should accept antislav-ery petitions. In 1798, a furor had erupted over a proposal to extend the Northwest Ordinance prohibition on slavery to Mississippi. In 1804, a new uproar had broken out over a proposal to bar new slaves from emigrating to Louisiana. In 1801 and again in 1814–1815, Federalists had protested the three-fifths compromise, which counted each slave as three-fifths of a person in apportioning representation in the House of Representatives.

But never before had passions been so heated or sectional antagonisms so overt. In the Northeast, for the first time, philanthropists like Elias Boudinot of Burlington, New Jersey, succeeded in mobilizing public opinion against the westward expansion of slavery. Mass meetings convened in a number of cities in the Northeast. The vehemence of anti-Missouri feeling is apparent in an editorial that appeared in the New York *Advertiser*: "THIS QUESTION INVOLVES NOT ONLY THE FUTURE CHARACTER OF OUR NATION, BUT THE FUTURE WEIGHT AND INFLUENCE OF THE FREE STATES. IF NOW LOST—IT IS LOST FOREVER."

Compromise resolved the crisis of 1819. The Senate narrowly voted to admit Missouri as a slave state. To preserve the sectional balance, it also voted to admit Maine, which had previously been a part of Massachusetts, as a free state, and to prohibit the formation of any further slave states from the territory of the Louisiana Purchase north of the 36° 30' north latitude. Henry Clay then skillfully steered the compromise through the House, where a handful of antislavery representatives, fearful of the threat to the Union, threw their support behind the proposals.

A second crisis erupted when the Missouri constitutional convention directed the state legislature to forbid the migration of free blacks and mulattoes into the state. This crisis, too, was resolved by compromise. Missouri agreed not to abridge the constitutional rights of any United States citizens—without specifically acknowledging that free blacks were U.S. citizens.

Compromise was possible in 1819 and 1820 because most northerners were apathetic to the Tallmadge Amendment and opponents of slavery were still disunited. Public attention was focused on the Panic of 1819 and the resulting depression. Leadership of the drive to restrict

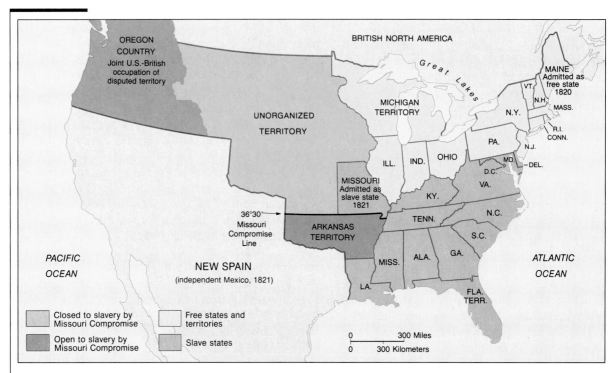

Missouri Compromise

The agreement reached in the Missouri Compromise temporarily settled the argument over slavery in the territories.

slavery in Missouri had been assumed by Presbyterian and Congregationalist churchmen, provoking widespread hostility from an anticlerical and anti-Federalist opposition.

Southerners won a victory in 1820, but they paid a high price. While many states would eventually be organized from the Louisiana Purchase area north of the compromise line, only two (Arkansas and part of Oklahoma) would be formed from the southern portion. If the South was to defend its political power against an antislavery majority, it had but two options in the future. It would either have to forge new political alliances with the North and West, or it would have to acquire new territory in the Southwest. The latter would inevitably reignite northern opposition to the further expansion of slavery.

The Era of Good Feelings ended on a note of foreboding. Although compromise had been achieved, it was clear that sectional conflict had

not been resolved, only postponed. Sectional antagonism, Jefferson wrote, "is hushed, indeed, for the moment. But this is a reprieve only, not a final sentence. A geographical line, coinciding with a marked principle, moral and political, once conceived and held up to the angry passions of men, will never be obliterated; and every new irritation will mark it deeper and deeper." John Quincy Adams agreed. The Missouri crisis, he wrote, is only the "title page to a great tragic volume."

CONCLUSION

The Era of Good Feelings came to a formal close on March 4, 1825, the day that John Quincy Adams was inaugurated as the nation's sixth president. Adams, who had served eight years as his predecessor's secretary of state, believed that James Monroe's terms in office would be

CHRONOLOGY
OF KEY EVENTS

1785 Oliver Evans opens the first automated flour mill

1786 John Fitch demonstrates his first steamboat

1793 Samuel Slater opens the first American textile mill at Pawtucket, Rhode Island

1807 Robert Fulton's *Clermont* demonstrates practicality of steam-powered navigation

1814 First factory to turn raw cotton into cotton cloth opens in Waltham, Massachusetts

1815 Congress declares war on Algiers

1816 Second Bank of the United States is chartered; Protective Tariff is passed; James Monroe is elected fifth president

1818 General Andrew Jackson invades Florida; Rush-Bagot convention between Britain and United States establishes American fishing rights and U.S.-Canadian boundary

1819 Panic of 1819; Spain cedes Florida to the United States and recognizes the western limits of the Louisiana Purchase in the Adams-Onis Treaty; *Dartmouth* v. *Woodward* upholds the sanctity of contracts; *McCulloch* v. *Maryland* upholds the constitutionality of the second Bank of the United States

1820 Missouri Compromise prohibits slavery in the northern half of the Louisiana Purchase; Missouri enters the union as a slave state and Maine as a free state

1822 Denmark Vesey's slave insurrection in South Carolina is exposed

1823 President James Monroe opposes any further European colonization or interference in the Americas, establishing the principle now known as the Monroe Doctrine

1825 Erie Canal opens

1837 Panic of 1837; *Charles River Bridge* v. *Warren Bridge*

1840 Congress passes Van Buren's Independent Treasury Act; William Henry Harrison, a Whig, is elected ninth president

1841 Harrison's death makes John Tyler the tenth president

1842 Dorr Rebellion against suffrage restrictions in Rhode Island

---

regarded by future generations of Americans as a "golden age." In his inaugural address, he spoke with pride of the nation's achievements since the War of 1812. A strong spirit of nationalism pervaded the nation and the country stood united under a single political party, the Republicans. The nation had settled its most serious disputes with England and Spain, extended its boundaries to the Pacific, asserted its diplomatic independence, encouraged the wars for national independence in Latin America, had developed a strong manufacturing system, and begun to create a system of transportation adequate to a great nation.

The Era of Good Feelings marked a period of dramatic growth and intense nationalism, but it also witnessed the emergence of new political divisions as well as growing sectional animosities. The period following the War of 1812 brought rapid growth to cities, manufacturing, and the factory system in the North, while the South's economy remained centered around slavery and cotton. These two great sections were developing along diverging lines. Whether the spirit of nationalism or the spirit of sectionalism would triumph was the great question that would dominate American politics over the next four decades.

SUGGESTIONS FOR FURTHER READING

OVERVIEWS AND SURVEYS

William Barney, *The Passage of the Republic: An Interdisciplinary History of Nineteenth-Century America* (1987); W. Elliot Brownlee, *Dynamics of Ascent: A History of the American Economy*, 2d ed. (1988); Stuart Bruchey, *The Roots of American Economic Growth, 1607–1861* (1965); George Dangerfield, *The Awakening of American Nationalism* (1965), and *The Era of Good Feelings* (1952); Robert Heilbroner, *The Economic Transformation of America*, 2d ed. (1984); John R. Howe, *From the Revolution Through the Age of Jackson* (1973); John Mayfield, *The New Nation, 1800–1845*, rev. ed. (1982); Douglas C. North, *The Economic Growth of the United States, 1790–1860* (1961); Sidney Ratner, James H. Soltow, and Richard Sylla, *The Evolution of the American Economy* (1979).

THE GROWTH OF AMERICAN NATIONALISM

Samuel Flagg Bemis, ed., *The American Secretaries of State and Their Diplomacy*, vol. 4 (1928); Edward M. Burns, *The American Idea of Mission: Concepts of National Purpose and Destiny* (1957); Robert K. Faulkner, *The Jurisprudence of John Marshall* (1968); Lloyd C. Gardner et al., *Creation of the American Empire: U.S. Diplomatic History* (1973); C. C. Griffin, *The United States and the Disruption of the Spanish Empire* (1937); George Lee Haskins and Herbert A. Johnson, *History of the Supreme Court of the United States, vol. 2, Foundations of Power: John Marshall, 1801–15* (1981); Ernest R. May, *The Making of the Monroe Doctrine* (1975); Frederick W. Merk, *Manifest Destiny and Mission in American History: A Reinterpretation* (1963), and *The Monroe Doctrine and American Expansionism, 1843–1849* (1966); Paul C. Nagel, *One Nation Indivisible: The Union in American Thought, 1776–1861* (1964); Dexter Perkins, *The Monroe Doctrine* (1927).

THE ROOTS OF AMERICAN ECONOMIC GROWTH

Richard A. Bartlett, *The New Country: A Social History of the American Frontier, 1776–1890* (1974); Alfred D. Chandler, Jr., ed., *The Railroads: The Nation's First Big Business* (1965), and *The Visible Hand* (1977); Howard Chudacoff, *The Evolution of American Urban Society* (1975); Victor S. Clark, *History of Manufactures in the United States, 1607–1860*, 2 vols. (1916–1928); Thomas C. Cochran, *Frontiers of Change: Early Industrialism in*

America (1981); Robert F. Dalzell, Jr., *Enterprising Elite: The Boston Associates and the World They Made* (1987); Clarence H. Danhof, *Change in Agriculture: The Northern United States, 1820–1870* (1969); Paul David, *Technical Choice, Innovation and Economic Growth* (1975); Lance Davis et al., *American Economic Growth: An Economist's History of the United States* (1972); Everett Dick, *The Lure of the Land: A Social History of the Public Lands* (1970); Joseph A. Durrenberger, *Turnpikes: A Study of the Toll Road Movement* (1968); John Faragher, *Sugar Creek* (1986); Albert Fishlow, *American Railroads and the Transformation of the Antebellum Economy* (1965); Paul W. Gates, *The Farmer's Age: Agriculture, 1815–1860* (1960); Sigfried Giedion, *Mechanization Takes Command* (1948); Carter Goodrich, ed., *Canals and American Economic Development* (1961), and *Government Promotion of American Canals and Railroads, 1800–1890* (1960); Ralph D. Gray, *The National Waterway: A History of the Chesapeake and Delaware Canal*, 2d ed. (1989); Erik F. Haites, James Mak, and Gary M. Walton, *Western River Transportation: The Era of Early Internal Development, 1810–1860* (1975); David Hamer, *New Towns in the New World: Images and Perceptions of the Nineteenth-Century Urban Frontier* (1990); Oscar and Mary Handlin, *Commonwealth: A Study of the Role of Government in the American Economy*, rev. ed. (1969); Louis Hartz, *Economic Policy and Democratic Thought* (1948); Morton Horwitz, *The Transformation of American Law, 1780–1860* (1977); David A. Hounshell, *From the American System to Mass Production* (1984); Louis C. Hunter, *Steamboats on the Western Rivers* (1949); James Willard Hurst, *Law and the Conditions of Freedom in the Nineteenth-Century United States* (1956), and *The Legitimacy of the Business Corporation in the Law of the United States, 1780–1970* (1970); David J. Jeremy, *Transatlantic Industrial Revolution: The Diffusion of Textile Technologies Between Britain and America, 1790–1830s* (1981); Arthur M. Johnson and Barry Supple, *Boston Capitalists and Western Railroads: A Study in the Nineteenth Century Railroad Investment Process* (1967); John F. Kasson, *Civilizing the Machine: Technology and Republican Values in America, 1776–1900* (1976); Darwin P. Kelsey, ed., *Farming in the New Nation* (1972); Susan Previant Lee and Peter Passell, *A New Economic View of American History* (1979); Leonard W. Levy, *The Law of the Commonwealth and Chief Justice Shaw* (1957); Timothy R. Mahoney, *River Towns in the Great West: The Structure of Provincial Urbanization in the American Mid-*

west, 1820–1870 (1990); Blake McKelvey, *American Urbanization: A Comparative History* (1973); Nathan Miller, *The Enterprise of a Free People: Aspects of Economic Development in New York State During the Canal Period, 1792–1838* (1962); Zane Miller, *The Urbanization of America* (1973); Eric H. Monkkonen, *America Becomes Urban: The Development of U.S. Cities and Towns* (1988); William Nelson, *The Americanization of the Common Law: The Impact of Legal Change on Massachusetts Society, 1760–1830* (1975); James D. Norris, *R. G. Dun and Co., 1841–1900* (1978); Douglas C. North, *Growth and Welfare in the American Past*, 2d ed. (1974); F. S. Philbrick, *The Rise of the West, 1754–1830* (1965); Glenn Porter and Harold C. Livesay, *Merchants and Manufacturers: Studies in the Changing Structure of Nineteenth-Century Marketing* (1971); J. Potter, "The Growth of Population in America, 1700–1860" in D. V. Glass and D. E. C. Eversley, eds., *Population in History* (1965); Allan R. Pred, *Urban Growth and the Circulation of Information* (1973); Malcolm J. Rohrbough, *The Land Office Business* (1960), and *The Trans-Appalachian Frontier* (1978); Nathan Rosenberg, *Technology and American Economic Growth* (1972); Harry Scheiber, *Ohio Canal Era: A Case Study of Government and the Economy, 1820–1861* (1969); Leo F. Schnore, ed., *The New Urban History: Quantitative Explorations by American Historians* (1975); Ronald E. Shaw, *Canals for a Nation: The Canal Era in the United States* (1990), and *Erie Water West: A History of the Erie Canal, 1792–1854* (1966); Carl Siracusa, *A Mechanical People: Perceptions of the Industrial Order in Massachusetts, 1815–1880* (1979); Merritt Roe Smith, *Harpers Ferry Armory and the New Technology* (1977); John R. Stilgoe, *Borderland: Origins of the American Suburb* (1988); John F. Stover, *Iron Road to the West: American Railroads in the 1850s* (1978), and *The Life and Decline of the American Railroad* (1970); George Rogers Taylor, *The Transportation Revolution* (1951); Jon C. Teaford, *The Municipal Revolution in America: Origins of Modern Urban Government, 1650–1825* (1975); Peter Temin, *Causal Factors in American Economic Growth in the Nineteenth Century* (1975), and *Iron and Steel in Nineteenth Century America* (1964); Stephan Thernstrom and Richard Sennett, eds., *Nineteenth-Century Cities: Essays in the New Urban History* (1969); Robert L. Thompson, *Wiring a Continent: The History of the Telegraph Industry in the United States, 1832–1866* (1947); Dale Van Every, *The Final Challenge: The American Frontier, 1804–1845* (1964); Richard C. Wade, *The Urban Frontier* (1959); Caroline F. Ware, *The Early New England Cotton Manufacture* (1931); Sam Bass Warner, Jr., *The Private City: Philadelphia in Three Periods of Its Growth* (1968), and *The Urban Wilderness* (1972); James W. Whitaker, ed., *Farming in the Midwest, 1840–1900* (1974).

THE GROWTH OF POLITICAL FACTIONALISM AND SECTIONALISM

David Brion Davis, *The Problem of Slavery in the Age of Revolution, 1770–1823* (1975); Don E. Fehrenbacher, *The South and Three Sectional Crises* (1980); Staughton Lynd, *Class Conflict, Slavery and the United States Constitution* (1967); Duncan J. MacLeod, *Slavery, Race, and the American Revolution* (1974); Glover Moore, *The Missouri Controversy* (1953); D. L. Robinson, *Slavery in the Structure of American Politics, 1765–1820* (1971); Murray N. Rothbard, *The Panic of 1819: Reactions and Policies* (1962).

BIOGRAPHIES

Harry Ammon, *James Monroe: The Quest for National Identity* (1971); Leonard Baker, *John Marshall: A Life in Law* (1974); Samuel Flagg Bemis, *John Quincy Adams and the Foundations of American Foreign Policy* (1949), and *John Quincy Adams and the Union* (1956); Richard Current, *Daniel Webster and the Rise of National Conservatism* (1955); Gerald T. Dunne, *Justice Joseph Story and the Rise of the Supreme Court* (1970); Clement Eaton, *Henry Clay and the Art of American Politics* (1957); Mary W. M. Hargreaves, *The Presidency of John Quincy Adams* (1985); John Horton, *James Kent: A Study in Conservatism* (1939); George A. Lipsky, *John Quincy Adams: His Theory and Ideas* (1950); J. H. Powell, *Richard Rush: Republican Diplomat* (1942); F. N. Stites, *John Marshall: Defender of the Constitution* (1981); Barbara M. Tucker, *Samuel Slater and the Origins of the American Textile Industry, 1790–1860* (1984); Glyndon G. Van Deusen, *The Life of Henry Clay* (1937); Charles M. Wiltse, *John C. Calhoun: Nationalist, 1782–1828* (1944).

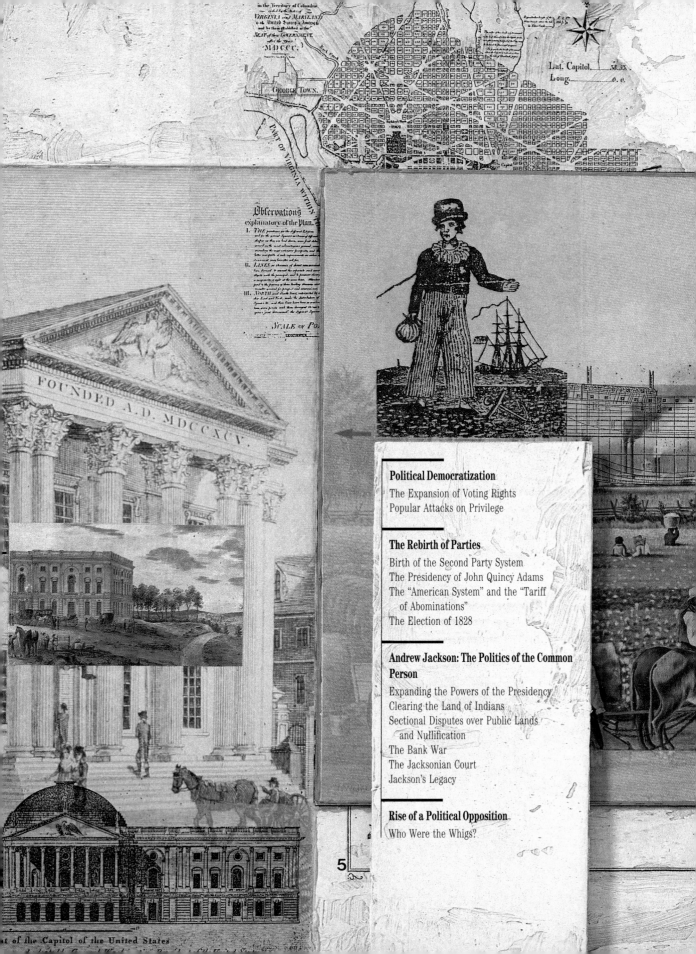

FOUNDED A.D. MDCCXCV.

5

t of the Capitol of the United States

CHAPTER 10

Power and Politics
in Jackson's America

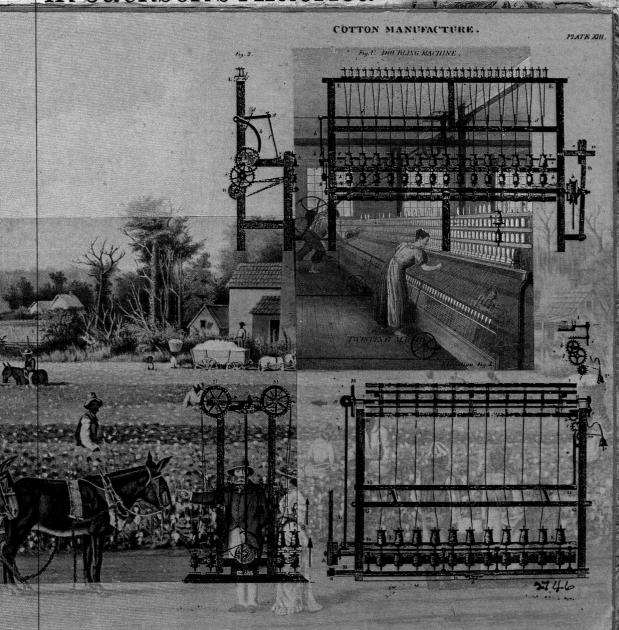

COTTON MANUFACTURE.

PLATE XIII.

PLATE 340.

*I*t was, without a doubt, one of the most exciting, colorful, and dirty presidential campaigns in American history. In 1840, William Henry Harrison, a military hero best known for fighting an alliance of Indians at the Battle of Tippecanoe in 1811, challenged the Democratic incumbent, Martin Van Buren, for the presidency.

Harrison's campaign began at 9:30 A.M., Monday, May 4, 1840. A huge procession, made up of an estimated 75,000 people, marched through the streets of Baltimore to celebrate Harrison's nomination by the Whig party convention. Although Harrison was college-educated and brought up on a plantation with a workforce of some 200 slaves, his Democratic opponents had already dubbed him the "log cabin" candidate, who was happiest on his backwoods farm sipping hard cider. In response, Harrison's supporters enthusiastically seized on this image and promoted it in a number of colorful ways. They distributed barrels of hard cider, passed out campaign hats and placards, and mounted eight log cabins on floats.

Harrison's campaign brought many innovations to the art of electioneering. For the first time, a presidential candidate spoke out on his own behalf. On the morning of Saturday, June 6, 1840, before a Columbus, Ohio, crowd of 25,000, Harrison gave the first campaign speech ever delivered by a candidate. Previous candidates had chosen to let others speak for them. Harrison's backers also coined the first campaign slogans: "Tippecanoe and Tyler Too," "Van, Van is a used up man," and "Matty's policy, 12½ cents a day and french soup, Our policy, 2 Dollars a day and Roast Beef." They staged log cabin raisings, including the erection of a 50-by-100-foot cabin on Broadway in New York City. They sponsored barbeques, including one in Wheeling, Virginia (now West Virginia), where a crowd devoured 360 hams, 26 sheep, 20 calves, 1500 pounds of beef, 8000 pounds of bread, 1000 pounds of cheese, and 4500 pies. Harrison's campaign managers even distributed whiskey bottles in the shape of log cabins, filled by the E.C. Booz Distillery of Philadelphia, thereby adding the word "booze" to the American vocabulary.

While defending their man as the "peoples'" candidate, Harrison's backers heaped an un-precedented avalanche of personal abuse on his Democratic opponent. The Whigs accused President Van Buren of eating off of golden plates and lace tablecloths, drinking French wines, perfuming his whiskers, and wearing a corset. Whigs in Congress denied Van Buren an appropriation of $3665 to repair the White House lest he turn the executive mansion into a "palace as splendid as that of the Caesars." The object of this rough and colorful kind of campaigning was to show that the Democratic candidate harbored aristocratic leanings, while Harrison truly represented the people.

The Harrison campaign provided a number of effective lessons for future politicians, most notably an emphasis on symbols and imagery over ideas and substance. Fearful of alienating voters and dividing the Whig party, the political convention that nominated Harrison agreed to adopt no party platform. Harrison himself said not a single word during the campaign about his principles or proposals. He closely followed the suggestion of one of his advisers that he "rely entirely on the past" (that is, his reputation as a general and victor over the Indians), and offer no indication "about what he thinks now, or what he will do hereafter."

The new campaign techniques produced an overwhelming victory. In 1840, voter turnout was the highest it had ever been in a presidential election: nearly 80 percent of eligible voters cast ballots. The log cabin candidate for president won 53 percent of the popular vote and a landslide victory in the Electoral College.

POLITICAL DEMOCRATIZATION

When James Monroe began his second term as president in 1821, he rejoiced at the idea that the country was no longer divided by political parties, which, he believed, were "the curse of the country," breeding disunity, demagoguery, and corruption. Yet even before Monroe's second term had ended, new political divisions had already begun to evolve, creating an increasingly democratic system of politics.

In 1821, American politics was still largely dominated by deference. Competing political parties were nonexistent and voters generally deferred to the leadership of local elites or lead-

In 1840 the Whig party tried to mobilize voter support for William Henry Harrison by distributing gaily colored handkerchiefs and whiskey bottles shaped like log cabins.

ing families. Political campaigns tended to be relatively staid affairs. Direct appeals by candidates for support were considered in poor taste. Election procedures were, by later standards, quite undemocratic. Most states imposed property and taxpaying requirements on the white adult males who alone had the vote, and conducted voting by voice. Presidential electors were generally chosen by state legislatures. Given the fact that citizens had only the most indirect say in the election of the president, it is not surprising that voting participation was generally extremely low, amounting to less than 30 percent of adult white males.

Between 1820 and 1840, a revolution took place in American politics. In most states, property qualifications for voting and officeholding were repealed; and voting by voice was largely eliminated. Direct methods of selecting presidential electors, county officials, state judges, and governors replaced indirect methods. Because of these and other political innovations, voter participation skyrocketed. By 1840 voting participation had reached unprecedented lev-

els. Nearly 80 percent of adult white males went to the polls.

A new two-party system, made possible by an expanded electorate, replaced the politics of deference to and leadership by elites. By the mid-1830s, two national political parties with marked philosophical differences, strong organizations, and wide popular appeal competed in virtually every state. Professional party managers used partisan newspapers, speeches, parades, rallies, and barbeques to mobilize popular support. Our modern political system had been born.

The Expansion of Voting Rights

The most significant political innovation of the early nineteenth century was the abolition of property qualifications for voting and officeholding. At the time of the Revolution, every American colony imposed formal restrictions on the right to vote and hold public office. Following the English principle that voters had to have a stake in the community, every colony required citizens to own a minimum amount of land or pay a minimal amount of taxes in order to qualify to vote. In the Carolinas and in Maryland, a voter had to own 50 acres of land. New Jersey voters had to own $250 worth of property. Aspirants for public office were often required to meet higher property qualifications. In North Carolina a senator was required to own at least 300 acres of land, and in South Carolina a representative had to own at least 500 acres and 10 slaves.

A number of the colonies also imposed a religious test for voting and officeholding. In South Carolina, voters had to believe in God and in divine punishment. In Connecticut, New Hampshire, New Jersey, and Vermont no atheist, Jew, or Roman Catholic was allowed to hold a public office.

In practice, restrictions on voting were not particularly burdensome. By European standards, a relatively large proportion of the population was qualified to vote because ownership of land was widespread. Moreover, curbs on voting were loosely enforced and easily evaded; men who did not meet property requirements were sometimes allowed to vote on grounds of "good character." Nevertheless, the

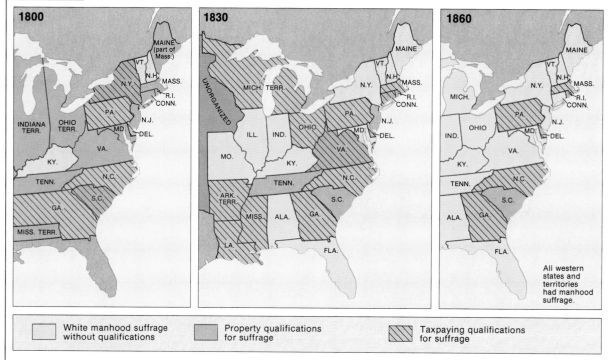

| White manhood suffrage without qualifications | Property qualifications for suffrage | Taxpaying qualifications for suffrage |

Extension of Male Suffrage

Some states and territories reserved the suffrage to white male property holders and taxpayers, while others permitted an alternative such as a period of residence.

laws barred a significant and growing segment of the adult white male population from voting.

During the last years of the eighteenth century and the early decades of the nineteenth century, virtually every state repealed many of the restrictions on voting. During the 1790s, South Carolina permitted Roman Catholics to vote for the first time, while New Hampshire extended the vote to all males over the age of 21.

Hard times resulting from the panic of 1819 led many people to demand an end to property restrictions on voting and officeholding. For example, in 1821, New York State debated the wisdom of extending voting rights to all white men over the age of 21. At the beginning of 1821 fewer than two adult males in five in New York could legally vote for senator or governor. Conservatives led by Federalist James Kent argued that universal suffrage was a bad idea, since men who owned no property had no stake in the well-being of society. Agricultural interests

also opposed the change. They feared that universal manhood suffrage would allow merchants and manufacturers to dominate state politics by controlling the votes of their employees. Proponents of universal manhood suffrage replied that "we are not a government of the people" so long as restrictions upon voting continued to exist.

Under the new constitution adopted in 1821, all adult white males were allowed to vote, so long as they paid taxes or had served in the militia (there was also unsuccessful agitation in the state legislature to enfranchise male African-Americans). Five years later, an amendment to the state's constitution eliminated the taxpaying and militia qualifications, thereby establishing universal white manhood suffrage.

By 1840, universal white manhood suffrage had largely become a reality. Only three states—Louisiana, Rhode Island, and Virginia—still restricted the suffrage to white male property owners and taxpayers.

The transition from property qualifications to universal white manhood suffrage occurred gradually, without violence and with surprisingly little dissension, except in Rhode Island, where lack of progress toward democratization provoked an episode known as the "Dorr War." In 1841, Rhode Island, still operating under a Royal Charter granted in 1663, restricted suffrage to landowners and their eldest sons. The charter lacked a bill of rights and grossly underrepresented growing industrial cities, such as Providence, in the state legislature. As Rhode Island grew increasingly urban and industrial, the state's landless population increased and fewer residents were eligible to vote. By 1841 just 11,239 out of 26,000 adult males were qualified to vote. In that year, Thomas W. Dorr, a Harvard-educated attorney, organized an extralegal convention to frame a new state constitution and abolish voting restrictions. The state's governor declared Dorr and his supporters guilty of insurrection, proclaimed a state of emergency, and called out the state militia. Dorr tried unsuccessfully to capture the state arsenal at Providence. He was arrested, found guilty of high treason, and sentenced to life imprisonment at hard labor. To appease popular resentment, the governor pardoned Dorr the next year, and the state adopted a new constitution with liberal suffrage provisions in 1843.

While universal white manhood suffrage was becoming a reality, restrictions on voting by blacks and women remained in force. Only one state, New Jersey, had given unmarried women property holders the right to vote following the Revolution, but the state rescinded this right at the time it extended suffrage to all adult white men. Most states also explicitly denied the right to vote to free blacks. By 1858 free blacks were eligible to vote in just four northern states: New Hampshire, Maine, Massachusetts, and Vermont.

Immigrant males, by contrast, were permitted to vote in most states if they had declared their intention to become citizens. During the nineteenth century, 22 states and territories permitted immigrants who were not yet naturalized citizens to vote.

In addition to removing property and tax qualifications for voting and officeholding, states also reduced residency requirements for voting and allowed voters to choose presidential electors, governors, and county officials. By 1824, only 6 of the nation's 24 states still chose presidential electors in the state legislature, and 8 years later the only state still to do so was South Carolina, which continued to do so until the Civil War. In order to encourage popular participation in politics, most states also instituted statewide nominating conventions, opened polling places in more convenient locations, extended the hours that polls were open, and eliminated the earlier practice of voting by voice. This last reform did not truly institute the secret ballot, which was only adopted beginning in the 1880s, since voters during the mid-nineteenth century usually voted with straight-ticket paper ballots prepared by the political parties themselves. Each party had a different colored ballot, which voters deposited in a publicly viewed ballot box, so that those present knew who had voted for which party.

Popular Attacks on Privilege

The democratic impulse that swept the country in the 1820s was also apparent in widespread attacks on special privilege and aristocratic pretension. Established churches, the bench, and the legal and medical professions all saw their elitist status diminished.

The judiciary was made more responsive to public opinion through the election, rather than the appointment, of judges. To open up the legal profession, many states dropped formal training requirements to practice law. Some states also abolished training and licensing requirements for physicians, allowing unorthodox "herb and root" doctors, including many women, to compete freely with established physicians.

In upstate New York democratic sentiment took the form of violent "antirent wars," which successfully undermined an old system of land tenure. Under the old system, landlords and land companies collected a yearly payment from farmers as well as a share of the proceeds from the sale of any farm, called a "quitrent." From 1839 to 1843, tenant farmers, disguised as Indians, tarred and feathered sheriffs and deputies, and successfully agitated for a new state constitution that prohibited this little revised form of feudal land tenure.

The surge of democratic sentiment had an important political consequence: the breakdown of deferential politics and its terminology. The eighteenth-century language of politics—which included such terms as "faction," "junto," and "caucus"—was rooted in an elite-dominated political order.

During the first quarter of the nineteenth century, however, this system disintegrated and the influence of local elites declined sharply. With this change, a new democratic political vocabulary emerged that drew its words from everyday language. Instead of "standing" for public office, candidates "ran" for office. Politicians "log-rolled" (made deals) or "straddled the fence" or promoted "pork barrel" legislation (programs that would benefit their constituents).

As the influence of local elites declined, they were replaced by professional politicians. In the 1820s, political innovators such as Martin Van Buren, the son of a tavernkeeper, and Thurlow Weed, a newspaper editor in Albany, New York, devised new campaign tools, such as torchlight parades, subsidized partisan newspapers, and nominating conventions. These political bosses and manipulators soon discovered that the most successful technique for arousing popular interest in politics was to attack a privileged group or institution that had used political influence to attain power or profit.

The "Anti-Masonic party" was the first political movement to win widespread popular following using this technique. In the mid-1820s, a growing number of people in New York and surrounding states had come to believe that members of the fraternal order of Freemasons, who seemed to monopolize many of the region's most prestigious political offices and business positions, had used their connections to enrich themselves. They noted, for instance, that Masons held 22 of the nation's 24 governorships.

Then, in 1826, in the small town of Batavia, New York, William Morgan, a former Mason, disappeared. Morgan had written an exposé of the organization in violation of the order's vow of silence, and rumor soon spread that he had been tied up with heavy cables and dumped into the Niagara River. When no indictments were brought against the alleged perpetrators of Morgan's kidnapping and presumed murder, many upstate New Yorkers accused local constables, justices of the peace, and judges, who were members of the Masons, of obstruction of justice.

By 1830, the Anti-Mason movement had succeeded in capturing half the vote in New York State and had gained substantial support throughout New England. In the mid-1830s, the Anti-Masons were absorbed into a new national political party, the Whigs.

THE REBIRTH OF PARTIES

As discussed in Chapter 7, the framers of the Constitution did not anticipate the development of organized political parties in the new nation that they created. In fact, they associated political parties with the kind of aristocratic alliances based on patronage that dominated eighteenth-century English politics. Organized political parties, they feared, would divide the nation and partisan spirit would detract from a sense of the public good.

Despite widespread opposition to the idea of parties, the first years of the new republic did give rise to two competing political parties, the Federalists and the Republicans (see pp. 219, 222). The first party system, however, differed in two important respects from the kinds of political parties Americans are familiar with today. First, the Federalists and Republicans tended to have a strong sectional character, with the Federalists dominant in New England and the Republicans dominant elsewhere. Furthermore, the two parties denied the legitimacy of parties and never accepted the principle of a loyal political opposition.

After the War of 1812, the nation reverted to a period of one-party government in national politics. The decline of the Federalist party created the illusion of national political unity, but appearances were deceptive. Without the discipline imposed by competition with a strong opposition party, the Republican party began to fragment into cliques and factions.

During James Monroe's presidency, the Republican party disintegrated as a stable national organization. Following his overwhelming victory in 1816, Monroe sought to promote the ideal expressed by George Washington in his Farewell Address: a nation free of partisan divisions. Monroe was hostile to the very idea of parties; he asserted that they were "not necessary for free government." Like Washington, he appointed rival factional leaders, such as John Quincy Adams and John C. Calhoun, to his cabinet. He refused to use federal patronage to strengthen the Republican party. He also took the position that Congress, not the president, was the best representative of the public will, and therefore should define public policy.

The absence of a strong leader, however, led to the fragmentation of the Republican party during Monroe's administration. Factional and sectional rivalries grew increasingly bitter and party machinery fell into disuse.

Birth of the Second Party System

Over time, local and personal factions began to coalesce into a new political party system. Three critical factors contributed to the creation of the second party system. The first was the financial panic of 1819 and the subsequent depression (see p. 286). Factories closed, laborers were left jobless, and banks called in their loans. The amount of currency in circulation fell from $100 million in 1817 to just $45 million in 1819. Production of staple crops fell by half and land values declined by 50 to 70 percent. "Such is the depreciation of the value of property," said one western newspaper, "that the accumulated labor of years is not now sufficient to pay a trifling debt, and property some years since which could have sold for eight to ten thousand dollars will scarcely, at this time, pay a debt of five hundred."

The panic resulted in significant political differences over such issues as debt relief, banking and monetary policy, and tariffs. Farmers, particularly in the South and West, demanded enactment of stay laws to postpone repayment of debts. In Mississippi, debtors asked the state to print additional paper money that could be used to pay off creditors. Ardent nationalists called for higher tariffs to protect infant industries and government-financed transportation improvements to reduce the cost of trade.

Many artisans and farmers blamed banks for causing the panic by printing an excessive amount of worthless paper money. They demanded that bank notes be replaced by hard money, gold and silver coinage. In Congress, Senator Thomas Hart Benton of Missouri gave voice to the growing antibank sentiment. "I know towns, yea cities," the senator declared, "where this bank already appears as an engrossing [a monopolizing] proprietor. All the flourishing cities of the West are mortgaged to this money power. . . . They are in the jaws of the monster!" During the 1820s, the Republican party in such states as Alabama, Georgia, Kentucky, New Hampshire, North Carolina, Ohio, Pennsylvania, and Tennessee divided over questions of debt relief, bank regulation, and state support for internal improvements.

A second source of political division was southern alarm over the slavery debates in Con-

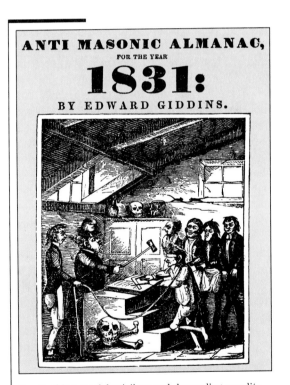

By attacking special privilege and demanding equality of opportunity for all citizens, the Anti-Masonic party won broad support in New York and other northern states.

gress in 1819 and 1820 (see pp. 286–288). At his home in Monticello, Thomas Jefferson worried that the debates might be the "[death] knell of the Union." Many Southern leaders feared that the Missouri crisis might spark a realignment in national politics along sectional lines. Such a development, John Quincy Adams wrote, was "terrible to the South—threatening in its progress the emancipation of all their slaves, threatening in its immediate effect that Southern domination which has swayed the Union for the last twenty years."

Anxiety over the slavery debates in 1819 and 1820 induced many southerners to seek political alliances with the North. As early as 1821, Old Republicans in the South—those who opposed high tariffs, a national bank, and federally funded internal improvements—had begun to form a loose alliance with Senator Martin Van Buren of New York and the Republican party faction he commanded, the Albany Regency.

The third major source of political division was the selection of presidential candidates. The "Virginia dynasty" of presidents, a chain that had begun with George Washington and included Thomas Jefferson, James Madison, and James Monroe, was at its end by 1824.

Traditionally, the Republican party's candidate was selected by a caucus of the Republican party's members of Congress. At the 1824 caucus, the members met in closed session and chose William Crawford, Monroe's secretary of the Treasury, as the party's choice. Not all Republicans, however, supported this method of nominating candidates. As a result, only one-quarter of the Republican senators and representatives bothered to attend the congressional caucus, and Republican members of Congress from eight states refused to participate. Explained John Quincy Adams: "A majority of the whole people of the United States and a majority of the States [are] utterly adverse to the nomination by Congressional caucus, thinking it adverse to the spirit of the Constitution and tending to corruption."

When the early favorite, Crawford, who had the support of Thomas Jefferson, suffered a stroke and was left partially disabled, four other candidates emerged—Secretary of State John Quincy Adams, the son of the nation's second

TABLE 10.1

Election of 1824			
Candidate	Party	Popular Vote	Electoral Vote
J. Q. Adams	No party	113,122	84
Jackson	designations	151,271	99
Clay		47,531	37
Crawford		40,856	41

president and the only candidate from the North; John C. Calhoun, Monroe's secretary of war, who had little support outside of his native South Carolina and decided to settle for the vice presidency; Henry Clay, the Speaker of the House, who was a staunch advocate of a national bank, a protective tariff to aid manufacturing, and government support of internal improvements in transportation; and General Andrew Jackson, the hero of the Battle of New Orleans and victor over the Creek and Seminole Indians. About the latter, Thomas Jefferson commented dryly, one might as well try "to make a soldier of a goose as a President of Andrew Jackson."

In the election of 1824, Jackson received the greatest number of votes both at the polls and in the Electoral College, followed (in electoral votes) by Adams, Crawford, and then Clay. But he failed to receive the constitutionally required majority of the electoral votes. As provided by the Twelfth Amendment of the Constitution, the election was therefore thrown into the House of Representatives, which was required to choose from among the top three vote-getters in the Electoral College. In the House, each state had one vote. There, Henry Clay persuaded his supporters to vote for Adams, commenting acidly that he did not believe "that killing two thousand five hundred Englishmen at New Orleans" was a proper qualification for the presidency. Adams was elected on the first ballot.

The Philadelphia *Observer* charged that Adams had made a secret deal to obtain Clay's support. Three days later, Adams's nomination of Clay as secretary of state seemed to confirm the charges of a "corrupt bargain." Jackson was outraged, since he could legitimately argue that he was the popular favorite. The general exclaimed, "The Judas of the West has closed the contract and will receive the thirty pieces of silver."

The Presidency of John Quincy Adams

John Quincy Adams was one of the most brilliant and well-qualified men ever to occupy the White House. A deeply religious, intensely scholarly man, he read Biblical passages at least three times a day —once in English, once in German, and once in French. Even before he entered Harvard at the age of 18, he had served as an assistant to American diplomats for five years and was fluent in seven foreign languages, including Greek and Latin. After graduation, he became an attorney, a diplomat, a United States senator, a Harvard professor of rhetoric and oratory, and one of the nation's ablest secretaries of state (he turned down a possible nomination to the Supreme Court). During his brilliant career as a diplomat and secretary of state, he negotiated the treaty that ended the War of 1812, acquired the Floridas, and conceived the Monroe Doctrine.

John Quincy Adams won the election of 1824 in the House of Representatives even though Andrew Jackson received the most popular votes.

Although one of the most capable men to serve as president, Adams lacked the political skills and personality necessary to create support for his program. Like his father, Adams lacked personal warmth. His adversaries mockingly described him as a "chip off the old iceberg." He described himself as "a man of reserved, cold, austere and forbidding manners," "a gloomy misanthrope," and "an unsocial savage."

But Adams's problems as president did not arise exclusively from his temperament. His misfortune was to serve as president at a time of growing partisan divisions and sectional tensions. The Republican party had split in two. Adams's supporters were known as National Republicans; their opponents would become the Jacksonian Democrats (from the Democratic-Republican label many had previously used). Adams's nationalistic vision of using the federal revenue to finance roads and canals and to promote science clashed with that of his opponents, who demanded a limited, cheap government. Above all, Adams's conception of the presidency as standing above partisan politics was unsuited to an era of rough-and-tumble politics.

As the only president to lose both the popular vote and the electoral vote, Adams faced hostility from the start. Jackson and his supporters accused the new president of "corruptions and intrigues" to gain Henry Clay's support. Only a heavy snowfall prevented a pro-Jackson crowd from disrupting the inaugural festivities by burning Adams in effigy.

Acutely aware of the fact that "two-thirds of the whole people [were] averse" to his election as president, Adams promised in his inaugural address to make up for this with "intentions upright and pure, a heart devoted to the welfare of our country." A staunch nationalist, Adams proposed an extraordinary program of federal support for science and economic development that included a national university, astronomical observatories ("lighthouses of the skies"), federal funding of roads and canals, and exploration of the country's territory—all to be financed by a high tariff.

Adams's advocacy of a strong federal government and a high tariff enraged defenders of slavery and states' rights advocates who clung to traditional Jeffersonian principles of limited government and strict construction of the Constitution. They feared that any expansion of federal authority might set a precedent for interference with slavery. Thomas Jefferson himself condemned Adams's proposals, declaring in a stinging statement that they would undermine the states and create a national elite—"an aristocracy . . . riding and ruling over the plundered ploughman and beggarded yeomanry."

Adams met with further frustration because he was unwilling to adapt to the practical demands of politics. Disapproving of the very idea of partisanship, Adams made no effort to use his patronage powers to build support for his proposals, and refused to fire federal officeholders who openly opposed his policies. During his entire term in office he removed just 12 incumbents, and these only for gross incompetence. He justified his actions by saying that he did not want to make "government a perpetual and intermitting scramble for office."

Adams's Indian policies also cost him supporters. Although he, like his predecessor Monroe, wanted to remove the southern Indians to the area west of the Mississippi River, he believed that the state and federal governments had a duty to abide by Indian treaties and to purchase, not merely annex, Indian lands. Adams's decision to repudiate and renegotiate a fraudulent treaty that stripped the Georgia Creek Indians of their land outraged land-hungry southerners and westerners.

Even in the realm of foreign policy, his strong suit prior to the presidency, Adams encountered difficulties. To strengthen ties with Latin America, he sent delegates to a Pan-American conference in Central America, but his representatives arrived too late to take part. His attempts to peacefully acquire Texas from Mexico failed, as did his efforts to persuade Britain to permit more American trade with the British West Indies.

The "American System" and the "Tariff of Abominations"

President Adams was committed to using the federal government to promote national economic development. His program included a high protective tariff to promote industry, the sale of public lands at low prices to encourage western settlement, federally financed transportation improvements, expanded markets for western grain and southern cotton, and a strong national bank to regulate the economy.

Adams's secretary of state, Henry Clay, called this economic program the "American system" because it was supposed to promote growth in all parts of the country. But the program infuriated southerners who believed that it favored northeastern industrial interests at

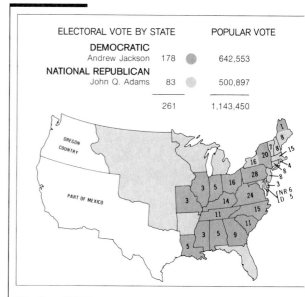

Election of 1828

their region's expense. Southerners particularly disliked a protective tariff, since it raised the cost of manufactured goods, which they did not produce.

Andrew Jackson's supporters in Congress sought to exploit the tariff question in order to embarrass Adams and help Jackson win the presidency in 1828. They framed a bill, which became known as the Tariff of Abominations, to win support for Jackson in Kentucky, Missouri, New York, Ohio, and Pennsylvania while weakening the Adams administration in New England. The bill raised duties on iron, hemp, and flax (which would benefit westerners), while lowering the tariff on woolen goods (to the detriment of New England textile manufacturers). John Randolph of Virginia accurately described the object of the bill as an effort to encourage "manufactures of no sort or kind, except the manufacture of a President of the United States."

The Tariff of Abominations created a political uproar in the South. The legislatures of Georgia, Mississippi, South Carolina, and Virginia denounced the tariff as unconstitutional and discriminatory. The tariff, southerners insisted, was essentially a tax on their region to

THE REBIRTH OF PARTIES

assist northern manufacturers. South Carolina expressed the loudest outcry against the tariff. At a public meeting in Charleston, protesters declared that a tariff was designed to benefit "one class of citizens [manufacturers] at the expense of every other class." One South Carolina representative asserted that the tariff would transfer the equivalent of 40 out of every 100 bales of cotton to northeastern capitalists. Some South Carolinians called for revolutionary defiance of the national government.

What should southern opponents of the tariff do? How could a minority region effectively protest the tariff and protect its economic and political interests short of secession? Vice President John C. Calhoun, a skilled logician well versed in political theory, offered an answer. Retreating from his early nationalistic position, the South Carolinian anonymously published an essay that advanced the principle of "nullification." A single state, Calhoun maintained, might overrule or "nullify" a federal law within its own territory, until three-quarters of the states had upheld the law as constitutional. In 1828, the state of South Carolina decided not to imple-

ment this doctrine but rather to wait and see what attitude the next president would adopt toward the tariff.

The Election of 1828

"J. Q. Adams who can write" squared off against "Andy Jackson who can fight" in the election of 1828, one of the most bitter campaigns in American history. Jackson's followers repeated the charge that Adams was an "aristocrat" who had obtained office as a result of a "corrupt bargain." The Jackson forces also alleged that the president had used public funds to buy personal luxuries, installed gaming tables in the White House, and served as a pimp for the czar while serving as minister to Russia. They even charged that Mrs. Adams had been born out of wedlock.

Adams's supporters countered by digging up an old story that Jackson had begun living with his wife before she was legally divorced from her first husband (which was technically true, although neither Jackson nor his wife

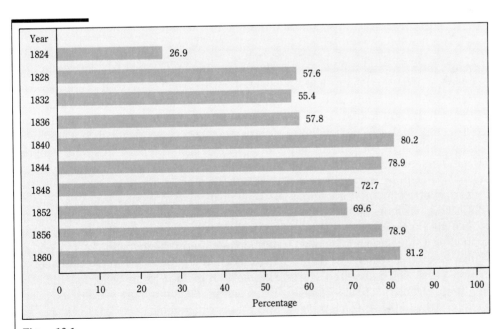

Figure 10.1
Voter population, 1824–1860

Twenty thousand people attended a reception for President Jackson at the White House, trampling rugs, breaking furniture, and stealing china.

Rachel knew her first husband was still living). They called the general a slave trader, a gambler, and a backwoods buffon who could not spell more than one word out of four correctly. One Philadelphia editor published a handbill picturing the coffins of 12 men allegedly murdered by Jackson in numerous duels.

The Jackson campaign in 1828 was the first to directly appeal for voter support through a professional political organization. Skilled political organizers, like Martin Van Buren of New York, Amos Kendall of Kentucky, and Thomas Ritchie of Virginia, created a vast network of pro-Jackson newspapers, which pictured the general as the "candidate of the people" and Adams as a Federalist in Republican clothing who believed that the "few should govern the many." Jackson supporters set up an extensive network of campaign committees and subcommittees to organize mass rallies, parades, and

barbecues, and to erect hickory poles, Jackson's symbol, "in every village as well as upon the corners of many city streets." Together, these new political techniques succeeded in transforming a broad heterogeneous political combination of former Federalists, Republicans, and supporters as well as opponents of banks, protective tariffs, and internal improvements into a successful political movement.

For the first time in American history, a presidential election was the focus of public attention, and voter participation increased dramatically. Twice as many voters cast ballots in the election of 1828 as in 1824, four times as many as in 1820. As in most previous elections, the vote divided along sectional lines. Jackson swept every state in the South and West and Adams won the electoral votes of every state in the North except Pennsylvania and part of New York.

Contemporaries interpreted Jackson's resounding victory as a triumph for political democracy. Jackson supporters called the vote a victory for the "farmers and mechanics of the country" over the "rich and well born." Even Jackson's opponents agreed that the election marked a watershed in the nation's political history, signaling the beginning of a new democratic age. One Adams supporter said bluntly, "a great revolution has taken place."

ANDREW JACKSON: THE POLITICS OF THE COMMON PERSON

Supporters of Adams regarded Jackson's victory with deep pessimism. A justice of the Supreme Court declared, "The reign of King 'Mob' seems triumphant." John Randolph of Virginia feared that "the country is ruined past redemption." But enthusiasts greeted Jackson's victory as a great triumph for the people. At the inaugural, a cable stretched in front of the east portico of the Capitol to keep back the throngs snapped under the pressure of the surging crowd. As many as 20,000 well-wishers attended a White House reception to honor the new president, muddying rugs, breaking furniture, and damaging china and glassware. "It was a proud day for the people," commented one Kentucky newspaperman. "General Jackson is their own President."

Although viewed by the public primarily as a military hero who had defeated the British at New Orleans, crushed the Creek Indians, and driven the Spanish out of Florida, Jackson was, in fact, the product of a more complicated background. In certain respects, Jackson was truly a self-made man. Born in 1767 in a frontier region along the North and South Carolina border known as the Waxhaws, he was the first president to be born in a log cabin. His father, a poor farmer from northern Ireland, died two weeks before his birth, while his mother and only two brothers died during the American Revolution. At the age of 13, Jackson volunteered to fight in the American Revolution, joining the mounted militia of South Carolina. He was taken prisoner and a British officer severely slashed Jackson's hand and head when the boy refused to shine the officer's shoes.

Jackson soon rose from poverty to a career in law and politics. He associated with individuals far removed from the common people. In 1788, a year after he was admitted to the bar, Jackson became public prosecutor for the western district of North Carolina, an area that included what would become the state of Tennessee. He then became Tennessee's first congressman, a senator, and judge on the state supreme court.

Known as a champion of the common people, President Jackson greatly expanded the powers of the presidency.

Although Jackson would later gain a reputation as the champion of the common people, in Tennessee he was allied by marriage, business, and political ties to the state's "beaver-hat" conservatives and against the "beaver-skinner" yeomanry. As a land speculator, cotton planter, and attorney, he accumulated a large personal fortune and acquired more than 100 slaves. His candidacy for the presidency was initially promoted by speculators, creditors, and elite leaders in Tennessee who hoped to exploit Jackson's popularity in order to combat anti-banking sentiment and fend off challenges to their dominance of state politics.

Few presidents have aroused as much controversy as Andrew Jackson. His admirers regarded him as a firm leader who strengthened the powers of the presidency, championed the rights of ordinary people, and attacked privilege to increase economic opportunity. His detractors accused him of weakening the economy, waging an anticapitalist assault on banks and other business corporations, needlessly killing Indians, and causing the financial panic of 1837. Yet, however one evaluates his presidency, there can be no doubt that he left an indelible stamp on the nation's highest office; indeed, on a whole epoch in American history.

Expanding the Powers of the Presidency

In office, Jackson greatly enhanced the power and prestige of the presidency. He was the first president to fire a cabinet officer, the first to use federal troops to put down a labor strike, the first to open diplomatic relations with the Far East, and the first to declare that the president, and not Congress, represented the people. He was also the first president to declare that the Union could not be peacefully dissolved. In the name of opposing special privilege, he declared war on the national bank, vetoed federal aid for internal improvements, paid off the national debt, and lowered the federal tariff. Few presidents ever aroused deeper passions than Andrew Jackson.

As president, Jackson convinced many Americans that their votes mattered. He espoused a political ideology of "democratic republicanism" that stressed the common peoples' virtue, intelligence, and capacity for self-government. He also expressed a deep disdain for the "better classes," which claimed a "more enlightened wisdom" than common men and women.

Endorsing the view that a fundamental conflict existed between working people and the "nonproducing" classes of society, Jackson and his supporters promised to remove any impediments to the ordinary citizen's opportunities for economic improvement. According to the Jacksonians, inequalities of wealth and power were the direct result of monopoly, favoritism, and special privileges, which made "the rich richer and the powerful more potent." Only free competition in an open marketplace would ensure that wealth would be distributed in accordance with each person's "industry, economy, enterprise, and prudence." The goal of the Jacksonians was to remove all obstacles that prevented farmers, artisans, and small shopkeepers from earning a greater share of the nation's wealth.

Nowhere was the Jacksonian ideal of openness made more concrete than in Jackson's theory of rotation in office, known as the "spoils system." In his first annual message to Congress, Jackson defended the principle that public offices should be rotated among party supporters in order to help the nation achieve its republican ideals. Performance in public office, Jackson maintained, required no special intelligence or training, and rotation in office would ensure that the federal government did not develop a class of corrupt civil servants set apart from the people. In the United States, Jackson noted, "where offices are created solely for the benefit of the people . . . no one has any more intrinsic right to official station than another." His supporters advocated the spoils system on practical political grounds, viewing it as a way to reward political party loyalists and build a stronger party organization. As Jacksonian Senator William Marcy of New York proclaimed, "To the victor belongs the spoils."

The spoils system opened government positions to many of Jackson's supporters, but it was neither as new nor as democratic as it appeared. During his first 18 months in office, Jackson replaced fewer than 1000 of the nation's 10,000 civil servants on political grounds, and fewer than 20 percent of federal officeholders were removed during his administration. Moreover, many of the men Jackson appointed to office had backgrounds of wealth and social eminence. Further, Jackson did not originate the spoils system. By the time he took office, a number of states, including New York and Pennsylvania, practiced political patronage.

During the Jacksonian era, land, tariff, and banking policies dominated national politics. In the heated political battles swirling around these questions, two competing national political parties emerged. Compared to the issues that dominated British politics during the same years—slave emancipation, factory regulation, and assistance to the poor—the questions Americans fought over might seem less important. Nevertheless, vital interests were at stake, relating to such fateful questions as equality of opportunity, the distribution of wealth, the balance of sectional power, and the proper role of government in the economy.

Clearing the Land of Indians

The first major political controversy of Jackson's presidency involved Indian policy. At the time

Jackson took office, 125,000 Native Americans still lived east of the Mississippi River. Cherokee, Choctaw, Chickasaw, and Creek Indians—60,000 strong—held millions of acres in what would become the southern cotton kingdom stretching across Georgia, Alabama, and Mississippi. The key political controversies were whether these Indian tribes would be permitted to block white expansion and whether the U.S. government and its citizens would abide by previously made treaties. By 1840, Jackson and his successor, Martin Van Buren, had answered these questions. All Indians east of the Mississippi had been uprooted from their homelands and forced to move westward, with the exception of rebellious Seminoles in Florida and small numbers of Indians living on isolated reservations in Michigan, North Carolina, and New York.

Since Jefferson's presidency, two conflicting Indian policies, assimilation and removal, had governed the treatment of Native Americans. The assimilation policy encouraged Indians to adopt white American customs and economic practices. The government provided financial assistance to missionaries in order to Christianize and educate Native Americans and convince them to adopt single-family farms. Proponents defended assimilation as the only way Native Americans would be able to survive in a white-dominated society. According to the American Board of Commissioners for Foreign Missions, "There is no place on earth to which they can migrate, and live in the savage and hunter state. The Indian tribes must, therefore, be progressively civilized, or successively perish."

By the 1820s, the Cherokee had demonstrated the ability of Native Americans to adapt to changing conditions while maintaining their tribal heritage. Sequoyah, a leader of these people, had developed a written alphabet. Soon the Cherokee opened schools, established churches, built roads, operated printing presses, and even adopted a constitution.

The other policy—removal—was first suggested by Thomas Jefferson as the only way to ensure the survival of Indian cultures. The goal of this policy was to encourage the voluntary migration of Indians westward to tracts of land

In 1809 a Cherokee named Sequoyah began to devise an alphabet consisting of letters based on English, Greek, and Hebrew. The Cherokee nation's weekly newspaper, the *Cherokee Phoenix*, was printed with this alphabet.

where they could live free from white harassment. As early as 1817, James Monroe declared that the nation's security depended on rapid settlement along the southern coast and that it was in the best interests of Native Americans to move westward. In 1825 he set before Congress a plan to resettle all eastern Indians on tracts in the West where whites would not be allowed to live.

Initially, Jackson followed the dual policy of assimilation and removal, promising remuneration to tribes that would move westward, while offering small plots of land to individual Indians who would operate family farms. After 1830, however, Jackson favored removal.

This shift in federal Indian policy came partly as a result of a controversy between the Cherokee nation and the state of Georgia. The Cherokee people had adopted a constitution asserting sovereignty over their land. The state responded by abolishing tribal rule and claiming that the Cherokee fell under its jurisdiction. The discovery of gold on Cherokee land triggered a land rush, and the Cherokee nation sued to keep white settlers from encroaching on their territory. In two important cases, *Cherokee Nation* v. *Georgia* in 1831 and *Worcester* v. *Geor-*

gia in 1832, the Supreme Court ruled that states could not pass laws conflicting with federal Indian treaties and that the federal government had an obligation to exclude white intruders from Indian lands. Angered, Jackson is said to have exclaimed: "John Marshall has made his decision; now let him enforce it."

The primary thrust of Jackson's removal policy was to encourage Indian tribes to sell all tribal lands in exchange for new lands in Oklahoma and Arkansas. Such a policy, the president maintained, would open new farm land to whites while offering Indians a haven where they would be free to develop at their own pace. "There," he wrote, "your white brothers will not trouble you, they will have no claims to the land, and you can live upon it, you and all your children, as long as the grass grows or the water runs, in peace and plenty."

Pushmataha, a Choctaw chieftain, called on his people to reject Jackson's offer. Far from being a "country of tall trees, many water courses, rich lands and high grass abounding in games of all kinds," the promised preserve in the west was simply a barren desert. Jackson responded by warning that if the Choctaw refused to move west, he would destroy their nation.

During the winter of 1831, the Choctaw became the first tribe to walk the "Trail of Tears" westward. Promised government assistance failed to arrive, and malnutrition, exposure, and a cholera epidemic killed many members of the nation. Then, in 1836, the Creek suffered the hardships of removal. About 3500 of the tribe's 15,000 members died along the westward trek. Those who resisted removal were bound in chains and marched in double file.

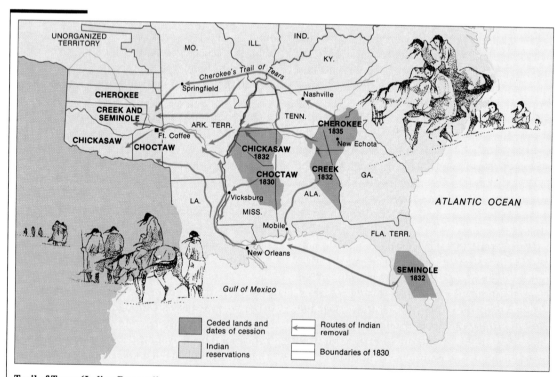

Trail of Tears (Indian Removal)
Andrew Jackson's Indian removal policy was known to many Native Americans as the Trail of Tears. Native Americans were herded westward off their lands in order to open the territory for expansion. The trek brought death to perhaps one-fourth of those who set out.

The Cherokee, however, were emboldened by the Supreme Court decisions declaring that Georgia law had no force on Indian territory. The nation resisted removal. Fifteen thousand Cherokee joined in a protest against Jackson's policy: "Little did [we] anticipate that when taught to think and feel as the American citizen . . . [we] were to be despoiled by [our] guardian, to become strangers and wanderers in the land of [our] fathers, forced to return to the savage life, and to seek a new home in the wilds of the far west, and that without [our] consent." The federal government bribed a faction of the tribe to leave the land in exchange for transportation costs and $5 million, but the majority of the people held out until 1838, when the army evicted them from their land. All told, 4000 of the 15,000 Cherokee died along the trail to Indian territory in what is now Oklahoma.

A number of other tribes also organized resistance against removal. In the Old Northwest, the Sauk and Fox Indians fought the Black Hawk War to recover ceded tribal lands in Illinois and Wisconsin. The Indians claimed that when they had signed the treaty transferring title to their land, they had not understood the implications of the action. "I touched the goose quill to the treaty," said Chief Black Hawk, "not knowing, however, that by that act I consented to give away my village." The United States army and the Illinois state militia ended the resistance by wantonly killing nearly 500 Sauk and Fox men, women, and children who were trying to retreat across the Mississippi River. In Florida, the military spent seven years putting down Seminole resistance at a cost of $20 million and 1500 casualties, and even then succeeding only after the treacherous act of kidnapping the Seminole leader Osceola during peace talks.

Black Hawk War

The Sauk and Fox resisted removal and fought the Black Hawk War to recover ceded lands in Illinois and Wisconsin. The U.S. army and the Illinois state militia ruthlessly suppressed the Native Americans.

By twentieth-century standards, Jackson's Indian policy was both callous and inhumane. Despite the semblance of legality—94 treaties were signed with Indians during Jackson's presidency—Indian migrations to the West almost always occurred under the threat of government coercion. Even before Jackson's death in 1845, it was obvious that tribal lands in the West were no more secure than Indian lands had been in the East. In 1851 Congress passed the Indian Appropriations Act, which sought to concentrate the western Native American population on reservations.

Why were such morally indefensible policies adopted? Simply because many white Americans regarded Indian control of land and other natural resources as a serious obstacle to their desire for expansion and as a potential threat to the nation's security. Even had the federal government wanted to, it probably lacked the resources and military means necessary to protect the eastern Indians from encroaching white farmers, squatters, traders, and speculators. By the 1830s, a growing number of missionaries and humanitarians agreed with Jackson that Indians needed to be resettled westward for their own protection. But the removal program was ill-fated from the start. Given the nation's commitment to limited government and its lack of experience with social welfare programs, removal was foredoomed to disaster. Contracts for food, clothing, and transportation were awarded to the lowest bidders, many of whom failed to fulfill their contractual responsibilities. Indians were resettled on semi-arid lands, unsuited for intensive farming. The tragic outcome was readily foreseeable.

The problem of preserving native cultures in the face of an expanding nation was not confined to the United States. Jackson's removal policy can only be properly understood when seen as part of a broader process: the political and economic conquest of frontier regions by expanding nation states. During the early decades of the nineteenth century, European nations were penetrating into many frontier areas, including the steppes of Russia, the plains of Argentina, the veldt of South Africa, the out-

(Text continues on p. 312)

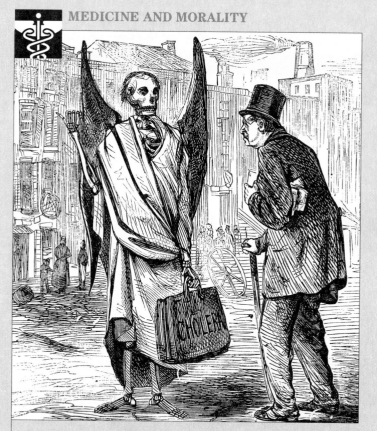

THE CHOLERA EPIDEMIC OF 1832: SINNERS AND SAINTS

In the spring of 1832, Americans braced themselves for an attack by cholera—what one historian has called "the classic epidemic disease of the nineteenth century." They knew it was coming. Throughout the preceding year, newspapers had reported with alarm the disease's escape from its Asian homeland and its westward march across Europe. The press had turned shrill when cholera crossed the Atlantic Ocean—the last great barrier that shielded the Americas from this horrible plague—and struck Canada in June 1832. Despite the certainty

that the disease would soon reach the United States, however, neither the federal, state, nor local governments did much to prevent or even prepare for an epidemic.

Nothing in their inventory of illnesses, not even the ravages of smallpox or malaria, had prepared Americans for the terror that seized them when cholera finally appeared. Their fear is easily understood: Cholera killed approximately half of those who contracted it, and it struck with unbelievable rapidity. A New Yorker who survived the 1832 epidemic testified that he was walk-

ing down the street when he suddenly fell forward on his face "as if knocked down with an axe."

Cholera's symptoms, which mimic those of severe arsenic poisoning, are indeed spectacular. The onset of the disease is marked by acute diarrhea, uncontrollable vomiting, and violent abdominal cramps. Within hours, this sudden and massive loss of fluids causes dehydration, and the victim's extremities feel cold, the face turns blue, and the feet and hands appear dark and swollen. Unless proper medical treatment is provided, death can follow within a few hours after the first symptoms appear, or, at most, within a few days. Even more than its devastating symptoms, it was the disease's ability to kill so swiftly that terrorized the public. "To see individuals well in the morning & buried before night, retiring apparently well & dead in the morning is something which is appalling to the boldest heart," exclaimed another survivor of America's first cholera epidemic.

The cause of cholera was not discovered until 1883 when Robert Koch, the famous scientist, led a commission to Egypt that isolated *Vibrio comma*, the guilty bacterium. These deadly germs settle in the intestines of their victims, following a journey along any one of several pathways that lead to the human digestive tract. Although dirty hands or raw fruits and vegetables often transmit the disease, most cholera epidemics are spread by polluted drinking water from sewage-contaminated water systems.

Unfortunately, America's cities in 1832 harbored more than enough filth to nurture an epidemic. New York was especially dirty. Residents were required by law to pile their garbage in the gutter in front of their homes for removal by the city, but it seldom got collected. (With their characteristic sense of humor, New Yorkers dubbed these piles of stinking, decomposing garbage "corporation pie.") The only effective "sanitary engineers" in New York were the thousands of swine that roamed the streets gorging themselves on the refuse.

Thanks to this filth, cholera unleashed a great plague of death when it reached New York. Thousands died in the epidemic, producing so many bodies that the undertakers could not keep up with the volume and had to stack corpses in warehouses and public buildings to await burial. In short, cholera hit New York with the same force with which yellow fever had knocked Philadelphia to its knees in 1793.

In the midst of their suffering, New Yorkers could not help but wonder why some people contracted the disease while others escaped it. To answer this question, America's physicians espoused a doctrine of predisposing causes. People who kept God's laws, they explained, had nothing to fear, but the intemperate and the filthy stood at great risk. In fact, physicians elaborated their warnings about "predisposing" or "exciting" causes into a jeremiad against sin. Impiety, imprudence, idleness, drunkenness, gluttony, and sexual excess all left their devotees weakened and "artificially stimulated," their bodies to be vulnerable to cholera.

Because the disease was "decidedly vulgar," physicians predicted that it would confine itself largely to the lower classes—specifically, to blacks and to the Irish, who were thought by upper-class individuals to be the most intemperate and debauched members of society. Here, then, was a classic example of how the medical profession appropriated social attitudes regarding class and race to blame the victims of disease for their suffering.

Again, the doctors appeared to be right, but for the wrong reasons. Cholera was indeed a "poor man's plague"; sin, however, was not the explanation. The upper classes suffered less because they fled the cities and dispersed to country homes and lodges where pure water and low population density prevented infection. The poor, by contrast, could not afford to leave: they had to remain and take their chances.

Typically, most of New York's lower classes lived in tiny, unvented apartments where entire families (and perhaps a boarder or two) occupied a single room, while the most wretched hoveled in unfurnished cellars whose walls glistened with sewage and slime every time it rained. Instead of pure water imported in hogsheads from fresh water springs in the countryside (the only water the wealthy would touch), poor people drew their drinking water from the river or from contaminated shallow wells. Though New Yorkers had long joked that their water was an excellent purgative, they might as well have called it "liquid death" when cholera swept the land.

Once cholera struck, physicians found that none of the traditional remedies of heroic medicine worked. In addition to bloodletting, they treated their patients with laudanum (the main ingredient of which was opium), tobacco smoke enemas, and huge doses of calomel, a chalky mercury compound employed as a cathartic. In desperation, one of New York's leading physicians (a practical thinker) even recommended plugging the patient's rectum with beeswax to halt the diarrhea.

Many Americans turned to quacks or treated themselves with home remedies. It made no difference. Those who survived the epidemic did so in spite of the medical care they received, not because of it.

Cholera receded from the land almost as quickly as it had come. By the fall of 1832 the epidemic had spent its fury, and by the winter it was gone. When it struck again in 1866, Americans had learned how to battle the disease. They no longer talked about cholera in moral terms as God's vengeance on the poor and the wicked. Instead, they approached it as a social problem amenable to human intervention. They imposed quarantines, opened emergency hospitals, increased the powers of health authorities, removed the trash and garbage from city streets, and cleaned up municipal water supplies. The contrast between 1832 and 1866 could not have been more complete.

Within the span of two generations, the public changed the way it viewed disease. American physicians became more scientific in handling and treating the sick— eloquent testimony to the medical advances in a modernizing society.

back of Australia, and the American West. In each of these regions, national expansion was justified on the grounds of strategic interest (to preempt settlement by other powers) or in the name of opening valuable land to white settlement and development. And in each case, expansion was accompanied by the removal or wholesale killing of native peoples.

Sectional Disputes over Public Lands and Nullification

Bitter sectional disputes arose during Jackson's presidency over public lands and the tariff. Sectional differences first appeared in a debate over the disposal of public lands. After the Revolutionary War, the federal government owned one-quarter billion acres of public land; the Louisiana Purchase added another half billion acres to the public domain. These public lands constituted the federal government's single greatest resource. Early in the new nation's history, the sale of public land served as a primary source of public revenue. By 1820, however, many Americans believed that land should be sold as rapidly and cheaply as possible in order to promote the establishment of farms.

In that year, Congress encouraged the rapid sale of public land by reducing the minimum land purchase to just 80 acres, at a price of $1.25 per acre. Still, a variety of groups favored even easier terms for land sales. Squatters, for example, who violated federal laws that forbade settlement prior to the completion of public surveys, pressured Congress to adopt preemption acts that would permit them to buy the land they occupied at the minimum price of $1.25 when it came up for sale. Urban workingmen—agitating under the slogan "Vote Yourself a Farm"—demanded free homesteads for any American who would settle the public domain. Transportation companies, which built roads, canals, and later railroads, called for grants of public land to help fund their projects.

In Congress, two proposals—"distribution" and "graduation"—competed for support. Under the distribution proposal, which was identified with Henry Clay, Congress would distribute the proceeds from the sale of public lands to the states, which would use it to finance

transportation improvements. Senator Thomas Hart Benton of Missouri offered an alternative proposal, graduation. He proposed that Congress gradually reduce the price of unsold government land and finally freely give away unpurchased land.

The debate on public lands soon became entangled in bitter sectional disputes over the tariff, states' rights, and John C. Calhoun's doctrine of nullification. At the end of 1829, a Connecticut senator proposed a cessation of public land sales. This transformed the debate over public lands into a sectional battle over the nature of the union. Senator Benton denounced the proposal as a brazen attempt by manufacturers to keep laborers from settling "the blooming regions of the West," fearing that westward migration would reduce the size of the urban workforce and therefore raise their wage costs. The northeastern program of high tariffs and opposition to cheap land, he claimed, was "a most complex scheme of injustice, which taxes the South to injure the West, to pauperize the poor of the North."

Benton's words touched off one of the most celebrated oratorical duels in American history. The debate featured two of the nation's most renowned orators—Daniel Webster of Massachusetts and Robert Y. Hayne of South Carolina. The issue they debated—whether the states or the federal government was sovereign—would haunt Americans for the next three decades. Senator Hayne spoke first. He accused the federal government of "constantly stealing power from the States." He then called on the South and West to unite in affirming the principle of nullification against attempts by the northeast to strengthen the powers of the federal government.

Daniel Webster of Massachusetts answered Hayne in one of the most famous speeches in American history. The United States, Webster proclaimed, was not simply a compact of the states. It was a creation of the people, who had invested the Constitution and the national government with ultimate sovereignty. If a state disagreed with an action of the federal government, it had a right to sue in federal court or seek to amend the Constitution, but it had no right to nullify a federal law. That would inev-

In his famous oration, Senator Daniel Webster answered Senator Robert Hayne's call for states' rights, proclaiming, "Liberty and Union, now and forever, one and inseparable."

itably lead to anarchy and civil war. It was delusion and folly to think that Americans could have "Liberty first and Union afterwards," Webster declared. "Liberty and Union, now and forever, one and inseparable."

Jackson did not reveal his position on the questions of states' rights and nullification until April 13, 1830. Asked to offer a toast at a Jefferson Day dinner, the president stood up, fixed his eyes on Vice President John C. Calhoun, and expressed his sentiments in ringing terms: "Our Union: It must be preserved." Calhoun responded to Jackson's challenge and offered the next toast: "The Union, next to our liberty, most dear. May we always remember that it can only be preserved by distributing equally the benefits and burdens of the Union."

Relations between Jackson and Calhoun had grown increasingly strained. Jackson had learned that when Calhoun was secretary of war under Monroe he had called for Jackson's court-martial for his conduct during the military occupation of Florida in 1818. Jackson was also angry because Mrs. Calhoun had snubbed the wife of Secretary of War John H. Eaton, because Mrs. Eaton was the twice-married daughter of

a tavern keeper. Jackson's own late wife Rachel had been snubbed by society (partly because she smoked a pipe, partly because she had unknowingly married Jackson before a divorce from her first husband was final), and the president had empathy for young Peggy Eaton. In 1831, Jackson reorganized his cabinet and forced Calhoun's supporters out. The next year, Calhoun became the first vice president to resign his office, when he became a senator from South Carolina.

In 1832, in an effort to conciliate the South, Jackson proposed a lower tariff. Revenue from the existing tariff (together with the sale of public lands) was so high that the federal debt was quickly being paid off; in fact on January 1, 1835, the United States Treasury had a balance of $440,000, not a penny of which was owed to anyone—the only time in U.S. history when the government was completely free of debt. The new tariff adopted in 1832 was somewhat lower than the Tariff of 1828 but still maintained the principle of protection. In protest, South Carolina's fiery "states' righters" declared both the Tariff of 1832 and the Tariff of 1828 null and void. In Charleston, South Carolinians flew banners that read "Nullification—the only rightful remedy of an injured state." To defend nullification, the state legislature voted to raise an army.

Jackson responded by declaring nullification illegal. In a "Proclamation to the People of South Carolina," he became the first president to declare the Union indissoluble. If the crisis went on, he wrote, "our country will be like a bag of meal with both ends open. Pick it up in the middle or endwise, and it will run out. I must tie the bag and save the country." He announced that nullification was illegal and then asked Congress to empower him to use force to execute federal law. Congress promptly enacted a Force Act. Privately, Jackson threatened to "hang every leader . . . of that infatuated people, sir, by martial law, irrespective of his name, or political or social position." He also dispatched a fleet of eight ships and a shipment of 5000 muskets to Fort Pinckney, a federal installation in Charleston harbor.

In Congress, Henry Clay, the "great compromiser" who had engineered the Missouri Compromise of 1820, worked feverishly to reduce South Carolina's sense of grievance. "He who loves the Union must desire to see this agitating question brought to a termination," he said. In less than a month, he persuaded Congress to enact a compromise tariff with lower levels of protection.

Although South Carolinians regarded Jackson's forceful actions as "the mad rages of a driveling dotard," they backed down, rescinding the ordinance nullifying the federal tariff. As a final gesture of defiance, however, the state adopted an ordinance nullifying the Force Act.

In 1830 and 1831 South Carolina stood alone. No other southern state yet shared South Carolina's fear of federal power or its militant desire to assert the doctrine of states' rights. South Carolina's anxiety had many causes. By 1831 declining cotton prices (from 31 cents a pound in 1818 to 8 cents a pound), a protracted depression, and growing concern about the future of slavery had turned the state from a staunch supporter of economic nationalism into the nation's most aggressive advocate of states' rights. Increasingly, economic grievances fused with concerns over slavery. In 1832, the Pal-

metto State was one of just two states whose population was made up of a majority of slaves. By that year events throughout the hemisphere made South Carolinians desperately uneasy about the future of slavery. In 1831 and 1832 militant abolitionism had erupted in the North, slave insurrections had occurred in Southampton County, Virginia, and Jamaica, and Britain was moving to emancipate all slaves in the British Caribbean.

By using the federal tariff as the focus of their grievances, South Carolinians found an ideal way of debating the question of state sovereignty without debating the morality of slavery. Following the Missouri Compromise debates (see pp. 286–288), a slave insurrection led by Denmark Vesey had been uncovered in Charleston in 1822. By 1832 South Carolinians did not want to stage debates in Congress that might bring the explosive slavery issue to the fore and possibly incite another slave revolt.

The Bank War

Although the tariff was important, the major political issue of Jackson's presidency was his war against the second Bank of the United States. To understand this battle, the nature of the banking system at the time Jackson assumed the presidency must be understood. It was completely different than it is today. At that time, the federal government coined only a limited supply of hard money and printed no paper money at all. The principal source of circulating currency—of paper bank notes—was private commercial banks (of which there were 329 in 1829), chartered by the various states. These private, state-chartered banks supplied the credit necessary to finance land purchases, business operations, and economic growth. The notes they issued were promises to pay gold or silver, but they were backed by a limited amount of precious metal and they fluctuated greatly in value.

In 1816, the federal government had chartered the second Bank of the United States partly in an effort to control the notes issued by state banks. By demanding payment in gold or silver, the national bank could discipline overspeculative private banks. But the very idea of a national bank was unpopular for various reasons. Many people blamed it for causing the Panic of 1819. Others resented its political influence. For example, Senator Daniel Webster was both the bank's chief lobbyist and a director of the bank's Boston branch. Wage earners and small businesspeople blamed it for economic fluctuations and loan restrictions. Private banks resented its privileged position in the banking industry. Still others, including President Jackson, believed it to be unconstitutional because, they said, Congress had no constitutional right to charter a private business. Also, said Jackson, the bank was a bastion of special privilege.

In 1832, Henry Clay, Daniel Webster, and other Jackson opponents in Congress, seeking an issue for that year's presidential election, passed a bill rechartering the second Bank of the United States. The bank's charter was not due to expire until 1836, but Clay and Webster wanted to force Jackson to take a clear probank or antibank position. Jackson had frequently attacked the bank as an agency through which speculators, monopolists, and other seekers after economic privilege cheated honest farmers and mechanics. Now, his adversaries wanted to force him either to sign the bill for recharter, alienating voters hostile to the bank, or veto it, antagonizing conservative voters who favored a sound banking system.

Jackson vetoed the bill in a forceful message that condemned the bank as a privileged "monopoly" created to make "rich men . . . richer by act of Congress." The bank, he declared, was "unauthorized by the Constitution, subversive of the rights of the States, and dangerous to the liberties of the people." In the presidential campaign of 1832, Henry Clay tried to make an issue of Jackson's bank veto, but Jackson swept to an easy second-term victory, defeating Clay by 219 electoral votes to 49.

Jackson interpreted his reelection as a mandate to undermine the bank still further. In September 1833, he ordered his Treasury secretary

As this anti-Jackson cartoon illustrates, defenders of the second Bank of the United States regarded Jackson's bank as a threat to destroy the nation's economic health.

to divert federal revenues from the Bank of the United States to selected state banks, which came to be known as "pet" banks. The secretary of the Treasury and his successor resigned rather than carry out the president's order. It was only after Jackson appointed a second new secretary that his order was implemented. Jackson's decision to divert federal deposits from the national bank prompted his adversaries in the Senate to formally censure the president's actions as arbitrary and unconstitutional. The bank's president, Nicholas Biddle, responded to Jackson's actions by reducing loans and calling in debts. Over the span of six months, the bank reduced loans by nearly $10 million in an attempt to pressure Jackson to approve a new charter. "This worthy President," said Biddle, "thinks that because he has scalped Indians and imprisoned Judges he is to have his way with the Bank. He is mistaken." Jackson retorted: "The Bank . . . is trying to kill me, but I will kill it."

On the other hand, Jackson's decision to divert funds drew strong support from many conservative businesspeople who believed that the bank's destruction would increase the availability of credit and open up new business opportunities.

Jackson, however, hated all banks, and believed that the only sound currencies were gold and silver. Having crippled the Bank of the United States, he promptly launched a crusade to replace all bank notes with hard money. Denouncing "the power which the moneyed interest derives from a paper currency," the president prohibited banks that received federal deposits from issuing bills valued at less than $5. Then, in the Specie Circular of 1836, Jackson prohibited payment for public lands in anything but gold or silver. That same year, in another antibanking measure, Congress voted to deprive pet banks of federal deposits. Instead nearly $35 million in surplus federal funds to the states was distributed to help finance internal improvements.

To Jackson's supporters, the presidential veto of the bank bill was a principled assault on a bastion of wealth and special privilege. His efforts to curtail the circulation of bank notes was an effort to rid the country of a tool used by commercial interests to exploit farmers and working men and women. To his critics, the veto was an act of economic ignorance that destroyed a valuable institution that promoted monetary stability, eased the long-distance transfer of funds, provided a reserve of capital on which other banks drew, and helped regulate the bank notes issued by private banks. Jackson's effort to limit the circulation of bank notes was a misguided act of a "backward-looking" president, who failed to understand the role of a banking system in a modern economy.

Jackson's banking policies still remain controversial, especially since an initial economic boom following his assault on the bank collapsed in the financial Panic of 1837. Land sales, canal construction, cotton production, and manufacturing boomed following Jackson's decision to divert federal funds from the bank. At the same time, however, state debts rose sharply and inflation increased dramatically. Prices climbed 28 percent in just three years. Then in 1837, just after the election of Jackson's successor Democrat Martin Van Buren, a deep financial depression struck the nation.

Cotton prices fell by half. In New York City, 50,000 people were thrown out of work and 200,000 lacked adequate means of support. From across the country came "rumor after rumor of riot, insurrection, and tumult." "Hard Times! is the cry from Madawaska to Galena," declared a New York newspaper. Mobs in New York broke into the city's flour warehouse. Orestes Brownson, one of the nation's most prominent authors and clergymen, announced that revolution was only waiting for the "signal to rush to the terrible encounter, if the battle has not already begun."

Who was to blame for the Panic of 1837? One school of thought holds Jackson responsible, arguing that his banking policies removed a vital check on the activities of state-chartered banks. Freed from the regulation of the second Bank of the United States, private banks rapidly expanded the volume of bank notes in circulation, contributing to the rapid increase in inflation. Jackson's Specie Circular of 1836, which sought to curb inflation by requiring that public land payments be made in hard currency, forced many Americans to exchange paper bills for gold and silver. Many private banks lacked sufficient reserves of hard currency and were forced to close their doors, triggering a financial crisis.

Another school of thought blames the panic on factors outside of Jackson's control. A surplus of cotton on the world market caused the price of cotton to drop sharply, throwing many southern and western cotton farmers into bankruptcy. Meanwhile, in 1836, Britain suddenly raised interest rates in order to curb a rapid outflow of gold and silver from the Bank of England into speculative investments in American canals and railroads. Higher interest rates in Britain and subsequently in the United States drastically reduced investment in the American economy and forced a number of states to default on loans from foreign investors.

If Jackson's policies did not necessarily cause the panic, they certainly made recovery more difficult. Jackson's handpicked successor, Martin Van Buren, responded to the economic depression in an extremely doctrinaire way. A firm believer in the Jeffersonian principle of limited government, Van Buren refused to provide government aid to business. "The less government interferes," Van Buren said, "the better for general prosperity."

Fearful that the federal government might lose funds it had deposited in private banks, Van Buren convinced Congress in 1840 to adopt an independent treasury system. Under this proposal, federal funds were locked up in insulated subtreasuries, which were totally divorced from the banking system. As a result the banking system was deprived of funds that might have aided recovery, and the country did not fully pull out of the depression until the mid-1840s.

The Jacksonian Court

Presidents' judicial appointments represent one of their most enduring legacies. In his two terms as president, Andrew Jackson appointed five of the seven justices on the Supreme Court. The death of John Marshall in 1835 not only allowed Jackson to name a new chief justice, it meant that he had now named a majority of the members of the Court. For chief justice, Jackson selected his Treasury secretary, Roger B. Taney,

the co-author of the president's bank veto message and the secretary who had agreed to remove deposits from the Bank of the United States. Taney, who would lead the court for nearly three decades, was the first chief justice to wear trousers instead of knee breeches. In many other ways, he broke with tradition and led the Court in new directions. Under Taney, the Court sought to extend Jacksonian principles of promoting national economic growth and individual opportunity by removing traditional restraints on competition in the marketplace. The Taney Court upheld the doctrine of limited liability for corporations and provided legal sanction to state subsidies for canals, turnpikes, and railroads. Taken together, the decisions of the Taney Court played a vital role in the emergence of the American system of free enterprise.

Shortly after his confirmation, the Taney Court heard the case of *Charles River Bridge* v. *Warren Bridge*. It raised an issue fundamental to the nation's future economic growth— whether state-granted monopolies would be allowed to block competition from new enterprises. In 1828, the state of Massachusetts chartered a company to build a bridge connecting Boston and neighboring Charlestown. The owners of an existing bridge sued, claiming that their 1785 charter included an implied right to a monopoly.

In its decision, the Court ensured that monopolistic privileges granted in the past would not be allowed to interfere with public welfare. The Court held that contracts conferred only explicitly stated rights. Any ambiguity in wording should be construed in the public interest. The decision epitomized the ideals of Jacksonian democracy: a commitment to removing artificial barriers to opportunity and an emphasis upon free competition in an open marketplace.

Jackson's Legacy

Andrew Jackson was one of the nation's most resourceful and effective presidents. In the face of hostile majorities in Congress, he carried out his most important policies, affecting banking, internal improvements, Native Americans, and tariffs. As president, Jackson used the veto power more often than all earlier presidents had together during the preceding 40 years, and used it in such a way that he succeeded in representing himself as the champion of the people against special interests in Congress. In addition, his skillful use of patronage and party organization and his successful manipulation of public symbols helped create the nation's first modern political party with truly national appeal.

And yet, despite his popular appeal, Jackson's legacy is a matter of great dispute among historians. His Indian policies, under which 45,000 Native Americans were uprooted from their tribal homelands and relocated west of the Mississippi, continue to arouse passionate criticism. Although Jackson has often been viewed as the president of the common man, his economic policies did little to help small farmers, artisans, and workingpeople. In fact, his policies actually weakened the ability of the federal government to regulate the nation's economy. Indeed, many historians now believe that slaveholders—not small farmers or workingpeople—benefited most from his policies. His Indian policy helped to open new lands for slaveowners, and his view of limited government forestalled federal interference with slavery.

RISE OF A POLITICAL OPPOSITION

During the 32 years following Andrew Jackson's election to the presidency in 1828, the Democratic party controlled the White House all but 8 years. Twice the opposition candidate won the election, only to die soon after taking office. It would be a mistake, however, to assume that the Jacksonians faced no effective opposition. Although it took a number of years for Jackson's opponents to coalesce into an effective national political organization, by the mid-1830s the Whig party, as the opposition came to be known, was able to battle the Democratic party on almost equal terms throughout the country. And by 1840, the Whigs were strong enough to oust a Democratic president, Martin Van Buren, from the White House.

The party was formed in 1834 as a coalition of National Republicans, Anti-Masons, and disgruntled Democrats, who were united by their hatred of "King Andrew" Jackson and his "usurpations" of congressional and judicial authority. The party took its name from the seventeenth-century British Whigs, who had defended English liberties against the usurpations of pro-Catholic Stuart Kings.

In 1836 the Whigs mounted their first presidential campaign. The party ran three regional candidates against Martin Van Buren: Daniel Webster, the senator from Massachusetts and an ardent defender of the Bank of the United States who had substantial appeal in New England; Hugh Lawson White, who had appeal in the South; and William Henry Harrison, who fought an Indian alliance at the Battle of Tippecanoe and appealed to the West and to Anti-Masons in Pennsylvania and Vermont. The party strategy was to throw the election into the House of Representatives, where the Whigs would unite behind a single candidate. Van Buren easily defeated all his Whig opponents, winning 170 electoral votes to just 73 for his closest rival.

The emergence of Martin Van Buren as Jackson's successor resulted in a major defection of southerners and conservative Democrats to the Whig party. Unlike the southern slaveowning Jackson, Van Buren was a "Yankee" from New York, and many southerners feared that he could not be trusted to protect slavery. As a result, the Whigs carried Georgia, Kentucky, Maryland, and Tennessee.

Ironically, as president, Van Buren supported a congressional rule—known as the Gag Rule—which quashed debate over antislavery petitions in the House of Representatives. His independent treasury scheme combined with his staunch opposition to any federal interference in the economy lured Calhoun and the southern nullifiers back to the Democratic party. Conversely, his attacks on paper money and his scheme to remove federal funds from the private banking system alienated many conservative Democrats who threw their support to the Whigs.

Following his strong showing in the election of 1836, William Henry Harrison received the united support of the Whig party in 1840. Benefiting from the Panic of 1837 and from a host of colorful campaign innovations, Harrison easily defeated Van Buren by a vote of 234 to 60 in the electoral vote.

Unfortunately, the 68-year-old Harrison caught cold while delivering a two-hour inaugural address in the freezing rain. Barely a month later he died of pneumonia, the first president to die in office. His successor, John Tyler of Virginia, was an ardent defender of slavery, a staunch advocate of states' rights, and a former Democrat, whom the Whigs had nominated in order to attract Democratic support to the Whig ticket.

A firm believer in the principle that the federal government should exercise no powers other than those expressly enumerated in the Constitution, Tyler rejected the entire Whig legislative program, which called for reestablishment of a national bank, an increased tariff, and federally funded internal improvements. "He is," commented John Quincy Adams, "a political sectarian of the slave-driving, Virginian, Jeffersonian school, principled against all improvement, with all the interests and passions and vices of slavery rooted in his moral and political constitution."

The Whig party was furious. An angry mob gathered at the White House, threw rocks through the windows, and burned the president in effigy. To protest Tyler's rejection of the Whig political agenda, all members of the cabinet but one resigned. Tyler had become a president without a party.

"His Accidency" vetoed nine bills during his four years in office, more than any previous one-term president. He thus frustrated not only the Whig plan to recharter the national bank, but also dashed the party's hopes of raising the tariff while simultaneously distributing proceeds of land sales to the states. In 1843 Whigs in the House of Representatives made Tyler the subject of the first serious impeachment attempt. On January 10, 1843, Whigs introduced resolutions of impeachment charging Tyler with gross usurpation of power. The resolutions were defeated by a vote of 127 to 83.

Curiously, it was during John Tyler's tumultuous presidency that the nation's new two-party system achieved full maturity. Prior to Tyler's ascension to office, the Whig party had been a loose conglomeration of diverse political

John Tyler's opponents mocked him as "His Accidency" because he was the first vice president to take office as president upon the death of his predecessor.

factions unable to agree on a party platform. Tyler's presidency increased unity among Whigs who found common cause in their opposition to his policies. Tyler's apostasy caused the Whigs to unite finally behind a specific political agenda and create an effective party organization. On important issues, four-fifths of all Whig members of Congress regularly voted together. At the same time, the Whigs created an elaborate network of party newspapers in all parts of the country. Never before had party identity been so high or partisan sentiment so strong.

Who Were the Whigs?

The Jacksonians made a great effort to to persuade voters to identify their own cause with Thomas Jefferson and their Whig opponents with Alexander Hamilton. A radical Jacksonian Democrat made the point bluntly. "The aristocracy of our country . . . continually contrive to change their party name," wrote Frederick Robinson. "It was first Tory, then Federalist, then no party, then amalgamation, then National Re-

CHRONOLOGY OF KEY EVENTS

1820 Land Act reduces price of public land to $1.25 per acre

1821 New York State Constitutional Convention eliminates property qualification for voting

1825 House of Representatives elects John Quincy Adams as sixth president; President Monroe calls for voluntary removal of eastern Indians to lands west of the Mississippi River

1826 Disappearance of William Morgan touches off Anti-Masonic movement in New York State

1828 John C. Calhoun's South Carolina Exposition and Protest spells out the doctrine of nullification; Congress passes Tariff of Abominations; Andrew Jackson is elected seventh president

1830 Indian Removal Act provides funds to purchase Indian homelands in exchange for land in present-day Oklahoma and Arkansas; Webster-Hayne debate on land policy and nature of the union; Anti-Masons hold the first national party convention

1832 Jackson vetoes the bill to recharter the second Bank of the United States; John C. Calhoun becomes the first vice president to resign; South Carolina nullifies the federal tariff; United States defeats the Sauk and Fox Indians in the Black Hawk War

1833 Congress adopts "Compromise Tariff," lowering tariff rates, but also passes "Force Bill," authorizing Jackson to enforce federal law in South Carolina

1835 Roger B. Taney succeeds John Marshall as chief justice

1836 Jackson issues the Specie Circular; Martin Van Buren is elected eighth president

1837 Panic of 1837; *Charles River Bridge* v. *Warren Bridge*

1840 Congress passes Van Buren's Independent Treasury Act; William Henry Harrison, a Whig, is elected ninth president

1841 Harrison's death makes John Tyler the tenth president

1842 Dorr Rebellion against suffrage restrictions in Rhode Island

---

publican, now Whig." In spite of Democratic charges to the contrary, however, the Whigs were not simply a continuation of the Federalist party. Like the Democrats, the Whigs drew support from all parts of the nation. Indeed, the Whigs often formed the majority of the South's representatives in Congress. Like the Democrats, the Whigs were a coalition of sectional interests, class and economic interests, and ethnic and religious interests.

Democratic voters tended to be small farmers, residents of less-prosperous towns, and the Scots-Irish and Catholic Irish. Whigs tended to be educators and professionals, manufacturers, business-oriented farmers, British and German Protestant immigrants, upwardly aspiring manual laborers, free blacks, and active members of Presbyterian, Unitarian, and Congregational churches. The Whig coalition included supporters of Henry Clay's American System, states' righters, religious groups alienated by Jackson's Indian removal policies, and bankers and businesspeople frightened by the Democrats antimonopoly and antibank rhetoric.

Whereas the Democrats stressed class conflict, Whigs emphasized the harmony of interests between labor and capital, the need for humanitarian reform, and leadership by men of talent. The Whigs also idealized the "self-made man," who starts "from an humble origin, and from small beginnings rise[s] gradually in the world, as a result of merit and industry." Finally, the Whigs viewed technology and factory enterprise as forces for increasing national wealth and improving living conditions.

In 1848 and 1852 the Whigs tried to repeat their successful 1840 presidential campaign by nominating military heroes for the presidency. The party won the 1848 election with General Zachary Taylor, an Indian fighter and hero of the Mexican War, who had boasted that he had never cast a vote in a presidential election. Like Harrison, Taylor confined his campaign speeches to uncontroversial platitudes. "Old Rough and Ready," as he was known, died after just 1 year and 127 days in office. Then, in 1852, the Whigs nominated another Indian fighter and Mexican War hero, General Winfield Scott, who carried just four states for his dying party. "Old Fuss and Feathers," as he was called, was the last Whig nominee to play an important role in a presidential election.

CONCLUSION

A political revolution occurred in the United States between 1820 and 1840. Property qualification for voting and officeholding were abolished, voting by voice was eliminated, voter participation increased, and a new party system emerged. Unlike America's first political parties, the Federalists and Republicans, the Jacksonian Democrats and the Whigs were parties with grass-roots organization and support in all parts of the nation.

Andrew Jackson, the dominant political figure of the period, spelled out the new democratic approach to politics. In the name of eliminating special privilege and promoting equality of opportunity, he helped institute the national political nominating convention, defended the spoils system, destroyed the second Bank of the United States, and opened millions of acres of Indian lands to white settlement. A strong and determined leader, Jackson greatly expanded the power of the presidency. When South Carolina asserted the right of a state to nullify the federal tariff, Jackson made it clear that he would not tolerate defiance of federal authority.

SUGGESTIONS FOR FURTHER READING
OVERVIEWS AND SURVEYS
James MacGregor Burns, *The Crosswinds of Freedom: The Vineyard of Liberty* (1982); Ronald P. Formisano, "Toward a Reorientation of Jacksonian Politics: A Review of the Literature, 1959–1975," *Journal of American History*, 63 (1976); Edward Pessen, *Jacksonian America: Society, Personality, and Politics*, rev. ed. (1978); Robert V. Remini, *The Revolutionary Age of Andrew Jackson* (1976); Arthur M. Schlesinger, Jr., *The Age of Jackson* (1945); Harry L. Watson, *Liberty and Power: The Politics of Jacksonian America* (1990).

POLITICAL DEMOCRATIZATION
Henry Christman, *Tin Horns and Calico: A Decisive Episode in the Emergence of Democracy* (1945); Ronald Formisano, *Transformation of Political Culture: Massachusetts Parties, 1790s–1840s* (1983); Paul Goodman, *Toward a Christian Republic: Antimasonry and the Great Transition in New England* (1988); Merrill Peterson, ed., *Democracy, Liberty and Property: The State Constitutional Conventions of the 1820s* (1966); Lorman Ratner, *Anti-Masonry: The Crusade and the Party* (1969); W. P. Vaughn, *The Antimasonic Party in the United States, 1826–1843* (1983); Chilton Williamson, *American Suffrage: From Property to Democracy, 1760–1860* (1960).

THE REBIRTH OF PARTIES
Lee Benson, *The Concept of Jacksonian Democracy: New York as a Test Case* (1961); James S. Chase, *Emergence of the Presidential Nominating Convention, 1789–1832* (1973); Donald B. Cole, *Jacksonian Democracy in New Hampshire, 1800–1851* (1970); Ronald Formisano, *The Birth of Mass Political Parties: Michigan, 1827–1861* (1971); Marvin E. Gettleman, *The Dorr Rebellion: A Study in American Radicalism, 1833–1849* (1973); M. J. Heale, *The Presidential Quest: Candidates and Images in American Political Culture, 1787–1852* (1982); Richard Hofstadter, *The Idea of a Party System: The Rise of Legitimate Opposition in the United States, 1780–1840* (1969); Robert Kelley, *The Cultural Pattern in American Politics: The First Century* (1979); Peter D. Levine, *The Behavior of State Legislative Parties in the Jacksonian Era, New Jersey, 1829–1844* (1977); Shaw Livermore, *The Twilight of Federalism: The Disintegration of the Federalist Party, 1815–1830* (1962); Richard P. McCormick, *The Second American Party System* (1966), and *The Presidential*

Game: The Origins of American Presidential Politics (1982); Edward Pessen, *Riches, Class, and Power Before the Civil War* (1973); Robert V. Remini, *The Election of Andrew Jackson* (1963), and *Martin Van Buren and the Making of the Democratic Party* (1959); Arthur M. Schlesinger, Jr., ed., *History of U.S. Political Parties, 1789–1860: From Factions to Parties* (1973); Arthur M. Schlesinger, Jr. and Fred L. Israel, eds., *History of American Presidential Elections, 1789–1968* (1971); J. Mills Thornton III, *Politics and Power in a Slave Society: Alabama, 1800–1860* (1977); Joel Silbey, *The American Political Nation, 1838–1893* (1991), and *The Partisan Imperative: The Dynamics of American Politics Before the Civil War* (1985); Harry L. Watson, *Jacksonian Politics and Community Conflict: The Emergence of the Second Party System in Cumberland County, North Carolina* (1981).

ANDREW JACKSON: THE POLITICS OF THE COMMON PERSON

William L. Anderson, ed., *Cherokee Removal: Before and After* (1991); John Ashworth, *"Agrarians" and "Aristocrats": Party Political Ideology in the United States, 1837–1846* (1983); Jean H. Baker, *Affairs of Party: The Political Culture of Northern Democrats in the Mid-Nineteenth Century* (1983); Amy Bridges, *A City in the Republic: Antebellum New York and the Origins of Machine Politics* (1984); Matthew A. Crenson, *The Federal Machine: Beginnings of Bureaucracy in Jacksonian America* (1975); James C. Curtis, *Andrew Jackson and the Search for Vindication* (1976); Angie Debo, *And Still the Waters Run: The Betrayal of the Five Civilized Tribes* (1940); A. H. DeRosier, Jr., *The Removal of the Choctaw Indians* (1970); B. W. Dippie, *The Vanishing American: White Attitudes and U.S. Indian Policy* (1982); Cecil Eby, *"That Disgraceful Affair": The Black Hawk War* (1973); Richard Ellis, *The Union at Risk: Jacksonian Democracy, States' Rights, and the Nullification Crisis* (1987); Daniel Feller, *Public Lands in Jacksonian Politics* (1984); William W. Freehling, *Prelude to Civil War: The Nullification Controversy in South Carolina, 1816–1836* (1966); Michael D. Green, *The Politics of Indian Removal: Creek Government and Society in Crisis* (1982); Charles G. Haines and Foster H. Sherwood, *The Role of the Supreme Court in American Government and Politics, 1835–1864* (1957); Bray Hammond, *Banks and Politics in America: From the Revolution to the Civil War* (1957); Stanley I. Kutler, *Privilege and Creative Destruction: The Charles River Bridge Case* (1971); Richard Latner, *The Presidency of Andrew Jackson: White House Politics, 1829–1837* (1979); John M. McFaul, *The Politics of Jacksonian Finance* (1972); R. C. McGrane, *The Panic of 1837* (1924); James H. Merrell, *The Indians' New World: Catawbas and Their Neighbors from European Contact Through the Era of Removal* (1989); Marvin Meyers, *The Jacksonian Persuasion* (1957); M. D. Peterson, *Olive Branch and Sword: The Compromise of 1833* (1982); F. P. Prucha, *American Indian Policy in the Formative Years* (1962); Fritz Redlich, *The Molding of American Banking: Men and Ideas* (1951); Robert Remini, *The Legacy of Andrew Jackson* (1988); Hugh Rockoff, *The Free Banking Era* (1975); Ronald N. Satz, *American Indian Policy in the Jacksonian Era* (1975); Bernard Schwartz, *From Confederation to Nation: The American Constitution, 1835–1877* (1973); W. G. Shade, *Banks or No Banks: The Money Issue in Western Politics, 1832–1865* (1972); J. R. Sharp, *The Jacksonians versus the Banks* (1970); W. B. Smith and A. H. Cole, *Fluctuations in American Business, 1790–1860* (1935); Paul Studenski and Herman E. Krooss, *Financial History of the United States*, 2d ed. (1963); Peter Temin, *The Jacksonian Economy* (1969); Richard H. Timberlake, Jr., *The Origins of Central Banking in the United States* (1978); J. Van Fenstermaker, *The Development of American Commercial Banking, 1782–1837* (1965); Herman J. Viola, *Thomas L. McKenney: Architect of America's Early Indian Policy* (1974); John William Ward, *Andrew Jackson: Symbol for an Age* (1955); Philip Weeks, *Farewell, My Nation: The American Indian & the United States, 1820–1890* (1990); Leonard D. White, *The Jacksonians: A Study in Administrative History, 1829–1861* (1954); Jean Alexander Wilburn, *Biddle's Bank: The Crucial Years* (1967).

RISE OF A POLITICAL OPPOSITION

Thomas Brown, *Politics and Statesmanship: Essays on the American Whig Party* (1985); Daniel Walker Howe, *The Political Culture of the American Whigs* (1979); Lawrence Frederick Kohl, *The Politics of Individualism: Parties and the American Character in the Jacksonian Era* (1989); Thomas H. O'Connor, *Lords of the Loom: The Cotton Whigs and the Coming of the Civil War* (1968).

BIOGRAPHIES

Irving H. Bartlett, *Daniel Webster* (1978); Maurice G. Baxter, *One and Inseparable: Daniel Webster and the Union* (1984); Norman D. Brown, *Daniel*

Webster and the Politics of Availability (1969); Alfred A. Cave, *An American Conservative in the Age of Jackson: The Political and Social Thought of Calvin Colton* (1969); William N. Chambers, *Old Bullion Benton: Senator from the New West* (1956); Oliver Perry Chitwood, *John Tyler: Champion of the Old South* (1939); Freeman Cleaves, *Old Tippecanoe: William Henry Harrison and His Time* (1939); Donald B. Cole, *Martin Van Buren and the American Political System* (1984); Richard N. Current, *Daniel Webster and the Rise of National Conservatism* (1955), and *John C. Calhoun* (1963); James C. Curtis, *The Fox at Bay: Martin Van Buren and the Presidency, 1837–1841* (1970); Robert F. Dalzell, Jr., *Daniel Webster and the Trial of American Nationalism, 1843–1852* (1973); Martin Duberman, *Charles Francis Adams, 1807–1886* (1961); Robert G. Gunderson, *The Log Cabin Campaign* (1957); Richard Hofstadter, *The American Political Tradition* (1948); Robert J. Morgan, *A Whig Embattled: The Presidency under John Tyler* (1954); Sydney Nathans, *Daniel Webster and Jacksonian Democracy* (1973); John Niven, *John C. Calhoun and the Price of Union* (1988); John Niven, *Martin Van Buren: The Romantic Age of American Politics* (1983); Robert V. Remini, *Andrew Jackson and the Course of American Empire, 1767–1821* (1977), *Andrew Jackson and the Course of American Freedom, 1822–1832* (1981), *Andrew Jackson and the Course of American Democracy, 1833–1845* (1984), and *Martin Van Buren and the Making of the Democratic Party* (1959); G. G. Van Deusen, *The Life of Henry Clay* (1937).

CHAPTER 11

Reforming American Society

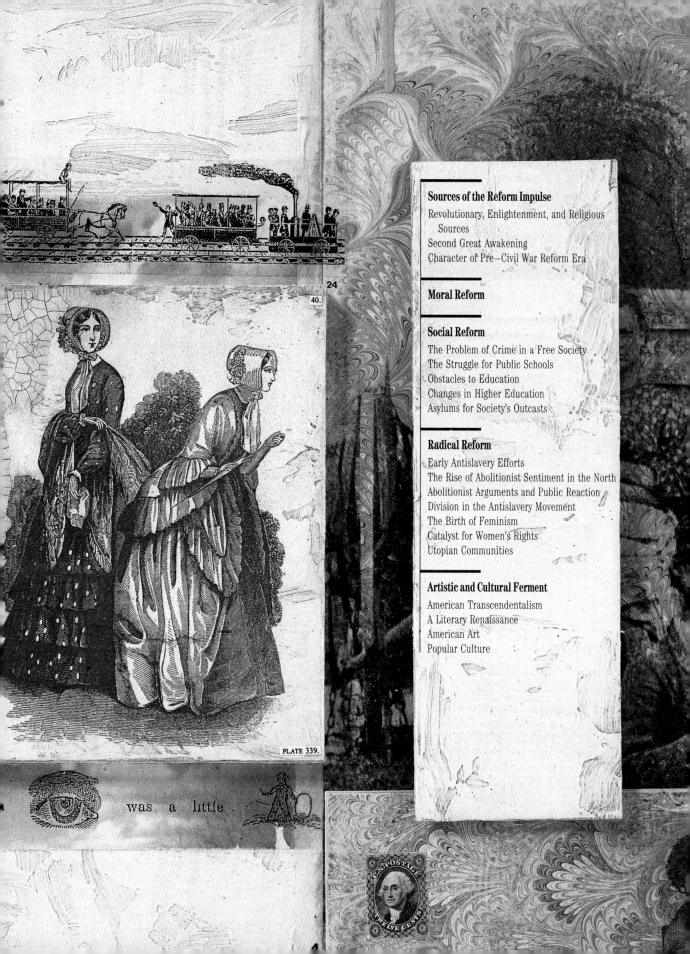

Many early nineteenth-century New Yorkers feared that their city was being overwhelmed by crime. In one highly publicized incident a little girl was stabbed to death over a penny she had begged. In another incident in 1849, 30 people died and another 100 were injured in a riot outside the city's Astor Place Opera House. Declared the city's mayor: "This city is invested by gangs of hardened wretches" who "patrol the streets making night hideous and insulting all who are not strong enough to defend themselves." Between 1814 and 1835, New York City's population doubled, but reports of crime increased fivefold.

Poverty and crime appeared to be epidemic. Young girls, dressed in rags, tried to support themselves by selling toothpicks. Journalists reported seeing little boys search the gutters for whiskey bottles, then drink the last drops. An estimated 10,000 prostitutes plied their trade, brazenly standing outside of fashionable hotels or strolling through theaters. Gangs, bearing such names as the Plug Uglies, Dead Rabbits, and the Bowery B'hoys, prowled the city streets, stealing from warehouses, junk shops, and private residences.

Critics decried a "carnival of murder." In 1857, six men were shot or stabbed in barroom brawls in a single night. In response to the apparent upsurge in crime, fearful citizens armed themselves, carrying guns and night sticks for their defense when they went outside at night. For added protection, many homeowners installed iron bars over their ground-floor windows.

During the decades before the Civil War, newspapers were filled with reports of crime, vice, and violence in the growing cities of the North, in the slave South, and on the frontier. In Vicksburg, Mississippi, on July 4, 1835, respectable citizens responded to an increase in gambling and prostitution with vigilantism. They raided gaming houses and brothels and lynched five gamblers.

In pre–Civil War America, incidents of crime and violence led many Americans to ask how a free society could maintain stability and moral order. Americans sought to answer this question through religion, education, and social reform.

During the years before the Civil War, newspapers were filled with graphic accounts of crime and violence, such as this drawing of a shooting in front of the Fifth Avenue Opera House in New York City. Americans sought solutions to problems of poverty, crime, and such violence in religious and social reform.

SOURCES OF THE REFORM IMPULSE

The first half of the nineteenth century witnessed an enormous effort to improve society through reform. Reformers launched unprecedented campaigns to assist the handicapped, rehabilitate criminals and prostitutes, outlaw alcohol, guarantee women's rights, achieve world peace, and abolish slavery. Our modern systems of free, public schools, prisons, and hospitals for the infirm and the mentally ill are all legacies of this first generation of American reform.

What were the sources of the reform impulse? Why was the "demon of reform," as Ralph Waldo Emerson called it, unleashed with such vigor in pre–Civil War America?

Revolutionary, Enlightenment, and Religious Sources

Reformers were inspired by the republican ideals enshrined in the Declaration of Independence. The Declaration's emphasis on natural rights, liberty, and equality led reformers to view their efforts as a continuation of political struggles begun during the Revolution. The principles of liberty and equality embodied in the Declaration led abolitionists like William Lloyd Garrison to challenge the justice of the institution of slavery and feminists like Elizabeth Cady Stanton to call for equal rights for women. The concept of natural rights set forth in the Declaration encouraged educational reformers like Horace Mann to work to improve the nation's educational system and humanitarians like Dorothea Dix to reform the treatment of the mentally ill.

The philosophy of the Enlightenment, with its belief in the people's innate goodness and its rejection of the inevitability of poverty and ignorance, was another important source of reform. By providing a more favorable moral and physical environment through the application of reason, reform could overcome social problems and antisocial behavior.

Religion further strengthened the reform impulse. Almost all the leading reformers were devoutly religious men and women, who wanted to deepen the nation's commitment to Christian principles. Two trends in religious thought—religious liberalism and evangelical revivalism—strengthened reformers' zeal. The first was an emerging humanitarian form of religion that rejected the harsh Calvinist doctrines of original sin and predestination. Its preachers stressed the basic goodness of human nature and each individual's capacity to follow the example of Christ.

William Ellery Channing (1780–1842) was America's leading exponent of religious liberalism. In 1815 the quiet and dignified young minister became involved in a conflict within New England Congregationalism that pitted traditionalists who believed that people were born with original sin against liberals who maintained that humankind was basically good. In Baltimore in 1819, Channing delivered a sermon entitled "Unitarian Christianity," which proclaimed principles that became the basis for American Unitarianism. The new religious denomination stressed individual freedom of belief, a united world under a single God, and the mortal nature of Jesus Christ, whom individuals should strive to emulate. Wits defined Unitarianism as a religion dedicated to "the fatherhood

of God, the brotherhood of man, and the neighborhood of Boston."

Channing's belief that the sole purpose of Christianity was "the perfection of human nature, the elevation of men into nobler beings" stimulated many reformers to work toward improving the conditions of the physically handicapped, the criminal, the pauper, and the enslaved. Religious liberals, such as Unitarians and Quakers, joined reform movements in far higher numbers than their percentage in the population would predict.

Second Great Awakening

The enthusiastic religious revivals that swept the country in the early nineteenth century were also a source of the reform impulse. On August 6, 1801, some 25,000 men, women, and children poured into the small frontier community of Cane Ridge, Kentucky, in search of religious salvation. Twenty-five thousand was a fantastically large number of people at a time when the population of the whole state of Kentucky was a quarter million, and the state's largest city, Lexington, had only 1795 residents. The Cane Ridge camp meeting went on for a week. Baptists, Methodists, and ministers of other denominations joined together to preach to the vast throng. Within three years, similar revivals had swept across Kentucky, Tennessee, and Ohio. This great religious fervor came to be called the Second Great Awakening.

The revivalists urged their followers to repent their sins and reject selfishness and materialism. To the revivalists, sin was not a metaphysical abstraction. Drinking and dueling were sins. Luxury, high living, indifference to religion, preoccupation with worldly and commercial matters—all these were denounced as sinful. Revivalists believed that the nation could only be redeemed if individuals truly repented their sins and accepted Jesus Christ as their personal savior. If men and women did not seek God through Christ, the nation would face divine retribution.

What explains the rapid rise of revivalism? The growing separation of church and state that followed the Revolution was now complete. At the same time that state governments deprived established churches of the colonial era of state support (Virginia ended state support for churches in 1785, Connecticut in 1818, and Massachusetts in 1833), the number of other denominations expanded. Revivals provided a vehicle for dramatically increasing church membership and ensuring that America would remain a God-fearing nation. By the 1830s perhaps three-quarters of the American people were members of a church.

Revivals also influenced the political rhetoric of pre–Civil War America. The evangelical themes of sin, sacrifice, repentance, rebirth, and national mission shaped political discourse. Above all, the revivals inspired a widespread sense that the nation was standing close to the millennium, a thousand years of peace and brotherhood, when sin, war, and tyranny would vanish from the earth. The revivals reinforced the conviction that each individual was personally responsible for sin and for eradicating moral evil. Evangelical revivals helped instill a belief that Americans had been chosen by God to

Americans turned to revival meetings in times of social and economic upheaval. These meetings, which stressed new birth conversions, could last for days.

lead the world toward "a millennium of republicanism."

Charles Grandison Finney (1792–1875), the "father of modern revivalism," led revivals throughout the Northeast. Finney grew up and studied law in western New York. In 1821 he underwent a conversion experience, which was as familiar to American Protestants as the Scriptural account of Paul's conversion on the road to Damascus. On a Sabbath evening Finney, then a prosperous young lawyer, thumbed through the pages of a Bible as part of his research on a court case. He soon began to read the text more closely, overwhelmed by questions he had never before considered. "What are you waiting for?" a voice seemed to be saying. "Are you leading a righteous life?" Gripped by fear, Finney worried that his heart was dead to God. But then it seemed as if he "met the Lord Jesus Christ face to face." The Holy Spirit seemed to be speaking to him, asking him, "Will you doubt?" Finney cried out, "No I will not doubt; I cannot doubt." Suddenly, his sense of guilt and sinfulness was gone. He had been born again.

Finney believed that he had "a retainer from the Lord Jesus Christ to plead his cause," and despite his rejection of formal theology training, he began to convert souls to Christ in the small towns of upstate New York. He introduced a series of "new measures" to win converts. He prayed for sinners by name; he held "protracted meetings" that lasted night after night for a week or more; he set up an "anxious bench" at the front of the meeting, where the almost-saved could receive special prayers. And he encouraged women to actively participate in revivals. Finney's message was that anyone could experience a redemptive change of heart and a resurgence of religious feeling. If only enough people converted to Christ, Finney told his listeners, the millennium would arrive within three years.

Revival meetings attracted both frontier settlers and city folk, slaves and masters, farmers and shopkeepers. The revivals had their greatest appeal among isolated farming families on the western and southern frontier, among upwardly mobile merchants, shopkeepers, artisans, and skilled laborers in the expanding commercial and industrial towns of the North. They drew support from social conservatives who feared that America would disintegrate into a state of anarchy without the influence of evangelical religion, and also enlisted followers among poorer whites and slaves in the South. Above all, revivals attracted large numbers of young women, who took an active role organizing meetings, establishing church organizations, and editing religious publications.

Character of Pre–Civil War Reform Era

During the first decades of the nineteenth century, America's revolutionary heritage, Enlightenment philosophy, and religious liberalism and revivalism all contributed to a spirit of optimism, a sensitivity to human suffering, and a boundless faith in humankind's capacity to improve social institutions. Church leaders encouraged their flocks to engage in works of "practical benevolence"—to save the nation from gambling, drinking, horseracing, atheism, and anarchy. Many middle-class women, particularly in the Northeast, took active public roles in temperance and antislavery movements, and led campaigns against the moral depravity found in saloons, houses of prostitution, and other centers of "lewd and lascivious" segregated male entertainment. Many members of the growing urban working class campaigned for public schools, penal reform, and abolition of imprisonment for debt. Each of these groups sought to influence politics and perfect human institutions.

Reformers varied widely in their motives. Some people turned to reform as a way of enforcing order in society. Others were motivated by a religious vision of creating a godly society on Earth. Still others viewed reform as a way of spreading the values associated with the Protestant Ethic: sobriety, punctuality, self-discipline, and personal responsibility.

Between the 1820s and the 1840s, reformers shifted from an emphasis on voluntary action to an increasing reliance on government action to achieve their objectives. By the 1840s, reformers did not try to persuade drinkers to abstain from alcohol or slaveowners to recognize the sinfulness of slavery. Rather, they called for prohibition laws to bar the manufacture and sale of liquor and for the abolition of slavery through political action.

MORAL REFORM

The earliest reformers wanted to persuade Americans to adopt more godly personal habits. They set up associations to battle profanity and Sabbath breaking, to place a Bible in every American home, to provide religious education for the children of the poor, and to curb the widespread heavy use of hard liquor. By discouraging drinking, gambling, and vulgar entertainments (such as bear baiting and cockfighting), and encouraging observance of the Sabbath, reformers hoped to "restore the government of God."

One of the most dramatic attempts at moral reform involved Magdalene societies, which sought in the 1830s and 1840s to rehabilitate prostitutes and discourage male solicitation. The New York Moral Reform Society had 15,000 members in 1837, and three years later had doubled the number of branches in New England and upstate New York. Members walked into brothels and prayed for the prostitutes, publicized in the newspapers the names of men who patronized prostitutes, visited prostitutes in jails, and lobbied for state laws that would make male solicitation of prostitutes a crime.

But, the most extensive moral reform campaign was against liquor. At the beginning of the nineteenth century, heavy drinking was an integral part of American life. Many people believed that downing a glass of whiskey before breakfast was conducive to good health. Instead of taking coffee breaks, people took a dram of liquor at 11 and again at 4 o'clock as well as drinks after meals "to aid digestion" and a nightcap before going to sleep. Campaigning politicians offered voters generous amounts of liquor during campaigns and as rewards for "right voting" on election day. On the frontier, one evangelist noted, "a house could not be raised, a field of wheat cut down, nor could there be a log rolling, a husking, a quilting, a wedding, or a funeral without the aid of alcohol."

By 1820 the typical adult American consumed more than 7 gallons of absolute alcohol a year (compared to 2.6 gallons today). Consumption had risen markedly in two decades, fueled by the growing amounts of corn distilled by farmers into cheap whiskey, which could be transported more easily than bulk corn.

(Text continues on p. 332)

GOUGING FIGHTS AND BACKCOUNTRY HONOR

Nobody ever called them pretty. Eastern and European travelers to the American southern backcountry employed many descriptive and emotive adjectives—disgusting, brutal, savage, uncivilized, disgraceful, barbaric, unsightly—but never once pretty. And, indeed, backcountry fights, whether called "gouging" matches, "rough-and-tumble" contests, or "no holds barred" battles, were not attractive affairs. Men fought all out, using fists, hands, feet, elbows, knees, teeth, and whatever other part of their anatomy promised to do bodily damage to their opponents. Capturing the temper of these battles, Anglican minister Charles Woodmason counseled, "I would advise you when You do fight Not to act like Tygers and Bears as these Virginians do—Biting one anothers Lips and Noses off, and *gouging* one another—that is, thrusting out one anothers Eyes,

and kicking one another on the Cods, to the Great damage of many a Poor Woman."

The goal of a gouging match was the disfigurement of one's opponent. This could be accomplished in any number of ways, but the most popular was eye gouging. Fighters manicured their fingernails hard and sharp so that they could use them as a fulcrum to pry out their adversary's eye. On seeing a renowned fighter badly mauled, a passerby remarked, " 'You have come off badly this time; I doubt?' 'Have I,' says he triumphantly, showing from his pocket at the same time an eye; which he had extracted during the combat, and preserved as a trophy."

Reading descriptions of these sanguinary contests provokes a series of questions. Who would engage in such activities? And why? Were the contests considered sports

or manifestations of blood feuds? And what of the spectators and the law—did they enjoy and allow and condone such barbarities? Finally, what do the contests tell us about the society in which they flourished?

Gouging centered in the region of rivers and largely untamed backcountry south of the Ohio River. It was a land of dangers and violence and early deaths. Organized Indian tribes threatened settlers. Wild animals roamed the heavily wooded forests. Outlaws practiced their professions almost unchecked by the law. High infant mortality rates, short life expectancies, dangerous occupations, and random violence stood as grim reminders that life in this region of nature was, as philosopher Thomas Hobbes once noted, "solitary, poor, nasty, brutish, and short."

The men who disfigured each other in gouging matches had been hardened by their environment and their occupations. Many worked on the rivers as roustabouts, rivermen, or gamblers. Others were hunters, herders, or subsistence farmers. No plantations dotted their world; no landed aristocrats dominated them. As Elliott J. Gorn, a leading historian of the subject, commented, "the upland folk lived in an intensely local, kin-based society. Rural hamlets, impassible roads, and provincial isolations—not growing towns, internal improvements, or international commerce—characterized the backcountry."

The work these men performed was physically demanding and dangerous. Working on a Mississippi barge or trapping game in the backcountry exposed men to all the forces of nature and did not foster a gentle view of life. Death and pain were everywhere to be seen. Mark Twain remembered such men from his boyhood experiences in a raw river town: "Rude, uneducated, brave, suffering terrific hardships with sailorlike stoicism; heavy drinkers, coarse frolickers . . . , heavy fighters, reckless fellows, every one, elephantinely jolly, foul witted, profane, prodigal of their money, bankrupt at the end of the trip, fond of barbaric finery, prodigious braggarts." They were not Jacksonian men on the make or respectable churchgoers. Rather they were men who worked hard, played hard, and drank hard.

Since they spent most of their lives in the company of other men, much of their sense of self-worth came from how their companions viewed them. They did not use money or piety as yardsticks for measuring the worth of a man. Bravery, strength, conviviality, and a jealous sense of personal honor determined the cut of a man. The ability to drink, boast, and fight with equal ability marked a backcountry Renaissance man.

Question a man's honor and you questioned in the most profound sense his manhood. If aristocratic Southerners dueled over such slights, backcountry laborers gouged over them. Northerners found this touchy sense of honor perplexing. Philip Vickers Fithian, a New Jerseyite who traveled to the South in the 1770s, commented about the reason for one fight, "I suppose either that they are lovers, and one has in Jest or reality some way supplanted the other; or has in a merry hour called him a *Lubber* or a *Thick-Skull*, or a *Buckskin*, or a *Scotsman*, or perhaps one has mislaid the other's hat, or knocked a peach out of his Hand, or offered him a dram without wiping the mouth of the Bottle." Any excuse, thought Fithian, could lead to mortal combat. But he misread the situation. In truth, any insult, no matter how slight, could be judged serious enough to provoke violence.

Once men exchanged angry words and angrier challenges, their combat provided entertainment for their companions. At the fights, drinking and boasting continued, and the line between participant and spectator was hazy. One fight often led to another and general melees were not uncommon. Were such contests sports? Probably not, but it was not a question that anyone would have posed. Just as there was little distinction between participant and spectator, there was little difference between sport and battery.

Gouging matches were certainly not civilized affairs, and as civilized behavior and culture penetrated the backcountry men ceased to settle their differences in such brutal contests. This is not to say that they stopped fighting. Rather they "defended their honor" in more "civilized" ways. Bowie knives, swords, and pistols replaced honed thumbnails and filed teeth as the weapons of choice. And these "affairs of honor" were held before a few solemn witnesses rather than a host of cheering friends. During an earlier time, it was considered an unmanly sign of fear for a person to carry a weapon. But more refined sensibilities reversed this notion. By the mid-nineteenth century weapon carrying had become an indication of manliness. "Thus," as Gorn observed, "progress . . . slowly circumscribed rough-and-tumble fighting, only to substitute a deadlier option. Violence grew neater and more lethal as men checked their savagery to murder each other."

But if gouging became a relic of another age, it remained a particularly telling relic. It provides an important clue to the values of the southern backcountry. How men fought—just as how they worked or played—indicates much about their lives. The men who gouged led strenuous, often violent lives. They were not the sort of men to turn pale at the sight of blood or even at the sight of an eyeless eye socket. They admired toughness, fearlessness, and even meanness—not piety, gentleness, and sensitivity. As Gorn so aptly noted, "Violent sports, heavy drinking, and impulsive pleasure seeking were appropriate for men whose lives were hard, whose futures were unpredictable, and whose opportunities were limited. Gouging champions were group leaders because they embodied the basic values of their peers."

The temperance movement of the 1830s and 1840s used religious revivalist tactics to frighten drinkers into taking the "pledge" to abstain from drinking.

In the 1820s, a gallon of whiskey cost just a quarter.

In their campaign, reformers sought to alter the cultural norms that encouraged alcohol consumption by identifying liquor as the cause of a wide range of social, family, and personal problems. Many middle-class women blamed alcohol for the abuse of wives and children and the squandering of family resources. Many businesspeople identified drinking with crime, poverty, and inefficient and unproductive employees.

The stage was clearly set for the appearance of an organized movement against liquor. In 1826 the nation's first formal national temperance organization was born: the American Society for the Promotion of Temperance. Led by socially prominent clergy and laypeople, the new organization called for total abstinence from distilled liquor. Within three years, 222 state and local antiliquor groups were laboring to spread this message.

By 1835 membership in temperance organizations had climbed to 1.5 million, and an estimated 2 million Americans had taken the "pledge" to abstain from hard liquor. Temperance reform drew support from many southern-

ers and westerners who were otherwise indifferent or hostile to reform. Temperance reformers did not rid the nation of the "Demon Rum," but they helped reduce annual per capita consumption of alcohol from 7 gallons in 1830 to just 3 gallons a decade later, forcing 4000 distilleries to close. Fewer employers provided workers with 11 o'clock or 4 o'clock drams, and some businesses began to fire employees who drank on the job.

The sudden arrival of hundreds of thousands of immigrants from "heavy drinking" cultures heightened the concerns of temperance reformers. Between 1830 and 1860, nearly 2 million Irish arrived in the United States along with an additional 893,000 Germans. In Ireland, land was in such short supply that many young men were unable to support a family by farming. The only solution was to delay marriage and socialize with other young men in "bachelor groups," a ritual that often involved heavy drinking. These immigrants probably drank no more than most native-born Americans prior to the 1830s, but increasingly the heavy drinking of immigrants was regarded as a sign of their supposed moral degeneracy.

The 1840s also saw two new approaches to

nineteenth century, most colleges offered their students, who usually enrolled between the ages of 12 and 15, only a narrow training in the classics designed to prepare them for the ministry. During the 1820s and 1830s, in an effort to adjust to the "spirits and wants of the age," colleges broadened their curricula to include the study of history, literature, geography, modern languages, and the sciences. The entrance age was also raised and the requirements demanded of students were broadened.

The number of colleges also increased. Most of the new colleges, particularly in the South and West, were church-affiliated, but several states, including Georgia, Tennessee, Virginia, and Michigan established state universities. Prior to the Civil War, 16 states provided some financial support to higher education, and in New York City by the 1850s, an education, from elementary schools to college, was available tuition free.

A few institutions of higher education opened their doors to blacks and women. In 1833 Oberlin College, where Charles G. Finney taught, became the nation's first coeducational college, and four years later, Mary Lyon established the first women's college, Mount Holyoke, to train teachers and missionaries. A number of western state universities also admitted women. In addition, three colleges for blacks were founded before the Civil War, and a few other colleges, including Oberlin, Harvard, Bowdoin, and Dartmouth admitted small numbers of black students.

Asylums for Society's Outcasts

A number of reformers devoted their attention to the problems of the mentally ill, the deaf, and the blind. In 1841, Dorothea Dix (1802–1887), a 39-year-old former schoolteacher, volunteered to give religious instruction to women incarcerated in the East Cambridge, Massachusetts, House of Correction. Inside the House of Correction, she was horrified to find mentally ill inmates dressed in rags and confined to a single dreary room without any source of heat. Shocked by what she saw, she embarked on a lifelong crusade to reform the treatment of the mentally ill.

After a two-year secret investigation of every jail and almshouse in Massachusetts, Dix issued a report to the Massachusetts state legislature. The mentally ill, she found, were mixed indiscriminately with paupers and hardened criminals. Many were confined "in cages, closets, cellars, stalls, pens! Chained, naked, beaten with rods and lashed into obedience." When keepers of institutions questioned the report's credibility, accusing Dix of "sensational and slanderous lies," Dix enlisted the support of such influential men as Horace Mann, who encouraged the state to construct a large addition for the insane to the state hospital.

Following her successes in Massachusetts, Dix carried her campaign for state-supported asylums nationwide, traveling 30,000 miles in ten years and persuading more than a dozen state legislatures to improve institutional care for the insane. Congress approved her proposal for a federal system of hospitals for the mentally ill, but President Franklin Pierce vetoed it on the grounds that it was unwise for the federal government to assume responsibility for the nation's poor.

Through the efforts of such reformers as Thomas Gallaudet and Samuel Howe, institutions to care for the deaf and blind began to appear. Thomas Hopkins Gallaudet (1787–1851), moved by the plight of a deaf-mute named Alice Cogswell, established in 1817 the nation's first school in Hartford, Connecticut, to teach deaf-mutes to read and write, read lips, and communicate through hand signals. Samuel Gridley Howe (1801–1876), the husband of Julia Ward Howe, composer of the "Battle Hymn of the Republic," accomplished for the blind what Gallaudet achieved for the deaf. He founded the country's first school for the blind in Boston and produced printed materials with raised type. He aroused national attention by his successful instruction of Laura Bridgman, a blind deaf-mute.

RADICAL REFORM

The initial thrust of reform—moral reform—was to rescue the nation from infidelity and intemperance. A second line of reform, social or humanitarian reform, sought to alleviate such sources of human misery as crime, cruelty, disease, and ignorance. A third line of reform, radical reform, sought national regeneration by eliminating slavery and racial and sexual discrimination.

Early Antislavery Efforts

Increasing antislavery sentiment resulted in the most influential of the radical reform movements, the struggle to abolish slavery. As late as the 1750s, no church had discouraged its members from owning or trading in slaves. The governments of Britain, France, Denmark, Holland, Portugal, and Spain openly participated in the slave trade. Slaves could be found in each of the 13 American colonies, and prior to the American Revolution, only one colony, Georgia, had temporarily sought to prohibit slavery (because the founders did not want a workforce that would compete with the convicts they planned to transport from England).

Within half a century, however, protests against the institution of slavery had become widespread. By 1804 nine states north of Maryland and Delaware had either emancipated their slaves or adopted gradual emancipation plans. Both the United States and Britain in 1807 outlawed the African slave trade. In 1833 Britain emancipated 780,000 slaves in the British West Indies, and in 1848 France and Denmark freed slaves in their New World colonies.

In the early nineteenth century, the emancipation of slaves in the northern states and the prohibition against the African slave trade generated optimism that slavery was dying. Congress in 1787 had barred slavery from the Old Northwest, the region north of the Ohio River to the Mississippi River. The number of slaves freed by their masters had risen dramatically in the upper South during the 1780s and 1790s, and more antislavery societies been formed in the South than in the North. At the present rate of progress, predicted one religious leader in 1791, within 50 years it will "be as shameful for a man to hold a Negro slave, as to be guilty of common robbery or theft."

By the early 1830s, however, the development of the Cotton Kingdom proved that slavery was not on the road to extinction. Despite the end the African slave trade, the slave population had continued to grow, climbing from 1.5 million in 1820 to over 2 million a decade later.

A widespread belief that blacks and whites could not coexist and that racial separation was necessary encouraged futile efforts at deportation and overseas colonization. In 1816 a group of prominent ministers and politicians formed the American Colonization Society to resettle free blacks in West Africa, encourage planters to voluntarily emancipate their slaves, and create a group of black missionaries who would spread Christianity in Africa. Various plans for African colonization gained the support of the nation's major political figures, including Thomas Jefferson, James Madison, James Monroe, and John Marshall. During the 1820s, Congress helped fund the cost of transporting free blacks to Africa—first to Sierra Leone and then, beginning in 1822, to Liberia. In the face of the strong political support for colonization, many staunch opponents of slavery confined their efforts to lobbying for state emancipation acts and measures to prevent the kidnapping and sale of free blacks.

A few blacks supported African colonization in the belief that it provided the only alternative to continued degradation and discrimination. Paul Cuffe (1759–1817), a Quaker sea captain who was the son of a former slave and an Indian woman, led the first experiment in colonization. In 1815 he transported 38 free blacks to Sierra Leone, on the western coast of Africa, and devoted thousands of his own dollars to the cause of colonization. By the 1820s, however, it was apparent that colonization was a wholly impractical solution to the nation's slavery problem. Each year the nation's slave population rose by roughly 50,000, but in 1830 the American Colonization Society succeeded in persuading just 259 free blacks to migrate to Liberia, bringing the total number of blacks colonized in Africa to just 1400.

The Rise of Abolitionist Sentiment in the North

The movement condemning colonization and northern discrimination against African-Americans was initially led by free blacks. As early as 1817, more than 3000 members of Philadelphia's black community staged a protest against colonization, at which they denounced the policy as "little more merciful than death." In 1829 David Walker (1785–1830), a free black owner of a second-hand clothing store in Boston, issued the militant *Appeal to the Colored Citizens of the World*. The appeal threatened insurrection and violence if calls for the abolition of slavery and improved conditions for free blacks were not realized. The next year, some 40 black delegates from 8 states held the first of a series of annual conventions that denounced slavery and called for an end to discriminatory laws in the northern states.

The idea of abolition received impetus from William Lloyd Garrison (1805–1879). In 1829 the 25-year-old white Bostonian added his voice to the outcry against colonization, denouncing it as a cruel hoax designed to promote the racial purity of the northern population while doing nothing to end slavery in the South. Colonization, Garrison insisted, was "a libel upon republicanism—a libel upon the Declaration of Independence—a libel upon Christianity." Instead, he called for "immediate emancipation." By immediate emancipation, he meant the immediate and unconditional release of slaves from bondage without compensation to slaveowners.

On January 1, 1831, he began publishing *The Liberator*, a militant abolitionist newspaper that was the country's first publication to demand an immediate end to slavery. On the front page of the first issue, he defiantly declared: "I will not equivocate—I will not excuse—I will not retreat a single inch—AND I WILL BE HEARD." Upset by Garrison's plea, the state of Georgia offered a $5000 reward to anyone who brought him to the state for trial.

Within four years, 200 antislavery societies had appeared in the North. They had mounted a massive propaganda campaign to proclaim the sinfulness of slavery. These societies distributed a million pieces of abolitionist literature and sent 20,000 tracts directly to the South.

The initial weapon of the abolitionists was moral suasion. Many abolitionists had labored in earlier movements for moral reform—movements to distribute Christian tracts; to enforce observance of the Sabbath; and to suppress vice, intemperance, and lotteries. They believed that direct appeals to conscience would convince slaveholders that slavery was a moral evil. Abolitionists sought "the destruction of error by the potency of truth—the overthrow of prejudice by the power of love—and the abolition of slavery by the spirit of repentance." To spread their ideas, they organized antislavery societies, distributed newspapers and tracts, and circulated petitions. They avoided concrete proposals for emancipation, fearful of becoming embroiled in debates over the details of specific plans.

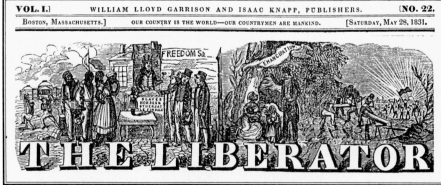

William Lloyd Garrison, the symbol of radical abolitionism, sought immediate freedom for slaves, without compensation to their owners.

Abolitionist Arguments and Public Reaction

Abolitionists attacked slavery for its illegality, immorality, and economic backwardness. Slavery was illegal because it violated the principles of natural rights to life and liberty embodied in the Declaration of Independence. Justice, said Garrison, required that the nation "secure to the colored population . . . all the rights and privileges that belong to them as men and as Americans." Slavery was sinful because slaveholders, in the words of abolitionist Theodore Weld, had usurped "the prerogative of God." Masters reduced a "God-like being" to a manipulable "THING." Slavery also encouraged sexual immorality and undermined the institutions of marriage and the family. Not only did slave masters sexually abuse and exploit slave women, abolitionists charged, but in some older southern states, such as Virginia and Maryland, they bred slaves for sale to the more recently settled parts of the Deep South.

Slavery was economically retrogressive because slaves, motivated only by fear, did not exert themselves willingly. By depriving their labor force of any incentive for performing careful and diligent work, by barring slaves from acquiring and developing productive skills, planters hindered improvements in crop and soil management. Abolitionists also charged that slavery impeded the development of towns, canals, railroads, and schools.

Antislavery agitation provoked a harsh public reaction in both the North and the South. Mobs led by "gentlemen of property and standing" attacked the homes and businesses of abolitionist merchants, destroyed abolitionist printing presses, disrupted antislavery meetings, and attacked black neighborhoods. Crowds pelted abolitionist reformers with eggs and even stones. During antiabolitionist rioting in Philadelphia in October 1834, a white mob destroyed 45 homes in the city's black community. A year later, a Boston mob dragged Garrison through the streets and almost lynched him before authorities removed him to a city jail for his own safety. That same year, the citizens of East Feliciana, Louisiana, offered a $50,000 reward for the capture, dead or alive, of Arthur Tappan, president of the American Anti-Slavery Society. States in both the North and the South debated "gag" laws to suppress antislavery agitation, and the U.S. postmaster general refused to deliver antislavery tracts to the South. In each session of Congress between 1836 and 1844 the House of Representatives adopted gag rules allowing that body to automatically table resolutions or petitions concerning the abolition of slavery. And each year, former president, now representative, John Quincy Adams, sponsored bills to accept the petitions and overturn the gag rules.

On November 7, 1837, the abolitionist movement acquired its first martyr. The Reverend Elijah P. Lovejoy was editor of a militant antislavery newspaper in Alton, Illinois, a town located across the Mississippi River from slaveholding St. Louis, Missouri. Three times mobs had destroyed Lovejoy's printing presses and attacked his house. When a fourth printing press arrived, Lovejoy armed himself and guarded the new press at the warehouse. The antiabolitionist mob set the warehouse on fire and shot Lovejoy as he fled the building. The following day, opponents of the abolitionists lined the streets and cheered as the mutilated corpse was dragged through the town.

Abolitionists never expected such a reaction. "When we first unfurled the banner of *The Liberator*," Garrison wrote, "we did not anticipate that . . . the free states would voluntarily trample under foot all order, law and government, or brand the advocates of universal liberty as incendiaries." This violent response produced division and fragmentation within the antislavery movement.

Division in the Antislavery Movement

By the late 1830s, questions of strategy and tactics increasingly divided the abolitionist movement. At the 1840 annual meeting of the American Anti-Slavery Society in New York, abolitionists split over such questions as women's right to participate in the administration of the organization and the advisability of nominating abolitionists as independent political candidates. Garrison won control of the organization, and his opponents promptly walked out. From this point on, no single organization could speak for abolitionism.

One group of abolitionists looked to politics

as the answer to ending slavery and founded political parties, such as the Liberty party, for that purpose. The Liberty party, founded in 1840 under the leadership of Arthur and Lewis Tappan, wealthy New York City businessmen, and James G. Birney, a native of Kentucky and former slaveholder who had moved to Cincinnati, called on Congress to abolish slavery in the District of Columbia, end the interstate slave trade, and cease admitting new slave states to the Union. The party also sought the repeal of local and state "black laws" in the North, which discriminated against free blacks, much as segregation laws would in the post-Reconstruction South. The Liberty party nominated Birney for president in 1840 and again in 1844, and although it gathered less than 7100 votes in its first campaign, it polled some 62,000 votes four years later and captured enough votes in Michigan and New York to deny Henry Clay the presidency.

In 1848 antislavery Democrats (known in New York State as Barnburners, because of their willingness to burn down the Democratic "barn" in order to rid the party of undesirable persons) and Conscience Whigs (in contrast to Cotton Whigs, who avoided the slavery issue) merged with the Liberty party to form the Free Soil party. Unlike the Liberty party, which was dedicated to the abolition of slavery and equal rights for blacks, the Free Soil party narrowed its demands to the abolition of slavery in the District of Columbia and exclusion of slavery from the federal territories. The Free Soilers also wanted a homestead law to provide free land for western settlers, high tariffs to protect American industry, and federally sponsored internal improvements. Campaigning under the slogan "free soil, free speech, free labor, and free men," the new party polled 300,000 votes in the presidential election of 1848 and helped to elect the Whig Zachary Taylor. Later the same slogan would be taken up by the new Republican party, which added the word "Frémont" (for Republican presidential nominee John C. Frémont) to the litany in 1856.

Other abolitionists, led by Garrison, took a more radical direction, advocating civil disobedience and linking abolitionism to such other reforms as women's rights, world government, and international peace. The radicals questioned whether the Bible represented the word of God because it condoned slavery, withdrew from membership in established churches that permitted slavery, and called for the voluntary dissolution of the Union. Taking the position that "it is the duty of the followers of Christ to suffer themselves to be defrauded . . . and barbarously treated, without resort to either their own physical energies, or the force of human law," Garrison and his supporters established the New England Non-Resistance Society in 1838. Members refused to vote, to hold public office, or to bring suits in court. In 1854 Garrison attracted notoriety by publicly burning a copy of the Constitution, which he called "a covenant with death and an agreement with Hell" because it acknowledged the legality of slavery.

African-Americans played a vital role in the abolitionist movement, staging protests against segregated churches, schools, and public transportation. In New York and Pennsylvania, free blacks launched petition drives for equal voting rights. Northern blacks also had a pivotal role in the "underground railroad," which provided escape routes for southern slaves through the northern states and into Canada. African-American churches offered sanctuary to runaways, and black "vigilance" groups in cities like New York and Detroit offered physical resistance to slave catchers.

Fugitive slaves, such as William Wells Brown, Henry Bibb, and Harriet Tubman, advanced abolitionism by publicizing the horrors of slavery. Their first-hand tales of whippings and separation from spouses and children combated the notion that slaves were contented under slavery and undermined belief in racial inferiority. Tubman risked her life by making 19 trips into slave territory in order to free as many as 300 slaves. Slaveholders posted a reward of $40,000 for the capture of the "Black Moses."

Frederick Douglass was the most famous fugitive slave and black abolitionist. His early life illustrated many of the cruelties of slavery. He was born in 1818, the son of a Maryland slave woman and an unknown white father. At the age of 6, he was sold away from his mother to work on a plantation owned by one of the largest slaveholders on Maryland's eastern shore. At the age of 15, he was sold again. Then, he was rented out to a local farmer known as a "Negro

Harriet Tubman, a fugitive slave who led 19 raids into slave territory, was a strong proponent of abolitionism. In 1841 Frederick Douglass gained public notice by giving a powerful speech against slavery. He opposed not only slavery but all forms of racial discrimination.

By the 1850s, many blacks had become pessimistic about defeating slavery. Colonizationist sentiment appeared again among African-Americans. In the 15 months following passage of the federal Fugitive Slave Law in 1850, some 13,000 free blacks fled the North for Canada. In 1854, Martin Delany (1812–1885), a Pittsburgh doctor who had studied medicine at Harvard, organized a National Emigration Convention to investigate possible sites for black colonization in Haiti, Central America, and West Africa.

Other blacks argued in favor of violence. Black abolitionists in Ohio adopted resolutions encouraging slaves to escape and called on their fellow citizens to violate any law that "conflicts with reason, liberty and justice, North or South." A meeting of fugitive slaves in Cazenovia, New York, declared that "the State motto of Virginia, 'Death to Tyrants,' is as well the black man's as the white man's motto." By the late 1850s, a growing number of free blacks had concluded that it was just as legitimate to use violence to secure the freedom of the slaves as it had been to establish the independence of the American colonies.

Over the long run, the fragmentation of the antislavery movement worked to the advantage of the cause. Henceforth, Northerners could support whichever form of antislavery best reflected their views. Moderates could vote for political candidates with abolitionist sentiments without being accused of radical Garrisonian views or of advocating violence for redress of grievances.

The Birth of Feminism

The women's rights movement was a major legacy of radical reform. At the outset of the century, women experienced political, social, and legal discrimination. Women were prohibited from voting or holding office in every state; they had no access to higher education and were excluded from professional occupations. American law was guided by the principle that a wife had no legal identity apart from her husband. She could not be sued, nor could she bring a legal suit, make a contract, or own property. She was not permitted to control her own wages or gain custody of her children in case of separa-

breaker." After repeated beatings and whippings at the hand of this cruel farmer, Douglass fought back and defeated him in a fist fight. After this, he was no longer punished. In 1838, at the age of 20, he escaped from slavery by borrowing the papers of a free black sailor.

In the North, Douglass became the first runaway slave to speak out on behalf of the antislavery cause. When many Northerners refused to believe that this eloquent orator could possibly have been a slave, he responded by writing an autobiography that identified his previous owners by name. Although he initially allied himself with William Lloyd Garrison, Douglass later started his own newspaper, *The North Star*, and supported political action against slavery.

tion or divorce, and under many circumstances she was even deemed incapable of committing crimes.

Broad social and economic changes, such as the development of a market economy and a decline in the birthrate, opened employment opportunities for women. Instead of bearing children at two-year intervals after marriage, as was the general case throughout the colonial era, early nineteenth-century women bore fewer children and ceased childbearing at younger ages. During these decades the first women's college was established, and some men's colleges first opened their doors to women students. More women were postponing marriage or not marrying at all; unmarried women gained new employment opportunities as "mill girls" and elementary school teachers; and a growing number of women achieved prominence as novelists, editors, teachers, and leaders of church and philanthropic societies.

While there were many improvements in the status of women during the first half of the century, women still lost political and economic status when compared with men. As the franchise was extended to larger and larger numbers of white males, including large groups of recent immigrants, the gap in political power between women and men widened. Even though women made up a core of supporters for many reform movements, men excluded them from positions of decision making and relegated them to separate female auxiliaries. Women also lost economic status as production shifted away from the household to the factory and workshop. During the late eighteenth century, the need for a cash income led women and older children to engage in a variety of household industries, such as weaving and spinning. Increasingly, in the nineteenth century, these tasks were performed in factories and mills.

The fact that changes in the economy tended to confine women to a sphere separate from men had important implications for reform. Since women were believed to be uncontaminated by the competitive struggle for wealth and power, many argued that they had a duty—and the capacity—to exert an uplifting moral influence on American society.

Catharine Beecher (1800–1878) and Sarah J. Hale (1788–1879) helped lead the effort to expand women's roles through moral influence. Beecher, the eldest sister of Harriet Beecher Stowe, was one of the nation's most prominent educators before the Civil War. A woman of many talents and strong leadership, she wrote a highly regarded book on domestic science and spearheaded the campaign to convince school boards that women were suited to serve as schoolteachers. Hale edited the nation's most popular women's magazines, the *Ladies Magazine* and *Godey's Ladies Book*. She led the successful campaign to make Thanksgiving a national holiday (during Lincoln's administration), and she also composed the famous nursery rhyme "Mary Had a Little Lamb."

Both Beecher and Hale worked tirelessly for women's education (Hale helped found Vassar College). They gave voice to the grievances of women—the abysmally low wages paid to women in the needle trades (12.5 cents a day for a 14-hour workday), the physical hardships endured by female operatives in the nation's shops and mills (where women workers were awakened at 5 A.M., required to work 14 hours a day by lamplight, standing all the while, breathing particles thrown off by the spindles and looms), and the minimizing of women's intellectual aspirations. Even though neither woman supported full equal rights, they were important transitional figures in the emergence of feminism. Each significantly broadened society's definition of "women's sphere" and assigned women vital social responsibilities: to shape the character of children, to morally uplift husbands, and to promote causes of "practical benevolence," including Sunday schools, playgrounds, and seamen's aid societies (which aided not sailors but abandoned wives, widows, and orphans).

Other women broke down old barriers and forged new opportunities in a more dramatic fashion. Frances Wright (1795–1852), a Scottish-born reformer and lecturer, received the nickname "The Great Red Harlot of Infidelity" because of her radical ideas about birth control, liberalized divorce laws, and legal rights for married women. In 1849 Elizabeth Blackwell (1821–1910) became the first American woman to receive a degree in medicine. A number of women became active as revivalists. Perhaps the most notable was Phoebe Palmer (1807–1874), a Methodist preacher who ignited religious fervor among thousands of Americans and Canadians.

Catalyst for Women's Rights

A public debate over the proper role of women in the antislavery movement, especially their right to lecture to audiences composed of both sexes, led to the first organized movement for women's rights. By the mid-1830s more than a hundred female antislavery societies had been created, and women abolitionists were circulating petitions, editing abolitionist tracts, and organizing antislavery conventions. A key question was whether women abolitionists would be permitted to lecture to "mixed" audiences of men and women. In 1837 a national women's antislavery convention resolved that women should overcome this taboo: "The time has come for women to move in that sphere which providence has assigned her, and no longer remain satisfied with the circumscribed limits which corrupt custom and a perverted application of Scripture have encircled her."

Angelina Grimké (1805–1879) and her sister Sarah (1792–1873)—two sisters from a wealthy Charleston, South Carolina, slaveholding family—were the first women to break the restrictions and widen women's sphere through their writings and lectures before mixed audiences. In 1837 Angelina gained national notoriety by lecturing against slavery to audiences that included men as well as women. Shocked by this breach of the separate sexual spheres ordained by God, ministers in Massachusetts called on their fellow clergy to forbid women the right to speak from church pulpits. Sarah Grimke responded with a pamphlet entitled *Letters on the Condition of Women and the Equality of the Sexes*, one of the first modern statements of feminist principles. She denounced the injustice of lower pay and denial of equal educational opportunities for women. Her pamphlet expressed outrage that women were "regarded by men, as pretty toys or as mere instruments of pleasure" and were taught to believe that marriage is "the *sine qua non* [indis-

A Quaker minister, feminist, and the mother of six children, Lucretia Mott was an ardent opponent of slavery and often faced angry and violent mobs.

pensable element] of human happiness and human existence." Men and women, she concluded, should not be treated differently, since both were endowed with inherent natural rights.

In 1840, after the American Anti-Slavery Society split over the issue of women's rights, the organization proceeded to name three female delegates to a World Anti-Slavery Convention to be held in London later that year. There, these women were denied the right to participate in the convention on the grounds that their participation would offend British public opinion. The convention relegated them to seats in a balcony.

Eight years later, Lucretia Mott, who earlier had been denied the right to serve as a delegate to the World Anti-Slavery Convention, and Elizabeth Cady Stanton organized the first women's rights convention in history. The convention was held in July 1848 at Seneca Falls, New York. It drew up a Declaration of Sentiments, modeled on the Declaration of Independence, that opened with the phrase "All men and women are created equal." It specified 15 specific inequities suffered by women, and after detailing "a history of repeated injuries and usurpations on the part of men toward woman," the document concluded that "he has endeavored, in every way that he could, to destroy her confidence in her own powers, to lessen her self-respect, and to make her willing to lead a dependent and abject life."

Among the resolutions adopted by the convention, only one was not ratified unanimously—that women be granted the right to vote. Of the 66 women and 34 men who signed the Declaration of Sentiments at the convention (including black abolitionist Frederick Douglass), only two lived to see the ratification of the women's suffrage amendment to the constitution 72 years later.

By midcentury women's rights conventions had been held in every northern state. Despite ridicule from the public press—the *Worcester* (Massachusetts) *Telegraph* denounced women's rights advocates as "Amazons"—female reformers contributed to important, if limited, advances against discrimination. They succeeded in gaining adoption of Married Women's Property Laws in a number of states, granting married women full control over their own income and property. A New York law passed in 1860 gave women joint custody over children and the right to sue and be sued, and in several states women's rights reformers secured adoption of permissive divorce laws. A Connecticut law, for example, granted divorce for any "misconduct" that "permanently destroys the happiness of the petitioner and defeats the purposes of the marriage relationship."

Utopian Communities

Between the 1820s and 1840s, hundreds of "utopian communities" were founded by individuals who believed in the perfectability of the social and political order. These experimental communal societies were called utopian communities because they provided blueprints for a perfectionist vision of an ideal society.

The characteristics of these communities varied widely. Shaker communities were rooted in the religious teachings of Mother Ann Lee, the English-born daughter of a blacksmith who believed that the millennium was at hand and that the time had come for people to totally renounce sin. She preached that God had both male and female aspects and that sexual intercourse was the basic cause of human sin.

In 1776, two years after she arrived in New York City, she established the first Shaker settlement northwest of Albany, New York. By 1800, there were 12 Shaker colonies. These communities placed Shaker men and women on a level of sexual equality and both sexes served as elders and deacons. Aspiring to live like the early Christians, the Shakers adopted communal ownership of property and a way of life emphasizing simplicity. Dress was kept simple and uniform. Shaker architecture and furniture are devoid of ornament—no curtains on windows, carpets on floors, or pictures on walls—but they are pure and elegant in form.

The two most striking characteristics of the Shaker communities were their dances and abstinence from sexual relations. The Shakers believed that religious fervor should be expressed through the head, heart, and mind, and their ritual religious practices included shaking, shouting, and dancing. The Shakers also adopted strict rules concerning celibacy. They attempted to replenish their membership by admitting volunteers and taking in orphans. Today, the Shakers have all but died out. Fewer than 20 survive in the early 1990s.

Another utopian effort was Robert Owen's experimental community at New Harmony, Indiana, which reflected the influence of Enlightenment ideas. Owen, a paternalistic Scottish industrialist, was deeply troubled by the social consequences of the industrial revolution. Inspired by the idea that people are shaped by their environment, Owen purchased a site in Indiana where he sought to establish common ownership of property and abolish religion. At New Harmony the marriage ceremony was reduced to a single sentence and children were raised outside of their natural parents' home. The community lasted just three years, from 1825 to 1828.

Some 40 utopian communities were inspired by the French theorist Charles Fourier, who hoped to eliminate poverty through the es-

Officially named "The United Society of Believers in Christ's Second Appearing," the Shakers received their popular name from the movements they made during their religious dances.

tablishment of scientifically organized cooperative communities called "phalanxes." Each phalanx was to be set up as a "joint-stock company," in which profits were divided according to the amount of money members had invested, their skill, and their labor. Fourier coined the term *feminism*, and in the phalanxes, women received equal job opportunities and equal pay, equal participation in decision making, and the right to speak in public assemblies. Although one Fourier community lasted for 18 years, most were unsuccessful.

The currents of radical antislavery thought inspired Frances Wright, a fervent Scottish abolitionist, to found Nashoba Colony in 1826, near Memphis, Tennessee, as an experiment in interracial living. She established a racially integrated cooperative community in which slaves were to receive an education and earn enough money to purchase their own freedom. Publicity about Fanny Wright's desire to abolish the nuclear family, religion, private property, and slavery created a furor, and the community dissolved after only four years.

Perhaps the most notorious and successful experimental colony was John Humphrey Noyes's Oneida Community. Noyes, who began his career as a lawyer, was converted in one of Charles Finney's revivals and proceeded to study theology for three years at Andover Theological Seminary and Yale. Convinced that the Second Coming of Christ had taken place in A.D. 70, Noyes believed that the final millennium would only occur when people strove to become perfect through an "immediate and total cessation from sin."

In Putney, Vermont, in 1835 and in Oneida, New York, in 1848, he established perfectionist communities that practiced communal ownership of property and "complex marriage." Complex marriage involved the marriage of each member of the community to every member of the opposite sex. Exclusive emotional or sexual attachments were forbidden, and sexual relations were arranged through an intermediary in order to protect a woman's individuality and give her a choice in the matter. Men were required to practice *coitus interruptus* (withdrawal) as a method of birth control, unless the group had approved of the couple's having offspring. After the Civil War, the community conducted experiments in eugenics, the selective control of mating in order to improve the hereditary qualities of children. Other notable features of the community were mutual criticism sessions and communal childrearing. Oneida flourished in its original form until 1880. Descendants can be found in the early 1990s working at the Oneida silverworks, which became a corporation after the dissolution of the community by Noyes.

ARTISTIC AND CULTURAL FERMENT

At the same time that educational reformers, abolitionists, and feminists sought to improve society through reform, thinkers, writers, and artists strove to create national art forms equal to those of Europe. During the early nineteenth century, Europeans treated American culture with contempt. They charged that America was too commercial and materialistic, too preoccupied with money and technology, to produce great art and literature. "In the four quarters of the globe," asked one English critic, "who reads an American book? or goes to an American play? or looks at an American picture or statue?"

In fact, the decades preceding the American Civil War are among the most creative in all of American cultural and intellectual history, producing some of this nation's greatest poets, novelists, and philosophers, including Ralph Waldo Emerson, Nathaniel Hawthorne, Herman Melville, Edgar Allen Poe, Harriet Beecher Stowe, Henry David Thoreau, and Walt Whitman.

At the beginning of the nineteenth century, many Americans wondered whether their country's infant democracy was capable of producing great works of art. During the late eighteenth and early nineteenth centuries, Europe created a remarkable legacy of great literature, art, music, and philosophy. It was the age of Wordsworth, Keats, and Shelley in poetry; of Jane Austen in literature; of Beethoven in music; of Hegel in philosophy.

The United States, in contrast, had few professional writers or artists. In part, the United States lacked a large class of patrons to subsidize the arts. It possessed few magazines and only a single art museum. Above all, America seemed to lack the traditions out of which artists and writers could create great works. The novelist Nathaniel Hawthorne complained about the absence of castles and moss-covered ruins to stir artists' imagination, so he used the gabled architecture of New England instead.

On August 31, 1837, a 34-year-old former Unitarian minister named Ralph Waldo Emerson (1803–1882) answered these critics. As he stood at the pulpit of the First Parish Church of Cambridge, Massachusetts—the very spot where Anne Hutchinson had been examined for heresy two centuries before—addressing Harvard College's Phi Beta Kappa Society, he delivered a talk, entitled "The American Scholar," that would be called America's "intellectual Declaration of Independence." In his address, Emerson urged Americans to cast off their "long apprenticeship to the learning of other lands" and abandon subservience to English models and create distinctly American forms of art rooted in the facts of American life.

Even before Emerson's call for a distinctly American culture, a number of authors had already begun to create literature emphasizing native scenes and characters. Washington Irving (1783–1859), who was probably the first American to support himself as a man of letters, demonstrated the possibility of creating art out of native elements in his classic tales "Rip Van Winkle" (1819) and "The Legend of Sleepy Hollow" (1820).

The poet Henry Wadsworth Longfellow was even more successful in transforming American legends into the stuff of art and reaching a broad popular audience. His narrative poems dramatizing scenes from America's past made such figures as Paul Revere, Miles Standish, John Alden, Priscilla Mullins, and Hiawatha household names. His simple evocative lines have been cherished by generations of American children:

> Under the spreading chest-nut tree
>   The village smithy stands;

> I shot an arrow into the air,
>   It fell to earth, I knew not where;

> There was a little girl
>   Who had a little curl
>   Right in the middle of her forehead.

Ironically, this popular poet was a "Boston Brahmin," an expert in linguistics, a professor of modern languages at Harvard, and a translator of the latest European poetry.

James Fenimore Cooper (1789–1851) was another successful mythmaker. His works gave us such staples of western fiction as the lone frontiersmen, the faithful Indian companion, and the kidnap, chase, and rescue. He also made such words and phrases as "paleface," "on the warpath," and "war paint" part of the American vocabulary.

Born in Burlington, New Jersey, the son of a land speculator, Cooper grew up in the frontier community of Cooperstown in central New York. At 13, he enrolled at Yale but was expelled for blowing open a classmate's door with a charge of gunpowder and roping a donkey onto a professor's chair. He then went to sea as a common sailor.

In 1819, following his return to Cooperstown, Cooper was reading a popular novel of the day aloud to his wife. He tossed the book aside and claimed that he could write a better one. His wife dared him to try, and during the remaining 32 years of his life he wrote 34 books.

In his second and third novels, *The Spy* (1821) and *The Pioneers* (1823), Cooper created one of the most enduring archetypes in American culture. His hero, the frontiersman Natty Bumppo (also known as Hawkeye, Leatherstocking, and Pathfinder) was an American knight errant at home in the wilderness. He became the prototype not only for future trappers and scouts, but also for countless cowboys, detectives, and superheroes found in popular American fiction and film. Part of Natty Bumppo's appeal was that he gave expression to many of the misgivings early nineteenth-century Americans felt about the cost of progress (his last words were "Let me sleep where I have lived—beyond the din of settlements"). An acute social critic, Cooper railed against the destruction of the natural environment, the violence directed at American Indians, and the rapaciousness and materialism of an expansive American society.

American Transcendentalism

On the afternoon of September 19, 1836, a number of Boston's leading young intellectuals met at the Boston home of the Reverend George Ripley. Ralph Waldo Emerson, who would shortly deliver his "American Scholar" address, was there, as was Bronson Alcott, the father of novelist Louisa May Alcott and a pioneering educational reformer. Orestes Brownson, a staunch advocate of the rights of workers, also attended. Their goal was "to see how far it would be possible for earnest minds to meet." Soon, other important thinkers joined the meetings, including the novelist Nathaniel Hawthorne, the feminist editor Margaret Fuller, the educator Elizabeth Peabody, and the pencil-maker and poet Henry David Thoreau. So abstract and incomprehensible were their conversations to those outside their circle that unkind wits dubbed the group the "Transcendentalist Club." The nickname stuck, and these important thinkers, authors, and reformers would be called the transcendentalists.

Natty Bumppo, the legendary American frontiersman created by James Fenimore Cooper, from the frontispiece to Cooper's *Last of the Mohicans*. Bumppo, the hero of Cooper's Leatherstocking tales, has been called the most famous character in American fiction.

The transcendentalists were a group of young New Englanders, mostly of Unitarian background, who found liberal religion too formal and rationalistic to meet their spiritual and emotional needs. Logic and reason, they believed, were incapable of explaining the fundamental mysteries of human existence. Where, then, could people find answers to life's fundamental problems? The deepest insights, the transcendentalists believed, were to be found within the human individual, through intuition.

The transcendentalists shared a common outlook: a belief that each person contains infinite and godlike potentialities; an emphasis on emotion and the senses over reason and intellect; and a glorification of nature as a creative, dynamic force in which people could discover their true selves and commune with the supernatural. Like the romantic artists and poets of Europe, they emphasized the individual, the subjective, the imaginative, the personal, the emotional, and the visionary.

The central figure in transcendentalism was Ralph Waldo Emerson. Trained, like his father, to be a liberal Unitarian minister, Emerson found his parents' faith unsatisfying. Unitarian theology and ritual, he wrote, was "corpse-cold"; it was the "thin porridge or cold tea" of genteel Bostonians. Emerson's life was marked by personal tragedy and illness—his father died when he was a boy; his first wife died after less than two years of marriage; his first-born son died at the age of five; a brother went insane. Consequently, Emerson could never believe that logic and reason offered answers to life's mysteries.

Essayist Ralph Waldo Emerson was one of the foremost intellectual figures of his era. His philosophy, called transcendentalism, espoused the belief that people can transcend ordinary understanding and find truth through intuition.

Appalled by the complacency, provinciality, and materialism of Boston's elite, the 29-year-old Emerson resigned as minister of the prestigious Second Church of Boston in 1832. Convinced that no external answers existed to the fundamental problems of life, he decided to look inward and "spin my thread from my own bowels."

In his essays and public lectures, Emerson distilled the essence of the new philosophy: All people contain seeds of divinity, but society, traditionalism, and lifeless religious institutions thwart the fulfillment of these potentialities. In his essay "Nature" (1836), Emerson asserted that God's presence is immanent within both humanity and nature and can best be sensed through intuition rather than through reason. In his essay "Self-Reliance" (1841), he called on his readers to strive for true individuality in the face of intense social pressures for conformity:

> Society everywhere is in conspiracy against the manhood of every one of its members. . . . The virtue in most request is conformity. . . . Whoso would be a man must be a nonconformist.

Although Emerson himself was not an active reformer (he once wrote that whenever he saw a reformer, he felt like asking, "What right, Sir, do you have to your one virtue?"), his philosophy inspired many reformers far more radical than he. His stress on the individual, his defense of nonconformity, and his vocal critique of the alienation and social fragmentation that had accompanied the growth of cities and industry led others to try to apply the principles of transcendentalism to their personal lives and to society at large.

Henry David Thoreau (1817–1862) was one of the transcendentalists who strove to realize Emersonian ideals in his personal life. A pencilmaker, surveyor, and poet, Thoreau, like Emerson, was educated at Harvard. He felt nothing but contempt for social conventions and wore a green coat to chapel because Harvard's rules required black. After college, he taught school and worked at his father's pencil factory, but these jobs brought him no fulfillment.

In March 1845, the 28-year-old Thoreau, convinced that his life was being frittered away by details, walked into the woods near Concord, Massachusetts, to live alone. He put up a cabin near Walden Pond as an experiment—to see if it was possible for a person to live truly free and uncommitted:

> I went into the woods because I wished to live deliberately, to front only the essential facts of life, and see if I could not learn what it had to teach, and not, when I came to die, discover that I had not lived.

The aim of his experiment was to break free from the distractions and artificialities of life, to shed himself of needless obligations and possessions, and to establish an original relationship with nature. His motto was "simplify, simplify."

During his 26 months at Walden Pond, he constructed his own cabin, raised his own food ("seven miles of beans"), observed nature, explored his inner self, and kept a 6000-page journal. He served as "self-appointed inspector of snow-storms and rain-storms," "surveyor of forest-paths and all across-lot routes," and protector of "wild-stock." He also spent a night in jail, for refusing to pay taxes as a protest against the Mexican War. This incident led him to write the classic defense of nonviolent direct action, "Civil Disobedience." (On Walden, see pp. 351–353; on "Civil Disobedience," see p. 430.)

Another figure who sought to realize transcendentalist ideals in her personal life was Margaret Fuller (1810–1850), editor of the transcendentalist journal *The Dial*. Often mocked as an egotist, she once said: "I know all the people worth knowing in America, and I find no intellect comparable to my own." She did indeed possess one of nineteenth-century America's towering minds. Her personal life was truly extraordinary. She was the first woman to use the Harvard College library and later became one of the nation's first woman journalists, writing for Horace Greeley's New York *Tribune*. A determined social reformer, she became a leading advocate of women's rights in 1845 by publishing *Women in the Nineteenth Century*. A partisan in Rome's revolution of 1849, she shocked Bostonians by taking an Italian revolutionary nobleman, 11 years her junior, as her lover, and bearing his child out of wedlock (later, they secretly married). She died in a shipwreck off Long Island, at the age of 40,

along with her husband and son. Edgar Allan Poe spoke for many Americans when he said of her: "Humanity is divided into men, women, and Margaret Fuller."

Another key figure in the transcendentalist circle was Bronson Alcott (1799–1888), a pioneer in the areas of child development and education. Often ridiculed—reviewers mockingly described one of his books as "clear as mud"— Alcott was far ahead of his time in his conception of education, which he viewed as a process of awakening and drawing out children's intellectual and moral capacities through dialogue, individualized instruction, nature study, and encouragement of creative expression through art and writing. Critics scoffed at his techniques, particularly his rejection of corporal punishment and his substitution of "vicarious atonement," a method of child discipline in which Alcott had naughty children spank him. When his own daughters misbehaved, Alcott went without dinner. Convinced that adults had a great deal to learn about children's physical, intellectual, and moral development, Alcott recorded 2500 pages of observations on the first years of his daughters' lives (including Louisa May who later wrote *Little Women* and *Little Men*). He also published his dialogues with pupils on such controversial topics as the meaning of the Christian gospel and the processes of conception and birth.

Two dramatic attempts to apply the ideas of transcendentalism to everyday life were Brook Farm, a community located near Boston, and Fruitlands, a utopian community near Harvard, Massachusetts. In 1841, George Ripley, like Emerson a former Unitarian clergyman, established Brook Farm in an attempt to substitute transcendentalist ideals of "brotherly cooperation," harmony, and spiritual fulfillment for the "selfish competition," class division, and alienation that increasingly characterized the larger society. "Our ulterior aim is nothing less than Heaven on Earth," declared one community member. Brook Farm's residents, who never numbered more than 200, supported themselves by farming, teaching, and manufacturing clothing. The most famous member of the community was Nathaniel Hawthorne, who based his 1852 novel *The Blithedale Romance*

(Text continues on p. 354)

PRIMARY SOURCE ESSAY

WALDEN

His neighbors considered him an idler, a loner, and an eccentric. The leading literary critics of the age denounced him as a misanthrope with a "morbid dislike of humanity," and a "skulker" who retreated to the woods rather than directly confront the great moral issues of the era. The famous philosopher Ralph Waldo Emerson said that his young friend lacked literary ambition, and "wanting this, instead of engineering for all America, he was the captain of a huckleberry party."

His name was Henry David Thoreau, and his life was marked by few great events. Born in 1817 in Concord, Massachusetts, he never married and lived only briefly away from his birthplace. He never held a steady job, and, at various times, worked as a teacher, a surveyor, a gardener, a farmer, a house painter, a carpenter, a mason, a day laborer, a pencilmaker, and a glassmaker. He published only two books during his lifetime, and neither attracted a broad readership. His first, *A Week on the Concord and Merrimack Rivers*, sold just 294 copies; his second, *Walden*, a mere 2000 copies.

And yet this man is now considered one of the supreme artists of American literature, and has become the personification of uncomprising nonconformity and environmental awareness. His words remain a source of inspiration to all who seek to live according to their own values and not, like the "mass of men," simply conform to society's dictates: "If a man does not keep pace with his companions, perhaps it is because he hears a different drummer. Let him step to the music which he hears, however measured or far away."

Walden, his masterpiece, is based on his experiences living for more than two years in a cabin two miles south of the Concord, Massachusetts, common. He moved, he explained, because he wanted to "live deep and suck out all the marrow of life, to live so sturdily and Spartan-like as to put to rout all that was not life." Rejecting the larger society's ideal of material success, he constructed a frame for a small cabin on the shore of Walden Pond in March 1845. He then purchased a shed from an Irish railroad worker and used the wood as siding for his cabin. He erected a chimney and covered the walls with plaster. The total cost of his one-room cabin was just $28.

To support himself, he raised two-and-a-half acres of beans, corn, peas, potatoes, and turnips. Altogether he spent about a dollar a month on food, drinking water and

Henry David Thoreau. Thoreau said he went to live in solitude in the woods because he wished to "front only the essential facts of life."

eating bread made of rye and Indian meal, potatoes, rice, molasses, and some salt pork. He reserved his time for reading, observing nature, and keeping a journal, which provided the raw material for his book *Walden*. In 1847, after 26 months at Walden, Thoreau left, declaring that he had other lives to live.

One of *Walden*'s harshest critics, the poet James Russell Lowell, considered Thoreau's depiction of a life of spartan simplicity and solitary contemplation a fraud. Thoreau's experiment was wholly dependent on the products of civilization, Lowell claimed: "He squatted on another man's land; he borrows an ax; his boards, his nails, his bricks, his mortar, his books, his lamp, his fishhooks, his plough, his hoe, all turn state's evidence against him as an accomplice in the sin of that artificial civilization which rendered it possible that such a person as Henry D. Thoreau should exist at all." And it is true that Thoreau visited his parents' home nearly every day; frequently dined with the Emersons; took his shoes to be repaired at a local cobbler's; and entertained many visitors at his cabin.

And yet, it would be a mistake of the highest order to dismiss *Walden* as a misrepresentation of Thoreau's experience. The book offers one of the most powerful statements ever written about the way that yearnings for material possessions and luxury threaten to keep individuals from realizing their own uniqueness. *Walden* establishes an ideal of a life of simplicity and self-sufficiency and intimacy with nature that has grown increasingly meaningful as life has grown more organized and bureaucratized and nature has become more and more developed.

WALDEN

I went to the woods because I wished to live deliberately, to front only the essential facts of life, and see if I could not learn what it had to teach, and not, when I came to die, discover that I had not lived. I did not wish to live what was not life, living is so dear; nor did I wish to practice resignation, unless it was quite necessary. I wanted to live deep and suck out all the marrow of life, to live so sturdily and Spartanlike as to put to rout all that was not life, to cut a broad swath and shave close, to drive life into a corner, and reduce it to its lowest terms, and, if it proved to be mean, why then to get the whole and genuine

This hut is believed to be Thoreau's forest residence during his sojourn at Walden Pond.

meanness of it, and publish its meanness to the world; or if it were sublime, to know it by experience, and be able to give a true account of it in my next excursion. For most men, it appears to me, are in a strange uncertainty about it, whether it is of the devil or of God, and have *somewhat hastily* concluded that it is the chief end of man here to "glorify God and enjoy him forever."

Still we live meanly, like ants. . . . Our life is frittered away by detail. An honest man has hardly need to count more than his ten fingers, or in extreme cases he may add his ten toes, and lump the rest. Simplicity, simplicity, simplicity! I say, let your affairs be as two or three, and not a hundred or a thousand; instead of a million count half a dozen, and keep your accounts on your thumb nail. . . . Simplify, simplify. Instead of three meals a day, if it be necessary eat but one; instead of a hundred dishes, five; and reduce other things in proportion. . . . Men think that it is essential that the *Nation* have commerce, and export ice, and talk through a telegraph, and ride thirty miles an hour, without a doubt, whether *they* do or not; but whether we should live like baboons or like men, is a little uncertain. . . .

—Where I Lived, and What I Lived for

The title page from the first edition of Thoreau's *Walden*, published in 1854.

Thoreau died in 1862 at the age of 44 after a long and painful struggle with tuberculosis. Three incidents that occurred toward the end of his life symbolize Thoreau's basic values and commitments. In one incident a relative asked him whether he had made his peace with God. Replied Thoreau: "I wasn't aware that we had quarrelled." Religious orthodoxy condemned American transcendentalism as "the latest form of infidelity," yet while Thoreau, like other transcendentalists, often criticized institutionalized religion, transcendentalism was very much a spiritual movement, dedicated to contact with the divine spirit that could be found in nature and within each individual.

In another incident, a relative asked the dying Thoreau whether he had caught a glimpse of the next world, Heaven. Thoreau answered: "One world at a time." Like other transcendentalists, Thoreau did not deny the existence of a spiritual realm, but he did not want it to serve as an escape from earthly affairs. At a time when fur trappers and traders were exploring the far western frontier, Thoreau saw himself as engaged in a process of discovery and exploration. His was an inner quest of self-discovery and self-observation, and it took place not in some distant frontier but in a cabin less than two miles from his parents' home.

The third incident took place on Thoreau's deathbed. As he slipped away, he muttered two words, "Moose, Indian." Living at a critical moment in the nation's history, at the very onset of rapid urban and industrial growth, Thoreau was acutely conscious that a vital link between people and their environment was being severed. Only through communion with nature could people achieve personal integration and contact with the divine.

At the young essayist's funeral, Ralph Waldo Emerson gave a remarkably accurate assessment of Thoreau's life and work. He told the assembled mourners that "the country knows not yet . . . how great a son it has lost," and he declared that the real tragedy of Thoreau's premature death was that he had only had 44 years to engage in his true "calling, the art of living well."

on his experiences there. The community lasted in its original form just three years.

In 1843, Bronson Alcott and others attempted to form a "New Eden" at Fruitlands—a community where they could achieve human perfection through high thinking, manual labor, and dress and diet reform. Practices at Fruitlands included communal ownership of property, frequent cold water baths, and a diet based entirely on native grains, fruits, herbs, and roots. Residents wore canvas shoes and linen tunics, so as not to have to kill animals for leather or use slave grown cotton. Sex roles, however, were untouched. Responsibility for housekeeping and food preparation fell on Alcott's wife Abba. Asked by a visitor if there were any beasts of burden at Fruitlands, Abba Alcott replied: "There is one woman."

A Literary Renaissance

Emerson's 1837 plea for Americans to cease imitating Europeans, speak with their own voices, and create art drawn from their own experiences coincided with an extraordinary burst of literary creativity. Nathaniel Hawthorne, Herman Melville, Edgar Allan Poe, Harriet Beecher Stowe, and Walt Whitman, like Emerson and Thoreau, produced literary works of the highest magnitude, yet in their own time many of their greatest works were greeted with derision, abuse, or indifference. It is a tragic fact that with the sole exception of Harriet Beecher Stowe, none of pre–Civil War America's greatest writers was able to earn more than a modest income from his or her books (On Harriet Beecher Stowe, see pp. 451–454.)

Edgar Allan Poe, shown here in a self-portrait, is known for his haunting stories and poems, his literary theories, and his invention of the modern detective story.

During his lifetime, Edgar Allan Poe (1809–1849) received far more notoriety from his legendary dissipation than from his poetry or short stories. The Boston-born son of two poor actors, Poe was raised by a Richmond, Virginia, merchant after his father abandoned the family and his mother died. For two years he went to the University of Virginia and briefly attended West Point, but drinking, gambling debts, and bitter fights with his guardian cut short his formal education. At the age of 24, he married a 13-year-old second cousin, who died a decade later of tuberculosis, brought on by cold and starvation. Found drunk and unconscious in Baltimore in 1849, Poe died at the age of 40.

Sorely underappreciated by contemporaries, Poe invented the detective novel; edited the *Southern Literary Messenger*, one of the country's leading literary journals; wrote incisive essays on literary criticism; and produced some of the most masterful poems and frightening tales of horror ever written. His literary techniques inspired a number of important French writers, including Charles Baudelaire, Stéphane Mallarmé, and Paul Valéry. Poe said that his writing style consisted of "the ludicrous heightened into the grotesque; the fearful coloured into the horrible; the witty exaggerated into the burlesque; the singular wrought into the strange and mystical."

Nathaniel Hawthorne (1804–1864), the author of *The Scarlet Letter* (1850), one of America's towering works of fiction, did not consider himself a novelist. He wrote "romances," he insisted—imaginative representations of moral problems, rather than novelistic depictions of social realities. A descendant of one of the Salem witch-trial judges, the Salem-born Hawthorne grew up in a somber and solitary atmosphere. His father, a sea captain, perished on a voyage when his son was just 4 years old, and Hawthorne's mother spent the remainder of her life in mourning. After attending Bowdoin College, where Henry Wadsworth Longfellow and future president Franklin Pierce were among his classmates, he began to write. It would not be until 1837, however, when he published *Twice-Told Tales*, that the 33-year-old Hawthorne first gained public recognition. He lived briefly at Brook Farm and participated in the transcendentalist circle, but did not share their idealistic faith in the innate goodness of man. Herman Melville observed of Hawthorne: "He says NO! in thunder; but the Devil himself cannot make him say yes."

In his fiction, Hawthorne, more than any other early nineteenth-century American writer, challenged the larger society's faith in science, technology, progress, and humanity's essential goodness. Many of his greatest works project nineteenth-century concerns—about women's roles, sexuality, and religion—on to seventeenth century Puritan settings. Some of his stories examine the hubris of scientists and social reformers who dare to tamper with natural environment and human nature.

Herman Melville (1819–1891), author of *Moby Dick* (1851), possibly America's greatest romance, had little formal education and claimed that his intellectual development did not begin until he was 25. By then, he had already seen his father go bankrupt and die insane, worked as a cabin boy on a merchant ship, served as a common seaman on a whale ship, deserted in the Marquessa Islands, escaped on an Australian whaler, and been imprisoned in Tahiti. He drew on these experiences in his first two books, *Typee* (1846) and *Omoo* (1847), which were popular successes, but his third book *Mardi* (1849), a complex blend of political and religious allegory, metaphysics, and cosmic romance, failed miserably, foreshadowing the reception of his later works.

Part of a New York literary circle called Young America, Melville dreamed of creating a novel as vast and energetic as the nation itself. In *Moby Dick*, he produced such a masterwork. Based on the tale of "Mocha-Dick," a gigantic white whale that sank a whaling ship, *Moby Dick* combined whaling lore and sea adventure into an epic drama of human hubris, producing an allegory that explores what happens to a people who defy divine limits. Tragically, neither *Moby Dick* nor Melville's later works found an audience, and Melville spent his last years as a deputy customs collector in New York. He died in utter obscurity, and his literary genius was only rediscovered in the 1920s.

In 1842, Ralph Waldo Emerson lectured in New York and called for a truly original American poet who could fashion verse out of "the

In the poem "Song of Myself" from the collection *Leaves of Grass*, Walt Whitman declared "the United States themselves are essentially the greatest poem." This "carpenter portrait" of the author accompanied the first edition of *Leaves of Grass*, published in 1855.

factory, the railroad, and the wharf." Sitting in Emerson's audience was a 22-year-old New York printer and journalist named Walt Whitman (1819–1892). A carpenter's son with only five years of schooling, Whitman soon became Emerson's very ideal of the native American poet with the publication of *Leaves of Grass* in 1855. "A mixture of Yankee transcendentalism and New York rowdyism," *Leaves of Grass* was, wrote Emerson, "the most extraordinary piece of wit & wisdom that America has yet contributed." Most reviewers, however, reacted scornfully to the book, deeming it "trashy, profane & obscene" for its sexual frankness. A sprawling portrait of America, encompassing every aspect of American life, from the steam-driven Brooklyn ferry to the use of ether in surgery, the volume opens not with the author's name but simply with his daguerreotype (a forerunner of the photograph). Unconventional in style—Whitman invented "free verse" rather than use conventionally rhymed or regularly metered verse—the volume stands out as a landmark in the history of American literature for its celebration of the diversity, the energy, and the expansiveness of pre–Civil War America.

American Art

If Americans could produce literary masterpieces, were they also capable of creating visual art that would rival that of Europe? At the end of the eighteenth century, this seemed doubtful. Artistic implements, such as paints, brushes, and canvases, were difficult to obtain, and professional artists were few in number. Although the last half of the eighteenth century witnessed the appearance of a number of talented portrait painters—including John Singleton Copley, Charles Willson Peale, and Gilbert Stuart—most painters were simply skilled craftspeople, who devoted most of their time to painting houses, furniture, or signs.

Perhaps the biggest obstacle to the development of the visual arts was the fact that the revolutionary generation associated art with luxury, corruption, sensual appetite, and aristocracy. Commented one person: "When a people get a taste for the fine arts, they are ruined."

During the early nineteenth century, however, artists succeeded in overcoming public hostility toward the visual arts. One way artists gained a degree of respectability was through historical painting. The American public hungered for visual representations of the great events of the American Revolution, and works such as John Trumbull's Revolutionary War battle scenes and his painting of the Declaration of Independence (1818) fed the public's appetite. Romantic landscape paintings also attracted a large popular audience. Portrayals of the American landscape by such artists such as Thomas Cole and the Hudson River school, Albert Bierstadt, and Frederic Church evoked a sense of the immensity, power, and grandeur of nature,

which had not yet been completely tamed by an expansive American civilization.

A more favorable public attitude toward art was also evident in public campaigns to erect patriotic monuments, to landscape homes, and to beautify cities by restoring town greens and commons, constructing the first urban parks, and building the first modern "park" cemeteries. At the beginning of the nineteenth century, public monuments and statues were rarities; town commons were muddy, ill-kept areas, often containing buildings and packs of animals; houses lacked lawns; and cemeteries were unlandscaped collections of graves located near town centers.

Beginning in 1825, when an obelisk was erected at Bunker Hill to commemorate that Revolutionary War battle, Americans began to construct patriotic monuments. Around the same time, homeowners began to beautify their homes with lawns and landscaping, while cities established the nation's first urban parks. Construction of Mount Auburn cemetery in the 1830s in a pastoral setting outside of Boston marked the beginning of the modern park cemetery, where the living could commune with the spirit of the dead (though the site was initially popular because it was a "green space" that could be used as a picnic ground). These beautification campaigns represented a response to the urban and industrial growth of cities that already threatened to destroy the physical beauty of city environments.

Popular Culture

Existing alongside the literary and artistic achievements of Emerson, Thoreau, and Melville was a vibrant popular culture. Consisting of penny newspapers, dime novels, minstrel shows, and other forms of popular amusement, this commercialized mass culture began to emerge just at the beginning of the nineteenth century. By the eve of the Civil War, however, mass-circulation newspapers, inexpensive popular novels, and popular theater had become staples of American life.

One important aspect of popular culture was the penny press. Prior to the American Revolution, newspapers were few in number, ex-

114.

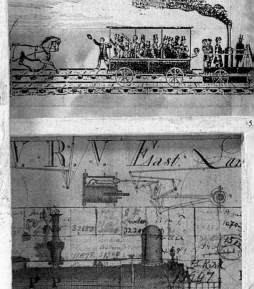

COTTON MANUFACTURE.

Fig. 1. DOUBLING MACHINE.

TWISTING MACHINE.

Elevation Fig. 4.

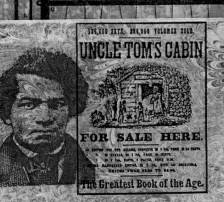

135,000 SETS. 270,000 VOLUMES SOLD.

UNCLE TOM'S CABIN

FOR SALE HERE.

The Greatest Book of the Age.

When was a little

In the early 1790s, slavery appeared to be a dying institution. Slave imports into the New World were declining and slave prices were falling because the crops grown by slaves—tobacco, rice, and indigo—did not generate enough income to pay for their upkeep. In Maryland and Virginia, planters were replacing tobacco, a crop grown by a slave labor force, with wheat and corn, which was not. At the same time, leading Southerners, including Thomas Jefferson, denounced slavery as a source of debt, economic stagnation, and moral dissipation. A French traveler reported that people throughout the South "are constantly talking of abolishing slavery, of contriving some other means of cultivating their estates."

Then Eli Whitney of Massachusetts gave slavery a new lease on life. Even as a teenager, Whitney was well known for his mechanical genius. At the age of 12, he produced a violin that "made tolerable good musick." At 15 he took over his father's workshop in Westborough, Massachusetts, and began manufacturing nails. By the time he was 18, he had begun to produce other items, including hat pins for women's bonnets and men's walking sticks. But young Whitney hoped to become something more than a clever mechanic, and at the age of 23 he abandoned his father's workshop and entered college at Yale.

In 1792, just after his graduation, Whitney made a fateful decision. He accepted a tutoring job on a South Carolina plantation. His journey south was filled with disasters. During the boat trip, he became seasick. Before he could recover, his boat ran aground on rocks near New York City. Then, while seeking another boat, he contracted smallpox. The only good thing to happen during his journey was that he was befriended by a charming Southern widow named Catharine Greene, whose late husband, General Nathanael Greene, had been a leading general during the American Revolution. When he arrived in the South, Whitney discovered that his promised salary as a tutor had been cut in half. So he quit the job and accepted Greene's invitation to visit her plantation near Savannah.

During young Whitney's visit, a group of planters visited the Greene plantation and bemoaned the sorry state of southern agriculture.

They desperately needed a money crop to pay off their debts. Cotton was the obvious choice, because England's expanding textile mills devoured every available bit of the crop. But the kind of cotton that grew best in Georgia—green seed, short staple—was useless because a person needed ten hours to separate one pound of lint from the small tough seeds. "Gentlemen," said Greene, "tell your troubles to Mr. Whitney, he can make anything."

From a slave known only by the name Sam, Whitney learned that a comb could be used to remove seeds from cotton. In just ten days, Whitney devised a way of mechanizing the comb. Within a month, Whitney's cotton engine (gin for short) could separate fiber from seeds faster than 50 people working by hand.

Whitney's invention revitalized slavery in the South. Between 1792, when Whitney arrived on the Greene plantation, and 1794, the price of slaves doubled. By 1825 field hands, who brought $500 apiece in

While seeking employment in the South, Yankee schoolteacher Eli Whitney developed a simple machine for separating cotton from its seeds. The "cotton gin" met the increasing demand for cotton and breathed new life into the institution of slavery.

1794, were worth $1500. As the price of slaves rose, so too did the number of slaves. During the first decade of the nineteenth century, the number of slaves in the United States increased by 33 percent; during the following decade (after the African slave trade became illegal), the slave population grew another 29 percent.

As the institution of slavery expanded in the South, it declined in the North. In 1780 Pennsylvania adopted the first emancipation law in the New World. Judicial decisions freed slaves in Massachusetts and New Hampshire, and other northern states adopted gradual emancipation acts. By the beginning of the nineteenth century, the new republic was fatefully divided into a slave section and a free section.

A DIVIDED CULTURE

By 1860 most Americans believed that the Mason-Dixon line divided the nation into two distinctive cultures: a commercial North and an agrarian South. Each region, so it was believed, had its own "manners, habits, customs, principles, and ways of thinking."

This belief—that the cultures of the North and South were fundamentally different—was not a new idea on the eve of the Civil War. During the bitter political battles of the 1790s, New England Federalists pictured the South as a backward, economically stagnant society in which manual labor was degraded and wealth was dissipated in personal luxury. Many Southern Republicans countered by denouncing the corrupt, grasping, materialistic society of the North.

Many factors contributed to this sense of sectional difference. Diction, work habits, diet, and labor systems distinguished the two sections. One section depended on slave-based agriculture; the other emphasized commercial agriculture based on family farms and a developing industrial sector resting on wage labor.

The population of the North was more than 50 percent greater than in the South. Urbanization was far more advanced, as European immigrants arrived in far greater numbers. In addition, commerce, financial institutions, manufacturing, and transportation were more developed. In contrast, the South had more primitive transportation facilities. Cities were smaller and fewer in number. Most important of all, a third of the South's population lived in slavery.

Despite these differences, the pre–Civil War North and the South were in certain respects strikingly similar. Both sections were predominantly rural. Both had booming economies and were engaged in speculation and trade. Both were rapidly expanding westward. Both enacted democratic political reforms and voted for the same national political parties. Nevertheless, most Americans thought of their nation as divided into two halves, a commercial civilization and an agrarian civilization, each operating according to entirely different sets of values.

In 1812, Rochester, New York, did not exist. Two decades later, as a result of the construction of the Erie Canal, Rochester was the fastest growing city in the United States.

THE EMERGENCE OF A NEW INDUSTRIAL ORDER IN THE NORTH

To all outward appearances, life in the North in 1790 was not much different than in 1740. The vast majority of the people—more than 90 percent—still lived and worked on farms or in small rural villages. Not 1 Northerner in 13 worked in either trade or manufacturing.

Conditions of life remained primitive. The typical house—a single-story one- or two-room log or wood frame structure—was small, sparsely furnished, and afforded little personal privacy. Sleeping, eating, and work spaces were not sharply differentiated, and mirrors, curtains, upholstered or padded chairs, carpets, desks, and bookcases were luxuries enjoyed only by wealthy families.

Even prosperous farming or merchant families lived simply. Many families ate meals out of a common pot or bowl, just as their ancestors had in the seventeenth century. Standards of cleanliness remained exceedingly low. Bed bugs were constant sleeping companions, and people seldom bathed or even washed their clothes or dishes.

Daily life was physically demanding. Most families made their own cloth, clothing, and soap. Because they lacked matches, they lit fires by striking a flint again and again with a steel striker until a spark ignited some tinder. As there was no indoor plumbing, chamber pots had to be used and emptied. Homes were usually heated by a single open fireplace and illuminated by candles. Housewives hand-carried water from a pump, well, or stream, and threw the dirty water or slops out the window. Family members hauled grain to a local grist mill or else milled it by hand. They cut, split, and gathered wood, and fed it into a fireplace.

But by 1860, even though the North remained predominantly a rural agricultural society, profound and far-reaching changes had taken place. Commercial agriculture had replaced subsistence agriculture. Household production had been supplanted by centralized manufacturing outside the home. And nonagricultural employment had begun to overtake agricultural employment. By 1860, nearly half of the North's population made a living outside of the agricultural sector.

These economic transformations are all aspects of the industrial revolution, a revolution that affected every aspect of life. It raised living standards, transformed the work process, and relocated hundreds of thousands of people across oceans and from rural farms and villages into fast-growing industrial cities.

The most obvious consequence of this revolution was an impressive increase in wealth, per capita income, and commercial, middle-class job opportunities. Between 1800 and 1860, output increased 12-fold, and purchasing power doubled. New middle-class jobs proliferated. Increasing numbers of men found work as agents, bankers, brokers, clerks, merchants, professionals, and traders.

Living standards rose sharply, at least for the rapidly expanding middle class. Instead of making cloth and clothing at home, families began to buy them. Instead of hand milling grains, an increasing number of families began to buy

processed grains. Kerosene lamps replaced candles as a source of light; coal replaced wood as fuel; friction matches replaced crude flints. Even poorer families began to cook their food on cast-iron cookstoves and to heat their rooms with individual-room heaters. The advent of railroads and the first canned foods brought variety to the northern diet year round.

Physical comfort increased markedly. Padded seats, spring mattresses, and pillows became more common. By 1860 many urban middle-class families had central heating, indoor plumbing, and wall-to-wall carpeting.

Houses became larger and more affordable. The invention in the 1830s of the balloon frame—a light-weight houseframe made up of boards nailed together—as well as prefabricated doors, window frames, shutters, and sashes—resulted in larger and more reasonably priced houses. The cost of building a house fell by 40 percent, and two-story houses, with four or five rooms, became increasingly common.

A revolution in values and sensibility accompanied these changes in the standard of living. Standards of cleanliness and personal hygiene rose sharply. People bathed more frequently, washed their clothes more often, and dusted, swept, and scrubbed their houses more regularly. Standards of propriety also rose. The respectable classes began to blow their noses into handkerchiefs, instead of wiping them with their sleeves, and to dispose of their spittle in spitoons.

Pre–Civil War Northerners regarded all of these changes as signs of progress. A host of northern political leaders, mainly Whigs and later Republicans, celebrated the North as a region of bustling cities, factories, railroads, and prosperous farms and independent craftsmen—a stark contrast to an impoverished, backward, slave South, suffering from soil exhaustion and economic and social decline.

Although the industrial revolution brought many material benefits, critics decried its negative consequences. Labor leaders deplored the bitter suffering of factory and sweatshop workers, the breakdown of craft skills, the vulnerability of urban workers to layoffs and economic crises, and the maldistribution of wealth and property. Conservatives lamented the disintegration of an older household-centered economy in which husbands, wives, and children had labored together. Southern writers, like George Fitzhugh, argued that the North's growing class of free laborers were slaves of the marketplace, suffering even more insecurity than the South's chattel slaves, who were provided for in sickness and old age.

During the early nineteenth century, the industrial revolution transformed northern society, altering the way people worked and lived and contributing to growing sectional differences between the North and South. How and why did the industrial revolution occur when it did? What were its consequences? How did it fuel sectional antagonisms?

The Eve of the Industrial Revolution

In 1790 most farm families in the rural North produced little more than they needed for themselves. Except for a few necessities such as iron goods, rum, salt, and sugar, families,

often with the assistance of neighbors, produced most of what they needed to live. Instead of using money to purchase necessities, families entered into complex exchange relationships with relatives and neighbors and used barter to acquire the goods they needed.

Skilled artisans, assisted by an apprentice or two and an occasional journeyman, produced specialized and luxury goods. Such crafts as blacksmithing, bootmaking, carriage building, leather working, papermaking, and woodworking were performed by hand in a small shop or home. The North's few industries were small. Iron foundries produced just 30,000 tons of iron a year. All the North's shoemakers produced barely 80,000 pairs of shoes annually.

Between 1790 and the 1820s, a new pattern emerged. Farmers increasingly began to grow cash crops for sale and used the proceeds to buy goods produced by others. The independent artisans of earlier years gave way to an increasingly industrial economy of wage laborers and salaried employees. As late as 1800, fewer than

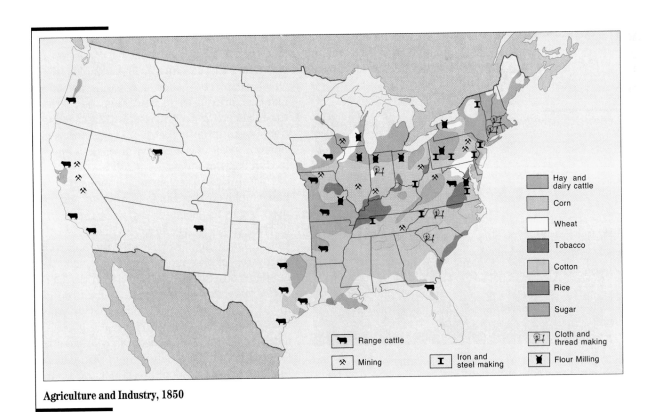

Agriculture and Industry, 1850

10 percent of the labor force was composed of "employees" who worked for wages. A decade later the number of wage-earning employees had quadrupled.

The Transformation of the Rural Countryside

In 1828 Dexter Whittemore, the owner of a small country store in rural Fitzwilliam, New Hampshire, discovered a new way to make money. Braided hats were the rage, and the New Hampshire shopkeeper knew that he could sell as many hats as he could acquire. So he arranged for local farm families to pick up split palm leaves from his store, braid the leaves into hats, and return them to the store, in exchange for credits on the store's ledgers. By the early 1830s Whittemore was marketing about 23,000 hats annually, and by the 1850s the figure had climbed to 80,000.

For cash-poor farm families, the opportunity to earn cash was a godsend. Roxanna Bowker Stowell, one of Whittemore's hatmakers, pleaded with the storekeeper for a chance to work. "Money is so very scarce and we must have some," she told him. Each month she earned a dollar by braiding five hats, money that could be used to pay off debts, finance farm improvements, purchase household goods, or send a child to school.

Opulent shops like L. J. Levy and Company's Dry Goods Store appeared in northern cities with increasing numbers during the 1850s.

Beginning in the late eighteenth century, household industries provided work for thousands of men, women, and children in rural areas. Shopkeepers or master craftspeople supplied farm families with raw materials, paid piece rates, and marketed the products. Among the goods produced were towels, sheets, table linens, coverlets, socks, gloves, carpets, thread, nails, and farm utensils. The quantity of goods produced was staggering. In New Hampshire 40 families produced 13,000 pounds of maple sugar annually. In 1809 farm families near Philadelphia produced more than 230,000 yards of cloth for sale, four times the amount of cloth produced by the area's textile factories. In Massachusetts farm households produced more than 100,000 pairs of shoes a year—more than all the nation's professional shoemakers made. As early as 1791, Alexander Hamilton reported that the rural areas surrounding America's cities had become "a vast scene of household manufacturing . . . in many instances to an extent not only sufficient for the supply of the families in which they are made, but for sale, and even for export."

Commercial agriculture replaced subsistence farming. Farm families raised their standard of living by producing goods for sale and using the earnings to buy candles, medicines, soap, and other necessities previously made by farm wives. In New Hampshire farmers raised sheep for wool; in western Massachusetts they began to fatten cattle and pigs for sale to Boston; in eastern Pennsylvania, they specialized in dairy products.

After 1820, the household industries that had employed thousands of women and children began to decline. They were replaced by manufacturing in city shops and factories. New England farm families began to buy their shoes, furniture, cloth, and sometimes even their clothes ready-made. Small rural factories closed their doors, and village artisans who produced for local markets found themselves unable to compete against cheaper city-made goods. As local opportunities declined, many long-settled farm areas suffered sharp population losses. Convinced that "agriculture is not the road to wealth, nor honor, nor to happiness," thousands of young people left the fields for cities.

The Disruption of the Artisan System of Labor

As late as the 1820s, skilled craftspeople, known as *artisans* or *mechanics*, performed most manufacturing in small towns and larger cities. They made shoes and men's clothing, built houses, and set type for printed material. These craftspeople manufactured goods in traditional ways—by hand in their own homes or in small shops located nearby—and marketed the goods they produced. Matthew Carey, a Philadelphia newspaperman, personified the early nineteenth-century artisan-craftsman. He not only wrote articles and editorials that appeared in his newspaper, he also set the paper's type, operated the printing press, and hawked the newspaper.

The artisan class was divided into three subgroups. At the highest level were self-employed master craftspeople. They were assisted by skilled journeymen, who owned their own tools but lacked the capital to set up their own shops, and by apprentices, teenaged boys who typically served a three-year term in exchange for training in a craft.

Urban artisans did not draw a sharp separation between home and work. A master shoemaker might make shoes in a 10-foot square shed located immediately in back of his house. A printer would bind books or print newspapers in a room below his family's living quarters. Typically, a master craftsperson lived in the same house with his assistants. The household of Everard Peck, a Rochester, New York, publisher, was not unusual. It included his wife, his children, his brother, his business partner, a day laborer, and four journeyman printers and bookbinders.

Nor did urban artisans draw a sharp division between work and leisure. Work patterns tended to be irregular and were frequently interrupted by leisure breaks during which masters and journeymen would drink whiskey or other alcoholic beverages. During slow periods or periodic layoffs, workers enjoyed fishing trips and sleigh rides, cockfights and bear-baiting, as well as drinking and gambling at local taverns. Artisans often took unscheduled time off to attend boxing matches, horseraces, and exhibitions by traveling musicians and acrobats.

The first half of the nineteenth century witnessed the decline of the artisan system of labor. Skilled tasks, previously performed by artisans, were divided and subcontracted out to less expensive unskilled laborers. Small shops were replaced by large "machineless" factories, which made the relationship between employer and employee increasingly impersonal. Many masters abandoned their supervisory role to foremen and contractors and substituted unskilled teenaged boys for journeymen. Words like *employer, employee, boss,* and *foreman*—descriptive of the new relationships—began to be widely used.

Between 1790 and 1850 the work process, especially in the building trades, printing, and such rapidly expanding consumer manufacturing industries as tailoring and shoemaking, was radically reorganized. The changes in the shoemaking industry in Rochester, New York, during the 1820s and 1830s illustrate this process. Instead of producing an entire shoe, a master would fit a customer, rough-cut the leather uppers, and then send the uppers and soles to a boarding house, where a journeyman would shape the leather. Then, the journeyman would send the pieces to a binder, a woman who worked in her home, who would sew the shoes together. Finally, the binder would send the shoe to a store for sale to a customer. Tremendous gains in productivity sprang from the division and specialization of labor.

By 1850, the older household-based economy, in which assistants lived in the homes of their employers, had disappeared. Young men moved out of rooms in their master's home into hotels and boarding houses in distinct working-class neighborhoods. The older view that each worker should be attached to a particular master, who would supervise his behavior and assume responsibility for his welfare, declined. The older paternalistic view was replaced by a new conception of labor as a commodity, like cotton, that could be acquired or disposed of according to the laws of supply and demand.

The Introduction of the Factory System

In 1789 the Pennsylvania legislature placed an advertisement in English newspapers offering a

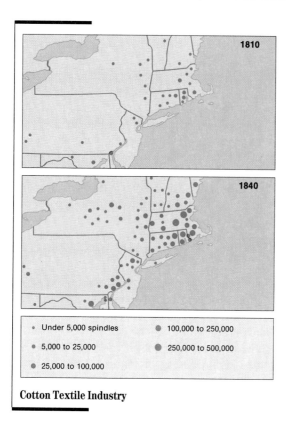

Cotton Textile Industry

dren attended a special school Slater founded for their education.

The opening of Slater's mill marked the beginning of a widespread movement to consolidate manufacturing operations under a single roof. During the last years of the eighteenth century, merchants and master craftspeople who were discontented with the inefficiencies of their work force created the nation's first modern factories. Within these centralized workshops, employers closely supervised employees, synchronized work to the clock, and punished infractions of rules with heavy fines or dismissal. In 1820, just 350,000 Americans worked in factories or mills. Four decades later, on the eve of the Civil War, the number had soared to 2 million.

Child labor offered one solution to the problem of acquiring an inexpensive and reliable factory labor force. During the early phases of industrialization, textile mills and agricultural tool, metal goods, nail, and rubber factories had a ravenous appetite for cheap teenage laborers. In many mechanized industries, from a quarter to over half of the work force was made up of young men or women under the age of 20.

During the first half of the nineteenth century, unmarried women made up a majority of the work force in cotton textile mills and a substantial minority of workers in factories manufacturing ready-made clothing, furs, hats, shoes, and umbrellas. Women were also employed in significant numbers in the manufacture of buttons, furniture, gloves, gunpowder, shovels, and tobacco.

Many women found the new opportunities exhilarating. Eleven-year-old Lucy Larcom went off to the Lowell textile mill enthusiastically: "The novelty of it made it seem easy, and it really was not hard, just to change the bobbins on the spinning-frames every three quarters of an hour or so. . . . The intervals were spent frolicking around among the spinning-frames, teasing and talking to the older girls, or entertaining ourselves with games and stories in a corner."

Unlike farmwork or domestic service, employment in a mill offered female companionship and an independent income. Wages were twice what a woman could make as a seamstress, tailor, or schoolteacher. Furthermore,

cash bounty to any English textile worker who would migrate to the state. Samuel Slater, who was just finishing an apprenticeship in a Derbyshire textile mill, read the ad. He went to London, booked passage to America, and landed in Philadelphia. There he learned that Moses Brown, a Quaker merchant, had just completed a mill in Pawtucket, Rhode Island, and needed a manager. Slater applied for the job and received it, along with a promise that if he made the factory a success he would receive all the business's profits, less the cost and interest on the machinery.

On December 21, 1790, the mill opened. Seven boys and 2 girls, all between the ages of 7 and 12, operated the little factory's 72 spindles. Slater soon discovered that these children, "constantly employed under the immediate inspection of a [supervisor]," could produce three times as much as whole families working in their homes. To keep the children awake and alert, Slater whipped them with a leather strap or sprinkled them with water. On Sundays the chil-

most mill girls viewed the work as only temporary before marriage. Most worked in the mills fewer than four years, and frequently interrupted their stints in the mill for several months at a time with trips back home.

By the 1830s, increasing competition among textile manufacturers caused deteriorating working conditions that drove native-born women out of the mills. Employers cut wages, lengthened the workday, and required mill workers to tend four looms instead of just two. Hannah Borden, a Fall River, Massachusetts, textile worker, was required to have her loom running at 5 A.M. She was given an hour for breakfast and half an hour for lunch. Her workday ended at 7:30 P.M., 14.5 hours after her workday had begun. For a 6-day work week, she received between $2.50 and $3.50.

The mill girls militantly protested the wage cuts. In 1834 and again in 1836, the mill girls went out on strike. An open letter spelled out the workers' complaints: "sixteen females [crowded] into the same hot, ill-ventilated attic"; a workday "two or three hours longer a day than is done in Europe"; and workers compelled to "stand so long at the machinery . . . that varicose veins, dropsical swelling of the feet and limbs, and prolapsus uter[us], diseases that end only with life, are not rare but common occurrences."

During the 1840s, fewer and fewer native-born women were willing to work in the mills. "Slavers," which were long, black wagons that criss-crossed the Vermont and New Hampshire countryside in search of mill hands, arrived in Rhode Island and Massachusetts milltowns empty. Increasingly, employers replaced the native-born mill girls with a new class of permanent factory operatives: immigrant women from Ireland.

Labor Protests

In 1806 journeymen shoemakers in New York City organized one of the nation's first labor strikes. The workers' chief demands were not higher wages and shorter hours. Instead, they protested the changing conditions of work. They staged a "turn-out" or "stand-out," as a strike was then called, to protest the use of

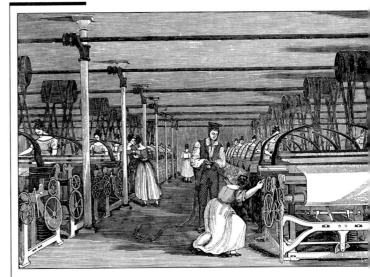

Young women made up the bulk of the work force in the early textile mills.

cheap unskilled and apprentice labor and the subdivision and subcontracting of work. To ensure that journeymen did not resume work, a "tramping committee" patrolled the shops. The strike ended when the city's largest shoe employers asked municipal authorities to criminally prosecute the shoemakers for conspiracy to obstruct trade. A court found the journeymen shoemakers guilty and fined them $1 plus court costs.

By the 1820s, a growing number of journeymen were organizing to protest employer practices that were undermining the independence of workers, reducing them to the status of "a humiliating servile dependency, incompatible with the inherent natural equality of men." Unlike their counterparts in Britain, American journeymen did not protest against the introduction of machinery into the workplace. Instead, they vehemently protested wage reductions, declining standards of workmanship, and the increased use of unskilled and semiskilled workers. Journeymen charged that manufacturers had reduced "them to degradation and the loss of that self-respect which had made the mechanics and laborers the pride of the world." They insisted that they were the true producers of wealth and that manufacturers, who did not engage in manual labor, were unjust expropriators of wealth.

In an attempt to raise wages, restrict hours, and reduce competition from unskilled workers, skilled journeymen formed the nation's first labor unions. In larger eastern cities like Boston, New York, and Philadelphia, as well as in smaller western cities like Cincinnati, Louisville, and Pittsburgh, they formed local trade unions and city trades' assemblies. House carpenters, handloom weavers, combmakers, shoemakers, and printers formed national societies to uphold uniform wage standards. In 1834 journeymen established the National Trades' Union, the first organization of American wage earners on a national scale. By 1836 union membership had climbed to 300,000.

These early unions encountered bitter employer opposition. To counter the influence of the newly formed unions, employers banded together in employers' associations, which claimed that union methods were "most ob-noxious, coercive, and detrimental to the peace, prosperity and best interests of the community."

Employers also requested prosecution of unions as criminal combinations. In 1806, in a case involving Philadelphia shoemakers, a Pennsylvania court established an important precedent by ruling that a labor union was guilty of criminal conspiracy if workers struck to obtain wages higher than those set by custom. Other court decisions declared unions illegal constraints on trade. In 1842, in the landmark case *Commonwealth* v. *Hunt*, the Massachusetts supreme court established a new precedent by recognizing the right of unions to exist and restricting the use of the criminal conspiracy doctrine.

In addition to establishing the nation's first labor unions, during the 1830s journeymen also formed political organizations, known as Working Men's parties, as well as mutual benefit societies, libraries, educational institutions, and producers' and consumers' cooperatives. Working men and women published at least 68 labor papers, and they agitated for free public education, reduction of the work day, and abolition of capital punishment, state militias, and imprisonment for debt. Following the Panic of 1837, land reform was one of labor's chief demands. One hundred sixty acres of free public land for those who would actually settle the land was the demand, and "Vote Yourself a Farm" became the popular slogan.

The Movement for a Ten-Hour Day

Labor's greatest success was a campaign to establish a ten-hour workday in most major northeastern cities. In 1835 carpenters, masons, and stonecutters in Boston staged a seven-month strike in favor of a ten-hour day. The strikers demanded that employers reduce excessively long hours worked in the summer and spread them throughout the year. Quickly, the movement for a ten-hour workday spread to Philadelphia, where carpenters, bricklayers, plasterers, masons, leather dressers, and blacksmiths went on strike. Parades and bands marched through the city carrying banners that read "From 6 to 6." Textile workers in Paterson, New

During the 1830s, rapid inflation and mounting competition for jobs encouraged the growth of unions. By the late 1830s, an estimated 300,000 American workers were union members.

Jersey, were the first factory operatives to strike for a reduction in work hours. Soon, women textile operatives in Lowell added their voices to the call for a ten-hour day, contending that such a law would "lengthen the lives of those employed, by giving them a greater opportunity to breathe the pure air of heaven" as well as provide "more time for mental and moral cultivation."

In 1840 the federal government introduced a ten-hour workday on public works projects. In 1847 New Hampshire became the first state to adopt a ten-hour day law. It was followed by Pennsylvania in 1848. Both states' laws, however, included a clause that allowed workers to voluntarily agree to work more than a ten-hour day. Despite the limitations of these state laws, agitation for a ten-hour day did result in a reduction in the average number of hours worked, to approximately 11.5 by 1850.

The Laboring Poor

In January of 1850, police arrested John McFeaing in Newburyport, Massachusetts, for stealing wood from the wharves. McFeaing pleaded necessity and a public investigation was conducted. Investigators found McFeaing's wife and four children living "in the extremity of misery. The children were all scantily supplied with clothing and not one had a shoe to his feet. There was not a stick of firewood or scarcely a morsel of food in the house, and everything betokened the most abject want and misery."

The quickening pace of trade and finance during the early nineteenth century not only increased the demand for middle-class clerks and shopkeepers, it also dramatically increased demand for unskilled workers, such as carters, coal heavers, day laborers, deliverypeople, dockworkers, draymen, longshoremen, packers, and porters. Such unskilled workers earned extremely low incomes and led difficult lives. In many of these families, wives and children were forced to work to maintain even a low standard of living.

In 1851 Horace Greeley, editor of the *New York Tribune*, estimated the minimum weekly budget needed to support a family of five. Essential expenditures for rent, food, fuel, and clothing amounted to $10.37 a week. In that year, a shoemaker or a printer earned just $4 to $6 a week, a male textile operative $6.50 a week, and an unskilled laborer just $1 a week. The only manual laborers able to earn Greeley's minimum were blacksmiths and machinists.

Frequent unemployment compounded the problems of the unskilled. In Massachusetts upward of 40 percent of all workers were out of a job for part of a year, usually for four months or more. Fluctuations in demand, inclement weather, interruptions in transportation, technological displacement, fire, injury, and illness all could leave workers jobless.

Typically, a male laborer earned just two-thirds of his family's income. The other third was earned by wives and children. Many married women performed work in the home, such as embroidery and making artificial flowers, tailoring garments, or doing laundry. The wages of children were critical for a family's standard of living. Children under the age of 15 contributed 20 percent of the income of many working-class families. These children worked, not because their parents were heartless, but because children's earnings were absolutely essential to the family's survival.

To provide protection against temporary unemployment, many working-class families scrimped and saved in order to buy a house or maintain a garden. In Newburyport, Massachusetts, many workers bought farm property on the edge of town. On New York City's East Side, many families kept goats and pigs. Ownership of a house was a particularly valuable source of security, since a family could always obtain extra income by taking in boarders and lodgers.

Immigrants: The New Working Class

During the summer of 1845, a "blight of unusual character" devastated Ireland's potato crop, the basic staple in the Irish diet. A few days after potatoes were dug from the ground, they began to turn into a slimy, decaying, blackish "mass of rottenness." Expert panels convened to investigate the blight's cause suggested that it was a result of "static electricity" or the smoke that billowed from railroad locomotives or "mortiferous vapours" rising from underground volcan-

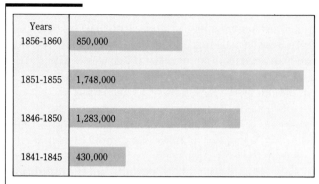

Figure 12.1
Total immigration, 1840–1860

oes. In fact, the cause was a fungus that had traveled from America to Ireland.

"Famine fever"—dysentery, typhus, and infestations of lice—soon spread through the Irish countryside. Observers reported seeing children crying with pain and looking "like skeletons, their features sharpened with hunger and their limbs wasted, so that there was little left but bones, their hands and arms." Masses of bodies were buried without coffins, a few inches below the soil.

Over the next ten years, 750,000 Irish died and another 2 million left their homeland for Great Britain, Canada, and the United States. Freighters, which carried American and Canadian timber to Europe, offered fares as low as $17 to $20 between Liverpool and Boston— fares subsidized by English landlords eager to be rid of the starving peasants. As many as 10 percent of the emigrants perished while still at sea. In 1847, 40,000 (or 20 percent) of those who set out from Ireland died along the way. "If crosses and tombs could be erected on water," wrote the U.S. commissioner for emigration, "the whole route of the emigrant vessels from Europe to America would long since have assumed the appearance of a crowded cemetery."

At the beginning of the nineteenth century, only about 5000 immigrants arrived in the United States each year. During the 1830s, however, immigration climbed sharply as 600,000 immigrants poured into the country. This figure jumped to 1.7 million in the 1840s, when harvests all across Europe failed, and reached 2.6 million in the 1850s. Most of these immigrants came from Germany, Ireland, and Scandinavia, pushed from their homelands by famine, evic-

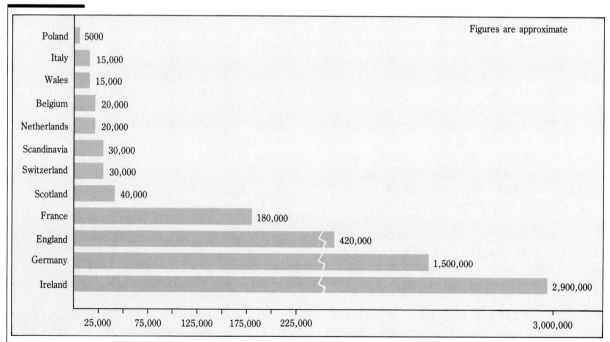

Figure 12.2
Immigration by country of origin, 1840–1860

tion from farm lands by landlords, political unrest, and the destruction of traditional handicrafts by factory enterprises. Attracted to the United States by the prospects of economic opportunity and political and religious freedom, many dispossessed Europeans braved the voyage across the Atlantic.

By the 1850s, the Irish comprised half the population of Boston and New York, and German immigrants made up a significant proportion of the populations in Cincinnati, Milwaukee, and St. Louis. The new immigrants found employment in construction work, domestic service, factories, foundries, and mining. As early as 1855, German and Irish immigrants constituted 96 percent of New York City's shoemakers and tailors.

The Divided North

During the decades preceding the Civil War, it was an article of faith among Northerners that their society offered unprecedented economic equality and opportunity, free of rigid class divisions and glaring extremes of wealth and poverty. It was a land where even a "humble mechanic" had "every means of winning independence which are extended only to rich monopolists in England." How accurate is this picture of the pre–Civil War North as a land of opportunity, where material success was available to all?

In fact, the percentage of wealth held by those at the top of the economic hierarchy appears to have increased substantially before the Civil War. While the proportion of wealth controlled by the richest 10 percent rose from 50 percent in the 1770s to 70 percent in 1860, the real wages of unskilled northern workers stagnated or, at best, rose modestly. By 1860 half of all free whites held fewer than 1 percent of the North's real and personal property, while the richest 1 percent owned 27 percent of the region's wealth—a level of inequality comparable to that found in early nineteenth-century Europe and greater than that found in the United States today. In towns as different as Stonington, Connecticut, and Chicago, Illinois, between two-thirds and three-quarters of all households owned no property.

The first stages of industrialization and ur-

The North's growing cities were characterized by sharp contrasts between wealth and squalor. Only a few blocks separated spacious, well-furnished New York City homes from damp, unlighted cellars where thousands of slum dwellers resided.

banization in the North, far from diminishing social inequality, actually widened class distinctions and intensified social stratification. At the top of the social and economic hierarchy was an elite class of families, linked together by intermarriage, membership in exclusive social clubs, and residence in exclusive neighborhoods, as rich as the wealthiest families of Europe. At the bottom were the working poor—immigrants, casual laborers, free blacks, widows, and orphans—who might be thrown out of work at any time. These poor, propertyless unskilled laborers comprised a vast floating population, which trekked from city to city in search of work. They congregated in urban slums like Boston's Ann Street and New York's Five Points, where starving children begged for pennies and haggard prostitutes plied their trade.

Between these two extremes were family farmers and a rapidly expanding urban middle class of northern shopkeepers, merchants, bankers, agents, and brokers. This was a highly mixed group which ranged from prosperous en-

(Text continues on p. 380)

POLICING THE PRE–CIVIL WAR CITY

During the mid-1830s, a wave of rioting without parallel in earlier American history swept the nation. In April 1834, in New York, three days of rioting pitting pro-Democrat against pro-Whig gangs erupted during municipal elections. In July, another New York mob stormed the house of a prominent abolitionist, carried the furniture into the street, and set it on fire. Over the next two days, a mob gutted New York's Episcopal African Church and attacked the homes of many of the city's free blacks. The state militia had to be called out to quell the disturbances.

Rioting was not confined to New York City. August 11, 1834, a mob composed of lower-class men and boys sacked and burned a convent in Charlestown, Massachusetts, near the site of Bunker Hill, following a series of impassioned anti-Catholic

sermons by the Reverend Lyman Beecher, the father of novelist Harriet Beecher Stowe. Two months later, a proslavery riot swept Philadelphia, destroying 45 homes in the city's black community.

Altogether there were at least 115 incidents of mob violence during the 1830s, compared to just 7 incidents in the 1810s and 21 incidents in the 1820s. *Niles' Register*, a respected newspaper of the time, reported that a "spirit of riot or a disposition to 'take the law into their own hands' prevails in every quarter." Abraham Lincoln, then a young Springfield, Illinois, attorney, echoed these sentiments. "Outrages committed by mobs," he lamented, had become "the everyday news of the times."

Mob violence during the 1830s had a variety of sources. A rate of urban growth faster than in any

previous decade was one major contributor to social turbulence during the 1830s. Urban populations grew by 60 percent and the sharp upsurge in foreign immigration heightened religious and ethnic tensions. The number of immigrants entering the country jumped from just 5000 a year at the beginning of the century to over 50,000 annually during the 1830s.

Another source of violence was abolitionism, which emerged at the beginning of the decade and produced a violent reaction. The belief that abolitionists favored miscegenation—interracial marriages of blacks and whites—enflamed antiblack sentiment. The mobs that attacked black homes and churches, burned white abolitionists' homes and businesses, and disrupted antislavery meetings were often led by "gentlemen of property and standing." These old-stock merchants and bankers feared that abolitionist appeals to the middle class and especially to women and children threatened their patriarchal position in local communities and even in their own families.

The birth of a new two-party political system also contributed to a growing climate of violence. Mob violence frequently broke out on election days as rival Democratic and Whig gangs tried to steal ballot boxes and keep the opposition's voters from reaching local polling places.

Traditional methods of preserving public order proved totally inadequate by the 1830s. Earlier in time, the nation's cities were "policed" by a handful of unpaid, untrained, ununiformed, and unarmed sheriffs, alderman, marshals, constables, and nightwatchmen. In New England towns, tithingmen armed with long black sticks tipped with brass patrolled streets searching for drunkards, disorderly children, and wayward servants.

These law officers were not a particularly effective deterrent to crime. Nightwatchmen generally held other jobs during the day and sometimes slept at their posts at night. Sheriffs, aldermen, marshals, and constables made a living not by investigating crimes or patrolling city streets but by collecting debts, foreclosing on mortgages, and serving court orders. Victims of crime had to offer a reward if they wanted these unpaid law officers to investigate a case.

This early system of maintaining public order worked in earlier decades when the rates of serious crime were extremely low and citizens had informal mechanisms that helped maintain order. Most cities were small and compact and lacked any distinct working-class ghettoes. Shopkeepers usually lived at or near their place of business and apprentices, journeymen, and laborers tended to live in or near the house of their master. Under these circumstances, the poor and the working class were subject to close supervision by their social superiors. By the mid-1830s, however, this older pattern of social organization had clearly broken down. Class-segregated neighborhoods grew increasingly common. Youth gangs, organized along ethnic and neighborhood lines, proliferated. Older mechanisms of social control weakened.

After 1830, drunken brawls, robberies, beatings, and murders all increased in number. Fear of crime led city leaders to look for new ways of preserving public order. Many municipal leaders regarded the new professional police force established in London in 1829 by the British Parliament as a model. London's police, nicknamed "bobbies" after Prime Minister Robert Peel, were trained, full-time professionals. They wore distinctive uniforms to make them visible to the public, patrolled regular beats, and lived in the neighborhoods they patrolled.

Initially, resistance to the establishment of professional police forces in American cities was intense. Taxpayers feared the cost of a police force. Local political machines feared the loss of the night watch as a source of political patronage. By the mid-1840s, however, continued rising crime rates overcame opposition to the establishment of a professional police force.

In New York City, the turning point came in 1841 following the unsolved murder of Mary Rogers, who worked in a tobacco shop. On July 25, 1841, she disappeared. Three days later, the body of the "beautiful cigar girl" was found in a river. The coroner said she had died not from drowning but from being abused and murdered by a gang of ruffians. The case aroused intense passion in New York City, prompting vocal demands for an end to waterfront gangs. But the city's constables said that they would only investigate the murder if they were promised a substantial reward. Public opinion was outraged. In 1844, the New York state legislature authorized the establishment of a professional police force to investigate crimes and patrol streets in New York City. Boston appointed its first police officers in 1838 and Philadelphia established a modern police department in 1854.

The life of a mid-nineteenth-century police officer was exceptionally hard. In many cities, members of gangs, like New York's Bowery B'hoys, Baltimore's Rip Raps, and Philadelphia's Schuylkill Rangers, actually outnumbered police officers. Young toughs regularly harrassed police officers. Many officers resisted wearing uniforms on the grounds that any distinctive dress made them readily identifiable targets for street gangs. In New York City, four officers were killed in the line of duty in a single year.

After 1850, in large part as a result of more efficient policing, the number of street disorders in American cities began to drop. Despite the introduction of the Colt revolver and other easily concealed and relatively inexpensive handguns during the middle years of the century, homicide rates, too, began to decline. By the eve of the Civil War, the nation's cities had become far less violent and far more orderly places than they had been two decades before.

trepreneurs and professionals to hard-pressed journeymen, who found their skills increasingly obsolete.

Does this mean that the pre–Civil War North was not the fluid, "egalitarian" society that Jacksonians claimed? The answer is a qualified "no." In the first place, the North's richest individuals, unlike Europe's aristocracy, were not ostentatiously rich; they were a working class, engaged in commerce, insurance, finance, shipbuilding, manufacturing, landholding, real estate, and the professions. Even more importantly, wealthy Northerners publicly rejected the older Hamiltonian notion that the rich and well-born were superior to the masses of people. During the early decades of the nineteenth century, wealthy Northerners shed the wigs, knee breeches, ruffled shirts, and white-topped boots that had symbolized high social status in colonial America and began to dress like other men, signaling their acceptance of an ideal of social equality. One wealthy Northerner succinctly summarized the new ideal: "These phrases, the higher orders, and lower orders, are of European origin, and have no place in our Yankee dialect."

Above all, it was the North's relatively high rates of economic and social mobility that gave substance to a widespread belief in equality of opportunity. Although few rich men were truly "self-made" men who had climbed from "rags to riches," there were many dramatic examples of upward mobility and countless instances of more modest climbs up the ladder of success. Industrialization rapidly increased the number of nonmanual jobs in commerce, industry, and the professions. There were new opportunities for lawyers, bookkeepers, business managers, brokers, and clerks. Giving additional reinforcement to the belief in opportunity was a remarkable rate of physical mobility. Each decade, fully half the residents of northern communities moved to a new town.

Even at the bottom of the economic hierarchy, prospects for advancement increased markedly after 1850. During the 1830s and 1840s, less than one unskilled worker in ten managed in the course of a decade to advance to a white-collar job. After 1850, the percentage doubled. The sons of unskilled laborers were even more likely to advance to skilled or white-collar employment. Even the poorest unskilled laborers often were able to acquire a house and a savings account.

It was the reality of physical and economic mobility that convinced the overwhelming majority of Northerners that they lived in a uniquely open society, in which differences in wealth or status were the result of hard work and ambition.

SOUTHERN DISTINCTIVENESS

In 1785 Thomas Jefferson jotted down a brief list of differences between North and South:

> In the North they are
>   cool
>   sober
>   laborious
>   independent
>   jealous of their own liberties and just to those
>   of others,
>   interested
>   chicaning
>   superstituous and hypocritical in their
>   religion.
> In the South they are
>   fiery
>   voluptuary
>   indolent
>   unsteady
>   zealous for their own liberties, but trampling
>   on those of others,
>   generous
>   candid
>   without attachment or pretensions to any re-
>   ligion but that of the heart.

Pre–Civil War Americans regarded Southerners as a distinct people, who possessed their own values and way of life. It was widely though mistakenly believed that the North and South had originally been settled by two distinct groups of immigrants, each with its own ethos. Northerners were said to be the descendants of seventeenth-century English Puritans, while Southerners were the descendants of England's country gentry. In the eyes of many pre–Civil War Americans this contributed to two distinct kinds of Americans: the aggressive, individualistic, money-grubbing Yankee and the southern cavalier. According to the popular stereotype, the cavalier, unlike the Yankee, was violently sensitive to insult, indifferent to money, and preoccupied with honor.

The Plantation Legend

During the three decades before the Civil War, popular writers created a stereotype, now known as the "plantation legend," that described the South as a land of aristocratic planters, beautiful southern belles, poor white trash, faithful black household servants, and superstitious fieldhands. Well known to anyone who has ever seen the movie *Gone With the Wind*, this stereotype was invented by authors from both the North and South, including Virginia Congressman George Tucker, Baltimore lawyer John Pendleton Kennedy, New Yorker James Kirk Paulding, and William Gilmore Simms of South Carolina.

This image of the South as "a land of cotton" where "old times" are "not forgotten" received its most popular expression in 1859 in a song called "Dixie," written by a Northerner named Dan D. Emmett to enliven shows given by a troupe of black-faced minstrels on the New York stage. In the eyes of many Northerners, uneasy with their increasingly urban, individualistic commercial society, the culture of the South seemed to have many things absent from the North—a leisurely pace of life, a clear social hierarchy, and an indifference to money.

The Old South: Images and Realities

Despite the strength of the plantation stereotype, the South was, in reality, a diverse and complex region. Though Americans today often associate the old South with cotton plantations, large parts of the South were unsuitable for plantation life. In the mountainous regions of eastern Tennessee and western Virginia, few plantations and few slaves were to be found. Nor did southern farms and plantations devote their efforts exclusively to growing cotton or other cash crops, such as rice and tobacco. Unlike the slave societies of the Caribbean, which produced crops exclusively for export, the

South devoted much of its energy to raising food and livestock.

The pre–Civil War South encompassed a wide variety of regions that differed geographically, economically, and politically. Such regions included the Piedmont, Tidewater, coastal plain, piney woods, Delta, Appalachian mountains, upcountry, and a fertile "black belt"—regions that clashed repeatedly over such political questions as debt relief, taxes, apportionment of representation, and internal improvements.

The white South's social structure was much more complex than the popular stereotype of proud aristocrats disdainful of honest work and ignorant, vicious, exploited poor whites. The old South's intricate social structure included many small slaveowners and relatively few large ones.

Actually, large slaveholders were extremely rare. In 1860 just 11,000 Southerners—three-quarters of one percent of the white population—owned more than 50 slaves; just 2358 owned as many as 100 slaves. However, although large slaveholders were few in number, they owned most of the South's slaves. Over half of all slaves lived on plantations with 20 or more slaves and a quarter lived on plantations with more than 50 slaves.

Slave ownership was relatively widespread. In the first half of the nineteenth century, one-third of all southern white families owned slaves, and a majority of white southern families either owned slaves, had owned them, or expected to own them. These slaveowners were a diverse lot. A few were black, mulatto, or Indian; one-tenth were women; and more than one in ten worked as artisans, businesspeople, or merchants rather than as farmers or planters. Few led lives of leisure or refinement. The average slaveowner lived in a log cabin rather than a mansion and was a farmer rather than a planter. The average holding varied between four and six slaves, and most slaveholders possessed no more than five.

White women in the South, despite the image of the hoop-skirted southern belle, suffered under heavier burdens than their northern counterparts. They married earlier, bore more children, and were more likely to die young. They lived in greater isolation, had less access

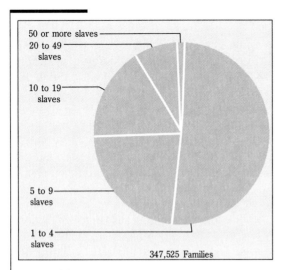

Figure 12.3
Slave-owning population, 1850

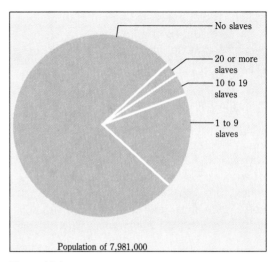

Figure 12.4
Southern white population, 1860

to the company of other women, and lacked the satisfactions of voluntary associations and reform movements. Their education was briefer and much less likely to result in opportunities for independent careers.

The plantation legend was misleading in still other respects. Slavery was neither dying nor was it unprofitable. In 1860 the South was richer than any country in Europe except England, and it had achieved a level of wealth unmatched by Italy or Spain until the eve of World War II. Instead of stagnating, per capita income was growing 30 percent more rapidly in the South than in the North between 1840 and 1860, and exceeded the income of the states in the West by 14 percent. Personal income lagged well behind the North's, in spite of the rapid growth rate. Per capita income in the South in 1860 was 25 percent lower than in the North.

The southern economy generated enormous wealth and was critical to the economic growth of the entire United States. Well over half of the richest one percent of Americans in 1860 lived in the South. Even more importantly, southern agriculture helped finance early nineteenth-century American economic growth. Prior to the Civil War, the South grew 60 percent of the world's cotton, provided over half of all U.S. export earnings, and furnished 70 per-

cent of the cotton consumed by the British textile industry. Cotton exports paid for a substantial share of the capital and technology that laid the basis for America's industrial revolution. In addition, precisely because the South specialized in agricultural production, the North developed a variety of business that provided services for the southern states, including textile factories and a meat processing industry. And since the South, like other slave societies, did not develop its own financial and commercial facilities, northern bankers, insurance agents, and cotton brokers developed substantial businesses.

Impact of Slavery on the Southern Economy

Although slavery was highly profitable, it had a negative impact on the southern economy. It impeded the development of industry and cities and contributed to high debts, soil exhaustion, and a lack of technological innovation. The philosopher and poet Ralph Waldo Emerson said that "slavery is no scholar, no improver; it does not love the whistle of the railroad; it does not love the newspaper, the mail-bag, a college, a book or a preacher who has the absurd whim of saying what he thinks; it does not increase the white population; it does not improve the soil; everything goes to decay." There appears to be a large element of truth in Emerson's observation.

The South, like other slave societies, did not develop urban centers for commerce, finance, and industry on a scale equal to those found in the North. Virginia's largest city, Richmond, had a population of just 15,274 in 1850. That same year, Wilmington, North Carolina's largest city, had just 7264 inhabitants, while Natchez and Vicksburg, the two largest cities in Mississippi, had fewer than 3000 white inhabitants.

Southern cities were small because they failed to develop diversified economies. Unlike the cities of the North, southern cities rarely became processing or finishing centers and southern ports rarely engaged in international trade. Their primary functions were to market and transport cotton or other agricultural crops, supply local planters and farmers with such necessities as agricultural implements, and produce the small number of manufactured goods, such as cotton gins, needed by farmers.

An overemphasis on slave-based agriculture led Southerners to neglect industry and transportation improvements. As a result, manufacturing and transportation lagged far behind the North's. In 1860 the North had approximately 1.3 million industrial workers compared to the South's 110,000, and northern factories manufactured nine-tenths of the industrial goods produced in the United States. The North produced 17 times as much cotton and woolen goods as the South, 30 times as many boots and shoes, 20 times as much pig iron, and 24 times as many locomotive engines.

The South's transportation network was primitive by northern standards. Traveling the 1460 overland miles from Baltimore to New Orleans in 1850 meant riding five different railroads, two stagecoaches, and two steamboats. Most southern railroads served primarily to transport cotton to southern ports, where the crop could be shipped on northern vessels to northern or British factories for processing.

Because of high rates of personal debt, Southern states kept taxation and government spending at much lower levels than in the North. As a result, Southerners lagged far behind Northerners in their support for public education. Illiteracy was widespread. In 1850, 20 percent of all southern white adults could not read or write. In contrast, the national figure for illiteracy was 8 percent (including the South) and 0.42 percent in New England. At midcentury, southern pupils attended 36 fewer days in class each year, spent fewer years in school, and were half again as likely to be truant as northern pupils.

Because large slaveholders owned most of the region's slaves, wealth was more stratified than in the North. In the deep South, the middle class held a relatively small proportion of the region's property, but wealthy planters owned a very significant portion of the productive lands and slave labor. In 1850, 17 percent of the farming population held two-thirds of all acres in the rich cotton-growing regions of the South.

There are indications that during the last decade before the Civil War slave ownership was increasingly concentrated in fewer and fewer hands. As soil erosion and exhaustion diminished the availability of cotton land, scarcity and heavy demand forced the price of land and slaves to rise beyond the reach of most, and in newer cotton-growing regions, yeomen farmers were pushed off the land as planters expanded their holdings. In Louisiana, for example, nearly half of all rural white families owned no land. During the 1850s, the percentage of the total white population owning slaves declined significantly. By 1860, the proportion of whites holding slaves had fallen from about one-third to one-fourth. As slave and land ownership grew more concentrated, a growing number of whites were forced by economic pressure to leave the land and move to urban centers.

Growth of a Distinctive Southern Identity

Beginning in the 1830s, the South developed a new and aggressive sense of "nationalism" that was rooted in its sense of distinctiveness and its perception that it was ringed by enemies. The South began to conceive of itself more and more as the true custodian of America's revolutionary heritage. Southern travelers who ventured into the North regarded it as a "strange and distant land" and expressed disgust about its vice-ridden cities and its grasping materialism.

At the same time, southern intellectuals began to defend slavery as a positive good. After 1830, white Southerners stopped referring to slavery as a necessary evil. Instead, they argued that it was a beneficial institution that created a hierarchical society superior to the leveling democracy of the North. By the late 1840s, a new more explicitly racist rationale for slavery had emerged.

With the emergence of militant abolitionism in the North, sharpened by slave uprisings in Jamaica and Southampton County, Virginia, the South began to see itself as surrounded by enemies. Southern leaders responded aggressively. On the Senate floor in 1837, John C. Calhoun pronounced slavery "a good—a positive good" and set the tone for future southern proslavery arguments. Prior to the 1830s, southern statements on slavery had been defensive; afterward, they were defiant.

In the 1840s, a growing number of southern ministers, journalists, and politicians began to denounce the North's form of capitalism as "wage slavery." The condition of free labor, they argued, was actually "worse than slavery," because slaveholders, unlike greedy northern employers, provide for their employees "when most needed, when sickness or old age has overtaken [them]." Northern workers, they declared, were simply "slaves without masters."

Writers like George Fitzhugh argued that slavery was a beneficient institution that permitted the development of an upper class devoted to high intellectual pursuits. The champions of slavery maintained that the South's hierarchical, organic society was superior to the individualistic, materialistic civilization of the North in which abolitionism, feminism, and labor unrest indicated that the social order was disintegrating.

During the 1840s, a growing number of Southerners defended slavery on explicitly racial grounds. In doing so, they drew on new pseudoscientific theories of racial inferiority. Some of these theories came from Europe, which was seeking justification of imperial expansion over nonwhite people in Africa and Asia. Other racist ideas were drawn from northern scientists, who employed an elaborate theory of "polygenesis" that claimed that blacks and whites were separate species.

The Decline of Antislavery Sentiment in the South

During the eighteenth century, the South was unique among slave societies in its openness to antislavery ideas. In Delaware, Maryland, and North Carolina, Quakers freed more than 1500 slaves and sent them out of state. Scattered Presbyterian, Baptist, and Methodist ministers and advisory committees condemned slavery as a sin "contrary to the word of God." As late as 1827, the number of antislavery organizations in the South actually outnumbered those in the free states by at least four to one.

The South's historical openness to antislavery ideas ended in the 1830s. Southern religious sects that had expressed opposition to slavery in the late eighteenth century modified their antislavery beliefs. Quakers and Unitarians who were strongly antagonistic to slavery emigrated. By the second decade of the century, antislavery sentiment was confined to Kentucky, the Piedmont counties of North Carolina, and the mountains in eastern Tennessee.

State law and public opinion stifled debate and forced conformity to proslavery arguments. Southern state legislatures adopted a series of laws suppressing criticism of the institution. Louisiana in 1830 made it a crime to make any statement that might produce discontent or insubordination among free blacks. Six years later, Virginia made it a felony for any member of an abolition society to come into the state and for any citizen to deny the legality of slavery.

The silent pressure of public opinion limited public discussion of the slavery question. College presidents or professors suspected of sympathizing with abolitionists lost their jobs. Mobs attacked editors who dared to print articles critical of slavery. One Richmond, Virginia, editor fought eight duels in two years. In Parkville, Missouri, and Lexington, Kentucky, crowds dismantled printing presses of antislavery newspapers. An "iron curtain" against the invasion of antislavery propaganda was erected.

Only once, in the wake of Nat Turner's famous slave insurrection in 1831, did a southern state openly debate the possibility of ending slavery. These debates in the Virginia legislature in January and February 1832 ended with the defeat of proposals to abolish slavery.

James G. Birney was one of many Southerners to discover that it was hopeless to work for slave emancipation in the South. Birney was born into a wealthy Kentucky slaveholding family, and, like many members of the South's slaveowning elite, educated at Princeton. After graduation, he moved to Huntsville, Alabama, where he practiced law and operated a cotton plantation. In Huntsville, he developed qualms about slavery and began to work as an agent for the American Colonization Society. Soon, his doubts about slavery had grown into an active hatred for the institution. He returned to Kentucky, emancipated his slaves, and in 1835 organized the Kentucky Anti-Slavery Society.

In Kentucky, Birney quickly discovered that public opinion vehemently opposed antislavery ideas. A committee of leading citizens in Danville informed him that they would not permit him to establish an antislavery newspaper in the city. When Birney announced that he would go through with his plans anyway, the committee bought out the paper's printer, and the town's postmaster announced that he would refuse to deliver the newspaper. In a final effort to publish his paper, Birney moved across the Ohio River into Cincinnati, but a mob destroyed his press while the city's mayor looked on.

After 1830 the defense of slavery also led to hostility toward all social reforms. One southern newspaper editor declared the South "has uniformly rejected the isms which infest Europe and the Eastern and Western states of this country." Many Southerners spoke proudly of the rejection of the reforms that flourished in the North. The South, said one South Carolina scientist, was "the breakwater which is to stay that furious tide of social and political heresies now setting toward us from the shores of the old world." Only the temperance movement made headway in the South.

"Reforming" Slavery from Within

Many white Southerners felt genuine moral doubts about slavery. For the most part, however, these doubts were directed into efforts to reform the institution by converting slaves to Christianity, revising slave codes to make them less harsh, and making slavery conform to the ideal depicted in the Old Testament.

During the early eighteenth century, ministers from such denominations as the Quakers, Moravians, and Anglicans launched the first concerted campaigns to convert slaves in the American colonies to Christianity. Missionaries established schools and taught several thousand slaves to read and recite Scripture. They stressed that Christian slaves would make more loyal and productive workers, less likely to stage insurrections. The Great Awakening of the 1730s and 1740s stimulated renewed efforts to promote Christianization, but it would not be until the early nineteenth century that most slaveowners expressed concern for converting their slaves to Christianity.

There were also early nineteenth-century efforts to ameliorate the harshness of the early slave codes. The eighteenth-century codes permitted owners to punish slaves by castration and cutting off limbs. Slaveholders had no specific obligations for housing, feeding, or clothing slaves, and many observers reported seeing slaves half-clothed or naked. Few eighteenth century masters showed any concern for slave marriages, families, or religion.

During the early nineteenth century, the southern states enacted new codes regulating the punishment of slaves and setting minimum standards for maintenance. State legislatures defined killing a slave with malice as murder and made dismemberment and some other cruel punishments illegal. Three states forbade the sale of young slave children from their parents, and four states permitted slaves to be taught to read and write.

Many of the new laws went unenforced, but they suggest that a new code of values and behavior was emerging. Paternalism was the defining characteristic of this new code. According to this new ideal, slaveholding was "a duty and a burden" carrying strict moral obligations. A humane master of a plantation was supposed to show concern for the spiritual and physical well-being of his slaves.

These minimal efforts to reform slavery were, however, accompanied by tighter restrictions on other aspects of slave life. Private manumissions were made illegal. Southern states instituted the death penalty for any slaves involved in plotting a rebellion. Most states prohibited slaves from owning firearms, horses, or drums, which might be used during an insurrection, placed tight restrictions on slave funerals, and barred black preachers from conducting religious services unless a white person was present. In order to restrict contact between free blacks and slaves, a number of southern states required manumitted slaves to leave the state. Other restrictive laws quarantined vessels containing black sailors and imprisoned those who stepped on shore.

Southern Economic, Literary, Religious, and Educational Movements

Seeking to free their region from cultural, economic, and religious dependence on the North, southern "nationalists" launched campaigns for economic diversification, new colleges, religious independence, and a uniquely southern literature. These southern "nationalists" sought to preserve the cultural and intellectual distinctiveness of the South and to insulate the Southern economy from the corrupting commercial and industrial values of the North.

The 1830s saw attempts to promote southern economic self-sufficiency, to create southern-oriented educational and religious institutions, and to develop a distinctive southern

literature. Beginning in 1837, southern leaders held the first of a series of commercial conventions in an attempt to diversify the southern economy and to rescue the South from northern "pecuniary and commercial supremacy." Manufacturing, wrote a Mobile, Alabama, editor, was "the only safe and effectual remedy against Northern oppression."

Efforts to develop the southern economy were surprisingly successful. Southern railroad mileage quadrupled between 1850 and 1860— although southern track mileage still trailed the free states' by 14,000. By 1860 Richmond manufactured more tobacco than any other American city and exported more goods to South America than any other American port, including New York.

Other southern nationalists strove to create southern-oriented educational institutions. As early as the 1820s, influential southern leaders argued that the South had to create its own institutions of higher learning in order to protect the young from, in Jefferson's words, "imbibing opinions and principles in discord" with those of the South. Schoolbooks, declared one southern magazine, "have slurs and innuendoes at slavery; the geographies are more particular in stating the resources of the Northern States; the

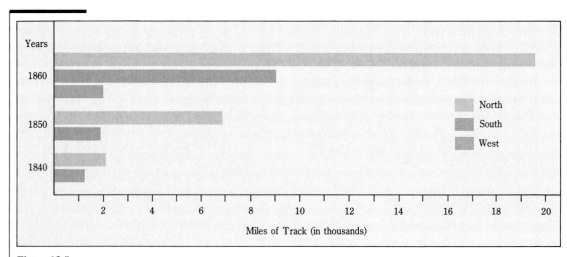

Figure 12.5
Railroad growth, 1840–1860. An overemphasis on slave-based agriculture led Southerners to neglect transportation improvements.

histories almost ignore the South; the arithmetics contain in their examples reflections upon the Southern states."

The struggle for independent southern colleges achieved considerable success. By 1860 Virginia had 23 colleges and Georgia had 32, while New York had 17 colleges and Massachusetts just 8. In 1856 the University of Virginia had 558 students, compared to just 361 at Harvard.

Regional independence was also called for in religion. Between 1835 and 1845, the slavery question had been raised at national meetings of the Baptist and Methodist churches, which included three-fourths of the southern population. A growing number of Southerners began to believe that the northern churches were "mixed up with the whole machinery of abolition and antislavery agitation and invasion." In 1844 southern delegates to the Methodist General Conference set up the Methodist Episcopal Church South to free themselves "from the oppressive jursidiction of the majority in the North." The next year, southern Baptists established a separate Southern Baptist Convention. In 1857, the Presbyterians split into northern and southern groups, partially over the slavery issue. In the early 1990s, only the Baptists remain divided.

At the same time that educators and church leaders denounced "Northern domination in Our Schools and Pulpits," southern sectionalists called for a distinctive and peculiarly southern literature. More than 30 periodicals were founded with the word "Southern" in their title, all intended to "breathe a Southern spirit, and sustain a strictly Southern character." Authors like Nathaniel Beverly Tucker and William Gilmore Simms called on the South to overcome the taunts of "Englishmen and Northernmen" that they were intellectually inferior and to write on southern themes.

Southern Radicalism

By the early 1850s, a growing number of aggressive Southerners had moved beyond earlier calls for separate southern factories, colleges, and churches. Militant nationalists called for the reopening of the slave trade and aggressive annexations of new slave territory in Latin America and the Caribbean.

In a bid to acquire new lands for slavery a filibustering expedition was launched from New Orleans in 1851 to secure Cuba for the South. After this failed, extreme southern nationalists supported the efforts of William Walker, "the gray-eyed man of destiny," to extend slave labor into Latin America. In 1853, with considerable southern support, Walker raised a private army and unsuccessfully invaded Mexico. Two years later, he launched the first of three invasions of Nicaragua. On his final foray in 1860, he was taken prisoner by a British officer, handed over to Honduran authorities, and, at the age of 36 executed by a firing squad. In the late 1850s, another group of ardent southern expansionists, the Knights of the Golden Circle, developed plans to create an independent slave empire stretching from Maryland and Texas to northern South America and the West Indies. The only practical effect of these schemes was to arouse northern opinion against an aggressive southern slaveocracy.

SLAVERY

The primary distinguishing characteristic of the South was its dependence on slave labor. During the decades before the Civil War, 4 million black Americans, one-third of the South's population, labored as slaves.

Two unrelated incidents suggest the complexity of the institution of slavery. The first took place in 1811. Lilburne and Isham Lewis, two nephews of Thomas Jefferson, ordered Lilburne's slaves to lash a slave named George to the kitchen floor of their southwest Kentucky farm. The 17-year old slave had run away, returned, and then broken a treasured pitcher. Enraged and probably drunk, Lilburne seized an axe and nearly decapitated the young slave. Then the brothers had their terrorized slaves dismember the victim and throw the pieces on the fire.

The second picture of slavery is from 1825. In that year, Joseph Davis, a Mississippi planter, met Robert Owen, the Scottish industrialist and utopian reformer. Inspired by Owen's vision of society operating according to the principles of voluntary cooperation, Davis attempted to reorganize his plantation at Davis Bend, 30 miles south of Vicksburg. Davis provided slave families with two-room cabins and supplied food freely. His most famous innovation was a form of self-government for the slave community. No slave of the more than 300 on his plantation could be punished without being tried and convicted by a jury of his peers. Later Joseph's younger brother, Jefferson Davis, the future president of the Confederacy, put a similar system into practice on his plantation.

During the early nineteenth century, abolitionists developed a devastating moral indictment of slavery. They attacked slaveowners for breaking marriages, selling children from parents, dividing families, systematically breeding slaves for sale, and taking slave mistresses as

Despite the physical harshness of life under slavery, slaves were able to sustain a sense of dignity and self-worth through their religious and cultural traditions.

concubines. They attacked masters for working slaves to death and inadequately feeding them. Slavery was "the sum of all villainies," they declared, because it encouraged every other sin.

Slavery's apologists responded to these charges, maintaining that, on the whole, masters were decent, slaves were contented, and slaves' living conditions were superior to those of many free workers in the North. Ardent proslavery writers asserted that planter paternalism and public opinion protected slaves from abuse. But several questions remain. How repressive was slavery in the United States? Under what conditions did slaves live?

In general, slaves were overworked, poorly clad, inadequately housed, and received the minimum of medical care. Debt, the death of a master, or merely the prospect of economic gain frequently tore slave husbands from wives and slave parents from children. And yet, as brutal and destructive as the institution of slavery was, slaves were not defenseless or emasculated victims. Slaves were able to sustain ties to their African past and to maintain a separate life. Through religion, folklore, music, and family life as well as more direct forms of resistance, slaves were able to sustain a vital culture supportive of human dignity.

The Legal Status of Slaves

Every southern state enacted a slave code that defined the slaveowners' power and the slaves' status as property. The codes stated that a slave, like a domestic animal, could be bought, sold, and leased. A master also had the right to compel a slave to work. The codes prohibited slaves from owning property, testifying against whites in court, or from making contracts. Slave marriages were not recognized by law. Under the slave codes, slavery was lifelong and hereditary, and any child born to a slave woman was the property of her master.

The slave codes gave slaves limited legal rights, but their primary purpose was to enforce discipline. In order to refute abolitionist contentions that slavery was unjust and inhumane, southern legislators adopted statutes regulating slaves' hours of labor and establishing certain minimal standards for slave upkeep. Most states

Hardworking slaves on a plantation pick and carry cotton while white overseers look on.

also defined the wanton killing of a slave as murder, prohibited cruel and unusual punishments, and extended to slaves accused of capital offenses the right to trial by jury and legal counsel. Whipping, however, was not regarded by southern legislatures as a cruel punishment, and slaves were prohibited from bringing suit to seek legal redress for violations of their rights.

The main goal of the slave codes, however, was to regulate slaves' lives. Slaves were forbidden from striking whites or using insulting language toward white people, holding a meeting without a white person present, visiting whites or free blacks, or leaving plantations without permission. The laws prohibited whites and free blacks from teaching slaves to read and write, gambling with slaves, or supplying them with liquor, guns, or poisonous drugs. Most of the time, authorities loosely enforced these legal restrictions, but whenever fears of slave uprisings spread, enforcement tightened.

Slave Labor

Simon Gray was a slave. He was also the captain of a Mississippi River flatboat and the builder and operator of a number of sawmills. Emanuel Quivers, too, was a slave. He worked at the Tredegar Iron Works of Richmond, Virginia. Andrew Dirt was also a slave. He was a black overseer.

Slaves performed all kinds of work. During the 1850s, half a million slaves lived in southern towns and cities, where they were hired out by their owners to work in ironworks, textile mills, tobacco factories, laundries, shipyards, and mechanics' homes. Other slaves labored as lumberjacks, as deckhands and fire tenders on river boats, and in sawmills, gristmills, and quarries. Many other slaves were engaged in construction of roads and railroads. Most slaves, to be sure, were fieldhands, raising cotton, hemp, rice, tobacco, and sugarcane. But even on plantations not all slaves were menial laborers. Some worked as skilled artisans such as blacksmiths, shoemakers, or carpenters; others held domestic posts, such as coachmen or house servants; and still others held managerial posts. At least two-thirds of the slaves worked under the supervision of black foremen of gangs, called drivers. Not infrequently they managed the whole plantation in the absence of their masters.

For most slaves, slavery meant backbreaking field work on small farms or larger plantations. On the typical plantation, slaves worked "from day clean to first dark." Solomon Northrup, a free black who was kidnapped and enslaved for 12 years on a Louisiana cotton plantation, wrote a graphic description of the work regimen imposed on slaves: "The hands are required to be in the cotton field as soon as it is light in the morning, and, with the exception of ten or fifteen minutes, which is given them at noon to swallow their allowance of cold bacon, they are not permitted to be a moment idle until it is too dark to see, and when the moon is full, they often times labor till the middle of the night." Even then, the slaves' work was not over; it was still necessary to feed swine and mules, cut wood, and pack the cotton. At planting time or harvest time, work was even more exacting, as planters required slaves to stay in the fields 15 or 16 hours a day.

To maximize productivity, slaveowners assigned each hand a specific set of tasks throughout the year. During the winter, field slaves ginned and pressed cotton, cut wood, repaired buildings and fences, and cleared fields. In the spring and summer, field hands plowed and hoed fields, killed weeds, and planted and cultivated crops. In the fall, slaves picked, ginned, and packed cotton, shucked corn, and gathered peas. Elderly slaves cared for children, made clothes, and prepared food.

Labor on large plantations was as rigidly organized as in a factory. Under the gang system, which was widely used on cotton plantations, field hands were divided into plow gangs and hoe gangs, each commanded by a driver. Under the task system, mainly used on rice plantations, each hand was given a specific daily work assignment.

Because slaves had little direct incentive to work hard, slaveowners combined a variety of harsh penalties with positive incentives. Some masters denied disobedient slaves passes or forced them to work on Sundays or holidays. Other planters confined disobedient hands to private or public jails, and one Maryland planter required a slave to eat worms he had failed to pick off tobacco plants. Chains and shackles were widely used to control runaways. Whipping was a key part of the system of discipline and motivation. On one Louisiana plantation, at least one slave was lashed every four-and-a-half days. In his diary, Bennet H. Barrow, a Louisiana planter, recorded flogging "every hand in the field," breaking his sword on the head of one slave, shooting another slave in the thigh, and cutting another with a club "in 3 places very bad."

But physical pain alone was not enough to elicit hard work. To stimulate productivity, some masters gave slaves small garden plots and permitted them to sell their produce. Others distributed gifts of food or money at the end of the year. Still other planters awarded prizes, holidays, and year-end bonuses to particularly productive slaves. One Alabama master permitted his slaves to share in the profits of the cotton, peanut, and pea crops.

Material Conditions of Slave Life

Deprivation and physical hardship were the hallmarks of life under slavery. It now seems clear that the material conditions of slave life may have been even worse than those of the poorest, most down-trodden free laborers in the North and Europe. Although the material conditions for slaves improved greatly in the nineteenth century, slaves remained much more likely than southern or northern whites to die prematurely, suffer malnutrition or dietary deficiencies, or lose a child in infancy.

Plantation records reveal that over half of all slave babies died during their first year of life—a rate twice that of white babies. Although slave children's death rate declined after the first year of life, it remained twice the white rate.

The average slave's small size indicates a deficient diet. At birth, over half of all slave children weighed less than $5\frac{1}{2}$ pounds—or what today is considered to be underweight. Throughout their childhoods, slaves were smaller than white children of the same age. The average slave children did not reach 3 feet in height until their fourth birthdays. At that age they were $5\frac{1}{2}$ inches shorter than a typical child today and about the same height as a child in present-day Bangladesh. At 17, slave men were shorter than 96 percent of present-day American men, and slave women were smaller than 80 percent of American women.

The slaves' diet was monotonous and unvaried, consisting largely of corn meal, salt pork, and bacon. Only rarely did slaves drink milk or eat fresh meat or vegetables. This diet provided enough bulk calories to ensure that slaves had sufficient strength and energy to work as productive field hands, but it did not provide adequate nutrition. As a result, slaves were small for their ages, suffered from vitamin and protein deficiencies, and were victims of such ailments as beriberi, kwashiorkor, and pellagra. Poor nutrition and high rates of infant and child mortality contributed to a short average life expectancy—just 21 or 22 years compared to 40 to 43 years for whites.

The physical conditions in which slaves lived were appalling. Lacking privies, slaves had to urinate and defecate in the cover of nearby bushes. Lacking any sanitary disposal of garbage, they were surrounded by decaying food. Chickens, dogs, and pigs lived next to the slave quarters, and in consequence, animal feces contaminated the area. Such squalor contributed to high rates of dysentery, typhus, diarrhea, hepatitis, typhoid fever, and intestinal worms.

Slave quarters were cramped and crowded. The typical cabin—a single, windowless room, with a chimney constructed of clay and twigs and a floor made up of dirt or planks resting on the ground—ranged in size from 10×10 feet to 21×21 feet. These small cabins were often quite crowded, containing five, six, or more occupants. On some plantations, slaves lived in single-family cabins; on others, two or more shared the same room. On the largest plantations, unmarried men and women were sometimes lodged together in barracks-like structures. Josiah Henson, the Kentucky slave who

served as the model for Harriet Beecher Stowe's Uncle Tom, described his plantation's cabins this way:

> We lodged in log huts. . . . Wooden floors were an unknown luxury. In a single room were huddled, like cattle, ten or a dozen persons, men, women, and children. . . . There were neither bedsteads nor furniture. . . . Our beds were collections of straw and old rags. . . . The wind whistled and the rain and snow blew in through the cracks, and the damp earth soaked in the moisture till the floor was muddy as a pig sty.

Slave Family Life

In 1858, after being sold away from his family, a Georgia slave named Abream Scriven wrote the following words to his wife: "Give my love to my dear father and mother and tell them good bye for me. . . . My dear wife for you and all my children my pen cannot express the grief I feel to be parted from you. I remain your true husband until death."

According to antebellum critics of slavery, the greatest evil inflicted by the "peculiar insti-

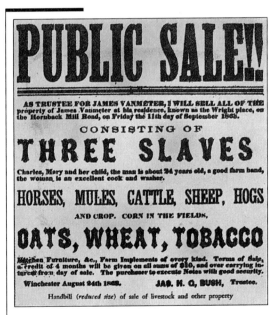

Slavery's worst evil was that it reduced people to the status of property. Under slavery, slaves could be bought, sold, leased, and traded from their families.

tution" was the havoc it inflicted on the slave family. In truth, slavery exacted a terrible toll on black family life. Members of a family were subject to sale and often lived on separate plantations. Parents lacked authority to protect children. Slave women were vulnerable to sexual abuse from masters and overseers. Deliberate and systematic efforts to breed slaves were not unknown.

And yet, despite the constant threat of sale and family breakup, African-Americans managed to forge strong family ties and personal relationships. Despite the fact that southern law provided no legal sanction for slave marriages, most slaves established *de facto* arrangements that were often stable over long periods of time. In spite of frequent family disruption, a majority of slaves grew up in families headed by a father and a mother. Nuclear family ties stretched outward to an involved network of extended kin. In large measure because of the strength and flexibility of their kin ties, black Americans were able to resist the psychologically debilitating effects of slavery.

Slavery severely strained black family life. Slave sales frequently broke up slave families. During the Civil War, nearly 20 percent of exslaves reported that an earlier marriage had been terminated by "force." The sale of children from parents was even more common. Over the course of a lifetime, the average slave had a 50–50 chance of being sold at least once and was likely to witness the sale of several members of his immediate family.

Even in instances in which marriages were not broken by sale, slave husbands and wives often resided on separate farms or plantations and were owned by different individuals. On large plantations, one slave father in three had a different owner than his wife and could visit his family only at his master's discretion. On smaller holdings, divided ownership occurred even more frequently. The typical farm and plantation were so small that it was difficult for many slaves to find a spouse at all. As one exslave put it, men "had a hell of a time getting a wife during slavery."

Other obstacles stood in the way of an independent family life. Living accommodations undermined privacy. Many slaves had to share their single-room cabins with relatives and other slaves who were not related to them. On larger plantations, food was cooked in a common kitchen and young children were cared for in a communal nursery while their parents worked in the fields. Even on model plantations, children between the ages of 7 and 10 were taken from their parents and sent to live in separate cabins.

Slavery imposed rigid limits on the authority of slave parents. Nearly every slave child went through an experience similar to one recalled by a young South Carolina slave named Jacob Stoyer. Jacob was being trained as a jockey. His trainer beat him regularly, for no apparent reason. Jacob appealed to his father for help, but his father simply said to work harder, "for I cannot do anything for you." When Jacob's mother argued with the trainer, she was whipped for her efforts. From this episode, Jacob learned a critical lesson: The ability of slave parents to protect their own children was sharply limited.

Of all the evils associated with slavery, abolitionists most bitterly denounced the sexual abuse suffered by slave women. Abolitionists claimed that slaveholders adopted deliberate policies to breed slaves for sale in the lower South—"like oxen for the shambles"—and kept "black harems" and sexually exploited slave women. Some masters did indeed take slave mistresses and concubines. One slave, Henry Bibb, said that a slave trader forced Bibb's wife to become a prostitute.

Planters also sought to increase slave birthrates through a variety of economic incentives. Many slaveholders gave bounties in the form of cash or household goods to mothers who bore healthy children and increased rations and lightened the workload of pregnant and nursing women.

But contrary to what early nineteenth-century abolitionists charged, the sexual life of slaves was not casual or promiscuous nor did slave women become mothers at a particularly early age. Some slave women, like some white women, engaged in premarital intercourse and bore children outside of marriage. But most slave women settled into a long-lasting monogamous relationship in their early twenties, which lasted, unless broken by sale, until she or her husband died.

Slave Cultural Expression

Despite the harshness and misery of life under slavery, it did not destroy the slaves' ability to develop a distinctive life and culture. Even under the weight of slavery, blacks developed a vital religion, music, and folklore. Through their families, their religion, and their cultural traditions, slaves were able to fashion an autonomous culture and community, beyond the direct control of their masters.

During the late eighteenth and early nineteenth centuries, slaves embraced Christianity, but they molded and transformed it to meet their own needs. Slave religious beliefs were a mixture of African traditions and Christianity. From their African heritage, slaves brought a hopeful and optimistic view of life, which contrasted sharply with evangelical Protestantism's emphasis on human sinfulness. In Protestant Christianity the slaves found an emphasis on love and the spiritual equality of all people that strengthened their ties to other blacks. Many slaves fused the concepts of Moses, who led his people to freedom, and Jesus, who suffered on behalf of all humankind, into a promise of deliverance in this world.

A major form of black religious expression was the spiritual. Slave spirituals, like "Go Down Moses" with its refrain "let my people go," indicated that slaves identified with the history of the Hebrew people, who had been oppressed and enslaved, but achieved eventual deliverance.

In addition to the spiritual, another major form of slave cultural expression was folklore. Slave folktales were much more than amusing stories; slaves used them to comment on the whites around them and to convey everyday lessons for living. Among the most popular slave folktales were animal trickster stories, like the Brer Rabbit tales, derived from similar African stories, which told of powerless creatures who achieve their will through wit and guile rather than power and authority. These tales taught slave children how they had to function in a white-dominated world and held out the prom-

This sketch of a slave dance in Lynchburg, Virginia, illustrates how slaves used their rare moments of leisure time and hints at the rich folk culture they tried to perpetuate.

ise that the powerless would eventually triumph over the strong.

Slave Resistance

It was a basic tenet of the proslavery argument that slaves were docile, contented, faithful, and loyal. "Our slave population is not only a happy one," said a Virginia legislator, "but it is a contented, peaceful, and harmless one."

In fact, there is no evidence that the majority of slaves were contented. One scholar has identified more than 200 instances of attempted insurrection or rumors of slave resistance between the seventeenth century and the Civil War. And many slaves who did not directly rebel made their masters' lives miserable through a variety of indirect protests against slavery, including sabotage, stealing, malingering, murder, arson, and infanticide.

Four times during the first 31 years of the nineteenth century, slaves attempted major insurrections. In 1800, a 24-year-old Virginia slave named Gabriel Prosser, who was a blacksmith, led a march of perhaps 50 armed slaves on Richmond. The plot failed when a storm washed out the road to Richmond, giving the Virginia militia time to arrest the rebels. White authorities executed Prosser and 25 other conspirators.

In 1811 in southern Louisiana, between 180 and 500 slaves, led by Charles Deslondes, a free mulatto from Haiti, marched on New Orleans, armed with axes and other weapons. Slaveowners retaliated by killing 82 blacks and placing the heads of 16 leaders on pikes.

In 1822 Denmark Vesey, a former West Indian slave who had been born in Africa, bought his freedom, and moved to Charleston, South Carolina. There he devised a conspiracy to take over the city on a summer Sunday when many whites would be vacationing outside the city. Using his connections as a leader in the African Church of Charleston, Vesey drew support from skilled black artisans, carpenters, harnessmakers, mechanics, and blacksmiths as well as from field slaves. Before the revolt could take place, however, a domestic slave of a prominent Charlestonian informed his master. The authorities proceeded to arrest 131 blacks and hang 37.

The most famous slave revolt took place nine years later in Southampton County in southern Virginia. On August 22, 1831, Nat Turner, a trusted Baptist preacher, led a small group of fellow slaves into the home of his master Joseph Travis and killed the entire Travis household. By August 23, Turner's force had increased to between 60 and 80 slaves and had killed more than 50 whites. The local militia counterattacked and killed about 100 blacks. Twenty more slaves, including Turner, were later executed. Turner's revolt sparked a panic that spread as far south as Alabama and Louisiana. One Virginian worried that "a Nat Turner might be in any family."

Slave uprisings were much less frequent and less extensive in the American South than in the West Indies or Brazil. Outright revolts did not occur more often because the chances of success were minimal and the consequences of defeat catastrophic. As one Missouri slave put it, "I've seen Marse Newton and Marse John Ramsey shoot too often to believe they can't kill" a slave.

The conditions that favored revolts elsewhere were absent in the South. In Jamaica, blacks outnumbered whites ten to one, whereas in the South whites were a majority in every state except Mississippi and South Carolina. In addition, slaveholding units in the South were much smaller than in other slave societies in the Western Hemisphere. Half of all U.S. slaves worked on units of 20 or less; in contrast, many sugar plantations in Jamaica had more than 500 slaves.

The unity of the white population in defense of slavery made the prospects for a successful rebellion bleak. In Virginia in 1830, 100,000 of the state's 700,000 whites were members of the state militia. Finally, southern slaves had few havens to which to escape. The major exception was the swamp country in Florida, where black "maroons" joined with Seminole Indians in resisting the U.S. army.

Recognizing that open resistance would be futile or even counterproductive, most plantation slaves expressed their opposition to slavery in a variety of subtle ways. Most day-to-day resistance took the form of breaking tools, feigning illness, doing shoddy work, stealing, and running away. These acts of resistance most commonly occurred when a master or overseer overstepped customary bounds. Through these acts, slaves tried to establish a right to proper treatment.

Free Blacks

In 1860, 488,000 black Americans were not slaves. After the American Revolution, slaveowners freed thousands of slaves, and countless others emancipated themselves by running away. In Louisiana, a large free black Creole population had emerged under Spanish and French rule, and in South Carolina a Creole population had arrived from Barbados. The number of free blacks in the deep South increased rapidly with the arrival of thousands of light-colored refugees from the black revolt in Haiti.

Free blacks varied greatly in status. Most lived in poverty, but in a few cities, such as New Orleans, Baltimore, and Charleston, free blacks worked as skilled carpenters, shoemakers, tailors, and millwrights. In the lower South, a few free blacks achieved high occupational status and actually bought slaves of their own. One of the wealthiest free blacks was William Ellison, the son of a slave mother and a white planter. As a slave apprenticed to a skilled artisan, Ellison had learned how to make cotton gins, and at the age of 26 bought his freedom with his overtime earnings. At his death in 1861, he had acquired the home of a former South Carolina governor, a shop, lands, and 63 slaves worth more than $100,000.

Free people of color occupied an uneasy middle ground between the dominant whites and the masses of slaves. Legally, courts denied them the right to serve on juries or to testify against whites. Some, like William Ellison, distanced themselves from those black people who remained in slavery and even bought and sold slaves. Others identified with slaves and poor free blacks and took the lead in establishing separate black churches.

In addition to the more than 250,000 free blacks who lived in the South, another 200,000 free blacks lived in the North. Although free blacks comprised no more than 3.8 percent of the population of any northern state, they faced intense legal, economic, and social discrimination, which kept them desperately poor. They were prohibited from marrying whites and were forced into the lowest paying jobs. Whites denied them equal access to education, relegated them to segregated jails, cemeteries, asylums, and schools, forbade them from testifying against whites in court, and, in all but four states—New Hampshire, Maine, Massachusetts, and Vermont—denied them the right to vote.

In the North as well as the South, most free blacks faced economic hardship and substandard living conditions. Northern free blacks typically lived in tenements, sheds, and stables. An 1847 visitor described the typical black dwelling in Philadelphia as "a desolate pen," 6 feet square, without windows, beds, or furniture, possessing a leaky roof and a floor so low in the ground "that more or less water comes in on them from the yard in rainy weather." According to the *New York Express*, the principal residence of a free black in that city was a house with eight or ten rooms, "and in these are crowded not infrequently two or three hundred souls."

While many free blacks lived in poverty, some worked as skilled carpenters, tailors, millwrights, or sawyers.

During the 1830s or even earlier, free blacks in both the North and South began to suffer from heightened discrimination and competition from white immigrants in both the skilled trades and such traditional occupations as domestic service. In the late 1850s, the plight of free blacks worsened. In states like South Carolina and Maryland, they faced a new crisis. White mechanics and artisans, bitter over the competition they faced from free people of color, demanded that the states legislate the reenslavement of free blacks. During the winter of 1859, politicians in the South Carolina legislature introduced 20 bills restricting the freedom of free blacks. None passed. The next summer, Charleston officials went house to house, demanding that free people of color provide documentary proof of their freedom and threatening to reenslave those who lacked evidence. A panic followed, and hundreds of free blacks emigrated to the North. Some 780 emigrated from South Carolina before secession; 2000 more left during the first month and a half of 1861.

CHRONOLOGY OF KEY EVENTS

1790 Samuel Slater opens the nation's first textile mill in Pawtucket, Rhode Island

1793 Eli Whitney obtains a patent for the cotton gin

1801 Gabriel Prosser's slave insurrection is uncovered in Richmond, Virginia

1806 Journeymen shoemakers in New York stage one of the nation's first labor strikes

1811 Charles Deslondes's slave insurrection in southern Louisiana is suppressed

1822 Denmark Vesey's slave rebellion is uncovered in South Carolina

1831 Nat Turner's slave insurrection in Southhampton County, Virginia

1832 Virginia legislature defeats proposal to abolish slavery

1834 National Trades' Union is organized; Massachusetts mill girls stage their first strike

1837 Panic of 1837 begins

1838 Boston establishes the nation's first modern police force

1840 Ten-hour day is established for federal employees

1842 Massachusetts supreme court, in *Commonwealth* v. *Hunt*, recognizes unions' right to exist

1843 Baptists split over the slavery issue

1844 Methodist church divides over slavery issue

1845 Potato blight strikes Ireland

1848 Revolutions in Europe; Free Soil party is organized to oppose expansion of slavery into new territories

1857 Hinton Helper publishes *The Impending Crisis of the South*

CONCLUSION

In 1857 Hinton Rowan Helper, the son of a western North Carolina farmer, published one of the most politically influential books ever written by an American. Entitled *The Impending Crisis of the South*, the book argued that slavery was incompatible with economic progress. Using statistics drawn from the 1850 census, Helper maintained that by every possible measure, the North was growing far faster than the South and that slavery was the cause of the South's economic backwardness.

Helper's thesis was that southern slavery was inefficient and wasteful, inferior in all respects to the North's free labor system. Helper argued that slavery was incompatible with economic progress; it impoverished the South, degraded labor, inhibited urbanization, thwarted industrialization, and stifled innovation. A rabid racist, Helper accompanied a call for the aboli-

tion of slavery with a demand for black colonization overseas. He concluded his book with a call for the South's nonslaveholders to overthrow the region's planter elite.

Helper's book created a nationwide furor. the *New York Tribune* distributed 500 copies a day, viewing the book as the most effective propaganda against slavery ever written. Many Southerners burned it, fearful that it would divide the white population and undermine the institution of slavery.

By 1857, when Helper's book appeared, the North and South had become in the eyes of many Americans two distinct civilizations, with their own distinctive set of values and ideals: one increasingly urban and industrial, the other committed to slave labor. Although the two sections shared many of the same ideals, ambitions, and prejudices, they had developed along diverging lines. In increasing numbers, Northerners identified their society with progress and believed that slavery was an intolerable obstacle to innovation, self-improvement, and commercial and economic growth. A growing number of Southerners, in turn, regarded their rural and agricultural society as the true embodiment of republican values. The great question before the nation was whether it could continue to exist half slave, half free.

SUGGESTIONS FOR FURTHER READING

OVERVIEWS AND SURVEYS

Daniel Boorstin, *The Americans: The National Experience* (1965); Russel B. Nye, *Society and Culture in America, 1830–1860* (1974); Edward Pessen, *Jacksonian America: Society, Personality, and Politics*, rev. ed. (1978).

THE EMERGENCE OF A NEW INDUSTRIAL ORDER IN THE NORTH

Hal S. Barron, *Those Who Stayed Behind: Rural Society in Nineteenth-Century New England* (1984); Mary H. Blewett, *Men, Women, and Work: Class, Gender, and Protest in the New England Shoe Industry* (1988); Stuart Blumin, *The Emergence of the Middle Class: Social Experience in the American City* (1989), and *The Urban Threshhold* (1976); John L. Brooke, *The Heart of the Commonwealth: Society and Political Culture in Worcester County, Massachusetts* (1989); Christopher Clark, *The Roots of Rural Capitalism: Western Massachusetts, 1780–1860* (1990); Dennis Clark, *The Irish in Philadelphia* (1973); Kathleen N. Conzen, *Immigrant Milwaukee, 1836–1860* (1976); Allen F. Davis and Mark H. Haller, eds., *The Peoples of Philadelphia* (1973); Alan Dawley, *Class and Community: The Industrial Revolution in Lynn* (1976); Hasia R. Diner, *Erin's Daughters in America* (1983); Robert Doherty, *Society and Power: Five New England Towns, 1800–1860* (1977); Thomas Dublin, *Women at Work: The Transformation of Work and Community in Lowell, Massachusetts, 1826–1860* (1979); Faye E. Dudden, *Serving Women: Household Service in Nineteenth-Century America* (1983); Robert Ernst, *Immigrant Life in New York City, 1825–1863* (1949); John Faragher, *Sugar Creek* (1986); Michael Feldberg, *The Turbulent Era: Riot and Disorder in Jacksonian America* (1980); Michael Frisch, *Town into City: Springfield, Massachusetts and the Meaning of Community, 1840–1880* (1972); *Philadelphia, 1800–1880* (1989); Richard Stott, J. Ritchie Garrison, *Landscape and Material Life in Franklin, Massachusetts, 1770–1860* (1991);

David A. Gerber, *The Making of an American Pluralism: Buffalo, New York, 1825–60* (1989); Howard M. Gitelman, *Workingmen of Waltham* (1974); Steven Hahn and Jonathan Prude, eds., *The Countryside in the Age of Capitalist Transformation* (1985); Oscar Handlin, *Boston's Immigrants*, rev. ed. (1959); Marcus L. Hansen, *The Atlantic Migration, 1607–1860* (1940); William F. Hartford, *Working People of Holyoke* (1990); Joel T. Headley, *Great Riots of New York, 1712–1873* (1970); Willard A. Heaps, *Riots, U.S.A., 1765–1970* (1970); Susan Hirsch, *Roots of the American Working Class: The Industrialization of Crafts in Newark, 1800–1860* (1978); Joan M. Jensen, *Loosening the Bonds: Mid-Atlantic Farm Women, 1750–1850* (1986); Maldwyn A. Jones, *American Immigration* (1960); Alice Kessler-Harris, *Out to Work: A History of Wage-Earning Women in the United States* (1982); Alexander Keyssar, *Out of Work: The First Century of Unemployment in Massachusetts* (1986); Peter R. Knights, *The Plain People of Boston, 1830–1860* (1971); Roger Lane, *Policing the City: Boston, 1822–1855* (1967), and *Violent Death in the City: Suicide, Accident and Murder in Nineteenth Century Philadelphia* (1979); Jack Larkin, *The Transformation of Everyday Life* (1989); Bruce Laurie, *Artisans into Workers* (1989), and *Working People of Philadelphia* (1980); Kerby A. Miller, *Emigrants and Exiles: Ireland and the Irish Exodus to North America* (1985); Brian C. Mitchell, *The Paddy Camps: The Irish of Lowell* (1988); Eric H. Monkkonen, *Police in Urban America* (1981); Edward Pessen, *Most Uncommon Jacksonians: Radical Leaders of the Early Labor Movement* (1967), and *Riches, Class and Power Before the Civil War* (1973); Jonathan Prude, *The Coming of Industrial Order: Town and Factory Life in Rural Massachusetts, 1810–1860* (1983); Leonard D. Richards, *"Gentlemen of Property and Standing": Anti-Abolitionist Mobs in Jacksonian America* (1970); James F. Richardson, *The New York Police: Colonial Times to 1901* (1970), and *Urban Police in the United States* (1974); W. J. Rorabaugh, *The Craft Apprentice* (1986); Steven J. Ross, *Workers on the Edge: Work, Leisure, and Politics in Industrializing Cincinnati* (1985); Billy G. Smith, *The "Lower" Sort: Philadelphia's Laboring People, 1750–1800* (1990); Lee Soltow, *Men and Wealth in the United States, 1850–1870* (1975); Christine Stansell, *City of Women: The Female Laboring Poor in New York, 1789–1860* (1986); Allen Steinberg, *The Transformation of Criminal Justice: Philadelphia, 1800–1880* (1989); Richard Stott, *Workers in the Metropolis: Class, Ethnicity, and Youth in Antebellum New York City* (1990); Philip

Taylor, *The Distant Magnet: European Emigration to the U.S.A.* (1971); Stephan Thernstrom, *Poverty and Progress, Social Mobility in a Nineteenth Century City* (1964), and *The Other Bostonians* (1973); Anthony F. C. Wallace, *Rockdale: The Growth of an American Village in the Early Industrial Revolution* (1978); Norman Ware, *The Industrial Worker, 1840–1860* (1924); Paul O. Weinbaum, *Mobs and Demogogues: The New York Response to Collective Violence* (1979); Sean Wilentz, *Chants Democratic: New York City and the Rise of the American Working Class, 1788–1850* (1984).

SOUTHERN DISTINCTIVENESS

Edward L. Ayers, *Vengeance and Justice: Crime and Punishment in the 19th Century American South* (1984); Fred Bateman and Thomas Weiss, *A Deplorable Scarcity: The Failure of Industrialization in the Slave Economy* (1981); Carol Bleser, ed., *In Joy and In Sorrow: Women, Family, and Marriage in the Victorian South* (1991); John B. Boles and Evelyn Thomas Nolen, *Interpreting Southern History* (1987); Blaine A. Brownell and David R. Goldfield, eds, *The City in Southern History* (1977); Dickson D. Bruce, Jr., *Violence and Culture in the Antebellum South* (1979); Orville Vernon Burton and Robert C. McMath, Jr., eds., *Class, Conflict and Consensus: Antebellum Southern Community Studies* (1982); Randolph B. Campbell, *A Southern Community in Crisis: Harrison County, Texas, 1850–1880* (1983); Randolph B. Campbell and Richard G. Lowe, *Wealth and Power in Antebellum Texas* (1977); Jane Turner Censer, *North Carolina Planters and Their Children, 1800–1860* (1984); Catherine Clinton, *The Plantation Mistress: Woman's World in the Old South* (1982); William J. Cooper, Jr., *South and the Politics of Slavery* (1978); William J. Cooper, Jr. and Thomas E. Terrill, *The American South: A History* (1990); Carl N. Degler, *The Other South: Southern Dissenters in the Nineteenth Century* (1974); Clement Eaton, *The Freedom-Of-Thought Struggle in the Old South*, rev. ed. (1964); Drew Gilpin Faust, *A Sacred Circle: The Dilemma of the Intellectual in the Old South* (1977), *The Ideology of Slavery, 1830–1860* (1981), and *James Henry Hammond and the Old South* (1982); James D. Foust, *The Yeoman Farmer and Westward Expansion of U.S. Cotton Production* (1975); Elizabeth Fox-Genovese, *Within the Plantation Household* (1988); George Fredrickson, *The Black Image in the White Mind* (1971); Alison Goodyear Freehling, *Drift Toward Dissolution: The Virginia Slavery Debate of 1831–1832* (1982); Jean E. Friedman, *The Enclosed Garden: Women and Community in the Evangelical South, 1830–1900* (1985); Eugene D. Genovese, *The Political Economy of Slavery* (1965), and *The World the Slaveholders Made* (1969); Kees Gispen, ed., *What Made the South Different?* (1990); David R. Goldfield, *Cotton Fields and Skyscrapers: Southern City and Region, 1607–1980* (1982); George D. Green, *Finance and Economic Development in the Old South* (1972); Kenneth S. Greenberg, *Masters and Statesmen* (1985); J. William Harris, *Plain Folk and Gentry in a Slave Society* (1985); Michael S. Hindus, *Prison and Plantation: Crime, Justice, and Authority in Massachusetts and South Carolina, 1767–1878* (1980); Rachel N. Klein, *Unification of a Slave State: The Rise of the Planter Class in the South Carolina Backcountry* (1990); Suzanne Lebsock, *The Free Women of Petersburg, 1784–1860* (1984); Raimondo Luraghi, *The Rise and Fall of the Plantation South* (1978); Edward Magdol and Jon L. Wakelyn, eds., *The Southern Common People* (1980); Donald G. Mathews, *Religion in the Old South* (1977); Robert E. May, *The Southern Dream of a Caribbean Empire, 1854–1861* (1973); John McCardell, *The Idea of a Southern Nation* (1979); John Hebron Moore, *The Emergence of the Cotton Kingdom in the Old Southwest* (1988); James Oakes, *The Ruling Race* (1982), and *Slavery and Freedom: An Interpretation of the Old South* (1990); Anne Firor Scott, *The Southern Lady: From Pedestal to Politics, 1830–1930* (1970); Steven M. Stowe, *Intimacy and Power in the Old South* (1987); Michael Tadman, *Speculators and Slaves: Masters, Traders, and Slaves in the Old South* (1989); Ronald T. Takaki, *A Pro-Slavery Crusade: The Agitation to Reopen the African Slave Trade* (1971); William R. Taylor, *Cavalier and Yankee: The Old South and the American National Character* (1961); Larry E. Tise, *Proslavery: A History of the Defense of Slavery* (1987); Jack K. Williams, *Dueling in the Old South* (1980); Harold D. Woodman, *King Cotton & His Retainers: Financing & Marketing the Cotton Crop of the South, 1800–1825* (1968); Ralph A. Wooster, *The People in Power: Courthouse and Statehouse in the Lower South, 1850–1860* (1969), and *Politicians, Planters, and Plain Folk: Courthouse and Statehouse in the Upper South, 1850–1860* (1975); Gavin Wright, *The Political Economy of the Cotton South* (1978); Bertram Wyatt-Brown, *Southern Honor: Ethics and Behavior in the Old South* (1982).

SLAVERY

Ira Berlin, *Slaves Without Masters: The Free Negro in the Antebellum South* (1974); Eugene H. Berwanger, *The Frontier Against Slavery: Western Anti-Negro Prejudice and the Slavery Extension Controversy* (1967); John W. Blassingame, *The Slave Community: Plantation Life in the Antebellum South*, rev. ed. (1979), and *Slave Testimony: Two Centuries of Letters, Speeches, Interviews, and Autobiographies* (1977); John B. Boles, *Black Southerners, 1619–1869* (1983); John H. Bracey, Jr., August Meier, and Elliott Rudwick, eds., *American Slavery: The Question of Resistance* (1971); James O. Breeden, ed., *Advice Among Masters: The Ideal in Slave Management in the Old South* (1980); Michael Craton, ed., *Roots and Branches: Current Directions in Slave Studies* (1979); Daniel J. Crowley, ed., *African Folklore in the New World* (1977); Leonard P. Curry, *The Free Black in Urban America, 1800–1850* (1981); Paul A. David et al., eds., *Reckoning with Slavery* (1976); Charles B. Dew, "The Slavery Experience," in *Interpreting Southern History*, John B. Boles and Evelyn Thomas Nolen, eds. (1987); Dena J. Epstein, *Sinful Tunes and Spirituals: Black Folk Music to the Civil War* (1977); Paul D. Escott, *Slavery Remembered* (1979); Robert William Fogel, *Without Consent or Contract: The Rise and Fall of American Slavery* (1989); Eugene D. Genovese, *From Rebellion to Revolution: Afro-American Slave Revolts in the Making of the Modern World* (1979), and *Roll, Jordan, Roll: The World the Slaves Made* (1974); Claudia D. Goldin, *Urban Slavery in the American South, 1820–1860* (1976); Herbert G. Gutman, *The Black Family in Slavery and Freedom, 1750–1925* (1976), and *Slavery and the Numbers Game* (1975); Janet Sharp Hermann, *The Pursuit of a Dream* (1981); Joseph E. Holloway, *Africanisms in American Culture* (1990); Michael P. Johnson and James L. Roark, *Black Masters: A Free Family of Color in the Old South* (1984), and eds., *No Chariot Let Down: Charleston's Free People of Color on the Eve of the Civil War* (1984); James Hugo Johnston, *Race Relations in Virginia & Miscegenation in the South, 1776–1860* (1970); Jacqueline Jones, *Labor of Love, Labor of Sorrow* (1985); Charles Joyner, *Down by the Riverside: A South Carolina Slave Community* (1984); Kenneth F. Kiple and Virginia Himmelsteib King, *Another Dimension to the Black Diaspora: Diet, Disease, and Racism* (1981); Lawrence Levine, *Black Culture and Black Consciousness* (1977); Ronald L. Lewis, *Coal, Iron, and Slaves* (1979); Leon Litwack, *North of Slavery: The Negro in the Free States* (1961); Donald G. Mathews, *Religion in the Old South* (1977); Gary B. Mills, *The Forgotten People: Cane River's Creoles of Color* (1977); Michael Mullin, ed., *American Negro Slavery* (1976); Gary B. Nash, *Forging Freedom: The Formation of Philadelphia's Black Community* (1988); Gary B. Nash and Jean R. Soderlund, *Freedom by Degrees: Emancipation and its Aftermath in Pennsylvania* (1991); Stephen B. Oates, *The Fires of Jubilee: Nat Turner's Fierce Rebellion* (1975); Leslie Howard Owens, *This Species of Property: Slave Life and Culture in the Old South* (1976); Peter J. Parish, *Slavery: History and Historians* (1989); Jane H. Pease and William H. Pease, *They Who Would Be Free: Blacks' Search for Freedom, 1830–1861* (1990); Richard Price, ed., *Maroon Societies: Rebel Slave Communities in the Americas*, 2d ed. (1979); Albert J. Raboteau, *Slave Religion: The "Invisible Institution" in the Antebellum South* (1978); George P. Rawick, *From Sundown to Sunup: The Making of the Black Community* (1972); Willie Lee Rose, ed., *A Documentary History of Slavery in North America* (1976), and *Slavery and Freedom* (1982); Todd L. Savitt, *Medicine and Slavery* (1978); William K. Scarborough, *The Overseer: Plantation Management in the Old South* (1966); Kenneth M. Stampp, *The Peculiar Institution: Slavery in the Antebellum South* (1956); Robert S. Starobin, ed., *Denmark Vesey: the Slave Conspiracy of 1822* (1970), and *Industrial Slavery in the Old South* (1970); Dorothy Sterling, ed., *We Are Your Sisters: Black Women in the Nineteenth Century* (1984); Sterling Stuckey, *Slave Culture* (1987); Mark Tushnet, *The American Law of Slavery, 1810–1860* (1981); William L. Van Deburg, *The Slave Drivers* (1979); Michael Vlach, *The Afro-American Tradition in Decorative Arts* (1978); Richard C. Wade, *Slavery in the Cities: The South, 1820–1860* (1964); Alan Watson, *Slave Law in the Americas* (1989); Thomas L. Webber, *Deep Like the Rivers: Education in the Slave Quarter Community, 1831–1865* (1978); Deborah Gray White, *Ar'n't I a Woman: Female Slaves in the Plantation South* (1985); Joel Williamson, *New People: Miscegenation and Mulattoes in the United States* (1980).

CHAPTER 13

Surge to the Pacific

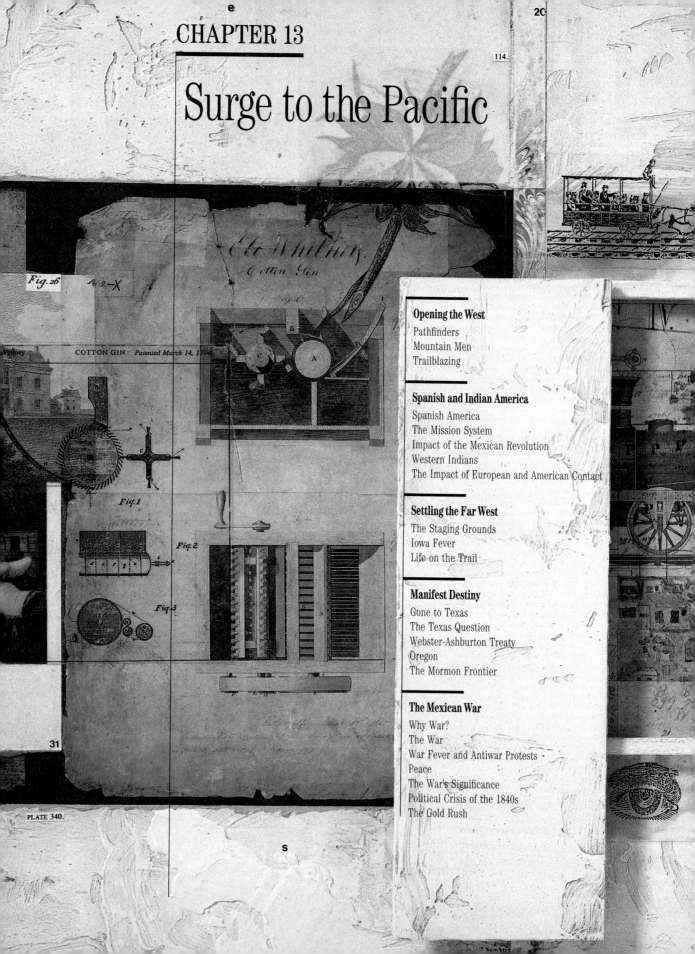

Early in April, 1846, 87 pioneers led by George Donner, a well-to-do 62-year-old farmer, set out from Springfield, Illinois, for California. As this group of pioneers headed westward, they never imagined the hardship and tragedy that awaited them. Like many emigrants, they were ill-prepared for the dangerous trek. The pioneers' 27 wagons were loaded not only with necessities but with fancy foods and liquor and such luxuries as built-in beds and stoves. George Donner's wife Tamsen had sewn $10,000 into a quilt and packed a wagon full of paints and schoolbooks for a young ladies' academy she planned to establish in California.

On July 20, at Fort Bridger, Wyoming, the party decided to take a shortcut. Lansford W. Hastings, an explorer, wagon train guide, and California booster, had suggested in a guidebook that pioneers could save 400 miles by cutting south of the Great Salt Lake. Hastings himself had never taken his own shortcut. He was trying to overthrow California's weak Mexican government and hoped to bring in enough emigrants to start a revolution. His misleading advice was designed to attract settlers to California.

At first, the trail was "all that could be desired." But soon huge boulders, arid desert, and dangerous mountain passes slowed the expedition to a crawl. During one stretch, the party traveled only 36 miles in 21 days. A desert crossing that Hastings said would take 2 days actually took 6 days and nights and forced the party to bury many of its valuables in the sand.

Twelve weeks after leaving Fort Bridger, the Donner party reached the eastern Sierra Nevada Mountains and prepared to cross Truckee Pass, the last remaining barrier before they arrived in California's Sacramento Valley. On October 31, they climbed the high Sierra ridges in an attempt to cross the pass, but early snows and 5-foot high drifts blocked their path. "The snow came on so suddenly," Leanna Donner wrote, "that we had barely time to pitch our tent, and put up a brush shed, as it were, one side of which was open."

Trapped by the early snow, the party built crude tents and tepees, covered with clothing, blankets, and animal hides, which were soon buried under 14 feet of snow. The pioneers intended to slaughter their livestock for food, but many of the animals perished in 40-foot snow drifts. To survive, the Donner party was forced to eat mice, their rugs, and even their shoes. In the end, surviving members of the party escaped starvation only by eating the flesh of those who died.

Finally in mid-December, a group of 12 men and 5 women made a last-ditch effort to cross the pass to find help. They took only a six-day supply of rations, consisting of finger-sized pieces of dried beef—two pieces a person per day. During a severe storm, two of the group died. The surviving members of the party "stripped the flesh from their bones, roasted and ate it, averting their eyes from each other, and weeping." More than a month passed before seven frost-bitten survivors reached an American settlement. By then, the rest had died and two Indian guides had been shot and eaten.

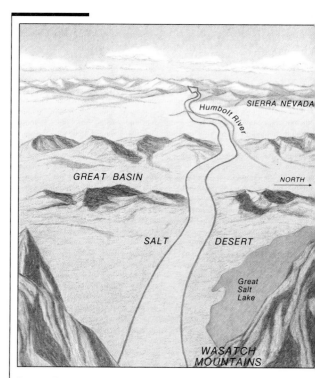

Donner Party
Western emigrants like the Donner party were ill-prepared for the dangers of travel to the Far West.

Relief teams immediately sought to rescue the pioneers still trapped near Truckee Pass. During the winter, four successive rescue parties broke through and brought out the survivors. The situation that the rescuers found was unspeakably gruesome. Thirteen were dead. Surviving members of the Donner party were delirious from hunger and overexposure. One survivor was found in a small cabin next to a cannibalized body of a young boy. Of the original 87 members of the party, only 47 survived.

It took Americans a century and a half to expand as far west as the Appalachian Mountains, a few hundred miles from the Atlantic coast. It took another 50 years to push the frontier to the Mississippi River. By 1830 fewer than 100,000 pioneers had crossed the Mississippi.

Only a small number of explorers, fur trappers, traders, and missionaries had ventured far beyond the Mississippi River. These trailblazers drew a picture of the American West as a land of promise, a paradise of plenty, filled with fertile valleys and rich land. During the 1840s, tens of thousands of Americans began the process of settling the West beyond the Mississippi River. Thousands of families chalked GTT ("Gone to Texas") on their gates or painted "California or Bust" on their wagons and joined the trek westward. By 1850, pioneers had pushed the edge of settlement all the way to Texas, the Rocky Mountains, and the Pacific Ocean.

OPENING THE WEST

Before the nineteenth century, mystery shrouded the Far West. Mapmakers knew very little about the shape, size, or topography of the land west of the Mississippi River. French, British, and Spanish trappers, traders, and missionaries had traveled the Upper and Lower Missouri River and the British and Spanish had explored the Pacific coast, but most of western North America was an unknown.

The popular conception of the West was largely a mixture of legend and guesswork. Educated men and women, like Thomas Jefferson, believed that the West was populated by primeval beasts and that a "Northwest Passage" connected the Missouri River with the Columbia

Margaret Reed was one of only 47 survivors of the original party of 81 pioneers to reach California.

River and the Pacific Ocean. They had only a primitive conception of the Rocky Mountains. They believed that only a single ridge of mountains, known as the "Shining Mountains" or "Stony Mountains" needed to be crossed before one could see the Pacific Ocean.

Pathfinders

Beginning in 1803, American explorers, hunters, soldiers, naturalists, trappers, and traders accumulated an enormous body of geographical information about the West. The first wave of exploration was touched off on July 5, 1803, when President Thomas Jefferson appointed his personal secretary, Meriwether Lewis, and William Clark to explore the Missouri and Columbia rivers as far as the Pacific. As a politician interested in the rapid settlement and commercial development of the West, Jefferson wanted Lewis and Clark to establish American claims to the region west of the Rocky Mountains, gather information about furs and minerals in the region, and identify sites for trading posts and settlements. As a scientist, the president also instructed the expedition to collect information covering the diversity of life in the West, ranging from climate, geology, and plant growth to fossils of extinct animals and Indian religions, laws, and customs.

In 1806, the year that Lewis and Clark returned from their 8000-mile expedition, a young

Meriwether Lewis, assisted by army captain William Clark, 34 soldiers, ten civilians, and an Indian woman guide named Sacajawea, led an expedition up the Missouri River, across the northern Rocky Mountains, and along the tributaries of the Columbia River to the Pacific Ocean.

army lieutenant named Zebulon Montgomery Pike left St. Louis to explore the southern border of the Louisiana Territory, just as Lewis and Clark had explored the territory's northern portion. Traveling along the Arkansas River, Pike saw the towering peak that bears his name. He and his party then traveled into Spanish territory along the Rio Grande and Red River. Pike's description of the wealth of Spanish towns, primarily Chihuahua and Santa Fe, in the Southwest brought some American traders to the region.

Pike's report of his expedition, published in 1810, helped to create one of the most influential myths about the Great Plains: This region was nothing more than a "Great American Desert," a treeless and waterless land of dust storms and starvation. "Here," wrote Pike, is "barren soil, parched and dried up for eight months of the year . . . [without] a speck of vegetation." This image of the West as a region of savages, wild beasts, and deserts received

added support from another government-sponsored expedition, one led by Major Stephen H. Long in 1820 in search of the source of the Red River. Long's report described the West as "wholly unfit for cultivation, and . . . uninhabitable by a people depending upon agriculture for their subsistence." This report helped implant the image of the Great American Desert even more deeply in the American mind, retarding western settlement for a generation.

The view of the West as a dry, barren wasteland was not fully offset until the 1840s when another government-sponsored explorer, John C. Frémont, nicknamed "The Pathfinder," mapped much of the territory between the Mississippi Valley and the Pacific Ocean. His glowing descriptions of the West as a paradise of plenty captivated the imagination of many midwestern families who, by the 1840s, were eager for new lands to settle.

Mountain Men

Traders and trappers were more important than government explorers in opening the West to white settlement. Trappers and traders were the first U.S. citizens to exploit the West economically. They trapped beaver and bartered with Indians for pelts. They blazed the great westward trails through the Rockies and Sierra Nevada and stirred the popular imagination with stories of redwood forests, geysers, and fertile valleys in California, Oregon, and other areas west of the Rocky Mountains. The men also undermined the ability of the western Indians to resist white incursions by encouraging intertribal warfare and making Indians dependent on American manufactured goods. They killed off animals that provided a major part of the Indian hunting and gathering economy, distributed alcohol, and spread disease.

When Lewis and Clark completed their expedition, they brought back reports of rivers and streams in the northern Rockies teeming with beaver and otter. Fur traders and trappers quickly followed in their footsteps. Starting in 1807, keel boats ferried fur trappers up the Missouri River. Called "mountain men," these trappers brought $3,750,000 worth of furs to St. Louis between 1815 and 1830. By the mid-1830s, these trappers had marked out the overland trails that would lead pioneers to Oregon and California.

The central figures in the opening of the western fur trade were two entrepreneurs, William Henry Ashley and Andrew Henry, who established the Rocky Mountain Fur Company in 1822. Instead of buying skins from the Indians, Ashley and Henry inserted ads in the St. Louis newspapers asking for white trappers willing to go to the wilderness. Among the adventurous trappers who answered the ad were Jedediah Strong Smith (the first U.S. citizen known to have entered California from the east) and James Bridger (discoverer of the Great Salt Lake), whose exploits were legendary even in their own time. In 1822 Ashley and Henry sent a hundred trappers out along the upper Missouri River. Three years later, Ashley and Henry introduced the "rendezvous" system, under which trappers met once a year at an agreed-upon meeting place to barter pelts for supplies. "The rendezvous," wrote one participant, "is one continued scene of drunkenness, gambling, and brawling and fighting, as long as the money

and the credit of the trappers last." The trappers' rendezvous was notorious for its buffalo chases, shooting matches, duels, and gambling.

The life of the mountain men was difficult, dangerous, and violent. The novelist Washington Irving said that they lived "a life of more continued exertion, peril, and excitement" than any other Americans of their time. They were threatened by dangerous animals as well as by floods, blizzards, and exposure to the elements. Trappers also faced competition from the British Hudson's Bay Company, which in 1824 had established a fort on the banks of the Columbia River in Oregon and sent brigades of traders into the northern Rocky Mountains to search for pelts. One trapper in five died on the trails.

At the same time that mountain men searched for beaver in the Rockies and along the Columbia River, other groups of trappers, led by Jedediah Smith and James Pattie, trapped furs in the Southwest, then part of Mexico. In 1827 Smith and a party of 15 trappers, after nearly dying of thirst, discovered a westward route to California. It led across the burn-

In 1826 Jedediah Smith led a party of trappers through Utah, across the Colorado River, then across the Mojave Desert and the San Bernardino Mountains to the Pacific.

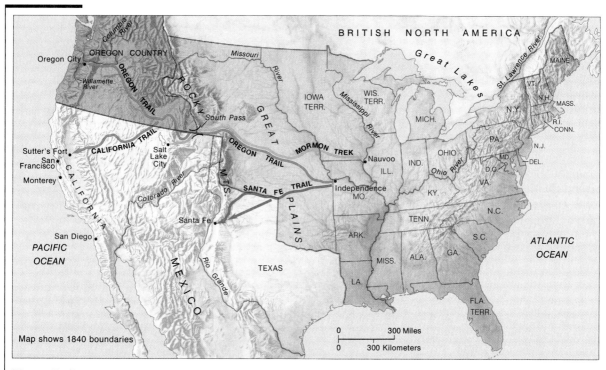

Western Trails

ing Mojave Desert and the San Bernardino Mountains to the Pacific Coast. Jim Beckwourth, a black mountain man who was the son of a Virginia slave, also discovered a pass through the Sierra Nevada that became part of the overland trail to California.

The western fur trade lasted only until 1840, when the last annual rendezvous was held. Beaver hats for gentlemen went out of style in favor of silk hats, bringing the romantic era of the mountain man, dressed in a fringed buckskin suit, to an end. Fur bearing animals had been trapped out, and profits from trading, which amounted to as much as 2000 percent during the early years, fell steeply. Instead of hunting furs, some trappers became scouts for the United States Army or pilots for the wagon trains that were beginning to carry pioneers to Oregon and California.

Trailblazing

The Santa Fe and Oregon trails were the two principal routes to the Far West. William Becknell, an American trader, opened the Santa Fe

Trail in 1821. Ultimately the trail tied the New Mexican Southwest economically to the rest of the United States and hastened American penetration of the region.

On September 1, 1821, Becknell left Arrow Rock, Missouri, with a band of men and $300 worth of goods on pack animals. Two months and nearly 800 miles later his caravan arrived in Santa Fe. During the journey, Becknell had been forced to drink the blood from a mule's ear and the contents of a buffalo's stomach to survive when he could find no water. A year later, Becknell took the first wagons across the same crude trail.

The Santa Fe Trail served primarily commercial functions. From the early 1820s until the 1840s, an average of 80 wagons and 150 traders used the Santa Fe Trail each year. Mexican settlers in Santa Fe purchased cloth, hardware, glass, books, and the region's first printing press. Many goods were shipped on to Chihuahua and California. On their return east, American traders carried Mexican blankets, beaver pelts, wool, mules, and Mexican silver coins. By the 1850s and 1860s, more than 5000 wagons a year took the trail across long stretches of desert, dangerous water crossings, and treacherous mountain passes.

From its beginnings, the Santa Fe Trail stirred the imaginations of Americans. Before Becknell blazed the Santa Fe Trail, few Americans had entered the Spanish Southwest. Although Santa Fe had served as the northern capital of Spain's vast American empire for 212 years, Spain had severely restricted the town's contact with Americans. Then, just weeks before Becknell arrived, Mexico proclaimed independence from Spain, and Americans began to trade with the area. By the 1830s, traders had extended the trail into California, with branches reaching Los Angeles and San Diego. The Santa Fe Trail made the Spanish Southwest economically dependent on the United States and first brought Americans into the areas that became Arizona, California, and New Mexico.

In 1811 and 1812 fur trappers marked out the Oregon Trail, the longest and most famous pioneer route in American history. This trail crossed about 2000 miles from Independence, Missouri, to the Columbia River country of Oregon. During the 1840s, 12,000 pioneers traveled the trail's entire length to Oregon. After gold was discovered in California in 1848, thousands of gold seekers took an offshoot of the Oregon Trail through the Sierra Nevada to the California gold fields. In the summer of 1850, the peak year of pioneering, 55,000 gold seekers followed that trail to California.

Travel on the Oregon Trail was a tremendous test of human endurance. The journey by wagon train took six months. Settlers encountered prairie fires, sudden blizzards, and impassable mountains. Cholera and other diseases were common, and food, water, and wood were scarce. Only the stalwart dared brave the physical hardship of the westward trek.

SPANISH AND INDIAN AMERICA

When Americans ventured westward, they did not enter virgin land. Large parts of the Far West were already occupied by Indians and Mexicans, who had lived in the region for hundreds of years and established their own distinctive ways of life.

Spanish America

Between 1528 and 1800, Spain established imperial claims and isolated outposts in an area extending from present-day Montana to Mexico and from California to the Mississippi River. Half a century before the first English colonists arrived at Jamestown, Spain had permanent settlements in the Far West, founded partly as a way to keep out other European powers. Then, in the late sixteenth century, Spain planted a colony in New Mexico and a century later built the first settlements in what is now Arizona and Texas. In the late eighteenth century, fears of British and Russian occupation of the Pacific Coast led Spain to also establish outposts in California.

The Mission System

The Spanish clergy, particularly Jesuits and Franciscans, played a critical role in settling the Southwest, using the mission system. Their missions were designed to spread Christianity among, and establish control over, native populations. In some areas, they forced Indians to live in mission communities, where the priests taught them weaving, blacksmithing, candle-making, and leather-working, and forced them

Between 1769 and 1823, Spain built 21 missions between San Diego and San Francisco. Here Native Americans perform a dance at the San Francisco mission in 1816.

to work in workshops, orchards, and fields for long hours. The missions were most successful in New Mexico (despite a successful Indian revolt in 1680) and California, and far less successful in Arizona and Texas.

Mission life reached its peak in California, an area that Spain did not begin to colonize, despite its closeness to Mexico, until 1769. In the mid-eighteenth century, Spain learned that Russian seal hunters and traders were moving south from Alaska into California. Determined to halt the Russian advance down the Pacific Coast, Spanish authorities dispatched Captain Gaspar de Portola to explore and settle the region. On his expedition de Portola discovered San Francisco Bay and established presidios (military forts) at San Diego and Monterey. Accompanying de Portola's expedition was a Franciscan father Junipero Serra, who established the first California mission, San Diego de Alacala, near the present-day site of San Diego. Between 1769 and 1823, Spain established 21 missions in California, extending from San Diego northward to Sonoma. By 1830, 30,000 of California's 300,000 Indians worked on missions, where they harvested grain and herded 400,000 cattle, horses, goats, hogs, and sheep.

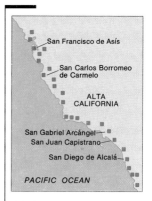

California Missions

Mission life reached its peak of development in California.

Impact of the Mexican Revolution

The Mexican Revolution (1810–1821) had important effects on the Southwest. It definitely encouraged American settlement in Texas and California and undermined the mission system. The revolution began in 1810 when Miguel Hidalgo y Costilla, a Mexican priest, led a revolt against Spanish rule. The uprising was suppressed, but it represented the beginning of Mexico's struggle for independence. Not until September 21, 1821, however, did Mexico finally win independence from Spain.

The Mexican Revolution marked the beginning of a period of far-reaching change in the Southwest. In New Mexico and Arizona, the collapse of Spanish authority allowed American traders to bring American goods into the area and trappers to hunt for beaver. In Texas, Mexican independence convinced many Americans that the province was theirs for the taking. In 1820 Moses Austin of Missouri successfully petitioned Spanish officials in San Antonio to allow Americans to colonize the sparsely populated province; in 1821 Mexican authorities reaffirmed the grant to Austin's son, Stephen. Then American adventurers staged a series of filibuster expeditions into Texas, which contributed to a general feeling that any American could move in. Under Mexican rule, California was also opened up to American commerce and settlement. By 1848 Americans made up about half of California's non-Indian population.

Mexican independence also led to the demise of the mission system in California. After

After it won its independence from Spain, Mexico secularized the missions and divided the land into ranchos. This painting shows a master of a rancho in the Mexican Southwest.

the revolution, the missions were "secularized"—broken up and their property sold or given away to private citizens. In 1833–1834 the Mexican government confiscated California mission properties and exiled the Franciscan friars. As a result, mission properties fell into private hands. By 1846 mission land and cattle had largely passed into the hands of 800 private landowners called rancheros, who controlled 8 million acres of land in units (ranchos) ranging in size from 4500 to 50,000 acres. The ranchos were run like feudal estates, and the Indians who worked on the estates had a status similar to that of slaves. Indeed, the death rate of Indians who worked on ranchos was twice as high as the rate among Southern slaves, and by 1848 one-fifth of California's Indian population had died.

Western Indians

In 1840, before large numbers of pioneers and farmers crossed the Mississippi, at least 300,000 Indians lived in the Southwest, on the Great Plains, in California, and on the northwest Pacific Coast. The Native American population was divided into more than 200 tribes. Their life-styles ranged from nomadic hunting and gathering to sedentary farming. Their social organization was equally diverse, with each tribe having its own language, religious beliefs, kinship patterns, and system of government.

The best-known of the western Indians are the 23 Indian tribes—including the Cheyenne and Sioux—who lived on the Great Plains and hunted buffalo, antelope, deer, and elk for subsistence. For many present-day Americans, the Plains Indians, riding on horseback, wearing a warbonnet, and living in a tepee, are regarded as the typical American Indians. In fact, however, the Plains Indians first acquired the horse from the Spanish in the sixteenth century. Not until the middle of the eighteenth century did these tribes have a large supply of horses and not until the early to mid-nineteenth century did most Plains Indians have firearms.

South and west of the Plains, in the huge arid region that is now Arizona and New Mexico, sophisticated farmers, like the Hopi, Zuni, and other Pueblo groups, coexisted with nomadic hunters and gatherers, like the Apache and Navajo. In the Great Basin, the harsh barren region between the Sierra Nevada and the Rocky Mountains, food was so scarce that nations like the Paiutes and the Gosiutes subsisted on berries, pine nuts, roots, insects, rabbits, reptiles, and mice.

More than 100,000 Indians still lived in California when the area was acquired by the United States in 1848. Most of these people occupied small villages during the winter but moved during the rest of the year gathering wild plants and seeds, hunting small game, and fishing in the rivers.

The large number of tribes living along the northwest Pacific Coast developed an elaborate social hierarchy based on wealth and descent. These people found an abundant food supply in the sea, coastal rivers, and forests. They took salmon, seal, whale, and otter from the coastal waters and hunted deer, moose, and elk in the forests.

The Impact of European and American Contact

Even before the Civil War, contact with white traders, trappers, and settlers caused a dramatic decline in Indian populations. In California disease and deliberate campaigns of extermination killed 70,000 Indians between 1849 and 1859. Many Indian women were forced into concubinage and many men into virtual slavery. One Indian hater expressed widespread sentiments: "We must kill them big and little, nits make lice" (nits are the eggs of lice). In the Great Basin, impoverished Gosiutes and Paiutes were shot by trappers for sport. In Texas, the Karankawas and many of the other original tribes of the area largely disappeared. Further west, Comanche, Kiowa, and Apache warriors bitterly resisted white encroachment on their land. White settlers accused these warriors of impaling women on fenceposts, staking men under the sun with their eyelids removed, and heaping burning coals on their genitals. Tribes in the Pacific Northwest and the northern Plains struggled desperately to slow the arrival of whites along the Oregon Trail. The Nez Percé and Flathead Indians expelled American mis-

Comanche Chasing Buffalo with Bows and Lances, by George Catlin. Catlin lived with many different tribes of the Plains and produced a faithful record of Native American life, both in his book *Letters and Notes on the Manners, Customs and Condition of the North American Indians*, published in 1841, and in hundreds of sketches, engravings, and paintings.

sionaries from their tribal lands, and the Snake, Cheyenne, Shasta, and Rogue River Indians tried futilely to cut emigrant routes. The federal government employed the army in protecting settlers and attacking the western Indians and forced the cession of 147 million acres of tribal lands to the United States between 1853 and 1857.

SETTLING THE FAR WEST

During the early 1840s, thousands of pioneers headed westward toward California and Oregon. In 1841 the first party of 69 pioneers left Missouri for California, led by an Ohio schoolteacher named John Bidwell. The members of the party knew little about western travel: "We only knew that California lay to the west." The hardships the party endured were nearly unbearable. They were forced to abandon their wagons and eat their pack animals, "half roasted, dripping with blood." American pioneering of the Far West had begun. The next year another 200 pioneers went west. Within two years, more than a thousand pioneers had crossed the Plains into California and Oregon. Who were these pioneers? What forces drove them to abandon civilization for the wilderness?

The Staging Grounds

The rugged pioneer life was not a new experience for most of these early western settlers. Most of the pioneers who migrated to the Far West came from the states that border the Mississippi River: Missouri, Arkansas, Louisiana, and Illinois. These states had only recently acquired statehood: Louisiana in 1812, Illinois in 1818, Missouri in 1821, and Arkansas in 1836.

Pioneering was a familiar experience for many of these people. Either they or their parents had already moved several times before reaching the Mississippi Valley. During the early nineteenth century, the Mississippi Valley seemed to many observers to be a region of restless energy, violence, and boisterous tall talk. It was a land where yeomen farmers and respectable traders lived alongside lawless gamblers, rivermen, and roustabouts.

Contemporary observers were shocked by the brutal pastimes of the Mississippi Valley, which included "rough-and-tumble" bare-fisted fighting in which combatants tried to gouge out an opponent's eyes and tear off his testicles. Mark Twain vividly described the kinds of men he had seen while growing up in Hannibal, Missouri: "Rude, uneducated, brave, suffering terrific hardships with sailor-like stoicism; heavy drinkers . . . heavy fighters, reckless fellows, every one, elephantinely jolly, foul witted, profane; profligal of their money . . . yet in the main, honest, trustworthy, faithful to promises and duty, and often picaresquely magnanimous."

The Mississippi Valley was filled with restless men and women, thirsty for adventure and eager to better themselves. In 1833, when Iowa was cleared of Indians and opened to settlement, thousands of families pulled up stakes and poured into the area.

Iowa Fever

In 1854 Horace Greeley, a newspaper editor, gave Josiah B. Grinnell, a New Yorker, a famous piece of advice. "Go West, young man, and grow up with the country," said Greeley. Grinnell took Greeley's advice, moved west, and later founded Grinnell, Iowa.

Before 1830 Iowa was Indian land, occupied by the Sauk, Fox, Missouri, Pottowatomi, and other Indian tribes. The defeat of the Sauk and Fox Indians in the Black Hawk War in 1832 opened the first strip of Iowa to settlement. Even before Iowa became a territory in 1838, settlers raced across the Mississippi and established farms and founded such cities as Davenport, Dubuque, and Iowa City. By 1840 Iowa's population had risen to 40,000.

Because no government land office was established in Iowa until 1838, many early settlers were squatters who set up farms on land that they did not own. Because they had cleared the land and built houses, they believed that the federal government would give them the right to purchase the land at minimum prices when it came up for sale. Unfortunately, later settlers, known as "claim-jumpers," tried to take the squatters' land away by outbidding them at public auctions or taking over their land when a family went to town for supplies. Squatters formed more than 100 land-claims associations—extra-legal associations of local settlers—to eliminate competitive bidding and protect their holdings when the lands were offered for sale.

In 1841 Congress passed the Preemption Bill of 1841, which recognized squatters' rights. The bill provided that squatters who lived on and made improvements on surveyed government land could have the first option to buy up to 160 acres for $1.25 an acre.

At the same time that settlers poured into Iowa, other emigrants migrated to Michigan, Minnesota, and Wisconsin. Lumberjacks and miners were the first to arrive. Soon they were followed by farmers and tradesmen. Even before this northern tier of states was filled, people in the Mississippi Valley leapfrogged treeless prairies, deserts, and mountains for the West Coast.

It was not until the 1870s and 1880s that pioneers settled on the prairies of Nebraska, Montana, and the Dakotas because these areas were much drier and settlers preferred well-watered regions near rivers and streams. Only when this land was no longer available did pioneers edge onto the more difficult prairies, using windmills to pump water and unplowed land or sod for their houses. Most of this settlement would occur after the Civil War.

Life on the Trail

Each spring, pioneers gathered at Independence and St. Joseph, Missouri, and Council Bluffs, Iowa, to begin a 2000-mile journey westward. For many families, the great spur for emigration was economic: the financial depression of the late 1830s, accompanied by floods and epidemics in the Mississippi Valley. Said one woman: "We had nothing to lose, and we might gain a fortune." Between 1841 and 1867, more than 350,000 trekked along the overland trails.

Except for fortune hunters heading to California, settlers traveled in family units. Even single men attached themselves to family groups. In virtually every recorded case, it was the husband, and not the wife, who made the decision to set out on the overland trail. Said one woman, "the thought of becoming a pioneer's wife never entered my mind."

At first, pioneers tried to maintain the rigid sexual division of labor that characterized early nineteenth century America. Men drove the wagons and livestock, stood guard duty, and hunted buffalo and antelope for extra meat. Women got up at four in the morning, collected wood and "buffalo chips" (animal dung used for fuel), hauled water, kindled campfires, kneaded dough, and milked cows. At the end of the day,

men expected women to fix dinner, make up beds, air out the wagons to prevent mildew, wash the clothes, and tend the children. The demands of the journey forced a blurring of gender role distinctions for women, who performed many chores previously reserved for men. They drove wagons, yoked cattle, and loaded wagons. Some men even did things such as cooking, previously regarded as women's work.

Accidents, disease, and sudden disaster were ever-present dangers. Children fell out of wagons, oxen hauling wagons became exhausted and died, and diseases such as typhoid, dysentery, and mountain fever killed many pioneers. Emigrant parties also suffered devastation from buffalo stampedes, prairie fires, and floods. Pioneers buried at least 20,000 emigrants along the Oregon Trail.

Still, despite the hardships of the experience, few emigrants ever regretted their decision to move west. As one pioneer put it: "Those who crossed the plains . . . never forgot the ungratified thirst, the intense heat and bitter cold, the craving hunger and utter physical exhustion of the trail. . . . But there was another side. True they had suffered, but the satisfaction of deeds accomplished and difficulties overcome more than compensated and made the overland passage a thing never to be forgotten."

MANIFEST DESTINY

In 1845 John L. O'Sullivan, editor of the *Democratic Review*, referred in his magazine to America's "Manifest Destiny to overspread the continent allotted by Providence for the free development of our yearly multiplying millions." One of the most influential slogans ever coined, *manifest destiny* expressed the romantic emotion that led Americans to risk their lives to settle the Far West.

The idea that America had a special destiny to stretch across the continent motivated many people to migrate West. The very idea of manifest destiny encouraged men and women to dream big dreams. "We Americans," wrote Herman Melville, one of this country's greatest novelists, "are the peculiar, chosen people—the Israel of our time." Manifest destiny inspired a 29-

Life along the westward trails was a tremendous test of human endurance. Pioneers encountered arid desert, difficult mountain passes, dangerous rivers, and quicksand.

year-old named Stephen F. Austin to talk grandly of colonizing the Mexican province of Texas with "North American population, enterprise and intelligence." It led expansionists, united behind the slogan "54° 40′ or fight!," to demand that the United States should own the entire Pacific Northwest all the way to the southern border of Alaska. Aggressive nationalists invoked the idea to justify Indian removal, war with Mexico, and American expansion into Cuba and Central America. More positively, the idea of manifest destiny inspired missionaries, farmers, and pioneers, who dreamed only of transforming plains and fertile valleys into farms and small towns.

Gone to Texas

In 1822, when the first caravan of American traders traversed the Santa Fe Trail and the first hundred fur trappers searched the Rocky Mountains for beaver, a small number of Americans followed trails to another frontier—Texas.

American settlement in Texas began with the encouragement of first the Spanish, and then Mexican, governments. In the summer of 1820 Moses Austin, a bankrupt 59-year-old Missourian, asked Spanish authorities for a large Texas land tract that he would promote and sell to American pioneers. Austin's request should have seemed preposterous. His background was that of a Philadelphia dry goods merchant, a Virginia mine operator, a Louisiana judge, and a Missouri banker. But early in 1821 the Spanish government gave him permission to settle 300 families in Texas. Spain welcomed the Americans for two reasons—to provide a buffer against illegal U.S. settlers, who were creating problems in east Texas even before the grant was made to Austin, and to help develop the land, since only 3500 native Mexicans had settled in Texas (which was part of the Mexican state of Coahuila y Tejas). Moses Austin did not live to see his dream realized. On a return trip from Mexico City, he died of exhaustion and exposure.

Before he died, his son Stephen promised to carry out the dream of colonizing Texas. In 1822 Stephen led the first group of 150 settlers to Texas. By the end of 1824, young Austin had

This 1879 painting by John Gast depicts the spirit of manifest destiny leading pioneers, farmers, railroads, and telegraphs across the continent.

attracted 272 colonists to Texas and had persuaded the newly independent Mexican government that encouragement of American immigration was the best way to develop Texas. To attract colonists, Mexico in 1825 gave land agents (called empresarios) 67,000 acres of land for every 200 families they brought to Texas. Mexico imposed two conditions on land ownership: Settlers had to become Mexican citizens and they had to convert to Roman Catholicism. By 1830 there were 16,000 Americans in Texas. At that time, Americans formed a 4-to-1 majority in the northern section of Coahuila y Tejas, but people of Hispanic heritage formed a majority in the state as a whole.

As the Anglo population swelled, Mexican authorities grew increasingly suspicious of the growing American presence. Mexico feared that the United States planned to use the Texas colonists to acquire the province by revolution. Finally, in 1827, the Mexican government sent General Manuel de Mier y Terán to investigate the situation.

In his report, Terán warned that unless the Mexican government took timely measures, American settlers in Texas were certain to rebel. Differences in language and culture, Terán believed, had produced bitter enmity between the colonists and native Mexicans. The colonists, he noted, refused to learn the Spanish language, maintained their own separate schools, and conducted most of their trade with the United States. They complained bitterly that they had to travel more than 500 miles to reach a Mexican court and resented the efforts of Mexican authorities to deprive them of the right to vote.

To reassert its authority over Texas, the Mexican government reaffirmed its constitutional prohibition against slavery throughout Mexico and established a chain of military posts occupied by convict soldiers, levied customs duties, restricted trade with the United States, and decreed an end to further American immigration. Initially, these actions might have provoked Texans to revolution. But in 1832 General Antonio López de Santa Anna, a Mexican politician and soldier, became Mexico's president. Colonists hoped that he would make Texas a self-governing state within the Mexican republic, separate from the much more populous Coahuila, south of the Rio Grande, thereby eliminating any reason for rebellion. Once in power, however, Santa Anna proved to be less liberal than many Americans had believed. In 1834 he overthrew Mexico's constitutional government, abolished state governments, and made himself dictator. When Stephen Austin went to Mexico City to try to settle the Texans' grievances, Santa Anna imprisoned him in a Mexican jail for a year.

As the situation in Texas grew increasingly tense, Santa Anna tried to tighten his grip on the province, by proposing to reinforce military garrisons in Texas. In the meantime, on November 3, 1835, American colonists adopted a constitution and organized a temporary government but voted overwhelmingly against declaring independence. A majority of colonists hoped to attract the support of Mexican liberals in a joint effort to depose Santa Anna and to restore power to the state governments, hopefully including a separate state of Texas.

One of the most colorful leaders of the struggle for Texas independence, Sam Houston lived for a time with the Cherokee Indians, was a popular hero of the Creek War, and later served as a congressman and governor of Texas.

While holding out the possibility of compromise, the Texans prepared for war by electing Sam Houston commander of whatever military forces he could muster. Houston, one of the larger-than-life figures who helped win Texas independence, had a remarkable background. At the age of 15, he had run away from home and lived for three years with the Cherokee Indians in eastern Tennessee. During the War of 1812, he had fought in the Creek War under Andrew Jackson. At 30 he was elected to the House of Representatives and at 34 he was elected governor of Tennessee. Many Americans regarded him as the heir apparent to Andrew Jackson.

Then, suddenly, in 1829 scandal struck. Houston married a woman 17 years younger than himself. Within three months, the marriage was mysteriously annulled. Depressed and humiliated, Houston resigned as governor. After wandering about the country as a near derelict, he returned to live with the Cherokee in present-day Arkansas and Oklahoma. During his stay with the tribe, Houston was instrumental in forging peace treaties among several warring Indian nations. In 1832 Houston traveled to Washington to demand that President Jackson live up to the terms of the removal treaty. Jackson did not meet Houston's demands, but instead apparently sent him unofficially to Texas to keep an eye on the American settlers and the growing anti-Mexican sentiment.

In the middle of 1835, scattered local outbursts erupted against Mexican rule. Then, a band of 300 to 500 Texas riflemen—who comprised the entire Texas army—captured Mexico's military headquarters in San Antonio. Revolution was underway.

Soon, the ominous news reached Texas that Santa Anna himself was marching north with 7000 soldiers to crush the revolt. In actuality, Santa Anna's army was not particularly impressive; it was filled with raw recruits and included many Indian troops who spoke and understood little Spanish. When Houston learned that Santa Anna's initial goal was to recapture San Antonio, he ordered San Antonio abandoned. But, 150 Texas rebels decided to defend the city and made their stand at an abandoned Spanish mission, the Alamo. The Texans were led by William Travis and Jim Bowie and included the frontier hero David Crockett.

For 12 days, Mexican forces lay siege to the Alamo. Travis issued an appeal for reinforcements, but only 32 men were able to cross Mexican lines. Legend has it that on the evening

(Continued on p. 418)

Texas Revolution

The revolution left Texas a lone republic, unrecognized by Mexico and unwanted by the United States.

By 8 A.M. on March 6, the fight at the Alamo was over. One hundred and eighty three defenders were dead, and three Mexican soldiers had fallen for each defender.

TEJANOS AT THE ALAMO

General Antonio López de Santa Anna, backed by some 2400 Mexican troops, put the Alamo under siege on February 23, 1836. On that day he ordered the hoisting of a red flag, meaning "no quarter," which only hardened the resolve of the Alamo's small contingent of defenders, including the legendary Jim Bowie, Davy Crockett, and William Barret Travis. Also inside the Alamo were men like Juan Seguin and Gregorio Esparza. They represented a handful of Tejano defenders. As native residents of Texas (named the province of Tejas in 1691 by the conquering Spanish), they despised Santa Anna for having so recently overthrown the Mexican Constitution of 1824 in favor of dictatorship.

San Antonio was a center of the Tejano population of Texas. Juan Seguin's father, Don Erasmo, was a wealthy local rancher who in earlier years had encouraged the opening of the Mexican province of Coahuila y Tejas to nonnative Anglos from the United States. Most of the Anglos settled far to the east of San Antonio, but those who traveled to the Tejano settlements knew Don Erasmo as a generous host who entertained lavishly at his hacienda, "Casa Blanca." His son Juan was also locally prominent and had helped immeasurably in driving Mexican troops under General Martin Perfecto de Cós, Santa Anna's brother-in-law, out of San Antonio late in 1835. His reward was a commission as a captain of Texas cavalry.

Much less is known about Gregorio Esparza. He lived with his wife and four children in San Antonio. Juan Seguin had recruited him for his cavalry company. When Santa Anna's advance troops appeared on February 23, Esparza quickly gathered up his family and rushed for protection behind the thick walls of the old Spanish mission known locally as the Alamo.

The Alamo defenders were in an all-but-impossible position, especially with Santa Anna tightening his siege lines every day. Inside the Alamo, the defenders looked to Jim Bowie for leadership, but he was seriously ill with pneumonia. So they accepted orders from William Barret Travis. With 1000 troops, Travis had argued, the Alamo would never fall. His numbers, however, were hardly more than 150. As a result, Travis regularly sent out couriers with urgent messages for relief. His words were direct. He would never "surrender or retreat." He would "die like a soldier who never forgets what is due to his own honor and that of his country." For those at the Alamo, the alternatives were now "VICTORY OR DEATH."

Late in February Travis, who would gain only 32 troops as reinforcements, prepared yet another appeal, this time addressed to Sam Houston, commander-in-chief of the Texas army. Time was running out, Travis wrote. "If they overpower us," he explained, "we hope posterity and our country will do our memory justice. Give me help, oh my country!" Travis handed the message to Juan Seguin, who borrowed Jim Bowie's horse and rode off with his aide, Antonio Cruz, under the cover of a driving rainstorm. They eventually found Houston, far to the east, but there was nothing anyone could do now to save those defenders still with Travis.

Early on the morning of March 6, 1836, the Alamo fell to 1800 attacking Mexican soldiers. The fighting was so brutal that 600 of Santa Anna's troops lay dead or wounded before the last of the 183 defenders faced mutilation from countless musket balls, bayonet thrusts, or summary executions after the battle. Gregorio Esparza was torn to shreds as the Mexicans reached the church inside the courtyard. Only women, children, Colonel Travis's slave Joe, and one Tejano, who claimed that he was a prisoner, survived. Later that day Mrs. Esparza got permission to bury her husband with Christian rites. Santa Anna issued orders to have the bodies of all other defenders heaped into piles and set on fire.

During the next several weeks Santa Anna's troops pushed steadily eastward with the goal of destroying another Texas army being hastily assembled by Sam Houston. The Seguins, father and son, played key parts in providing resistance. Don Erasmo worked furiously to collect needed food supplies, and Juan led troops in harassing and delaying the Mexican column, all of which aided in the staging of Houston's stunning victory over Santa Anna at the Battle of San Jacinto on April 21, 1836—the day the Republic of Texas secured its independence.

As the Texas Revolution gained momentum in late 1835 and early 1836, Tejanos had to choose which side to support. Some hoped that uniting with the Anglos would force Santa Anna to renounce his dictatorship in favor of the liberal 1824 constitution. Few actually favored independence because they knew that Anglos held them in contempt, which caused men like Gregorio Esparza's brother to join Santa Anna's army and fight against the Alamo defenders. He suspected that heavy-handed rule under the Mexican dictator could not be worse and might well be better than living under culturally and racially intolerant Anglos from the United States.

From the very outset, Anglos entering Texas spoke of Tejanos and Mexicans as debased human beings, comparable in many ways to Indian "savages" blocking the westward movement of white European civilization. In 1831 colonizer Stephen F. Austin wrote: "My object, the sole and only desire of my ambitions since I first saw Texas, was to . . . settle it with an intelligent, honorable, and enterprising people." Four years later Austin still wanted to see Texas "Americanized, that is settled by a population that will harmonize with their neighbors on the East, in language, political principles, common origin, sympathy, and even interest." The success of the Texas Revolution, from Austin's point of view, would assure that Anglo-Americans pouring into the region would not be ruled by what they considered an inferior native populace.

Increasingly before and after 1836, Anglo migrants employed terms of racial and cultural derision to describe the native Tejanos. They were the most "lazy, indolent, poor, starved set of people as ever the sun shined upon"; they were "slaves of popish superstitions and despotism"; and they would "spend days in gambling to gain a few bits" rather than "make a living by honest industry." With their mixture of blood from Spanish, Indian, and black parents, the native populace represented a "mongrel" race, a "swarthy looking people much resembling . . . mulattoes."

Worse yet, according to the Anglos, they behaved at times like depraved, violent, less-than-human creatures as personified by Santa Anna at the Alamo and by Mexican troops later at Goliad, where nearly 400 captured rebels were systematically shot to death. Wrote one Anglo veteran of the Texas Revolution late in life: "I thought that I could kill Mexicans as easily as I could deer and turkeys." He apparently did so while shouting: "Remember the Alamo! Remember Goliad!"

This veteran, like so many others looking back at the days of the Texas Revolution, only recalled selected portions of the Alamo story. They talked of the bravery of Bowie, Crockett, and Travis but ignored the courage of Tejanos like Don Erasmo and Juan Seguin and Gregorio Esparza. Nor did they remember that Juan Seguin received an honorable military discharge before serving as mayor of San Antonio until 1842 when Anglo rumormongers accused him of supporting an attempted military invasion from Mexico.

To save himself, Seguin had to flee across the border. Eventually he returned to his native Texas and quietly lived out his days far removed from the public limelight. No doubt Seguin wondered whether he had made the right decision in not joining the side of Santa Anna, especially as he experienced the racial and cultural malice directed at Mexican-Americans as the United States surged forward toward the Pacific. Although his thoughts are not known, it is fortunate that his story and those of other Tejano resisters have not been forgotten. Surely they too deserve remembrance as heroes of the Alamo and the Texas Revolution.

of March 5, 1836, Travis, realizing that defense of the Alamo was futile, drew a line in the dirt with his sword. Only those willing to die for Texas independence, Travis announced to the garrison, should step across the line and defend the Alamo. All but 2 men did. One refused to cross the line, and another, Jim Bowie, too sick to move from his cot, called over some friends and had them carry him across Travis's line.

At 5 A.M., March 6, Mexican troops scaled the mission's walls. By 8 A.M., the fighting was over. One hundred eighty-three defenders lay dead—including several Mexican defenders who had fought for Texas independence. (Seven defenders surrendered and were immediately executed, and approximately 15 persons survived, including an American woman and her child.) Mexican forces soaked the defenders' bodies in oil, stacked them like cordwood outside the mission, and set them ablaze. But if the Alamo was a military defeat, it was a psychological victory. Santa Anna's troops suffered 600 casualties—4 Mexican soldiers killed or wounded for every defender. "Remember the Alamo" became the battle cry of the Texas war of independence.

One disaster after another followed the Alamo. A Texas detachment at San Patricio was overwhelmed. Then, two weeks after the defeat at the Alamo, James Fannin and his men surrendered to Mexican forces outside of Goliad with the understanding that they would be treated as prisoners of war. But Santa Anna set aside the agreement. Instead, he ordered more than 350 Texans shot.

The defeats, however, had an unexpected side effect. They gave Sam Houston time to raise and train an army. Volunteers from the American South flocked to his banner. On April 21, his army of less than 800 men surprised Santa Anna's army as it camped out on the San Jacinto River, east of present-day Houston. The Texas rebels, who suffered 9 dead and 30 wounded, killed 630 of the enemy and captured 730. The next day, Houston's army captured Santa Anna himself and forced him to sign a treaty granting Texas its independence—a treaty that was never ratified by the Mexican government because it was acquired under duress.

For most Mexican settlers in Texas, defeat meant that they would be relegated to second-class social, political, and economic positions. The new Texas constitution denied citizenship and property rights to those who failed to support the revolution. All persons of Hispanic ancestry were considered in the "denial" category unless they could prove otherwise. Consequently, many Mexican landowners fled the region.

Texas grew rapidly following independence. In 1836 5000 immigrants arrived in Texas, boosting its population to 30,000. By 1847 its population had reached 140,000. The region also grew economically. Although cotton farming dominated the Texas economy, cattle were becoming an increasingly important industry. Many Mexican landowners abandoned cattle after the Texas Revolution, and by the 1840s, large numbers of wild cattle roamed the range. By 1850 the first American cowboys were driving 60,000 cattle a year to New Orleans and California.

These cowboys borrowed the clothing, customs, and even the songs of earlier Mexican

The first American cowboys borrowed the clothing and customs of Mexican cowhands known as *vaqueros*.

cowhands, known as *vaqueros*. Like the *vaqueros*, the cowboy used a rope known as a lariat (*reata*) to corral cattle and utilized a special saddle (now known as a "western" saddle) with a horn. The cowboys also borrowed the *vaqueros*' clothing, including the wide-brimmed hat, the high-heel pointed-toe boots, and leather leggings, known as chaps (short for *chaparreras*), that protected the cowboy's legs. Their nickname, wrangler, came from a Spanish word, *catallerango*. Many cowboy songs, like "The Streets of Laredo," were actually translations of Mexican ballads.

The Texas Question

Texas had barely won its independence when it decided to become a part of the United States. A referendum held soon after the Battle of San Jacinto showed Texans favoring annexation by a vote of 3277 to 93.

The annexation question became one of the most controversial issues in American politics in the late 1830s and early 1840s. The issue was not Texas but slavery. The admission of Texas to the Union would upset the sectional balance of power in the U.S. Senate, just as the admission of Missouri had threatened 15 years earlier. President Andrew Jackson, acutely conscious of the opposition to admitting Texas as a slave state, agreed only to recognize Texan independence. In 1838 John Quincy Adams, now a member of the House of Representatives, staged a 22-day filibuster that successfully blocked annexation. It appeared that Congress had settled the Texas question. For the time, Texas would remain an independent republic.

At this point, proslavery Southerners began to popularize a conspiracy theory that would eventually bring Texas into the Union as a slave state. In 1841 John Tyler, an ardent defender of slavery as a positive good, succeeded to the presidency on the death of William Henry Harrison. Tyler and his fourth secretary of state, John C. Calhoun, argued that Great Britain was scheming to annex Texas and transform it into a haven for runaway slaves. According to this theory, British slave emancipation in the West Indies had been a total economic disaster, and the British now hoped to undermine slavery in

the American South by turning Texas into a British satellite state. (In fact, British abolitionists, but not the British government, were working to convince Texas to outlaw slavery in exchange for British foreign aid.) Sam Houston played along with this ploy by conducting highly visible negotiations with the British government. If the United States would not annex Texas, Houston warned, Texas would seek the support of "some other friend."

The Texas question was the major political issue in the presidential campaign of 1844. James Polk, the Democratic candidate, ardently supported annexation. His victory encouraged Tyler to submit a resolution to Congress calling for annexation. (There were not enough votes in the Senate to ratify a treaty by the required two-thirds majority; a congressional resolution required only a simple majority.) Congress, fearing British intentions, narrowly approved the resolution in 1845, making Texas the twenty-eighth state.

Webster-Ashburton Treaty

Today, the 4000-mile United States–Canadian border is one of the most peaceful international boundaries in the world. During the decades before the Civil War, however, the border between the United States and British America was the scene of constant tensions. One source of contention was the eastern boundary. In 1837 many Americans viewed an insurrection in eastern Canada as an opportunity to annex the country. Americans who lived near the Canadian border aided the rebels, and in one incident several hundred western New Yorkers crossed into Canada and staged an abortive attack on a band of British soldiers. After British forces suppressed the uprising, New Yorkers provided safe haven for the insurrection's leaders. When the rebels began to launch raids into Canada from western New York State, Canadian officials crossed the U.S. border, killed a Canadian rebel, and burned an American ship, the *Caroline*, which had supplied the rebels. When Americans demanded an apology and reparations, Canadian officials refused. Almost immediately, another dispute erupted over the Maine boundary, as American and Canadian lumberjacks and farmers battled for possession of northern Maine and western New Brunswick.

The Webster-Ashburton Treaty of 1842 settled these controversies. The treaty awarded the United States seven-twelfths of the disputed territory in Maine and New Brunswick, and adjusted the Canadian–United States boundary between Lake Superior and Lake of the Woods. In addition, Britain expressed regret "that some explanation and apology . . . was not immediately made" for the burning of the *Caroline* (without explicitly apologizing for the incident). The treaty also settled other disputes between the United States and Britain. Most notably, the United States agreed to station ships off the coast of West Africa to apprehend illegal slave trading vessels carrying the American flag. The Webster-Ashburton Treaty left one major border controversy unresolved: the Canadian-American boundary in the Pacific Northwest.

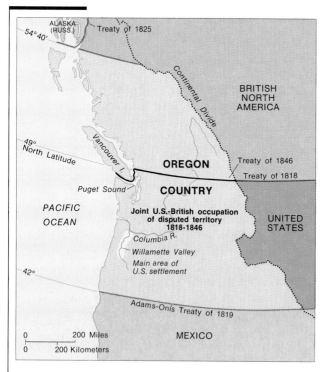

Oregon Country, Pacific Northwest Boundary Dispute
The United States and Great Britain nearly came to blows over the disputed boundary in Oregon.

Oregon

Disputes between the United States and Britain over the "Oregon" country emerged early in the nineteenth century. In 1810 John Jacob Astor, an American who had made a fortune in the Great Lakes fur trade, decided to open a trading post, named Astoria, at the mouth of the Columbia River. He hoped the post would secure a monopoly over the western fur trade, and then ship the furs to eager customers in China.

Astor sent two expeditions to the Far West—one by land and one by sea. Both met with disaster. The sea expedition ran aground on a sandbar at the entrance to the Columbia River, killing eight men. Then, after dropping several passengers off at Astoria, the ship proceeded northward, where Indians destroyed it and massacred the crew. The land expedition was nearly as unlucky. After setting out from St. Louis in 1811, the expedition tried to navigate the rapids of the Snake River and cross the Utah desert on foot. By the time the weary survivors reached Astoria, they found that the British already controlled the fur trade. When the War of 1812 began, the British navy made it impossible to supply Astoria, and Astor sold the post to Canadian traders.

For nearly two decades, Britain dominated the Pacific Northwest. The British Hudson's Bay Company established a well-defended and well-supplied fort at the mouth of the Columbia River that had a dock for ocean-going ships. It scattered smaller forts and trading posts throughout the Pacific Northwest. To ensure that the region was self-sufficient in food, the company set up farms, orchards, and ranches.

As British fur traders expanded their activities in the Pacific Northwest, American politicians grew alarmed that Britain, and not the United States, would gain sovereignty over the region. American diplomats moved quickly to try to solidify American claims to Oregon. Spain, Russia, Britain, and the United States all claimed rights to the Pacific Northwest. In 1818 British and American negotiators agreed that nationals of both countries could trade in the region; this agreement was renewed in 1827. In 1819 the United States persuaded Spain to cede its claims to Oregon to the United States, and two years later Secretary of State John Quincy Adams warned Russia that the United States would oppose any Russian attempts to occupy the territory.

But U.S. politicians, merchants, and fur traders were unsuccessful in promoting American settlement of Oregon. In the end, it was neither commerce nor politics, but religion that led to American settlement of Oregon. In 1831 three chiefs of the Nez Percé tribe and another from the Flathead nation arrived in St. Louis to learn "the true mode of worshipping the great Spirit." The result was increased interest in missionary activity in the Pacific Northwest. The *Christian Advocate*, a leading religious newspaper, declared: "Let the Church awake from her slumbers and go forth in her strength to the salvation of those wandering our native forests."

The first missionaries arrived in Oregon in 1834. In the spring of that year, the Reverend Jason Lee and his nephew Daniel joined a fur trading expedition and trekked to Oregon. There, the Hudson's Bay Company, fearful that missionaries would upset the profitable fur trade with the Indians, convinced the Lees to found their mission in the fertile Willamette Valley, near present-day Salem, where few Indians lived.

Other missionaries soon followed. The most famous western missionaries were Marcus Whitman, a young doctor, and his wife, Narcissa Prentiss Whitman, who were sent west in 1836 by the Methodists. The couple founded a mission at Waiilatpu, near present-day Walla Walla, Washington, where they taught the Cayuse Indians how to till fields, irrigate their crops, and build mills to grind corn and wheat. A fellow missionary described their goal: "We point them with one hand to the Lamb of God, with the other to the hoe as the means of saving their famishing bodies." The Whitmans persisted in their efforts to convert the Indians to Christianity until 1847, when a severe epidemic of measles broke out in the area. Many Indians blamed the epidemic on the white missionaries, and the Whitmans and 12 others were murdered.

Before his death, Marcus Whitman made an epic 3000-mile journey to Boston, during which he publicized the attractions of the Pacific Northwest and warned easterners of the need

to offset British influence in the region. On his return trip to Oregon in 1843, Whitman guided nearly 900 immigrants along the Oregon Trail. The "great western migration," as this journey was known, generated enormous national interest and convinced hundreds of families that it was safe to travel over the Oregon Trail. "The Oregon fever," reported *Niles' Weekly Register*, "is raging in almost every part of the Union." By the mid-1840s, 6000 Americans had moved to Oregon.

The rapid influx of a large number of land-hungry Americans into Oregon in the mid-1840s forced Britain and the United States to decide the status of Oregon. In the presidential election of 1844, the Democratic party demanded the "re-occupation" of Oregon and annexation of the entire Pacific Northwest coast up to the edge of Russian-held Alaska, which was fixed at 54° 40′. This demand helped Democratic candidate James Polk win the presidency in 1844.

In truth, Polk had little desire to go to war with Britain. As an ardent proslavery Southerner, he did not want to add new free states from the Pacific Northwest to the Union. Furthermore, he believed that the northernmost portions of the Oregon country were unsuitable for agriculture. Therefore, in 1846—despite the expansionist slogan "54° 40′ or fight"—he readily accepted a British compromise on the boundary dispute to extend the existing United States–British American boundary along the 49th parallel from the Rocky Mountains to the Pacific Ocean.

The Mormon Frontier

Pioneers migrated to the West for a wide variety of reasons. Some were driven westward by the hope of economic and social betterment, others by a restless curiosity and an urge for adventure. The Mormons moved west for an entirely different reason—to escape religious persecution.

In the history of religion, few stories are more dramatic than that of the Mormons. It is a story with the haunting Biblical overtones of divine revelations and visitations, of persecution and martyrdom, of an exodus two-thirds of the way across a continent, and of ultimate success in establishing a religious society in an uninhabited desert. This story, however, did not take place in a foreign land and in the distant past. It took place in the United States during the nineteenth century.

The Mormon church had its beginnings in upstate New York, which, during the early nineteenth century, was a hotbed of religious fervor. Methodist, Baptist, Presbyterian, Universalist, and Campbellite preachers all eagerly sought converts. Fourteen-year-old Joseph Smith, Jr., the son of a farmer, listened closely to these preachers but was uncertain which way to turn. "So great were the confusion and strife among the different denominations," Smith later recalled, "that it was impossible for a person, young as I was . . . to come to any certain conclusion who was right and who was wrong,"

In the spring of 1820, Smith went into the woods near Palmyra, New York, to seek divine guidance. Suddenly, he was "seized upon by some power that entirely overcame me." According to his account, a brilliant light revealed to him "two personages," who announced that they were God the Father and Christ the Savior. They told him that all existing churches were false and that the true church of God was about to be reestablished on earth.

Three years later, young Smith underwent another supernatural experience. On the evening of September 21, 1823, "a personage" visited his bedroom and said "that God had work for" him to do. The spectral visitor told him of the existence of a set of buried golden plates that contained a lost section from the Bible describing a tribe of Israelites that had lived in America. The next morning, Smith said, he made his way to nearby Hill Cumorah and proceeded to unearth the golden plates that were deposited in a stone box. He was forbidden to remove them or reveal their existence for four years. Finally, in 1827 Smith received the plates and with the aid of magic stones, translated them into English. In 1830, the messages on the plates were published as the *Book of Mormon.*

For Mormons, the visions and revelations received by Joseph Smith, Jr., beginning in 1820, marked the dawn of a new age in human history. They signaled the end of "the Great Apostasy" of 1400 years, during which Catholic and Protestant churches had deluded the world. On April 6, 1830, Smith formally founded the Church of Christ, later renamed the Church of Jesus Christ of Latter-Day Saints, and he committed the church to establishing the Kingdom of God on earth.

At first, members of the church were mainly relatives and neighbors. Soon, Smith attracted several thousand followers largely from isolated rural parts of New England, New York, and Pennsylvania, and the frontier Midwest. The converts to Mormonism were usually small farmers, mechanics, and tradesmen who had been displaced by the growing commercial economy and who were repelled by the rising tide of liberal religion and individualism in early nineteenth-century America.

Because Joseph Smith said that he conversed with angels and received direct revelations from the Lord, local authorities threatened to indict him for blasphemy. He and his followers responded by moving to Kirtland, Ohio, near Cleveland, where they built their first temple. It was in Kirtland that the Mormons first experimented with an economy planned and controlled by the church. In this economy, church trustees controlled the property of church members and put members to work building a temple and other community structures. Meanwhile, the Mormons set up an unauthorized wildcat bank—a venture that nearly destroyed the church when it failed during the Panic of 1837.

From Kirtland, the Mormons moved to Independence, Missouri, and then to a town called Far West, in northern Missouri. Disputes broke out almost immediately between Mormons and "gentiles," as non-Mormons were called. Beginning in 1832, proslavery mobs attacked the Mormons, accusing them of inciting slave insurrection. They burned several Mormon settlements and seized Mormon farms and houses. At the "massacre at Haun's Hill," 18 Mormon men and a boy were killed. Joseph Smith, Jr., was arrested for treason and sentenced to be shot, but he managed to escape several months later. Fifteen thousand Mormons fled from Missouri to Illinois after Governor L. W. Boggs proclaimed them enemies who "had to be exterminated, or driven from the state."

Saints [Mormons] *Driven from Jackson County, Missouri,* by C. C. A. Christensen. Mormon settlements in Missouri were repeatedly attacked and destroyed by mobs between 1832 and 1839, when the Mormons moved to Illinois.

After years of warfare in Missouri, in 1839 communities of Mormons, including many converts from Britain and northern Europe, resettled along the east bank of the Mississippi River in the town of Commerce, Illinois. They changed the name of the town to Nauvoo, and it soon grew into the second largest city in the state. Both Illinois Whigs and Democrats eagerly sought support among the Mormons. In exchange for their votes, the state legislature awarded Nauvoo a special charter that made the town an autonomous city-state, complete with its own 2000-man militia, armed with guns provided by the state.

But trouble arose again. A group of anti-Mormons led by a young lawyer named Thomas C. Sharp accused the Mormons of sending secret diplomatic missions to France, Russia, and the Republic of Texas; practicing polygamy; and instituting theocratic rule by setting up a secret Council of Fifty. These accusations divided the Mormon church, and on June 7, 1844, a dissident group within the church published a newspaper denouncing the practice of polygamy and attacking Joseph Smith for trying to become "king or lawgiver to the church."

On Smith's orders, the city marshal and Mormon legionnaires destroyed the dissidents' printing press. Authorities charged Smith with treason, but the Illinois governor gave Smith his pledge of protection. Smith and his brother were then confined to a Carthage, Illinois, jail cell. Late in the afternoon of June 27, 1844, a mob of prominent citizens, aided by jail guards, broke into Smith's cell, shot him and his brother, and threw their bodies out of a second-story window. The Mormon prophet was dead.

Why did the Mormons seem so menacing? Why did many western settlers agree with the Reverend Finis Ewing when he said that "the

Polygamy helped absorb single and widowed women into Mormon communities.

'Mormons' are the common enemies of mankind and ought to be destroyed"? Today, it is hard to believe that Mormons could ever have been regarded as subversive, since they are known for their abstinence from tobacco and alcohol and their stress on family and community responsibility. Why were they subjected to continuing persecution?

Anti-Mormonism was rooted in a struggle for economic and political power. Individualistic frontiersmen feared the Mormons, who voted as their elders told them to do and who controlled land as a bloc. Many early nineteenth-century Americans feared that the nature of the Mormon community created an unfair advantage in the struggle for wealth and power.

Mormonism was also denounced as a threat to fundamental social values. Protestant ministers railed against it as a threat to Christianity since Mormons rejected the legitimacy of established churches and insisted that the *Book of Mormon* was Holy Scripture, equal in importance to the Bible. They attacked Mormonism as a preposterous hoax that was played on naive and superstitious minds. The Mormons were also accused of corrupt moral values, especially after rumors about the practice of polygamy began to spread after 1842. Indeed, Mormons did

practice polygamy for half a century before the leader of the denomination had a vision that led to a change in church rules in 1890. It was justified theologically as an effort to reestablish the patriarchal Old Testament family. Polygamy also served an important social function by absorbing single or widowed women into Mormon communities. Critics denounced polygamy as "a slavery which debases and degrades womanhood, motherhood and family," but contrary to popular belief it was not widely practiced. Altogether, only 10 to 20 percent of Mormon families were polygamous and nearly two-thirds involved a man and two wives.

After the murder of Joseph Smith, the Mormons decided to migrate across a thousand miles of unsettled prairie, plains, and arid desert to a new refuge outside the boundaries of the United States. They finished their temple in Nauvoo (which the poet John Greenleaf Whittier called "the most splendid and imposing architectural monument in the new world") and conducted religious rituals before beginning their exodus to the Far West.

The Mormon church appeared to be on the point of splintering. But then a new leader, Brigham Young, emerged, and he led the Mormons to a new Zion where they might live in safety. Young had begun his career as an uneducated carpenter, printer, and glazier, but he had found in Mormonism the inspiration that would transform him into the leader whose efforts enabled the church to survive. In February 1846 the first Mormon wagons left Nauvoo. By fall, 15,000 Mormons had reached the west bank of the Missouri River, where they learned that an Illinois mob had burned their temple to the ground.

Early in April, the first wagons began to move again. On July 23, Young looked out upon the Great Salt Lake and said, "This is the right place." More than 85,000 Mormon migrants followed in the steps of Young's trek. By the time of his death in 1877, 125,000 Mormons lived in Utah.

As governor of the Mormon state of Deseret and later as governor of Utah, Young oversaw the building of Salt Lake City and 186 other Mormon communities, developed church-owned businesses, and established the first cooperative irrigation projects. He also publicly preached polygamy in 1852 and had 27 wives and 56 children. In 1857 public outrage over polygamy led President James Buchanan to replace Young with a non-Mormon governor and to send an army of 2500 men to force the Mormons to obey federal law. Young responded by mobilizing a Mormon militia and blocking the route of advancing U.S. troops. This episode, known as the Mormon War or "Buchanan's Blunder," ended in 1858, when the Mormons accepted the new governor and Buchanan issued a general pardon.

Today, the Mormon church is the fastest growing religious group in the United States, and its members are known for their industriousness, sobriety, and thrift. A century ago, anti-Mormons regarded the church as a fundamental threat to American values. Early nineteenth-century American society attached enormous importance to individualism, secularism, monogamous marriage, and private property, and the Mormons were believed to threaten each of these values. But in a larger sense, the Mormons' aspirations were truly American. They sought nothing less than the establishment of the Kingdom of God on earth—a dream that was, of course, not new in this country. In seeking to build God's kingdom, the Mormons were carrying on a quest that had been begun by their Puritan ancestors two centuries before.

THE MEXICAN WAR

When Brigham Young led the Mormons west, he was seeking a homeland outside the boundaries of the United States. But even before he arrived at the Great Salt Lake during the summer of 1847, Utah as well as California, Nevada, and parts of Arizona, Colorado, New Mexico, and Wyoming, became part of the United States as a result of the war with Mexico.

Why War?

Fifteen years before the United States was plunged into Civil War, it fought a war against Mexico that added half a million square miles of

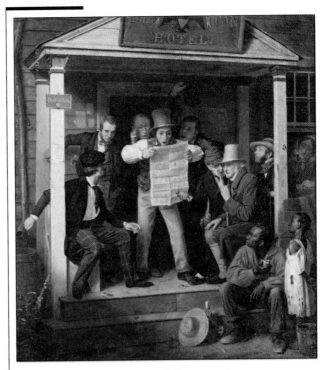

The Mexican War was the nation's first war to be reported in newspapers as it actually happened.

territory to the United States. Not only was it the first American war fought almost entirely outside the United States, it was also the first American war to be reported, while it happened, by daily newspapers. It was also a controversial war that bitterly divided American public opinion. Finally, it was the war that gave young officers named Ulysses S. Grant, Robert E. Lee, Thomas ("Stonewall") Jackson, William Tecumseh Sherman, and George McClellan their first experience in a major conflict.

The underlying cause of the Mexican War was the inexorable movement of American pioneers into the Far West. As Americans marched westward, they moved into land claimed by Mexico, and inevitably Mexican and American interests clashed.

The immediate reason for the conflict was the annexation of Texas in 1845. After the defeat at San Jacinto in 1836, Mexico made two abortive attempts in 1842 to reconquer Texas. Even after these defeats, Mexico refused to recognize Texan independence and warned the

United States that the annexation of Texas would be tantamount to a declaration of war. In early 1845, when Congress voted to annex Texas, Mexico expelled the American ambassador and cut diplomatic relations. But it did not declare war.

Polk told his commanders to prepare for the possibility of war. He ordered American naval vessels in the Gulf of Mexico to position themselves outside Mexican ports. Secretly, he warned the Pacific fleet to prepare to seize ports along the California coast in the event of war. And he dispatched American forces in the Southwest to Corpus Christi, Texas.

Peaceful settlement of the two countries' differences still seemed possible. In the fall of 1845, the president sent John Slidell as "envoy extraordinary and minister plenipotentiary" to Mexico City with a proposal to peacefully resolve the disputes. The most significant controversies concerned Texas's boundary and the Mexican government's failure to compensate American citizens for losses due to revolution and theft. Slidell was authorized to cancel the damage claims and pay $5 million in reparations if the Mexicans agreed to recognize the Rio Grande as the southwestern boundary of Texas (earlier, the Spanish government had defined the Texas boundary as the Nueces River, 130 miles north and east of the Rio Grande). No Americans lived between the Nueces and the Rio Grande, although many Hispanics lived in the region.

Polk not only wanted to settle the boundary and claims disputes, he also wanted to acquire Mexico's two northwestern provinces, New Mexico and California. He directed Slidell to offer up to $5 million for the province of New Mexico—which included Nevada and Utah and parts of four other states—and up to $25 million for California.

Polk was anxious to acquire California because in mid-October 1845 he had been led to believe that Britain was on the verge of making California a protectorate. This was supported by the fact that in 1839 Britain and France had used military action in an effort to force Mexico to pay its debt. It was widely believed that Mexico had agreed to cede California to Britain as payment.

Immediate preventive action seemed necessary. Polk therefore instructed his consul in Monterey to encourage Californians to agitate for annexation by the United States. He also dispatched a young Marine Corps lieutenant, Archibald H. Gillespie, to California, apparently to foment revolt against Mexican authority.

The Mexican government, already incensed over the annexation of Texas, refused to negotiate. The Mexican president, José Herrera, refused to receive Slidell and ordered his leading commander, General Mariano Paredes y Arrillaga, to assemble an army and reconquer Texas. Paredes proceeded to topple Herrera's government and declare himself president. But he also refused to receive Slidell.

The failure of Slidell's mission led Polk to order Brigadier General Zachary Taylor to march 3000 troops southwest from Corpus Christi, Texas, to "defend the Rio Grande." Late in March of 1846, Taylor and his men set up camp along the Rio Grande, directly across from the Mexican city of Matamoros, on a stretch of land claimed by both Mexico and the United States.

On April 25 a Mexican cavalry force crossed the Rio Grande and clashed with a small American squadron, forcing the Americans to surrender after the loss of several lives. Polk used this episode as an excuse to declare war. "Hostilities may be considered to have commenced," Taylor wrote to President Polk. "American blood has been spilled."

On May 8, the day before he had received word of the skirmish, Polk and his cabinet had already decided to press for war with Mexico. On May 11, after he received word of the border clash, Polk asked Congress to acknowledge that a state of war already existed "by the act of Mexico herself . . . notwithstanding all our efforts to avoid it." "Mexico," the president announced, "has passed the boundary of the United States, has invaded our territory and shed American blood upon the American soil." Congress responded with a declaration of war.

The Mexican War was extremely controversial. Its supporters argued that the nation was destined to expand "to cover the whole northern, if not the southern continent." They blamed Mexico for the hostilities because it had severed relations with the United States, threatened war, refused to receive an American emissary, or to pay the damage claims of American citizens. In addition, Mexico had "invaded our territory and shed American blood upon the American soil." Opposition leaders denounced the war as an immoral land grab by an expansionistic power against a weak neighbor that had been independent barely two decades. The war's critics claimed that Polk deliberately provoked Mexico into war by ordering American troops into disputed territory. A Delaware senator declared that ordering Taylor to the Rio Grande was "as much an act of aggression on our part as is a man's pointing a pistol at another's breast."

Critics argued that the war was an expansionist power play dictated by an aggressive Southern slaveocracy intent on acquiring more land for cotton cultivation and more slave states to better balance the Northern free states in the U.S. Senate. "Bigger pens to cram with slaves," was the way poet James Russell Lowell put it. Others blamed the war on expansion-minded westerners who were hungry for land, and on eastern trading interests, which dreamed of establishing "an American Boston or New York" in San Francisco to increase trade with Asia. Mexicans denounced the war as a brazen attempt by the United States to seize Mexican territory.

The War

American strategy was based on a three-pronged attack. Colonel Stephen Kearny had the task of securing New Mexico and occupying California, while naval forces under Commodore John D. Sloat blockaded the California Coast and General Zachary Taylor invaded Mexico. Kearny easily accomplished his mission. In less than two months, he marched his 1700-man army more than a thousand miles. On August 18, 1846, he occupied Santa Fe and declared New Mexico's 80,000 inhabitants American citizens.

Meanwhile, American settlers in California's Sacramento Valley, fearful that Mexican authorities were about to expel them from the region, revolted. At dawn on June 10, 1846, a small group of buckskin-clad Americans led by frontiersman Ezekiel Merritt seized Sonoma, Spain's northernmost settlement in California, proclaimed an independent Republic of California, and raised a flag showing a grizzly bear facing a red star. As a result, the revolt was known as the Bear Flag Rebellion.

In early July, the Bear Flag was replaced by the stars and stripes. On July 7, 1846, U.S. naval forces under Commodore Sloat captured the California town of Monterey and proclaimed California a part of the United States. In January 1847 U.S. troops under Kearny and Commodore Robert F. Stockton won the Battle of San Gabriel near Los Angeles, completing the American conquest of California.

Although the American invasion of Mexico's northernmost provinces was completely successful, the Mexican government did not surrender. Switching strategy, Polk ordered the army to push deeper into Mexican territory. In June 1846 Colonel A. W. Doniphan led 856 Missouri cavalry volunteers 3000 miles across mountains and desert into the northern Mexican province of Chihuahua. He occupied El Paso and then captured the capital city of Chihuahua. Meanwhile, 6000 volunteers under the command of Zachary Taylor defeated a Mexican force of 15,000 at the battle of Buena Vista on February 22 and 23, 1847.

Despite the unbroken string of American victories, Mexico refused to negotiate. In disgust, Polk ordered General Winfield Scott to invade central Mexico from the sea, march inland, and capture Mexico City. On March 9, 1847, the Mexicans allowed Scott and a force of 10,000 men to land unopposed at the garrison of Veracruz on the Gulf of Mexico. As American soldiers encircled the fortress, ships and land-based mortars lobbed shells into the seaport. Three weeks later the garrison surrendered. Scott's losses totaled 13 killed and 55 wounded.

Scott's forces then began to march on the Mexican capital. On April 18, at a mountain pass near Jalapa, a 9000-man American force met 13,000 Mexican troops and in bitter hand-to-hand fighting, forced the Mexicans to flee. As Scott's army pushed on toward Mexico City, it stormed a Mexican fortress at Contreras and then routed a large Mexican force at Churubusco on August 19 and 20. For two weeks, from

August 22 to September 7, Scott observed an armistice to allow the Mexicans to consider peace proposals. When the negotiations failed, Scott's 6000 remaining men attacked El Molino del Rey—the King's Mill—and stormed Chapultepec, a fortified castle guarding Mexico City's gates. On September 14, 1847, the Americans entered the Mexican capital. At 7 A.M., the American flag was raised over Mexico City—an event memorialized in the Marine Corps hymn with the line "from the halls of Montezuma."

Despite the capture of their capital, the Mexicans refused to surrender. Hostile crowds staged demonstrations in the streets, and snipers fired shots and hurled stones and broken bottles from the tops of flat-roofed Mexican houses. To quell the protests, General Scott ordered the streets "swept with grape and cannister" and artillery "turned upon the houses whence the fire proceeded." Outside the capital, belligerent civilians attacked army supply wagons, and guerrilla fighters harassed American troops. Senator Daniel Webster of Massachusetts expressed the prevailing sentiment: "Mexico is an ugly enemy. She will not fight—and will not retreat."

War Fever and Antiwar Protests

During the first few weeks following the declaration of war a frenzy of prowar hysteria swept the country. Two hundred thousand men responded to a call for 50,000 volunteers. Novelist Herman Melville observed that in his hometown of Lansingburgh, New York, "a military ardor pervades all ranks. . . . Nothing is talked about but the halls of the Montezumas." In New York, placards bore the slogan "Mexico or Death." Many newspapers, especially in the North, declared that the war would benefit the Mexican people by bringing them the blessings of democracy and liberty. The *Boston Times* said that an American victory "must necessarily be a great blessing," because it would bring "peace

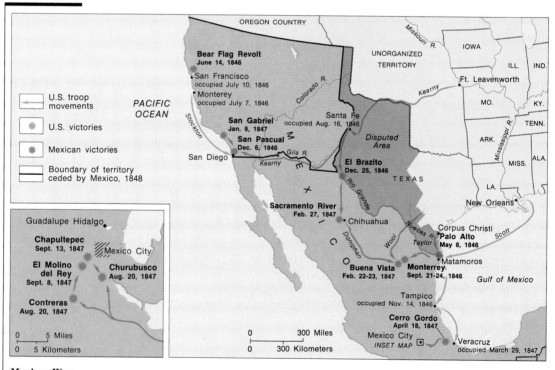

Mexican War
The Mexican War would increase the nation's size by one-third.

into a land where the sword has always been the sole arbiter between factions" and would introduce "the reign of law where license has existed for a generation."

In Philadelphia, 20,000 turned out for a pro-war rally, and in Cincinnati, 12,000 celebrated Zachary Taylor's victories with cannon salutes, parades, and speeches. In Tennessee, 30,000 men volunteered for 3000 positions as soldiers, prompting one applicant to complain that it was "difficult even to purchase a place in the ranks." Poet Walt Whitman, then editor of the *Brooklyn Eagle*, echoed the prevailing mood: "Yes, Mexico must be chastised." The war was particularly popular in the West. Of the 69,540 men who were accepted for service, more than 40,000 were from the western states.

But from the war's very beginning, a small but highly visible group of intellectuals, clergymen, pacifists, abolitionists, and Whig and Democratic politicians denounced the war as brutal aggression against a "poor, feeble, distracted country."

Literary and reform circles were particularly vocal in their opposition to the war. Congregationalist minister Theodore Parker declared that if the "war be right then Christianity is wrong, a falsehood, a lie." Abolitionist William Lloyd Garrison's militant newspaper, the *Liberator*, expressed open support for the Mexican people: "Every lover of Freedom and humanity throughout the world must wish them the most triumphant success."

Most Whigs supported the war—in part because two of the leading American generals, Zachary Taylor and Winfield Scott, were Whigs, and in part because they remembered that opposition to the War of 1812 had destroyed the Federalist party. But many prominent Whigs, from the South as well as the North, openly expressed opposition. Thomas Corwin of Ohio denounced the war as merely the latest example of American injustice to Mexico: "If I were a Mexican I would tell you, 'Have you not room enough in your own country to bury your dead.' " Henry Clay declared, "This is no war of defense, but one of unnecessary and offensive aggression." Daniel Webster, a frequent Whig presidential candidate, mockingly described the conflict as a "war of pretexts"—the pretext that

Mexico had refused to receive an American emissary, had refused to pay Americans financial claims, and had invaded American territory.

A freshman congressman from Illinois named Abraham Lincoln lashed out against the war, calling it immoral, proslavery, and a threat to the nation's republican values. In Congress, he proposed the so-called Spot Resolution, demanding that President Polk identify the precise spot on which Mexicans had "shed American blood upon the American soil." One of Lincoln's constituents branded him "the Benedict Arnold of our district," and he was denied renomination by his own party.

As newspapers informed their readers about the hardships and savagery of life on the front, public enthusiasm for the war began to wane. The war did not turn out to be the romantic exploit that Americans envisioned. Troops complained that their food was "green with slime" and "acted as an instanteous emetic." Their meat, they said, would stick "if thrown against a smooth plank." Diarrhea, amoebic dysentery, measles, and yellow fever ravaged American soldiers. Seven times as many Americans died of disease and exposure as died of battlefield injuries. Of the 90,000 Americans who served in the war, only 1721 died in action. Another 11,155 died from disease and exposure to the elements.

Public support for the war was further eroded by reports of brutality against Mexican civilians. Newspaper reporters claimed that the chapparal was "strewn with the skeletons of Mexicans sacrificed" by American troops. After one of their members was murdered, the Arkansas volunteer cavalry surrounded a group of Mexican peasants and began an "indiscriminate and bloody massacre of the poor creatures." A young lieutenant named George G. Meade reported that volunteers in Matamoros robbed the citizens, stole their cattle, and killed innocent civilians "for no other object than their own amusement." If only a tenth of the horror stories were true, General Winfield Scott wrote, it was enough "to make Heaven weep, & every American of Christian morals blush for his country."

During wartime, the party in power has often lost support. The Mexican War was no exception. In the congressional election of 1846, which took place half a year after the outbreak of war, the Democrats lost control of the House of Representatives to the Whigs.

Dissent even made its way to the battlefield. A group of enlisted Irish-Catholic Americans, apparently shocked by the desecration of Catholic churches, deserted to the Mexican side, formed the San Patricio Battalion, and fought against the American army. At Churubusco, 65 members of the battalion (which also consisted of foreign nationals resident in Mexico) were captured. Fifty were executed and 11 others were punished with 50 lashes apiece and the letter D (for deserter) branded on their cheeks.

A young essayist and poet named Henry David Thoreau staged the best known act of protest against the Mexican War. On July 23, 1846, the constable of Concord, Massachusetts, arrested the transcendentalist poet for failure to pay the state poll tax (a head tax on male citizens between the ages of 21 and 70). The constable actually offered to pay the tax if Thoreau was short of money, but Thoreau insisted that he refused to pay on principle, as a protest against his country's involvement in the Mexican War. The constable then placed Thoreau in the local jail. Thoreau spent only a single night in jail because his tax was paid, much to his disgust, by one of his relatives.

In response to his arrest Thoreau wrote an essay that became a source of inspiration for Leo Tolstoi, Mahatma Gandhi, and Martin Luther King, Jr. Thoreau entitled his essay "Civil Disobedience." In it he declared that if all citizens who opposed the Mexican War followed his example and went to jail for their beliefs, the government could be forced to end the conflict. It was the duty of every individual to protest a government policy, even though it had been adopted with majority consent, when it conflicted with moral law. "Any man more right than his neighbor," he wrote, "constitutes a majority of one." So how should an individual protest a moral wrong? Here Thoreau was at his most creative. He described a type of disobedience that disrupted the everyday workings of society and dramatized the moral issues at stake, without resorting to violence. Individual acts of protest, he argued, would awaken the conscience of those people whose consciences could still be stirred.

Out of Thoreau's jailing grew a legend. Ralph Waldo Emerson, America's greatest philosopher, visited Thoreau in jail. Emerson asked, "Henry, why are you here?" Thoreau replied, "Why are you not here?"

Peace

Difficult negotiations followed the war. After American troops entered the Mexican capital, Santa Anna, the Mexican president resigned and the Mexican Congress retreated to a provincial capital to try to reorganize. Not until mid-November 1847 was a new civilian government able to gain control over the country and name a peace negotiator.

As Americans waited impatiently for a final peace settlement, they grew increasingly divided over their war aims. Ultra-expansionists, who drew support from such cities as Baltimore, New York, and Philadelphia as well as from the West, wanted the United States to annex all of Mexico. Many Southerners, led by John C. Calhoun, called for a unilateral withdrawal to the Rio Grande. They opposed annexation of any of Mexico below the Rio Grande because they did not want to extend American citizenship to Mexicans. Most Democratic party leaders, however, wanted to annex at least the one-third of Mexico south and west of the Rio Grande.

Then suddenly on February 22, 1848, word reached Washington that a peace treaty had been signed. On February 2, 1848, Nicholas Trist, a Spanish-speaking State Department official, signed the Treaty of Guadalupe Hidalgo, ending the Mexican War. Trist had actually been ordered home two months earlier by Polk, but he had continued negotiating anyway, fearing that his recall would be "deadly to the cause of peace."

According to the treaty, Mexico ceded to the United States only those areas that Polk had originally sought to purchase. Mexico ceded California, Nevada, Utah, New Mexico, and parts of Arizona, Colorado, Kansas, and Wyoming to the United States for $15 million and the assumption of $3.25 million in debts owed to Americans by Mexico. The treaty also settled the Texas border dispute in favor of the United States, placing the Texas-Mexico boundary at the Rio Grande.

Ultra-expansionists called on Polk to throw out the treaty. William Tecumseh Sherman called the treaty "just such a one as Mexico might have imposed on us had she been the conqueror." But a war-weary public wanted peace. Polk quickly submitted the treaty to the Senate, which ratified it overwhelmingly. The war was over.

The War's Significance

The story of America's conflict with Mexico tends to be overshadowed by the story of the Civil War, which began only a decade and a half later. In fact, the conflict had far-reaching consequences for the nation's future. It increased the nation's size by a third, but it also created deep political divisions that threatened the country's future.

The most significant result of the Mexican War was to reignite the question of slavery in the western territories—the very question that had divided the country in 1819. Even before the war had begun, philosopher Ralph Waldo Emerson had predicted that the United States would "conquer Mexico, but it will be as the man who swallows the arsenic which will bring him down in turn. Mexico will poison us." The war convinced a growing number of Northerners that Southern slaveowners had precipitated the war in order to open new lands to slavery and acquire new slave states. And most significant of all, the war weakened the party system and made it increasingly difficult for congressional leaders to prevent the issue of slavery from dominating congressional activity.

Political Crisis of the 1840s

Prior to the Mexican War, the major political issues that divided Americans were questions of tariffs, banking, internal improvements, and land. Political positions on these issues largely divided along party lines. After the outbreak of war with Mexico, a new issue began to dominate American politics—the extension of slavery in the western territories. Public opinion began to polarize and party cohesion began to break down as party factional and sectional divisions grew more important than traditional party coalitions.

The question of slavery burst into the public spotlight one summer evening in 1846. Congressman David Wilmot, a Pennsylvania Democrat, introduced an amendment, known as the Wilmot Proviso, to a war appropriations bill. The proviso forbade slavery in any territory acquired from Mexico. The states of New York, Massachusetts, Michigan, and Vermont adopted resolutions endorsing the Wilmot Proviso. Throughout the North, thousands of workingmen, mechanics, and farmers feared that free workers would be unable to successfully compete against slave labor. "If slavery is not excluded by law," said one Northern congressman, "the presence of the slave will exclude the laboring white man."

Southerners denounced the Wilmot Proviso as "treason to the Constitution." The state Democratic party in Alabama denied that Congress had the authority to limit slavery in the territory and threatened secession if the Wilmot Proviso were enacted. Polk tried to quiet the debate between "Southern agitators and Northern fanatics" by assuring moderate Northerners that slavery could never take root in the arid southwest, but his efforts were to no avail. With the strong support of westerners, the amendment passed the House twice, but was defeated in the Senate. Although the Wilmot Proviso did not become law, the issue it raised—the extension of slavery into the western territories—continued to contribute to the growth of political factionalism.

Meanwhile, at the very moment that Congress was debating the Wilmot Proviso, another sectional dispute flared up over the tariff. In 1846 President Polk persuaded Congress to enact the Walker Tariff, a low tariff that delighted Southerners, but infuriated Northerners who favored tariff protection for industry.

Growing sectional tensions were also evident in the founding of the Free Soil party in 1848. This sectional party opposed the westward expansion of slavery and favored free land for western homesteaders. Much more popular than the Liberty party, an earlier antislavery po-

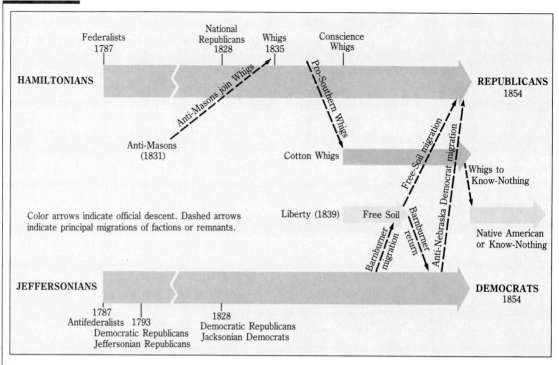

Figure 13.1

Chronological development of American political parties to 1854

litical party, the Free Soil party drew support from dissident New England Whigs (known as "conscience" Whigs because of their opposition to slavery), antislavery New York Democrats (known as "Barnburners"), and former members of the Liberty party. Under the slogan "free soil, free speech, free labor, and free men," the party nominated ex-President Martin Van Buren as its presidential nominee in 1848 and polled 291,000 votes. This was enough to split the Democratic vote and throw the election to Whig candidate Zachary Taylor.

Up until the last month of 1848, the debate over slavery in the Mexican cession seemed academic. Most Americans thought of the newly acquired territory as a wasteland filled with "broken mountains and dreary desert." William Tecumseh Sherman summed up prevailing sentiment when he said he would not trade two eastern counties for all the Far West. Then in his farewell address, Polk electrified Congress with the news that gold had been discovered in California—and suddenly the question of slavery was inescapably important.

The Gold Rush

On January 24, 1848, less than 10 days before the signing of the peace treaty ending the Mexican War, James W. Marshall, a 36-year-old carpenter and handyman, noticed several bright bits of yellow mineral near a sawmill that he was building for John A. Sutter, a Swiss-born immigrant who owned one of the great ranches that dotted California's Sacramento Valley. To test if the bits were "fool's gold," which shatters when struck by a hammer, or gold, which is malleable, Marshall "tried it between two rocks, and found that it could be beaten into a different shape but not broken." He told the men working with him: "Boys, by God, I believe I have found a gold mine."

On March 15 a San Francisco newspaper, the *Californian*, printed the first account of

CHRONOLOGY OF KEY EVENTS

1803 Louisiana Purchase

1804 Lewis and Clark Expedition sets out from St. Louis to explore the Louisiana Purchase

1810 Mexican War for Independence against Spanish rule begins; John Jacob Astor attempts to plant a trading post in Oregon

1811–1812 Fur trappers mark out the Oregon Trail

1818 United States and Britain agree to joint occupation of Oregon

1819 Spain cedes its claims to Oregon to the United States

1821 Mexico gains independence from Spain; first American traders traverse the Santa Fe Trail; Stephen Austin founds American colony in Texas

1822 William Henry Ashley and Andrew Henry begin to send trappers into the frontier

1830 Joseph Smith, Jr., founds Church of Jesus Christ of Latter-Day Saints

1833–1834 Mexican government confiscates California missions

1834 Santa Anna overthrows Mexico's constitutional government and makes himself dictator; first American missionaries arrive in Oregon

1835 Scattered local outbursts erupt in Texas against Mexican rule

1836 Texas Revolution

1838 John Quincy Adams's filibuster defeats move to annex Texas

1841 First party of pioneers leaves Missouri for California; Congress recognizes squatters' rights in the Preemption Bill

1844 Joseph Smith, Jr., assassinated at Carthage, Illinois

1845 Texas is admitted as twenty-eighth state; Mexican government breaks off diplomatic relations with the United States

1846 The United States declares war on Mexico; Britain and the United States divide Oregon along 49th parallel; Donner party becomes trapped in Sierra Nevada; Brigham Young leads the Mormons to the Great Salt Lake Valley

1847 U.S. forces complete the American conquest of California

1848 Gold is discovered at Sutter's Mill in California; Treaty of Guadalupe Hidalgo ends the Mexican War

1849 Gold Rush brings 80,000 49ers to California

Marshall's discovery. Within two weeks, the paper had lost its staff and was forced to shut down its printing press. In its last edition it told its readers: "The whole country, from San Francisco to Los Angeles . . . resounds with the sordid cry of Gold! Gold! Gold! while the field is left half-planted, the house half-built, and everything neglected but the manufacture of picks and shovels."

In 1849, 80,000 men arrived in California—half by land and half by ship around Cape Horn or across the Isthmus of Panama. Only half were Americans; the rest came from Britain, Australia, Germany, France, Latin America, and China. Platoons of soldiers deserted; sailors jumped ship; husbands left wives; apprentices ran away from their masters; farmers and businesspeople deserted their livelihoods. By July, 1850, sailors had abandoned 500 ships in San Francisco Bay. Within a year, California's population had swollen from 14,000 to 100,000. The population of San Francisco, which stood at 459 in the summer of 1847, reached 20,000 within a few months.

During the early years of the gold rush, men traveled alone to California. Few women arrived during the early years—for example, only 700 in 1849. In 1850 women made up only 8 percent of California's population. In mining areas, they made up less than 2 percent.

The gold rush transformed California from a sleepy society into one that was wild, unruly, ethnically diverse, and violent. Philosopher Josiah Royce, whose family arrived in the midst of the gold rush, declared that the Californian was "morally and socially tried as no other American ever has been tried." In San Francisco alone there were more than 500 bars and 1000 gambling dens. In the span of 18 months, the city burned to the ground six times. There were a thousand murders in San Francisco during the early 1850s, but only one conviction. Forty-niners (the nickname of the immigrants who traveled to California in 1849) slaughtered Indians for sport, drove Mexicans from the mines on penalty of death, and sought to restrict the immigration of foreigners, especially the Chinese. Since the military government was incapable of keeping order, leading merchants formed vigilance committees, which attempted to rule by lynch law and the establishment of "popular" courts.

The rapid influx of miners into California led to a frenzy of price gouging. A bottle of molasses or a pint-and-a-half of vinegar sold for a dollar. Pork was $5 a pound. Eggs went for as much as $4 a dozen. Toothpicks were sold for 50 cents apiece. The value of real estate exploded. A lot in San Francisco purchased in 1847 for $16.50 sold for $6000 in the spring of 1848 and was later resold for $48,000.

The gold rush era in California lasted less than a decade. By the mid-1850s, the lone miner who prospected for gold with a pick, a shovel, and a washpan was already an anachronism. Mining companies using heavy machinery replaced the individual prospector. Systems of dams exposed whole river bottoms. Drilling machines drove shafts 700 feet into the earth. Hydraulic mining machines blasted streams of water against mountainsides. The romantic era of California gold mining had come to a close.

Territorial Growth to 1853

CONCLUSION

By 1860 the gold rush was over. Prospectors had found more than $350 million worth of gold. Certainly, some fortunes were made—one prostitute claimed to have made $50,000 after a year's work—but few struck it rich.

Ironically, the two men most responsible for the gold rush died penniless. James W. Marshall, who discovered the first gold bits, eventually became a blacksmith in Kelsey, California, and died in poverty. John A. Sutter, on whose ranch gold was discovered, was left bankrupt as a result of the gold rush. His workmen deserted to hunt gold; his crops rotted in the fields; and forty-niners trespassed on his land and stole his cattle. He died in 1880 in Pennsylvania while lobbying Congress to reimburse him for the losses he had suffered because of the discovery of gold on his land.

By 1850 the American flag flew over an area that stretched from sea to sea. In the span of just five years, the United States had increased in size by a third and acquired an area that now includes the states of Arizona, California, Colorado, Idaho, Nevada, New Mexico, Oregon, Texas, Utah, Washington, and Wyoming.

First to carry the American flag into the Far West were a small coterie of government explorers, fur trappers, traders, and missionaries. These were the people who found the fertile valleys and great forests of the West, marked trails, and stirred the imagination of many midwesterners eager for adventure. Ranchers, farmers, and tradesmen followed, taking the overland trails across treeless plains, dangerous mountains, and arid deserts, into Texas, Oregon, and California. The United States acquired Texas through annexation. Negotiations with Britain gave the United States half of the Oregon country. California and the great Southwest became part of the United States as a result of war with Mexico.

The exploration and settlement of the Far West is one of the great epics of nineteenth-century history. But America's dramatic territorial expansion also created severe problems. In addition to providing the United States with its richest mines, greatest forests, and most fertile farm land, the Far West intensified the sectional conflict between the North and South and raised the fateful and ultimately divisive question of whether slavery would be permitted in the western territories. Could democratic political institutions resolve the question of slavery in the western territories? That question would dominate American politics in the 1850s.

SUGGESTIONS FOR FURTHER READING

OVERVIEWS AND SURVEYS

Ray A. Billington, *The Far Western Frontier, 1830–1860* (1956), and *Westward Expansion*, 5th ed. (1982); Bernard DeVoto, *The Year of Decision: 1846* (1943), and *Across the Wide Missouri* (1947); Richard Drinnon, *Facing West: The Metaphysics of Indian-Hating and Empire-Building* (1980); Thomas R. Hietala, *Manifest Design: Anxious Aggrandizement in Late Jacksonian America* (1985); Reginald Horsman, *Race and Manifest Destiny: The Origins of American Racial Anglo-Saxonism* (1981); Anne Farrar Hyde, *An American Vision: Far Western Landscape and National Culture* (1990); Howard R. Lamar, ed., *Reader's Encyclopedia of the American West* (1977); Patricia Nelson Limerick, *The Legacy of Conquest: The Unbroken Past of the American West* (1987); Frederick Merk, *History of the Westward Movement* (1978); Martin Ridge and Ray A. Billington, eds., *America's Frontier Story* (1969); Albert K. Weinberg, *Manifest Destiny* (1935).

OPENING THE WEST

Gloria G. Cline, *Exploring the Great Basin* (1963); William Cronon, *Nature's Metropolis: Chicago and the Great West* (1991); R. L. Duffus, *The Santa Fe Trail* (1930); William H. Goetzmann, *Army Exploration in the American West, 1803–1863* (1959), and *Exploration and Empire: Explorer and Scientist in the Winning of the West* (1966); Michael P. Malone, ed., *Historians and the American West* (1983); Dale L. Morgan, *Jedediah Smith and the Opening of the West* (1953); Francis Parkman, *The Oregon Trail* (1849); Gerald Rawling, *The Pathfinders* (1964); Richard Slotkin, *The Fatal Environment: The Myth of the Frontier in the Age of Industrialization* (1985); David J. Wishart, *The Fur Trade of the American West* (1979).

SPANISH AND INDIAN AMERICA

Rodofo Acuña, *Occupied America: A History of Chicanos*, 3d ed. (1988); Robert F. Berkhofer, Jr., *The White Man's Indian: Images of the American In-

dian from Columbus to the Present (1978); Albert Camarillo, *Chicanos in California* (1984); John R. Chávez, *The Lost Land* (1984); Arnoldo De León, *The Tejano Community, 1836–1900* (1982), and *They Called Them Greasers: Anglo Attitudes Toward Mexicans in Texas, 1821–1900* (1983); Sarah Deutsch, *No Separate Refuge: Culture, Class, and Gender on an Anglo-Hispanic Frontier in the American Southwest* (1987); Edward P. Dozier, *The Pueblo Indians of North America* (1970); Harold E. Driver, *Indians of North America*, 2d ed. (1969); Fred Eggan, *The American Indian* (1966); Jack Forbes, *Native Americans of California and Nevada*, rev. ed. (1982); Thomas D. Hall, *Social Change in the Southwest, 1350–1880* (1989); Robert F. Heizer and Alan Almquist, *The Other Californians* (1971), and with M. A. Whipple, eds., *California Indians*, 2d ed. (1971); Alice Kehoe, *North American Indians: A Comprehensive Account* (1981); Robert H. Lowie, *Indians of the Plains* (1963); Cecil Robinson, *Mexico and the Hispanic Southwest in American Literature* (1977); Robert Rosenbaum, *Mexicano Resistance in the Southwest* (1981); Robert F. Spencer and Jesse D. Spencer, *The Native Americans: Ethnology and Backgrounds of the North American Indians*, 2d ed. (1977); W. R. Swagerty, ed., *Scholars and the Indian Experience: Critical Reviews of Recent Writings in the Social Sciences* (1984); Wilcomb Washburn, *The Indian in America* (1975); David J. Weber, *The Mexican Frontier, 1821–1846: The American Southwest under Mexico* (1982).

SETTLING THE FAR WEST

John Mack Faragher, *Women and Men on the Overland Trail* (1979); Julie Roy Jeffrey, *Frontier Women: The Transmississippi West, 1840–1880* (1979); Sandra L. Myres, *Westering Women and the Frontier Experience, 1800–1915* (1982); Glenda Riley, *The Female Frontier* (1988); Lillian Schlissel, *Women's Diaries of the Westward Journey* (1982), and with Byrd Gibbens and Elizabeth Hampsten, *Far from Home: Families of the Western Journey* (1989); Joanna Stratton, *Pioneer Women* (1981); John Unruh, *The Plains Across: The Overland Emigrants and the Trans-Mississippi West* (1979).

MANIFEST DESTINY

Leonard J. Arrington, *Great Basin Kingdom* (1958), and with Davis Bitton, *The Mormon Experience* (1979); Gunther Barth, *Instant Cities: Urbanization and the Rise of San Francisco and Denver* (1975); William C. Binkley, *The Texas Revolution* (1952); Robert Calvert and Arnoldo De León, *The History of Texas* (1990); Malcolm Clark, Jr., *Eden Seekers: The Settlement of Oregon, 1818–1862* (1981); Robert B. Flanders, *Nauvoo: Kingdom on the Mississippi* (1965); Norman F. Furniss, *The Mormon Conflict, 1850–1859* (1960); Robert Gottlieb and Peter Wiley, *America's Saints: The Rise of Mormon Power* (1984); Norman A. Graebner, *Empire on the Pacific* (1955); Klaus Hansen, *Quest for Empire: The Political Kingdom of God and the Council of Fifty in Mormon History* (1967); Robert F. Heizer and Alan J. Almquist, *The Other Californians: Prejudice and Discrimination under Spain, Mexico, and the United States* (1971); Marvin S. Hill and James B. Allen, eds., *Mormonism and American Culture* (1972); Frederick Merk, *Fruits of Propaganda in the Tyler Administration* (1971), *The Oregon Question: Essays in Anglo-American Diplomacy and Politics* (1967), and *Slavery and the Annexation of Texas* (1972); William Mulder and A. Russell Mortensen, eds., *Among the Mormons: Historic Accounts by Contemporary Observers* (1958); David M. Pletcher, *The Diplomacy of Annexation: Texas, Oregon, and the Mexican War* (1973); Earl Pomeroy, *The Pacific Slope: A History* (1965); Jan Shipps, *Mormonism: The Story of a New Religious Tradition* (1985); Wallace Stegner, *The Gathering of Zion: The Story of the Mormon Trail* (1964); Philip Taylor, *Expectations Westward: The Mormons and the Emigration of Their British Converts in the Nineteenth Century* (1966).

THE MEXICAN WAR

K. Jack Bauer, *The Mexican War, 1846–1848* (1974); Walton Bean, *California: An Interpretive History*, 3d ed. (1978); Warren A. Beck and David A. Williams, *California: A History of the Golden State* (1972); Paul H. Bergeron, *The Presidency of James K. Polk* (1987); Gene M. Brack, *Mexico Views Manifest Destiny, 1821–1846: An Essay on the Origins of the Mexican War* (1975); Kinley J. Brauer, *Cotton Versus Conscience: Massachusetts Whig Politics and Southwestern Expansion, 1843–1848* (1967); William R. Brock, *Parties and Political Conscience, 1840–1850* (1979); Seymour V. Connor and Odie B. Faulk, *North America Divided: The Mexican War, 1846–1848* (1971); Eric Foner, "The Wilmot Proviso Revisited," *Journal of American History*, 56 (1969); Paul W. Gates, ed., *California Ranchos and Farms, 1846–1862* (1967); Neal Harlow, *California Conquered: War and Peace on the Pacific, 1846–1850* (1982); J. S. Holliday, *The World Rushed In* (1981); Robert

Johannsen, *To the Halls of the Montezumas: The Mexican War in the American Imagination* (1985); Rudolph M. Lapp, *Blacks in Gold Rush California* (1977); James M. McCaffrey, *Army of Manifest Destiny: The American Soldier in the Mexican War* (1992); Frederick Merk, "Dissent in the Mexican War," in *Dissent in Three American Wars*, Samuel E. Morison et al., eds. (1970); Robert Ryal Miller, *Shamrock and Sword: Saint Patrick's Battalion in the U.S.-Mexican War* (1989); C. W. Morrison, *Democratic Politics and Sectionalism: The Wilmot Proviso Controversy* (1967); Rodman W. Paul, *California Gold: The Beginning of Mining in the Far West* (1947), and *Mining Frontiers of the Far West, 1848–1880* (1963); R. H. Peterson, *Manifest Destiny in the Mines: A Cultural Interpretation of Anti-Mexican Nativism in California,* *1848–1853* (1975); Andrew F. Rolle, *California: A History*, 4th ed. (1987); Alexander Saxton, *The Indispensable Enemy: Labor and the Anti-Chinese Movement in California* (1971); John H. Schroeder, *Mr. Polk's War: American Opposition and Dissent* (1973); Kevin Starr, *Americans and the California Dream, 1850–1915* (1973); John E. Weems, *To Conquer a Peace: The War Between the United States and Mexico* (1974).

BIOGRAPHIES

Leonard J. Arrington, *Brigham Young: American Moses* (1985); Richard L. Bushman, *Joseph Smith and the Beginnings of Mormonism* (1984); K. Jack Bauer, *Zachary Taylor* (1985); Charles G. Sellers, *James K. Polk: Continentalist* (1966).

CHAPTER 14

The House Divided

2

*E*arly in 1864, a New York economist named John Smith Dye published a book entitled *The Adder's Den or Secrets of the Great Conspiracy to Overthrow Liberty in America.* In his volume, Dye set out to prove that for more than 30 years a ruthless Southern "slave power" had engaged in a deliberate, systematic plan to subvert civil liberties, pervert the Constitution, and extend slavery into the western territories.

In Dye's eyes, the entire history of the United States was the record of repeated Southern plots to expand slavery. An arrogant and aggressive "slave power," he maintained, had entrenched slavery in the Constitution, caused financial panics to sabotage the Northern economy, dispossessed Indians from their native lands, and fomented revolution in Texas and war with Mexico in order to expand the South's slave empire. Most important of all, he insisted, the Southern slaveocracy had secretly assassinated two presidents by poison and unsuccessfully attempted to murder three others.

According to Dye, this campaign of political assassination began in 1835 when John C. Calhoun, outraged by Andrew Jackson's opposition to states' rights and nullification, encouraged a deranged man named Richard Lawrence to kill Jackson. This plot failed when Lawrence's pistols misfired. Six years later, in 1841, Dye argued, a successful attempt was made on William Henry Harrison's life. After he refused to cooperate in a Southern scheme to annex Texas, Harrison died of symptoms resembling arsenic poisoning. This left John Tyler, a strong defender of slavery, in the White House.

The next president to die at the hands of the slave power, according to Dye, was Zachary Taylor. A Louisiana slaveowner who had commanded American troops in the Mexican war, Taylor had shocked Southerners by opposing the extension of slavery into California. Just 16 months after taking office, Taylor was stricken by acute gastroenteritis, caused, claimed Dye, by arsenic poisoning. (This theory was disproved by a 1991 postmortem examination of Taylor's remains.) He was succeeded by Vice President Millard Fillmore, who was more sympathetic to the Southern cause. Just three years later, Dye maintained, another attempt was

made on a president's life. The slave power considered Franklin Pierce, a New Hampshire Democrat, unreliable. On the way to his inauguration, Pierce's railroad car derailed and rolled down an embankment. The president and his wife escaped injury, but their 12-year-old son was killed. In the future, Pierce toed the Southern line.

In 1857, Dye claimed, yet another attempt was made to kill a president. On February 23, 1857, President-elect James Buchanan, a Pennsylvania Democrat, dined at Washington's National Hotel. Buchanan had won the Democratic presidential nomination in the face of fierce Southern opposition, and, in Dye's view, the slaveocracy wanted to remind Buchanan who was in charge. Southern agents sprinkled arsenic on the lump sugar used by Northerners to sweeten their tea. Because Southerners drank coffee and used granulated sugar, no Southerners were injured. But, according to Dye, 60 Northerners were poisoned, including the president, and 38 died. Frightened by this near bout with death, Buchanan proved to be a reliable tool of the slave power.

In fact, no credible evidence supports any of John Smith Dye's sensational allegations. Historians have uncovered no connection between John C. Calhoun and the assassination attempt on Andrew Jackson; nor have they found any proof that Harrison's and Taylor's deaths resulted from poisoning or that Southern agents derailed Pierce's train; nor have they located any evidence at all that 60 Northerners were poisoned at the dinner for President-elect Buchanan. Yet even if his charges were without foundation, Dye was not alone in interpreting events in conspiratorial terms. His book *The Adder's Den* was only one of the most extreme examples of conspiratorial charges that had been made by abolitionists since the late 1830s. By the 1850s, a growing number of Northerners had come to believe that an aggressive Southern slave power had seized control of the federal government and threatened to subvert republican ideals of liberty, equality, and self-rule. At the same time, an increasing number of Southerners had begun to believe that antislavery radicals dominated Northern politics and would "rejoice" in the ultimate consequences of abo-

section and in every state in the country. Voter participation was extremely high, and in presidential elections neither party was able to gain more than 53 percent of the popular vote. Then, in the space of just five years, the two-party system began to disintegrate in response to two issues: massive foreign immigration and the reemergence of the issue of the expansion of slavery.

The first sign of the breakdown of the party system occurred during the debates over the Compromise of 1850. Whigs in the Deep South—convinced that their party was no longer firm on the slavery question—joined the Democratic party in large numbers. The political system was further fragmented by the sudden rise of the Know Nothings, an anti-immigrant, anti-Catholic third party in many states. By 1856 the Whig party had collapsed and been replaced by a new sectional party, the Republicans.

The Know Nothings

Four times in American history the emergence of a small, vigorous third party has led to a major realignment of the American political system. In the 1820s the rise of the Anti-Masonic party opened the way to the creation of a party system dominated by the Democratic and Whig parties. In the 1890s the emergence of the Populist party among Southern and Midwestern farmers generated a shift in voting among the Democratic and Republican parties. And in 1968 George Wallace's American Independent party led to a massive shift of voters away from the Democratic party into the Republican party.

The most momentous shift in party sentiment in American history, however, took place in the early 1850s following the rise of a party vigorously opposed to immigrants and Catholics. This party, which was known as the American party or Know Nothing party, crippled the Whig party, weakened the Democratic party, and made the political system incapable of resolving the growing crisis over slavery.

Hostility toward immigrants and Catholics had deep roots in American culture. The Protestant religious revivals of the 1820s and 1830s stimulated a "No Popery" movement. Promi-

After Philadelphia's Catholic bishop convinced the city's board of education in 1844 to use both the Catholic and Protestant versions of the Bible in schools, a vicious anti-Catholic riot erupted.

nent Northern clergymen, mostly Whig in politics, accused the Catholic Church of conspiring to overthrow democracy and subject the United States to Catholic despotism. Popular fiction offered graphic descriptions of priests seducing women during confession and nuns cutting unborn infants from their mothers' wombs and throwing them to dogs. A popular children's game was called "break the Pope's neck." Anti-Catholic sentiment culminated in mob rioting and in the burning of churches and convents. In 1834, for example, a Philadelphia mob rampaged through Irish neighborhoods, burning churches and houses.

A massive wave of immigration from Ireland and Germany after 1845 led to a renewed outburst of antiforeign and anti-Catholic sentiment. Between 1846 and 1855, more than three million foreigners arrived in America. In cities such as Chicago, Milwaukee, New York, and St. Louis immigrants actually outnumbered native-born citizens. Nativists—ardent opponents of immigration—capitalized on deep-seated Protestant antagonism toward Catholics, working-class fear of economic competition from cheaper immigrant labor, and resentment among native-born Americans of the growing political power of foreigners. Nativists charged that Catholics were responsible for a sharp increase in poverty, crime, and drunkenness and were subser-

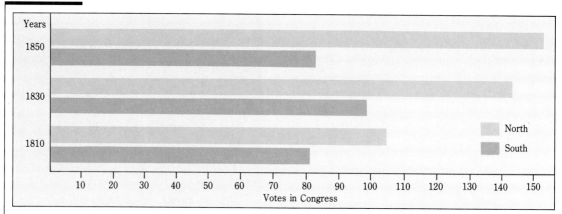

Figure 14.1
Number of votes in Congress, North versus South

vient to a foreign leader, the Pope. Thousands of native-born Americans were outraged when Catholic Archbishop John Hughes of New York declared, "Everyone should know that we have for our mission to convert the world—including the inhabitants of the United States—the people of the cities and the people of the country, the officers of the navy and the marines, commanders of the army, the legislatures, the Senate, the Cabinet, the President, and all!"

To native-born Protestant workers, the new immigrants posed a tangible economic threat. The late 1840s and early 1850s were a period of disruptive economic change. Rapid inflation followed the discovery of gold in California. The growth of railroads disrupted local markets and eliminated jobs in river and canal transportation. Economic slumps in 1851 and 1854 resulted in severe unemployment and wage cuts. Native workers blamed Irish and German immigrants for their plight. Complained one resentful New Yorker: "Are American mechanics to be borne down, crushed, or driven to western wilds?" The immigrants also posed a palpable political threat. Concentrated in the large cities of the eastern seaboard, Irish and German immigrants voted as blocs and quickly built up strong political organizations.

In 1849 a New Yorker named Charles Allen responded to this anti-Catholic hostility by forming a secret fraternal society made up of native-born Protestant working men. Allen called this secret society "The Order of the Star

Spangled Banner," and it soon formed the nucleus of a new political party known as the Know Nothing or the American party. The party received its name from the fact that when members were asked about the workings of the party, they were supposed to reply, "I know nothing."

By 1855 the Know Nothings had captured control of the legislatures in New England except in Vermont and Maine and were the dominant opposition party to the Democrats in New York, Pennsylvania, Maryland, Virginia, Tennessee, Georgia, Alabama, Mississippi, and Louisiana. In the presidential election of 1856, the party supported Millard Fillmore and won more than 21 percent of the popular vote and 8 electoral votes. In Congress, the party had 5 senators and 43 representatives. Between 1853 and 1855, the Know Nothings replaced the Whigs as the nation's second largest party.

Respectable public opinion spoke out vehemently against the dangers posed by the party. In 1855 an Illinois Whig politician named Abraham Lincoln denounced the Know Nothings in eloquent terms:

> I am not a Know-Nothing. How could I be? How can any one who abhors the oppression of Negroes be in favor of degrading classes of white people? Our progress in degeneracy appears to me pretty rapid, as a nation we began by declaring "all men are created equal." We now practically read it, "all men are created equal, except Negroes." When the Know-Nothings get control,

it will read "all men are created equal, except Negroes, and foreigners, and Catholics." When it comes to this I should prefer emigrating to some country where they make no pretense of loving liberty—to Russia, for example, where despotism can be taken pure and without the base alloy of hypocrisy.

By 1856, however, the Know Nothing party was already in decline. Many Know Nothing officeholders were relatively unknown men with little political experience. In the states where they gained control, the Know Nothings proved unable to enact their legislative program, which included a 21-year residency period before immigrants could become citizens and vote, a limitation on political officeholding to native-born Americans, and restrictions on the sale of liquor.

After 1855 the Know Nothing party was supplanted in the North by a new and explosive sectional party, the Republicans. By 1856 Northern workers felt more threatened by the Southern slave power than by the Pope and Catholic immigrants. At the same time, fewer and fewer Southerners were willing to support a party that ignored the question of the expansion of slavery. As a result, the Know Nothing party rapidly dissolved.

Nevertheless, the Know Nothings left an indelible mark on American politics. The Know Nothing movement eroded loyalty to the national political parties, helped destroy the Whig party, and undermined the capacity of the political system to contain the divisive issue of slavery.

Young America

For nearly four years following the Compromise of 1850, agitation over the question of the expansion of slavery abated. Most Americans were weary of the continuing controversy and turned their attention away from politics to focus instead on railroads, cotton, and trade. The early 1850s were dominated by dreams of greater American influence abroad—in areas such as Asia, the Caribbean, and Central America. Majestic clipper ships raced from New York to China in as few as 104 days. Steamship and railroad promoters launched ambitious schemes to build transit routes across Central America to link California and the Atlantic Coast. Expansionists sponsored filibustering expeditions into Cuba, Mexico, and Nicaragua.

The whole world appeared to be opening up to American influence. In 1853 Commodore Matthew Perry sailed into Tokyo Bay with two steam frigates and two sailing ships, thereby ending Japan's era of isolation from the western world. The next year, Perry forced the Japanese to accept the Treaty of Kanagawa, which permitted the United States to open a consulate in Japan, opened some Japanese ports to American trade, and established low import duties. This, in turn, led to Japanese decisions in the 1860s and 1870s to industrialize in order to prevent Westerners from controlling Japan's future.

Yet the appearance of sectional calm was deceptive. Both the Democratic and Whig parties were deeply divided. In the presidential election of 1852, six different candidates had run. Although Franklin Pierce, a New Hampshire Democrat, scored an impressive Electoral College victory, 254–42, his margin in the popular vote was just 44,000 votes. He actually received 14,000 fewer votes in the North than his opponents.

At his inauguration as the nation's fourteenth president in March 1853, Pierce voiced the popular longing for a new era of sectional peace. "I fervently hope," he declared, "that the [slavery] question is at rest, and that no sectional or ambitious or fanatical excitement may again threaten the durability of our institutions or obscure the light of our prosperity."

In office, Pierce tried to unite the country with an aggressive program of foreign expansion called "Young America." As president, he sought to annex Hawaii, expand American influence in Honduras and Nicaragua, and acquire new territory from Mexico and Spain. He announced that his administration would not be deterred "by any timid forebodings of evil" raised by the slavery question. But each effort to expand the country's boundaries only provoked new sectional disputes because any acquisition would have posed the question of its status with regard to slavery.

Pierce was the first "doughface" president. He was, in the popular phrase, "a Northern man with Southern principles." Many Northerners

(Text continues on p. 460)

AMERICA AND THE WORLD
COMMODORE PERRY ENCOUNTERS JAPAN

This watercolor painting, *First Landing at Kurihama, July 14, 1853*, by Japanese artist Gessan Ogata depicts Commodore Perry's arrival in Japan. In the background are the "black ships" of Perry's squadron.

Young Matthew Calbraith Perry (1794–1858) loved the sea. Born in Newport, Rhode Island, he took a midshipman's commission when only 15 years old. He gained combat experience while serving under the command of his older brother, Oliver Hazard Perry, a naval hero of the War of 1812. Young Perry devoted the remainder of his life to naval affairs. He was an early advocate of an all-steam American navy; he was among the founders of the United States Naval Academy at Annapolis, Maryland; and he commanded naval forces in support of U.S. troops during the Mexican War of the 1840s. By 1850 he ranked among the best known U.S. naval officers of his generation.

When in 1843 the United States sent an envoy, Congressman Caleb Cushing of Massachusetts, to the Orient to negotiate a commercial treaty with China, Perry took note. The Cushing Treaty gained Senate ratification in

1845 and resulted in an explosion in U.S. trade with the Chinese. The value of American trade goods sent to China rose from $9 million in 1845 to $22 million in 1860. Perry saw in trading relationships a benevolent basis for sharing the blessings of American civilization with other peoples.

Like so many citizens of his era, Perry was an expansionist who believed it was part of America's "manifest destiny" to spread the blessings of freedom and liberty throughout the world. More practically, his interest in promoting the use of steamships helped pique his interest in the Orient. Early steamers lost much cargo space because their inefficient engines required the consumption of large amounts of coal. As such, finding local supplies of coal as well as securing fueling stations were essential to the further development of trade in the Far East. Japan supposedly had huge coal deposits, described by an American official as "a gift of Providence, deposited . . . in the depths of the Japanese islands, for the benefit of the human family."

The need for coal, fueling bases, and the desire to expand the booming Oriental trade were matters that appealed to Perry's expansionist impulses with respect to Japan. So too were factors relating to religion and politics. Two centuries earlier the Japanese, in an effort to preserve their cultural and religious values from what they considered the contaminating effects of European explorers, traders, and missionaries, had expelled all foreigners from their land. Only the Dutch retained any commercial privileges—restricted to an annual cargo delivered to the tiny island of Deshima at the port of Nagasaki. Meantime, the *shogun*, or ranking warlord, ruled Japan with an iron will. During this period Japan's emperors were ceremonial figureheads.

From what little knowledge early nineteenth-century Americans possessed about the Japanese, they perceived them as victims of a brutal, hierarchical political system (the Tokugawa *shogunate*), what one writer called an "inveterately vicious absurdity." Their religion, declared another, represented "the grossest paganism" in reference to Shintoism because of its emphasis on multiple gods. What was lacking, exclaimed a third commentator, was some means to "convert their selfish government into a liberal republic in a short time." The proper method for doing so was to open Japan to western trade, insisted an ardent expansionist, since it was "the mission of commerce to civilize the world" and "to carry those principles of liberty and enterprise ... to the other races and nations of mankind."

The self-assured Perry subscribed to all of these notions. What he did not foresee was the central part he would play as the chief emissary of manifest destiny in prying open Japan. In 1852 Perry was anxious to gain command of the Mediterranean fleet as a capstone to his naval career. When the secretary of the navy named him commodore of the Asian fleet, he despaired but only for a moment. He soon learned that his assignment had as its focus the negotiation of a treaty with Japan.

Perry, known as "Old Bruin" by his sailors because of his gruff, bear-like manner, was fully capable of conveying in his person, as he wrote of his mission, "some imposing manifestation of power." President Millard Fillmore, however, warned him against warlike acts of any kind unless for "self-defense in the protection of the vessels and crews under his command." Fillmore commissioned him as a special diplomatic envoy charged with gaining protection for American seamen whose ships had been wrecked among the islands making up Japan, with securing a fuel depot, and with opening at least one Japanese port to American commerce. On his own Perry stocked up with goods—a telegraph system, a small steam locomotive with rail cars and track, and numerous firearms manufactured by Samuel Colt among other items—to impress the Japanese with American technology. He got pretty much everything he wanted, except a fleet of 12 ships. He would have to impress the Japanese with only four vessels—two well-armed steam frigates and two sloops.

On July 8, 1853, Perry's squadron brushed aside various smaller Japanese craft and swept into Tokyo Bay. The audacious commodore then dropped anchor a mile closer to the capital city than any foreigner had ever dared before. Japanese officials exhorted Perry to go to Nagasaki, but he refused. They could do nothing since their weapons were primitive in their firepower by comparison to those of the tiny American fleet. Six days later amid much pomp and pageantry, the two sides met formally for a brief period. With great solemnity Perry presented the American demands before returning to his squadron. He also announced that he would soon reappear with a larger fleet to receive Japan's reply. As a final bold statement, Perry ignored a request to leave at once. The next morning he scouted the inner bay before finally withdrawing. Certainly Perry had placed the shogunate in a perplexing position regarding how to maintain

Japan's seclusion in the face of so technologically superior ships and weapons.

Perry's early version of "gunboat" diplomacy had the desired impact. The shogun called together his inner council of advisors who disagreed on the proper reaction. One group favored a policy of *joi*, summarized in the phrase "expel the barbarians" at all costs. The other group preferred the strategy of *kaikoku*, or to "open the country" with limited concessions. They wanted to learn as much as possible about western military technology and ways of making war so that Japan could, in time, become powerful enough to defend itself against foreign barbarians. Their position won out.

When Perry returned to Tokyo Bay on February 12, 1854, this time with a more impressive fleet of nine warships, he found Japanese officials in a more receptive mood. After prolonged negotiations and gift giving—the Japanese were particularly impressed with the steam locomotive—the commodore signed an agreement, the Treaty of Kanagawa, on March 31, 1854. The shogunate promised to take good care of stranded American sailors and allowed two ports, Hakodate and Shimoda, to serve as trading and fueling stations. Japan also agreed to the presence of an American consul to facilitate ongoing diplomatic relations.

News about Perry's success thrilled expansionist-minded Americans. His mission, wrote a delighted editorialist, represented "the entering wedge that will, ere long, open to us the interior wealth of these unknown lands." The treaty, stated a ranking U.S. government official, would likewise "advance the cause of civilization, liberty, and religion" as defined by the West. A few even spoke of an American empire that would someday encompass China and Japan.

In reality, Commodore Perry's encounter with Japan turned out to have very different consequences. The Japanese learned as much as possible about western technology and rushed forward with programs of industrial modernization. By the early twentieth century they could do much more than keep foreigners at bay; Japan had emerged as a major expansionist power in its own right, one that engaged the United States in World War II rather than see its own territorial ambitions checked in the Far East. Wrote Admiral Isoroku Yamamoto, who planned the attack on Pearl Harbor: "I wanted to return Commodore Perry's visit." Certainly, too, the postwar infusion of Japanese trade goods into the American marketplace attests to the ironic effects of Commodore Perry's opening of Japan for the expansion of American commerce.

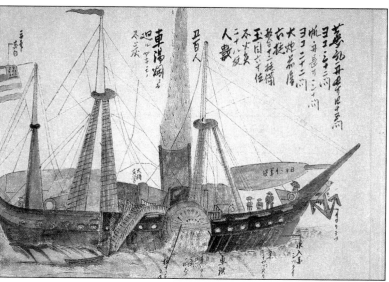

Commodore Matthew Perry's display of armor and technology led Japan to accept the Treaty of Kanagawa, opening Japanese ports to American trade. These drawings were done by artists dispatched by Japanese officials to keep a visual record of Perry's activities.

suspected that Pierce's real goal was the acquisition of new territory for slavery. This suspicion was first raised in 1853, when the president instructed James Gadsden, his minister to Mexico, to purchase as much Mexican territory as possible, to provide a route for a southern railroad from New Orleans to California. Antislavery senators forced Pierce to reduce the size of the Gadsden Purchase (to 45,535 acres and a price of $10 million), but they were unable to prevent the deal from being completed.

Cuba was the next object of Pierce's ambitions. Southern slaveholders coveted Cuba's 300,000 slaves. Other Americans wanted to free Cuba's white population from Spanish rule. In 1854 Pierce instructed his ambassador to Spain to offer $130 million for Cuba, but Spain refused the offer. That same year, at a meeting in Ostend, Belgium, three of Pierce's diplomatic ministers (including a future Democratic president, James Buchanan) sent a dispatch, later titled the Ostend Manifesto, to the secretary of state. It urged the military seizure of Cuba if Spain continued to refuse to sell the island. The Ostend Manifesto outraged Northerners, who regarded it as a brazen attempt to expand U.S. slavery in defiance of Spain's sovereign rights.

The Kansas-Nebraska Act

In 1854, less than four years after the Compromise of 1850, a piece of legislation was introduced in Congress that revived the issue of the expansion of slavery, shattered all illusions of sectional peace, and reordered the political landscape by destroying the Whig party, dividing the Democratic party, and creating the Republican party. Ironically, the author of this legislation was Senator Stephen A. Douglas, the very man who had pushed the earlier compromise through Congress—and a man who had sworn after the passage of the Compromise of 1850 that he would never make a speech on the slavery question again.

In January 1854 Douglas, the chairman of the Senate Committee on Territories, proposed that the area west of Iowa and Missouri—which had been set aside as a permanent Indian reservation—be organized as the Nebraska territory and opened to white settlement. Douglas had sought to achieve this objective since 1844, but Southern congressmen had objected because Nebraska was located in the northern half of the Louisiana Purchase where the Missouri Compromise prohibited slavery. In order to forestall Southern opposition, Douglas's original bill ignored both the Missouri Compromise and the status of slavery in the Nebraska territory. It simply provided that Nebraska, when admitted as a state, could enter the Union "with or without slavery," as its "constitution may prescribe."

Southern senators, however, refused to allow Douglas to evade the slavery issue. They demanded that he add a clause specifically repealing the Missouri Compromise and stating that the question of slavery would be determined on the basis of popular sovereignty. For reasons still in dispute, Douglas relented to Southern pressure. "By God, Sir," Douglas said, "you are right. I will incorporate it in my bill, though I know it will raise a hell of a storm." In its final form, Douglas's bill created two territories, Kansas and Nebraska, and declared that the Missouri Compromise was "inoperative and void" because it was "inconsistent with the principles of nonintervention by Congress with slavery in the States and Territories, as recognized by the legislation of 1850." With solid support from Southern Whigs and Southern Democrats

and the votes of half of the Northern Democratic congressmen, the measure passed. On May 30, 1854, President Pierce signed the measure into law.

Why did Douglas risk reviving the slavery question? His critics accused him of yielding to the Southern pressure because of his presidential ambitions and a desire to enhance the value of his holdings in Chicago real estate and western lands. They charged that the Illinois senator's chief interest in opening up Kansas and Nebraska was to secure a right of way for a transcontinental railroad that would make Chicago the transportation center of mid-America.

Douglas's supporters, on the other hand, pictured him as a statesman laboring for western development and a sincere believer in popular sovereignty as a solution to the problem of slavery in the western territories. Douglas had long insisted that the democratic solution to the slavery issue was to allow the people who actually settled a territory to decide whether slavery would be permitted or forbidden. Popular sovereignty, he believed, would allow the nation to "avoid the slavery agitation for all time to

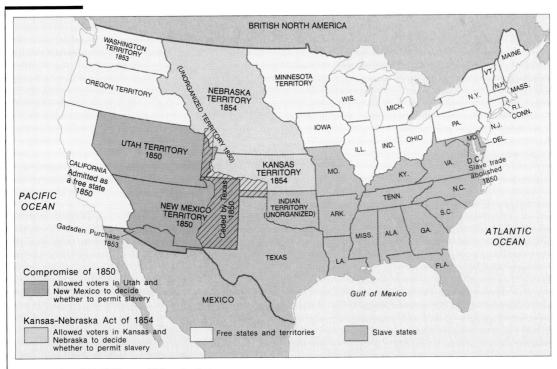

Compromise of 1850/Kansas-Nebraska Act

come." Moreover, he believed that because of climate and geography slavery could never be extended into Kansas and Nebraska anyway.

In order to understand why Douglas introduced the Kansas-Nebraska Act, it is important to realize that by 1854 political and economic pressure to organize Kansas and Nebraska had become overwhelming. Midwestern farmers agitated for new land. A southern rail route had been completed through the Gadsden Purchase in December 1853, and promoters of a northern route for a transcontinental railroad viewed territorial organization as essential. Missouri slaveholders, already bordered on two sides by free states, believed that slavery in their state was doomed if they were surrounded by a free territory. All wanted to see the region opened to settlement.

Revival of the Slavery Issue

Neither Douglas nor his Southern supporters anticipated the extent and fury of Northern opposition to the Kansas-Nebraska Act. Opponents denounced it as "a gross violation of a sacred pledge; as a criminal betrayal of precious rights" and part of a secret plot "to exclude from a vast unoccupied region, immigrants from the Old World and free laborers from our own States, and convert it into a dreary region of despotism, inhabited by masters and slaves." Abraham Lincoln said that when he read the provisions of the bill in the newspaper, he was "thunderstruck and stunned" and aroused "as he had never been aroused before." Opponents burned so many figures of Douglas from trees, the Illinois senator joked, "I could travel from Boston to Chicago by the light of my own effigy."

Douglas predicted that the "storm will soon spend its fury," but it did not subside. Northern Free Soilers regarded the Missouri Compromise line as a "sacred compact" that had forever excluded slavery from the northern half of the Louisiana Purchase. Now, they feared that under the guise of popular sovereignty, the Southern slave power threatened to spread slavery across the entire western frontier. Five Northern state legislatures adopted resolutions condemning the act.

No single piece of legislation ever passed by Congress had more far-reaching political consequences. The Kansas-Nebraska Act led conservative Whigs to abandon their party and join the Democrats, while it led Northern Democrats with free soil sentiments to repudiate their own elected representatives. In the elections of 1854, 44 of the 51 Northern Democratic representatives who voted for the act were defeated. In that election, the Democrats lost every free state except California and New Hampshire and saw the number of Northern Democratic congressmen fall from 93 to 27.

Across the North, anti-Nebraska groups sprouted up, uniting dissident Democrats, Free-Soilers, Whigs, and Know Nothings, to protest the repeal of the Missouri Compromise. On February 28, 1854, in Ripon, Wisconsin, a leading Whig named Alvan E. Bovay led a meeting that proposed that anti-Nebraska groups join together and adopt the name "Republican." Not only was this the term used by Thomas Jefferson and his followers, it also reflected a desire to place the national interest above sectional interests. In Washington, a caucus of 30 antislavery Whig and Democratic congressmen endorsed the proposal for formation of a new party opposed to the expansion of slavery.

On July 13, 1854, the anniversary of the Northwest Ordinance, which had outlawed slavery in the Old Northwest, Republican conventions were held in Indiana, Ohio, and Vermont. In the fall of 1854, the new party contested congressional elections for the first time and won 46 seats in the House of Representatives, compared to just 84 seats for the Democrats and 62 seats for the Know Nothings.

The new party, a combination of diverse elements, stood for the belief that slavery must be barred from the western territories. It contained antislavery radicals, moderate and conservative Free Soilers, old-line Whigs, former Jacksonian Democrats, nativists, and antislavery immigrants. It included a number of men, like William H. Seward of New York, who believed that blacks should receive civil rights including the right to vote. But the new party also attracted many individuals, like Salmon P. Chase and Abraham Lincoln, who favored colonization as the only workable solution to slavery. Despite their differences, however, all of these groups shared a conviction that the west-

Holman Hamilton, *Prologue to Conflict: the Crisis and Compromise of 1850* (1964); Joseph G. Rayback, *Free Soil: The Election of 1848* (1970).

DISINTEGRATION OF THE PARTY SYSTEM

Thomas Alexander, *Sectional Stress and Party Strength* (1967); Carleton Beales, *Brass Knuckles Crusade: The Great Know-Nothing Conspiracy* (1960); Ray Allen Billington, *The Protestant Crusade, 1800–1860* (1938); Eric Foner, *Free Soil, Free Labor, Free Men: the Ideology of the Republican Party* (1970); Paul W. Gates, *Fifty Million Acres: Conflicts over Kansas Land Policy, 1854–1890* (1954); William E. Gienapp, *Origins of the Republican Party* (1987); Charles G. Hamilton, *Lincoln and the Know-Nothing Movement* (1954); Michael F. Holt, *Forging a Majority: The Formation of the Republican Party in Pittsburgh, 1848–1860* (1969); James C. Malin, *The Nebraska Question, 1852–1854* (1953); Stuart C. Miller, *The Unwelcome Immigrant* (1969); John R. Mulkern, *The Know-Nothing Party in Massachusetts* (1990); Alice Nichols, *Bleeding Kansas* (1954); Roy F. Nichols, "The Kansas-Nebraska Act: A Century of Historiography," *Mississippi Valley Historical Review*, 43 (1956); W. Darrell Overdyke, *The Know-Nothing Party in the South* (1950); James A. Rawley, *Race and Politics: "Bleeding Kansas" and the Coming of the Civil War* (1969); Joel H. Silbey, *The Shrine of Party: Congressional Voting Behavior, 1841–1852* (1967), and *The Transformation of American Politics, 1840–1860* (1967); Mark W. Summers, *The Plundering Generation: Corruption and the Crisis of the Union* (1987).

THE GATHERING STORM

Dale Baum, *The Civil War Party System: The Case of Massachusetts, 1848–1876* (1984); Robert M. Cover, *Justice Accused* (1975); Don E. Fehrenbacher, *The Dred Scott Case: Its Significance in American Law and Politics* (1978); Paul Finkelman, *An Imperfect Union: Slavery, Federalism and Comity* (1981); Eric Foner, *Free Soil, Free Labor, Free Men: The Ideology of the Republican Party before the Civil War* (1970); A. Leon Higginbotham, Jr., *In the Matter of Color: Race and the American Legal Process* (1978); Michael F. Holt, *Forging a Majority: The Formation of the Republican Party in Pittsburgh, 1848–1860* (1969); Stanley I. Kutler, *The Dred Scott Decision* (1967); Stephen E. Maizlish, *The Triumph of Sectionalism:*

The Transformation of Ohio Politics (1983); Thomas D. Morris, *Free Men All: The Personal Liberty Laws of the North* (1974); Arthur M. Schlesinger, Jr., and Fred L. Israel, eds., *History of U.S. Political Parties* (1973); Hans L. Treffouse, *The Radical Republicans* (1969).

CRISIS OF THE UNION

Jules Abels, *Man on Fire: John Brown and the Cause of Liberty* (1971); Elizabeth Ammons, ed., *Critical Essays on Harriet Beecher Stowe* (1979); Hannah Page Wheeler Andrews, *Time and Variations: Uncle Tom's Cabin as Book, Play, and Film* (1979); R. O. Boyer, *The Legend of John Brown* (1973); Don E. Fehrenbacher, *Prelude to Greatness: Lincoln in the 1850s* (1962); Charles H. Foster, *The Rungless Ladder: Harriet Beecher Stowe and New England Puritanism* (1970); Thomas F. Gossett, *Uncle Tom's Cabin and American Culture* (1985); Theodore R. Hovet, *The Master Narrative: Harriet Beecher Stowe's Subversive Story of Master and Slave* (1988); Henry V. Jaffa, *Crisis of the House Divided: An Interpretation of the Issues in the Lincoln-Douglas Debates* (1959); Ellen Moers, *Harriet Beecher Stowe and American Literature* (1978). Truman Nelson, *The Old Man: John Brown at Harper's Ferry* (1973); Benjamin Quarles, *Allies for Freedom: Blacks and John Brown* (1974), and *Blacks on John Brown* (1972); Jeffrey Rossbach, *Ambivalent Conspirators: John Brown, the Secret Six, and a Theory of Slave Violence* (1982); Louis Ruchames, ed., *John Brown: The Making of a Revolutionary* (1969); Kenneth M. Stampp, *America in 1857* (1990); David Zarefsky, *Lincoln, Douglas, and Slavery* (1990).

BIOGRAPHIES

John R. Adams, *Harriet Beecher Stowe* (1989); Richard Current, *The Lincoln Nobody Knows* (1963); Robert W. Johannsen, *Stephen A. Douglas* (1973); William S. McFeely, *Frederick Douglass* (1991); Samuel Eliot Morison, *"Old Bruin": Commodore Matthew C. Perry, 1794–1858* (1967); William L. Neumann, *America Encounters Japan: From Perry to MacArthur* (1963); Stephen B. Oates, *To Purge This Land with Blood: A Biography of John Brown*, 2d ed., (1984), and *With Malice Toward None: The Life of Abraham Lincoln* (1977); William E. Parrish, *David Rice Atchison of Missouri* (1961); Damon Wells, *Stephen Douglas: The Last Years, 1857–1861* (1971).

Election News.
Lincoln elected—

PONY
NOV
ST. JOSEPH
THE CENTRAL OVERLAND CALIFORNIA
& PIKES PEAK
EXPRESS COMPANY
NOV 8
ST. JOSEPH, MO

Benham
Jules bur
for the Rocky Mountains

CHAPTER 15

A Nation Shattered by Civil War, 1860–1865

*L*ooking eastward from Sharpsburg into the mountains of western Maryland, General Robert E. Lee uttered the fateful words: "We will make our stand." Behind him was the Potomac River and to his front was Antietam Creek. Having invaded Union territory in early September 1862, Lee dispersed his Army of Northern Virginia, some 50,000 strong, across the countryside to capture strategic points like Harpers Ferry and to rally the citizens of this border, slaveholding state behind the Confederate cause. Now he issued orders for his troops to reassemble with all haste at Sharpsburg. A major battle was in the making. General George B. McClellan's Army of the Potomac, numbering nearly 100,000 soldiers, was rapidly descending upon Lee's position.

Early on the morning of September 17, the great battle began. As the day progressed, Union forces attacked in five uncoordinated waves, which allowed Lee to maneuver his heavily outnumbered troops from point to point in warding off federal assaults. As usual, Lee calculated his opponent's temperament correctly. McClellan was too timid to throw everything into the battle at once. As darkness fell, the Confederates still held their lines. Lee knew, however, that if McClellan attacked again the next morning, the Southern army might well be annihilated.

Among those rebel troops who marched into Maryland was 25-year-old Thomas Jefferson Rushin. He had grown up secure in his social station as the second son of Joel Rushin, a prospering west Georgia cotton planter who owned 21 slaves. Young Thomas was anxious to show those far-off "Black Republican" Yankees that Southern gentlemen would never shrink from battle in defense of their way of life. He enlisted in Company K of the Twelfth Georgia Volunteers in June 1861. At 5:30 A.M. on September 17, 1862, Sergeant Rushin waited restlessly north of Sharpsburg—where the first Union assault occurred.

As dawn beckoned, Rushin and his comrades first heard skirmish fire, then the booming of cannons. Out in an open field they soon engaged Yankee troops appearing at the edge of a nearby woods. The Twelfth Georgia Volunteers

stood their ground until they pulled back at 6:45 A.M. By the time that order came, 62 of the Georgians lay dead or wounded, among them the lifeless remains of Thomas Jefferson Rushin.

To the south of Sharpsburg, the battle would soon heat up. At 9:00 A.M. General Ambrose E. Burnside's Union soldiers prepared to cross a stone bridge over Antietam Creek. On the other side was sharply rising ground, on top of which troops in gray waited, ready to shoot at any person bold enough to venture onto what became known as Burnside Bridge.

The Eleventh Connecticut Volunteers were among those poised for the advance. Included in their number was 18-year-old Private Alvin Flint, Jr., who had enlisted a few months before in Company D. He was from Hartford where his father, Alvin, Sr., worked in a paper-making factory. Flint's departure from home was sorrowful because his mother had just died of consumption. A few weeks later he received word that his younger sister had succumbed to the same disease.

Flint's own sense of foreboding must have been overwhelming as he charged toward the bridge. In an instant, he became part of the human carnage, as minié balls poured down from across the bridge. Bleeding profusely from a mortal wound, he died before stretcher-bearers from the Ambulance Corps could reach him.

Flint never knew that his father and younger brother had recently joined another Connecticut regiment, affording Alvin, Sr., the chance to visit the battlefield a month later in search of his son's remains. Deeply distressed, his father wrote the *Hartford Courant* and decried the loss of "my boy" who "was brutally murdered" because of this "hellish, wicked rebellion." "Oh how dreadful was that place to me," he wrote in agony, where his son "had been buried like a beast of the field!"

Fifty-three-year-old Alvin Flint, Sr., gave up, returned to his regiment, and marched toward Fredericksburg, Virginia, where another major battle took place on December 13, 1862. A month later the two remaining Flints died of typhoid fever, a disease then raging through the Army of the Potomac.

As the human toll mounted higher and higher, Civil War battlefields became hallowed

The human toll of the Civil War was overwhelming for contemporaries and remains so for later generations. Thomas Jefferson Rushin (left) and Alvin Flint, Jr. (right), were young casualties at the Battle of Antietam.

ground. Southerners named these sites after towns while Northerners named them for nearby landmarks like rivers and streams. In the South the Battle of Sharpsburg symbolized a valiant stand against overwhelming odds. In the North the Battle of Antietam represented a turning point in the war because Union troops, at last, controlled the field of combat after Lee, astonished that McClellan did not continue the fight, ordered a retreat back into Virginia on the evening of September 18.

Different names could not change the results. With 23,000 dead and wounded soldiers, Antietam turned out to be the bloodiest one-day action of the Civil War. And before the slaughter ended in 1865, total casualties reached 1.2 million people, including 620,000 dead—more than the total number of United States troops who lost their lives in World Wars I and II combined. Back in April 1861 when the Confederates fired on Fort Sumter, no one foresaw such carnage. No one imagined bodies as "thick as human leaves" decaying in fields around Sharpsburg, or how "horrible" looking would be "the faces of the dead."

The coming of the Civil War could be compared to a time bomb ready to explode. The fundamental issue was slavery, or more specifically whether the "peculiar institution" would be allowed to spread across the American landscape. Southerners likewise feared that Northern lead-

ers would use federal authority to declare slavery null and void throughout the land. The South made its stand on the principle of states' rights and voted to secede. The North, in response, went to war to save the Union, but always lurking in the background was the issue of permitting the continued existence of slavery. The carnage of the war settled the matter. A few days after Antietam, President Abraham Lincoln announced the Emancipation Proclamation, which transformed the Civil War into a struggle to end slavery—and the way of life it supported—as a means of destroying Confederate resistance and preserving the federal Union.

FROM SECESSION TO FULL-SCALE WAR

On April 23, 1860, the Democratic party gathered in Charleston, South Carolina, to select a presidential candidate. No nominating convention faced a more difficult task. The delegates argued bitterly among themselves. In a rehearsal of what was to come, many Southern delegates left the convention. The breaking up of the Democratic party cleared the way for Lincoln's election, which in turn provoked the secession of seven Southern states by February 1861. As the Union came apart, all Americans watched closely to see how "Honest Abe," the "Railsplitter" from Illinois, would handle the secession crisis.

Electing a New President

Even before the Democratic convention met, there was evidence that the party was crumbling. Early in 1860 Jefferson Davis of Mississippi introduced a series of resolutions in the U.S. Senate calling for federal protection of slavery in all western territories. More extreme "Fire-eaters," such as William L. Yancey of Alabama, not only embraced Davis's proposal but announced that he and others would leave the convention if the party did not defend their inalienable right to hold slaves and nominate a Southerner for president. Playing to cheering galleries in Charleston, the center of secessionist sentiment, delegates from eight Southern states walked out after the convention rejected an extreme proslavery platform.

Those who remained tried to nominate a candidate, but after dozens of ballots no one received a two-thirds majority. So the delegates gave up and agreed to reconvene in Baltimore in another six weeks. But that convention also failed to produce a consensus. Finally, in two separate meetings, Northern delegates named Stephen A. Douglas as their candidate while Southern delegates chose John C. Breckinridge of Kentucky.

To confuse matters further, a short-lived party, the Constitutional Unionists, emerged. This coalition of former Whigs, Know Nothings, and Unionist Democrats adopted a platform advocating "no political principle other than the Constitution of the country, the union of the states, and the enforcement of the laws." They nominated John Bell of Tennessee, and he enjoyed some support in the border states, drawing votes away from both Douglas and Breckinridge and making it easier for the sectional Republican party to carry the election.

When the Republicans gathered in Chicago during mid-May, they were very optimistic, especially with the Democrats hopelessly divided. Delegates constructed a platform with many promises, including high tariffs in an appeal to gain the support of Northern manufac-

turers and a homestead law in a bid to win the backing of citizens wanting free farmland. On the slave expansion issue there was no hint of compromise. "The normal condition of all the territory of the United States is that of freedom," the platform read, and no federal, state, or local legislative body could ever "give legal existence to slavery in any territory." The platform, however, did not call for an end to the institution of slavery in states where it already existed.

To ensure victory, Republican party regulars sought a candidate, as one of them stated, "of popular origin, . . . who had no record to defend and no radicalism of an offensive character." This left out Senator William H. Seward, the front-runner, who was widely known as a strong antislavery advocate. Seward fell short of a majority on the first ballot. Then the skilled floor managers of Abraham Lincoln, the local favorite from Illinois—a state that the Republican party had failed to carry in 1856—started what became a landslide for their candidate.

The 1860 presidential campaign took place in a lightning-charged atmosphere of threats and fears bordering on hysteria. Rumors of slave revolts, town burnings, and the murder of women and children swept the South. Newspapers reported the imminence of John Brown–style invasions and of slaves stockpiling strychnine to poison water supplies. In one Alabama town, a mob hanged a stranger, thinking him to be an abolitionist. Across the South militia companies armed themselves and started to drill just in case that "black-hearted abolitionist fanatic" Lincoln won the election.

According to custom, Lincoln stayed at home during the campaign and let others speak for him. His supporters inflamed sectional tensions by bragging that slavery would never survive their candidate's presidency. Stephen Douglas, desperately trying "to save the Union," announced that "I will go South." He embarked on the first nationwide speaking tour of a presidential nominee. Once underway, Southern Democrats asked Douglas to withdraw from the election in favor of Breckinridge, whom they thought had a better chance to beat Lincoln. Douglas refused, maintaining a public posture that only he could defeat the Republican candidate.

This 1860 cartoon shows Abraham Lincoln, "the fittest of all candidates," outdistancing his opponents.

On election day, November 6, 1860, Lincoln won only 39.9 percent of the popular vote, but he received 180 Electoral College votes, 57 more than the combined total of his opponents. The vote was purely sectional; Lincoln's name did not appear on the ballots of ten Southern states. Even when totaling all the popular votes against him, Lincoln still would have won in the Electoral College by 17 votes because he carried the most populous states—all in the North. His election dramatically demonstrated to Southerners their minority status.

Secession Rends the Union

Lincoln told one friend during the campaign that Southerners "have too much good sense, and good temper, to attempt the ruin of the government." He explained to others that he would support a constitutional amendment protecting slavery where it already existed, but Southerners believed otherwise. Northerners, especially abolitionists, stated a Georgian, were "a troublesome . . . set of meddlers." The choice for the South, as the Mississippi secession convention framed the alternatives, was either to "submit to degradation, and to the loss of [slave] property worth four billions," or to leave the Union. No matter what, "the South will never submit" was the common refrain. Secession, then, meant liberation from the oppression of Black Republicans.

South Carolina led the way when its legislature, in the wake of Lincoln's victory, unanimously called for a secession convention. On December 20, 1860, the delegates voted 169 to 0 to leave the Union. The rationale had long since been developed by John C. Calhoun. State authority was superior to that of the nation, and as sovereign entities, states could as freely leave as they had freely joined the Union. South Carolina, as the delegates announced, had "resumed her position among the nations of the world."

By early February 1861 the Deep South states of Georgia, Florida, Alabama, Mississippi, Louisiana, and Texas had also voted for secession. Representatives from the seven states first met in Montgomery, Alabama, on February 8 and proclaimed a new nation, the Confederate States of America. They elected Jefferson Davis

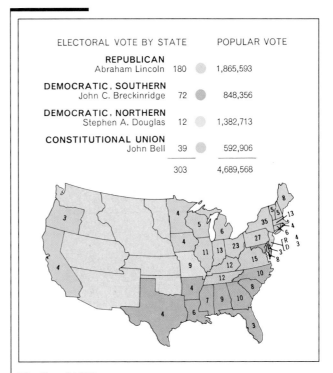

ELECTORAL VOTE BY STATE	POPULAR VOTE
REPUBLICAN Abraham Lincoln 180	1,865,593
DEMOCRATIC, SOUTHERN John C. Breckinridge 72	848,356
DEMOCRATIC, NORTHERN Stephen A. Douglas 12	1,382,713
CONSTITUTIONAL UNION John Bell 39	592,906
303	4,689,568

Election of 1860

provisional president and wrote a plan of government, which except for emphasizing states' rights they modeled on the federal Constitution. The Southern government would consist of an executive branch headed by a president, a two-house Congress, and a Supreme Court. The Confederate constitution limited the president to a single six-year term, required a two-thirds vote of Congress to admit new states or enact appropriations bills, and forbade protective tariffs and government funding of internal improvements.

For some Northerners, such as newspaper editor Horace Greeley of the *New York Tribune*, the intelligent course was to let the "wayward sisters" of the South "depart in peace." A more conciliatory approach, as suggested by Senator John J. Crittenden of Kentucky, was to enshrine the old Missouri Compromise line of 36° 30′ in a constitutional amendment that would also promise no future restrictions on slavery where it existed. Neither alternative appealed to Lincoln. Secession was unconstitutional, he maintained, and appeasement, especially any plan endorsing the spread of slavery,

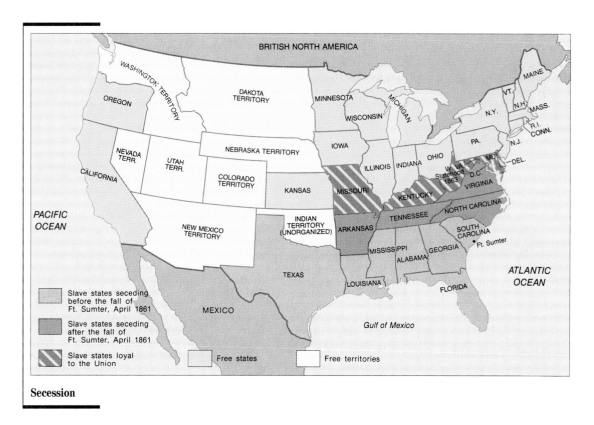

Secession

was unacceptable. "On the territorial question," he stated, "I am inflexible." These words killed the Crittenden Compromise.

President-elect Lincoln, enduring pressure from all sides to do something, decided instead to do nothing until after his inauguration. He continued to hope that pro-Unionist sentiment in the South would win out over secessionist feelings. Also, eight slave states remained in the Union; controversial statements might have pushed some or all of them into the Confederate camp. Lincoln would make his moves prudently, indeed so carefully that some leading Republicans misread him as a bumbling, inept fool. William Seward, his future secretary of state, even politely offered to run the presidency on Lincoln's behalf.

Lincoln Takes Command

On February 11, 1861, Lincoln left his beloved home of Springfield, Illinois, for the last time. All the way to the nation's capital, as his special train stopped in town after town, the president-elect spoke in vague, conciliatory terms. Be-

tween stops, he worked on his inaugural address, which embodied his plan.

On March 4 Lincoln raised his hand and swore to uphold the Constitution as the nation's sixteenth president. Then he read his inaugural address, with its powerful but simple message. The Union was "perpetual," and secession was illegal. To resist federal authority was both "insurrectionary" and "revolutionary." As president, he would support the Union by maintaining possession of federal properties in the South. Then Lincoln appealed to the Southern people: "We are not enemies, but friends." And he warned: "In your hands, my dissatisfied countrymen, and not in mine, is the momentous issue of civil war. . . . You can have no conflict without yourselves being the aggressors."

Even as he spoke, Lincoln knew that the seceding states had taken possession of all federal military installations within their borders—with the principal exceptions of Fort Sumter, guarding the entrance to Charleston harbor, and Fort Pickens along the Florida coast at Pensacola. The next day Lincoln received an ominous report. Major Robert Anderson, in command of Fort Sumter, was running out of provisions and would have to abandon his position within six weeks unless resupplied.

Lincoln had a month to back off or decide upon a showdown. He consulted his cabinet, only to get sharply conflicting advice. Finally, he sent an emissary to South Carolina to gather intelligence. At the end of March he received a distressing report. South Carolinians, the agent informed him, had "no attachment to the Union" and were anxious for war. Now Lincoln realized how grossly he had overestimated the extent of pro-Union feeling in the South. The president would stand firm.

Knowing full well the implications of his actions, Lincoln ordered the navy to take provisions to Fort Sumter. Just before the expedition left, he sent a message to South Carolina's governor, notifying him that "if such attempt be not resisted, no effort to throw in men, arms, or ammunition, will be made." It was up to the rebels, from the president's point of view, to decide whether they wanted war.

Before the supply expedition arrived, Confederate General P. G. T. Beauregard presented Major Anderson with a demand that he and his troops withdraw from Fort Sumter. Anderson replied that he would do so, if not resupplied. Knowing that help was on the way, Confederate officials ordered the cannonading of Fort Sumter. The firing commenced at 4:30 A.M. on April 12, 1861. Thirty-four hours later, Major Anderson surrendered. On April 15 Lincoln announced that an "insurrection" existed and called for 75,000 volunteers to put down the Southern rebellion. The Civil War had begun.

An Accounting of Resources

The firing on Fort Sumter caused both jubilation and consternation. Most citizens thought that a battle or two would quickly end the conflict, so they rushed to enlist, not wanting to miss the action. The emotional outburst was particularly strong in the South where up to 200,000 enthusiasts tried to join the fledgling Confederate military machine. Several thousand had to be sent home because it was impossible to muster them into the service in so short a time with even the bare essentials of war—uniforms, weapons, camp equipment, and food rations.

Professional military men like Lieutenant Colonel Robert E. Lee, who had experienced combat in the Mexican War, were less enthusiastic. "I see only that a fearful calamity is upon us," he wrote. Lee was anxious "for the preservation of the Union," but he felt compelled to defend the "honor" of Virginia, should state leaders vote for secession. If that happened, he would resign his military commission and "go back in sorrow to my people and share the misery of my native state."

Virginians seceded (April 17) in direct response to Lincoln's declaration of an insurrection. By late May, North Carolina, Tennessee, and Arkansas had also voted to leave the Union, meaning that 11 states containing a population of nearly 9 million people, including 3.5 million slaves, ultimately proclaimed their independence. On the other hand, four slaveholding states bordering the North—Delaware, Maryland, Kentucky, and Missouri—equivocated about secession. Lincoln understood that sustaining the loyalty of the border states was critical. Besides making it more difficult for the Confederates to carry the war into the North, their presence gave the Union, with 23 million people, a decisive population edge, a major asset should there be a prolonged military struggle.

Set in this frame, Robert E. Lee's gloom reflected more than a personal dilemma about conflicting loyalties; it also related to a realistic appraisal of what were overwhelming Northern advantages going into the war. The value of Northern property was twice that of the South; the banking capital advantage was ten to one, and it was eight to one in investment capital. The North could easily underwrite the production of war goods, whereas the South would have to struggle, given its scarce capital resources and an industrial capacity far below that of the North. In 1861 there were just 18,000 Confederate manufacturing establishments employing 110,000 workers. By comparison, the North had 110,000 establishments utilizing the labor of 1.3 million workers.

By other crucial resource measures, such as railroad mileage, representing the capacity to move armies and supplies easily, the Union was far ahead of the Confederacy. The North had 22,000 miles of track, as compared to 9000 for the South. In 1860 U.S. manufacturers produced 470 locomotives, only 17 of which were built in the South. That same year the North produced 20 times as much pig iron, 17 times the clothing, and 32 times as many firearms. Indeed, Northern factories manufactured nearly 97 percent of all firearms, a major reason why the Confederacy could not absorb all those enthusiasts who wanted to enlist in the spring of 1861. The South went to war with a serious weapons shortage.

With this imbalance, it is incredible that the South performed so well in the early going, coming so close to securing independence, and that the North fared so poorly. Among the Southern assets, at least in 1861, was sheer geographic size. As long as the Confederacy maintained a defensive military posture, the North would have to demonstrate an ability to win more than an occasional battle. It would have to conquer a massive region, and this factor alone emboldened Southern leaders. In analogies alluding to the American Revolution, they discussed how the British, with superior resources, had failed to reconquer the colonies. If Southerners main-

tained their resolve, something more likely to happen when soldiers were defending homes and families, nothing, it appeared, could extinguish their desire for national independence.

In addition, the South held an initial advantage in generalship. When secession occurred, regular army officers, some of them trained at West Point, had to decide which side to serve. Most, like Robert E. Lee, stood with their states. There were about 300 available West Pointers, and some 120 joined the Confederate army. Of those senior in age, the South gained more initial talent with Lee (54), Joseph E. Johnston (54), and Albert Sidney Johnston (58), when compared to the North's draw of Henry W. Halleck (46), Joseph Hooker (47), and George G. Meade (46).

As mature senior commanders, men like the two Johnstons and Lee quickly gravitated to the top of the new Confederate command structure. The Union structure, however, was already in place, with the aging hero of the Mexican War, "Old Fuss and Feathers" Winfield Scott (74) serving as general-in-chief in April 1861.

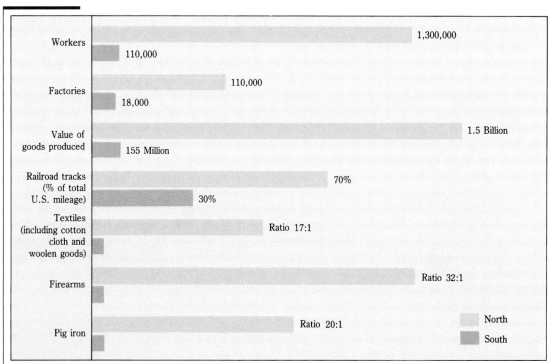

Figure 15.1
Resources, North and South

Despite valiant Southern efforts to produce war goods, the advantage of material resources in the North took its toll. This photograph shows the equipment used by General Grant during his campaigns in the South.

Jefferson Davis was named provisional president of the Confederate States of America in 1861. He faced the difficulty of establishing a new government while at the same time fighting an ongoing war.

president. "He bears the marks of greatness," wrote an admirer in 1862, because "above all, the gentleman is apparent, the *thorough, high-bred,* polished gentleman."

Appearances, however, were deceptive. Davis was a hard-working but ineffective administrator. He would not delegate authority and became tangled up in details; he surrounded himself with weak assistants; he held strong opinions on all subjects; and he was invariably rude with those who disagreed with him. Perhaps worst of all, he was not an inspirational leader, something the South desperately needed after war weariness set in. A close associate aptly described Davis in 1865: "Few men could be more chillingly, freezingly cold."

Abraham Lincoln, by comparison, lacked the outward demeanor of a cultured gentleman. Republican campaign literature of 1860 stated: "We know Old Abe does not look very handsome, but if all the ugly men in the U.S. vote for him, he will surely be elected." Worse yet, his credentials were unimpressive. He had little formal schooling; he spent an impoverished childhood in Kentucky and Indiana before moving to Illinois and succeeding as a country lawyer; he had served only one term in Congress; and he had virtually no military experience, except for brief duty as a militia captain during the Black Hawk War (1832). As Lincoln liked to joke, he "fought, bled, and came away" barely alive—not because of contact with "fighting Indians" but because of "many bloody struggles with the mosquitoes."

Many Northerners shook their heads as Lincoln entered the White House. With his tall, thin frame and long legs, he seemed to stumble as he walked, half hunched over in baggy clothes. When he listened, he appeared to be daydreaming; yet he did listen, and when he spoke in re-

Younger West Pointers, such as Ulysses S. Grant (39), William Tecumseh Sherman (41), and George B. McClellan (34), were not even in the service. Grant had developed a drinking problem after the Mexican War and was running a general store in Illinois; Sherman had fared poorly as a banker in San Francisco and was heading a military academy in Louisiana; and McClellan was in the railroad business. Even with West Point credentials, it took Grant and Sherman time to work through the pack of lackluster military professionals in line ahead of them.

Then there was the matter of civilian leadership. At the outset the South appeared to have the advantage. Jefferson Davis, the Confederacy's new president, possessed superb qualifications. Besides being a wealthy slaveholder, he had a West Point education, had fought in the Mexican War, had served in Congress, and had been Franklin Pierce's secretary of war (1853–1857). Further, he looked like a

turn, stated one newspaper reporter, "the dull, listless features dropped like a mask." Citizens soon found that Lincoln viewed himself as a man of the people, eager to do anything necessary to save the Union. They saw him bear up under unbelievable levels of criticism. Even those who disagreed with him came to admire his ability to reflect and think through the implications of proposed actions—then move forward decisively. As "Old Abe" or "Father Abraham," he emerged as an inspirational leader in the North's drive for victory.

"FORWARD TO RICHMOND!" AND "ON TO WASHINGTON!"

War hysteria was pervasive after Fort Sumter, and Southerners exuded confidence. As a Virginian wrote, "all of us are . . . ripe and ready. . . . I go for taking Boston and Cincinnati. I go for wiping them out." Another, having sent forth

five sons, offered his daughter who "desires me to say . . . that if you will furnish her with *suitable arms* she will undertake deeds of daring that will astonish many of the sterner sex." Northerners were equally delirious with war fever. In New York a woman reported on "the terrible excitement" of a city full of "excited crowds" reveling in "the incessant movement and music of marching regiments." It was a bittersweet time with loved ones parting, she said in describing a "young wife . . . packing a regulation valise for her husband"; the courageous wife "doesn't let him see her cry."

The populace clearly wanted a fight. Throughout the North the war cry was "Forward to Richmond!," referring to the Virginia city 100 miles south of Washington that had been selected as the permanent capital of the Confederacy. Throughout the South anyone shouting "On to Washington!" could expect to hear cheering voices in return. The land between the two capitals soon became a major

The departure of the Seventh Regiment from New York conveys the sense of enthusiasm everyone had early in the war.

combat zone, and the bloodshed began after President Lincoln, bowing in mid-July to pressure for a demonstration of Union superiority in arms, ordered General Irvin McDowell and 30,000 half-trained "Billy Yanks" to engage General P. G. T. Beauregard and his "Johnny Rebs," who were gathering at sleepy Manassas Junction, lying near a creek called Bull Run 25 miles southwest of the federal capital.

The Battle of Bull Run (First Manassas) occurred on Sunday, July 21. Citizens of Washington packed picnic lunches and went out to observe the engagement. Because the battlefield soon became shrouded in smoke, they saw little except Union soldiers finally breaking off and fleeing past them in absolute panic for their lives. Bull Run had its glorious moments, such as when Virginians under Thomas J. Jackson held onto a key hill, despite a crushing federal assault. This earned Jackson his nickname, "Stonewall," and he became the South's first authentic war hero. There were no heroes for the North. As Union troops straggled back into Washington, they "looked pretty well whipped." Bull Run, with 2700 Union and 2000 Confederate casualties, proved to Lincoln that the warring sections were in for a long-term struggle.

Planning the Union Offensive

Bull Run showed the deficiencies of both sides. Union troops had not been trained well enough to stand the heat of battle. The Confederates were so disorganized after sweeping their adversaries from the field that they could not take advantage of the rout and strike a mortal blow at Washington. Lincoln now realized, too, that he had to develop a comprehensive strategy— a detailed war plan—to break the Southern will of resistance. Also, he needed to find young, energetic generals who could organize Union forces and guide them to victory. Devising a war strategy proved to be much easier than locating military leaders with the capacity to execute those plans.

Well before Bull Run, Lincoln turned to Winfield Scott for an overall strategic design, and the general came up with the "Anaconda Plan"—which like the snake was capable of squeezing the resolve out of the Confederacy. The three essential coils included a full naval

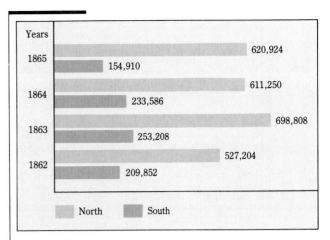

Figure 15.2
Comparative troop strength, North and South

blockade of the South's coastline to cut off shipments of war goods and other supplies from Europe; a campaign to gain control of the Mississippi River, thereby splitting the Confederacy into two parts; and a placement of armies at key points to ensure that Southerners could not wiggle free of the squeeze. Once accomplished, Scott predicted, pro-Unionists would rise up, discredit secessionist hotheads, and lead the South back into the Union, all in a year's time.

Lincoln liked certain features. He ordered the blockade, a seemingly impossible assignment, given a southern coastline stretching for 3550 miles and containing 189 harbors and navigable rivers. In early 1861 the U.S. Navy had only 7600 seamen and 90 warships, 21 of which were unusable. But with a burst of energy under Secretary Gideon Welles, the navy expanded to 20,000 sailors and 264 ships by late 1861 and continued building to 650 vessels and 100,000 sailors thereafter. Lincoln's "paper blockade," as detractors called it, became more effective with each passing month, and it also was a political success. Neutral powers generally respected the blockade, which seriously hampered Southern efforts to gain essential war matériel from abroad.

Lincoln also concluded that splitting the Confederacy was critical. He ordered Generals Henry W. Halleck, headquartered in St. Louis, and Don Carlos Buell, based in Louisville, to build great armies for the western theater. The president likewise worked with the Navy De-

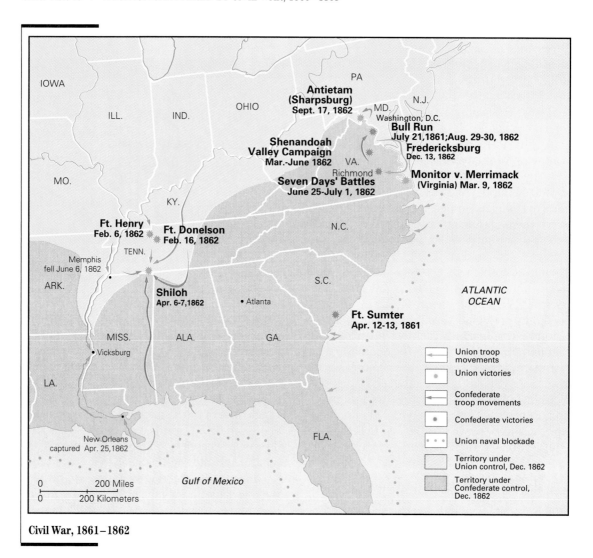

Civil War, 1861–1862

partment to devise the means to gain control of the Mississippi River. The latter effort resulted in the risky campaign of Captain David G. Farragut, whose fleet of 24 wooden ships and 19 mortar vessels captured New Orleans on April 25, 1862. Farragut's triumph was a major first step in cutting the South apart and crippling dreams of independence.

The third aspect of the Anaconda Plan, Lincoln thought, was naive. Fort Sumter convinced him that the slaveholding elite had too powerful a grip on the Southern populace to expect any significant rallying of pro-Unionists. Nor should armies sit on the sidelines or train endlessly and wait for a decisive battle. After all, Bull Run had accomplished little except to embarrass Lin-

coln. By July 1861 the president was talking about truly muscular federal armies, mightier than anything the South, with its limited resources, could ever muster. After Bull Run he got Congress to authorize the enlistment of 500,000 additional volunteer troops, far beyond the number recommended by Scott.

For a man with no formal training in military strategy, Lincoln was way ahead of the generals immediately surrounding him. As he explained to one of them, "we have the *greater* numbers," and if "superior forces" could strike "at *different* points at the *same* time," breakthroughs would occur, and the South could then be disemboweled from the inside. Lincoln's thinking pointed toward unrestrained total war, implying the complete destruction of the South, if need be, to save the Union. What the former militia captain needed were ranking officers of like mind.

Lincoln hoped that he found such a person in George B. McClellan, whom he brought to Washington to replace McDowell. McClellan happened to be in the public eye because he had just directed a small force in saving the territory of western Virginia from Confederate raiders. (West Virginia joined the Union as a separate state in 1863.) McClellan turned out to be one of Lincoln's mistakes.

Yankee Reverses and Rebel Victories in the East

George McClellan was a man of great bravado who had finished second in his West Point class and authored a book on the art of war. He could organize and train troops like no one else, as evidenced by his work with the Army of the Potomac. He was also an inspiring leader, adored by his troops. With his usual brashness McClellan told Lincoln: "I can do it all." Unfortunately, the cocksure commander was incapable of using effectively what he had built.

Lincoln gave McClellan everything necessary to do the job. Not only did the president name him commander of the Army of the Potomac, which at peak strength numbered 150,000 troops, but he made him general-in-chief after Winfield Scott retired in the fall of 1861. The problem was McClellan's unwillingness to move his showcase force into combat. When Lincoln called for action, McClellan demanded more soldiers. The rebels, he claimed from spy reports, had 220,000 troops at Manassas Junction—the actual number was closer to 36,000. To counter this mythical force, McClellan wanted at least 273,000 men before entering the field.

To give McClellan his due, his approach to the war was different from Lincoln's. He intended to maneuver his army but avoid large battles. He wanted to save soldiers' lives, not expend them, and he thought that he could threaten Southerners into submission by getting them to realize the futility of standing up to so superior a force—and so brilliant a general in command. In time he would catch the rebels

off guard and seize Richmond. Then, he believed, the game would be over, as if everyone were participating in a chess tournament.

For Lincoln, now convinced that only crushing victories orchestrated along several fronts could break the Confederate will, McClellan had contracted a bad case of "the slows." In January 1862 the angry president laughed and told a friend, "I am thinking of taking the field myself." By March he no longer covered his feelings. So that McClellan would concentrate on campaigning, Lincoln removed him as general-in-chief and ordered him to use the Army of the Potomac.

What followed was McClellan's Peninsula campaign. He transported his army down through Chesapeake Bay, landing between the York and James rivers, about 75 miles to the southeast of Richmond. In May his army moved forward at a snail's pace, which allowed the Confederates time to mass 70,000 troops before him. By the end of the month his advance units were approaching the outskirts of Richmond. Rebel forces under Joseph E. Johnston struck the main Union army near the Chickahominy River on May 31 and June 1. The Battle of Seven Pines cost a total of 10,000 casualties, among them a seriously wounded General Johnston.

Johnston's misfortune opened the way for Robert E. Lee, then advising President Davis on military matters, to assume command of the Army of Northern Virginia. Evaluating his opponent, Lee called in "Stonewall" Jackson's corps from the Shenandoah Valley and went after the Union army aggressively. McClellan all but panicked. Insisting that his army now faced 200,000 rebels (the number was 90,000), he retreated after two inconclusive fights north of the Chickahominy. What ensued was the Battle of the Seven Days (June

At first, Robert E. Lee was an advisor to Jefferson Davis. Then, on June 1, 1862, Davis appointed him to command the Confederate Army of Northern Virginia. After the war, Lee encouraged reconciliation between the North and South.

25–July 1) in which combined casualties reached 30,000, two-thirds sustained by the Confederates. Still, Lee's offensive punches prevailed—and saved Richmond. McClellan soon boarded his troops on waiting transport ships and returned to Washington.

The aggressive Lee, meantime, sensed other opportunities. In defending Richmond the rebels had abandoned their advanced post at Manassas Junction. A Union force numbering 45,000 under General John Pope had moved into position there. Having just come in from the western theater, Pope was as blind to danger as McClellan was cautious. He thought the enemy a trifle and kept exhorting his officers to "study the probable lines of retreat of our opponents." What he did not factor in was the brilliance of Lee, who, once sure of McClellan's decision to retreat, wheeled about and rushed northward straight toward Pope.

Lee broke all the rules by dividing his force and sending Jackson's corps in a wide, looping arc around Pope. On August 29, Jackson began a battle known as Second Bull Run (Second Manassas). When Pope turned to face Jackson, Lee hit him from the other side. The battle raged for another day and ended with Union troops again fleeing for Washington. Combined casualties were 19,000 (10,000 for the North).

Even with another monstrous body count, the Army of the Potomac had gained nothing in over a year's campaigning. A tired, frustrated Lincoln said: "We might as well stop fighting." Somehow, the president knew, he had to get the war off dead center; he was already working on plans to that effect, which included an emancipation proclamation. Lee gave Lincoln the opportunity to use that document when he led his victorious army into Maryland in early September, moving toward Antietam and yet another rendezvous with McClellan.

Federal Breakthrough in the West

The two Union western commanders, Henry W. Halleck and Don Carlos Buell, also suffered from "the slows." Neither responded to Lincoln's pleas for action. Halleck, however, was not afraid to let his subordinates take chances. Brigadier General Ulysses S. Grant had a good idea about how to break through 50,000 Confederate troops—under the overall command of General Albert Sidney Johnston—spread thinly along a 150-mile line running westward from Bowling Green, Kentucky, to the Mississippi River. The weak points were the two rebel forts, Henry and Donelson, guarding the Tennessee and Cumberland rivers in far northern Tennessee.

Ulysses S. Grant was criticized for his command tactics early in the war, but Lincoln remained supportive of him throughout. Grant later became the eighteenth president of the United States.

Grant sensed that a combined land and river offensive might reduce these forts, thereby cutting through the rebel defensive line and opening states like Tennessee to full-scale invasion. Working with Flag Officer Andrew H. Foote, who commanded the Union gunboats, the Federals captured both forts in February 1862. Grant even earned the nickname "Unconditional Surrender" when he told the commander of Fort Donelson to choose between capitulation or annihilation, which netted the Union cause 15,000 rebel prisoners.

After breaking the Confederate line, Grant's army of 40,000 poured into Tennessee, following after Johnston, who retreated all the way to Corinth in northern Mississippi. Cautioned by Halleck "to strike no blow until we are strong enough to admit no doubt of the result," Grant settled his army in at Pittsburg Landing, 25 miles north of Corinth along the Tennessee River—with advanced lines around a humble log church bearing the name Shiloh. There he waited for reinforcements marching south under General Buell. Flushed with confidence, Grant did not bother to order a careful posting of picket guards.

When Johnston received additional troops under General Beauregard, he decided to attack. At dawn on April 6, 40,000 rebels overran Grant's outer lines, and for two days the battle raged before the Federals drove off the Confederates. The Battle of Shiloh (Pittsburg Landing) resulted in 20,000 combined casualties. General Johnston died the first day from a severe leg wound, which cost the South a valued commander. Grant, so recently hailed as a war hero, now faced severe criticism for not having secured his lines. Some even claimed that he was dead drunk when the rebels first struck, undercutting—at least for the moment—thoughts of elevating him to higher command.

With other Union victories along the Mississippi corridor, and with Farragut's capture of New Orleans, the Union western offensive was making headway. The only portion of the Mississippi River yet to be conquered was a 110-mile stretch running north from Port Hudson, Louisiana, to Vicksburg, Mississippi. Since the rebels had powerful artillery batteries trained on the river, Union gunboats could not pass through this strategic zone and complete the dissection of the Confederacy. General Grant would redeem his reputation in 1863 by conquering Vicksburg after a prolonged siege.

TO AND FROM EMANCIPATION: THE WAR ON THE HOME FRONT

Rarely a man of humor, Jefferson Davis laughed when he read a letter from a young woman demanding that her soldiering boyfriend be sent home to wed her. Even though "I is willin'" to marry him, she wrote, the problem was "Jeem's capt'in," who "ain't willin'" to let him leave the front. She begged President Davis to intervene, promising that "I'll make him go straight back when he's done got married and fight just as hard as ever." Thinking it good for morale, Davis ordered the leave. True to his bride's word, "Jeem," once married, did return to his unit in one of thousands of incidents involving ordinary citizens who were trying to maintain the normal rhythms of life in the midst of a terrible war.

Keeping up morale—and the will to endure at all costs—was a major challenge for both sides, once citizens at home accepted the reality of a long and bloody conflict. Issues threatening to erode popular resolve were different in the North and the South. How civilian leaders handled these problems had a direct bearing on the outcome of the conflict; and Northern leaders, drawing upon greater resources, proved more adept at finding solutions designed to keep up morale while breaking the Southern will to continue the war.

An Abundance of Confederate Shortages

With their society lacking an industrial base, Southern leaders understood the need for securing material aid from Europe, just as the American colonists had received foreign support to sustain their rebellion against Britain. Secession enthusiasts thought that Europe's dependence on cotton would assure them unofficial assistance, if not diplomatic recognition as an independent nation. "Cotton," predicted the *Charleston Mercury*, "would bring England to her knees." It did not. There was already a glut in the European marketplace, and textile manufacturers after 1861 turned to Egypt, India, and Brazil as sources for new supplies of cotton.

The British decided to stay out of the conflict, and Queen Victoria declared their neutrality in May 1861. Despite concerted diplomatic efforts, other European nations followed Britain's lead and officially ignored the Confederacy. What secessionist enthusiasts had not fully considered was that European countries were just as dependent on Northern grain crops to help feed their populace. In addition, nations like Britain, having long since abandoned slavery, had serious moral qualms about publicly recognizing a slave power.

The Confederacy, however, received small amounts of secret aid from Europe. By 1865 blockade runners brought an estimated 600,000 European-produced weapons into Southern ports, and in 1862 English shipyards built two commerce raiders, the *Florida* and *Alabama*, before protests from the Lincoln administration ended such activity. The Richmond government also received about $710 million in foreign loans, secured by promises to deliver cotton; but the tightening Union naval blockade made the exportation of cotton difficult, discouraging further European loans because of the mounting risk of never being paid back.

Although neither the *Monitor* (foreground) nor the *Merrimack* won a decisive victory when they met, they helped introduce a new era in naval warfare by demonstrating the superior capacity of ironclads over wooden vessels.

From the very outset Union naval superiority was a critical factor in isolating the South. There was a moment of hope in March 1862 when a scuttled U.S. naval vessel, the *Merrimack*, now covered with iron plates, given a huge ram, and renamed the CSS *Virginia*, steamed out into Norfolk Bay and battered a fleet of wooden Union blockade vessels. Losing engine power, the *Virginia* retreated, then returned the next day to discover a new adversary, the USS *Monitor*, also clad in iron and ready to fight. The *Virginia* held its own in the ensuing battle but finally backed away, as if admitting that whatever the South tried, the North could counter it effectively. The Confederacy simply lacked the funds to build a fleet of any consequence, which allowed the Union navy to dominate the sea lanes.

The effects of cutting the South off from external support were profound. By the spring of 1862 citizens at home were experiencing many shortages—and getting mad about it.

Such common items as salt, sugar, and coffee had all but disappeared, and shoes and clothing were at a premium. In 1863 bread riots broke out in several Southern cities, including Richmond, where citizens demanded basic food because, as they shouted, "we are starving." Shortages abetted rapid inflation, as did the overprinting of Confederate dollars. The central government put a total of $1.5 billion into circulation to help pay for the war. Between 1861 and 1865 prices spiraled upward on the average of 7000 percent.

Once it was obvious that cotton would not bring significant foreign support, Jefferson Davis tried to turn adversity to advantage by urging citizens to raise less cotton and grow more food. Farm women, thrown into new roles as heads of households with husbands and older sons off at war, did so, but then Richmond-based tax collectors appeared and started seizing portions of these crops—wheat, corn, and peas—to feed the armies. For struggling wives, this was too much. Many wrote their husbands and begged them to come home; and some did, which only aggravated an increasing desertion problem.

Most Southerners, in trying to comprehend so many difficulties, blamed their central government. When the Confederate Congress, for example, enacted a conscription act in April 1862—the first draft law in U.S. history—because of rapidly declining enlistments, a North Carolina soldier wrote: "I would like to know what has been done to the main principle for which we are now fighting—*States' Rights!*—Where is it? . . . When we hear men comparing the despotism of the *Confederacy* with that of the Lincoln government—*something must be wrong.*" The fault lay with power-hungry leaders like Davis, many argued, not with a political philosophy inherently at odds with the need for effective, centralized military planning to defeat the Northern war machine.

In the months that followed accusations of political high-handedness in Richmond could be heard everywhere. The draft law, for example, allowed individuals to purchase substitutes, and with rapid inflation, avoiding service became a wealthy man's prerogative—the right of those "whose relatives are conspicuous in society," as a Mississippian complained to President Davis. When the central government in October 1862 exempted from the draft all those managing 20 or more slaves, ordinary citizens were furious with their planter leaders. Some started referring to the contest as "a rich man's war and a poor man's fight."

These were very serious problems. As a means of protecting their slave property, wealthy planters had shouted states' rights to rally their more humble neighbors on behalf of independence. With all the shortages and sacrifices, however, disaffection with these same planters was on the rise because they violated the tenets of states' rights and wrote laws favoring their class. Working in combination with a dawning realization that the North had overpowering resources and numbers, some South-

---

TABLE 15.1

Previous Occupations of Sampled White Union and Confederate Soldiers*

Civil War soldiers came rather evenly from all occupational categories, an indication that fighting the war did not fall disproportionately on any one economic group. Confederate claims to the contrary, Union armies were not made up heavily of the foreign born. Although 31 percent of all white Northern males of military age were foreign born, only 26 percent of white Union soldiers were nonnatives. By comparison, some 10 percent of all Southern troops were foreign born, even though only 7.5 percent of Confederate males of military age were nonnatives. The South, then, drew more heavily on its supply of foreign-born residents than did the North, just as the Confederacy called upon a far greater proportion of its eligible population (90 percent as compared to 40 percent for the Union) to fight the war. Running out of troops by late 1864, the only source left for the South was the slave population.

Occupational Categories	Union Troops	Total Male Population North (1860 census)	Confederate Troops	Total Male Population South (1860 census)
Farmers and farm laborers (includes Southern planters)	47.5	42.9	61.5	57.5
Skilled laborers	25.1	24.9	14.1	15.7
Unskilled laborers	15.9	16.7	8.5	12.7
White collar and commercial	5.1	10.0	7.0	8.3
Professional	3.2	3.5	5.2	5.0
Miscellaneous and unknown	3.2	2.0	3.7	0.8

*All numbers are in percentages.
Source: *Ordeal by Fire: The Civil War and Reconstruction* by James M. McPherson. Copyright © 1982 by Alfred A. Knopf, Inc. Reprinted by permission.

erners concluded, even before the end of 1862, that "the enemy is superior to us in everything but courage." Courage, especially when leaders in Richmond appeared to be so self-serving, could only be sustained for so long.

Directing the Northern War Effort

Although Abraham Lincoln focused most of his energies on military matters, he did not neglect other vital areas, including diplomatic relations with foreign powers and domestic legislation. His diplomatic objective was to keep European nations from supporting the Confederacy, and his domestic goal was to maintain high levels of popular support for the war effort. Lincoln was successful on both counts, but he took many risks, the most dramatic being his announcement of an emancipation proclamation.

Unlike Jefferson Davis, Lincoln delegated authority whenever he could. In foreign affairs he relied heavily on Secretary of State William Seward, whom European leaders came to regard as hotheaded but effective. Early in the war, for example, Lord John Russell, Britain's foreign secretary, met briefly—and unofficially—with fire-eating William L. Yancey, who was in London to seek diplomatic recognition for the Confederacy. When informed of the meeting, Seward drafted a strong letter, which Lincoln toned down, all but threatening the British with war. Russell never saw the text, but he learned about it and decided not to meet again with commissioners of the Confederacy. "For God's sakes," Russell stated, "let us if possible, keep out of it," since Britain really had nothing to gain by recognizing—and supporting—the Confederacy.

There were some intense diplomatic moments, such as in November 1861 when the U.S. warship *San Jacinto* intercepted a British packet vessel, the *Trent*, and seized two Confederate envoys, James M. Mason and John Slidell, who were on their way to the courts of Europe. England vehemently protested such an overt violation of maritime law—stopping and searching neutral vessels on the high seas. The often bellicose Seward took these threats seriously, and he and Lincoln, with the skillful help of U.S. Ambassador to England Charles Francis Adams, the son and grandson of two former

presidents, smoothed matters over by apologizing for the *Trent* affair and releasing the envoys from jail.

Then a few months later, Seward received reports that English shipyards were completing two ironclad ram vessels, similar to the CSS *Virginia*. This time the United States threatened serious repercussions, and British officials confiscated the ironclads, thus averting another crisis. All in all, Seward and Lincoln helped convince the major European powers that they could "commit no graver error than to mix . . . in our affairs." With Europe maintaining a posture of neutrality the North could fully focus its energies on defeating the South.

Also helping the Yankee cause was wartime prosperity, which Lincoln and a Republican-dominated Congress tried to sustain. In 1862 Congress passed the Homestead Act, which granted 160 acres free to individuals who agreed to farm that land for at least five years; the Morrill Land Grant Act, which offered huge parcels of public land to states that established agricultural colleges; and the Pacific Railway Act, which laid the basis for constructing a transcontinental railroad after the war. Under the leadership of Lincoln's treasury secretary, Salmon P. Chase, Congress approved National Banking acts in 1863 and 1864, which clamped down on irresponsible financial practices and provided for a uniform national currency. Also, the Republican Congress, to protect the North's manufacturing interests from foreign competition, approved tariff acts that raised import duties nearly 50 percent.

Under the watchful eye of Secretary Chase, the government likewise resorted to various expedients to finance the war effort. In 1861 Congress approved a modest income tax with rates that only fell on the wealthy. The government also taxed the states, borrowed heavily (around $2.2 billion), and issued "greenbacks," a fiat currency that, like Confederate dollars, had no backing in gold or silver but held its value better because of slowly growing confidence in the Union war effort. At no time did the Lincoln administration need to confiscate farm goods, a morale booster in and of itself.

Historians have debated whether the economic boom in the North generated by the Civil War sped up the process of industrialization in the United States. By some measures, such as the annual rate of economic growth during the 1860s, the war injured the economy. No decade in American history before the Great Depression years of the 1930s saw less economic growth, but most of this pattern had to do with the destruction of the Southern economy. By war's end in 1865, two-fifths of all Southern livestock had been killed; more than half of the Confederacy's farm machinery had been destroyed; and countless plantations and family farms had been ruined. In the North, by comparison, per capita commodity output rose by 56 percent during the decade of the 1860s, and the amount of working capital to underwrite business activity increased by 50 percent. Entrepreneurs, John D. Rockefeller and Andrew Carnegie among them, made monumental profits from war contracts. Their new-found capital base and ideas about the advantages of large-scale business organization certainly foreshadowed the rapid postwar transition to a full-scale industrial economy (see Chapter 17).

The intense level of governmental activity resulted in charges that Lincoln's true purpose was to become a dictator. These accusations started soon after Fort Sumter when the new president, acting by himself since Congress was not then in session, declared an insurrection and began a military buildup. Shortly thereafter, secessionist-minded Marylanders attacked Yankee troops moving through Baltimore to the federal capital. To quell such turbulence, Lincoln suspended the writ of habeas corpus in Maryland and ordered the arrest and jailing of leading advocates of secession, including Baltimore's mayor and several state legislators.

Whether the president had the power to violate fundamental civil rights, even when facing wartime emergencies, quickly produced a response from Supreme Court Chief Justice Roger B. Taney, a Marylander himself. In a federal circuit court case, *Ex Parte Merryman* (1861), Taney proclaimed Lincoln's action illegal by arguing that only Congress had the authority to suspend writs of habeas corpus in times of rebellion. Lincoln ignored Taney's ruling, and John Merryman, one of those arrested, languished in a military prison with no set trial date on vague charges of having incited Marylanders to secede from the Union.

During the war Lincoln authorized the arrest of some 14,000 dissidents and had them jailed without any prospect for trials. He was careful, however, not to go after his political opponents, particularly leading members of the Democratic party. The president worked to have open and fair elections, operating on a distinction between legitimate dissent in support of the nation and willful attempts to subvert the Union. Most agree that Lincoln, given the tense wartime climate, showed sensitivity toward basic civil rights. At the same time he clearly tested the limits of presidential powers.

Some of his political opponents, mostly Peace Democrats who favored negotiating an end to the war and letting the South leave the Union, regularly described Lincoln as a doer of all evil. These "Copperheads," as their detractors called them, had some support in the Midwest. They rallied around individuals like Congressman Clement L. Vallandigham of Ohio. In 1863 Union military officials arrested him on nonspecific charges, but Lincoln ordered him set free and banished to the South. Vallandigham then moved to Canada where he conducted a vigorous election campaign to become governor of Ohio, which he decisively lost. Lincoln wisely ignored the matter, hoping that Vallandigham and other Peace Democrats, who most of all liked to bewail the Emancipation Proclamation, could not muster enough popular support to undermine the Union cause.

Issuing the Emancipation Proclamation

Abraham Lincoln believed fervently in the ideals of the Declaration of Independence, which gave Americans "the right to rise" out of poverty, as he described his own experience, and "get through the world respectably." He also admired the Declaration's emphasis on human liberty, which made chattel slavery inconsistent with the ideals of the Revolution. Slavery, he wrote as early as 1837, was "founded both on injustice and bad policy."

After becoming president Lincoln promised not to interfere with slavery in established Southern states. When the fighting commenced, he seemed to move with indecisive steps toward emancipation. His only war aim, he claimed well into the spring of 1862, was to save the Union.

(Text continues on p. 498)

In this lithograph, John Bull, representing Britain, chooses between his country's need for cotton from the American South and Britain's abhorrence of slavery. Distaste for slavery ultimately outweighed dependence on cotton; thus the South failed to win Britain's support in the U.S. Civil War.

From the beginning of the conflict, both Northern and Southern leaders recognized the importance of Europe to the outcome of the Civil War. Lacking an industrial base, the South needed a steady infusion of supplies and materials from abroad. A successful Northern blockade of Southern ports would cut the vital lifeline to Europe and bring the South to its knees in a long war. The European powers, especially the British, had the power to break the blockade, and active support of the Confederacy could tip the scales decisively toward the South. Thus diplomatic success was crucial.

How the British would respond to the hostilities was the most serious diplomatic question. At first the Confederates were cocky, believing that British support for the South was inevitable. One confident Confederate wrote in early 1861, "Great Britain, France, and Russia will acknowledge us at once in the family of nations."

Southern confidence was understandable. In 1855 David Christy had published the book *Cotton Is King*. Its title became the rallying cry of the Confederacy. Because approximately one-fifth of the English population made its living directly or indirectly from the production of cotton cloth, Southerners reasoned that the British would move quickly to protect its cotton supplies.

The sentiments of most upper-class English citizens were also pro-South. The elite had long found the idea of a democratic republic repugnant. With the planter aristocracy, they shared a worldview of a natural hierarchy

to the president, shouting that "they would hug him to death" if he would "come out of that palace" and greet them. For African-Americans the Civil War at last meant liberation.

Up until this point blacks had found the war frustrating. Federal officials had blocked their attempts to enlist. Not wanting to stir up racial violence, Lincoln had danced around the issue. Most early black enlistments were in the navy. Finally in 1862 Secretary of War Edwin M. Stanton, with the president's backing, called for the enlistment of blacks—North and South. In a model program, Colonel Thomas Wentworth Higginson, one of the financial sponsors of radical abolitionist John Brown, worked with former slaves in the Sea Island region of South Carolina, an area under Union control, to mold them into a well-trained regiment (the 1st South Carolina Volunteers). They fought effectively in the coastal region running south to Florida.

The success of Higginson's troops broke down some racial stereotypes by demonstrating that blacks could master the art of war. No regiment proved that more dramatically than the 54th Massachusetts Infantry. Like all other black regiments, the 54th trained separately from white units and received its commands from white officers. The 54th Massachusetts, which included among its enlistees two sons of Frederick Douglass, prepared itself for combat during the spring of 1863 under 25-year-old Robert Gould Shaw, the scion of a wealthy Boston antislavery family. Then the regiment shipped out to the front lines in coastal South Carolina.

On July 18, 1863, the 54th Massachusetts led an early evening assault against more than twice its numbers that were defending Fort Wagner, a major bastion protecting Charleston harbor for the Confederacy. Eventually repulsed after fierce fighting, the 54th experienced more than a 40 percent casualty rate that evening. Gould, who had complete confidence in his troops, was shot dead in the charge. After the battle the rebel defenders tried to mock Gould, even in death as a Confederate stated, by burying him in a common grave "with his niggers!" Their attempted insult failed. Gould became a martyred war hero in the North, and his surviving troops, wrote one of them, swore "Revenge for our galant Curnel." The 54th still ex-

Despite an excellent record in combat, black soldiers often found themselves the victims of discrimination. Black regiments were kept separate from white units and were commanded by white officers.

pected "to Plant the Stars and Stripes on the Sity of Charleston" or die in the effort, this soldier also declared with conviction.

Before the war ended, 179,000 blacks served in the Union army (10 percent of the total), and another 29,000 were in the navy (25 percent of the total). Some 135,000 were former slaves, delighted to be free at last of their masters. Some 44,000 died fighting to save the Union and to defend the prize of freedom for black Americans. Twenty-four received the Congressional Medal of Honor for extraordinary bravery in battle. Among them was Sergeant William H. Carney of the 54th Massachusetts, whose citation praised him for grabbing the regimental flag after its bearer was shot down and leading the troops forward into the outer works of Fort Wagner. Carney, a runaway slave from Virginia, then planted the flag and engaged in hand-to-hand combat. Severely wounded, he reluctantly retreated with flag in hand, not suspecting that he would become the first black Medal of Honor recipient in the Civil War—and American history.

Because of the Emancipation Proclamation, African-Americans thus could "march through . . . fine thoroughfares," explained one black observer, as "Negro soldiers!—with banners flying." Still, as they marched, they received lower pay until protests ended such discrimination in 1864; and they quite often drew menial work assignments, such as digging latrines and burying the dead after battle. Emancipation, blacks soon realized, was just the beginning of an awesome struggle that lay ahead—beyond the Civil War—to overcome the prejudice and hatred that had locked them in slavery for over two centuries.

BREAKING CONFEDERATE RESISTANCE, 1863–1865

During the spring of 1863 Union war sentiment sagged to a new low point. Generals kept demanding more troops; yet with the exception of black enlistees, there were few new volunteers. Congress faced up to reality in March and passed a Conscription Act, which provided for the drafting of males between the ages of 20 and 45. Draftees could buy exemptions for

$300.00—an average wage for half a year—or hire substitutes. All told, federal conscription produced 166,000 soldiers, roughly three-fourths of whom were substitutes.

Conscription infuriated many Northerners, particularly day laborers who lacked the income to buy their way out of the service. Riots took place in several cities, and the worst were in New York where Irish workers, sensing a plot to force them into the Union army so that newly freed slaves would get their jobs, vented their rage in mid-July 1863. The rampaging started when workers assaulted a building in which a draft lottery was taking place. For a week the streets were not safe, particularly for blacks, who in a few cases were beaten to death or hanged by roaming mobs. Only the intervention of federal troops ended the New York draft riots, but not before 100 or more persons had died.

Moderate Republicans wondered whether the Northern war effort could outlast such serious turmoil on the home front, but Lincoln would not back down on emancipation. As a Senate leader said of him, "he is stubborn as a mule when he gets his back up." Lincoln kept approaching the war effort with the same grim determination, even as he continued his search for a commanding general with the capacity and tenacity to achieve total military victory.

The Tide Turns: Gettysburg and Vicksburg

Even before he relieved McClellan of command, Lincoln had named a new general-in-chief, Henry W. Halleck. "Old Brains," as the soldiers called him because of his West Point education and voluminous writings on military strategy, moved to Washington from the western theater in the summer of 1862. Life in the field was one thing; life in the nation's capital was another. The pressures of office caused Halleck to have a nervous breakdown.

Lincoln did not replace Halleck but functioned as his own general-in-chief until the spring of 1864. His greatest frustration was with commanders of the Army of the Potomac, which the masterful Robert E. Lee kept subjecting to embarrassing defeats. After dismissing McClellan, Lincoln named General Ambrose E. Burnside, famous for his huge sideburns, to head the eastern army. Burnside did not have

it to her hearts content." In systematic fashion Sherman's army broke the southern capacity to keep fighting by burning and leveling everything in sight.

As word of Sherman's devastating march reached Lee's troops in the Petersburg trenches, they deserted in droves, wanting to get back home to protect their loved ones. By late March Lee's Army of Northern Virginia had fewer than 35,000 troops, compared to Grant's total of 115,000. The situation was all but hopeless, so the Confederate commander ordered a retreat to the west, and Richmond fell on April 3. Grant's soldiers moved quickly to encircle the disintegrating rebel army, and they soon had their prey entrapped.

On April 9, 1865, Lee met with Grant and surrendered at Appomattox. The two generals reminisced for a few moments about their serving in the Mexican War. They said goodbye, but not before Grant graciously allowed the Confederates to keep their horses—they had to give up their arms—so that they could more easily plow their fields and plant crops after returning home. Lee's surrender served as a signal to other Confederate commanders to lay down their arms and accept military defeat. The Civil War, at long last, had ended.

CONCLUSION

At noon on Good Friday, April 14, 1865, a crowd gathered to watch Major General Robert Anderson raise over Fort Sumter the very same U.S. flag that he had surrendered four years before. A genuinely moved Anderson said: "I thank God that I have lived to see this day." Then he hoisted up the "weather-beaten, frayed, and shell-torn old flag" as Union naval vessels out in Charleston harbor fired their cannons in salute. Citizens at the fort wept and cheered, realizing that the national tragedy was finally over, a tragedy that had forever sealed the fate of secession. The states, while far from reunited, would continue together as a nation.

Just a few hours later another shot rang out, this time in the nation's capital. John Wilkes Booth, a Confederate sympathizer and racist fanatic who hated Abraham Lincoln for eman-

cipating black Americans, gained access to the presidential box at Ford's Theater and assassinated the president at point blank range. At 7:22 A.M. the next morning, four years to the day after he had declared an insurrection and called up federal troops, Lincoln died quietly at the age of 56.

In his last days Lincoln felt the elation of knowing that a war begun to preserve the Union had achieved its objective. Further, in recognition of the horrible price in lives maimed and destroyed, he took pride in the elimination of slavery from the American landscape, which he called the "act" that would put "my name . . . into history." Lincoln had also started to speak openly of citizenship for blacks as part of his reconstruction plans. Even as the American people mourned his passing, they too turned to the difficult task of how best to bring the South—defeated, destroyed, but still with a resolute streak of defiance—back into the nation.

SUGGESTIONS FOR FURTHER READING
OVERVIEWS AND SURVEYS
William L. Barney, *Flawed Victory* (1975); Bruce Catton, *The Centennial History of the Civil War*, 3 vols. (1961–1965); Henry S. Commager, ed., *The Blue and the Gray*, 2 vols., rev. ed. (1973); David Donald, *Liberty and Union* (1978), and ed., *Why the North Won the Civil War* (1960); Shelby Foote, *The Civil War*, 3 vols. (1958–1974); Richard M. McMurry, *Two Great Rebel Armies: An Essay in Confederate Military History* (1989); James M. McPherson, *Battle Cry of Freedom: The Civil War Era* (1988), and *Ordeal by Fire: The Civil War and Reconstruction* (1982); Allan Nevins, *The War for the Union*, 4 vols. (1959–1971); Phillip Shaw Paludan, *"A People's Contest": The Union and Civil War, 1861–1865* (1988); Peter J. Parish, *The American Civil War* (1975); Charles P. Roland, *The American Iliad: The Story of the Civil War* (1991); Emory M. Thomas, *The Confederate Nation, 1861–1865* (1979).

FROM SECESSION TO FULL-SCALE WAR
Michael C. C. Adams, *Our Masters the Rebels* (1978); Bern Anderson, *By Sea and By River* (1962); William L. Barney, *The Road to Secession* (1972), and *The Secessionist Impulse: Alabama and Mississippi in 1860* (1974); Steven A. Channing, *Crisis of Fear: Secession in South Carolina* (1970); Rich-

ard N. Current, *Lincoln and the First Shot* (1963); Randall C. Jimerson, *The Private Civil War: Popular Thought During the Sectional Conflict* (1988); Michael P. Johnson, *Toward a Patriarchal Republic: The Secession of Georgia* (1977); Charles R. Lee, *The Confederate Constitutions* (1963); David M. Potter, *Lincoln and His Party in the Secession Crisis*, 2d ed. (1962); Donald E. Reynolds, *Editors Make War: Southern Newspapers in the Secession Crisis* (1970); Kenneth M. Stampp, *And the War Came; The North and the Secession Crisis, 1860–1861* (1950); Emory M. Thomas, *The Confederacy as a Revolutionary Experience* (1971); Bell I. Wiley, *The Road to Appomattox* (1956); Ralph A. Wooster, *The Secession Conventions of the South* (1962).

"FORWARD TO RICHMOND!" AND "ON TO WASHINGTON!"

Michael Barton, *Goodmen: The Character of Civil War Soldiers* (1981); Thomas L. Connelly and Archer Jones, *The Politics of Command: Factions and Ideas in Confederate Strategy* (1973); Paul D. Escott, *After Secession: Jefferson Davis* (1978); Joseph A. Frank and George A. Reaves, *"Seeing the Elephant": Raw Recruits at the Battle of Shiloh* (1989); William A. Frassanito, *America's Bloodiest Day: Antietam* (1978); Paddy Griffith, *Battle Tactics of the Civil War* (1989); Earl J. Hess, *Liberty, Virtue, and Progress: Northerners and Their War for the Union* (1988); Archer Jones, *Civil War Command and Strategy* (1992); Gerald F. Linderman, *Embattled Courage: Combat in the American Civil War* (1987); Reid Mitchell, *Civil War Soldiers: Their Expectations and Experiences* (1988); James I. Robertson, *Soldiers Blue and Gray* (1988), and *The Stonewall Brigade* (1963); Frank E. Vandiver, *Rebel Brass: The Confederate Command System* (1956); Ezra J. Warner, *Generals in Gray* (1959), and *Generals in Blue* (1964); Bell I. Wiley, *The Life of Johnny Reb* (1943), and *The Life of Billy Yank* (1952); T. Harry Williams, *Lincoln and His Generals* (1952), and *McClellan, Sherman, and Grant* (1962).

TO AND FROM EMANCIPATION: THE WAR ON THE HOME FRONT

Thomas B. Alexander and Richard E. Beringer, *The Anatomy of the Confederate Congress* (1972); Curtis A. Amlund, *Federalism in the Southern Confederacy* (1966); Dale Baum, *The Civil War Party System* (1984); Herman Belz, *A New Birth of Freedom: The Republican Party and Freedmen's Rights* (1976); Stuart L. Bernath, *Squall Across the Atlantic: Civil War Prize Cases* (1970); Allan G. Bogue, *The Congressman's Civil War* (1989), and *The Earnest Men: Republicans of the Civil War Senate* (1981); Dudley T. Cornish, *The Sable Arm: Negro Troops in the Union Army*, 2d ed. (1987); LaWanda Cox, *Lincoln and Black Freedom* (1981); Beth G. Crabtree and James M. Patton, eds., *"Journal of a Secesh Lady"* (1979); David P. Crook, *The North, the South, and the Powers, 1861–1865* (1974), and *Diplomacy During the American Civil War* (1975); Drew Gilpin Faust, *The Creation of Confederate Nationalism* (1988); Eric Foner, *Politics and Ideology in the Age of the Civil War* (1980); Norman B. Ferris, *The Trent Affair* (1977); John Hope Franklin, *The Emancipation Proclamation* (1963); George M. Fredrickson, *The Inner Civil War* (1965); J. Matthew Gallman, *Mastering Wartime: A Social History of Philadelphia During the Civil War* (1990); Louis Gerteis, *From Contraband to Freedman: Federal Policy Toward Southern Blacks, 1861–1865* (1973); Brian A. Jenkins, *Britain & the War for the Union*, 2 vols. (1974–1980); Jacqueline Jones, *Labor of Love, Labor of Sorrow* (1985); Frank L. Klement, *The Copperheads in the Middle West* (1960); Leon F. Litack, *Been in the Storm So Long* (1979); James M. McPherson, *The Struggle for Equality* (1964), and *Abraham Lincoln and the Second American Revolution* (1990); Clarence L. Mohr, *On the Threshold of Freedom: Masters and Slaves in Civil War Georgia* (1986); Robert M. Myers, ed., *The Children of Pride: Georgia and the Civil War* (1972); Mark E. Neely, Jr., *The Fate of Liberty: Abraham Lincoln and Civil Liberties* (1991); Frank L. and Harriet Owsley, *King Cotton Diplomacy*, rev. ed. (1959); Benjamin Quarles, *The Negro in the Civil War* (1953); George C. Rable, *Civil Wars: Women and the Crisis of Southern Nationalism* (1989); Willie Lee Rose, *Rehearsal for Reconstruction: The Port Royal Experiment* (1964); Joel H. Silbey, *A Respectable Minority: The Democratic Party in the Civil War Era* (1977); Richard C. Todd, *Confederate Finance* (1954); Hans L. Trefousse, *The Radical Republicans* (1969); Maris A. Vinovskis, ed., *Toward a Social History of the American Civil War* (1990); V. Jacque Voegeli, *Free But Not Equal: The Midwest and the Negro* (1967); Gordon H. Warren, *Fountain of Discontent: The Trent Affair* (1981); T. Harry Williams, *Lincoln and the Radicals* (1941); Forrest G. Wood, *Black Scare: Racist Response to Emancipation and Reconstruction* (1968); C. Vann Woodward, ed., *Mary Chesnut's Civil War* (1981), and with Elisabeth Muhlenfeld, eds., *The Private Mary Chesnut* (1984); Wilfred B. Yearns, *The Confederate Congress* (1960).

BREAKING CONFEDERATE RESISTANCE, 1863–1865

Richard E. Beringer, Herman Hattaway, Archer Jones, and William N. Still, Jr., *Why the South Lost the Civil War* (1986); Iver Bernstein, *The New York City Draft Riots* (1990); David W. Blight, *Frederick Douglass' Civil War* (1989); Robert F. Durden, *The Gray and the Black* (1972); William A. Frassanito, *Gettysburg* (1975), and *Grant and Lee* (1983); Joseph T. Glatthaar, *The March to the Sea and Beyond* (1985), and *Forged in Battle: The Civil War Alliance of Black Soldiers and White Officers* (1990); U.S. Grant, *Personal Memoirs*, 2 vols. (1885–1886); Edward Hagerman, *The American Civil War and the Origins of Modern Warfare* (1988); Herman Hattaway and Archer Jones, *How the North Won* (1983); Lawrence L. Hewitt, *Port Hudson: Confederate Bastion on the Mississippi* (1987); Jay Luvaas, *The Military Legacy of the Civil War* (1959); Grady McWhiney and Perry D. Jamieson, *Attack and Die: Civil War Military Tactics and the Southern Heritage* (1982); Phillip Shaw Paludan, *A Covenant with Death: Equality in the Civil War Era* (1975); James L. Roark, *Masters Without Slaves* (1977); Charles Royster, *The Destructive War: Sherman, Jackson, and the Americans* (1991); Steven E. Woodworth, *Jefferson Davis and His Generals: The Failure of Confederate Command in the West* (1990).

BIOGRAPHIES

Thomas L. Connelly, *The Marble Man: Robert E. Lee* (1977); David Donald, *Lincoln Reconsidered* (1956); Martin Duberman, *Charles Francis Adams* (1961); Douglas S. Freeman, *R. E. Lee: A Biography*, 4 vols. (1934–1935); William S. McFeely, *Frederick Douglass* (1991), and *Grant: A Biography* (1981); James M. Merrill, *William Tecumseh Sherman* (1971); Alan T. Nolan, *Lee Considered: General Robert E. Lee and Civil War History* (1991); Stephen B. Oates, *With Malice Toward None: Abraham Lincoln* (1977), and *Abraham Lincoln: The Man Behind the Myths* (1984); Stephen W. Sears, *George B. McClellan: The Young Napoleon* (1988); Brooks D. Simpson, *Let Us Have Peace: Ulysses S. Grant* (1991); Benjamin P. Thomas, *Abraham Lincoln* (1953); Emory M. Thomas, *Bold Dragoon: J. E. B. Stuart* (1986); Hans L. Trefousse, *Andrew Johnson: A Biography* (1989); Frank E. Vandiver, *Mighty Stonewall* (1957).

CHAPTER 16

The Nation Reconstructed:
North, South, and the West, 1865–1877

& Co.

Fig.4

4

2

Washington City D.C
April 15. 1865.—

Sir:

Abraham Lincoln, President
United States, was shot by an a[s]-
[sas]sin this evening, at Ford's Theater
City, and died at the hour of 22[m]

About the same time at abo[ut]
President was shot, an Assassin
the [ba]ck chamber of the Hon W[m] H
Secretary of State, and stabbed him
several places, in the throat, neck,
face, [illegible] mortally wounde[d]

e

G

*A*s Thomas Pinckney approached El Dorado, his plantation on the Santee River in South Carolina, he felt a quiver of apprehension. Pinckney, a captain in the defeated Confederate army, had stayed the night with neighbors before going to reclaim his land. "Your negroes sacked your house," they reported, "stripped it of furniture, bric-a-brac, heirlooms, and divided these among themselves. They got it in their heads that the property of whites belongs to them." Pinckney remembered the days when his return home had been greeted with slaves' chants of "Howdy do, Marster! Howdy do, Boss!" Now he was welcomed with an eerie silence. He did not even see any of his former slaves until he went into the house. There, a single servant seemed genuinely glad to see him, but she pleaded ignorance as to the whereabouts of the other freedmen. He lingered about the house until after the dinner hour. Still no one appeared, so he informed the servant that he would return in the morning and expected to see all his former slaves.

On his ride back the next day, Pinckney nostalgically recalled his days as a small boy when the slaves had seemed happy to see him as he accompanied his mother on her Saturday afternoon rounds. He could not believe he had any reason to fear his "own people" whom he "could only remember as respectful, happy and affectionate." He probably mistook their previous displays of submissiveness as expressions of a genuine affection that would not be altered by freedom. Yet he was armed this time, and after summoning his former slaves, he quickly noticed that they too were armed. Their sullen faces reflected their defiant spirits.

Pinckney told them, "Men, I know you are free. I do not wish to interfere with your freedom. But I want my old hands to work my lands for me. I will pay wages." The freedmen remained silent as he gave further reassurances. Finally one responded, "O yes, we gwi wuk! We gwi wuk fuh ourse'ves. We ain' gwi wuk fuh no white man." Pinckney was confused and asked how they expected to support themselves and where they would go. They quickly informed him that they intended to stay and work "right here on de lan' whar we wuz bo'n an' whar belongs tuh us." One former slave, dressed in a Union army uniform, stood beside his cabin, brought his rifle down with a crash, and declared, "I'd like tuh see any man put me outer dis house."

Pinckney had no intention of allowing the freedman to work the land for themselves. He joined with his neighbors in an appeal to the Union commander at Charleston, who sent a company of troops and addressed the blacks himself. They still refused to work under his terms, so Pinckney decided to "starve" them into submission. He denied them access to food and supplies. Soon his head plowman begged food for his hungry family, claiming he wanted to work, "But de other niggers dee won' let me wuk." Pinckney held firm, and the man returned several days later saying, "Cap'n, I come tuh ax you tuh lemme wuk fuh you, suh." Pinckney pointed him to the plow and let him draw his rations. Slowly, his other former slaves drifted back to work. "They had suffered," he later recalled, "and their ex-master had suffered with them."

All over the South this scenario was acted out with variations, as former masters and former slaves sought to define their new relationships. Whites tried to keep the freedmen a dependent labor source; African-Americans struggled to win as much independence as possible. Frequently Union officials were called upon to arbitrate; the North had a stake in the final outcome. At the same time the other sections of the nation faced similar problems of determining the status of heterogeneous populations whose interests were sometimes in conflict with the majority. The war had reaped a costly harvest of death and hostility, but at the same time it accelerated the modernization of the economy and society. Western expansion forced Americans to deal with the often hostile presence of the Plains Indians; the resumption of large-scale immigration raised issues of how to adapt to an increasingly pluralistic society made up of many different ethnic and religious groups. More and more the resolution of conflicting interests became necessary: farmer versus industrialist, whites versus blacks, Republicans versus Democrats, Indians versus settlers, North versus South, management versus labor, immigrant versus native born, men

Although freedmen hoped that emancipation would release them from supervised gang labor in cotton fields, many were forced to sign yearly labor contracts and work under conditions similar to slavery.

versus women, one branch of government versus another. Complicating these issues were unresolved questions about federal authority, widespread racial prejudice in both North and South, and strongly held beliefs in the sanctity of property rights.

Reconstruction offered an opportunity to balance conflicting interests with justice and fairness. In the end, however, the government was unwilling to establish ongoing programs and permanent mechanisms to protect the rights of minorities. As on Pinckney's plantation, economic power usually became the determining factor in establishing relationships. Authorities sacrificed the interests of both African-Americans and the Indians of the West to the goals of national unity and economic growth. In 1865 a planter predicted the outcome, using a reference to the black Shakespearean character Othello. "Where shall Otello go? Poor elk—poor bufaloe—poor Indian—poor Nigger—this is indeed a white man country." Yet in the ashes of failure were left two cornerstones on which the future could be built—the Fourteenth and Fifteenth amendments to the Constitution.

POSTWAR CONDITIONS AND ISSUES

General William T. Sherman proclaimed, "War is all hell." Undoubtedly it was for most soldiers and civilians caught up in the actual throes of battle and for the families of the 360,000 Union and 258,000 Confederate soldiers who would never return home. The costs of war, however, were not borne equally. Many segments of the Northern economy were stimulated by wartime demands, and with the once powerful Southern planters no longer there, Congress enacted programs to aid industrial growth. Virtually exempt from the devastation of the battlefield, the North built railroads and industries and increased agricultural production at the same time that torn-up Southern rails were twisted around trees, Southern factories were put to the torch, and Southern farmland lay choked with weeds.

In 1865 Southerners were still reeling from the bitter legacy of total war. General Philip Sheridan announced that after his troops had finished in the Shenandoah Valley even a crow would have to carry rations to fly over the area.

One year after the war, Carl Schurz noted that along the path of Sherman's march the countryside still "looked for many miles like a broad black streak of ruin and desolation." Southern cities suffered the most. A Northern reporter described Columbia, South Carolina, as a "wilderness of ruins ... blackened chimneys and crumbling walls." Atlanta, Richmond, and Charleston shared the same fate. Much of what was not destroyed was confiscated, and emancipation divested Southerners of another $2 billion to $4 billion in assets. The decline of Southern wealth has been estimated at more than 40 percent during the four years of war.

The War's Impact on Individuals

Returning soldiers and their wives had to reconstruct relationships disrupted by separation—and the assumption of control by the women on farms and plantations. War widows envied them that adjustment. While the homeless wandered, one plantation mistress moaned, "I have not one human being in the wide world to whom I can say 'do this for me.'" Another noted, "I have never even so much as washed out a pocket handkerchief with my own hands, and now I have to do all my work." Southerners worried about how to meet their obligations; Confederate currency and bonds were worthless except as collectors' items—and even as collectors' items, they were too plentiful to have much value. One planter remarked drily that his new son "promises to suit the times, haveing remarkably large hands as if he might one day be able to hold plough handles." Many white Southerners, rich and poor, suffered a self-induced paranoia. They imagined the end of slavery would bring a nightmare of black revenge, rape, and pillage unless whites retained social control.

For four million former slaves, emancipation had come piecemeal, following the course of the Northern armies. It was not finalized until the ratification of the Thirteenth Amendment in December 1865. By then most border states had voluntarily adopted emancipation, but the amendment destroyed the remnants of slavery in Delaware and Kentucky. Most slaves waited patiently for the day of freedom, continuing to work the plantations but speaking up more boldly. Sometimes the Yankees came, proclaimed them free, and then left them to the mercy of their masters. Most, therefore, reacted cautiously to test the limits of their new freedom.

Many African-Americans had to leave their plantations, at least for a short time, to feel liberated. A few were confused as to the meaning of freedom and thought they would never have to work again. Soon, most learned they had gained everything—and nothing. As Frederick Douglass, the famous black abolitionist, noted, the freedman "was free from the individual master but a slave of society. He had neither money, property, nor friends. He was free from the old plantation, but he had nothing but the dusty road under his feet. He was free from the old quarter that once gave him shelter, but slave to the rains of summer and the frosts of winter. He was turned loose, naked, hungry, and destitute to the open sky."

The wartime plight of homeless and hungry blacks as well as whites impelled Congress to take unprecedented action, establishing on March 3, 1865, the Bureau of Refugees, Freedmen, and Abandoned Lands, within the War Department. The bureau was to provide "such issues of provisions, clothing, and fuel" as were needed to relieve "destitute and suffering refugees and their wives and children." Never before had the national government assumed responsibility for relief. Feeding and clothing the population had not been deemed its proper function. Considered drastic action, warranted only by civil war, the bureau was supposed to operate for just a year.

Under Commissioner Oliver O. Howard, the bureau had its own courts to deal with land and labor disputes. Agents in every state provided rations and medical supplies and helped to negotiate labor contracts between freedmen and landowners. The quality of the service rendered to the freedmen depended on the ability and motivation of the individual agents. Some courageously championed the freedmen's cause; others sided with the former masters. One of the most lasting benefits of the Freedmen's Bureau was the schools it established, frequently in cooperation with such Northern agencies as the American Missionary Association. During and after the war, African-Americans of all ages flocked to these schools to taste the previously forbidden fruit of education. The freedmen shrewdly recognized the keys to the planters' power—land, literacy, and the vote. The white South legally denied all three to African-Amerians in slavery, and many freedmen were determined to have them all.

Some former bondsmen had a firmer grasp of reality than their "liberators." Southern whites had long claimed to "know our Negroes" better than outsiders could. Ironically, this was proven false, but the reverse *was* true. Ex-slaves knew their ex-masters very well. One freedman pleaded, "Gib us our own land and we can take care ourselves; but widout land, de ole massas can hire us or starve us, as dey please." The events on Pinckney's plantation proved the wisdom of that statement.

Later generations have laughed at the widespread rumor among freedmen that they were to receive "forty acres and a mule" from the government, but the rumor did have some basis.

During the war, General Sherman was plagued with swarms of freedmen following his army, and in January 1865 he issued Special Field Order 15 setting aside a strip of abandoned coastal lands from Charleston, South Carolina, to Jacksonville, Florida, for the exclusive use of freedmen. African-Americans were to be given "possessory titles" to 40-acre lots. Three months later, the bill establishing the Freedmen's Bureau gave the agency control of thousands of acres of abandoned and confiscated lands to be rented to "loyal refugees and freedmen" in 40-acre plots for three-year periods with an option to buy at a later date. By June 1865, 40,000 African-Americans were cultivating land. In the Sea Islands and elsewhere, they proved they could be successful independent farmers. Yet land reform was not a popular cause among whites. Although a few congressmen continued to advocate land confiscation and redistribution, the dream of "forty acres and a mule" was a casualty of the battle for control of Reconstruction when Andrew Johnson's pardons returned most confiscated lands. Indeed, the is-

(Text continues on p. 522)

Freedmen realized that education was one key to real freedom and flocked to schools opened by the Freedmen's Bureau, the American Missionary Association, and various religious and rights groups.

DAY OF JUBILO:
SLAVES CONFRONT EMANCIPATION

Rooted in Africa, the oral tradition became one of the tools slaves used to maintain a sense of self-worth. Each generation heard the same stories, and story-telling did not die with slavery. The day that slaves first learned of their emancipation remained vivid in their own minds and later in those of their descendants. The great-grandchildren of a strong-willed woman named Caddy relished the family account of her first taste of freedom:

> Caddy threw down that hoe, she marched herself up to the big house, then she looked around and found the mistress. She went over to the mistress, she flipped up her dress and told the white woman to do some thing. She said it mean and ugly. This is what she said: *Kiss my ass!*

Caddy's reaction was not typical. There was no typical response. Reminiscences of what was called the "Day of Jubilo" formed a tapestry as varied as the range of personality. Some, however, seem to have occurred more frequently than others. Many freedmen echoed one man's description of his and his mother's action when their master announced their emancipation: "Jes like tarpins or turtles after 'mancipation. Jes stick our heads out to see how the land lays."

Caution was a shrewd and realistic response. One of the survival lessons in slavery had been not to trust whites too much. This had been reinforced during the war when Union troops moved through regions proclaiming emancipation only to depart, leaving blacks at the mercy of local whites. One elderly slave described the aftermath to a Union correspondent. "Why, the day after you left, they jist had us all out in a row and told us they was going to shoot us, and they did hang two of us; and Mr. Pierce, the overseer, knocked one with a fence rail and he died the next day. Oh, Master! we seen stars in de day time."

Environment played a role in slaves' reactions to the Day of Jubilo. Urban slaves frequently enjoyed more freedom than plantation slaves. Even before emancipation such black social institutions as schools and churches emerged in many cities. When those cities were liberated, organized celebrations occurred quickly. In Charleston 4000 black men and women paraded before some 10,000 spectators. Two black women sat in one mule-drawn cart while a mock auctioneer shouted, "How much am I offered?" In the next cart a black-draped coffin was inscribed with the words "Slavery is Dead." Four days after the fall of Richmond blacks there held a mass rally of some 1500 people in the First African Church.

Knowledge of their freedom came in many forms to the slaves. Rural slaves were less likely to enjoy the benefits of freedom as early as urban slaves. Many heard of the Emancipation Proclamation through the slave grapevine or from Union soldiers long before its words became reality for them. Masters sometimes took advantage of the isolation of their plantations to keep their slaves in ignorance or to make freedom seem vague and frightening. Their ploys usually failed, but learned patterns of deference made some freedmen unwilling to challenge their masters. Months after emancipation one North Carolina slave continued to work without compensation, explaining to a Northern correspondent, "No, sir; my mistress never said anything to me that I was to have wages, nor yet that I was free; nor I never said anything to her. Ye see I left it to her honor to talk to me about it, because I was afraid she'd say I was insultin' to her and presumin', so I wouldn't speak first. She ha'n't spoke yet." There were, however, limits to his patience; he intended to ask her for wages at Christmas.

Numerous freedmen described the exuberance they felt. One elderly Virginia black went to the barn, jumped from one stack of straw to another, and "screamed and screamed!" A Texas man remembered, "We all felt like horses" and "everybody went wild." Other blacks recalled how slave songs and spirituals were updated, and "purty soon ev'ybody fo' miles around was singin' freedom songs."

Quite a few slaves learned of freedom when a Union officer or Freedmen's Bureau agent read them the Emancipation Proclamation—often over the objections of the master. "Dat one time," Sarah Ford declared, "Massa Charley can't open he mouth, 'cause de captain tell him to shut up, dat he'd do the talkin'." Some masters, however, still sought to have the last word. A Louisiana planter's wife announced immediately after the Union officer departed, "Ten years from today I'll have you all back 'gain."

Fear did not leave all slaves as soon as their bondage was lifted. Jenny Proctor of Alabama recalled that her fellow slaves were stunned by the news. "We didn' hardly know what he means. We jes' sort of huddle 'round together like scared rabbits, but after we knowed what he mean, didn' many of us go, 'cause we didn' know where to of went." James Lucas, a former slave of Jefferson Davis, explained, "folks dat ain' never been free don' rightly know de *feel* of bein' free. Dey don' know de meanin' of it."

Freedmen quickly learned that one could not eat or wear freedom. "Dis livin' on liberty," one declared, "is lak young folks livin' on love after they gits married. It just don't work." They searched for the real meaning of liberty in numerous ways. Some followed the advice of a black Florida preacher, "You ain't none 'o you, gwinter feel rale free till you shakes de dus ob de Ole Plantashun offen you feet," and moved. Others declared their independence by legalizing their marriages and taking new names or publicly using surnames they had secretly adopted while in slavery. "We had a real sho' nuff weddin' wid a preacher," one recalled. "Dat cost a dollar." When encouraged to take his old master's surname, a black man declared, "Him's nothing to me now. I don't belong to he no longer, an' I don't see no use in being called for him." Education was the key for others. "If I nebber does do nothing more while I live," a Mississippi freedman vowed, "I shall give my children a chance to go to school, for I considers education next best ting to liberty."

Most came to a good understanding of the benefits and limits of their new status. One explained, "Why, sar, all I made before was Miss Pinckney's, but all I make now is my own." Another noted, "You could change places and work for different men." One newly freed slave wrote his brother, "I's mightly well pleased tu git my eatin' by de 'sweat o' my face, an all I ax o' ole masser's tu jes' keep he hands off o' de Lawd Almighty's property, fur *dat's me*." A new sense of dignity was cherished by many. An elderly South Carolina freedman rejoiced, "Don't hab me feelins hurt now. Used to hab me feelins hurt all de times. But don't hab em hurt now, no more." Charlie Barbour exulted over the fact "dat I won't wake up some mornin' fer fin' dat my mammy or some ob de rest of my family am done sold." Most agreed with Margrett Millin's answer when she was asked decades later whether she had liked slavery or freedom better. "Well, it's dis way. In slavery I owns nothin'. In freedom I's own de home and raise de family. All dat cause me worryment and in slavery I has no worryment, but I takes de freedom."

sue of economic security for the freedman was obscured by other questions that seemed more important to whites.

Unresolved Issues

At war's end some issues had been settled, but at a terrible cost. As historian David Potter noted, "slavery was dead, secession was dead, and six hundred thousand men were dead." A host of new problems had arisen from the nature of civil war and the results of that war as well as the usual postwar dislocations. Many questions remained unanswered. Reconstruction was shaped by the unresolved issues.

The first of these concerned the status of the freedmen. They were indeed free, but were they citizens? The Dred Scott decision (1857) had denied citizenship to all African-Americans. Even if it were decided that they were citizens, what rights were conferred by that citizenship? Would they be segregated as free blacks in the antebellum North had often been? Also, citizenship did not automatically confer suffrage; women were proof of that. Were the freedmen to be given the ballot? These weighty matters were complicated by racial prejudice as well as constitutional and partisan questions.

The Constitution had been severely tested by civil war, and many felt it had been twisted by the desire to save the Union. Once the emergency was over, how were constitutional balance and limits to be restored? Except during the terms of a few strong presidents, Congress had been the most powerful branch of government during the nation's first 70 years. Lincoln had assumed unprecedented powers, and Congress was determined to regain its ascendency. The ensuing battle directly influenced Reconstruction policies and their implementation.

Secession was dead, but what about states' rights? Almost everyone agreed that a division of power between the national and state governments was crucial to the maintenance of freedom. The fear of centralized tyranny remained strong. There was reluctance to enlarge federal power into areas traditionally controlled by the states, even though action in some of those areas was essential to craft the kind of peace many desired. Hesitation to reduce

states' rights produced timid and compromised solutions to such issues as suffrage. Also troubling many was federal action in the realm of social welfare—an idea so new that it failed to win lasting acceptance by that generation.

Another constitutional question concerned the status of the former Confederate states and how they were to be readmitted to the Union. There was no constitutional provision for failed secession, and many people debated whether the South had actually left the Union or not. The query reflected self-interest rather than an intellectual inquiry. Ironically, Southerners and their Democratic sympathizers now argued that the states had never legally separated from the rest of the nation, thus denying validity to the Confederacy in order to quickly regain their place in the Union. Extremists on the other side—Radical Republicans—insisted that the South had reverted to the status of conquered territory, forfeiting all rights as states. Under territorial governments, Representative Thaddeus Stevens declared, Southerners could "learn the principles of freedom and eat the fruit of foul rebellion." Others, including Lincoln, believed that the Confederate states had remained in the Union but had forfeited their rights. This constitutional hair-splitting grew out of the power struggle between the executive and legislative branches to determine which had the power to readmit the states and on what terms. It also reflected the hostility of some Northerners toward the "traitorous rebels" and the unwillingness of some Southerners to accept the consequences of defeat.

Republican Representative Thaddeus Stevens of Pennsylvania was among those who thought that the Southern states had forfeited their rights. He believed they should revert to the status of territories and be required to reapply for statehood in the Union.

Lingering over all these questions were partisan politics. Although not provided for in the Constitution, political parties had played a major role in the evolving American government. The road to war had disrupted the existing party structure—killing the Whig party, dividing the Democratic party, and creating the Republican party. The first truly sectional party, the Republican party had very few adherents in the South. Its continued existence was dubious in the face of the probable reunion of the Northern and Southern wings of the Democratic party. Paradoxically, the political power of the South, and in turn the Democratic party, was increased by the abolition of slavery. As freedmen, all African-Americans would be counted for representation; as slaves only three-fifths of them had been counted. Thus the Republican party's perceived need to make itself a national party also colored the course of Reconstruction.

PRESIDENTIAL RECONSTRUCTION

Early in the conflict, questions regarding the reconstruction of the nation were secondary to winning the war—without victory there would be no nation to reconstruct. Nonetheless, Lincoln had to take some action as Union forces pushed into the South. Authority had to be imposed in the reclaimed territory, so the president named military governors for Tennessee, Arkansas, and Louisiana in 1862 after federal armies occupied most of those states. He also began formulating plans for civilian government for those states and future Confederate areas as they came under the control of Union forces. The result was a Proclamation of Amnesty and Reconstruction issued in December of 1863 on the constitutional basis of the president's power to pardon.

Lincoln's Plan

Called the 10 percent plan, Lincoln's provisions were incredibly lenient. Rebels could receive presidential pardon by merely swearing their future allegiance to the Union and their acceptance of the end of slavery. In other words, former Confederates were not required to say they were sorry—only to promise they would be good in the future. A few people were excluded

from pardons: Confederate military and civilian officers; United States judges, congressmen, and military officers who had resigned their posts to serve the Confederacy; and those accused of failing to treat captured black Union soldiers as prisoners of war. Nevertheless, Lincoln did not require the new state governments to bar such people from future voting or office-holding. Moreover after only 10 percent of the number who had voted in 1860 had taken the oath, a state could form a civilian government. When such states produced a constitution outlawing slavery, Lincoln promised to recognize them as reconstructed. He did not demand any provisions for protecting black rights or allowing black suffrage.

Tennessee, Arkansas, and Louisiana met Lincoln's requirements and soon learned they had only cleared the first barrier in what became a long obstacle course. Radical Republicans, such as Representative Thaddeus Stevens of Pennsylvania and Senator Charles Sumner of Massachusetts, were outraged by the president's generosity. They thought the provisions did not adequately punish Confederate treason, restructure Southern society, protect the rights of African-Americans, or aid the Republican party. The Radicals were in a minority, but many moderate Republicans were also dismayed by Lincoln's leniency, and shared the Radical view that Reconstruction was a congressional, not a presidential, function. As a result Congress recognized neither the three states' elected congressmen nor their electoral votes in the 1864 election.

After denying the president's right to reconstruct the nation, Congress drew up a plan for reconstruction: the Wade-Davis Bill. Its terms were much more stringent, yet not unreasonable. A majority, rather than 10 percent, of each states' voters had to declare their allegiance in order to form a government. Only those taking "ironclad" oaths of their past Union loyalty were allowed to participate in the making of new state constitutions. Barely a handful of high-ranking Confederates, however, were to be permanently barred from political participation. The only additional requirement imposed by Congress was the repudiation of the Confederate debt; Northerners did not want Confederate bondholders to benefit from their "investment in treason" at a cost to loyal taxpayers. Congress would determine when a state had met these requirements.

Constitutional collision was postponed by Lincoln's pocket veto of the bill and his assassination on April 14, 1865. While most of the nation mourned, some Radicals rejoiced at the results of John Wilkes Booth's action. Lincoln had been a formidable opponent and had articulated his position on the South in his second inaugural address. Calling for "malice toward none" and "charity for all," he proposed to "bind the nation's wounds" and achieve "a just and lasting peace." His successor, Andrew Johnson, on the other hand, had announced, "Treason is a crime, and crime must be punished." Johnson was a Tennessee Democrat and Unionist; he had been the only Southerner to remain in the Senate after his state seceded. Placed on the 1864 Republican "Union" ticket as a gesture of unity, Johnson's political affiliation was less

than clear, but some considered him a weaker opponent than Lincoln. Radical Senator Benjamin Wade proclaimed, "By the gods there will be no trouble now in running this government."

Radicals found comfort in, but miscalculated, Johnson's hatred of the planters. He hated them for their aristocratic domination of the South, not for their slaveholding. Born of humble origins in Raleigh, North Carolina, and illiterate until adulthood, Johnson entered politics in Tennessee as a successful tailor. A champion of the people, he called the planters a "cheap purse-proud set . . . not half as good as the man who earns his bread by the sweat of his brow." Favoring free public education and a homestead act, Johnson was elected mayor, congressman, governor, and senator, before being appointed military governor of Tennessee and then becoming vice president. Although he shared the Radicals' hatred and distrust of the planters, he was a firm believer in black inferiority and did not support the Radical aim of black legal equality. He also advocated strict adherence to the Constitution and strongly supported states' rights.

Johnson's Plan

In the end Johnson did not reverse Lincoln's lenient policy. Congress was not in session when Johnson became president so he had about eight months to pursue policies without congressional interference. He issued his own proclamation of amnesty in May 1865 that barred everyone with taxable property worth more than $20,000. Closing one door, he opened another by providing for personal presidential pardons for excluded individuals. By year's end he had issued about 13,000 pardons. The most important aspect of the pardons was Johnson's claim that they restored all rights, including property rights. Thus many freedmen with crops in the ground suddenly found their masters back in charge—a disillusioning first taste of freedom that foreclosed further attempts at widespread land redistribution.

Johnson's amnesty proclamation did not immediately end the Radicals' honeymoon period with him, but his other proclamation issued on the same day caused deep concern. In it, he announced plans for the reconstruction of

Andrew Johnson, a former governor and a senator from North Carolina, was the only senator from a seceding state to remain loyal to the Union. In 1862 Lincoln appointed him military governor of Tennessee, and in 1864 Johnson was selected as Lincoln's running mate.

North Carolina—a plan that would set the pattern for all Southern states. A native Unionist was named provisional governor with the power to call a constitutional convention elected by loyal voters. Omitting Lincoln's 10 percent provision, Johnson did eventually require ratification of the Thirteenth Amendment, repudiation of Confederate debts, and state constitutional provisions abolishing slavery and renouncing secession. He also recommended limited black suffrage, primarily to stave off congressional attempts to give the vote to all black males.

The presidential plan fell short of the Radicals' hopes, but many moderates might have accepted it if the South had complied with the letter and the spirit of Johnson's proposals. Instead, Southerners seemed determined to ignore their defeat, even to make light of it. The state governments, for the most part, met the minimum requirements (Mississippi and South Carolina refused to repudiate the debt and Mississippi declined to ratify the Thirteenth Amendment). Their apparent acceptance, however, grew out of a belief that very little had actually changed, and Southerners proceeded to show almost total disregard for Northern sensibilities. Presenting themselves, like prodigal sons, for admission to Congress were four Confederate generals, six Confederate cabinet officials, and as the crowning indignity, Confederate Vice President Alexander H. Stephens. Most Northerners were not exceedingly vindictive. Although Union soldiers had sung, "We'll hang Jeff Davis in a sour apple tree," he, and only he, served more than a few months in prison, and the only execution was not for treason, but for alleged war crimes at the Confederate prison camp in Andersonville, Georgia. Still the North did expect some sign of change and hoped for some indication of repentence by the former rebels.

Black Codes in the South

At the very least, Northerners expected adherence to the abolition of slavery, and the South was blatantly forging new forms of bondage. African-Americans were to be technically free, but Southern whites expected them to work and live as they had before emancipation. To accomplish this, the new state governments enacted a

The freedom of ex-slaves was sharply curtailed through Black Codes and vagrancy laws. This sketch shows the provost guard in New Orleans rounding up vagrant blacks in 1864.

series of laws known as the Black Codes. This legislation granted certain rights denied to slaves. Freedmen had the right to marry, own property, sue and be sued, and testify in court. Complex legalisms, however, often took away what was apparently given. Black Codes in all states prohibited racial intermarriage. Some forbade freedmen to own certain types of property, such as alcoholic beverages and firearms. Most so tightly restricted black legal rights that they were practically nonexistent. Black Codes imposed curfews on African-Americans, segregated them, and outlawed their right to congregate in large groups.

The Black Codes did more than merely provide means of racial control; they also sought to fashion a labor system as close to slavery as possible. Some required that African-Americans obtain special licenses for any job except agricultural labor or domestic service. Most mandated the signing of yearly labor contracts, which sometimes required African-Americans to call the landowner "master" and allowed withholding wages for minor infractions. To accomplish the same objective, Mississippi prohib-

Southern whites frequently vented their frustrations on blacks. In the New Orleans riot of July 30, 1866, 37 blacks and three white sympathizers were killed after a Radical Republican meeting.

ited black ownership or even rental of land. Mandatory apprenticeship programs took children away from their parents, and vagrancy laws allowed authorities to arrest blacks "wandering or strolling about in idleness" and use them on chaingangs or rent them out to planters for as long as a year.

When laws failed, some Southern whites resorted to violence. In Memphis, whites resented the presence of black troops at nearby Fort Pickering. A local paper asserted "the negro can do the country more good in the cotton field than in the camp" and chastised "the dirty, fanatical, nigger-loving Radicals of this city." In May 1866 a street brawl erupted between white policemen and recently discharged black soldiers. That night, after the soldiers had returned to the fort, white mobs attacked the black section of the city, with the encouragement of the police and local officials, one of whom urged the mob to "go ahead and kill the last damned one of the nigger race." The reign of terror lasted

over 40 hours and left 46 blacks and 2 whites dead. This and other outbreaks of violence disgusted Northern voters.

Most Northerners would not have insisted on black equality or suffrage, but the South had regressed too far. Some Black Codes were even identical to the old slave codes, with the word negro substituted for slave. At the same time, reports of white violence against blacks filtered back to Washington. It is no wonder that upon finally reconvening in December 1865, Congress refused to seat the representatives and senators from the former Confederate states and instead proceeded to investigate conditions in the South.

CONGRESSIONAL RECONSTRUCTION

To discover what was really happening in the South, Congress established the Joint Committee on Reconstruction, which conducted inquiries and interviews that provided graphic and chilling examples of white repression and brutality toward African-Americans. Prior to the committee's final report, even moderates were convinced that action was necessary. In early 1866 Congress passed a bill to extend the life of the Freedmen's Bureau. The bill also granted the agency new powers to establish special courts for disputes concerning freedmen and to promote black education. Johnson vetoed it, claiming that the bureau was constitutional only in wartime conditions. Now, he claimed, the country had returned "to a state of peace and industry."

At first Johnson prevailed; his veto was not overridden. Then he made a mistake. In an impromptu speech on Washington's birthday, Johnson launched into a bitter attack on the Joint Committee on Reconstruction. Even moderates were offended. In mid-March 1866 Congress passed the Civil Rights Act. It declared that "all persons born in the United States and not subject to any foreign power, excluding Indians not taxed," were citizens and entitled to "full and equal benefit of all laws." Congress was responding to the Black Codes, but Johnson deemed the bill both unconstitutional and unwise. He vetoed it. This time, however, Congress overrode the veto. It then passed a slightly revised Freedmen's Bureau bill in July and enacted it over Johnson's veto. Even though the South had ignored much of Johnson's advice, such as granting limited suffrage to blacks, he stubbornly held to his conviction that reconstruction was complete and labeled his congressional opponents as "traitors."

His language did not create a climate of cooperation. Congress was concerned about the constitutional questions he raised and his challenge to congressional authority. To protect its handiwork and establish an alternate program of reconstruction, it drafted the Fourteenth Amendment. Undoubtedly the most significant legacy of Reconstruction, the first article of the amendment defined citizenship and its basic rights. Every person born in the United States and subject to its jurisdiction is declared a citizen. It also forbids any state from abridging "the privileges and immunities" of citizenship, from depriving any person of "due process of law," and from denying citizens the "equal protection of the laws." Although 100 years passed before its provisions were enforced as intended, the amendment has been interpreted to mean that states as well as the federal government are bound by the Bill of Rights—an important con-

TABLE 16.1

Reconstruction Amendments, 1865–1870

Amendment	Main Provisions	Congressional Passage (⅔ majority in each house required)	Ratification Process (¾ of all states including ex-Confederate states required)
13	Slavery prohibited in United States	January 1865	December 1865 (27 states, including 8 southern states)
14	1. National citizenship 2. State representation in Congress reduced proportionally to number of voters disfranchised 3. Former Confederates denied right to hold office	June 1866	Rejected by 12 Southern and border states, February 1867 Radicals make readmission of Southern states hinge on ratification Ratified July 1868
15	Denial of franchise because of race, color, or past servitude explicitly prohibited	February 1869	Ratification required for readmission of Virginia, Texas, Mississippi, Georgia Ratified March 1870

stitutional change that paved the way for the civil rights decisions and laws of the twentieth century.

The remaining four sections of the amendment spelled out Congress's minimum demands for postwar change and was the South's last chance for a lenient peace. A creation of the congressional moderates, the amendment did not require black suffrage but reduced the "basis of representation" proportionately for those states not allowing it. Former Confederate leaders were also barred from holding office unless pardoned by Congress—not the president. Finally, neither Confederate war debts nor compensation to former slaveholders were ever to be paid. The amendment, which passed Congress in June 1866, was then sent to the states for ratification.

President Johnson bridled at this assault on his perceived powers and urged the Southern states not to ratify the amendment. All but Tennessee decided to take his advice and wait for further congressional action. They and Johnson miscalculated; both hoped that the public would repudiate the amendment in the 1866 congressional elections. Johnson hit the campaign trail, urging people to oust the Radicals. His "swing around the circle" was met with heckling and humiliation. The campaign was vicious, characterized by appeals to racial prejudice by the Democrats and charges of Democratic treason by the Republicans. Although few elections are referenda on any single issue, the Republicans won overwhelming victories, which they interpreted as a mandate for congressional reconstruction.

"Radical" Reconstruction

The election results along with Southern intransigence finally gave the Radicals an upper hand. In 1867 Congress passed the Military Reconstruction Act that raised the price of readmission. The act declared all existing "Johnson governments," except Tennessee's, void and divided the South into five military districts headed by military governors granted broad powers to govern. Delegates to new constitutional conventions were to be elected by all qualified voters—a group that by congressional

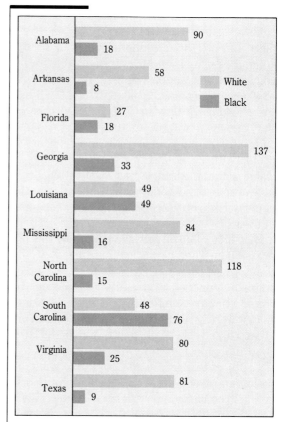

Figure 16.1
Composition of state constitutional conventions under congressional reconstruction

stipulation included black males and excluded former Confederate leaders. Following the ratification of a new state constitution providing for black suffrage, elections were to be held and the state would be required to ratify the Fourteenth Amendment. When that amendment became part of the Constitution and Congress approved the new state constitutions, the states would be granted representation in Congress once again.

Obviously, Johnson was not pleased with the congressional plan; he vetoed it, only to see his veto overridden. Nevertheless, as commander-in-chief he reluctantly appointed military governors, and by the end of 1867 elections had been held in every state except Texas. Because many white Southerners boycotted the elections, the South came under the control of Republicans supported by Union forces. In a way, however, Southerners had brought more radical measures upon themselves by their inflexibility. As the *Nation* declared in 1867,

> Six years ago, the North would have rejoiced to accept any mild restrictions upon the spread of slavery as a final settlement. Four years ago, it would have accepted peace on the basis of gradual emancipation. Two years ago, it would have been content with emancipation and equal civil rights for the colored people without the extension of suffrage. One year ago, a slight extension of the suffrage would have satisfied it.

Congress realized the plan it had enacted was unprecedented and subject to challenge by the other two branches of government. To check Johnson's power to disrupt, Congress took two other actions on the same day it passed the Military Reconstruction Act. The Command of the Army Act limited presidential military power. The Tenure of Office Act required Senate consent for the removal of any official whose appointment had required the Senate's confirmation. It was meant in part to protect Secretary of War Edwin M. Stanton, who supported the Radicals.

The Supreme Court had also shown its willingness to challenge Reconstruction actions in two important cases of 1866. In *Ex parte Milligan* the justices struck down the conviction of a civilian by a military tribunal in an area where civil courts were operating. Another decision ruled as void a state law barring ex-Confederates from certain professions on the basis that the act was *ex post facto*. Nevertheless, other decisions reflected a hesitation to tackle some of the thornier issues of Reconstruction. Important cases were pending, and Congress acted in March 1868 to limit the court's power to review cases. Because the congressional action was clearly constitutional, the Supreme Court acquiesced and in *Texas* v. *White* (1869) even acknowledged congressional power to reframe state governments.

President Johnson was not so accommodating. He sought to sabotage military reconstruction by continuing to pardon former Confederates, removing military commanders who were Radical sympathizers, and naming former Confederates to federal positions. Congress was

angry but could not find adequate grounds for impeachment. Johnson did not attempt to mend fences. In August 1867, during a congressional recess, he tried to replace Secretary of War Stanton with Ulysses S. Grant. When the Senate refused confirmation, however, Grant returned the office to Stanton. Johnson did not surrender; on February 21 he named Lorenzo Thomas to the cabinet position. Stanton also refused to surrender and barricaded himself in his office. On February 24 the House voted impeachment.

The Senate was given 11 articles of impeachment for its trial of the president. Eight related to the violation of the Tenure of Office Act and another to a violation of the Command of the Army Act. Only the last 2 reflected the real reasons for congressional action. Those articles accused Johnson of "inflammatory and scandalous harangues" against Congress and of "unlawfully devising and contriving" to obstruct congressional will. The heated and bitter trial lasted from March 5 to May 26. Johnson did not attend, but his lawyers made a good legal case that he had not

Andrew Johnson was the only president of the United States to be impeached. His successful defense centered on the legitimate uses of his executive powers.

technically violated the Tenure of Office Act since Stanton had been appointed by Lincoln. They tried to keep the trial focused on indictable offenses. Radical prosecutors continued to argue that Johnson had committed "high crimes and misdemeanors," but they also asserted that a president could be removed for political reasons, even without being found legally guilty of crimes—a position James Madison had supported during the drafting of the Constitution.

The vote for conviction fell one short of the required two-thirds majority, when seven Republicans broke ranks and voted against conviction. This set the precedent that a president must be guilty of serious misdeeds to be removed from office. The outcome was a political blow to the Radicals, costing them some support. The action, however, did make Johnson more cooperative for the last months of his presidency.

Black Suffrage

In the 1868 presidential election, the Republicans won with Ulysses S. Grant, whose Civil War victories made his name a household word. He ran on a platform that endorsed congressional reconstruction, urged repayment of the national debt, and defended black suffrage in the South as necessary but supported the right of each Northern state to restrict the vote. His slogan, "Let us have peace," was appealing, but his election was less than a ringing endorsement for Radical policies. The military hero who had seemed invincible barely won the popular vote in several key states.

While Charles Sumner and a few other Radicals had long favored national black suffrage, only after the Republicans' electoral close call in 1868 did the bulk of the party begin to consider a suffrage amendment. Many were swayed by the political certainty that the black vote would be theirs and might give them the margin of victory in future close elections. Others were embarrassed by the hypocrisy of forcing black suffrage on the South while only 7 percent of Northern African-Americans could vote. Still others believed that granting African-Americans the vote would relieve whites of any further responsibility to protect black rights.

Suffrage supporters faced many objections to such an amendment. One was based on the lack of popular support. At that time only seven Northern states granted blacks the right to vote, and since 1865, referendum proposals for black suffrage in eight states had been voted down. In fact, only in Iowa and Minnesota (both containing minuscule black populations) had voters supported the extension of the vote. The amendment was so unpopular that, ironically, it could never have won adoption without its ratification by the Southern states, where black suffrage already existed.

A more serious challenge was the question of whether Congress could legislate suffrage at all. Before Reconstruction the national government had never taken any action regarding the right to vote; suffrage had been considered not a right but a privilege which only the states could confer. The Radical answer was that the Constitution expressly declared that "the United States shall guarantee to every State in this Union a republican form of government." Charles Sumner further asserted that "anything for human rights is constitutional" and that black rights could only be protected by black votes.

Senator George Vickers sarcastically asked, "does not the doctrine of human rights asserted by the senator apply as well to females as to males?" Although he was "no advocate for woman suffrage," he noted that "if the Congress of the United States had been composed exclusively of women we should have had no civil war. We might have had a war of words, but that would have been all." When one senator did propose female suffrage, a colleague informed him that "to extend the right of suffrage to negroes in this country I think is necessary for their protection; but to extend the right of suffrage to women is not necessary."

Some women, such as Elizabeth Cady Stanton and Susan B. Anthony, did not want to rely upon their fathers, brothers, or husbands to protect their rights. As leaders of the Women's Loyal League, both had worked hard for the adoption of the Thirteenth Amendment, only to be rewarded by inclusion of the word "male" in the Fourteenth Amendment of the Constitution—the first time that word appears. Some women, such as Lucy Stone of the American Woman Suffrage Association, accepted the plea of long-time woman suffrage supporter Frederick Douglass that it was the "Negro's hour," and worked for ratification. Anthony, however, vowed to "cut off this right arm of mine before I will ever work for or demand the ballot for the Negro and not the woman." Such differences played a role in splitting the women's movement in 1869 between those working for a national suffrage amendment and those who concentrated their efforts on the state level. Anthony and Stanton founded the National Woman Suffrage Association to battle for a constitutional amendment and other feminist reforms. Others

Susan B. Anthony (left) moved from temperance work to join with Elizabeth Cady Stanton in 1869 to form the National Woman Suffrage Association.

became disillusioned with that approach and established the American Woman Suffrage Association, which focused on obtaining suffrage on a state-by-state basis.

Actually, women did not lose much by not being included in the Fifteenth Amendment. To meet the various objections, compromise was necessary. The resulting amendment did not grant the vote to anyone. It merely stated that the vote could not be denied "on account of race, color, or previous condition of servitude." Suffrage was still essentially to be controlled by the states, and other bases of exclusion were not deemed unconstitutional. These loopholes would eventually allow white Southerners to make a mockery of the amendment.

Although congressional reconstruction was labeled "Radical," compromise had instead produced another essentially moderate plan. What Congress did *not* do is as important as what it did. It did not even guarantee the right to vote. There was only one execution for war crimes and only Jefferson Davis was imprisoned for

more than a few months. For all but a handful, ex-Confederates were not permanently barred from voting or holding office. By 1872 only about 200 were still denied the right to hold office. Most local Southern governments were undisturbed. Land as well as rights were restored to former rebels, eliminating the possibility of extensive land redistribution. Most areas that had traditionally been the states' domain remained so, free from federal meddling. For example, no requirements were placed on the states to provide any education to freedmen. The only attempt by the national government to meet the basic needs of its citizens was the temporary Freedmen's Bureau—justified only as an emergency measure. The limited nature of Reconstruction doomed it as an opportunity to provide means for the protection of minority rights.

Such congressional moderation reflected the spirit of the age. Enduring beliefs in the need for strict construction of the Constitution and in states' rights presented formidable barriers to truly radical changes. Property rights were considered sacrosanct—even for "traitors." Cherished ideals of self-reliance and the conviction that a person determined his or her own destiny led many to support Horace Greeley's so-called root, hog, or die approach to the black problem. By ending the threat of slavery, he argued, "we may soon break up our Freedmen's Bureaus and all manner of coddling devices and let the negroes take care of themselves." Few agreed with Charles Sterns who argued that even a hog could not root without a snout—that there could be no equality of opportunity where one group had long been allowed an unfair advantage. Many instead sided with an editorialist for the *New York Herald* who wrote of the bill to extend the life of the Freedmen's Bureau: "The bill ought to be called an act to support the negroes in idleness by the honest labor of white people, or an act to establish a gigantic and corrupt political machine for the benefit of the radical faction and a swarm of officeholders." Clearly the idea of affirmative action or even equal opportunity had even less support then than it did 100 years later.

Tainting every action was the widespread conviction that African-Americans were not equal to whites. Many Northerners were more concerned with keeping blacks in the South than with abstract black rights. In 1866, for example, New York Senator Roscoe Conkling catered to the Northern fear of black immigration while calling for support of the Fourteenth Amendment:

> Four years ago mobs were raised, passions were aroused, votes were given, upon the idea that emancipated negroes were to burst in hordes upon the North. We then said, give them liberty and rights in the South, and they will stay there and never come into a cold climate. We say so still, and we want them let alone, and that is one thing that this part of the amendment is for.

Even Radical Representative George Julian admitted to his Indiana constituents, "the real trouble is that *we hate the negro*. It is not his ignorance that offends us, but his color."

Northerners who engaged in politics in the South before or after the war were called carpetbaggers. This cartoon shows Grant and Union soldiers propping up carpetbag rule with bayonets, while the "Solid South" staggers under the weight.

The plan for Reconstruction evolved fitfully, buffeted first one way and then another by the forces of the many unresolved issues at war's end. If permanent changes were very limited, nonetheless precedents had been set for later action, and for a brief time congressional reconstruction brought about the most democratic governments the South had ever seen— or would see for another hundred years.

RECONSTRUCTION IN THE SOUTH

Regardless of the specific details hammered out in Washington, any dictated peace would probably have been unpalatable to Southern whites. They were especially leery of any action that seemed to threaten white supremacy—whether or not that was the intended result. Even before the war, suspicion greeted every Northern move. Southerners continued to see a radical abolitionist behind every bush.

The Freedmen's Bureau established during the last year of the war operated for five years in the South. Most Southerners criticized and condemned the bureau from its first day to its last. Many believed its agents were partial to African-Americans. As one Mississippi planter declared, "The negro is a sacred animal. The Yankees are about negroes like the Egyptians were about cats." Actually there was a great diversity in the background and goals of bureau agents. Some were idealistic young New Englanders who, like the Yankee schoolmarms, came south to aid in the transition to freedom. Others were army officers whose first priority was to maintain order—often by siding with the landowners. All were overworked, underpaid, and under pressure.

The results of bureau actions were mixed in regard to conditions for African-Americans. The agents helped to negotiate labor contracts that African-Americans were forced to sign to obtain rations. Frequently the wages were well below the rate at which slaves had been hired out by their owners before the war. While it should be remembered that money was scarce at the time, these contracts helped to keep African-Americans on the farm—someone else's farm. On the other hand, between 1865 and

1869 the bureau issued over 21 million rations, of which about 5 million went to whites. Thus it showed that the government could establish and administer a massive relief program, as it would again do during the depression of the 1930s. The bureau also operated more than 40 hospitals, opened hundreds of schools, and accomplished the herculean task of resettling some 30,000 people displaced by the war.

Carpetbaggers, Scalawags, and Black Republicans

Until the passage of the Reconstruction Acts in 1867, Southern governments were much the same as they had been before the war. Afterwards, however, Republican officeholders joined bureau agents in directing the course of Reconstruction. Despised by many whites, these men, depending on their origins, were derisively labeled "carpetbaggers," "scalawags," and "nigrahs." Opponents considered all three groups despicable creatures whose "black and tan" governments were tyrannizing native whites, while engaged in an orgy of corruption. Myths created about Southern Republicans lingered long after the restoration of Democratic party rule.

Northerners who came to the South during or after the war and became engaged in politics were called carpetbaggers. They supposedly arrived with a few meager belongings in their carpetbags, which would expand to hold ill-gotten gains from looting an already devastated South. Probably what most infuriated whites was the carpetbaggers' willingness to cooperate with African-Americans. Calling them "a kind of political dry-nurse for the negro population," native whites accused the carpetbaggers of cynically exploiting the freedmen for their own gain. Many agreed with the charge that the carpetbaggers were standing "right in the public eye, stealing and plundering, many of them with both arms around negroes, and their hands in their rear pockets, seeing if they cannot pick a paltry dollar out of them."

White Southerners who voted for Republicans were labeled scalawags. The term, said to be derived from Scalloway, "a district in the Shetland Islands where small, runty cattle and horses were bred," had been used previously as a "synonym for scamp, loafer, or rascal." Thus Southern white Republicans were depicted as people "paying no taxes, riding poor horses, wearing dirty shirts, and having no use for soap." Such men were said to have "sold themselves for office" and become a "subservient tool and accomplice" of the carpetbaggers.

Most detested by white Southerners were the black Republicans. Having long characterized African-Americans as inferior creatures dependent on white management for survival, Southerners loathed the prospect of blacks in authority. They feared that the former slaves would exact payment for their years of bondage. Democrats also knew that racism was their best rallying cry to regain power. Thus Reconstruction governments were denounced for "Ethiopian minstrelsy, Ham radicalism in all its glory." Whites claimed ignorant freedmen, incapable of managing their own affairs, were allowed to run the affairs of state with disastrous results. A former governor of South Carolina observed, "All society stands now like a cone on its Apex, with base up."

Such legends persisted for a long time, despite contrary facts. Southern whites had determined even before Reconstruction began that it would be "the most galling tyranny and most stupendous system of organized robbery that is to be met with in history." The truth was, as W. E. B. Du Bois later wrote, "There is one thing that the white South feared more than negro dishonesty, ignorance, and incompetency, and that was negro honesty, knowledge, and efficiency." To a surprising degree they got what they most feared.

Black voters were generally as fit to vote as the millions of illiterate whites enfranchised by Jacksonian democracy. Black officials as a group were as qualified as their white counterparts. In South Carolina two-thirds of them were literate, and in all states most of the acknowledged leaders were well educated and articulate. They usually had been members of the Northern or Southern free black elite or part of the slave aristocracy of skilled artisans and household slaves. Hiram Revels, a U.S. senator from Mississippi, was the son of free blacks who had sent him to college in the North. James Walker Hood,

In a historic first, seven African-Americans were elected to the Forty-first and Forty-second Congresses. Between 1869 and 1901, two African-Americans became senators and 20 served in the House.

the presiding officer of the North Carolina constitutional convention of 1867, was a black carpetbagger from Pennsylvania who came to the state as an African Methodist Episcopal Zion missionary. Some, such as Francis Cardoza of South Carolina, were the privileged mulatto sons of white planters. Cardoza had been educated in Scottish and English universities. During Reconstruction 14 such men served in the U.S. House of Representatives and 2 in the Senate. By 1901 6 others were elected to the House, before Southern black political power was effectively demolished.

Even if black Republicans had been incompetent, they could hardly be held responsible for the perceived abuses of so-called black reconstruction. Only in South Carolina did African-Americans have a majority of the delegates to the constitutional convention provided for by the Reconstruction Acts. Neither did they dominate the new governments; only for a two-year period in South Carolina did blacks control both houses of the legislature. None were elected governor, although P. B. S. Pinchback, the lieutenant governor of Louisiana, did serve as acting governor for a short time. When the vote was restored to ex-Confederates, African-Americans comprised only one-third of the voters of

the South, and only in two states did they have a majority.

Actually, carpetbaggers dominated most Republican governments to an extent not warranted by their numbers. They accounted for less than one percent of the party's voters but held a third of the offices. Their power was especially obvious in the higher offices. Over half of all Southern Republican governors and almost half of the Republican congressmen and senators were former Northerners. Although some carpetbaggers did resemble their stereotypes, most did not. Many had come south before black enfranchisement and could not have predicted political futures based on black votes. Most were Union veterans whose wartime exposure to the region convinced them that they could make a good living there without having to shovel snow. Some brought with them much needed capital for investment in their new home. A few came with a sense of mission to educate blacks and reform Southern society.

Obviously, if African-Americans constituted only a third of the population and carpetbaggers less than one percent, those two groups had to depend on the votes of a sizable number of native white Southerners to obtain office in some regions of the South. Those men came from diverse backgrounds. Some scalawags were members of the old elite of bankers, merchants, industrialists, and even some planters who, as former Whigs, favored the "Whiggish" economic policies of the Republican party and hoped to control and use the black vote for their own purposes. On discovering their inability to dominate the Republican governments, most of these soon drifted into alliance with the Democrats. The majority of Southern white Republican voters were yeoman farmers and poor whites from areas where slavery had been unimportant. They had long resented planter domination and had opposed secession.

To win their vote the Republicans appealed to class interests. In Georgia they proclaimed, "Poor White men of Georgia: Be a Man! Let the Slave-holding aristocracy no longer rule you. Vote for a constitution which educates your children free of charge; relieves the poor debtor from his rich creditor; allows a liberal homestead for your families; and more than all, places you on a level with those who used to boast that for every slave they were entitled to three-fifths of a vote in congressional representation." Many accepted such arguments and joined African-Americans to put Republicans into office. The coalition, however, was always shaky, given the racism of poor whites. The scalawags actually represented a swing vote that finally swung toward the Democratic party of white supremacy later in the 1870s.

Character of Republican Rule

While the coalition lasted, the Republican governments became the most democratic that the South had ever had. More people could vote for more offices, all remaining property requirements for voting and officeholding were dropped, representation was made fairer through reapportionment, and more offices became elective rather than appointive. Salaries for public officials made it possible to serve without being wealthy. Most important, universal male suffrage was enacted with the support of black legislators. Ironically, by refusing to deny Southern whites what had been denied to them—the vote—African-Americans sowed the seeds of their own destruction.

The Republican state constitutions, which brought the South firmly into the mainstream of national reform, often remained in effect years after the end of Reconstruction. Legislatures abolished automatic imprisonment for debt and reduced the use of the death penalty. More institutions for the care of the indigent, orphans, mentally ill, deaf, and blind were established. Tax structures were overhauled, reducing head taxes and increasing property taxes to relieve somewhat poorer taxpayers. At the same time, Southern railroads, harbors, and bridges were rebuilt.

Reforms also affected the status of women, increasing their rights in the possession of property and divorce. Although giving women legal control of their property was mainly intended to protect the families of their debt-ridden husbands, African-Americans in particular pushed for more radical changes. When William Whipper's motion to give South Carolina women the

African-Americans eagerly participated in politics when allowed. In this 1867 election in the nation's capital, they served as polling place judges and lined up as early as 2 A.M. to vote.

vote did not receive a second, he persevered and declared:

> However frivolous you may think it, I know the time will come when every man and woman in this country will have the right to vote. I acknowledge the superiority of woman. There are large numbers of the sex who have an intelligence more than equal to our own. Is it right or just to deprive these intelligent beings of the privileges which we enjoy? The time will come when you will have to meet this question. It will continue to be agitated until it must ultimately triumph.
>
> However derisively we may treat these noble women, we shall yet see them successful in the assertion of their rights.

The area in which black legislators had the most success was laying the foundations for public education. Antebellum provisions for

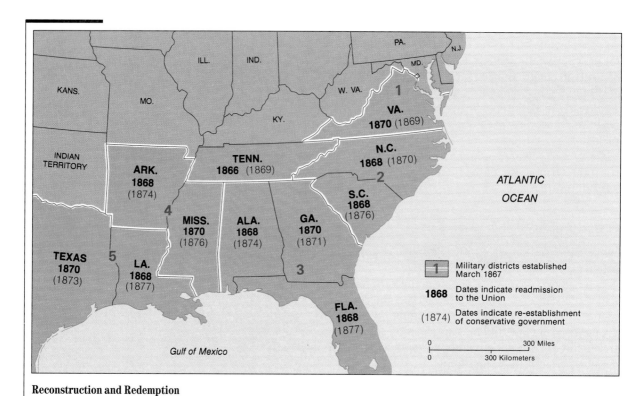

Reconstruction and Redemption

public schools below the Mason-Dixon line were meager to nonexistent. In every state African-Americans were among the main proponents of state-supported schools, but most accepted segregated facilities as necessary compromises. Some black parents did not even desire integration; they believed their children could not flourish in environments tainted by white supremacy. By 1877 some 600,000 blacks were in schools, but only the University of South Carolina and the public schools of New Orleans were integrated.

As desirable as many of the new social services were, they required money and money was scarce. The war had destroyed not only railroads and bridges but also much of the Southern tax base. The necessary tax increases were bound to be unpopular, as were soaring state debts. Both were blamed on corruption, with some justification. Louisiana governor Henry C. Warmouth netted some $100,000 dollars in a year in which his salary was only $8000. A drunken South Carolina governor signed an issue of state bonds for a woman in a burlesque show.

One black man was paid $9000 to repair a bridge with an original cost of only $500. Contracts for rebuilding and expanding railroads, subsidies to industries, and bureaucracies for administering social services offered generous opportunities for graft and bribery. When these occurred, Southern whites loudly proclaimed that they knew it would happen if shifty former slaves were given the keys to the till.

Actually, although African-Americans received a large share of the blame, they received little of the profit. A smaller percentage of blacks than whites were involved in the scandals. Also the corruption that the Democrats denounced at every turn was rather meager compared with the shenanigans of such contemporary Northern Democratic regimes as the Boss Tweed Ring of New York. There seemed to be an orgy of national corruption that infected both parties. Indeed, in the South a Democratic state treasurer who came to office after Reconstruction deserves the dubious distinction of being the largest embezzler of the era.

The "tyranny" that so distressed Southern whites did not include wholesale disfranchisement or confiscation of their lands. In fact, the demands of most African-Americans were quite reasonable and moderate. Their goals were expressed by the declarations of the many postwar black conventions, such as a Virginia one in 1865 that declared, "All we ask is an *equal chance* with the white *traitors* varnished and japanned with the oath of amnesty."

Black and White Economic and Social Adaptation

Just as the ex-slaves on Thomas Pinckney's plantation had learned, freedmen everywhere soon realized that the economic power of whites had diminished little. If anything, land became more concentrated in the hands of a few. In one Alabama county, the richest 10 percent of landowners increased their share of landed wealth from 55 to 63 percent between 1860 and 1870. Some African-Americans, usually through hard work and incredible sacrifice, were able to obtain land. The percentage of blacks owning property increased from less than 1 to 20 percent. Indeed, African-Americans seemed to fare better than poor whites. One observer noted, "The negro, bad as his condition is, seems to me, on the whole, to accommodate himself more easily than the white to the change of situation." The truth of his assertion is reflected in the fact that the percentage of whites owning land dropped from 80 to 67 percent. Increasingly, poor blacks and whites became agricultural laborers on someone else's land.

The black landless farmers, like the slaves before them, were not mere pawns. If they could not control their destinies, at least they could shape them. As one Northern observer wrote, "They have a mine of strategy to which the planter sooner or later yields." Through strikes and work slowdowns, African-Americans resisted contract and wage labor because working in gangs under white supervision smacked too much of slavery. When they could not own land, they preferred to rent it, but the few who had the cash to do so found few Southern whites would risk the wrath of their neighbors by breaking the taboo against renting to blacks.

Sharecropping emerged both as a result of black desire for autonomy and whites' lack of cash. Landowners gave blacks as well as poor whites a plot of land to work in return for a share of the crops. Freedom from white supervision was so desirable to freedmen that they sometimes hitched mule teams to their old slave cabins and carried them off to their assigned acres. To put distance between themselves and slavery, many black men would not allow their wives and children to work in the fields.

Sharecropping at first seemed to be a good bargain for African-Americans because they frequently negotiated their way to a half share of the crops. Their portion of the profits from Southern agriculture, including all provisions, rose from 22 percent under slavery to 56 percent by the end of Reconstruction. Moreover, they were making more for working less. Fewer family members worked and black men labored shorter hours; as a group African-Americans worked one-third fewer hours than under slavery. Per capita black income increased quickly after the war to about one-half that of whites, but then it stagnated.

African-Americans obtained a little more freedom to control working conditions under the sharecropping system, but their poverty limited their ability to acquire machinery. Many relied on "human power" for plowing.

Sharecropping later proved to be disastrous for most blacks and poor whites. They needed more than land to farm; they also required seeds, fertilizers, and provisions to live on until they harvested their crops. To obtain these they often borrowed against their share of the crops. Falling crop prices, high credit rates, and sometimes cheating by creditors left many to harvest a growing burden of debt with each crop. In many states, when the Democrats regained power, laws favoring creditors were passed. These led to debt peonage for many sharecroppers.

If most freedmen did not win economic freedom, they benefited from freedom in other ways. It was no longer illegal to learn to read and write, and African-Americans pursued education with much zeal. Many even paid as much as 10 percent of their limited incomes for tuition. They began to learn the fundamentals, and a growing number also sought higher education. Between 1860 and 1880 over 1000 African-Americans earned college degrees. Some went north to college, but most went to 1 of the 13 Southern colleges established by the American Missionary Association or by black and white churches with the assistance of the Freedmen's Bureau. Such schools as Howard and Fisk were a permanent legacy of Reconstruction.

African-Americans were also able to enjoy and expand their rich cultural heritage. Religion was a central focus for most, just as it had been in slavery. Withdrawing from white congregations with segregated pews and self-serving sermons on the duty of servants to their masters, freedmen everywhere established separate black churches. The membership in such antebellum denominations as the African Methodist Episcopal soared. In essence, black Christians declared their religious independence, and their churches became centers of political and social activities as well as religious ones. As one carpetbagger noted, "The colored preachers are *the great power* in controlling and uniting the colored vote." The churches also functioned as vehicles for self-help and sources of entertainment.

Most African-Americans desired racial intermingling no more than whites. Many could not feel free until they had removed themselves and their children as far as possible from white arrogance. They created separate congregations and acquiesced to segregated schooling. Nevertheless, they did not want to be publicly humiliated by such measures as separate railroad cars. They frequently used their limited political power to protect civil rights through clauses in state constitutions and legislation, as well as by appeals for the enforcement of national laws. Consequently, black Southerners did enjoy the use of public facilities to a greater degree than they would during the 75 years following Reconstruction.

The very changes that gave African-Americans hope during Reconstruction distressed poor whites. Black political equality rankled them, but much more serious was their own declining economic status. As their landownership declined, more whites became dependent on sharecropping and low wage jobs, primarily in the textile industry. Even these meager opportunities were eagerly greeted; as one North Carolina preacher proclaimed, "Next to God, what this town needs is a cotton mill." Economic competition between poor whites and blacks was keen, but their common plight also favored cooperation based on class interest. The economic pressures applied by the white elite frequently hurt both groups as well as middle-class yeoman farmers, and for brief periods during Reconstruction they warily united in politics. Invariably, however, these attempts were shattered by upper-class appeals to white supremacy and racial unity.

Ironically, although poor whites were perceived by nearly everyone as the group most hostile to blacks, the two shared many aspects of a rich Southern cultural heritage. Both groups developed colorful dialects. For each, aesthetic expression was based on utility—reflecting their need to use wisely what little they had. Their quilts were not merely functional but often quite beautiful. In religion and recreation, their experiences were similar. At camp meetings and revivals, poor whites practiced a highly emotional religion, just as many black Southerners did. Both groups spun yarns and sang songs that reflected the perils of their existence and provided folk heroes. They also shared many superstitions as well as useful folk remedies. Race, however, was a potent wedge between them that upper-class whites frequently exploited for their own political and economic goals.

Planters no longer dominated the white elite; sharecropping turned them and others into absentee landlords. The sons of the old privileged families joined the growing ranks of lawyers, railroad entrepreneurs, bankers, industrialists, and merchants. In some ways, the upper and middle classes began to merge, but in many places the old elite and their sons still enjoyed a degree of deference and political leadership. Their hostility toward African-Americans was not as intense, largely because they possessed means of control. When their control slipped, however, they also became ranting racists.

So strongly were all Southern whites imbued with a belief in white superiority that most could not imagine total black equality. A Freedmen's Bureau agent reported in 1866 that "a very respectable old citizen . . . swore that, if he could not thrash a negro who insulted him, he would leave the country." White attitudes toward blacks were as irrational as they were generalized. Most whites exempted the blacks they knew from such generalizations. As an Alabama planter declared in 1865, "If all were like some of mine I wouldn't say anything. They're as intelligent and well behaved as anybody. But I can't stand free niggers anyhow!"

Violent White Resistance

Large numbers of whites engaged in massive resistance to Reconstruction. Unlike the resistance of Southern blacks 100 years later, however, this brand of resistance was not passive but very aggressive. In 1866, some bored young men in Pulaski, Tennessee, organized a social club with all the trappings of fraternal orders—secret rituals, costumes, and practical jokes. They soon learned that their antics intimidated African-Americans; thenceforth the Ku Klux Klan grew into a terrorist organization, copied all over the South under various names. A historian of the Klan asserts that it "whipped, shot, hanged, robbed, raped, and otherwise outraged Negroes and Republicans across the South in the name of preserving white civilization." A major goal of the Klan was to intimidate Republican voters and restore Democrats to office.

The Ku Klux Klan and other white terrorist groups used violence to eliminate black gains. This 1874 cartoon and others like it helped arouse the public to demand action against the Klan.

In South Carolina, when blacks working for a scalawag began to vote, Klansmen visited the plantation and "whipped every nigger man they could lay their hands on." The group's increasing lawlessness alarmed many people and led to congressional action. The Klan was broken up by three Enforcement Acts (1870–1871) that gave the president the right to suspend habeas corpus against "armed combinations" interfering with any citizen's right to vote. In 1871 Grant did so in nine South Carolina counties. Disbanding the Klan, however, did little to decrease Southern violence or the activities of similar terrorist groups.

Some blacks Southerners were probably never allowed to vote freely. At the peak of Reconstruction, fewer than 30,000 federal troops were stationed in the entire South—hardly enough to protect the rights of 4.5 million African-Americans. As troops were being withdrawn, Democrats sought to regain control of their states. They made appeals to white supremacy and charged the Republicans with corruption. Without secret ballots landowners could threaten sharecroppers with eviction for "improper" voting. In addition to economic intimidation, violence against freedmen escalated in most states as the Democrats increased their political power. When victory seemed close, Democrats justified any means to the desired end that they called "redemption." A South Carolina Democratic campaign plan in 1876 urged, "Never threaten a man individually. If he deserves to be threatened, the necessities of the times require that he should die. A dead Radical is very harmless." One Democratic candidate for governor in Louisiana proclaimed, "We shall carry the next election if we have to ride saddle-deep in blood to do it." In six heavily black counties in Mississippi such tactics proved highly successful—reducing Republican votes from more than 14,000 in 1873 to only 723 in 1876. Beginning with Virginia and Tennessee in 1869, by 1876 all but three states—Louisiana, Florida, and South Carolina—had Democratic "Redeemer" governments. The final collapse of Reconstruction became official the following year with the withdrawal of federal troops from the three unredeemed states.

RECONSTRUCTION IN THE NORTH AND WEST

In the end, the South could be said to have lost the war but won the peace. After 1877 Southern whites found little resistance to their efforts to forge new institutions to replace both the economic benefits and racial control of slavery. By 1910 they had devised a system of legalized repression that gave whites many of the benefits of slavery without all the responsibilities. Surely this was not what the North had envisioned after Appomattox. How did it happen? Much of the answer is found in events occurring in the North and West.

Northern Shifts in Attitudes

The basic cause for the decline of Reconstruction can be seen in an 1874 conversation between two Northern Republicans during which one declared that the people were "tired out with this wornout cry of 'Southern Outrages!!!' Hard times and heavy taxes make them wish the

. . . 'everlasting nigger' were in [hell] or Africa. . . . It is amazing the change that has taken place in the last two years in the public sentiment." A shifting political climate, economic hard times, increasing preoccupation with other issues, and continued racism combined to make most Northerners wash their hands of the responsibility for the protection of black rights.

When Grant won the presidency in 1868, the nation appeared to reject the Democratic charge that the Republican Congress had "subjected ten states, in the time of profound peace, to military despotism and Negro supremacy." In reality the voters had chosen a war hero who had no political record or experience. They voted not so much for a program, but for Grant's campaign slogan: "Let us have peace."

The victorious general proved to be a poor choice for the presidency. Not only was he politically inexperienced, but he also lacked a taste for politics. Haunted by a fear of failure and socially insecure, Grant was too easily influenced by men of wealth and prestige. He made some dismal appointments and remained loyal to individuals who did not merit his trust. The result was a series of scandals. Grant was not personally involved, but his close association with the perpetrators blemished both his and his party's image. The first major scandal involved Crédit Mobilier, a dummy construction company used to milk money from railroad investors in order to line the pockets of a few insiders, including Vice President Schuyler Colfax and a number of other prominent Republicans. Later, bribes and kickback schemes surfaced that involved Indian trading posts, post office contracts, and commissions for tax collection. Such revelations as well as the corruption in some Southern Republican governments did little to enhance the public image of the party, and Democrats were quick to make corruption a major issue in both the North and the South.

Although by the 1872 presidential election, there had only been a hint of scandal, some Republicans were disenchanted. In that election the Republican party was split; a number, calling themselves Liberal Republicans, formed a separate party. They supported their own candidate, *New York Tribune* editor Horace Greeley, rather than Grant. Among Greeley's campaign pledges was a more moderate Southern policy. Even with the Democrats also nominating Greeley, Grant easily won reelection, but the fear of disgruntled Republicans merging with Democrats remained. By 1874 Republicans were becoming aware that the black vote would not save them. That year the Democrats captured the House and gained in the Senate, following further revelations of Republican corruption.

At least as detrimental to Republican political fortunes was a depression that followed the panic of 1873, which was caused by overinvestment in railroads and risky financial deals. Lasting six years, it was the most serious economic downturn the nation had yet experienced. Whatever their cause, depressions usually result in "voting the rascals out." Democratic fortunes were bound to rise as the people's fell. Yet economic distress had an even wider impact on Reconstruction. People's attention became focused on their pocketbooks rather than on abstract ideals of equality and justice. Economic scrutiny brought such issues as currency and tariffs to the forefront. As the depression deepened, many questioned Republican support for "sound money" backed by gold and the retirement of the legal tender "greenback" paper money that had been issued during the war.

Those greenbacks had increased the money supply needed to finance postwar economic expansion. Yet many Republicans were suspicious of any money not backed by specie—that is, gold or silver. One of the last actions of the Republican-controlled Congress was to pass the Resumption Act of 1875. It provided for the gradual redemption of greenbacks in gold. The resulting deflation favored creditors over debtors because debtors were forced to repay loans with money that was worth more than it had been when they borrowed it. Many Americans, especially farmers, were in debt, and deflation coupled with a depression brought economic distress.

Actually, the panic of 1873 merely brought into clearer focus the vast changes occurring in the North during Reconstruction. The South had never had the undivided attention of the rest of the nation. Such events as the comple-

tion of the first transcontinental railroad in 1869 often overshadowed reports of "Southern outrages." The United States was experiencing the growing pains of economic modernization and western expansion. The Republican platform of 1860 had called for legislation favoring both of these as well as stopping the expansion of slavery. Comprised of diverse interest groups, the party went through a battle for its soul during Reconstruction. For a while the small abolitionist faction had gained some ascendancy due to postwar developments. By the late 1870s, however, the Republican party had foresaken its reformist past to become a protector of privilege rather than a guarantor of basic rights. In effect, Republicans and Democrats joined hands in conservative support of railroad and industrial interests.

Racism and American Indians

The major reason for the decline of Reconstruction was the pervasive belief in white supremacy. There could be little determination to secure equal rights for those who were considered unequal in all other respects. Reconstruction became a failed opportunity to resolve justly the status of one minority, and the climate of racism almost ensured failure for others as well. Western expansion not only diverted attention from Reconstruction but also raised the question of what was to be done about the Plains Indians. They, too, were considered inferior to whites. William H. Seward, who later became secretary of state, spoke for most white Americans when in 1860 he described blacks as "a foreign and feeble element like the Indians, incapable of assimilation." Indeed, while Reconstruction at first offered hope to African-Americans, for the American Indian hope was fading.

In the end, African-Americans were oppressed; Native Americans were exterminated or separated into shrinking reservations. From the white viewpoint the reason was obvious. As a so-called scientific treatise of the 1850s explained, "The *Barbarous* races of America . . . although nearly as low in intellect as the Negro races, are essentially untameable. Not merely have all attempts to civilize them failed, but also every endeavor to enslave them. Our Indian tribes submit to extermination, rather than wear the yoke under which our negro slaves fatten and multiply." Because most Africans, like Europeans, depended on agriculture rather than hunting, they adapted more easily to agricultural slavery. Black labor was valuable, if controlled; Indians were merely barriers to expansion.

When settlers first began moving onto the Great Plains, they encountered about 250,000 Plains Indians and 13 million buffalo. Some tribes, including the Zuni, Hopi, Navaho, and Pawnee, were fairly settled and depended on gardening and farming. Such tribes as the Sioux, Apache, and Cheyenne, however, were nomadic hunters who followed the buffalo herds over vast tracts of land. These herds played a crucial role in most Plains Indians' culture—providing almost all the basic necessities. Indians ate the buffalo meat, made clothing and tepees out of the hides, used the fats for cosmetics, fashioned the bones into tools, made thread from the sinews, and even burned dried buffalo droppings as fuel. To settlers, however, the buffalo were barriers to western expansion. The herds interfered with construction, knocked over telegraph poles and fences, and could derail trains during stampedes.

Other cultural differences caused misunderstandings between settlers and Native Americans. Among Anglo-Americans, capitalism fostered competition and frontier living promoted individualism. On the other hand, Plains Indians lived in tribes based on kinship ties. As members of an extended family that included distant cousins, Indians were taught to place the welfare of the group over the interests of the individual. The emphasis within a tribe was on cooperation rather than competition. Some tribes might be richer than other tribes, but there was seldom a large gap between the rich and the poor within a tribe.

Power as well as wealth was usually shared. Tribes were loosely structured rather than tightly organized. Chiefs seldom had much individual power. The Cheyenne, for example, had a council of 44 to advise the chief. Instead of having a lot of political power, chiefs were generally religious and ceremonial leaders. Anglo-Americans did not always understand

their limited power. Whites incorrectly believed that an individual Indian could make decisions and sign agreements that would be considered legal by their fellow Indians.

Another major cultural difference between the newly arriving settlers and the Plains Indians was their attitudes toward the land. Most Indians had no concept of private property. Chief Joseph of the Nez Percé eloquently expressed the Indian view: "The earth was created by the assistance of the sun, and it should be left as it was. . . . The country was made without lines of demarcation, and it is no man's business to divide it."

Chief Joseph of the Nez Percé expressed the views of Native Americans who had no concept of owning the earth. He proclaimed, "The earth and myself are of one mind."

The Indians refused to draw property lines and borders because of how they viewed the place of people in the world. Whites tended to see land, plants, and animals as resources to be exploited. Indians, on the other hand, stressed the unity of all life—and its holiness. As Chief Joseph said, "The earth and myself are of one mind." Thus people were not meant to dominate the rest of nature; they were a part of it.

Most of the Plains Indians believed that land could be utilized, but never owned. The idea of /owning land was as absurd as owning the air people breathed. To some, the sacredness of the land made farming against their religion. Chief Somohalla of the Wanapaun explained why his people refused to farm. "You ask me to plow the ground! Shall I take a knife and tear my mother's bosom? . . . You ask me to cut grass and make hay and sell it, and be rich like white men! But how dare I cut off my mother's hair?"

Indians had great reverence for all land. In addition, some particular pieces of land were considered especially sacred or holy. Certain bodies of water were seen as sources of healing and sites for worship. Some areas were burial grounds, where the spirits of ancestors were believed to reside. White settlers had little understanding of or respect for such Indian sentiments. The results could be tragic where interests collided.

From the white viewpoint, the most significant characteristic of many of the Plains Indian tribes, such as the Cheyenne, Sioux, and Arapaho, was their ability as mounted warriors. Using horses introduced by the Spanish, they had resisted white encroachment for two centuries. Most had no desire for assimilation; they merely wanted to be left alone. "If the Indians had tried to make the whites live like them," one Sioux declared, "the whites would have resisted, and it was the same way with the Indians."

Although some tribes could coexist peacefully with settlers, the nomadic tribes had a way of life that was incompatible with miners, railroad developers, cattle ranchers, and farmers. To Anglo-Americans the Indians were barriers to expansion. They agreed with Theodore

Roosevelt that the West was not meant to be "kept as nothing but a game reserve for squalid savages." Thus U.S. Indian policy focused on getting more territory for white settlement. Prior to Reconstruction this was done by signing treaties that divided land between Indians and settlers and restricted the movement of each on the lands of the other. Frequently Indian consent was fraudulently obtained, and white respect for Indian land depended on how desirable it was for settlement. As the removal of the Southern Cherokees to Oklahoma had shown in the 1830s, compatibility of cultures did not protect Native Americans from the greed of whites.

During the Civil War, Sioux, Cheyenne, and Arapaho braves rejected the land cessions made by their chiefs. Violence against settlers erupted as frontier troop strength was reduced to fight the Confederacy. The war also provided an excuse to nullify previous treaties and pledges with the tribes resettled in Oklahoma by Andrew Jackson's Indian removal. Some did sup-

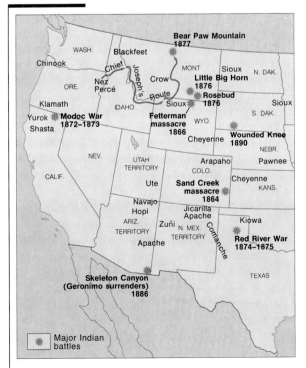
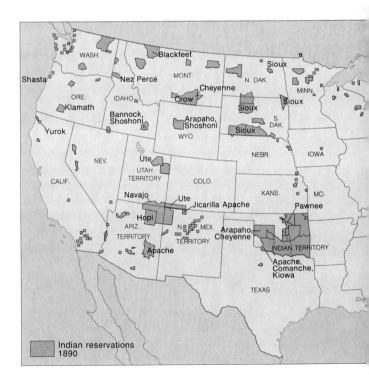

Indian Battles and Reservations

port the Confederacy, but all suffered the consequences of Confederate defeat. Settlers moved into the most desirable land, pushing the Indians farther south and west. Some Indians began to resist.

By the close of the Civil War, Indian hostility had escalated, especially after an 1864 massacre. The territorial governor of Colorado persuaded most of the warring Cheyennes and Arapahoes to come to Fort Lyon on Sand Creek, promising them protection. Colonel J. M. Chivington's militia, however, attacked an Indian camp flying a white flag and the American flag and killed hundreds of Indian men, women, and children. The following year Congress established a committee to investigate the causes of conflict. Its final report in 1867 led to the creation of an Indian Peace Commission charged with negotiating settlements. At two conferences in 1867 and 1868, Indian chiefs were asked to restrict their tribes to reservations in the undesirable lands of Oklahoma and the Black Hills of the Dakotas in return for supplies and assistance from the government.

Most Indians did not consider the offer very generous. Some acquiesced and others resisted, but in the end federal authorities subdued or killed them all. Several factors made their resistance unsuccessful. Railroads had penetrated the West, bringing in both settlers and federal troops more rapidly. Most important, however, was the destruction of the buffalo herds. Just as modern Americans would be helpless without oil or electricity, the Plains Indians' culture could not survive the near extinction of the buffalo by professional and sport hunters. In 1872 the Indian commissioner accurately forecasted that in a few years the "most powerful and hostile bands of today" would be "reduced to the condition of supplicants for charity."

In 1876, the final year of Reconstruction, Lieutenant Colonel George A. Custer's defeat at Little Bighorn called attention to the "Indian problem." The stage was set for this confrontation with Chief Sitting Bull's Sioux warriors and their Cheyenne allies two years earlier when gold was discovered in the Black Hills. The territory suddenly became tempting, and miners began pouring into the lands guaranteed to the Indians only five years before. "The white

man is in the Black Hills just like maggots," one Indian lamented.

Despite Sitting Bull's victory, the die had been cast during Reconstruction. All that remained were "mopping up" exercises. Federal authorities solved the Indian problem by reducing the number of Indians to a level that posed no threat. Still, white Americans would not leave the Indians alone. The exact nature of the Indians' status, like that of African-Americans, would be determined after Reconstruction was over. The treatment of both, as well as of immigrants, would be justified by the increasingly virulent racism of whites, which was given "scientific" support by the scholars of the late nineteenth century. One thing was clear in 1876: Northerners who believed that the only good Indian was a dead Indian could hardly condemn Southern whites for their treatment of African-Americans. The patriotism engendered by the 1876 centennial of the Declaration of Independence also fostered a desire for unity among white Americans at the expense of nonwhites.

Final Retreat from Reconstruction

By 1876, fewer Americans championed black rights than had at the close of the war. Some of the old abolitionist Radicals had grown tired of what had become a protracted and complex problem. They therefore justified their withdrawal from the fight by the failures of some Southern Reconstruction governments. Those least likely to do so, such as Thaddeus Stevens and Charles Sumner, were dead. Until his death in 1874, Sumner had struggled to get Congress to pass a civil rights act that would spell out more specifically the guarantees of the Fourteenth Amendment. He proposed that segregation of all public facilities, including schools, be declared illegal and the right of African-Americans to serve on juries specified. After his death, in part as a tribute to him but mostly as one provision of a larger political bargain, Congress enacted the Civil Rights Act of 1875. The act did not include Sumner's clause on schools and did not provide any means of enforcement. For African-Americans it was a paper victory that marked an end of national action on their behalf. Never effectively enforced, the act was

In this 1898 watercolor, an Indian participant in the Battle of Little Bighorn depicts its aftermath. As Sitting Bull and others stand watching, Sioux and Cheyenne warriors ride horseback over the corpses of Custer (left center) and his troops.

rendered totally impotent by Supreme Court decisions of the late nineteenth century.

By 1876 all the elements were present for a national retreat on Reconstruction: the distraction of economic distress, a deep desire for unity among whites, the respectability of racism, a frustrated weariness with black problems by former allies, a growing conservatism on economic and social issues, a changing political climate featuring a resurgence of the Democratic party, and finally a general public disgust with the failure of Reconstruction. The presidential election of that year sealed the fate of Reconstruction and brought about an official end to it.

Corruption was a major issue in the 1876 election and the Democrats chose Samuel J. Tilden, a New Yorker whose claim to fame was breaking up the notorious Boss Tweed Ring. The Republicans nominated Rutherford B. Hayes, a man who had offended few—largely by doing little. Although Hayes had been elected governor of Ohio three times, to one observer he was "a third rate nonentity, whose only rec-

ommendation is that he is obnoxious to no one." As would become typical of most elections during the decades following Reconstruction, the campaign did not focus on any burning issues. The Democrats ran against Republican corruption. The Republicans ran against Democratic violence in the South. "Our strong ground," Hayes wrote, "is the dread of a solid South, *rebel rule*, etc., etc.... It leads people away from 'hard times'; which is our deadliest foe."

The election itself was so riddled with corruption and violence that no one can ever know what would have happened in a fair election. One thing is certain. The Democrats gained strength. Tilden won the popular vote and led Hayes in undisputed electoral votes 184 to 165. However, 185 votes were needed for election, and 20 votes were disputed—19 of them from Louisiana, Florida, and South Carolina. They were the only Southern states still under Republican rule with the backing of federal troops. In each, rival election boards sent in different returns.

With no constitutional provision for such an occurrence, the Republican Senate and Democratic House established a special commission to decide which returns were valid. The 15-member Electoral Commission had 5 members each from the House, the Senate, and the Supreme Court. At first it was evenly divided with 7 Republicans and 7 Democrats; politically independent Supreme Court Justice David Davis was the swing vote. Illinois Democrats then made a mistake and selected Davis as their senator. Thus, a Republican justice was appointed to replace him on the Electoral Commission, which proceeded to vote along party lines, 8 to 7, to give all the disputed votes to Hayes. Democrats were outraged, and a constitutional crisis seemed in the making if a united Democratic front in the House voted to reject the commission's findings.

A series of agreements between Hayes's advisors and Southern Democratic congressmen averted the crisis. In what came to be called the "Compromise of 1877," Hayes agreed to support federal aid for Southern internal improvements, especially a transcontinental railroad. He also promised to appoint a Southern Democrat to his cabinet and to allow Southern Democrats a say in the allocation of federal offices in their region. Most important, however, was his pledge to remove the remaining federal troops from the South. In return Southern Democrats promised to protect black rights and to support the findings of the Electoral Commission. On March 2, the House voted to accept the report and declare Hayes the presidential winner by an electoral vote of 185 to 184. After taking office, Hayes removed the troops, and the remaining Republican governments in the South soon collapsed.

Scholars once considered the Compromise of 1877 an important factor in the end of Reconstruction. Actually, its role was more symbolic than real; it merely buried the corpse. The battle for the Republican party's soul had been lost by its abolitionist faction well before the election of 1876. The Democratic party had never sought to extend or protect blacks' rights. The Supreme Court began to interpret the Fourteenth and Fifteenth amendments very narrowly, stripping them of their strength. Thus African-Americans were left with a small number of allies, and one by one many of their rights were lost during the next four decades.

CONCLUSION

As the Civil War ended, many unresolved issues remained. The most crucial involved the status of the freedmen and of the former Confederate states. The destinies of both were inextricably intertwined. Anything affecting the status of either influenced the fate of the other. Quick readmission of the states with little change would doom black rights. Enforced equality of African-Americans under the law would create turbulence and drastic change in the South. This difficult problem was further complicated by constitutional, economic, and political considerations, ensuring that the course of Reconstruction would be chaotic and contradictory.

Presidential Reconstruction under both Lincoln and Johnson favored rapid reunification

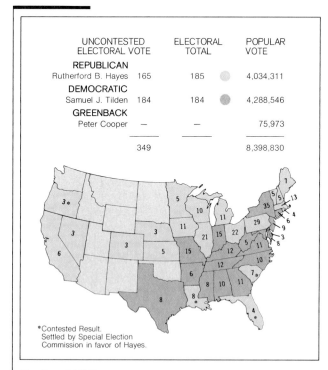

	UNCONTESTED ELECTORAL VOTE	ELECTORAL TOTAL	POPULAR VOTE
REPUBLICAN			
Rutherford B. Hayes	165	185	4,034,311
DEMOCRATIC			
Samuel J. Tilden	184	184	4,288,546
GREENBACK			
Peter Cooper	–	–	75,973
	349		8,398,830

*Contested Result.
Settled by Special Election
Commission in favor of Hayes.

Election of 1876

CHRONOLOGY
OF KEY EVENTS

1863 Lincoln proclaims 10 percent plan for Reconstruction, which requires states to abolish slavery and have 10 percent of the citizens who had voted in the 1860 election subscribe to an oath to support the Constitution and the Union

1864 Lincoln vetoes Wade-Davis Bill on grounds that it imposes too severe conditions on the readmission of the seceded states; Sand Creek Massacre of Indians in Colorado

1865 Congress establishes Freedmen's Bureau to aid former slaves and refugees; Confederate army surrenders at Appomattox; John Wilkes Booth assassinates Lincoln at Ford's Theater in Washington, D.C.; Andrew Johnson becomes seventeenth president; Thirteenth Amendment is ratified, abolishing slavery

1866 Civil Rights Act provides that all persons born in the United States are citizens and possess equal legal and property rights; Fourteenth Amendment is proposed

1867 Reconstruction Act, passed over Johnson's veto, divides the South into five military districts, each governed by an army general. Requires each state to adopt a constitution disqualifying former Confederate officials from holding office; grant black citizens the right to vote; and ratify the Fourteenth Amendment

1868 House of Representatives impeaches President Johnson; he escapes conviction in the Senate by one vote; Fourteenth Amendment is ratified; it guarantees citizenship to black Americans; Indian peace conference leads to establishment of reservations in Oklahoma and the Black Hills of the Dakotas; Ulysses S. Grant is elected eighteenth president

1870 Fifteenth Amendment is ratified; outlaws the exclusion from voting on the basis of race

1870–1871 Ku Klux Klan Acts are passed, which outlaw use of force to prevent people from voting and authorize use of federal troops to enforce the laws; Tweed Ring in New York City is exposed

1872 Crédit Mobilier scandal is exposed

1876 Custer is defeated at Little Bighorn; disputed presidential election between Tilden and Hayes

1877 Electoral commission awards disputed ballots to Republican Rutherford B. Hayes, who becomes nineteenth president

---

and white unity more than changes in the racial structure of the South. The South, however, refused to accept a meaningful end of slavery, as was blatantly demonstrated by the Black Codes. Congressional desire to reestablish legislative supremacy and the Republican need to build a national party combined with this Southern intransigence to unite Radical and moderate Republicans on the need to protect black rights and to restructure the South. What emerged from congressional reconstruction were Republican governments that expanded democracy and enacted needed reforms but were deeply resented by many Southern whites. At the core of that resentment was not disgust over incompetence or corruption but hostility to black political power in any form.

Given the pervasiveness of racial prejudice, what is remarkable is not that the Freedmen's Bureau, the constitutional amendments, and the civil rights legislation did not produce permanent change but that these actions were taken at all. Cherished ideas of property rights, limited government, and self-reliance, as well as an almost universal belief in black inferiority, almost guaranteed that the experiment would fail. The first national attempt to resolve fairly and justly the question of minority rights in a pluralistic society was abandoned in less than a decade. Indians, blacks, and women saw the truth of the Alabama planter's words of 1865: "Poor elk—poor buffaloe—poor Indian—poor Nigger—this is indeed a white man country." Nevertheless, less than a century later seeds planted by the amendments would finally germinate, flower, and be harvested.

SUGGESTIONS FOR FURTHER READING

OVERVIEWS AND SURVEYS

Eric Anderson and Alfred A. Moss, Jr., *The Facts of Reconstruction: Essays in Honor of John Hope Franklin* (1992); Mary Francis Berry and John W. Blassingame, *Long Memory: The Black Experience in America* (1982); Eric Foner, *Reconstruction: America's Unfinished Revolution, 1863–1877* (1988); Jay R. Mandle, *Not Slave, Not Free: The African-American Experience Since the Civil War* (1992); James McPherson, *Ordeal by Fire* (1982); James G. Randall and David Donald, *The Civil War and Reconstruction*, 2d ed. (1969); Kenneth M. Stampp, *The Era of Reconstruction, 1865–1877* (1965).

POSTWAR CONDITIONS AND ISSUES

Herman Belz, *Emancipation and Equal Rights: Politics and Constitutionalism in the Civil War Era* (1976); John H. Cox and LaWanda Cox, *Politics, Principles, and Prejudice* (1963); W. E. B. DuBois, *Black Reconstruction* (1935); John Hope Franklin, *Reconstruction After the Civil War* (1961); Peter Kolchin, *First Freedom: The Responses of Alabama's Blacks to Emancipation and Reconstruction* (1972); J. Morgan Kousser and James McPherson, eds., *Region, Race, and Reconstruction* (1982); Leon Litwack, *Been in the Storm So Long* (1979); Rembert W. Patrick, *Reconstruction of the Nation* (1967); James Roark, *Masters Without Slaves* (1977); Willie Lee Rose, *Rehearsal for Reconstruction* (1964); James Sefton, *The United States Army and Reconstruction, 1865–1877* (1967); Ted Tunnell, *Crucible of Reconstruction* (1984).

PRESIDENTIAL RECONSTRUCTION

Richard H. Abbott, *The Republican Party and the South, 1855–1877: The First Southern Strategy* (1986); Michael Les Benedict, *A Compromise of Principle* (1974); William R. Brock, *An American Crisis* (1963); LaWanda Cox, *Lincoln and Black Freedom* (1981); David Donald, *The Politics of Reconstruction* (1965); William B. Hesseltine, *Lincoln's Plan of Reconstruction* (1960); Peyton McCrary, *Abraham Lincoln and Reconstruction* (1978); Eric McKitrick, *Andrew Johnson and Reconstruction* (1960); James M. McPherson, *The Struggle for Equality: Abolitionists and the Negro in the Civil War and Reconstruction* (1964); Patrick W. Riddleberger, *1866: The Critical Year Revisited* (1979); Hans L. Trefousse, *The Radical Republicans* (1969).

CONGRESSIONAL RECONSTRUCTION

Michael Les Benedict, *The Impeachment of Andrew Johnson* (1973); Ellen DuBois, *Feminism and Suffrage* (1978); William Gillette, *The Right to Vote* (1969); Harold M. Hyman, *A More Perfect Union* (1973); Joseph James, *The Framing of the Fourteenth Amendment* (1956); Stanley I. Kutler, *The Judicial Power and Reconstruction Politics* (1968); Hans L. Trefousse, *The Impeachment of a President* (1975).

RECONSTRUCTION IN THE SOUTH

Dan T. Carter, *When the War Was Over: The Failure of Self-Reconstruction in the South, 1865–1867* (1985); Stephen J. DeCanio, *Agriculture in the Postbellum South* (1974); Paul D. Escott, *Many Excellent People* (1985); Barbara Jeanne Fields, *Slavery and Freedom on the Middle Ground: Maryland During the Nineteenth Century* (1985); Eric Foner, *Nothing but Freedom* (1983); Herbert G. Gutman, *The Black Family in Slavery and Freedom* (1976); Steven Hahn, *The Roots of Southern Populism* (1983); William C. Harris, *The Day of the Carpetbagger* (1979); Thomas Holt, *Black over White* (1977); Gerald Jaynes, *Branches Without Roots: Genesis of the Black Working Class in the American South, 1862–1882* (1986); Jay R. Mandle, *The Roots of Black Poverty* (1978); Robert C. Morris, *Reading, 'Riting and Reconstruction* (1981); Otto H. Olsen, ed., *Reconstruction and Redemption in the South* (1980); Michael Perman, *The Road to Redemption: Southern Politics, 1869–1879* (1984); Lawrence N. Powell, *New Masters: Northern Planters During the Civil War and Reconstruction* (1980); Howard Rabinowitz, *Race Relations in the*

Urban South (1978); George C. Rable, *But There Was No Peace: The Role of Violence in the Politics of Reconstruction* (1984); Peter J. Rachleff, *Black Labor in the South: Richmond, Virginia, 1865–1890* (1984); Roger L. Ransom and Richard Sutch, *One Kind of Freedom: The Economic Consequences of Emancipation* (1977); Joe Gray Taylor, *Louisiana Reconstructed* (1974); Allen Trelease, *White Terror* (1971); Ted Tunnell, *Crucible of Reconstruction* (1984); Jonathan M. Wiener, *Social Origins of the New South: Alabama, 1860–1885* (1978); Sarah Woolfolk Wiggins, *The Scalawag in Alabama Politics* (1977); Joel Williamson, *After Slavery: The Negro in South Carolina During Reconstruction* (1965), and *A Rage for Order: Black-White Relations in the American South Since Emancipation* (1986).

RECONSTRUCTION IN THE NORTH AND WEST

Ralph K. Andrist, *The Long Death: The Last Days of the Plains Indians* (1964); Robert F. Berkhofer, *The White Man's Indian* (1978); Eugene H. Berwanger, *The West and Reconstruction* (1981); Charles Fairman, *Reconstruction and Reunion*, 2 vols. (1971–1987); David A. Gerber, *Black Ohio and the Color Line, 1860–1915* (1976); William Gillette, *Retreat from Reconstruction* (1979), and *The Right to Vote* (1969); Norris Handley, Jr., ed., *The American Indian* (1974); Nell Irvin Painter, *The Exodusters* (1977); Keith Ian Polakoff, *The Politics of Inertia* (1973); Francis Paul Prucha, *American Indian Policy in Crisis* (1975); Ronald T. Takaki, *Iron Cages* (1979); Mark W. Summers, *Railroads, Reconstruction and the Gospel of Prosperity* (1984); Wilcomb E. Washburn, *The Indian in America* (1975), and *Red Man's Land/White Man's Law* (1971); C. Vann Woodward, *Reunion and Reaction* (1951).

BIOGRAPHIES

Fawn M. Brodie, *Thaddeus Stevens* (1959); David Donald, *Charles Sumner and the Rights of Man* (1970); Erik S. Lunde, *Horace Greeley* (1980); William S. McFeely, *Yankee Stepfather: General O. O. Howard and the Freedmen* (1968), and *Grant: A Biography* (1981), and *Frederick Douglass* (1990); John G. Neihardt, *Black Elk Speaks* (1932); Hans L. Trefousse, *Andrew Johnson* (1989).

CHAPTER 17

Emergence as an Economic Power

Fig. 16

On a cold winter's night in December 1900, 75 of the richest, most influential American businessmen gathered at the New York University Club. They met for a dinner to honor Charles Schwab, president of Carnegie Steel Company. Seated to the honoree's right was J. P. Morgan, the powerful investment banker and consolidator of industry. He had been placed there so that he would not miss a word of Schwab's speech. When Schwab finally rose, he delivered a veiled threat instead of a speech. With pretended innocence he rhapsodized over a bright future of low prices and stability for the steel industry. This future was to be ushered in by the formation of a scientifically integrated firm—one that combined all phases of the industry from the production of raw steel to the manufacture of finished products.

Morgan did not miss the point. Previously, Carnegie Steel had limited its operations to making raw steel. For several years Morgan and others had been busily creating trusts among the producers of such finished steel products as tubes and wire. Trusts were attempts to unite smaller competing firms in order to control market and raise prices. Trusts often used their combined power to put remaining competitors out of business. The steel products trusts, however, had a problem. Andrew Carnegie's company was the largest supplier of raw steel and he hated trusts. Thus when American Tin Plate Company threatened to cancel its orders with Carnegie unless he refused to sell to its competitors, he decided to beat them at their own game. He joined several informal arrangements to fix prices, known as "pools," only to sabotage them from within. Morgan and his cohorts soon realized that depending on Carnegie for raw steel would doom their consolidation schemes. Consequently, in July 1900 National Tube, American Steel and Wire, and American Hoop canceled all their contracts with Carnegie. They were going to produce their own steel or buy it from others—and put Carnegie out of business.

Rather than surrender, Carnegie telegraphed instructions to his company's officers: "Crisis has arrived, only one policy open; start at once hoop, wire, nail mills ... Extend coal and coke roads, announce these; also tubes ...

Have no fear as to result, victory certain. Spend freely for finishing mills, railroads, boat lines." By continuing his policy of spending money to make money, Carnegie knew he could produce superior products at cheaper prices. After Schwab assured him that they could manufacture tubes at a price $10 a ton cheaper than National Tube, he decided to pay no dividends on common stock and began plans to build a $12 million tube plant.

The antiquated and scattered plants of his competitors would have been no match for Carnegie's new ones. Panicked promoters scurried to J. P Morgan in the weeks before the testimonial dinner. Few doubted Federal Steel president Elbert Gary's assertion that Carnegie could "have driven entirely out of business every steel company in the United States." Carnegie, however, wanted to retire. Schwab's speech was aimed at producing a bargain, not a war. After the dinner Morgan fired dozens of questions at Schwab. Later they held an all-night session at Morgan's house. In the early hours of the next day Morgan finally said, "Well, if Andy wants to sell, I'll buy. Go find his price."

Schwab approached Carnegie on the golf course, where he might be more inclined to cooperate. Carnegie listened and asked Schwab to return the next day for an answer. At that time Carnegie handed him a slip of paper with his asking price of $480 million written in pencil. When Schwab gave Morgan the offer, he glanced at it and replied, "I accept the price." A few days later Morgan stopped by Carnegie's office, shook hands on the deal and stated, "Mr. Carnegie, I want to congratulate you on being the richest man in the world."

Two of the best had locked in combat, and both were victors. Carnegie had his millions to endow libraries, and anything else that struck his fancy. Morgan founded United States Steel Corporation. A colossus even among the existing giants of American industry, it was capitalized at $1.4 billion, a figure three times larger than the annual budget of the United States. The fates of Carnegie and Morgan reflected the momentous changes after the Civil War. Moving from the ranks of second-rate industrial powers, by 1900 the nation was the leader—with a manufacturing output exceeding the combined total of Great Britain, France, and Germany. The speed with which this happened seems more suited to fairy tales than reality. As Andrew Carnegie exclaimed in 1886, "The old nations of the earth creep on at a snail's pace; the Republic thunders past with the rush of an express."

Many yardsticks supported his assertion. Between 1870 and 1914 railroad mileage increased from 53,000 to 250,000—more than the combined mileage of the rest of the world. Almost every sector of the economy grew in multiples of two or more from the 1860s to 1900. Land under agricultural production doubled; the gross national product was six times larger; the amount of manufactured goods per person tripled.

This phenomenal growth resulted from the foundations laid by antebellum industrial development, the abundance of the land and its people, technological breakthroughs, and a favorable business climate—ideologically, financially, legally, and politically. The rapidity of change produced chaotic conditions, which led to new managerial styles and finally to economic consolidation and the rise of such supercorporations as United States Steel.

The forces of economic modernization swept through all sections and all segments of the economy. The results were profound alterations of the social order that touched virtually every aspect of life. Much of what is now commonplace—electric lights, petroleum, the telephone, the skyscraper, the hand-held camera, the typewriter—was largely unknown prior to the Civil War. The natures of work and marketing were drastically transformed, affecting all social relationships. The new order produced a few big winners, such as Carnegie and Morgan, but there were losers, too.

AMERICA: LAND OF PLENTY

In 1847 Walt Whitman boasted, "Yankeedoodledom is going ahead with the resistless energy of a sixty-five-hundred-horse-power steam engine. . . . Let the Old World wag on under its cumbersome load of form and conservatism; we are of a newer, fresher race and land. And all we have to say is, to point to fifty years hence

Lavish displays of wealth were common in the business world, as in this 1901 dinner meeting of officials of the Carnegie Steel Company to celebrate the formation of U.S. Steel.

and say, 'Let those laugh who win.'" By 1897 Americans were laughing. Their victory was facilitated by the abundance of the nation's new land, new people, and new ideas.

Mineral and Geographic Possibilities

Explorers and early settlers in what would become the United States were disappointed not to find an abundance of gold and silver such as had enriched their Spanish neighbors to the south. Only in the nineteenth century did Americans begin to realize the vast wealth that their expansion had brought. Most spectacular was the discovery of gold in California in the 1840s. It sparked frenzied prospecting all through the West. Each new discovery led to "rushes," creating mining towns almost overnight. Between 1850 and the 1880s thousands of men and women of almost every ethnic background helped create makeshift social institutions whenever and wherever strikes were made in California, Nevada, Montana, Idaho, Colorado, and the Black Hills of the Dakotas.

Wherever it moved, the mining frontier tended to follow the same pattern. Adventurous optimists searched for the elusive glint of precious metals. After living weeks or months at subsistence level, many went home poorer. A few, however, did strike it rich—usually as discoverers rather than miners. Inexpensive and inefficient placer mining (washing loose ore from gravel) quickly exhausted the easily obtainable supplies of precious metals. Extracting ore from beneath the ground and in veins of quartz was expensive. It required large capital investments best raised by mining syndicates, which were frequently financed by eastern and European investors. Prospectors usually sold their claims to these companies for a fraction of their value.

As mining became an organized business, its focus moved to less exotic but more useful minerals such as copper, lead, talc, zinc, quartz, and oil. These fed the growing demands of the industrializing East. By the 1880s mining no longer represented easy riches for pioneering individuals; it had become an integrated part of the modernizing, industrial economy of the nation.

The extraction of the nation's mineral resources played an important role in the rise of basic industry. Prior to the Civil War, manufacturing centered mainly on such consumer goods as textiles, paper, and flour, which were processed from farm or forest materials. Emerging basic industries such as steel, petroleum, and electric power depended on large supplies of various minerals, which seemed to become available as needed. Sometimes new deposits were found; other times new uses for minerals spurred the mining of known deposits.

Iron working was extensive prior to the war, and major deposits were found from 1850 onward in Michigan and Minnesota. Wrought iron could be forged into plows and other implements. It was limited, however, by its lack of durability and could be used successfully only on farms and in small businesses. Then Andrew Carnegie and others employed new technology to produce large quantities of relatively cheap and durable steel. The availability of steel opened new manufacturing vistas, and between 1870 and 1900 the output of steel grew from 850,000 tons to over 10.5 million tons.

The same pattern developed in the mining of other minerals. Copper had been found in Michigan prior to the war and in Arizona in the 1870s. A much richer copper deposit was discovered in Butte, Montana, in 1881. At first mainly used for household products, copper became a key ingredient in such new fields as oil refining, electrical generation and conduction, and telephone communications. Most went into the miles and miles of wiring that electrified the cities. The new uses for copper modernized America and increased demand for the mineral. Its output grew from 8000 tons in 1860 to 800,000 tons in 1914, and by 1900 the annual value of copper production almost equaled that of gold and silver combined.

Coal mining had also been a minor enterprise before 1850, but its production grew from about a half million tons in 1860 to 270 million tons in 1900. Its spectacular rise was generated by the increased use of coal-burning steam engines to power machinery and locomotives. In 1876 visitors to the Philadelphia Centennial Exhibition were awed by the massive Corliss reciprocating engine with its 30-foot fly wheel. Its size was no more impressive than the change it symbolized. As late as 1869 almost half of all power used in manufacturing came from water wheels; by 1900 coal-burning steam engines supplied 80 percent of such power. Earlier dependence on water supplies had forced manufacturers to locate along rivers—often in rather sparsely populated rural areas. The steam engine, and later gasoline engines and electric motors, allowed new freedom in selecting plant sites, and manufacturing began to move to the cities that supplied both workers and transportation connections.

Even more dramatic was the rise of the importance of petroleum. Many people were aware of large reserves in Pennsylvania, which seeped into streams and springs. Demand, however, was mainly limited to such uses as patent medicines of dubious value. In 1855 Pennsylvania businessman George Bissell decided to explore other possible uses. He sent a sample to a Yale professor who hailed its potential use as both a lighting source and lubricating oil. Encouraged by that report, Bissell funded drilling efforts, and in 1859 his employee, Edwin L. Drake, tapped the first oil well in Titusville,

Pennsylvania. Commonly labeled "Drake's folly," it marked the beginning of another growing industry. Oil was needed to lubricate the increasing number of machine parts, and in the 1870s about 20 million barrels were being produced annually. After John D. Rockefeller and others began refining oil into kerosene, it also provided a popular form of illumination, displacing candles before being replaced by electricity.

An officer in Rockefeller's Standard Oil Company is reputed to have volunteered to drink all the oil ever found outside of Pennsylvania. He was fortunate that no one held him to his word. Although for the rest of the century most of the nation's oil continued to come from the Appalachian area and the Midwest, growing demand led to the search for "liquid gold" in the Southwest. In 1901 a well shot a 160-foot stream of oil into the air at Spindletop, Texas. New sources were thus available for the development of the gasoline engine in the twentieth century. Abundant natural resources and technology often interacted—each shaping the evolution of the other.

Technological Change

Seldom has a single generation experienced such rapid change as in the late nineteenth century. Technology dramatically transformed much of people's lives. Bewildering as the changes sometimes were, the public generally welcomed new inventions with wide-eyed awe. Some of the most important public events were like mass rituals to the new god of technology. Completion of the first transcontinental railway at Promontory Point, Utah, on May 10, 1869, was greeted with parades and thanksgiving services as well as the ringing of the Liberty Bell. Awed sightseers crammed expositions celebrating "progress." At the Philadelphia Centennial Exposition, visitors confronted for the first time not only the Corliss engine but also bicycles, the typewriter, the elevator, Alexander Graham Bell's telephone, and even the "floor covering of the future"—linoleum. By the time of the World's Columbian Exposition at Chicago in 1893, the Corliss engine was obsolete, and many of the miracles of 1876 were commonplace "necessities." At the 1893 exposition

Called "Drake's folly," the first oil well was drilled in Titusville, Pennsylvania, in 1859. Edwin Drake (in top hat) got his inspiration from watching salt-well drilling operations.

everything was powered by electricity, including 5000 arc lamps and 100,000 incandescent bulbs.

These mass rituals reflected a nationalistic pride, voiced by the commissioner of patents in 1892: "America has become known the world around as the home of invention." The patent record definitely supported his contention. Whereas only 276 inventions had been recorded during the Patent Office's first decade in the 1790s, during the single year of the Columbian Exposition 22,000 patents were issued.

The impact of new inventions was enormous. In 1889 an economist wrote that to catalog "what the world did not have half a century ago is almost equivalent to enumerating all those things which the world now regards as constituting the dividing lines between civilization and barbarism." Technological change af-

The Columbian Exposition of 1893 in Chicago celebrated the enormous technological progress of the late nineteenth century. In the Palace of Electricity many visitors saw their first electric lamp.

fected the lives of individuals far more than any political or philosophical development of the era. Even a select list of late-nineteenth-century inventions would fill numerous pages. Offices became mechanized with the invention of the typewriter in 1867 and the development of a practical adding machine in 1888. As clerical work became more needed as well as requiring less skill, it was classed as women's work with lower pay scales. Numerous inventions such as George Westinghouse's airbrake, which made longer, faster trains possible, revolutionized railroad transportation. Later, electric street-cars profoundly changed the character of urban development by accelerating the move to the suburbs.

Along with transportation changes, communication innovations welded a unified nation from a collection of island communities. Links with the rest of the world also increased when an Atlantic telegraphic cable was completed in 1866. New inventions in the field of printing made popular newspapers with wide circulations a reality—along with mass advertising.

Photographic advances culminated in George Eastman's Kodak hand-held camera in 1888. However, few, if any, inventions rivaled the importance of Bell's 1876 "toy." Telephones rapidly became necessities—more than one and one-half million were installed by 1900.

Increasingly, new inventions such as the telephone relied on cheap and efficient sources of electricity. Here the name of Thomas Edison stands above the rest. Beginning his career at an early age by peddling candy and newspapers on trains, he soon became a telegrapher and invented various improvements. The success of his ideas convinced him to go into the "invention business." Establishing a research lab at Menlo Park, New Jersey, in 1876, he promised to produce "a minor invention every ten days and a big thing every six months or so." He pretty much kept his promise, inventing the phonograph in 1877 and the incandescent light bulb in 1879, as well as hundreds of other devices such as a better telephone, the dictaphone, the mimeograph, the dynamo, motion pictures, and electric transmission. With backing from banker J. P. Morgan, he created the first electric company in 1882 in New York City and formed the Edison General Electric Company in 1888 to produce light bulbs.

As in all research, Edison followed a number of blind alleys, but his only serious mistake was the choice of direct electrical current. This limited the range of transmission to a radius of about two miles. George Westinghouse's development of an alternating current system in 1886 soon supplanted direct current, forcing even Edison's companies to make the switch. Westinghouse also acquired and improved an electric motor that had been invented by a Croatian immigrant named Nikola Tesla in 1888.

While a handful of inventors struck it rich, more often inventions paved the way to vast fortunes for such entrepreneurs as Carnegie. The success of most of the captains of industry came from their effective exploitation of new technology. Carnegie invented no new product but utilized such advances as the Bessemer and open-hearth processes to produce cheap and plentiful steel. In like manner, Rockefeller built his industrial empire on new refining methods, and Gustavus Swift's meat-packing operation depended on the invention of the refrigerated railroad car. Eventually machine-made, inter-

In his Menlo Park, New Jersey, laboratory, Thomas Edison aimed at practicality in his inventions. He eventually obtained over 1000 patents. Here he is listening to his phonograph in 1888.

changeable parts revolutionized every industry engaged in mass production.

The course of U.S. industrialization was profoundly influenced by both the relative abundance of natural resources and scarcity of manpower. In the beginning, Americans burned wood extravagantly. Later, seemingly inexhaustible supplies of coal and metal ores continued the bias toward labor-saving and material-consuming technology. Thus while population only tripled, industrial output grew nine times larger between 1860 and 1914. Population changes and growth, however, played an important role in the expanding economy.

Population Patterns and the New Industrial Work Force

Technology produced machines that displaced many skilled craftspeople and farmers, but paid employment also increased. For example, by the 1890s mechanization allowed one farmer to harvest 18 times as much wheat as he had done by hand in 1830. Nevertheless, the needs of a rapidly expanding population created so many new markets that the agricultural work force still grew by 50 percent. At the same time nonagricultural employment rose 300 percent. As early as 1880 the number of people employed in manufacturing, transportation, and construction grew to 5 million from only 1.5 million a generation earlier. During the next decade, farmers became a minority for the first time, and by 1900 six out of every ten Americans made their living outside of agriculture.

Those not engaged in farming increasingly concentrated in the cities. Between 1860 and 1900 urban residents increased from 6 million to 24 million. This clustering of population was essential to the expansion of industry—both feeding it and being fed by it. Some economic historians contend that of all the factors spurring industrial growth none was more important than the rise of an American mass market. Both the urban population boom and the transportation revolution created markets unparalleled in vastness and accessibility.

Mass markets would not have inevitably led to mass production and mass marketing without the public's acceptance of standardized goods.

Many people were lured to the cities with the promise of excitement, modern conveniences, and better, higher-paying jobs.

Several factors made Americans more receptive than Europeans to such goods. Class distinctions, though not absent, were more blurred and became increasingly so with the availability of ready-made clothing. Also, physical mobility broke down many of the local loyalties so prevalent in Europe. Such factors created opportunities that modern mass advertising exploited. Nowhere were changes greater than in the food industry. Food processors originally produced limited quantities for nearby markets. As transportation advances widened distribution areas, producers first relied on wholesale merchants and agents to sell their goods to the public. Then the marketing of consumer goods underwent a remarkable transformation. The communication revolution allowed manufacturers to peddle their wares directly to the consumer. Rather than selling nonperishable foods by the barrel to wholesalers, they now packaged them in smaller containers of standard size and weight. By 1900, $90 million was being spent annually to convince Americans of the advantages of specific brand names; modern advertising had embarked on its persistent quest to shape the tastes of the public.

Advertising increased demand for many products, creating more industrial jobs for ur-ban consumers. The dramatic expansion of this industrial workforce was fed mainly by massive migration to the cities. Although more people were being born than were dying in American cities, the natural increase of the urban population accounted for no more than one-fifth of its growth. This was true for several reasons. A declining birthrate reduced the number of children produced by the average woman from over 7 in 1800 to 3.6 in 1900, and this decline was most pronounced in the cities, where more women worked outside the home and had access to birth control information. Also, infectious disease led to higher death rates in the cities; an 1890 report revealed that 24 percent of the babies born in cities died in their first year.

Four-fifths of the new city residents moved there. Some 8 or 9 million of the 18 million of them were probably migrants from rural America. They came to cities for a variety of reasons. One was an increasing surplus of young men and women in the countryside. Rural birthrates remained high while mechanization decreased the number of hands needed to produce a crop. Such surpluses naturally "pushed" people from rural areas, but the cities also "pulled" them with the promise of more excitement, variety, and modern conveniences. Urban jobs also paid more; in 1890 clerical workers earned more than three times as much as farm laborers. While the average agricultural laborer earned $244 a year, clerical workers averaged $848.

Internal migration, however, did little to meet the fivefold increase in demand for industrial labor. Even before the Civil War native-born Americans could no longer be lured in sufficient numbers to work in factories. Rural white Americans more frequently joined the growing ranks of white-collar workers. Rural African-Americans would have gladly taken even the lowest factory job. However, because of the persistent notions of black inferiority, they were passed over in favor of foreign workers. Thus in 1890 only 7 percent of black males worked in factories, and as late as 1900 about 90 percent of African-Americans remained in the South—the least urbanized section of the nation.

Unlike industrializing European nations, therefore, the United States did not rely primarily on its own population to produce its industrial work force. Instead large numbers of immigrants manned the factories. The "pull" of job opportunities combined with factors "pushing" Europeans out of their native countries to produce a virtual flood of immigration. Some European villages lost half their residents as millions of people came to the United States. The large numbers facilitated industrialization but eventually produced a backlash from native-born Americans (see Chapter 18).

An Expanding Railroad Network

Americans developed a love/hate relationship with the railroads. The same locomotive that inspired Walt Whitman's rhapsody to its "fierce throated beauty" was described by Frank Norris in 1901 as "the leviathan, with tentacles of steel clutching into the soil, the soulless Force, the iron-hearted Power, the Master, the Colossus, the Octopus." There might be differing visions, but no one doubted the importance of the railroads. "The generation between 1865 and 1895 was already mortgaged to the railroads," Henry Adams wrote, "and no one knew it better than the generation itself."

The railroads provoked strong emotions because of their crucial role in forging a new society. More than anything else, railroads transformed a continent of isolated communities into a unified nation with an interdependent economy. Their rails brought raw materials to population centers, making possible large factories that mass produced goods. Those goods could then be shipped to national mass markets over the same rails. Changes were required, however, before railroads could meet the needs of an expanding economy.

The early railroads were strictly local affairs. By 1865 there were already 35,000 miles of rails, but few linked up in any rational way. Eleven different gauges of rail caused both goods and passengers to be unloaded from one set of cars and reloaded on another set—sometimes at a depot on the opposite side of town. Between New York and Chicago, cargo had to be unloaded and reloaded as many as six times. In some cases the inefficiency was intentional. Many small antebellum roads purposely adopted different gauges and conflicting schedules to prevent being swallowed up by larger, powerful competitors.

Unlike many European rail systems, American railroads grew with little advance planning or regulation by government. Their development was far from orderly, and they sprouted like weeds in populous areas where immediate profits could be made. Especially in the antebellum South, too many small lines serviced the same places. Four hundred companies sprang up—each with an average track length of a mere 40 miles. Twenty competing lines provided service between Atlanta and St. Louis.

While too many railroads served some sections in the East, prior to 1869 no transcontinental lines linked the East and West coasts. Financing their construction was the major problem. The construction of the railroads of the East required large amounts of capital, but a return on the investment came quickly. This was not true in the West. There railroads often preceded settlement and, therefore, traffic for their lines. Because of the need for transcontinental routes, land grants became the solution.

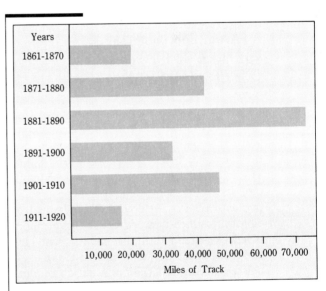

Figure 17.1

Railroad construction, 1861–1920. By 1865 there were 35,000 miles of railroad, but few lines connected in any logical way to provide direct routes from one location to another. Source: U.S. Bureau of the Census, 1975.

Contemporary and later analysts have questioned the size of those grants, but they undoubtedly had the desired effect. By the turn of the century there were five transcontinental routes.

At the same time, after some fierce competitive battles, a few eastern railroad companies gained control of many of the numerous local lines. When the dust settled, there were four main trunklines in the Northeast and five in the Southeast. The average track length of a railroad grew from a mere 100 miles in 1865 to over 1000 in two decades. Seven major groups controlled over two-thirds of the nation's railroad mileage. Gauges were standardized and a more efficient rail system emerged.

America's "newer, fresher race and land" provided the material basis for economic expansion. The "Land of Plenty" produced resources, people, and machinery in seemingly inexhaustible amounts and railroads tied them together. Nevertheless, even such wealth does not adequately explain the phenomenal mushrooming of American industry or the rise of large corporations. Less tangible developments nurtured the fantastic growth rate.

A FAVORABLE CLIMATE: THE ROLE OF IDEOLOGY, POLITICS, AND FINANCE

People, materials, and machinery were the "seeds" of industrialization. For a good harvest, however, good soil, favorable climatic conditions, and adequate fertilization were required. The bountiful economic harvest of the late nineteenth century depended on the "good soil" of popular support fostered by intellectual and cultural justifications. Favorable governmental policies created a desirable climate, while legal and financial developments provided the needed "fertilizer." The combination produced not only more industries but also larger industries. In 1870 shops and factories employed an average of 8 workers. Thirty years later the average work force was four times as large, and approximately 1450 factories employed 500 or more workers.

Social Darwinism and the Gospel of Wealth

Expanding economic opportunities fostered cutthroat competition from which fewer and fewer winners emerged. The road to wealth taken by the new captains of industry was strewn with ruined competitors and broken labor movements. Ruthlessness not only became increasingly necessary, it was also transformed into a virtue by the twin ideologies of Social Darwinism and the Gospel of Wealth.

For such men as Andrew Carnegie the works of Social Darwinists Herbert Spencer and William Graham Sumner helped to relieve any unwelcome guilt. "I remember that light came as in a flood and all was clear," Carnegie later recalled about his reaction to Spencer's writings. Spencer and his followers applied the biological concepts of Charles Darwin to the workings of society. Just as competition for survival ensured that the fittest of a species would live longer and produce more offspring, a similar process of natural selection in society was said to cause the fittest individuals to survive and flourish in the marketplace. Survival of the fittest supposedly enriched not only the winners but also society as a whole. Human evolution would produce what Spencer called "the ultimate and inevitable development of the ideal man" through a culling process. "If [individuals] are sufficiently complete to live, they do live," he wrote, "and it is well that they should live. If they are not sufficiently complete to live, they die and it is best they should die."

According to the Social Darwinists, poverty and slums were as inevitable as the concentration of wealth in the hands of the "fittest." Spencer pleaded that "there should not be a forcible burdening of the superior for the support of the inferior." His disciple Sumner declared, "If we do not like the survival of the fittest, we have only one possible alternative, and that is the survival of the unfittest." In other words, governmental or charitable intervention to improve the conditions of the poor was said to interfere with the functioning of natural law and prolonged the life of "defective gene pools" to the detriment of society as a whole.

The so-called fittest naturally greeted "scientific" endorsement of their elite positions with eagerness. John D. Rockefeller told his Baptist Sunday school class, "The growth of large business is merely the survival of the fittest. This is not an evil tendency in Business. It is merely the working out of a law of nature and a law of God." His statement illustrates that the captains of industry did not rely solely on science for justification; they also looked to religion. Indeed, although some business leaders used the jargon of Darwinism, Andrew Carnegie was one of the few actually to read and understand the dense, obtuse writings of Spencer.

Few business leaders were intellectuals, and some who understood Darwinist principles found the ruthlessness of the theory an unpalatable justification for their ruthless actions. They sought their solace in religious rationales for the accumulation of great wealth. Since colonial times, the Protestant work ethic had denounced idleness and viewed success as evidence of being among the "elect"—God's chosen people. Building upon this base, apologists constructed the "Gospel of Wealth." Some simply and boldly announced God's sanction of their wealth; Rockefeller asserted, "God gave me my riches." Not surprisingly, Carnegie was the one to produce a written, logically argued rationale. "Not evil, but good, has come to the race," he wrote, "from the accumulation of wealth by those who have the ability and energy that produces it." The masses would waste extra income "on the indulgence of appetite." On the other hand, "Wealth, passing through the hands of the few," Carnegie wrote, "can be a much more potent force for the elevation of our race than if it had been distributed in small sums to the people themselves." In other words, the "fittest" at the top could decide for people what they needed better than they could decide for themselves. In Carnegie's case, he took that responsibility seriously, distributing some $300 million to such philanthropic causes as founding libraries.

Among the most effective apologists for the wealthy, however, were religious leaders of the era. In 1901 Bishop William Lawrence proclaimed, "Godliness is in league with riches." Not only did the elite deserve their riches, but the poor also were responsible for their status. The eminent preacher Henry Ward Beecher ar-

gued that "no man suffers from poverty unless it be more than his fault—unless it be his sin." Perhaps the most popular evangelist for the Gospel of Wealth was Russell Conwell, who delivered his celebrated "Acres of Diamonds" speech approximately 6000 times between 1861 and 1925. In it he declared that anyone could get rich and asserted, "I say that you ought to get rich, and it is your duty to get rich." To those preaching sacrifice and vows of poverty, Conwell proclaimed, "It is a mistake of these pious people to think you must be awfully poor in order to be pious." Instead he asserted,

> Money is power, and you ought to be reasonably ambitious to have it. You ought because you can do more good with it than you could without it. Money printed your Bible, money builds your churches, money sends your missionaries, and money pays your preachers. . . . The man who gets the largest salary can do the most good with the power that is furnished to him.

Thus the maldistribution of wealth was not only inevitable but also desirable according to both scientific and religious thought. Probably more important was the support provided by popular culture. *McGuffey Readers* continued to stress the virtue of hard work and its inevitable rewards in poems such as "Try, Try Again." Novelist Horatio Alger penned many stories whose heroes rose from poverty to comfortable middle-class status through a combination of diligence and good luck. Thus popular literature reinforced the idea that success always came to those who deserved it in America, the land of opportunity. Finally, economic theory also lent respectability to greed and to the idea that government should not intervene in the economy.

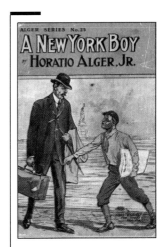

Popular culture at the turn of the century reinforced the American dream. In the Horatio Alger stories, the hero always escapes poverty through hard work and good fortune and joins the middle class.

Laissez-Faire in Theory and Practice

In 1776 Adam Smith's *The Wealth of Nations* presented arguments that would long be used to explain the workings of a free economy and to prescribe government's role in that economy. Smith asserted that the market was directed and controlled by an "invisible hand" composed of a multitude of individual choices. If government did not meddle, competition engendered by an unregulated market naturally led to the production of desired goods and services at reasonable prices. Short supply of a good in demand increased the price of that good, thereby encouraging more people to produce it in order to reap large profits. This increased production eventually caused the price to fall as supply equaled or even exceeded demand. In short, if everyone were left free to act according to self-interest, the result would be an economy best suited to meet the needs of general society.

Acceptance of the "invisible hand" of supply and demand economic theory naturally led to a policy called "laissez-faire." Government's proper role was to leave the economy alone. Apologists maintained that any governmental interference inevitably disrupted the operation of the natural forces that ordered the economy—thus producing a disorderly, inefficient market. Business leaders naturally endorsed the theory's rejection of governmental regulation. At the same time, however, they saw no contradiction in asking for government aid and subsidies to foster industrialization. To a large extent the industrialists got what they wanted—a laissez-faire policy that left them alone, except to help. Ironically, this distortion of theory helped to produce an economy where business consolidation wreaked havoc

Following the Civil War, government did little to regulate business. As a result, no laws protected consumers from fraudulent services or products like this claim for patent medicine.

upon the very competition needed for natural regulation of the economy.

Absolute free enterprise never really existed. There was plenty of governmental activity—just not in the area of regulation. Indeed the freedom of action given to businesspeople following the Civil War boggles the modern mind. No laws protected the consumer from adulterated foods, spurious claims for ineffective or even dangerous patent medicines, the sale of stock in nonexistent companies, or unsafe and overpriced transportation services. No national regulating agency existed prior to the establishment of the Interstate Commerce Commission in 1887. The proclamation "Let the buyer beware" asked people to make decisions and choices without adequate access to the information needed to protect their interests.

While denying support and protection to consumers or workers, government at all levels aided businesspeople. Alexander Hamilton's vision of an industrializing nation fostered by favorable governmental action never entirely died and was rejuvenated by the Republican party. Among the party's many promises in 1860 were pledges to enact higher tariffs, to subsidize the completion of a transcontinental railroad, and to establish a stable national banking system. The victory of Republican ideology undoubtedly helped to create a favorable environment for rapid industrialization. There was no sharp break with the past, however; nor was there a great victory by business over agriculture. The pattern of governmental aid to business was, as one historian has noted, "like certain kinds of embroidery . . . boldly visible but not of simple design." No form of aid was without antebellum precedents. Many concessions to business had wide public support that crossed party lines, often because other groups also benefited. Both the motives behind many actions and their results were mixed. In addition, the gains from some probusiness legislation were larger on paper than in practice. At the same time, agriculture was far from unrepresented and powerless, as can be seen by the passage of the Homestead and Morrill Land Grant acts, which provided free land to settlers and financed agricultural education.

Tariffs had a long history. Two days before Lincoln took office, Democratic President Buchanan signed the Morrill Tariff, marking the first tariff increase since 1842. That inaugurated an upward, practically uninterrupted, rise in tariff rates for the remainder of the century. At first, such American industries as steel needed to be protected from European competition to survive. Yet even after Carnegie and others were able to greatly reduce the cost of steel production, the tariff remained—allowing higher profits at the expense of consumers. As the average rate approached 50 percent, the duties on some commodities exceeded 80 percent of foreign manufacturers' prices. Without foreign competition, businesspeople were able to charge more for goods. Consumers came to resent these higher prices. Such bonanzas should not, however, obscure the fact that tariffs were widely viewed as serving the national interest by fostering economic independence from the British and others.

Additional forms of subsidy were also meant to serve the public good. Dwarfing all others were the land grants to railroads. In 1862 and 1864 Congress granted 20 square miles of public land in alternating sections for each mile of track laid by the Union Pacific and Central Pacific railroads in order to speed the completion of a transcontinental route. Only the scale of these grants was new; prior to the war railroads had already received nearly 20 million acres of federal land. By the time the grants ended, a total of 130 million acres of federal land went to various railroads, along with some 51 million acres of state land. Congress gave all those acres to a handful of people—creating some of America's wealthiest families. Nevertheless, as the 1869 celebrations of the completion of the first transcontinental line reflected, the public was not outraged. After all, even that incredible number of acres constituted less than 7 percent of the national domain in the West. In return the government paid only half fare to move troops and supplies. In addition, the value of the remaining land increased, and the uniting of the East and West spurred the entire economy. Only a decade after the grants' ceased were they denounced.

Business also benefited from favorable labor and financial legislation as well as low-interest loans. Individuals exploited these policies for personal gain, and the results were not uniformly positive. Aid to business, however, was never unlimited or unrestricted, and it enjoyed wide public support at first. Indeed nationalism and patriotism accompanied the process of industrialization. Many Americans took pride in the nation's growing economic power. When John D. Rockefeller explained his business activities by saying, "I wanted to participate in the work of making our country great," his words fell on sympathetic ears. Only after the problems of industrialization became more apparent did the public begin to cry "foul."

Corporations and Capital Formation

Such governmental aid as high tariffs, land grants, low interest loans, and lack of regulation provided rich fertilizer for economic expansion. The harvest brought both blessings and problems. The same is true of the rise of the corporation and decline of individual ownership and partnerships.

Corporations were certainly not new; they had long been used to finance ventures too expensive or too risky for a single individual to undertake—such as the English colonization of the New World. There were many advantages to incorporation for large-scale enterprises. By selling "shares" to a multitude of individual investors, the great sums of capital needed by modern industry could be amassed. Corporations did not risk the disruption of operation due to death of a partner or arguments between partners. Individuals could also hedge their bets. Rather than using all one's capital to buy a single ship, for example, one could buy a 10 percent interest in ten ships. Thus a hurricane or pirates could not wipe out one's investment with a bout of bad luck.

Despite the long history of corporations, changes dating from the Jacksonian period paved the way for their postwar domination of the economy. The first of these changes was the shift from the old practice of states issuing individual charters to each corporation. Under that system a corporation had to apply to a state legislature for a charter. New standard corporation laws allowed businesspeople to incorporate on their own, provided they met the requirements of the laws. Following the Civil War, courts also began to affirm the principle of "limited liability." Previously, bankruptcy could bring not only the loss of one's investment but also seizure of personal property by creditors. A corporation's liability finally became limited to its assets—making investment a safer and more desirable venture. One knew just how much could be lost.

One favorable court decision, *Santa Clara County* v. *The Southern Pacific Railroad* (1886), was a perversion of the Fourteenth Amendment. The Supreme Court ruled that a corporation was a legal "person" and therefore entitled to all the protections granted by the amendment. States could not deny corporations "equal protection of the law" or deprive them of their rights or property without "due process" of the law. In other words, all regulations had to apply equally to flesh-and-blood persons and to corporations. Corporations were eventually granted the "right" to "reasonable" profits—to be determined by the courts, not the state.

Instead of receiving "equal protection," corporations actually became privileged members of society. Real people whose rights were protected by the Constitution were also held personally responsible for illegal activities. There were no handcuffs or jail cells large enough for "corporate persons." Punishing individuals for corporate crimes was also difficult because corporate directors acted merely as employees of the company. A popular saying noted that a corporation had neither a soul to be damned nor a body to be kicked. Such advantages helped to spur the growth of corporations; by 1904 almost 70 percent of all manufacturing employees worked for corporations.

Perhaps the greatest advantage of corporations remained the ability to raise large amounts of capital. The expansion of industry in the late nineteenth century required big infusions of money. Every sector of the economy demanded capital: Farmers needed new machinery to increase productivity; manufacturers needed new plants to utilize the latest technology; cities needed new construction to service the needs of the urban population.

From where was all this money to come? Some, of course, was generated by the rising gross national product—the total value of goods and services produced in one year—which grew from $225 per person in 1870 to nearly $500 in 1900. New technology increased productivity and put more money into the hands of people— "extra money" not required to meet physical needs. Their collective decision on its use laid the foundations for the modern American economy. Many chose to use their extra money, or capital, to make more money by investment. The result was "capital deepening." An increasing share of the national income was invested rather than spent for personal consumption. Indeed the proportion of income going to capital formation almost doubled from 15 percent at the time of the Civil War to 29 percent in the 1880s.

Increasing amounts of this capital were invested in manufacturing. One reason was that investment bankers, such as J. P. Morgan, marketed corporate stocks and bonds. Foreign investment was also important; by 1900 Europeans had $3.4 billion invested in the United States, which represented approximately one-third of the almost $10 billion invested in manufacturing. This was rich fertilizer indeed for growth.

The net result of the favorable conditions of the late nineteenth century was industrial supremacy. Americans reveled in their nation's transformation to a colossus outproducing the entire world. Vast mineral wealth, technological breakthroughs, population changes, railroads, popular support, beneficial government policies, liberal corporation laws, and the availability of capital fostered this transformation. Many of these factors influenced not only the speed and size of the industrial "harvest" but also the nature of the fruit. At first the favorable conditions worked like overfertilized land—producing too many plants for the available space and resources. In this overgrown industrial garden competition created chaos until such entrepreneurs as Andrew Carnegie found ways to prune away their rivals.

THE RISE OF BIG BUSINESS

"You might as well endeavor to stay the formation of clouds, the falling of rains, the flowing of streams, as to attempt . . . to prevent the or-

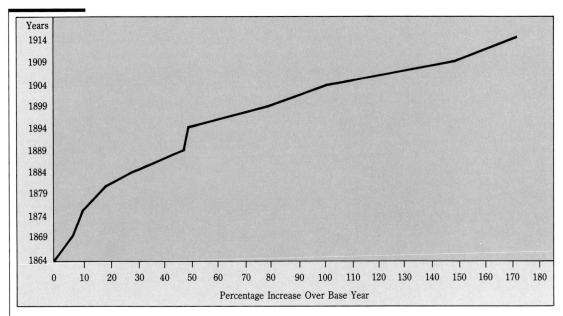

Figure 17.2
Index of manufacturing production, 1864–1914

ganization of industry." These words of John D. Rockefeller's attorney described what he considered to be the inevitable domination of entire industries by large corporations such as U.S. Steel. In industry after industry men like Rockefeller, Morgan, and Carnegie eliminated competitors and controlled markets. Methods of domination were refined and perfected over the course of time. The impact of this consolidation of industry was enormous. As companies grew larger, new management styles and more white-collar workers were needed. Mass production began to rise—profoundly changing the nature of work for industrial laborers. Also giant corporations amassed great power over production, people, and politics.

Controlling Competition

Most business leaders did not really advocate free enterprise fueled by competition. To them competition meant chaos, and they sought to eliminate it. J. P. Morgan, one historian wrote, "felt that the American economy should ideally be like a company organizational chart, with each part in its proper place, and the lines of authority clearly designated. He did not really believe in the free enterprise system, and like

most ardent socialists, he hated the waste, duplication, and clutter of unrestrained competition." To men like Morgan too many companies glutted the markets—producing chaos and cutthroat competition.

As America's first big business, the railroad industry was the first to confront the problems of competition. Most incurred gigantic debts to finance construction costs and expensive machinery. Debt payments were "fixed costs" that stayed the same regardless of how much business they received. As the 20 separate lines between Atlanta and St. Louis indicate, in many areas too many companies were after the same traffic. Thus railroads desperately sought to woo shippers to their lines by giving lower rates for bulk shipments and long hauls. To some preferred customers they also gave "rebates"—secret kickbacks below their published prices. They sought to make up for the lost revenue by overcharging smaller shippers.

Such tactics did not really solve the railroads' problems, especially when rate wars broke out. In the 1870s some railroad managers tried cooperation as a cure for competition. They formed regional federations to divide traffic equitably and to raise rates to increase profits. Such "pools," however, were not legally

After a period of intense competition in the railroad industry, a few rail barons consolidated lines by often using unscrupulous methods, seemingly carving up the nation at will.

enforceable. Greed frequently overcame scruples, dooming many such agreements.

For the railroads consolidation rather than cooperation became the key to controlling competition. Ruthless tactics sometimes accompanied consolidation. The former shipping magnate Cornelius Vanderbilt gained control of the New York Central Railroad in 1867 by buying two key lines that connected with it. He then refused to accept any rail cars going to or from the Central. His embargo worked but was much criticized. Vanderbilt's response was, "Can't I do what I want with my own?" He proceeded to acquire more lines to connect New York with Chicago and beyond. The net result of his ruthlessness was a personal fortune and an efficient, well-constructed railway system. Elsewhere buyouts and mergers eventually reduced the number of competitors—especially after depressions in the 1870s and 1890s.

Another weapon in the arsenal against competition was the "trust." John D. Rockefeller developed this device because the oil industry suffered from similar problems as the railroads. The relatively low cost of drilling oil wells at first encouraged the proliferation of so many small companies that output and prices fluctuated dramatically. After entering the oil business in 1862, John D. Rockefeller founded the Standard Oil Company of Ohio in 1870. This giant corporation was capitalized at $41 million. Competition, however, still created chaos, and Rockefeller lamented that "the butcher, the baker, and the candlestick maker began to refine oil."

Before creating the trust, Rockefeller tried a combination of pooling and rebates. In 1872 he organized the South Improvement Company. It was a combination of oil refiners and railroad directors aimed at dividing the oil carriage trade

John D. Rockefeller used ruthless techniques to eliminate competition and consolidate the oil-refining industry.

between the railroads. In return for a guaranteed share of the shipments, Rockefeller convinced the railroads to give rebates. Eventually Rockefeller was able to obtain rebates not only on the oil he shipped but also on the shipments of his competitors. Thus Rockefeller could undersell his competitors, whom he often bought out during times of economic depression.

Such techniques allowed Rockefeller to control 90 percent of the oil business, but legal problems arose from Standard Oil's far-flung holdings. His solution was the trust. In 1882 he convinced the major stockholders in a number of refineries to surrender their stock to a board of nine trustees. In return they received trust certificates that entitled them to a share of the joint profits of all the refineries. The benefits of this device were readily apparent. Pools had no legal standing and could be manipulated by some members to the detriment of other members. In a trust, however, competitive actions were of no benefit. Everyone shared all losses and gains.

Soon trusts began popping up like crabgrass throughout the economy. By 1888 a corporate lawyer wrote:

It is currently reported and believed that the "Trust" monopolies have drawn within their grasp not only kerosene oil and cotton seed oil, but sugar, oatmeal, starch, white corn meal, straw paper, . . . whiskey, rubber, steel, . . . wrought iron, pipes, iron nuts, stoves, lead, copper, envelopes, paper bags, paving pitch, cordage, coke, reaping and binding and mowing machines, plows, glass, and water works. And the list is growing day by day. Millions of dollars, in cash and property, are being drawn into the vortex.

Andrew Carnegie disliked pools and trusts, but found other ways to gain a competitive edge. One of these was "vertical integration." Buying the sources of his raw materials—iron ore and coke—he both lowered their cost to him and controlled his supplies. Not content merely with this "backward integration," he also practiced "forward integration" by acquiring many of the transportation facilities needed to distribute his product. This vertical integration lowered final prices by cutting out profit-taking by suppliers and shippers.

The key to Carnegie's success was his ability to cut costs without lowering quality. He used such traditional measures as wage cuts and increased hours for workers, but he also constantly explored new methods to increase productivity. When told that a plant had broken all records the previous week, he replied, *"Congratulation! Why not do it every week?"* By not focusing on short-term profits, he was willing to invest in expensive new technology to lower long-term costs of production. Reportedly, he opened one board meeting with the question, "Well, what shall we throw away this year?"

Carnegie often boasted that he knew almost nothing about steel. He hired experts to do that. What he did know was how to run a company and make money. His shrewdness took all variables into account. For example, he built his steel mill in Homestead—just outside the Pittsburgh city limits—which unlike the city was serviced by two railroads. He could therefore wrangle over rates, an opportunity not shared by his competitors in the city.

Carnegie effectively used all the economies of scale available to large firms. Soon he was able to undersell and destroy most of the dozens of steel companies that had blossomed

Andrew Carnegie rose from an immigrant textile mill worker to control the U.S. steel industry.

in response to the increased demand by railroads and industry. He also was a master at exploiting downturns in the business cycles. Most of his acquisitions were made during depressions, when prices were lower.

Competitors and labor movements suffered from Carnegie's actions, but the result was better steel at cheaper prices. As Carnegie once noted, "Two pounds of ironstone mined upon Lake Superior and transported nine hundred miles to Pittsburgh; one pound and one half of coal, mined and manufactured into coke, and transported to Pittsburgh; a small amount of manganese ore mined in Virginia and brought to Pittsburgh . . . these four pounds of materials [are] manufactured into one pound of steel, for which the consumer pays one cent." Such cheap steel aided the expansion of the railroads and the rise of other industries.

Of course, Carnegie was well-paid for these benefits—receiving almost a half billion dollars when he sold Carnegie Steel to J. P. Morgan. That sale illustrates another factor in consolidation: the role of bankers. Morgan and other bankers often stepped in during economic panics to reorganize bankrupt companies. They chewed up failing companies and railroads and spat them out as single supercorporations. The result was a more orderly economy, but at the price of centralizing vast economic power into the hands of a few unelected individuals. As one wit quipped when U. S. Steel was formed, "God created the world in 4004 B.C. and J. P. Morgan reorganized it in 1901."

New Managerial Styles and an Expanding Middle Class

The consolidation of companies into giant corporations created the need for new management techniques. Again, the railroads pioneered. As railroad companies grew larger, their activities covered hundreds of miles and employed thousands of workers. Safety and market conditions also required the entire system to operate as a single unit under a tight schedule. These conditions caused managerial problems. In the beginning, as one railroad expert wrote, "management had been personal and autocratic; the superintendent, a man gifted with energy and clearness of perception, molded the property to his own will. But as the properties grew, he found himself unable to give his personal attention to everything. Undaunted, he sought to do everything and do it well. He ended by doing nothing."

Railroad management required a level of coordination previously unknown in business. In the 1850s Erie Railroad employee Daniel McCallum sought answers. For the longer roads, he asserted, "I am fully convinced that in the want of system lies the true secret of their failure." Seeking to create system by establishing a formal administrative structure, he knew he was breaking new ground. "We have no precedent or experience upon which we can fully rely." The result was the first organizational table for an American company. McCallum drew up a chart with a chain of command moving from local train agents through five branches representing main operating divisions to the president and board of directors. Responsibilities were divided on a functional basis. Top management was separate from daily operations.

Better accounting procedures were also needed to keep track of the monies collected and paid out by numerous conductors as well as station and freight agents. On the Baltimore and Ohio railroad the management and accounting of funds were given to new divisions: the controller's office and the treasurer's office. Later the Louisville and Nashville Railroad adopted a cost-accounting system to provide accurate data to judge the performance of their lines.

Other large-scale businesses began to adopt the accounting methods, hierarchical administrative structures, and divisions of responsibilities pioneered by the railroads. The result was the creation of "middle management," who coordinated the operations of far-flung local plants and reported to the top executives. Big businesses were now run by bureaucracies staffed by white-collar workers, who had no role in founding the companies they served but who began to work their way up the bureaucratic ladder.

A profound consequence of the new economic order was the expansion of the middle

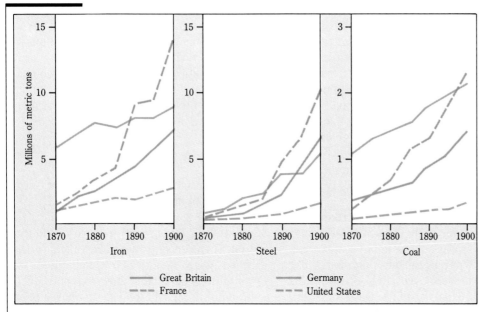

Figure 17.3

Iron, coal, and steel production, 1870–1900. Source: Carl N. Degler, *The Age of Economic Revolution.*
Copyright © 1977 by Scott, Foresman and Co.

class. Corporations needed accountants, middle managers, clerical workers, and sales representatives. The urban growth that accompanied industrialization also created demands for the services of professionals, shopkeepers, and government employees. The earnings of the middle class rose nearly 30 percent between the Civil War and the 1890s. By 1900 more than a third of urban families owned their homes. Although its members were sometimes dissatisfied with the new economic order, the middle class clearly derived benefits from and had a stake in it.

Mass Marketing, Assembly Lines, and Mass Production

Drastic transformations occurred in consumer industries as well as basic industry, as can be seen in the meat-packing business. There the interplay of new technology and new organization also ushered in new marketing techniques. Once again, the railroads played a key role by opening up the grazing ranges of the Great Plains. Because of its rail network, Chicago quickly became the major funnel through which

cattle were distributed from West to East. From its Union Stock Yards, cattle were shipped to abattoirs, or slaughterhouses, on the outskirts of eastern cities. The meat from the slaughtered animals was then distributed through local butchers to city residents.

There were several problems with such a distribution system, chief of which was the deterioration of the stock during long train journeys. Until the development of the refrigerated car, however, the only alternative was pickling or curing meat—processes that had already made Chicago the pork-packing center, but which were not as well suited to beef. Cattle dealer Gustavus Swift realized the possibilities opened up by refrigerated cars. Not only could fresh beef and pork be shipped more safely, but by centralizing slaughtering, waste products could be utilized. Profits were increased by making horns into buttons and hooves into glue. Eventually Swift formed glue, fertilizer, soap, and glycerine factories. People said that Swift used every part of a pig except the squeal.

Local butchers and wholesalers usually lacked refrigerated storage facilities, so Swift established his own warehouses, bypassing wholesale distributors and their cut of the profits. Swift had to overcome consumer resistance to the idea of buying meat weeks after the animal was slaughtered in a distant city. Local butchers often fed consumer distrust; New York shops frequently displayed signs reading "No Chicago beef sold here." Swift responded with a major advertising campaign stressing the superiority of western beef. His mass-marketing tactics proved successful. By the late 1890s six packers supplied almost 90 percent of all meat shipped in interstate commerce, and abattoirs virtually disappeared.

Swift also pioneered in mass production, employing assembly lines. The slaughtering and packing process was subdivided into numerous distinct jobs. Workers repeated one particular action as carcasses moved along on overhead conveyor belts. There was little wasted motion, and, as one of Swift's superintendents noted, "If you need to turn out a little more, you speed up the conveyor a little and the men speed up to keep pace."

Motion picture star Charlie Chaplin later parodied such tactics in the movie *Modern Times.* In it, a too-rapid conveyor created comic chaos. The waste of time, however, was no laughing matter to industrial managers. Engineer Frederick W. Taylor laid the foundations of "scientific management" with his time-and-motion studies. Stopwatch in hand, Taylor observed the workers and then divided the manufacturing process into units that allowed for little wasted motion. He believed his ideas would benefit labor as well as management. Instead, his aim "to induce men to act as nearly like machines as possible" promoted monotony and displaced workers—especially higher paid skilled ones.

In meat packing, machinery did not replace workers; their work was merely subdivided to increase efficiency. In other industries, after the work had been broken down into simple, repetitive tasks, machines were created to replace hand labor. Mass production by machine worked best on products made from standardized, interchangeable parts. The idea of standardized parts was not new; they had been used before the Civil War to make such products as guns. The early machines that cut the

parts were not very precise. Workers had to hand file most metal pieces before they were fit together. As in other businesses, inventions improved the machine tool industry. The turret lathe automatically made a series of complex cuts in metal with great speed and accuracy. The ingredients were now in place to mass produce large numbers of standardized goods.

The Power of Bigness

The creation of the gigantic U.S. Steel Corporation was not an isolated occurrence. By 1904 a single firm in each of 50 different industries accounted for 60 percent or more of the total output. Such concentrations of economic power alarmed many Americans. Competition was never entirely eliminated, however, and consolidation did bring such benefits as lower prices and higher standards of living. Nevertheless, the transition from local, independently owned shops and factories to giant national corporations with impersonal boards of directors dramatically altered the work and leisure time of the American people (Chapter 18). The transition was often painful for individuals and not always smooth. The economy experienced a frightening cycle of boom and bust. Three se-

Because the emergence of gigantic trusts concentrated economic power into relatively few hands, many people saw the trusts as the real "bosses of the Senate."

This portrait of the family of William Astor illustrates the lavish life-style of the rich. Parties of the wealthy were especially ostentatious; at one, guests smoked cigarettes rolled in one hundred dollar bills after drinking coffee.

vere depressions (1873–1879, 1882–1885, and 1893–1897) rocked the nation, causing widespread unemployment and business failures.

Big business also created a class of millionaires who flaunted ostentatious homes and lavish life-styles. For example, during the depression in 1897 Mr. and Mrs. Bradley Martin decided to give a costume ball. They invited most of the richest people in New York to the Waldorf-Astoria Hotel, which was redecorated to resemble the palace at Versailles in France. The hostess dressed as Mary Queen of Scots and wore an enormous ruby necklace that had once adorned Queen Marie Antoinette. One guest came in a $10,000 suit of armor inlaid with gold. Those few hours of entertainment cost the Martins $369,000.

When one realizes that in 1890 about 11 million of the 12.5 million families in the United States averaged less than $380 a year in income, it is obvious that all did not share equally in the economic expansion of the era. Wealth had al-

ways been concentrated and industrialization continued the trend. In 1890 the richest 9 percent of Americans owned nearly three-quarters of the nation's wealth.

Many people resented or envied the life-styles such wealth provided, but they feared the power it produced. Big business grew while government and organized labor remained relatively small. Thus business leaders wielded enormous power over many phases of American life. Some actions benefited the nation but were taken in a high-handed manner. For example, before the 1880s each location determined its time by the position of the sun. Even in cities fairly close together clocks were set differently; New York City and Boston were 12 minutes apart. To simplify schedules, in 1883 railroad owners established four time zones—without consulting any branch of government.

Such arbitrary power alarmed the American public. Some of the freewheeling railroad barons aggravated fears. Vanderbilt once re-

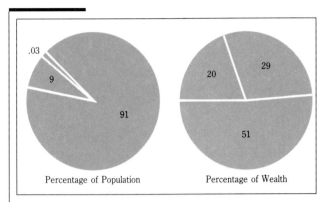

Percentage of Population   Percentage of Wealth

Figure 17.4
Distribution of wealth, 1890. The bulk of the wealth
was concentrated in less than 10 percent of the population, while 0.03 percent of the population controlled
20 percent of the wealth. Source: George K. Holmes,
"The Concentration of Wealth," *Political Science Quarterly*, vol. 8, no. 4, December 1893, p. 593.

marked, "What do I care about the law? Hain't
I got the power?" Another time a member of the
Pennsylvania legislature reportedly said, "Mr.
Speaker, I move we adjourn unless the Pennsylvania Railroad has some more business to
conduct." The railroad industry pioneered the
accumulation and use of economic power. Others followed in its footsteps, often corrupting
politics. Popular outcries eventually forced
congressional action to curb their excesses
(Chapter 21).

ECONOMIC MODERNIZATION IN THE SOUTH AND WEST

Although most industrialization occurred in the
Northeast, all regions experienced profound
changes as a national, interdependent economy
emerged. In that process a world based on personal relationships was displaced by a more impersonal world based on contractual relationships. Just as the local cobbler was replaced by
large factories mass producing shoes, the
largely self-sufficient farmer who sold a little
surplus locally to buy the cobbler's shoes gave
way to cash-crop farmers who bought factory-
made shoes by mail-order catalog—never

seeing the people who made or sold them. At
the same time, his crops went to feed urban
masses hundreds of miles away—none of whom
he knew personally.

Some of the forces feeding the growth of
industry also fueled agricultural expansion. Rural population kept growing, although not as
rapidly as urban population. Both the number
of farms and farmers more than doubled at the
same time that farmers became a minority of
the population. Most of these new farmers were
in the West, which was being tamed and exploited in the late nineteenth century. Demand
by the urban masses for food sparked a farming
revolution based on mechanization and scientific agriculture. One region, however, did not
share equally in the benefits of economic modernization. For a variety of reasons, the South
failed to keep pace with the rest of the nation.
Despite numerous efforts to forge a "New
South," the region slipped further and further
behind.

Western Expansion

The transcontinental railroads were not originally meant to "open up" the West. They were
laid across what was called the "Great American
Desert" in order to link the East and West
coasts. The perceived worthlessness of the
Plains was reflected in the willingness to give
much of it away—to the Indians and later to the
railroads. The mining frontier first altered perceptions of the region's value. Confrontations
between miners and Indians foreshadowed the
expulsion of the Indians from land that had
been "given" them "forever" before whites realized its real worth.

Miners starred in the first act of the drama
of western expansion and were followed by
other casts of actors. The railroads played a significant role in creating new ways to exploit the
land. In addition to mineral wealth, the region
had two other plentiful resources: grass and cattle. Railroads provided the means to get the cattle to eastern cities, where urban residents
wanted more meat to eat. The result was the
birth of western ranching.

At first, ranching, like placer mining, did not
require much capital. Both the cows and the

grass were free. By 1860 some five million head of wild Texas longhorns had descended from cattle imported by Spanish colonists. They displaced the buffaloes that were being hunted to virtual extinction. In fact, cattle were so plentiful that they were considered almost worthless in the West. However, steers sold for $30 to $50 a head in Chicago. All that was needed was a way to get them there.

Joseph G. McCoy realized the potential for profit and established the first "cowtown" at Abilene, Kansas, where he built stock pens and loading chutes. Cowboys drove cattle there for shipment by rail to Chicago. Other cowtowns arose as some six million head of cattle endured the "long drive" to those sites between 1866 and 1888.

As longhorns could not be easily captured or herded on foot, the methods of the Mexican vaquero were copied and the American cowboy was born. Herding cattle while mounted on horses was hard, dirty work. One participant wrote, "It was tiresome grimy business for the attendant punchers, who travelled over in a cloud of dust, and heard little but the constant chorus from the crackling of hoofs and ankle joints, from the bellows, lows, and bleats of the trudging animals." Romantic stories both whitened as well as glorified the cowboy. At least one-third were Mexicans and African-Americans. Actually, the heyday of the cowboy was rather brief, for ranching, like mining, was soon transformed into an organized business.

Profits from a successful drive were very good—about 40 percent. This naturally attracted eastern investors, and soon the long drives declined as better methods were found. The lean, rangy longhorns were better suited to enduring the long drive than to producing choice, juicy steaks. They became even less desirable after being herded long distances. As the rail network expanded into Texas, ranchers switched from rounding up stray cattle to raising and breeding the longhorns with superior imported stock to improve the quality of the beef.

The cattle breeders needed large tracts of grassland for grazing and usually just appropriated land from the public domain. Most centered their operations around stream banks and claimed all the adjoining grasslands. During this open-range era, high profits attracted even

(Text continues on p. 576)

In the heyday of the open range, thousands of wild cattle were rounded up to be driven to cowtowns for shipment to the East.

$5,000 REWARD

JESSE JAMES
For Train Robbery

THE WILD WEST

At 6 P.M. April 5, 1892, a mysterious train, its shades tightly drawn, pulled out of Cheyenne, Wyoming, the state capital, bound for Casper, 200 miles to the northwest. Aboard the trains were 46 heavily armed vigilantes who carried an impressive array of weapons including army rifles, dynamite, and strychnine. The train had been chartered by Wyoming's cattle kings. The vigilantes' mission: to kill Johnson County settlers suspected of cattle rustling.

For more than two decades, the cattlemen had accused homesteaders of land grabbing and cattle theft. Juries refused to convict the small stockmen, and the cattle barons responded by taking the law into their own hands. In one incident, on the night of July 20, 1889, 10 cattlemen captured 2 homesteaders and hanged them from a stunted pine tree. Altogether 6 or 7 suspected rustlers were shot or hanged. Despite lynchings and shootings, rustling continued, and in the summer of 1891, the cattle barons decided to launch an armed invasion of Johnson County and kill the most notorious rustlers. Members of the Wyoming Stock Growers' Association were asked to provide names of suspected rustlers. They compiled a list of 70 purported cattle thieves.

On Saturday, April 9, 1892, the vigilantes shot and killed 2 suspected rustlers at K C Ranch near the southern edge of Johnson County. Word of the killings quickly spread to Buffalo, Wyoming, the county seat, 46 miles to the north. There, 200 small stockmen formed a posse to avenge the murders. At the T A Ranch, 14 miles south of Buffalo, the posse surrounded the vigilantes.

Before the invaders could be captured, however, Wyoming's acting governor and the state's senators sent frantic telegrams to President Benjamin Harrison declaring that a state of insurrection existed in Johnson County and asking that the U.S. cavalry be sent in to quell the disturbances. Early on Wednesday, April 13, the cavalry rode to the rescue and escorted the invaders out of Johnson County. The vigilantes, who included several federal marshals and state officials, were charged with first degree murder, but the charges eventually were dropped. The Johnson County war was over.

Today, it is commonly assumed that the roots of violence in American society lie in our frontier heritage of violence and lawlessness. According to popular mythology—disseminated by dime novels, pulp newspapers, and television and movie westerns—the frontier was a lawless land populated by violent men: outlaws, stagecoach robbers, gunslingers, highwaymen, vigilantes, claim jumpers, cattle rustlers, horse thieves, Indian fighters, border ruffians, and mule skinners.

How violent was the Wild West? Certain forms of violence and lawlessness were indeed common: warfare between Indians and whites, attacks on Chinese and Mexican minorities, vigilantism, rowdyism, drunkenness, opium addiction, gambling, vigilante executions, stagecoach robberies, and gunfights. Racially motivated acts of brutality represented the ugliest side of frontier violence. In 1871, in one of the most gruesome incidents, ranchers in California's Sacramento Valley tracked 30 Digger Indians into a cave and shot them, saving the children for last because they "could not bear to kill them with [a] 56-calibre Spencer rifle. 'It tore them up so bad.'" Instead, they were shot with a 38-calibre Smith and Wesson revolver.

Chinese immigrants faced particular hostility. In Los Angeles, on October 24, 1871, a white mob stormed the city's Chinatown district and murdered between 20 and 25 Chinese men and women. In Rock Springs, Wyoming Territory, on September 2, 1885, a heavily armed white mob attacked the town's Chinatown, set fire to the Chinese coal miners' shacks, and fired bullets at fleeing workers, killing 50, 10 percent of the town's Chinese population. A few days later, in Seattle, Washington Territory, a mob killed Chinese hop pickers while they were asleep in their tents. In November, a Tacoma mob routed Chinese immigrants out of their dwellings and loaded them into wagons and dumped them outside of town.

African-Americans and Hispanics also encountered frontier violence. In 40 Texas counties, at least 373 black freedmen were lynched or murdered between June 1865 and June 1868. In California, some 15,000 Mexican, Chilean, and Peruvian gold hunters were driven out of the gold fields by threats of lynching, branding, whippings, and ear croppings. Said one white miner: "Give 'em a fair jury trial and rope 'em with all the majesty of the law."

Vigilante lynchings represented another widespread form of frontier violence. The lack of courts of law and police forces in the West gave rise to committees of vigilance—extralegal committees organized to suppress and punish crime summarily—in frontier regions. These committees banded together to punish murderers, counterfeiters, corrupt government officials, and horse and cattle thieves. In a single year in California, 1855, 47 people were executed by mobs, 9 by legal tribunals, and 10 by sheriffs or police officers. Between 1865 and 1890, 27 vigilante movements arose in Texas pursuing outlaws like John Wesley Hardin. A final wave of vigilantism originated in rural southern Indiana in 1887. Known as the White Cap movement, local rural committees flogged drunks, prostitutes, and men who failed to support their families.

The most notorious perpetrators of frontier violence were the outlaws and gunmen, like Belle Starr, Billy the Kid, Black Bart, Frank and Jesse James, John Wesley Hardin, the Younger brothers, Butch Cassidy and the Sundance Kid, and the Dalton Gang, who held up stagecoaches and trains, robbed banks, and stole horses and cattle. Hardin and the Jameses—who ironically were the sons of ministers—as well as the Younger brothers learned outlaw strategy as Confederate guerrillas during the Civil War. Hardin, who was probably the most prolific murderer, shot and killed over 20 men between 1868, when he was 15, and 1878, when he was finally captured and incarcerated in a Texas prison. Frank and Jesse James, America's most renowned bank and train robbers, staged at least 26 daring robberies between 1866 and 1881 in Missouri, taking in half a million dollars. Black Bart (born Charles E. Boles) robbed 27 stagecoaches in 28 attempts in California between 1875 and 1882, using an empty shotgun as his only weapon.

Most popular accounts of Western banditry, however, appear to be grossly exaggerated and romanticized. Bat Masterson, who, according to legend, killed 30 men in gunfights, actually killed 3. Billy the Kid, who supposedly killed 1 man for each of his 21 years of life, also apparently killed 3.

Kansas's cattle towns, legend holds, witnessed a killing every night. But in fact in Abilene, Caldwell, Dodge City, Ellsworth, and Wichita, a grand total of 45 homicides took place during a 15-year span, 1.5 homicides per cattle trading season, never exceeding 5 in one year. In Deadwood, South Dakota, where Wild Bill Hickok was shot in the back while playing poker in 1876, only four homicides—and no lynchings—took place in the town's most violent year. And in Tombstone, Arizona, the "town too tough to die" and the site of the shootout at the OK Corral, where Marshall Virgil Earp and his brothers Wyatt and Morgan, backed up by gambler Doc Holliday, hurled the Clanton brothers "into eternity in the duration of a moment," only 5 men were killed during the city's deadliest year.

Despite the omnipresence of rifles, knives, and revolvers and the prevalence of saloons, gambling houses, and bordellos, rape, robbery, and burglary were relatively rare. "We could go to sleep in our cabins," wrote one miner, "with our bag of gold dust under our pillows minus locks, bolts or bars, and feel a sense of absolute security."

more investors. Eventually the ranchers joined other segments of the economy that were out-producing demand. As the Plains became over-grazed, beef prices dropped from $30 to $10 a head in 1885 and 1886. Poorer producers were driven out by these low prices, challenges to their land claims by sheepherders and farmers, and bad weather. A winter of terrible blizzards following the scorching summer in 1886 led to the death of 90 percent of western cattle.

After sometimes bloody battles for suprem-acy between these economic competitors, the "Wild West" was largely tamed by the 1890s. Ranchers who remained established legal title to their grazing lands, fenced them in with barbed wire, and practiced scientific breeding and feeding of their stock. The forces of eco-nomic consolidation had reached ranching—making it a business requiring large amounts of capital.

Land legislation of the era aided the mon-opolization of ranching by a relatively few "cat-tle barons." Large tracts of public lands were given away or sold cheaply through such acts as the Homestead Act of 1862, the Timber Culture Act of 1873, and the Desert Land Act of 1877. Enacted to promote socially desirable goals, all had large loopholes that were exploited by cat-tlemen and land speculators. To promote settle-ment, the Homestead Act gave 160 free acres to those who would cultivate it for five years. The Desert Land Act granted 640 acres at $1.25 an acre to anyone who would irrigate the land. The Timber Culture Act, based on the theory that the trees increased rainfall, awarded 160 acres to anyone who would plant trees on a quarter of the land. Cattlemen and speculators fraudulently claimed to have met the terms of the grants or hired dummy entrymen to stake claims for them. A bucket of water was some-times the only basis for claims of irrigation. Lumber barons in California, Nevada, Oregon, and Washington similarly utilized other land-granting laws. Thus much of the newly discov-ered wealth of the West ended up in hands of a few winners in the great land lottery.

While the mining, cattle, and lumber fron-tiers offered some quick, easy riches before being transformed into capital-intensive busi-nesses, the farming frontier required more pa-tience to make any profits. By the time farmers

arrived in the new West, much of the best land had already been appropriated. Most of the 274 million acres distributed under the terms of the Homestead Act were eventually purchased by bona fide settlers from speculators and cattle-men. Other farmers bought land from the rail-roads, which promoted settlement to increase traffic in isolated areas. To lure settlers railroad companies often provided easy credit terms and extolled western opportunities in flyers and speeches.

Many farming pioneers soon learned that railroad propaganda sometimes overstated the promise of the West. When they arrived, they discovered a shortage of wood and water but an overabundance of severe weather, insects, and social isolation. The houses they built of "bricks" cut from thick prairie sod were func-tional but bleak. At first, many farmers managed only to eke out a bare subsistence. Eventually, however, western farmers were caught up in the forces of change that transformed agriculture as dramatically as other sectors of the economy.

The Changing Nature of Farming

When Congress passed the Homestead Act in 1862, most of the arable land east of the Missis-sippi was already taken. The established farm-ers of the Old Northeast adapted fairly well to the changing economy and were generally pros-perous. Most did not try to compete with the new wheat and corn areas of the West. Instead they turned their efforts to supplying the rap-idly growing urban areas with fresh vegetables, dairy products, poultry, and pigs. They also prof-ited from rising land values by selling extra acres to residential and industrial developers at high prices. Although they may not have liked all the changes, most received a reasonable share of the fruits of economic expansion. The same could not be said for many farmers in the West and South.

The challenges of farming were much greater in the West, and when they were finally met, overproduction depressed prices. Cultiva-tion of the West required new agricultural tech-niques and adaptations to the environment. The scarcity of trees not only dictated the building of sodhouses but also made the cost of fencing prohibitive. Until the development of barbed

Because of the scarcity of trees on the Plains, settlers built homes from "bricks" of sod. With walls 2 to 3 feet thick, the houses were gloomy but provided cozy and solid protection from the elements.

wire in 1874, crops were not easily protected from the millions of roaming cattle.

A more serious problem was the lack of water. Farmers came to believe they had found solutions by using new varieties of seed, pumping water from far below the ground surface with windmills, and using cultivation techniques known as "dry farming." In reality their success resulted mainly from abnormally wet summers in the 1870s, as they learned when conditions returned to normal. During the good times, however, optimism flourished. As one Kansas official noted: "Most of us crossed the Mississippi with no money but with a vast wealth of hope and courage. Haste to get rich has made us borrowers, and the borrowing has made booms, and the booms have made men wild, and Kansas became a vast asylum covering 50,000 square miles." Then came the droughts. By 1900 two-thirds of the homesteaders had failed, and farmers returned east with signs saying, "In God We Trusted; in Kansas We Busted."

In the South, the Civil War brought several changes that crippled agriculture. Wartime devastation destroyed half the region's farm equipment and killed one-third of its draft animals. The death of slavery also ended the plantation system, and replacements had to be found. The number of farms doubled from 1860 to 1880, but the number of landowners remained the same. The size of the average farm dropped from 347 acres to 156 acres, as sharecropping and tenancy rose. The farms were not only smaller but also frequently worked by people who did not own them. In other words, at the very time the rest of the economy was consolidating, Southern agriculture was marching off in the opposite, less efficient direction. Another problem was a shortage of cash, which forced Southern farmers to borrow against future crops. Crop liens and high credit costs kept a lot of black and white farmers trapped in a cycle of debt and poverty.

Many Plains and Southern farmers became losers in the economic modernization of agriculture. Nevertheless, both the winners and the losers were playing essentially the same game. That game was the commercialization of farming. Most of the rules were the same as those for manufacturers: specialization, new technology, mechanization, expanded markets, heavier capital investment, and reliance on interstate transportation. Most of these changes were wholeheartedly embraced by farmers of that generation until they fell behind their industrial cousins in the expanding economy.

Most farmers agreed with a farm journal's assertion: "Agriculture, like all other business, is better for its subdivision, each one growing that which is best suited for his soil, climate, and market." Specialization became apparent in the decline of subsistence farming and the growing importance of cash crops. Although general farming continued, most farmers planted more of their acreage in the single crop best suited for their land and market. Outside of the South, cash crops were usually supplemented by small gardens and stock raising. In Dixie cotton reigned supreme, and tenant farmers were often forced by landowners and merchants to plant all available acres with cotton. Most, however, specialized by choice.

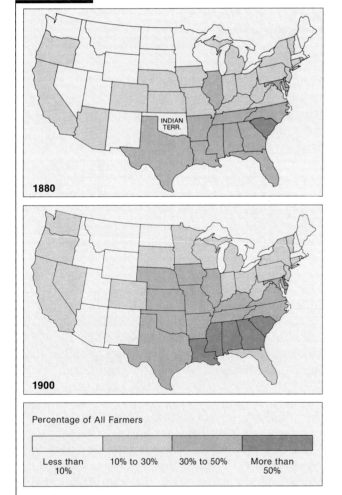

1880

1900

Percentage of All Farmers

| Less than 10% | 10% to 30% | 30% to 50% | More than 50% |

Rise of Tenancy

Technology and mechanization also revolutionized agriculture. Inventions came to the farms as rapidly as to the factories and increased productivity just as dramatically. After the mechanization of wheat farming, the hours required to farm an acre dropped from 61 to 3, and the per acre cost of production fell from $3.65 to $0.66. Machines entered every phase of agriculture, and by 1890 some 900 companies were manufacturing such items as hay loaders, cord binders, seeders, rotary plows, mowers, and combines. Farmers began to learn "scientific agriculture" at land-grant colleges that Congress established under the Morrill Land Grant Act of 1862. Agricultural researchers explored ways to increase production and found new uses for overabundant crops at agricultural experiment stations funded by the Hatch Act of 1887. Obviously, farmers were not opposed to all government aid to the economy.

As in manufacturing, mechanization brought economies of scale to agriculture, but they were not as easily exploitable. Although some bonanza farmers in the Dakotas cultivated 100,000 acres and more, the average farm remained 150 acres. The farms of the West were usually much larger than average because dry-farming techniques produced low yields per acre. To succeed, a western farmer needed more acres, and to work those acres he needed more machines; both cost money. Thus, like businesspeople, farmers needed access to capital. Unable to sell shares in their enterprise, most obtained personal loans using their land, machinery, and crops as collateral. Unfortunately, as production increased, prices fell, and to counteract lower profits farmers further expanded production in a self-defeating downward spiral. Mortgage indebtedness grew 2.5 times faster than agricultural wealth.

One solution to overproduction was to expand markets, which required cheap and reliable transportation facilities. Railroads, therefore, had as much impact in agriculture as in industry. Instead of selling surplus food to the local cobbler, American farmers fed distant urban masses at home and abroad; 20 percent of agricultural production was exported. This also meant that farmers' profits hinged on many factors beyond their control—such as the size of harvests in Argentina. Marketing became a key

G. Bogue, *From Prairie to Corn Belt* (1963); Orville Vernon Burton and Robert C. McMath, Jr., eds., *Towards a New South?: Post-Civil War Southern Communities* (1982); David L. Carlton, *Mill and Town in South Carolina, 1880–1920* (1982); Thomas D. Clark, *Frontier America*, 2d ed. (1969), with Albert D. Kirwan, *The South Since Appomattox* (1967); William C. Culberson, *Vigilantism: Political History of Private Power in America* (1990); Edward E. Dale, *The Range Cattle Industry, 1865 to 1925*, rev. ed. (1969); Pete Daniel, *Breaking the Land: The Transformation of Cotton, Tobacco, and Rice Cultures Since 1880* (1985); David Dary, *Cowboy Culture* (1981); Everett Dick, *The Sod-House Frontier, 1854–1890* (1937); Philip Durham and E. L. Jones, *The Negro Cowboys* (1965); Robert R. Dykstra, *The Cattle Towns* (1968); John S. Ezell, *The South Since 1865*, 2d ed. (1975); Gilbert C. Fite, *The Farmer's Frontier, 1865–1900* (1966); Paul Gaston, *The New South Creed* (1970); P. W. Gates, *History of Public Land Law Development* (1968); Dewey Grantham, Jr., *The Democratic South* (1963); Melvin Greenhut and W. Tate Whitman, eds., *Essays in Southern Economic Development* (1964); William S. Greever, *Bonanza West: Western Mining Rushes* (1963); Steven Hahn, *The Roots of Southern Populism: Yeoman Farmers and the Transformation of the Georgia Upcountry, 1850–1890* (1983); Robert Higgs, *Competition and Coercion: Blacks in the American Economy, 1865–1914* (1977); Robert V. Hine, *The American West*, 2d ed. (1984); W. Eugene Hollon, *Frontier Violence: Another Look* (1974); Julie Roy Jeffrey, *Frontier Women* (1979); Terry G. Jordan, *Trails to Texas: Southern Roots of Western Cattle Ranching* (1981); J. Morgan Kousser, *The Shaping of Southern Politics* (1974); Howard R. Lamar, *The Far Southwest, 1846–1912* (1966); Patricia Nelson Limerick, *The Legacy of Conquest: The Unbroken Past of the American West* (1987); Roger D. McGrath, *Gunfighters, Highwaymen, and Vigilantes: Violence on the Frontier* (1984); Melton A. McLaurin, *Paternalism and Protest: Southern Cotton Mill Workers and Organized Labor* (1971); Rodman W. Paul, *Mining Frontiers of the Far West, 1848–1880* (1963); Earl Pomeroy, *The Pacific Slope* (1965); Roger Ransom and Richard Sutch, *One Kind of Freedom: The Economic Consequences of Emancipation* (1977); R. M. Robbins, *Our Landed Heritage* (1942); J. M. Shagg, *The Cattle Trading Industry* (1973); Fred A. Shannon, *The Farmer's Last Frontier* (1945); Duane M. Smith, *Rocky Mountain Mining Camps* (1967); Henry Nash Smith, *Virgin Land: The West as Symbol and Myth* (1950); Frederick Jackson Turner, *The Frontier in American History* (1920); C. Vann Woodward, *Origins of the New South, 1877–1913* (1951), and *The Strange Career of Jim Crow*, 3d ed. (1974); Gavin Wright, *Old South, New South* (1986).

BIOGRAPHIES

Andy Adams, *Log of a Cowboy* (1927); Frederick Lewis Allen, *The Great Pierpont Morgan* (1949); Robert V. Bruce, *Bell: Alexander Graham Bell and the Conquest of Solitude* (1973); Alfred D. Chandler, Jr., *Pierre S. du Pont and the Making of the Modern Corporation* (1971); Robert F. Durden, *The Dukes of Durham* (1975); Julius Grodinsky, *Jay Gould* (1957); Louis R. Harlan, *Booker T. Washington: The Making of a Black Leader, 1856–1901* (1972), and *Booker T. Washington: The Wizard of Tuskegee, 1901–1915* (1983); David F. Hawke, *John D.: Founding Father of the Rockefellers* (1950); Maury Klein, *The Life and Legend of Jay Gould* (1986); Harold C. Livesay, *Andrew Carnegie and the Rise of Big Business* (1975); Allan Nevins, *Study in Power: John D. Rockefeller*, 2 vols. (1953); Raymond B. Nixon, *Henry W. Grady: Spokesman of the New South* (1943); Andrew Sinclair, *Corsair: The Life of J. Pierpont Morgan* (1981); Robert M. Utley, *Billy the Kid* (1989); Joseph F. Wall, *Andrew Carnegie* (1970), and *Alfred I. du Pont: The Man and His Family* (1990); George Wheeler, *Pierpont Morgan and Friends* (1973).

CHAPTER 18

Immigrants and Workers in Industrial America

In 1862, while the nation was locked in the grip of a terrible Civil War, Congress authorized the most ambitious building project that the country had ever contemplated: construction of a transcontinental railroad. The price tag was staggering: $136 million, more than twice the federal budget of 1861. The challenge was enormous: 1800 miles across arid plains and desert and the rugged granite walls of the Sierra Nevada and the Rocky Mountains.

Two companies undertook the actual construction: The Union Pacific began laying track westward from Omaha, Nebraska, and the Central Pacific commenced eastward from Sacramento, California. Of the two companies, the Central Pacific faced the more arduous task. It had to carve a rail bed through the high Sierra Nevadas. It also faced the more severe labor shortages. Managers constantly complained that they had too few workers and that too many of the few they had were unreliable.

In early 1865, the Central Pacific decided to dip into a new labor pool. Charles Crocker, chief of construction, persuaded his company to employ Chinese immigrants, arguing that the people who built the Great Wall of China and invented gunpowder could help build a railroad. Although the Chinese were paid less than white laborers, they fully vindicated Crocker's decision, earning reputations as tireless and extraordinarily reliable workers. Within two years, 12,000 of the Central Pacific's 13,500 employees were Chinese immigrants. Often working with pickaxes, hammers, and crowbars, the workers labored high in the mountains and inside tunnels. Explosions, avalanches, and other accidents left an estimated 1200 Chinese workers dead.

Despite their heroic labors, California's Chinese immigrants faced discrimination and racial violence. White Americans criticized their attachment to their homeland and questioned their loyalty to the United States. Perhaps Charles Wolcott Brooks, who spent several years in China, best articulated the views of Californian authorities. He was asked: "Do you think they have any particular love for our [American] institutions?" He replied:

"I don't think they have any at all. They come purely as a matter of gain—as a matter of dollars and cents. If it is profitable, they will come. If it is not profitable, they will not come. The very fact of their retaining their own dress and customs, and keeping themselves so entirely separate, as a people, shows that they have not. . . . The Chinese come abroad not to spend, but to accumulate. They maintain their own customs and language. . . . The Chinese . . . hate us most cordially."

Many Chinese may not have developed any emotional attachment to America or its institutions. After all, most never planned to stay in the United States. They loved the villages that they left behind, and they valued their own ageless Chinese customs. In America they sought the opportunity to work—not voting rights, education, or assimilation—and no work was beneath them. They resignedly accepted the most menial jobs in the mines, on the railroad construction gangs, and in the booming western cities.

For a large portion of the Chinese immigrants in the United States, home was always thousands of miles away. Since they only came to America to accumulate money, the Chinese immigrants lived as inexpensively as possible. They slept in huge halls, where as many as 1000 men could sleep on matted floors. Often 3 men would share one mat, sleeping in 8-hour shifts. By this method, a Chinese man could reduce the cost of his room to 10 cents a month. When not sleeping, he worked, and he sent most of his earnings back to his family in China, to whom he intended to return someday.

The majority left their wives in China. In America, there were 20 Chinese men for every Chinese woman. Occasionally the men would return to China long enough to impregnate their wives, but then it was back to America again for more "coolie" labor and Yankee dollars. If a Chinese man survived this difficult existence until he was 50 or 60 years old, he would return to China for good, respected by his family and village. If, as often happened, he died young in America, his bones would be sent back to China, and they too would be respected by his family and village.

Immigration, then, could in no way be interpreted as a rejection of China. In reality, it was a defense of the Chinese way of life, for the money sent home helped preserve the tradi-

Scorned and ridiculed for their "different" looks and customs, Chinese laborers demonstrated remarkable strength, courage, and endurance in helping build the railroads crisscrossing the country in the late nineteenth century.

tional order. America was not a sacred idea, but a means to an end, and, of course, sometimes a very lonely country. It was no wonder that opium, prostitution, and suicide were shadowy attractions of San Francisco's Chinatown.

Americans failed to understand the mind of the Chinese immigrant. To them, the Chinese were just non-Western, non-Christian, and nonwhite aliens. Although railroad builders and mine owners regarded the Chinese as good, inexpensive laborers, native-born American workers believed they brought down wages for all workers. Every major American labor organizer of the period, from T. V. Powderly and Samuel Gompers to Eugene V. Debs and Henry George, called for federal action to restrict Chinese immigration. Some leaders charged that the "coolies" so depressed wages that women in white

working families had to resort to prostitution to avoid starvation.

Labor leaders were joined by Irish-American politicians, the Catholic church, Eastern editorialists, and California workers in their crusade against Chinese laborers. All agreed, the Chinese should—*must*—be excluded from the United States as undesirable, unassimilable aliens. In 1882, Congress responded with the Chinese Exclusion Act, which suspended Chinese immigration. It was the first time that America closed its doors to any immigrants for ethnocultural reasons.

Later, other immigrant groups shared experiences similar to the Chinese. Native-born Americans saw other ethnic groups as beyond reform, as not having the "right stuff" to become Americans. Again and again labor leaders, religious authorities, and old-line Americans joined forces in opposition to certain groups of immigrants. The entire process toward restriction culminated in 1924 with the passage of the National Origins Act.

Yet immigrants contributed greatly to the growth of industrial America. They and their fellow workers—native-born white and black Americans—built the railroads that crisscrossed the country; mined the gold and silver that made other men rich; and labored in the oilfields, steel mills, coal pits, packing plants, and factories that made such names as Rockefeller, Carnegie, Swift, and Westinghouse famous. Without these men and their companions, there would have been no industrialization. In the process they made the United States an ethnically rich nation.

HUDDLED MASSES AT THE GOLDEN DOOR

On October 28, 1886, President Grover Cleveland traveled to New York Harbor to watch the unveiling of the Statue of Liberty. A gift from France, Frederic Auguste Bartholdi's grand statue was meant to symbolize solidarity between the two republics, but that was not how Americans and incoming immigrants interpreted the sculpture. For them it was a simple symbol of welcome, with the statue's torch lighting the path to a better future. A poem, written by Emma Lazarus and eventually placed at the base of the statue, emphasized the promise of America:

> Give me your tired, your poor,
> Your huddled masses yearning to breathe free,
> The wretched refuse of your teeming shore.
> Send these, the homeless, tempest-tossed to me,
> I lift my lamp beside the golden door!

In popular theory, the promise of America exerted a powerful pull on Europe and Asia. The United States stood for political freedom, social mobility, and economic opportunity. Since the first settlers landed in Jamestown, millions of immigrants had responded to the American magnet. At no time was immigration as great as in the late nineteenth and early twentieth centuries. Between 1860 and 1890, more than 10 million immigrants arrived on America's shores. Between 1890 and 1920 over 15 million more arrived.

America was not the only country to lure immigrants from Europe. Millions more immigrated to Australia, New Zealand, South Africa, Canada, Brazil, Argentina, and other underpopulated areas of the globe. In truth, seen in its worldwide context, the United States' pull was less powerful than Europe's push. During the nineteenth century, almost every European country experienced a dramatic population increase. Advances in medicine and public health standards reduced infant mortality rates and increased life expectancies, but available land and food could not increase to meet the new population demands. Almost every European country, from Ireland in the northwest to Greece in the southeast, experienced the same phenomenon. First came a population boom; 20 years later, when the baby boomers reached maturity, emigration increased sharply.

Historians have divided immigration to the United States into two categories: old and new. The source of the old immigration was northern and western Europe—England, Ireland, France, Germany, and Scandinavia. The immigrants were mostly Protestants (except for the Irish Catholics) and always white; a majority were literate and had lived under constitutional forms of government. Assimilation for them was a relatively easy process. The new immigration came from eastern and southern Europe. Greeks, Poles, Russians, Italians, Slavs, Turks—these people found assimilation more difficult. Politically, religiously, and culturally, they differed greatly from both the earlier immigrants and native-born Americans.

The shift from "old" to "new" occurred during the 1880s. For example, in 1882, when 788,992 immigrants arrived in America, most were German, British, and Scandinavian; 87 percent came from northern and western Europe. By 1907 this pattern had changed. That year when 1,285,349 immigrants landed in America, more than 80 percent were from southern and eastern Europe.

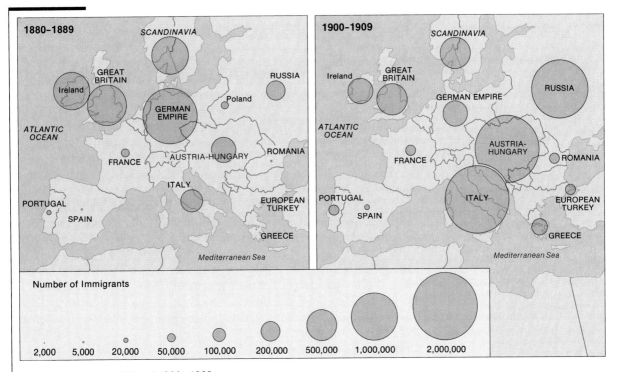

Immigration, 1880–1889 and 1900–1909
The source of old immigration was primarily northern and western Europe—England, Ireland, Germany, and Scandinavia. By the late 1890s a wave of new immigrants began to arrive from eastern and southern Europe.

Certainly, a geographic shift in origin of immigration to the United States took place, but more than geography differentiated the old and the new immigrants. Their reasons for leaving Europe, visions of America, settlement patterns, and occupational choices varied dramatically.

By the late nineteenth century, the motives and the opportunity to immigrate to America were present in southern and eastern Europe. With the abolition of serfdom, peasants were free to emigrate; and with the rise in population, young men faced job, land, and food shortages. Finally, railroads and steamships made travel faster and less expensive. During the 1880s, British and German steamships carried immigrants across the Atlantic for as little as $8, and by the turn of the century the trip only took five and a half days. In short, the conditions were right for the push to America.

"Birds of Passage"

Essentially two types of immigrants came to America. Permanent immigrants formed one group; migrant workers comprised the other. The people in the second group, often called birds of passage, were like the Chinese. They never intended to make the United States their home. Unable to earn a livelihood in their home countries, they came to America, worked and saved, and then returned home. Most were young men in their teens and twenties. They left behind their parents, young wives, and children, indications that their absence would not be too long. Before 1900, an estimated 78 percent of Italian immigrants and 95 percent of Greek immigrants were men. Many of them traveled to America in the early spring, worked until the late fall, and then returned to the warmer climates of their southern European homes for the winter. Some immigrants came to America fully intending to return home, but for one reason or another—love, hardship, early death—did not. Overall, 20 to 30 percent of all immigrants did return home.

The activity of the birds of passage can be clearly seen in Italian immigration patterns. Starting in the 1870s, Italian birthrates began to rise and mortality rates fell. Population pressure became severe, especially in *Il Mezzogiorno*, the southern and poorest provinces of Italy. Known as "the land that time forgot," the social customs and family patterns of *Il Mezzogiorno* seemed timeless. Life revolved around *la famiglia* (the family), and *l'ordine della famiglia* (the rules of family behavior and responsibility) was a sacred code. Unfortunately for the people in *Il Mezzogiorno*, the central government, dominated by northerners and concerned only with northern interests, did not forget the impoverished southern provinces. Heavily taxed and hurt by high protective tariffs on northern industrial goods, southern Italians sank deeper into poverty. Cynically, but realistically, they noted the sad truth of the old expression "*la legge va contra i cristiani*" (the law works against the people).

The law and population pressures already worked against the region; soon nature also joined the opposition. Natural disasters rocked southern Italy during the first decade of the twentieth century. Earthquakes caused untold devastation in the provinces of Basilicata and Calabria. Vesuvius erupted and buried a town near Naples. Then Etna erupted. The most cruel blow came in 1908 when an earthquake and tidal wave swept through the Strait of Messina between Sicily and the Italian mainland. The disaster destroyed hundreds of villages and killed hundreds of thousands of people. In the city of Messina alone, more than 100,000 people perished.

The kinds of jobs that Italian men sought reflected their attitude toward America. They did not look for careers. Occupations that provided opportunity for upward economic mobility were alien to them. Unlike most of the earlier immigrants to America, they did not want to farm in America or even own land, both of which implied a permanence that did not figure in

their plans. Instead, Italians headed for the cities, where labor was needed and wages were relatively good. Few jobs were beneath them. Native-born Americans commented that the Italian birds of passage readily accepted "work no white man could stand." Expecting their stay in America to be short, they lived as inexpensively as possible under conditions that native-born families considered intolerable.

Italians were particularly attracted to heavy construction jobs. One study of Italians in America noted in 1905 that Italians gravitated toward "work that is simple and monotonous . . . that can be performed by men disposed in a gang, under the more or less military supervision of a foreman, so that the worker becomes himself like a part of a machine." Contracted out by a professional labor broker known as a *padrone*, Italians supplied the muscle that dug tunnels and canals, laid railroad tracks, and constructed bridges and roads. So important were they to

Most of the miners from Pennsylvania to California were immigrants from Europe and Asia. Anxious to improve their standard of living in their homeland, these immigrants would accept dangerous, but high-paying jobs.

the construction business that in 1905 the Industrial Commission concluded that "it would be a difficult thing . . . to build a railroad of any considerable length without Italian labor." As early as 1890, 90 percent of New York's public works employees and 99 percent of Chicago's street workers were Italian.

While they received good wages, their homes in Italy were seldom forgotten. One nostalgic Italian admitted, "Doctor, we brought to America only our brains and our arms. Our hearts stayed there in the little house in the beautiful fields of our Italy." And for women, adjustment to America was even more difficult. They often wore black clothing, an old country practice that symbolized self-sacrifice, misery, and determination. Edward Corsi, the son of immigrants who became President Franklin Roosevelt's commissioner of immigration, recalled that his mother never adjusted to America: "She loved quiet, and hated the noise and confusion. . . . She spent her days, and the waking hours of the nights, sitting at one outside window staring up at the little patch of sky above the tenements. She was never happy here, though she tried."

Italians were not the only birds of passage. The same forces—population pressure, unemployment, hunger, and the breakdown of agrarian societies—sent Greeks, Slavs, Chinese, Japanese, Mexicans, French Canadians, and inhabitants of scores of other nations to the United States. Seeking neither permanent homes nor citizenship, they desired only an opportunity to work for a living, hoping to save enough money to return to a better life in the country of their birth. Always the land they coveted was some distant home not in the United States.

Slavs, and especially Poles, dramatized this pattern of temporary migration—the desire to use America as a means of improving their lot in their home country. Strong and determined, they preferred the work that paid the best— usually the most dangerous and physically exhausting. After disembarking at East Coast ports, Slavs generally headed directly to the mill and mining towns of Pennsylvania and the Midwest. They found the wages they were after in the stockyards of Chicago, the coal mines of Scranton, and the steel mills of Pittsburgh and Buffalo. In 1910 a Pittsburgh steel worker earned between $2.28 and $2.41 for a 12-hour day; a miner in the same area earned between $2.40 and $3.00 for 8 hours of work. For an unskilled laborer, who usually made less than a dollar a day for other jobs, that was considered good pay.

Unlike the Italians who preferred to work in sociable gangs and above ground, Poles readily accepted the hard lonely labor of the mines and steel mills. The extra money was enough compensation for the danger of underground or indoor work. Employers quickly noted this Slavic inclination. In 1909 a Pittsburgh newspaper advertisement solicited "Tinners, Catchers, and Helpers. To work in open shops. Syrians, Poles, and Romanians Preferred." Such an advertisement attracted hundreds of hardy Slavs in search of good wages and the fast route home.

In Search of a New Home

In contrast to the birds of passage, several million other immigrants came to America with no intention of ever returning to the land of their birth. These were the permanent immigrants, for whom America offered political and religious freedom as well as economic opportunity. The promise of America was especially appealing to members of ethnic and religious minorities who were persecuted, abused, and despised in their homelands. Germans from Slavic countries, Greeks from Romania, Serbs from Hungary, Turks from Bulgaria, Poles from Russia—for these men and women home held few warm associations.

A fine case in point is Czarist Russia, a country notoriously and historically inhospitable to many minorities. In 1907, 250,000 "Russians" emigrated from Russia. But who were these "Russians?" More than 115,000 were Jews, and another 73,000 were Poles. Others were Finns, Germans, and Lithuanians. Only a small percentage of the Russian emigrants were of Russian ethnic stock. In short, emigration from Russia was generally an alternative for minorities.

The Jews were the prototypical true immigrants. Like the Irish Catholics a generation before, they fled nearly unbearable hardships.

Hester Street, 1907, on New York City's Lower East Side was home to thousands of Jewish immigrants from Russia and eastern Europe. The immigrants crowded into the tenements lining the street, which bustled with peddlers and pedestrians.

From the thirteenth century, millions of Jews had maintained a relatively stable communal life in Poland. Then during the eighteenth century Russia, Prussia, and Austria conquered and divided Poland. Most of the Polish Jews lived under Russian rule, and the quality of their lives took an immediate, drastic, downward turn. Russian authorities drove Jews out of commerce and forced them into an area known as the Pale of Settlement, where over 90 percent of Russian Jews lived. There they toiled as farmers of the poor soil of the steppes or earned a living as artisans or craftsmen in impoverished villages. There, too, Russian officials burned their books, disrupted their religious practices, and occasionally even broke up their families. Particularly painful were the Russian conscription laws, which took thousands of boys between the ages of 12 and 18 for periods of military service up to 25 years.

Starting in 1881, when the liberal Russian Czar Alexander II was assassinated, conditions for Jews in Russia rapidly deteriorated from bad to worse to intolerable. Laws restricted Jewish businesses, prevented Jewish land ownership, and limited Jewish education. Pogroms, a form of legally sanctioned mob attack against Jews, killed and injured thousands of persons. Sometimes at the whim of authorities, Russian Cossacks burned Jewish houses and destroyed Jewish possessions.

For Jews, then, emigration offered a chance for a far better life than existed for them in the Pale of Settlement. Dr. George M. Price, one of the several million Jews who left Russia for America during the late nineteenth century, expressed the feelings of these immigrants for their homeland. In his diary he wrote: "Sympathy for Russia? How ironical it sounds! Am I not despised? Am I not urged to leave? Do I not hear the word zhid (Jew) constantly? Can I even think that some consider me a human capable of thinking and feeling like others? Do I not rise daily with the fear lest the hungry mob attack me? . . . It is impossible . . . that a Jew should regret leaving Russia." He voiced his feelings for America, his new home, in his booklet *Yidn in America* (1891) where he described the Atlantic crossing as "a kind of hell that cleanses a man of his sins before coming to the land of Columbus." Compared to Russia, the United States seemed like heaven to Price.

Because they came to the United States to stay, the form of Jewish immigration differed substantially from that of the birds of passage. For them, immigration was not simply a young man's alternative. Jews, as all other permanent immigrants, tended to come to America in family units. Men and women, young and old—they were all represented. They brought their life savings and most valuable possessions with them, never expecting to see again what they left behind. As a result, the move to America was financially and physically taxing. And once in America, whole families had more expenses than the young male birds of passage.

Since America was now their home, Jewish men looked for jobs offering future opportunities rather than simply the opportunity to work for wages. They were not drawn to the steel mills and mines or even to jobs in construction. They desired skilled, not unskilled, labor. Many Jews had skills, for the uncertain life of the Russian Pale had taught them not to depend on land or commerce. In the Pale a Jew's greatest possession was the ability to do something that could not be taken away. This meant a skilled craft. In the Pale and in America, Jews were tailors and seamstresses, cigar makers and toy makers, tanners and butchers, carpenters, joiners, roofers, and masons, coppersmiths and blacksmiths. They had the knowledge and ability to perform the thousands of skilled tasks needed in an urban environment. The available statistical evidence reinforces this point. Where 75 percent of Italians and Poles entering the United States between 1899 and 1910 were unskilled laborers or farmers, 67 percent of all Jews were skilled workers.

NATIVISM: THE ANTI-IMMIGRANT REACTION

Sometimes an isolated event, by itself not historically important, can illuminate like a flash of lightning the social landscape and beliefs of a particular time. Certainly this is true with the *Hennessy* case. In 1890 a feud between gangs on the New Orleans docks turned violent. Joe and Pete Provenzano were arrested and tried for attempting to massacre the rival gang. The trial took a sensational turn when David Hennessy, the New Orleans superintendent of police, asserted in 1891 that he had evidence that a secret Sicilian organization known as the Mafia was involved in the affair. Shortly after Hennessy made his bold charges, five armed men gunned him down. Before he died, Hennessy was heard to say, "The dagos shot me."

The crime raised a hue and cry against Sicilians, and local police arrested scores, urged on by Mayor Joseph Shakespeare's instructions to "arrest every Italian you come across, if necessary." The mayor told the public, "We must teach these people a lesson that they will not forget for all time." Eleven Sicilians were brought to trial, but a jury failed to convict them. Undaunted, a local mob promptly took matters into its own hands and shot or clubbed to death nine and hanged two of the suspects. As far as most natives of New Orleans were concerned, justice had been done.

Many Americans seemed to agree. Editorialists praised the mob action and damned the vile "un-American" Italians. Soon the affair sent ripples across diplomatic waters. Italy protested the mob assault, but Washington refused to take any action. Anti-Italian rhetoric became ugly, and wild rumors ricocheted like bullets. Some said that the Italian fleet was headed toward America's east coast; others claimed that uniformed Italians were going through military drills in the streets of New York City. One thing was clear, noted an editorialist in the *Review of Reviews*, Congress had to pass immigration legislation to keep out "the refuse of the murderbreeds of Southern Europe."

The *Hennessy* case soon faded from the front pages of American newspapers. Italy did not attack the United States, and Congress did not immediately push through a restrictive immigration policy. But the emotions it generated and revealed were very real. Native-born Americans harbored deep suspicions of and resentments toward immigrants, especially those from southern and eastern Europe. If American industrialists saw in the immigrants a bottomless pool of dependable inexpensive labor, other Americans saw something far different and much less promising. Workers saw competition. Protestants saw Catholics and Jews. Educators saw illiterate hordes. Politicians saw peasants, unfamiliar with the workings of republicanism, democracy, and constitutionalism, and, what was even worse, perhaps contaminated by a belief in socialism, communism, or anarchism. Social Darwinists saw a mass of dark-skinned, thick-browed, bent-backed people who were far "below" northern and western Europeans on the evolutionary ladder. In short, native-born Americans, heirs of a different culture, religion, and complexion, saw something alien and inferior, perhaps even dangerous.

They reacted accordingly. They posted signs: "No Jews or Dogs Allowed." They called the Chinese "coolies," and the Mexicans "bean heads." Overall, they created an atmosphere of hostility that too often spilled over into open violence. In 1891 in a New Jersey mill town, 500 tending boys in a glassworks rioted when the management hired 14 young Russian Jews. During an 1895 labor conflict in the southern Colorado coal fields, a group of American miners killed 6 Italians. When Slavic coal miners went on strike in 1897 in eastern Pennsylvania, local citizens massacred 21 Polish and Hungarian workers. On the West Coast, Chinese workers were subject to regular and vicious attacks. Especially during economic hard times, native-born Americans lashed out against the new immigrants.

Sources of Conflict

Nativism, as this anti-immigrant backlash was called, took many forms. Racial nativism, the subject of thousands of books and articles, is the best remembered. University professors such as Wisconsin's Edward Alsworth Ross and popular writers such as Madison Grant decried the new immigrants as biologically less advanced than the Americans who traced their ancestry back to northern and western Europe. "Observe immigrants," Ross wrote in *The Old World in the New*, "in their gatherings, washed, combed, and in their Sunday best. You are struck by the fact that from ten to twenty percent are hirsute, low-browed, big-faced persons of obviously low mentality. . . . These ox-like men are descendants of those who always stayed behind." Using such criteria as complexion, size of cranium, length of forehead, and slope of shoulders, the immigrants from southern and eastern Europe were judged inferior to most native-born Americans. That university professors and scientists accepted such theories of innate racial and ethnic inferiority gave credibility to these notions. And popular writers readily accepted these stereotypes. Jacob Riis, a Danish immigrant who became an urban reformer in America and wrote the popular book *How the Other Half Lives* (1890), characterized Italians as "born gamblers" who lived destitute and disorderly lives; Chinese as secretive and addicted to every vice; and Jews as "enslaved" by their pursuit of gold and living amidst filth.

Religious differences reinforced ethnic variations. Overwhelmingly Catholic and Jewish, the new immigrants challenged the Protestant orthodoxy in America. Anti-Catholicism, noted a leading student of nativism, "blossomed spectacularly" during the late nineteenth century. Many Americans regarded the pope as the anti-Christ and Catholics as his evil minions. And it was widely believed that the authoritarian bent of the Catholic mind made it incompatible with democratic institutions. As the Reverend Josiah Strong observed in his best-selling book, *Our Country: Its Possible Future and the Present Crisis* (1885), there was "an irreconcilable difference between papal principles and the fundamental principles of our free institutions."

Native-born Americans viewed Jews with even greater suspicion, attributing the characteristics of Shakespeare's Shylock to Jews as a whole. "Money is their God," wrote leading journalist and social critic Jacob Riis. Other writers commented that Jews were tactless, tasteless, and pushy. Eventually many social clubs, country clubs, hotels, and universities excluded Jews, arguing that money alone could not purchase respectability.

The *Leo Frank* case painfully demonstrated the ubiquitous anti-Semitism in American society. Frank, a Cornell University graduate and a son of a wealthy New York merchant, managed an Atlanta pencil factory. In 1914 one of the factory hands, Mary Phagan, was found murdered on the premises. Frank was tried and convicted on flimsy evidence, but the case soon became an international cause célèbre. After reviewing the case, the governor of Georgia commuted Frank's death sentence to life imprisonment. The decision outraged native Georgian whites. They boycotted Jewish merchants and clamored for Frank's blood. Finally, a group of citizens from Mary Phagan's home town took Leo Frank from a state prison, transported him 175 miles across the state, and coldly hanged him. As news of the hanging spread, people gathered to gaze at the sight and shout "Now we've got you! We've got you now!" In the 1980s, new evidence in the Phagan case proved Frank innocent, and Georgia's Board of Pardon's granted him a posthumous pardon. But dispassionate justice was scarce in the weeks after Frank's death.

Orators used the *Leo Frank* case as an object lesson. Tom Watson, the fiery Georgia politician, warned listeners, "From all over the world, the Children of Israel are flocking to this country, and plans are on foot to move them from Europe *en masse* . . . to empty upon our shores the very scum and dregs of the *Parasite Race*." Like Josiah Strong and Edward Alsworth Ross, Tom Watson believed that Congress should stop the flow of immigrants before America was flooded by the waves of eastern and southern Europeans.

Many congressmen agreed with Watson. They too harbored strong suspicions of the new immigrants. For them, political fears mixed naturally with racial and religious misgivings. They tended to equate immigration with radicalism and suspected that every boat that docked at Ellis Island contained a swarm of socialists, communists, and anarchists prepared to foment revolution. As unfounded as their fears were, they could always point to isolated cases of radicalism among immigrants. They drew attention, for example, to Leon Czolgosz, born only months after his eastern European immigrant parents arrived in America. Discontented and unable to adjust to American life, Czolgosz became a convert to revolutionary anarchism. On September 6, 1901, he attended the Pan-American Exposition in Buffalo and waited patiently in a receiving line to shake hands with President William McKinley. When he reached McKinley, Czolgosz smiled, lifted up a gun, and shot the president twice through his tuxedo vest. Questioned about his action, Czolgosz confessed, "I don't believe in the Republican form of government and I don't believe we should have any rulers. It is right to kill them." Such actions and statements seemed to confirm the worst fears of antiradical nativists.

The strongest resentments against the new immigrants, however, were purely economic. American workers, particularly the unskilled, believed that the immigrants depressed wages by their willingness to "work cheap." An iron worker complained, "Immigrants work for almost nothing and seem to be able to live on wind—something which I can not do." Even skilled workers maintained that the birds of passage immigrants were unwilling to support any union efforts to improve working conditions in America. Samuel Gompers, head of the American Federation of Labor, said that the immigration problem in America was "appalling." He believed that the immigrants from eastern and southern Europe and from Asia were ignorant, unskilled, and unassimilable. Calling for strong restrictive legislation, he said, "Some way must be found to safeguard America."

In short, by the 1890s, when a terrible depression had disrupted the normal economic and social course of America, the new immigrants became a convenient scapegoat for the nation's myriad ills. Americans were swept along by a wave of xenophobic fear. It was a time when people elevated racial prejudice and rumors to universal truths. Native-born Americans blamed crime on Italians and prostitution on the Chinese; they claimed that the social ills of America's expanding cities—corruption, poor sanitation, violence, crime, disease, pollution—were the fault of the new immigrants.

In 1882 Congress passed the Chinese Exclusion Act, which barred Chinese laborers from entering the United States for ten years.

And they looked to the federal government for relief and protection.

Closing the Golden Door

The first immigrants attacked were those who were the most different from native-born Americans and the most unskilled—the Chinese. Between 1868 and 1882, more than 160,000 Chinese entered the United States. They laid down railroad tracks and mined for gold, silver, and coal. Unlike native-born Americans and most members of other immigrant groups, they did not consider cooking, washing, and ironing as "women's work," and in these areas they were particularly successful. Perhaps even too successful.

Lee Chew, who as a boy in China dreamed of obtaining wealth in "the country of the American wizards," immigrated as a young man to the United States. In America he found opportunity. He worked and saved and sacrificed. In America he also discovered that the Chinese were subject to the worst forms of exploitation and abuses. As they did with blacks in the South and Indians in the West, white Americans cheated and sometimes violently attacked the Chinese. "Americans are not all bad," Lee noted, "nor are they wicked wizards. Still . . . their treatment of us is outrageous."

During the depression of the mid-1870s the Chinese came under increasingly bitter and violent attack. At the forefront of the nativistic onslaught were the Irish, themselves recent immigrants, who competed with the Chinese for unskilled jobs. Irish political leaders in America demanded an end to Chinese immigration into the United States. But by the provisions of the Burlingame Treaty (1868) with China, the Chinese were free to immigrate and to establish American citizenship.

Eventually Congress responded to the pressure for restriction. In 1880, China gave the United States the right "to regulate, limit or suspend," though not to prohibit, the immigration of workers. Quickly the golden door slammed shut. In 1882 the Chinese Exclusion Act suspended Chinese immigration for ten years and drastically restricted the rights of the Chinese already in the United States. In 1892 Congress extended the act for another ten years, and then in 1902 extended it indefinitely. The legislation established a precedent for the future exclusion of other immigrants. By the 1890s most Americans agreed that the country should restrict "undesirable" immigrants. But how, for example, could Congress close America's door to southern and eastern Europeans while leaving it open for northern and western Europeans? To achieve this end, politicians advocated a literacy test. As early as the late 1880s economist Edward W. Bemis proposed that the United States exclude all male adults who could not read and write their own language. He maintained that such a law would effectively stop the flow of eastern and southern Europeans into America. The idea soon had the backing of the influential Republican Senator Henry Cabot Lodge of Massachusetts and the equally important Immigration Restriction League.

In 1896 Lodge pushed through Congress a literacy test bill, which would have excluded any adult immigrant unable to read 40 words in his language. Lodge's timing was poor. The bill reached the desk of Democratic President Grover Cleveland two days before his second term expired. Cleveland promptly vetoed the measure. The bill, Cleveland suggested, tested prior opportunities and America stood for open opportunities. In short, the bill fell pitifully below American ideals.

Cleveland's veto did not end the demand for restrictive legislation, nor did it even kill the idea of a literacy test. Presidents William Howard Taft and Woodrow Wilson vetoed similar pieces of legislation. In 1917, on the eve of America's entry into World War I, Wilson vetoed a literacy test bill on the grounds that it was "not a test of character, of quality, or of personal fitness." Nevertheless Congress passed the act over Wilson's veto.

World War I chilled an already cold climate for immigrants from southern and eastern Europe. Those who were born in the polyglot Austro-Hungarian Empire were now considered the enemy. Others were watched with deep suspicion. This was especially true after the 1917 Bolshevik Revolution in Russia. Once again American authorities regarded Jews from Russia as potential revolutionaries. Responding to this fear, in 1918 and 1920 Congress passed legislation to exclude or deport anarchists and other "dangerous radicals."

The generation-long battle over restriction ended with a clear victory for nativism. In the early 1920s Congress discovered its own solution: the quota system. The Emergency Quota Act (1921) limited immigration according to a nation-based quota system. It provided that no more than 3 percent of any given nationality in America in 1910 could annually immigrate to the United States. In 1924 the National Origins Act lowered the quota to 2 percent of each nationality residing in America in 1890. By using 1890 as the base year, the act was clearly aimed at restricting eastern and southern Europeans, for there were far fewer of the new immigrants

in America in 1890 than in 1910. Although in 1927 the base year was changed to 1920, the National Origins Act had achieved its desired result. The golden door was no longer fully open to eastern and southern Europeans, and it was completely closed to Asians. An important era in American history had ended.

Nativism and Native Americans

Immigrants were not the only people affected by nativist impulses. In a cruel irony, American Indians also felt the impact of nativist theories and prejudices. During the 1860s, 1870s, and 1880s, Indians were forced onto reservations by the federal government. The process was not peaceful. At almost every step Indian tribes resisted. From Texas and the Great Plains to California and the Pacific Northwest, Indian tribes clashed with federal troops in bloody confrontations. Occasionally the Indians won small victories in individual battles. But after the Battle of the Little Bighorn (1876), where Sitting Bull and Crazy Horse joined forces to annihilate Lieutenant Colonel George A. Custer and 264 of his men (see Chapter 16), Indian victories were few and small.

The last major bloody confrontation occurred during the cold December of 1890 on the Pine Ridge Reservation (Sioux) in South Dakota. Poorly fed and supplied on the reservation, dissatisfied with their present, and longing for the glories of their past, members of the Teton Sioux took up the "Ghost Dance," a harmless ritual that promised the faithful the mystical disappearance of the whites and the return of their lands. An inept government agent overreacted, calling in troops to suppress the Ghost Dance and arrest the Sioux leader Sitting Bull, who the government considered the focal point of Indian resistance. When Indian police killed Sitting Bull, some Sioux took up arms and left the reservation. Near Wounded Knee Creek, U.S. soldiers, armed with rapid-fire Hotchkiss guns, attempted to disarm the Indians. When one Indian resisted, soldiers opened fire, killing more than 300 men, women, and children. The Battle of Wounded Knee, which resembled more a slaughter than a battle, ended the violent era of Indian and white relations.

At the Cheyenne/Arapaho Reservation in Darlington, Oklahoma, Arapaho followers of the Ghost Dance religion, some in a trance, perform the Circle Dance.

The violent confrontations caused Americans to search for a solution to the "Indian problem." Most believed that the Indians had to be removed from rich American land. An editor for the *New York Herald* claimed, "It is inconsistent with our civilization and with common sense to allow the Indian to roam over a country as fine as that around the Black Hills, preventing its development in order that he may shoot game and scalp his neighbors. That can never be. The region must be taken from the Indian." Others had even more radical solutions. L. Frank Baum, who in 1900 became famous for writing *The Wizard of Oz*, noted in the Aberdeen *Saturday Pioneer* in 1890 that the "nobility of the Redskin is extinguished" and that the whites "are masters of the American continent." To end any lingering problems, Baum proposed "the total annihilation of the few remaining Indians . . . Their glory has fled, their spirits broken, their manhood effaced; better that they should die than live the miserable wretches that they are."

By the time of Wounded Knee, however, the U.S. government had embarked on its own solution to the Indian problem, one which emphasized ethnocide rather than genocide. An assault on tribalism, ethnocide—the calculated destruction of a culture—was an attempt by white Americans to force Indian Americans to assimilate into their culture. Although not as bloody as the Indian wars, ethnocide was even more destructive to Indian societies.

At the heart of this new policy was the destruction of the reservation system. Reservations encouraged tribal unity, and, as such, distinctiveness from white American society. Congress believed that the solution was to treat Indians less like members of individual tribes and more like autonomous individuals. As a first step, in 1871 Congress had ruled that no Indian tribe "shall be acknowledged or recognized as an independent nation, tribe or power, with whom the United States may contract by treaty." Then in an attempt to destroy Indian culture, in 1887 Congress passed the Dawes Severalty Act, which authorized the president to divide tribal lands and redistribute the lands among tribal members, giving 160 acres to each head of a family and lesser amounts to bachelors, women, and children. Although the plots would be held in trust for 25 years to prevent Indians from immediately selling the land, the object of the legislation was to make Indians individual landowners. In addition, all Indians receiving land grants were also made citizens of the United States.

Dawes was motivated by what he believed were the best interests of the Indians. Like other reformers, he believed that the most effective solution to the Indian problem was to assimilate Indians into mainstream white American culture. To this end, other reformers opened Indian schools to teach Indian children to be mechanics and farmers and to train them for citizenship. Richard Pratt, an army officer who founded the Carlisle Indian Industrial School in Pennsylvania in 1879, maintained that the fastest and surest way to assimilate Indians was to remove Indian children from reservations and send them to boarding schools in the East. By 1905 there were 25 boarding schools patterned after Carlisle. The schools emphasized ruthless assimilation. The "Rules for Indian Schools" called for compulsory observation of the Christian Sabbath, all formal and casual conversation in English, and instruction in "the sports and games enjoyed by white youth, such as baseball, hopscotch, croquet, marbles, bean bags, dominoes, checkers." Even more boarding schools were established on reservations to serve the same ends. What surprised reformers the most, however, was the failure of these schools to break tribal loyalties or destroy Indian culture.

While the reformers opened schools, Congress continued its efforts to break up the reservations. The Curtis Act of 1898 ended tribal sovereignty in Indian Territory, voiding tribal control of mineral rights, abolishing tribal laws and courts, and imposing the laws and courts of the United States on the Indians. The Dead Indian Act (1902) permitted Indians to sell allotted lands they had inherited, thereby circumventing the 25 year trust period imposed by the Dawes Act. Four years later, Congress continued its assault on the trust period with the Burke Act, which eliminated the trust period altogether and allowed the secretary of interior to decide when Indians were competent to manage their own affairs. Finally, in 1924 Congress enacted the Snyder Act, which granted all Indians born in the United States full citizenship. As far as Congress was concerned, the United States had now assimilated its true natives.

Reformers believed that these acts would end the tribal system and lead to assimilation. The legislation, however, served only the land interests of white Americans. By 1932 the allotment program had taken 90 million acres of land away from tribal control, and as late as 1981 a U.S. district court decision branded the program "probably one of the best-intended grievous errors in the history of American policymaking." Far from being assimilated, Indians saw their own culture attacked and partially destroyed, while at the same time they were never fully accepted into the dominant American culture.

WORKING IN INDUSTRIAL AMERICA

If during the 1920s advocates of immigration restrictions and Indian assimilation won an important battle, they lost their self-proclaimed war. They longed for a rural, white, Protestant, ethnically homogeneous America, but the war they waged took the form more of a rear guard action than an offensive. Between 1870 and 1920 America had changed dramatically. It became a richly complex, ethnically diverse, industrial country. In fact, even before 1900 its cities were the most cosmopolitan in the world. In 1880 more than 87 percent of the inhabitants of Chicago were immigrants and their children. In other major American cities the statistics were similar: Milwaukee and Detroit, 84 percent; New York and Cleveland, 80 percent; St. Louis and San Francisco, 78 percent. By contrast, 94 percent of the inhabitants of London in 1910 came from England and Wales.

These new immigrants provided the muscle for America's spectacular industrial growth. They laid railroad tracks, built bridges and roads, mined coal, silver, and gold, and made steel. Once again, statistics tell at least part of the story. In 1919 more than 90 percent of the anthracite coal miners were immigrants from eastern and southern Europe. Of the 14,359 workers in Carnegie's steel plants in the Pittsburgh area, 11,694 were eastern and southern Europeans. Indeed, without immigrant labor American industrialization would have moved forward at a far slower pace.

Wages, Hours, and Standard of Living

Was it worth it after all? Was the price paid by native-born and immigrant labor for industrialization worth the benefits they received? This is not a simple question to answer; in fact, each laborer might have answered it differently. But in their answers there would have been common themes. Unquestionably industrialization extracted a heavy toll from the laborers, who suffered psychologically and emotionally in industrial America. It changed not only how, when, and where they worked but also how they regarded work and how they perceived themselves. Equally unquestionably, however, industrialization transformed the United States into the most prosperous country in the world. To some degree, laborers shared in that prosperity and increase in material comfort.

Wages played an important role in a laborer's attitude toward work. In general, wages rose and prices fell during the late nineteenth and early twentieth centuries. Exactly how much is a question of heated historical debate. Clarence Long, an economic historian, in his study of wages and earnings in the late nineteenth century, estimated that when adjusted for changes in the price level, real daily wage rates rose from about $1 in 1860 to $1.50 in 1890, and real annual earnings increased from approximately $300 in 1860 to more than $425 in 1890. Other students of the subject believe Long's estimates are overly optimistic and that wages tended to stagnate, especially in the large textile industries. Even Long, however, admits that the pace of wages and earnings lagged well behind the spectacular growth in the American economy.

Even with the modest improvements in wages, laborers fought a continual battle with poverty. More often than not, the prosperity of a family depended on how many members of that family worked. Carroll D. Wright, chief of the Massachusetts Bureau of the Statistics of Labor, expressed the matter plainly in 1882: "A family of workers can always live well, but the man with a family of small children to support, unless his wife works also, has a small chance of living properly."

Take, for example, the case of 2 coal miners studied in 1883 by agents for the Illinois Bureau of Labor Statistics. Both were hardworking union men who earned wages of $1.50 per day. The first worked only 30 weeks in 1883, and his total income was $250. He lived with his wife and five children in a $6 per month, 2-room tenement apartment. During the year, he spent only $80 on food, mainly bread, salted meat, and coffee. His apartment was crowded but neat, and his children attended public school. In 1883, at least, he made barely enough to allow his family to maintain a minimal standard of living. His existence was precarious. Strikes, layoffs, sickness, or injury could easily throw him and his family into abject poverty.

The second miner worked full time in 1883 and earned $420. He had a wife and four children, 3 of whom were also miners, and they brought home an additional $1000. They lived comfortably in their own 6-room house perched on an acre of land. They ate well, spending $900 a year on food. Steak, butter, potatoes, bacon,

and coffee comprised a typical breakfast. They bought books and enjoyed a full leisure life. The material quality of life, then, often depended on circumstances other than occupation or wages.

The most important factor in determining the economic well-being of a working-class family was how many members of the family worked. Fathers and sons, mothers and daughters, and often aunts, uncles, and grandparents—all contributed to the "family economy." To be sure, the nature of the family economy created concern. Carroll D. Wright in the United States Census of 1880 warned, "the factory system necessitates the employment of women and children to an injurious extent, and consequently its tendency is to destroy family life and ties and domestic habits, and ultimately the home."

In truth, the opposite was probably true. Without the income earned by wives and children, families faced greater threats to their unity. Economically, families worked as a single entity; the desires of any particular individual often had to be sacrificed for the good of the family. This meant that women and children worked, families took in boarders, and all earnings were used for a common end. Far from destroying the family, the family economy often strengthened it.

During the first decade of the twentieth century, social workers conducted numerous studies to determine how much a family or a single individual needed to sustain a typical working-class existence for a year. Estimates for New York City ranged between $800 and $876 for a family of four, $505 for a single man, and $466 for a working woman. Many of New York's laborers fell painfully below the recommended minimum. Single women lived particularly difficult lives. A New York study concluded that women earned about half as much as men, and that the majority made less than $300 per year. One woman worker described her meager existence: "I didn't live, I simply existed. I couldn't live that [which] you could call living. . . . It took me months and months to save up money to buy a dress or a pair of shoes. . . . I had the hardest struggle I ever had in my life."

What was true for women was equally valid for blacks, Asians, and Mexicans in America. They were given the most exhausting and dan-

The family economy was an important part of survival in America. This family earned extra money by arranging artificial flowers at home.

gerous work, paid the least, and were fired first during economic hard times. For a black sharecropper farming a patch of worked-over soil in Mississippi, or a Chinese miner carrying nitroglycerin down a hole in a Colorado mountain, or a Mexican working on a Texas ranch, $300 per year would have seemed a kingly sum.

There were clear divisions even among workers. At the top ranks were the highly skilled laborers. Mostly English-speaking, generally Protestant, and almost exclusively white, they were paid well, had good job security, and considered themselves elite craftsmen. Below them were the semiskilled and unskilled workers. Most were immigrants from southern and eastern Europe, spoke halting if any English, and were Catholics or Jews. They lacked job security and had to struggle for a decent existence. At the bottom of the semiskilled and unskilled category were the nonwhite and women workers, for whom even a decent existence was normally out of reach.

Like wages, hours varied widely. The central question workers asked was, "How much of a person's life should be devoted to work?" Long hours were not a new phenomenon tied to industrial America. Farm workers and artisans often labored from sunup to sundown, but the tempo and quality of their labor was different. Farm work was governed by the season and the weather. During summer months and harvest, work was intense, but it slowed down during the shorter days of winter. There was always time for fishing, horse racing, visiting, and tavern-going. The rhythms of the preindustrial workshop similarly mixed work with fellowship. If the work days were long, they were also sociable. As they worked, laborers talked, joked, laughed, and even drank. In fact, laborers considered rum drinking an integral aspect of work. As Richard O'Flynn recalled, "The rum barrel was always near the work—ready for distribution, by this means they kept the men hard at work all day."

Nor was time measured out in teaspoons for the preindustrial laborer. Punctuality was not the golden virtue it became during industrialization. In the early nineteenth century, house-

(Text continues on p. 606)

HOUSEWORK IN VICTORIAN AMERICA

Housework in nineteenth-century America was harsh physical labor. Preparing even a simple meal was a time- and energy-consuming chore. Prior to the twentieth century, cooking was performed on a coal- or wood-burning stove. Unlike an electric or a gas range, which can be turned on with the flick of a single switch, cast-iron and steel stoves were exceptionally difficult to use.

Ashes from an old fire had to be removed. Then, paper and kindling had to be set inside the stove, dampers and flues had to be carefully adjusted, and a fire lit. Since there were no thermostats to regulate the stove's temperature, a woman had to keep an eye on the contraption all day long. Any time the fire slackened, she had to adjust a flue or add more fuel.

Throughout the day, the stove had to be continually fed with new supplies of coal or wood—an average of 50 pounds a day. At least twice a day, the ash box had to be emptied, a task which required a woman to gather ashes and cinders in a grate and then dump them into a pan below. Altogether, a housewife spent four hours every day sifting ashes, adjusting dampers, lighting fires, carrying coal or wood, and rubbing the stove with thick black wax to keep it from rusting.

It was not enough for a housewife to know how to use a cast-iron stove. She also had to know how to prepare unprocessed foods for consumption. Prior to the 1890s, there were few factory-prepared foods. Shoppers bought poultry that was still alive and then had to kill and pluck the birds. Fish had to have scales removed. Green coffee had to be roasted and ground. Loaves of sugar had to be pounded, flour sifted, nuts shelled, and raisins seeded.

Cleaning was an even more arduous task than cooking. The soot and smoke from coal- and wood-burning stoves blackened walls and dirtied drapes and carpets. Gas and kerosene lamps left smelly deposits of black soot on furniture and curtains. Each day, the lamp's glass chimneys had to be wiped and wicks trimmed or replaced. Floors had to scrubbed, rugs beaten, and windows washed. While a small minority of well-to-do families could afford to hire cooks at $5 a week, waitresses at $3.50 a week, laundresses at $3.50 a week, and cleaning women and choremen for $1.50 a day, in the overwhelming majority of homes, all household tasks had to be performed by a housewife and her daughters.

Housework in nineteenth-century America was a full-time job. Gro Svendsen, a Norwegian immigrant, was astonished by how hard the typical American housewife had to work. As she wrote her parents in 1862:

> We are told that the women of America have much leisure time but I haven't yet met any woman who thought so! Here the mistress of the house must do all the work that the cook, the maid and the housekeeper would do in an upper class family at home. Moreover, she must do her work as well as these three together do it in Norway.

Before the end of the nineteenth century, when indoor plumbing became common, chores that involved the use of water were particularly demanding. Well-to-do urban families had piped water or a private cistern, but the overwhelming majority of American families got their water from a hydrant, a pump, a well, or a stream located some distance from their house. The mere job of bringing water into the house was exhausting. According to calculations made in 1886, a typical North Carolina housewife had to carry water from a pump or a well or a spring eight to ten times each day. Washing, boiling, and rinsing a single load of laundry used about 50 gallons of water. Over the course of a year she walked 148 miles toting water and carried over 36 tons of water.

Homes without running water also lacked the simplest way to dispose of garbage: sinks with drains. This meant that women had to remove dirty dishwater, kitchen slops, and, worst of all, the contents of chamberpots from their house by hand.

Laundry was the household chore that nineteenth-century housewives detested most. Rachel Haskell, a Nevada housewife, called it "the Herculean task which women all dread" and "the great domestic dread of the household."

On Sunday evenings, a housewife soaked clothing in tubs of warm water. When she woke up the next morning, she had to scrub the laundry on a rough washboard and rub it with soap made from lye, which severely irritated her hands. Next, she placed the laundry in big vats of boiling water and stirred the clothes about with a long pole to prevent the clothes from developing yellow spots. Then she lifted the clothes out of the vats with a washstick, rinsed the clothes twice, once in plain water and once with bluing, wrung the clothes out, and hung them out to dry. At this point, clothes would be pressed with heavy flatirons and collars would be stiffened with starch.

The last years of the nineteenth century witnessed a revolution in the nature of housework. Beginning in the 1880s, with the invention of the carpet sweeper, a host of new "labor-saving" appliances were introduced. These included the electric iron (1903), the electric vacuum cleaner (1907), and the electric toaster (1912). At the same time, the first processed and canned foods appeared. In the 1870s, H. J. Heinz introduced canned pickles and sauerkraut; in the 1880s,

Franco-American Co. introduced the first canned meals; and in the 1890s, Campbell's sold the first condensed soups. By the 1920s, the urban middle class enjoyed a myriad of new household conveniences, including hot and cold running water, gas stoves, automatic washing machines, refrigerators, and vacuum cleaners.

Yet despite the introduction of electricity, running water, and "labor-saving" household appliances, time spent on housework did not decline. Indeed, the typical full-time housewife today spends just as much time on housework as her grandmother or great-grandmother. In 1924, a typical housewife spent about 52 hours a week in housework. Half a century later, the average full-time housewife devoted 55 hours to housework. A housewife today spends less time cooking and cleaning up after meals, but she spends just as much time as her ancestors on housecleaning and even more time on shopping, household management, laundry, and childcare.

How can this be? The answer lies in a dramatic rise in the standards of cleanliness and childcare expected of a housewife. As early as the 1930s, this change was apparent to a writer in the *Ladies Home Journal*:

> Because we housewives of today have the tools to reach it, we dig every day after the dust that grandmother left to spring cataclysm. If few of us have nine children for a weekly bath, we have two or three for a daily immersion. If our consciences don't prick us over vacant pie shelves or empty cookie jars, they do over meals in which a vitamin may be omitted or a calorie lacking.

hold clocks were rare and many of them possessed only a single hand. Large-scale production of household clocks did not begin in America until the 1830s, and it was not until the Civil War that cheap, mass-produced pocket watches became readily available. Certainly the idea of punching a time clock exactly on time was alien to the preindustrial worker, who might think in terms of hours but not in terms of minutes.

Preindustrial labor, then, had a more relaxed atmosphere. This is not meant to romanticize it. Farm work and shop labor could be hard and dangerous, but there were not sharp lines between labor and leisure. Gambling, storytelling, singing, debating, and drinking formed a crucial part of the work day. Thrift, regularity, sobriety, orderliness, punctuality—hallmarks of an industrial society—were virtues not rigorously observed.

The new concept of time changed not only how people worked, but also how they regarded labor. The great architectural feature of nineteenth- and early twentieth-century New England mill towns was the giant, looming bell towers of the factories. At George Pullman's model factory outside Chicago, the bell tower was a solid Victorian structure whose clock face reflected in a pool in front of it. Before clocks and watches, the bell towers served a utilitarian function. They told the laborers when to get out of bed, be at work, eat lunch, and go home. The importance of time was literally drilled home in a brochure prepared by the International Harvester Corporation to teach Polish laborers the English language. "Lesson One" read:

> I hear the whistle. I must hurry.
> I hear the five minute whistle.
> It is time to go into the shop.
> I take my check from the gate board and hang it on the department board.
> I change my clothes and get ready to work.
> The starting whistle blows.
> I eat my lunch.
> It is forbidden to eat until then.
> The whistle blows at five minutes of starting time.
> I get ready to go to work.
> I work until the whistle blows to quit.
> I leave my place nice and clean.
> I put all my clothes in the locker.
> I must go home.

The lesson perfectly describes the ideal industrial worker. He is at work on time, labors continuously until a whistle tells him to eat, keeps himself and his workplace clean, and goes straight home after work. In short, he is punctual, hardworking, clean, and sober. He does not show up at work late, retire to a saloon for lunch, and gamble his weekly pay on Saturday night.

Given this new standard of work and time demanded by factory owners, laborers were reluctant to work the preindustrial dawn-to-dusk day. In 1889 hundreds of trade unionists paraded through the streets of Worcester, Massachusetts, behind a banner which read: "Eight Hours for Work, Eight Hours for Rest, Eight Hours for What We Will." That was their goal, and a popular song of the day captured the ideal.

> We mean to make things over;
> We're tired of toil for naught;
> We may have enough to live on,
> But never an hour for thought.
>
> We want to feel the sunshine,
> We want to smell the flowers;
> We are sure that God has willed it,
> And we mean to have eight hours.

The reality, however, fell far short of the ideal. It is difficult to generalize about hours because they varied considerably from occupation to occupation. In 1890, for example, bakers averaged over 65 hours a week, steelworkers over 66, and canners nearly 77. Working in a steel mill blast furnace was a 12-hour-a-day, 7-day-a-week job, including one 24-hour continuous shift and 1 day off every 2 weeks. Even as late as 1920, skilled workers still averaged 50.4 hours a week and the unskilled 53.7 hours. Before the 1930s, workers regarded the idea of an 8-hour day or even a 10-hour day as an unattainable dream.

For women, the new ideals of industrial America created even more work. The increased emphasis on cleanliness led to a greater demand for tidy homes. As a result, women devoted more time to cleaning, dusting, and scrubbing. In addition, the growing availability of washable cotton fabrics increased the amount of laundering housewives performed. Finally, more varied diets meant women spent more

Factory owners demanded standards of work, behavior, and punctuality that left the industrial worker little leisure time. During the late nineteenth century, workers campaigned unsuccessfully for an eight-hour workday.

more than 4000; and in 1916 the plant housed 15,000 workers. During that latter year, the Ford Motor Company works at Highland Park, Michigan, employed 33,000 workers. Increasingly, giant industries dominated the American economy.

These huge plants demanded an organized, disciplined work force. The informality of the preindustrial workshop, with only a handful of employees, was an inevitable casualty. During those earlier times, for example, a cigar maker might go to the shop early in the morning, sip his *café con leche*, and roll 50 cigars, including a few smokes for himself. At noon he retired to a saloon and played pinochle while eating a leisurely lunch and then returned to his bench for another four hours. There he talked and joked with his fellow workers with the hum of the other voices and the click of the cutting blade as background. In the industrial factories workers were carefully regulated to ensure maximum productivity. Work became formalized and structured, and between the owner and the worker several levels of bureaucrats emerged.

Mechanization of work led to both the large factories and the incredible boom in productivity. It also caused an erosion of certain skilled trades. Imaginative inventors designed machines that performed tasks previously done by skilled artisans. A simple cigar mold, for example, allowed an unskilled worker to bunch cigar tobacco, a job once handled by a skilled tobacco roller. Where once a single tailor took a piece of cloth, cut it, fashioned it, sewed it, and made it into a pair of pants, by 1859 a Cincinnati clothing factory had divided the process into 17 different semiskilled jobs. The replacement of highly skilled workers by semiskilled laborers was a characteristic of the factory system. As one historian has observed, "the typical factory hand became a machine operator or fractionated workman, toiling at a single bit of the manufacturing process."

By the end of the century, it appeared to many observers that all work was being mechanized and moving toward the factory mode. Even farmers followed the mechanization march. By the early 1880s, one Dakota Territory wheat farm—or "food factory" as a critic called it—stretched over 30,000 acres, used 20 reapers and 30 steam-powered threshers, and em-

time plucking feathers from chickens, soaking and blanching hams, roasting coffee beans, grinding whole spices and sugar, and cooking meals. By 1900 the typical housewife worked 6 hours a day on just 2 tasks: meal preparation and cleaning. This was in addition to the time they spent on other household tasks.

The Lost Crafts

Although workers complained regularly about wages and hours, they were equally disturbed by several other results of industrialization. The late-nineteenth-century industries differed from the preindustrial workshop in four important areas: size, discipline, mechanization, and displacement of skill. The new factories were huge; they employed hundreds, even thousands, of laborers. In 1850 the McCormick reaper plant in Chicago employed about 150 workers; in 1900 the work force had grown to

Workers at Swift's meat-packing plant wield huge cleavers as they impassively go about their tasks. A slip of the cleaver could mean the loss of a limb or even death for a worker.

ployed 1000 field hands. Workers did not know their bosses, but this impersonality of labor was offset by a remarkable increase in output.

Worker Discontent

In the long run, industrialization brought much to many. Between 1860 and 1920 the volume of manufactured goods increased almost 14-fold. Consumer goods, which once only the rich could afford, came into the purchasing range of the middle class. Newspapers and magazines advertised, and department stores displayed, a wide variety of factory products.

From a worker's perspective, however, industrialization was often an inhumane process. Factory labor tended to be monotonous, and machines made work more dangerous. Industrial accidents were alarmingly common, and careless or tired workers sacrificed their fingers, hands, arms, and sometimes even lives. Describ-

ing the hazards of work in the Chicago stock-yards, one historian noted, "Each job had its own dangers: the dampness and cold of the packing rooms and hide cellar; the sharp blade of the beef boner's knife; the noxious dust of the wool department and fertilizer plant; the wild charge of a half-crazed steer on the killing floor." Frequent speedups increased the chances of injury. In one year at Armour's meat-packing plant in Chicago, 22,381 workers were injured or became ill.

To make matters even worse, owners often assumed an uncaring attitude toward their laborers. Concerned with production quotas and cost efficiency, owners seemed insensitive to workers' needs; and in fact, many *were* insensitive. As one factory manager proclaimed, "I regard my people as I regard my machinery. So long as they can do my work for what I choose to pay them, I keep them, getting out of them all I can. What they do or how they fare outside my walls I don't know, nor do I consider it my business to know. They must look out for themselves as I do myself."

Where once workers determined their production and work pace, now factory managers with stopwatches made laborers account for their time by seconds. Workers particularly resented scientific time-motion experts who strove to get the maximum production out of every laborer. One worker expressed the feelings of many others: "We don't want to work as fast as we are able to. We want to work as fast as we think it's comfortable for us to work. We haven't come into existence for the purpose of seeing how great a task we can perform through a lifetime."

Workers did not passively accept industrialization and the changes caused by that enormous process. At almost every step they resisted change, and they had formidable weapons at their disposal. On one level, resistance entailed a simple, individual decision not to change completely. Factory managers demanded a steady, dependable work force, but they were plagued by chronic absenteeism. Immigrant workers refused to labor on religious holidays, and in some towns factories had to shut down on the day the circus arrived. Across America, heavy drinking on Sunday led to "blue Mondays," a term used to described absenteeism.

Another form of individual protest was simply quitting. Most industrial workers changed jobs at least every three years, and in many industries the annual turnover rate was over 100 percent. Some quit because they were bored, "forced to work too hard," or because they were struck by spring wanderlust and simply wanted to move. Others quit because of severe discipline, unsafe working conditions, or low wages. Compulsive quitting was a clear indication that perhaps 20 percent of the work force never came to terms with industrialization.

Quick to quit, workers were similarly quick to take collective action. The late nineteenth century witnessed the most sustained and violent industrial conflict in the nation's history. Strikes were as common as political corruption during the period. Between 1881 and 1890, the Bureau of Labor Statistics estimated that 9668

strikes and lockouts had occurred. In 1886, 1432 strikes and 140 lockouts involved 610,024 workers. Although most of the conflicts were relatively peaceful, some were so violent that citizens across the nation feared that America was moving toward another revolution.

Early Labor Violence

An examination of several conflicts indicates clearly the relative power of industrialists and workers. An early violent conflict occurred in the anthracite coal region of eastern Pennsylvania. The late 1860s and early 1870s were troubled times for this socially and ethnically divided area. Mine owners competed ruthlessly against each other, and they all distrusted the miners and their union, the Workingmen's Benevolent Association (WBA). Added to economic and class tensions, the area was torn by ethnic conflicts. American-born and Protestant Scots-Irishmen owned most of the mines, and Welshmen and Englishmen served as mine superintendents. Increasingly, however, the miners were Irish-Catholic immigrants. Old World prejudices thus mingled with New World economics.

Matters became worse when the depression of the mid-1870s hit the area. Led by Franklin B. Gowen, president of the Reading Railroad, a company that owned considerable mining land and made a large profit hauling coal to market, the mine owners came together and agreed to observe common policies regarding prices, wages, and union negotiations. Competition thus reduced, the owners cut wages and increased workloads. This sort of oppression was nothing new to the Irish, and they responded much as they had in the Old Country. More important than the WBA were the Ancient Order of Hibernians, a secret fraternal society of Irish immigrants, and its inner circle, the Molly Maguires. While the WBA battled the owners at the negotiation table, the Molly Maguires waged a violent guerrilla war. They disrupted the operation of several mines and attacked a handful of mining officials.

Because it was secretive, little is known about the Mollies. However, Gowen and the owners were able to infiltrate the group with a secret agent, James McParlan. McParlan was one of Ireland's own. Born in County Armagh, he was a Catholic who had been raised to hate informers. But he agreed to inform on his fellow Irishmen for the Pinkerton agency. While McParlan was gathering information, the WBA went on strike. Disorder and violence followed. Using the local press, Gowen convinced much of the community that a direct link existed between the WBA, the Mollies, and the bloodshed. His tactic worked and the strike was broken.

A short time later, Gowen used McParlan's testimony to destroy both the Mollies and the WBA. Altogether, 20 Mollies were convicted and executed. Throughout their sensational trials, Gowen again linked Molly activities with the WBA. It was a scenario that industrialists would use again and again. The greatest weapon against strikers was the community's fear of violence. If an industrialist could convince the public that unions promoted violence, then they could characterize their own union-busting tactics as a sincere defense of law and order. Gowen used the tactic successfully in 1875 and 1876.

The same depression that convulsed the Pennsylvania coal fields shook the rest of the country as well. To keep from going under, many businessmen cut rates and attempted to recoup their losses by reducing labor costs. This was true especially in the highly competitive railroad business. Repeatedly, workers suffered wage cuts, and usually unskilled wages were slashed more than the skilled. Workingmen, one railroad worker declared in 1877, "know what it is to bring up a family on ninety cents a day, to live on beans and cornmeal week in and week out, to run in debt at the stores until you cannot get trusted any longer, to see the wife breaking down under privation and distress, and the children growing up sharp and fierce like wolves day after day because they don't get enough to eat." And that knowledge drove many workers to desperate lengths.

During the dog days of mid-July 1877, the Baltimore and Ohio Railroad (B&O) announced its third consecutive 10 percent wage cut. Angry, frustrated, hot, hungry, and led by the new Trainmen's Union, railroad workers along the line went on strike. When trouble followed, Baltimore and Ohio workers seized an important

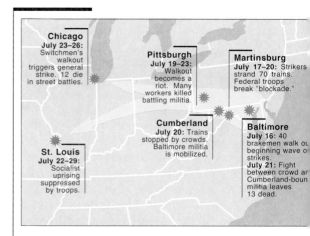

The Great Railroad Strike, 1877
The spontaneous uprising that followed the railroad strike of 1877 paralyzed two-thirds of the nation's trackage for two weeks and destroyed millions of dollars worth of railroad property.

junction at Martinsburg, West Virginia. The state militia and local sheriffs sympathized with the workers and could not end the strike. As a result, President Rutherford B. Hayes sent in federal troops to protect an army of strikebreakers.

From Martinsburg the strike spread north and west. Railroad workers walked off their jobs, and trains, which were vital to the American economy and the very symbols of progress during the nineteenth century, sat unused and deserted. The strike paralyzed transportation in the Midwest and much of the industrial northeast. It seemed there was violence and destruction everywhere. In Baltimore the state militia shot into a mob and killed ten persons; in Pittsburgh rioters burned 2000 freight cars, looted stores, and torched railroad buildings; in Buffalo, Chicago, and Indianapolis workers and police engaged in bloody battles.

When local police and state militiamen failed to quell the problems, President Hayes ordered more federal troops to do the job. Eventually, superior force restored peace and the trains started rolling again, but not before more than a hundred strikers were killed. Like most spontaneous strikes, the Great Strike of 1877 failed. But the anger it revealed frightened America. Although some authorities labeled the disturbances as the work of communist agita-

nized, he maintained, labor could deal with capital on equal terms.

Gompers's approach toward working with capital and organizing labor proved successful in the long run. Before 1900, however, the AFL was not more successful than the Knights or the NLU. In fact, workers benefited little from unions before the turn of the century. All together fewer than 5 percent of American workers joined trade unions, and the major areas of industrial growth were the least unionized. Nevertheless, the experimentation during the late nineteenth century taught workers valuable lessons. To combat the power of capital, labor needed equal power. During the twentieth century labor would move closer to that power.

CONCLUSION

In 1986 the Statue of Liberty was given a good cleaning. Its copper was shined as much as copper turned green can be shined, and its structure was refortified. America celebrated, and television newscasters recited once again Emma Lazarus's poem "The New Colossus"—or as one commentator called it "her 'huddled masses' poem." Few asked the question, "What are we celebrating?"

What America celebrated was nothing less than the emergence of modern America. In 1876 when France shipped the Statue of Liberty to the United States, the country, despite a recent civil war, was remarkably uniform. Most Americans traced their ancestry to Great Britain, worshiped in a Protestant church, and lived on farms or in small villages. If they were divided, it was along political and economic lines, not along ethnic and religious ones. The United States was not a world leader. Its navy was small, its diplomats uninfluential, and its industry still largely underdeveloped.

By 1900 America had changed radically. Unprecedented immigration had transformed the country into the most diverse nation in the world. Italians, Slavs, Serbs, Greeks, Chinese—a host of immigrants crowded into American cities. Catholics and Jews worked alongside Protestants in the country's expanding industries. For some it was an exciting, hopeful time; for others a painful, disillusioning one. Old America gave way to a New America with startling speed. In fact, most Americans in 1900 had not yet adjusted to the massive changes. What role would the new immigrants play in American life? What rights did workers have in the large industries? These and other questions would be answered in the next century.

SUGGESTIONS FOR FURTHER READING

OVERVIEWS AND SURVEYS

Thomas J. Archdeacon, *Becoming American: An Ethnic History* (1983); John Bodnar, *The Transplanted: A History of Immigrants in Urban America* (1985); Roger Daniels, *Coming to America: A History of Immigration and Ethnicity in American Life* (1990); Leonard Dinnerstein and David Reimers, *Ethnic Americans* (1975); Harold U. Faulkner, *Politics, Reform, and Expansion* (1959); John Garraty, *The New Commonwealth* (1968); Ray Ginger, *The Age of Excess* (1965); Oscar Handlin, *The Uprooted*, 2d ed. (1973); Samuel Hays, *The Response to Industrialism, 1885–1914* (1957); Jacqueline Jones, *The Dispossessed: America's Underclasses from the Civil War to the Present* (1992); Maldwyn Allen Jones, *American Immigration*, 2d ed. (1992); Alan M. Kraut, *The Huddled Masses* (1982); James S. Olson, *The Ethnic Dimension in American History* (1979); Rudolph J. Vecoli and Suzanne M. Sinke, eds., *A Century of European Migrations, 1830–1930* (1991); Robert Wiebe, *The Search for Order, 1877–1920* (1967).

HUDDLED MASSES AT THE GOLDEN DOOR

Rodolfo Acuña, *Occupied America: A History of Chicanos*, 3d ed. (1988); Josef J. Barton, *Peasants and Strangers* (1975); Rowland Berthoff, *British Immigrants in Industrial America, 1790–1950* (1953); John W. Briggs, *The Italian Passage* (1978); Jack Chen, *The Chinese of America* (1980); Alexander DeConde, *Half Bitter, Half Sweet: An Excursion into Italian-American History* (1971); Hasia R. Diner, *Erin's Daughters in America: Irish Immigrant Women in the Nineteenth Century* (1983); John Duff, *The Irish in the United States* (1971); David M. Emmons, *The Butte Irish* (1989); Elizabeth Ewen, *Immigrant Women in the Land of Dollars: Life and Culture on the Lower East Side* (1985); Richard Gambino, *Blood of My Blood* (1974); Mario García, *Desert Immigrants* (1981); Susan A. Glenn, *Daughters of the Shtetl: Life and Labor in* the *Immigrant Generation* (1990); Caroline Golab, *Immigrant Destinations* (1977); Irving Howe, *World of Our Fathers* (1976); Yuji Ichioka, *The Issei: The World of the First Generation Japanese Americans, 1885–1924* (1988); Maldwyn Allen Jones, *American Immigration* (1960), and *Destination America* (1976); Thomas Kessner, *The Golden Door* (1977); Harry Kitano, *Japanese Americans*, 2d ed. (1976); Helen Znaniecka Lopata, *Polish Americans* (1976); Joseph Lopreato, *Italian Americans* (1970); Carey McWilliams, *North from Mexico* (1948); Ande Manners, *Poor Cousins* (1972); Kerby A. Miller, *Emigrants and Exiles: Ireland and the Irish Exodus to North America* (1985); Charles C. Moskos, Jr., *Greek Americans*, 2d ed. (1989); Cecyle S. Neidle, *America's Immigrant Women* (1975); Humbert Nelli, *Italians in Chicago, 1880–1930* (1970), and *The Business of Crime* (1976); William Petersen, *Japanese Americans* (1971); Moses Rischin, *The Promised City: New York's Jews, 1870–1914* (1962); Andrew Rolle, *The Immigrant Upraised* (1968), and *The Italian Americans* (1980); Theodore Saloutos, *The Greeks in the United States* (1964); Philip Taylor, *The Distant Magnet* (1971); Stephan Thernstrom, *Poverty and Progress* (1964), and *The Other Bostonians* (1973); Maurice Violette, *The Franco Americans* (1976); Sydney Weinberg, *The World of Our Mothers: Lives of Jewish Immigrant Women* (1988); Joseph Wytrawal, *America's Polish Heritage* (1961), and *The Poles in America* (1969); Virginia Yans-McLaughlin, *Family and Community: Italian Immigrants in Buffalo, 1880–1930* (1977); Olivier Zunz, *The Changing Face of Inequality* (1982).

NATIVISM: THE ANTI-IMMIGRANT REACTION

David H. Bennett, *The Party of Fear: From Nativist Movements to the New Right in American History* (1988); Robert Carlson, *The Quest for Conformity* (1975); Leonard Dinnerstein, *The Leo Frank Case* (1968); Milton M. Gordon, *Assimilation in American Life* (1964); Mark Haller, *Eugenics* (1963); Leo Hershkowitz, *Tweed's New York* (1977); John Higham, *Strangers in the Land* (1955); Gerd Korman, *Industrialism, Immigrants, and Americanizers* (1967); Richard M. Linkh, *American Catholicism and European Immigrants, 1900–1924* (1975); Seymour Mandelbaum, *Boss Tweed's New York* (1965); Paul McBride, *Culture Clash* (1975); Stuart Creighton Miller, *The Unwelcome Immigrant* (1969); Thomas J. Pavlak, *Ethnic Identification and Political Behavior* (1976); Diane Ravitch, *The Great School Wars* (1974); Alexander Saxton, *The Indispensable Enemy* (1971).

WORKING IN INDUSTRIAL AMERICA

Paul Avrich, *The Haymarket Tragedy* (1984); James R. Barrett, *Work and Community in the Jungle: Chicago's Packinghouse Workers, 1894–1922* (1987); Susan Porter Benson, *Counter Cultures: Saleswomen, Managers, and Customers in American Department Stores, 1890–1940* (1986); John Bodnar, *Immigration and Industrialization* (1977); Jeanne Boydston, *Home and Work: Housework, Wages, and the Ideology of Labor in the Early Republic* (1990); Paul Boyer, *Urban Masses and Moral Order in America, 1820–1920* (1978); David Brody, *Steelworkers in America* (1960); Wayne G. Broehl, Jr., *The Molly Maguires* (1964); Robert V. Bruce, *1877: Year of Violence* (1959); John R. Commons, et al., *History of Labour in the United States*, 4 vols. (1918–1935); Ruth Schwartz Cowan, *More Work for Mother: The Ironies of Household Technology* (1983); Melvyn Dubofsky, *Industrialism and the American Worker*, 2d ed. (1985), and *We Shall Be All: A History of the Industrial Workers of the World* (1969); Leon Fink, *Workingmen's Democracy: The Knights of Labor and American Politics* (1983); Victor Greene, *The Slavic Community on Strike* (1968); Gerald Grob, *Workers and Utopia* (1961); Herbert Gutman, *Work, Culture, and Society in Industrializing America* (1976); Jacqueline Hall, et al., *Like a Family: The Making of a Southern Cotton Mill World* (1987); Tamara Hareven and Randolph Langenbach, *Amoskeag: Life and Work in an American Factory-City* (1979) and Hareven, *Family, Time, and Industrial Timer* (1982); Alice Kessler-Harris, *Out to Work: A History of Wage-Earning Women in the United States* (1982); William H. Harris, *The Harder We Run: Black Workers Since the Civil War* (1982); David Katzman, *Seven Days a Week: Women and Domestic Service in Industrializing America* (1978); Stuart B. Kaufman, *Samuel Gompers and the Origins of the AFL* (1973); Susan Kennedy, *If All We Did Was to Weep at Home: A History of White Working-Class Women in America* (1979); S. J. Kleinberg, *The Shadow of the Mills: Working-Class Families in Pittsburgh, 1870–1907* (1989); Susan Levine, *Labor's True Woman, Carpet Weavers, Industrialization, and Labor Reform in the Gilded Age* (1984); Harold Livesay, *Samuel Gompers and Organized Labor in America* (1978); Glenna Matthews, *"Just a Housewife": The Rise and Fall of Domesticity in America* (1987); David Montgomery, *Beyond Equality* (1967), *Workers' Control in America* (1979), and *The Fall of the House of Labor, 1865–1925* (1987); Stephen H. Norwood, *Labor's Flaming Youth: Telephone Operators and Worker Militancy, 1878–1923* (1990); Annegret S.

Ogden, *The Great American Housewife: From Helpmate to Wage Earner* (1986); Daniel T. Rodgers, *The Work Ethic in Industrial America, 1850–1920* (1978); Gerald Rosenblum, *Immigrant Workers* (1973); Roy A. Rosenzweig, *Eight Hours for What We Will* (1983); Nick Salvatore, *Eugene V. Debs, Citizen and Socialist* (1982); David Shannon, *The Socialist Party of America* (1955); Peter Shergold, *Working-Class Life* (1982); Susan Stras-ser, *Never Done: A History of American Housework* (1982); Sharon Hartman Strom, *Beyond the Typewriter: Gender, Class, and the Origins of Modern American Office Work* (1992); Leslie W. Tentler, *Wage-Earning Women* (1979); Daniel J. Walkowitz, *Worker City, Company Town: Iron and Cotton-Worker Protest in Troy and Cohoes, New York, 1855–84* (1978); Norman Ware, *The Labor Movement in the United States, 1860–1895* (1929).

Fig. 16

VII

eric Cople Jaher, *The Urban Establishment* (1982); Maury Klein and Harvey A. Kantor, *Prisoners of Progress: American Industrial Cities, 1850–1920* (1976); Roger Lane, *Policing the City: Boston, 1822–1885* (1967), and *Violent Death in the City* (1979); Blake McKelvey, *American Urbanization* (1973); Clay McShane, *Technology and Reform* (1974); Harold M. Mayer and Richard C. Wade, *Chicago* (1969); Martin V. Melosi, *Garbage in the Cities* (1982), and (ed.) *Pollution and Reform in the American Cities, 1870–1930* (1980); Gilbert Osofsky, *Harlem: The Making of a Ghetto* (1966); Harold L. Platt, *The Electric City: Energy and the Growth of the Chicago Area, 1880–1930* (1991); Bradley R. Rice, *Progressive Cities* (1977); Christine M. Rosen, *The Limits of Power: Great Fires and the Process of City Growth in America* (1986); Martin J. Schiesl, *The Politics of Efficiency* (1977); Allan H. Spear, *Black Chicago* (1967); John Stilgoe, *Borderland: Origins of the American Suburb, 1820–1939* (1988); Joel A. Tarr, "Transportation Innovation and Changing Spatial Patterns in Pittsburgh, 1850–1934" in *Essays in Public Works History* (1978); Jon C. Teaford, *The Municipal Revolution in America* (1975), *City and Suburb* (1979), and *The Unheralded Triumph: City Government in America, 1870–1900* (1984); David Ward, *Cities and Immigrants* (1971); Sam Bass Warner, Jr., *Streetcar Suburbs* (1962); William S. Worley, *J. C. Nichols and the Shaping of Kansas City* (1991).

CITY CULTURE

Lois W. Banner, *Women in Modern America* (1974), and *American Beauty* (1983); Gunther Barth, *City People* (1980); Susan P. Benson, *Counter Cultures: Saleswomen, Managers, and Customers in American Department Stores, 1890–1940* (1986); Burton J. Bledstein, *The Culture of Professionalism* (1976); Paul Boyer, *Urban Masses and Moral Order in America, 1820–1920* (1978); Carl W. Condit, *The Chicago School of Architecture* (1964), and *The Rise of the Skyscraper* (1952); Carl N. Degler, *At Odds: Women and the Family in America from the Revolution to the Present* (1980); Blanche H. Gelfant, *The American City Novel* (1954); James Gilbert, *Perfect Cities: Chicago's Utopias of 1893* (1991); Alfred Kazin, *On Native Grounds* (1942); Neil Leonard, *Jazz and the White Americans* (1962); Lawrence W. Levine, *Highbrow/Lowbrow: the Emergence of Cultural Hierarchy in America* (1988); William L. O'Neill, *Divorce in the Progressive Era* (1967); David J. Pivar, *Purity Crusade: Sexual Morality and Social Control, 1868–1900* (1973); W. J. Rorabaugh, *The Alcoholic Republic* (1979); Sheila M. Rothman, *Woman's Proper Place* (1978); Lewis O. Saum, *The Popular Mood of America, 1860–1890* (1990); William J. Schafer and Johannes Riedel, *The Art of Ragtime* (1973); Thomas J. Schlereth, *Victorian America* (1991); Vincent Scully, *American Architecture and Urbanism* (1969); Larzer Ziff, *The American 1890s* (1966).

ENTERTAINING THE MULTITUDES

Melvin L. Adelman, *A Sporting Time* (1986); Reid Badger, *The Great American Fair* (1979); David F. Burg, *Chicago's White City of 1893* (1976); Dominick Cavallo, *Muscles and Morals: Organized Playgrounds and Urban Reform, 1880–1920* (1981); John E. DiMeglio, *Vaudeville U.S.A.* (1973); Perry Duis, *The Saloon* (1983); Lewis A. Erenberg, *Steppin' Out: New York Nightlife and the Transformation of American Culture, 1890–1930* (1981); Charles E. Funnell, *By the Beautiful Sea* (1975); Warren Goldstein, *Playing for Keeps: A History of Early Baseball* (1989); Elliott Gorn, *The Manly Art* (1986); Allen Guttmann, *A Whole New Ball Game: An Interpretation of American Sports* (1988); Stephen Hardy, *How Boston Played: Sport, Recreation, and Community, 1865–1915* (1982); John F. Kasson, *Amusing the Millions, Coney Island at the Turn of the Century* (1978), and *Rudeness & Civility: Manners in Nineteenth-Century Urban America* (1990); T. J. Jackson Lears, *No Place of Grace: Antimodernism and the Transformation of American Culture, 1880–1920* (1981); Lary May, *Screening Out the Past: The Birth of Mass Culture and the Motion Picture Industry* (1980); Donald J. Mrozek, *Sport and American Mentality, 1880–1910* (1983); James D. Norris, *Advertising and the Transformation of American Society, 1865–1920* (1990); Russel B. Nye, *The Unembarrased Muse* (1970); Kathy Peiss, *Cheap Amusements: Working Women and Leisure in Turn-of-the-Century New York* (1986); Steven A. Riess, *Touching Base: Professional Baseball and American Culture in the Progressive Era* (1980); Robert Sklar, *Movie-Made America* (1975); Dale A. Somers, *The Rise of Sports in New Orleans, 1850–1900* (1972).

BIOGRAPHIES

Neil Harris, *Humbug: The Art of P. T. Barnum* (1973); Michael T. Isenberg, *John L. Sullivan and His America* (1988); Justin Kaplan, *Mr. Clemens and Mark Twain* (1966); Peter Levine, *A. G. Spalding and the Rise of Baseball* (1985); Randy Roberts, *Papa Jack: Jack Johnson and the Era of White Hopes* (1983), and *Jack Dempsey: The Manassa Mauler* (1979); Laura Wood Roper, *FLO: A Biography of Frederick Law Olmsted* (1973); Elizabeth Stevenson, *Park Maker: A Life of Frederick Law Olmsted* (1977).

CHAPTER 20

Imperial America, 1870–1900

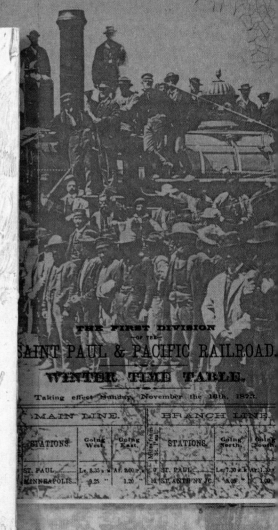

*D*reams of expansion came easily to Americans during the nineteenth century. For most of the century they expanded westward, moving into Texas and Kansas, pushing across the Great Plains, and occupying California and the Pacific Northwest. But they did not restrict their dreams to the millions of acres between Mexico and Canada. They cast covetous eyes toward Central America and the islands of the Caribbean and the Pacific. Plans to annex Nicaragua, Cuba, Santo Domingo, the Virgin Islands, Hawaii, and Samoa fired politicians' imaginations. Before the Civil War, the debate over slavery blocked these larger expansionist efforts. Once the Union was preserved, however, expansionists returned to their plans with revived energy and enthusiasm.

President Ulysses S. Grant had a pet expansionist project of his own. He eyed the Dominican Republic, the eastern two-thirds of the Caribbean island of Santo Domingo. Annexation, he maintained, would benefit America in a number of ways. The island was rich in mineral resources, possessed an important natural harbor, and its inhabitants were eager to buy American products. Most importantly for Grant, who was ever mindful of America's race problem, the Dominicans were black. The island could serve as a frontier for black Americans, a retreat from Ku Klux Klan harassment.

With so much to gain, Grant put his full political weight behind annexation. His conduct was less than presidential. First, he sent his personal secretary and close friend Orville Babcock to Santo Domingo on a "fact finding" mission. Unimpressed by the islanders, Babcock reported: "The people are indolent and ignorant. The best class of people are the American Negroes who have come here from time to time." But Babcock was convinced that the Dominican Republic was a commercial and strategic prize worthy of annexation. What was more, Buenaventura Baez, the unscrupulous president of the republic, was anxious to sell his country. With the money he would make from the transaction, Baez hoped to move and establish residence in Paris or Madrid, because, as Babcock noted, the Dominican Republic was "a dull country."

Unrest at home added fuel to Baez's willingness to sell. His government was threatened both by neighboring Haiti and a strong force of Dominican rebels. So difficult was Baez's position that Babcock had to order a United States Navy ship to protect the Baez government during the annexation negotiations, which were completed in the late fall of 1869. The promise of American dollars had convinced Baez that his country should belong to the United States.

Grant was pleased. The treaty of annexation, however, would have to be ratified by the Senate, a body more difficult to satisfy than Baez's government. An informal man, Grant decided to forgo presidential protocol and personally visit Charles Sumner, the chairman of the Senate Foreign Relations Committee. On the evening of January 2, 1870, Grant made an unannounced call at Sumner's Washington home on Lafayette Park. Later Sumner recalled that Grant was drunk. Drunk or sober, Grant was certainly in earnest. He energetically discussed the need to annex the Dominican Republic. Sumner listened then replied: "Mr. President, I am an Administration man, and whatever you do will always find in me the most careful and candid consideration." Grant departed for his short walk back to the White House believing he had won Sumner's full support. In fact, he had only won the powerful Massachusetts senator's "candid consideration."

After consideration and considerable investigation, Sumner decided that the entire annexation scheme was distasteful. He was disturbed by Babcock's and Baez's unethical financial dealings and was enraged that the United States Navy had been used to keep the Dominican president in power. Sumner was not a man to mince words. Labeled "probably the most intolerant man that American history has ever known," he accused Grant of being "a colossus of ignorance." Finally by a vote of 5 to 2, the Foreign Relations Committee voiced its disapproval of the treaty of annexation.

Grant was furious. His son later recalled, "I never saw Father so grimly angry." Known for his bulldog tenacity during the Civil War, Grant was not about to quit. He hinted that if the United States did not take the Dominican Republic, one of the European powers would, and he reported the results of a rigged plebiscite in which the Dominicans supposedly supported annexation by the suspiciously lopsided vote of 15,169 to 11, but Grant's efforts failed. On June 30, 1870, the Senate rejected the treaty. Defining America's duty toward the island, Sumner said, "Our duty is as plain as the Ten Commandments. Kindness, beneficence, assistance, aid, help, protection, all that is implied in good neighborhood, these we must give freely, bountifully, but their independence is as sacred to them as is ours to us."

The failed attempt to annex the Dominican Republic is important for the themes it underscored. It demonstrated both the desire for expansion by the president and his advisors and the power of Congress in foreign affairs. During the remainder of the century the scenario would be repeated again and again, often with different results. Gradually during this period, presidents wrested more control over foreign affairs from Congress. And Congress, for its part, accepted a more expansionist foreign policy. As presidents and Congress found common ground, America expanded outward into the Caribbean and the Pacific. The expansion took different forms. Sometimes the United States annexed countries outright. Other times America remained content to exercise less forceful control over nominally independent countries. The results were the same. The United States ultimately acquired an overseas empire and expanded its influence over the Western Hemisphere.

Area of Grant's Expansionist Scheme

During the turn of the century, the United States increasingly tried to influence world affairs. Here, Uncle Sam assumes a forceful attitude.

CONGRESSIONAL CONTROL AND THE REDUCTION OF AMERICAN POWER

Foreign Service

In 1869 when Grant took office, congressmen and other Americans held the State Department and the diplomatic service in low esteem. No majestic building housed the State Department. Instead the department was headquartered in a former orphan asylum. Nor was the post of sec-

retary of state as great a prize as it had been. Once regarded as a stepping-stone to the presidency, politicians increasingly viewed the post as a reward for outstanding party men or the refuge for defeated presidential aspirants. Even the diplomats themselves did not escape criticism. One newspaper editor said the diplomatic service was too often used as "gilt edged pigeon holes for filing away Americans, more or less illustrious, who are no longer particularly wanted at home."

The irreverent treatment of the State Department reflected a congressional and national mood. Concerns over the currency, civil service reform, Reconstruction, taxation, the tariff, Indian fighting, and railroad building dwarfed interest in foreign affairs. As late as 1889, Henry Cabot Lodge, whose interests in foreign affairs were great, could write: "Our relations with foreign nations today fill but a slight place in American politics, and excite . . . a languid interest. We have separated ourselves so completely from the affairs of other people." During the

1870s and 1880s, when a powerful Congress largely dictated foreign policy, the spirit of Washington's Farewell Address and the Monroe Doctrine guided the country. Washington had counseled America to steer clear of foreign entanglements and Monroe had made isolationism a national obsession. Separated from a powerful Europe by the cold North Atlantic, Congress saw no reason to spend time or money on the State Department or foreign affairs.

Using its control over the budget as a sword, Congress trimmed the State Department to the bone. In 1869, Congress allowed the State Department a paltry 31 clerks; by 1881 presidential efforts had succeeded in raising that number to a still inadequate 50. Politicians who considered the foreign service "a nursery of snobs" viewed diplomats as an expensive, nearly useless luxury. A few reformers even advocated the abolition of the foreign service. They argued that two oceans protected America and they could hire international lawyers to handle really serious international crises.

Reduction of the Military

The sword that trimmed the State Department was also used on America's army and navy. When the Civil War ended and peace returned to the country, Congress quickly reduced America's military might. The result made the United States a weaker country. In 1865 America had the largest and perhaps the most powerful navy in the world. To be sure, it was a ragtag navy, composed of just about any vessel that would float. Ranging from the powerful *Monitor*-class ironclads to modest yachts, the United States Navy numbered 971 vessels. Within nine months of Appomattox, the fleet was reduced to 29.

As Congress watched unconcerned, the navy declined intellectually as well as physically. To begin with, there were far too many officers. Although after the post–Civil War reductions America's navy was less than one-tenth as large as Great Britain's, it contained over half as many officers. With promotions based strictly upon length of service, any officer who lived long enough could become an admiral. The system almost guaranteed poor leadership. While the world's best navies converted to steel and steam, American naval leaders remained tied to wood and sails. As one American officer from the period recalled, "To burn coal was so grievous an offense in the eyes of the authorities that for years the coal-burning captain was obliged to enter in the logbook in *red ink* his reasons for getting up steam and starting the engines." Quickly the American navy became a joke. In 1881 authorities claimed, with some justification, that a single modern ship of the Chilean navy could destroy the entire United States fleet.

The men appointed as the secretaries of the navy did nothing to help matters. They were mostly political appointees who knew little and cared less about ships. One historian noted that Richard W. Thompson of Indiana, whom Rutherford B. Hayes appointed secretary of the navy, was "so densely ignorant of naval affairs as to express surprise upon learning that ships were hollow."

The power and effectiveness of the army were similarly reduced. On May 23, 1865, with the Civil War just ended, Union bluecoats marched down Pennsylvania Avenue in a victory parade. There were over 100,000 soldiers. It took an hour for General Meade's cavalry to pass the reviewing stand. "Marching twelve abreast, the general's infantry consumed another five hours." The next day thousands of General Sherman's men repeated the performance, marching briskly "like the lords of the world!"

The sight would not be repeated for over 50 years. Demobilization occurred quickly and haphazardly. In May 1865 the army contained 1,034,064 volunteers; by November 1866 only 11,043 remained in uniform. Eventually Congress slashed the number of even the regular troops. By the end of Reconstruction, Congress had reduced the army to a distant echo of its former self. In 1876 the maximum strength stood at 27,442 troops.

Certainly in 1876 the United States did not need an active foreign service and a powerful army and navy to secure its borders. No countries threatened America. Geography defended the United States, and the European balance of power discouraged foolish European designs on

H. Wayne Morgan, *From Hayes to McKinley* (1969), ed. *The Gilded Age*, rev. ed. (1970), and *America's Road to Empire* (1965); Louis Pérez, Jr., *Cuba under the Platt Amendment, 1902–1934* (1986); Julius W. Pratt, *Expansionists of 1898* (1936); Goran Rystad, *Ambiguous Imperialism* (1975); Daniel B. Schirmer, *Republic or Empire* (1972); E. Berkeley Tompkins, *Anti-Imperialism in the United States* (1970); David F. Trask, *The War with Spain in 1898* (1981); Richard E. Welch, Jr., *Response to Imperialism* (1979); Leon Wolff, *Little Brown Brother* (1961).

BIOGRAPHIES

David Donald, *Charles Sumner and the Rights of Man* (1970); John A. Garraty, *Henry Cabot Lodge* (1953); H. Wayne Morgan, *William McKinley and His America* (1963); Allan Nevins, *Grover Cleveland* (1932), and *Hamilton Fish*, rev. ed. (1957); Ernest N. Paolino, *The Foundations of the American Empire: William Henry Seward and U. S. Foreign Policy* (1973); Ronald Spector, *Admiral of the New Empire: The Life and Career of George Dewey* (1974); John M. Taylor, *William Henry Seward* (1991).

End of the Century Crisis

On July 9, 1896, William Jennings Bryan rose to speak to the delegates at the Democratic National Convention in Chicago. "I thought I had never seen a handsomer man," a reporter wrote, "young, tall, powerfully built, clear-eyed, with a mane of black hair which he occasionally thrust back with his hand." Thirty-six years old, Bryan was the son of a circuit court judge. His father was a Baptist deacon and his mother was a devout Methodist. Steeped in both religion and politics from an early age, Bryan was elected to Congress from Nebraska in 1890.

As the cry for "free silver" swept the rural areas of the West and South, Bryan took up the cause. "I don't know anything about free silver," he admitted. "The people of Nebraska are for free silver and I am for free silver. I will look up the arguments later." In the 1890s the slogan referred to expanding the amount of money in circulation by coining more silver dollars. Farmers believed such inflation of the currency would raise crop prices and alleviate their heavy debt burdens. Many rural residents felt the national government had not been responsive to their needs—that both political parties had been captured by industrialists, railroad owners, and bankers. In 1896 silver was a symbol for popular grievances. Among other things, silver represented rural values, the common people, and a growing discontent with northeastern political domination.

By the time of the Democratic convention the Republicans had nominated William McKinley and adopted a platform calling for the gold standard—or currency backed entirely by gold supplies in the federal treasury. The Democrats were divided between the "silverites" and the "Gold Democrats," monetary conservatives who supported President Grover Cleveland. Control of the party by the northeast was being challenged by southern and western delegates when Bryan finally rose to speak.

Called "the Great Commoner," Bryan voiced the frustrations of farmers with the failure of traditional politicians to meet their needs. "We have petitioned," he cried, "and our petitions have been scorned; we have entreated, and our entreaties have been disregarded; we have begged, and they have mocked when our calamity came. We beg no longer; we entreat no more; we petition no more. We defy them!"

He enthralled the crowd from the beginning, but his closing words created pandemonium. "We will answer the demand for a gold standard," he roared, "by saying to them: 'You shall not press down upon the brow of labor this crown of thorns, you shall not crucify mankind upon a cross of gold.'" As he spoke his fingers first traced the course of imaginary trickles of blood from his temples. He closed with his arms outstretched as if he were nailed to a cross.

When he dropped his arms, he had won the Democratic nomination and cinched the victory of the party's silverites. The Cleveland supporters left Chicago unwilling to accept Bryan's "foul pit of repudiation, socialism, [and] anarchy," as one declared. Another said, "I am a Democrat still—very still." Because many party regulars deserted him and nearly half the Democratic newspapers opposed him, Bryan was only able to raise the meager sum of about $500,000. Taking his campaign directly to the people, he appealed to sectional and class animosities: "Probably the only passage in the Bible read by some financiers is that about the wise men of the East. They seem to think that wise men have been coming from that direction ever since."

Low on funds, Bryan relied on his oratorical genius and electrifying charisma. Between August and November he had traveled more than 18,000 miles, visiting 27 states and giving 600 speeches. His youth sustained him as he made his own travel arrangements, bought his own tickets, carried his own bags, rode in public cars, and walked from train stations to hotels late at night. He was often called upon to give unscheduled speeches; when one Indiana crowd awakened him, he spoke in his nightshirt.

With a Republican campaign fund of more than $3.5 million, McKinley wisely refused to follow Bryan's course. "I might just as well put up a trapeze in my front lawn and compete with some professional athlete as to go out speaking against Bryan," he said. Between June and November, McKinley left his home in Canton, Ohio, for only three days. Railroads provided cheap excursion rates to Canton so that every day except Sunday, crowds of up to 50,000 thronged

In the 1896 election, Republicans sought to convince voters that Bryan was a radical who threatened American values and institutions, while McKinley (shown in the campaign poster above) would guarantee stability, order, and integrity.

to McKinley's lawn. There he conducted his "front porch" campaign. The gatherings were hardly spontaneous. His staff organized the groups by occupation or interest, screened each delegation's remarks, and planned each event in detail down to brass bands and banners.

Unlike Bryan's speeches, McKinley's were calm and dispassionate, stressing national unity rather than division. "We are all dependent on each other, no matter what our occupation may be," he declared. "All of us want good times, good wages, good markets; and then we want good money always." From his front porch he addressed some 750,000 people from 30 states. The Republicans also spent more for printing than Bryan raised for his entire campaign. By the campaign's end Republicans sent 200 million pamphlets in several languages to 15 million voters and some 250 paid speakers toured 27 states.

On election day Bryan and his wife rose at 6:30 A.M. and voted at a local fire station in Omaha, Nebraska. He then gave seven speeches in his hometown before collapsing, exhausted, in bed that evening. McKinley walked to his poll-

ing place and stood in line to vote. He then returned home to wait for the returns—his lawn and porch in worse shape than he was. All over the nation politicians and just plain people waited to find out which man and party would preside over the dawning of the twentieth century.

The election came in a decade of turbulence that saw violence toward the labor movement, rising racial tensions, militant farmers, and discontented unemployed workers—all of which intensified after a major depression began in 1893. The social fabric seemed to be unraveling rapidly, which is why the election of 1896 was considered so important. For the first time since the 1870s voters were given a clear choice between two very different candidates and platforms.

Following Reconstruction, national politics were colorful but not very significant. No important policy differences separated the two major parties, the campaigns revolved around personalities, gimmicks, emotional slogans, and local issues. As elections were trivialized, they also became a major source of entertainment, and voters turned out in record numbers. This triumph of style over substance in politics, as well as culture, caused the era to be labeled the "Gilded Age." By 1890 both the Democratic and Republican parties had lost touch with the sentiments of large blocks of voters. The losers in the great national race toward economic modernization began to question its assumptions. Their voices rose in the 1890s, but unable to unite around a viable agenda, they failed to win many battles at that time. The issues they raised, however, appeared regularly on political agendas in the twentieth century.

EQUILIBRIUM AND INERTIA: THE NATIONAL POLITICAL SCENE

American politics have often seemed odd to Europeans. Never was this more true than in the closing decades of the nineteenth century. American political parties bewildered them. In his 1898 book, *The American Commonwealth*, Lord James Bryce wrote that "neither party has any principles, any distinctive tenets. Both have traditions. Both claim to have tendencies. Both have certainly war cries, organizations, interests enlisted in their support. But those interests are in the main the interests of getting or keeping the patronage of government. . . . All has been lost, except office or the hope of it."

Patronage, or the granting of political favors and offices, became more important than issues to the two major parties for many reasons. Close elections caused the parties to be careful not to alienate potential supporters. Most people also believed in limited government. Political parties were therefore organized more to win offices than to govern. The result was a failure by government to deal effectively with the enormous changes wrought by industrialization and urbanization.

Divided Power: The Parties and the Federal Government

After Reconstruction both the Democratic and Republican parties emerged with sizable and stable constituencies. For the 20 years between 1876 and 1896 they shared a rare equality of political power. Elections were so close that until 1896 no president won office with a majority of the popular vote. Two (Hayes and Harrison) even entered the presidency without a plurality. The average popular vote margin was 1.5 percent. Republicans occupied the White House for 12 years, Democrats for 8. Only during three 2-year periods did the same party control the presidency and both houses of Congress— Democrats once and Republicans twice. Most of the time Congress itself was split, with Democrats generally taking the House and the Republicans the Senate. Very few seats shifted parties in any given election.

The party division of Congress inevitably weakened the presidents of the era. None was elected to consecutive terms. Calling them "the lost Americans," one observer noted that "their gravely vacant and bewhiskered faces mixed, melted, swam together" in the public mind. Lord Bryce claimed none of them "would have been remembered had he not been President." To be fair, all were competent men, some with distinguished war records, most with considerable public service. One reason they were so forgettable was the era's concept of the presidency. Many agreed with Cleveland's assertion that the office "was essentially executive in nature." "I did not come here to legislate," he said. Presidents were only supposed to implement efficiently and honestly laws passed by Congress—occasionally vetoing ill-advised legislation. Even though these presidents were able to turn back many of the encroachments on presidential authority that began in Andrew Johnson's term, none considered it his duty to propose legislation.

Some found the office frustrating. After James Garfield moved from leadership roles in the House of Representatives to the presidency, he lamented, "I have heretofore been treating of the fundamental principles of government, and here I am considering all day whether A or B should be appointed to this or that office." Even representatives and senators were frequently frustrated, however, because congressional action was often stalemated. In the House, outdated, complex rules hampered action. Party discipline was practically impotent in both houses, and since neither controlled both houses for more than a two-year term, there was little possibility of formulating and enacting any coherent legislative program.

The lack of legislative action did not seem to be a serious problem at the start of the Gilded Age. Most people rejected the idea of an activist government. Widely accepted doctrines of laissez-faire and Social Darwinism limited what people expected of government. The Social Darwinist William Graham Sumner once proclaimed that government had "at bottom . . . two chief things . . . with which to deal. They are the property of men and the honor of women. These it has to defend against crime." Both parties basically accepted a narrow vision of federal responsibility. When vetoing a small appropriation for drought relief in Texas, Democrat Cleveland asserted that "though the people support the Government, the Government should not support the people." Republican leader Roscoe Conkling claimed that the only duty of government was "to leave every class and every individual free and safe in the exertions and pursuits of life."

Such antigovernment sentiment tended to increase the power of the judicial branch. Many saw the courts as a bastion against governmental interference in the economy, and they certainly fulfilled that role. On the basis of the Fourteenth Amendment, judges were especially active in striking down state laws to regulate business. The courts narrowly interpreted the Constitution on federal authority—ruling that the power to tax did not extend to personal incomes and that the power to regulate interstate commerce applied only to trade, not manufacturing. Congress also indirectly gave judges more power by enacting vague laws that relied upon the courts for both definition and enforcement.

Subtle Differences: The Bases of Party Loyalty

One consequence of the equality of power shared by the Democrats and Republicans was the reluctance of either party to chance losing voters by taking clear positions on most contemporary issues. Perhaps this reluctance was also based on the memories of the divisive 1860 election and its devastating impact on party and national unity. In addition, during the early

stages few Americans criticized industrialization and economic modernization, and there was widespread agreement on many issues.

Most members of both parties did not question the pace or cost of industrialization. They also saw little need for the federal government to play a major role in regulating the economy. When a Democratic president replaced a Republican one in 1893, one of Andrew Carnegie's managers wrote him, "I cannot see that our interests are going to be affected one way or another by the change in administration." Indeed business leaders had so little to fear from either party that they contributed generously to both.

Until 1896 the parties did share numerous similarities. Both were led by wealthy men but still tried to appeal to wage earners and farmers as well as merchants and manufacturers. Most members of both parties believed in protective tariffs and "sound currency." Both rejected economic radicalism and positive programs to aid workers. Presidents of both parties sent federal troops to break up strikes.

Ironically, for all their similarities the parties evoked fierce loyalty from a heterogeneous mix of people. One reason party platforms were so innocuous as to be interchangeable is that both parties were composed of factions and coalitions of "strange bedfellows." Because of its past and abolitionist connection the Republican party retained the support of activist reformers, idealists, and African-Americans. Yet most Republicans came from established "old stock" families. The more wealth a man had, the more likely he was to vote Republican. The party therefore was a curious combination of "insiders" and "outsiders."

The Democrats were even more mixed. The party's constituents sometimes seemed united mainly by opposition to the Republicans on various grounds. One Republican leader complained, "The Republican party does things, the Democratic party criticizes; the Republican party achieves, the Democratic party finds fault." Several generations later humorist Will Rogers quipped, "I don't belong to an organized party; I'm a Democrat." His words were certainly true of the Gilded Age. The party contained such disparate elements as Southern whites, immigrants, Catholics, and Jews.

For historical and cultural reasons, party

loyalty was frequently determined by the three factors of region, religion, and ethnic origin. The regional factor was most evident in the support white Southerners gave to the Democratic party. To vote for the party of abolition and Reconstruction was considered treason and a threat to white supremacy. On the other hand, the Republicans could count on heavy support from New England for the opposite reasons. To New Englanders, the Democrats were members of the party of traitorous rebellion against the Union. Because the Republicans could not expect to receive southern white votes, this was one issue they did need to tiptoe around. They frequently "waved the bloody shirt," reminding Northerners that the Democrats had caused the Civil War. In 1876 one Republican declared, "Every man that tried to destroy this nation was a Democrat. . . . Soldiers, every scar you have on your heroic bodies was given you by a Democrat."

For various reasons immigrants had long gravitated toward the Democratic party. Many were members of the poorest classes, which traditionally voted Democratic. In the 1850s anti-immigration Know Nothing party members joined the Republican ranks, reinforcing immigrants' ties to the Democrats. Most of the "new immigrants" of the Gilded Age settled in cities controlled by Democratic political machines that won their loyalty by meeting the immigrants' needs. As immigration swelled, increasing Democratic strength, Republicans became more and more restrictionist. In fact, immigration policy was one of the very few substantive issues on which the parties took clearly different stands.

Religious affiliations also helped determine party loyalty—partly because of the positions on immigration. Many of the late-nineteenth-century immigrants were Catholics and Jews who were suspicious of the Protestant-dominated Republican party. There were also fundamental differences in the religious orientation of most Republicans and Democrats. Republicans tended to belong to *pietistic* sects that based salvation on good works and moral behavior. Democrats, on the other hand, leaned toward *ritualistic* religions based on faith and observance of church rituals. Pietistic Republi-

cans frequently sought to legislate morality, supporting prohibition of alcohol and enforcement of Sunday blue laws, which barred various activities on the sabbath—including baseball. Many Democrats did not believe that personal morality could or should be a matter of state concern. A Chicago Democrat explained, "A Republican is a man who wants you t' go t' church every Sunday. A Democrat says if a man wants t' have a glass of beer on Sunday he can have it."

The roots and constituencies of the parties created differences in their outlooks. The Republicans became the "party of morality," the Democrats the "party of personal liberty." Democrats not only rejected government interference in their personal life; in the nineteenth century, they were also more suspicious of government action of any sort. Some quoted Democrat Albert Gallatin's dictum: "We are never doing as well as when we are doing nothing."

Because of their mixed constituencies, however, the differences and divisions *within* parties were as great, and sometimes greater, than those between them. Democrats could count on the South for all its electoral votes, but southern Democrats frequently broke party ranks when voting on legislation. They sometimes voted with western Republicans on acts favorable to farmers. They were, however, fundamentally conservative men of whiggish tendencies who usually voted with northern Republicans on financial and economic issues, as well as on immigration restriction. In a bizarre political arrangement, southern Democrats also voted with northern Republicans at times in order to receive a share of the patronage.

The Republicans were even more deeply divided into factions. One group, led by Roscoe Conkling of New York, was labeled the "Stalwarts." Followers of James G. Blaine of Maine were called "Half-breeds." The only significant item of dispute between the two was who would receive the numerous jobs appointed by the president. The distribution of patronage was a prime function of both parties of the era. Thus the division was bitter. When Conkling was asked if he intended to campaign for Blaine for president in 1884, he snapped that he did not engage in criminal activities.

There was one faction of the Republican party that did have some ideological basis. It was composed of reformers whose primary concern was honest and effective government. They had bolted the party in 1872 because of the corruption of the Grant regime, and they bolted again in 1884. Party regulars ridiculed them, calling them "goo-goos" for their idealistic good government crusade. They were finally labeled "Mugwumps," and a joke asserted that they had their "mugs" on one side of the fence and their "wumps" on the other.

The divisions in the Republican party reflected the fact that the politicians of the day were less concerned with issues and ideology than with winning office and distributing patronage. Lord Bryce observed that American politicians could be distinguished from European ones by the fact "that their whole time is frequently given to political work, that many of them draw an income from politics . . . that . . . they are proficient in the acts of popular oratory, of electioneering, and of party management."

The Business of Politics: Party Organization

Gilded Age politicians were very serious about their careers. They worked hard at both "party management" and "electioneering." The result was the largest voter turnout in the nation's history. In the elections from 1860 to 1900 an average of 78 percent of eligible voters cast ballots. Outside of the South (where blacks were increasingly prevented from voting and where the Democratic nomination determined the general election), the turnout sometimes reached 90 percent.

Party organization was geared to get out the vote. The parties were structured like pyramids with ward or precinct meetings at the base. At these all party members were allowed to attend. They generally elected representatives to county committees, which then sent members to the state committees that conducted the ongoing business of the party and nominated state candidates for office. At the top were the national committees. National conventions, where representation was based on the electoral votes of the states, met every four years to select na-

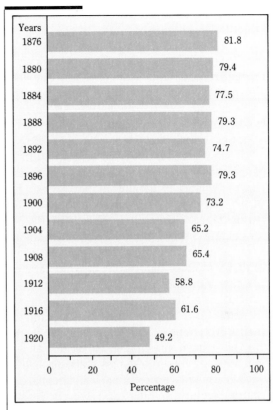

Figure 21.1
Voter participation in presidential elections, 1876–1920

tional candidates, draft platforms, and vote on party rules.

There was one main difference in Republican and Democratic party organization. Republicans generally depended on strong state organizations, and Democrats tended to rely on urban political machines to win and control votes. Since city governmental structures did not keep pace with the huge population increases, machines based on ward captains provided many of the services for which government would later be held responsible. The machine also helped immigrants and rural migrants to adjust to city life. One ward boss noted: "There's got to be in every ward somebody that any bloke can come to—no matter what he's done—and get help. Help, you understand, none of your law and justice, but help." The politicians were paid in votes from the people, bribes from legal and illegal businesses, and graft from contractors. The system worked so well that the Democrats usually carried the big cities.

For both parties recruiting and maintaining party voters was a game for professionals. In Pennsylvania, Republican workers compiled a list of 800,000 voters with notations as to their reliability as voters. Politics was also a rough and frequently corrupt game. Conkling warned, "Parties are not built by deportment, or by ladies' magazines, or gush." In 1888 when Benjamin Harrison proclaimed, "Providence has given us the victory," Republican party boss Matt Quay snorted, "Providence hadn't a damn thing to do with it." Quay then added that Harrison "would never know how close a number of men were impelled to approach the gates of the penitentiary to make him president." Electoral corruption was not limited to one party. In the same year a Mississippi Democrat admitted: "It is no secret that there has not been a full vote and a fair count in Mississippi since 1875, that we have been preserving the ascendancy of white people by revolutionary methods. In other words, we have been stuffing ballot boxes, committing perjury, and here and there in the state carrying the elections by fraud and violence."

Gilded Age politics was not dull. One could almost claim that the business of politics was entertainment. One observer remarked, "What the theatre is to the French, or the bull fight . . . to the Spanish . . . [election campaigns] and the ballot box are to *our* people." The drama of emotional tent meetings rivaled circuses. The pageantry of parades also provided excitement. Almost everyone got caught up in the elections, frequently displaying such paraphernalia as buttons, handkerchiefs, hats, banners, and posters emblazoned with their party's symbol or slogan. In 1888 one tobacco company enclosed pictures similar to baseball cards of the 25 presidential hopefuls in its packages. Politics was undoubtedly the prime form of mass entertainment.

Many politicians surely must have enjoyed their status as "media stars" and folk heroes. For some, whose ethnic or class backgrounds closed conventional doors of opportunity, politics provided a vehicle of upward social mobility, similar to professional entertainment and athletics or trade union leadership. Yet politics as a vocation offered other rewards. Elected and appointed officials not only received salaries but also openly accepted gifts from lobbyists and free passes from railroads. They sometimes used their governmental status to promote their private interests. James G. Blaine of Maine expressed no qualms about accepting stock concessions from an Arkansas railroad that he had aided in getting a federal land grant. One quip claimed that the United States had the best Congress money could buy.

The Struggle for Inclusion: Women and Politics

Politics could be a rough and dirty business—one that many considered an inappropriate activity for women. Increasingly women disagreed and sought inclusion. After an 1869 split in the suffrage movement, the National Woman Suffrage Association, (NWSA) led by Elizabeth Cady Stanton and Susan B. Anthony, fought for the vote on the national level through the courts and a proposed constitutional amendment. At the same time the American Woman Suffrage Association (AWSA) sought victories at the state level.

By 1890, when the groups merged to form the National American Woman Suffrage Association (NAWSA), the victories of both groups were limited. NWSA lost an 1874 Supreme

Gimmicks in Gilded Age political campaigns, such as this Bryan donkey, stirred public interest, resulting in the highest voter turnouts in the nation's history.

Court decision resulting from a suit filed by Virginia Minor against a St. Louis registrar for denying her the right to vote. The Court ruled that citizenship did not automatically confer the vote and that suffrage could be denied specific groups, such as criminals, the insane, and women. In 1878 Anthony did succeed in getting a constitutional amendment introduced into the Senate that stated that "the right to vote shall not be denied or abridged by the United States or by any state on account of sex." It continued to be submitted for the next 18 years but was usually killed in committee and only rarely reached the floor of the Senate.

There was more success on the state and local level. By 1890 19 states allowed women to vote on school issues, and 3 states extended women the franchise on tax and bond issues. Referenda were held in 11 states, but only the territory of Wyoming had granted women full political equality. Three states—Colorado, Utah, and Idaho—adopted women's suffrage during the 1890s, but then the movement seemed to lose steam. As male resistance mounted, no other state acted until 1910. Many men agreed with a Texas senator that "equal suffrage is a repudiation of manhood."

In 1869 Wyoming became the first territory to allow women to vote in all territorial elections. It later refused to enter the Union without women's suffrage.

STYLE OVER SUBSTANCE: GOVERNMENT IN THE GILDED AGE, 1877–1892

Politics provided great entertainment, but there were always people who wanted more. Often local political activity was considerably more vibrant than the political inertia at the national level. As discontent arose, many problems were first tackled on the city, county, and state levels before becoming a part of the national agenda. Such issues as the currency and tariffs could only be solved at the national level. Others such as demands for clean government were undertaken at all levels. On the whole, the states responded more vigorously than the national government to the problems created by economic changes—only to have the Supreme Court sometimes tie their hands. People began to look to Washington for solutions. The presidents and Congress responded timidly. National elections still focused mainly on trivial issues. When backed to the wall, Congress would enact laws to quiet popular cries for action, but such laws were often limited in scope and unenforceable. Style triumphed over substance, and most problems remained unsolved.

Hayes and the "Money Question"

After the disputed election of 1876 almost created a constitutional crisis, the presidency was snatched from Democrat Samuel J. Tilden and given to Rutherford B. Hayes. A series of bargains was needed for the acceptance of the 8 to 7 vote of the electoral commission that named Hayes president. Thus from the start, his administration was tainted with snide references to him as "His Fraudulence" and "Old 8 to 7." He was actually honest, competent, and did much to establish the Republican party as the "party of morality" after the corruption of the Grant regime. His wife also helped to link Republicans with morality by refusal to serve strong drinks—earning her the label of "Lemonade Lucy." One guest at a White House party remarked in disgust that "the water flowed like champagne."

Hayes is now probably best remembered for removing the remaining federal troops from the South—marking the end of Reconstruction. At the time, however, economics rather than race relations occupied the public's mind. Hayes came into office more than three years into an economic depression that began with the panic of 1873. That depression raised the "money question" and the currency issue would continue to crop up for more than two decades. The issue was as complex as it was heated.

At its root was a long period of deflation following the Civil War. The level of prices dropped because the production of goods was growing faster than the supply of money. More goods than the money with which to buy them reduced prices. Farmers are not necessarily hurt by a general deflation if all prices fall

equally and their debt level is low. Wheat, corn, and cotton prices, however, declined more than other prices in the late nineteenth century. Farmers had also borrowed heavily to expand production, and they were caught in a debt squeeze with their mortgage payments remaining high while the prices they received fell. For example, a farmer who borrowed $1000 to buy a farm in 1868 on a 25-year mortgage found that he had to produce over twice as much cotton to make the mortgage payment in 1888. Although he received virtually nothing for doubling his efforts, his creditor received not only interest for the use of his money but also an additional bonanza—dollars worth twice as much as the ones he lent.

Debtors of all occupations began blaming their problems on deflation and saw inflation of the currency as the cure. For them inflation was a moral issue—a question of justice. One way this could happen was to increase the number of legal tender paper "greenbacks" first issued during the war. Supporters of that solution or-

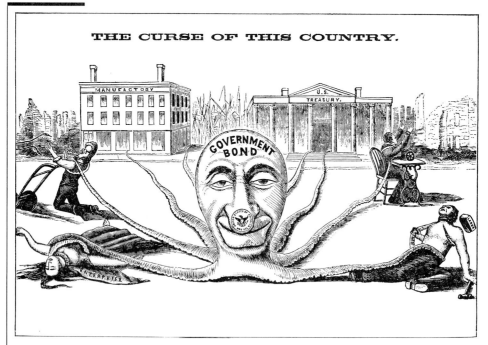

In this Greenback party cartoon from the 1870s, a gold-nosed government octopus puts a stranglehold on U.S. farmers, laborers, and small businesses. Greenbackers, who organized with the aim of distributing more money to more of the American people, opposed specie (gold) payments on bonds.

ganized the Greenback party in 1874. Instead, two years before Hayes entered the White House, Congress enacted the Resumption Act of 1875 to eliminate paper money not backed by gold or silver.

With the defeat of greenbackism, some inflationists turned their attention to silver. Before the issuance of greenbacks, the nation had been on a bimetallic standard since the 1790s. The dollar was based on both gold and silver, and for years dollars were coined at a 16 to 1 mint ratio. In other words a dollar contained 16 times as much silver as gold. By the 1870s this ratio did not reflect the market prices of the metals. Silver prices were so high that producers sold it on the open market rather than take it to the mint to be coined. Unable to buy silver at that ratio, Congress had passed the Coinage Act of 1873 that halted the minting of silver dollars.

Soon after, the discovery of large deposits of silver drove prices down. Then it was in the interest of both silver miners and inflationists to return to the coining of silver at 16 to 1. Together they formed a large lobby that wrested minor concessions from Congress. The Bland-Allison Act of 1878 required the government to buy between $2 and $4 million worth of silver each month. Like much of the legislation of the Gilded Age, the Bland-Allison Act proved to be a cosmetic answer to popular demands. It neither raised silver prices nor inflated the currency significantly. Thus inflationists remained unhappy, and the Greenback party nominated James B. Weaver in the 1880 election.

Garfield, Arthur, and the Patronage Issue

In the 1880 election neither of the two major parties focused on substantial issues but instead relied upon slogans and gimmicks to win votes. The battle for the Republican nomination was between the Half-Breed and Stalwart factions. Hayes had sought to set some standards for federal officeholders; his actions, however, mainly alienated fellow Republicans, and he refused to run for a second term in 1880. Stalwarts hoped to run Grant again, but the Republican convention became deadlocked. On the thirty-sixth ballot the party picked James A. Garfield, a veteran but relatively unknown Ohio congressman.

To conciliate the Stalwarts, Chester A. Arthur, a Conkling henchman, became the vice-presidential nominee.

The Democrats nominated an even more obscure figure, General Winfield Scott Hancock, whose only claim to fame was being a hero of the Battle of Gettysburg. He was described as "a good man weighing 250 pounds." Garfield was also bland, but he had the advantage of a log cabin birth and a brief career on a canal towpath—which gave rise to a popular Republican campaign slogan, "From the towpath to the White House." The 1880 election was one of the closest of the century in popular vote. Garfield received a mere 39,000 vote plurality out of almost 10 million ballots cast. Greenback nominee Weaver came in a distant third, gaining only 3.4 percent of the popular vote.

The currency question was overshadowed by the issue of patronage because of returning prosperity and a tragic event. Only four months after Garfield's inauguration he was shot twice by a deranged office seeker named Charles Guiteau, who explained, "I am a Stalwart. Arthur is now President of the United States." A native of Vermont, Arthur attended Union College, became an abolitionist lawyer, and then held a series of appointed offices. Considered by many to be a party hack, Arthur surprised them by becoming a champion of governmental reform.

The mugwumps and others had become increasingly concerned with corruption in government. In an 1873 novel that gave the era its label of the Gilded Age, Mark Twain and Charles Dudley Warner wrote, "The present era of indelible rottenness is not Democratic, it is not Republican, it is national. Politics are not going to cure more ulcers like these, nor the decaying body they fester upon." Because of the pervasiveness of the corruption, some saw no way out. "All being corrupt together," E. L. Godkin, editor of *The Nation*, wrote, "what is the use of investigating each other?"

Some reformers believed that one answer to the problem of corruption was reforming the "spoils system" of patronage. Since the early 1800s government jobs had been considered the "spoils" of political victory to be awarded to loyal party workers regardless of their qualifications. Problems grew between 1865 and 1891 as federal positions tripled, from 53,000 to

Charles Guiteau shoots President Garfield as Secretary of State Blaine looks on in horror. After suffering for two and a half months, the President died on September 19, 1881. Guiteau, whose behavior during his trial suggested insanity, was convicted on January 25, 1882, and hanged on June 30.

166,000. Indeed, presidents spent much of their time making some 100,000 appointments—most of which were in the postal service. That number of jobs provided incentives to precinct and ward bosses to get out the vote, but such inventions as the typewriter required government workers to have skills other than getting people to vote.

Hayes's actions to improve the quality of political appointees lost him his party's support, and not until after the revulsion at Garfield's assassination did Congress finally take action. With the support and encouragement of President Arthur, Congress enacted the Pendleton Act in 1883. It outlawed political contributions by appointed officeholders and established competitive examinations for federal positions to be given by the Civil Service Commission. The act was rather timid—only applying to about 10 percent of government employees. It was also not passed from purely unselfish motives. Since it was to apply only to future appointees and protect incumbents, the Democrats called it "a bill to perpetuate in office the

Republicans who now control the patronage of the Government." In the same manner, every president after its enactment increased the number of positions protected from political removal—usually to prevent his appointees from being removed. The political system was becoming modernized, but some questioned whether it was being improved.

Cleveland, the Railroads, and Tariffs

When 1884 brought the next presidential election, Arthur's actions had won him more favor from the public than from his party. The Republicans bypassed him and nominated James G. Blaine, who was far from bland. He was so handsome and charismatic that a colleague's wife once remarked, "Had he been a woman, people would have rushed off to send expensive flowers." Indeed, Blaine had almost all the qualities of a successful presidential candidate: a phenomenal memory for names and faces, eloquent oratory, and a quick wit. He was, however, a tainted political commodity. While in

Congress he had become very rich without any visible means of outside income. Copies of letters circulated that seemed to indicate Blaine was up for sale to the railroads. He was more than the mugwumps could stomach and they could not support him.

Realizing the potential advantage of a mugwump defection, the Democrats selected Grover Cleveland, a reform governor of New York. He was neither physically attractive nor charismatic. He did have one appealing quality, however. He was honest. As one supporter explained, "We love him for the enemies he has made." Yet Cleveland and Blaine did not disagree on the major issues. Therefore, their campaign revolved around personalities and became one of the most scurrilous in the nation's history.

Blaine's tainted past was obvious fodder for the Democrats' campaign. At torchlit rallies Democrats chanted: "Blaine! Blaine! James G. Blaine! Continental liar from the state of Maine!" Unable to find a shred of evidence to challenge Cleveland's honesty, Republicans publicized a more personal scandal. As a bachelor, Cleveland had supported an illegitimate child since 1874, even though his paternity was questionable. Thus Republicans countered Democratic chants with "Ma! Ma! Where's my pa? Going to the White House? Ha! Ha! Ha!" In the end Cleveland's victory may have come as the result of an indiscretion by a Blaine supporter who labeled the Democrats as the party of "rum, Romanism, and rebellion." Even though Blaine's mother was Catholic, Democrats were able to rally Catholic voters to win key states.

The major legislation of Cleveland's first presidency came as the result of public pressure and actions of the courts. The power and discriminatory rates of the railroads scared and angered many Americans, and actions to regulate the railroads had started at the state level. Beginning with the establishment of a regulatory commission in Massachusetts in 1869, 14 states had railroad commissions by 1880. The most active advocate of regulation was the Patrons of Husbandry—a farmers' group organized into local chapters called "granges." The Grangers and their allies, especially in the Midwest, got stronger legislation enacted that set maximum rates and charges within their states.

The railroad men naturally attacked these so-called Granger laws through the courts. At first they lost. In the 1877 *Munn* v. *Illinois* decision, the Supreme Court ruled that when "private property is affected with a public interest it . . . must submit to be controlled by the public for the common good." Nevertheless, it was difficult for states to regulate railroads chartered by other states and doing business across state lines. Then in the 1886 *Wabash, St. Louis & Pacific Railway Company* v. *Illinois* case the Supreme Court took away their rights to even try by ruling that only Congress had the right to regulate interstate commerce.

Pressure began to build for federal action, and Congress responded to the demands with the Interstate Commerce Act, which Grover Cleveland signed in February 1887. It prohibited pools, rebates, and rate discriminations; provided that all charges by the railroads should be "reasonable and just"; and established the Interstate Commerce Commission (ICC). The commission was significant as the first federal regulatory agency, but its power was woefully limited. It could investigate charges against the railroads and issue "cease and desist" orders, which could only be enforced by the courts.

In this cartoon, Grover Cleveland's illegitimate child is used to impugn "Grover the Good's" well-known political integrity.

Public anger over railroad power finally pushed Congress to pass the Interstate Commerce Act in 1887.

Conservative courts soon nullified 90 percent of the commission's orders, and between 1887 and 1905 the Supreme Court decided against the ICC in 15 of 16 cases. By 1892 railroad attorney Richard S. Olney wrote, "The Commission, as its functions have now been limited by the Courts, is, or can be made of great use to the railroads. It satisfies the popular clamor for a government supervision of railroads, at the same time that such supervision is almost entirely nominal . . . It thus becomes a sort of protection against hasty and crude legislation hostile to railroad interests. . . . The part of wisdom is not to destroy the Commission but to utilize it." One railroad executive admitted, "There is not a road in the country that can be accused of living up to the rules of the Interstate Commerce Commission."

The Interstate Commerce Act temporarily satisfied "popular clamor" without alienating railroad owners. It therefore did not become a partisan issue for either party. However, during Cleveland's term, a major issue on which

Democrats and Republicans actually differed emerged: the tariff. Both parties supported these taxes on imports in order to raise revenue and to protect American products from being undersold by foreign competitors. The question was merely how high these tariffs should be. Regardless of party, congressmen voted their constituents' interests, which made few of them consistent on the issue. "I am a protectionist for every interest which I am sent here by my constituents to protect," one Democratic senator explained. Supporters of protectionism were those who sold on the domestic markets; opponents depended on foreign markets. Both groups included some farmers and manufacturers from every region.

Like most Democrats, Cleveland had long been less enthusiastic about high tariffs than Republicans. While in office he found that existing tariff rates were producing treasury surpluses that tempted congressmen to propose programs and appropriations which he considered dangerous expansions of federal activities. A moralistic man, Cleveland was deeply opposed to governmental involvement in the economy and social issues. Thus he became an advocate of tariff reduction. In 1887 at his urging, the Democratic House enacted moderate reductions, but the Republican Senate blocked the bill. Cleveland then proceeded to make the tariff a focus of his reelection bid in 1888.

Harrison and Big Business

In 1888 the Democrats renominated Cleveland and wrote tariff reduction into their platform. The Republicans chose Benjamin Harrison and cheerfully picked up the gauntlet—denouncing Cleveland's "free trade" as unpatriotic. They also promised generous pensions to veterans. Voters at last were given some choice on a real issue. The result was a viciously corrupt and close election. Harrison's campaign chairman, Matt Quay, proceeded to "put the manufacturers of Pennsylvania under the fire and fry all the fat out of them." He asked them to make large contributions to the Republican party as insurance premiums against lowered tariff rates. When Cleveland lost, many blamed his defeat on taking too clear a stand on an issue. Republicans erroneously interpreted his narrow defeat as a mandate for protectionism. Congress then enacted the McKinley Tariff, which raised the average duties to the highest level yet. The Republicans misread public sentiment; the McKinley Tariff was very unpopular.

Both high tariffs and trusts were becoming distasteful to many Americans. Popular demand for legislative action against trusts had been growing during the 1880s. Again action started on the state level; 15 southern and western states had passed antitrust legislation by the mid-1880s. Of course, companies simply incorporated in more sympathetic states. The laws were both ineffective and likely to be overturned by federal courts, but they did reflect popular distaste for the monopolies. Congress responded to these rumblings by enacting the Sherman Antitrust Act in 1890. On the surface it seemed to doom the trusts, prohibiting any "contract, combination in the form of trust or otherwise, or conspiracy in restraint of trade or commerce." As with the Interstate Commerce Act appearances were deceiving, but not to all the congressmen who passed it. One senator explained that the congressmen had wanted to pass "some bill headed 'A bill to Punish Trusts' with which to go to the country" to aid their reelection.

Until 1901 the act was virtually unenforced; the Justice Department instituted only 14 suits and failed to get convictions in most of them. The Supreme Court also emasculated the law in *United States* v. *E. C. Knight Co.* (1895), ruling that it applied to commerce but not manufacturing. Thus the subject of the suit, a sugar trust controlling 98 percent of the industry, was not in violation. Indeed, the only effective use made of the act in its first decade was as a tool to break up labor strikes by court injunctions.

The Sherman Antitrust Act of 1890 was designed to quiet "public clamor." In that same year popular pressure led to further action on the currency question. Following the Bland-Allison Act of 1878, the money supply continued to grow too slowly for the expanding economy. By 1890 pressure to coin more silver was growing, and Congress responded with the Sherman Silver Purchase Act. It required the government to buy 4.5 million ounces of silver

each month at the unrealistic ratio of 16 to 1. Paper money to pay for the purchases was redeemable in gold or silver, keeping the inflationary impact minimal. The act was a compromise that satisfied no one; the silver issue grew more heated in the 1890s.

During Harrison's presidency Congress was more active than previously—passing the McKinley Tariff, the Sherman Antitrust Act, the Sherman Silver Purchase Act, and the first billion dollar budget. At the same time the Republican party was becoming alienated from its abolitionist past and more closely tied to big business.

Legislative Activity on Minority Rights and Social Issues

To African-Americans the Republicans remained the party of black rights, but following the election of 1876 the party did less and less to earn that label. By 1890, however, conditions finally moved some Republicans to action. Dismayed by increasing southern assaults on the black vote, Senator Henry Cabot Lodge and others drafted a federal elections bill. The Lodge Bill sought to protect voter registration and guarantee fair congressional elections by establishing mechanisms to investigate charges of voting fraud and to deal with disputed elections.

Southern white response was rapid and bitter. The *Florida Times-Union* charged: "The gleam of federal bayonets will again be seen in the South." The *Mobile Register* warned that the bill "would deluge the South in blood." Northern Democrats lent their support to southern outrage. Cleveland exclaimed, "It is a dark blow at the freedom of the ballot." Although in 1890 Republicans controlled both houses of Congress, they finally bartered away the Lodge Election Bill to gain support for the McKinley Tariff. Protection of manufacturers was more important to them than the protection of African-Americans.

In that same year Republicans also let the Blair Education Bill die. It would have provided federal aid to schools, mostly black, that did not get a fair share of local and state funds. The Blair Bill marked the last glimpse of the party's dying abolitionist roots as well as the dethronement of party idealism. The Fifty-first Congress was seeking to alleviate treasury surpluses to protect tariffs, but in the end the only group to receive substantial aid was Union Army veterans, who were voted pensions by the so-called Billion Dollar Congress in 1890.

Other measures of the era affected minorities—but usually in a negative way. Southern white Democrats enacted discriminatory legislation against blacks at the local and state level. A movement for immigration restriction, usually initiated by Republicans, led to the Chinese Exclusion Act of 1882 and other legislation banning certain categories of immigrants and giving the federal government control of overseas immigration. In 1887 the Dawes Act attacked the tribal roots of American Indian culture by trying to make Native Americans homesteading farmers, and resulted unintentionally in making them dependent wards of the state.

Although most social issues received short shrift at the federal level, at the local and state level some received passionate attention. The two main ones—education and prohibition— were essentially Republican issues. An Iowa Republican slogan called for "a school house on every hill, and no saloon in the valley." Many were alarmed by the increased use of alcohol— annual consumption of beer rose from 1.6 to 6.9 gallons per capita from 1850 to 1880. Republicans moved beyond the educative temperance movement to attempt to make drinking alcohol a crime. They also sought to increase compulsory school attendance, but their efforts were often linked to moves to undermine parochial schools and schools that taught immigrants in their native tongues. In most areas these Republican actions backfired, losing more voters than they gained. For example, Republicans had once predicted "Iowa will go Democratic when Hell goes Methodist," but in 1890 the state fell to their opponents.

By 1890 very little effective legislation had been adopted to deal with the problems arising from a pluralistic society experiencing rapid social and economic change. This resulted partly from a political equilibrium that bred inertia. At the same time concepts of the limited nature of governmental responsibility did not provide impetus for action. Nevertheless, public demands for change were growing. No group challenged the status quo more than the farmers.

THE FARMERS REVOLT

Cries for change naturally came from the losers in the new economic order. Among the greatest losers were American farmers. Their failure to thrive in the expanding economy convinced many that the cards had been stacked against them. After seeking various solutions to their problems, farmers turned to politics—taking up Populist leader Mary E. Lease's cry "to raise less corn and more hell." Their success was limited, but they led the first American mass movement to reject Social Darwinism and laissez-faire. They also promoted the "radical" idea that "it is the duty of government to protect the weak, because the strong are able to protect themselves." Some even questioned basic tenets of industrial capitalism.

Grievances: Real and Imagined

In 1887 North Carolina editor Leonidas L. Polk summed up the views of many farmers: "There is something radically wrong in our industrial system. There is a screw loose. . . . The railroads have never been so prosperous, and yet agriculture languishes. The banks have never done a better . . . business, and yet agriculture languishes. Manufacturing enterprises never made more money, . . . and yet agriculture languishes. Towns and cities flourish and 'boom,' . . . and yet agriculture languishes."

The basic cause of the farmers' problems was the decline of agricultural prices—primarily because of overproduction. Farmers had a hard time believing, however, that they could produce too much. Kansas governor Lorenzo Dow Lewelling wondered how "there were hungry people . . . because there was too much bread" and "so many . . . poorly clad . . . because there was too much cloth."

Overproduction was an abstract, invisible enemy; many farmers sought more tangible, personal villains—the railroads, bankers, and monopolists. As "Sockless" Jerry Simpson claimed, "It is a struggle between the robbers

Midwest (1971); Morton Keller, *Affairs of State: Public Life in Nineteenth Century America* (1977); Paul Kleppner, *The Cross of Culture: A Social Analysis of Midwestern Politics, 1850–1900* (1970), and *The Third Electoral System, 1853–1892* (1979); Michael E. McGerr, *The Decline of Popular Politics: The American North, 1865–1928* (1986); Robert D. Marcus, *GOP: Political Structure in the Gilded Age, 1880–1896* (1971); Horace S. Merrill, *Bourbon Democracy in the Middle West, 1865–1896* (1953); H. Wayne Morgan, *From Hayes to McKinley* (1969); David J. Rothman, *Politics and Power: The United States Senate, 1869–1901* (1966); Leonard D. White, *The Republican Era, 1869–1901* (1958); R. Hal Williams, *Years of Decision: American Politics in the 1890s* (1978).

STYLE OVER SUBSTANCE: GOVERNMENT IN THE GILDED AGE, 1877–1892

Mary R. Dearing, *Veterans in Politics* (1952); Vincent P. DeSantis, *Republicans Face the Southern Question, 1877–1897* (1959); Justus D. Doenecke, *The Presidencies of James A. Garfield & Chester A. Arthur* (1981); Eleanor Flexner, *Century of Struggle: The Women's Rights Movement in the United States,* rev. ed. (1975); Margaret Forster, *Significant Sisters: The Grassroots of Active Feminism, 1839–1939* (1984); Lewis L. Gould, *The Presidency of William McKinley* (1980); Stanley P. Hirshson, *Farewell to the Bloody Shirt: Northern Republicans and the Southern Negro* (1962); Ari A. Hoogenboom, *Outlawing the Spoils: The Civil Service Reform Movement* (1961); Aileen Kraditor, *The Ideas of the Woman's Suffrage Movement, 1890–1920* (1965); Gerald W. McFarland, *Mugwumps, Morals, and Politics 1884–1920* (1975); Michael McGerr, *The Decline of Popular Politics* (1986); Walter T. K. Nugent, *Money and American Society* (1968); Arnold M. Paul, *Conservative Crisis and the Rule of Law: Attitudes of Bar and Bench, 1887–1895* (1969); John G. Sproat, *The Best Men: Liberal Reformers in the Gilded Age* (1968); Tom E. Terrill, *The Tariff, Politics, and American Foreign Policy, 1874–1901* (1973); Allen Weinstein, *Prelude to Populism: Origins of the Silver Issue, 1867–1878* (1970).

THE FARMERS REVOLT

Peter H. Argersinger, *Populism and Politics: William Alfred Peffer and the People's Party* (1974); Allan G. Bogue, *Money at Interest: The Farm Mortgage on the Middle Border* (1955); Paul W. Glad, *McKinley, Bryan, and the People* (1964); Lawrence Goodwyn, *Democratic Promise: The Populist Moment in America* (1976); Sheldon Hackney, *Populism to Progressivism in Alabama* (1969); Steven Hahn, *The Roots of Southern Populism* (1983); John D. Hicks, *The Populist Revolt* (1931); Richard Hofstadter, *The Age of Reform* (1955); Robert McMath, Jr., *Populist Vanguard: A History of the Southern Farmers' Alliance* (1975); Walter T. K. Nugent, *The Tolerant Populists* (1963); Bruce Palmer, *Man over Money: The Southern Populist Critique of American Capitalism* (1980); Norman Pollack, ed., *The Populist Mind* (1967), and *The Populist Response to Industrial America* (1962); Barton C. Shaw, *The Wool-Boys: Georgia's Populist Party* (1984).

DEPRESSION AND TURBULENCE IN THE 1890s

John P. Diggins, *The American Left in the Twentieth Century* (1973); Robert F. Durden, *The Climax of Populism: The Election of 1896* (1965); Charles Hoffmann, *The Depression of the Nineties: An Economic History* (1970); Stanley L. Jones, *The Presidential Election of 1896* (1964); J. Morgan Kousser, *The Shaping of Southern Politics: Suffrage Restriction and Establishment of the One-Party South, 1880–1910* (1974); Paul Krause, *The Battle for Homestead, 1880–1892* (1992); Charles Lofgren, *The Plessy Case: A Legal-Historical Interpretation* (1987); Donald L. McMurry, *Coxey's Army* (1929); Samuel T. McSeveney, *The Politics of Depression* (1972); Howard N. Rabinowitz, *Race Relations in the Urban South, 1865–1890* (1978); C. Vann Woodward, *The Strange Career of Jim Crow,* rev. ed. (1974).

BIOGRAPHIES

Paolo Coletta, *William Jennings Bryan: Political Evangelist* (1964); Ray Ginger, *Bending Cross: A Biography of Eugene Victor Debs* (1949); Paul W. Glad, *The Trumpet Soundeth: William Jennings Bryan and His Democracy* (1960); Louis Koenig, *Bryan* (1971); Allan Nevins, *Grover Cleveland: A Study in Courage* (1932); Allan Peskin, *Garfield* (1978); Thomas Reeves, *Gentlemen Boss: The Life of Chester Alan Arthur* (1975); Martin Ridge, *Ignatius Donnelly* (1962); Nick Salvatore, *Eugene V. Debs: Citizen and Socialist* (1982); Charles Morrow Wilson, *The Commoner: William Jennings Bryan* (1970); C. Vann Woodard, *Tom Watson: Agrarian Rebel* (1938).

Fig. 16

THE FIRST DIVISION
—OF THE—
SAINT PAUL & PACIFIC RAILROAD.
—
WINTER TIME TABLE.
—
Taking effect Sunday, November the 16th, 1873.

Miles from St. Paul	MAIN LINE.			Miles from St. Paul	BRANCH LINE.		
	STATIONS.	Going West.	Going East.		STATIONS.	Going North.	Going South.
0	ST. PAUL	Le. 8.35 a m	Ar. 8.00 p m	0	ST. PAUL	Le. 7.30 a m	Ar. 1.30 p m

CHAPTER 22

The Progressive Struggle

*T*imes had changed by 1902 when George F. Baer declared "anthracite mining is business and not a religious, sentimental or academic proposition." Those tough-minded words might have won public approval at an earlier time, but many believed that Baer, spokesperson for mine owners in Pennsylvania, was merely pig-headed. His words were in response to a request by John Mitchell of the United Mine Workers (UMW) for arbitration of a labor dispute. There was an unusual amount of support for the coal miners' position. Exposés had increased popular awareness of miserable working conditions, and the union's demands seemed reasonable: a 9-hour day, recognition of the union, a 10 to 20 percent increase in wages, and a fair weighing of the coal mined. Mitchell repeatedly stated the miners' willingness to accept arbitration, both before and after 50,000 miners walked out of the pits in May 1902.

Skillfully led, the coal miners stood firm month after month. By September, coal reserves were running short and prices were rising. With winter approaching, empty coal bins began multiplying, even in schools and hospitals. Baer remained stubborn. "The rights and interests of the laboring man," he declared, "will be protected and cared for—not by the labor agitators, but by the Christian men to whom God in his infinite wisdom has given the control of property interests in this country." This proclamation of the Gospel of Wealth fell on deaf ears. Newspaper after newspaper expressed disgust with the mine owners, and some tentatively suggested government ownership of the mines.

On October 3, President Theodore Roosevelt, temporarily in a wheelchair as a result of an accident, presided over a conference in the White House. Attending were Mitchell, Baer, Attorney General Philander C. Knox, and other labor leaders and mine operators. Baer was not in a mood to be cooperative. "We object to being called here to meet a criminal," he told a reporter, "even by the President of the United States." Refusing to speak directly to Mitchell, Baer urged Roosevelt to prosecute UMW leaders under the Sherman Antitrust Act and to use federal troops to break the strike, just as Cleveland had done in the 1894 Pullman strike. While Mitchell "behaved like a gentleman" according to Roosevelt, Baer was obstinate, concluding one diatribe against unions by calling "free government . . . a contemptible failure if it can only protect the lives and property and secure comfort of the people by compromise with violators of law and instigators of violence and crime."

Irritated with Baer, Roosevelt declared, "If it wasn't for the high office I hold I would have taken him by the seat of the breeches and the nape of the neck and chucked him out of that window." When the owners returned to Pennsylvania, they took actions that indicated they might use force to break the strike. Roosevelt's response was to begin preparations to send 10,000 federal troops to take over and operate the mines. This action jolted opponents of state socialism, who induced banker J. P. Morgan to get involved. Serving as a broker, Morgan was able to patch together a compromise under which the miners returned to work and Roosevelt appointed a commission to arbitrate the dispute.

The commission and its findings illustrate a number of aspects of the turn-of-the-century reforms labeled "progressivism." Originally, the commission was to consist of an army engineer, a mining engineer, a businessperson "familiar with the coal industry," a federal judge, and an "eminent sociologist"—reflecting a progressive tendency to call upon "experts" to conduct public affairs. Its composition was also decidedly probusiness, and even the addition of two other members and the appointment of a labor leader as the "eminent sociologist" did not redress this imbalance. As a result, its findings were essentially conservative: a 10 percent wage increase and reduction of working hours to 8 a day for a handful of miners and to 9 for most. The union did not receive recognition, and the traditional manner of weighing coal was continued. The commission also suggested a 10 percent increase in the price of coal. Business influence on other progressive responses to social problems generally produced similar moderate solutions that frequently brought industrialists as many benefits as losses.

Nevertheless, Roosevelt's actions did add some new rules to the game. For the first time, a president did not give kneejerk support to business. Government became not merely a

President Roosevelt, surrounded here by coal miners after their 1902 strike, set a precedent by threatening the use of force against management rather than labor.

champion of the status quo, but also an arbiter of change. This retreat from laissez-faire was motivated by the demands of the middle class and workers. By 1902 many middle-class citizens had rejected the heavy-handed tactics of management, which often ended in chaos and conflict. They sought a more orderly, stable, and just society through government intervention. Workers also began to flex their political muscles, electing sympathetic mayors in a number of cities. Like the coal miners, Americans of all classes were learning the limits of individualism and joining together in organizations to accomplish their goals. National leaders such as Roosevelt began to recognize the need for change in order to preserve stable government and the capitalistic system. Roosevelt justified his actions in 1902 to save "big propertied men . . . from the dreadful punishment which their folly would have brought upon them." He stood, he declared, "between them and socialistic action." For a variety of motives, a plethora of legislation was enacted—sometimes with unintended results.

THE PROGRESSIVE IMPULSE

Americans exalted progress as a basic characteristic of their nation's distinctiveness. Technology was reshaping the human environment in dramatic ways. The pace of change was dizzying. Then in the late 1890s, people seemed to stop, catch their breath, and look around at their brave, new world. Much filled them with pride, but some of what they saw seemed outmoded or disruptive. Problems, however, appeared eminently solvable. Modern minds were explaining and harnessing natural forces. Could they not also understand and control human behavior? Could they not eliminate conflict and bring harmony to competing interests through some simple adjustments in the system? Americans increasingly answered "Yes" and called themselves "progressives." Many agreed with Thomas Edison's observation, "We've stumbled along for awhile, trying to run a new civilization in old ways, but we've got to start to make this world over."

America in 1901

The twentieth century opened with a rerun of the 1896 election between William Jennings Bryan and William McKinley. Although the outcome was the same, much was different. "I have never known a Presidential campaign so quiet," Senator Henry Cabot Lodge noted. By 1900 the crises of the 1890s had largely passed. Prosperity had returned and was shared by many. The nation also reveled in its new-found international power following the Spanish-American War. The social fabric seemed to be on the mend, but memories of the depression still haunted Americans, and society's blemishes appeared more and more intolerable to many.

As the nation reached adulthood, a number of ugly moles and warts had indeed erupted. Unequal distribution of wealth and income persisted. One percent of American families possessed nearly seven-eighths of its wealth. Four-fifths of Americans lived on a subsistence level, while a handful lived in incredible opulence. In

Breaker boys employed by the mines worked in dirty, dismal, and dangerous surroundings that robbed them of their childhood.

1900, Andrew Carnegie's income was $23 million; the average working man earned $500. The wealth of a few was increased by the exploitation of women and children. One out of five women worked to earn money for food, rather than for personal fulfillment, earning wages as low as $6 a week. The sacrifice of the country's young to the god of economic growth was alarming. One reporter undertook to do a child's job in the mines for one day and wrote, "I tried to pick out the pieces of slate from the hurrying stream of coal, often missing them; my hands were bruised and cut within a few minutes; I was covered from head to foot with coal dust, and for many hours afterwards I was expectorating some of the small particles of anthracite I had swallowed."

Working conditions were equally horrifying in other industries, and for many Americans housing conditions were as bad or worse. One investigator described a Chicago neighborhood, remarking on the "filthy and rotten tenements, the dingy courts and tumble down sheds, the foul stables and dilapidated outhouses, the broken sewer pipes, the piles of garbage fairly alive with diseased odors." At the same time the Vanderbilts summered in a "cottage" of 70 rooms, and wealthy men partied in shirts with diamond buttons worth thousands of dollars.

The middle class experienced neither extreme. Its members did have their economic grievances, however. Prosperity increased the cost of living by 35 percent in less than a decade, while many middle-class incomes remained fairly stable. Such people were not poor, but they believed they were not getting a fair share of the prosperity. Many came to blame the monopolies and watched with alarm as trusts, proving to be immune from the Sherman Act, proliferated rapidly. Nearly three-fourths of all trusts in 1904 had been created since 1898. Decreasing competition seemed to threaten America's status as the land of opportunity.

People came to believe that they had to find political solutions to the nation's problems. To achieve that goal they had to wrestle government from the hands of a few and return it to the "people." The great democratic experiment seemed to have run afoul. Wealthy industrialists bought state and federal legislators; urban political machines paid for votes with money from bribes; southern elections had become both bloody and corrupt.

Most problems were not new in 1901; neither were the proposed solutions. What came to be called progressivism was rooted in the Gilded Age. Whereas reform had been a sideshow earlier, it now became a national preoccupation. Progressivism was more broadly based and enjoyed greater appeal than any previous reform movement. The entire nation had experienced war or depression, never reform. One reason it did so was the diversity and pervasiveness of the voices calling for change.

Voices for Change

By 1900, Americans had done nothing less than reinterpret their understanding of their world. Under the old, classical interpretation, the universe was governed by absolute and unchangeable law. There was divine logic to all and truth was universal—the same at all times and in all places. Humanity's chore was to discover these truths, not to devise new ones. Under this vision, public policy should be aligned with natural laws; to attempt to change the course of those laws through man-made law was to court disaster. Such logic justified the concentration of wealth as well as the lack of governmental regulation of business and assistance to the poor and weak.

Social Darwinism, laissez-faire economics, and the Gospel of Wealth never enjoyed total acceptance. Throughout the Gilded Age, challenges and alternative visions had chipped away at their bases of support. The earlier challengers offered rather radical or simplistic alternatives. In 1879 Henry George wrote *Progress and Poverty*. As the title implies, he early recognized the unequal distribution of the fruits of economic growth. His solution was a "single tax" on what he called the "unearned increment" of land values. He wanted to tax those who benefited from land speculation and rising property values without producing anything. In essence he attacked the premise of capitalism that one could use money to make more money without providing other goods or services. In *Looking Backward* (1888) Edward Bellamy provided a

glimpse of a utopian society based upon a state-controlled economy propelled by cooperation rather than competition. The writings of such people profoundly influenced the Populists, the Socialists, and many who called themselves progressive.

Although critics dismissed the likes of George as crackpots, some respectable voices arose from the arts and literature, academia, the legal world, organized religion, and journalism. Realist writers described the world as it was, not as it should be. Instead of romantic heroes battling for abstract ideals, their characters were ordinary people dealing with concrete problems. The naturalists portrayed the powerlessness of the individual against the uncaring forces of urbanization and industrialization. Artists of the "ashcan" school painted urban scenes teeming with problems as well as life. Thus art and literature became mirrors of social concerns (see Chapter 19).

A revolution was also taking place in the academic world. Two of the most important changes were the democratization of higher education and the revolt against formalism. From 1870 to 1910 the number of colleges and universities nearly doubled, and their enrollment grew from 52,000 in 1870 to 600,000 in 1920. Higher education became less elitist, white, religious, and male, as women came to account for 47.3 percent of students in 1920 and black enrollment grew to over 20,000. Their professors became increasingly middle class as well. Such students and teachers had less interest in supporting the status quo.

Also undermining the status quo was the revolt against formalism. Previous academics had sought to explain the world by formulating abstract, universal theories. The new scholars, especially in the emerging social sciences, turned this approach on its head. They began instead by collecting concrete data. In field after field that data did not support the so-called natural laws propounded by their predecessors. Knowledge, philosopher and educator John Dewey proclaimed, was "no longer an immobile solid; it has been liquefied."

Theories had prescribed limits to human action; facts became weapons for change. Classical economists asserted that self-interested

These women in a physics class illustrate the growing presence of women in college during the Progressive Era.

economic decisions by individuals in a freely competitive economy provided natural regulation of markets through the laws of supply and demand. The new economists, calling themselves "institutional economists," conducted field research to learn how the economy actually worked. Their findings challenged the laissez-faire doctrines of the classicists on two levels: that free competition existed and that human decisions were based on purely economic motivations. To continue policies based on competition was absurd in an economy dominated by monopolies. In *Theory of the Leisure Class* (1899) and *The Instinct of Workmanship* (1914), economist Thorstein Veblen demonstrated the power of noneconomic motives. For example, vanity prompted the newly rich to indulge in "conspicuous consumption" well beyond their economic needs. For many economists "natural laws" were, in the words of Richard T. Ely, "used as a tool in the hands of the greedy."

A group of sociologists called themselves "Reform Darwinists" and rejected Spencer's Social Darwinism as another tool of exploitation. They accepted evolutionary principles and the influence of environment but denied that people were merely pawns manipulated by natural forces. Human intelligence was an active factor that could control and change the environment, especially when people worked together. A leading Reform Darwinist, Lester Frank Ward, thus proclaimed, "The individual has reigned long enough. The day has come for society to take its affairs into its own hands and shape its own destinies."

Ward's call for "rational planning" and "social engineering" in his *Dynamic Sociology* (1883) was echoed by Frederick W. Taylor, an efficiency advisor to management. His time and motion studies led to lowered production costs, and he asserted, "The fundamental principles of scientific management are applicable to all kinds of human activities." The goal of most such social scientists was a more orderly society, as was expressed by Walter Lippmann, who called on society "to introduce plan where there has been clash, and purpose into the jungles of disordered growth."

Legal scholars joined the assault on formalism in both books and court decisions. During the Gilded Age, courts had read laissez-faire principles into their interpretation of the Constitution. Decisions striking down regulatory and reform legislation invoked such abstract principles as the sanctity of property rights and contracts. In theory all such rights were equal before the law; reality was a different matter. For example, in *Lochner* v. *New York* (1905) the Supreme Court struck down a New York law limiting bakers' working hours. The law, the Court ruled, violated the bakers' rights to bargain freely and to make contracts. Most workers, however, had no real power to bargain and maintaining that myth merely increased management's already overwhelming advantage.

A new breed of jurist, many of whom were disciples of Dean Roscoe Pound of the Harvard Law School, challenged laissez-faire justice. Pound advocated "sociological jurisprudence," calling for "the adjustment of principles and doctrines to the human conditions they are to govern rather than assumed first principles." Supreme Court Justice Oliver Wendell Holmes, Jr., agreed. He rejected the idea that laws had ever been the logical result of pure, universal principles. "The life of the law has not been logic;" he wrote, "it has been experience." Laws had been and should be based on "the felt necessities of the time." Lawyer Louis D. Brandeis successfully argued these ideas in 1908. That year the Supreme Court upheld a ten-hour law for women working in Oregon laundries in *Muller* v. *Oregon*, primarily because of social research documenting the damage done to women's health by long hours.

As Americans began to reject absolute truths and universal principles, the question remained of how to determine right from wrong and good from bad. The answer came from philosopher William James with his doctrine of pragmatism. Ideas, he argued, were to be judged by their results. An idea that produced a socially desirable end was right and good. Philosophical thought was useless unless it was directed at solving problems. Pragmatism was a distinctly American philosophy and found many adherents. One of them, John Dewey, applied its principles to education. Earlier schools that stressed rote memorization of a static body of facts, he believed, were unable to meet the needs of individuals in a dynamic, changing environment. Instead, education should be based on experience and directed toward personal growth. In schools modeled after Dewey's Lab-

oratory School at the University of Chicago, students engaged in activities that taught problem solving by doing rather than reading.

The literary and intellectual currents of the era helped to set the stage for reform by combining optimism, idealism, and a tough-minded practicality. Yet the educated elite were probably reflecting rather than shaping public opinion. Priests and preachers influenced far more people than professors. The impact of organized religion on progressivism was profound. It was no coincidence that Teddy Roosevelt's supporters marched around the hall singing "Onward Christian Soldiers" at their 1912 convention.

The confrontation between the church and the city produced the Social Gospel movement. The impact of environment was brought home to urban clergymen who saw bodies ravaged before souls could be saved. As a young Baptist minister in the dismal New York neighborhood "Hell's Kitchen," Walter Raushenbusch described the poor coming to his church for aid. "They wore down our threshold, and they wore away our hearts . . . one could hear human virtue cracking and crunching all around."

For Raushenbusch and many others like him, there was no conflict between science and religion. "Translate the evolutionary theses into religious faith," he declared, "and you have the doctrine of the Kingdom of God." Following the lead of William Graham Taylor at the Chicago Theological Seminary, theology schools added courses in Christian sociology to teach "the application of our common Christianity to . . . social conditions." The Social Gospelers used the tools of scientific inquiry to root out and solve human problems in order to usher in the "Kingdom of God on Earth." Many settlement house workers, such as Jane Addams, sought to put their faith into action for "the joy of finding the Christ that lieth in man, but which no man

In 1889 Jane Addams founded Hull House, a social settlement in Chicago. A "Social Gospeler," Addams turned to Christian ideals to solve social problems.

can unfold save in fellowship." The Social Gospelers advocated a kind of sacred humanism.

Progressivism was dominated by, but not limited to, Protestantism. The 1891 encyclical, *Rerum Novarum*, by Pope Leo XIII inspired such Catholic priests as Father John A. Ryan to declare "a small number of very rich men have been able to lay upon the masses of people a yoke little better than slavery itself" and "no practical solution of this question will ever be found without the assistance of the church." Such Catholics as Alfred E. Smith and Robert F. Wagner became prominent progressive politicians. Others such as Jewish lawyer Louis Brandeis illustrated that the reform sentiment was not exclusively Christian either.

The Muckrakers

A final spark that ignited public interest in reform was popular journalism. The expansion of education and cities provided a mass audience for low-priced magazines. Such journals as *Collier's* and *McClure's* sold for only 10 cents and could only succeed if large numbers of people bought them. Their editors quickly rediscovered people's fascination with evil and launched series of exposés. Investigative reporters peeked beneath all sorts of rocks and brought to light corruption in almost every facet of society. Their vivid, indignant accounts sold magazines, but appalled some of the elite such as Teddy Roosevelt, who compared the writers to the character in John Bunyan's *The Pilgrim's Progress*, who was too engrossed in raking muck to look up and accept a celestial crown. Thus these chroniclers came to be called muckrakers.

Most of the exposés came out serially in magazines. Others were published as books, but all titillated the public. John Spargo wrote on child labor, "Statistics cannot express the withering of child lips in the poisoned air of factories; the tired strained look of child eyes that never dance to the glad music of souls tuned to Nature's symphonies." The U.S. Senate, according to David Graham Phillips, "betrayed the public to that cruel and vicious spirit of Mammon [money] which has come to dominate the nation." Further, he argued, "The United States Senate is a larger factor than your labor and intelligence, you average American, in determining your income. And the Senate is a traitor to you!" State legislatures were little better, as was shown by William Allen White's investigation in Missouri. "The legislature met biennially, and enacted such laws as the corporations paid for and such as were necessary to fool the people." In *Following the Color Line* Ray Stannard Baker exhorted, "Whether we like it or not the whole nation . . . is tied by unbreakable bonds to its Negroes, its Chinamen, its slum-dwellers, its thieves, its murderers, its prostitutes. We cannot elevate ourselves by driving them back either with hatred, violence or neglect; but only by bringing them forward: by service." Ida Tarbell called Standard Oil "one of the most gigantic and dangerous conspiracies ever attempted." In similar, stirring words Lincoln Steffens denounced urban politics in *The Shame of the Cities*, and the socialist Upton Sinclair described the horrifying conditions in the meat-packing industry in *The Jungle*.

One might believe these men and women were cynical mudslingers, but that was not how they saw themselves. "We muckraked," said Baker, "not because we hated our world, but because we loved it. We were not hopeless, we

Ida Tarbell became one of the most influential muckrakers after the 1904 publication of her *History of the Standard Oil Company*.

were not cynical, we were not bitter." The public sometimes missed the intended message. Sinclair's goal in *The Jungle* was a socialist critique of the exploitation of labor in the meatpacking industry, but as he ruefully noted, "I aimed at the nation's heart and hit it in the stomach." After a few years, muckraking tended to degenerate into sloppy research and wild, unsubstantiated charges. Yet the publishers of the more than 2000 muckraking books and articles who aimed at the nation's pocketbooks hit a number of Americans in the heart.

PROGRESSIVES IN ACTION

Voices of change echoed a genuine transformation of popular sentiment. Americans of all classes began calling themselves "progressives" and sought to reform whichever social evil captured their attention. Most believed problems could be legislated away; their typical response to injustice or sin was "There ought to be a law." At the same time they rejected the individualism of Social Darwinism and believed that progress would come through cooperation rather than competition. Thus they organized themselves by droves into groups that shared their own particular vision of human progress.

The diversity of the organizations founded reflects the breadth of reform activity. Indeed, so varied were the aims of people calling themselves progressive that to call progressivism a movement is a mistake. There was little unity except in the idea that people could improve society. Most progressives, however, were middle-class moderates who abhorred radical solutions. Motivated by a fear and hatred of class conflict, such progressives sought to save the capitalists from their own excesses and thereby salvage the system. Their goal was an orderly and harmonious society.

The Drive to Organize

Organizing was a major activity at the turn of the century. Such professional groups as the American Medical Association (AMA) and the American Historical Association began to emerge in modern form. These groups reflected the rise of a new professionalism that helped to create a body of "experts" to be tapped by progressives wanting to impose order and efficiency on social institutions. The organizations themselves also acted to bring change. The AMA was reorganized in 1901, and by 1910 its membership had increased from 8400 to more than 70,000. Its major goal was to improve professional standards. The government assisted by enacting laws that required licenses to practice medicine. In 1910 a Carnegie Foundation study recommended minimum standards for medical education. The widespread acceptance of its report closed the doors of dozens of marginal medical schools, several of which trained minority doctors. The result of the new professionalism in most fields was to limit the number of practitioners. Although this did help weed out incompetents, it also increased the incomes of the remaining practitioners and often reduced minority participation. In other words, order, stability, and improved standards were achieved at the cost of decreased opportunity.

Given the religious bent of progressive thought, a number of church-related organizations also arose. One of the most important was the Federal Council of Churches of Christ in America. Founded in 1908, it was an interdenominational group that advocated safer working conditions, the abolition of child labor, shorter work weeks and higher wages, workmen's compensation, old-age pensions, and "the most equitable division of the products of industry that can ultimately be devised."

To a large extent, middle-class women led in the organization of reform. Technology and domestic help lessened the burdens of running a home for these women, but a stigma remained on paid employment. Women's clubs provided an outlet for the energies and abilities of many competent and educated women. Local organizations flourished and, in 1890 joined to form the General Federation of Women's Clubs. In the next two decades, reform groups founded and led mainly by women sprang up.

The majority of activist, middle-class women became involved in movements closely linked to their assigned social roles as guardians of morality and nurturers of the family. Many worked through such religious groups as the

(Text continues on p. 732)

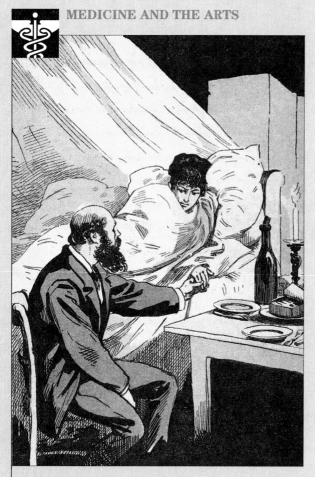

THE WHITE PLAGUE

of infections caused by tubercle bacilli, isolated in 1882 by Robert Koch, the famous German scientist. The most common (and most feared) is pulmonary tuberculosis, a chronic, debilitating disease of the lungs; it can kill its victims in a few months but usually requires several years to complete the task. Other common forms of the disease include meningeal TB, which produces an inflammation of the membranes surrounding the brain; TB of the spine, which causes a hunchback deformity of the spine; lupus, TB of the skin; and miliary TB, a generalized infection that occurs when the tubercle bacilli are distributed by the bloodstream throughout the body, producing small nodules on most organs.

Because the term "tuberculosis" did not appear in print until around 1840, most Americans knew the disease as consumption, which seemed the perfect metaphor for describing how the victims of the disease gradually wasted away from debilitating fever, weight loss, night sweats, chronic cough, and copious sputum, decorated toward the end with the bright red blood spots that denoted advanced pulmonary tuberculosis.

In less polite society, "consumptives" were called "lungers," a term of derision. Throughout the nineteenth century, many people associated TB with poverty and attached a social stigma to the disease. Others believed that TB was caused by some hereditary defect. For them, the perplexing problem was why the disease hit some families harder than others. In Ralph Waldo Emerson's family, for example, he and three of his brothers suffered from the disease, while his fellow transcendentalist, Henry David Thoreau,

During the Progressive Era, the rise of scientific ways of thinking cleared the way for reformers and health officers to launch a campaign against the disease most identified with industrialization—tuberculosis (TB). During the nineteenth century, TB was aptly called "the Captain of All the Men of Death." It killed more people and caused more sickness than any other disease in the western world. Its very name conjures up images of fetid sweatshops and sulfurous mills where men, women, and children had their

health broken by long working hours and physical exhaustion; of urban slums and overcrowded tenements rotten with disease; and, finally, of emaciated, ghostlike wretches, feverish with infection, gasping for breath, coughing up mouthfuls of blood, and staring hollow-eyed into space waiting for death.

In a sense, TB mirrors the complexity of the industrial revolution, for just as the transformation of the economy was multifaceted, TB is not one but many diseases. TB is merely the generic name for a host

lost a father, a sister, and a grand-father to TB before dying from the disease himself.

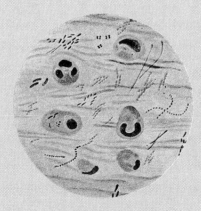

Paradoxically, despite its dreadful symptoms and terrifying ability to wipe out entire families, TB was romanticized on both sides of the Atlantic. For many writers, it became a metaphor for comparing decay in nature to disease in man. Thus, Henry Thoreau, upon seeing the first splashes of red in the green maple leaves of autumn, could write in 1852 in his *Journal Intime*: "Decay and disease are often beautiful, like ... the hectic glow of consumption."

In fact, the Age of Romanticism's much heralded "doom and gloom" may have derived at least in part from the sadness and melancholy caused by the deaths of loved ones from TB—especially the death of young adults for whom the disease had a special affinity. John Keats, the quintessential romantic poet, succumbed to TB at 26; Emily Brontë, author of the powerful *Wuthering Heights*, was cut down tragically at 30. The novels of the day, Charles Dickens's *David Copperfield*, for one, are positively littered with the corpses of people killed in the bloom of youth by the "White Plague."

The disease also broke its share of hearts in the theater and at the opera. Alexander Dumas lamented the death from TB of a beautiful heroine in *La Dame aux Camelias*, which in its English translation became the play, *Camille, or the Fate of a Coquette*, later adapted by Verdi for the opera as *La Traviata*. An identical fate befell the heroine in the play, *La Boheme*, which inspired Puccini's opera of the same name.

Under the spell of this heart-wrenching romanticism, writers, poets, and artists created a new and profoundly twisted ideal of feminine beauty: the dying angel, smitten by consumption, whose physical appeal was somehow enhanced by her malady. One gravely ill woman confided to her diary, "I cough continually! But for a wonder, far from making me look ugly, this gives me an air of languor that is very becoming." As depicted by writers, the dying female consumptive was, to her fingertips, an exquisitely fragile creature, the very embodiment of both the romantic and the Victorian ideal of frail feminine beauty. Her languid pallor was rendered even more pale by the generous application of whitening powders; and her slender body, with its swanlike neck and elongated limbs, was adorned in thin, sheer white clothing of cotton or linen, giving her appearance an ethereal quality, as a spirit not quite of this earth.

Numerous artists struggled to capture this image on canvas, including Gabriel Rossetti of the Pre-Raphaelite school, who idealized tall, slender women "with cadaverous bodies and sensual mouths." Reducing this image to a word portrait, Henry James described

Janet Burden, one of the leading Pre-Raphaelite models, as "strange, pale, livid, gaunt, silent, and yet in a manner graceful and picturesque." To another observer the same woman looked "as if she had walked out of an Egyptian tomb at Luxor."

As the nineteenth century drew to a close, however, the romantic view of life gradually lost its hold on the public's imagination. Instead of celebrating TB, writers, joined by health reformers, saw TB through the lens of realism. They linked the disease to poverty, unsafe working conditions, overcrowded housing, poor diet, and the failure of government to safeguard the public's health. Rather than glorifying consumptives, this change in attitude depicted them as the victims of a cruel, punishing illness. TB was no longer something to spark the artistic imagination; it was now a microbial insult to mankind and an indictment against the society that tolerated it.

Young Women's Christian Association. Numerous others joined in a resurgence of prohibitionism. Americans had always drunk a lot of alcohol, and consumption had been increasing since the Civil War. By the 1890s, earlier movements to control consumption had faded, leaving only three states with prohibition laws. After a quarter of a century of inactivity, the Woman's Christian Temperance Union revived and by 1898 had 10,000 local branches. It was assisted by the Anti-Saloon League (organized in 1893) and such church organizations as the Temperance Society of the Methodist Episcopal church.

Some of the prohibitionists were Protestant fundamentalists who considered the consumption of alcohol a sin; others were concerned with its social impact. Urban reformers constantly saw the consequences of alcohol abuse in domestic violence, accidents, and pauperism. Alcohol was the root of so many social problems that to ignore it was like "bailing water out of a tub with the tap turned on; letting the . . . liquor traffic run full blast while we limply stood around and picked up the wreckage." The AMA reported the physically devastating effects of alcoholism. Many in the Anti-Saloon League were also dismayed by the part played by drinking establishments in machine politics.

The idea of legislating morality for the good of society spilled over into the sexual sphere. A major area of concern was prostitution, and its opponents had a variety of motivations. Some stressed its role in the spread of venereal disease. Others deplored the exploitation of women and the double standard that allowed only men sexual freedom. For some it was morally wrong; to others it was just one more social evil—a product of environment rather than original sin. Many linked it with immigration as they did alcohol abuse. The crusade against this age-old problem had deep roots, but at the turn of the century it followed a typically progressive path. Muckraking journalists enraged the public with lurid accounts of "white slavery" rings that kidnapped young women and forced them into prostitution. The first step toward eliminating the problem was to pressure local governments to establish commissions to study the issue. Most reports stressed the economic roots. One prostitute asked an investigator, "Do you suppose I am going back to earn five or six dollars a week in a factory, when I can earn that amount any night and often much more?"

Some people believed prostitution was merely a symptom of a larger disease, and they became "purity crusaders." Dr. Will K. Kellogg wrote "The exorbitant demands of the sexual appetites encountered among civilized people are not the result of a normal instinct, but are due to the incitements of an abnormally stimulating diet, including alcohol, the seduction of prurient literature and so-called art, and the temptations of impure associations." After a national Purity Congress in 1895, the purity crusaders lobbied not only for the prohibition of alcohol and prostitution but also for such things as censorship and the regulation of narcotics.

Progressive social reform had two aims: control and justice. Women were deeply involved in social justice as well as control movements like prohibition. Middle-class women had long dominated humanitarian work, but during the 1890s their work took on a new aggressiveness. Women came to believe that aid to the poor was an inadequate response to society's ills; they wanted to attack the causes of poverty. They sought to improve wages and working conditions, especially for women, and to protect children from exploitation. To this end, they started several organizations. The National Consumers League, led by former Illinois factory inspector Florence Kelly, lobbied for protective legislation for women and children as well as better working and living conditions for all. Kelly became a leading advocate of child labor laws and was joined in this cause by Alabama clergyman Edgar Gardner Murphy, who proposed the formation of the National Child Labor Committee in 1904. Like most progressives, child labor reformers gathered data and photographs to document horrors for legislators at the local, state, and finally federal level.

A similar path was followed by many organizations that studied various urban problems and proposed solutions. The National Municipal League (1895) was a forum for improving city government. The National Housing Association (1910), seeking to obtain building codes with at least minimum health and safety standards, proposed federally subsidized housing. The American Association for Labor Legislation and the American Association for Old-Age Security lob-

Alarmed by the unhealthy child-care practices of many immigrants, visiting nurses went to immigrant homes to teach such things as the proper bathing of babies.

bied for protective legislation for labor and pension plans.

Some reformers were not content to be merely advocates for the poor and the weak; they wanted to become directly involved with such people in an effort to educate them and organize them to help themselves. Here again middle-class women played a key role. Foremost among such activities was the settlement house movement. Following the lead of Jane Addams of Hull House in Chicago, many young college-educated women moved into slum neighborhoods to live and work with those they sought to help. "From the first," Addams wrote, "it seemed understood that we were ready to perform the humblest neighborhood services. We were asked to wash the newborn babies, and to prepare the dead for burial, to nurse the sick, and to 'mind the children.' "

More than unselfishness motivated such women. One worker confessed that settlement houses gratified her "thirst to know how the other half lives." Some educated women wanted more freedom than marriage and part-time volunteer work seemed to offer. One appeal of settlement work was that men did not control it.

The result was a growing social feminism that cut across class lines. An example was the founding of the National Women's Trade Union League in 1905. Through it, wealthy supporters organized women workers, joined their strikes, and trained leaders.

At first such activity seemed to draw attention away from the suffrage movement. Women's roles in progressive reforms, however, convinced many people that women not only deserved the right to vote but also that their political participation would be socially beneficial. Jane Addams asserted, "If women have in any sense been responsible for the gentler side of life which softens and blurs some of its harsher conditions may they not have a duty to perform in our American cities?" Arguments based on women's "special role," however, cut both ways. In articles with such titles as "Famed Biologist's Warning on the Peril in Votes to Women," writers charged that voting was so "unnatural" for women that pregnant women would miscarry and nursing mothers' milk would cease to flow. As during the fight for ratification of the Equal Rights Amendment in the 1970s, not all opponents were male. Mrs. A. J. George of the National Association Opposed to Woman Suffrage declared, "The Woman-suffrage movement is an imitation-of-man movement, and as such, merits the condemnation of every normal man and woman."

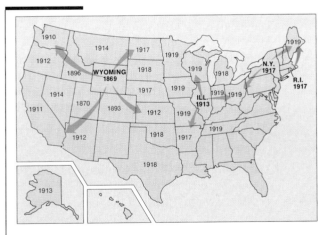

Women's Suffrage
Between 1869 and 1919, states gradually allowed women to vote in presidential elections, foreshadowing the Nineteenth Amendment.

Women employed a variety of tactics in their fight for the vote. Here Dr. Anne Shaw and Carrie Chapman Catt lead 20,000 marchers down Fifth Avenue in New York City.

In the face of such opposition, suffragists began to escalate their demands for the vote. Many became convinced that only national action could be effective. Thus the National American Woman Suffrage Association, led by Carrie Chapman Catt after 1915, began a broad-based campaign for a federal amendment to the Constitution. More militant women followed the young Quaker, Alice Paul, who founded the National Woman's party in 1914. She preferred the tactics of British suffragists who had picketed, gone on hunger strikes, and actively confronted both politicians and police.

Another group in the social justice movement sought to improve relations between blacks and whites. White Southerners had continued to devise forms of racial control to replace slavery. Their solution became a three-legged stool: legal segregation, disfranchisement, and violence. From the beginning, blacks resisted white efforts to suppress them. In city after city, African-Americans utilized almost every tool and tactic that would prove successful in the 1960s. They marched, they lobbied legislative bodies, they petitioned, they challenged discriminatory legislation in courts, and they boycotted segregated streetcars. Under the leadership of Booker T. Washington, they also tried conciliation. Nothing stemmed the rising tide of racism.

As conditions grew worse, Booker T. Washington seemed to grow even more accommodating, at least in public. Behind the scenes, however, he supported protest activities, using code names and secret funds. Educated African-Americans, however, became increasingly disenchanted with his public performance. They also resented his suppression of dissent by his fellow blacks. His influence with white politicians and philanthropists as well as his control of much of the black press gave him incredible power, which he used ruthlessly on occasion. The so-called anti-Bookerite radicals found their spokesperson in W. E. B. Du Bois. Unlike Washington, who had been born into slavery and educated at an industrial school, Du

Bois was born to free parents in Massachusetts and became the first African-American to receive a doctorate from Harvard.

Gifted with staggering intellectual brilliance, Du Bois expressed the frustrations and dreams of his fellow blacks in *The Souls of Black Folks* (1903). Of being black in America, he wrote, "one ever feels his twoness—an American, a Negro, two souls, two thoughts, two unreconciled strivings, two warring ideals in one dark body." In that book he also penned a polite but devastating critical analysis of Washington's leadership. Among other things, he objected to Washington's failure to recognize the importance of the vote, his emphasis on industrial education at the expense of higher education, his reluctance to criticize as well as praise white actions, and his willingness to give up previously won rights.

Relations between the two men deteriorated steadily after 1903, even though only immediate methods and not ultimate goals separated them. Both wanted the full acceptance of African-Americans as first-class citizens. To Washington, the best route was self-help and educating the masses. To these ends, he made Tuskegee Institute into an impressive institution staffed entirely by blacks. Du Bois, on the other hand, was more integrationist and believed the key to black advancement was in cultivating what he called the "Talented Tenth." To him, more of the limited education funds should go to train the ablest 10 percent of African-Americans for leadership through liberal arts and professional schooling.

By 1905 their differences were so great that Du Bois joined William Monroe Trotter in forming the Niagara Movement, an organization devoted to two main objectives: opposition to Washington's leadership and demands for "full manhood rights." Only about 50 educated African-Americans—mainly Northerners—joined, and the movement struggled to exist in the face of unrelenting sabotage by Washington. It played an important role, however, in convincing northern white progressives that an alternative to Washington was desirable. When a white mob in Springfield, Illinois, went on a rampage against African-Americans, concerned whites joined with Du Bois to found the National

Association for the Advancement of Colored People (NAACP) in 1909. At first the group was led and dominated by whites; Du Bois was the only African-American to hold a responsible position, as editor of its journal *The Crisis*. The organization became more black over time, but the focus of its activities remained essentially the same: education and propaganda, court challenges to discrimination, and lobbying for such legislation as a federal antilynching law.

Immigration policy became another source of organizational activity. The American Protective Association (1887) sought to control and limit the access of the "teeming masses yearning to breathe free." Members lobbied for literacy tests and quotas. One described a boatload of immigrants, saying "in every face there was something wrong—lips thick, mouth coarse, upper lip too long, cheek bones too high, chin poorly formed, the bridge of the nose hollowed, the base of the nose tilted, or else the whole face prognathous." While many Americans recoiled from the nation's pluralistic nature, others welcomed it. One wrote, "our dream of the United States ought not to be a dream of monotony," but instead an "orchestration of mankind." Thus some progressives formed the North American League for Immigrants to "protect the newcomers from unscrupulous bankers, steamship captains and fellow countrymen."

Even if most were middle class, progressives obviously came from all classes, and within classes there was a diversity of responses to the modernization of society and the economy. Many businesspeople organized to fight regulatory and labor legislation in such groups as the National Association of Manufacturers and the American Anti-Boycott Association. Others, however, joined such moderate reform groups as the Reform Municipal Voters League and the Chamber of Commerce. Some viewed labor unionism as more desirable than government regulation. The National Civic Federation was founded in 1901 with wealthy Republican politician Mark Hanna as president and labor leader Samuel Gompers as vice president. The group accepted unionization and sought to bring together employers, employees, and the general public to discuss industrial problems.

W. E. B. Du Bois, shown here in the editorial offices of the *Crisis* at the New York headquarters of the NAACP, was at first the only African-American to hold a significant office in the organization.

The drive to organize pervaded all of society, creating such diverse groups as the Boy Scouts of America (1910), the Rotary Club (1915), the National Collegiate Athletic Association (1906), the National Birth Control League (1915), and even the Aero Club of America (1905) to popularize "ballooning as a sport, especially among the more wealthy class." Americans came to believe in cooperative efforts to reach goals. In unprecedented numbers they also began to look to government for answers—starting at the city level and moving up to Washington.

Urban Beginnings

Progressivism was largely a response to modernization, and it first confronted the most visible problems, most of which were found in the cities. Incredibly rapid increases in urban populations outpaced the ability of "small-town" governments to meet the challenges. Political machines provided needed services but came under attack in the 1890s as inefficient and corrupt. Progressivism began to emerge in cities even while most attention was still focused on the rural-based Populists. Middle- and upper-class reformers demanded that governments operate "on a strict business basis" and be run "not by partisans, either Republican nor Demo-

cratic, but by men who are skilled in business management and social service."

Urban reformers' victories included the secret ballot and voter registration in some cities. Then in 1900, a model for efficient, nonpartisan city government emerged from the chaos created when a devastating hurricane killed more than 6000 people in Galveston, Texas. Local government broke down and the state legislature appointed a five-man commission to run the city. The idea spread to over 400 cities by World War I. A refinement was added in 1913, when in the wake of a disastrous flood, the government of Dayton, Ohio, hired a city manager to run the city on a day-to-day basis.

The cost of efficiency was decreased democracy. Indeed, some urban reformers were openly antidemocratic. One wrote in 1901, "Ignorance should be excluded from control. City business should be carried on by trained experts selected on some other principle than popular suffrage." The ward system, under which aldermen were elected by district, was seen as a problem because, as a Chicago businessman noted in 1911, "Men of successful experience and ability large enough to do justice to public affairs will seldom live and bring up families in the poorer wards." Such reformers naively sought to take "politics" out of government, but by "politics" they often meant the voice of people not like themselves. Nevertheless, these goals contradicted broader support for democracy, and by 1914 most city commissioners were required to run for election—often, however, in at-large elections rather than by district.

Middle-class progressives sometimes found their will thwarted by lower-class voters. Breaking up urban machines often destroyed the informal welfare networks that met the needs of the poor. When that happened, the poor rejected the new efficiency. In 1901, the Tammany Hall machine recaptured New York with the campaign slogan "To hell with reform." Poor immigrants did not accept that their ignorance and "foreign ways" were at the root of urban problems. "It is not so much the under crust," one declared, "as the upper crust that endangers the interests of the people."

In a number of cities, voters elected mayors who sympathized with working-class desires. Tom L. Johnson, elected mayor of Cleveland in 1901, rejected Americanization efforts to impose middle-class morality on the poor. "I am not trying to enforce Christianity," he proclaimed, "only make it possible." To this end he expanded social services and brought about the public ownership of the waterworks, gas and electric utilities, and public transportation, thereby reducing their costs to the poor. After his election 1899, Mayor Samuel "Golden Rule" Jones sought to establish the "Cooperative Commonwealth, the Kingdom of Heaven on Earth," in Toledo, Ohio. Until his death in 1904, he worked to provide free kindergartens, free playgrounds, free golf courses, and free concerts. He also reformed the police department, substituting light canes for the heavy clubs carried by patrolmen and prohibiting the jailing of people without charges. He made some powerful enemies and once declared, "Everyone is against me but the people." Most urban liberals depended on working-class voters.

The move toward public ownership of utilities was most avidly supported by the Socialists, who showed growing strength on the local level. In 1910 a Socialist was elected mayor of Milwaukee, and in the next year 70 others were elected in towns and cities across the nation. By 1912 about 1000 held offices in 33 states and 160 cities. Their rising power, however, helped trigger a backlash by middle-class voters, who favored regulatory commissions to public ownership of utilities.

Urban progressivism was obviously not a coherent, unified movement. Different groups at different times succeeded in different cities. Social services were cut to lower business taxes in some cities and expanded in others. In most cities the evils of overcrowded, unhealthy tenements were attacked with varying degrees of success with such measures as building codes. By the turn of the century, however, more and more people began to look to the states to solve problems.

Reform Reaches the State Level

Regardless of their objectives, many urban reformers eventually dabbled in state politics. The city had little power and the federal government seemed too remote. Thus the states became major battlegrounds for reform. The form and leadership of state progressivism were as diverse and complex as urban progressivism. In the South, most progressives worked through the Democratic party; in the Midwest and on the Pacific Coast, progressives captured the Republican party. In the industrial Northeast, progressives emerged in both major parties, but the Democrats were the more successful. In some cases progressive governors, such as Al Smith of New York, were the products of urban machines that embraced reform to hold onto their electorates. Others, such as Robert La Follette of Wisconsin, were Republican regulars who bypassed party leaders to ride reform to power. In the South, reform governors were elected by startlingly diverse constituencies. In Mississippi, small-town lawyer and editor James K. Vardaman was elected by the "redneck" vote of poor farmers. In Georgia, the urban middle class was the main supporter of Hoke Smith, publisher of the *Atlanta Journal*.

State progressives pursued four major goals: establishing "direct democracy," protecting the public by regulating the economy, increasing state services, and social control. Reformers passed many laws, but the impact of legislation was not always what they expected.

One progressive creed was dramatically stated by William Allen White: "The voice of the people is indeed the will of God." By World War I many states had adopted political procedures designed to give the people a more direct say in running the government. An initiative allowed voters to propose legislative changes, usually by petition; a referendum gave the public a mechanism for voting directly on controversial legislation; recall provided a way to remove elected officials. Many states also established direct primaries. Other states adopted measures to cleanse electoral procedures, including the secret ballot, voter registration, and corrupt practices legislation. The drive for direct democracy culminated in the Seventeenth Amendment to the Constitution (1913), which substituted the popular election of senators for their election by state legislatures.

The victories of women suffragists at the state level also expanded democracy. After the 1890s their efforts seemed to stall, and no new state gave women the vote until Washington did so in 1910. California acted the next year, and four other western states followed suit by 1916.

Born on a Montana ranch in 1880 and graduated from the University of Montana in 1902, Jeannette Rankin was elected to Congress in 1916.

That year Jeannette Rankin was elected to Congress from Montana. These victories encouraged the efforts to obtain a constitutional amendment allowing women to vote.

Clearly, progressive actions to protect the public and regulate the economy took many forms. In the West, especially, the emphasis was on regulating railroads and utilities, reflecting the region's Populist heritage. Legislatures created commissions to regulate the rates charged by both. At the same time, taxes on corporations were increased. For example, after La Follette's election in Wisconsin in 1900, state revenues from taxes on railroads grew from $1.9 million to $3.4 million.

In the industrialized states, workmen's compensation became a major goal. Horror stories about industrial accidents had long abounded, and muckrakers further inflamed the public. Then in 1911 a major tragedy chilled the hearts of Americans. A fire broke out at the Triangle Shirtwaist Company in New York just 30 minutes before closing time. The doors were locked to prevent the women who worked there from leaving early, and many fire escape ladders were either broken or missing. By the time the flames were doused, 147 workers, mainly women and girls, had lost their lives—47 had jumped to their deaths, littering the street with bodies. The Triangle fire was the worst example of escalating industrial accident rates. The only recourse for most maimed workers or their widowed spouses was to sue the company, which for many was not a realistic option. Some did get large settlements, however, which represented an unpredictable cost to businesses. Thus, the idea of mandatory insurance grew in popularity with support of many factory owners. Between 1910 and 1916, 32 states enacted workmen's compensation laws.

The work of the National Child Labor Committee and other organizations moved states to legislate protection for women and children. Progressives gathered evidence of the harm done to both by long working hours and unsafe, unhealthy conditions. State action was necessary, they argued, for two reasons: Women and children could not protect themselves and the nation's future depended on the health of both. By 1916, 32 states had laws regulating the hours worked by women and children, 11 had specified minimum wages for women, and every state regulated child labor in some manner. Other protective legislation included building and sanitary codes.

A number of states also expanded social services. Because of lobbying by settlement house workers, by 1914 some 20 states had provided mother's pensions to widows or abandoned wives with dependent children. The sums paid were meager, ranging from $2 to $15 a month for the first child and lesser amounts for the rest.

Funding for education also increased. A major area of reform was the expansion of compulsory education to the high school level. Support often came from businesses, which saw public education as a means of preparing individuals for life in an industrial society. As a result, very few public schools were modeled on John Dewey's progressive educational doctrines. Instead of promoting personal development, education, in the industrialists' minds, should inculcate discipline and punctuality. Hence school bells trained one for factory whistles and letter grades taught the value of individual initiative. Governments also made school organization more businesslike with increased power given to school superintendents and principals, who were expected to be trained in management techniques.

The flip side of state social justice legislation was increased efforts at social control. Prohibitionists won many victories in the states, especially in the South. That region provided fertile soil because of the strength of Protestant fundamentalism and the so-called race problem. One southern prohibitionist argued that blacks were "a child race in the South, and if drunkenness causes three-fourths of the crime ascribed to it, whiskey must be taken out of the Negro's hands," and that it was the duty "of the stronger race to forego its own personal liberty for the protection of the weaker race." Between 1907 and 1909 Georgia, Mississippi, North Carolina, Tennessee, and Alabama adopted state prohibition, and 14 other states had joined them by 1916.

The move toward social control infected all regions. Between 1907 and 1917, 16 states passed laws authorizing sterilization of various categories of allegedly unfit individuals. Social control measures were usually directed at minorities, so the South naturally offered the most extreme examples, but California progressives excluded Asians almost as ruthlessly. Southern whites trumpeted segregation as a reform, and they had the approval of many northern progressives. Even race relations muckraker Ray Stannard Baker wrote, "As for the Jim Crow laws in the South, many of them, at least, are at present necessary to avoid clashes between the ignorant of both races." Segregation was often enacted under progressive governors—a paradox only if the general progressive tendency toward social control is ignored.

In most ways, southern progressivism was for whites only. Increased school funding was common, but the bulk went to educating white children. The discrepancies between the amounts spent accelerated, making even more of a lie of the *Plessy* v. *Ferguson* (1896) formula of "separate but equal" facilities. In 1919 southern states spent an average of $12.16 per white student and $3.29 per black student. Racism remained a potent force. As governor of Mississippi from 1903 to 1907, James K. Vardaman pursued progressive reforms in such areas as convict-lease, school funding, and railroad regulation. At the same time he defended lynching, saying "We would be justified in slaughtering every Ethiopian on earth to preserve unsullied the honor of one Caucasian home."

The legacy of progressivism in the states was mixed, as were the motives of reformers. Regardless of their goals, most came to look to the federal government for help. One reformer expressed their frustration. "When I was in the city council . . . fighting for a shorter work day, [my opponents] told me to go to the legislature; now [my fellow legislators] tell me to go to Congress for a national law. When I get there and demand it, they will tell me to go to hell."

PROGRESSIVISM MOVES TO THE NATIONAL LEVEL

When McKinley was reelected in 1900, few expected a national reform leader; but for a quirk of fate they would have been right. As the 1900 Republican convention rolled around, party leaders realized they had a problem. Theodore Roosevelt had become a national hero in the wake of the Spanish-American War, but he had angered party regulars by supporting regulatory legislation as governor of New York. When they decided to "bury" Roosevelt in the vice presidency, Mark Hanna warned, "Don't you realize that there's only one life between that madman and the White House?" On September 6, 1901, anarchist Leon Czolgosz shot McKinley. Eight days later that one life was gone, and Roosevelt was president. It was not immediately apparent, however, that he would usher in reform. Many remembered that during the Pullman strike Roosevelt had suggested shooting the strikers. Most therefore did not expect the action he took in the 1902 coal strike. That year, however, became the first in a decade and a half of snowballing reform that would result in a massive amount of legislation and four constitutional amendments by 1920.

Roosevelt and New Attitudes Toward Government Power

Roosevelt became the most forceful president since Lincoln, but few men have looked or sounded less presidential. He was short, nearsighted, beaver-toothed, and talked in a high-pitched voice. A frail, asthmatic child, he seemed intent on proving his manliness. Thus his life became a robust adventure of sports, hunting, and camping. Once while president he took a foreign diplomat skinny-dipping in the Potomac. His exuberance, vitality, and wit captivated most Americans. They called him "Teddy" and named a stuffed bear after him. To understand him, an observer declared, one had to remember "the president is really only six years old." He was not a simple man, however. His hobbies included writing history books, and he displayed a keen intellect that he had honed at Harvard.

Born into an aristocratic Dutch family in New York, Roosevelt rejected a leisurely life for the rough and tumble world of politics, which his friends declared was an occupation for saloonkeepers and such. "I answered," he wrote in his autobiography, "that if this were so it merely meant that the people I knew did not belong to the governing class, and that I intended to be one of the governing class." His privileged background made him an unlikely candidate for a reformer, yet he ended up making reform both fun and respectable. He saw himself as a conservative, but declared, "The only true conservative is the man who resolutely sets his face toward the future." To preserve what was vital, one had to reform. The conservatives of his time, however, rejected his call for change and continued to insist on laissez-faire policies and limited government.

Roosevelt, on the other hand, shared two progressive sentiments. One was that government should be efficiently run by able, competent people. The other was that industrialization had created the need for expanded governmental action. "A simple and poor society," he observed, "can exist as a democracy on the basis of sheer individualism. But a rich and complex society cannot so exist." As a result of these two sentiments, Roosevelt reorganized and revitalized the executive branch, modernized the army command structure and the consular service, and pursued the federal regulation of the economy that has characterized twentieth-century America.

Although he was later remembered more for his "trust-busting" and "Square Deal," Roosevelt considered conservation his greatest domestic accomplishment. It was the topic of his first presidential address. "We are prone to think of the resources of this country as inexhaustible; this is not so," he later warned Congress. In 1902 he backed the Newlands Reclamation Act, which set aside the proceeds from public land sales for irrigation and reclamation projects. He also used presidential power to add almost 150 million acres to national forests and to preserve valuable coal and water sites for national development. With his ally, chief forester, Gifford Pinchot, he sponsored a National Conservation Congress in 1908.

Some businesspeople already disliked Roosevelt for his conservation policies, but he aggravated others by two actions in 1902. The first was his handling of the coal strike, which served notice that the government could no longer be counted on to come automatically to the aid of management in labor disputes. The

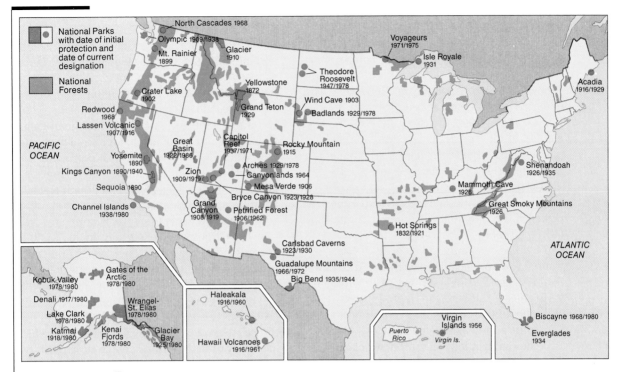

National Parks and Forests

Under the presidency of Theodore Roosevelt, who considered conservation his most important domestic achievement, millions of acres of land were set aside for national parks and forests.

second was a suit against Northern Securities Company under the Sherman Antitrust Act. Roosevelt's trust-busting was an answer to progressive prayers. Antimonopoly was a strong component of progressivism. Most agreed with Louis Brandeis that "If the Lord had intended things to be big, he would have made men bigger—in brains and character." Antitrust action had not been undertaken on a large scale in the cities and states only because federal action seemed necessary.

Northern Securities was a wise choice for action. It was a highly unpopular combination of northwestern railroad systems engineered by such heavyweights as James J. Hill and J. P. Morgan. The suit infuriated Hill, who complained, "It seems hard that we should be compelled to fight for our lives against the political adventurers who have never done anything but pose and draw a salary." In 1904 the Supreme Court ordered the company's dissolution. That same year, in a case against the major meat

packers, the Court also reversed the *E. C. Knight* ruling that exempted manufacturing from federal antitrust law.

The rulings pleased Roosevelt, who rejected the Court's earlier narrow, strict interpretations of the Constitution. Instead, he believed that the Constitution "must be interpreted not as a straight-jacket . . . but as an instrument designed for the life and healthy growth of the Nation." In his desire to expand federal power, he was once credited with asking "What's the Constitution between friends?" Yet Roosevelt was not a true convert to trust-busting.

"This is an age of combination," he wrote, "and any effort to prevent all combination will be not only useless, but in the end vicious." At the same time he believed "of all the forms of tyranny the least attractive and the most vulgar is the tyranny of mere wealth." Thus he attacked trusts that abused their power and left alone trusts that acted responsibly. He preferred to negotiate differences, and to do so he established in 1904 a Bureau of Corporations within the Department of Commerce and Labor, which had been created the year before.

Campaigning on the promise to provide a "Square Deal" to all Americans, Roosevelt easily defeated the Democratic candidate Alton B. Parker in the 1904 presidential election. Now elected in his own right, he launched into expanding the regulatory power of the federal government. His top priority over the objection of conservative Republican senators was effectively to control the railroads by expanding the power of the Interstate Commerce Commission (ICC). Although the Elkins Act, passed in 1903, had already eliminated rebates, Roosevelt wanted to go further and give the ICC the power to set rates. Through shrewd political maneuvering he got this with the Hepburn Act of 1906, although he had to give up his demand for limited court review of rate decisions.

The publication of Upton Sinclair's *The Jungle* in that same year caused a consumer uproar for regulation of the food and drug industries. A chemist in the Agriculture Department, Harvey W. Wiley had long been analyzing food products for chemical adulteration by testing additives on volunteers known as the "Poison Squad." His data were supplemented by an investigation of the meat-packing industry ordered by Roosevelt, which proved the truth of Sinclair's charges of filth and contamination. As a result, Congress passed the Pure Food and Drug Act and the Meat Inspection Act on the same day in 1906. By 1908 Roosevelt had left his indelible mark on the nation and decided not to run for reelection. He cast his support to William Howard Taft, who easily defeated William Jennings Bryan, the Democratic nominee and loser for the third time. Roosevelt then retired and went to hunt lions in Africa, a move that led J. P. Morgan to toast "Health to the Lions."

Taft and Quiet Progressivism

William Howard Taft brought to the presidency a distinguished record of public service. An Ohio lawyer, he had served as a federal judge, the first civil governor of the Philippines, and secretary of war. He did not, however, look presidential; he weighed more than 350 pounds

and this lead to rumors that a special bathtub was to be installed in the White House. Unlike his predecessor, he was far from charismatic and indeed quite shy. Legalistic and precise, he was neither a fiery writer nor speaker. In short, he was incapable of rallying public support for any cause, and reformers were especially skeptical about him. As a judge he had been called the "injunction standard bearer" by labor leaders. When soldiers shot into the crowd at the Haymarket riot, he confided, "they have only killed six as yet. This is hardly enough to make an impression."

Indeed Taft was essentially more conservative than Roosevelt, especially in his view of governmental power. "The lesson must be learned," he argued, "that there is only a limited zone within which legislation and governments can accomplish good." Further, he declared, "We can, by passing laws which cannot be enforced, destroy that respect for laws . . . which has been the strength of people of English descent everywhere." On the other hand, his respect for the law extended to the Sherman act.

Without federal regulation, meat packers exploited workers and allowed rats and other contaminants to be processed with meat to make sausage.

"We are going to enforce that law or die in the attempt," he promised, and far more cases were prosecuted in his administration than during the so-called trust-buster Roosevelt's tenure.

In his own quiet way Taft was as sympathetic to reform as Roosevelt. He supported the eight-hour day and favored legislation to improve mine safety. He also urged passage of the Mann-Elkins Act of 1910, which increased the rate-setting power of the ICC and extended its jurisdiction to telephone and telegraph companies. The Sixteenth and Seventeenth amendments were initiated under his presidency. Purity crusaders also won a victory in 1910 with the passage of the Mann Act, which made it illegal to transport women across state lines for "immoral purposes."

Nevertheless, Taft was not forceful enough to preside effectively over the growing divisions within the Republican party. The conservatives, led by the powerful Senator Nelson W. Aldrich, were determined to draw the line against further reform. At the same time, progressive Republicans such as Robert La Follette and George Norris were growing rebellious. Conflict came on several fronts. The first was the tariff. In his campaign Taft had promised a lower tariff, but in the end he accepted the much compromised Payne-Aldrich Tariff. While placing many nonessential items on the duty-free list, it actually raised some key duties. It disappointed reformers immensely. Listing such duty-free items as silkworm eggs, canary birdseed, hog bristle, leeches, and skeletons, the political humorist Finley Peter Dunne had his fictional bartender, Mr. Dooley, proclaim, "The new tariff puts these familyer commodyties within the reach iv all." Taft had suffered a defeat, but foolishly did not admit it. He called the tariff the "best" ever passed. In reality he backed down on his pledges because he believed the president should not interfere unduly with the legislative branch. He also simply had an accommodating personality. One Republican griped, "The trouble with Taft is that if he were Pope he would think it necessary to appoint a few Protestant Cardinals."

Caught in the middle of several conflicts, Taft eventually alienated the progressive wing of his party as well as Teddy Roosevelt. He first supported and then abandoned party insur-

At his inauguration in 1909, William Howard Taft did not realize the challenges he would face in Congress from a divided Republican party.

gents who challenged the power of conservative Speaker of the House "Uncle Joe" Cannon. Later, when Gifford Pinchot protested a sale of public lands by Secretary of the Interior Richard A. Ballinger, Taft fired him. That action infuriated both conservationists and Roosevelt, who was also irritated by Taft's antitrust prosecutions. Roosevelt believed that a case had been pursued against U.S. Steel to embarrass him. The investigation exposed a deal he made with J. P. Morgan in 1907 in return for the banker's aid in stemming a financial panic.

By 1912 progressive Republicans were ready to bolt the party if Taft were renominated, and Roosevelt declared his intention to run. The fight for the nomination became bitter. Taft called Roosevelt's supporters "political emotionalists or neurotics." Roosevelt labeled Taft's people as "men of cold heart and narrow mind, who believe we can find safety in dull timidity and dull inaction." As president, Taft was able to control the convention. The defeated Roosevelt walked out with his supporters and formed a third party, known as the Progressive or Bull Moose party.

Robert La Follette in Cumberland, Wisconsin, in 1897. La Follette, known for progressive reforms as governor of and U.S. senator from Wisconsin, was part of the split in the Republican party between progressives rebelling against Taft and conservatives opposing further reforms.

CRAVEN COLLEGE

Many leading reformers attended the Progressive convention, which often resembled a religious revival with hymn singing and marches. Its platform endorsed such wide-ranging reforms as abolition of child labor; federal old-age, accident, and unemployment insurance programs; an eight-hour day; and women's suffrage. At Roosevelt's request, however, a plank supporting black equality was deleted. Calling the major parties "husks with no real soul," he accepted its nomination.

With the Republicans divided, Democratic chances of recapturing the White House increased. A former Republican senator lamented that the only unanswered question was "Which corpse gets the most flowers?" The scent of victory led to a hard fight for the Democratic nomination, which New Jersey's progressive governor, Woodrow Wilson, won on the forty-sixth ballot. The Socialist party nominated Eugene V. Debs, making it a four-way race.

As soon became apparent, the real battle was between Wilson and Roosevelt. It was marked by an unusually high level of debate over the proper role of government in a modern, industrialized society. Wilson declared, "What this country needs above everything else is a body of laws which will look after the men who are on the make rather than the men who are already made." Labeling his program "New Freedom," his aim was the restoration of competition and his tool was to be trust busting. Roosevelt, on the other hand, believed that big business was not necessarily bad, but proclaimed, "Somehow or other we shall have to work out methods of controlling the big corporations without paralyzing the energies of the business community." His answer was "New Nationalism"—the expansion of federal regulatory activities to control rather than dismantle the trusts. Big government would offset the power of big business. Their rhetoric differed sharply, but in their presidencies each practiced a little of both "New Freedom" and "New Nationalism."

Election of 1912

Woodrow Wilson did not receive a majority of the popular vote, but the split in the Republican party gave him the majority of the votes in the Electoral College.

The split in the Republican party enabled the Democrats to capture not only the White House but also the Senate. Democrats also consolidated their control of the House, so Wilson entered the presidency with his party solidly in power. Nevertheless, Wilson did not receive a majority of the popular vote. He got 6.3 million votes, Roosevelt 4.1 million, Taft 3.5 million, and Debs nearly 1 million. In the Electoral College, however, Wilson won an impressive 435 votes to Roosevelt's 88 and a mere 8 for Taft.

Wilson and Moral Progressivism

As the third Progressive-Era president, Woodrow Wilson differed from his predecessors in both appearance and leadership style. He looked very much like the moralistic professor he was. The son and grandson of Presbyterian ministers, Wilson was raised in the South and practiced law in Atlanta before receiving his doctorate from Johns Hopkins University in Baltimore. His book *Congressional Government* was published in 1895, and he became president of Princeton University in 1902 before being elected governor of New Jersey. His religion was an important factor in his personality. "My life would not be worth living," he declared, "if it were not for the driving power of religion."

Wilson was not the kind of man whom people named stuffed animals after or gave nicknames. His self-righteousness was not endearing. One politician noted that when Wilson "said something to me . . . I didn't know whether God or him was talking." Although much less charismatic, Wilson did resemble Roosevelt in being a better speaker than Taft and in his view of the role of the president. Roosevelt had called the presidency a "bully pulpit," and Wilson agreed that the president should be the "political leader of the nation" because "his is the only national voice in politics." Unlike Taft, he argued that the president must be "as much concerned with the guidance of legislation as with the just and orderly execution of the laws."

Wilson's activism coincided with growing demands for further reform. Investigations and amendments launched earlier came to fruition during his presidency. The result was an outpouring of legislation. In 1913, his first year in office, the Sixteenth Amendment was ratified,

A distinguished professor, Woodrow Wilson brought both competence and a grim moral determination to the presidency.

allowing the imposition of a federal income tax. It appeared as a provision of the Underwood Tariff, which was passed in a special session of Congress that year. Wilson called the session to redeem a campaign pledge to lower duties as part of the New Freedom goal of restoring competition. During the tariff hearings, lobbyists were so plentiful Wilson complained, "a brick wouldn't be thrown without hitting one of them." This time, however, they did not all prevail. Congress significantly lowered duties for the first time since the Civil War. To recoup lost revenues, a graduated tax of from 1 to 6 percent was placed on personal incomes of $3000 and over.

Congress passed banking reform the same year. Following the panic of 1907, congressional investigations were launched into its causes. Everyone, including bankers, had come to believe the nation's banking system needed to be stabilized by governmental action. The question was *how* to do it. Wall Street wanted a centralized system owned and controlled by bankers. Others wanted a more decentralized system owned or controlled by the government. The Federal Reserve Act of 1913 was a compromise. It established the Federal Reserve System of 12 regional banks owned by bankers but under the control of a presidentially appointed Federal Reserve Board.

Prohibitionists won their first national victory with the Webb-Kenyon Act of 1913. It allowed dry states to interfere with the transportation of alcohol across their state lines. The next year those concerned with the large amounts of narcotics in patent medicines rejoiced over the passage of the Harrison Narcotic Act. It required a doctor's prescription for the sale of a list of controlled substances. Congress also compelled manufacturers of these drugs to register with the government and maintain sales records.

In 1914 Congress also took actions to deal with monopolies and to regulate business. In September it established the Federal Trade Commission to replace the Bureau of Corporations. The five-person body was charged with investigating alleged violations of antitrust law and could issue "cease and desist" orders against corporations found guilty of unfair trade practices. The next month the Clayton Antitrust Act sought to close some of the loopholes of the Sherman act and prohibited a number of business practices such as price discrimination. One provision declared that labor unions were not to be considered illegal combinations in restraint of trade—a move designed to undermine the use of court injunctions against strikers.

At that point Wilson believed he had accomplished his agenda. He was not a supporter of further labor legislation or farm-credit plans. A firm opponent of paternalism, he said, "The old adage that God takes care of those who take care of themselves is not gone out of date. No federal legislation can change that thing. The minute you are taken care of by the government you are wards, not independent men." As the election of 1916 approached, however, progressives reminded Wilson of the importance of the farm and labor vote. Legislation to win those votes soon followed. Farmers were given the Federal Farm Loan Act, which provided low-interest credit, and legislation giving federal supplemental funding for agricultural specialists in each county. Labor got the Keating-Owen

Child Labor Act, which barred goods made by children under 16 from interstate commerce; the Adamson Act, which established an eight-hour day for railroad workers; and the Workman's Compensation Act, which provided protection to federal employees. Progressives were also pleased by Wilson's appointment of Louis Brandeis to the Supreme Court. All of these actions helped to ensure victory over the Republican nominee Charles Evans Hughes in 1916.

PROGRESSIVISM IN THE INTERNATIONAL ARENA

Many progressives did not believe that progress was limited by national boundaries. In their eyes, human beings had the capacity to create a more just and orderly society both at home and abroad. The progressive spirit was optimistic, and progressive victories on the home front merely expanded Americans' confidence in their ability to solve problems—even on the international level. This confidence was further bolstered by the nation's economic growth and victory in the Spanish-American War.

Everyone agreed that by 1900, America's status in the world had changed. How to respond to those changes was the unanswered question. Just as people differed over what alterations, if any, were required in domestic policies, various visions of a new American foreign policy also emerged. For some, progressivism simply redefined and reinvigorated the old ideas of manifest destiny. The United States would solve its problems at home and then remake the world in its own image. Such a new world order would also open up new markets for America's industrial and agricultural surpluses. Other progressives believed that democratic principles required that all people, even foreigners, be free to determine their own destinies. Order and justice were two progressive goals that sometimes conflicted. The conflict was also apparent in the international arena.

Big Stick Diplomacy

The first Progressive-Era president was Theodore Roosevelt, and his foreign policy reflected the same kind of vigor he displayed in everything else. His "macho" foreign policy followed his belief that a man's mission was to "work, fight, and breed." He believed progress and order could benefit the world as well as the nation. He also asserted Congress was "not well fitted for the shaping of foreign policy" and expanded presidential power in the conduct of diplomacy. It was his destiny to deal with the legacies of increased power and influence from the Spanish-American War. Order having been restored in Cuba and Philippines by 1903, Roosevelt launched the United States into the role of policeman. His doctrine was to "speak softly and carry a big stick," but he really only lived up to the second half of the slogan.

Possession of the Philippines brought with it concern over turbulent Asian politics. Most alarming was the emergence of Japan after its unexpected victories in the Russo-Japanese War (1904–1905). Often playing the role of arbiter at home, Roosevelt now shifted his arena and mediated the crisis at the Portsmouth, New Hampshire, conference in August 1905—an action that won him a Nobel Peace Prize. Japan remained a formidable rival, however, and agreements were reached to respect each other's Asian interests. In the Pacific, Roosevelt's "big stick" was displayed by conspicuous stops there during a 1907–1909 tour of America's "Great White Fleet." He meant to intimidate the Japanese, but he failed to halt their growing power.

Within the Western Hemisphere, Roosevelt was even less reluctant to threaten or use force. In 1906 he responded to Cuban demonstrations against the Platt Amendment and insurrection by sending in marines, who stayed until 1909. "I am doing my best," he declared, "to persuade the Cubans that if only they will be good, they will be happy. I am seeking the very minimum of interference necessary to make them good." The marines could be very persuasive.

Progress and strategic considerations also demanded that a canal in Central America link the Atlantic and Pacific oceans. Roosevelt was determined to make it happen. There were two possible routes: one through Nicaragua and one across the Panamanian isthmus, which belonged to Colombia. A start had been made in Panama by a French company, which ran out of funds and was reorganized as the New Panama

Canal Company. The new company's major asset was its concession from Colombia that extended to 1904.

Three commissions appointed to determine the route recommended Nicaragua, primarily because the New Panama Canal Company demanded $190 million for its rights, property, and previous work. Its stockholders, mainly Americans, were frantic to convince Congress to choose the Panamanian route. They dropped their demand to $40 million, contributed profusely to campaign funds, and hired a full-time lobbyist—Philippe Bunau-Varilla, the

Panama Canal
The Panama Canal provided a strategic link between the Atlantic and the Pacific oceans.

French chief engineer of the original company. In June 1902, Congress authorized efforts to secure the rights to a Panamanian canal. The Hay-Herran Treaty provided the United States with rights to a 6-mile-wide zone in return for a $10 million payment to Colombia and an annual rental fee of $250,000 to begin 9 years after the ratification of the treaty. As in America, ratification required the consent of the Colombian senate, which in August 1903 rejected the treaty unanimously. Its motive was probably to delay the treaty until 1904, when the New Panama Canal Company's concession expired and Colombia might receive some of the $40 million originally earmarked for the company.

Roosevelt was furious. "The blackmailers of Bogota," he roared, should not be allowed "permanently to bar one of the future highways of civilization." He drafted a message to Congress proposing to take the canal zone by force, but never delivered it. A different solution was found. Bunau-Varilla engineered a Panamanian revolution by providing people with a national constitution, flag, and anthem as well as assurances that the United States would not let their revolt fail. He was right. Most Colombian troops were prevented from even getting to the so-called revolution by the USS *Nashville*. Three days after its start, Roosevelt recognized the independence of the Republic of Panama. The

American secretary of state and the French citizen Bunau-Varilla, who had demanded to be made ambassador to the United States, then quickly drafted the Hay-Bunau-Varilla Treaty with essentially the same terms as the Hay-Herran Treaty—only now the payment went to the rebels, not Colombia.

American actions enraged people all over the world. At first Roosevelt denied any part in the revolution, but he eventually admitted, "I took the Canal Zone and let Congress debate; and while the debate goes on the Canal does also." In 1914, the canal, a monument to both progress and Yankee imperialism, was completed. It was a big investment, one that required protection from foreign military vessels.

At the same time, Latin American countries sometimes fell behind in debt payments to such European powers as Britain and Germany. As a result those two nations blockaded Venezuela in 1902–1903. A year later, Roosevelt announced that the United States would assume the responsibility of seeing that the nations of the Caribbean behaved themselves and paid their debts. European intervention, therefore, would not be necessary. Known as the Roosevelt Corollary to the Monroe Doctrine, this policy justified U.S. intervention in such places as the Dominican Republic, Nicaragua, and Haiti. Roosevelt's "big stick" diplomacy established America as the "police of the Western Hemisphere"—a role that would last long into the twentieth century.

Dollar Diplomacy

Before becoming president, William Howard Taft had served as governor-general in the Philippines and as Roosevelt's troubleshooter in Cuba. These experiences convinced Taft of two principles. The first was the need for order and stability. The second was the limited capacity of armed force for solving problems. He also realized that the United States had a new source of power—its economic clout. From 1898 to 1909, American overseas investments had risen from about $800 million to more than $2.5 billion.

Called "dollar diplomacy," Taft's approach was to use dollars instead of bullets to ensure

stability and order. He wanted American capital to replace European capital in Latin America in order to increase U.S. influence there. When British bondholders wanted to collect their debts from Honduras in 1909, Taft asked American financiers to assume the debt. In 1910 he convinced New York bankers to take over the assets of the National Bank of Haiti. When needed, however, Taft also wielded a big stick. He refused to recognize a revolution in Nicaragua until the leaders agreed to accept American credits to pay off British debts and sent marines to punctuate his point.

Missionary Diplomacy

As in domestic policies, Woodrow Wilson's foreign policy differed more in style than substance from his predecessors. Wilson's moralism did not stop at national boundaries. Indeed his sermonistic foreign policy has sometimes been called "missionary diplomacy." His gospel was American-style democracy. "When properly directed," he declared, "there is no people not fitted for self-government." That direction was to come from the United States. He spoke of "releasing the intelligence of America for the service of mankind" and proclaimed "every nation needs to be drawn into the tutelage of America."

The rhetoric was different from his predecessors, but the results were the same. Renouncing both big stick and dollar diplomacy, Wilson continued to maintain stability and order in the Caribbean by similar measures. He sent marines to the Dominican Republic and Haiti, and kept them in Nicaragua. His interventionism ran into more trouble in Mexico, where the overthrow of long-time dictator Porfirio Diaz in 1911 began a cycle of revolution. Just before Wilson entered office Victoriano Huerta came to power through assassination—an action that repulsed the moralistic Wilson. To the surprise of many, Wilson refused to extend diplomatic recognition to Huerta's government. Such recognition was generally routine whenever a government could demonstrate control; it did not imply approval.

Wilson simply refused to accept what he

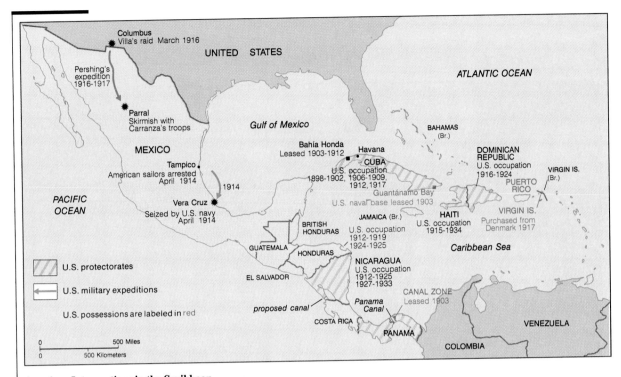

American Interventions in the Caribbean

Early in the twentieth century, the United States policed the Western Hemisphere and often took action when it judged Latin American countries were not running their affairs properly.

called a "government of butchers." He wrote one diplomat, "The United States intends not merely to force Huerta from power but to exert every influence it can to secure Mexico a better government under which all contracts and business concessions will be safer than they have ever been." Americans considered protection of contracts and concessions very important, and they controlled 75 percent of Mexico's mines, 60 percent of its oil, and 70 percent of its rubber. Wilson's tactics escalated from diplomatic pressure to landing troops at Veracruz, a move that infuriated Mexicans more than Huerta's despotism. Even after Huerta was overthrown, civil war continued between the government forces of Venustiano Carranza and rebels led by Pancho Villa.

In an attempt to draw America into the fracas, Villa launched a raid into New Mexico in March 1916. The tactic worked, and Wilson sent an expedition to capture Villa. Led by General John Pershing, American troops failed to find him. Soon they were 300 miles deep into Mexican territory, and as a result, on the brink of war with Carranza's government in January 1917. By then, however, America was being drawn into World War I, and Wilson decided to withdraw the troops. In the end he got basically the kind of government he wanted for Mexico, but Mexicans continued to believe that their government was their business and deeply resented the American intervention.

American involvement in World War I diverted attention from more than Mexico. Domestic reform took a backseat to "making the world safe for democracy." Yet war always brings changes on the home front. Thus the nation shifted gears, but progressivism did not entirely die. Indeed prohibitionists, woman suffragists, and immigration restrictionists won their greatest victories in the wake of war.

(Text continues on p. 752)

AMERICA AND THE WORLD
VERACRUZ: AN AFFAIR OF HONOR

U.S. Marines march into Veracruz to occupy the city while at the same time U.S. warships blockade the port to prevent delivery of weapons shipments from Europe. The occupation forces withdrew from Veracruz in November 1914, but U.S. troops remained in Mexico until 1917, when the United States finally recognized the new Mexican government established by Venustiano Carranza.

"It would be the irony of fate if my administration had to deal chiefly with foreign affairs," Woodrow Wilson remarked a few days before his inauguration as president in 1913. Wilson spoke the truth, as his own background had been limited almost exclusively to domestic affairs. In his career as a scholar, he had devoted years to the study of congressional government, and during his two-year stint as governor of New Jersey he had acquired first-hand knowledge of domestic affairs; but prior to entering the White House Wilson had evinced only a casual interest in international relations and knew very little about the workings or history of foreign affairs. As president, Wilson would face the ultimate test of his skills as a diplomatist in World War I, but his first challenge in foreign affairs came in revolution-torn Mexico, where he confronted warring political factions that demanded his attention from the day he entered office.

The problems in Mexico were as old as the nation. After winning independence from Spain in 1821, Mexico entered a period of profound political instability. More than a hundred governments came and fell during Mexico's first 50 years as a nation, as two factions, one conservative, the other liberal, fought for power. In broad terms, the conservative faction was composed of wealthy landowners who were aligned with the Catholic church and favored an aristocratic oligarchy (or even monarchy), and the liberal faction represented Mexico's nascent middle class and various peasant groups who favored democratic government and land reform.

Out of the constant clashes between these factions emerged General Porfirio Díaz, who ruled Mexico with an iron hand from the early 1870s to 1910. Díaz was a political strong man (*caudillo*) who drew his support from the military, wealthy landowners, and the Catholic church. As dictator, Díaz ended the political chaos and brought order to his nation, and he proved extremely adept at capitalizing on Mexico's new-found stability. He opened Mexico to foreign investors. Under his protective hand a flood of foreign businesspeople rushed in to tap Mexico's rich mineral wealth, to build railroads, and to exploit the agricultural sector of its economy. On the eve of World War I, American businesspeople valued their holdings in Mexico at one billion dollars. Yet only a handful of wealthy Mexicans benefited from the economic development of their nation, and the political stability Díaz brought to Mexico came at the expense of individual liberties. He crushed political opposition and turned a deaf ear to pleas for land reform.

In 1910, liberal opponents revolted and to the world's amazement Díaz proved to be a paper tiger. Unable to extinguish a series of small revolts that sprang up across Mexico, he fled the country and went into exile in France. Mexico's new leader was Francisco I. Madero, an idealist who championed the middle class's aspirations for democracy and the peasant class's demands for land reform. Madero had hardly settled into the presidency before new revolts broke out, plunging Mexico into political chaos. On February 22, 1913, less than two weeks before William Howard Taft's term as president ended, Madero and his vice president were assassinated by federal troops under the command of General Victoriano Huerta, who immediately proclaimed himself Mexico's new ruler. Despite the urgent recommendations of his ambassador to Mexico, Henry Lane Wilson, who was strongly identified with the Republican administration's "dollar diplomacy," President Taft did not extend diplomatic recognition to Huerta's government, leaving the issue to be resolved by the president-elect, Thomas Woodrow Wilson.

President Wilson refused to recognize Huerta's government. Wilson regarded Mexico's new strong man as a murderer and a usurper, a ruler who symbolized all that was wrong with Latin American governments. To Wilson's legalistic mind, diplomatic recognition implied moral approval, and he could never sanction a government that had seized power by substituting bullets for ballots. Moreover, no less than his claims to legitimacy, Huerta's claims to power were shaky. Following Madero's assassination, several political factions in Mexico revolted against Huerta. Emiliano Zapata led an army against federal troops in Morelos, a mountainous state in southern Mexico. In the north, Venustiano Carranza, the governor of Coahuila, declared himself the first chief of the Constitutionalist forces and won the allegiance of several powerful regional leaders, including Pancho Villa, Alvaro Obregon, and Pablo Gonzalez.

Because Huerta was not able to defeat his opponents in battle, his claim to controlling Mexico was suspect; and his apparent weakness only strengthened President Wilson's decision to withhold diplomatic recognition. In truth, Wilson wanted Huerta's government to fall, and American policy was designed to aid Huerta's opponents, particularly Carranza. As the self-proclaimed first chief of the Constitutionalist forces, Carranza appealed strongly to Wilson, who was anxious to find a tool for restoring democracy to Mexico. As Wilson confided to a British diplomat, "I am going to teach the South American republics to elect good men."

However noble his ambition, Wilson allowed his animus against Huerta to trigger an American invasion of Mexico. In April 1914, Mexican officials arrested several American sailors in Tampico, detained a mail courier, and delayed an official Department of State dispatch. Wilson used these minor incidents to precipitate a showdown with Huerta's government, and less than two weeks later American troops invaded the port city of Veracruz. At least 200 Mexicans died in the fighting that followed and another 300 were wounded, most of whom were noncombatant civilians. American troops remained in Veracruz for six months.

None of Mexico's warring factions approved the invasion and subsequent occupation of Veracruz. In fact, no issue has produced more bitterness in Mexico against the United States—not even the Mexican War. To Mexicans their defeat in the 1840s inflicted a serious wound to their national pride, but they saw the war as a lesson in power politics. Manifest destiny was a harsh policy, but Mexicans could understand the motives from which it sprang. Americans wanted American land, and they took it. What made the invasion of Veracruz so galling was that President Wilson clothed American aggression, in the words of one historian, "with the sanctimonious rainment of idealism." Because he insisted his acts were moral, Wilson "aroused both the hatred and the scorn of the Mexicans—hatred over the invasion but a deep scorn for what they saw as his hypocrisy."

In one sense, Wilson got what he wanted in Mexico. Huerta's government collapsed in 1915, and Carranza became the new president. In the larger sense, however, the United States was the big loser in Mexico. Mexicans deeply resented Wilson's arrogant assumption that he had the right to intervene in their internal affairs. Perhaps the ultimate lesson to be learned from Wilson's Mexican policy was that good intentions are no substitute for respecting the territorial integrity and independence of other nations.

PROGRESSIVE ACCOMPLISHMENTS, PROGRESSIVE FAILURES

The twentieth century began with great optimism about the power of human beings to shape their destinies. Progress, people believed, could be legislated. Efficient, noncorrupt government could provide order and stability, promote social justice, and improve personal morals. Groups organized to promote their goals, and more and more of them began to win their objectives. In the 1920s, however, some realized that legislation had not always had its desired effect, that not everyone had benefited equally, and that change had been far from radical.

The Impact of Legislation

Measured by direct results most progressive reforms proved disappointing. In some cases unintended consequences actually worked against the intended goals of laws. This often occurs when ideals confront reality. Solving one problem frequently creates another. Nevertheless, progressives established important precedents that opened doors to later, more effective reform.

Attempts to promote direct democracy were among the least effective. Direct election of senators did not seem to alter the kinds of people elected. Initiative, referendum, and recall were rarely used, and then not by people in general. The expense and organization needed for petition drives were beyond the reach of any but well-financed pressure groups. An unintended result of democratization was to increase the power of urban machines. Bosses may have had to work a little harder, but most were still able to dominate primaries as well as elections. The move toward popular voting increased the political power of populous cities and the machines that controlled them. The greatest failing of the movement was a dramatic drop in voter participation. Nevertheless, in some states, such as Wisconsin, government did become more responsive to public needs, and urban machines often adopted reform measures to maintain power.

Other kinds of urban reforms had varying results. In some, government did indeed become more efficiently and economically run. The competency and honesty of officials generally increased. An occasional consequence, however, was cuts in social services in less affluent neighborhoods. This was more likely to happen where the commissioner-manager system was adopted—usually in midsize cities without a tradition of machine politics. In other cities municipally owned utilities lowered rates, which provided real relief for the poor.

Attempts to regulate the railroads on either the state or national level rarely produced dramatic benefits for the general public. The chief advocates and beneficiaries of railroad regulation were frequently large shipping interests that did not share lower costs with consumers. With the Hepburn Act, Roosevelt did accomplish his primary goal of giving the ICC the power to set rates. The provision allowing court review of its decisions, however, made the act more significant as a precedent for expanded governmental power than as an immediate solution to problems. The courts ruled in favor of the railroads in most rate disputes.

Antimonopoly actions also did not always produce the intended results. For example, the breakups of Standard Oil and the American Tobacco Company did not increase competition or lower prices. Perhaps the only legislation to fulfill the promise of New Freedom was the Underwood Tariff, and it was reversed by the tariff legislation of the 1920s. The Clayton Antitrust Act was widely, and correctly, considered too vague for effective enforcement. The general counsel of the American Anti-Boycott Association analyzed the provision to exempt labor organizations from antitrust legislation and declared that the law "makes few changes in existing law as relating to labor unions, injunctions and contempts of court, and those are of slight practical importance." Later, the court decisions proved his assessment accurate.

The Federal Trade Commission (FTC) did not become an aggressive watchdog either. One of Wilson's cabinet members reported that the president viewed it as "a counsellor and friend to the business world," rather than as a "policeman to wield a club over the head of the business community." His appointments were fairly probusiness, and the appointments of the 1920s were even more so. In the end, the FTC proved beneficial to big business by protecting firms from unexpected suits and by outlawing many "unfair trade practices," many of which had promoted competition at the expense of stability. On the other hand, the FTC was also an important precedent.

Proclaimed victories for labor frequently turned out to be more symbolic than real. In the arbitration of the 1902 coal strike, for example, what the United Mine Workers did not receive is very significant: The union did not win recognition. As the 1920s would show, organized labor did not emerge from the progressive era any stronger. Yet the symbolism can be important. The precedent that the government would not automatically support the demands of management was later built upon during the New Deal of the 1930s.

Some labor legislation brought benefits but also produced unintended results. Child labor laws in combination with compulsory education legislation decreased the number of children from ages 10 to 15 who were working for wages from 1 in 5 in 1900 to 1 in 20 by 1930. During those same years, the number of students enrolled in secondary education increased by 800 percent. Both were desirable results, but in the short run at least, the poor received a mixed blessing. The incomes of a family's children were often crucial to its welfare, and no alternatives were provided. As one historian noted, "Child labor laws treated the symptoms and made the disease—poverty—worse." Much the same can be said about limits imposed on women's working hours. Laws establishing minimum wages for women helped somewhat to offset earning losses resulting from child labor legislation. In any event, laws such as the Child Labor Act were declared unconstitutional in the 1920s.

Workmen's compensation laws were an improvement over existing procedures but were not an unqualified victory of labor over management. Indeed, businesspeople eventually welcomed the relief from the growing number of suits instituted by hungry lawyers on a contingency fee basis. By agreeing to take a percentage of any damage awards and to charge no fee for lost cases, attorneys made it possible for poor workers to take legal action. The award schedule in most compensation plans provided payments far below what some lawyers had been winning in court. Workers, however, were guaranteed at least some compensation. For the industrialists, a predictable premium replaced the uncertainty of court actions, decreasing the risks and increasing stability in the cost of doing business.

The establishment of the Federal Reserve System also enhanced order and stability. Everyone benefited from the maintenance of cash reserves for emergencies, a more flexible currency, and national check clearing facilities. The banking system became more resistant to panics but, as 1929 would prove, not immune to them. Wall Street was not a big loser. Three of the five seats on the Federal Reserve Board went to large bankers, and the New York Federal Reserve bank quickly came to dominate the system. The new system, in other words, was a significant improvement, but far from a radical change.

From the consumer's point of view, the Pure Food and Drug Act and the Meat Inspection Act were great victories. After the rise of mass production and mass marketing, only federal action could provide adequate protection from adulteration of the nation's foodstuffs. Unintended beneficiaries, however, were the large drug and meat-packing companies that could more easily afford the increased expenses of meeting required production standards. Thus the effect was anticompetitive. Lobbying by the big meat packers also affected the final form of the legislation. Their victories included government payment of inspection costs and the deletion of the requirement to date canned meat. Like much progressive legislation, the final act did provide protection for consumers, but in a way agreeable to big business. Swift, one of the largest meat packers, even endorsed its passage in an advertisement declaring, "It is a wise law."

Other progressive legislation left mixed legacies. Roosevelt's conservation measures prevented wanton squandering of resources, but also aided the larger lumber companies. Morality legislation made undesirable activities illegal but at the same time more profitable for organized crime. It also fostered widespread disrespect for the law. With a maximum rate of 6 percent, the income tax did little to redistribute the huge fortunes of such men as J. P. Morgan but did establish an important tool for later use. A significant precedent was set by the Adamson Act, through which the federal government first dabbled in wage and in hour legislation. Many other progressive reforms were illusory or short lived. In the 1920s, lax enforcement and hostile court decisions reversed many of them. Nevertheless, laissez-faire had suffered an irreversible blow. That was a major accomplishment and perhaps as much as many progressives wanted.

Winners and Losers

Before the era was ended, people from almost every class and occupation had sought to take advantage of the climate of change to promote their interests. Obviously not all were equally successful. Few were unqualified winners or losers, but some gained far more than others, and some lost more than they gained. Clearly, large corporations were among the biggest winners. One historian labeled the movement "the triumph of conservatism." Given the basic moderation of all three presidents and most congressmen, as well as the resources and influence of big business, this may have been inevitable. It was not, however, the original intention of all legislation. To label most progressives as conservative is a gross mistake. They rejected the strict laissez-faire principles of nineteenth-century conservatives and embraced a vision of a more activist government.

Other winners included members of the growing body of middle-class technocrats. At all levels of government the search for orderly, efficient management created new job opportunities for engineers, health professionals, trained managers, and other experts. Reforms that diminished the influence of political parties also increased the power of special interest groups working for particular social and economic goals. Consumers of all classes shared benefits from government regulation.

In general most of the winners were white, urban, Protestant, and middle class. This was true even though working-class ethnics won victories in some cities and states. They and small businesspeople were among those who both lost and gained. African-Americans came closest to being unqualified losers. For them, the only lasting advances came from establishing organiza-tions. The NAACP survived to become an important force later in the century, and self-help organizations provided aid to many. Other victories were mainly token; the defeats were concrete.

In the South, and often in the North as well, African-Americans were clearly losers on the local level. At the same time black relations with the federal government also deteriorated. Of the three presidents, Roosevelt was the most sympathetic to blacks. In 1901, he invited Booker T. Washington to dine at the White House, consulted with him on some southern appointments, and named a few African-Americans to federal positions. His actions hardly reflected an acceptance of black equality, however. He believed, "as a race and in the mass they are altogether inferior to whites." One of his speeches to Congress seemed to condone lynching. Most disturbing to African-Americans

Theodore Roosevelt gave the appearance of supporting African-Americans when he invited Booker T. Washington to the White House, but like many white leaders, he did not promote equality between blacks and whites.

CHRONOLOGY
OF KEY EVENTS

1879 Henry George's *Progress and Poverty* proposes a tax on land as a means of controlling illegitimate profits

1888 Edward Bellamy's *Looking Backward* depicts a utopian society guided by cooperation rather than competition

1889 Jane Addams founds Hull House

1901 President William McKinley is assassinated; Theodore Roosevelt becomes the twenty-sixth president

1902 Oregon, South Dakota, and Utah become first states to adopt initiative and recall; Roosevelt threatens to use troops to run coal mines when owners refuse to negotiate; Roosevelt charges Northern Securities with violating the Sherman Antitrust Act—in 1904, the U.S. Supreme Court orders the company's breakup

1903 In *The Souls of Black Folks*, W. E. B. Du Bois attacks Booker T. Washington for abandoning the goal of equal rights; Wisconsin becomes the first state to adopt primary elections; Elkins Act bars railroad rebates

1904 Lincoln Steffins's *Shame of the Cities* exposes corruption in city government; United States obtains right to build the Panama Canal; announcement of Roosevelt Corollary to the Monroe Doctrine, asserting the right of the United States to exercise international police power in the Caribbean

1905 Roosevelt helps negotiate an end to a war between Russia and Japan—he wins the Nobel Peace Prize for his efforts

1906 Upton Sinclair's *The Jungle* exposes unsanitary conditions in the meat-packing industry; Meat Inspection Act enforces health and sanitary standards in meat-packing industry; Pure Food and Drug Act prohibits the use of harmful additives and misleading advertisements of drugs; Hepburn Act gives the Interstate Commerce Commission the right to set maximum freight rates

1907 Roosevelt dispatches 16 battleships ("the great white fleet") on an around-the-world cruise

1908 Staunton, Virginia, hires the first city manager

1909 National Association for the Advancement of Colored People (NAACP) is founded to protect the rights of black Americans

1910 Mann-Elkins Act allows Interstate Commerce Commission to regulate railroad rates even without complaints from shippers

1912–1917 12 states adopt minimum wage laws for women; 30 states adopt industrial accident insurance

1912 Roosevelt and his supporters launch the Progressive party; Democrat Woodrow Wilson is elected the twenty-eighth president

1913 Sixteenth Amendment gives Congress the power to levy an income tax; Underwood-Simmons Tariff substantially lowers duties on imports and imposes a graduated income tax; Seventeenth Amendment requires direct election of senators; Federal Reserve System is created to supervise banking system and regulate money supply

1914 Federal Trade Commission is established to preserve economic competition by preventing unfair business practices; Clayton Antitrust Act prohibits interlocking corporate directorates and predatory pricing policies; U.S. Navy captures Mexican port of Veracruz

1915 U.S. marines are dispatched to Haiti

1916 U.S. troops enter Mexico to search for Pancho Villa; U.S. marines are sent to Dominican Republic

1919 Eighteenth Amendment prohibits manufacture and sale of liquor

1920 Nineteenth Amendment grants women the right to vote

was his handling of an incident in Brownsville, Texas, in 1906. There, a shoot-out occurred between white townspeople and black soldiers. No one could determine exactly what happened, but that did not deter Roosevelt from ordering dishonorable discharges for 167 black soldiers without court martial.

When Taft became president, he approved of southern disfranchisement and appointed white-supremacist Republicans to federal jobs. These actions by the two Republicans convinced some African-Americans, including W. E. B. Du Bois, to support Wilson in 1912. They made a mistake. The influence of Wilson's southern upbringing and advisors became apparent when he allowed his cabinet to segregate federal employees and to demote black office-holders, especially those "who boss white girls." Jim Crow moved to Washington, and Wilson's defense of these actions indicated the blindness and paternalism of many white progressives on race:

> It is true that the segregation of the colored employees in the several departments was begun upon the initiative and at the suggestion of the heads of departments, but as much in the interest of the negroes as for any other reason, with the approval of some of the most influential negroes I know, and with the idea that the friction, or rather the discontent and uneasiness, which had prevailed in many departments would thereby be removed. It is as far as possible from being a movement against the negroes. I believe it to be in their interest.

It seems that white progressives often seemed to feel they knew the best interests of those not like them, at home and abroad.

CONCLUSION

At the start of the new century, Americans confronted the urban squalor, poverty, powerful monopolies, corrupt and inefficient government, disorder, and despair that had accompanied the forces of modernization. They were determined to do something to achieve more social justice and stability. Numerous solutions were proposed and victories won. In the end, however, Americans rejected radicalism and ignored major problems.

Once again the nation resolutely refused to come to terms with its ethnic and cultural diversity. Rather than protect minorities, most actions infringed on their personal liberties and sought to control rather than accommodate their differences. Women won some victories, but the majority of Americans did not accept the radical feminists' vision of true equality. Socialists' dreams of a peaceful, democratic redistribution of the country's wealth fell on deaf ears. In the end, there was no significant change in the distribution of either wealth or power. The United States had weeded and tidied up its social garden, not replanted it. Although that garden produced bitter fruit for some people, many Americans benefited. Also, the vigor and diversity of progressive actions brought to light many problems and provided later generations with a body of experience in dealing with them.

SUGGESTIONS FOR FURTHER READING

OVERVIEWS AND SURVEYS

John W. Chambers, *The Tyranny of Change: America in the Progressive Era* (1980); Robert M. Crunden, *Ministers of Reform: The Progressives' Achievement in American Civilization* (1982); Arthur Ekrich, *Progressivism in America* (1974); Richard Hofstadter, *Age of Reform* (1955); Arthur S. Link and Richard L. McCormick, *Progressivism* (1983); Robert Wiebe, *The Search for Order* (1967).

THE PROGRESSIVE IMPULSE

Richard Abrams, *The Burdens of Progress* (1978); Jerold S. Auerbach, *Unequal Justice: Lawyers and Social Change in Modern America* (1976); Robert M. Crunden, *Ministers of Reform: The Progressives' Achievement in American Civilization, 1889–1920* (1982); Harold U. Faulkner, *The Quest for Social Justice, 1898–1914* (1931); Louis Filler, *The Muckrakers*, rev. ed. (1976); Samuel Haber, *Efficiency and Uplift: Scientific Management in the Progressive Era* (1964); Thomas Haskell, *The Emergence of Professional Social Science* (1977); William R. Hutchison, *The Modernist Impulse in American Protestantism* (1976); James T. Kloppenberg, *Uncertain Victory: Social Democracy and Progressivism in European and American Thought, 1870–1920* (1986); Samuel Konefsky, *The Legacy of Holmes and Brandeis* (1956); David W. Marcell, *Progress and Pragmatism* (1974); David W. Noble, *The Progressive Mind*, rev. ed. (1981);

Frank Tariello, *The Reconstruction of American Political Ideology* (1982); John L. Thomas, *Alternative America: Henry George, Edward Bellamy, Henry Demarest Lloyd, and the Adversary Tradition* (1983); Laurence Veysey, *The Emergence of the American University* (1970); James Weinstein, *The Corporate Ideal in the Liberal State, 1900–1918* (1968); Morton White, *Social Thought in America: The Revolt Against Formalism* (1975); Harold S. Wilson, *McClure's Magazine and the Muckrakers* (1970).

PROGRESSIVES IN ACTION

John D. Buenker, *Urban Liberalism and Progressive Reform* (1973); Norman H. Clark, *Deliver Us From Evil: An Interpretation of Prohibition* (1976); Allen F. Davis, *Spearheads for Reform: The Social Settlements and the Progressive Movement, 1890–1914* (1967); Rene J. Dubos, *The White Plague: Tuberculosis, Man, and Society* (1952); Nancy S. Dye, *As Equals and Sisters: Feminism, the Labor Movement, and the Women's Trade Union League of New York* (1980); Dewey Grantham, *Southern Progressivism: The Reconciliation of Progress and Tradition* (1983); Sheldon Hackney, *Populism to Progressivism in Alabama* (1969); Melvin G. Holli, *Reform in Detroit: Hazen S. Pingree and Urban Politics* (1969); Charles F. Kellogg, *NAACP* (1967); Ellen Condliffe Lagemann, *A Generation of Women: Education in the Lives of Progressive Reformers* (1979); Roy Lubove, *The Progressives and the Slums, 1890–1917* (1962); Richard L. McCormick, *From Realignment to Reform: Political Change in New York State, 1893–1910* (1981); August Meier, *Negro Thought in America, 1880–1915* (1963); George E. Mowry, *California Progressives* (1951); Bradley R. Rice, *Progressive Cities: The Commission Government Movement* (1977); Ruth Rosen, *The Lost Sisterhood: Prostitution in America, 1900–1918* (1982); Bruce M. Stave, *Urban Bosses, Machines, and Progressive Reformers*, 2d ed. (1984); David P. Thelen, *The New Citizenship: Origins of Progressivism in Wisconsin* (1972); James H. Timberlake, *Prohibition and the Progressive Movement* (1963); Walter I. Trattner, *Crusade for the Children* (1970); Irwin Yellowitz, *Labor and the Progressive Movement in New York State* (1965).

PROGRESSIVISM MOVES TO THE NATIONAL LEVEL

John D. Buenker, *The Income Tax and the Progressive Era* (1985); Paolo E. Coletta, *The Presidency of William Howard Taft* (1973); Lewis L. Gould, *Reform and Regulation: American Politics from Roosevelt to Wilson* (1986); James Holt, *Congressional Insurgents and the Party System* (1969); James Penick, Jr., *Progressive Politics and Conservation: The Ballinger-Pinchot Affair* (1968); James Oliver Robertson, *No Third Choice: Progressives in Republican Politics, 1916–1921* (1983).

PROGRESSIVISM IN THE INTERNATIONAL ARENA

P. Edward Haley, *Revolution and Intervention: The Diplomacy of Taft and Wilson with Mexico, 1910–1917* (1970); Walter LaFeber, *The Panama Canal*, rev. ed. (1989); Lester Langley, *The United States and the Carribean* (1980); Dana G. Munro, *Intervention and Dollar Diplomacy in the Caribbean, 1900–1921* (1964); Whitney Perkins, *Constraints of Empire: The United States and Caribbean Interventions* (1981); Robert E. Quirk, *An Affair of Honor: Woodrow Wilson and the Occupation of Veracruz* (1962); John Womack, *Zapata and the Mexican Revolution* (1968).

PROGRESSIVE ACCOMPLISHMENTS, PROGRESSIVE FAILURES

Paul D. Casdorph, *Republicans, Negroes, and Progressives in the South, 1912–1916* (1981); John Dittmer, *Black Georgia in the Progressive Era, 1900–1920* (1977); Jack Temple Kirby, *Darkness at the Dawning: Race and Reform in the Progressive South* (1972); Gabriel Kolko, *The Triumph of Conservatism* (1963); Robert Wiebe, *Businessmen and Reform* (1962).

BIOGRAPHIES

Howard K. Beale, *Theodore Roosevelt and the Rise of America to World Power* (1956); John M. Blum, *The Republican Roosevelt*, 2d ed. (1977), and *Woodrow Wilson and the Politics of Morality* (1956); John Milton Cooper, Jr., *The Warrior and the Priest: Woodrow Wilson and Theodore Roosevelt* (1983); Allen F. Davis, *American Heroine: Jane Addams* (1973); William Harbaugh, *The Life and Times of Theodore Roosevelt*, rev. ed. (1963); Louis R. Harlan, *Booker T. Washington: The Making of a Black Leader, 1856–1901* (1972), and *The Wizard of Tuskegee, 1901–1915* (1983); Arthur S. Link, *Wilson*, 5 vols. (1947–1965), and *Woodrow Wilson and the Progressive Era* (1954); Daniel Nelson, *Frederick W. Taylor and the Rise of Scientific Management* (1980); David Riesman, *Thorstein Veblen* (1953); Elliott M. Rudwick, *W. E. B. Du Bois* (1960); David P. Thelen, *Robert LaFollette and the Insurgent Spirit* (1976).

126

a

900 Die
400 An
Was

EUROPE VIA LIVERPOOL
LUSITANIA

Fig. 55

Production Possibility
Curve 2

1914

1918

1914   1918

Guns

CHAPTER 23

The United States and World War I

The Road to War
American Neutrality
Allied Violations of Neutrality
Submarine Warfare
Preparedness Campaign
The Election of 1916
The End of Neutrality

American Industry Goes to War
Voluntarism
"Hooverizing"
Peace with Labor
Financing the War

The American Public Goes to War
Selling the War
Political Repression
Wartime Reform
Blacks and the Great Migration

The War Front
The War at Sea
Raising an Army
The Defeat of Germany

Social Unrest After the War
Labor Unrest and the Red Scare

The Treaty of Versailles
The Fourteen Points
Discord Among the Victors
The Struggle for Ratification
The Election of 1920

*D*isillusioned writers of the 1920s honored Randolph Bourne as "the intellectual hero of World War I," yet his appearance was anything but heroic. Theodore Dreiser called Bourne "as frightening a dwarf as I had ever seen." An unusually messy forceps delivery crushed one side of Bourne's skull at birth, leaving him with a misshapen ear, a partially paralyzed face, and a mouth permanently askew in a horrible grimace. Then, when he was four, an attack of spinal tuberculosis twisted his frame and left him a hunchback dwarf.

Bourne's brain, however, was razor sharp. He started reading at the age of 2, and by the time he entered school, he had devoured entire books, including the Bible. A brilliant student, Bourne attended Columbia University where he studied under Franz Boaz, the father of cultural anthropology; John Dewey, the famed educator and apostle of pragmatism; and Charles A. Beard, the historian who stressed the economic motives of the founding fathers.

Bourne left college on the eve of World War I determined to become a writer. Drawn by the intense intellectual ferment of the day, he settled in New York's Greenwich Village, where self-styled literary radicals had declared war on the smugness and the optimism of American culture. Bourne contributed to new magazines, such as *The New Republic*, *The Seven Arts*, and *The New Masses*. While his interests ranged wide and far, he made his reputation as a critic of America's entrance into World War I.

Bourne loathed President Woodrow Wilson, whom he labeled "an indubitably intellectualized president," but he directed his choicest barbs at fellow intellectuals who supported Wilson's policies. In effect, he accused them of not doing their job as thinkers—of not subjecting the president's high-sounding rhetoric to the fierce scrutiny required to sharpen public debate. Instead of questioning Wilson's policies, they had betrayed their duty by "opening the sluices and flooding the public with the sewage of the war spirit." When his colleagues accused Bourne of not understanding the realities of war, he replied: "In a time of faith, skepticism is the most intolerable of all insults."

Bourne refused to endow the war with lofty purposes. Hardly a knee-jerk pacifist, he knew that some wars were unavoidable, perhaps even necessary. In his judgment, however, World War I was not a struggle to make the world safe for democracy; it was nothing more than "frenzied mutual suicide." To those who argued that this war would be different, that this war could somehow be converted into an instrument of progress and democracy, Bourne replied that World War I would unleash "all the evils that are organically bound up with it." America's allies would reject Wilson's call for a "peace without victory," Bourne cautioned, because "war determines its own end—victory." Eschewing a just peace, they would try to win the war and "then grab what they can."

On the home front there would be "clumsily levied taxes and the robberies of imperfectly controlled private enterprises," warned Bourne, and the suppression of civil liberties and the growth of big government. "War is the health of the State," he declared in one of his most famous lines. "It automatically sets in motion

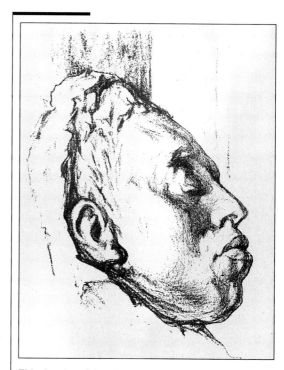

This drawing of American critic, essayist, and pacifist Randolph Silliman Bourne was done by Arthur G. Dove from the death mask by James Earle Fraser.

October 1915 to permit loans to belligerents, a decision that favored Great Britain and France far more than Germany. By 1917 American loans to the Allies had soared to $2.25 billion; loans to Germany stood at a paltry $27 million. The United States became a creditor nation for the first time, giving Americans a strong economic interest in an Allied victory.

Yet the marketplace did not drive America into the Allies' waiting arms. Ultimately, submarines broke the peace between the United States and Germany.

Submarine Warfare

Given Britain's overwhelming naval superiority, Germany had no chance of winning a conventional sea war. Therefore, Germany decided to rely on a new weapon, the submarine, and on February 4, 1915 Germany proclaimed a "war zone" around the British Isles. Henceforth all enemy merchant ships that entered the zone would be torpedoed without warning, and neutral ships would not be guaranteed safe passage. Germany was bluffing. It had only four submarines in the area, but Germany intended to use the threat of submarine warfare to terrorize and intimidate its enemies until it could build enough ships to enforce its threats.

A new development in naval technology, the submarine posed serious challenges to international law. The law required ships that attacked other vessels on the high seas to warn their intended victims, allow time for passengers to reach lifeboats and clear the area, and then rescue survivors after the sinking. Moreover, merchant vessels suspected of transporting contraband had to be "visited and searched" before being attacked. By its very nature, the submarine could not abide by these regulations. A silent assassin whose effectiveness depended on the element of surprise, it had to strike from below the surface. Therefore, Germany ignored international law and authorized its submarines to kill without warning.

Nothing in President Wilson's makeup prepared him to accept submarine warfare. He was not a student of naval history or international affairs. His own experience as a scholar and as a progressive governor had been limited to do-

The German U-boat (*Unterseeboot*) violated an international law that required a warship to warn a passenger or merchant vessel before attacking. The U-boat struck silently and without warning.

mestic politics, and he wanted to apply the same principles of liberal reform to foreign affairs. Wilson's approach to foreign affairs was both legalistic and moralistic. He expected nation-states to behave like gentlemen; and, above all, that meant living up to the letter of international law and respecting the rights of every nation.

To Wilson's legalistic mind, German submarines committed criminal acts. In contrast to British violations of American neutrality, which merely resulted in property losses, submarine warfare threatened to kill innocent civilians. In unusually blunt language, he warned Berlin that it would be held "strictly accountable" for American lives lost to submarine attacks. While international law did not guarantee the safety of neutrals who traveled on belligerent ships, Wilson acted as though it did. With the United States demanding that Germany treat a single

American passenger as a shield for an entire merchant ship, a German diplomat in Washington warned "there will be hell to pay."

On March 28, 1915, a German submarine torpedoed the *Falaba*, a British liner, killing 104 passengers, including one American. "PIRACY," "SHOCKING BLOODTHIRSTINESS," "BARBARISM RUN MAD," screamed the American press in banner headlines. Wilson was outraged, but Secretary of State Bryan reminded the president of numerous British violations of American neutrality in her attempt to blockade Germany. "Why be shocked at the drowning of a few people," asked Bryan, "if there is no objection to the starving of a nation?"

While Wilson and Bryan debated America's response, the German Embassy on May 1 took out ads in New York newspapers warning Americans not to travel on Allied ships. Undeterred, 197 Americans sailed for the British Isles on board the *Lusitania*, the queen of the British-owned Cunard fleet. On May 7, 1915, a German submarine torpedoed the *Lusitania* off the coast of Ireland. She sank in 18 minutes, killing 1198 persons, 128 of them Americans. The public was shocked and outraged. The *New York Nation* called the sinking "wholesale murder on the high seas," and a small minority of Americans, led by Theodore Roosevelt, demanded war. It did not seem to matter that the *Lusitania* (like the *Falaba*) was transporting munitions in her hull and had secret orders to ram submarines on sight.

Here was a harsh test of America's neutrality, and the president rose to the challenge. In a sharply worded dispatch, Wilson ordered Germany to apologize for the sinking, compensate the victims, and pledge to stop attacking merchant ships. When Berlin equivocated, Wilson sent a second *Lusitania* note repeating his demands. This time the Germans met him halfway. In February 1916 they expressed regret over the *Lusitania* and agreed to pay an indemnity. However, the Imperial Government refused to stop sinking merchant ships without warning, explaining that Germany's survival depended on full use of the submarine.

Though Wilson's handling of the *Lusitania* crisis had been far from bellicose, Bryan resigned from the cabinet on June 8 to protest what he saw as a dangerous tilt toward Great Britain in American policy. From the outset, he had urged the president to try to end the war through mediation and arbitration; but, as the war progressed, Bryan had become convinced that Wilson's policies would lead to war with Germany. While Bryan's resignation permitted the president to replace him as secretary of state with Robert Lansing, who shared Wilson's views, it also freed Bryan to plead his case for strict neutrality before the public.

For his part, Wilson felt relieved to put the *Lusitania* incident behind him, Bryan's resignation notwithstanding. Still, Wilson knew that the issue of submarine warfare had not been resolved. "I can't keep the country out of war," he admitted privately. "Any little German lieutenant can put us into war at any time by some calculated outrage."

Events soon showed how right he was. On March 24, 1916, a submarine attacked the *Sussex*, an unarmed French passenger ship. The *Sussex* reached port, but more than 80 people died in the attack and 7 Americans sustained severe wounds. While Secretary Lansing insisted that the time for writing notes had ended, Wilson tempered his response. He threatened to sever diplomatic relations unless Germany promised to stop sinking all merchant and passenger ships without warning. Anxious to keep the United States neutral, Berlin agreed. The so-called *Sussex* pledge reduced tensions between the United States and Germany for the remainder of 1916, but the fragile peace depended solely on German restraint.

Preparedness Campaign

As the submarine threatened to draw the United States into the fighting, the American people and their leaders debated whether or not to make ready for war. Initially, Wilson's policy toward preparedness reflected cautious hostility. In December 1914 he told Congress, "We never have had, and while we retain our present principles and ideals we never shall have, a large standing army."

Many Americans saw the issue differently. Wilson increasingly found himself assailed by prominent and highly vocal critics who insisted that the best way to preserve peace was to prepare for war. The pugnacious Theodore Roosevelt called the president "the popular pacifist hero," while another critic sneered that the Germans were "standing by their torpedoes, the British by their guns, and Wilson by strict accountability." As Tin Pan Alley produced songs with titles such as "I Did Not Raise My Boy to Be a Coward," the National Security League, headed by General Leonard Wood, organized volunteer military training programs across the country.

Yet Wilson felt pressured by groups opposed to war. Socialists such as Eugene V. Debs and Morris Hillquit dismissed the war as a struggle for assets among capitalist nations. Radicals such as anarchist Emma Goldman and "Big Bill" Haywood, head of the Industrial Workers of the World, shared this view and advocated violent resistance to preparedness. Liberal reformers such as Randolph Bourne and Oswald Garrison Villard feared that war would destroy the spirit of progressivism. Pacifists such as social worker Jane Addams and Hamilton Holt, head of the League to Enforce Peace, opposed the war on moral grounds. And most troubling of all, Wilson had to worry about groups within his own party that wanted no part of Europe's war. Speaking for the peace Democrats, former Secretary of State William Jennings Bryan warned that a preparedness campaign would transform the United States into "a vast armory with skull and crossbones above the door."

In the end, Wilson shifted ground and threw his support behind a moderate preparedness program. Throughout January and February 1916, he stumped the country pleading for a military force powerful enough to protect the nation's honor. In June 1916 Congress passed the National Defense Act (Hay Act), increasing the army from 90,000 to 175,000 men. A few months later Congress passed the Naval Construction Act, appropriating more than $500 million for new ships. Though of small importance militarily (Teddy Roosevelt dismissed the measures as a "shadow program" of "half preparedness"), both acts drew fire from the anti-preparedness forces in Congress who predicted that armaments would lead to war.

At the height of the preparedness controversy, Wilson had to beat back a serious challenge to his control of American foreign policy. During the early months of 1916, Congress considered separate resolutions sponsored by Senator Thomas Gore of Oklahoma and Representative Jeff McLemore of Texas. Fearing that Wilson's defense of neutral rights would draw the United States into the conflict, the Gore-McLemore resolutions sought to prevent future incidents by prohibiting Americans from traveling on ships owned by belligerent nations and by prohibiting American vessels or neutral vessels from transporting American citizens and contraband "at one and the same time." Both resolutions enjoyed strong support in Congress, and for a while their passage appeared inevitable, but Wilson threw his power and prestige into a furious attack on both measures, insisting that if the United States accepted any abridgment of neutral rights "many other humiliations would follow." In the end, Congress accepted his argument and the Gore-McLemore resolutions went down to defeat.

The Election of 1916

Foreign affairs dominated the election of 1916. The Republicans chose Charles Evans Hughes as their candidate over the fiery Theodore Roosevelt. A member of the progressive wing of the GOP, Hughes was a former governor of New York and a Supreme Court justice who had earned a solid reputation as a liberal. His nomination demonstrated the GOP's determination to regain progressive support and avoid the split that had put Wilson in the White House four years earlier. Though his campaign speeches criticized the president soundly, Hughes had a hard time explaining how his policies differed.

Wilson, by contrast, ran squarely on his record. The Democratic platform, which Wilson wrote in advance of the convention, stressed the president's legislative victories for progressive reform, his patient handling of the Mexican crisis, and his steadfast insistence on American neutrality. While the delegates responded warmly to the first two items, they burst into thunderous applause as they heard speakers praise the president for keeping the nation at peace.

Profoundly influenced by the demonstrations, Wilson decided to make peace the key issue in 1916. For the remainder of the campaign, he labeled the Republicans the party of war and charged that Hughes' election would plunge the United States into Europe's madness. Despite his support for military preparedness and his battles with Congress, Wilson ran as the peace candidate in the election of 1916, and "He kept us out of war" became the Democrats' rallying cry.

The race was extremely close. On election eve the *New York Times* and the *New York World* both awarded victory to Hughes, who went to bed believing he had won. He ran well in traditional Republican strongholds such as the Midwest (he won Illinois, Indiana, and Michigan) and the large eastern states. However, Wilson won in the Electoral College by a vote of 277 to 254, with a popular vote margin of 9.1 million to Hughes's 8.5 million.

A careful analysis of Wilson's victory reveals that the Democrats won because they managed to fuse progressivism with the cause of peace. Wilson carried the Solid South, Ohio, Maryland, and New Hampshire, but he owed his victory to voters west of the Mississippi River, where he took every state except Oregon, Iowa, South Dakota, and Minnesota. This was the section of the country where peace sentiment ran high and the opposition to preparedness was the strongest. Moreover, the Democratic party's strength in 1916 clearly rested on an ethnic-worker-farmer coalition. Wilson captured the Solid South, the labor vote in the Northeast and Midwest, the old-line progressives, and substantial numbers of western farmers.

The End of Neutrality

Interpreting his reelection as a vote for peace, Wilson attempted to mediate. On December 18, 1916, he asked the belligerents to list their war aims and state their terms for peace. The following month he called for both sides to embrace his call for "peace without victory." Neither side welcomed his overtures. The Germans announced they would not permit neutrals at the conference table, while the British politely rejected Wilson's offer. Privately, a high-ranking British official confided to Walter Hines Page, the American ambassador: "Everybody is mad as hell," and called Wilson an "ass." Randolph Bourne was right. Above all else, the belligerents wanted victory.

Any hope for a negotiated settlement ended when Germany announced that after February 1, 1917, all vessels caught in the war zone, neutral or belligerent, armed or unarmed, would be sunk without warning. Driven to desperation by the British blockade and unable to break the impasse on land, Germany had decided to risk everything on a furious U-boat campaign designed to starve Britain into submission. The German high command expected the United States to declare war in retaliation, but they believed their submarines could deliver a knockout blow before America could mobilize.

Here, then, was the ultimate test of "strict accountability." Members of his cabinet pressed Wilson to declare war, but he broke diplomatic relations instead. Though critics accused the president of shaking first his fist and then his finger, Wilson refused to budge. Viewing war as the defeat of reason, he could not bring himself to act. For weeks he seemed indecisive and confused, unable to accept the fact that "strict accountability" demanded war once the Germans started sinking American ships.

The Zimmermann telegram snapped Wilson out of his daze. On January 16 British cryptographers intercepted a secret message from Arthur Zimmermann, the German foreign minister, to the German ambassador to Mexico, proposing an alliance between Germany and Mexico in the event Germany went to war with the United States. Germany promised to help Mexico recover the territory it had lost in the 1840s, roughly the present-day states of Texas, New Mexico, California, and Arizona. The British revealed the scheme to Wilson on February 24, hoping to draw the United States into the war.

The Zimmermann telegram convinced Wilson that German militarism threatened American security. For years the United States had been concerned about Germany's economic penetration of world markets, as well as her strong military tradition. The Zimmermann telegram persuaded millions of Americans that Germany would stop at nothing to satisfy her ambitions and that those ambitions posed a serious danger to America's rights and security.

Late in February Wilson asked Congress for permission to arm American merchant ships. The House approved, but 11 pacifists in the Senate filibustered against the bill. Dismissing his Senate opponents as "a little band of willful men, representing no opinion but their own," Wilson issued an executive order on March 12, arming merchant ships and instructing them to shoot submarines on sight.

At this critical juncture, with the United States and Germany virtually at war, the Russian Revolution erupted. Suddenly, the czar's government was swept away, and in its place stood the provisional government of a Russian Republic, complete with a representative parliament. Given his penchant for framing issues in moral terms, Wilson could now view the Allies in a new light: With the only autocratic regime among the Allies transformed overnight into a fledgling democracy, the war now truly seemed to pit the forces of democracy against the forces of despotism.

Pale and solemn, Wilson delivered his war message to Congress on April 2. The United States "had no quarrel with the German people," he insisted, but their "military masters" had to be defeated in order to make the world "safe for democracy." Congress interrupted his address several times with thunderous applause. The next day the Senate approved the war resolution, 82 to 6; the House followed on April 6, 373 to 50. The president signed the declaration on April 7, 1917, and America was at war.

For more than two years Wilson had worked frantically to keep the United States at peace: Why did he now lead the nation to war? True, cultural ties with Great Britain predisposed the United States to favor the Allies, and enormous volumes of trade and loans strengthened those ties. Yet cultural bonds and money did not decide the issue. Wilson drew the sword, although reluctantly, because of his devotion to the rule of law.

In the end, Wilson concluded that German submarines violated international law and made a mockery of America's long-standing commitment to freedom of the seas. Therefore, his strong defense of neutral rights left him no choice but to declare war once Germany resumed its attacks on American ships.

One additional factor weighed heavily on Wilson—his desire to help shape the peace. By entering the war, the United States would be guaranteed a place at the peace table. "I hate this war," an anguished Wilson confided to one of his aides, "and the only thing I care about on earth is the peace I am going to make at the end of it."

Most Americans supported Wilson's call to arms. John Dewey, the famed educator, spoke for progressives when he described war as an ugly reality that had to be converted into an instrument for benefiting mankind. Randolph Bourne disagreed. "If the war is too strong for you to prevent," he asked pointedly, "how is it going to be weak enough for you to control and mould to your liberal purposes?"

AMERICAN INDUSTRY GOES TO WAR

At first administration officials believed America's major contribution to the war would be economic, not military. Production had to be raised to supply the Allies. Yet no one, in or out of government, had a thorough understanding of the economy. Wilson looked skeptical when a leading economist at Columbia University estimated the war might cost as much as $10 billion in its first year. Wilson badly underestimated both the size and the cost of the task at hand.

Voluntarism

Thanks to the strength of the peace forces, the United States entered the Great War unprepared. The problems went far beyond the puny size of the military forces. Americans themselves had no idea of what the war would ask of them as a society. Decisions had to be made about mobilization, but the public had not formed a consensus on the proper role of government in society. One group of progressives demanded more government regulation, but another group simply wanted to break up the large industrial monopolies and then let market forces govern the economy. Conservatives opposed any growth of government power at the expense of business. Caught between these differing views, Wilson hesitated to mobilize by decree. Instead, he tried to create a system of economic incentives that would encourage Americans to support the war in a spirit of voluntarism.

It took nearly a year to organize an effective war administration. Wilson established a war cabinet with six key boards, conferring broad power on the central government. The War Industries Board (WIB), organized early in 1918 under the leadership of Bernard M. Baruch, a Wall Street financier, assumed the task of managing the economy. Baruch's team of 100 businessmen (many of them volunteer "Dollar-A-Year" men) fixed prices, set priorities, and reduced waste. To increase production, they appealed to the profit motive. Baruch reasoned that "you could be forgiven if you paid too much to get the stuff, but you could never be forgiven if you did not get it, and lost the war." The WIB set prices artificially high, permitting profits to triple during the war. One steel executive confessed: "We are all making more money out of this war than the average human being ought to."

The Fuel Administration, the War Trade Board, the Shipping Board, and the U.S. Railroad Administration adopted similar policies. Under the slogan "Mine More Coal," the Fuel Administration increased production by two-fifths and conserved supplies through voluntary "lightless nights" and "gasless Sundays." The Railroad Administration ended the chaos that had snarled the rail system during the early months of the war, spending more than $500 million on equipment and repairs. By offering large profits to railroads and high wages to workers, it established a rail system under national control.

"Hooverizing"

Agricultural production came under the jurisdiction of the Food Administration, headed by Herbert Hoover, a mining engineer and self-made millionaire who had served with distinction as director of relief operations in Belgium. Appealing to the spirit of patriotism, he preached "the gospel of the clean plate." Americans "Hooverized" with wheatless Mondays and Wednesdays, meatless Tuesdays, and porkless Thursdays and Saturdays.

No foe of profits, Hoover set farm prices at high levels to encourage production. He stabilized the grain market by guaranteeing farmers a minimum price, and he purchased raw sugar

and then sold it to refineries at a fixed rate. The policies worked. Overall, real farm incomes rose 30 percent during the war; and, despite bad wheat crops in 1916 and 1917, food production increased by one-quarter, domestic food consumption fell, and America's food shipments to the Allies tripled.

Peace with Labor

The government also made concessions to labor. At his own request, Wilson addressed the American Federation of Labor (AFL) convention in November 1917, the first time a president had so honored the trade union movement. Flanked by a guard of soldiers to dramatize the solemnity of the occasion, he delivered an eloquent plea for industrial peace. Important policy shifts followed. Gradually, Wilson recognized labor's right to organize and engage in collective bargaining, and he sanctioned other key demands, including the eight-hour workday. To settle labor disputes, Wilson created the National War Labor Board (WLB), with ex-president William Howard Taft and Frank B. Walsh, a liberal lawyer, as its chairmen. Though it lacked legal authority, the WLB had the president's backing and a commitment from industry and labor to accept its decisions. During the war the WLB heard 1241 cases affecting 711,500 workers.

While Wilson embraced the AFL, his administration opposed militant unions like the Industrial Workers of the World (IWW or the "Wobblies"). From the textile mills of New England to the logging camps of the Pacific Northwest, the Wobblies demanded higher wages and better working conditions, and they went out on strike to win them. Because the Wobblies frequently employed the rhetoric of class warfare to dramatize their demands, their strikes frightened many Americans who feared social revolution. Warning that strikes would cripple the war effort, shrewd businessmen played upon these fears to demand suppression of the so-called radical unions. The Wobblies were "traitors," they sneered, and the IWW stood for "I Won't Work."

Samuel Gompers, president of the AFL, shrewdly separated his union from the militant workers. He seized Wilson's olive branch and

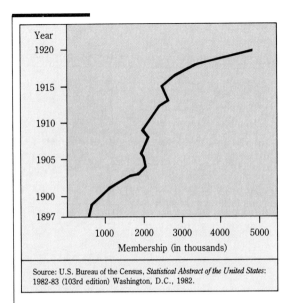

Figure 23.1
Labor union membership, 1897–1920

Source: U.S. Bureau of the Census, *Statistical Abstract of the United States:* 1982-83 (103rd edition) Washington, D.C., 1982.

pledged not to strike for the duration of the war. The AFL supported the war like superpatriots and joined the administration's attack on socialist critics. Gompers's policies paid handsome dividends. The AFL won a voice in homefront policy, and union men occupied seats in wartime agencies where they pushed for the 8-hour day and staved off pressure from employers bent on preserving the open shop. Real income of manufacturing workers and coal miners rose by one-fifth between 1914 and 1918. By 1919 almost half of the American labor force had achieved a 48-hour week (compared to one-eighth in 1915). Finally, the AFL expanded its membership from 2.7 million in 1916 to 4 million in 1919.

Financing the War

While business and labor both profited from the war, neither group could agree on how it should be financed. By 1920 the war had cost $33.5 billion—33 times the federal government's revenues in 1916. Conservatives favored a regressive tax policy—consumption taxes, borrowing, and, if necessary, a slight increase in income taxes. Reformers and radicals demanded a progressive tax policy—inheritance and excess profits taxes coupled with higher income taxes. Wilson walked the middle ground, but the heaviest burdens fell on the wealthy through taxes on large incomes, corporate profits, and estates. By 1919 the tax burden in the highest income brackets had risen to 77 percent.

World War I brought an important change in the sources of federal tax revenues. Before the war nearly three-quarters of federal revenues had come from excise and customs taxes; the remainder came from a modest income tax and from other duties on wealth such as estate taxes. After the war, the ratios were reversed. America's tax structure shifted from taxing consumption to taxing wealth, proof that progressives had won an important victory in the struggle to make upper-income groups pay a large share of the cost of government. On the tax issue Randolph Bourne was wrong.

THE AMERICAN PUBLIC GOES TO WAR

Wilson opposed any action that might alter the nation's economic system. A fiscal conservative at heart, he wanted to keep the government's hands off the economy. Like most of his contemporaries, he preferred to see real authority and control exercised by the private sector. In the end, however, Wilson presided over the expansion of federal powers during World War I.

Selling the War

Wilson's decision to substitute voluntarism for state controls had profound social consequences. By refusing to impose statutory controls on industry, he placed the burden of supporting the war on the profit motive and the public's sense of patriotism. To be sure, this policy avoided the clash between Wilson and industry that would have resulted from strict government control over the economy, but it did so at a huge cost to civil liberties.

Throughout the war the government directed its coercion at people rather than industries. Because he doubted the loyalty of many ethnic Americans, Wilson established the Committee on Public Information (CPI) to mobilize public support for the war. Its chairman, George

Wilson's administration opposed militant labor unions like the Industrial Workers of the World (IWW), shown here striking against Oliver Steel in Pennsylvania. Such strikes did little to help the war effort at home. Samuel Gompers, who wanted to separate members of the American Federation of Labor (AFL) from more militant workers, pledged not to strike until the war was over.

W. Creel, an able and energetic journalist, created America's first propaganda agency. Creel immediately drafted a voluntary censorship agreement with newspapers that permitted them to cover the war but kept sensitive military information out of print. The CPI hired hundreds of musicians, writers, and artists to stage a patriotic campaign, and it sponsored 75,000 speakers who delivered 4-minute war pep talks in vaudeville and movie theaters across the country. During the war, Americans could not watch a movie without being told to love their country and hate the enemy.

Indeed, the CPI found a powerful ally in Hollywood. Quick to perceive the link between patriotism and profits, studio moguls cranked out scores of war films with titles such as *The Prussian Cur, The Claws of the Hun*, and *To Hell with the Kaiser*. Crude propaganda pieces all, these films reduced World War I to a conflict between good and evil, with the Allies cast as heroes and the Central Powers as villains. Moreover, movie stars such as Douglas Fairbanks, Mary Pickford, and Charlie Chaplin toured the country selling war bonds, while songwriters did their best to foster patriotism by pumping out a series of catchy tunes with titles like "Keep the Home Fires Burning" and "Over There."

Popular culture reflected the CPI's influence. Truth became the first casualty; language lost meaning, and stereotypes abounded. Suddenly, dissent meant treason, Germans devolved into Huns, and German-Americans all spied for the fatherland. It did not matter that the vast majority of German-Americans supported the United States; the CPI consistently attacked their loyalty. At its best the CPI may have sold war bonds, discouraged war stoppages, and convinced the public to support the war; at its worst the CPI fostered a witch-hunt.

As passions rose, Americans lashed out at all things German. In the name of patriotism, musicians no longer played Bach and Beethoven, and schools stopped teaching the German language. Americans renamed sauerkraut "liberty cabbage"; dachshunds, "liberty hounds"; and German measles, "liberty measles." Cincinnati, with its large German-American population, even removed pretzels from the free lunch counters in saloons. More alarming, vigilante groups attacked anyone suspected of being unpatriotic. German-speaking families feared talking on the street, and not without reason; many became the victims of mob violence. Workers who refused to buy war bonds often suffered harsh retribution, and attacks on labor protesters were nothing short of brutal. The legal system backed the suppression. Juries routinely released defendants accused of violence against individuals or groups critical of the war.

Hollywood and Tin Pan Alley did their parts to encourage patriotism by putting out scores of war films and a large number of music pieces like the one shown here.

Political Repression

The government fueled the hysteria. In June 1917 Congress passed the Espionage Act, which gave postal officials the authority to ban newspapers and magazines from the mails and threatened individuals convicted of obstructing the draft with $10,000 fines and 20 years in jail. The following year, Congress clamped down harder. The Sedition Act of 1918 made it a federal offense to use "disloyal, profane, scurrilous, or abusive language" about the Constitution, the government, the American uniform, or the flag. The government prosecuted over 2100 people under these acts. Randolph Bourne's prediction that civil rights would fall victim to the power of the state rang true.

Political dissenters bore the brunt of the repression. Eugene V. Debs, who urged socialists to resist militarism, went to prison for nearly three years. The IWW never recovered from government attacks during World War I. In September 1917 the Justice Department staged massive raids on IWW officers, arresting 169 of its veteran leaders. The administration's purpose was, as one attorney put it, "very largely to put the IWW out of business." Many observers thought the judicial system would protect dissenters, but the courts handed down stiff prison sentences to the Wobblies.

The Supreme Court later approved the attacks on civil liberties. Oliver Wendell Holmes, the court's leading champion of civil liberties, upheld the Espionage Act in *Schenck* v. *United States* (1919) by comparing the denial of free speech during the war to the prohibition against "a man falsely shouting fire in a theater and causing panic." In a second case, *Abrams* v. *United States* (1919), Holmes reversed himself and argued against the Sedition Act, returning to his support for "free trade in ideas." He was outvoted seven to two.

World War I did not cause repression; it merely intensified old fears. Many Americans clung to the image of the United States as a strong, isolated country, inhabited by old stock, white, middle-class Protestants. Their vision no longer reflected reality, but the war offered them a chance to lash out at those who had changed America. Immigrants, radical labor organizers, socialists, anarchists, Communists, and critics of any kind became victims of intolerance.

Wartime Reform

The war hysteria bred a curious alliance between superpatriots and old style reformers. Prohibitionists had little difficulty turning World War I to their advantage. They had been winning victories at the state level since the middle of the nineteenth century, but they did not enjoy any success at the federal level until 1917 when Congress prohibited the use of grain for the production of alcoholic beverages, insisting that foodstuffs must be used to feed America's soldiers and Allies. To supply an additional push, prohibitionists joined the anti-German craze, portraying America's enemies as beer-guzzling Huns and warning that German-Americans controlled the nation's breweries. Congress passed the Eighteenth Amendment in 1917 and the final state ratified the amendment two months after the Armistice. The Volstead Act, which banned the manufacture, transportation, and sale of alcoholic beverages, took effect one year later.

Like prohibition, women's suffrage benefited from the emergency atmosphere of World War I. Although radical suffragists, led by Alice Paul of the National Woman's Party, refused to back the war as long as women could not vote, most women's organizations supported the war effort. Wilson appointed suffragists Carrie Chapman Catt and Anna Howard Shaw as directors of the Women's Committee of the Council of National Defense. As blue-collar female workers started pouring into defense industries, middle-class women showed support for the war by volunteering to help the sick and the wounded. Thousands of women joined the Red Cross and the American Women's Hospital Service and served overseas as nurses, physicians, clerks, and ambulance drivers, and thousands more enlisted in the military after the army established the Army Corps of Nurses in 1918.

Suffragists demanded the vote in return for their support of the war. Wilson had long opposed women's suffrage, but political reality ultimately forced his hand. Most western states had granted women the vote before he entered

Members of the National Woman's Party, led by Alice Paul (on the balcony), celebrate their right to vote at their headquarters in Washington, D.C., in 1920.

During the war, many women took jobs previously held by men. Here a group of women assemble an automobile in a factory.

the White House. When Illinois fell in line in 1914, followed by Rhode Island and New York in 1917, pressure started building for national action. Alice Paul, head of the National Woman's Party, pressed the issue by organizing around-the-clock picketing in front of the White House. Determined to prevent women's suffrage from becoming a political issue in the congressional elections of 1918, Wilson told the Senate that the vote for women "is vital to the winning of the war." In 1919, shortly after the Armistice, Congress passed the Nineteenth Amendment, granting women the right to vote. Ratification followed in the summer of 1920.

Apart from voting rights, World War I brought few permanent changes for women. Women had hoped the war would open new jobs for them. Instead, employment opportunities proved meager and brief. Of the one million women who found work in war-related industries, the majority had held jobs before the war. Labor unions opposed hiring women and tolerated their presence solely as a wartime necessity. Industrial jobs, the unions insisted, belonged to men and should be returned to them as soon as the war ended. As the Central Federated Union of New York put it: "the same patriotism which induced women to enter industry during the war should induce them to vacate their positions after the war." Fewer than half of the women who took jobs in heavy industry during the war still held them in 1919, and the number of women who remained in the work force in 1920 dropped below the 1910 figures.

Blacks and the Great Migration

Like women, blacks wanted to use the war to improve their status. While the government had given blacks little reason to shed their blood, most black newspapers backed the war. The militant black intellectual W. E. B. Du Bois urged blacks to "close ranks" with whites, declaring, "If this is our country, then this is our war." Du Bois hoped that blacks, by demonstrating patriotism and bravery, could win public respect and earn better treatment after the war.

At first military leaders even denied blacks the right to fight for their country. The marines accepted no blacks; the navy used them only as mess boys; and the army planned to make them laborers and stevedores. When the National Association for the Advancement of Colored People (NAACP) and other black organizations protested, however, the army agreed to compromise. Following the Civil War example, the army created black regiments commanded almost exclusively by white officers. Black regiments committed to battle fought bravely, but most black soldiers in Europe never got the chance to prove their valor. Instead, they were assigned to move supplies. While two-thirds of the American Expeditionary Force saw combat, only one-fifth of the black troops did so.

Back home the record was equally mixed. In the decades following the Civil War a steady trickle of blacks had left the South to search for jobs in northern cities. During World War I the trickle became a flood. Plagued by the boll weevil, low cotton prices, and unrelenting white repression, sharecroppers longed for change. When labor agents appeared in 1916 promising jobs in the North, blacks responded eagerly. By November 1918 the "Great Migration" had brought half a million southern blacks to the "Land of Hope."

Many found jobs in northern factories and packing houses. The labor force in Chicago's packing houses had been 97 percent white in 1901, but by 1918 they employed 10,000 blacks—over 20 percent of the work force. The labor force in the northern steel industry had been virtually all white in 1900, but by 1920 blacks held 10 percent of those jobs. Still, regardless of the industry, discrimination forced blacks to the bottom of the ladder, where they took over the menial, backbreaking jobs that had been vacated by Slavic and Italian workers, the most recent wave of immigrants.

The Great Migration angered southern whites. The price of cotton tripled during the war; southern planters, fearing the loss of their labor force, resorted to intimidation and mob violence to stop the exodus. A mob in Mississippi, for example, derailed a train to prevent blacks from leaving. Like their ancestors who had taken the underground railroad to freedom, many blacks who moved to the North during World War I had to travel under cover of darkness.

Northern whites opposed the Great Migration, too. Manufacturers welcomed cheap black

The 369th Infantry Regiment returned from the war in February 1919. They were awarded the *Croix de Guerre* (war cross) for bravery in the Meuse-Argonne.

THE WAR FRONT

The United States entered World War I without a large army or the ships to transport one to Europe. Six weeks before Congress declared war, the army had not even drafted plans to organize a large military force. Confident the Allies were winning, Wilson hoped to limit America's contribution to supplies, financial credits, and moral support. In truth, the Allies were ready to collapse. The French army was in the throes of mutiny. Soldiers were tired of suicidal assaults ordered by inept generals, and the submarine offensive had reduced Britain to a six-week supply of food. (Allied losses for 1917 stood at 6.5 million tons of shipping.)

The War at Sea

Faced with a desperate situation, Wilson ordered the United States Navy to act immediately. American ships relieved the British of patrolling the Western Hemisphere while another portion of the fleet steamed to the north Atlantic to combat the submarine menace. Six destroyers reached Ireland on May 4; 35 ships had arrived by July; and 343 ships patrolled the seas surrounding England by the war's end.

American and British commanders disagreed sharply on how best to defend merchant ships. The British believed in the "needle in the haystack" theory—dispersing individual vessels widely at sea and then shooting them through carefully patrolled channels for the last leg of the journey. The policy had not worked. In April alone shipping losses totaled 881,027 tons. The Americans proposed a convoy system—using warships to escort merchant ships to Great Britain. The British reluctantly agreed, and by December the convoy system had cut losses in half.

Raising an Army

Wilson responded more cautiously to the Allies' cries for land forces. His choice to lead the American Expeditionary Force (AEF) was Major General John J. "Black Jack" Pershing. Despite urgent requests from Allied commanders, Pershing refused to send raw recruits to the

labor (especially as strikebreakers), but most Northerners felt threatened by the newcomers. Middle-class whites feared changes in the racial composition of their society, while immigrants resented the competition for jobs and housing. Increasingly, Northerners turned to segregation, discrimination, and violence; and blacks, hoping for a better life in the North, fought back. Race riots erupted in 26 cities in 1917, with the most serious violence occurring in East St. Louis, where at least 39 blacks died in the fighting.

Clearly, World War I meant different things to different groups: for the administration, a test of the limits of voluntarism; for businessmen and technocrats, a chance to pull the levers of government; for nativists and superpatriots, an excuse to lash out at "undesirable" elements; for radicals and dissenters, repression and hardship; for manufacturers and farmers, high profits; for reformers, victories on women's suffrage and prohibition; for trade unions, the right to organize for better pay; and for blacks, a chance to escape from southern poverty.

At the January peace conference in Paris, Wilson met with Prime Minister David Lloyd George, Premier Vittorio Orlando, and Premier Georges Clemenceau.

broke them. Wilson gave us his Fourteen Points—we shall see."

Premier Vittorio Orlando of Italy, the most urbane of the delegates, was bent on pressing Italy's territorial ambitions in the Tyrol and on the Adriatic. When Wilson refused to sanction Italy's sovereignty over the largely Yugoslav population near Fiume, Orlando stormed out of the peace conference in disgust. The final important negotiator was Count Nobuaki Makino, the ambitious spokesman for Japan, who demanded control over German interests in the Far East. In addition, he complicated peace negotiations by insisting upon a statement of racial equality in the League of Nations charter.

The Russians were conspicuously absent at Versailles. Allied leaders, furious at the Bolsheviks for negotiating a separate peace with Germany at Brest-Litovsk in March 1918, refused to assign V. I. Lenin's "Red" government a place at the peace conference. Indeed, the Allies had earlier decided to intervene militarily in the Russian Revolution, and even as their spokesmen met in Versailles, Allied armies were fighting in Russia on the side of the "White," or anti-Communist, forces.

Personally, Wilson despised the Bolsheviks (too undemocratic), and, in keeping with his response to Huerta's regime in Mexico, he refused to extend diplomatic recognition to Lenin's government. Moreover, much as he had with Mexico, Wilson did not stop to ponder how Russians would react to finding American soldiers on their soil. To help rescue Czech troops trapped by the Germans in northern Russia, Wilson sent 5000 American soldiers to the Soviet Union in 1918, where they joined British troops. The following year Wilson sent 9000 American troops to Siberia to help evacuate Czech troops through Vladivostok. Wilson hoped American troops in Russia would save the Czechs and discourage any Japanese designs on Siberia. In addition, he wanted this show of force to bolster the anti-Communist forces in Russia by weakening the Bolsheviks' claims to power. Consequently, the United States dragged its feet and did not withdraw its last troops from Russia until 1920.

American Military Forces in Russia, 1918

The Bolsheviks deeply resented these heavy-handed efforts to undermine their regime. Yet the invasion of Russian soil by American troops was not the only reason for the intense hatred that developed between Lenin and Wilson. As the architect of the Bolshevik Revolution, Lenin emerged as Wilson's chief rival for world leadership. Where Wilson offered liberal democracy and limited social change, Lenin championed communism, social revolution, and swift changes. Wilson was determined to see his vision of the future, not Lenin's, carry the day at Versailles.

To achieve any treaty at all, Wilson had to compromise. Though he fought gallantly, he could not overcome the combined strength of his opponents. In the end he tried to scale down their demands and pinned his hopes on the League of Nations. Under the territorial compromise, the Allies gained control of Germany's colonies as "mandates" under the League of Nation's supervision. Japan acquired Germany's Pacific islands under mandate and assumed Germany's economic interest in China's Shantung peninsula. In eastern Europe, the delegates created the nation states of Poland, Yugoslavia, Czechoslovakia, Estonia, Latvia, Lithuania, and Finland. Europe's political map for the first time roughly resembled its linguistic and cultural map.

Security proved more difficult to negotiate. Over the misgivings of most delegates, Wilson insisted on making the League of Nations an integral part of the final treaty. France remained dubious that any international organization could protect French borders and demanded a buffer zone. To satisfy Clemenceau, the delegates gave France control over Alsace-Lorraine for 10 years and placed the coal-rich Saar Basin under the League of Nations for 15 years. After Wilson and Lloyd George both signed security treaties guaranteeing these arrangements, France grudgingly agreed to join the League of Nations.

Despite promises of a just peace, the treaty imposed a harsh settlement on Germany, burdening the country with a $34 billion reparations bill, far more than Germany could pay. In addition, Germany lost territories that contained German people: Alsace-Lorraine to France, the Saar Basin to a League protectorate, a corridor containing the port of Danzig to Poland, and Upper Silesia to Czechoslovakia. Moreover, under the terms of the war guilt clause in the reparations bill, Germany accepted the blame for World War I, agreed to dismantle its war machine, and pledged not to rearm in the future.

Germany felt betrayed. Clearly, this was not a peace based upon the Fourteen Points. Rather, it brought to life Bourne's prediction of victors who "grab what they can."

Wilson derived no joy from the Treaty of Versailles. He accepted the treaty's territorial and punitive provisions in order to ensure the adoption of the League of Nations, which he hoped would secure world peace and eventually redress the treaty's inequities. The League consisted of an assembly that included all member states and an executive council composed of the United States, Great Britain, France, Italy, Japan, and four other states to be elected by the assembly. But the heart of the League was clearly Article 10, which pledged all members "to respect and uphold the territorial integrity and independence of all members of the

Europe after World War I

League." It embodied Wilson's dream of an international organization that would keep the peace by giving all nations (large and small) equality and protection.

The Struggle for Ratification

Wilson knew the treaty faced stiff opposition back home. In February 1919, 39 Senate Republicans had signed a petition warning they would not approve the League in its present form. To court domestic support, Wilson persuaded the delegates in Europe to acknowledge the Monroe Doctrine, omit domestic issues from the League's purview, and permit member states to withdraw after two years' notice. Though he worked to include provisions the Senate wanted, Wilson refused to separate the League from the treaty. In March he warned: "When the treaty comes back, the gentlemen on this side will find the covenant not only in it, but so many threads of the treaty tied to the covenant that you cannot dissect the covenant from the treaty without destroying the whole vital structure."

Senate opposition broke into three groups, each reflecting different visions of the future role the United States should play in world affairs. The first, the 14 "irreconcilables," were staunch isolationists who wanted the United States to remain unaligned and uninvolved. Led by Senator William Borah of Idaho, they were opposed to a League of Nations in any form. Though their attack was broad-based, they concentrated their fire on Article 10, which called for the mutual protection of the territorial integrity of all member states.

Henry Cabot Lodge of Massachusetts spoke for the second group of critics known as the "strong reservationists." Parodying Wilson's "Fourteen Points," Lodge offered 14 amendments, called the "Lodge" reservations. Of these the second reservation was the most important, as it struck at Article 10, the heart of the proposed League of Nations. The second Lodge reservation decreed that the United States "assumes no obligation" to protect the independence or territory boundaries of any other nation, or to send American troops for such purposes unless Congress should so order. Yet Lodge and his followers were basically in favor of the treaty

and could have been won over if Wilson agreed to their modifications.

The third group of opponents, the "limited reservationists," in all probability spoke for the majority of Americans. Steeped in the diplomatic legacy of the nineteenth century, these limited reservationists favored a middle ground between Senator Borah's acute isolationism and President Wilson's ardent internationalism. They instinctively approached international affairs as cautious nationalists, favoring an independent foreign policy as the best tool for protecting American interests. They, too, had doubts about Article 10 but could have been won over by relatively minor alterations. With their backing and the support of Senate Democrats, the treaty would have passed easily.

As Wilson sailed back to the United States, polls suggested that most Americans favored the League in some form. All he had to do was compromise and the treaty would pass. Instead, Wilson descended on Washington in July itching for a fight, and he grew more stubborn and frustrated as the summer wore on. He made little effort to mask his contempt for critics who questioned the treaty.

Wilson was determined to make the United States assume a leading role in world affairs. Dismissing his opponents as "blind and little provincial people," he declared that the "Senate must take its medicine." His use of a medical metaphor was telling, for Wilson's health had deteriorated under the strain of the war. In fact, in Paris he had suffered what doctors diagnosed as a severe bout of indigestion. In all probability, however, the attack was a mild stroke.

Fearing Senate debate had eroded popular support for the treaty, Wilson decided to take his case directly to the people. Against his doctor's advice, he launched a nationwide tour in September 1919, covering 8000 miles in 33 days and delivering 32 major addresses. He started in the Midwest where opposition to the treaty was strongest, gradually moving west where he met cheering crowds. Totally exhausted, Wilson collapsed on September 25 in Pueblo, Colorado. Four days after returning to Washington, he suffered a severe stroke that paralyzed the left side of his body. In all probability, Wilson sustained enough neurological damage to warp his personality and impair his judgment. Unable to

The refusal of the Senate to ratify the Treaty of Versailles and join the League of Nations is satirized in this cartoon.

work, he did not meet his cabinet for more than six months. Since the law made no provision for removing an incapacitated president, Wilson's second wife, Edith Bolling Wilson, assisted by a few close aides, ran the government, operating under a cloak of silence about the president's condition.

As the Senate vote on the treaty drew near, Wilson remained adamant, telling his wife: "Better a thousand times to go down fighting than to dip your colours to dishonorable compromise." He ordered all Democrats to vote against the treaty if it contained any changes. The treaty came to a vote one year, one week, and one day after the Armistice. The Senate defeated the revised version of the treaty, 55 to 39; a few minutes later the Senate defeated the treaty without changes, 39 to 53. The "irreconcilables" were delighted.

The Senate's failure to reach a compromise must be blamed on Wilson. When the treaty's supporters tried again in March, many of the Democrats disobeyed the president and voted for a revised version of the treaty. But 23 Democrats followed Wilson's orders, and the treaty fell 7 votes short of adoption. Elated by their

victory, Republicans proclaimed (in a parody of Wilson's 1916 slogan), "He kept us out of peace." Yet it would be wrong to interpret the treaty's defeat as an endorsement of isolationism. In essence, the Senate rejected both isolationism and Wilsonian internationalism in favor of preserving a nationalistic foreign policy that would allow the United States to act independently.

An admirer of the British parliamentarian system, Wilson then hatched a bizarre scheme that showed how badly he had lost contact with reality. He asked his Senate opponents to resign and stand immediately for reelection. If pro-League senators replaced them, Wilson would have his ratification; if a majority won reelection, Wilson would resign the presidency. At the urging of advisors, Wilson finally dropped the proposal.

The Election of 1920

Unable to accept defeat, Wilson decided to make the election of 1920 a "solemn referendum" on the League: The election of a Democrat would signify approval of the treaty; a Republican victory would mean the treaty's death. At best the president's proposal offered a dubious test of the public's support for the treaty. National elections rarely turn on a single issue. Instead, they involve a myriad of issues, most of which are quite local in character.

When the Democratic convention met in San Francisco, the delegates ignored Wilson's pathetic anglings for a third term and nominated Governor James M. Cox of Ohio. To round out the ticket, they selected the assistant secretary of the navy, Franklin D. Roosevelt, for vice president, largely to capitalize on the magic Roosevelt name. The Republicans nominated Senator Warren G. Harding of Ohio. A stalwart party regular on domestic issues, Harding had voted for the Treaty of Versailles with the Lodge reservations.

While Cox barnstormed the country, Harding campaigned from his front porch in Ohio. His campaign managers refused to turn him loose on the election circuit for fear of what he might say. As one wag put it, "Thank God only one of them can be elected." Cox campaigned unequivocally for the League of Nations and the

Treaty of Versailles. Harding, by contrast, waffled shamelessly, announcing that he opposed the League but favored an "association of nations." Thus, the election of 1920 did not provide a "solemn referendum" on the League because the issue was hopelessly confused.

Indeed, the League had become a dead issue. Most voters wished to preserve America's options in the coming decades by pursuing an independent foreign policy. Tired of foreign crusades, they wanted to repudiate Wilson's ardent internationalism, and they did just that, giving Harding the largest electoral victory (61 percent of the popular vote) since Washington's election. Harding received 16,152,200 votes to Cox's 9,147,353. Eugene V. Debs, the Socialist candidate, won 919,799 votes (at the time he was serving a prison term in the Atlanta federal penitentiary for opposing American involvement in the war). In the Electoral College, Harding trounced Cox 404 to 127.

The Republicans won because Wilson's fragile coalition of 1916 fell apart. Many Democrats, disillusioned by the costs of the war, either stayed at home or switched parties. Angered by the Treaty of Versailles, ethnic Americans (Germans, Italians, and the Irish in particular) abandoned the Democrats in droves. Their defection cost Democrats the nation's urban centers. Western states and the Midwest went Republican as well, for despite their wartime prosperity, many farmers believed that Wilson's agricultural policies had favored cotton growers in the South over grain producers of the Midwest. The Solid South remained a bastion of Democratic strength, but it did not have nearly enough votes to elect a president.

Harding interpreted his victory as a mandate to reject the League. America never joined the League of Nations, opening the way for those who later blamed the United States for the rise of fascism in Italy and Nazism in Germany. Critics went so far as to claim that America's failure to join the League caused World War II. If the United States had only joined, they insisted, the League would have been able to deter German and Japanese aggression by presenting a united front.

But what good was a united front if its members refused to fight? Critics failed to realize that the French and the English were not willing to use force to impose collective security. Neither was the United States, in or out of the League. Congress played the dominant role in foreign policy until the very eve of World War II, and it was determined to prevent the United States from being drawn into another European war. The war's main legacy, then, was not peace without victory, but bitterness and suspicion.

CONCLUSION

World War I made Randolph Bourne a prophet. The changes in American life between 1914 and 1919 bore out his fear that war obliterates idealism and brings out the dark side of the human spirit. Before the war, the United States had been an isolated, Western Hemisphere country, preoccupied with life on this side of the Atlantic. The industrial revolution had largely transformed the economic landscape, but many Americans still farmed their own land for a living. Although the progressive movement had attempted to use government to eliminate gross economic abuses, federal power remained miniscule compared to the private sector. And while it is true that many old-stock Americans felt threatened by cultural pluralism, they still thought they lived in a country that had more consensus than confusion, more accord than conflict.

World War I altered everything. It accelerated social and economic changes, unleashing extraordinary fears that led to attacks on labor unions, blacks, immigrants, Socialists, and Communists. Similar confusion gripped America's foreign policy. The United States emerged from the Great War as the premier economic power on earth, with global interests requiring protection. Those responsibilities terrified a country that had been lulled into a sense of security by three centuries of geographic isolation. Tired and disillusioned, Americans attempted to flee their responsibilities. Rather than make global political commitments commensurate with their new economic interests, they refused to ratify the Treaty of Versailles or join the League of Nations.

The result was an upsurge in isolationist sentiment in the United States during the 1920s and 1930s that made it very difficult for Amer-

CHRONOLOGY OF KEY EVENTS

1914 World War I begins in Europe

1915 U.S. marines are dispatched to Haiti; German submarine sinks the British passenger ship *Lusitania*, killing 1198 passengers including 128 Americans

1916 Germany suspends unannounced submarine attacks

1917 Germany resumes submarine attacks; Zimmermann telegram, secret note to German minister in Mexico, urges Mexico and Japan to join Central Powers if the United States enters the war in Europe; United States enters the war; Espionage Act passed, imposing fines and jail sentences for aiding the enemy or obstructing recruitment; Russian Revolution begins; War Industries Board is created to coordinate industrial production

1918 Wilson's Fourteen Points outline a plan for peace; National War Labor Board is created to arbitrate disputes between labor and management; Sedition Act passes, punishing any expression of disloyalty to the American government or flag; Germany surrenders

1919 Treaty of Versailles ends World War I

1920 Palmer raids arrest suspected Communists; Senate rejects Treaty of Versailles; Nineteenth Amendment grants women the right to vote; Republican Warren Harding is elected twenty-ninth president

---

ica's leaders to respond strongly to the rise of despotic governments in Europe and the Far East. The Great War did not make the world "safe for democracy." It left humankind a legacy of bitterness, hatred, and suspicion, creating rich soil for the seeds of future conflicts.

In 1920, however, most Americans felt too tired and too disillusioned to give much thought to the future. When Harding promised a return to "normalcy," he struck a responsive chord. Millions of Americans thought he meant resurrecting rural villages and a small farm economy, restoring Anglo-Protestant culture, and forgetting about the rest of the world. The 1920s proved they were in for a surprise.

SUGGESTIONS FOR FURTHER READING

OVERVIEWS AND SURVEYS

Randolph S. Bourne, *War and the Intellectuals: Collected Essays, 1915–1919* (1964); Foster R. Dulles, *America's Rise to World Power, 1898–1954* (1955); Robert H. Ferrell, *Woodrow Wilson and World War I, 1917–1921* (1985); Lloyd C. Gardner, *Safe for Democracy: The Anglo-American Response to Revolution, 1913–1923* (1984); Otis L. Graham, Jr., *The Great Campaigns: Reform and War in America, 1900–1928* (1971); Ellis W. Hawley, *The Great War and the Search for a Modern Order: A History of the American People and Their Institutions, 1917–1933* (1979); William E. Leuchtenburg, *The Perils of Prosperity, 1914–32* (1958); Emily S. Rosenberg, *Spreading the American Dream: American Economic and Cultural Expansion 1890–1945* (1982); Bernadotte Schmitt and Harold C. Vedeler, *The World in the Crucible: 1914–1919* (1984); Daniel M. Smith, *The Great Departure: The United States and World War I, 1914–1920* (1965).

THE ROAD TO WAR

John M. Cooper, Jr., *The Vanity of Power: American Isolationism and the First World War, 1914–1917* (1969) and *The Warrior and the Priest: Woodrow Wilson and Theodore Roosevelt* (1983); Patrick Devlin, *Too Proud to Fight: Woodrow Wilson's Neutrality* (1974); Ross Gregory, *The Origins of American Intervention in the First World War* (1971); George F. Kennan, *The Decision to Intervene* (1958) and *Russia Leaves the War* (1956); N. Gordon Levin, Jr., *Woodrow Wilson and World Politics: America's Response to War and Revolution* (1968); Arthur S. Link, *Woodrow Wilson:*

Revolution, War and Peace (1979); Ernest R. May, *The World War and American Isolation, 1914–1917* (1959); Barbara Tuchman, *The Guns of August* (1962).

AMERICAN INDUSTRY GOES TO WAR

Valerie Jean Conner, *The National War Labor Board: Stability, Social Justice, and the Voluntary State in World War I* (1983); Robert D. Cuff, *The War Industries Board: Business-Government Relations During World War I* (1973); Charles Gilbert, *American Financing of World War I* (1970); Maurine Weiner Greenwald, *Women, War, and Work: The Impact of World War I on Women Workers in the United States* (1980); Stephen Skowronek, *Building a New American State: The Expansion of National Administrative Capacities, 1877–1920* (1982); Neil A. Wynn, *From Progressivism to Prosperity: World War I and American Society* (1986).

THE AMERICAN PUBLIC GOES TO WAR

Rodolfo Acuña, *Occupied America*, 3d ed. (1988); Allan M. Brandt, *No Magic Bullet: A Social History of Venereal Disease in the United States Since 1880* (1985); Wayne Cornelius, *Building the Cactus Curtain: Mexican Migration and U.S. Responses from Wilson to Carter* (1980); James R. Grossman, *Land of Hope: Chicago, Black Southerners, and the Great Migration* (1989); David M. Kennedy, *Over Here: The First World War and American Society* (1980); K. Austin Kerr, *Organized for Prohibition: A New History of the Anti-Saloon League* (1985); Daniel J. Kevles, *In the Name of Eugenics: Genetics and the Uses of Human Heredity* (1985); Frederick C. Luebke, *Bonds of Loyalty: German-Americans and World War I* (1974); Carole Marks, *Farewell—We're Good and Gone: The Great Black Migration* (1989); John F. McClymer, *War and Welfare: Social Engineering in America, 1890–1925* (1980); Paul L. Murphy, *World War I and the Origin of Civil Liberties in the United States* (1979); H. C. Peterson and Gilbert C. Fite, *Opponents of War 1917–1918* (1957); William Preston, Jr., *Aliens and Dissenters: Federal Suppression of Radicals, 1903–1933* (1963); John A. Thompson, *Reformers and War: American Progressive Publicists and the First World War* (1987); Stephen Vaughn, *Holding Fast the Inner Lines: Democracy, Nationalism, and the Committee on Public Information* (1980).

THE WAR FRONT

Arthur E. Barbeau and Florette Henri, *The Unknown Soldiers: Black American Troops in World War I* (1974); Edward M. Coffman, *The War to End Wars: The American Military Experience in World War I* (1968); Harvey DeWeerd, *President Wilson Fights His War: World War I and the American Intervention* (1968); Russell F. Weigley, *The American Way of War: A History of United States Military Strategy and Policy* (1973).

SOCIAL UNREST AFTER THE WAR

Wesley M. Bagby, *The Road to Normalcy: The Presidential Campaign and Election of 1920* (1962); David Brody, *Labor in Crisis: The Steel Strike of 1919* (1965); Richard C. Cortner, *A Mob Intent on Death: The NAACP and the Arkansas Riot Cases* (1988); Paul Fussell, *The Great War and Modern Memory* (1975); Christine A. Lunardini, *From Equal Suffrage to Equal Rights: Alice Paul and the National Woman's Party, 1910–1928* (1986); Robert K. Murray, *The Red Scare: A Study in National Hysteria, 1919–1920* (1955); Burl Noggle, *Into the Twenties: The United States from Armistice to Normalcy* (1974); Francis Russell, *A City in Terror: 1919, the Boston Police Strike* (1975); Arthur M. Schlesinger, Jr., *The Crisis of the Old Order, 1919–1933* (1957); William Tuttle, Jr., *Race Riot: Chicago and the Red Summer of 1919* (1970).

THE TREATY OF VERSAILLES

Thomas A. Bailey, *Woodrow Wilson and the Great Betrayal* (1945), and *Woodrow Wilson and the Lost Peace* (1944); Warren F. Kuehl, *Seeking World Order* (1969); N. Gordon Levin, Jr., *Woodrow Wilson and World Politics: America's Response to War and Revolution* (1968); Herbert F. Margulies, *The Mild Reservationists and the League of Nations Controversy in the Senate* (1989); Arno J. Mayer, *Politics and Diplomacy in Peacemaking: Containment and Counterrevolution at Versailles, 1918–1919* (1967) and *Wilson vs. Lenin: Political Origins of the New Diplomacy, 1917–1918* (1959); Ralph A. Stone, *The Irreconcilables: The Fight Against the League of Nations* (1970); William C. Widenor, *Henry Cabot Lodge and the Search for an American Foreign Policy* (1980).

BIOGRAPHIES

Robert W. Cherny, *A Righteous Cause: The Life of William Jennings Bryan* (1985); Kendrick A. Clements, *William Jennings Bryan, Missionary Isolationist* (1982); Stanley Coben, *A. Mitchell Palmer: Politician* (1963); Lawrence W. Levine, *Defender of the Faith: William Jennings Bryan, The Last Decade, 1915–1925* (1965); Arthur S. Link, *Wilson* (5 vols., 1947–1965); James R. Vitelli, *Randolph Bourne* (1981); Edwin A. Weinstein, *Woodrow Wilson: A Medical and Psychological Biography* (1981).

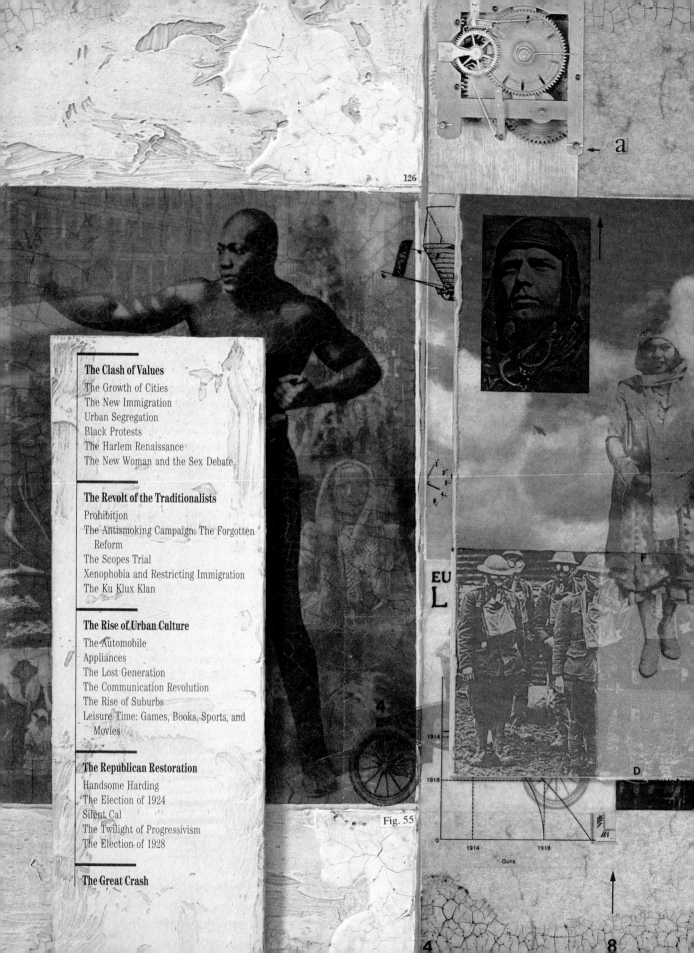

a

EU
L

Fig. 55

1914

1918

1914   1918

Guns

4

D

F

4   8

CHAPTER 24

Modern Times, the 1920s

*I*n 1898 the Physicians Club of Chicago held a symposium on "sexual hygiene" to give its members some practical tips on marriage counseling. Confronted by an increasing number of married women who wanted information on birth control, Chicago physicians offered this advice: "Get a divorce and vacate the position for some other woman, who is able and willing to fulfill all a wife's duties as well as to enjoy her privileges."

Most Americans shared this view. They did not believe sex should be separated from procreation. To the male custodians of morality, birth control challenged patriarchy. It would lead to sexual promiscuity and an epidemic of venereal diseases, they charged, while others feared it would weaken the family by raising the divorce rate. Many women condemned birth control just as soundly. Taught from childhood to embrace the cult of domesticity, they accepted childbearing as their "biological duty" and rejected birth control as immoral and radical.

Yet by 1950 most Americans regarded birth control as a public virtue rather than a private vice. The person most responsible for this amazing transformation was Margaret Sanger (1879–1966), a tireless crusader who possessed an iron will and the soul of a firebrand. From 1914 to 1937 Sanger campaigned to make birth control morally acceptable. She built a network of clinics where women could get accurate information about contraception and obtain inexpensive, reliable birth control devices. After World War II, she helped organize the international planned parenthood movement and played a key role in the development of "the pill." Through her birth control work, Margaret Sanger probably had a greater influence on the world than any other American woman of her day.

Sanger's mother, Margaret Higgins, bore 11 children, all 10 pounders or more. Michael Higgins, her father, was a free-thinking Irishman who worked as a stonecutter but preferred to hang around pubs proclaiming his faith in socialism and doubts about God. Her mother died of pulmonary tuberculosis at 43; her father lived to 84. For the rest of her life, Sanger blamed her mother's suffering on the absence of effective family planning.

An unhappy marriage also pushed Sanger toward reform. While still in nursing school, she married William Sanger, an architect and would-be artist, and they set up housekeeping in Greenwich Village, a bohemian colony in New York City. After bearing three children in rapid succession, Sanger overcame her own struggle with tuberculosis, finished school, and began a nursing career. Through her husband, she met an amazing group of radicals in New York, including the anarchist Emma Goldman and the Wobbly William D. "Big Bill" Haywood. Feeling trapped by married life and determined to achieve her own identity, Margaret plunged into New York's labor movement. As her marriage to William slowly dissolved, she devoted herself to the working poor.

Convinced large families placed a terrible economic burden on poor people, Sanger sympathized with the countless women, rich and poor, who desperately wanted to control their fertility. After watching several working-class women bleed to death from back-alley abortions, she came to regard family planning as the most important issue of her day because birth control would make abortion, as well as unwanted babies, unnecessary. When male labor leaders refused to add contraception to their reform agenda, Sanger left the labor movement, resolving to make birth control her life's work.

On the eve of World War I, Sanger launched a one-woman crusade. She lectured to anyone who would listen and offered birth control devices to anyone in need. In 1921 she organized the American Birth Control League, which opened scores of clinics in major American cities. Next Sanger recruited physicians and social workers to agitate for repeal of the Comstock Act of 1873, a federal law making it illegal to send birth control information or devices through the mail. In addition, she attracted several wealthy feminists to the birth control movement and used their support to finance research on the relative safety and effectiveness of different kinds of contraceptives.

Sanger played a key role in the transition to modern times. Her career illustrates how the reform spirit of the Progressive Era survived the conservative climate of the 1920s to touch the lives of future generations. Whereas most reforms pursued political agendas, birth control

Margaret Sanger, a nurse who had watched many women suffer from unwanted births and die from illegal abortions, was one of the founders of the modern American birth control movement. After spending a year studying medical literature and learning about contraceptives, Sanger began publishing the journal *The Woman Rebel.*

developed into a social movement that involved feminists, philanthropists, social workers, physicians, and scientists. No legacy of progressivism was more far-reaching. The birth control movement reformed sexual mores, redefined women's role in society, and redistributed power within the family. But the birth control movement represented just one symptom of a society in flux, one in which urban growth, ethnic diversity, and economic development set the stage for controversy on almost every imaginable topic—race, sex, religion, alcohol, even the family automobile.

THE CLASH OF VALUES

Many Americans found the 1920s a confusing decade. In the wake of the Great War's carnage and failed promises, they disagreed on a host of issues. Wets battled drys, atheists ridiculed fundamentalists, white, Anglo-Saxon Protestants (WASPs) denounced the "new immigrants," whites lashed out against blacks, and practically everyone sensed a decline in morality. Rural folks debated the dubious morals of city dwell-ers, while farmers glowered at industrialists. Midwesterners and Southerners voiced their skepticism about the Golden East, with its sprawling cities teeming with immigrants.

Yet none of these disputes was new. Each was a continuing, if sharpening, controversy that had been building for decades. At bottom these conflicts reflected more uncertainty than rancor, as a society in transition debated which of its traditional values to preserve and which to modify or abandon. Because the choices seemed so disconcerting, few Americans recognized these conflicts for what they were—unavoidable growing pains of a nation struggling to come to grips with cultural pluralism and changing values.

The Growth of Cities

Cities underwent dramatic and visible changes. According to the census of 1920, more Americans dwelled in cities than in the country for the first time in the nation's history. Most urbanites lived in small towns and cities, but a surprising number resided in metropolitan areas—large cities with 50,000 or more people. During the 1920s nearly 15 million Americans moved to cities. The South remained largely rural, but its rate of urbanization outstripped other areas, rising from 25 percent in 1920 to 32 percent in 1930, a clear indication of what the future held in store for the "Sun Belt."

Most new city dwellers came from the country. Farms lost over 10 million residents between 1920 and 1940. Even people who remained on the land did not escape the city's influence. Electrical power scattered industries over broad areas, and as the automobile increased labor's mobility, many rural folk commuted to jobs in nearby mill towns and cities.

Urban growth drove up land values and reshaped the skyline of America's cities, especially in central business districts. In New York and Chicago, office space more than doubled during the 1920s. Skyrocketing land prices forced architects to build "up" instead of "out," launching the first great era of skyscrapers. Builders completed New York's ornate Woolworth Building, rising 55 stories and 760 feet above ground level, in 1913, offering the prototype for the new "Woolworth Gothic" sky-

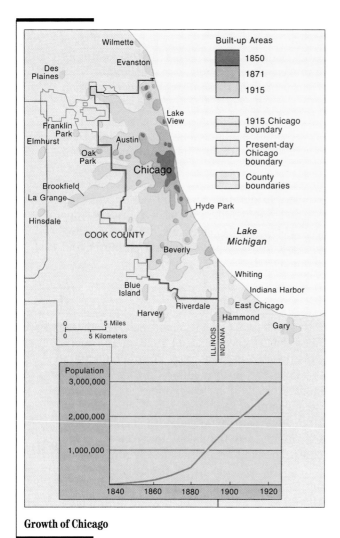

Growth of Chicago

migrants included large numbers of Roman Catholics, Jews, and members of the Greek Orthodox faith. Old-stock Americans had grown accustomed to immigrants from Ireland and Scandinavia, but they felt threatened by the arrival of Poles, Lithuanians, Czechs, Slovaks, Magyars, Ukrainians, Russians, Serbians, Croatians, Italians, Greeks, and Armenians.

The new immigrants poured into the industrial cities of the Northeast and Midwest, filling them with new sights, sounds, and smells that many old-stock Americans found offensive. World War I briefly stopped the flow of immigrants, but in 1919 the trickle again became a flood. Between 1919 and 1926, more than 3.2 million immigrants poured into the United States. Protestants resented the influx of Catholics and Jews; labor unions feared the competition for jobs; and eugenicists feared old-stock Americans would be outbred by the newcomers, with disastrous consequences for the nation.

Urban Segregation

In 1910 three out of every four black Americans lived on farms, and nine out of ten lived in the South. World War I changed that profile. Hoping to escape the tenant farming, sharecropping, and peonage of the South, 1.5 million blacks moved to cities in the 1920s. Some went to southern cities such as Houston, Memphis, Atlanta, and Birmingham, but most settled in major northern metropolises such as New York, Philadelphia, Cleveland, and Chicago. By 1930, one of five black Americans lived in the North.

Black migration intensified housing shortages, making competition for limited housing a source of friction between blacks and whites. In city after city, whites closed ranks against blacks, blocking access to white neighborhoods. Cities passed municipal residential segregation ordinances, white realtors refused to show blacks houses in white areas, and white property owners formed "neighborhood improvement associations." Above all, these associations stressed keeping blacks out. After the Supreme Court declared municipal residential segregation ordinances unconstitutional in 1917, however, whites resorted to the restrictive convenant, a formal deed restriction binding white property owners in a given neighbor-

scrapers that quickly dominated Manhattan's skyline. Soon Chicago had its 34-story, Gothic-topped Tribune Tower on Michigan Avenue, and other skyscrapers dotted the landscapes in Pittsburgh, Cleveland, Kansas City, and San Francisco. Cities throughout the United States were starting to look alike.

The New Immigration

America's cities attracted large numbers of new immigrants. Immigration patterns to the United States began to change in the 1880s, with fewer and fewer people arriving from northern and western Europe and more and more coming from southern and eastern Europe. Instead of bringing more Protestants, the new waves of im-

hood not to sell to blacks. Whites who broke these agreements could be sued by "damaged" neighbors. Not until 1948 did the Supreme Court strike down restrictive covenants, rendering them impossible to enforce, even if their language survived in many deeds.

Zoning laws offered a more subtle means of segregating blacks. Originally designed to keep businessmen and industries out of residential neighborhoods, zoning laws were upheld by the Supreme Court in 1926. By 1930, 981 American cities had adopted zoning ordinances. These new zoning laws addressed not only land usage but the height and shape of buildings, specifying rigid construction requirements that precluded low-income groups from building or buying homes in well-to-do neighborhoods. By the 1930s zoning restrictions had become the tool of choice for segregating people on the basis of wealth.

Racial animosity, restrictive covenants, and zoning restrictions confined blacks to certain neighborhoods. Between World War I and World War II, scores of American cities developed black cores. By 1930 New York and Chicago, the cities with the largest black populations, had wards that registered 95 percent black. Cities within cities, these "black metropolises" resembled ethnic ghettos of the late nineteenth and early twentieth centuries, with one major difference: Racial prejudice made it all but impossible for their residents to escape to the suburbs.

Black Protests

Black protests heightened the fears of many old-stock Americans. In the 1920s several black organizations stepped up their protests against discrimination. Closely identified with Booker T. Washington's conciliatory approach to race relations, the National Urban League, organized in 1911 by social workers, white philanthropists, and conservative blacks, concentrated on finding jobs for urban blacks. During the 1920s the League touted the new opportunities increased prosperity would bring to urban blacks, but a report from the Atlanta League on training blacks to become better janitors revealed the true employment picture. Blacks made scant progress on the job front during the 1920s.

Leaving economic issues to the Urban League, the National Association for the Advancement of Colored People (NAACP), formed in 1909, concentrated on civil rights and legal action. The NAACP won important Supreme Court decisions against the grandfather clause (1915) and restrictive covenants (1917). Except for W. E. B. Du Bois, who became the director of publicity, white liberals served as the NAACP's top officers during its early years. After World War I, however, the leadership gradually shifted to blacks.

Under the capable direction of James Weldon Johnson, its first black secretary, the NAACP fought school segregation in northern cities during the 1920s, and lobbied hard,

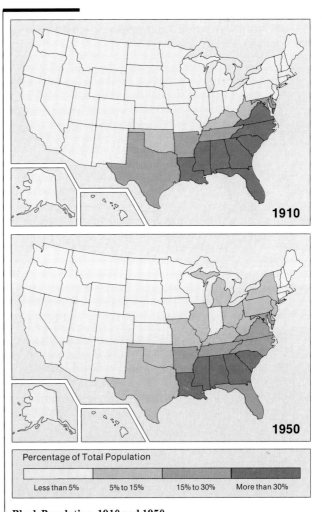

Black Population, 1910 and 1950

though unsuccessfully, for a federal antilynching bill. Though progress on these fronts did not come until after World War II, the NAACP consolidated its position between the wars as the nation's leading civil rights organization.

Black radicals dismissed the Urban League and the NAACP as too conservative. A. Philip Randolph, the brilliant editor of the militant Socialist monthly, the *Messenger*, saw prejudice as the inevitable consequence of a capitalist system that drove a wedge between black and white workers. To end discrimination and achieve racial equality, he called for a "New Negro" who would meet violence with violence. Randolph also urged blacks to seek admission into trade unions. To promote this goal he organized the Brotherhood of Sleeping Car Porters in the 1920s. After years of bitter opposition, the Pullman Company recognized the Brotherhood in 1937 as the porters' bargaining agent. Though Randolph addressed the black masses, he appealed to the college educated, black elite. Most blacks neither read nor understood his intellectual theories.

Marcus Garvey spoke for the black masses. A flamboyant and charismatic figure from Jamaica, Garvey rejected integration and preached racial pride and black separatism. He declared that God and Jesus were both black men and exhorted his followers to glorify their African heritage and to revel in the beauty of their black skin.

In 1914 Garvey organized the Universal Negro Improvement Association (UNIA) to promote black migration to Africa. Under the slogan, "Africa for the Africans, at home and abroad," the UNIA opened branches in many American cities and in several foreign countries after World War I. Its Black Star Steamship Line sold stock to thousands of members, promising to help blacks migrate to Africa. Garvey also advocated economic self-sufficiency for blacks who remained in the United States. To enable his followers to buy only from black-owned businesses, the UNIA opened a chain of laundries, groceries, restaurants, a hotel, a doll factory (whose products all had black bodies), and a printing plant.

The UNIA collapsed in the mid-1920s after the Black Star Line went bankrupt. Garvey was charged with mail fraud, jailed, and finally deported, but this "Black Moses" left behind a rich legacy. At a time when magazines and newspapers overflowed with advertisements for hair straighteners and skin lightening cosmetics, Garvey's message of racial pride struck a responsive chord in many black Americans.

Marcus Garvey, a charismatic Jamaican, encouraged black pride. His Universal Negro Improvement Association (UNIA) included one million members worldwide.

The Harlem Renaissance

The movement for black pride found its cultural expression in the Harlem Renaissance. Located in New York's upper Manhattan, Harlem attracted black intellectuals who migrated from small towns or rural areas where they had felt stifled and oppressed. Langston Hughes, poet laureate of the Harlem Renaissance, captured the exhilaration of arriving in Harlem: "I can never put on paper the thrill of the underground ride to Harlem. I went up the steps and out into the bright September sunlight. Harlem! I stood there, dropped my bags, took a deep breath, and felt happy again."

By the 1920s the Harlem Renaissance was in bloom. Langston Hughes probed the past in his elegant poem, "The Negro Speaks of Rivers," while Countee Cullen struck an ironic note in "Yet Do I Marvel," where he pondered God's ways and declared: "Yet do I marvel at this curious thing: To make a poet black and bid him sing." In *Cane*, a compilation of short stories, poems, and vignettes, Jean Toomer, perhaps the most gifted prose writer of the renaissance, explored the lives of blacks who toiled in Georgia's sawmills in the 1880s.

Yet for all its artistic promise, the Harlem Renaissance had little influence on the black masses, most of whom never knew it existed. "The ordinary Negroes hadn't heard of the Negro Renaissance," Hughes later lamented. "And

Artist Archibald Motley, Jr., one of the black painters of the 1920s Harlem Renaissance, celebrated the energy and excitement of the era in *Black Belt* (1934).

if they had, it hadn't raised their wages any." Moreover, the Harlem Renaissance often reflected the stereotypes of its white patrons, who wished to dabble in the cult of the primitive, which came into vogue during the 1920s. White liberals underwrote the Harlem Renaissance by providing scholarships, prizes, and grants to aspiring young black artists who all too often felt pressured to reinforce white stereotypes of black culture. Leaders of the Harlem Renaissance shied away from controversial social issues such as "passing" and all but ignored jazz, one of the most important black contributions to American popular culture.

The New Woman and the Sex Debate

"If all girls at the Yale prom were laid end to end, I wouldn't be surprised," sighed Dorothy Parker, the official wit of New York's smart set. Parker's quip captured the public's perception that America's morals had taken a nose-dive. As early as 1913 an editor for *Current Opinion* complained that America had struck "Sex O' Clock," and a few years later a writer for *The Atlantic* warned of the "obsession of sex which has set us all a-babbling about matters once excluded from the amenities of conversation." Practically every newspaper featured articles on prostitution, venereal disease, sex education, birth control, and the rising divorce rate—not to mention somber warnings against "racial suicide" by eugenicists who feared "inferior stocks of people" might take over the country by outbreeding their social betters.

City life nurtured new sexual attitudes. With its crowded anonymity, urban culture eroded sexual inhibitions by relaxing community restraints on individual behavior. Cities also promoted secular, consumer values, and city people seemed to tolerate, if not welcome, many forms of diversity.

If cities spawned a new environment for sexual values, the new psychology of Sigmund

The image of the "flapper," who bobbed her hair, bared her knees, and smoked and drank in public, alarmed a public still clinging to Victorian codes of morality.

Freud provided the ideas. A Vienna physician, Freud revolutionized academic and popular thinking about human behavior by arguing that unconscious sexual anxieties cause much of human behavior. Freud also explained how sexual fears develop in infancy and stay with people throughout their lives. During the 1920s, Freud precipitated countless arguments as physicians, academics, advice columnists, women's magazines, and preachers debated his theories.

The image of the "flapper" said it all—the liberated woman who bobbed her hair, painted her lips, raised her hemline, and danced the Charleston. The public's anxiety about "fast" women reached all the way down to adolescent girls. One fretful mother told sociologists Robert and Helen Lynd, "My son has been asked to a dance by three different girls and there is no living with him," while another complained, "It's the girls' clothing. We can't keep our boys decent when girls dress that way."

Women's behavior raised more eyebrows than hemlines. When Lewis Terman, a distinguished psychologist at Stanford University, questioned 777 middle-class women in 1938, he discovered that 74 percent of those born between 1890 and 1900 remained chaste until marriage, while the figure dropped to 32 percent among those born after 1910. Alfred C. Kinsey's research revealed a similar pattern. Between 1938 and 1956 Kinsey and his co-workers at Indiana University interviewed 5940 white females from all social classes. Women born after 1900 were twice as likely to have had premarital sex as their mothers, with the most pronounced changes occurring in the generation reaching maturity at the end of World War I and in the early 1920s.

Sexual permissiveness had eroded Victorian values, but the "new woman" posed less of a challenge to traditional morality than her critics feared. Far from being promiscuous, her sexual experience before marriage was limited (a woman usually had no more than one or two partners, one of whom she married), and she shared the older generation's commitment to marriage. In practice, this narrowed the gap between men and women and moved society toward a single standard of morality. Instead of turning to prostitutes, men made love with their sweethearts, who in many instances became their wives.

Moreover, the sexual revolution did not redefine gender roles for women. The "new woman" embraced the traditional roles of wife and mother. In fact, the most striking theme of women's history in the 1920s was its continuity with the past. Whether one looked at politics, the workplace, or the home, the status of women remained much the same.

Nowhere was the absence of change more evident than in politics. Most feminists had viewed politics as the key to ending discrimination against women, arguing the vote would bring other reforms in its train. After the Nineteenth Amendment passed, reformers talked about female voters uniting to clean up politics, improve society, and end discrimination in the marketplace.

None of these dreams came true during the 1920s. Women failed to organize into a bloc vote, and apart from a few state and local elections where the female vote did prove decisive, women did not vote differently than men. Even more galling to feminists, substantial numbers of women failed to vote at all. Throughout the 1920s significantly fewer women showed up at the polls than men.

Nor did women win new opportunities in the marketplace. According to the census of 1920, the American work force included over 8 million women (the figure rose to more than 10 million by 1930), employed in 437 different types of jobs. But black and foreign-born women comprised 57 percent of the female work force, and domestic service remained the largest occupation, followed by secretaries, typists, and clerks—all low-paying jobs. Though female workers made significant progress in organizing the garment industry, they failed to make inroads in other industries. The American Federation of Labor (AFL) remained openly hostile to women because it did not want females competing for male jobs.

Female professionals, too, made little progress. They consistently received less pay than their male counterparts. Moreover, while the proportion of women in the professions rose from roughly 12 to 14 percent between 1920 and 1930, three-quarters of female professionals concentrated in "female" occupations— teaching and nursing. The percentage of female lawyers and architects remained constant between 1910 and 1930 (about 3 percent), while the total number of female doctors declined from 9015 to 6825. The United States had only 60 female certified public accountants and 151 female dentists in the late 1920s.

Most Americans regarded working women as an anomaly. Young women could work during the interlude between leaving home and marriage, but they were expected to make homemaking their career after marriage. While economic necessity forced many poor women to continue working after marriage, most middle-class women of the 1920s abandoned any hope of combining careers with marriage. If anything, the 1920s saw feminism decline and domesticity surge. As one article put it, "the office woman,

no matter how successful, is a transplanted posey." The proper role for women, one college president advised, was "to strengthen and beautify and sanctify the home."

America had not resolved the basic conflict between equal rights for women and the sexual division of labor that continued to confine women to the domestic sphere. Feminists had secured the vote, not true equality.

THE REVOLT OF THE TRADITIONALISTS

Teeming cities, crowded ghettos, unfamiliar immigrants, black migration, civil rights protests, and new sexual mores all proved deeply threatening to traditional white Protestants. During

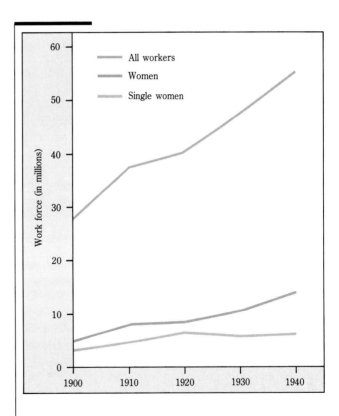

Figure 24.1

Women in the work force, 1900–1940. Although the number of women in the workplace rose from 1900 to 1940, they were concentrated in low-paying and traditionally "female" jobs.

(Text continues on p. 804)

THE SEXUAL REVOLUTION
OF THE EARLY 1900s

During the 1800s, public sexual attitudes in the United States were rooted in a moral code known as "civilized sexual morality." This sexual code condemned public discussion of sexual matters, held that sexual relations outside marriage were the blackest of sins, and declared that the only legitimate purpose of sexual relations was reproduction. Foreign travelers were invariably struck by Americans' sexual prudery. In the United States, they reported, a chicken breast was called a bosom and a piano leg was called a limb and was covered with lace trousers.

This strict sexual code drew support from a large medical literature that declared that any violation of the tenets of civilized morality would be detrimental to a person's health. Respected physicians insisted that loss of semen through masturbation or excessive sexual intercourse would produce "urinary difficulties, disorders of the genital organs, spinal diseases, weakness of the brain, loss of memory, epilepsy, insanity, apoplexy, abortions, premature births, and extreme feebleness, morbid predispositions, and an early death of offspring." Medical authorities also

warned that women were too frail physically and too sensitive spiritually to engage in frequent intercourse and that "the majority of women (happily for them) are not very much troubled with sexual feelings of any kind." Above all, physicians warned that individuals who had sexual relations outside of marriage ran a high risk of contracting incurable venereal diseases.

The Victorian sexual code was a public ideal, not an accurate description of reality. Prostitution flourished in turn-of-the-century America. Every large city had at least one red-light district. In New York, there was the Tenderloin; in Chicago, the Levee; in New Orleans, Storyville; in San Francisco, the Barbary Coast. Early twentieth-century vice commissions estimated that there were "not less" than a quarter of a million prostitutes in the country. In Chicago, an estimated quarter of the city's males visited prostitutes annually, and paid them $15 million a year. Pornography was also widespread.

Nor were nineteenth-century women necessarily the prudish, asexual, sexually ignorant figures popularized in Victorian mythology.

An early sexual survey of the attitudes of 45 well-educated women, mainly born before 1870, reported that most enjoyed intercourse and experienced orgasm.

Nevertheless, the values of civilized sexual morality dominated polite society and received strong public backing from the broad-based crusade to suppress vice. A "purity crusade" had arisen in the 1860s and 1870s in response to proposals to legalize and regulate prostitution. In almost every major city in the country, former abolitionists like William Lloyd Garrison, feminists like Susan B. Anthony, temperance advocates, and ministers joined forces to defeat legalized prostitution. Prostitution, they argued, was a menace "to the chastity of our women and the sanctity of the home." It exploited poor women to satisfy male lust and endangered respectable women, who were often infected with syphilis and gonorrhea by their husbands.

In later years, the purity forces broadened their aims. In addition to fighting prostitution, they also sought to protect the family by outlawing abortion, restricting the sale of alcohol, stamping out pornography, censoring nudity in the arts, enforcing the Sabbath through enactment of "blue laws," suppressing the use of narcotics, and stopping the flow of birth control information through the mails.

The self-appointed leader of the purity forces was a staunch crusader named Anthony Comstock. Born on a farm in New Canaan, Connecticut, Comstock, as a youth, had been so upset by an impulse to masturbate that he feared he might be driven to commit suicide. While serving with a Connecticut regiment in the Civil War he had been appalled by the pornographic French postcards circulated among soldiers. After the war he moved to New York, where he became active in the Young Men's Christian Association and was shocked by the prevalence of prostitutes and of vendors selling obscene books.

In 1873, Comstock persuaded Congress to pass a federal law banning from the mails "every obscene lewd, lascivious or filthy book, pamphlet, paper, letter, writing, print or other publication of an indecent character." Comstock was then appointed special agent of the Post Office and made responsible for arresting those who used the mail in violation of the law. "Morals, not art or literature," was Comstock's motto. He took credit for hounding 16 persons to their deaths.

By 1910, Comstock and the purity forces had achieved many of their legislative goals. They had successfully pushed for state laws to restrict divorce; raised the age of consent for sexual intercourse (from 7, in some states, to 18); imposed tests for venereal disease prior to marriage; and criminalized abortion. The purity crusaders also won passage of a federal statute that defined the mailing of birth control information a felony.

The years just before World War I witnessed a series of sharp challenges to the nineteenth-century code of sexual purity. Radical new ideas about marriage were publicized and debated. Swedish feminist Ellen Key preached a scheme of "unwed motherhood"; Edith Ellis, wife of British sex researcher Havelock Ellis, advocated trial marriage and "semi-detached marriage" in which each spouse occupied a separate domicile; still others advocated "serial marriage" and easier divorce. Greenwich Village bohemians and political radicals advocated, and to some extent practiced, free love. Psychologists, including Havelock

Ellis, G. Stanley Hall, and Sigmund Freud, attacked the notion that women lacked sexual impulses.

Sexual conduct was also changing rapidly. The first scientific sex surveys indicated that women who came to maturity after the turn of the century were much more likely than their mothers to engage in sex before marriage and outside it. Women who were born around 1900 were two to three times as likely to have premarital intercourse compared to women born before 1900. They were also more likely to experience orgasm. Among men, premarital sexual experience did not increase, but it occurred less often with prostitutes and more frequently with other women.

Public alarm over the changes occurring in American sexual experience culminated in the first decade of the 1900s in an explosion of concern over "white slavery"—prostitution—and the "black plague"— venereal disease. Many lurid books appeared—with such titles as *The Traffic in Souls*, *The House of Bondage*, and *The Shame of a Great Nation*—which explained how innocent young girls were seduced by panderers and, through the use of a chloroformed cloth, a hypodermic needle, or a drugged drink, forced into prostitution. Congress attacked the problem of "white slavery" in 1910 by adopting the Mann Act, which made it a crime to transport women across state lines for immoral purposes. During World War I, Congress provided states with federal funds to set up facilities to detain and rehabilitate women apprehended as prostitutes. Fifteen thousand women were detained during the war. Sex was becoming a subject of open public debate and direct government involvement.

During the 1920s, the drift toward sexual liberalization continued.

Journalists wrote in bewilderment about a new social phenomenon, the flapper, the independent assertive, pleasure-hungry young woman, "making love lightly, boldly, and promiscuously." Systematic sex surveys showed that the incidence of premarital intercourse was continuing to rise and that an increasing number of young women had slept with men other than their future husband. Half of those women born in the first decade of the twentieth century and two-thirds of those born in the second decade had engaged in intercourse before marriage. Meanwhile, contraceptive practices were also changing dramatically. Instead of relying heavily on douching or coitus interruptus as a form of birth control, younger women were using the more effective and less disruptive diaphragms.

Growing sexual permissiveness evoked a sharp reaction. Purity forces renewed their crusade to discourage indecent styles of dancing, immodest dress, and impure books and films. Religious journals denounced popular dance styles as "impure, polluting, corrupting, debasing, destroying spirituality, [and] increasing carnality." A bill was introduced in the Utah state legislature to fine and imprison women who wore skirts on the streets "higher than three inches above the ankle." In the Ohio legislature it was proposed that cleavage be limited to two inches and that the sale of any "garment which unduly displays or accentuates the lines of the female figure" be prohibited. Four states and many cities established censorship boards to review films, and many other cities broke up red-light districts and required licenses for dance halls. But despite these efforts, a sexual revolution had begun that has continued until this day.

the 1920s, old-stock Americans vented their fears and frustrations by attacking alcohol, smoking, evolution, immigrants, and radicals.

Prohibition

Like the sex debate, prohibition exposed deep fissures in American society. The issue turned on the class, ethnic, and religious makeup of individual communities, not merely on whether the community was rural or urban.

At first prohibition's apparent success muted its critics. Distilleries and breweries shut down, saloons locked their doors, arrests for drunkenness declined, and alcohol-related deaths all but disappeared. Compliance, however, had less to do with piety and public support than the law of supply and demand: Since illegal liquor remained in short supply, its price rose beyond the average worker's means.

Private enterprise filled the void. Smugglers supplied wealthy imbibers who could afford the best liquor and wine, but the less affluent had to rely on small-time operators who produced for local consumption. Due to high shipping and storage charges, it cost more to produce beer or wine, so the price of liquor, relative to other alcoholic beverages, dropped. Drinking habits shifted accordingly: The consumption of hard liquor rose, while beer and wine sales declined.

Much of this booze ran the gamut from swill to poison. According to one widely circulated story, a potential buyer who sent a liquor sample to a laboratory for analysis was shocked when the chemist replied: "Your horse has diabetes." For others the problem of "killer batches" was no laughing matter. Hundreds, perhaps thousands, died from drinking concoctions with names like "Jackass Brandy" and "Soda Pop Moon."

Neither federal nor state authorities had enough funds to enforce prohibition. The Federal Prohibition Bureau began the 1920s with 1520 agents, and by 1930 the number had grown to only 2836. Lax enforcement, coupled with huge profits, enticed large-scale operators to enter bootlegging. Organized crime, of course, had long been a fixture of urban life, with gambling and prostitution as its base, but small-time, local operators managed these vices. Liquor demanded production plants, dis-tribution networks, and sales forces, attracting large-scale operators with the capital and business skills to tackle big-time bootlegging.

Bootlegging turned into a gold mine for organized crime. By the late 1920s syndicates sold 150 million quarts of liquor each year, generating revenue in excess of $2 billion annually (more than 2 percent of the gross national product). Chicago's Al Capone had a gross income of $60 million in 1927 and employed an army of workers. A ruthless figure accused of ordering numerous gangland killings, he preferred to think of himself as a businessman. "All I do is supply a public demand," he insisted. "I do it in the best and least harmful way I can."

From the outset, cynics insisted prohibition could not be enforced. They were right. Where the public backed prohibition, it had teeth; where it lacked support, particularly in large cities, people openly flaunted it. On more than one occasion journalists saw President Warren Harding's bootlegger drive to the back door of the White House and unload cases of liquor in broad daylight.

In 1923 New York became the first state to repeal its enforcement law, and by 1930 six more states had followed suit. Others remained firmly committed to prohibition, prompting Walter Lippmann to conclude: "The high level of lawlessness is maintained by the fact that Americans desire to do so many things which they also desire to prohibit." Not until the 1930s, when the Great Depression gave the country something really serious to worry about, did prohibition lose steam. After a presidential commission reported prohibition could not be enforced, Congress finally repealed it in 1933, making liquor control a state and local matter, precisely the jurisdictions where many Americans thought it belonged.

The Antismoking Campaign: The Forgotten Reform

"Prohibition is won," exclaimed the evangelist Billy Sunday in 1920, "Now for tobacco!" Sunday's challenge became the battle cry for religious groups, educators, moral crusaders, and health advocates who wanted to follow up their victory over demon rum with a crusade against "our Lady Nicotine."

Opposition to tobacco was hardly new. King James I denounced smoking in 1603 as "a custom loathsome to the eye, hateful to the nose, harmful to the brain, dangerous to the lungs." During the nineteenth century, the antitobacco campaign remained an appendage of the temperance movement, and critics of the "vile weed" denounced pipes, cigars, plugs, and snuff with equal venom. After the introduction of machine-made cigarettes in the 1880s, however, opponents concentrated their fire on the "little white slavers," insisting cigarettes damaged the public's health more than previous forms of tobacco because smokers inhaled fumes filled with poison.

As early as the Civil War, a few cities had banned smoking in restaurants, theaters, public buildings, trolleys, and railway cars. After antismokers organized the National Anti-Cigarette League in 1903, scores of prominent leaders joined the crusade, including David Starr Jordan, the president of Stanford University, who told audiences, "Boys who smoke cigarettes are like wormy apples"; and the lecturer Elbert Hubbard who declared, "Cigarette smokers are men whose future lies behind them." Between 1896 and 1923, 14 states, mainly in the Midwest, outlawed the sale of cigarettes, prompting calls for a constitutional amendment for national prohibition.

Smokers had little to fear. By the end of the 1920s every state had repealed its law against cigarette sales. The crusade against tobacco was the last hurrah of the prohibition movement, and it failed because prohibition devolved into a legal fiasco and because the public considered smoking the lesser vice. Nor did the style of the antismokers help their cause. Many Americans dismissed them as moral zealots and opponents of individual liberty who wanted to expand the power of the state over private behavior.

Largely because a national consensus had not formed against tobacco, smokers had no difficulty defending their right to smoke. The tobacco industry supported them by opposing every effort to restrict the sale of cigarettes and by spending millions of dollars on advertisements to reassure the public smoking was sophisticated, sexy, and even healthy. Industry spokesmen hammered home the message that

smoking should be left to individuals to decide, with no interference from the state. Not until the 1950s, when scientists linked smoking to lung cancer, did reformers win public support for their war against what one scholar has called "slow motion suicide."

The Scopes Trial

Many custodians of small-town morality also fretted over the teaching of evolution in public schools, and they got their day in court in the celebrated "Monkey Trial." In 1925 the Tennessee legislature passed a bill that prohibited the teaching of evolution in public schools. Immediately after the new law took effect, the officers of the American Civil Liberties Union offered to challenge the law in court, and George Rappelyea, a young mining engineer in Dayton, Tennessee, decided to accept the offer. He persuaded the town's 24-year-old science teacher, John Scopes, to provoke a test case by declaring publicly he taught biology from an evolutionary standpoint.

GATHERING DATA FOR THE TENNESSEE TRIAL

When biology teacher John Scopes taught evolutionary theory to his class, the state of Tennessee brought him to trial. The well-publicized trial emphasized the split between religious fundamentalists and those who advocated scientific and academic freedom.

Scopes was brought to trial in the summer of 1925. At the request of the World's Christian Fundamentals Association, William Jennings Bryan, rural America's defender of the faith, agreed to join the team of prosecutors, and Clarence Darrow, the celebrated trial lawyer and self-proclaimed agnostic, volunteered his services to the legal team retained by the American Civil Liberties Union to defend Scopes.

The trial opened on July 10, 1925, with the Honorable John T. Raulston, a fundamentalist judge from Gizzard's Cove, Tennessee, presiding. As Holy Rollers from the surrounding regions held revivals and as religious zealots carried signs telling people to read their Bibles and escape damnation, more than a thousand people jammed into the stifling courthouse to watch Bryan and Darrow do combat. Following a week of testimony, the judge grew concerned the building might collapse beneath the weight of all those spectators and conducted the final day of trial on the courthouse lawn, where the cries of hot dog vendors added to the carnival atmosphere.

The outcome was never in doubt. Scopes admitted he had broken the law. He was convicted and fined $100. (Tennessee's supreme court later upheld the case but rescinded the fine on a technicality.) What gave the trial its drama was the clash between Bryan and Darrow and the opposite images of America they represented. As one observer remarked, the trial "was a battle between two types of mind—the rigid, orthodox, accepting, unyielding narrow, conventional mind, and the broad liberal critical, cynical, skeptical and tolerant mind."

Near the end of testimony the defense surprised everyone by asking Bryan to take the stand as an expert witness on the Bible. Bryan's simple, direct answers to Darrow's sarcastic questions revealed an unshakable faith in the literal truth of the Bible. Though Darrow sought to belittle his testimony as "fool ideas that no intelligent Christian on earth believes," Bryan insisted "it is better to trust in the Rock of Ages than to know the ages of rocks." At one point tempers flared and both men leaped to their feet shaking their fists at one another.

Throughout the trial Eastern journalists ridiculed Bryan, but he defied their scorn. Bryan, who died five days after the trial ended, left the courtroom believing he had carried the day, and many fundamentalists for whom he spoke agreed. Bryan's opponents, however, thought he had been humiliated and proclaimed the Scopes trial a victory for academic freedom. In the end, the Scopes trial merely illustrated how little tolerance secular and fundamentalist groups had for each other.

Xenophobia and Restricting Immigration

Cultural fears unleashed a new wave of nativism in the 1920s. A broad band of Americans believed the new immigrants posed a grave threat to the United States: Organized labor, bent upon protecting high wages, resented competition from cheap labor; staunch nativists and superpatriots warned that foreign influences would corrupt the American character; social workers argued that their caseload of disadvantaged people was already at the breaking point; eugenicists made grave predictions about "racial suicide"; and assorted businessmen denounced immigrants as dangerous radicals.

To protect the United States these groups demanded drastic changes in the nation's immigration policy. After a stopgap immigration law in 1921 failed to halt the flow, Congress passed the National Origins Act of 1924. It established an annual immigration quota of 2 percent of each national group counted in the 1890 census. Since southern and eastern Europeans did not begin arriving in large numbers until the turn of the century, the law gave western and northern Europeans a big edge over the "new immigrants." Great Britain and Ireland, for example, could send 65,731 a year, but Italy only 5802.

Asians suffered the harshest treatment. Bowing to pressure from the West Coast, Congress excluded them entirely, even though earlier agreements with China and Japan had virtually stopped immigration from the Far East. (For example, the quota system would have allowed fewer than 150 Japanese to enter the United States annually.) The Japanese people deeply resented the insult. Japan boycotted American goods, a patriotic Japanese committed hara-kiri in front of the American Embassy in Tokyo, and the Japanese ambassador in Washington resigned in protest.

Hostility to immigrants also surfaced in the Sacco and Vanzetti case. On April 15, 1920, two unidentified gunmen robbed a payroll messenger from a shoe factory in South Braintree, Massachusetts, murdering a paymaster and a guard. The crime occurred at the peak of the Red Scare in the United States when the Justice Department was investigating two Italian immigrants, Nicola Sacco and Bartolomeo Vanzetti, both avowed anarchists, for distributing leaflets calling for a rally to protest the infamous Palmer raids. Justice Department officials worked hand-in-glove with local authorities in Massachusetts, and on May 5 police arrested the men, charging them with robbery and murder. Although the state failed to prove its case, it did present strong evidence against one of the defendants and prosecutors succeeded in parading the political views of both men before the jury. On July 14, 1921, Sacco and Vanzetti were convicted and sentenced to death.

The trial brought a storm of protest from Italian-Americans, liberals, and civil rights advocates. Sacco-Vanzetti defense funds sprang up in the United States and Europe, attracting distinguished supporters such as Albert Einstein, Felix Frankfurter, H. G. Wells, and George Bernard Shaw. Protesters demanded a review of the case, claiming Sacco and Vanzetti had been convicted not with facts but with their political views.

For six years the state granted stays of execution. Early in July 1927 Governor Alvan T. Fuller of Massachusetts appointed a blue-ribbon commission, headed by Harvard University president Abbott Lawrence Lowell, to investigate the case. After a month's work, the commission upheld the conviction. Sacco and Vanzetti, asserting their innocence to the end, went to the electric chair on August 23, 1927, with the words, "This is our career, and our triumph." Following their deaths, mobs attacked American embassies across Europe. Nor did the controversy fade with time. The debate about their guilt or innocence has reverberated down to this day.

The Ku Klux Klan

Fear of political radicals and ethnic minorities found its most strident voice during the 1920s in the Ku Klux Klan, a secret organization that stood for "100 percent pure Americanism" and limited its membership to white, native-born

Many people felt that Sacco and Vanzetti, Italian-born admitted anarchists, were persecuted for their immigrant status and radical views rather than for any real crime. Their trial, shown here in a painting by Ben Shahn, became an important symbol in the fight for civil liberties and brought about violent protest in America and abroad.
(Ben Shahn, *Bartolomeo Vanzetti and Nicola Sacco* (1931–32). Tempera on paper over composition board, $10\frac{1}{2} \times 14\frac{1}{2}''$. Gift of Mrs. John D. Rockefeller, Jr./The Museum of Modern Art, New York.)

Protestants. Organized on Thanksgiving night, 1915, in a ceremony beneath a burning cross on a mountaintop in Georgia, the revived Klan was, in the words of its founder and imperial wizard, Colonel William Joseph Simmons, a "living memorial" to the Klan of Reconstruction days. An insurance salesman, part-time Methodist minister, and perennial booster of fraternal societies, Simmons had no political agenda. Under his inept leadership, the Klan attracted fewer than 5000 members during its first few years and remained a small southern organization teetering on the edge of bankruptcy.

That changed in 1920 when Simmons hired two advertising specialists, Edward Young Clark and Elizabeth Tyler, to market the Klan. They did nothing to change the product. The Klan remained, as before, a loosely knit web of vigilante groups, with no national program. Klan policy was set at the local level, varying from community to community to accommodate local prejudices, be they directed at blacks, Catho-

The Ku Klux Klan exploited postwar confusion and fear of things "un-American." Although the Klan had flourished in small, rural towns across the South, during the 1920s it spread to working-class and middle-class neighborhoods of large cities, where people felt threatened by the influx of African-American and immigrant workers.

lics, Jews, Mexicans, Orientals, foreigners, or "Reds." Clark and Tyler hired an army of organizers to canvas the country selling memberships in the Klan. (Membership cost $10; the sheet was $4 extra.) Working on commission and molding their pitch to match their clientele, they enjoyed astounding success. By 1921 the Klan had become a national organization with over 90,000 paying members; by 1925 it claimed a membership of 5 million! An amazed southern newspaper editor called the "idea of selling people their own prejudices almost equal to the old bunco game of selling a hick the Capitol."

Yet the Klan's membership was not limited to rednecks. True, the Klan was strongest (and most violent) in the South, but the Klan had a large following in the Southeast, the Far West, and the Midwest. Moreover, the Klan showed considerable strength in several large urban areas, including Chicago, Indianapolis, and Detroit. Its natural habitat was not the countryside, but middling towns and small cities. Most members were not "poor white trash," but members of the lower middle class from old-stock, respectable families.

In its heyday (1921–1926), the Klan was a political force to reckon with. At the state level, it controlled or influenced the election of governors and legislators in Alabama, Georgia, Arkansas, Texas, Oklahoma, California, Oregon, Indiana, and Ohio. In fact, the Klan's strength extended into Pennsylvania, New York, and parts of New England. Regardless of where it rose to power, however, the Klan's vision was essentially negative. Except for an Oregon statute requiring Catholic children to attend public schools (later declared unconstitutional), the Klan did not inspire a single law.

Night ridings, cross burnings, tar and featherings, public beatings, and lynchings formed the Klan's stock in trade, but the Klan did not limit its wrath to ethnic and religious offenders. The Klan's victims reflected the public's anxieties about the decline in private behavior. The Klan lashed out against wife beaters, drunkards, bootleggers, gamblers—anyone who violated time-honored standards of morality.

In the end, poor leadership and the absence of a political program destroyed the Klan. Once they attained office, Klan-supported officials offered no constructive legislation. Even more damaging, several Klan leaders became involved in sex scandals, and several more were indicted for corruption. By 1930 voters had turned Klansmen out of office, Klan membership had fallen to 50,000, and the forces of nativism were in full retreat. The country had abandoned a grass-roots movement that purported to stand for Americanism but smacked of fascism. The white sheets and cross burnings vanished from public view, to return again in a few decades when the civil rights movement challenged white supremacy.

THE RISE OF URBAN CULTURE

Despite all the upheavals, a new force for social cohesion was drawing Americans together during the 1920s. The United States was rapidly evolving a consumer culture that blunted regional differences and imposed similar tastes and life-styles. Centered in the cities and propelled by revolutions in transportation, advertising, communications, and entertainment, a new consumer society emerged during the 1920s, enshrining materialism and self-indulgence as the dominant cultural motifs of prosperity's decade.

The Automobile

"Why on earth do you need to study what's changing this country," a Midwesterner asked the sociologists Robert and Helen Lynd in 1924. "I can tell you what's happening in just four letters: A-U-T-O!" The man was right. In 1900 only 8000 motor vehicles were registered in the United States and the automobile was little more than a rich man's toy; by 1920 Americans owned more than 9 million automobiles. By 1925 Henry Ford had lowered the price of his sturdy Model Ts to less than $300, about three-months pay for the average urban worker. That year registrations reached 19,940,724, and by 1930 registrations had risen to 26,531,999 (more than one automobile for every five people).

No previous form of transportation (except walking) had been so widely available. In Muncie, Indiana, a town of 11,000, only 125 families owned a horse and carriage in 1890. Most people walked. By the time of the Lynds' study in 1924, however, two out of three families in Muncie owned an automobile. The great American love affair with the automobile had begun. One working-class housewife told the Lynds, "I'll go without food before I'll see us give up the car."

Enthusiasts claimed the automobile promoted family togetherness through evening rides, picnics, and weekend excursions. Critics decried family squabbles between parents and teenagers over use of the automobile, an apparent decline in church attendance resulting from all-day Sunday outings, and budget pressures working families faced to support their automobile habit. Others felt uneasy about the blurring of class lines (blue-collar families riding around just like rich folks). Worst of all, charged critics, automobiles gave young people freedom and privacy. Enclosed sedans constituted nearly 90 percent of the automobiles sold in the United States by 1927. These "portable bedrooms" removed courtship from the family parlor and gave couples a private room they could take anywhere.

Critics also blamed the automobile for undermining the public's devotion to thrift. In the past, people had been taught to live within their means. That meant paying cash for consumer goods or doing without. The automobile eroded this thrift ethic. An ad in a midwestern newspaper showed a kindly banker advising a young couple to buy an automobile on time, predicting the purchase would raise their horizons, which, in turn, would boost their earning power. Long before New Dealers started quoting John Maynard Keynes, Madison Avenue was telling Americans to spend themselves rich.

Appliances

Madison Avenue struck another bonanza in appliances, and electricity offered the key to this vast new market. Prior to World War I only one-fifth of America's households had electricity, but by 1929 the proportion had risen to two-thirds, and by 1940, to over four-fifths. Electric refrigerators, washing machines, vacuum cleaners, and toasters quickly took hold. By 1929 one in four homes had electric vacuum cleaners; one in five had toasters.

Appliances eased the sheer physical drudgery of housework, but they did not shorten the average housewife's work week. Women had to do more because the standards others told them to meet kept rising. In the 1920s and 1930s housewives fell under the spell of advice columnists, the ads of soap manufacturers who brought their favorite "soap" operas into their homes, and the precepts of appliance manufacturers. All equated cleanliness with motherly love, hoping to make women who did not keep spotless homes feel like failures. Sheets had to be changed weekly; the house had to be vacuumed daily.

In short, social pressure expanded household chores to keep pace with the new technology. Nor did the irony stop there. Touted as labor-saving devices, household appliances actually stopped the trend toward the centralization of certain jobs, like laundry and baking. Far from liberating women, appliances imposed new standards and pressures.

The Lost Generation

While most Americans embraced the consumer culture, others found it thoroughly disgusting. Disillusioned by the collapse of Wilsonian idealism, the hypocrisy of prohibition, and the upsurge of nativism, a new generation of American writers felt alienated. To these cultural critics, America had become a nation of conspicuous consumption, awash in materialism and devoid of spiritual vitality. Writers of the so-called Lost Generation despised the narrow-mindedness of small town life, with its complacency, its conformity, and, above all, its devotion to the all-mighty dollar.

No author captured these themes better than Sinclair Lewis, the first American to win the Nobel Prize for literature (1930). In *Main Street* (1920), he mingled satire with caricature when he declared: "Main Street is the climax of civilization. That this Ford might stand in front of the Bon Ton Store, Hannibal invaded Rome and Erasmus wrote in Oxford cloisters." In *Babbitt* (1922), a biting portrait of America's businessmen, Lewis attacked the spiritual conformity that drove Americans to follow the crowd.

H. L. Mencken mounted a scathing attack on his countrymen. As editor of *Mercury* magazine, he wrote hundreds of essays mocking practically every aspect of American life. He called the South "the Sahara of the Bozart," a "gargantuan paradise of the fourth rate," and the middle class the "booboisie." Mencken directed his choicest barbs at reformers, whom he blamed for the bloodshed of World War I and the gangsters of the 1920s. "If I am convinced of anything," he snarled, "it is that Doing Good is in bad taste."

F. Scott Fitzgerald and Ernest Hemingway made the same points more obliquely. In novels such as *The Great Gatsby* (1925) and *Tender Is the Night* (1929), Fitzgerald exposed the decadence and materialism of American culture. Hemingway lionized toughness and "manly virtues" as a counterpoint to the softness of American life. In *The Sun Also Rises* (1926) and *A Farewell to Arms* (1929), he emphasized meaningless death and the importance of facing stoically the absurdities of the universe.

The Communication Revolution

In 1897 the United States had less than one telephone for every hundred residents, by 1914 the number had risen to one in ten, and by 1930 it stood at one in six. Americans averaged over 64 million calls per day in 1929, and a person in New York could talk with someone in London

Members of the "Lost Generation" of writers felt disillusioned with an American culture obsessed with money and devoid of spiritual vitality. Two of the Lost Generation's most prominent members were Ernest Hemingway (left) and F. Scott Fitzgerald (right).

for about $10 a minute that same year. The telephone hastened the transition from the written to the electronically transmitted word, brought the home in closer contact with the outside world, and reduced household visiting among neighbors as friends picked up the phone instead of dropping in.

Radio had an even greater impact. It drew the nation together by bringing news, entertainment, and advertisements to millions of listeners. With the organization of the National Broadcasting Corporation (NBC) in 1926 and the Columbia Broadcasting System (CBS) the following year, radio developed into a national industry, offering the same programs from coast to coast. In 1929 over 10 million households owned radios (well over one-third of the families in the country), and in that same year Americans spent a staggering $85 million on radio equipment.

The radio offered something for everyone. Not only did it report news events minutes after they happened, it brought politics to life as Americans listened to the voices of their political leaders and heard Will Rogers poke gentle fun at them. Serial adventures such as "The Green Hornet" and "The Lone Ranger" appealed to the entire family, while producers pitched sports broadcasts at male audiences. The "soaps" dominated weekday programming as millions of housewives listened to "Portia Faces Life" and "Life Can Be Beautiful."

Radio programs helped create mass culture by blunting regional differences. Listeners heard the same news reporters, serial shows, and sporting events delivered in the same dialect. They heard the same advertisements telling them what to buy, when to buy it, and how much to pay for it. Moreover, no other media had the power to create folk heroes so quickly. When Charles Lindbergh, the "Lone Eagle," became the first person to fly nonstop across the Atlantic from New York to Paris in 1927, the radio brought this incredible feat into American homes and made him a celebrity overnight.

Yet radio waves also brought the nation decidedly unheroic images. "Amos and Andy," which first aired in 1929, was one of the most popular shows of the depression. Its portrait of black life spread vicious racial stereotypes into homes whose white occupants knew little about black people. Other minorities fared no better. The Italian gangster, the bloodthirsty Indian, the Mexican with the sing-song voice, the tight-fisted Jew, and the Irish thug became stock characters in radio programming.

The Rise of Suburbs

Americans who bought the same products and listened to the same programs also shared new housing arrangements. The 1920s saw a spectacular growth in suburbs. Havens for the wealthy and upper middle class and home to a variety of white ethnic groups, suburbs expanded at a much faster rate than inner cities. Between 1920 and 1930 the population of Beverly Hills, a Los Angeles suburb, increased 2485 percent; Shaker Heights, a Cleveland suburb, 1000 percent; and Elmwood Park, a Chicago suburb, 717 percent.

New forms of transportation made the suburbs possible. For much of the nation's history, cities could not grow larger because workers had to live within walking distance of their jobs. Public transportation simply did not exist. After the Civil War, however, trolleys and streetcars greatly expanded labor's mobility, permitting workers to move beyond the walking radius surrounding factories. Metropolitan growth followed the trolley tracks as suburbs sprang up along the commuter lines. The automobile opened up vast new regions for housing, giving workers numerous options about where to live. Though suburbs had once been the exclusive domain of the well-to-do, the automobile enabled working-class families to move there, too.

Yet optimists who hoped to escape the city's congestion by moving to the suburbs got fooled. The sharp rise in road construction following the Federal Highway Act of 1916 produced complicated lateral traffic flows within cities and traffic congestion became worse. City planners counterattacked with traffic circles, synchronized stoplights, divided dual highways, and grade separation of highways from city streets, but nothing could free motorists from rush hour and holiday traffic jams. Whether one looked at the size and shape of cities or the flow of people within them, automobile tracks could be seen on virtually every inch of America's urban landscape.

Leisure Time: Games, Books, Sports, and Movies

Thanks to the unprecedented prosperity of the 1920s, Americans had more money for leisure activities than ever before. Spending for entertainment more than doubled during the 1920s, reaching $4.3 billion in 1929. The average worker devoted seven hours a week to play. Much of the time and money went for parlor games—mahjong sets, crossword puzzles, and the like. Contract bridge became the most durable of the new pastimes, followed closely by photography. Americans hit golf balls, played tennis, and bowled. Dance crazes swept the country. The fox trot made way for the Charleston, which in turn gave way to the jitterbug.

While Lewis, Mencken, Fitzgerald, and Hemingway found a wide audience, millions of Americans preferred the new popular literature, largely because it resolved rather than explored cultural tensions. In 1914, Edgar Rice Burroughs published *Tarzan of the Apes*, which immediately became a runaway bestseller. During the next 20 years, he wrote 40 other novels, most about Tarzan. For readers who felt concerned about urbanization and industrialization, the adventures of a lone white man in "dark Africa" revived the spirit of the frontier and individualism.

Zane Grey's novels enjoyed even greater popularity. His *Riders of the Purple Sage* appealed to readers who wished to celebrate their frontier heritage as a time when life seemed simple. Grey used a tried but true formula: romance, action, and a moralistic struggle between good and evil, all put in a western setting. Between 1918 and 1934, Grey wrote 24 books and became the best-known writer of popular fiction in the country.

While many readers demanded virtuous heroes and old-time values in their fiction, others wanted to be titillated. The 1920s saw a boom in "confession magazines." Urban values, liberated women, and Hollywood films had all relaxed Victorian standards, and confession magazines rushed to fill the vacuum, purveying stories of romantic success and failure, divorce, fantasy, and adultery. Of this genre, the most successful magazine was *True Story*, whose subscriptions soared from 10,000 in 1919 to more than 2 million in 1926. Writers survived the censors' cuts by placing moral tags at the end of their stories, advising readers to avoid similar mistakes in their own lives.

Spectator sports attracted vast audiences in the 1920s. The country yearned for heroes in an increasingly impersonal, organized society, and sports provided them. Prizefighting enjoyed a huge following, especially in the heavyweight division, where hard punchers like Jack Dempsey became national idols. Team sports flourished in colleges and high schools, but Americans focused on individual superstars, people whose talents or personalities made them appear larger than life. While Notre Dame emerged as a college football powerhouse in the 1920s, it was head coach Knute Rockne, with his "pep talks" on dedication and persistence, who got woven into the fabric of American popular culture. Harold "Red" Grange, the "Galloping Ghost" halfback for the University of Illinois, raised professional football to new heights when he signed a contract with the Chicago Bears in 1926.

Baseball drew even bigger crowds than football. George Herman "Babe" Ruth, the "Sultan of Swat," ruled as the sport's undisputed superstar. The public loved Ruth for his fabulous skills. As a member of the Boston Red Sox, Ruth set the major league record for the most scoreless innings pitched in a World Series. Ruth then went on to lead the New York Yankees to victory in four World Series by setting four home run records, hitting 60 in his best year. Yet quite apart from his pitching and hitting, the public adored Ruth for his gargantuan appetite and for his capacity to drink himself into a stupor. Die hard fans admired his beer belly almost as much as his swing.

Ruth transformed baseball in the 1920s because the public wanted change. Until the 1920s, Ty Cobb's brand of baseball dominated the sport—defense, base hits, and stolen bases. Ruth revolutionized the game in 1919 when he hit 29 home runs, the most ever in a single season, followed by an astonishing 54 in 1920. Between 1915 and 1930, the total number of home runs in major league baseball increased from 384 a year to 1565. Stolen bases dropped by one-half. Baseball became the game of the big hitter, the superstar, and no hitter was bigger,

Spectator sports became popular in the 1920s: Heroes of the day included men like "Red" Grange of the University of Illinois and "Babe" Ruth of the New York Yankees.

literally or figuratively, than Babe Ruth: He made baseball the "national pastime" as fans spent countless hours calculating, memorizing, and quizzing one another on baseball statistics.

Despite the mania for athletics, Americans shelled out ten times more money on movies than on spectator sports. By 1929, 90 million Americans went to the movies every week, out of a population of 120 million. Movies had become big business, and Hollywood could afford to produce huge spectacles. Cecil B. DeMille's *Ten Commandments* with its "cast of thousands" and dazzling special effects, demonstrated the new medium's ability to hold audiences spellbound. Comedies enjoyed great popularity as well, whether highly sophisticated pieces such as *Sinners in Silk*, featuring young men and women sharing in new sexual freedom, or slapstick masterpieces starring Charlie Chaplin, Buster Keaton, or Harold Lloyd. Ironically, slapstick comedies delivered the most significant social commentary of the 1920s, spoofing the pretensions of the wealthy and presenting sympathetic portraits of the poor.

Like radio and sports, movies helped create a new popular culture, with common speech, dress, behavior, and heroes. And like radio, Hollywood did its share to reinforce vicious racial stereotypes by denigrating minority groups. Mexicans appeared as sleepyeyed peasants, while the only parts for blacks went to actors like Stepin Fetchit, who got rich playing superstitious, blithering idiots. The wooden box and the silver screen both molded and mirrored mass culture.

THE REPUBLICAN RESTORATION

National politics looked backward during the 1920s. When Republican leaders promised to restore prosperity, most Americans embraced the conservative rhetoric, hoping to find in politics the stability they found lacking in their culture.

Talk about trust-busting and regulating big business gave way in "New Era" politics to calls for a partnership between government and industry, one that would promote the interests of American corporations at home and abroad. Politicos of the 1920s saw themselves as managers who understood economic growth. In place of government regulation, they put their faith in cooperation through the exchange of information among voluntary associations in every segment of the economy.

The Republican party dominated American politics in the 1920s, and its victories rested squarely on the votes of traditional Republicans. Though strongest in the rural states of the Midwest, Republicans enjoyed firm support in the Far West and in much of New England. Socially, the GOP remained the choice of old-stock, Protestant, middle-, upper-middle-, and upper-class Americans; occupationally, it drew its strength from bankers, professionals, business managers, and large farmers.

Handsome Harding

By and large the presidents of the New Era were mediocre figures. Senator Warren G. Harding of Ohio, who led off the decade, suited the times perfectly. Handsome enough to be a movie star, he not only looked great, but told the voters what they wanted to hear. Harding promised a return to "normalcy," which meant "not heroism but healing, not agitation but adjustment, not surgery but serenity." Democrat William McAdoo, the son-in-law of Woodrow Wilson and former secretary of the treasury, derided Harding's speeches as "an army of pompous phrases moving over the landscape in search of an idea," but McAdoo missed the point: Americans listened to Harding's words and felt reassured. He appeared to be a moderate, responsible leader who would avoid extremes and guide the country into a decade of prosperity. Harding trounced the Democratic candidate, Governor James M. Cox of Ohio, 16,143,407 to 9,130,328, carrying every state outside the Democratic South.

Harding remained in office what he had been before, a fun-loving man who liked to hit golf balls, play poker, drink whiskey, and shoot the breeze with old pals. He left government to his cabinet members and the Supreme Court, staffed by political conservatives all. They approached public service as managers, equating the people's interests with those of big business. Secretary of State Charles Evans Hughes championed American business interests abroad with unbridled enthusiasm; Andrew Mellon, secretary of the treasury, denounced government regulation and slashed taxes on the rich; and

Henry Wallace, the secretary of agriculture, organized conferences between farmers and bureaucrats under the Bureau of Agricultural Economics.

Business leaders had contributed $8 million to the GOP's campaign chest in 1920; in return they expected the federal government to roll back the gains organized labor had made during World War I. The courts led the attack. In 1921 Harding named William Howard Taft as chief justice of the Supreme Court. Taft's judicial philosophy embraced the sanctity of private property as the highest ideal of the republic. Under Taft, the Court took a narrow view of federal power, assigning the responsibility for protecting individual citizens to the states. During the 1920s the Court outlawed picketing, upheld the yellow-dog contract, overturned national child labor laws, and abolished minimum wage laws for women.

The decade's most capable figure was Herbert Hoover, secretary of commerce under both Harding and his successor, Calvin Coolidge. A world-famous engineer and self-made millionaire, Hoover abhorred destructive competition and waste in the economy, which he proposed to eliminate through "associationism." Hoover called for voluntary trade associations to foster cooperation in nearly every major industry and agricultural commodity through educational conferences, research commissions, trade practice controls, and ethical standards. By 1929 more than 2000 trade associations were busily at work implementing Hoover's vision of a stable and prosperous economy. Hoover also converted the Commerce Department into a planning agency for businesspeople. Working in cooperation with private groups, such as the National Bureau of Economic Research, the Commerce Department conducted studies and compiled statistics to aid corporate planning. No other Harding appointment matched Hoover's talent and vision.

In fact, several of Harding's appointees proved to be disasters. His own father once chided Harding: "It's a good thing you weren't born a girl. Because you'd be in a family way all the time. You can't say no." Harding found it especially hard to say no to old friends and cronies, members of the so-called Ohio Gang, when they asked for government jobs. In the end, this motley assortment of political hacks and hangers-on plunged his administration into disgrace.

Within two years after Harding assumed office, major scandals (involving bribes and kickbacks) erupted in the Justice Department and in the Veterans Bureau. Shortly after these disclosures, Harding died of a cerebral embolism on August 2, 1923. Immediately after his death, more misdeeds came to light, including the infamous Teapot Dome oil scandal. Albert B. Fall, a wealthy senator from New Mexico whom Harding had appointed as secretary of the interior, was convicted of accepting $360,000 in bribes in exchange for leasing drilling rights on federal naval oil reserves. He became the first cabinet member in American history convicted for crimes in office. Nor did the corruption in high places end there. After authorities accused Attorney General Harry Daugherty of accepting payoffs for selling German chemical patents controlled by the Alien Property Office, Daugherty resigned in disgrace.

In retrospect, two facts stand out about the scandals. First, none involved partisan attacks on private individuals or on political opponents, tactics associated with the Watergate scandal that brought down the presidency of Richard Nixon half a century later. Harding simply appointed men who were personally corrupt. Second, the public seemed indifferent to the scandals. Harding's successor, Calvin Coolidge, managed to convert the scandals into a political asset by convincing the public he had moved swiftly to punish the wrongdoers.

The Election of 1924

The election of 1924 symbolized, in a variety of ways, the tensions and concerns of the 1920s. Despite the Harding scandals, President Calvin Coolidge remained extremely popular, largely because the nation was awash in prosperity. Meeting in New York to nominate their candidate, the Democrats split their support between Alfred Smith, the governor of New York, and William Gibbs McAdoo. McAdoo represented the southern, rural wing of the party, which opposed immigration and evolution and supported prohibition, Protestantism, and the Ku Klux Klan. Smith spoke for the northern urban wing, which opposed immigration restriction, prohi-

Harding's administration was fraught with scandals involving bribes and kickbacks within his cabinet and inner circle.

bition, and the Ku Klux Klan. After 102 ballots in the sweltering heat of Madison Square Garden, the Democrats nominated a compromise candidate, John W. Davis, a Wall Street attorney. But by that time, the Democrats were so badly divided they had no chance for victory, at least not in 1924.

A coalition of labor leaders, social workers, and former progressives bolted both major parties and formed the Progressive party, which nominated Wisconsin Senator Robert La Follette for president. Their platform called for government ownership of natural resources, abolition of child labor, elimination of monopolies, and increased taxes on the rich. In the end, no issue could match the GOP's prosperity crusade. Coolidge won the election with 15,725,016 votes to Davis's 8,385,586 and La Follette's 4,822,856.

Silent Cal

Coolidge was a stern-faced, tight-lipped New Englander, whom Alice Roosevelt Longworth (Theodore Roosevelt's daughter) said looked like he had been "weaned on a pickle." Born in Plymouth Notch, Vermont, where five generations of Coolidges had worked the same family farm, he epitomized the rural values threatened by immigration, urbanization, and industrialization. After graduating from Amherst College, Coolidge opened a law office in Northampton, Massachusetts, where he embarked on a political career that led to the governorship of the Bay State. After crushing the Boston police strike in 1919 by calling out the National Guard, Coolidge gained a reputation as a staunch conservative. His reward came in 1920 when Republicans gave him the number two slot on their ticket.

Coolidge had no desire to be a strong president in the tradition of a Teddy Roosevelt or a Woodrow Wilson. In the words of Irving Stone, "He aspired to become the least President the country had ever had; he attained his desire." Coolidge went to bed early, slept ten hours a night, napped every afternoon, and seldom worked more than four hours a day. In part his sloth stemmed from a metabolic need for rest, but it also derived from a deep philosophical belief in the wisdom of inactivity. "Four-fifths of all our troubles in this life would disappear," sighed Coolidge, "if we would only sit down and keep still."

Harding and Coolidge both idealized rich businessmen, but Coolidge was positively consumed by his reverence for the corporate elite. "The man who builds a factory builds a temple," said Coolidge. "The man who works there, worships there." It followed, then, that government should do everything in its power to promote business interests. While Coolidge set the tone for his administration, he left it to his cabinet members, the courts, and Congress to devise strategies for consummating the marriage between business and government.

The Twilight of Progressivism

The government's tilt toward business signaled a retreat from progressivism. With the Democrats in disarray and Teddy Roosevelt's wing of the GOP all but dead, conservative Republicans were riding high. Still, the reform impulse did not disappear entirely during the 1920s. A small band of beleaguered reformers, led by Robert

La Follette of Wisconsin and George Norris of Nebraska, kept progressivism alive in Congress, where they worked for farm relief, child labor laws, and regulation of wages and working hours for women.

In 1922, Congress passed the Capper-Volstead Act, which exempted farm cooperatives from antitrust prosecution, clearing the way for production restrictions and price-fixing. Yet the farm bloc failed to enact the McNary-Haugen Bill, which would have raised farm prices by having the government purchase farm surpluses and then sell them in foreign markets. Congress passed the bill twice, but Coolidge vetoed it both times. Progressives did manage to defeat an attempt by private investors (led by Henry Ford) to build a hydroelectric dam across the Tennessee River at Muscle Shoals, Alabama, thus preserving the task of developing electricity in the region for the federal government.

Welfare advocates won a few temporary victories at the national level. In 1912 President William Howard Taft created the Children's Bureau in the Department of Labor to compile information on a variety of problems involving the nation's youth. In 1918 the bureau reported that 16,000 women had died in childbirth that year and 250,000 children had failed to survive their first year. Armed with these figures, reformers demanded federal action to improve prenatal and neonatal care. Social workers, joined by Margaret Sanger and other birth control advocates, supported the idea, and although the American Medical Association opposed it, Harding backed it. In 1921 Congress passed the Sheppard-Towner Act, which appropriated $1.5 million in 1922 for state hygiene instruction programs. The program died seven years later when Coolidge refused to renew its funding.

In keeping with their historic pattern, progressives had better luck at the state and local level. Once again, social workers and women's groups spearheaded the campaigns, sponsoring a broad range of welfare legislation. By 1930, 43 states had passed laws providing assistance to women with dependent children, and 34 states had adopted workers' compensation laws. Under the leadership of Governor Alfred Smith, New York granted women a 41-hour work week and instituted the nation's first public housing program.

Welfare opponents counterattacked, arguing labor reforms would increase production costs and leave states that passed welfare legislation at a competitive disadvantage with states without such laws. Asked to choose between social welfare programs and jobs, Congress, along with most states, opted for jobs. Moreover, the public did not seem to care. As one coed told a pollster: "We're not out to benefit society . . . or to make industry safe. We're not going to suffer over how the other half lives."

The Election of 1928

Coolidge announced his retirement from politics in 1928 with the terse statement, "I do not choose to run." Following his exit, the Republicans nominated Herbert Hoover, while the Democrats turned to Alfred E. Smith. Since both parties adopted nearly identical platforms, the election turned on personalities and images. Few elections have pitted opponents who better defined the two faces of America—one rural, the other urban.

A native of Iowa, Hoover depicted himself as a simple farmboy who, through hard work and pluck, had grown up to become wealthy and famous. During the campaign he told folksy tales of an idyllic boyhood spent in rural America, replete with nostalgic glimpses of swimming holes, hunting and fishing trips, and moonlit romps in fresh snow. In truth, his childhood had been far from perfect. Orphaned as a boy, Hoover was shuttled back and forth among a variety of relatives until he went to Stanford University. After graduating with a degree in mining engineering in 1893, Hoover labored in the mines during the depression that year before landing an engineering job with an international firm. Brilliant, hard working, and focused, he was a millionaire 12 years later. As a self-made man, Hoover presented a portrait of a safe, reassuring world.

Herbert Hoover, the consummate self-made man, was in office only a few months when the stock market crashed.

Yet Hoover was also a spokesman for the future. A leading advocate of scientific progressivism, he accepted the reality of industrialization, technology, governmental activism, and global markets. In contrast to Harding and Coolidge, Hoover believed the president should lead the nation. He thought the federal government had a responsibility to coordinate the competing interests of a modern economy. According to Hoover, technology, logic, and expertise, in both the public and private sectors, would make economic prosperity a permanent feature of American life.

Smith offered voters a clear choice. The son of immigrants, he was an Irish Catholic from Hell's Kitchen in New York City who had started public life with nothing and had climbed the political ladder as a faithful son of Tammany Hall. Smith sported his eastern accent and mannerisms with the same pride that he tipped his brown derby hat. A foe of prohibition, he spoke for urban, ethnic Americans. Yet Smith, too, represented the future, not so much in terms of science, technology, and organization, but in terms of cultural pluralism and urbanization. America's future lay with her cities, and the cities contained large groups of ethnic Americans struggling for acceptance and their share of the good life. Trapped between its past and the future, the Democratic party might be badly divided between its rural and urban wings, but Smith made no bones about his loyalties.

Not that it made much difference who the Democrats ran. Thanks to the booming economy, the Republicans were unbeatable in 1928. Smith was hurt by his failure to bridge the North-South, urban-rural split in the party; by anti-Catholic sentiment; and by his own attacks on prohibition. Aided by prosperity, religious bigotry, and the dry vote, Hoover coasted to an easy victory, swamping Smith by 21,392,190 votes to 15,016,443. The Democrats were so divided that six states from Dixie abandoned the Solid South and defected to Hoover.

Yet even in defeat, Smith's campaign revealed the most significant political change of the 1920s—the growing power of urban and ethnic voters within the Democratic party. Smith carried the 12 largest cities in the United

States by a margin of 38,000 votes. Equally important, many voters cast ballots for the first time in the election, as total voter turnout rose from 49 percent in 1924 to 57 percent in 1928. In large measure, the new voters came from industrial, urban communities in the North. This meant that hyphenated Americans were rapidly acquiring the habit of voting, and they were voting Democratic, shrinking the influence of the rural element in the party, as well as in the nation.

Herbert Hoover's election marked the climax of New Era politics. As president he advocated total cooperation between government and business. "Given a chance to go forward with the policies of the last eight years," he declared shortly after entering the White House, "we shall soon with the help of God be in sight of the day when poverty will be banished from this nation." Optimistic businesspeople, bankers, and stockbrokers applauded Hoover's promises, predicting a future of prosperity and progress. Ironically, the stock market crashed before their cheers had stopped echoing.

THE GREAT CRASH

Economic historians have been hard pressed to explain why "prosperity's decade" ended in financial disaster. Employment was high, prices were stable, and production was soaring. Manufacturing output nearly doubled between 1921 and 1929, and the real wages of industrial workers rose by about 17 percent. Not everyone prospered, to be sure. Strapped with long-term debts, high taxes, and a sharp drop in crop prices, farmers lost ground throughout the decade, never matching their income of 1920. Most blacks and Hispanics lived in poverty, large numbers of poor whites haunted southern Appalachia, and virtually every large American city had its ghetto. Still, more people were comfortable, well-to-do, or rich during the 1920s than ever before in American history.

The upper income groups included many Americans who became downright greedy, displaying what the economist John Kenneth Galbraith called an "inordinate desire to get rich quickly with a minimum of physical effort."

Many speculators sought to make their fortune in the Florida land boom of 1925–1926, the most spectacular monument to investment irresponsibility of the decade. Land prices in Florida rose exponentially until two devastating hurricanes in 1926 showed, in the words of Frederick Lewis Allen, "what a Soothing Tropic Wind could do when it got a running start from the West Indies." After the wind and the rain washed away the land boom, prices fell back to earth, bringing financial disaster to those who thought providence had selected Florida's marshlands as the perfect instrument for making them wealthy.

The Great Bull Market offered even more Americans the chance to vent their passion for speculation. Beginning in the last six months of 1924 the price of securities began to rise. While there were periodic dips over the next few years, the stock market continued to climb upward until 1928 when the rate of increase switched from measured steps to vaulting leaps. In March of 1928 alone, the value of stocks shot up more than ten percent. With the price of individual stocks rising as much as 20 percent in a single day and 5 million shares changing hands, the ticker tapes often ran 2 hours behind.

Credit provided the yeast for the Great Bull Market. Margin buying allowed the purchaser of securities to pay only a fraction of their face value. The actual securities would then be left with the broker as collateral for the loan that paid for them, but the purchaser retained full title to them at their face value, including the right to sell them at a profit as the market rose. Speculators could get all the benefits of ownership without paying the full purchase price. In 1926 trading in the stock market stood at $451 million; by 1929 it had leaped to $1.1 billion. Brokers' loans stood at $3.5 billion in 1926; by 1929 they had jumped to $8.5 billion, showing how investment borrowing had transmuted itself into an orgy of speculation. Contrary to later mythology, the masses did not join in the fun. Most speculators were wealthy people or members of the upper middle class. Most working-class Americans did not own stocks, let alone play the market.

While the Federal Reserve Board was supposed to prevent such shenanigans, board members found themselves in a real dilemma. If they raised interest rates to stifle speculation, they risked slowing down the economy and creating unemployment. If they lowered interest rates to stimulate the economy, they risked making securities speculation worse. Confused and uncertain, the Federal Reserve Board pursued contradictory policies. Between 1927 and 1929 the board raised and lowered interest rates several times in a futile attempt to slow Wall Street down without harming the economy. In the end, private greed and government impotence combined to create a catastrophe.

A few days before he left office in 1929, Coolidge reassured the public stocks were "cheap at current prices." Critics disagreed. Financial analysts for the *New York Times* warned investors that the huge gap between stock prices and the rate of economic growth was bound to end in disaster. The bubble burst in September and October of 1929 when the market finally crashed. By November the value of the average stock had dropped 50 percent, reducing private wealth in the United States by an estimated $30 billion. Following a brief flirtation with stability in 1931, the market continued its downward spiral for the next several years. Overall, the index of common stocks dropped from a high of 26 points in 1929 to a low of 6.9 points in 1932.

But the Great Crash did not cause the Great Depression. Whole segments of the American economy, including agriculture, banking, manufacturing, and foreign trade, were shaky long before the stock market collapsed. Farm prices had been depressed ever since the end of World War I. Burdened by the heavy debts needed to finance wartime production increases, farmers could not compete on the world market when European agriculture revived. Following World War I, global farm production rose and commodity prices dropped. Caught with declining incomes, farmers tried to recover their losses and make their debt payments by increasing production. The collective result of millions of farmers raising output was larger surpluses and lower prices, a vicious cycle that persisted throughout the decade. Moreover, the decline in farm income reverberated throughout the economy: Rural consumers stopped buying farm implements, tractors, automobiles, furniture, and consumer goods from the mail order houses.

Millions of farmers defaulted on their debts, placing tremendous pressure on the banking system. Between 1920 and 1929 more than 5000 of the country's 30,000 banks failed. Afraid to put their money in banks, large numbers of people began hoarding cash, which by 1930 removed more than $1 billion from circulation. Following the stock market crash in 1929 and the continued downward spiral through 1933, the banking system saw more of its assets destroyed. Between 1929 and 1933, when the entire banking system collapsed, another 5000 banks went under. Small wonder many bankers became frightened and cautious, refusing to make loans even to worthy borrowers.

Thanks to the banking crisis, thousands of small businesspeople failed because they could not secure working capital loans. Thousands more failed because they had lost their working capital in the stock market. Instead of plowing some of their profits during the 1920s back into

This newspaper headline from October 25, 1929, tried to reassure the public that the economy was fundamentally sound, but the downward spiral continued through 1932, when prices were 80 percent below their 1929 highs.

their businesses and expanding capacity, many gambled on the securities markets. When the crash came in 1929, they lost money that should have gone into new factories, technologies, and distribution systems. Unable to raise their own cash or borrow funds, these small businesses shut their doors and laid off workers.

Labor formed another weak link in the chain. Because wage increases during the 1920s failed to keep pace with rising corporate profits, purchasing power could not absorb the supply of consumer goods. While business leaders promoted the consumer culture through advertising, they refused to give workers the wage increases needed to buy products. Like farmers, workers did not have enough purchasing power to sustain the economy.

Installment buying also weakened the economy. Between 1919 and 1927 term debt increased from $100 million to $7 billion. Consumers went on a spending binge, encouraged by "buy now and pay later" advertising. As demand for automobiles and furniture rose higher and higher, those industries expanded rapidly in the early 1920s. Later in the decade, consumer demand for cars and furniture reached the saturation point. By 1927 both industries found themselves with excess capacity and had to lay off workers.

Finally, Republican tariff policies damaged the economy by depressing foreign trade. Anxious to protect American industries from foreign competitors after World War I, Congress passed the Emergency Tariff Act of 1921, the Fordney-McCumber Tariff of 1922, and the Hawley-Smoot Tariff of 1930, each of which raised tariff rates to unprecedented levels. Along with serious weaknesses in the European economies, American tariffs stifled international trade and deepened the economic malaise, making it difficult for European nations to pay off their debts to creditor nations such as the United States.

Declining purchasing power created a vicious cycle. Drops in consumer spending led inevitably to reductions in production and worker layoffs. Unemployed workers then spent less and the cycle repeated itself. Business bankruptcies increased and even healthy firms postponed investment.

All these factors sapped the economy, leaving it ripe for disaster. Yet the depression did not strike instantly; it infected the country gradually, like a slow-growing cancer. From Maine to California, in numbers that seemed incredible, businesses failed, banks folded, and corporations slashed production, cut wages, and laid off employees. The national income dropped from $88 billion in 1929 to $40 billion in 1933, by which time 13 million Americans (25 percent of the work force) had lost their jobs.

Measured in human terms, the Great Depression was the greatest economic catastrophe in American history. It hit urban and rural areas, blue- and white-collar families alike. In the nation's cities, unemployed men took to the streets to sell apples or shine shoes. By the end of 1930, New York City had 33 soup kitchens, serving lines of hungry families that stretched for blocks. Thousands of men, many of whom deserted their wives and children, hopped freight trains and wandered from town to town looking for jobs or handouts.

Unlike most of western Europe, the United States had no federal system of unemployment insurance. The relief burden fell on state and municipal governments working in cooperation with private charities, such as the Red Cross and the Community Chest. Created to handle temporary emergencies, these groups lacked the resources to alleviate the massive suffering created by the Great Depression. The rural South had virtually no relief funds. A social worker in Alabama considered herself fortunate when the county appropriated $300 to serve 5000 unemployed, starving people.

Urban centers in the North fared little better. Most city charters did not permit public funds to be spent on work relief. Philadelphia provided relief to only one needy family in five, and those families lucky enough to receive assistance got less than $20 a month. New York paid less than $10 a month per family. Relative to the cost of living, these subsidies were meager, yet most small and medium-sized cities offered no assistance. By the fall of 1931 relief programs had collapsed in most cities. Adding insult to injury, several states disqualified relief clients from voting, while other cities forced them to surrender their automobile license plates. "Prosperity's decade" ended in economic disaster.

CHRONOLOGY OF KEY EVENTS

1914 Marcus Garvey organizes the Universal Negro Improvement Association (UNIA) to promote black migration to Africa

1915 Ku Klux Klan is revived and claims 4 million members by 1924

1917–1925 Some 600,000 black Americans migrate to northern industrial cities

1919 Labor unrest includes a nationwide steel strike, a coal miners strike, a general strike in Seattle, and a police strike in Boston; Race riots erupt in over 20 cities; Eighteenth Amendment bans the manufacture and sale of alcoholic beverages

1920 Palmer raids arrest suspected Communists; Massachusetts trial of two Italian anarchists, Nicola Sacco and Bartolomeo Vanzetti, begins on charges of murder and results in their execution in 1927; Sinclair Lewis's *Main Street* exposes the complacency of small-town life

1921 Warren Harding's inauguration as the twenty-ninth president begins 12 years of Republican control of the presidency; Revenue Act slashes taxes on higher incomes; European immigration is restricted to a quota of 3 percent of the population of a nationality living in the United States in 1910

1922 Fordney-McCumber Tariff raises duties on imports

1923 President Harding dies; Calvin Coolidge becomes the thirtieth president

1924 Congress reduces immigration quota to 2 percent of the population of a nationality living in the United States in 1890; Senate committee begins an investigation of Teapot Dome oil-leasing scandal

1925 Scopes trial, the celebrated "Monkey Trial," attacks the teaching of evolution in public schools; F. Scott Fitzgerald's *The Great Gatsby* criticizes the American success ethic

1926 New revenue act further reduces tax rates on high incomes

1929 Herbert Hoover is inaugurated as the thirty-first president; annual quota of immigrants is reduced to about 152,000; stock market crashes

1930 Hawley-Smoot Tariff raises import duties to unprecedented levels

CONCLUSION

Janus, the two-faced god of antiquity, offers an intriguing symbol for America in the 1920s. The nation's image was divided, with one profile looking optimistically to the future and the other staring longingly at the past. Caught between the disillusionment of World War I and the economic malaise of the Great Depression, the 1920s witnessed a gigantic struggle between an old and a new America, a time when the past was visibly, almost palpably laboring to give birth to the future.

No longer a land of farms and villages, the United States had become a nation of factories and cities. The Protestant culture of rural America was threatened by the secular values of urban society. Yet throughout the 1920s tradition gave way to accommodation as a modern society began to take shape. Country against city, native against immigrant, worker against farmer, Protestant against Catholic and Jew, fundamentalist against liberal, conservative against progressive, wet against dry, Victorian against libertarian—all these issues reflected different images of the same battle: a colossal identity crisis that saw the United States struggling to come to terms with secular values and cultural pluralism. But what World War I started, the Great Depression interrupted. The intense cultural upheavals of the 1920s gave way to the equally intense economic debates of the 1930s as cultural politics took a backseat to the politics of survival.

SUGGESTIONS FOR FURTHER READING

OVERVIEWS AND SURVEYS

Frederick Lewis Allen, *Only Yesterday: An Informal History of the Nineteen-Twenties* (1931); Paul A. Carter, *Another Part of the Twenties* (1977) and *The Twenties in America*, 2d ed. (1975); Ellis Hawley, *The Great War and the Search for Modern Order* (1979); John D. Hicks, *Republican Ascendancy, 1921–1933* (1960); William E. Leuchtenburg, *The Perils of Prosperity, 1914–32* (1958); Geoffrey Perrett, *America in the Twenties: A History* (1982).

THE CLASH OF VALUES

Houston A. Baker, Jr., *Modernism and the Harlem Renaissance* (1987); Albert Camarillo, *Chicanos in a Changing Society: From Mexican Pueblos to American Barrios in Santa Barbara and Southern California, 1848–1930* (1979); William H. Chafe, *The American Woman: Her Changing Social, Economic, and Political Role* (1972); Mark Thomas Connelly, *The Response to Prostitution in the Progressive Era* (1980); John D'Emilio and Estelle B. Freedman, *Intimate Matters: A History of Sexuality in America* (1988); Peter G. Filene, *Him/Her/Self: Sex Roles in Modern America* (1986); David H. Fischer, *Growing Old In America* (1978); Ellen Fitzpatrick, *Endless Crusade: Women Social Scientists and Progressive Reform* (1990); Penina Migdal Glazer and Miriam Slater, *Unequal Colleagues: The Entrance of Women into the Professions, 1890–1940* (1987); Linda Gordon, *Woman's Body, Woman's Right: A Social History of Birth Control in America* (1976); John B. Holway, *Black Diamonds: Life in the Negro Leagues From the Men Who Lived It* (1989); Nathan Huggins, *Harlem Renaissance* (1971); Ira Katznelson, *Black Men, White Cities* (1973); Kenneth Kusmer, *A Ghetto Takes Shape: Black Cleveland, 1870–1930* (1976); J. Stanley Lemons, *The Woman Citizen: Social Feminism in the 1920s* (1973); David Levering Lewis, *When Harlem Was in Vogue* (1981); Gilbert Osofsky, *Harlem: The Making of a Ghetto: Negro New York, 1890–1930*, 2d ed. (1971); James Reed, *From Private Vice to Public Virtue: The Birth Control Movement and American Society Since 1830* (1978); Ricardo Romo, *East Los Angeles: History of a Barrio* (1983); Ruth Rosen, *The Lost Sisterhood: Prostitution in America, 1900–1918* (1982); Leslie W. Tentler, *Wage-Earning Women: Industrial Work and Family Life in the United States, 1900–1930* (1979); Theodore Vincent, *Black Power and the Garvey Movement* (1971); Winifred D. Wandersee, *Women's Work and Family Values, 1920–1940* (1981); Nancy Weiss, *The National Urban League, 1910–1940* (1974).

THE REVOLT OF THE TRADITIONALISTS

David Chalmers, *Hooded Americans: The First Century of the Ku Klux Klan, 1865–1965* (1965); Robert A. Divine, *American Immigration Policy, 1924–1952* (1957); Norman Furniss, *The Fundamentalist Controversy, 1918–1931* (1954); Ray Ginger, *Six Days or Forever? Tennessee v. John Thomas Scopes* (1958); Vivian Gornick, *The Romance of American Communism* (1977); John Higham, *Strangers in the Land: Patterns of American Nativism, 1860–1925* (1955); Kenneth T. Jackson, *The Ku Klux Klan in the City, 1915–1930* (1967); Don S. Kirshner, *City and Country: Rural Responses to Urbanization in the 1920s* (1970); Andrew Sinclair, *Prohibition* (1962); William Young and David E. Kaiser, *Postmortem: New Evidence in the Case of Sacco and Vanzetti* (1985).

THE RISE OF URBAN CULTURE

Loren Baritz, ed., *The Culture of the Twenties* (1970); Erik Barnouw, *A Tower of Babel: A History of Broadcasting in the United States to 1933* (1966); Robert Crunden, *From Self to Society: 1919–1941* (1972); Paula Fass, *The Damned and the Beautiful: American Youth in the 1920s* (1977); James J. Flink, *The Car Culture* (1975); Lewis F. Fried, *Makers of the City* (1990); Frederick Hoffman, *The Twenties: American Writing in the Postwar Decade*, rev. ed. (1962); Kenneth T. Jackson, *Crabgrass Frontier: The Suburbanization of the United States* (1985); Peter J. Ling, *America and the Automobile: Technology, Reform, and Social Change* (1990); Fred J. MacDonald, *Don't Touch That Dial!* (1979); Roderick Nash, *The Nervous Generation: American Thought, 1917–1930* (1970); Daniel Pope, *The Making of Modern Advertising* (1983); John B. Rae, *The Road and the Car in American Life* (1971); Robert Sklar, *Movie-Made America: A Cultural History of American Movies* (1975).

THE REPUBLICAN RESTORATION

LeRoy Ashby, *The Spearless Leader: Senator Borah and the Progressive Movement in the 1920s* (1972); Gary Dean Best, *The Politics of American Individualism: Herbert Hoover in Transition, 1918–1921* (1976); David Burner, *The Politics of Provincialism: The Democratic Party in Transition, 1918–1932* (1968); Clarke Chambers, *Seedtime of Reform, 1918–1932* (1963); Paula Eldot, *Governor Alfred E. Smith: The Politician as Reformer* (1983); John D. Hicks and Theodore Saloutos, *Twentieth Century Populism: Agricultural Discontent in the Midwest, 1900–1939* (1951); Allan Lichtman, *Prejudice and the Old Politics: The Presidential Election of 1928* (1979); Robert K. Murray, *The Harding Era: Warren G. Harding and His Administration* (1969) and *The Politics of Normalcy* (1973); Burl Noggle, *Teapot Dome: Oil and Politics in the 1920s* (1962); Robert H. Zieger, *Republicans and Labor, 1919–1929* (1969).

THE GREAT CRASH

William J. Barber, *From New Era to New Deal: Herbert Hoover, the Economists, and American Economic Policy, 1921–1933* (1985); Irving Bernstein, *The Lean Years: A History of the American Worker, 1920–1933* (1960); David Brody, *Workers in Industrial America: Essays on the Twentieth Century Struggle* (1980); Alfred Chandler, *Strategy and Structure: Chapters in the History of the Industrial Enterprise* (1962); Martin L. Fausold, *The Presidency of Herbert Hoover* (1985); John Kenneth Galbraith, *The Great Crash, 1929* (1955); Ellis W. Hawley, *The Great War and the Search for a Modern Order* (1979); Sanford M. Jacoby, *Employing Bureaucracy: Managers, Unions, and the Transformation of Work in American Industry, 1900–1945* (1985); David C. Jones, *Empire of Dust: Settling and Abandoning the Prairie Dry Belt* (1987); C. P. Kindleberger, *The World in Depression, 1929–1939* (1973); Jim Potter, *The American Economy Between the World Wars*, rev. ed. (1985); James Prothro, *The Dollar Decade: Business Ideas in the 1920s* (1954); Albert U. Romasco, *The Poverty of Abundance: Hoover, the Nation, and the Depression* (1965); Jordan A. Schwarz, *Interregnum of Despair: Hoover, Congress, and the Depression* (1970); Robert Sobel, *The Great Bull Market* (1968); George Soule, *Prosperity Decade: From War to Depression, 1917–1929* (1947); Peter Temin, *Did Monetary Forces Cause the Great Depression?* (1976).

BIOGRAPHIES

David Burner, *Herbert Hoover: A Public Life* (1979); Ellen Chesler, *Woman of Valor; Margaret Sanger and the Birth Control Movement in America* (1992); William Harbaugh, *Lawyer's Lawyer: The Life of John W. Davis* (1973); Matthew Josephson and Hannah Josephson, *Al Smith: Hero of the Cities* (1969); David Kennedy, *Birth Control in America: The Career of Margaret Sanger* (1970); Lawrence Levine, *Defender of the Faith: William Jennings Bryan, the Last Decade, 1915–1925* (1965); Richard Lowitt, *George W. Norris* (1971); Manning Marable, *W. E. B. Du Bois: Black Radical Democrat* (1986); Donald R. McCoy, *Calvin Coolidge: The Quiet President* (1967); George Nash, *The Life of Herbert Hoover—the Engineer*, vol. 1 (1983); Randy Roberts, *Jack Dempsey, the Manassa Mauler* (1979); Francis Russell, *The Shadow of Blooming Grove: Warren G. Harding in His Times* (1968); Andrew Sinclair, *The Available Man: The Life Behind the Masks of Warren Gamaliel Harding* (1965); Richard N. Smith, *An Uncommon Man: The Triumph of Herbert Hoover* (1984); David P. Thelen, *Robert M. La Follette and the Insurgent Spirit* (1976); William Allen White, *A Puritan in Babylon: The Story of Calvin Coolidge* (1938).

The Age of Roosevelt

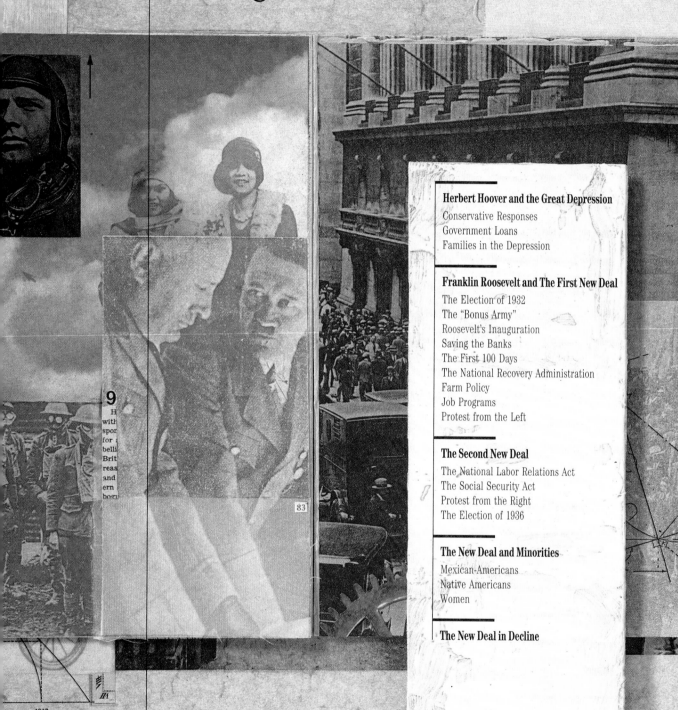

Locust. 52

2

Fig. 113(b)

true form

Fig. 113(bb)

To fans of authentic folk music, Woodrow Wilson "Woody" Guthrie was a "Shakespeare in overalls," the finest American frontier balladeer of the twentieth century. Yet Guthrie himself downplayed his importance, insisting "All you can write is what you see." He must have seen plenty, for according to Alan Lomax, the distinguished musicologist, Guthrie knew America's plain folk better than anyone. His singing voice (droning, nasal, and high-pitched) was definitely an acquired taste, but the words of Guthrie's songs spun pure poetry. In lyrics at once simple and penetrating, he sang of vagabonds who wandered the land in search of work, of union men who saw their comrades on the picket lines knocked to the ground by company goons, and of farmers who watched with horror as their land dried up, blew away, and turned the skies of the Southwest into a dust bowl. In short, he put to music the hardships and struggles of working-class Americans trapped in the Great Depression.

Guthrie drew his material from his life. Born in 1912, Woody (his mother named him after Woodrow Wilson who won the Democratic nomination a week before his birth) grew up in Oklahoma and the Texas Panhandle in a family star-crossed by disasters. When he was still a boy his older sister died from setting herself on fire after an argument with their mother; his father, once a prosperous land speculator, sank into alcoholism as land prices plummeted following the collapse of the oil boom; and his mother slipped slowly into madness and had to be committed to the state mental hospital where she died of Huntington's chorea, the illness that later claimed Woody.

In the face of these tragedies the Guthrie household simply dissolved, leaving Woody pretty much on his own. By nature shy and a bit of a loner, he passed the time by learning to play the guitar and harmonica. Guthrie soon discovered he had a natural talent for music and for making people laugh, and he started playing on street corners for the small change people tossed into his cigar box. Eventually, he dropped out of school and became a drifter, driven by an internal restlessness that kept him on the road for the rest of his life.

Guthrie spent the Great Depression riding the rails, playing his music on a revolving stage of one-night stands and visiting "his" people, the "Okies" and "Arkies" along the boxcars, hobo jungles, and squalid migrant camps from Oklahoma to California. As he crisscrossed the country, he saw families sleeping on the ground and children with distended bellies who cried from hunger while guards hired to protect the orchards prevented them from eating fruit that lay rotting on the ground. Over time a quiet anger began to eat at him and he blamed the nation's "polli-Tish-uns" for not doing more to relieve the people's suffering. In private he even spoke of strapping on six-guns, robbing banks, and giving the money to the poor, like the Robin Hood figure, "Pretty Boy Floyd," in one of his ballads.

By 1940, Guthrie had made his debut in New York City, where he recorded several albums and quickly became a cult figure. By this time his repertoire of Dust Bowl ballads had grown to include a variety of protest ballads, including an endless assortment of union songs. His home-grown radicalism made him an instant hit with Socialist and Communist intellectuals and entertainment figures who saw his music as a powerful weapon in the class struggle. They saw Guthrie as an authentic folk hero, the very embodiment of the proletarian artist.

In truth, Guthrie held more radical political views than most Americans. Nevertheless, he

Woody Guthrie often inscribed the phrase, "This machine surrounds hate and destroys it" on his guitars.

aptly fulfilled his role as the "voice of the people" by putting to music the most important themes to emerge in American life during the 1930s—the common man's defiant pride, his will to survive in the face of adversity, and the extraordinary love Americans felt for their country. In the opening verse of "Dust Can't Kill Me," for example, Guthrie has an anguished mother proclaim:

> That old dust storm killed my baby,
> But it won't kill me, lord.
> No, it won't kill me.

In "God Blessed America" (which later generations of Americans would recognize by its first line, "This land is your land, this land is my land"), Guthrie sang of "endless skyways," "golden valleys," "diamond deserts," and "wheat fields waving," evoking the country's grandeur with a poet's sense of beauty. What gave the song its power, however, was the idea that America belonged to the people: Every verse closed with the refrain, "God blessed America for me."

Thus, even in the depths of the Great Depression, Guthrie found much of enduring value in America. Somehow the nation was surviving without blowing itself apart, and he gave much of the credit to America's plain folks. In ballad after ballad, he celebrated their fortitude, dignity, and strength. Woody Guthrie was right to praise the people. They provided the glue that held things together while President Franklin D. Roosevelt experimented with policies and programs designed to promote relief, recovery, and reform.

HERBERT HOOVER AND THE GREAT DEPRESSION

When the Great Depression struck, most political and economic leaders regarded recessions as inevitable. The prevailing economic theory held that government intervention was both unnecessary and unwise. Periodic dips, economists argued, formed a natural part of the business cycle. Financial panics in 1837, 1857, 1873, 1893, and 1907 had failed to elicit much response from government; and many economists

in 1929 continued to extol the virtues of inaction. Left to itself, they counseled, the economy would recover. President Hoover disagreed. Though Hoover saw the Great Crash as a temporary slump in a fundamentally healthy economy, he believed the president should try to facilitate economic recovery.

Conservative Responses

First, Hoover resorted to old-fashioned "jawboning." Shortly after the stock market crashed, he summoned business and labor leaders to the White House for a series of meetings. In response to the president's pleas to sustain prices, wages, and employment, industrial leaders promised to maintain prices and wages, and labor spokesmen pledged not to strike or demand higher wages. While Hoover remained hopeful voluntary measures would suffice, businesspeople could not maintain employment.

Next, the president tried cheerleading. The contrast between Hoover's speeches and conditions in the country was jarring. In the spring of 1930, just before unemployment figures rose sharply, he assured Americans: "The worst effects of the crash upon unemployment will have passed during the next sixty days." According to Hoover, the economy was fundamentally sound, hard times were nearly over, and recovery was just around the corner. After listening to his rosy pronouncements, critics accused Hoover of being insensitive to the unemployed and the dispossessed, and the public gradually came to share this view. Cynics called the shantytown slums on the edges of cities "Hoovervilles." Newspapers became "Hoover blankets" and empty pockets turned inside out, "Hoover flags."

Neither cruel nor insensitive, Hoover was a humane man who felt tormented by poor people's suffering. Yet he could not bring himself to sanction large-scale federal public works programs because he honestly believed recovery depended on the private sector, because he wanted to maintain a balanced budget, and because he feared the "dole" (his derisive term for federal relief programs) would undermine individual character by making the recipient dependent on the state. He did not realize the sheer size and complexity of the nation's economic problems rendered meaningless old shibboleths like "self-reliance" and "rugged individualism."

Government Loans

When jawboning and cheerleading failed to revive the economy, Hoover reluctantly adopted other measures. In 1932 Congress created the Reconstruction Finance Corporation (RFC) and authorized it to loan $2 billion to banks, savings and loan associations, railroads, and life insurance companies. Blaming the depression on tight credit, Hoover believed federal loans would "trickle down" through the money markets to businesses, enabling them to increase production and hire workers. The same principle applied to the Federal Home Loan Bank System (FHLBS), created by Congress in July 1932 to lend up to $500 million to savings and loan associations to revive the construction industry.

Yet by early 1933 Hoover's antidepression agencies had exhausted their resources without making a dent in the Great Depression. The money from the RFC and FHLBS had not trickled down because the real problem was not tight credit but the soft demand for goods, a problem that flowed both from the chronic low wages paid to the bulk of American workers and the massive layoffs following the Great Crash. It was a vicious cycle. Unemployed workers could not buy goods, so businesspeople cut back production and laid off additional workers. Businesspeople did not ask banks for working capital loans because they had no interest in increasing production. Therefore, government-sponsored loans, which Hoover had hoped would revive the economy, simply rotated back and forth between financial institutions and the RFC and FHLBS. In the meantime, thousands of banks across the country went bankrupt, the unemployment rate climbed to 25 percent, and life got worse for millions of people.

Down to the bitter end, Hoover refused to admit people were starving in America, even though his opponents placed the responsibility squarely at the White House door. Here was proof Hoover was a great engineer, sneered one

Bank failures wiped out the life savings of many prudent Americans.

critic, for "in a little more than two years he has drained, ditched, and damned the United States."

Families in the Depression

The Great Depression did not affect people equally. Many rich people, insulated by their wealth, maintained their opulent life-styles, and perhaps as many as 40 percent of Americans made it through these years without experiencing real hardships. Still, the majority of Americans saw the Great Depression as a wolf at the door. "Mass unemployment," as one journalist observed, "is both a statistic and an empty feeling in the stomach." The unemployment figures reveal how many Americans felt these hunger pains: When Franklin D. Roosevelt took office in 1933, one-quarter of the nation's families had no breadwinner. That figure fluctuated during the 1930s, but it did not drop below 14.3 percent until 1941.

For all but the most fortunate, the Great Depression reduced family income. In 1929 the average American family earned $2300; by 1933 the figure had declined to $1500, a 35 percent drop. Most of the loss resulted from unemployment, but it also reflected reduced wages for those who kept their jobs. By 1933 nine out of ten companies had cut wages (some by as much as 50 percent), and more than half of all employers had converted their work force from full- to part-time jobs, averaging roughly 60 percent of the normal work week.

These reductions devastated workers. As late as 1870, half the work force was self-employed (on farms, for the most part), but by 1923 three out of four Americans worked for salaries or wages, leaving them vulnerable to economic changes. The depression forced Americans to develop a new category of poor people. In addition to the traditional poor, who included single parents, the elderly, tenant farmers, and the disabled, officials now spoke of the "new" poor—middle- and working-class people who had lost their jobs and slid into poverty as a result of the depression.

The depression had a powerful impact on families. It forced couples to delay marriage, lowered the divorce rate (many couples could not afford to maintain separate households or pay legal fees to obtain divorces), and drove the birthrate below the replacement level for the first time in American history.

The depression also altered traditional roles within the family. Many unemployed fathers saw their status lowered by the Great Depression. With no wages to punctuate their authority, they lost power as primary decision makers. In fact, large numbers of men who could not fulfill their roles as breadwinners lost self-respect, became immobilized, and stopped looking for work, while others turned to alcohol and became self-destructive or abusive to their families. Still others walked out the door, never to return. A survey in 1940 revealed that more than 1.5 million married women had been deserted by their husbands.

In contrast to men, many women saw their status rise during the depression. Despite the historic opposition to outside employment for wives, married women entered the work force in large numbers. (Black women, in particular, found it easier than black men to find jobs.) Most women worked as domestic servants, clerks, secretaries, salespersons, textile workers, and the like. But regardless of their jobs, the fact they were employed elevated their po-

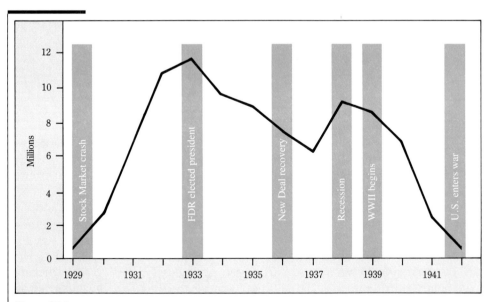

Figure 25.1
Unemployment, 1929–1942

TABLE 25.1

Depression Shopping List: 1932–1934

Automobiles		**Household Items**		**Toys**	
Pontiac Coupe	$585.00	Silverplate flatware,		Doll carriage	$ 4.98
Chrysler Sedan	995.00	26 pieces	$ 4.98	Sled	1.45
Dodge	595.00	Double-bed sheets	.67	Tricycle	3.98
Studebaker	840.00	Bath towel	.24	Bicycle	10.95
Packard	2150.00	Wool blanket	1.00	Fielder's glove and ball	1.25
Chevrolet ½-ton pick-up truck	650.00	Wool rug (9′ × 12′)	5.85		
				Food	
Clothing		**Appliances**			
				Sirloin steak/lb	$ .29
Women's		Electric iron	$ 2.00	Rib roast/lb	.22
		Electric coffee percolator	1.39	Bacon/lb	.22
Mink coat	$585.00	Electric mixer	9.95	Ham/lb	.31
Leopard coat	92.00	Vacuum cleaner	18.75	Chicken/lb	.22
Cloth coat	6.98	Electric washing machine	47.95	Pork chops/lb	.20
Wool dress	1.95	Gas stove	23.95	Salmon (16 oz can)	.19
Wool suit	3.98	Electric sewing machine	24.95	Milk (quart)	.10
Wool sweater	1.69			Butter/lb	.28
Silk stockings	.69	**Furniture**		Eggs (dozen)	.29
Leather shoes	1.79			Bread (20 oz loaf)	.05
		Dining room set, 8-piece	$46.50	Coffee/lb	.26
Men's		Lounge chair	19.95	Sugar/lb	.05
		Double bed and mattress	14.95	Rice/lb	.06
Overcoat	$ 11.00	Mahogany coffee table	10.75	Potatoes/lb	.02
Wool suit	10.50	Chippendale sofa	135.00	Tomatoes (16 oz. can)	.09
Trousers	2.00	Louis XV walnut dining table	124.00	Oranges/dozen	.27
Shirt	.47	Wing chair	39.00	Cornflakes (8 oz. box)	.08
Pullover sweater	1.95	Grand piano	395.00		
Silk necktie	.55			**Air Travel**	
Stetson hat	5.00				
Shoes	3.85			New York to Chicago,	
				round trip	$86.31
				Chicago to Los Angeles,	
				round trip	207.00

sition within the family. Bringing home paychecks gave women economic power and this, in turn, strengthened their voices in family decisions.

The depression hit older Americans especially hard. The number of senior citizens had increased sharply since the Civil War. In 1860, for example, only 1 American in 40 was 65 or older; by 1940, the figure had risen to 1 in 15. For most senior citizens, a longer life span meant financial dependency. According to a government survey in 1937, less than 35 per-

cent of elderly Americans enjoyed financial security; nearly half had to rely upon relatives for support.

Despite the hardships it inflicted, the Great Depression drew some families closer together. As one observer noted, "Many a family has lost its automobile and found its soul." Families had to devise strategies for getting through hard times because their survival depended on it. Their stories, as Woody Guthrie knew instinctively, shed as much light on the Great Depression as anything that happened in Washington.

Consider the case of the Jewell Jones family of Bauxite, Arkansas, a small mining town near the center of the state. Though they never went hungry, the Joneses depended on contributions from each family member. The father brought home $3 a week for one day's work in the mines, while the mother earned $2 a week scrubbing floors in the company hospital. The couple's two sons added a few extra dollars by working as caddies at a nearby golf course, and their three daughters helped tend the family garden, can produce, and slaughter chickens and a calf each year.

The family's meager income supported few luxuries. The father made toys for the children, and the mother sewed most of their clothes, which were carefully mended and handed down from child to child. Shoes were an exception. The Jones children each got a pair of "store-bought" shoes when school began in the fall (plenty large so they would fit all year). When the soles wore out, they continued to wear the tops even though their bare feet touched the ground. Looking back on those hard times 50 years later, Cornelia, one of the daughters, recalled:

> One year there came a terrible snowstorm and Mamma wouldn't let me go to school because my shoes were worn out and my feet would freeze. I cried and cried because I had a perfect attendance that year. So I was just bawling when Winfred [the older brother] took Mamma into the kitchen, talked to her, and then came out smiling. "Don't cry, Sissy," he said. "You can go to school." He carried me the whole way [about three miles round trip] on his back. You see, he was a football star in high school, and the company had bought him football shoes. So he could walk on the snow.

Like many other American families, the Joneses made it through the depression by pulling together.

In a sense, the Joneses were lucky because they managed to hold their own. Others, like Benjamin Isaac's family of Chicago, Illinois, lost ground. Prior to the depression, Ben had earned a comfortable living selling clothing door-to-door on credit, collecting by the week. Most of his customers, he recalled, were middle-class folks who bought freely and paid their bills promptly. After the depression struck, however, Ben watched his weekly collections drop from $400 to $15. Suddenly, he could not pay the rent and had to move his wife and three children out of their spacious apartment into a $15 a month flat. "I'm telling you," he lamented, "today a dog wouldn't live in that place. Such a dirty, filthy, dark place."

Shortly after they moved in, their landlord abandoned the building and the city turned off the water. For the next two months, his wife had to carry water from another building to cook, wash, bathe, and flush the toilet. Their diet suffered, too. Though they managed to buy a good cut of meat on occasional Sundays, their meat ration for the rest of the week was half a pound of baloney.

Ben's most painful memory was going on relief. Over time they lost all their family resources, including their car, which had to be sold to buy food. Unemployed and destitute, Ben finally asked for help:

> I didn't want to go on relief. Believe me, when I was forced to go to the office . . . the tears were running out of my eyes. I couldn't bear myself to take money from anybody for nothing. If it wasn't for those kids I tell you the truth—many a time it came to my mind to go commit suicide [rather] than go ask for relief. But somebody had to take care of those kids.

Ben did not find a steady job for the remainder of the depression. After their public assistance ran out, he turned to selling razor blades and shoe laces door-to-door. Some days his total earnings did not exceed 50 cents. Yet somehow the Isaac family held together and survived.

Like the Joneses and the Isaacs, other families pooled their incomes, moved in with relatives in order to cut expenses, bought day-old bread, ate in souplines, and did without. Many families drew comfort from their religion, sustained by the hope things would turn out well in the end, while others placed their faith in themselves, in their own dogged determination to survive that so impressed observers like Woody Guthrie. But many Americans no longer believed the problems could be solved by people acting alone or through voluntary associations. Increasingly, they looked to the federal government for help.

FRANKLIN ROOSEVELT AND THE FIRST NEW DEAL

The Election of 1932

Franklin D. Roosevelt won the Democratic nomination in June 1932. At first glance he did not look like a man who could relate to other peoples' suffering, for Roosevelt had spent his entire life in the lap of luxury. A fifth cousin of Teddy Roosevelt, he was born in 1882 to a wealthy family in Dutchess County, New York. Roosevelt enjoyed a privileged youth. He attended Groton, an exclusive private school, Harvard (where his professors did not regard him as a serious student), and Columbia Law School. Blessed with a famous political family name, Roosevelt entered public service in 1910 as a state senator in New York. President Wilson appointed him as assistant secretary of the navy in 1913, and his status as the rising star of the Democratic party was confirmed when James Cox chose Roosevelt as his running mate in the presidential election of 1920.

Roosevelt was charming and charismatic, and many people felt he was genuinely interested in their concerns. Here Roosevelt meets with a miner during his 1932 campaign.

Handsome and outgoing, Roosevelt seemed to have a bright political future. Then disaster struck. In 1921 he was stricken with polio. The disease left him paralyzed from the waist down and confined to a wheelchair for the rest of his life. Instead of retiring, however, Roosevelt threw himself into a rehabilitation program and labored diligently to return to public life. "If you had spent two years in bed trying to wiggle your toe," he later declared, "after that anything would seem easy."

Buoyed by an exuberant optimism and devoted political allies, Roosevelt won the governorship of New York in 1928, one of the few Democrats to survive the Republican landslide. As governor, he surrounded himself with able advisors, including several college professors and social workers who had spent their lives fighting urban poverty. Together they converted New York into a laboratory for testing political reforms, involving conservation, old age pensions, public works projects, and unemployment insurance—reforms that presaged how Roosevelt would later attack the depression as president.

In his acceptance speech before the Democratic convention in Chicago, Roosevelt promised "a New Deal for the American people." As the band struck up "Happy Days Are Here Again," the delegates cheered wildly. In truth, Roosevelt had not given them much to yell about, for his speech contained few concrete proposals. Many intellectuals remained suspicious. Walter Lippmann described Roosevelt as "a pleasant man who, without any important qualifications for the office, would very much like to be President."

The people saw Roosevelt differently. During the campaign, he calmed their fears, raised their spirits, and gave them hope. A member of Hoover's administration admitted: "The people seem to be lifting eager faces to Franklin Roosevelt, having the impression that he is talking intimately to them." Charismatic and utterly charming, Roosevelt radiated confidence. He even managed to turn his lack of a blueprint into an asset. Instead of offering plans, he advocated the experimental method. "It is common sense to take a method and try it," he declared, "if it fails, admit it frankly and try another."

The Republicans stuck with Hoover. Dejected and embittered, he projected despair and failure. (One observer quipped that "if you put a rose in Hoover's hand, it would wilt.") Advocating the same measures that had failed to bring relief since 1929, Hoover's campaign slogan was "It could have been worse." No doubt this was true, but it did not reassure the public that Hoover had any idea how to make things better. At any rate, when Hoover challenged Roosevelt to a debate, Roosevelt remained silent and watched Hoover end what little chance he had for reelection by his callous treatment of the "Bonus Army."

The "Bonus Army"

The "Bonus Army" was a bedraggled collection of unemployed veterans and their families who marched on Washington in the spring of 1932. Calling themselves the Bonus Expeditionary Force (BEF), a parody of the American Expeditionary Force (AEF), they asked Congress for immediate payment of their war service bonuses, which did not come due until 1945. More than 15,000 strong, they erected a shantytown, camped out in vacant lots, and occupied empty government buildings. Though the House gave them what they wanted, the Senate killed the bill after Hoover lobbied against it, prompting one angry veteran to shout in disgust, "We were heroes in 1917, but we're bums today."

Most of the veterans then left Washington, D.C., but a few thousand stayed behind because they had no place to go. At Hoover's request, Congress appropriated $100,000 to help pay their expenses home. Late in July, however, the District of Columbia police tried to evict some bonus marchers from government buildings and a riot broke out in which two policemen and two marchers died.

Secretary of War Patrick Hurley urged Hoover to declare martial law, but he refused. Hoover did not want to harm the veterans. Instead, he told Hurley to order General Douglas MacArthur to use federal troops to remove them from the government buildings. MacArthur exceeded these orders badly. Using tanks, tear gas, rifle fire, sabers, and torches, he attacked and drove the veterans from the city.

Bonus army recruits poured into Washington, D.C., from every part of the country during the spring and summer of 1932.

Newsmen captured the melee in vivid photographs papers carried the next day.

Hoover was appalled by what happened. Privately, he blamed both Hurley and MacArthur; publicly, he accepted the responsibility but endorsed MacArthur's charge that the bonus marchers included dangerous radicals who wanted to overthrow the government. Yet most Americans felt outraged by the government's harsh treatment of the Bonus Army, and Hoover encountered bitter resentment everywhere he campaigned. In Detroit crowds of unemployed auto workers chanted, "Down with Hoover, Slayer of Veterans." Upon learning of the Bonus Army incident, Franklin D. Roosevelt remarked: "Well, this will elect me."

Roosevelt buried Hoover in November. He won 22,809,638 votes to Hoover's 15,758,901, and 472 to 59 electoral votes. In addition, the Democrats swept Congress: 311 to 119 seats in the House (including 131 freshmen Democrats from Republican districts) and 60 to 35 in the Senate.

Roosevelt appealed to a wide range of voters. A Protestant, he returned the South to the Democratic fold. In addition, he attract-

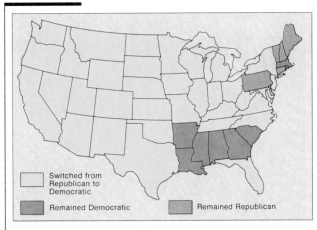

Electoral Shift, 1928 and 1932

ed new groups of voters, including young people, women, and ethnic Americans. Moreover, Roosevelt carried every state but seven in the Northeast (Pennsylvania was the only large state he lost). Here careful analysis reveals that Roosevelt's support was strongly non-Protestant. Urban Catholics, Jews, and members of the Eastern Orthodox Church voted overwhelmingly for Roosevelt, the first of many elections to come in which the Democratic party's fortunes would be strongly affected by these groups.

While many Republicans apparently boycotted the election, the vast majority of Americans stayed within the two-party system, despite their disdain for Hoover. The Socialist nominee received only 880,000 votes; the Communist party's candidate, only 100,000.

Roosevelt's Inauguration

The New Deal was a jumble of hastily improvised legislation and executive orders, which in the words of one historian somehow added up to "more than the sum of its parts." Most of the legislation was economic and came in three spurts: the first in 1933, the second in 1935, and the last in 1938. From beginning to end, the New Deal represented an intensely personal enterprise unified only by Roosevelt's personality. The ideas behind particular measures came from his advisors, for Roosevelt never pretended to be an original thinker. In place of a

well-defined political philosophy, he pursued a vague commitment to moderate reform, leavened with keen political instincts and a desire to help people.

Roosevelt's greatest asset was his ability to persuade, and no president has ever encountered a Congress so eager to follow. As one representative confessed, "I had as soon start a mutiny in the face of a foreign foe as . . . [go] against the program of the President." Even Senator Arthur H. Vandenberg, a leading Republican conservative, insisted the situation called for a "dictator." No one knew what Roosevelt should do, but the country preferred anything to inaction. On inauguration day Will Rogers exclaimed: "If he burned down the Capitol we would cheer and say, 'Well, at least he got a fire started anyhow.'"

In his inaugural address on March 4, 1933, Roosevelt told the public, "the only thing we have to fear is fear itself." Promising decisive action, he called Congress into special session and demanded "broad executive power to wage a war against the emergency, as great as the power that would be given me if we were in fact invaded by a foreign foe." His ringing speech summoned the nation to battle, and across the nation people held their breaths waiting to see what the new president would do.

Saving the Banks

Roosevelt attacked the banking crisis first. In the months before he took office, America's banking system had all but disintegrated. Hundreds of banks had collapsed, wiping out the life savings of nearly 10 million people. Thirty-eight states had closed their banks, while banks in the remaining states operated on reduced schedules. On March 5 Roosevelt declared a national bank holiday, stopping all banking transactions. A few days later he sent Congress the Emergency Banking Relief Bill, a conservative set of reforms drafted with the assistance of Hoover's advisors. Immediately approved by Congress, the new law permitted solvent banks to reopen under government supervision. More important, it allowed the RFC to buy the stock of troubled banks and keep them open until they could be reorganized. Fi-

(Text continues on p. 839)

PRIMARY SOURCE ESSAY
THE FIRST "FIRESIDE CHAT"

On the eve of Franklin D. Roosevelt's inauguration America's banking system was in shambles. In the first three years following the Great Crash some 5500 banks had closed, and only a handful of those that remained open were solvent. With less than $6 billion in cash against $41 billion in deposits, banks were vulnerable to a wholesale run. If depositors demanded their money, banks would be forced to sell their assets (securities and mortgages) at a fraction of their former value to raise funds.

In the weeks before Roosevelt took office, the run began. Warned that Detroit's Union Guardian Trust Company was about to collapse and drag other banks down with it, Governor William A. Comstock declared a banking moratorium throughout Michigan on February 14, 1933. As news of Michigan's horrors spread, long lines of depositors demanding their money appeared in banks across the land. Banks in Indiana, Ohio, and Kentucky tried to weather the storm by limiting withdrawals to five percent of balances, but many states followed Michigan's lead. By March 1, 17 states had declared so-called "banking holidays." During the next two days every bank in Kansas and Minnesota closed its doors, and the closings quickly spread into North Carolina and Virginia. On the eve of Roosevelt's inauguration, rumors spread that the largest banks in New York City and Chicago were teetering. With its two most important financial strongholds in jeopardy, the nation's financial system was truly on the brink of disaster.

Within days after taking office, Roosevelt moved to restore the public's confidence in banks. The first bill he sent to Congress addressed the nation's banking crisis, and on March 12, 1933, Roosevelt held his first "Fireside Chat" to explain his actions directly to the American people. He spoke not as some remote politician on high but as a straightforward man who understood the public's concerns and could relate to their fears. Above all, he spoke with simple language and profound confidence. When the banks reopened the following morning, the long lines disappeared, as people demonstrated their confidence by returning far more money to their accounts than they withdrew. In the Federal Reserve districts alone, deposits outstripped withdrawals by more than $10 million dollars in a single day.

President Franklin Delano Roosevelt, Jr., used the relatively new broadcast medium of radio to deliver a message of reassurance to the American public.

The following are excerpts from the president's speech. Notice his word choice, his gift for simplifying complicated issues, and his ability to banish "the phantom of fear" from peoples' hearts:

I want to talk for a few minutes with the people of the United States about banking—with the comparatively few who understand the mechanics of banking but more particularly with the overwhelming majority who use banks for the making of deposits and the drawing of checks. I want to tell you what has been done in the last few days, why it was done, and what the next steps are going to be. . . .

First of all, let me state the simple fact that when you deposit money in a bank the bank does not put the money into a safe deposit vault. It invests your money in many different forms of credit—bonds, commercial paper, mortgages and many other kinds of loans. . . . In other words, the total amount of all the currency in the country is only a small fraction of the total deposits in all of the banks.

What, then, happened during the last few days of February and the first few days of March? Because of undermined confidence on the part of the public, there was a general rush by a large portion of our population to turn bank deposits into currency or gold—a rush so great that the soundest banks could not get enough currency to meet the demand. . . .

By the afternoon of March 3d scarcely a bank in the country was open to do business. . . .

It was then that I issued the proclamation providing for the nationwide bank holiday and this was the

The threat of bank runs, like that pictured here, in which depositors demanded their funds from banks unable to produce their money, prompted FDR's first fireside chat.

bank puts your money to work to keep the wheels of industry and of agriculture turning around. A comparatively small part of the money you put into the bank is kept in currency--an amount which in normal times is wholly sufficient to cover the cash needs of the average citizen. In other words the total amount of all the currency in the country is only a ~~comparatively~~ small ~~proportion~~ _fraction_ of the total deposits in all of the banks.

What, then, happened during the last few days of February and the first few days of March? Because of undermined confidence on the part of the public, there was a general rush by a large portion of our population to turn bank deposits into currency or gold. -- A rush so great that the soundest banks could not get enough currency to meet the demand. The reason for this was that on the spur of the moment it was, of course,

This page is a reproduction of the actual radio script FDR used in his fireside chat of March 12, 1933.
Note the handwritten changes made to simplify the address even further.

first step in the Government's reconstruction of our financial and economic fabric.

The second step was the legislation promptly and patriotically passed by the Congress confirming my proclamation and broadening my power so that it became possible in view of the requirement of time to extend the holiday and lift the ban of that holiday gradually. . . .

The third stage has been the series of regulations permitting the banks to continue their functions to take care of the distribution of food and household necessities and the payment of payrolls. . . .

A question you will ask is this: why are all the banks not to be reopened at the same time? The answer is simple. Your Government does not intend that the history of the past few years shall be repeated. We do not want and will not have another epidemic of bank failures.

As a result, we start tomorrow, Monday, with the opening of banks in the twelve Federal Reserve bank cities—those banks which on first examination by the treasury have already been found to be all right.

This will be followed on Tuesday by the resumption of all their functions by banks already found to be sound in cities where there are recognized clearing houses. . . .

On Wednesday and succeeding days banks in smaller places all through the country will resume business, subject, of course, to the Government's physical ability to complete its survey. . . .

The success of our whole great national program depends, of course, upon the cooperation of the public—on its intelligent support and use of a reliable system. . . .

It has been wonderful to me to catch the note of confidence from all over the country. . . .

. . . Confidence and courage are the essentials of success in carrying out our plan. You people must have faith; you must not be stampeded by rumors or guesses. Let us unite in banishing fear. We have provided the machinery to restore our financial system; it is up to you to support and make it work.

It is your problem no less than it is mine. Together we cannot fail.

Few political speeches have enjoyed more success than President Roosevelt's first "Fireside Chat." Before he addressed the nation, there were over $7.5 billion in circulation; the figure declined by $1.25 billion during the remainder of March and an additional $2 billion by the end of August. The money returned to banks derived from hoarded funds rather than general circulation, as most deposits came in the larger bills ($50 or over) not generally used in day-to-day transactions.

The flow of money back into banks saved them. Three days after the banking holiday ended, 4507 national banks and 567 state banks reopened for business, an impressive 76 percent of all the member banks of the Federal Reserve System. By the middle of April, 7400 nonmember banks (approximately 72 percent of the total of such banks) had been licensed by state authorities. By the end of 1933, the banks that had reopened had been strengthened with new capital, either from local interests or funds supplied by the Reconstruction Finance Corporation. The U.S. banking system had survived its greatest challenge in history, thanks in no small part to the superb communication skills and resolute action of President Roosevelt.

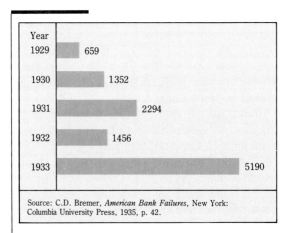

Year	
1929	659
1930	1352
1931	2294
1932	1456
1933	5190

Source: C.D. Bremer, *American Bank Failures*, New York: Columbia University Press, 1935, p. 42.

Figure 25.2
Bank failures, 1929–1933

nally, the law gave the president broad powers over the Federal Reserve System.

To generate support for his programs, Roosevelt appealed directly to the people. On March 12, he conducted the first of many "fireside chats" over a national radio network heard by 60 million Americans. Using the radio the way later presidents exploited television, he explained what he had done in plain, simple terms and told the public to have "confidence and courage." Roosevelt's serene assurance paid handsome dividends. When the banks reopened the following day, people demonstrated their faith by making more deposits than withdrawals. One of Roosevelt's key advisors did not exaggerate when he later boasted, "Capitalism was saved in eight days."

Three months later Congress passed the Glass-Steagall Banking Act of 1933. The law gave the federal reserve banks greater power to curb the lending practices of member banks. To protect depositors from risky projects, the law separated investment banking from commercial banking. It also established the Federal Deposit Insurance Corporation (FDIC), which addressed a chronic problem in America's banking system. During the 1920s and early 1930s, panic-stricken depositors made numerous "runs" on banks, forcing bankers to liquidate assets or default. By guaranteeing all deposits up to $2500 (raised to $5000 in 1934, to $10,000 in 1950, to $15,000 in 1966, to $20,000 in 1969, and

most recently to $100,000), the FDIC hoped to restore the public's confidence in banks.

The First 100 Days

Banking reform was just the beginning. During the first "100 Days" of Roosevelt's term, Congress rammed through 15 major bills, more legislation than any preceding session had passed in history. Most of the early bills were conservative and deflationary. During his first days in office, Roosevelt opposed deficit spending to finance government programs. Cutting federal spending, placing a consumer tax on beer, and helping large bankers at the expense of small bankers—these were measures that Hoover could have supported. In fact, no less than his predecessor, Roosevelt hoped to maintain a balanced budget.

The later bills of the 100 Days marked a change in direction. Distancing himself from Hoover's tight-money policies, Roosevelt provided relief to debtors and exporters by devaluing the dollar, abandoning the gold standard, and ordering the Federal Reserve System to ease credit. This shift reflected the declining clout within his administration of conservatives like Lewis Douglas, the budget director, and the growing influence of advisors who came to be known as the "brain trust."

TABLE 25.2

Legislation Enacted During the Hundred Days, March 9–June 16, 1933	
March 9	Emergency Banking Relief Act
March 20	Economy Act
March 22	Beer-Wine Revenue Act
March 31	Unemployment Relief Act
March 31	Civilian Conservation Corps Act
May 12	Agricultural Adjustment Act
May 12	Federal Emergency Relief Act
May 18	Tennessee Valley Authority Act
May 27	Securities Act of 1933
June 5	Gold Repeal Joint Resolution
June 13	Home Owners' Refinancing Act
June 16	Farm Credit Act
June 16	Banking Act of 1933
June 16	Emergency Railroad Transportation Act
June 16	National Industrial Recovery Act

Drawing upon the talents of a bright young group of economists and college professors whose members included Rexford G. Tugwell (generally regarded as the architect of the first New Deal), Raymond Moley, and Adolph A. Berle, Jr., the brain trust supplied Roosevelt with economic ideas and oratorical ammunition. Harking back to the position of Theodore Roosevelt, they saw "bigness" as the natural product of a mature industrial economy. Instead of busting trusts, they believed government should accept consolidation, impose national economic planning on private corporations, and enforce regulations designed to promote open and fair competition. Under their tutelage, Roosevelt launched two major reforms, one directed at industry, the other at agriculture.

The National Recovery Administration

Roosevelt called the National Recovery Administration (NRA), established by the National Industrial Recovery Act (NIRA), "the most important and far-reaching legislation ever passed by the American Congress." The NRA distilled three decades of federal efforts to define a working relationship between government and industry. Philosophically, the NRA had much in common with Teddy Roosevelt's "New Nationalism"; it rejected Woodrow Wilson's "New Freedom" because the New Dealers thought Wilson had attempted to regulate industry too closely; it copied its labor policies from Bernard Baruch's experiences with the War Industries Board of World War I; and it embraced Hoover's trade association movement, although he opposed the NRA because it replaced voluntary cooperation with government coercion.

The NRA proposed to resolve the major causes of economic instability (ruinous competition, overproduction, labor-management confrontations, and price fluctuations) through economic planning. Under the NRA, boards of industrial leaders, labor representatives, and government officials would draft codes of competition to limit production, assign quotas among individual producers, and impose strict price guidelines. Participation in the NRA was purely voluntary, but businesses that joined were exempted from antitrust prosecution. In practice, this meant that the codes offered businesspeople the chance to fix prices. To attract labor's support, Section 7A of the NIRA guaranteed maximum hours, minimum wages, and collective bargaining. In short, the NRA proposed to restore economic health by letting industry regulate itself and by conferring the government's blessing on labor unions.

General Hugh Johnson, Roosevelt's choice to head the new agency, worked hard to win support for the NRA, and under his tireless prodding, the new agency got off to a promising start. By midsummer 1933, over 500 industries had signed codes covering 22 million workers. By the end of the summer the nation's ten largest industries had been won over, as well as hundreds of smaller businesses ranging from dog food producers to burlesque houses. All across the land businesses displayed the "Blue Eagle," the insignia of the NRA, in their windows, and General Johnson remained confident the public would boycott businesses that refused.

The NRA's success was short-lived. Johnson proved to be an overzealous leader who alienated many businesspeople by attacking NRA critics as "chiselers." Instead of creating a smooth-running corporate state, Johnson presided over a chorus of endless squabbling. Since representatives of big business dominated the boards, the boards drafted codes that favored their interests over those of small competitors. Aware the NRA lacked the staff to monitor compliance with the codes, many small businesses simply ignored them. Moreover, even though they controlled the new agency from the outset, many leaders of "big business" opposed the NRA. At bottom, the NRA allowed government to tell businesspeople what to do and they resented it.

For labor the NRA was a mixed blessing. On the positive side, the codes abolished child labor and established the precedent of federal regulation of minimum wages and maximum hours. In addition, the NIRA boosted the labor movement by drawing large numbers of unskilled workers into unions. For example, John L. Lewis of the United Mine Workers (UMW), which merged with the garment trade unions in 1938

John L. Lewis, one of the nation's most influential labor leaders, expanded the membership of the United Mine Workers Union (UMW) under the National Industrial Recovery Act.

to form the Congress of Industrial Organizations (CIO), pointed to Section 7A as proof of Roosevelt's support for organized labor. During the NRA's first year, Lewis expanded the UMW's membership from 150,000 to 500,000. On the negative side, however, the NRA codes set wages in most industries well below what labor demanded, and large occupational groups, such as farm workers, fell outside the codes' coverage. In the end, the "National Run Around" pleased no one.

The NIRA also tried to promote industrial recovery through "pump-priming," a favorite scheme of the "brain trusters." They advocated large public works construction projects to stimulate the economy. Title II of the NIRA appropriated $3.3 billion for public projects, but the administration moved too slowly. A cautious administrator who insisted upon meticulous planning, Harold Ickes, secretary of the interior and director of the Public Works Administration (PWA), was obsessed with eliminating waste and political influence from the public projects. While the PWA eventually pumped $3 billion into the economy, Ickes's prudence prevented the funds from being spent fast enough to have any measurable impact.

Backing Ickes fully, Roosevelt allowed public construction to lag because he wanted to return unspent PWA funds to the federal budget. As late as 1936 federal spending on new construction reached only 60 percent of its predepression level. Other New Deal agencies followed the same pattern as the PWA. While the New Deal was remarkably scandal free, the government often worked at cross purposes with itself, permitting concern for potential corruption to hamper prompt and decisive action.

Farm Policy

The Great Depression all but destroyed America's farmers. Between 1929 and 1933 farmers saw their income fall 60 percent, leaving them with crops they could not sell and mortgages they could not pay. To make matters worse, their current woes followed a decade of hard times in the 1920s. Small wonder farmers looked back wistfully to the brief period of prosperity they had enjoyed on the eve of World War I and tried to regain it through their repeated calls for "parity," a pricing policy that would have allowed farm prices to occupy the same position relative to industrial prices that had existed in 1914.

The New Deal attacked farm problems through a variety of programs. As late as 1935 more than 6 million of America's 6.8 million farms had no electricity. Unlike their sisters in the city, farm women had no washing machines, refrigerators, or vacuum cleaners. As one historian has noted, farm wives "performed their backbreaking chores like peasant women in a preindustrial age." Nor did private utility companies intend to change things. Estimating it would cost as much as $5000 per mile to build power lines to individual farms, private companies insisted electrical service could never be brought to rural areas.

Roosevelt disagreed. Aware that hydroelectric power generated most of America's electricity, he agreed with the critic who asked, "Who and what should own a river, if not the people as a whole?" Roosevelt wanted to break the private monopoly of electric power in rural areas, and he envisioned a future in which electric power would serve broader goals, including flood control, soil conservation, reforestation, diversification of industry, and a general improvement in the quality of life for rural Americans. Settling on the 40,000 square-mile valley of the Tennessee River as his test site, Roosevelt decided to put the government into the electric business.

Two months after he took office, Congress passed a bill creating the Tennessee Valley Authority (TVA). The bill authorized the TVA to build 21 dams to generate electricity for tens of thousands of farm families. In 1935 Roosevelt signed an executive order creating the Rural Electrification Administration (REA) to bring electricity generated by government dams to America's hinterland. As the poles with their silvery lines paralleled county roads, as lines stretched from poles to homes, and as homes got wired, the sense of anticipation became almost unbearable while people waited for the electricity to be turned on. In the Texas hill country, for example, a family returned home after dark one evening and the mother exclaimed, "Oh my God, the house is on fire." "No Mamma," her daughter replied. "The lights are on." Between 1935 and 1942 the lights came on for 35 percent of America's farm families.

Nor was electricity the only benefit the New Deal bestowed on farmers. The Soil Conservation Service helped farmers battle erosion; the Farm Credit Administration provided some relief from farm foreclosures; and the Commodity Credit Corporation permitted farmers to use stored products as collateral for loans. Roosevelt's most ambitious farm program, however, was the Agriculture Adjustment Act (AAA).

Like the NRA, the AAA sought a partnership between the government and major producers. Together the new allies would raise prices by reducing the supply of farm goods. Secretary of Agriculture Henry Wallace borrowed the idea from farmers in the Midwest who had experimented with "farm holidays," hoping to boost prices by holding goods off the market. Under the AAA, the large producers, acting through farm cooperatives, would agree upon a "domestic allotment" plan that would set total output by assigning acreage quotas to each producer. Participation would be voluntary. Farmers who thought they could make it without government subsidies could go their own way, but those who cut production to comply with the quotas would be paid for land left fallow. These payments, in turn, would be financed by a tax on middlemen and processors, making the AAA largely self-supporting.

Unfortunately for its backers, the AAA got off to a horrible start. Because the 1933 crops had already been planted by the time Congress established the AAA, the administration ordered farmers to plow their crops under. Farmers collected over $100 million for mowing down 10 million acres of cotton. To forestall a glut in the hog market, the government purchased and slaughtered 6 million shoats and 200,000 pregnant sows, burying over 9 million pounds of pork. True, the government salvaged one million pounds for the needy, but the public neither understood nor forgave the waste. While future reductions came from planning rather than destruction, the AAA's image never recovered. The AAA remained a public relation's disaster, as most Americans never forgave the agency for destroying food while jobless people went hungry.

Overall, the AAA's record was mixed. Farm income doubled between 1933 and 1936, but large farmers reaped most of the profits. The AAA did little to help sharecroppers and tenant farmers, the groups hardest hit by the agricultural crisis. The South had more than 700,000 sharecroppers and tenant farmers who rented land in return for money or a share of the harvest. After they signed acreage reduction contracts, landlords threw more than 50,000 tenant families off the land. Between 1932 and 1935, 3 million Americans abandoned farming and moved to the city.

Nor did the AAA succeed in solving overproduction. Thanks to technological breakthroughs, such as the widespread use of chemical fertilizers and the increased mechanization of farm tasks, dramatic increases in crop yields per acre more than offset reductions produced by allotment plans. The pattern of subsidy and surplus so familiar to post-World War II America was already in place by the late 1930s.

Job Programs

Even the most optimistic New Dealers knew the NRA and the AAA would not end the depression overnight. To provide short-term assistance for the unemployed, Roosevelt reluctantly turned to welfare programs. In March 1933 Congress created the Civilian Conservation Corps (CCC) to offer young people jobs in national parks. By midsummer, the government had hired 300,000 young men between the ages of 18 and 25 who went to work planting saplings, building fire towers, stocking depleted streams, and restoring historic battlefields. All told, the CCC built 2650 camps and by 1942, 2.5 million men had served in Roosevelt's "Tree Army."

No New Deal program enjoyed greater popularity. The CCC offered young men fresh air, exercise, healthy food, and educational programs. In addition to room and board, they received a modest wage, most of which went home to their families or got set aside in savings accounts to help finance college. Though clearly a public relations triumph, the CCC's economic impact was small. It excluded women, imposed rigid quotas on blacks, and offered employment to only a small number of the young people who needed work.

The Civil Works Administration (CWA), established in November 1933, sponsored truly ambitious relief programs. At its helm stood Harry Hopkins, the unorthodox social worker who had headed Roosevelt's relief program in New York State. Hopkins did not fit the traditional "Jane Addams" image of the social worker. He was divorced, played the horses, and cursed fluently, but even his critics admitted Hopkins knew how to get things done. When he arrived for work and found his office under construction, he set up a desk in the hallway and spent $5 million dollars in two hours channeling relief funds through state and local agencies. Within a month, the CWA put 2.6 million men to work, and within two months it employed 4 million men building 250,000 miles of road, 40,000 schools, 150,000 privies, and 3700 playgrounds.

In March 1934, however, Roosevelt scrapped the CWA because he (like Hoover) did not wish to create a permanent dependent class. In a rare display of poor judgment, Roosevelt blithely observed: "No one is going to starve during warm weather." Official statistics later revealed that 110 Americans starved to death in 1934.

Roosevelt badly underestimated the crisis. As government funding slowed down and economic indicators leveled off, the depression deepened in 1934, triggering a series of violent strikes. Communists agitated among farm workers from coast to coast; a general strike closed down San Francisco for four days; and a British correspondent reported that Toledo was "in the

For $30 a month, workers in the Civilian Conservation Corps (CCC) planted trees and dug drainage ditches. Such federal work relief programs helped many retain their self-respect.

grip of civil war." On Labor Day, 1934, garment workers launched the single largest strike in the nation's history. All across the land, critics attacked Roosevelt for not doing enough to combat the depression, charges that did not go unheeded in the White House.

The congressional elections of 1934 put more pressure on the president. The Democrats won 13 new House seats and 9 new Senate seats, a clear mandate for bolder action. After the elections, the Republicans controlled less than one-third of the seats in Congress and a paltry 7 governorships. Many newly elected Democrats had campaigned as reformers, prompting an elated Harry Hopkins to exclaim: "Boys—this is our hour. We've got to get everything we want—a works program, social security, wages and hours, everything—now or never."

Following the elections, Roosevelt abandoned his hopes for a balanced budget. He had lost faith in government planning and the proposed alliance with business, which left only one other road to recovery—government spending. Privately, he called the dole "a narcotic, a subtle destroyer of the human spirit." Yet no other choice seemed possible. Encouraged by the CCC's success, he decided to create more federal jobs for the unemployed.

In January 1935 Congress created the Works Progress Administration (WPA), Roosevelt's program to employ 3.5 million workers at a "security wage"—twice the level of welfare payments but well below union scales. To head the new agency, Roosevelt again turned to Harry Hopkins. Since the WPA's purpose was to employ men quickly, Hopkins opted for labor-intensive tasks, creating jobs that were often makeshift and inefficient. Jeering critics said the WPA stood for "We Piddle Along," but the agency built many worthwhile projects. In its first five years alone, the WPA constructed or improved 2500 hospitals, 5900 schools, 1000 airport fields, and nearly 13,000 playgrounds. By 1941 it had provided jobs to 40 percent of the nation's unemployed, pumping $11 billion into the economy.

The WPA sponsored several cultural programs. With the economy in shambles, America seemed all the more precious, and the public wanted to preserve it. While folksingers like Woody Guthrie honored the nation in ballads, other artists were hired to catalog it, photograph it, paint it, record it, and write about it. In photojournalism, for example, the Farm Security Agency (FSA) employed scores of talented photographers, including Dorothea Lange, Walker Evans, and Ben Shahn, to create a pictorial record of the land and its people. They produced a raft of "I've seen America" books, and among the 27,000 photographs they shot, only a handful showed people who appeared broken in health or in spirit. Most of the faces belonged to survivors, people in whom determination had triumphed over despair.

In fact, the celebration of "the people" became the New Deal's dominant cultural motif. Under the auspices of the WPA, the Federal Writers Project sponsored an impressive set of state guides and dispatched an army of folklorists into the backcountry in search of tall tales and other "American Stuff." Oral historians collected slave narratives, and musicologists compiled an amazing collection of folk music. (Woody Guthrie was the subject of an extensive interview and three-album recording session.)

Other WPA programs included the Theatre Project, which produced the "living newspaper," a running commentary on everyday affairs, and the Art Project, which decorated the nation's libraries and post offices with murals of muscular workmen, bountiful wheatfields, and massive machinery. Since their subject matter had to be approved by local authorities, these murals reveal how communities saw themselves and how they wished to be seen by others. This was especially true in the South, where local leaders, sensitive to the image of their region as a benighted land, forced artists to paint murals that presented sympathetic portraits of southern life, promoting what one historian has called "a gentle reconstruction."

Valuable in their own right, the WPA's cultural programs had the added benefit of providing work for thousands of writers, artists, actors, and other creative people. In addition, these programs established the precedent of federal support to the arts and the humanities, laying the groundwork for future federal programs to promote the life of the mind in America.

Protest from the Left

The WPA marked the zenith of Roosevelt's influence over Congress. Following its passage, Congress dallied for several months over the remainder of his program. Opposition came from both the right and the left. Conservatives attacked the NRA and New Deal labor policy, while liberals accused Roosevelt of not doing enough to help poor people. Not one but three figures stepped forward to challenge Roosevelt: Huey Long, a Louisiana senator; Father Charles Coughlin, a Catholic priest from Detroit; and Francis Townsend, a retired California physician.

Of the three, Huey Long attracted the widest following. For those who insisted America needed a dictator, Louisiana's self-styled "Kingfish" was the man of the hour. Long took his nickname from one of the characters on the hit radio show, "Amos and Andy." Rotten with ambition, endowed with supernatural energy, and totally devoid of scruples, Long was a fiery, spellbinding orator in the tradition of southern populism. As governor and then senator, he ruled Louisiana with an iron hand. Yet the people of Louisiana loved him because he attacked the big oil companies, increased state spending on public works, and improved public schools. Although he backed Roosevelt in 1932, Long quickly abandoned the president and opposed the New Deal as too conservative.

Early in 1934 Long announced his "Share Our Wealth" program. Vowing to make "Every Man a King," he promised to soak the rich by imposing a stiff tax on inheritances over $5 million and by levying a 100 percent tax on annual incomes over $1 million. The confiscated funds, in turn, would be distributed to the people, guaranteeing every American family an annual income of no less than $2000, in Long's words more than enough to buy "a radio, a car, and a home." By February 1935 Long's followers had organized over 27,000 "Share Our Wealth" clubs. Roosevelt had to take him seriously, for a Democratic poll revealed the "Kingfish" could attract three to four million voters to an independent presidential ticket.

Like Long, Father Charles Coughlin was an early supporter who turned sour on the New Deal. Known as the "radio priest," he spoke to the nation from his Catholic parish in Royal Oak, Michigan, a Detroit suburb. By 1934 Coughlin's weekly mail was larger than the president's and his radio audience was estimated at 30 million. In a rich, warm voice, he blamed the depression on greedy bankers and challenged Roosevelt to solve the crisis by nationalizing banks and inflating the currency. When Roosevelt refused to heed his advice, Coughlin stopped referring to the New Deal as "Christ's Deal" and denounced it as the "Pagan Deal." In 1934 he broke with Roosevelt and formed the National Union for Social Justice.

Roosevelt's least strident opponent was Dr. Francis Townsend, a decent man whose opposition to the New Deal flowed less from personal ambition than from honest disagreements. As a public health officer in Long Beach, California, he found himself unemployed at the age of 67, with only $100 in savings. Townsend saw many people in similar straits in California, el-

The WPA program employed artists like Jackson Pollock, Willem de Kooning, and Ben Shahn to decorate public buildings with murals that celebrated American culture.

derly migrants from the Midwest with no jobs and no resources. What finally drove him to act, however, was the sight of three old women rummaging through garbage cans for scraps of food. Their plight, coupled with his own financial difficulties, made Townsend embrace old age relief as the key to ending the depression.

In January 1934 Townsend announced his plan for "Old Age Revolving Pensions, Limited," demanding a $200 monthly pension for every citizen over the age of 60. In return, recipients had to retire and spend their entire pension every month within the United States. As explained by Townsend, younger adults would inherit the jobs vacated by senior citizens, and the economy would be stimulated by the increased purchasing power of the elderly. Critics lambasted Townsend, arguing it was ludicrous to spend $24 billion out of a national income of only $40 billion to benefit a mere 9 percent of the population. Yet those Americans who found his plan refreshingly simple no doubt agreed with Townsend when he replied, "I'm not in the least interested in the cost of the plan." By 1936 Townsend claimed to have 3.5 million followers.

Roosevelt could not afford to ignore his critics. Acting alone, Long, Coughlin, and Townsend might not have enough support to defeat Roosevelt, but their challenge was real. In a close election, they commanded more than enough votes to tip the scales in favor of a Republican candidate. To remain in office, Roosevelt had to shift policies.

THE SECOND NEW DEAL

Alarmed by his critics, Roosevelt slowly abandoned his dream of building a coalition that would unite all Americans behind the New Deal. Previously, he had seen himself as an honest broker attempting to reconcile the conflicting demands of widely diverse interest groups. Now Roosevelt stopped trying to please everyone and started inching toward the left.

The Supreme Court shoved Roosevelt further in this direction. On May 26, 1935, the Court struck down the NRA in *Schechter* v. *United States*—the famous "sick chicken" case. In *Schechter* the Court held unanimously the federal government did not have the power to regulate the sale of poultry in Brooklyn, delivering a stinging rebuke both to Roosevelt and the Congress for expanding federal authority where it did not belong. Denying the transaction could be deemed interstate commerce, the Court ruled the sale a purely local transaction that Congress could not regulate without violating the separation of powers. Roosevelt was furious. He accused the court of returning the nation "to the horse-and-buggy definition of interstate commerce." In June Roosevelt refused to dismiss Congress for summer vacation, vowing to make its members swelter in the Washington heat until they passed his new legislative agenda. The result was the "Second Hundred Days."

The National Labor Relations Act

The National Labor Relations Act (Wagner Act) came first. Senator Robert F. Wagner of New York, the bill's sponsor, seized the opportunity to replace Section 7A of the NIRA with what he called "labor's Magna Carta." Down to this point Roosevelt had resisted any drastic change in government labor policy, but once the Wagner Act's passage seemed assured he gave it his belated blessing. The bill passed overwhelmingly, delivering the government's most important concession to labor to date. It guaranteed labor's right to organize by creating the National Labor Relations Board (NLRB), which had the power to conduct labor elections, determine bargaining units, and restrain business from "unfair labor practices."

The Wagner Act inspired an unprecedented burst of labor organizing. Philip Murray of the United Mine Workers (UMW) organized the Steel Workers' Organizing Committee; Sidney Hillman established the Textile Workers' Organizing Committee; and late in 1936 Walter Reuther and the United Automobile Workers (UAW) launched their famous "sit-down" strikes in which workers occupied factories but refused to work. The automobile companies responded with violence, but the union prevailed. In February 1937 General Motors recognized the union, and UAW membership increased from 30,000 members to more than 400,000 in less than a year.

Union organizers made inroads in other industries as well. When the Steel Workers' Organizing Committee signed up 350,000 workers by 1937, the United States Steel Corporation capitulated to the union's demands. The new umbrella organization for the UMW, the UAW, the Steel Workers' Organizing Committee, the Textile Workers' Organizing Committee, and the Amalgamated Clothing Workers (and other unions) was the Congress of Industrial Organizations (CIO), formed in 1938 under the leadership of John L. Lewis, who was active in drafting labor legislation and in promoting industrial unionism. The Wagner Act had put the full force of the federal government behind labor's right to bargain collectively.

The Social Security Act

The Social Security bill came next. A goal of reformers since the Progressive Era, the bill was aimed at alleviating the plight of America's visible poor—dependent children, the elderly, and the handicapped. Senator Robert Wagner of New York and Congressman David Lewis of Pennsylvania, both of whom had firsthand knowledge of poverty, sponsored the bill, and Roosevelt signed it on August 15, 1935.

A major political victory for Roosevelt, the Social Security Act was a triumph of social legislation. It stole Francis Townsend's thunder by offering workers 65 or older monthly stipends based on previous earnings (with payments due to start in 1940), and it gave the indigent elderly small relief payments, financed by the federal government and the states. In addition, the act provided assistance to blind Americans and those with other handicaps, and to dependent children who did not have a wage-earning parent. The act also established the nation's first federally sponsored system of unemployment insurance. Mandatory payroll deductions levied equally on employees and employers financed both the retirement system and the unemployment insurance.

Yet the Social Security Act was profoundly disappointing to reformers who demanded "cradle to grave" protection as the birthright of every American. According to its critics, the new system authorized pitifully small payments (initially, they ranged from $10 to $85 a month); its retirement system left huge groups of workers uncovered, as it excluded such occupations as migrant workers, civil servants, domestic servants, merchant seamen, day laborers, and employees of charitable, religious, and educational institutions; its budget came from a regressive tax scheme that placed a disproportionate tax burden on the poor; and, most troubling of all, it failed to provide health insurance. According to conservatives, however, the act placed the United States on the road to socialism by making the government responsible for duties that belonged to individuals or to their families.

Despite criticisms from the left and the right, the Social Security Act introduced a new era in American history. It committed the government to a social welfare role by providing the first federally sponsored "floor" for elderly, disabled, dependent, and unemployed Americans. By so doing, the act greatly expanded the public's sense of entitlement, the support people expected the government to give all citizens. Defending the compromises he made as "politics all the way through," Roosevelt boasted that because the program was financed by both employers and employees through payroll deductions, "no damn politician can ever scrap my social security program." He was right. Over the next few decades, the Social Security system assumed the status of a "sacred cow" in American politics.

The remaining "must legislation" of the Second Hundred Days included utilities regulation, banking reform, and a new tax proposal. Yet none of these measures represented a drastic change in American politics. On the whole, the Second New Deal merely sought to make capitalism more humane. William Allen White, a distinguished American journalist, described these measures as a "belated attempt to bring the American people up to the modern standards of

TABLE 25.3

Later New Deal Legislation	
1934	Farm Mortgage Refinancing Act
	Gold Reserve Act
	Civil-Works Emergency Relief Act
	Home Owners' Loan Act
	Farm Mortgage Foreclosure Act
	Bank Deposit Insurance Act
	Silver Purchase Act
	Securities Exchange Act
	Labor Dispute Joint Resolution
	Railway Pension Act
	Communication Act
1935	Emergency Relief Appropriation Act
	National Labor Relations Act
	Social Security Act
	Public Utility Holding Company Act
	Work Relief Act
1937	National Housing Act
	Bankhead-Jones Farm Tenancy Act
1938	Fair Labor Standards Act

English-speaking countries." Roosevelt never contemplated, much less achieved, a social revolution. He made no attacks on private property; the well-to-do retained their privileges; wealth was not redistributed; the poor remained poor.

The majority of Americans did not want dramatic changes. Despite severe economic hardships, they still supported capitalism. How else can one explain the phenomenal success of Monopoly, the new board game introduced in 1935 by the Parker Brothers? In the true spirit of rapacious capitalism, this new real estate game required players to acquire private property, convert their property into monopolies, and then drive their competitors to the wall through exorbitant rents. An instant hit, Monopoly went on to become the most popular board game in American history.

Protest from the Right

To hear many wealthy conservatives tell it, however, Roosevelt was a wild-eyed radical who threatened the very foundation of capitalism. William Randolph Hearst ordered his newspapers to substitute the words "Raw Deal" for "New Deal." Firmly committed to a balanced budget, conservatives viewed heavy government spending as sacrilege, and they were appalled by the growth of the bureaucracy in Washington, D.C. In 1932 the number of civilian federal employees in the nation's capital stood at 73,445, but by 1936 the number had climbed to 122,937. (By 1940 it had risen to 139,770, nearly double what it had been in 1932.) Conservatives feared government's growth would increase federal power at the expense of states' rights and individual liberties, and they believed Roosevelt would raise rich people's taxes to finance his relief programs for the poor.

Viewing Roosevelt as a traitor to his class, many wealthy Americans saw the election of 1936 as their chance to save the country. Mark Sullivan, a conservative journalist, warned his readers that 1936 might be "the last presidential election America may ever have," and confessed his despair over the public's failure "to see that the New Deal is to America what the early phase of Nazism was to Germany."

The Election of 1936

To carry its banner in 1936, the GOP picked Alfred M. Landon of Kansas, the only Republican governor who survived the 1934 elections. As their campaign song, the Republicans chose Stephen Foster's "Oh! Susanna." Clearly, nostalgia was the primary appeal of the soft-spoken, sincere "Kansas Coolidge." Yet Landon was far more liberal than many of his backers. He had opposed the KKK, backed business regulation, and supported many New Deal programs. A poor public speaker, Landon offered few alternatives to Roosevelt's programs.

To win in 1936 the GOP needed help from a third party. Assistance from this quarter never arrived. Huey Long's organization fell apart following his assassination in 1935, and Roosevelt's swift reconciliation with Louisiana Democrats became known as the "Second Louisiana Pur-

"Mother, Wilfred wrote a bad word!"

Some Americans felt capitalism was threatened under Roosevelt's New Deal. This 1938 *Esquire* cartoon captures the mood of disapproval prevalent among many at the time.

chase." Francis Townsend's campaign, already weakened by passage of the Social Security Act in 1935, collapsed in the spring of 1936 under charges of corruption; and by 1936 Father Coughlin had been reduced to an abusive name-caller who had been publicly rebuked by the Catholic church. By the time the remnants of their followers formed the Union party and nominated William Lemke, the farm radical from North Dakota, as their candidate, Roosevelt's critics on the left no longer posed a threat.

Always a brilliant campaigner, Roosevelt enjoyed the race. Embracing the rhetoric of the left, he lashed out at "economic royalists" who opposed the New Deal. Economic indicators supported the Democrats. In 1936 industrial output more than doubled its 1933 figures, and the national income rose half again as much. When Landon heard the third-quarter economic report he privately conceded defeat.

On election night Roosevelt's inner circle gathered at Hyde Park to hear the news: Approximately 61 percent of the eligible voters had cast ballots—27,752,869 for the president, 16,674,665 for Landon, and 882,479 for Lemke. Roosevelt carried every state but Maine and Vermont. James A. Farley, the president's political manager, joked, "As Maine goes, so goes Vermont," while another New Dealer boasted: "If Roosevelt had given one more speech he would have carried Canada." Democrats won an equally lopsided victory in the congressional races: 331 to 89 in the House and 76 to 16 in the Senate. The election swept so many Democrats into Congress that 12 freshman senators had to sit on the Republican side.

The Democrat's victory rested on a broad base of support. Roosevelt's backers included poor people, organized labor, urban ethnics, the Democratic South, blacks, and many intellectuals. A formidable alliance of diverse groups, Roosevelt's New Deal coalition would shape the contours of American politics for decades to come.

THE NEW DEAL AND MINORITIES

Among Roosevelt's supporters, blacks benefited least from the New Deal. From a purely political

standpoint, Roosevelt at first had little reason to reward blacks. In the election of 1932 he received only 21 percent of the black vote; the overwhelming majority of black voters showed their traditional loyalty to the party of Lincoln. By the end of Roosevelt's first administration, however, one of the most dramatic voter shifts in American history had occurred, and in 1936, 75 percent of black voters supported the Democrats.

Blacks turned to Roosevelt in part because his spending programs gave them a measure of relief from the depression and in part because the GOP had done little to repay their earlier support. Still, Roosevelt's record on civil rights must have made many blacks wonder why they bothered to change. Instead of using New Deal programs to promote civil rights, the administration consistently bowed to discrimination. Neither major party placed a high priority on equal rights for blacks; and the vast majority of white Americans did not think race relations required any changes. In that sense Roosevelt reflected his times.

Politics shaped Roosevelt's approach to the race issue. In order to pass major New Deal legislation, he needed the support of southern Democrats. Vigorous promotion of civil rights for blacks, Roosevelt feared, would alienate southern whites. Time and time again, he backed away from equal rights to avoid antagonizing southern whites, although his wife, Eleanor, did take a public stand in support of civil rights.

Most New Deal programs discriminated against blacks. The NRA, for example, not only offered whites the first crack at jobs but authorized separate and lower pay scales for blacks. To disillusioned blacks, the NRA stood for "Negroes Ruined Again." The Federal Housing Authority (FHA) refused to guarantee mortgages for blacks who tried to buy in white neighborhoods, and the CCC maintained segregated camps. Furthermore, the Social Security Act excluded precisely those job categories blacks traditionally filled. One NAACP writer became so disgruntled with Roosevelt's record he dismissed the New Deal as "the same raw deal."

The story in agriculture was particularly grim. Since 40 percent of all black workers made
(Text continues on p. 852)

THE TUSKEGEE SYPHILIS STUDY

The South in the 1930s was the section of the United States that most resembled the underdeveloped nations of the world. Its people (white and black) remained mostly rural; they were less well-educated than other Americans; and they made decidedly less money.

As a group, black Americans in the South were among the poorest of the poor—virtual paupers, chronically unemployed, without benefit of sanitation, adequate diet, or the rudiments of hygiene. They suffered from a host of diseases, including tuberculosis, syphilis, hookworm, pellagra, rickets, and rotting teeth; and their death rate far exceeded that of whites.

Despite their need, few blacks received proper medical care. In fact, many black Americans lived outside the world of modern medicine, going from cradle to grave without ever seeing a doctor. There

was a severe shortage of black physicians, and many white physicians refused to treat black patients. In addition, there were only a handful of black hospitals in the South, and most white hospitals either denied blacks admission or assigned them to segregated wings that were often overcrowded.

But poverty was as much to blame as racism for the medical neglect of black Americans. Medical care in the United States was offered on a fee-for-services basis, and the simple truth was that many blacks were too poor to be able to afford medical care.

To combat these and other problems, the federal government in 1912 united all its health-related activities under the Public Health Service (PHS). Over the next few decades, the PHS distinguished itself by launching attacks on hookworm, pellagra, and a host of other

illnesses. In no field was it more active than in its efforts to fight venereal diseases.

Health reformers knew that syphilis was a killer, and that it was also capable of inflicting blindness, deafness, and insanity on its victims. Furthermore, they saw the disease as a serious threat to the family because they associated it with prostitution and with loose morals in general, which added a moral dimension to their medical concerns.

Taking advantage of the emergency atmosphere of World War I, progressive reformers pushed through Congress in 1918 a bill to create a special Division of Venereal Diseases within the PHS. The PHS officers who launched this new offensive against syphilis began with high motives, and their initial successes were impressive. By 1919, they had established over 200 health clinics, which treated over 64,000 patients who could not otherwise have afforded health care.

In the late 1920s, the PHS joined forces with the Rosenwald Fund (a private philanthropic foundation based in Chicago) to develop a syphilis control program for blacks in the South. Most doctors assumed that blacks suffered a much higher infection rate than whites because blacks abandoned themselves to sexual promiscuity. And once infected, the argument went, blacks remained infected because they were too poor and too ignorant to seek medical care.

To test these theories, PHS officers selected communities in six different southern states, examined the local black populations to ascertain the incidence of syphilis, and offered free treatment to those who were infected. This pilot program had hardly gotten underway, however, when the stock market collapse forced the Rosenwald Fund to terminate its support, and the PHS was left without sufficient funds to follow up its syphilis control work among blacks in the South.

Macon County, Alabama, was the site of one of those original pilot programs. Its county seat, Tuskegee, was the home of the famed Tuskegee Institute. It was in and around Tuskegee that the PHS had discovered an infection rate of 35 percent among those tested, the highest incidence in the six communities studied. In fact, despite the presence of the Tuskegee Institute, which boasted a well-equipped hospital that might have provided low-cost health care to blacks in the region, Macon County was home to the worst poverty and the most sickly residents the PHS uncovered anywhere in the South. It was precisely this ready-made laboratory of human suffering that prompted the PHS to return to Macon County in 1932. Since they could not afford to treat syphilis, the PHS officers decided to document its damage on its victims by launching a scientific study of the effects of untreated syphilis on black males. Many white Southerners (including physicians) believed that although practically all blacks had syphilis, it did not harm them as severely as it did whites. PHS officials knew that syphilis was a serious threat to the health of black Americans, and they intended to use the results of the study to pressure southern state legislatures into appropriating funds for syphilis control work among rural blacks.

Armed with these good motives, the PHS launched the Tuskegee Study in 1932. It involved approximately 400 black males, who tested positive for the disease, and 200 nonsyphilitic black males to serve as controls. In order to secure cooperation, the PHS told the local residents that they had returned to Macon County to treat people who were ill. The PHS did not inform them that they had syphilis. Instead, the men were told that they had "bad blood," a catch-all phrase rural blacks used to describe a host of ailments.

While the PHS had not intended to treat the men, state health officials demanded, as the price of their cooperation, that the men be given at least enough medication to render them noninfectious. Consequently, all of the men received a little treatment. No one worried much about the glaring contradiction of offering treatment in a study of untreated syphilis because the men had not received enough treatment to cure them. Thus, the experiment was scientifically flawed from the outset.

Although the original plan called for a one-year experiment, the Tuskegee Study continued until 1972— partly because many of the health officers became fascinated by the scientific potential of a long-range study of syphilis. No doubt others rationalized the study by telling themselves that the men were too poor to afford proper treatment, or that too much time had passed for treatment to be of any benefit. The health officials, in some cases, may have seen the men as clinical material rather than human beings.

At any rate, the Tuskegee Study killed approximately 100 black men who died as a direct result of syphilis, scores went blind or insane, and still others endured lives of chronic ill health from syphilis-related complications. Throughout their suffering, the PHS made no effort to treat the men, and on several occasions took steps to prevent them from getting treatment on their own. As a result, the men did not receive penicillin when that "wonder drug" became widely available after World War II.

During those same four decades, however, civil protests raised America's concern for the rights of black people, and the ethical standards of the medical profession changed dramatically. These changes had no impact on the Tuskegee Study. PHS officials published no fewer than 13 scientific papers on the experiment (several of which appeared in the nation's leading medical journals), and the PHS routinely presented sessions on it at medical conventions. The Tuskegee Study ended in 1972 because a "whistle-blower" in the PHS named Peter Buxtun leaked the story to the press. At first health officials tried to defend their actions, but public outrage quickly silenced them, and they agreed to end the experiment. As part of an out-of-court settlement, the survivors were finally treated for syphilis. In addition, the men, and the families of the deceased, received small cash payments.

The 40-year deathwatch had finally ended, but its legacy can still be felt today. In the wake of its hearings, Congress enacted new legislation to protect the subjects of human experiments. The Tuskegee Study left behind a host of unanswered questions about the social and racial attitudes of the medical establishment in the United States. It served as a cruel reminder of how class distinctions and racism could negate ethical and scientific standards.

their living as sharecroppers and tenant farmers, the AAA acreage reduction hit blacks hard. White landlords could make more money by leaving land untilled than by putting land into production. As a result, the AAA's policies forced more than 100,000 blacks off the land in 1933 and 1934. Moreover, many black sharecroppers and tenants who remained on the land received no AAA payments because the money had to pass through the hands of white landlords before it reached them. In 1934 white liberals and black leaders organized the Southern Tenant Farmers Union (STFU) to protest the plight of sharecroppers, including blacks, but when the STFU demanded direct AAA payments to tenants, white commercial farmers protested and the administration backed down.

Even more galling to black leaders, the president failed to support an antilynching bill and a bill to abolish the poll tax. When questioned by Walter White, head of the NAACP, about the antilynching bill, Roosevelt pleaded political necessity, telling critics "I just can't take that risk." Conservative southern Democrats had seniority in Congress and controlled many committee chairmanships, he explained, and if he tried to fight them on the race question, they would block his bills.

Yet the New Deal did record a few gains in civil rights. Roosevelt named Mary McLeod Bethune, a black educator, to the advisory committee of the National Youth Administration (NYA), and thanks to her efforts, blacks received a fair share of NYA funds. The WPA was color-blind, and blacks in northern cities benefited from its work relief programs. Harold Ickes, a strong supporter of civil rights, poured federal funds into black schools and hospitals in the South. True, black leaders would have preferred integrated facilities, but most agreed that separate facilities beat no facilities. Ickes's department quickly became the home of the much publicized "Black Cabinet," including Clark Foreman as his personal assistant and Robert C. Weaver and William H. Hastie, two bright young lawyers. Together they lobbied the administration at every turn (if unsuccessfully) to end segregation.

Still, most blacks appointed to New Deal posts served in token positions as advisors on

Mary McLeod Bethune, a member of the advisory committee for the National Youth Administration, meets here with Eleanor Roosevelt.

black affairs in one department or another. At best they achieved a new visibility in government. No longer called in from the outside for consultations and then sent home, they now had permanent positions within the administration.

Mexican-Americans

During the 1930s most Mexican-Americans lived in California or the Southwest. Like blacks, they reaped few benefits from the New Deal. AAA acreage reduction programs affected migrant workers in much the same way as sharecroppers and tenant farmers. Many Mexican-Americans lost their jobs due to acreage reductions or competition in the fields from unemployed whites.

Still, the New Deal offered Mexican-Americans a little help. The Farm Security Administration established camps for migrant farm workers in California, and the CCC and WPA hired unemployed Mexican-Americans on relief jobs. Yet many Mexican-Americans did not qualify for relief assistance because they worked as migrant workers and did not live in the same place long enough to meet residency requirements. Furthermore, agricultural workers were not eligible for benefits under workers' compensation, Social Security, and the National Labor Relations Act.

Mexican-Americans also faced serious opposition from organized labor. As unemployment rose, labor unions resented competition from Mexican workers. Unions demanded deportation, and federal, state, and local authorities surrendered to the pressure. Los Angeles deported Mexicans and Mexican-Americans alike to prevent them from applying for relief. "The Mexicans are trash," declared one California official. "They have no standard of living. We herd them like pigs." All told, the United States deported more than 400,000 people of Mexican descent during the 1930s. Since this group included many citizens of the United States (American-born husbands, wives, and children of Mexican aliens), the deportations constituted a gross violation of civil liberties.

Native Americans

The so-called "Indian New Deal" was the only bright spot in the administration's treatment of minorities. In 1933 Roosevelt appointed John Collier as commissioner of Indian affairs. At Collier's request, Congress created the Indian Emergency Conservation Program (IECP), a CCC-type project for the reservations. By the time World War II broke out, the IECP had employed more than 85,000 Indians, building 1742 dams and reservoirs, 12,230 miles of fence, 91 lookout towers, and 9737 miles of fire trails. In addition, Indian workers conducted pest control projects on 1,315,870 acres of land and removed poisonous weeds from 263,129 acres of reservation farm and grazing land. Collier also made certain that the PWA, WPA, CCC, and NYA hired Native Americans.

Collier had long been an opponent of the 50-year-old government allotment program, in which tribal lands had been broken up and distributed to individual Native Americans and whites. In 1934 Congress passed the Indian Reorganization Act, which terminated the allotment program of the Dawes Severalty Act of 1887; provided funds for tribes to purchase new land; offered government recognition of tribal constitutions; and repealed prohibitions on the use of Native American languages, tribal ceremonies, and traditional dress on reservations. That same year, the Johnson-O'Malley Act provided federal grants to local school districts, hospitals, and social welfare agencies to assist Native Americans.

Women

Women achieved measured progress under the New Deal. Prior to the depression, women had dominated both social work and the voluntary associations that provided charity for the poor and unemployed. Since the same skills were needed to combat the depression, women joined the throngs of professionals who rushed to Washington to work in the New Deal.

Once there, women formed a tightly knit network of professionals who supported each other's careers. Frances Perkins, the secretary of labor and the first woman in American history to hold a cabinet appointment, brought many women into government; and Molly Dewson, the director of the Women's Division of the Democratic Committee, helped place women throughout the administration. By 1939 women held one-third of all positions in the independent agencies and almost one-fifth of the jobs in the executive departments.

Eleanor Roosevelt deserves much of the credit for the progress made by minorities. The first president's wife to stake out an independent public position, she provided the social conscience of the New Deal. Few people knew how much she hated making public appearances. She had to overcome an almost pathological shyness to voice her sympathies and convictions, but overcome it she did. In 1933 alone the First Lady traveled 40,000 miles, visiting families, investigating work conditions, and checking welfare programs. In fact, she seemed to pop up everywhere: a *New Yorker* cartoon of the 1930s showed a startled coal miner at the bottom of a pit exclaiming: "For gosh sakes, here comes Mrs. Roosevelt!"

The First Lady worked tirelessly to persuade her husband and the heads of government agencies to hire well-qualified women and blacks. More courageous than her husband and less restricted politically, she did not hesitate to take a public stand on civil rights. When the Daughters of the American Revolution refused in 1939 to grant the black contralto Marian Anderson permission to sing in Constitution Hall, Mrs. Roosevelt arranged for a concert on the steps of the Lincoln Memorial on Easter Sunday.

Philosophically, the president appeared to move closer to his wife's vision of society after the election of 1936. In his second inaugural address, he promised to press for new social legislation. "I see one-third of a nation ill-housed, ill-clad, ill-nourished," he told the country. Yet instead of pursuing new reforms, Roosevelt allowed his second term to bog down in political squabbles. He wasted his energies on an ill-conceived battle with the Supreme Court and an abortive effort to purge the Democratic party.

THE NEW DEAL IN DECLINE

As Roosevelt's first term drew to a close, the Supreme Court turned on the New Deal. In 1935 the Court ruled the NRA unconstitutional in *Schechter* v. *United States*; and in 1936 it struck down the AAA in *Butler* v. *United States*. Hitting as they did at the heart of the New Deal, these decisions convinced Roosevelt the Supreme Court was at odds with the other two branches of government. The president therefore decided to make his opponents on the Supreme Court resign so he could replace them with justices more sympathetic to his policies. On February 5, 1937, Roosevelt announced a plan to add one new member to the Supreme Court for every judge who had reached the age of 70 without retiring (six justices were over 70). To offer a carrot with the stick, Roosevelt also outlined a generous new pension program for retiring federal judges.

The court-packing scheme was a political disaster. Conservatives and liberals alike de-

nounced Roosevelt for attacking the separation of powers, and critics accused him of trying to become a dictator. Fortunately, the Court itself ended the crisis by shifting ground—"the switch in time that saved nine," as one wit quipped. In two separate cases, each decided by five-to-four votes, the Court upheld the Wagner Act and approved a Washington state minimum wage law (much like the one it had overthrown in New York). Two more close decisions (one upholding compulsory unemployment insurance, the other old age pensions) furnished added proof the Court had softened its opposition to the New Deal.

Yet Roosevelt remained too obsessed with the battle to realize he had won the war. He lobbied for the court-packing bill until the end of July, squandering his strength on a struggle that had long since become a political embarrassment. In the end, the only part of the president's plan to gain congressional approval was the pension program. Once it passed, Justice Willis Van Devanter, the most obstinate New Deal opponent on the Court, resigned. By 1941 Roosevelt had named five justices to the Supreme Court, including Hugo Black and William O. Douglas. Few legacies of the president's leadership proved more important, for the new "Roosevelt Court" significantly expanded the government's role in the economy and in civil liberties.

Roosevelt's second blunder in 1937 involved fiscal policy. One group within his administration, led by Secretary of the Treasury Henry Morganthau, demanded severe spending cuts to balance the federal budget and to restore business confidence. A second group, led by WPA head Harry Hopkins, wanted the administration to follow the teachings of the British economist, John Maynard Keynes. A proponent of vigorous government action, Keynes recommended tax cuts and new spending programs to combat the depression. Reassured by good economic news in 1936, Roosevelt sided with the budget balancers. Late in 1937 he slashed government spending.

The budget cuts knocked the economy into a tailspin. By early 1938 economic indicators dipped nearly as low as they had been in 1932, and just as he had reaped credit for the recovery of 1936, Roosevelt got blamed for the depression of 1937–1938. Republicans, bone-sick of hearing about "Hoover's depression," relished the chance to decry "Roosevelt's depression." Finally, on April 14, 1938, Roosevelt reversed himself and asked Congress to resume spending. Congress responded with huge appropriations for the PWA and increased welfare funds for the states. As before, public spending blunted the worst effects of the troubled economy, but it took the massive federal budgets of World War II to end the depression and restore economic health to the nation.

The third (and final) mistake of Roosevelt's second term was the president's futile attempt to purge the Democratic party of conservative senators who had opposed the New Deal. In the congressional elections of 1938, Roosevelt campaigned against five southern senators, all of whom won reelection. The abortive purge intensified the conservative-liberal split within the Democratic party by showing conservatives they could defy the president with impunity. It also weakened the Democratic coalition at a time when Roosevelt badly needed conservative support for military preparedness to meet the growing threat from Europe.

By the end of 1938 the reform spirit was gone. Even Harry Hopkins admitted Americans had become "bored with the poor, the unemployed, and the insecure." In Congress a conservative alliance of southern Democrats and northern Republicans blocked all efforts to expand the New Deal. Yet if Roosevelt could not pass any new measures, neither could his opponents dismantle his programs. The New Deal ended in stalemate, but with several reforms ensconced as permanent features of American politics.

CONCLUSION

From a purely economic perspective, the New Deal barely made a dent in the Great Depression. Roosevelt's programs suffered from poor planning and moved with considerable caution. By 1939 national productivity had barely reached 1929 levels, and 10 million men and

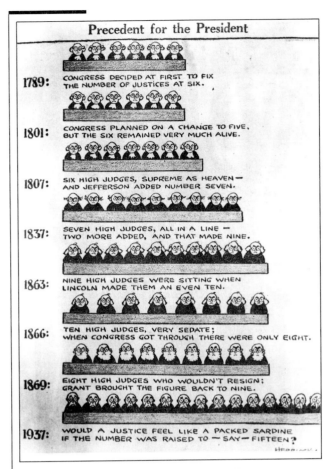

Roosevelt's court-packing scheme, designed to fill the court with justices sympathetic to his policies, outraged both liberals and conservatives because it seemed to attack the separation of powers doctrine.

women remained unemployed. Roosevelt simply could not bring himself to support huge federal budgets. Government expenditures stayed below $10 billion a year, with annual deficits on the scale of $4 billion. Indeed, despite the handwringing and wailing of conservatives, huge deficits did not become a feature of the federal budget until World War II, when federal spending leaped to $95 billion a year, with deficits over half that amount. World War II, not the New Deal, snapped America out of the depression, for then and only then did the economy recover and unemployment disappear.

Yet whatever its economic shortcomings, the New Deal blunted the worst effects of the

CHRONOLOGY
OF KEY EVENTS

1928 Herbert Hoover is elected thirty-first president

1929 Stock market crashes

1930 Hawley-Smoot Tariff raises import duties to unprecedented levels

1932 Congress creates Reconstruction Finance Corporation to lend money to banks, railroads, and insurance companies; to revive the construction industry, Congress creates the Federal Home Loan Bank System to lend money to savings and loan associations; Bonus Army, a group of veterans demanding immediate payment of World War I bonuses, is dispersed by federal troops in Washington, D.C.; Franklin Roosevelt is elected thirty-second president

1933 Emergency Banking Relief Act addresses banking crisis; Roosevelt conducts the first of many "fireside chats" over national radio; Civilian Conservation Corps puts young people to work conserving natural resources; Federal Emergency Relief Act provides relief payments to the unemployed through local and state welfare agencies; Civil Works Administration offers employment to over 4 million people; Agricultural Adjustment Act sets up a system of farm price supports and production limits; National Industrial Recovery Act authorizes industrial codes regulating production, prices, and working conditions and provides funds for public works projects; Tennessee Valley Authority constructs dams and hydroelectric plants in the Tennessee River valley; Twenty-first Amendment repeals prohibition; Glass-Steagall Act creates the Federal Deposit Insurance Corporation to insure savings accounts against bank failure; Farm Credit Administration and Home Owners' Loan Corporation provide low-interest loans to farmers and home owners

1934 Dr. Francis Townsend proposes a $200 monthly pension for every citizen over 60; the "radio priest" Father Charles Coughlin breaks with Roosevelt and forms the National Union for Social Justice; Senator Huey Long of Louisiana announces his "Share Our Wealth Program" to provide every American family with a guaranteed annual income; Indian Reorganization Act provides funds for tribes to purchase land, offers recognition of tribal constitutions, and repeals prohibitions on Native American customs

1935 *Schechter* v. *United States* declares National Industrial Recovery Act unconstitutional; Emergency Relief Appropriation Act creates Works Progress Administration and National Youth Administration; National Labor Relations Act guarantees workers' right to organize and bargain collectively; Public Utility Holding Company Act is passed to prevent monopolies in gas and electricity distribution; Social Security Act creates a federal system of old age pensions and state-run unemployment compensation programs

1937 Roosevelt proposes his "court-packing" scheme

1938 Fair Labor Standards Act bans child labor and establishes minimum wages and maximum hours

Great Depression. Through economic reforms and public works projects Roosevelt managed to preserve the public's faith in capitalism and in democratic government at a time when both seemed on the verge of destruction. Most of the New Deal's economic reforms were modest in scope, but they strengthened the public's faith in the government as their agency of action and reform. Roosevelt accomplished this, in large measure, by reaching out to groups that Washington had largely neglected in the past. The Social Security program, while it ignored many, made the government responsible for old age pensions and welfare payments to citizens who could not support themselves. The NIRA and the Wagner Act encouraged the growth of unions; minimum wage laws put an economic floor under many workers; and child labor was finally abolished in industry (though it remained in agriculture). While the New Deal stopped far short of providing equal treatment under the law for black Americans, it offered them a measure of relief from the depression and a new visibility in government.

The New Deal encouraged Americans to look to the White House for strong executive leadership. When Roosevelt took office the situation required decisive action, and he responded in kind. A compassionate man and a bold leader, Roosevelt had little difficulty persuading Congress to pass his programs. More and more, the public expected the other branches of government to support presidential initiatives. Roosevelt's administrative style, creating special agencies to handle specific problems and placing people in charge who answered directly to him, further enhanced presidential power. Moreover, on a purely partisan level, the New Deal benefited the Democratic party mightily by forging the Roosevelt coalition, a powerful alliance of labor, blacks, urban ethnics, intellectuals, and southern whites that helped shape American politics for the next several decades.

Above all the New Deal made the federal government responsible for safeguarding the nation's economic health. Prior to the 1930s if people were asked how the government affected them, they probably thought in terms of the state government, or even their local gov-

ernment. Federal policies simply did not impinge that much on the public. The New Deal changed all that. FDR's alphabet soup of programs and agencies made the federal government such a daily presence in people's lives they now expected Washington to involve itself in everything from farm subsidies to the sale of stocks and securities.

Finally, there is the question of federal fiscal policy. Anyone comparing the political economy of 1920 and 1940 notices two dramatic changes. First, by 1940 the federal government had claimed responsibility for stable prices and full employment, and second, Keynesian fiscal policies had largely replaced older theories on how the government should approach the economy. For better or for worse, the New Deal had dramatically altered the government's fiscal policy.

SUGGESTIONS FOR FURTHER READING

OVERVIEWS AND SURVEYS

James M. Burns, *Roosevelt: The Lion and the Fox* (1956); Sean Dennis Cashman, *America in the Twenties and Thirties: The Olympian Age of Franklin Delano Roosevelt* (1989); Paul K. Conkin, *The New Deal*, 2d ed. (1975) and *The Southern Agrarians* (1988); Otis L. Graham, Jr., *The New Deal: The Critical Issues* (1971); Robert L. Heilbroner and Aaron Singer, *The Economic Transformation of America* (1977); Jack Temple Kirby, *Rural Worlds Lost: The American South, 1920–1960* (1987); William E. Leuchtenburg, *Franklin D. Roosevelt and the New Deal* (1963) and *The Perils of Prosperity, 1914–32* (1958); James T. Patterson, *America's Struggle Against Poverty* (1981); Albert U. Romasco, *The Politics of Recovery: Roosevelt's New Deal* (1983); Studs Terkel, *Hard Times: An Oral History of the Great Depression* (1970).

HERBERT HOOVER AND THE GREAT DEPRESSION

William J. Barber, *From New Era to New Deal; Herbert Hoover, the Economists, and American Economic Policy, 1921–1933* (1985); Andrew Bergman, *We're in the Money: Depression America and Its Films* (1971); Roger Daniels, *The Bonus March: An Episode of the Great Depression* (1971); Glen H. Elder, Jr., *Children of the Great Depression: Social Change in Life Experience* (1974); Martin L.

Fausold, *The Presidency of Herbert Hoover* (1985); Donald J. Lisio, *The President and Protest: Hoover, Conspiracy, and the Bonus Riot* (1974); Albert U. Romasco, *The Poverty of Abundance: Hoover, the Nation, the Depression* (1965); Jordan A. Schwarz, *Interregnum of Despair: Hoover, Congress, and the Depression* (1970); Winifred D. Wandersee, *Women's Work and Family Values, 1920–1940* (1981).

FRANKLIN ROOSEVELT AND THE FIRST NEW DEAL

Sue Bridwell Beckham, *Depression Post Office Murals and Southern Culture: A Gentle Reconstruction* (1989); Bernard Bellush, *The Failure of the NRA* (1975); Donald R. Brand, *Corporatism and the Rule of Law: A Study of the National Recovery Administration* (1988); David E. Conrad, *The Forgotten Farmers: The Story of the Sharecroppers in the New Deal* (1965); Frank Freidel, *Launching the New Deal* (1973); Robert F. Himmelberg, *The Origins of the National Recovery Administration* (1976); R. Douglas Hurt, *The Dust Bowl: An Agricultural and Social History* (1981); Jerre Mangione, *The Dream and the Deal: The Federal Writers' Project, 1935–1943* (1972); Robert S. McElvaine, *The Great Depression: America, 1929–1941* (1984); David Milton, *The Politics of U.S. Labor: From the Great Depression to the New Deal* (1982); Michael Parrish, *Securities Regulation and the New Deal* (1970); John Salmond, *The Civilian Conservation Corps, 1933–1942: A New Deal Case Study* (1967); Ronald W. Schatz, *The Electrical Workers: A History of Labor at General Electric and Westinghouse, 1923–1960* (1983).

THE SECOND NEW DEAL

Alan Brinkley, *Voices of Protest: Huey Long, Father Coughlin, and the Great Depression* (1982); Robert F. Burk, *The Corporate State and the Broker State: The Du Ponts and American National Politics, 1925–1940* (1990); Keith Dix, *What's a Coal Miner to Do? The Mechanization of Coal Mining* (1988); Sidney Fine, *Sit-Down: The General Motors Strike of 1936–1937* (1969); Philip J. Funigiello, *Toward a National Power Policy: The New Deal and the Electric Utility Industry, 1933–1941* (1973); Ellis Hawley, *The New Deal and the Problem of Monopoly: A Study in Economic Ambivalence* (1966); James A. Hodges, *New Deal Labor Policy and the Southern Cotton Textile Industry, 1934–1941* (1986); Harvey Klehr, *The Heyday of American Communism: The Depression Decade* (1984); Roy

Lubove, *The Struggle for Social Security, 1900–1935*, 2d ed. (1986); Thomas McCraw, *TVA and the Power Fight, 1933–1939* (1971); James T. Patterson, *Congressional Conservatism and the New Deal* (1967); Richard Polenberg, *Reorganizing Roosevelt's Government, 1936–1939* (1966).

THE NEW AND MINORITIES

Dan T. Carter, *Scottsboro: A Tragedy of the American South*, rev. ed. (1979); William H. Chafe, *The American Woman: Her Changing Social, Economic, and Political Role, 1920–1970* (1972); Cletus E. Daniel, *Bitter Harvest: A History of California Farmworkers, 1870–1941* (1981); Sara M. Evans, *Born for Liberty: A History of Women in America* (1989); Suzanne Forrest, *The Preservation of the Village: New Mexico's Hispanics and the New Deal* (1989); Mario T. García, *Mexican Americans: Leadership, Ideology, & Identity, 1930–1960* (1989); Nancy L. Grant, *TVA and Black Americans: Planning for the Status Quo* (1990); William H. Harris, *Keeping the Faith: A. Philip Randolph, Milton P. Webster, and the Brotherhood of Sleeping Car Porters, 1925-1937* (1977); Abraham Hoffman, *Unwanted Mexican Americans in the Great Depression, Repatriation Pressures, 1929–1939* (1974); James H. Jones, *Bad Blood: The Tuskegee Syphilis Experiment, A Tragedy of Race and Medicine*, rev. ed. (1992); Lawrence C. Kelly, *The Assault on Assimilation: John Collier and the Origins of Indian Policy Reform* (1983); Harry A. Kersey, Jr., *The Florida Seminoles and the New Deal, 1933–1942* (1989); Alice Kessler-Harris, *Out to Work: A History of Wage-Earning Women in the United States* (1982); Kenneth Philp, *John Collier's Crusade for Indian Reform, 1920-1954* (1977); Mark Reisler, *By the Sweat of Their Brow: Mexican Immigrant Labor in the United States, 1900–1940* (1976); Lois Scharf, *To Work and to Wed: Female Employment, Feminism, and the Great Depression* (1980); Susan Ware, *Beyond Suffrage: Women in the New Deal* (1981); Nancy J. Weiss, *Farewell to the Party of Lincoln: Black Politics in the Age of FDR* (1983); Raymond Wolters, *Negroes and the Great Depression: The Problem of Economic Recovery* (1970); Robert L. Zangrando, *The NAACP Crusade Against Lynching, 1909–1950* (1980).

BIOGRAPHIES

John Barnard, *Walter Reuther and the Rise of the Auto Workers* (1983); David Burner, *Herbert Hoo-*

ver: A Public Life (1979); Melvyn Dubofsky and Warren Van Tine, *John L. Lewis: A Biography* (1977); Steven Fraser, *Labor Will Rule: Sidney Hillman and the Rise of American Labor* (1991); Thomas Kessner, *Fiorello H. La Guardia and the Making of Modern New York* (1989); Joe Klein, *Woody Guthrie: A Life* (1980); Joseph Lash, *Eleanor and Franklin* (1971); Arthur Schlesinger, Jr., *The Age of Roosevelt*, 3 vols. (1957–1960); Richard N. Smith, *An Uncommon Man: The Triumph of Herbert Hoover* (1984); Geoffrey C. Ward, *A First-Class Temperament: The Emergence of Franklin Roosevelt* (1989); T. Harry Williams, *Huey Long* (1969).

CHAPTER 26

The End of Isolation: America Faces the World,

1920–1945

9

1918

Guns

48b

When he saw the production figures on American industry during World War II, Winston Churchill smiled broadly and exclaimed, "Nothing succeeds like excess!" Great Britain's bulldog of a prime minister was right: Allied armies won the decisive battles of World War II, but the Allied victory rested squarely on America's economic might. The gross national product rose from $91 billion in 1939 to $166 billion in 1945, and industrial production soared by an astonishing 96 percent. By 1943 America's productivity outstripped all its enemies combined; by 1944 it was twice as great.

No one symbolized this economic miracle better than Henry J. Kaiser. A man of stout frame, formidable jowls, and a pronounced paunch, Kaiser excelled at making money. Before the war his Six Companies consortium built Boulder Dam and sank the piers for the Golden Gate Bridge. Spectacular feats of engineering such as these more than supported the boasts of his son, Edgar, who proudly declared: "We are building an empire." When World War II erupted, Kaiser immediately used his experience with government contracts and officials to become one of the leading industrial architects of the Allied victory.

Kaiser built ships—tankers, small aircraft carriers, troop ships, and Liberty ships, the basic cargo carrier of the war. Speed was his watchword, and he would not tolerate delays in production schedules. In 1941 it took 355 days to build a Liberty ship. With prefabricated parts and assembly-line methods, Kaiser trimmed that time down to 56 days in 1943. By 1945 his 10 shipyards feasted on more than $3 billion in government contracts and turned out a ship a day. With enemy submarines sinking everything in sight, Kaiser stressed speed and large-scale production, not efficiency, cost, or quality.

Kaiser's shipyards formed a microcosm of American society. Teeming with migrants from farms and small towns, they employed 125,000 men and women who faced problems ranging from overcrowded housing to nonexistent child care. Kaiser devised ingenious ways to attract workers. He paid good wages, built a modern hospital or clinic near every shipyard, enrolled workers and their families in an excellent health plan, and experimented with round-the-clock nurseries and child-care centers.

After the war Kaiser praised himself as the embodiment of rugged individualism and dynamic capitalism, but in truth his success derived from "welfare capitalism." Government loans financed his shipyards, and cost-plus government contracts guaranteed his profits. In that sense, he was a charter member of the military-industrial complex. Yet his concern for workers and their families tempered capitalism with compassion, creating a model of corporate management that survived long after the last of his ships went into mothballs.

DIPLOMACY BETWEEN THE WARS

World War I's horrible casualties, disappointments over the Treaty of Versailles, the United States' failure to join the League of Nations, and the Red Scare left the public suspicious of foreign crusades. Americans wanted to retreat from world affairs. "The people have had all the

One of the biggest producers of war goods was Henry Kaiser. Almost one quarter of America's entire wartime output of merchant shipping came from his shipyards.

war, all the taxation, and all the military service they want," declared President Calvin Coolidge in 1925. During the 1920s and much of the 1930s, the United States concentrated on improving its status in the Western Hemisphere and on avoiding European entanglements.

The Isolationist Mirage

Throughout the 1920s, Republican leaders debated and ultimately refused to join the League of Nations or the World Court. Such commitments, they feared, might involve the United States too deeply in global politics. Yet Washington remained keenly interested in preserving international stability and tried to promote world peace through diplomatic means.

In December 1921 Secretary of State Charles Evans Hughes convened a disarmament conference in Washington, D.C., which produced the Five-Power Naval Treaty the following year. The treaty established a ten-year moratorium on the construction of battleships and set current tonnage for battleships at a ratio of 5:5:3 for the United States, Great Britain, and Japan; 1.75 for France and Italy. To win support for what the Japanese delegates called a ratio of "Rolls-Royce, Rolls-Royce, Ford," the United States and Great Britain agreed not to improve their fortifications in the Far East, especially in the Philippines. In 1922 the United States also signed the Nine-Power Treaty, an agreement to preserve the "Open Door" in China, and the Four-Party Treaty, which committed the United States, Great Britain, France, and Japan to consult before going to war in Asia.

Several years later the United States and France launched an international crusade to banish war from world affairs. In 1928 the French foreign minister, Aristide Briand, and Secretary of State Frank B. Kellogg negotiated the Kellogg-Briand Pact, which renounced war as an instrument for resolving international disputes and symbolized the post–World War I era's disillusionment with naked force. If attacked, however, the signatories, 62 in all, could defend themselves by force. While it raised hopes for peace and earned Kellogg the Nobel Peace Prize, the Kellogg-Briand Pact had no chance of preventing future bloodshed. Since the pact was without an enforcement mechanism, the pledges it rested upon were like pie crusts—easily formed and easily broken.

The Good Neighbor Policy

During the 1920s Republican administrations inched away from gunboat diplomacy and tried to develop better relations with Latin America. True, progress was uneven and Washington's policies occasionally reverted to heavy-handed interventions, but the thrust of Republican diplomacy during the 1920s clearly anticipated the shift toward improved relations with Latin America, which the Democrats dubbed the "Good Neighbor Policy" in the 1930s.

In 1924, for example, the United States pulled the marines out of the Dominican Republic, and the following year American troops left Nicaragua, only to be sent back a few months later when a revolution broke out. But the real test of the United States' desire for improved relations came in Mexico.

Following Alvaro Obregon's election as president of Mexico in 1920, the Mexican government threatened to expropriate American-owned oil properties. The oil companies demanded government intervention, but in 1927 President Calvin Coolidge appointed Dwight Morrow, a partner in the firm of J. P. Morgan and Company, as ambassador. Mexicans expected the worst; one newspaper declared, "after Morrow come the marines." They were wrong. Morrow liked Mexico. One of his first actions was to change the sign on the embassy to read "United States Embassy" rather than "American Embassy." It was a small gesture, but it was not lost on the Mexicans, who had long resented the United States' arrogance in appropriating a continental adjective. Morrow's diplomacy paid handsome dividends, and in 1927 Mexico once again recognized American-owned oil properties.

President Herbert Hoover continued the diplomacy of reconciliation. He announced plans to withdraw marines from Nicaragua and Haiti, and he resisted pressure from Congress to establish a customs receivership in El Salvador when the government there defaulted on its bonds. In 1930 Hoover approved a document

(Text continues on p. 866)

AMERICA AND THE WORLD
MARTIANS, WIZARDS, AND THE BATTLE OVER ISOLATIONISM

In *The Great Dictator*, his first talking film, Charlie Chaplin appeared as both the ranting "furore," a parody of Adolf Hitler, and the well-known little tramp character in the guise of a Jewish banker who pleads with the dictator for decency.

In 1938 Halloween came one day early. At 8 P.M. on Sunday, October 30, Orson Welles's Mercury Theater went on the air as usual to the strains of the Tchaikovsky Piano Concerto in B Flat Minor. Perhaps a million Americans listened to the opening of the CBS radio show. Far more—around 11 million—had their radios tuned to NBC's "Chase and Sanborn Hour," featuring the popular comedian and ventriloquist Edgar Bergen and his wooden, red-headed dummy Charlie McCarthy. At 8:12—right after Bergen finished his first skit, Chase and Sanborn began its first commercial, and listeners across

America started to fidget with their dials to see what else was on the radio—something strange happened on CBS's Mercury Theater. Breaking from the music of Ramon Raquello at the Meridian Room in New York's Hotel Park Plaza, the show shifted to the town of Groves Mills, New Jersey, for a special bulletin.

Something strange, terribly strange, was going on. Announcer Carl Phillips and Professor Pierson of Princeton were examining an object of unknown origin that had plummeted to earth from outer space. As they debated whether the smooth, cylindrical object was a meteorite or something totally new, the top of the object began to rotate. Tentacles, "wriggling out of the shadow like a gray snake," appeared, followed by a creature of sinister ugliness. Sobbing and retching, Phillips announced: "There, I can see the thing's body. It's large as a bear and it glistens like wet leather. But the face. It ... it's indescribable. I can hardly force myself to keep looking at it. The eyes are black and gleam like a serpent. The mouth is V-shaped with saliva dripping from its rimless lips that seem to quiver and pulsate. . . ."

The monster was followed by others, "the vanguard of an invading army from planet Mars." Equipped with flame throwers and poison gases, the Martians destroyed the New Jersey state police and National Guard and march on New York City. Each lightning strike was covered live by CBS radio. At 9:45 when CBS took a commercial break, the regular announcer informed his audience that it was listening to the Mercury Theater's production of H. G. Wells's *War of the Worlds*. But for many Americans the announcement came too late, for gripped in panic they had already left their radio sets. They had taken to the streets, fleeing the phantom invaders. They crammed churches and city halls, imploring God and politicians for help. A study conducted after the broadcast estimated that 1.7 million people believed the broadcast. Listeners who had not completed grammar school and who had been out of work for more than three years were the most vulnerable. But rich and well-educated Americans also fell under the show's spell.

Why? Part of the answer was radio itself. Americans had grown accustomed to radio announcers interrupting a broadcast with a special bulletin. And studies indicated that most Americans trusted radio commentators more than print journalists. Edward R. Murrow, Raymond Gram Swing, Elmer Davis, H. V. Kaltenborn, and other radio commentators were familiar, trusted voices. Part of the answer was the times. It was an uncertain age. Hitler was on the move in Europe. Talk of bombs and invasions, wars and crises, filled the air waves. Only a month before the broadcast, the Munich Pact was signed, ending the tense Czechoslovakian crisis that most Americans had believed would lead to another European war. But even with the Munich Pact, millions of Americans believed that the United States was headed toward a war. The *War of the Worlds* broadcast was made all the more believable because Americans had come to expect a crisis.

If world events could color the way Americans listened to and interpreted a radio show, mass media could influence the way Americans understood world events. During the 1930s, movies dominated the mass media. Eighty million Americans—two-thirds of the nation's population—went to the movies each week.

Throughout most of the 1930s the film industry ignored the rise of fascism in Europe, ignored the violent anti-Semitism and expansionist foreign policies of Hitler and Mussolini. The primary reason for this was that 40 to 50 percent of the industry's revenues came from foreign distribution and exhibition. If Germany, Italy, or any major country prohibited Hollywood's only product, the film industry would suffer. When Hollywood did touch, however obliquely, on foreign policy matters, it suggested that isolationism was the best solution for the United States. Released in 1939, the year Europe went to war, *The Wizard of Oz* underscored the theme, "There's no place like home."

Economic changes in the film industry, however, soon silenced such isolationist impulses. By the end of 1940 Hollywood's European market had all but vanished. Germany and Italy banned all American films in the areas they controlled. Only Great Britain remained as a solid market for American films, and Great Britain was at war with Germany. In short, the economic motive *not* to offend the Fascist dictatorships was removed.

Hollywood responded with a series of films emphasizing internationalism. One of the earliest internationalist films, *Blockade*, articulated the new position in Hollywood. The film tells of the barbarities committed by the Fascists during the Spanish Civil War. *Confessions of a Nazi Spy* (1939) condemned Nazi aggression and brutality and identified Germany as a real threat to the United States. Charlie Chaplin's *The Great Dictator* (1940) poked fun at Hitler and fascism. *Pastor Hall* (1940) vividly portrayed the brutality of Nazi Germany. Other anti-Nazi films followed—*The Mortal Storm* (1940), *Four Sons* (1940), *Escape* (1940), *I Married a Nazi* (1940), and *Man Hunt* (1941). All condemned Germany, Hitler,

and Nazism. Still other films glorified America's own military traditions. *Sargeant York* (1941), perhaps the most stirring of the latter group, reminded Americans that there were issues worth fighting for. This story of America's most publicized World War I hero amplified the theme of aggressive internationalism.

The power of Hollywood's newly found internationalism was not lost on politicians in Washington. President Roosevelt, who was working in support of Britain's war efforts, applauded films that cast Britain in the best possible light. Isolationists in Congress, however, charged that Hollywood had become a propaganda mill determined to push America into another European war. Senator Gerald P. Nye of North Dakota, one of the country's most vocal isolationists, told a national radio audience that Hollywood had "ceased to be an instrument of entertainment" and had become the home of propaganda and warmongers whose motive was to "rouse the war fever in America." The films glorified and sanitized war, Nye maintained. Instead of showing men "crouching in the mud . . . English, Greek, and German boys disemboweled, blown to bit," the films showed soldiers "marching in their bright uniforms, firing the beautiful guns at distant targets."

Isolationists in Congress demanded an investigation of Hollywood. In the late summer of 1941 a special subcommittee of the Senate Interstate Commerce Committee held hearings stemming from the charge that Hollywood had "been extensively used for propaganda purposes designed to influence the public mind in the direction of participation in the European war." Chaired by isolationist Bennett C. Clark of Missouri and stacked with other isolationists, the subcommittee had its sights set on changing the internationalist mood in Hollywood.

Hollywood fought back. The film industry hired Wendell L. Willkie, who had run for the presidency in 1940 on the Republican ticket, as their chief legal counsel. Willkie and such witnesses from Hollywood as Harry Warner, one of the Warner brothers, argued that the anti-Nazi films were factually accurate and that Hitler *was* a threat to the United States. "The motion picture industry and its executives are opposed to the Hitler regime," Willkie said. Nazism is "an evil force," Warner added. Hollywood's vigorous defense silenced the isolationists. The subcommittee adjourned the hearings on September 26 without issuing a report.

Two and a half months later the isolationists' charges became moot. The Japanese bombed Pearl Harbor and America went to war. And Hollywood was quickly enlisted to support the war effort. Movies had helped prepare America for war. Now they would help win the war.

written by Undersecretary of State J. Reuben Clark. The Clark Memorandum repudiated the Roosevelt Corollary to the Monroe Doctrine, which for 25 years had justified U.S. intervention in Latin America.

In his first inaugural address, President Franklin D. Roosevelt dedicated the United States "to the policy of the good neighbor," bestowing a name on the new relationship with Latin America. Secretary of State Cordell Hull stunned Latin America in December 1933 at the Seventh Pan-American Conference by declaring, "no state has the right to intervene in the international or external affairs of another." The marines left Nicaragua in 1933 and Haiti in 1934. In the Hull-Alfara Treaty of 1934, the United States finally gave Panama its political independence and surrendered the right to intervene in its affairs. Furthermore, when Mexico finally expropriated foreign oil properties in 1938, Roosevelt rejected calls to send in troops and let the action stand. The Good Neighbor Policy did not solve all the problems with Latin America. Fears of Yankee military power and economic might still remained, but the Good Neighbor Policy promoted better relations just when the United States needed hemispheric solidarity to meet the threat of global war.

THE COMING OF WORLD WAR II

Conflict in the Pacific

The first major threat to international stability following World War I came in the Far East, with Japan as the aggressor. Chronically short of raw materials and desperate to establish political and cultural hegemony in Asia, the Japanese looked enviously at Manchuria, China, Indochina, and the East Indies, where they could find iron ore, coal, rice, rubber, and petroleum. In September 1931 Japan invaded Manchuria, reducing the province to a puppet state, renamed Manchukuo in 1932. While Japan's aggression violated the League of Nations, the Treaties of Washington (1921–1922), and the Kellogg-Briand Pact, President Hoover, a peaceful man, refused to take strong actions in the Far East, explaining his policy was not to allow "under any circumstances anybody to deposit that baby in our lap."

Having rejected military intervention, Hoover also refused to impose economic sanctions against Japan, fearing such reprisals might hurt American exports or, worse yet, lead to war. Instead, Hoover applied the Stimson Doctrine (named after Secretary of State Henry L. Stimson), which revived the Wilsonian policy of refusing to recognize governments based on force. Expecting bolder measures, Japan ignored this slap on the wrist and concluded the United States would not use military might to oppose her designs on the Far East, a misapprehension for which Japan paid dearly in the next decade.

In 1933 the League of Nations condemned Japan's aggression in Manchuria. Determined to rival the colonial powers of Europe, Japan responded by withdrawing from the League of Nations. Justifying this action, one Japanese leader complained that Europe's leaders had taught Japan the game of poker but, having acquired all the chips, Europe now condemned poker as immoral and proposed to take up contract bridge.

Japan preferred to gamble. The following year, 1934, Japan terminated the Five-Power Naval Treaty of 1922, which had limited its naval power in the Pacific. When Japan walked out of the London Naval Conference in 1935, naval disarmament was dead, leaving Japan free to build an Asian empire, confident the Western powers, including the United States, would not use force to oppose her actions.

At first President Roosevelt seemed to follow Hoover's Far Eastern policy. The new administration continued to withhold recognition from Manchukuo, and Roosevelt's secretary of state, Cordell Hull, peppered Japan with diplomatic notes on the sanctity of treaties. Yet these measures obscured subtle policy changes. Instead of concentrating on Japan, the United States attempted to strengthen China, largely through technical and financial aid. The idea was to build China into an effective counterweight to Japan. By 1935, however, the United States acknowledged Japan's overwhelming superiority in the Far East and adopted a neutral posture toward China.

In 1937 Japan invaded China, a clear violation of the Nine-Power Treaty, the Kellogg-Briand Pact, and the Four-Party Treaty. The fighting erupted in the north and then spread quickly to the south where Japan attacked Shanghai, China's largest port. Furious fighting followed in Nanking, where Japanese troops routed the Chinese in less than a month, after which the Japanese occupied the city and perpetrated the "rape of Nanking," an orgy of looting and murder. In response to Japan's renewed aggression, the League of Nations sponsored a conference of the Nine-Power Treaty members (and others) at Brussels in November 1937. As the delegates debated whether or not to impose economic sanctions against Japan, the United States announced it would not support sanctions. The conference adjourned after passing a report that mildly criticized Japan for violating the Nine-Power Treaty.

Any doubts regarding the U.S. desire to avoid war vanished a few weeks later. In December 1937 Japanese aircraft bombed the *Panay*, a U.S. gunboat stationed on the Yangtze River near Nanking, killing 3 Americans and injuring 43 more. While the attack angered the public, few calls for war rang out similar to those following the sinking of the *Maine* or the *Lusitania*. If anything, Americans remained pensive and calm, as though they were determined to avoid what they regarded as earlier mistakes. Senator William E. Borah, chairman of the Foreign Relations Committee, called the incident "just one of those regrettable things," while Senator Henrik Shipstead of Minnesota thought Americans should "get the hell out of China war zones." Secretary Hull sent sharply worded protests to Tokyo, but the United States quickly accepted Japan's "profound apology," which included indemnities for the injured and relatives of the dead, promises against future attacks, and punishment of the pilots responsible for the bloodshed. In short, by the end of 1937, as one historian has noted, "America's Far Eastern Policy had retreated to inaction."

The Rome-Berlin Axis

The modern world had never known a leader like Adolf Hitler. Of course, he was a charismatic personality and a spellbinding orator, but history had seen such men before. What made Hitler unique was his ability to articulate a nation's darkest fears and hatreds and then turn them to his own twisted purposes. Winston Churchill offered a profound truth when he described Hitler as the "monstrous product of former wrongs and shame."

Hitler exploited the psychological injuries inflicted on Germans by World War I. Rare indeed was the German who did not feel stunned by his country's sudden, unexpected defeat or who did not seethe with anger over the harsh peace imposed by the victors. In truth, most Germans felt humiliated by their defeat and despised the Treaty of Versailles. Hitler's great genius (and history's great tragedy) was his ability to tap into his countrymen's anger and resentment. Exploiting the ugly strain of anti-Semitism in German culture, he blamed many of the nation's economic woes on German Jews, reducing them to scapegoats. In addition, he attacked the Treaty of Versailles, telling his countrymen they would regain their national honor only if they repudiated the war's verdict and abrogated the treaty. Purged of so-called Jewish traitors, cleared of the blame for causing the war, freed from onerous reparation payments, and rescued from emasculating disarmament, Germany would rise anew and reclaim her position as a world leader.

The 1920s had prepared Germans to embrace any leader who promised to restore national pride. The Treaty of Versailles had saddled Germany with a reparations bill of $34 billion in 1921. Unable to make the interest payments, let alone the principal, Germany staggered beneath the burden until its economy dissolved into severe unemployment and hyperinflation.

Confronted by Germany's imminent economic collapse, the United States offered a measure of relief. In 1924 Charles Dawes, a prominent American banker, worked out a proposal (the Dawes Plan) that reduced the reparations bill and provided Germany with an American loan. In 1929 the so-called Young Plan, developed by another American banker, Owen D. Young, cut reparations to $2 billion, but even that proved too much when the Great

Depression struck. Germany entered the 1930s with its economy in shambles. Poverty-stricken and chafing under the blame for World War I, Germans desperately wanted to reclaim their self-respect. Adolf Hitler vowed to restore this and more.

Hitler came to power in 1933, promising to repudiate the Treaty of Versailles and reassert German military might in Europe. True to his word, he immediately pulled Germany out of the League of Nations. In 1935 he rearmed Germany and started a peacetime draft, clear violations of the Treaty of Versailles. Recognizing Germany's right to rearm, Great Britain and France did not oppose Hitler's actions.

Next Hitler concentrated on forging alliances. When Benito Mussolini, whose Fascist party had won control of Italy in 1922, attacked helpless Ethiopia in 1935, Hitler recognized a kindred spirit and made overtures to Italy. As these negotiations went forward, Germany and Japan signed the Anti-Comintern Pact (forerunner of a full-scale military alliance) in 1936. Shortly thereafter Germany and Italy formed the Rome-Berlin Axis. That same year German troops reoccupied the Rhineland, the German-speaking region between the Rhine River and France. Once again, France and Great Britain did not oppose Hitler's bold advance, for they believed (or wanted to believe) the Rhineland would satisfy his ambitions.

But the Rhineland only whetted Hitler's appetite. Intent on reuniting all German-speaking peoples of Europe under the "Third Reich," Hitler annexed Austria in 1938. Once again, the British and the French acquiesced, hoping Austria would be Hitler's last stop. Later that year he seized the Sudentenland, the German-speaking region of western Czechoslovakia.

This time France and Great Britain felt compelled to act. In September 1938 Edouard Daladier, the premier of France, and Neville Chamberlain, Britain's prime minister, met with Hitler in Munich, Germany, to demand whether he had further designs on Europe. Fearing they could not count on each other to use force, British and French leaders eagerly accepted Hitler's promises not to seek additional territory in Europe. Upon arriving in England, Chamberlain told his anxious countrymen he had returned with an agreement that guaranteed "peace in our time." In less than a year, Munich would become synonymous with shameful appeasement and Chamberlain would be vilified for believing Hitler's lies.

By 1938, then, Hitler had kept his promise to avenge the humiliations Germans had suffered at Versailles. Germany's frontiers were larger than they had been in 1914, Germany was rearmed, and German national pride had been restored. In addition, Germany had acquired powerful allies in Japan and in Italy, whose military forces had demonstrated their taste for aggression by attacking China and Ethiopia.

All this had transpired virtually unopposed by the victors of World War I. The League of Nations had failed to act and its member states had offered only feeble protests. Their caution reflected the mood of a war-weary world. Everyone hoped the Germans, Italians, and Japanese would be satisfied with their acquisitions and stop expanding. In retrospect, such hopes were clearly wrong, but at the time they did not appear unfounded. Western leaders assumed they were dealing with reasonable and responsible men: They had no way of knowing appeasement would only fuel the Axis dictators' appetites for expansion.

Benito Mussolini and Adolf Hitler share their diplomatic triumph over France and England in Munich in 1938.

Axis Takeovers in Europe, 1936–1939

The United States responded to Europe's turmoil with caution. Preoccupied with the Great Depression, President Roosevelt had little time or energy to deal with foreign affairs. Yet America's timidity also reflected the strength of isolationist sentiment. Congress, not the president, played the dominant role in foreign affairs for much of the 1930s, and Congress was determined to keep the United States out of another European conflict.

Roosevelt's first diplomatic initiative involved the Soviet Union. Hoping to expand foreign trade and to use the Soviet Union to balance Japan in the Far East, he formally recognized the Soviet Union in 1933, provoking the wrath of isolationists and anti-Communists alike. In addition, Roosevelt raised eyebrows by refusing to cooperate with international efforts to combat the global depression. Instead of supporting the London Economic Conference of 1933, which tried to stabilize international currencies, Roosevelt shocked Western leaders by taking the United States off the gold standard. Outraged by Roosevelt's economic nationalism, the British accused the United States of under-

mining international efforts to restore economic stability to the world's markets.

Meanwhile, isolationist forces were gaining strength in the Senate. In 1934 Gerald P. Nye, a Republican from North Dakota, accused international bankers and weapons manufacturers of manipulating the United States into World War I in order to increase profits. While Nye never substantiated his charges, he held hearings for three years, feeding the public's fears the United States had been suckered into World War I by "merchants of death" who put profits above the national interest. If only Wilson's government had withheld foreign loans, clamped an embargo on trade with the belligerents, and kept Americans off ships in war zones, the argument went, the United States could have remained at peace.

Privately, Roosevelt opposed the retreat into isolation. In his view, the United States, like it or not, had to play an important role in world affairs because it had become a major power. But Roosevelt's freedom to act was severely limited by isolationists in Congress. Unlike Wilson, who had successfully resisted the challenge to his control over foreign affairs embodied in the Gore-McLemore resolutions, Roosevelt could not prevent Congress from converting its own commitment to peace into binding legislation.

Between 1935 and 1937, Congress passed three separate neutrality laws that clamped an embargo on arms sales to belligerents, forbade American ships from entering war zones and prohibited them from being armed, barred Americans from traveling on belligerent ships, and restricted trade with belligerents on non-embargoed exports to a "cash and carry" basis. Clearly, Congress was determined not to repeat what it regarded as the mistakes that had plunged the United States into World War I.

The neutrality laws troubled Roosevelt. Convinced these laws posed a serious threat to presidential power, he looked for opportunities to reassert his leadership. In a speech delivered in Chicago in October 1937, Roosevelt spoke of the need to "quarantine the aggressors," but he immediately retreated into silence when it became clear the public did not support vigorous action. This was where matters stood when Hitler decided to take advantage of the world's indecisiveness.

Conflict in Europe

On August 24, 1939, Germany and the Soviet Union signed the Nazi-Comintern Pact, a non-aggression treaty. In exchange for the pact, Hitler agreed to grant the Soviet Union a sphere of influence over eastern Poland, Estonia, Latvia, Finland, and Bessarabia (northeastern Romania), while Stalin approved Germany's designs on western Poland and Lithuania. His eastern flank protected, Hitler invaded Poland on September 1, 1939. Two days later, France and Great Britain honored their treaty obligations to defend Poland and declared war on Germany. World War II had formally begun.

Poland was no match for Germany. Though its people fought bravely, Poland fell in a few weeks, and then the land fighting in Europe stopped for several months. The Sitzkrieg (Phony War or Bore War) ended in April 1940, when German tanks swept through Denmark and Norway. Hitler's next victim was the Netherlands, which fell in five days.

Most observers expected Germany to stop there. If German troops marched again, they would have to confront France, with her army of 3 million men poised behind the Maginot line, a military engineering feat of miles of concrete underground installations. Undeterred, Germany attacked France in May. Hitler outflanked the supposedly invincible Maginot line by slicing his tank divisions through the Ardennes Forest. France surrendered in June, and only the heroic boatlift at Dunkirk saved 300,000 British and French troops from capture. With his homeland now controlled by pro-German sympathizers who installed a new government called Vichy France, Charles de Gaulle fled to London, declared himself the leader of Free France, and established a government in exile.

Following France's defeat, Great Britain braced herself for invasion. To soften her up, Hitler ordered his Luftwaffe (air force) to bomb Britain mercilessly. British fighter pilots ultimately won the Battle of Britain, establishing control of the air space over the British Isles; and as 1940 ended, Great Britain, though knocked to her knees and badly bloodied, had survived.

Americans watched the bloodshed with the gravest concern. During the first year of the war

Hitler's armies devastated Poland with their tremendous force and firepower. Here soldiers drive through a town battered by repeated bombings.

bookstores sold out their entire stock of Rand McNally's European maps as people tried to keep abreast of the German Blitzkrieg (lightning war). Throughout the fall of 1940, CBS's Edward R. Murrow, speaking from the rooftops of London, kept Americans glued to their radios with stirring reports of the dog fights.

Like Wilson before him, Roosevelt responded to Europe's war by declaring America's neutrality. Unlike the idealistic Wilson, however, he did not ask his countrymen to be "neutral in thought as well as in action." After France fell, Roosevelt feared a German victory would threaten America's future security, and he resolved to save England at all costs—including war.

Before he could rescue Britain, however, Roosevelt first had to regain control of American foreign policy. Soon after Germany invaded Poland, he pushed a fourth Neutrality Act through Congress. It modified the earlier legislation by permitting belligerents to purchase war materials, provided they paid cash and carried the goods away in their own ships. This act was pro-British because England controlled the Atlantic. Using private companies as go-betweens and acting on his own authority, Roosevelt then rushed thousands of planes and guns to Britain. In September 1940 he persuaded Congress to pass the first peacetime draft in American history and signed an executive agreement with Great Britain transferring 50 destroyers in exchange for 99 year leases on eight British bases in the Western Hemisphere. Most Americans supported the destroyers-for-bases deal. When the first ships slipped out of Boston harbor, motorists on the Charleston Bridge blew their horns, while pedestrians cheered from the shore.

Fearing Roosevelt was duplicating Wilson's mistakes, isolationists opposed the tilt toward Britain. Strongest in the Midwest, they represented the entire spectrum of political thought, including Republicans such as Senators Arthur Vandenberg of Michigan and Robert Taft of Ohio; Democrats such as Joseph Kennedy, ambassador to Great Britain; and progressives such as Wisconsin's Senator Robert La Follette. Isolationists offered several antiwar arguments, some compelling, others specious. Betraying a deep strain of anti-Semitism, aviator Charles Lindbergh accused Jews of trying to push the United States into war with Germany. Vandenberg warned against the growth of executive power, anticipating later concerns about the "imperial presidency." Yet their most powerful argument was that Europe's war did not threaten "fortress America." Germany had no designs on the Western Hemisphere, they insisted. Therefore, the United States should sit this war out because Germany did not endanger America's security.

Isolation and the Election of 1940

The war dominated the election of 1940. Roosevelt easily won renomination for an unprecedented third term and proceeded to dump Vice President John Garner, who had opposed a third term for the president. As his new running mate, Roosevelt picked Secretary of Agriculture

Henry A. Wallace. The Republicans passed over their front runners (isolationists all) to nominate a dark horse candidate, Wendell L. Willkie of Indiana. Head of a large public utilities holding company, Willkie was a liberal Republican who had been a Democrat most of his life.

Few American elections have been so dirty. Willkie faced such a barrage of missiles when he spoke in the big Democratic cities the *New York Times* issued daily reports of the objects thrown and the hits registered. (The projectiles ranged from rotten eggs to a five-pound steel wastebasket that split open the head of a teenage girl.) At first Willkie tried to attract voters by saying the New Deal amounted to socialism; but when this charge failed, he accused Roosevelt of trying to maneuver the United States into war. Stung by these attacks, Roosevelt assured American parents on the eve of the election: "I have said this before, but I shall say it again and again: Your boys are not going to be sent into any foreign wars."

Not since 1916 had a presidential election been decided by such a narrow popular vote. Roosevelt defeated Willkie 27 million votes to 22 million votes, and 449 electoral votes to 82. Democrats gained 7 seats in the House, but Republicans picked up 5 in the Senate. As New York City Mayor Fiorello La Guardia put it, Americans preferred "Roosevelt with his known faults to Willkie with his unknown virtues."

After the election, Churchill informed Roosevelt that England had run out of money and no longer could purchase war supplies. Consequently, the president replaced "cash and carry" with "lend-lease." In a press conference, he compared lend-lease to offering a garden hose to a neighbor whose house was on fire, explaining that after the fire had been extinguished, the neighbor would return the hose. Isolationists saw things differently. "Lending war equipment is a good deal like lending chewing gum," snarled Senator Taft of Ohio. "You don't want it back."

Roosevelt submitted the lend-lease bill to Congress in January 1941, setting off months of debate. The nastiest comment came from Senator Burton Wheeler, who called lend-lease a "Triple A foreign policy that would plow under every fourth American boy." Americans argued about lend-lease in barber shops, board meetings, and grocery stores across the country. Early in March, Congress passed the bill and Roosevelt signed it on March 11, 1941. With "this legislation," he declared, "our country has determined to do its full part in creating an adequate arsenal of democracy."

To cement the Anglo-American bond, Roosevelt met with Churchill in August 1941 on board the USS *Augusta* off the coast of Newfoundland. There they negotiated the Atlantic Charter, which pledged mutual support for democracy, freedom of the seas, arms reductions, and a just peace. In everything but name the United States and Great Britain were now allies.

While the public strongly supported aid for Great Britain, many Americans balked at helping the Russians. After Hitler invaded Russia in June 1941, the Soviet Union had no choice but to join the Grand Alliance against Germany. Roosevelt immediately offered lend-lease aid to the Soviet Union. While critics denounced Roosevelt, Churchill, who knew wars often made strange bedfellows, supported the decision wholeheartedly. "If Hitler invaded Hell," declared Churchill, "I would make at least a favorable reference to the Devil in the House of Commons." In November 1941, the United States allocated $1 billion in lend-lease to the Soviets. By 1945 America's allies had received $50 billion, four times the amount loaned to the allies in World War I.

In April 1941 the United States went beyond financial assistance by constructing bases in Greenland. During the summer American destroyers began escorting convoys as far as Iceland. To protect convoys the rest of the way, the American navy started tracking German submarines and signaling their locations to British destroyers. In September a German submarine attacked the *Greer*, the American destroyer that had been shadowing it. Assuring the public the *Greer* had been on an innocent mail run to Iceland, Roosevelt then ordered the navy to "shoot on sight" any German ships in the waters surrounding Iceland. Yet the president stopped short of asking Congress for a for-

Kneeling in prayer near the Capitol in Washington, D.C., members of the "Mother's Crusade" against the lend-lease bill plead for Congress not to pass the measure.

mal declaration of war; for a few more months the United States maintained the fiction of neutrality.

Pearl Harbor

Thanks to the public's preoccupation with Europe, Roosevelt had a relatively free hand in the Far East. Here the problem centered on Japan's march to acquire colonies. Japan wanted to build what it called the Greater East Asia Co-Prosperity Sphere, an empire that would encompass large parts of China, Southeast Asia, and the western Pacific. Yet Japan's dream of expansion clashed with the two main pillars of America's Far Eastern policy—preserving the "Open Door" for trade, and protecting China's territorial integrity.

After Japan invaded China in 1937, relations between Washington and Tokyo deteriorated rapidly. The United States pressured Japan to withdraw, but Tokyo refused, insisting the United States must drop all aid to Chiang Kai-shek, the leader of the Chinese government. In July 1939 Secretary of State Cordell Hull, aware American exports fueled Japan's war machine, threatened to impose economic sanctions. While Hull also considered clamping an embargo on all war materials, Roosevelt held back, fearing Japan would attack the Dutch East Indies to secure the oil it needed.

Events quickly forced Roosevelt's hand. After Germany defeated France in 1940, Vichy France "invited" Japan to occupy northern Indochina, an obvious step toward the Dutch East Indies. Roosevelt now believed Japan wanted to bring all of Asia under its control, threatening America's quest for free markets. Late in September he placed an embargo on scrap iron and steel, hoping economic sanctions would strengthen moderates in Japan who wished to avoid conflict with the United States. Following the embargo, however, Japan promptly negotiated the Tripartite Pact with Germany and Italy. To protect its northern flank, Japan then signed a five-year nonaggression pact in April 1941 with the Soviet Union. Japan punctuated these diplomatic maneuvers by occupying bases in southern Indochina.

Roosevelt's response was swift and decisive. As Japan tightened the noose around the Dutch East Indies, the Philippines, and British Malaya, Roosevelt retaliated in July 1941 by freezing Japanese assets in the United States and cutting off steel, oil, and aviation fuel exports to Japan.

The sanctions hurt Japan. Striving to secure the materials her military needed, Japan negotiated with the United States throughout 1941. Instead of compromising, however, the United States asked Japan to withdraw immediately from Indochina and China, concessions that would have ended Japan's dream of economic and military hegemony in Asia.

In a last ditch effort to avoid war, Japan promised not to march further south, not to attack the Soviet Union to the north, and not to declare war against the United States if Germany and America went to war. In return, Japan asked the United States to abandon Chiang Kaishek. Roosevelt refused. In October 1941 the Japanese government fell and General Hideki Tojo, the leader of the militants, seized power. War was imminent.

In November 1941 Tokyo offered to compromise if Washington would soften its demands, but Secretary of State Hull remained adamant. Having already decided on war if the United States rejected this last olive branch, Japan issued the final order on December 2 for an air strike on Pearl Harbor. More than a year earlier American cryptographers had broken Japan's highest diplomatic code (the Purple Cipher), though not the military code. In early December the volume of diplomatic cables increased, raising American suspicions, and on December 6 the United States intercepted a hostile sounding message from Tokyo to Japan's ambassador in Washington.

Most military experts expected Japan to attack the Dutch East Indies to secure oil and rubber. Before striking there, however, Japan moved to neutralize American power in the western Pacific. At 8:00 A.M. on Sunday morning, December 7, 1941, Japanese planes hit Pearl Harbor, executing the most daring surprise attack in military history. In less than two hours, Japan reduced the base to flames, sank two battleships, and heavily damaged six others. The remainder of the fleet was either damaged or destroyed. The United States lost more than 2400 dead, while Japan's sustained minimal losses.

Yet Japan had won a costly victory. Her planes failed to destroy America's aircraft carriers, as routine maneuvers had taken the flattops out to sea before the attack. More important, the attack united the American public as nothing else could have. Opposition to Roosevelt simply evaporated. Speaking for his fellow isolationists, Senator Wheeler shouted: "The only thing to do now is to lick the hell out of them." On December 8 Congress declared war on Japan with but one dissenting vote. Germany declared war on the United States on December 11.

AMERICA AT WAR

Practically everyone agreed what had to be done: Jump-start the economy, raise an army, and win the war. Yet the economic challenges facing the United States were truly mind-boggling. New plants had to be built and existing ones expanded; raw materials had to be procured and distributed where needed; labor had to be kept on the job; production had to be raised; and all this had to be accomplished without producing soaring inflation.

Economic Mobilization

Following Pearl Harbor, Roosevelt made the switch from reformer to war leader with ease, telling reporters that "Dr. New Deal" had to be replaced by "Dr. Win-the-War." Like Wilson before him, Roosevelt wished to avoid government controls. He, too, would fail. World War II created a huge (and apparently permanent) federal bureaucracy.

In January 1942 Roosevelt created the War Production Board (WPB) to "exercise general responsibility" over the economy. To lead the agency, he selected Donald Nelson, the highly respected head of Sears, Roebuck and Company. Yet Roosevelt refused to make Nelson the "czar" of American industry, reserving real power for himself.

Business leaders responded coolly to Nelson's call for economic conversion. With profits already booming because of the war in Europe, many industrialists did not wish to jeopardize their position in the domestic market by converting factories to military production. Others worried about getting stuck with inflated capacity after the war ended. As one executive cautioned, "Guns are not windshield wipers."

Detroit provided the test case for economic conversion. Not only did automobile makers possess the capacity to produce badly needed tanks and planes, their assembly lines consumed 80 percent of the nation's rubber, 18 percent of its steel, and 14 percent of its copper. Yet when Roosevelt called for 50,000 airplanes a year, Detroit ran for cover. Automotive sales had shot up by 40 percent in 1941, and industry executives did not want to risk profits.

To gain their support, Washington offered even greater returns. The armed services suspended competitive bidding, offered cost-plus contracts, guaranteed low-cost loans for retooling, and paid huge subsidies for plant construction and equipment. Lured by huge profits, Detroit made the switch. Aircraft production leaped from 6000 planes in 1940 to 47,000 in 1942; by 1943 production had jumped to 86,000; and by the end of the war it exceeded 100,000, more than doubling Roosevelt's goal. Secretary of War Henry Stimson defended Detroit's huge profits, explaining "in a capitalist country, you have to let business make money out of the process or business won't work."

Consumer industries prospered, too. Robert W. Woodruff of Coca-Cola made his 5-cent drink the most widely distributed consumer product in the world by convincing the army that soldiers needed Coke to refresh their fighting spirit. Backed by government subsidies, Woodruff built an international network of plants, and then purchased them at a fraction of their cost after the war, ensuring Coca-Cola's postwar supremacy in the soft drink industry.

Most military contracts went to big businesses because large-scale production simplified buying. At Roosevelt's insistence the Justice Department stopped prosecuting antitrust violators shortly after Pearl Harbor, despite clear evidence international cartels (particu-

In a little more than an hour, the surprise attack at Pearl Harbor had killed more than 2400 American sailors and damaged or sunk eight battleships, including the USS *Arizona* pictured here.

larly those involved in developing synthetic rubber) had impeded the war effort. Not until 1944 did Roosevelt allow the Justice Department to resume antitrust prosecutions. Moreover, he did so not to protect small businesspeople or consumers but to block business arrangements that might endanger national defense in the future.

Government policies accelerated business consolidations. Overall, industrial profits doubled, but small industries got crowded away from the federal trough. In 1940 the top 100 companies had produced 30 percent of America's industrial output; by 1943, they produced 70 percent and the other 175,000 companies the rest. After congressional hearings, chaired by Senator Harry S Truman from Missouri, accused conglomerates of squeezing out small businesses, Congress established the Smaller War Plants Corporation in 1943, but small companies simply lacked the capital to convert to war production and the political connections to borrow enough money to retool.

Research, supported by government grants, developed into a major new industry during World War II. When the war began, Germany enjoyed scientific and technological superiority, especially in tanks and artillery. To counter this advantage, Roosevelt created the Office of Scientific Research and Development (OSRD) in 1942. Its most ambitious project was the the atomic bomb. Alerted by Albert Einstein of Hitler's interest in developing nuclear weapons, Roosevelt put over $2 billion and 500,000 workers into the Manhattan Project, the atomic bomb's code name.

Federal funds also supported the development of radar, flame throwers, antiaircraft artillery, rockets, and penicillin. New blood plasma techniques permitted 13 million pints of blood to be collected. Moreover, antimalarial drugs and insecticides, including DDT, dramatically reduced the incidence of mosquito-carried diseases among troops in the Mediterranean and Pacific. Thanks to these advances, the death rate of wounded soldiers who reached medical installations was half that of World War I. Even more amazing, the noncombat-related death rate among troops was virtually the same as the domestic death rate.

No less than industry, American agriculture performed impressively during World War II. To encourage production, Roosevelt allowed farmers to make large profits by setting crop prices at 110 percent of parity, defined as the ratio between agricultural prices and manufactured goods prices during the agricultural boom years of 1910 to 1914. Good weather, mechanization, and a dramatic increase in the use of fertilizers did the rest. Cash income for farmers jumped from $2.3 billion in 1940 to $9.5 billion in 1945.

The distribution of profits in agriculture followed the same pattern as industry: The "big guys" flourished, while the "little guys" floundered. Most profits went to large-scale operators who could afford expensive machinery and fertilizers. Many small farmers, saddled with huge debts from the depression, abandoned their farms for jobs in defense plants or the armed services. Over 5 million farm residents (17 percent of the total) left rural areas during the war.

Overall, the war brought unprecedented prosperity to Americans. Per capita income rose from $373 in 1940 to $1074 in 1945, and total personal income went from $81 billion to $182 billion during the same years. Workers never had it so good. The total income of families increased dramatically as large numbers of women joined the work force, creating millions of two-income families.

In fact, World War II brought Americans more money than they could spend, for the production of consumer goods could not keep pace with the new buying power. During 1942 the gap between disposable income and available goods approached $17 billion. Hair curlers, toaster, dishes, diapers, spoons—everything was in short supply. As early as 1943 many manufacturers started accepting postwar orders. General Electric's ad the month of the Normandy invasion announced, "Now we'll be glad to put your name down for earliest available data on postwar air conditioning and refrigeration equipment."

Steeped in the values of a consumer society, Americans emerged from the depression with a backlog of desires only to face empty shelves. Most people accepted the deprivations stoically, but others hoarded what they could—shoes, canned goods, used tires, and other scarce products. If stores did not have what they wanted, some customers grabbed anything. On December 7, 1944, the third anniversary of Pearl Harbor, Macy's set a new sales record as many of its stores sold down to the bare shelves.

Controlling Inflation

The shortages led to inflation. Prices rose 18 percent between 1941 and the end of 1942, with an increase of 11 percent in food prices alone in 1942. Fearing inflation would destroy the economy, Congress created the Office of Price Administration (OPA) in January 1942 to control prices. The OPA quickly defined the ceiling for individual merchants as the highest price they had charged for a particular item in March 1942.

Since the success of price controls depended on the rationing of scarce goods, the OPA also introduced ten major rationing programs in 1942. For staple products in short supply, the OPA issued ration cards and coupons to more than 120 million people. To purchase sugar, meat, butter, bacon, cheese, alcohol, canned goods, and shoes, shoppers had to hand coupons to retailers, who found the whole system hopelessly cumbersome. The government rationed gasoline, too, allowing drivers a mere three gallons a week. To a society intoxicated with the automobile, three gallons a week posed a real hardship.

Relying on voluntarism and patriotism, the OPA extolled the virtues of self-sacrifice, telling people to "Use it up, wear it out, make it do, or do without." Yet the response to rationing often reflected old-fashioned Yankee ingenuity. When the OPA ordered a 10 percent cut in the cloth for women's bathing suits, manufacturers introduced the two-piece bathing suit. A bare midriff had suddenly become patriotic.

In addition to rationing, Washington attacked inflation by reducing the public's purchasing power. The administration targeted war bond sales directly at working-class families. Secretary of the Treasury Henry Morgenthau rejected a poster that showed a woman in a mink coat buying war bonds. He told the artist to draw a woman in overalls. The plan worked. War bonds not only helped finance the war; by 1944 they absorbed more than 7 percent of the real personal income of Americans.

The government also attacked inflation through tax reforms. Fewer than four million Americans had filed tax returns in 1939, and most blue-collar workers that year had paid no income taxes at all. To cool off consumer purchasing power, Congress passed the Revenue Act of 1942, which raised corporate taxes, increased the excess profits tax from 60 to 90 percent, and levied a flat 5 percent withholding tax on anyone who earned more than $642 a year. By mid-1943 most American workers had taxes deducted weekly from wages, and the number of tax returns at the end of the year leaped to 30 million. Tax reform during World War II reduced the public's buying power, forced citizens to pay more than 40 percent of the war's total cost as the war progressed, and laid the foundation for postwar tax policies.

Wage controls offered another tool for controlling inflation. The War Labor Board (WLB), established in 1942, had the power to set wages, hours, and working conditions. Because it had to proceed on a case-by-case basis, however, wage disputes quickly swamped the WLB. The government needed a test case to establish national guidelines, and steel workers provided such a case.

In the summer of 1942, workers in several steel mills demanded a dollar-a-day raise. In response, the WLB adopted what came to be called the "Little Steel" formula. Using January 1, 1941, as the starting point, the Little Steel formula permitted wages to rise by 15 percent to compensate for the cost of living increases up to May 1942, but additional pay increases were prohibited for the duration of the war. This meant the steel workers received only a 5.5 percent raise (about 44 cents a day) because they had already won pay hikes earlier in the year. The Little Steel formula was not inflationary because workers in other industries had already secured the maximum increase.

In practice, however, the Little Steel formula did not freeze wages. It applied only to hourly wages, not weekly totals. Thus, while

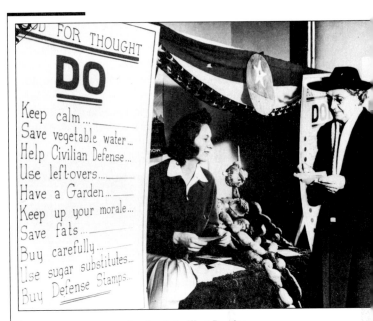

At a consumer conservation booth in West Dundee Township, Illinois, women offered "food for thought" in an attempt to help the war effort.

wage rates increased a modest 24 percent during the war, the weekly paychecks of workers, thanks to overtime, rose 70 percent.

Though price controls offered another effective weapon against inflation, the government refused to use them until labor demanded action. In October 1942 Roosevelt appointed James F. Byrnes, his chief all-purpose advisor, head of the Office of Economic Stabilization, later renamed the Office of War Mobilization. Byrnes instituted broad price freezes in the spring, and by the summer prices had stopped climbing. To placate consumers still further, Byrnes rolled back prices 10 percent on selected agricultural products, including meat and butter.

Working together, these programs brought inflation under control. After 1942 the annual inflation rate did not exceed 1.5 percent. Still, the administration's methods pleased no one. Everyone groused about taxes; manufacturers and farmers denounced price controls as an attack on their profits; and labor officials condemned wage freezes as an assault on their incomes.

Yet American workers clearly reaped a bonanza from World War II. Because the war created 17 million new jobs at the exact moment when 15 million men and women entered the armed services, unemployment virtually disappeared. In 1939 over 8 million people (17 percent of the work force) remained unemployed, but between 1939 and 1941 most traditional breadwinners got their jobs back. After Pearl Harbor, labor soared to an absolute premium, drawing into the work force previously unemployed and underemployed groups such as women, teenagers, blacks, senior citizens, and the handicapped.

The war also gave labor unions a lift. Under the benevolent hand of government protection, unions rebounded from their sharp decline of the 1920s and early 1930s. Union membership jumped from 10.5 million to 14.75 million during the war. The WLB enforced "maintenance of membership" agreements in all shops with defense contracts. Newly hired workers had 15 days to resign from the union. If they did not, the company had to collect their union dues. This represented a compromise between management's insistence upon an open shop (workers could join or drop the union at will) and labor's demand for a closed shop (all employees had to belong to the union).

Despite these gains, labor unrest increased throughout the war. After Pearl Harbor union officials pledged not to strike until the war ended, but inflation and wage restrictions quickly eroded their goodwill. Work stoppages rose from 2960 in 1942 to 4956 in 1944, though most ended quickly and did not harm the war effort. In 1943, however, coal miners went on strike and railroad workers threatened to follow. According to John L. Lewis, the fiery president of the United Mine Workers, the reason for the strike was simple: The average mine worker earned only $1700 in 1942 (well below the national average) and deserved a raise.

Lewis won a hefty pay increase for his men. By 1944 their wages averaged $2535 a year, the first time in American history coal miners earned more than most manufacturing workers. Yet labor's victory did not come cheaply. Most Americans condemned strikes as unpatriotic, and Roosevelt considered drafting or jailing the strikers. Lewis had supported Wendell Willkie in 1940, so there was no love lost between the president and the union leader. Privately,

Roosevelt offered to resign as president if Lewis promised to commit suicide, but publicly Roosevelt was a model of restraint with labor leaders. After all, labor formed a vital element of the New Deal coalition.

In contrast to the president, Congress took a hostile stand toward labor. Over Roosevelt's veto, it passed the Smith-Connally Act, which banned strikes in war industries, authorized the president to seize plants useful to the war effort, and limited political activity by unions. "In doing so," declared *Time* magazine, "it dealt Franklin Roosevelt the most stinging rebuke of his entire career, his worst domestic defeat of World War II." The Smith-Connally Act failed to end labor unrest. The bill's supporters blamed strikes on a handful of unruly labor barons, but in reality the pressure for strikes came from rank-and-file workers.

The Smith-Connally Act reflected a resurgence of conservatism, both in Congress and in the country at large. Democratic voters failed to turn out in large numbers in the congressional elections of 1942, as full employment seemed to weaken blue-collar voting. In addition, Congress did not allow soldiers away from home to vote. Though the Democrats continued to maintain a thin majority in both houses of Congress throughout the war, a coalition of Republicans and conservative Democrats after 1942 could defeat any measure. Secretary of the Treasury Morgenthau spoke the truth when he complained: "I can get all my New Dealers in the bathtub now."

Beginning in 1943 Roosevelt's opponents led a successful attack against the New Deal, refusing to fund the Civilian Conservation Corps, the Works Progress Administration, the National Youth Administration, and the National Resources and Planning Board. According to conservatives, these agencies had dangerously expanded federal power and deserved to die.

Election of 1944

With reform in retreat, the Republicans expected to win the election of 1944. Thomas E. Dewey, the dapper young governor of New York, won his party's nomination on the first ballot. (Harold Ickes quipped that the 42-year-old Dewey had thrown his diaper into the ring.)

While Dewey accepted the New Deal as part of American life, he opposed its expansion. No distance separated the two major candidates on foreign affairs: Dewey supported Roosevelt's foreign policy initiatives.

Despite his declining health, Roosevelt easily captured his party's nomination for a fourth term. In March 1944 doctors discovered he suffered from high blood pressure, creating special concern about his choice of a running mate. He dumped Vice President Henry Wallace, the ardent internationalist who promised to build "the Century of the Common Man" after the war ended. As his replacement, Roosevelt selected Harry S Truman, the little known senator from Missouri who had chaired the Senate hearings on wartime industrial profits.

The campaign revitalized Roosevelt. After delivering a flurry of vague speeches about ending poverty at home, he unveiled plans for a "GI Bill of Rights," promising liberal unemployment benefits, educational support, medical care, and housing loans for veterans. Congress approved it overwhelmingly in 1944. Fearing a Democratic windfall, Republicans again rallied their forces to defeat a federal voting bill permitting soldiers to cast absentee ballots. A Bill Mauldin cartoon aptly captured the disappointment of GIs, as Willie consoled his buddy by saying, "That's okay, Joe, at least we can take bets."

The smart money backed FDR, as the president easily won reelection. Unwilling to switch leaders while at war, the public stuck with Roosevelt to see the crisis through. The president received 25,611,936 votes to Dewey's 22,013,372, and he won in the Electoral College by 432 to 99.

Molding Public Opinion

Having witnessed the mistakes of World War I, Roosevelt did not want government propaganda to arouse or fuel false hopes. Shortly before Pearl Harbor, he created the Office of Facts and Figures under Archibald MacLeish, the Librarian of Congress. A gentle poet, MacLeish became embroiled in bureaucratic struggles with government agencies, the armed services, and the Office of Strategic Services. By 1944 the government had all but abandoned its efforts to shape public opinion about the war.

Private enterprise filled the void. Movies, comic strips, newspapers, books, and advertisements reduced the war to a struggle between good and evil as the Allies engaged in mortal combat with Japan and Germany. The Japanese bore the brunt of the propaganda, especially during the first two years of fighting. Caricatured with thick glasses and huge buck teeth, public portraits of the Japanese grew more ugly and vicious as deeply ingrained racism fed the stereotypes, reviving old fears of the "yellow peril."

Germans, by contrast, elicited more complex attitudes in Americans, largely because racism did not inflame passions. At first, Americans blamed Hitler for the war. As eyewitness accounts of German atrocities began to filter back from the front, however, the public's views shifted. Gradually, Americans came to blame not just the Nazis, but all Germans for the war.

Motion pictures emerged as the most important instrument of propaganda during World War II, but Hollywood made little effort to confront the war's complexities. Instead, the industry churned out a series of simple morality plays. War films featured exhausted, shell-shocked troops who battled the enemy to the end. Movies such as *Back to Bataan*, *Thirty-Seconds over Tokyo*, and *Guadalcanal Diary* showed a few Americans outfighting Japanese hordes. Hollywood also produced sympathetic portraits of America's allies, including the sentimental *Mrs. Miniver*, which won seven Academy Awards in 1942. Hollywood produced 982 movies during the war, enough for three new movies each week at the neighborhood theater.

Popular culture both fed and reflected the public's desire to win the war and get the boys back. Soldiers abroad wanted to return to Mom, and, as one GI told cartoonist Bill Mauldin, to a "piece of blueberry pie." Mauldin's characters, Willie and Joe, fought because they had to. They did not talk about building a new world; all they wanted was to go home to the good life in America—baths, steaks, and wives.

SOCIAL CHANGES DURING THE WAR

World War II produced important changes in American life, some subtle, others profound.

"Joe, yestiddy ya saved my life an' I swore I'd pay ya back. Here's my last pair of dry socks."

Bill Mauldin's cartoon characters, Willie and Joe, were popular not only at home but also among soldiers abroad.

Above all it set families in motion, pulling them off farms, out of small towns, and packing them into large urban areas. Urbanization had virtually stopped during the depression, but the war saw the number of city dwellers leap from 46 to 53 percent.

War industries sparked the urban growth. Detroit's population exploded as the automotive industry switched to war vehicles. Washington, D.C., became another boomtown, as tens of thousands of new workers staffed the swelling ranks of the bureaucracy. The most dramatic growth occurred in California. Of the 15 million civilians who moved across state lines during the war, over 2 million went to California to work in defense industries.

Women

The war had a dramatic impact on women. Easily the most visible change involved the sudden appearance of large numbers of women in uniform. The military organized women into auxiliary units with special uniforms, their own officers, and, amazingly, equal pay. By 1945 over 140,000 women had joined the Women's Army Corps (WAC); 60,000 the Army Nurses Corps; 100,000 the Women Accepted for Voluntary Emergency Service (WAVES); 14,000 the Navy Nurses Corps; 23,000 the marines; and 13,000 the Coast Guard. Most women who joined the armed services either filled traditional women's roles, such as nursing, or replaced men in non-combat jobs.

Women also substituted for men on the home front. For the first time in history married working women outnumbered single working women as 6.3 million women entered the work force during the war. Yet the majority of married women still did not work outside the home. Though women composed 37 percent of the civilian work force in 1945, only 22 percent of married women worked for wages. Nevertheless, the war challenged the conventional image of female behavior, as "Rosie the Riveter" became the popular symbol of women who abandoned traditional female occupations to work in defense industries.

Most observers expected women to retreat to the kitchen when the men returned home. Yet when the Women's Bureau surveyed working women in 1943, 70 percent said they hoped to keep their jobs after the war. Many women liked the economic freedom wages brought (sales of women's clothing doubled during the war), while others insisted they had to work to improve their family's standard of living, anticipating arguments for the two-income family after the war.

Women paid a high price for their economic independence. Outside employment did not free wives from domestic duties. The same women who put in full days in offices and factories went home to cook, clean, shop, and care for children. They had not one job, but two, and the only way they could fill both was to become "superwomen" who sacrificed relaxation, recreation, and sleep.

Yet not even a "superwoman" could be two places at once, which raised the question that troubled many Americans, "Who's minding the children?" A few industries, such as Kaiser Steel, offered day-care facilities, but most women had to make their own arrangements. Whether relatives or babysitters filled the void, child-care problems often arose, with a corresponding rise in the incidence of "latchkey" children.

Social critics had a field day attacking women. Social workers blamed working mothers for the rise in juvenile delinquency during the war, while other critics condemned women for their immodesty, self-indulgence, drinking, dress standards, and sexual promiscuity. "Choose any set of criteria you like," wrote the famous anthropologist Margaret Mead in 1946, "and the answer is the same: women and men are confused, uncertain and discontented with the present definition of women's place in America."

Amid this confusion, many women elected to cling to the familiar by embracing the traditional roles of housewives and mothers. From 1941 to 1945, the marriage rate oscillated between 93 and 105 per 1000 women between the ages of 17 and 29, well above the 89.1 for women of that age group during the "normal" years of 1925 to 1929. The birthrate increased, too, rebounding sharply from the all-time low of 18 to 19 per 1000 people during the depression. In 1943 the birthrate jumped to 22.7, and by 1946 it reached 25, where it remained with modest fluctuations for the rest of the decade. Overall, the "baby boom" did not signal a return to large families; rather, the birthrate rose because women married at younger ages and had their families earlier in life.

Hasty marriages between young partners often proved brittle. Wartime separations forced newlyweds to develop new roles and become self-reliant, and many couples later found it difficult to reestablish their relationships. Rather than remain in unhappy marriages, they often opted for divorce. In 1946 the American courts granted a record 600,000 divorces. By 1950 the divorce rate stood at one-quarter of the marriages, well above the prewar levels.

Yet Americans had not soured on marriage. The divorce rate had been climbing steadily (except during the depression years when many people could not afford to get married or divorced) since 1900. Furthermore, most Americans who divorced during the 1940s promptly remarried. They had rejected their mates, not marriage.

During the war, a growing number of women not only joined the armed services, but also helped out in the labor force at home by filling jobs normally held by men.

Minorities

World War II accelerated long-developing social trends for blacks. The war changed where many blacks lived and worked, as they moved to cities and found jobs in factories. Indeed, more than one million blacks migrated to the North during the war (twice the number who did so in World War I), and more than two million found work in defense industries. Yet blacks continued to be the last hired and the first fired, and other forms of discrimination remained blatant, especially in housing and employment.

Black leaders fought discrimination vigorously. In the spring of 1941 (months before America entered the war), the president of the Brotherhood of Sleeping Car Porters, A. Philip Randolph, with strong backing from the National Association for the Advancement of Colored People (NAACP), called for 150,000 blacks to march on Washington to protest discrimination in defense industries. Embarrassed and concerned, Roosevelt issued an executive order prohibiting discrimination in defense industries and creating the Fair Employment Practices Commission (FEPC). But the FEPC's tiny staff lacked the power and resources to enforce its decisions. During the war the FEPC did not even process most complaints, and contractors ignored 35 of the 45 compliance orders it issued.

Blacks fared no better in the public sector. Most blacks in the federal bureaucracy worked as janitors, and the armed services treated blacks as second-class citizens. The marines excluded blacks; the navy used them as servants; and the army created separate black regiments commanded mostly by white officers. The Red Cross even segregated blood plasma.

Not surprisingly, racial tensions deepened during the war. The number of black GIs rose from 100,000 in 1941 to 700,000 in 1944. Many joined the armed services hoping to find social mobility. Instead, they encountered segregation and discrimination. They resented white officials who denounced Nazi racism but remained silent about discrimination against blacks. Northern blacks stationed in the South found race relations shocking. Signs on buses in Charleston, South Carolina, read: "Avoid Friction. Be Patriotic. White passengers will be seated from front to rear, colored passengers from rear to front."

Conditions in the civilian sector were no better. As urban areas swelled with defense workers, housing and transportation shortages exacerbated racial tensions. In 1943 a riot broke out in Detroit in a federally sponsored housing project. Polish-Americans wanted blacks barred from the new apartments named, ironically, in honor of Sojourner Truth, the black abolitionist and poet. White soldiers from a nearby base joined the fighting, and other federal troops had to be brought in to disperse the mobs. The violence left 35 blacks and 9 whites dead.

Similar conflicts erupted across the nation, exposing in each instance the same jarring contradiction: White Americans espoused equality abroad but practiced discrimination at home. One black soldier told Swedish social scientist Gunnar Myrdal, "just carve on my tombstone, here lies a black man killed fighting a yellow man for the protection of a white man." A 1942 survey showed many black Americans sympathized with the Japanese struggle to expel white colonialists from the Far East. Significantly, the same survey revealed a majority of white industrialists in the South preferred a German victory to racial equality for blacks.

Many blacks responded to the rising tensions by joining civil rights organizations. During World War II, the NAACP intensified its legal campaign against discrimination, and its membership grew from 50,000 to 500,000 as large numbers of blacks and middle-class whites demanded racial equality.

Some blacks, however, considered the NAACP too slow and too conciliatory. Rejecting legal action, the Congress of Racial Equality (CORE), founded in 1942, organized a series of "sit-ins." Civil disobedience produced a few victories in the North, but the South's response was brutal. In Tennessee, for example, angry whites savagely beat Bayard Rustin, who became a prominent civil rights leader in the 1950s, for refusing to move to the back of the bus. While black activists won few gains during World War II, they forged new demands and tactics that shaped the civil rights movement after the war.

Federal officials did little to advance civil rights. Personally, Roosevelt sympathized with blacks, but he feared losing the Solid South's support if he moved too rapidly on the race issue. Thus, while he admitted black leaders to the White House to hear their grievances, Roosevelt seldom took action. Eleanor Roosevelt remained the conscience of the administration, voicing her sympathy for civil rights at every juncture, but the president refused to take the political risks needed to end discrimination and promote racial equality.

World War II affected Mexican-Americans no less than blacks. Almost 400,000 Mexican-Americans served in the armed forces. As soldiers, they expanded their contacts with Anglo society, visiting new parts of the country and meeting for the first time large groups of people who held few prejudices against them. For Mexican-Americans in the civilian sector, jobs in industry provided an escape hatch from the desperate poverty of migratory farm labor. In New Mexico, for example, about one-fifth of the rural Mexican-American population left for war-related jobs.

The need for farm workers rose dramatically after Pearl Harbor. To meet the demand, the United States established the *bracero* (work hands) program in 1942, and by 1945 several hundred thousand Mexican workers had immigrated to the Southwest. Commercial farmers welcomed them, but labor unions resented the competition, leading to animosity and discrimination against Mexicans and Mexican-Americans alike.

In Los Angeles, ethnic tensions erupted into violence. Anglo society both feared and resented newly formed Mexican-American youth gangs, whose members celebrated their ethnicity by wearing flamboyant "zoot suits" and by tattooing their left hands. In June 1943 hundreds of Anglo sailors on liberty from nearby naval bases invaded downtown Los Angeles. Eager to put down the Mexican-American youths, they attacked the "zooters" and riots broke out for several nights. The local press blamed Mexican-American gangs, and the riots did not end until military police ordered sailors back to their ships.

Despite the outbursts of violence and discrimination, World War II benefited the poor of all races. Thanks to full employment and progressive taxation, people at the bottom saw income redistributed in their favor. Americans who occupied the top 5 percent economically saw their share of disposable income fall from 23 percent in 1939 to 17 percent in 1945. Before the war there were 12 families with an income under $2000 for every family with an income over $5000; after the war the ratio was almost even. Still, the gains made by poor people came from the state of the economy (the need for soldiers and workers), not from federal policies or the efforts of organized labor.

Fear of Enemy Aliens

On December 8, 1941, Roosevelt issued an executive order regarding enemy aliens. It suspended naturalization proceedings for Italians, Germans, and Japanese immigrants, required them to register, restricted their mobility, and prohibited them from owning items that might be used for sabotage, such as cameras and shortwave radios. In practice, however, the government did not accord enemy aliens the same treatment: Italian and German aliens received lenient treatment, while Japanese aliens suffered gross injustices.

Approximately 600,000 Italian aliens lived in the United States in 1940. In general, the government treated them well throughout the war, administering the enemy alien laws with compassion. On Columbus Day, 1942 (just before the congressional elections), Roosevelt lifted the enemy alien designation for Italians and established simplified naturalization procedures. Moreover, German aliens received similar treatment. Though less numerous (264,000) and not as politically important to the Democrats, Roosevelt's administration treated them fairly throughout the war.

Jewish refugees complicated the German question. Reflecting a nasty strain of anti-Semitism, Congress in 1939 refused to raise immigration quotas to admit 20,000 Jewish children fleeing Nazi oppression. As the wife of the U.S. commissioner of immigration remarked at a cocktail party, "20,000 children would all too soon grow up to be 20,000 ugly adults."

Instead of relaxing immigration quotas, American officials worked in vain to persuade Latin American countries and Great Britain to admit Jewish refugees. Other officials, such as

Assistant Secretary of State Breckinridge Long, the chief administrator for immigration policy, insisted that winning the war offered the best means for rescuing European Jews. Bitterly anti-Semitic in his private views, Long argued that any relaxation of the quota system would permit Nazi spies to slip into the country along with legitimate refugees.

Nazi Concentration Camps

While the futile debates dragged on, Hitler's death camps killed helpless victims at the rate of 2000 an hour. As late as 1944, American officials who knew the ghastly truth publicly downplayed reports of genocide in the press. Air reconnaissance missions had taken scores of photographs of the death camp at Auschwitz, and military intelligence officers had learned the locations of several other concentration camps.

Finally, in January 1944, Secretary of the Treasury Henry Morgenthau, forced the issue to a head. The only Jew in the Cabinet, Morgenthau presented to Roosevelt the "Report to the Secretary on the Acquiescence of this Government in the Murder of the Jews." Shamed into action, Roosevelt created the War Refugee Board, which, in turn, set up refugee camps in Italy, North Africa, and the United States. But America's response offered too little, too late. During the 18 months of the War Refugee Board's existence, Hitler killed far more Jews than the War Refugee Board saved.

Like Jews, Japanese-Americans got a bitter taste of discrimination during World War II. Barred from immigrating to the United States by the Immigration Act of 1924, they comprised a tiny portion of the population in 1941, totaling no more than 260,000 people, of whom 150,000 lived in Hawaii, with the remaining 110,000 concentrated on the West Coast, where they worked mostly as small farmers or businesspeople serving the Japanese community. After Pearl Harbor, rumors spread about Japanese troops preparing to land in California, where they allegedly planned to link up with Japanese-Americans and Japanese aliens poised to strike as a fifth column for the invasion.

On February 19, 1942, Roosevelt authorized the Department of War to designate military areas and to exclude any or all persons from them. Armed with this power, military authorities immediately moved against Japanese aliens. In Hawaii, where residents of Japanese ancestry formed a large portion of the population and where the local economy depended on their labor, the military did not force Japanese-Americans to relocate. On the West Coast, however, military authorities ordered the Japanese to leave, drawing no distinction between aliens and citizens. Forced to sell their property for pennies on the dollar, most Japanese-Americans suffered severe financial losses. Relocation proved next to impossible, as no other states would take them. The governor of Idaho opposed any migration, declaring: "The Japs live like rats, breed like rats and act like rats. We don't want them."

When voluntary measures failed, Roosevelt created the War Relocation Authority. It resettled 100,000 Japanese-Americans in ten camps scattered across seven western states. Called relocation camps, they resembled minimum security prisons. In these concentration camps, American citizens who had committed no crimes were locked behind barbed wire, crowded into ramshackle wooden barracks where they lived one family to a room furnished with nothing but cots and bare light bulbs, forced to endure bad food, inadequate medical care, and poorly equipped schools.

Japanese-American Internment Camps

Nearly 18,000 Japanese-American men won release from those camps to fight for the United States Army. Most served with the 100th Infantry Battalion and the 442nd Regimental Combat Team. In Italy, the 442nd sustained nearly 10,000 casualties, with 3600 Purple Hearts, 810 Bronze Stars, 342 Silver Stars, 123 divisional citations, 47 Distinguished Service Crosses, 17 Legions of Merit, 7 Presidential Unit Citations, and 1 Congressional Medal of Honor. In short, they fought heroically, emerging as the most decorated military unit in World War II. In one of the most painful scenes in American history, Japanese-American parents, still locked inside concentration camps, received posthumous Purple Hearts for their sons.

Japanese-Americans protested their treatment, claiming numerous civil rights violations. Citing national security considerations, the Supreme Court backed the government six to three in *Korematsu* v. *U.S.* (1944). But in a dissenting opinion, Frank Murphy admitted federal policy had fallen "into the ugly abyss of racism." On December 18, 1944, in the *Endo* case, the Supreme Court ruled a civilian agency, the War Relocation Authority, had no right to incarcerate law-abiding citizens. Two weeks later the federal government began closing down the camps, ending one of the most shameful chapters in American history.

THE WAR IN EUROPE

The Grand Alliance

Following Pearl Harbor, the Axis Powers of Germany, Japan, and Italy faced the Grand Alliance, composed of the United States, Great Britain, Free France, and the Soviet Union. Yet from the beginning the Grand Alliance was an uneasy coalition, born of necessity and filled with tension. Apart from the need to defeat the enemy, the Allies found it difficult to agree on anything.

Great Britain's gaze fell on Europe, where Churchill approached international affairs in spheres-of-influence, balance-of-power terms. He wanted the war to weaken all the other continental powers, allowing Great Britain to play a major role in redrawing the postwar map of Europe, especially in Poland and the Balkans, where the British hoped to erect a barrier against Soviet expansion. In addition, Churchill intended for Britain to emerge from the war with her empire intact.

France's goals reflected the vision of one man—General Charles de Gaulle. Above all, de Gaulle wanted to restore France to greatness. By nature aloof, enigmatic, suspicious, and

Japanese-Americans of all ages, tagged like pieces of luggage, awaited their relocation to one of ten detention camps in seven western states. This family was from Hayward, California.

stubborn, he was equally charismatic and forceful. Like Churchill, he fought to retain his country's empire, and as the war progressed American officials came to regard de Gaulle as a political extremist. In policy disputes, he often sided with Britain to oppose American and Soviet demands.

Joseph Stalin spoke for the Soviet Union. The son of a cobbler, Stalin rose to power by crushing all political rivals during the turbulent years following the Bolshevik revolution. Iron-willed, deeply paranoid, and bold as a thief, "Uncle Joe" enjoyed a well-deserved reputation as a formidable negotiator. Throughout World War II, he pressed for a postwar settlement that would guarantee the Soviet Union's future security and open new lands for communism. To protect the Soviet Union from future attacks, Stalin insisted upon Germany's total destruction. As additional insurance, he demanded parts of Poland and Finland and all of the Baltic states. Eastern Europe would then form a buffer against future aggression from the West, provide colonies for rebuilding the Soviet economy, and add new territory to the communist world map.

Roosevelt had his own ideas about how the world should look after the war. In broad terms, he opposed colonialism and the spread of communism; and he supported open markets, democratic elections to counter spheres of influence, and a new League of Nations to promote world peace. Among these objectives, anticolonialism and support for free markets were his top priorities, and both goals reflected Roosevelt's remarkable ability to join political principle with economic advantage.

No less than his counterparts, Roosevelt's personality shaped his policies. Of all the Allied leaders he had the most exaggerated sense of his abilities as a diplomat. The basic problem was his temperament. Because he disliked the rough and tumble of hard bargaining, Roosevelt tried to avoid clashes with other leaders by postponing difficult decisions and by relying too heavily on his personal charm. In addition, Roosevelt's pragmatic approach to problem solving made him seek compromises whenever possible, which meant that he often sacrificed principles in order to preserve Allied cooperation.

From the outset, then, dissent riddled the Grand Alliance. In pursuit of its own national interest, each ally had a separate agenda, its own set of demands, and its own vision of the how the world map should look when the war ended. Given these conflicts, the Allies could look forward not to harmony but to clashes over military strategy throughout the war, bitter debates over peace terms at the war's end, and decades of international strife in the postwar era.

Early Axis Victories

After Pearl Harbor, the United States had to prepare for global war. Before the conflict ended, the United States had troops and supplies scattered around the world. The war would cost America one million casualties, and over 300,000 deaths. The financial price was equally high: $350 billion in all—about $250 million a day at the peak of the fighting.

During the first six months of combat Japan looked unbeatable. Japanese forces captured Guam, Wake Island, the Philippines, Hong Kong, and Malaya and slashed deep into Burma, cutting the Burma Road, China's lifeline to the West. General Douglas MacArthur, though vowing to return, was driven from the Philippines

in March 1942. In a matter of months Japanese troops had conquered a vast expanse extending from the Gilbert Islands through the Solomons and from New Guinea to Burma, leaving India and Australia vulnerable to attack.

Nor did the Allied cause look any brighter in Europe. During the first ten months of 1942, German submarines sank over 500 American merchant ships. With its lend-lease supplies threatened, Great Britain stood in danger of collapsing before the United States could mobilize. On the Russian front, German troops pressed toward Stalingrad, making short work of Stalin's divisions in their path. The news from North Africa was equally bleak. On May 26, 1942, German Field Marshal Erwin Rommel, the famous "Desert Fox," began his sweep toward the Suez Canal. A brilliant strategist, he slashed almost to Alexandria before the British managed to halt him.

In short, World War II opened badly for the Allies. Axis victories in the Pacific, Europe, and Africa served notice the war would be long and costly.

Stemming the German Tide

Roosevelt decided to assign Germany top priority for two reasons: First, he doubted Hitler could be dislodged from Europe if Britain fell; and, second, Roosevelt wanted to placate Stalin. Throughout the war, Stalin remained suspicious, fearing his allies planned to let Germans and Russians kill one another off so both nations would emerge from the war as second-rate powers. As the Germans drove deep into Soviet territory in 1942, Stalin demanded a second front in France to force Germany to divide her armies, thereby relieving some of the pressure on the Soviet Union. As one observer remarked, Soviet Foreign Minister V. M. Molotov knew only four words of English: "yes," "no," and "second front."

By the autumn of 1942 the tide was beginning to turn on the eastern front. In September Germany lost 12 divisions at Stalingrad, and in November the Red Army launched a furious counterattack, beginning the long drive to push the Germans back across the Ukraine. Despite Soviet victories and Stalin's repeated pleas for a second front, the Allies, at Churchill's insistence, decided to attack the Germans in North

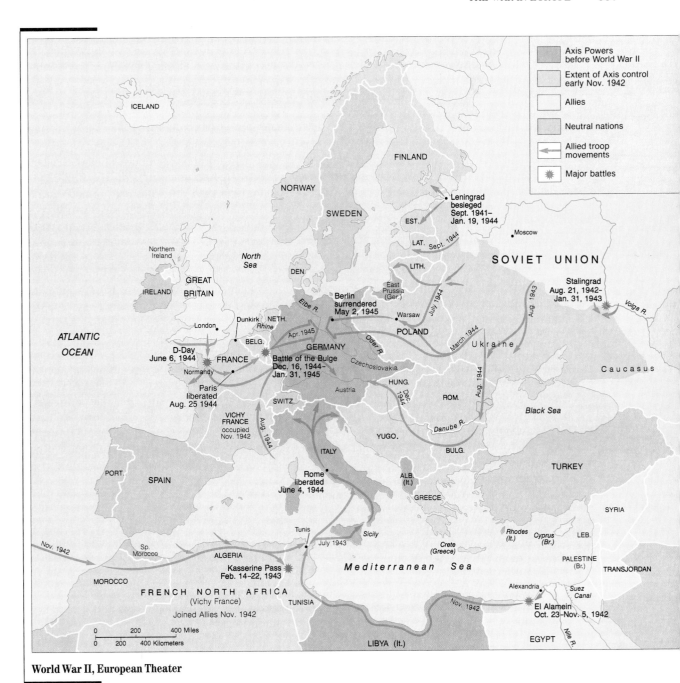

World War II, European Theater

Africa instead of France. Stalin saw this as a betrayal and his suspicions deepened.

Allied victories in Africa seemed to confirm Churchill's wisdom. British Field Marshal Sir Bernard Montgomery drove the Germans back to Tunis in October, and in November 1942 General Dwight David Eisenhower led a force of 400,000 Allied soldiers in a full-scale invasion of

North Africa (Operation TORCH). The German and Italian forces fought bravely. By the end of the campaign the Axis armies had lost 349,000 soldiers killed or captured, while the Allies had suffered only 70,000 casualties. Complete victory in North Africa came on May 12, 1943, when the remnants of the Axis armies surrendered. Germany and Italy had suffered a major defeat and Allied shipping could now cross the Mediterranean in safety.

Cheered by the North African victory, Allied leaders paused to select the next target. In January 1943 Churchill and Roosevelt met in Casablanca, French Morocco, without Stalin, who was invited but refused to attend, explaining he could not leave the Soviet Union at this critical juncture of the war. Haunted by ghastly memories of World War I and fearing a premature invasion of France might bog down into trench-style warfare, Churchill pushed hard for an attack on Sicily and then Italy. The United States initially opposed the plan (Operation HUSKY), arguing it would delay the invasion of France without accomplishing any decisive results, but Churchill prevailed. As one American military advisor remarked at the time: "We came, we listened, and we were conquered."

With the promised invasion of France again put on hold, Churchill and Roosevelt moved to reassure Stalin. The Casablanca conference yielded a renewed pledge for a second front in Europe, and Roosevelt and Churchill vowed to make peace with the Axis powers only on the basis of unconditional surrender. While the two leaders announced their "unconditional surrender" agreement to the public on the last day of the conference, they kept Stalin in the dark for several months about other agreements reached at Casablanca, including their decision to postpone the second front.

Sicily fell in August 1943 after a campaign of slightly more than a month. Shortly before its surrender, Italian dissidents, anticipating an Allied invasion of their homeland, deposed Mussolini and placed him under arrest. (German paratroopers later rescued Mussolini in a daring assault and installed him as head of the Italian government in German-occupied Italy.) To head Italy's new government, King Victor Emmanuel III then appointed Marshal Pietro Badoglio, an old fascist who had led the Italian invasion of Ethiopia. Under Badoglio, Italy promptly surrendered on September 8, 1943, immediately switched sides, and declared war on Germany.

The Allied victory in Italy did not come cheaply. The terrain was mountainous, and the Germans offered savage resistance. Though the Italian campaign secured the Mediterranean,

depleted German troops, and secured air bases for flights over central Europe, Stalin deeply resented the commitment of Allied troops there instead of France. Furthermore, he held Badoglio in contempt and opposed his sudden rehabilitation as an ally. Did Churchill and Roosevelt intend to allow other former Fascists to head Allied-dominated governments?

Stalin's protests fell on deaf ears. Since Soviet troops had not fought in the Italian campaign, Roosevelt and Churchill refused to permit Stalin to participate in organizing an occupation government in Italy. Stalin learned his lesson well. The next time he wanted a voice in a region he made certain to have his armies on site.

Meanwhile, Soviet troops were winning the war on the eastern front. By October 1943 they had recorded stunning victories at Leningrad and Stalingrad. American aid did not arrive in time to help win these victories, but American weapons, vehicles, clothing, and food contributed mightily to subsequent Soviet offensives. Keeping the Soviets supplied was no longer a problem because the Allies had won the Battle of the Atlantic. Radar, air patrols, and destroyer escorts neutralized the German submarines, lowering shipping losses from 514,744 tons in March 1943 to 199,409 tons in May.

The Teheran Conference

In November 1943 Roosevelt, Churchill, and Stalin held their first face-to-face conference, meeting in Teheran, the capital of Iran. Buoyed by military success, Stalin sounded conciliatory as they discussed the long-awaited second front and the shape of the postwar world. In response to Stalin's demands, the leaders set May 1944 as the target date for Operation OVERLORD, the code name for the invasion of France. To increase the odds for success, Stalin promised to coordinate Russia's spring offensive with the invasion.

Once the leaders turned to postwar issues, however, the conference dissolved into bitter controversy. Stalin demanded Soviet control over Eastern Europe and insisted Germany be divided into several weak states. Opposing both demands, Churchill proposed democratic governments for Eastern Europe, especially in Po-

On August 7, 1942, the 1st Marine Division attacked Guadalcanal in the Solomon Islands. Marines captured the air strip on Guadalcanal, and in February, following months of bloody fighting, they drove the Japanese troops into the sea, securing the Allied supply line to Australia. In addition, the victory at Guadalcanal protected the Allies' eastern flank, allowing General Douglas MacArthur, commander of southwest Pacific forces, to continue his march through New Guinea back to the Philippines.

Japanese advances in China proved more difficult to halt. While Allied troops had to cut a new road through the mountainous terrain of Burma to supply Chiang Kai-shek's army, the real problems stemmed from China's civil war. Chiang fought harder against the Communist forces headed by Mao Tse-tung than he did against the Japanese. Lieutenant General Joseph W. Stilwell ("Vinegar Joe"), the head of Allied forces in China, became so disillusioned he nicknamed Chiang "Peanut," but Roosevelt continued to regard Chiang as a strong ruler, destined to lead a powerful country.

Despite setbacks in China, the Allies won major victories in the South Pacific, where they squeezed Japan from two directions. In the southwest Pacific, General MacArthur seized Lae on the northern coast of New Guinea in September 1943. Then, instead of assaulting Japanese strong points head-on, he leapfrogged up the coast, capturing isolated positions and forcing Japanese troops to abandon their fortifications to attack. Japanese commanders ex-

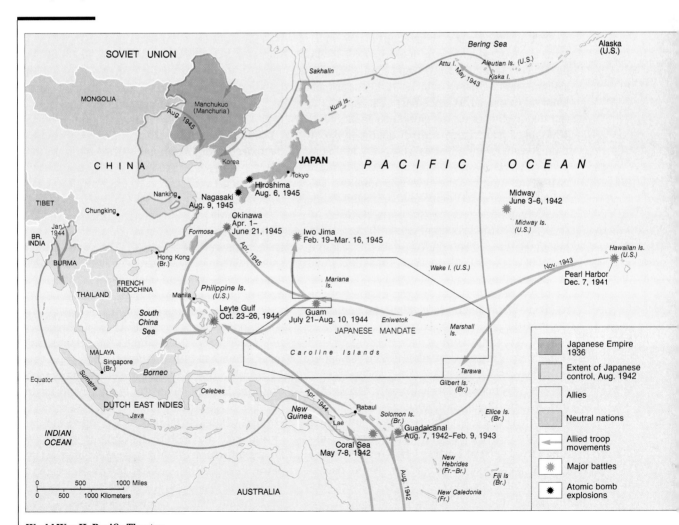

World War II, Pacific Theater

pected MacArthur to assault their impregnable 100,000-man fortress at Rabaul on New Britain. Instead, he cut its supply lines and bypassed it. By July 1944 MacArthur's forces controlled all of New Guinea.

Meanwhile, Admiral Chester Nimitz's naval and marine forces in the Central Pacific were "island hopping" toward Japan, capturing important positions, building airstrips, and then moving on to the next island. Their first target was the Gilbert Islands. In late November 1943, the marines attacked Tarawa, a tiny island 3 miles long and 600 yards wide. In the bloody 3-day battle that followed, Japanese troops fought to the death, inflicting 3301 casualties on American marines.

With the Gilberts secured, Nimitz invaded the Marshall Islands in February 1944. The Japanese offered only light resistance because they planned to make their stand at the Marianas Islands, prizes worth defending. Here the fighting centered on three large islands, Saipan, Tinian, and Guam, which the Americans planned to use as advance naval bases. Saipan, the major objective, was closest to Japan. Only 1200 miles from Tokyo (much nearer to Japan than Hawaii is to California), Saipan could supply airbases that would bring the main Japanese islands into range of the new B-29 bombers. Determined to protect their homeland against air-raids, Japanese commanders resolved to defend the islands to the last man. The battle for Saipan began on June 15 and ended on July 9. When it was over, 14,000 American troops had been killed or wounded, 30,000 of the island's 32,000 Japanese defenders lay dead, and 6000 of the island's 12,000 Japanese civilians had committed suicide rather than surrender. Tinian and Guam fell to the Americans in early August, and B-29s began regular bombing raids over Japan in November 1944.

On October 21, 1944, General MacArthur invaded the Philippines, splashing ashore with the 96th Division for the benefit of photographers. That same month the navy won a stunning victory at the Battle of Leyte Gulf, where the Japanese lost four carriers, three battleships, eight destroyers, and nine cruisers, virtually their entire remaining battle fleet. American submarines now controlled Pacific shipping lanes, sealing the Japanese Islands off from mil-

itary and food supplies. In January, Allied forces invaded Luzon, the main island of the Philippines, and Allied troops claimed victory five months later. All told 240,000 Japanese soldiers died in the fighting.

While MacArthur was reclaiming the Philippines, Nimitz was bearing down on Iwo Jima. Its capture would enable fighter planes to link up with B-29s heading out of the Marianas, providing fighter escorts for their raids on Japan. The 3d, 4th, and 5th Marine Divisions attacked Iwo Jima in February 1945, and by early March the island fell into American hands. Four thousand marines died in the battle.

With Iwo Jima safely under American control, fighter planes joined the B-29s over Japan, allowing bomber squadrons to reduce armaments and increase bombloads. American commanders made a strategic decision to shift to firebombing. By the end of the war American pilots had dropped 160,000 tons of bombs on Japan. Japan's population density, combustible building materials, and limited industrial capacity made firebombing more effective than in Europe. Bombs killed over 330,000 civilians (86,000 in the firebombing of Tokyo alone) and destroyed over 40 percent of the buildings in 65 cities. Japan's war production fell dramatically: oil refining by 83 percent and aircraft engines by 75 percent.

On April 1, 1945, American troops attacked Okinawa, 350 miles southwest of Japan. Japanese resistance was fierce. Kamikaze attacks (suicide flights by Japanese pilots) rose dramatically. Of the 4000 planes lost by the Japanese at Okinawa, kamikaze missions numbered 2800. Japan's soldiers fought just as bravely. Indeed, many fought to the death rather than surrender. Okinawa fell in June, after 70,000 Japanese soldiers had died defending it.

Confronted with certain defeat, many moderate leaders in Japan wanted to avoid an invasion. With the peace party growing in strength, Hideki Tojo resigned in July 1944, but strong factions within the military vowed to keep fighting. In an effort to save Japan, the Emperor switched his support to the peace party in February 1945. He then sent out peace feelers to Stalin, who in turn conveyed them to Truman at the Potsdam Conference in July 1945.

Truman and the Dawn of the Atomic Age

Few presidents have been asked to conduct diplomacy with less preparation than Harry S Truman. He had risen to power as a loyal machine politician in Kansas City. As vice president and former senator from Missouri he knew next to nothing about foreign affairs. Roosevelt had kept Truman largely in the dark, neither seeking his counsel nor confiding in him. When Roosevelt's death elevated him to the White House, Truman told reporters: "I felt like the moon, the stars, and all planets had fallen on me." Yet Truman brought certain assets to the challenge. A man who possessed the courage of his convictions, he fully intended to be a strong president and to make decisions resolutely.

Truman's first test came at Potsdam, a suburb of Berlin, where the Allied leaders convened in July 1945 for their last wartime meeting. Though new to the job, Truman had been in office long enough to believe Roosevelt had been too soft on Stalin. Truman viewed Stalin as a liar and a bully who only understood force. Yet like his predecessor Truman did not wish to risk a showdown over Eastern Europe, largely because his military advisors insisted the United States still needed the Soviet Union's help against Japan.

While Truman stopped short of picking a fight over Eastern Europe, he pushed Stalin hard at Potsdam. During the negotiations, Truman received word American scientists had successfully tested the first atomic bomb. Hoping to impress Stalin, Truman told him in a conversation one evening the United States now possessed a new weapon of awesome power. Stalin blithely replied he trusted the United States would make good use of it against Japan. Thus, Truman's first effort at "nuclear diplomacy" ended in failure. Far from being intimidated, Stalin had stood his ground.

Deadlocked on Eastern Europe, Truman and Stalin turned their attention to Japan. The Potsdam Declaration of July 26 (the conference's sole accomplishment) demanded immediate "unconditional surrender," warning that any other action would lead to "prompt and utter destruction."

Despite its apocalyptic tone, the Potsdam Declaration failed to give Japan ample warning,

On October 21, 1944, General MacArthur, commander of the Southeast Pacific forces, splashed ashore in the Philippines with the 96th Division.

and over the next several days, opponents of nuclear warfare pleaded with Truman not to use the bomb. Many scientists who had helped develop the bomb, joined by several key political figures, opposed the bomb because they foresaw its implications for a postwar arms race with the Soviet Union. Others, arguing from a moral position, wanted the United States to warn the Japanese about the bomb's terrifying power, giving them a chance to surrender. As a compromise, others advised Truman to conduct a demonstration. The United States could drop the bomb on an uninhabited Pacific island, before an audience of neutral observers (at a safe distance) who would tell Japan's leaders what they had witnessed.

Truman rejected these alternatives. The atomic bomb was the most jealously guarded secret of World War II, and Truman had no intention of divulging it to the enemy. Moreover, he rejected a test demonstration because his scientists could not guarantee the bomb would explode and because the United States had only three bombs in its nuclear arsenal. In the end, Truman decided to drop the bomb.

(Text continues on p. 899)

HIROSHIMA AND NAGASAKI

On July 16, 1945, the Atomic Age became reality. The place was Alamogordo Air Force Base in the southern desert region of New Mexico. The occasion was the first successful detonation of an atomic bomb. Observers witnessed "a blinding flash that lighted the entire northwestern sky." Next came "a huge billow of smoke," followed by "an enormous ball of what appeared to be fire and closely resembled a rising sun." Dr. J. Robert Oppenheimer, the chief scientist in charge of the team that designed the weapon, was so astonished by the scale of the blast that he recalled the Hindu quotation: "I am become death, shatterer of worlds."

Back in 1939 two brilliant scientists, Albert Einstein and Enrico Fermi, both of whom had fled fascism and anti-Semitism in Europe, warned President Roosevelt that German nuclear physicists under

Adolf Hitler's control might well be trying to develop such a bomb. Roosevelt realized the implications; he set in motion what became the "Manhattan Project," a top-secret effort involving civilian scientists and army engineers to apply the theory of nuclear fission to a bomb. Hitler's scientists never succeeded, but in July 1945, with the war over in Europe, the United States now had a weapon with the potential to threaten civilization itself. The question was whether the bomb would be used against Japan, the last of the Axis powers still at war.

The Japanese were a formidable foe. Since 1942 U.S. troops had been rolling back their empire, all the way to the shores of Japan and the Chinese mainland by the summer of 1945. The toll in casualties was horrendous. Japanese soldiers fought with a sense of personal honor that struck Americans as

fanatical. They would not surrender when beaten but would fight to their death. To do otherwise would be to disgrace themselves, their families, and their emperor, whom they considered a god.

At first, in defending Pacific islands such as Guadalcanal (August 1942–February 1943), Japanese soldiers mounted suicidal *banzai* charges. They ran forward in waves at U.S. troops, inflicting massive damage before being shot down. Later, on islands such as Iwo Jima (February–March 1945), they used elaborate networks of underground bunkers to wreak havoc, so much so that U.S. casualties started to reach the 50 percent range. By 1945 the Japanese were unleashing kamikaze raids in which pilots sacrificed themselves for the glory of the empire by dive bombing their planes into U.S. naval vessels. In the bloody battle of Okinawa (April–June 1945), kamikaze pilots flew some 2800 planes into American ships, inflicting 10,000 casualties and sinking 28 vessels, besides damaging 325 other ships.

American soldiers, as well as the U.S. public at large, neither understood nor respected Japanese martial values. Explained a Marine Corps general, to shoot "a Jap . . . was like killing a rattlesnake." A Guadalcanal veteran stated that the Japanese soldier "possessed considerable cleverness; he could not be classified as an intellectual. He was more of an animal. He could live on a handful of rice." Almost universally Americans used terms of racial derision to describe an enemy that had not only mounted the "sneak attack" on Pearl Harbor but now refused to surrender when beaten.

Such attitudes affected the development of a comprehensive U.S.

war plan, known as Operation DOWNFALL, constructed on the assumption that only a full-scale invasion of Japan would bring total victory in the Pacific. The first phase of the plan, called Operation OLYMPIC, involved an assault on Kyushu, the southernmost island of Japan, to begin in November 1945. The Joint Chiefs of Staff presented OLYMPIC to President Truman in June and stated that American casualties could reach 268,000 (out of 767,000 participants). The Japanese still had 2.3 million soldiers ready to fight and another 4 million citizens trained in the use of arms. If they battled to the death, as they had so far, American casualties, the Joint Chiefs predicted, would exceed 1 million by the time U.S. troops conquered the main island of Honshu in 1946 or 1947.

Because of the bloody price everyone expected to pay, high-ranking American officials were anxious to involve Russia—to attack through Manchuria and Korea—in the final crushing of Japan. At Yalta in February 1945 President Roosevelt secured pledges of Soviet assistance. Then at Potsdam in July, President Truman seemed much less interested. Having just learned of the test results in New Mexico, Truman told Joseph Stalin of "a new weapon of unusual destructive force." Stalin, however, would not be cast aside. He still wanted the territory (the lower half of Sakhalin Island, the Kurile islands, and certain considerations in Manchuria) promised at Yalta. The Soviet leader thus "hoped" the United States "would make good use" of the weapon "against the Japanese"; but the Russians would not be denied their part in the invasion or the promised territory.

Meanwhile, a committee of American scientists and military officers were at work in selecting possible targets. Some advocated a demonstration at a preannounced neutral site as a way of cajoling the Japanese into surrender, but others feared what might happen should the bomb prove to be a dud. All leverage would then be lost. Finally, with great reluctance, these advisors agreed that there was "no acceptable alternative to direct military use" of the bomb.

In public, Truman never admitted to any qualms about the decision to employ the new weapon, but in private he wondered how "we as the leader of the world for the common welfare" could drop "this terrible bomb." Still, he accepted the responsibility for many reasons. He hoped to save thousands of American lives by avoiding a full invasion of Japan against soldiers who fought like "savages, ruthless, merciless, and fanatic." Likely, too, Truman and his advisors feared the expansionism of the Communist regime of Joseph Stalin. Using the bomb might prove a great point of leverage in dealing with the Soviets in the days ahead.

While Truman and others considered the alternatives, a select unit of the Army Air Force, flying B-29s, made a series of practice bomb runs over Japan. Since these planes did not attack, as they had so often before in firebombing cities like Tokyo, no one paid much attention. Then on August 6, 1945, at a few minutes past 8:00 A.M., three B-29s at 31,600 feet of altitude appeared over Hiroshima. Colonel Paul Tibbets, piloting the lead bomber, *Enola Gay*, turned the controls over to Major Thomas Ferebee, the bombardier officer, who completed the run. It took 45 seconds, as *Enola Gay* banked away quickly, for the atomic bomb to reach the ground. As the fireball erupted toward the sky, nearly 100,000 people, including thousands of soldiers at the headquarters of Japan's Second General Army just 2000 yards from ground zero, died instantly. Three days later, in the absence of a firm willingness to surrender, a second bomb flattened Nagasaki and killed about 35,000 people. Thousands more perished later from serious burns, radiation poisoning, and other devastating effects of the two bombings.

Dropping the atomic bombs gave peace advocates in Japan the muscle they needed to overcome the militarists. When on August 10 Emperor Hirohito agreed to seek peace terms, the war faction reluctantly acceded, but only after General Anami Korechika, the war minister, upheld his honor on August 14 by committing suicide. He could not bear hearing Hirohito's proclamation of surrender.

When American troops training for Operation OLYMPIC heard about the surrender, they rejoiced. "We would not be obliged to run up the beaches near Tokyo assault-firing while being mortared and shelled," wrote one soldier. "We are going to live. We are going to grow up to adulthood after all." They did not realize how different the world would be with nuclear weapons in the hands of the two superpowers to emerge from World War II. For a moment, however, General Douglas MacArthur understood. After the Japanese surrender ceremony on September 2, 1945, he stated: "We have had our last chance. If we do not devise some greater and more equitable system, Armageddon will be at our door."

1921 Washington Naval Conference places limits on construction of large warships

1922 Mussolini seizes power in Italy

1924 Dawes Plan to help Germany pay reparations

1928 Kellogg-Briand Pact renounces war "as an instrument of national policy"; Clark Memorandum states that the United States does not have a right to intervene militarily in the affairs of Latin American nations

1931 Japan invades Manchuria

1932 Stimson Doctrine declares that the United States would not recognize Japanese territorial gains in China

1933 Adolf Hitler is appointed chancellor of Germany; Roosevelt announces Good Neighbor Policy, withdraws marines from Haiti, and nullifies Platt Amendment

1935 Neutrality Act allows president to bar arms sales to nations at war; is extended in 1936 to bar loans to belligerents and in 1937 to bar shipments of nonmilitary goods

1936 German troops reoccupy the Rhineland; Spanish Civil War begins

1937 Japan invades China

1938 Germany annexes Austria; Munich Pact hands over a third of Czechoslovakia to Nazi Germany

1939 Soviet Union and Germany sign a non-aggression pact; World War II begins following Germany's invasion of Poland

1940 United States transfers 50 destroyers to Britain in exchange for bases in New-foundland and the Caribbean; United States institutes first peacetime military draft; Roosevelt is elected to third term

1941 Lend-Lease Act allows United States to lend war materials to Britain; Roosevelt issues order prohibiting discrimination in defense industries; Hitler's army invades USSR; United States sets embargo on scrap metal, oil, and fuel to Japan; Japan attacks Pearl Harbor, killing over 2400 U.S. soldiers and sailors; United States enters World War II

1942 Congress creates the Office of Price Administration to control prices and ration scarce goods; President Roosevelt authorizes internment of 112,000 West Coast Japanese-Americans; Philippine Islands surrender; U.S. navy wins a major victory at Midway Island in the central Pacific; British and U.S. forces land in French North Africa

1943 British and U.S. forces defeat Axis forces in North Africa; U.S. marines secure control of Guadalcanal in the Solomon Islands; Soviets halt German drive into Soviet Union; Allies invade Italy; Mussolini is overthrown and new Italian government surrenders to Allies

1943–1944 U.S. marines and navy seize islands of Tarawa, Kwajalein, Wake, and Guam in Central Pacific and New Guinea in the South Pacific

1944 U.S. Supreme Court upholds the legality of the forced relocation of Japanese-Americans; D-Day: Allies launch amphibious invasion of northern France; U.S. forces begin an invasion of Philippine Islands and aerial attacks on Japan; Bretton Woods conference draws up plans for International Monetary Fund and International Bank to finance postwar economic recovery; Dumbarton Oaks conference makes plans for creation of United Nations; German troops launch counteroffensive in the Ardennes Forest along Belgium-Luxembourg border

1945 At Yalta, Roosevelt, Churchill, and Stalin discuss Soviet entry into the war against Japan, the postwar division of Europe, and plans for the United Nations; Roosevelt dies; Harry S Truman becomes thirty-third president; Germany surrenders; Potsdam conference plans postwar settlement in Europe and final attack on Japan; United States drops atomic bombs on Hiroshima and Nagasaki; Japan surrenders

Military considerations played a large role in his decision. According to the best intelligence reports, an invasion of the Japanese Islands might cost one million Allied casualties, with the Japanese suffering several times that figure. Ironically, the bomb had the potential to save countless lives on both sides by ending the war immediately. Yet Truman's decision to drop the bomb also reflected his growing frustration with the Soviet Union. He wanted to demonstrate the bomb's awesome power to impress Stalin so the Soviets would be easier to deal with after the war.

Following Japan's rejection of the Potsdam Declaration, Truman gave the final order. On August 6 three B-29s flew over Hiroshima and the lead bomber, the *Enola Gay*, dropped an atomic bomb that destroyed 4.4 square miles and killed 100,000 people instantly. Two days later the Soviets entered the war against Japan, making good on Stalin's promise at Yalta. Because Japan failed to surrender immediately, Truman ordered a second atomic strike. On August 9 Nagasaki was obliterated, killing another 35,000 Japanese. The following day Japan asked for peace.

The news that peace negotiations were going forward triggered spontaneous celebrations in the United States as tens of millions of Americans filled the streets in mass demonstrations of joy and relief. V-J Day (Victory in Japan) came on September 2, 1945, when Japanese officials surrendered unconditionally to General MacArthur aboard the battleship *Missouri* in Tokyo Bay. Truman refused to permit the Soviets to attend the ceremony or to play any role in creating an occupation government for Japan.

World War II was over. The fascist governments had been destroyed, their military machines crushed, their economies shattered, their major cities reduced to rubble, and their people ravaged by disease and starvation. Yet the war left the Allies hardly less devastated, except for the United States, which emerged from the fighting stronger than ever. Much of the world had to be reordered and rebuilt, but the conflicts between the United States and the Soviet Union that festered throughout the war raised grave doubts about the prospects for future cooperation.

This photo of the remains of the Nagasaki Medical College shows the almost total destruction by the atomic blast. The buildings that remained standing were made of reinforced concrete.

CONCLUSION

When World War II erupted in Europe, Roosevelt knew most Americans supported the Allies. So did he, but isolationists in Congress severely limited his freedom to act. For more than two years, Roosevelt struggled to preserve the fiction of neutrality while constructing programs to assist the Allies. After the attack on Pearl Harbor, isolationist opposition crumbled and the public united behind the war. The United States joined the Grand Alliance with Great Britain, Free France, and the Soviet Union to defeat the Axis Powers—Germany, Japan, and Italy. Yet apart from the need to crush the enemy, the Allies agreed upon little. Throughout the war, they clashed over military strategy and peace terms, disagreements that foreshadowed the conflicts of the postwar era.

World War II had an immediate and spectacular impact on the economy: It ended the Great Depression. Fueled by government contracts, the economy expanded dramatically, soaring to full employment and astounding the world with its productivity. The war accelerated corporate mergers and the trend toward large-scale units in agriculture. Labor unions also grew during the war as the government adopted pro-union policies, continuing the New Deal's sympathetic treatment of organized labor. Moreover, Keynesian economic principles took root as public policy during World War II, presaging the postwar growth of a large federal bureaucracy.

The Democrats reaped a political windfall from the war. Roosevelt rode the wartime emergency to unprecedented third and fourth terms, preserving the New Deal coalition so effectively that many people wondered if the Republicans would ever elect another president. Despite political victories, however, the Democrats could not rekindle congressional support for liberal reforms. The reform spirit had waned, a victim, it seemed, of the country's unmistakable swing to the right in politics.

The war's social effects varied from group to group. For most people, it had a disruptive influence—separating families, overcrowding housing, and creating a shortage of consumer goods. The war also set people in motion, accelerating the movement from the countryside to the cities; and it challenged gender and racial roles, opening new opportunities for women and minority groups. Yet sexual and racial barriers remained, highlighting reforms left unfinished at home even as American troops fought totalitarian forces abroad.

Presidential power expanded enormously during World War II, anticipating the rise of what postwar critics termed the "imperial presidency." Much of the president's energy went into formulating and directing a revolution in American foreign policy. Gone forever was the notion of fortress America, isolated and removed from world affairs. In its place stood a strong internationalist state, determined to exercise power on a global scale. Second only to the victory the Allies won for freedom, the war's most important legacy was the end of isolation and the rise of America's commitment to international security.

SUGGESTIONS FOR FURTHER READING

OVERVIEWS AND SURVEYS

Selig Adler, *The Uncertain Giant: American Foreign Policy Between the Wars* (1969); Albert R. Buchanan, *The United States and World War II*, 2

vols. (1964); Sean Dennis Cashman, *America, Roosevelt and World War II* (1989); Martha Hoyle, *A World in Flames: A History of World War II* (1970); Robert Leckie, *The Wars of America*, rev. ed., 2 vols. (1981); Studs Terkel, ed., *"The Good War"? An Oral History of World War Two* (1984); Russell F. Weigley, *The American Way of War: A History of United States Military Strategy and Policy* (1973); Gordon Wright, *The Ordeal of Total War 1939–1945* (1968).

DIPLOMACY BETWEEN THE WARS

Charles Chatfield, *For Peace and Justice: Pacifism in America 1914–1941* (1971); Charles De-Benedetti, *Origins of the Modern American Peace Movement, 1915–1929* (1978); Michael Dunne, *The United States and the World Court, 1920–1935* (1988); Robert H. Ferrell, *Peace in Their Time* (1953); Irwin F. Gellman, *Good Neighbor Diplomacy: United States Policies in Latin America, 1933–1945* (1979); Manfred Jonas, *Isolationism in America, 1935-1941* (1966); Joan Hoff-Wilson, *American Business and Foreign Policy, 1920–1933* (1971); John E. Wiltz, *In Search of Peace: The Senate Munitions Inquiry, 1934–36* (1963); Bryce Wood, *The Making of the Good Neighbor Policy* (1961).

THE COMING OF WORLD WAR II

Thomas A. Bailey and Paul B. Ryan, *Hitler vs. Roosevelt: The Undeclared Naval War* (1979); Robert J. Butow, *Tojo and the Coming of the War* (1961); Warren I. Cohen, *America's Response to China: A History of Sino-American Relations*, 3d ed. (1990); Wayne S. Cole, *America First: The Battle Against Intervention, 1940–1941* (1953), and *Roosevelt and the Isolationists, 1932–45* (1983); James V. Compton, *The Swastika and the Eagle: Hitler, the United States, and the Origins of World War II* (1967); Robert Dallek, *Franklin D. Roosevelt and American Foreign Policy, 1932–1945* (1979); Robert A. Divine, *Illusion of Neutrality* (1962), and *Second Chance: The Triumph of Internationalism During World War II* (1967); Herbert Feis, *The Road to Pearl Harbor: The Coming of the War Between the United States and Japan* (1950); Robert Edwin Herzstein, *Roosevelt & Hitler: Prelude to War* (1989); Akira Iriye, *After Imperialism: The Search for a New Order in the Far East, 1921–1931* (1965); Warren F. Kimball, *The Most Unsordid Act: Lend-Lease, 1939–1941* (1982); William L. Langer and S. Everett Gleason, *The Challenge to Isolation: The World Crisis of 1937–1940 and American Foreign Policy* (1952); Joseph P. Lash, *Roosevelt and Churchill, 1939–1941: The Partnership that Saved the West* (1976); Martin V. Melosi, *The*

Shadow of Pearl Harbor: Political Controversy over the Surprise Attack, 1941–1946 (1977); Keith L. Nelson, *Victors Divided: America and the Allies in Germany, 1918–1923* (1975); Gordon W. Prange, *At Dawn We Slept: The Untold Story of Pearl Harbor* (1981); David Reynolds, *The Creation of the Anglo-American Alliance, 1937–41: A Study in Competitive Co-operation* (1982); Bruce Russett, *No Clear and Present Danger: A Skeptical View of the United States Entry into World War II* (1972); Michael Schaller, *The U.S. Crusade in China, 1938–1945* (1979); John E. Wiltz, *From Isolation to War, 1931–1941* (1968); Roberta Wohlstetter, *Pearl Harbor: Warning and Decision* (1962).

AMERICA AT WAR

John Morton Blum, *V Was for Victory: Politics and American Culture During World War II* (1976); Eliot Janeway, *Struggle for Survival* (1951); William K. Klingaman, *1941: Our Lives in a World on the Edge* (1988); Paul A. C. Koistinen, *The Hammer and the Sword: Labor, the Military, and Industrial Mobilization, 1920-1945* (1979); Nelson Lichtenstein, *Labor's War at Home: The CIO in World War II* (1982); Richard Lingeman, *Don't You Know There's a War On? The American Home Front, 1941–1945* (1970); Richard Polenberg, *The War and Society: The United States, 1941–1945* (1972); Harold G. Vatter, *The U.S. Economy in World War II* (1985); Gerald T. White, *Billions for Defense: Government Financing by the Defense Plant Corporation During World War II* (1980).

SOCIAL CHANGES DURING THE WAR

Karen Anderson, *Wartime Women: Sex Roles, Family Relations, and the Status of Women During World War II* (1981); Allan Berube, *Coming Out under Fire: The History of Gay Men and Women in World War Two* (1990); A. Russell Buchanan, *Black Americans in World War II* (1977); Dominic J. Capeci, Jr., *Race Relations in Wartime Detroit: The Sojourner Truth Housing Controversy of 1942* (1984); Richard M. Dalfiume, *Desegregation of the U.S. Armed Forces: Fighting on Two Fronts, 1939–1953* (1969); Roger Daniels, *Concentration Camps USA: Japanese Americans and World War II* (1971); Richard Drinnon, *Keeper of Concentration Camps: Dillon S. Myer and American Racism* (1987); Charity Adams Earley, *One Woman's Army: A Black Officer Remembers the WAC* (1989); Audrie Girdner and Anne Loftig, *The Great Betrayal: The Evacuation of the Japanese-Americans During World War II* (1969); Sherna Berger Gluck, *Rosie the Riveter Revisited: Women, the War, and Social Change* (1987); Anne Bosanko Green, *One Woman's War: Letters Home from the Women's Army Corps, 1944–1946* (1989); Chester W. Gregory, *Women in Defense Work During World War II: An Analysis of the Labor Problem and Women's Rights* (1974); Susan M. Hartmann, *The Home Front and Beyond: American Women in the 1940s* (1982); Peter H. Irons, *Justice at War: The Story of the Japanese American Internment Cases* (1983); Mauricio Mazón, *The Zoot-Suit Riots: The Psychology of Symbolic Annihilation* (1984); August Meier and Elliot Rudwick, *CORE, 1942–1968* (1973); Gunnar Myrdal, *An American Dilemma* (1944); Robert Shogan and Thomas Craig, *The Detroit Race Riot* (1964); Neil Wynn, *The Afro-American and the Second World War* (1976).

THE WAR IN EUROPE

James MacGregor Burns, *Roosevelt: Soldier of Freedom* (1970); Diane Shaver Clemens, *Yalta* (1970); Kent Roberts Greenfield, *American Strategy in World War II: A Reconsideration* (1963); Eric Larrabee, *Commander in Chief: Franklin Delano Roosevelt, His Lieutenants, and Their War* (1987); Ronald Schaffer, *Wings of Judgment: American Bombing in World War II* (1985); Bradley F. Smith, *The Shadow Warriors: O.S.S. and the Origins of the C.I.A.* (1983); Gaddis Smith, *American Diplomacy During the Second World War, 1941–1945* (1965); John Snell, *Illusion and Necessity: The Diplomacy of Global War, 1939–1945* (1963); Mark A. Stoler, *The Politics of the Second Front: American Military Planning and Diplomacy in Coalition Warfare, 1941–1943* (1977).

THE WAR IN THE PACIFIC

Gar Alperovitz, *Atomic Diplomacy: Hiroshima and Potsdam*, rev. ed. (1985); Robert Butow, *Japan's Decision to Surrender* (1954); Herbert Feis, *The Atomic Bomb and the End of World War II* (1966); Gregg Herkin, *The Winning Weapon: The Atomic Bomb in the Cold War, 1945–1950* (1980); Robert Jungk, *Brighter than a Thousand Suns: A Personal History of the Atomic Scientists* (1958); Dan Kurzman, *Day of the Bomb: Countdown to Hiroshima* (1986); Martin J. Sherwin, *A World Destroyed: The Atomic Bomb and the Grand Alliance* (1975); Ronald H. Spector, *Eagle Against the Sun: The American War with Japan* (1985).

BIOGRAPHIES

Saul Alinsky, *John L. Lewis* (1949); Mark S. Foster, *Henry J. Kaiser: Builder in the Modern American West* (1989); Michael Schaller, *Douglas MacArthur: The Far Eastern General* (1989); Barbara Tuchman, *Stilwell and the American Experience in China, 1911–45* (1971).

Containing the Russian Bear

Origins of the Cold War
A World Divided
Tough Talk
The Truman Doctrine
The Marshall Plan: "Saving Western Europe"

The Containment Policy

Berlin Test
Troubling Times
The Korean War

The Cold War at Home

Adjusting to Peace
Confronting the Demands of Labor
Failure of the Fair Deal
Searching for the Enemy Within
The Rise and Fall of Joseph McCarthy

The Paranoid Style

HUAC Goes to Hollywood
"What's Wrong with Our Kids Today?"

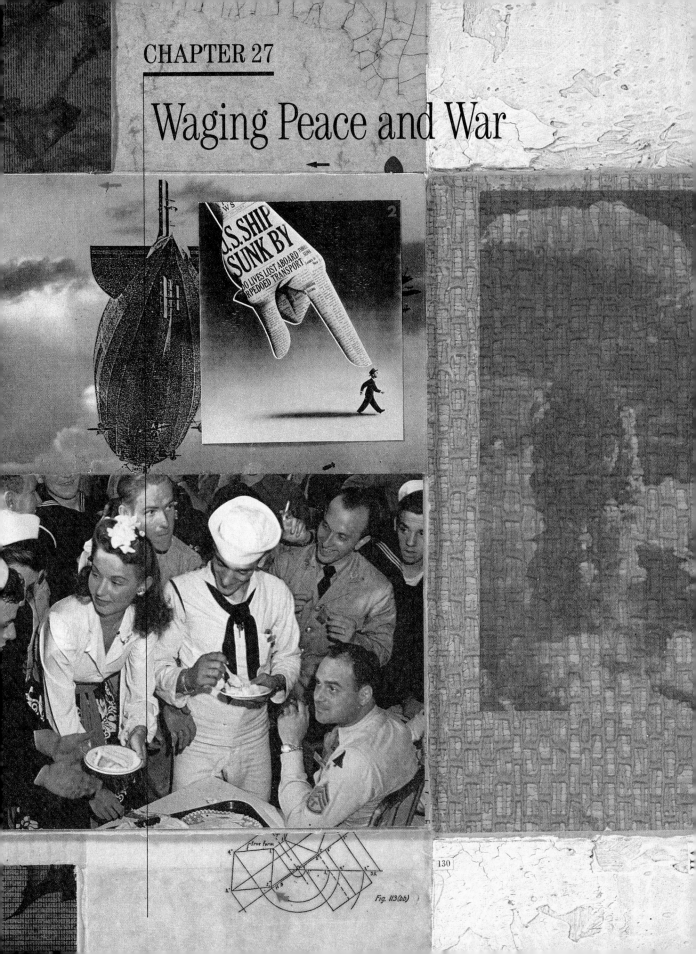

CHAPTER 27

Waging Peace and War

It was Sunday, August 27, 1948. Whittaker Chambers appeared calm as he answered questions on "Meet the Press," a weekly radio news show. The appearance, like most of Chambers's life, was a deception. He knew he was on enemy ground and that questions were the ammunition of the war. "I sought not to let myself be crowded," he later recalled, "not to lose my temper during the baiting." Chambers sat very still, waiting for the inevitable question. He didn't have to wait long. Edward T. Folliard, a reporter for the *Washington Post*, asked, "Are you willing to say now that Alger Hiss is or ever was a Communist?" Chambers paused a second before answering, for the answer could open him up to a slander or libel suit. Then came his terse, important reply: "Alger Hiss was a Communist and may be now." Like his questioners, Chambers also knew how to use words as weapons.

The road to "Meet the Press" had begun for Chambers a generation and a lifetime before 1948. It was paved with unhappiness. His father, Jay, was almost a stranger in his own house. For a time Jay left his wife Laha; after three years he returned. He demonstrated no love or affection for his wife or children. Whittaker remembers that Jay—who never allowed his children to call him "Papa"—dined alone and seldom spoke, except perhaps to say "don't." Home experiences left Chambers rebellious and feeling unwanted. He was forced to withdraw from Columbia for writing a mildly sacrilegious play, and he flirted with radical political philosophies, moved through a succession of love affairs, and kicked about Europe. In 1926 his brother Richard committed suicide. It was the most painful event in Chambers's life. For several months he was inconsolable. Almost as a form of therapy, he committed himself fully to another family— the Communist party. During his time of troubles, it gave his life a direction and a purpose.

During the late 1920s and early 1930s, as the United States sank deeper and deeper into the Great Depression, other Americans joined Chambers in the Communist party. Feeling betrayed by the capitalist order, they looked toward the Soviet Union for economic and political inspiration. Under Joseph Stalin, the Soviet Union appeared less affected by the depression than the capitalist West. Still more Americans joined the Communist party because only the Soviets seemed to be standing up against the Fascist threat posed by Hitler, Mussolini, and Franco. For Chambers and his comrades, then, the Red Star represented the future and the best hope of the world.

Chambers met Alger Hiss in 1934, when they both belonged to the same Communist "cell" in Washington, D.C. In appearance and personality they were almost perfect opposites. Chambers was overweight and sloppy; his clothes always seemed rumpled, and his face had a sleepy, slightly disinterested cast. Hiss was cut from different cloth. Handsome, thin, aristocratic looking, Hiss's career was marked by ambition and achievement. He was an honors student at Johns Hopkins and Harvard Law School; he was a favorite of future Supreme Court justice Felix Frankfurter; he clerked for the legendary Oliver Wendell Holmes. Popular with influential superiors and his co-workers, Hiss obviously had been singled out as one of the best and brightest, as one who would succeed. And he did. He acted as a counsel for the Agricultural Adjustment Administration, worked for the Senate committee investigating the munitions industry, went to the Yalta Conference with President Roosevelt, helped to organize the United Nations, and served as the president of the Carnegie Endowment for International Peace.

During his impressive career, Hiss worked with Whittaker Chambers for the Communist party. While Hiss served as a legal assistant for the Senate committee investigation of the munitions industry, he became close friends with Chambers. Hiss allowed Chambers to use his Washington, D.C., apartment for two months, gave him an automobile, and even permitted him to stay in his home on several occasions. Although Hiss would later deny that he knew Chambers—and then admit that he knew him slightly under a different name—the evidence is clear on one point: The bureaucrat and spy had formed a close friendship. It was during that period of friendship in the mid-1930s, Chambers later testified, that Hiss began to give him secret government documents.

Like many of his American comrades, Chambers abandoned the ideology of communism and lost faith in the Soviet Union during

On March 12, 1947, Truman appeared before a joint session of Congress and described the Greek and Turkish situations as battles between the forces of light and the legions of darkness. "At the present moment in world history nearly every nation must choose between alternative ways of life," he said. "One way of life is based upon the will of the majority, and is distinguished by free institutions, representative government, free elections, guarantees of individual liberty, freedom of speech and religion, and freedom from political oppression. The second way of life is based upon the will of a minority forcibly imposed upon the majority. It relies upon terror and oppression." Congress sounded its approval as Truman came to his climactic sentence: "I believe that it must be the policy of the United States to support free peoples who are resisting attempted subjugation by armed minorities or outside pressures." Labeled the Truman Doctrine, the statement set the course U.S. foreign policy would follow during the next generation.

Specifically, Truman called for economic and financial aid to "save" Greece and Turkey.

Congress responded by appropriating $400 million. By later standards it was a paltry sum, but it was a significant beginning. In the future, America would send billions of dollars in economic and military aid to countries fighting communism, even though the leaders of some of those nations were themselves dictators. In Truman's morality play, however, "anti-Communists" and "free peoples" became synonymous.

Although Truman succeeded in getting aid for Greece and Turkey and in arousing the American public, a few foreign policy experts believed that his scare tactics did more harm than good. George Kennan deplored the sweeping language of the Truman Doctrine, which placed U.S. aid to Greece "in the framework of a universal policy rather than in that of a specific decision addressed to a specific set of circumstances."

The Marshall Plan: "Saving Western Europe"

The millions of dollars sent to Greece and Turkey stabilized the pro-American governments of the two countries. But at the same time America was losing support in Western Europe, a far more vital region. Although the war had ended in the spring of 1945, Europe's problems continued. It lacked the money to rebuild its war-torn economies and scarred cities. To make matters worse, the winters of 1946 and 1947 were brutally cold. News reports from early 1947 told the sad story. Snow buried thousands of sheep in northern England; between December 1 and February 8, 40 residents of Berlin and 68 of Hamburg died from the cold; Holland was short of food; Italy was inundated by floods; and across the continent the weather report was always the same: "cold or very cold." The winter hardships fueled the Communist party, which made marked gains. American leaders assumed that economic distress would continue to breed political extremism. Anne O'Hare McCormick told Americans in the *New York Times:* "The extent to which democratic government survives on [the] continent depends on how far this country is willing to help it survive." Truman concurred, and so did his advisors. They were

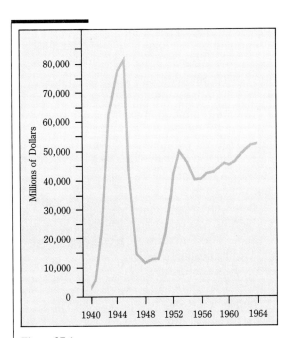

Figure 27.1
National defense budgets, 1940–1964

upset by the growth of anti-Americanism in Europe, an area that figured prominently in their postwar economic plans. The image of America had changed from loyal ally to selfish exploiter. Describing the typical occupation soldier in Germany, an army chaplain wrote, "There he stands in his bulging clothes, fat, overfed, lonely, a bit wistful, seeing little, understanding less—the Conqueror, with a chocolate bar in one pocket and a package of cigarettes in the other. . . . The chocolate bar and the cigarettes are about all that he, the Conqueror, has to give the conquered."

At the Harvard University commencement on June 5, 1947, Secretary of State George C. Marshall announced a plan to give Europe more. After describing the severe problems facing Europe, Marshall suggested that America could not afford to send a Band-Aid to cover the deep European wounds. "A cure rather than a mere palliative" was in order. Europe needed massive economic blood transfusions. He told his audience that the cost might seem high. Without America's help, however, "economic, social, and political deterioration of a very grave character" would result. And from a more selfish point of view, America needed a strong democratic Europe to provide rich markets for American goods and to act as a check against Soviet westward expansion.

In early 1948 Congress appropriated $17 billion to be spent over the next four years for the European Recovery Program (ERP), more popularly called the Marshall Plan. The program put food in the mouths of hungry children, coal in empty furnaces, and money in near-empty banks. More importantly, it rebuilt the economic infrastructure of Western Europe and restored economic prosperity to the region. In the process it created stable markets for American goods. Americans were proud of the Marshall Plan, and Europeans were moved by it. Winston Churchill judged it "the most unsordid act in history." And Hugh Gaitskell, British chancellor of the exchequer, noted: "We are not an emotional people . . . and not very articulate, but these characteristics should not . . . hide the real and profound sense of gratitude toward the American people." All told, the Marshall Plan greatly restored America's prestige abroad.

The Marshall Plan also fostered the economic integration of Western Europe by curbing nationalistic economic policies. American policy makers believed that only by functioning as a single economic unit could Western Europe enjoy real prosperity. "A healthy Europe," John Foster Dulles remarked, could not be "divided into small compartments." Although the process toward economic integration was slow and occasionally painful, it did move forward. The European Payments Union was created in 1950, the European Coal and Steel Authority in 1951, and the European Economic Community (Common Market) in 1958. In the final analysis, the Marshall Plan served both America's Cold War strategy and plans for a economic internationalism.

THE CONTAINMENT POLICY

Money, even billions of dollars, could not substitute for a concrete foreign policy to guide U.S. actions: an explicit policy that mixed the international idealism of the Truman Doctrine and the economic realism of the Marshall Plan with the will to meet the real or perceived Soviet threat. The policy was not long in coming. In July 1947, the journal *Foreign Affairs* contained an article entitled "The Sources of Soviet Conduct" by "Mr. X." The article provided a blueprint for the policy of containment, which would influence American foreign policy for at least the next generation.

"Mr. X" was George Kennan, the government's foremost authority on Russian history. Educated at Princeton University, Kennan had spent his adult life in the U.S. foreign service where he carefully stud-

George Kennan's analysis of United States-Soviet relations encouraged U.S. "containment" of the Russians and played a major role in the intensification of the Cold War.

ied the Soviet scene. During World War II he was stationed in Moscow, and was able to observe Soviet political behavior. Although he believed Russians were a "great and appealing people," he distrusted the Soviet government. In February 1946, he expressed his views of the Soviet Union in an 8000-word telegram to his superiors in Washington, and in the 1947 *Foreign Affairs* article, Kennan made his views public. He believed that Soviet communism was driven by two engines: the need for a repressive dictatorship at home and the belief there could never be any sense of community or true accord with the capitalist West. In fact, the Kremlin used the supposed threat from capitalism to justify its continued dictatorship. But, Kennan argued, Stalin and the leaders in the Kremlin were more interested in security than expansion. Soviets would only expand when allowed by American weakness. It could be *contained* to its present borders by a politically, economically, and militarily active United States. What was needed was "the adroit and vigilant application of counter-force at a series of constantly shifting geographical and political points, corresponding to the shifts and maneuvers of Soviet policy." Kennan even suggested that if the United States was firm in its resolve to contain Soviet expansion, "the possibility remains . . . that Soviet power . . . bears within it the seeds of its own decay." In short, Kennan held out the hope of complete victory in the Cold War.

Although Kennan later remarked that he was talking about the political containment of a political threat, in 1947 his article was read as primarily a military blueprint. As such, it satisfied hard-liners but was challenged by many other politicians and respected political commentators. Walter Lippmann challenged Kennan's policy in a series of newspaper articles later published as *The Cold War: A Study in U.S. Foreign Policy* (1947). Containment, Lippmann commented, allowed the Soviet Union largely to decide when and where its battles against America would take place, and it promised to tie the United States to small unstable "client" countries that would be a political, economic, and military drain on America. Seeing that the plan was primarily focused on Western European problems, Lippmann suggested that if followed it might well lead America into a land war in Asia where the idea of victory would be a cruel delusion. America, Lippmann maintained, was not in the military, economic, or strategic position to implement containment. Lippmann found it "hard to understand how Mr. X could have recommended such a strategic monstrosity."

Containment involved confronting the spread of communism across the globe and as Americans soon learned, it came with a heavy price. It meant supporting our allies around the world with billions of dollars in military and economic aid, and it meant thousands of Americans dying in foreign lands. Since containment was a defensive policy, it involved permanent Cold War without any hope of ultimate victory. Unlike World War I and World War II, the Cold War emphasized the doctrine of limited wars fought for limited goals. And in this arrangement, Kennan noted, "Man would have to recognize . . . that the device of military coercion would have . . . only relative—never an absolute—value in the pursuit of political objectives." It was a policy bound to breed frustration and anxiety—certain to influence domestic as well as foreign policy.

Berlin Test

During the late 1940s containment seemed to fit American needs. American-Soviet tensions centered particularly on the future of Germany. The United States maintained that the economic revival of Western Europe depended on a reindustrialized and prosperous Germany. The Soviets believed that a reindustrialized Germany was a dangerous Germany. An early test of the two different viewpoints came in Berlin, a divided city located in the heart of East Germany, deep within the Soviet zone. Future Soviet Premiere Nikita Khrushchev called democratic West Berlin a "bone in the throat" of Russia. In June 1948, Stalin decided to remove the bone by stopping all road and rail traffic between West Germany and Berlin. It was a crisis tailor-made for the containment policy. Stalin had picked the time and place. Now Truman had to decide upon a response.

He chose the sky. Stalin could close highways and railways, but he could not effectively close the skyways. For almost one year America and Britain kept West Berlin alive and democratic by a massive airlift. Food, coal, clothing, and all other essentials were flown daily into Berlin. It was an heroic feat, a triumph of technology. Western pilots logged 277,264 flights into West Berlin; they hauled in 2,343,315 tons of food, fuel, medicine, and clothing. Finally on May 12, 1949, Stalin lifted his blockade of West Berlin. For Stalin, the success of the airlift had become an embarrassment for the Soviet Union. In the West, containment had passed an important test.

Troubling Times

Truman scored a series of triumphs during 1947 and 1948. The Truman Doctrine, the Marshall Plan, and the Berlin Airlift strengthened his popularity at home and U.S. prestige abroad. In the election of 1948 Truman won a remarkable upset victory over Thomas E. Dewey. Then in 1949 eleven of the Western democracies joined the United States in signing the North Atlantic Treaty Organization (NATO), a mutual defense pact. NATO signified America's position as the leader of the Western Alliance, and it con-

formed to the containment policy. But difficult times for Truman, containment, and America lay ahead. In late August 1949, American scientists detected traces of radioactive material in the Soviet atmosphere. The cause was as clear as a mushroom-shaped cloud. The Soviets had the bomb—a full decade before American intelligence expected it.

On September 22 Truman told the public: "We have evidence that an atomic explosion occurred in the USSR." Although the press tried to downplay the story, a wave of anxiety swept the country. Physicist Harold C. Urey told reporters, "There is only one thing worse than one nation having the atomic bomb—that's two nations having it." There was another thing even worse: One of the nations that had the bomb also had the Red Army.

Between 1945 and 1949 the threat of the bomb had given teeth to American policy. It was America's check to the Red Army, and U. S. policy makers seldom allowed Soviet leaders to forget it. In 1945 then Secretary of State James F. Byrnes told his Soviet counterpart V. M. Molotov, "If you don't cut out all this stalling and let us get down to work, I am going to pull an atomic bomb out of my hip pocket and let you have it." Now Molotov had one in his hip pocket.

During 1948 and 1949, an American and British airlift brought close to 7000 tons of food and fuel each day to Soviet-blockaded West Berlin.

Truman responded by asking his scientists to accelerate the development of a hydrogen bomb; and Congress responded by voting appropriations for Truman's latest defense requests. Of such events and decisions arms races have their humble origins.

On the heels of the Soviet bomb came more unwelcome news—the establishment of the Communist government in China after a bitter civil war. The war between Mao Zedung's (Mao Tse-tung) and Chou En-lai's Communists and Jiang Jieshi's (Chiang Kai-shek) Nationalists had been raging since the 1930s. The United States had strongly backed Jiang during the civil war, providing him with more than $3 billion in aid between 1945 and 1949. But the aid was unable to prop up a government that was structurally unsound, inefficient, and corrupt. In the first week of May 1949, Jiang fled across the Formosa Strait to Taiwan, and on September 21, Mao proclaimed Red China's sovereignty. With Jiang in Taiwan and Mao on the mainland, China became a tale of two countries.

The Truman administration tried to put the best face possible on the turn of events. Secretary of State Dean Acheson issued a thousand-page White Paper explaining how Mao had won the civil war. It detailed the rampant corruption in the Nationalist government and Jiang's many mistakes. Assessing the role of the United States in the outcome of the conflict Acheson concluded, "Nothing that this country did or could have done within the reasonable limits of its capabilities could have changed that result . . . it was the product of internal Chinese forces, forces which this country tried to influence but could not."

For the American public, however, that explanation was not good enough. The China most Americans knew, as one historian put it, was associated with novelist "Pearl Buck's peasants, rejoicing in the good earth . . . dependable, democratic, warm, and above all pro-American." It was an image that American missionaries confirmed during the 1920s and 1930s and one that journalists supported during World War II. Americans were told that there were two types of Asians—the good Chinese and the evil Japanese. In 1941 *Time* magazine even ran an article entitled "How to Tell Your Friends From the Japs." It confidently reported, "the Chinese

The celebration of the first anniversary of Mao Zedung's rule in 1950 brought many to the streets of Peking.

expression is likely to be more placid, kindly, open; the Japanese more positive, dogmatic, arrogant."

Republicans and supporters of Jiang in America blamed Truman for "losing" China. Led by Henry Luce, the influential publisher of *Time* and *Life* who was the China-born son of American missionaries, an informal group known as the China Lobby blasted the Truman administration. They claimed "egg-sucking phony liberals" had "sold China into atheistic slavery." The China Lobby believed that America had far more influence than it actually had, that a country that contained 6 percent of the earth's population could control the other 94 percent. They were wrong, but millions of Americans took their loud cries seriously.

"China lost itself," Acheson countered. "We picked a bad horse," Truman admitted. But given the political pressure at home, Truman was not about to change mounts in the middle of the race. Reversing America's traditional policy of recognizing de facto governments whether approved or not, Truman refused to recognize the Communist People's Republic of China. Instead he insisted that Jiang's Nationalist government on Taiwan was the legitimate government of China. It was an unrealistic policy, but one that future presidents found politically difficult to reverse. The United States and the People's Republic of China did not establish formal relations until 1979.

The Korean War

The rhetoric of the Truman administration tended to simplify complex issues, intensify the Cold War rivalry, and tie foreign policy to domestic politics. Failure abroad could have calamitous consequences for politicians at home. "If you can't stand the heat, get out of the kitchen," Truman often said. By 1950 the kitchen had become hotter. After "China fell," Truman was more than ever determined to contain communism.

The mood of the Truman administration is clearly evident in National Security Council Paper Number 68 (NSC-68), one of the most important documents of the Cold War. Completed in April of 1950, it expressed the views of foreign policy planner Paul Nitze and Dean Acheson that communism is a monolithic world movement directed from the Kremlin; it advocated "an immediate and large-scale build-up in our military and general strength of our allies with the intention of righting the power balance and in the hope that through means other than all-out war we could induce a change in the nature of the Soviet system." NSC-68 extended the Truman Doctrine and called for America to protect the world against the spread of communism. The cost would be great—NSC-68 estimated it at 20 percent of the gross national product or over a 300 percent increase in military appropriations—but planners warned that without the commitment America faced the prospect of a world moving toward communism.

Truman realized that NSC-68 "meant a great military effort in time of peace. It meant doubling or tripling the budget, increasing taxes heavily, and imposing various kinds of economic controls." And he doubted whether Congress would accept such a peacetime buildup. He never got a chance to find out, for in June 1950 America went to war in Korea.

Korea, like Germany, was a divided country. When the Japanese surrendered its forces in Korea after World War II, Soviet troops accepted the surrender north of the 38th parallel, American troops south of that line. With the deepening of the Cold War, the temporary division line became permanent. North of the 38th parallel, Communist Kim Il Sung governed North Korea. Supported by the Soviet Union, Kim forged a modern, disciplined army during the late 1940s. In South Korea, 75-year-old President Syngman Rhee, who received strong aid and support from the United States, opposed any reconciliation with Communist North Korea. But, as Secretary of State Acheson noted in an unfortunate speech before the National Press Club on January 12, 1950, South Korea lay outside America's primary "defense perimeter." As far as military security of South Korea was concerned, Acheson emphasized, should "an attack occur the initial resistance" must come from "the people attacked."

On June 25, 1950, the attack occurred. In an orderly, coordinated offensive, North Korea sent 90,000 men across the 38th parallel into South Korea. They faced a weak, disorderly South Korean army, aptly described as "little more than a constabulary." It was a mismatch of epic proportions, and South Korean troops quickly mounted an all-out retreat. As the monsoon rains drenched the rice paddies and mountains, Korea moved swiftly toward unification under Kim's Communist government.

Why did North Korea attack? At the time, the Truman administration believed that the Soviets directed the assault. It regarded Kim as little more than a puppet whose strings were manipulated in Moscow. There is little evidence, however, to support this contention. More likely internal Korean politics dictated the course of events. Kim's position in North Korea was by no means secure. He faced organized opposition from a Democratic Front for the Unification of the Fatherland. The invasion of South Korea, therefore, may have been launched to undercut that movement. Certainly Kim informed Stalin of the impending invasion, but the idea and the timing were probably his own.

Truman had just finished a Saturday dinner in Independence, Missouri, when Acheson telephoned him with news of the invasion. His reaction was as rapid and as certain as North Korea's attack. Since both Koreas were technically wards of the United Nations, the Truman administration took the matter to the Security Council. With the Soviet Union absent (it was boycotting the United Nations over the refusal of the organization to seat the People's Republic of China), the Security Council by a 9 to 0 vote condemned the North Korean assault and demanded an immediate cease-fire. Encouraged by the United Nations's prompt action and without consulting Congress, Truman pledged American support to South Korea and strengthened the military position of the United States in Asia.

Truman termed the conflict a "UN police action" and, in fact, a number of UN members sent troops, but for all practical purposes it was a war that initially matched the United States and South Korea against North Korea. Air force advisors told Truman that they could stop the North Korean advance by bombing the Communist supply line. They convinced Truman that ground forces would not be needed. Truman's advisors seemed convinced that the Asians would turn and run at the first show of Western force. Although the bombs destroyed miles of roads and bridges, they did not slow the North Korean advance.

On June 30, Truman took the fateful step of ordering American occupation troops sta-

tioned in Japan to proceed to Korea. They soon joined their South Korean allies in a headlong retreat. For six weeks the allies fell steadily back until they stabilized a perimeter in southeast Korea around the port city of Pusan. With their offensive halted, North Korean troops mounted a siege. To the surprise of the world, the Pusan perimeter held firm.

For American soldiers it had been a painful and disappointing two months. They were fighting in an unfamiliar country for an unsatisfactory objective. Truman's announced goal was simply to restore the 38th parallel as the border between the two Koreas. Victory then was defined as a stalemate. Corporal Stephen Zeg of Chicago expressed the feeling of other soldiers when he commented, "I'll fight for my country, but I'll be damned if I see why I'm fighting to save this hellhole."

But fighting they were, and General Douglas MacArthur was determined to reverse the military situation of the war. A bold, even arrogant man, firmly fixed in his opinions and certain of his ability to command in battle, MacArthur decided to split his forces and launch a surprise attack against the North Koreans' rear. On the morning of September 15, 1950, American marines began an amphibious attack on In-

American occupation troops stationed in Japan joined South Korean allies in a retreat to the southeast area of Korea, where they managed to hold off the North Korean forces.

chon, a port city, wrote one historian, "about as large as Jersey City, as ugly as Liverpool, and as dreary as Belfast." MacArthur's military advisors warned him against the move, noting that Inchon possessed every natural and geographic handicap. MacArthur, however, was confident of victory. It was a bold, risky maneuver—a bold, risky, successful maneuver.

Faced with an enemy to their front and their rear, North Korean troops retreated across the border. By the beginning of October those North Korean soldiers who were not captured or killed were above the 38th parallel. Truman had achieved his stated objective. But the warrior in MacArthur wanted more—he wanted victory on the battlefield. And he said so, loudly and publicly. In private the Truman administration was moving toward MacArthur's position. Containment was giving way to a policy of liberation. After receiving MacArthur's reassurances at a private meeting on Wake Island, Truman decided to allow U.S. forces to move across the 38th parallel and "liberate" North Korea. Like MacArthur's Inchon landing, it was a bold plan, predicated on the widely held American belief that Red China would not intervene in the conflict.

This time boldness failed. North Korea was a difficult country to invade. The American army had no reliable maps and mountainous terrain rendered traditional military tactics impossible. In addition, as MacArthur's forces moved recklessly north toward Manchuria, Chinese officials sent informal warnings to the United States that unless the advance stopped, their country would enter the fray. MacArthur ignored Chinese warnings and his own intelligence reports and kept moving.

Communist China struck in late November. Over 300,000 troops poured across the border and attacked unprepared American forces. An advance force of marines near the Chosin Reservoir was cut off from the main army. They made the best of a bad situation. "The enemy is in front of us, behind us, to the left of us, and to the right of us," Colonel Lewis B. "Chesty" Puller told his regiment. "They won't escape *this* time." Puller's bravado, however, could not hide the terrible truth. The entry of Communist China into the conflict had radically altered the nature of the war.

Victory was now out of the question. Only MacArthur continued to talk about an absolute victory. If a nation was going to fight a war, he sermonized, it should fight to win. In Washington, however, the Truman administration was shifting back to the pre-Inchon policy of containment. When MacArthur publicly criticized the administration's newest approach, an angry Truman recalled him and replaced him with General Matthew B. Ridgway. In America Truman's sacking of Mac raised a firestorm of protest. An April 1951 Gallup poll reported that 66 percent of Americans disapproved of Truman's firing of the general, and then in October, 56

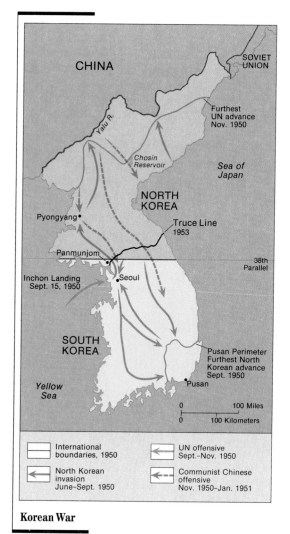

Korean War

percent indicated that they believed Korea was a "useless war."

The Korean War dragged on until July 10, 1951, when formal peace negotiations began, but it proved to be a long, difficult process. While diplomats talked, American soldiers fought and died. Altogether, 34,000 Americans were killed and 103,000 wounded during the Korean War. When Truman left office in early 1953 the carnage still continued. Finally on July 26, 1953, the war ended as it began, with North Koreans above the 38th parallel and South Koreans below it. It was a victory for Truman's containment policy, but for millions of Americans it somehow tasted like defeat.

THE COLD WAR AT HOME

Commie for a day. It was a theme idea. It answered the question, "What would it be like to live under a Soviet-type, communist dictatorship?" On May Day 1950, at Mosinee, Wisconsin, American Legionnaires disguised themselves as Soviet soldiers and staged a mock Communist takeover of their town. They arrested and summarily locked up the mayor and clergymen, nationalized all businesses, confiscated all firearms, and rid the library of rows of objectionable books. They even forced Mosinee residents to alter their eating habits. The local restaurants served only potato soup, dark bread, and black coffee, and only Young Communist Leaguers were permitted to eat candy. Eventually Mosinee patriots "liberated" their town, and at dusk they held a mass democratic rally amidst much patriotic music and the burning of Communist literature.

For most of Mosinee's citizens it was an edifying experiment. "We really learned about what 100 percent communism would be like," one resident observed. They concluded that life under communism was hardly worth living. Many found intolerable the lack of such basic freedoms as privacy, speech, press, religion, and decent food. One participant confessed, "I know some people who even drove to [neighboring] Wausau to get something to eat. In Russia I guess you wouldn't be able to get anything else anywhere."

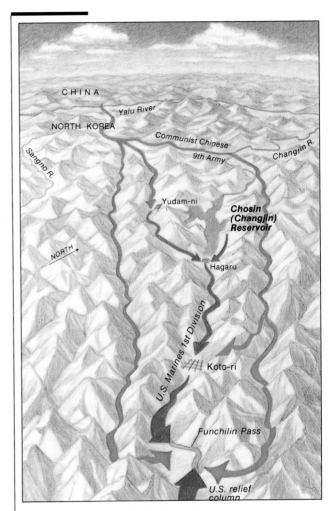

Marine Breakout from Chosin Reservoir
The Communist Chinese forces (100,000) had set a trap for the Marines (20,000) at Chosin Reservoir. The Marines doggedly fought their way out of the mountains in weather that ranged from −30°F at night to about 0° during the day.

There is an element of humor to Mosinee's Red May Day. But behind the events was a national mood that was far from funny. As Truman waged the Cold War abroad, Cold War issues gradually came to dominate the American domestic scene. During the ensuing Red Scare, the fear of communism disrupted American life, and the freedoms that Americans took for granted came under attack. At home as well as abroad, Americans battled real and imagined Communist enemies.

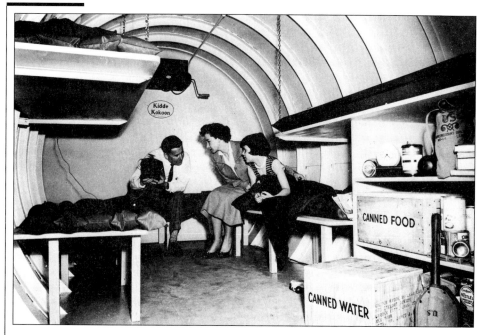

H-bomb shelters could take care of a family for three to five days and were big selling items in the 1950s. This deluxe model came equipped with five bunks and air mattresses.

Adjusting to Peace

Truman and his advisors approached the end of World War II with their eyes on the past. They were uneasy about the future. Memories of the Great Depression and the painful social and economic adjustment after World War I clouded their thinking. They knew that massive wartime spending, not the New Deal, had ended the decade of depression, and they worried that peace might bring more economic suffering. Peace with prosperity was their goal.

The solution to the problems of converting back to a peacetime economy, Truman believed, lay in the continuation, at least for a time, of wartime government economic controls. During the war the Office of Price Administration (OPA) had controlled prices and held inflation in check. After Japan surrendered, Truman asked Congress to continue price controls and outlined a program for economic reconversion. To ensure future prosperity, Truman advocated such economic measures as a 65-cents-an-hour minimum wage, nationalization of the housing industry, and stronger fair employment practices legislation.

Congress responded half-heartedly. It did pass the Employment Act of 1946. Although it was less than Truman had requested, it did provide the institutional framework for more government control over the economy. The act created the Council of Economic Advisors to help "promote free competitive enterprise, to avoid economic fluctuations . . . and to maintain employment, production, and purchasing power." During the decades after 1946, the council exerted a powerful influence over economic policy.

On the other hand, Republicans and southern Democrats balked against a return to more "New Dealism." One influential congressman even accused Truman of "out-dealing the New Deal." Instead, Congress destroyed the OPA by relaxing its controls, a policy that created immediate inflation. Congress's refusal to pass Truman's economic package did not tumble America into another depression. In truth, the American economy was basically sound. Wartime employment and wartime saving had created a people whose money was burning holes in their pockets. They wanted peacetime goods—automobiles, houses, Scotch whiskey, nylon stockings, and red meat. Given the demand and the short supply, inflation was inevitable. In addition, the short supply of consumer goods increased black market activities. Americans offered bribes for preferential treatment from car salesmen, butchers, and landlords. But as industries converted to peacetime production, consumer supplies rose to meet the new demands.

Confronting the Demands of Labor

The death of the OPA led to demands for higher wages as well as higher prices. During the war labor unions had taken "no strike" pledges, and through their efforts America became the "arsenal of democracy." Workers labored long and hard, agreeing to speedups and higher production quotas. Virtually no production time was lost to strikes.

The end of the war signaled the start of the strike season as workers demanded rewards for their wartime efforts and their loss of overtime pay. During 1946 over 4.5 million laborers struck, and 107,476,000 workdays were lost to strikes. If labor's cause was just, its timing was disastrous. After clashing repeatedly with an obstreperous Congress, Truman was in no mood to coddle labor. When two national railway brotherhoods threatened to disrupt the transportation system, Truman proposed to draft the workers. On national radio he announced, "The crisis at Pearl Harbor was the result of action by a foreign enemy. The crisis tonight is caused by a group of men within our country who place their private interests above the welfare of the nation." Confronted by hostile public opinion and an unsympathetic president, the brotherhoods went back to work.

Labor was angry. United Mine Workers leader John L. Lewis told reporters, "You can't mine coal with bayonets." As winter approached, Lewis took his men out on strike. The prospect of a cold winter created anxiety, and Truman reacted angrily. He threatened to take over the mines and lashed out publicly at the defiant Lewis. Finally Truman appealed directly to the miners, asking them to go back to work for the good and warmth of the nation. It worked. Lewis called off the strike. Truman's prestige and confidence soared.

Truman's gains were labor's losses. The congressional elections of 1946, which brought the conservative Republican-controlled Eightieth Congress, added to labor's problems. Led by Robert Taft, Congress pushed through the Labor-Management Relations Act of 1947 (better known as the Taft-Hartley Act), which was passed over Truman's veto. It outlawed the closed shop (a business or industry in which all the employees were required to join a union), gave presidents power to delay strikes by declaring a "cooling-off" period, and curtailed the political and economic power of organized labor. The act signified the conservative mood of the country.

It was a bad period for all workers, but for female workers it was especially hard. During the war they had filled a wide range of industrial jobs, but returning soldiers quickly displaced them. Some accepted the change and returned to their prewar occupations. Others resented the loss of their relatively high-paying jobs. What was worse, when new jobs opened employers hired and trained younger males rather than rehire the experienced females. Thus while male workers complained about the antilabor mood of the country, many unemployed women laborers lamented the antifemale prejudices among employers.

Failure of the Fair Deal

Political experts expected America to vote Republican in the 1948 presidential elections. Truman's policies had angered liberals, labor, Southerners, and most of Congress. Moreover, Democrats had occupied the White House since 1933. Republicans reasoned that it was time for a change. They nominated Thomas E. Dewey of New York, the GOP candidate in 1944. The Democrats stayed with Truman, even though large numbers of Southerners and liberals deserted the party to follow third-party movements. Southerners, angered by Truman's support of civil rights, formed the States' Rights Democratic party—better known as the Dixiecrats—and nominated Governor J. Strom Thurmond of South Carolina for president. Liberals joined with Communists to form the Progressive party, which nominated FDR's former vice president Henry A. Wallace for president.

SAID SOMETHING!

Most pollsters predicted that Republican candidate Thomas E. Dewey would win the 1948 presidential election, but in a stunning political upset the voters re-elected President Truman.

An underdog from the start, Truman rolled up his sleeves and took his cause to the people. His train was the 17-car "Presidential Special." The rear car was the *Ferdinand Magellan,* the bulletproof, steel-and-concrete reinforced presidential car that had been made for Roosevelt during the war. It weighed 285,000 pounds—enough to crush every other car in the train had the engineer stopped suddenly. It moved across the country, and at each stop Truman blasted the "do-nothing" Eightieth Congress. "If you send another Republican Congressman to Washington, you're a bigger bunch of suckers than I think you are," he lectured. "Give 'em hell, Harry!" was the popular refrain. By contrast, Dewey sat tight, seemingly more concerned with his fastidious appearance than his bland speeches. His cold personality failed to move American voters. "I don't know which is

the chillier experience—to have Tom ignore you or shake your hand," noted a Truman supporter. "You have to get to know Dewey to dislike him," added another.

By election day Truman had closed the gap. The old Roosevelt coalition—midwestern farmers, urban ethnics, organized labor, blacks, and Southerners—remained sufficiently strong to send Truman back to the White House. Neither the Dixiecrats nor the progressives hurt Truman in any substantial way. Most Democrats chose to remain in the center of the party with Truman rather than drift toward the radical fringes. The election was a testimony to the legacy of FDR as well as Truman's scrappiness, and to the often overlooked fact that Democrats outnumbered Republicans in the nation.

"Keep America Human With Truman," read one of his campaign posters. In 1949 he announced a plan to do just that. Known as the Fair Deal, the legislative package included an expansion of Social Security, federal aid to education, a higher minimum wage, federal funding for public housing projects, a national plan for medical insurance, civil rights legislation for minorities, and other measures to foster social and economic justice. As Truman explained, "I expect to give every segment of our population a fair deal." At the core of the Fair Deal was the belief that government-controlled economic expansion blunts extremism from the right and left and ensures prosperity.

Congress took Truman's package, stripped off the wrapping, threw away some of the contents, and sent it back to the president for his signature. Congress did extend Social Security, raise the minimum wage to 75 cents an hour, and further develop several New Deal programs. But the more original proposals of the Fair Deal—civil rights legislation, a national health insurance program, an imaginative farm program, and federal aid to education—were rejected by a Congress that opposed anything defined as "creeping socialism."

Truman, as well as Congress, contributed to the ultimate failure of the Fair Deal to achieve its objectives. To be sure, Republicans and Southerners joined forces in opposition to civil rights and government spending programs. But on domestic issues Truman demonstrated an al-

witnesses testified before the committee, but public interest centered on the alleged boss of the New York underworld Frank Costello, alias Francisco Castaglia, alias Frank Severio. Costello was purportedly head of the organized crime family previously run by Vito Genovese and Charles Luciano.

In his initial appearance before the committee, Costello's lawyer objected to having his client's face televised. Technicians proceeded to focus the cameras on Costello's hands. The result was television at its most powerful. As committee counsel Rudolph Halley fired questions, Costello was seen nervously ripping sheets of paper to shreds, drumming his fingers on the table top, and clenching his fist.

During the New York hearings, the daytime television audience grew from a miniscule 1.5 percent of homes to a phenomenal 26.2 percent. In the New York metropolitan area an average of 86.2 percent of all individuals watching television watched the hearings, twice the number that had watched the World Series the previous October. The New York City electric company had to add a generator to supply power for all the television sets in use. Commented *Life* magazine: "The week of March 12, 1951, will occupy a special place in history. . . . [People] had suddenly gone indoors into living rooms, taverns and clubrooms, auditoriums and backoffices. There, in eerie half-light, looking at millions of small frosty screens, people sat as if charmed. . . . Never before had the attention of the nation been riveted so completely on a single matter."

The Kefauver committee failed to produce effective crime fighting legislation, but it did heighten public awareness of the problem of political corruption and organized crime and generated pressure to enforce existing law. In the aftermath of the committee's investigation, more than 70 local crime commissions were established. The Special Rackets Squad of the FBI launched 46,000 investigations, and by 1957, federal prosecutors had won 874 convictions and recovered $336 million. The committee's hearings were largely responsible for the defeat of proposals to legalize gambling in Arizona, California, Massachusetts, and Montana.

The investigation was important in one other respect. The Kefauver committee played a vital role in popularizing the myth that organized crime in the United States was an alien import, brought to the United States by Italian, and especially by Sicilian, immigrants in the form of the Mafia, a highly centralized, secret organization, which used violence and deceit to prey on the weaknesses and vices of the public. In its report, the committee asserted that much of the responsibility for gambling, loan sharking, prostitutions, and narcotics trafficking lay in two major syndicates.

In fact, the committee's conclusion—that organized crime was rooted in a highy centralized ethnic conspiracy—was in error. Most organized crime in the United States is organized on a municipal and regional, rather than a national, basis. And despite the image portrayed in such epics as Mario Puzo's *The Godfather*, diverse ethnic groups have participated in such sophisticated crimes as large-scale gambling, loan sharking, narcotics trafficking, and labor racketeering.

Today, the power of the nation's traditional Mafia families appears to be dwindling. Since the mid-1980s, more than 100 top Cosa Nostra leaders have been sentenced to long prison terms. In Detroit, Kansas City, Milwaukee, New England, New Jersey, Philadelphia, and St. Louis, where Mafia gangs once influenced the construction, trucking, trash collection, and garment manufacturing industries, Mafia strength has sharply declined. Nevertheless, the decline of the mob does not mean the end of organized crime; rival crime groups have stepped in and taken over activities such as illegal gambling and drug trafficking.

It is, above all, a way of seeing the world and of expressing oneself. . . . The distinguishing thing about the paranoid style is . . . that its exponents see . . . a "vast" or "gigantic" conspiracy as *the motive force* in historical events. . . . The paranoid spokesman sees the fate of this conspiracy in apocalyptic terms—he traffics in the birth and death of whole worlds, whole political orders, whole systems of human values. . . . Since what is at stake is always a conflict between absolute good and absolute evil, the quality needed is not a willingness to compromise but the will to fight things out to the finish.

The nature of the fight against communism contributed to the paranoid style. Politicians warned Americans that communism silently and secretly destroyed a country from within. Although directed from Moscow, its aim was subversion through the slow destruction of a country's moral fiber. No one knew which institution it would next attack, or when. It might be the State Department or the YMCA; it might be the presidency, the army, the movie industry, or the Cub Scouts. Politicians counseled vigilance. They told Americans to watch for the unexpected, to suspect everyone and everything. As a result, between 1945 and 1955 a broad spectrum of institutions, organizations, and individuals came under suspicion. Whether it was the Mafia or the fluoridation of drinking water, Americans sought the answers to complex problems in the workings of conspiracies.

HUAC Goes to Hollywood

The House of Representatives established the Un-American Activities Committee (HUAC) in the late 1930s to combat subversive right-wing and left-wing movements. Its history was less than distinguished. From the first it tended to see subversive Communists everywhere at work in American society. HUAC even announced that the Boy Scouts were Communist infiltrated. During the late 1940s and the early 1950s HUAC picked up the tempo of its investigations, which it conducted in well-publicized sessions. Twice during this period HUAC traveled to Hollywood to investigate Communist infiltration in the film industry.

HUAC first went to Hollywood in 1947. Al-

though it didn't find the party line preached in the movies, it did call a group of radical screen writers and producers into its sessions to testify. Asked if they were Communists, the "Hollywood Ten" refused to answer questions about their political beliefs. As Ring Lardner, Jr., one of the ten, said, "I could answer . . . but if I did, I would hate myself in the morning." They believed that the First Amendment protected them. In the politically charged late 1940s, however, their rights were not protected. Those who refused to divulge their political affiliations were tried for contempt of Congress, sent to prison, and blacklisted.

HUAC went back to Hollywood in 1951. This time it called hundreds of witnesses from both the political right and the political left. Conservatives told HUAC that Hollywood was littered with "Commies." Walt Disney even recounted attempts to have Mickey Mouse follow the party line. Of the radicals, some talked but most didn't. To cooperate with HUAC entailed "naming names"—that is, informing on one's friends and political acquaintances. Again, those who refused to name names found themselves unemployed and unemployable.

The House Un-American Activities Committee conducted an investigation of Communist activities in Hollywood that included testimony by such notable actors as Ronald Reagan.

The HUAC hearings and blacklisting convinced Hollywood producers to make strongly anti-Communist films. Between 1947 and 1954 they released more than 50 such films. Most were second-rate movies, starring third-rate actors. The films assured Americans that Communists were thoroughly bad people—they didn't have children, they exhaled cigarette smoke too slowly, they murdered their "friends," and they went berserk when arrested. As one film historian has commented, the Communists in these anti-Communist films even looked alike; most were "apt to be exceptionally haggard or disgracefully pudgy," and there was certainly "something terribly wrong with a woman if her slip straps showed through her blouse."

If the films were bad civics lessons, they did have an impact. They seemed to confirm HUAC's position that Communists were everywhere, that subversives lurked in every shadow. They reaffirmed the paranoid style and helped to justify McCarthy's harangues and Truman's Cold War rhetoric.

Movies like *Rebel Without a Cause*, starring James Dean, depicted the futility and hopelessness of American youth in the 1950s.

"What's Wrong with Our Kids Today?"

At the same time it turned out films about serious but bumbling Communists, Hollywood produced movies that contributed to the fear that something was terribly wrong with the youth of America. Films such as *The Wild One* (1954), *Blackboard Jungle* (1955), and *Rebel Without a Cause* (1955) portrayed adolescents as budding criminals, emerging homosexuals, potential Fascists, and pathological misfits—everything but perfectly normal kids. On close inspection, cultural critics concluded that something was indeed wrong with American youth, who like Tony in *I Was a Teenage Werewolf* (1957) seemed closer to uncontrollable beasts than civilized adults. As Tony tells a psychiatrist, "I say things, I do things—I don't know why."

FBI reports and congressional investigations reinforced the theme of adolescent moral decline. J. Edgar Hoover, head of the FBI, linked the rise in juvenile delinquency to the decline in the influence of family, home, church, and local community institutions. Youths had moved away from benign authority toward temptations of popular culture, which, Hoover said, "flout indecency and applaud lawlessness."

Frederic Wertham, a psychiatrist who studied the problem extensively, agreed, emphasizing particularly the pernicious influence of comic books. He believed that crime and horror comic books fostered racism, fascism, and sexism in their readers. In his book *Seduction of the Innocent* (1954), Wertham even linked homosexuality to the reading of comics. Describing how the comic *Batman* could lead to homosexuality, Wertham quoted one of his male patients: "I remember the first time I came across the page mentioning the 'secret bat cave.' The thought of Batman and Robin living together and possibly having sex relations came to my mind . . . I felt I'd like to be loved by someone like Batman or Superman." Far from being an unheard voice, Wertham's attack generated congressional investigations of and local attacks against the comic book industry. In response, the comic book industry passed several self-regulatory codes designed to restrict the violent and sexual content of comic books.

For a number of critics, sports were an antidote to the ills of wayward youths. "Organized sport is one of our best weapons against juvenile delinquency," remarked J. Edgar Hoover. Youths who competed for championship trophies felt no inclination to compete for "wrist watches, bracelets and automobiles that belong to other people." Nor would they turn to communism. As Senator Herman Welker of Idaho bluntly put it, "I never saw a ballplayer who was a Communist."

Given these widespread beliefs, the sports scandals of the early 1950s shocked the nation and raised fresh questions about the morality of American adolescents. In February 1951 New York authorities disclosed that players for the City College of New York (CCNY) basketball team had accepted money to fix games. By the time the investigations ended, Long Island University, New York University, Manhattan College, St. John's, Toledo, Bradley, and Kentucky were implicated in the scandal, which involved forging transcripts and paying players as well as fixing games.

In August 1951 the scandal moved to football. This one involved academic cheating, not point shaving, and was confined to one school—the United States Military Academy at West Point. Altogether, academy officials dismissed 90 cadets, half of them football players, for violations of the school's honor code. "These acts," said Senator Harry F. Byrd of Virginia, "have struck a blow at the morals of the youth of the country which will last for a long time."

The West Point scandal especially struck at the nation's heart, for half a world away in Korea American soldiers were battling to contain communism. What of their moral fiber? They too had read comics, watched films written by left-wing screen writers, and been exposed to the "subversive" influences. Did they have the "right stuff"? These questions swirled around the Korean prisoner of war (POW) controversy. Early reports suggested the American POWs in Korea were different from, and inferior to, those of World War II. Journalists portrayed them as undisciplined, morally weak, susceptible to "brainwashing," uncommitted to traditional American ideals, and prone to collaborate with their guards. POW experiences seemed to confirm that something indeed was wrong with the kids of America.

What was wrong? Who was corrupting the youth of America? The Republican *Chicago Tribune* blamed the affair on the New Deal. The Communist *Daily Worker* said it was the fault of Wall Street, bankers, and greedy politicians. The paranoid style, after all, had no party affiliation. Other Americans, without being too specific, simply felt that there was some ominous force working within America against America.

Adherents to the paranoid style dealt more with vague perceptions than concrete facts. They reacted more to what seemed to be true than to what actually was true. In fact, sociologists and historians have demonstrated that Korean POWs behaved in much the same way as POWs from earlier wars. And during the late 1940s and 1950s juvenile delinquency was not on an upswing. Alien subversive forces were not undermining American morality. In retrospect, we know this. But the rhetoric of the Cold War and McCarthyism created a political atmosphere that proved fertile for the paranoid style.

CONCLUSION

By 1953 and 1954 there were indications of a thaw in the Cold War. First came the death of Joseph Stalin, which was officially announced on March 5, 1953. Shortly thereafter Georgi Malenkov told the Supreme Soviet, the highest legislative body of the Soviet Union: "At the present time there is no disputed or unresolved question that cannot be settled peacefully by mutual agreement. . . . This applies to our relations with all states, including the United States of America." That summer the Korean War ended in a stalemate that allowed both the United States and the Communist forces to save face. In America, 1954 saw the fall of McCarthy. Certainly these events did not end the paranoid style in either America or the Soviet Union, but they did ease the tension.

In addition, by 1954 both the United States and the Soviet Union had become more comfortable in their positions as world powers. Leaders in both countries had begun to realize that neither side could readily win the Cold War. Between 1945 and 1954 each had carved out

CHRONOLOGY
OF KEY EVENTS

1938 House Un-American Activities Committee (HUAC) is created to investigate Fascist or Communist subversion

1945 United Nations is founded

1947 Truman Doctrine declares that the United States will provide military and economic aid to allies faced by external aggression or internal subversion; Truman establishes a federal program to investigate the loyalty of government employees; Marshall Plan provides $17 billion over four years to aid Western Europe's economic recovery; Taft-Hartley Act passed over President Truman's veto bans the closed shop, restricts union political contributions, and allows courts to delay strikes threatening health or safety; HUAC investigates Communist infiltration of the film industry

1948 State of Israel proclaimed; United States, Britain, and France merge their zones of occupation in Germany to form an independent nation, West Germany; Soviet Union blockades Berlin; ex-Communist Whittaker Chambers charges former State Department official Alger Hiss of giving him secret government documents

1949 NATO is founded; Berlin blockade ends; Mao Tse-tung's Communist forces win China's civil war; Soviet Union successfully tests an atomic bomb

1950 NSC-68 argues that the United States must commit itself to whatever military steps are necessary to stop the spread of communism; Senator Joseph McCarthy claims he has the names of 205 State Department employees who were members of the Communist party; North Korean troops cross the 38th parallel, beginning the Korean War; UN forces invade North Korea; Chinese troops enter North Korea and force UN troops to retreat across the 38th parallel

1951 Negotiations to work out a cease-fire in Korea begin; HUAC conducts a second investigation of Communist subversion in Hollywood; Ethel and Julius Rosenberg are sentenced to death for atomic espionage

1953 Dwight D. Eisenhower is inaugurated thirty-fourth president; cease-fire in Korean War

1954 Army-McCarthy hearings; U.S. Senate censures McCarthy for "conduct unbecoming a member"

spheres of influence. The Soviet Union and its sometime-ally China dominated most of Eastern Europe and the Asian mainland. America and its allies controlled Western Europe, North and South America, most of the Pacific, and to a lesser extent Africa, the Middle East, and Southeast Asia. Throughout much of the Third World, however, emerging nationalistic movements challenged both U.S. and Soviet influences.

In the United States, the containment policy was seldom even debated. The Truman Doctrine and muscular internationalism governed foreign policy decisions, but economic and political questions lingered. How much would containment cost? Where would the money come from? Which Americans would pay the most? Would it mean the end of liberal reform? During the next decade American leaders would wrestle with these and other questions.

SUGGESTIONS FOR FURTHER READING

OVERVIEWS AND SURVEYS

Stephen E. Ambrose, *Rise to Globalism: American Foreign Policy since 1938*, 5th ed. (1988); H. W. Brands, *Inside the Cold War* (1991); William H. Chafe, *The Unfinished Journey*, 2d ed. (1991), and *The American Woman* (1972); Alexander DeConde, *A History of American Foreign Policy* (1963); Robert H. Ferrell, *American Diplomacy* (1959); John Lewis Gaddis, *The United States and the Cold War* (1992); Alonzo Hamby, *The Imperial Years* (1976); Godfrey Hodgson, *America in Our Time* (1976); Michael J. Lacey, ed., *The Truman Presidency* (1989); Walter LaFeber, *America, Russia, and the Cold War*, 5th ed. (1985); R. W. Leopold, *The Growth of American Foreign Policy* (1962); William Leuchtenburg, *A Troubled Feast*, rev. ed. (1983); William Manchester, *The Glory and the Dream* (1974); Thomas J. McCormick, *America's Half-Century* (1989); Thomas G. Paterson et al., *American Foreign Policy*, 3d ed., 2 vols. (1988), and with Robert J. McMahon, *The Origins of the Cold War*, 3d ed. (1991); Richard Polenberg, *One Nation Divisible* (1980); Emily and Norman Rosenberg, *In Our Times*, 4th ed. (1991); Frederick F. Siegel, *A Troubled Journey* (1984); William A. Williams, *The Tragedy of American Diplomacy*, 2d ed. (1972), and *The Roots of the Modern American Empire* (1969); Lawrence Wittner, *Cold War America*, rev. ed. (1978); Howard Zinn, *Postwar America, 1945–1971* (1973).

CONTAINING THE RUSSIAN BEAR

Gar Alperovitz, *Atomic Diplomacy*, rev. ed. (1985); Terry H. Anderson, *The United States, Great Britain and the Cold War, 1944–1947* (1981); James Aronson, *The Press and the Cold War* (1970); Stanley D. Bachrack, *The Committee of One Million: "China Lobby" Politics, 1953–1971* (1976); Richard J. Barnet, *The Giants: Russia and America* (1977); Ronald J. Caridi, *The Korean War and American Politics* (1969); Gordon H. Chang, *Friends and Enemies: The United States, China, and the Soviet Union, 1948–1972* (1990); Bernard C. Cohen, *The Public's Impact on Foreign Policy* (1972); Bruce Cumings, *The Origins of the Korean War*, 2 vols. (1981–1990); Lynn Etheridge Davis, *The Cold War Begins: Soviet-American Conflict over Eastern Europe* (1974); A. W. DePorte, *Europe Between the Superpowers: The Enduring Balance*, 2d ed. (1986); Herbert Feis, *From Trust to Terror: The Onset of the Cold War* (1970); Richard B. Finn, *Winners in Peace: MacArthur, Yoshida, and Postwar Japan* (1992); D. F. Fleming, *The Cold War and Its Origins*, 2 vols. (1961); John L. Gaddis, *The United States and the Origins of the Cold War, 1941–1947* (1972), and *Strategies of Containment: A Crucial Appraisal of Postwar American National Security Policy* (1982); Lloyd C. Gardner, *Architects of Illusion: Men and Ideas in American Foreign Policy, 1941–1949* (1970); Marshall I. Goldman, *Detente and Dollars: Doing Business with the Soviets* (1975); Michael Hogan, *The Marshall Plan* (1987); Akira Iriye, *The Cold War in Asia* (1974); Howard Jones, *A New Kind of War: America's Global Strategy and the Truman Doctrine in Greece* (1989); Burton Kaufman, *Trade and Aid* (1982); Joyce and Gabriel Kolko, *The Limits of Power: The World and U.S. Foreign Policy, 1945–1954* (1972); Bennett Kovrig, *The Myth of Liberation; East-Central Europe in U.S. Diplomacy and Politics Since 1941* (1973); Bruce Kuklick, *American Policy and the Division of Germany* (1972); Melvyn P. Leffler, *A Preponderance of Power: National Security, the Truman Administration, and the Cold War* (1991); Ralph B. Levering, *The Public and American Foreign Policy, 1918–1978* (1978), and *The Cold War, 1945–1987*, 2d ed. (1988); Louis Liebovich, *The Press and the Origins of the Cold War, 1944–1947* (1988); Vojtech Mastny, *Russia's Road to the Cold War, 1941–1945* (1979); Ernest R. May, *The Truman Administration and China, 1945–1949* (1975); Thomas Paterson, *On Every Front: The Making and Unmaking of the Cold War*, rev. ed. (1992); David Rees, *Korea: The Limited War* (1964); Martin Sherwin, *A World Destroyed: The Atomic Bomb and the Grand Alliance* (1975); John W. Spanier, *The Truman-MacArthur Controversy and the Korean War* (1959); Hugh Thomas, *Armed Truce: The Beginnings of the Cold War* (1986); Adam B. Ulam, *Expansion and Coexistence: The History of Soviet Foreign Policy, 1917–73*, 2d ed. (1974); William Welch, *American Images of Soviet Foreign Policy* (1970); Allen S. Whiting, *China Crosses the Yalu: The Decision to Enter the Korean War* (1960); Lawrence Wittner, *American Intervention in Greece, 1943–1949* (1982); Daniel Yergin, *Shattered Peace* (1977).

THE COLD WAR AT HOME

Edwin R. Bayley, *Joe McCarthy and the Press* (1981); Jeff Broadwater, *Eisenhower and the Anti-Communist Crusade* (1992); David Brody, *Workers in Industrial America* (1980); David Caute, *The Great Fear: The Anti-Communist Purge under Truman and Eisenhower* (1978); Alistair Cooke, *A Generation on Trial* (1950); Richard Freeland, *The Truman Doctrine and the Origins of McCarthyism*

(1972); Richard M. Fried, *Men Against McCarthy* (1976), and *Nightmare in Red* (1990); Walter Goodman, *The Committee* (1968); Robert Griffith, *The Politics of Fear*, 2d ed. (1987); Alonzo Hamby, *Beyond the New Deal: Harry S. Truman and American Liberalism* (1973); Susan M. Hartmann, *Truman and the 80th Congress* (1971); Fred Inglis, *The Cruel Peace: Everyday Life and the Cold War* (1991); Richard S. Kirkendall, *Harry S. Truman, Korea, and the Imperial Presidency* (1975); Stanley I. Kutler, *The American Inquisition: Justice and Injustice in the Cold War* (1982); R. Alton Lee, *Truman and Taft-Hartley* (1966); Samuel Lubell, *Future of American Politics* (1952); Maeva Marcus, *Truman and the Steel Seizure Case* (1977); Allen J. Matusow, *Farm Policies and Politics in the Truman Years* (1967); Michael Rogin, *The Intellectuals and McCarthy* (1967); Athan Theoharis, *Seeds of Repression: Harry S. Truman and the Origins of McCarthyism* (1971); Allen Weinstein, *Perjury: The Hiss-Chambers Case* (1978); Theodore Wilson, "The Kefauver Committee" in *Congress Investigates,* vol. 5, Arthur M. Schlesinger, Jr., and Roger Bruns, eds. (1975).

THE PARANOID STYLE

Larry Ceplair and Steven Englund, *The Inquisition in Hollywood* (1980); Stephen Fox, *Blood and Power: Organized Crime in Twentieth Century America* (1990); Eric Goldman, *The Crucial Decade and After* (1961); Richard Hofstadter, *The Paranoid Style in American Politics and Other Essays* (1965); William Howard Moore, *The Kefauver Committee and the Politics of Crime* (1974); Victor Navasky, *Naming Names* (1980); Nora Sayre, *Running Time: Films of the Cold War* (1982); Stephen J. Whitfield, *The Culture of the Cold War* (1991).

BIOGRAPHIES

Dean Acheson, *Present at the Creation: My Years in the State Department* (1969); Charles E. Bohlen, *Witness to History, 1929-1969* (1973); Robert J. Donovan, *Conflict and Crisis* (1977), and *Tumultuous Years* (1982); Robert H. Ferrell, *George C. Marshall* (1966), and *Harry S Truman and the Modern American Presidency* (1983); Charles L. Fontenay, *Estes Kefauver* (1980); Joseph Bruce Gorman, *Kefauver* (1971); Walter L. Hixson, *George F. Kennan* (1989); David S. McLellan, *Dean Acheson* (1976); David M. Oshinsky, *A Conspiracy So Immense: The World of Joe McCarthy* (1983); James T. Patterson, *Mr. Republican: A Biography of Robert A. Taft* (1972); Thomas C. Reeves, *The Life and Times of Joe McCarthy* (1982); Richard R. Rovere, *Senator Joe McCarthy* (1959); Edward L. and Frederick H. Schapsmeier, *Prophet in Politics: Henry A. Wallace and the War Years, 1940–1965* (1971); Gaddis Smith, *Dean Acheson* (1972); Ronald Steel, *Walter Lippmann and the American Century* (1980); Anders Stephanson, *Kennan and the Art of Foreign Policy* (1989); Mark A. Stoler, *George C. Marshall* (1989); Harry S Truman, *Memoirs*, 2 vols. (1955–1956).

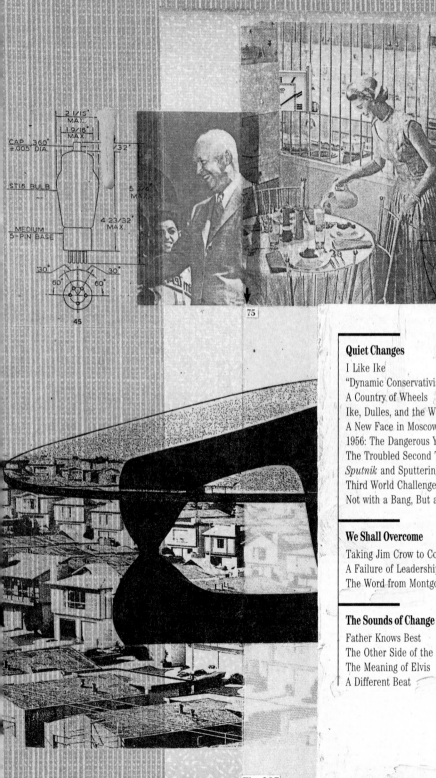

75

Fig. 287

103

COMPANY

CHAPTER 28

Ike's America

Figure 1-3. Equator, Latitude, and Parallels of Latitude

20c

*M*ose Wright stood and surveyed the courtroom. Most of the faces he saw were white. The two accused men were white. The 12 jurors were white. The armed guards were white. Slowly, Wright, a 64-year-old black sharecropper, extended his right arm. "Thar he," Wright answered, pointing at J. W. Milam. He then pointed at Roy Bryant, the second defendant. In essence, Wright was accusing the two whites of murdering Emmett Till, his 14-year-old nephew—accusing them in a segregated courtroom in Sumner, Mississippi. Wright later recalled that he could "feel the blood boil in hundreds of white people as they sat glaring in the courtroom. It was the first time in my life I had the courage to accuse a white man of a crime, let alone something as terrible as killing a boy. I wasn't exactly brave and I wasn't scared. I just wanted to see justice done."

It was 1955, but the march of racial justice in the South had been painfully slow. In 1954 the Supreme Court of the United States in the landmark *Brown* v. *Board of Education of Topeka* decision had ruled that segregated schooling was "inherently unequal." News of the *Brown* decision drew angry comments and reactions from all corners of the Jim Crow South. Mississippi Senator James Eastland told his constituents that the decision destroyed the Constitution of the United States and counseled, "You are not obliged to obey the decisions of any court which are plainly fraudulent." Throughout Dixie, Klansmen burned crosses while other white leaders hastily organized Citizens' Councils. Self-proclaimed protectors of white America vowed "to make it difficult, if not impossible, for any Negro who advocates desegregation to find and hold a job, get credit, or renew a mortgage."

Into this racially charged atmosphere came Emmett Till in August 1955. Taking a summer vacation from his home on the South Side of Chicago, he rode a train to visit relatives living near Money, Mississippi. Emmett had known segregation in Chicago, but nothing like what he discovered in Money, where shortly before his arrival a black girl had been "flogged" for "crowding white people" in a store.

Emmett's mother told him what to expect and how to act: "If you have to get on your knees and bow when a white person goes past, do it

willingly." But Emmett had a mind and a mouth of his own. In Chicago, he told his cousins, he was friends with plenty of white people. He even had a picture of a white girl, *his* white girl, he said. "Hey," challenged a listener, "there's a [white] girl in that store there. I bet you won't go in there and talk to her."

Emmett accepted the challenge. He entered Bryant's Grocery and Meat Market, browsed about, and bought some bubble gum. As he left, he said, "Bye, Baby" to Carolyn Bryant and gave a "wolf call" whistle. Outside an old black man told Emmett to scat before the woman got a pistol and blew "his brains out." The advice sounded sage enough, so Emmett beat a hasty retreat.

A few days later Roy Bryant returned to Money after hauling shrimp from Louisiana to Texas. What his wife told him is unknown, but it was enough to make him angry. After midnight that Saturday night, he and his half-brother, J. W. "Big" Milam, drove to Mose Wright's unpainted cabin. They demanded the "boy who done the talkin'." Mose tried to explain that Emmett was from "up nawth," that he "ain't got good sense" and was unfamiliar with southern ways. The logic of the argument was lost on the two white men, one of whom told Mose that if he caused trouble he would never see his next birthday.

Various stories have been told about what happened during the next few hours. One thing is for certain: Emmett Till did not live much past daybreak. According to Milam and Bryant's account, they had only meant to scare the northern youth. But Emmett did not beg for mercy. Therefore they *had* to kill him. "What else could we do? " Milam asked. "He was hopeless. I'm no bully; I never hurt a nigger in my life. I like niggers in their place. I know how to work 'em. But I just decided it was time a few people got put on notice."

Three days later Emmett's badly beaten body was found in the Tallahatchie River. A gouged out eye, crushed forehead, and bullet in his skull gave evidence to the beating he took. Around his neck, attached by barbed wire, was a 75-pound cotton gin fan. At the request of his mother, the local sheriff sent the decomposing body to Chicago for burial.

Mamie Bradley, Emmett's mother, grieved

openly and loudly. Contrary to the wishes of Mississippi authorities, she held an open casket funeral. Thousands of black Chicagoans attended the viewing, and the black press closely followed the episode. *Jet* magazine even published a picture of the mutilated corpse. In the black community the Till murder case became a cause célèbre. In a land that valued justice, would any be found in Mississippi?

In Money, white Southerners rallied to Bryant and Milam's side. Supporters raised a $10,000 defense fund, and southern editorials labeled the entire affair a "Communist plot" to destroy southern society. By the time the trial started, American interest seemed focused on Mississippi. Few people, however, expected that Bryant and Milam would be judged guilty because few expected any blacks would testify against white men in Mississippi.

Mose Wright proved the folly of common wisdom. He dramatically testified against the white men. So did several other relatives of Emmett Till. But in his closing statement, John C. Whitten, one of the five white attorneys, told the all-white, all-male jury: "Your fathers will turn over in their graves if [Milam and Bryant are found guilty] and I'm sure that every last Anglo-Saxon one of you has the courage to free these men in the face of that [outside] pressure."

The jury returned a "not guilty" verdict in one hour and seven minutes. "If we hadn't stopped to drink a pop, it wouldn't have taken that long," one juror commented. On that day in 1955 there was no justice in Sumner, Mississippi. Michigan Congressman Charles Diggs, who sat with other blacks in the rear section of the segregated courtroom, recalled, "I certainly was angered by the decision, [but] I was not surprised by it. And I was strengthened in my belief that something had to be done about the dispensation of justice in that state." Roy Wilkins of the NAACP remarked that "there is in the entire state no restraining influence of decency, not in the state capital, among the daily newspapers, the clergy, not among any segment of the so-called lettered citizens."

But if there was no justice that day, there were clear signs of change. A black man had demanded justice in white-controlled Mississippi. Soon—very soon—other voices would

Mose Wright and his three boys, seated in the "colored" section of the courtroom, attended the trial of Bryant and Milam, accused of killing Emmett Till in Mississippi.

join Mose Wright's. Their peaceful but insistent cries would be heard over the surface quiet of Dwight Eisenhower's America. They would force America to come to terms with its own ideology. After an heroic struggle against fascism and during a cold conflict against communism, Americans no longer could ignore racial injustice and inequality at home.

It was time for a change. During the late 1940s and the 1950s the process began. Slow, painful, poignant, occasionally uplifting—the march toward justice moved forward. It was part of other significant social and economic changes taking place in America. Against the backdrop of Eisenhower's calm assurances, a new country was taking shape.

QUIET CHANGES

Most white Americans during the late 1940s and the early 1950s were unconcerned about the struggles of their black compatriots. Perhaps some admired Jackie Robinson's efforts on the baseball field, but few made the connection between integration in sports and civil rights throughout society. Other concerns seemed more urgent. In November 1952 the Korean War was dragging into its third year, and the chances for a satisfactory peace were fading. Joseph McCarthy was still warning Americans about the Communist infiltration of the U.S. government. Political corruption had stained the Truman administration. At the polls Americans were ready to vote for change.

I Like Ike

Republicans certainly felt it was time for change. The Democrats had occupied the White House for the previous 20 years. In 1952 they ran Governor Adlai Stevenson of Illinois for the presidency. A political moderate and a vocal anti-Communist, the witty, sophisticated Stevenson was burdened by Truman's unpopularity. His Republican opponent was Dwight David Eisenhower, a moderate, anti-Communist war hero. The Republican campaign strategy was summarized in a formula—K_1C_2. Eisenhower promised that if elected he would first end the war in Korea then battle communism and corruption at home. The nation responded. Eisenhower was swept into office. He even carried several southern states and cut into the urban-ethnic coalition of the Democrats.

The country responded to Eisenhower. "I Like Ike" campaign buttons and posters captured the public sentiment. And there was much to like. Few people had advanced so far while making so few enemies. Ike's was the classic Horatio Alger success story. Although born in Texas, he was raised in Abilene, Kansas, the northern terminus of the Chisholm Trail. An accomplished athlete and a good student, Ike earned an appointment to West Point, where he graduated in 1915 among "the class on which the stars fell." (Fifty-nine of the 164 graduates of the class would rise to the rank of brigadier general or higher.)

As an army officer, Eisenhower demonstrated rare organizational abilities and a capacity for complex detail work. If by 1939 he had only risen to the rank of lieutenant colonel, he had impressed his superiors. With the outbreak of World War II, he was promoted with startling rapidity. In fact, in 1942 General George Mar-

shall passed over 366 more senior officers to promote Eisenhower to major general and appoint him commander of the European Theater of Operations. It was Ike who planned and oversaw America's invasions of North Africa, Sicily, and Italy and who led the combined British-American D-Day invasion of France. By the end of the war, Ike was a four-star general and an international hero.

Ike's ability to win the loyalty of others and work with people of diverse and difficult temperaments would serve him well as a politician. But during the early postwar years, he expressed no interest in holding political office. "I cannot conceive of any set of circumstances that could drag out of me permission to consider me for any political post from dog catcher to Grand High Supreme King of the Universe," he told a reporter in 1946. And indeed there is no evidence that Ike had ever voted or had any party affiliation before running for the presidency on the Republican ticket in 1952.

Eisenhower did have strong beliefs concerning America's domestic and foreign policies. His fiscal conservativism led him to the Republican party, and his internationalism convinced him to run for the presidency. He did not want to see an isolationist Republican elected in 1952, and the early front-runner was isolationist Robert Alphonso Taft, the powerful Ohio senator. Once Ike had defeated Taft for the nomination, his victory over Stevenson was almost anticlimactic.

Almost overnight the image of Eisenhower was transformed from one of a master military organizer to one of mumbling, bumbling, smiling incomprehensibility. Reporters commented on his friendly smile, engaging blue eyes, and his mangled syntax. As a young officer he wrote striking speeches for Douglas MacArthur, and as a World War II general he impressed reporters with the precision of his thought. Commenting on Ike's speaking style, FDR's press secretary said, "He knows his facts, he speaks freely and frankly, and he has a sense of humor, he has poise, and he has command."

Had Eisenhower somehow sunk into senility on taking office? Certainly not. He sensed that the country needed a rest from 20 years of active presidents. Rather than an earth shaker, the country needed a "dirt smoother." The result was the "hidden hand leadership" of Ike. In public he seemed everyone's favorite grandfather and golfing buddy, friendly, outgoing, quick to please, but only slightly interested in being president. Although he had read widely in both military history and the classics, he insisted publicly that he only read westerns, and those not too closely. But throughout his eight years in office, Eisenhower focused closely on his two major priorities: U.S.-Soviet relations and a balanced budget. These issues, not civil rights or other important social concerns, occupied most of his attention.

"Dynamic Conservativism"

Eisenhower brought the military chain of command system to the White House. He was in charge, and he kept the major decisions of his administration in his own hands. But he left the detail work and the political battling to his subordinates. The most important person after Eisenhower in this command structure was Sherman Adams, the former governor of New Hampshire who served as Ike's chief of staff. Adams determined who got to see the president and what issues were placed before him. Although forced to resign in 1958 for influence peddling (he had accepted an Oriental rug and a vicuña coat from a New England textile magnate), Adams pioneered modern White House administration.

Ike saw himself as a forward-looking Republican. He called himself a conservative, "but an extremely liberal conservative," one who was concerned with fiscal prudence but not at the expense of human beings. Ike termed his approach "modern Republicanism" and "dynamic conservatism," by which he meant, "conservative when it comes to money matters and liberal when it comes to human beings." In practice this approach led the Eisenhower administration to cut spending but not to attempt any rollback of New Deal social legislation.

George Humphrey, a conservative Ohio industrialist, served as Eisenhower's treasury secretary. More conservative than Eisenhower, Humphrey believed that the federal government should shift more fiscal responsibilities to the state and private sectors. He did succeed in getting Congress to abolish the Reconstruction

Finance Corporation (see Chapter 24) and turn over off-shore oil rights to the seaboard states. The *New York Times* called this latter piece of legislation, the Submerged Land Act, "one of the greatest and surely the most unjustified give-away programs in all the history of the United States." On the whole, however, Eisenhower's domestic programs were hardly reactionary.

During Ike's two terms the country made steady and at times spectacular economic progress. In 1955 the minimum wage was raised from 75 cents to $1 per hour, and during the 1950s the average family income rose 15 percent and real wages were up 20 percent. And work was plentiful. During the decade, unemployment averaged only 4.5 percent per year, a figure close to the magical 4 percent economists considered "full employment." Stable prices, full employment, and steady growth were the economic hallmarks of the 1950s. "American labor has never had it so good," AFL-CIO chief George Meany told his associates in 1955. Although the population increased by 28 million people, the country was on the whole better housed and fed than ever before. The output of goods and services rose 15 percent. Especially for white Americans, "modern Republicanism" seemed a viable alternative to New Dealism.

A Country of Wheels

If Eisenhower labored to curtail the role of the federal government in some areas, he expanded it in other places. As an expert on military logistics, Ike frequently expressed concern about the sad state of the American highway system. During World War II he had been impressed by Hitler's system of *Autobahnen*, which allowed the German dictator to deploy troops to different parts of Germany with incredible speed. From his first days in office, Eisenhower worked for legislation to improve America's highway network.

The highway lobby agreed. A loose collection of pressure groups formed the lobby, including representatives from the automobile, trucking, bus, oil, rubber, asphalt, and construction industries. Following the philosophy that what was good for General Motors was good for the country, the highway lobby pushed for a new federally subsidized interstate highway system. Not only would such a project provide millions of new jobs, it would contribute to a safer America by making it easier to evacuate major cities in the event of a nuclear attack.

As a result of presidential and lobby pressure, in 1956 Congress passed the National System of Interstate and Defense Highways Act, the most significant piece of domestic legislation enacted under Eisenhower. As planned, the system would cover 41,000 (later expanded to 42,500) miles, cost $26 billion, and take 13 years to construct. Although it took longer to complete and cost far more than Congress projected, it did provide the United States with the world's most extensive superhighway system. Secretary of Commerce Sinclair Weeks estimated that the act would create 150,000 new construction jobs and rank as "the greatest public works program in history."

More than any other piece of legislation, it also changed America. After Congress passed the 1956 bill, cultural critic Lewis Mumford wrote, "When the American people, through their Congress, voted . . . for a $26 billion highway program, the most charitable thing to assume is that they hadn't the faintest notion of what they were doing." Mumford realized that this commitment to internal combustion engines would alter the culture and landscape of America; and it has. It accelerated the decline of the inner city and the flight to the suburbs. The downtown portions of cities, once thriving with commerce and excitement, rapidly turned into ghost towns. As downtown businesses, hotels, and theaters closed, suburban shopping malls with multi-screen cinemas and roadside motels began to dot the American highway landscape. Drive-in theaters, gasoline service stations, mobile homes, and multicar garages signified the birth of a new extended society, one without center or focus. Indeed, highway construction was simply one expression of Americans' obsession with the automobile during the 1950s and 1960s. After being deprived of new cars during the war—when the maximum speed limit was 35 miles per hour—Americans adopted the new automobile philosophy of bigger is better and the biggest and fastest is the best. In 1952 over 52 million cars crowded

American roads, and that number doubled during the next 20 years.

Home architecture exemplified America's mobile-minded culture. The garage, once separated from and located behind the house, achieved a new position. By the 1960s the average home devoted more space to the family automobiles than to individual family members. With access to the house itself—usually through the kitchen—the garage had become an integrated part of the house and the car an important member of the family. Home architects in the 1960s and 1970s showed the growing importance of the automobile by placing the garage in a prominent position in the front of the house.

America's commitment to highways and cars created numerous problems. Mass transportation suffered most conspicuously. Street cars and commuter railroads languished, as did the country's major interstate railroads. Since highway construction was financed by a nondivertible gasoline tax, government often ignored mass transit. In the years since the end of World War II, 75 percent of government expenditures for transportation have gone for highways as opposed to 1 percent for urban mass transit. As a result, those without the use of automobiles—the old, the very young, the poor, the handicapped—became victims of America's automobile obsession.

Ike, Dulles, and the World

For Eisenhower, "modern Republicanism" was more than simply a domestic economic credo. It also implied an internationalist foreign policy. As with domestic policy, in foreign policy Ike preferred to operate behind the scenes. But he did make all major foreign policy decisions.

The point man for Ike's foreign policy was Secretary of State John Foster Dulles. When Eisenhower asked Dulles to head the State Department, he remarked, "You've been training yourself to be Secretary of State ever since you were nine years old." And so he had. An interest in foreign affairs was part of the Dulles heritage. Dulles's maternal grandfather had served as Benjamin Harrison's secretary of state, and one of his uncles, Robert Lansing, had occupied the

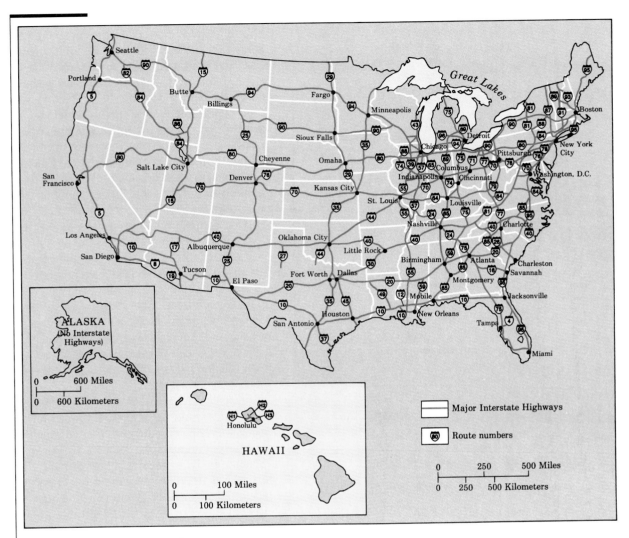

United States Interstate Highway System
The 1956 plan to create an interstate highway system drastically changed America's landscape and culture.

same post under Woodrow Wilson. In 1919 as a young man, Dulles had been part of the American delegation to the Versailles Peace Conference, and later, as a member of the prestigious Wall Street law firm of Sullivan and Cromwell, he represented clients with international interests. After World War II, he helped organize and then served as a delegate to the United Nations. In addition, throughout his life Dulles was a careful student of foreign affairs and international politics. Eisenhower noted, there was "only one man I know who has seen *more* of the world and talked with more people and *knows* more than [Dulles] does—and that's me."

Dulles's experience and knowledge were somewhat offset by his rigidity and excessive moralism. If Americans felt comfortable calling President Eisenhower "Ike," not even close friends called Dulles "Jack." Plain and as unpolished as granite, Dulles took himself, his Presbyterian religion, and the world seriously. "His face," commented an associate, "was permanently lined with an expression of unhappiness mingled with faint distaste—the kind of

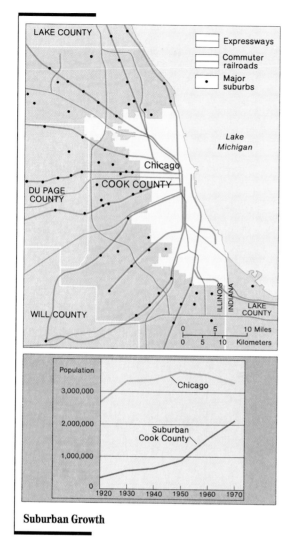

Suburban Growth

Although Eisenhower and Dulles had strikingly different public styles, they shared a common vision of the world. Both were internationalists and cold warriors who believed that the Soviet Union was the enemy and that the United States was and should be the protector of the free world. Peace was their objective—but never a peace won by appeasement. To keep honorable peace, both were willing to consider the use of nuclear weapons and go to the brink of war. As Dulles said in 1956, "You have to take some chances for peace, just as you must take chances in war."

Occasionally Dulles's impassioned anti-Communist rhetoric obscured the actual policies pursued by the Eisenhower administration. In public Dulles rejected the containment doctrine as a "negative, futile and immoral policy" and advocated the "liberation" of Eastern Europe. It was time to "roll back" the Iron Curtain, he said, and if nuclear weapons were needed to achieve America's objectives—well, then, so be it. In public Dulles constantly flexed his—and America's— muscles.

In reality, Eisenhower's objectives were far more limited and his approach toward foreign policy much more cautious. Eisenhower supported containment, but not as practiced by Truman. In Eisenhower's eyes, Truman's approach was unorganized and far too expensive. Like political journalist Walter Lippmann in the late-1940s, Ike believed that the United States could not support every country that claimed to be fighting communism. As historian Charles C. Alexander noted, "The chief lesson Eisenhower and his associates drew from Korea was that limited wars, fought with conventional weaponry on the periphery of the Communist world, only drained the nation's resources and weakened its allies' resolve." If America continued Truman's shotgun policies, the costs would soon become higher than Americans would be willing to pay. A change, Ike maintained, was needed.

Eisenhower termed his adjustments of the containment doctrine the "New Look." Ike's program began with the idea of saving money. To do this he decided to emphasize nuclear weapons over conventional weapons, assuming that the next major war would be a nuclear conflict. This "more bang for the buck" program

face that, on those rare occasions when it was drawn into a smile, looked as though it ached in every muscle to get back into its normal shape." One Washington correspondent described him as "a card-carrying Christian," and he frequently delivered lectures on the evils of "atheistic, materialistic Communism." He tended to see opposition to communism in religious terms. A friend recalled a conversation in which China's Jiang Jieshi (Chiang Kai-shek) and South Korea's Syngman Rhee were criticized. Offended, Dulles announced: "No matter what you say about them, those two gentlemen are modern-day equivalents of the founders of the church. They are Christian gentlemen who have suffered for their faith."

drew angry criticism. Congressional hawks claimed that Eisenhower was "putting too many eggs in the nuclear basket," and liberals suggested that the program would inevitably lead to nuclear destruction.

Whatever the criticisms, the New Look did save money. While air and missile forces were expanded, the army's budget was trimmed of all of its fat and much of its bone. In fact, if Eisenhower had had his way, the army would have been completely reorganized. The results of Eisenhower's approach were dramatic. In 1953 defense cost $50.4 billion. By 1956 Eisenhower had reduced the defense budget to $35.8 billion. In addition, during the same period troop levels were reduced by almost one-third.

Future presidents did not so much reverse Eisenhower's approach as enlarge it. They continued the nuclear buildup started by Eisenhower, and at the same time insisted on increased spending on conventional weapons. The result was an ever escalating defense budget.

The New Look took an unconventional approach to conventional warfare. Ike had learned from Truman's mistakes in Korea. America could not send weapons and men to all corners of the world to contain communism. It was a costly, deadly policy. Instead, the New Look emphasized the threat of massive retaliation to keep order, and reinforced America's position with a series of foreign alliances that encouraged indigenous troops and peoples to resist Communist expansion. Finally, Eisenhower used the CIA as a covert foreign policy arm. Through timely assassinations and political coups engineered by the CIA, Eisenhower was able to prevent—or at least forestall—the emergence of anti-America regimes. While historians argue about the morality of the CIA's covert operations, they were very much a part of the New Look.

A New Face in Moscow

The world changed dramatically a few months after Eisenhower took office. On March 5, 1953, Joseph Stalin, the Soviet dictator whom Ike knew personally, died. Always fearful of rivals, Stalin did not groom a successor. The result was

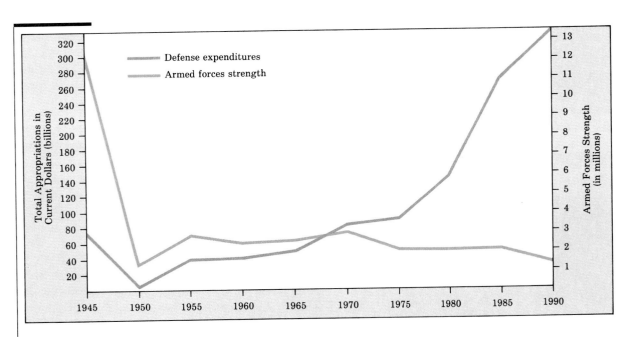

Figure 28.1
Defense expenditures, armed forces strength, 1945–1990

a power struggle within the Kremlin, from which Nikita Khrushchev emerged as the winner.

Khrushchev looked like a cross between a Russian peasant and Ike himself. Short, rotund, and bald, he had a warm smile and alert eyes. Unlike Stalin, Khrushchev enjoyed meeting people, making speeches, and traveling abroad. If occasionally he lost his temper and uttered belligerent remarks—he once even took off his shoe and pounded it on a table at the United Nations—Khrushchev did try to lessen the tensions between the Soviet Union and the United States.

Ike shared Khrushchev's dream for peaceful coexistence between the two world leaders. In fact, Eisenhower used Stalin's death as an opportunity to extend an olive branch. The Soviet Union peacefully responded. During 1955 the nations resolved several thorny issues: the Soviets repatriated German prisoners of war who had been held in the Soviet Union since World War II, established relations with Greece and Israel, and gave up claims to Turkish territory. The Soviet Union's most significant action was to withdraw from its occupation zone of Austria. Until the massive changes in Eastern Europe in 1990 and 1991, it was the only time that the Soviet Union withdrew from territory that it had seized during the war.

The cold winter of the Cold War seemed to be over. Khrushchev condemned Stalin's excesses, and Eisenhower talked guardedly about a new era of cooperation. In July 1955, the two leaders met in Geneva, Switzerland, for a summit conference. During the meeting, Eisenhower suggested that the United States and the Soviet Union allow aerial surveillance and photography of each other's nations to lessen the chance of a possible surprise attack. Khrushchev rejected this "open skies" proposal, calling it "a very transparent espionage device." Actually, the meeting achieved few tangible results, but the two leaders seemed to be working toward the same peaceful ends. Against Dulles's advice, Eisenhower even smiled when posing for pictures with the Soviets. "A new spirit of conciliation and cooperation" had been achieved, Ike announced. Unfortunately, "the Spirit of Geneva" would not survive the confrontations ahead.

At the Twentieth Congress of the Communist party in the Soviet Union, a worker from the Kiev region greets Soviet Premier Nikita Khrushchev.

1956: The Dangerous Year

Neither Eisenhower nor Khrushchev was completely candid. While working for "peaceful coexistence," both still had to satisfy critics at home. In Washington, Dulles continued to call for the "liberation" of Eastern Europe and to hint that the United States would rally behind any Soviet-dominated country that struck a blow for freedom. In reality, Eisenhower was not about to risk war with the Soviet Union to come to the defense of Poland, Hungary, or Czechoslovakia.

At the same time, Khrushchev's speeches often promised more than he would or could deliver. On February 24, 1956, for example, Khrushchev delivered a remarkable speech before the Twentieth Party Congress. For four hours in his "Crimes of Stalin" speech, he condemned the former dictator's domestic crimes and foreign policy mistakes, endorsed "peaceful coexistence" with the West, and indicated that he was willing to allow greater freedom behind the "iron curtain." Although the speech was supposed to be secret, the CIA obtained copies and distributed them throughout Eastern Europe.

Poland took Khrushchev at his word and moved in a more liberal, anti-Stalinist direction. Wladyslaw Gomulka, who represented the nationalistic wing of the Polish Communist party, gained power in Poland and moved his country away from complete Soviet domination. Claiming that "there is more than one road to socialism," Gomulka announced that Poles would defend with their lives their new freedoms. Since Poland did not attempt to withdraw from the Soviet bloc, Khrushchev allowed Poland to move along its more liberal course.

What Poland had won, Hungary wanted—and perhaps a bit more. On October 23, 1956, students and workers took to the streets in Budapest loudly demanding changes. They knocked over a gigantic statue of Stalin and desecrated it with freedom slogans and graffiti. As in Poland, they forced a political change. Independent Communist Imre Nagy replaced a Stalinist leader. The Soviets peacefully recognized the new government. Pressing his luck, Nagy then announced that he planned to pull Hungary out of the Warsaw Pact—the Soviet-dominated defense community that was created in response to the signing of the NATO Pact—and allow opposition political parties.

Khrushchev sent Soviet tanks and soldiers into Budapest to crush what he now termed a "counterrevolution" and the work of "fascist reactionary elements." Students with bricks and hastily made Molotov cocktails were no match for the Red Army. The Soviets kidnapped Nagy (and later executed him), killed hundreds of demonstrators, and brutally restored their control over Hungary. All the while, the Eisenhower administration just watched, demonstrating that the notion of "liberation" was mere rhetoric, not policy. Ike even refused a CIA request to parachute weapons and supplies to the Hungarian freedom fighters. Hungary, said Ike, was "as inaccessible to us as Tibet."

Actually, at the time of the Soviet move into Budapest, Eisenhower was more concerned with the troubled Western alliance. The source of the problem was Egypt, whose nationalistic leader, President Gamal Abdel Nasser, was struggling to remain neutral in the Cold War.

The United States had attempted to win Nasser's favor by promising to finance the construction of the Aswan High Dam on the Nile. But when Nasser recognized the People's Republic of China and pursued amicable relations with the Soviet Union, the Eisenhower administration withdrew the proposed loan. Neither Dulles nor Eisenhower was happy with Nasser's fence-sitting diplomacy.

Nasser struck back. On July 26, he nationalized the Suez Canal, the waterway linking the oil rich Gulf of Suez and the Mediterranean. Half of Western Europe's oil came through the Suez Canal, which Ike believed was essential to the security of Western Europe. "And it will be run by Egyptians," Nasser added in an emotional message to the world. If Eisenhower was upset, British and French leaders were outraged, loudly claiming that the seizure threatened their Middle Eastern oil supplies. Eisenhower counseled caution, but Britain, France, and Israel resorted to "drastic actions." On October 29, Israel invaded Egypt and Britain and France used the hostilities as a pretext to seize the Suez Canal.

Eisenhower was furious. He interrupted his reelection campaign to return to Washington. One observer reported, "The White House crackled with barracks-room language." Ike told Dulles to inform the Israelis that "goddamn it, we're going to apply sanctions, we're going to the United Nations, we're going to do everything that there is so we can stop this thing." And in a severe "tongue-lashing" he reduced British Prime Minister Anthony Eden to tears.

Eisenhower stood on the high ground, where he was uncomfortably aligned with the Soviet Union. Without law there can be no peace, he claimed, adding, "and there can be no law—if we were to invoke one code of international conduct for those who oppose us—and another for our friends." Cut off from American support and faced with angry Soviet threats, Britain, France, and Israel halted their operations on November 6, the same day Eisenhower overwhelmingly defeated Adlai Stevenson and was reelected for a second term.

Taken together, the Hungarian and the Suez crises strained America's relations with both the Soviet Union and Western Europe. "The spirit of Geneva" was being replaced by a

Before the crushing Soviet onslaught on November 4, 1956, Hungarian freedom fighters rushed toward Budapest in an attempt to fight off Soviet forces.

more hostile mood. Nowhere was this better seen than in the 1956 Olympic Games, held in Melbourne, Australia, only two weeks after the November incidents. Egypt, Lebanon, and Iraq refused to take part in any Games that included Britain, France, and Israel. And in the water polo competition, a match between the Soviet Union and Hungary quickly deteriorated into a form of aquatic warfare. The pool ran red with blood and the contest had to be halted before its official end.

The Troubled Second Term

In foreign affairs, Eisenhower's second term was less successful than his first. Although he restrained military spending and shrewdly utilized information gathered by U-2 spy missions, his actions received more criticism at home and abroad. Age and health may have contributed to this turn of events. During his first four years in office, Ike suffered a heart attack and a bout with ileitis, which entailed a serious operation. During his second term, he was more apt to take vacations and play golf and bridge with his close friends. John Foster Dulles's health was also declining. During the Suez crisis doctors discovered that he had cancer. Acute physical pain punctuated his last years as secretary of state and he died in 1959.

Sputnik and Sputtering Rockets

More than ill health plagued Ike's foreign policy. Soviet technological advances created a mood of edginess in American foreign policy and military circles. In 1957 the Soviet Union successfully placed a tiny transmitter encased in a 184-pound steel ball into an orbit around earth. They called the artificial satellite *Sputnik*—Russian for "fellow traveler of Earth"—but the humor of the name was lost on most Americans, who were too concerned about Soviet rocket advances to laugh.

Less than one month later, the Soviet Union launched its second *Sputnik*, this one built on a larger and grander scale. It weighed 1120 pounds, contained instruments for scientific research, and carried a small dog named Laika who was wired with devices to gauge the effects of extragravitational flight on animal functions. If the first *Sputnik* demonstrated that the Soviets had gained the high ground, the second indicated that they intended to go higher and to place men in space.

Before the end of 1957, the United States tried to respond with a satellite launch of its own. Code-named *Vanguard*, the satellite was placed on the top of a three-stage navy rocket that was ignited on December 6. Describing the "blast off," a historian wrote, "It wobbled a few feet off the pad and exploded. The grapefruit-sized American rival to *Sputnik* fell to the ground and beeped its last amid geysers of smoke." It was the first of a series of highly publicized American rocket launches that ended with the sputtering sound of failure.

Sputnik forced Americans to question themselves and their own values. Had the country become soft and overly consumer oriented? While Soviet students were studying calculus, physics, and chemistry, had American students spent too much time in shop, home economics, and driver education classes? More importantly, did *Sputnik* give the Soviet Union a military superiority over the United States? If a Soviet rocket could put a thousand-pound ball in orbit could the same rocket armed with nuclear warhead hit a target in the United States? Such questions disturbed ordinary Americans and U.S. policymakers alike.

In truth, Americans overrated the importance of *Sputnik*. It was not all that it seemed. As Wernher von Braun, one of America's leading German rocket scientists, would later demonstrate, launching a satellite was no great accomplishment. It simply took rockets with great thrust. Delivering a warhead to a specific target was quite another matter. That entailed sophisticated guidance systems, which the Soviet Union had certainly not developed.

Sputnik then did not demonstrate Soviet technological superiority. It did, however, indicate the willingness of Soviet leaders to place military advancement ahead of the physical well-being of their citizens. As a French journalist noted, the price of *Sputnik* was "millions of pots and shoes lacking." Then, as well as today, the Soviet Union lagged behind the West in diet, health care, education, housing, clothing, and transportation.

American policymakers reacted to the illusion of Soviet success. Congress appropriated more money for "defense-related" research and funneled more dollars into higher education in the United States. In fact, *Sputnik* was a tremendous boon for education. In an attempt to improve science and mathematics skills, Con-

U.S. efforts to compete with the Soviet Union's space advances suffered a major setback when the *Vanguard* exploded two seconds after takeoff on December 6, 1957.

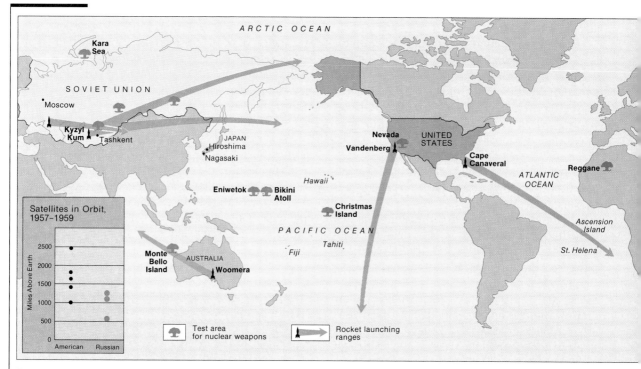

Rockets and Satellites, 1957–1959
The U.S. reaction to *Sputnik* led to a proliferation of rockets and satellites in both the USSR and the United States in the late 1950s.

gress passed the National Defense Education Act (1958) to help finance the undergraduate and graduate educations of promising students. The Eisenhower administration jumped into the "space race" determined to be the swiftest. A leading historian of space measured the success of Eisenhower's effort by noting, "more new starts and technical leaps occurred in the years before 1960 than in any comparable span. Every space booster and every strategic missile in the American arsenal, prior to . . . the 1970s, date from these years."

Third World Challenges

If *Sputnik* was largely an illusionary challenge, nationalist movements in the Third World created more serious problems. Eisenhower's response to such movements varied from case to case. On the one hand, he opposed Britain and France's efforts to use naked physical aggression to whip Egypt into line. On the other hand, Ike employed covert CIA operations to achieve his foreign policy goals. In 1953 the CIA planned and executed a coup d'état which replaced a popularly elected government in Iran with a pro-American regime headed by Shah Mohammad Reza Pahlavi. The reason for the coup was that the elected government had taken over Iranian oil resources that the British had been exploiting. One year later the CIA masterminded the overthrow of a leftist government in Guatemala and replaced it with an unpopular but strongly pro-American government.

To keep order in what he believed were areas vital to American interests, Eisenhower would even resort to armed intervention. In 1958, Lebanese Moslems backed by Egypt and Syria, threatened a revolt against the Beirut government dominated by the Christian minority. President Camille Chamoun appealed to Eisenhower for support. Concerned with Middle Eastern oil, Ike ordered marines from America's Sixth Fleet into Lebanon. Watching from the beaches of Beirut, sunbathers and ice-cream vendors cheered the American show of force.

Once order was restored and Lebanese politicians had agreed on a successor to Chamoun, Ike withdrew American troops from Lebanon. But like the CIA activities in Guatemala and Iran, short-term benefits came with long-term costs. Increasingly, the United States became identified with unpopular, undemocratic, and intolerant right-wing regimes. Such actions tarnished America's image in the Third World.

The problems of Eisenhower's approach toward the Third World were clearly seen in his handling of the Cuban Revolution. In 1959, revolutionary Fidel Castro overthrew Fulgencio Batista, a right-wing dictator who had encouraged American investments in Cuba at the expense of the Cuban people. Before the revolution, in fact, American companies owned 90 percent of Cuban mining operations, 80 percent of its utilities, and 40 percent of its sugar operations. Castro quickly set about to change the situation. He confiscated land and properties in Cuba owned by Americans, executed former Batista officials, built hospitals and schools, ended racial segregation, improved workers' wages, and moved leftward. Before long, Castro had begun to jail writers and critics, hold public executions, postpone elections, and condemn the United States as the "vulture ... feeding on humanity."

Instead of waiting for Cuba's anti-American feelings to subside, Eisenhower decided to move against Castro. He gave the CIA permission to plan an attack on Cuba by a group of anti-Castro exiles, a plan that would culminate with the disastrous Bay of Pigs invasion (see Chapter 29). As one of his last acts as president, in 1961 Eisenhower severed diplomatic relations with Cuba. Such actions only increased Castro's anti-American resolve and further drove him into the arms of the Soviet Union.

Ultimately, the Truman and Eisenhower brands of containment were unsuccessful in dealing with nationalistic independence movements. Such movements dominated the post–World War II world. Between 1944 and 1974, for example, 78 countries won their independence. These included more than one billion people, or close to one-third of the world's population. By using a political yardstick to evaluate these movements, American presidents since Truman have made critical mistakes that have lowered the image of the United States in the Third World and given ammunition to Third World politicians who have pandered to anti-American emotions.

Not with a Bang, But a Whimper

Going into his last year in office, Eisenhower hoped to improve on the foreign policy record of his second term. Since his last meeting with Khrushchev in Geneva, the Cold War had intensified. In particular, the Soviets were once again threatening to cut off Western access to West Berlin, an action Eisenhower feared might lead to a nuclear war. To solve the problem—or at least to neutralize it—Khrushchev visited the United States. He toured Iowa farms, visited Hollywood, and was generally warmly received by the American people. His biggest disappointment was that for security reasons he could not visit Disneyland. Turning to politics, he spent two days in private talks with Eisenhower at Camp David, where the two agreed to a formal summit meeting set for May 1960 in Paris.

The two world leaders never again had serious talks. Just before the meeting the Soviets shot down an American U-2 spy plane over their territory. So sophisticated was the plane's surveillance equipment, it could read a newspaper headline from 10 miles above the earth's surface or take pictures of the earth's surface 125 miles wide and 3000 miles long. During the previous few years, U-2 missions had kept Eisenhower abreast of Soviet military developments and convinced him that *Sputnik* posed no military threat to the United States. Nevertheless, the existence of such planes was a military secret, and U-2 pilots had strict orders to self-destruct their planes rather than be forced down in enemy territory. (For crash landings in neutral countries, the pilots carried a silk banner with the same statement in 14 languages: "I bear no malice toward your people. If you help me you will be rewarded.")

Assuming that the pilot had followed orders, Eisenhower responded to the Soviet charges of spying by publicly announcing that the Soviets had shot down a weather plane that had blown off course. Unfortunately for Ike, the pilot, Francis Gary Powers, had not followed orders, and the Soviets had him and the wreckage of his plane. Trying to save the summit, Khrushchev offered Eisenhower a way to save face. The Soviet leader indicated that he was sure that Eisenhower had not known about the flights. Eisenhower, however, accepted full personal responsibility and refused to apologize for actions he deemed were in defense of America. Rather than appear soft himself, Khrushchev refused to engage in the Paris summit.

Eisenhower's presidency ended on this note of failure. A chance to improve Soviet-American relations had been lost. But the end of his presidency should not obscure his positive accomplishments. He had ended one war, kept America out of several others, limited military spending, and presided over seven and a half years of relative peace. Like George Washington, when Eisenhower left office he issued warnings to America about possible future problems. In particular, he noted, the "military-industrial complex"—an alliance between government and business—could threaten the democratic process in the country. As Eisenhower remarked early in his presidency, "Every gun that is made, every warship launched, every rocket fired signifies, in the final sense, a theft from those who hunger and are not fed, those who are cold and are not clothed."

WE SHALL OVERCOME

When Dwight Eisenhower took office in early 1953 almost everywhere in the United States racism—often institutionalized, sometimes less formal—was the order of the day. Below the Mason-Dixon line it reached its most virulent form in the Jim Crow laws that governed the everyday existence of southern blacks. Whites framed the Jim Crow laws to separate the races and to demonstrate to all white superiority and black inferiority. Jim Crow dictated that whites and blacks eat in separate restaurants, drink from separate water fountains, sleep in separate hotels, and learn in separate schools. In some states, the separate schoolbooks of black and white children were stored in separate closets so as to avoid contamination by touch.

Jim Crow subjected blacks to daily bouts of degradation and soul-destroying humiliation. Blacks had to give way on sidewalks to whites, tip their hats, and speak respectfully. Blacks addressed whites of all ages as Mr., Mrs., or Miss; whites addressed blacks of all ages by their first names. Although the underpinning of the Jim Crow laws was the "separate but equal" doctrine enunciated in *Plessy* v. *Ferguson* (1896), both blacks and whites realized that subjuga-

The U-2 spy plane's sophisticated surveillance equipment kept President Eisenhower informed about Soviet military developments including nuclear testing.

tempted to attend school, they were inhospitably greeted by an angry mob chanting, "two, four, six, eight, we ain't going to integrate."

Television turned the ugly episode into a national drama. Millions of Americans for the first time witnessed violent racism as angry whites moved around the defenseless black children like hungry sharks. Television gave a face to racism, a concept that for many white Americans was still an abstraction. It showed the reality of hate and racism in the South. For the first but not last time, television aided the cause of civil rights by conveying the human suffering caused by racism.

To restore order, Eisenhower federalized the Arkansas National Guard and sent one thousand paratroopers from the 101st Airborne Division to Little Rock. It was the first time since Reconstruction that a president ordered troops to the South. Although their presence desegregated Central High in 1957, the following year Faubus closed Little Rock's public schools, declaring "I stand now and always in opposition to integration by force or at bayonet point." Taken together, Faubus's shortsighted political moves and Eisenhower's refusal to take action until public order had been disrupted created a crisis that more thoughtful leadership might have avoided.

The Word from Montgomery

The failure of white leaders convinced blacks that court orders would not magically produce equal rights. The fight would be difficult, the march long. Many blacks realized this even before the Little Rock crisis. On a cold afternoon in 1955 in Montgomery, Alabama, Rosa Parks, a well-respected black seamstress who was active in the NAACP, took a significant stride toward equality. She boarded a bus and sat in the first row of the "colored" section. The white section of the bus quickly filled, and according to Jim Crow rules, blacks were expected to give up their seats rather than force whites—male or female—to stand. The time came for Mrs. Parks

Paratroopers escorted black students to and from school in Little Rock, Arkansas, after violence erupted when the schools were instructed to desegregate.

to give up her seat. She stayed seated. When told by the bus driver to get up or he would call the police, she said, "You may do that." Later she recalled that the act of defiance was "just something I had to do." The bus stopped, the driver summoned the police, and Rosa Parks was arrested.

Rosa Parks's arrest for refusing to move to the back of a bus led to citywide bus boycotts throughout 1956. Martin Luther King, Jr., was one of the first to ride the buses when the bus systems were integrated.

Black Montgomery rallied to Mrs. Parks's side. Like her, they were tired of riding in the back of the bus, tired of giving up their seats to whites, tired of having their lives restricted by Jim Crow. Local black leaders decided to organize a boycott of Montgomery's white-owned and white-operated bus system. They hoped that economic pressure would force changes that court decisions could not. For the next 381 days, more than 90 percent of Montgomery's black citizens participated in a heroic and successful demonstration against racial segregation. The common black attitude toward the protest was voiced by an elderly black woman when a black leader offered her a ride. "No," she replied, "my feets is tired, but my soul is rested."

To lead the boycott, Montgomery blacks turned to the new minister of the Dexter Avenue Baptist Church, a young man named Martin Luther King, Jr. Reared in Atlanta, the son of a respected and financially secure minister, King had been educated at Morehouse College, Crozier Seminary, and Boston University, from which he earned a doctorate in theology. King was an intellectual, excited by ideas and deeply influenced by the philosophical writings of Henry David Thoreau and Mahatma Gandhi as well as the teachings of Christ. They believed in the power of nonviolent, direct action.

King's words as well as his ideas stirred people's souls. At the start of the Montgomery boycott he told his followers:

> There comes a time when people get tired. We are here this evening to say to those who have mistreated us so long that we are tired—tired of being segregated and humiliated, tired of being kicked about by the brutal feet of oppression . . . We've come here tonight to be saved from the patience that makes us patient with anything less than freedom and justice . . . If you protest courageously and yet with dignity and Christian love, in the history books that are written in future generations, historians will have to pause and say "there lived a great people—a black people—who injected a new meaning and dignity into the veins of civilization."

In King, civil rights had found a genuine spokesman, one who preached a doctrine of change guided by Christian love not racial hatred. "In our protest," he observed, "there will be no cross burnings. No white person will be taken from his home by a hooded Negro mob and brutally murdered. There will be no threats and no intimidation."

The success of the Montgomery boycott inspired nonviolent black protests elsewhere in the South. Increasingly, young blacks took the lead. Violence and biased law enforcement did not stop the protesters. Indeed, within a few months of the successful conclusion of the Montgomery boycott, demonstrations erupted in 54 cities in 9 states. The protesters were arrested, jailed, beaten, and even knocked off their feet by high-pressure fire hoses, but still they protested.

The protests were widely reported in the country's newspapers and televised nightly on the news shows. They confronted Americans everywhere with the stark reality of segregation. Ignorance of the situation became an impossibility; and as the violence continued, pressure mounted on white national politicians to take decisive action. By the early 1960s the word from Montgomery had reinforced the *Brown* decision. It was time for freedom to become a reality. (See Chapter 30 for fuller treatment of civil rights.)

THE SOUNDS OF CHANGE

Beginning in the 1970s, American advertisers started to market a new commodity—the fifties. They marketed it as a Golden Decade, a carefree time before the assassination of John F. Kennedy, the Vietnam War, and Watergate. According to the popular myth, kids in the 1950s thought "dope" referred to a dull-witted person, parents married for life, and major family problems revolved around whether or not sis had a date for the prom. This image of the decade has taken different forms. "Happy Days" presented it on television; *American Grafitti* and *Diner* (set in the early sixties) detailed it on the silver screen. It was an age of innocence, tranquility, and static charm. In truth, however, that carefully packaged Golden Decade never

Television programs of the 1950s often centered around a happy, well-adjusted suburban family with two or three children.

existed. Instead, the decade was alive with dynamic, creative tensions.

Father Knows Best

The stock television situation comedy of the 1950s centered on a white family with a happily married husband and wife and two—or sometimes three—well-adjusted children. Most often, the family lived in a white, two-story suburban home, from which the father ventured daily to his white-collar job. The wife did not work outside the house—there was no need since the husband made a comfortable living. In any case, the shows emphasized, wives were also mothers, and mothers were supposed to stay home and tend the children. "Father Knows Best" was the classic example of this genre. It ran from 1954 to 1962 and signaled an optimistic outlook through its title song, "Just Around the Corner There's a Rainbow in the Sky."

The picture these sitcoms presented of America was not entirely inaccurate. Starting after World War II, Americans moved steadily toward the suburbs, which during the 1950s grew six times faster than cities. Several factors contributed to this migration. The high price of urban real estate had driven industries out of the cities, and as always in American history, the population followed the jobs. By 1970 suburban areas had more manufacturing jobs than the central cities. In addition, developers built abundant, inexpensive homes, which newly married couples, aided by VA and FHA loans, purchased. Of the 13 million homes constructed during the 1950s, 11 million were built in the suburbs.

Nor was the television image of predominantly white suburban families misleading. A far greater percentage of whites than blacks moved to the suburbs. In 1950 blacks comprised 12.5 percent of America's urban population and 4.9 percent of the country's suburban population. By 1970 the urban figure had climbed to 20.5 percent and the suburban number declined modestly to 4.8 percent. Housing and job restrictions worked to keep blacks in the central cities while allowing whites to fill the suburban areas.

Even the image of the suburban housewife preoccupied with her husband and her family was socially sanctioned. American women in the 1950s had babies as never before. The population of the United States increased by under 10 million in the 1930s, 19 million in the 1940s, and a staggering 30 million in the 1950s. During the 1950s the nation's growth rate approached that of India. The best-sellers list even indicated America's concern with children. Between 1946 and 1976 the pocket edition of Dr. Benjamin Spock's *Baby and Child Care* sold over 23 million copies, ranking it behind only the Bible and the combined works of Mickey Spillane and Dr. Seuss.

During the age of remarkable fertility, popular writers glorified the role of the mother. The best-seller *Modern Woman: The Lost Sex* went as far as to say that an independent woman was "a contradiction in terms." The ideal woman, writers observed, was content being a wife and a mother or, in a word, a homemaker. "Women must boldly announce," wrote novelist Sloan Wilson, "that no job is more exacting, more necessary, or more rewarding than that of housewife and mother." In the 1950s women married younger and had children sooner than they had in the previous two decades.

The Other Side of the Coin

"Father Knows Best" and other shows portrayed an ideal world where serious problems seldom intrude and where life lacks complexity. In fact, the move to suburbia and the changes in family life forced Americans to reevaluate many of their beliefs.

Cultural critics, for example, claimed that life in suburbia fostered mindless conformity. Lewis Mumford described suburbs as "a multitude of uniform, unidentifiable houses, lined up inflexibly, at uniform distances, on uniform roads, in a treeless communal wasteland, inhabited by people of the same class, the same income, the same age group." And a popular song called the suburban homes:

> Little boxes on the hillside,
> Little boxes made of ticky tacky
> Little boxes on the hillside,
> Little boxes all the same.

Some writers feared the United States had become a country of unthinking consumers driven by advertisers to desire only the latest gadget. Americans bought automobiles, houses,

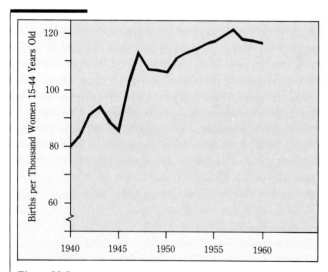

Figure 28.2
American birthrate, 1940–1960

(Text continues on p. 964)

PRIMARY SOURCE ESSAY

EDWARD R. MURROW AND
THE FUNCTION OF TELEVISION

During the 1940s and the 1950s, Edward R. Murrow (1908–1965) was the soul of radio and television news. His crisp, laconic style was as familiar to American listeners as his darting eyes and ever-present cigarette were to American viewers. Murrow entered the radio news business in the mid-1930s and he helped to determine its course and development. In 1938 when Hitler's determination to take the Sudetenland threatened war in Europe, Murrow and his roving reporter William L. Shirer brought the crisis to the American people with a series special broadcasts. During World War II Murrow—with his familiar "This . . . is London"—broadcast reports from rooftops, streets, and air-raid shelters, amid falling bombs and flying debris. After the war Murrow took his professional news skills to television. In 1951 his "See It Now" aired for the first time. This weekly half-hour show probed the important issues, policies, and personalities of the day. In 1954 "See It Now" even took on Senator Joseph McCarthy. From 1953 to 1959 Murrow also hosted the popular "Person to Person," an entertainment program that featured interviews with Hollywood celebrities and world leaders. But Murrow was always first a journalist and only second an entertainer. He deplored the shift in television from education to entertainment. Defeated by the forces of escapism and profit, he left broadcasting in 1961.

Edward R. Murrow at the microphone of his CBS-TV program, September 1957. Murrow believed in the instructional value of television and deplored the fact that most televised entertainment insulated the viewing public from reality.

REPRINTED IN *THE REPORTER* (NOV. 13, 1958), PP. 32–36

Our history will be what we make it. And if there are any historians about fifty or a hundred years from now, and there should be preserved the kinescopes for one week of all three networks, they will there find recorded in black-and-white, or color, evidence of decadence, escapism, and insulation from the realities of the world in which we live. I invite your attention to the television schedules of all networks between the hours of eight and eleven P.M. Eastern Time. Here you will find only fleeting and spasmodic reference to the fact that this nation is in mortal danger. There are, it is true, occasional informative programs presented in that intellectual ghetto on Sunday afternoons. But during the daily peak viewing periods, television in the main insulates us from the realities of the world in which we live. If this state of affairs continues, we may alter an advertising slogan to read: "Look Now, Pay Later." For surely we shall pay for using this most powerful instrument of communication to insulate the citizenry from the hard and demanding realities which must be faced if we are to survive. I mean the word—"survive"—literally. If there were to be a competition in indifference, or perhaps in insulation from reality, then Nero and his fiddle, Chamberlain and his umbrella, could not find a place on an early-afternoon sustaining show. If Hollywood were to run out of Indians, the program schedules would be mangled beyond all recognition. Then some courageous soul with a small budget might be able to do a documentary telling what, in fact, we have done—and are still doing—to the Indians in this country. But that would be unpleasant. And we must at all costs shield the sensitive citizens from anything that is unpleasant.

One of the basic troubles with radio and television news is that both instruments have grown up as an incompatible combination of show business, advertising, and news. Each of the three is a rather bizarre and demanding profession. And when you get all three under one roof, the dust never settles. The top management of the networks, with a few notable exceptions, has been trained in advertising, research, sales, or show business. But by the nature of the corporate structure, they also make the final and crucial decisions having to do with news and public affairs. Frequently they have neither the time nor the competence to do this. It is not easy for the same small group of men to decide whether to buy a new station for millions of dollars, build a new building, alter the rate card, buy a new Western, sell a soap opera, decide what defensive line to take in connection with the latest Congressional inquiry, how much money to spend on promoting a new program, what additions or deletions should be made in the existing covey or clutch of view-presidents, and at the same time—frequently on the same long day—to give mature, thoughtful consideration to the manifold problems that confront those who are charged with the responsibility for news and public affairs.

Edward R. Murrow addresses news reporters at a special press conference following Senator Joseph McCarthy's filmed rebuttal to Murrow's exposé of the senator on the journalist's "See It Now" program. Murrow gave up "See It Now" airtime to allow McCarthy to respond to the exposé.

In 1958 the Radio-Television News Directors Association (RTNDA) invited Murrow to address their annual meeting. The organization did not care about the subject of his address; they wanted Murrow for his name not for his thoughts on any particular subject. To the surprise of the organization, Murrow accepted the invitation. His speech "may do neither of us any good," he told RTNDA's program chairman. But he did have something that needed saying.

Murrow was the most famous television and radio journalist in America. No one else was even close. On CBS, "See It Now" had made as well as reported the news. In 1954 "See It Now" had courageously and successfully defended Lieutenant Milo Radulovich, an officer in the Air Force Reserve, who had been dismissed because of his associations with suspected radicals. The suspected radicals were his father and his sister. After Murrow's show on the case, the air force reinstated Radulovich. That same year, Murrow had taken on Joe McCarthy, and the show helped to break the grip of terror McCarthy had on America. Ending the show, Murrow told his viewers, "We proclaim ourselves—as indeed we are—the defenders of freedom, ... but we cannot defend freedom abroad by deserting it at home. The actions of the junior Senator from Wisconsin have caused alarm and dismay amongst our allies abroad and given considerable comfort to our enemies, and whose fault is it? Not really his. He didn't create this situation of fear; he merely exploited it, and rather successfully. Cassius was right: 'The fault, dear Brutus, is not in the stars but in ourselves . . .'"

But with fame came controversy and problems, especially with the management of CBS. Television is a commercial medium. It depends on advertising by sponsors for its revenues. And sponsors fear shows that generate controversy, for controversy can create a negative image that might defeat the objective of advertising itself. Alcoa, the sponsor of "See It Now," worried about the impact of the show, and this in turn concerned CBS president Frank Stanton and chairman of the board William S. Paley. In short, CBS was caught in the classic conflict of commercial television: programming freedom versus the demands of the sponsor. Murrow believed that the news division should not be constrained editorially by the profit motive. Stanton and Paley were not so sure. By 1958 Murrow could see that he was losing the fight, and he wanted to warn America before the contest was completely over.

Murrow's speech before RTNDA had a sense of urgency. "We are currently wealthy, fat, comfortable, and complacent," he said. "We have currently a built-in allergy to unpleasant or disturbing information. Our mass media reflect this. But unless we get up off our fat surpluses and recognize that television in the main is being used to distract, delude, amuse, and insulate us, then television and those who finance it, those who look at it and those who work at it, may see a totally different picture too late." He believed in the possibilities of television, but he knew that it could only be as good as the people who controlled the networks and stations: "This instrument can teach, it can illuminate; yes, it can even inspire. But it can do so only to the extent that humans are determined to use it to those ends. Otherwise it is merely wires and lights in a box."

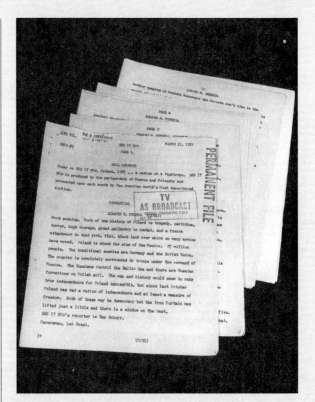

The script from Edward R. Murrow's "See It Now" broadcast, March 31, 1957.

Murrow lost the fight. In less than three years he was gone from CBS. But what he said was as true in 1958 as it is today. When asked why he criticized the industry that brought him fame and fortune, Murrow responded, "I've always been on the side of the heretics against those who burned them because the heretics so often proved right in the long run. Dead—but right." Murrow, the heretic, lost his electronic pulpit because he told the truth.

TABLE 28.1

Population of Metropolitan Areas by Region, Size, and Race, 1950–1970				
Year		Inner City	Suburbs	Black Population as Percent of Inner City	Black Population as Percent of Suburbs
1950	White	43,001,634	33,248,836		
	Black	6,194,948	1,736,521	12.5	4.9
	Other	216,210	102,531		
1970	White	49,430,443	71,148,286		
	Black	13,140,331	3,630,279	20.5	4.8
	Other	1,226,169	843,303		

Historical Statistics of the United States, Bicentennial Edition, vol. 1, p. 40.

and electrical appliances as never before. Thirty percent more Americans owned homes in 1970 than in 1940. Between 1945 and 1960 the number of cars in the country increased by 133 percent and the use of electricity tripled. Perhaps the symbol of this consumerism was the Barbie doll. Introduced to the American public in 1958, Barbie cost only $3 dollars, but her full wardrobe cost over $100. Indeed, the buying of homes, cars, televisions, and electrical appliances fueled the tremendous economic growth between 1945 and 1970. Clearly buying was good for the American economy, but was it beneficial to the individuals who spent more and more of their time in their cars and watching their televisions? Cultural observers despaired.

Some women also expressed frustration about their roles as wives and mothers. One poll of the 1934 graduates of the best women's colleges reported that one out of every three women felt unfulfilled. Although many women worked, cultural stereotyping prevented most of them from rising to the higher paying, more prestigious positions. In addition, Betty Friedan, a leader in the women's rights movement, noted that those women who did place a career above marriage or family were regarded as abnormal.

The problems of suburban life were explored in numerous films, novels, articles, and advice books. The film *Invasion of the Body Snatchers* (1956) is an outstanding example of the fear that suburbia had created a nation of conformists. In the movie, the inhabitants of the town Santa Mira are turned into emotionless shells by giant pods from outer space. Like abusers of Miltown or Thorazine—the most popular adult drugs of the 1950s—the pod-people utterly lack individuality. As one explains, podism means being "reborn into an untroubled world, where everyone's the same." In that world, "there is no need for love or emotion." For such cultural critics as David Riesman, author of *The Lonely Crowd* (1955), America's acceptance of conformity threatened to make podism a form of reality.

The critics, however, overreacted to the "suburban threat." If the houses looked the same, the people were individuals—even if they often banded together to try to form suburban communities. In the suburbs, white working-class families could afford for the first time to purchase homes and live middle-class lives. This was a real accomplishment. The problems that critics observed in the suburbs—the tendency toward conformity, cultural homogeneity, materialism, and anxiety over sex roles—were urban problems as well.

The Meaning of Elvis

The harshest critics of "suburban values" were American youths. Their criticism took different forms. Some of it was thoughtful and formalized, the result of the best efforts of young intellectuals. At other times it took a more visceral form, a protest that came from the gut rather than the mind. Of the second type of protest, none was more widely embraced by youths—or roundly attacked by adults—than rock and roll.

Rock and roll was the bastard mulatto child of a heterogeneous American culture. It combined black rhythm and blues with white country music. It was made possible by the post–World War II demographic changes. The movement of southern blacks and whites to the cities of the upper South and North threw together different musical traditions and forged an entirely new sound. Its lyrics and heavy beat challenged the accepted standards of "good taste" in music. Giving voice to this challenge, black rock-and-roll artist Chuck Berry sang:

> Well, I'm gonna write a little letter, gonna mail it to my local D.J.
> Yes, it's a jumpin' little record I want my jockey to play
> Roll over Beethoven, I gotta hear it again today
> You know my temp'rature's risin' and the jukebox blowin' a fuse
> My heart's beatin' rhythm and my soul keeps singin' the blues
> Roll over Beethoven and tell Tchaikovsky the news.

Confronting conventional morality, rock and roll was openly vulgar. The very term—"rock 'n' roll"—had long been used in blues songs to describe lovemaking, and early black rock-and-roll singers glorified physical relationships. Little Richard sang:

> Well, Long Tall Sally she's built for speed, she got
> Everythin' that Uncle John needs.

And in another song, he boasted:

> I'm gonna RIP IT UP!
> I'm gonna rock it up!
> I'm gonna shake it up. I'm gonna ball it up!
> I'm gonna RIP IT UP and ball tonight.

From its emergence in the early 1950s, rock and roll generated angry criticism. In the South, white church groups attacked it as part of an NAACP plot to corrupt the morals of southern youths and foster integration. In Hartford, Connecticut, Dr. Francis J. Braceland described rock and roll as "a communicable disease, with

Elvis Presley, one of the great pioneers of rock-and-roll music, was the target of much controversy throughout his life.

music appealing to adolescent insecurity and driving teenagers to do outlandish things . . . It's cannibalistic and tribalistic." Particularly between 1954 and 1958, there were numerous crusades to ban rock and roll from the airways.

Most of the critics of rock and roll focused on Elvis Presley, who more than any other artist most fully fused country music with rhythm and blues. In his first record, he gave the rhythm-and-blues song "That's All Right Mama" a country feel and the country classic "Blue Moon over Kentucky" a rhythm-and-blues swing. It was a unique exhibition of genius. In addition, Presley exuded sexuality. When he appeared on the Ed Sullivan Show, network executives instructed cameramen to avoid shots of Elvis's suggestive physical movements. Finally, Presley upset segregationists by performing "race music." Head of Sun Records Sam Phillips had once claimed, "If I could find a white man who had the Negro sound and the Negro feel, I could make a million dollars." Presley was that white man.

In the end, however, the protests implicit in Elvis Presley and rock and roll were largely coopted by middle-class American culture. Record producers, most of whom were white, smoothed the jagged edges of rock and roll. Sexually explicit black recordings were rewritten and rerecorded—a process known as "covering"—by white performers and then sold to white youths. Black singer Joe Turner, for example, recorded "Shake, Rattle and Roll" for a black audience. Its lyrics ran:

> Get out of that bed,
> And wash your face and hands.
> Get into the kitchen,
> Make some noise with the pots and pans.
> Well you wear low dresses,
> The sun comes shinin' through.
> I can't believe my eyes,
> That all of this belongs to you.

The white group Bill Haley and the Comets "covered" the song for a white audience. The new version stated:

> Get out in that kitchen,
> And rattle those pots and pans.
> Roll my breakfast
> 'Cause I'm a hungry man.
> You wear those dresses,
> Your hair done up so nice.
> You look so warm,
> But your heart is cold as ice.

In the second recording all references to beds and bodies have been eliminated; by 1959 rock and roll had become an accepted part of mainstream American culture.

A Different Beat

Rock-and-roll artists never rejected the idea of success in America. If they challenged conventional sexual mores and tried to create a unique sound, they accepted the rewards of success in a capitalistic society. Elvis Presley translated success into a steady stream of Cadillacs and conventional, unchallenging films. Not all youth protests, however, were so easily absorbed into middle-class culture. The Beat movement, for example, questioned the values at the heart of that culture.

The Beat Generation extolled the very thing that ·conventional Americans abhorred, and they rejected what the others prized. Beats scorned materialism, traditional family life, religion, sexuality, and politics. They renounced the American Dream. Instead, they valued spontaneity and intuition, searching for truth through Eastern mysticism and drugs. Although whites formed the rank and file of the Beat Generation, they glorified the supposedly "natural" life of black Americans, a life representing (at least for whites) pure instinctual drives. They adopted black music and the jive words of the black lexicon. *Cat, solid, chick, Big Apple, square,* were all absorbed into the Beat vocabulary.

Allen Ginsberg was the leading poet of the Beat Generation. A graduate of Columbia University, where he was influenced by the lifestyle of New York City lowlifes and artists, Ginsberg moved to San Francisco in the mid-1950s. There, surrounded by kindred souls, Ginsberg came to accept his homosexuality and preached a life based on experimentation. He also developed an authentic poetic voice. In 1955 he wrote "Howl," the prototypical Beat poem. Written under the influence of drugs, "Howl" is a literary kaleidoscope, a breathless succession of stark images and passionate beliefs. In a unique but soon to be widely imitated style, Ginsberg declared,

Allen Ginsberg was educated at the University of California, Berkeley, and at Columbia University. His poems expressed the Beat Generation's dissatisfaction with conventional middle-class values.

CHRONOLOGY
OF KEY EVENTS

1944 GI Bill of Rights grants veterans financial aid for education and government loans for building houses and starting businesses

1947 25-year-old Jackie Robinson becomes the first black player in major league baseball

1948 President Truman bans segregation in armed forces

1953 Dwight D. Eisenhower becomes thirty-fourth president; Stalin dies; Nikita Khrushchev emerges as leader of the Soviet Union; CIA helps bring Shah Mohammad Reza Pahlavi to power in Iran

1954 CIA masterminds overthrow of leftist government of Guatemala; *Brown* v. *Board of Education of Topeka* decision holds that "separate educational facilities are inherently unequal"

1955 Emmett Till murder; black residents of Montgomery, Alabama, organize a bus boycott to protest segregation; Eisenhower and Khrushchev hold summit in Geneva, Switzerland

1956 Soviet troops crush Hungarian uprising; Suez crisis; United States begins interstate highway system

1957 Eisenhower sends troops to Little Rock, Arkansas, to allow black students to enroll in formerly all-white public schools; Soviet Union launches the first satellite, *Sputnik*

1958 U.S. marines intervene in Lebanon; Congress passes the National Defense Education Act to provide federal aid to schools and colleges

1959 Fidel Castro leads Cuban Revolution against the regime of Fulgencio Batista

1960 U-2 spy plane is shot down over the Soviet Union

> I saw the best minds of my generation destroyed by madness, starving hysterically naked, dragging themselves through the negro streets at dawn looking for an angry fix . . .

Ginsberg even questioned accepted Cold War beliefs. He wrote:

> America you don't really want to go to war.
> America it's them bad Russians.
> Them Russians them Russians and them Chinamen. And them Russians.
> Them Russians want to eat us alive.
> America this is quite serious.
> America this is the impression I get from looking in the television set.
> America is this correct?

Ginsberg and Jack Kerouac, the leading Beat novelist, outraged adults but discovered followers on college campuses and in cities across America. They tapped an underground dissatisfaction with the prevailing blandness of conventional culture. In this their appeal was similar to that of rock and roll. Both were scattering seeds that would bear fruit during the next decade.

CONCLUSION

Ike's America was both more and less than what it seemed. In foreign and domestic affairs, Eisenhower appeared to allow his subordinates to run the country, when in reality he made the important decisions. Whether it was national highways or the Middle East, Eisenhower's vision of order helped shape American policy. He was more influential than most Americans during the 1950s realized.

If Eisenhower was more active than he appeared, then the country was more dynamic than it seemed on the surface. Although critics railed against the conformity of suburban America, everywhere there were signs of change. During the 1950s blacks quickened the pace of their struggle for equality and youths experimented with alternatives to traditional behavior. And increasingly these two rebellions merged to form a distinct subculture. During the 1960s, the war in Vietnam would give a political edge to that subculture.

SUGGESTIONS FOR FURTHER READING

OVERVIEWS AND SURVEYS

Stephen E. Ambrose, *Rise to Globalism: American Foreign Policy Since 1938*, 5th ed. (1988); William H. Chafe, *The Unfinished Journey*, 2d ed. (1991), and *The American Woman* (1972); Alexander DeConde, *A History of American Foreign Policy* (1963); Robert H. Ferrell, *American Diplomacy* (1959); Alonzo Hamby, *The Imperial Years* (1976); Godfrey Hodgson, *America in Our Time* (1976); Walter LaFeber, *America, Russia, and the Cold War*, 5th ed. (1985); R. W. Leopold, *The Growth of American Foreign Policy* (1962); William Leuchtenburg, *A Troubled Feast*, rev. ed. (1983); William Manchester, *The Glory and the Dream* (1974); Thomas G. Paterson et al., *American Foreign Policy*, 3d ed., 2 vols. (1988); Richard Polenberg, *One Nation Divisible* (1980); Emily and Norman Rosenberg, *In Our Times*, 4th ed. (1991); Frederick F. Siegel, *A Troubled Journey* (1984); William A. Williams, *The Tragedy of American Diplomacy*, 2d ed. (1972), and *The Roots of the Modern American Empire* (1969); Lawrence Wittner, *Cold War America*, rev. ed. (1978); Howard Zinn, *Postwar America, 1945–1971* (1973).

QUIET CHANGES

Charles Alexander, *Holding the Line: The Eisenhower Era, 1952–1961* (1975); Chester L. Cooper, *The Lion's Last Roar: Suez, 1956* (1978); Robert A. Divine, *Eisenhower and the Cold War* (1981); Fred I. Greenstein, *The Hidden-Hand Presidency: Eisenhower as Leader* (1982); Peter L. Hahn, *The United States, Great Britain, and Egypt, 1945–1956* (1991); Richard Immerman, *The CIA in Gua-*

temala (1982); Madeleine Kalb, *The Congo Cables: The Cold War in Africa—from Eisenhower to Kennedy* (1982); Richard Melanson and David Mayers, eds., *Reevaluating Eisenhower: American Foreign Policy in the 1950s* (1987); John B. Rae, *The Road and the Car in American Life* (1971); Mark H. Rose, *Interstate: Express Highway Politics, 1939–1989*, rev. ed. (1990); Walt W. Rostow, *The Stages of Economic Growth: A Non-Communist Manifesto*, 2d ed. (1971); Stephen Schlesinger and Steven Kinzer, *Bitter Fruit: The Untold Story of the American Coup in Guatemala* (1982); James Sundquist, *Politics and Policy: The Eisenhower, Kennedy, and Johnson Years* (1968); Richard Welch, Jr., *Response to Revolution: The United States and the Cuban Revolution, 1959–1961* (1985).

WE SHALL OVERCOME

Numan V. Bartley, *The Rise of Massive Resistance: Race and Politics in the South During the 1950s* (1969); Jack Bass, *Unlikely Heroes: The Dramatic Story of the Southern Judges of the Fifth Circuit* (1981); Sally Belfrage, *Freedom Summer* (1965); William Berman, *The Politics of Civil Rights in the Truman Administration* (1970); Albert Blaustein and Clarence Clyde Ferguson, Jr., *Desegregation and the Law*, 2d ed. (1962); William H. Chafe, *Civilities and Civil Rights: Greensboro, North Carolina, and the Black Struggle for Equality* (1980); Robert Conot, *Rivers of Blood, Years of Darkness* (1967); Richard Dalfiume, *Desegregation of the U.S. Armed Forces: Fighting on Two Fronts, 1939–1953* (1969); David Garrow, *Protest at Selma* (1978); Richard Kluger, *Simple Justice: The History of Brown v. Board of Education and Black America's Struggle for Equality* (1976); Steven Lawson, *Black Ballots: Voting Rights in the South, 1944–1969* (1976), and *Running for Freedom: Civil Rights and Black Politics in America since 1941* (1991); Manning Marable, *Race, Reform, and Rebellion: The Second Reconstruction in Black America, 1945-1990* (1991); Donald R. McCoy and Richard T. Ruetten, *Quest and Response: Minority Rights and the Truman Administration* (1973); Melton A. McLaurin, *Separate Pasts: Growing Up White in the Segregated South* (1987); Neil R. McMillen, *The Citizens' Council: Organized Resistance to the Second Reconstruction, 1954–64* (1971); August Meier and Elliott Rudwick, *CORE: A Study in the Civil Rights Movement, 1942–1968* (1973); Benjamin Muse, *The American Negro Revolution* (1968); Gunnar Myrdal, *An American Dilemma*, 2 vols. (1944); William L. O'Neill, *American High: The Years of Confidence, 1945–1960* (1986);

James Peck, *Freedom Ride* (1962); Howell Raines, *My Soul Is Rested: Movement Days in the Deep South Remembered* (1977); Harvard Sitkoff, *The Struggle for Black Equality* (1981); Morton Sosna, *In Search of the Silent South: Southern Liberals and the Race Issue* (1977); Howard Zinn, *The Southern Mystique* (1964).

THE SOUNDS OF CHANGE

Kent Anderson, *Television Fraud* (1978); Erik Barnouw, *Tube of Plenty*, 2d ed. (1990); Carl Belz, *The Story of Rock*, 2d ed. (1972); Paul A. Carter, *Another Part of the Fifties* (1983); William H. Chafe, *Women and Equality* (1977); Bruce Cook, *The Beat Generation* (1971); Marcus Cunliffe, *The Literature of the United States*, 4th ed. (1986); John D'Emilio and Estelle Freedman, *Intimate Matters: A History of Sexuality in America* (1988); Scott Donaldson, *The Suburban Myth* (1969); James Flink, *The Car Culture* (1975); Betty Friedan, *The Feminine Mystique* (1963); John Kenneth Galbraith, *The Affluent Society*, 4th ed. (1984); Herbert Gans, *The Levittowners* (1967); Charlie Gillett, *The Sound of the City: The Rise of Rock and Roll*, rev. ed. (1984); Michael Harrington, *The Other America: Poverty in the United States* (1962); Molly Haskell, *From Reverence to Rape: The Treatment of Women in the Movies*, 2d ed. (1987); Will Herberg, *Protestant, Catholic, Jew* (1955); Jerry Hopkins, *The Rock Story* (1970); Kenneth Jackson, *The Crabgrass Frontier: The Suburbanization of the United States* (1985); Pauline N. Kael, *I Lost It at the Movies* (1965); Marcus Klein, comp., *The American Novel since World War II* (1969); W. T. Lhamon, Jr., *Deliberate Speed: The Origins of a Cultural Style in the American 1950s* (1990); David Marc, *Demographic Vistas: Television in American Culture* (1984), Greil Marcus, *The Mystery Train*, 3d ed. (1990); Douglas Miller and Marion Nowak, *The Fifties: The Way We Really Were* (1977); James T. Patterson, *America's Struggle Against Poverty, 1900–1980* (1981); Ned Polsky, *Hustlers, Beats, and Others* (1967); David M. Potter, *People of Plenty: Economic Abundance and the American Character* (1954); David Riesman, *The Lonely Crowd* (1950); Stephen M. Rose, *The Betrayal of the Poor: The Transformation of Community Action* (1972); Lynn Spigel, *Make Room for TV: Television and the Family Ideal in Postwar America* (1992); I. F. Stone, *The Haunted Fifties* (1963); Michael Wood, *America in the Movies* (1975).

BIOGRAPHIES

Stephen E. Ambrose, *Eisenhower*, 2 vols. (1983–1984); Jervis Anderson, *A. Philip Randolph* (1973); Robert A. Caro, *The Power Broker: Robert Moses and the Fall of New York* (1974); Robert J. Donovan, *Eisenhower* (1956); David Garrow, *Bearing the Cross: Martin Luther King, Jr., and the Southern Christian Leadership Conference* (1986); Peter Goldman, *The Death and Life of Malcolm X*, 2d ed. (1979); Alex Haley, *Autobiography of Malcolm X* (1965); Townsend Hoopes, *The Devil and John Foster Dulles* (1973); David L. Lewis, *King*, 2d ed. (1978); Peter Lyon, *Eisenhower: Portrait of the Hero* (1974); Anne Moody, *Coming of Age in Mississippi* (1968); Stephen B. Oates, *Let the Trumpet Sound: The Life of Martin Luther King, Jr.* (1982).

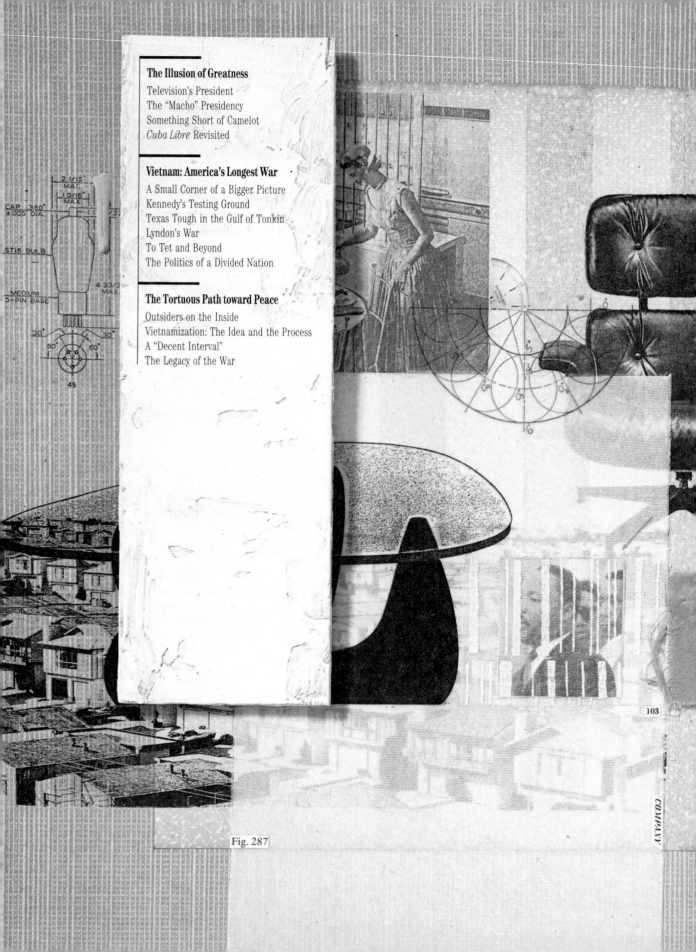

Fig. 287

103

COMPANY

CHAPTER 29

Vietnam and the Crisis of Authority

Ho Chi Minh was born roughly 9000 miles from America, but he might as well have come from a different planet. Ho was a tiny man, a frail, thin splinter of a man. He was gentle, and in public always deferential. Even after he had come to sole power in North Vietnam, he steadfastly avoided all the trappings of authority. Instead of uniforms or the white sharkskin suit of the mandarin, Ho favored the simple shorts and sandals worn by the Vietnamese peasants. He was sure of who he was—certain of his place in Vietnamese history—and he had no desire to impress others with his position. To his followers, he was "Uncle Ho," the kind, bachelor relative who treated all Vietnamese citizens like the children he never had. But in the pursuit of Vietnamese independence and the realization of a Communist nation, Ho could be cold-blooded and ruthless.

Ho was born in 1890 in a village in a central province of Vietnam and originally named Nguyen Sinh Cung. In 1912 Ho left Vietnam and began a generation-long world odyssey. Signing aboard a French freighter, he moved from one port to the next. For a time he stayed in the United States, visiting Boston, New York City, and San Francisco. He was amazed not only by America's skyscrapers but also by the fact that immigrants in the United States enjoyed the same legal rights as American citizens. He was also struck by the impatience of the American people, their expectations of immediate results. (Later, during the Vietnam War, Ho would say to his military leaders, "Don't worry, Americans are an impatient people. When things begin to go wrong, they'll leave.")

After three years of almost constant travel, Ho settled in London, where he worked at the elegant Carlton Hotel. He lived in squalid quarters and learned that poverty existed even in the wealthiest, most powerful countries. Then it was on to Paris, where he came in contact with the French left. There he studied, and his nationalist ambitions became tinged with revolutionary teachings. He was still in Paris when the Great War ended and the world leaders came to Versailles for the Peace Conference. Inspired by Woodrow Wilson's call for national self-determination, Ho wrote that "all subject peoples are filled with hope by the prospect that an era of right and justice is opening to them . . . in the struggle of civilization against barbarism." Ho wanted to meet Wilson; he wanted to plead for independence for his country. Wilson ignored his request; Vietnam remained France's colony. Ho moved on—farther east and further left.

Disillusioned with France and socialism, Ho traveled to Moscow, where Lenin had declared war against imperialism. In the Soviet Union Ho embraced communism. In the ideology he saw a road to his ultimate goal, the liberation of Vietnam. By the early 1920s he was actively organizing Vietnamese exiles into a revolutionary force. He continued to travel—to Western Europe, back to Russia, to China, back to Russia, to Thailand, back to the West. He lived a life of secrecy, moving from place to place, changing his name, renouncing anything even remotely resembling a personal life. No wife, no children, few friends—only a cause. As he advised one Vietnamese returning to the homeland, "The colonialists will be on your trail. Keep away from our friends' homes and don't hesitate to pose as a degenerate if it will help put the police off the scent."

In 1941 Ho returned to Vietnam. The time was right, he believed, to free Vietnam from colonial domination. During the early part of World War II, the Japanese had won control of the country from the French; now Ho and his followers would force out the Japanese. Once again Ho allied himself with the United States. Working alongside American Office of Strategic Services (OSS) agents, Ho proved his mettle. He impressed the OSS agents with his bravery, intelligence, and unflagging devotion to his cause. On September 2, 1945, borrowing passages from the American Declaration of Independence, Ho declared Vietnamese independence.

Ho Chi Minh was influenced by French socialism and Soviet communism in his goal to liberate Vietnam from the French.

The French, who returned to Vietnam after the war, had different plans for Vietnam, but Ho's struggle continued. In candid moments he admitted that he didn't expect to live to see Vietnam fully independent. Yet he knew that the struggle of others would eventually secure independence. Ho had patience. It was a quality that the West—first France and then the United States—found difficult to understand.

That was only one of the qualities of Ho and of the Vietnamese that the West did not understand. A deep intellectual chasm divided Vietnam and the West. The West viewed history as a straight line in which progress was the governing principle. Emphasizing technological advancements and material improvements, Westerners glorified change and prized individualism.

The Vietnamese were products of different beliefs. Notions of competition, individualism, and technological change were anathema to traditionbound Vietnamese. For a thousand years they had survived using the same rice cultivating methods. Often, however, the margin between survival and death was a razor's edge. Unlike the United States, Vietnam did not have fertile frontier areas to settle. To make do with the land they had, the Vietnamese organized life around villages and practiced cooperative existence. Rich people were considered selfish because their wealth *had* to be gained at the direct expense of others. As one authority explained, "the idea remains with the Vietnamese that great wealth is antisocial, not a sign of success but a sign of selfishness."

Like wealth, individualism threatened the corporate nature of village life, based on duties, not individual rights, and on social harmony more than individual justice. Even their language excluded the idea of individualism. Vietnamese has no personal pronoun equivalent to the Western *I, je, ich*. A person speaks of oneself in relationship to the person being addressed—for example, as "your teacher," "your brother," "your wife."

Nor did Vietnamese believe in intellectual freedom, which fostered debate and discord, rather than community stability. Americans considered Soviet communism evil because it discouraged the exchange of free ideas; Ho Chi Minh was drawn to the doctrine because it provided a set of answers not subject to questioning. Ho Chi Minh was the product of that closed world. America was the prophet of an open world. Motivated by the Cold War, during the period between 1954 and 1973, U.S. officials became convinced that they had to "save" Vietnam from Ho Chi Minh and his Communist brand of nationalism. Given Vietnamese leadership, traditions, and desire for independence, the American intervention in Vietnam was almost certain to fail.

THE ILLUSION OF GREATNESS

Television's President

John Fitzgerald Kennedy was made for television. His tall, thin body gave him the strong vertical line that cameras love, and his weatherbeaten good looks appealed to women without intimidating men. He had a full head of hair, and even in the winter he maintained a tan. Complementing his appearance was his attitude. He was always "cool" in public. This too was tailor-made for the "cool medium" television. Wit, irony, and understatement, all delivered with a studied nonchalance, translate well on television. Table thumping, impassioned speech, and even earnest sincerity often just do not work on television.

In the 1960 presidential race Kennedy challenged his Republican opponent Richard M. Nixon to a series of television debates. At the time, Kennedy faced an uphill battle. Young, handsome, and wealthy, Kennedy was considered by many too young, too handsome, and too wealthy to make an effective president. His undistinguished political record stood in stark contrast to Nixon's work in Congress and eight years as Eisenhower's vice president. In addition, Kennedy was Catholic, and Americans had never elected a Catholic president. Behind in the polls, Kennedy needed a dramatic boost. Thus the challenge. Against the advice of his campaign manager, Nixon accepted.

The first debate was held in Chicago on September 26, 1960, only a little more than a month before the election. Nixon arrived looking ill and weak. During the previous six weeks he had banged his kneecap, which became infected, spent several weeks at the Walter Reed

During the Kennedy-Nixon debates, John F. Kennedy demonstrated that for television politics, style was as important as substance.

Hospital, and then caught a bad chest cold that left him hoarse and weak. All and all, by the day of the debate he looked like a nervous corpse—pale, 20 pounds underweight, and haggard. Makeup experts offered to hide his heavy beard and soften his jowls, but Nixon accepted only a thin coat of Max Factor's "Lazy Shave," a pancake cosmetic.

Kennedy looked better, very much better. He didn't need makeup to appear healthy, nor did he need special lighting to hide a weak profile. He did, however, change suits. He believed that a dark blue rather than a gray suit would look better under the bright lights. Kennedy was right, of course, as anyone who watches a nightly news program must realize.

The debate started. Kennedy spoke first. Although he was nervous, he intentionally slowed down his delivery. His face was controlled and cool. He smiled with his eyes and perhaps the corners of his mouth, and his laugh was a mere suggestion of a laugh. His body language was perfect. As for what he said, Kennedy disregarded the prearranged ground rules and shifted what was supposed to be a debate on domestic issues to one on foreign policy.

Nixon fought back. He perspired, scored debating points, produced memorized facts, and struggled to win; but his efforts were "hot"—bad television. Instead of hearing a knowledgeable candidate, viewers saw a nervous, uncertain man, one whose clothes did not fit and whose face looked pasty and white. In contrast, what Kennedy said sounded statesmanlike, and he *looked* very good. Kennedy was the clear winner. Only later did Nixon realize that the telecast had been a production, not a debate.

The polls registered the results. For the first time during the campaign, Kennedy inched ahead of Nixon in a Gallup poll. Republicans realized the impact of the debate. Republican Senator Barry Goldwater called it "a disaster." Most of the people who were undecided before watching the debate voted for Kennedy. That proved to be the margin of victory. Only one-tenth of one percent separated the two candidates. Perhaps the most important result of the election, however, was not Kennedy's victory but the demonstration of the power of television. It came into its own in 1960.

The "Macho" Presidency

In his inaugural address Kennedy issued threats and challenges as well as making promises. Proud to be the first American president born in the twentieth century, proud to be the torchbearer for "a new generation," Kennedy wanted the world to know where he stood: "Let every nation know, whether it wishes us well or ill, that we shall pay any price, bear any burden, meet any hardship, support any friend, oppose any foe to assure the survival and the success of liberty." And who would pay, bear, meet, support, and oppose? On this point too Kennedy was clear: "And so, my fellow Americans: ask not what your country can do for you—ask what you can do for your country."

After the blandness and mangled syntax of Eisenhower's addresses, here was a speaker of rare ability, here were speeches beautifully phrased. Kennedy probably asked for more sacrifice and promised more rewards than any other president since Woodrow Wilson. Only years after his death did people begin to ask if he was serious or if he was more concerned with

dhist monks engaged in self-immolation. In full view of American reporters and cameras, one burned himself to death on a busy, downtown Saigon intersection. Although the gruesome sight shocked Americans, Diem's sister-in-law, Madame Nhu, laughed at the "barbecues," offering gasoline and matches for more fiery deaths.

More fiery deaths followed. Protests mounted. Outside of Saigon, Diem exerted little influence. Such insightful American reporters as Davis Halberstam, Neil Sheehan, Peter Arnett, and Stanley Karnow argued that the Diem regime was isolated and paranoid, that a stable democracy would never develop as long as Diem held power. Rather than talk with reporters, Diem delivered five-, six-, even ten-hour monologues. One reporter recalled that during these sessions Diem's "face seemed to be focused on something beyond me. . . . The result was an eerie feeling that I was listening to a monologue delivered at some other time and in some other place—perhaps by a character in some allegorical play."

The Kennedy administration soon reached the conclusion that without Diem South Vietnam had serious problems, with Diem the country was doomed. In sum, Diem had to go. Behind the scenes, Kennedy encouraged Vietnamese generals to overthrow Diem. On November 1, 1963, Vietnamese army officers arrested and murdered Diem and his brother. Although Kennedy did not approve of the assassination, the United States quickly aided the new government.

Three weeks later Kennedy was assassinated in Dallas. Several friends of Kennedy have suggested that he had begun to reevaluate his Vietnam policy and that after the 1964 election he would have started the process of American disengagement. In a moment of insight, Kennedy himself had observed, "The troops will march in; the bands will play; the crowds will cheer; and in four days everyone will have forgotten. Then we will be told we have to send more troops. It's like taking a drink. The effect wears off, and you have to take another." But whatever Kennedy's plans or insights, he had increased U.S. involvement in Vietnam.

Unfortunately for Kennedy's successor, the prospects for South Vietnam's survival were less than they had been in 1961. By 1963 South Vietnam had lost the fertile Mekong Delta to the Vietcong and with it most of the country's rural population. From the peasants' perspective, the Saigon government stood for heavy taxes, no services, and military destruction; and increasingly they identified the United States with Saigon. Such was the situation Lyndon Johnson inherited.

Texas Tough in the Gulf of Tonkin

Lyndon Baines Johnson was a complex man—shrewd, arrogant, intelligent, sensitive, vulgar, vain, and occasionally cruel. He loved power, and he knew where it was, how to get it, and how to use it. "I'm a powerful sonofabitch," he told two Texas congressmen in 1958 when he was the most powerful legislator on Capitol Hill. Everything about Johnson seemed to emphasize or enhance his power. He was physically large, and seemed even bigger than he was, and he used his size to persuade people. The "Johnson treatment" involved "pressing the flesh"— a backslapping, hugging sort of camaraderie. He also used symbols of power adroitly, especially the telephone, which had replaced the sword and pen as the symbol of power. "No gunman," remarked one historian, "ever held a Colt .44 so easily" as Johnson handled a telephone.

A legislative genius, Johnson had little experience in foreign affairs. Reared in the poverty of the Texas hill country, educated at a small teachers' college, and concerned politically with domestic issues, before becoming president LBJ had expressed little interest in foreign affairs. "Foreigners are not like the folks I am used to," he often said, and whether it was a joke or not he meant it. He was particularly uncomfortable around foreign dignitaries and ambassadors, often receiving them in groups and scarcely paying attention to them. "Why do I have to see them?" he once asked. "They're [Secretary of State] Dean Rusk's clients, not mine."

Yet to say Johnson had little experience in foreign affairs is not to suggest that he did not have strong opinions on the subject. Like most politicians of the period, Johnson was an unquestioning Cold Warrior. In addition, along with accepting the domino theory—the idea that if Vietnam fell, other nations would also fall to communism—and a monolithic view of communism, Johnson cherished a traditionally southern notion of honor and masculinity. It was his duty, he maintained, to honor commitments made by earlier presidents. "We are [in Vietnam] because . . . we remain fixed on the pursuit of freedom, a deep and moral obligation *that will not let us go.*" Leaving Vietnam, Johnson believed, would be a dishonorable act, dangerous for the nation's future. Raised in an area where the frontier was still visible, Johnson approached foreign policy like a frontier sheriff. To show weakness and back down was worse than cowardly—it was unmanly. As he often said, "If you let a bully come into your front yard one day, the next day he will be up on your porch and the day after that he will rape your wife in your own bed."

Furthermore, Johnson believed that any retreat from Vietnam would destroy him politically. Soon after becoming president, he told America's ambassador to Vietnam, "I am not going to be the President who saw Southeast Asia go the way China went." No, he would not "lose" Vietnam and allow Republican critics to attack him as they had Truman. "I knew," LBJ later noted, "that Harry Truman and Dean Acheson had lost their effectiveness from the day the communists took over China." Johnson was determined to win the war, to "nail the coonskin to the wall."

Before winning in Vietnam, however, he had to win in the United States. The presidential election in 1964 was his top priority. He was pitted against Barry Goldwater, the powerful Arizona senator from the Republican Right. "Extremism in the defense of liberty is no vice," Goldwater said, and if elected he promised to defend South Vietnam at any cost. He also preached against the welfare state, Social Security, the Nuclear Test Ban Treaty of 1963, and any rapprochement with the Soviet Union or China. Democrats transformed his campaign slogan "In Your Heart, You Know He's Right," to "In Your Heart, You Know He Might," by which they meant that Goldwater might start a nuclear war. Goldwater did little to discourage such thinking. In his campaign he labored to make "nukes" socially acceptable, even coining the

In the presidential campaign of 1964, Republican candidate Barry Goldwater, a U.S. senator from Arizona, promised to defend South Vietnam regardless of the price.

uncomfortably comforting phrase "conventional nuclear weapon."

Johnson's campaign strategy was to appear as the thoughtful, strong moderate. He would not lose Vietnam, he told voters, but neither would he use nuclear weapons or "send American boys nine or ten thousand miles from home to do what Asian boys ought to be doing themselves." Johnson promised that if elected he would create a "Great Society" at home and honor American commitments abroad. As usual, he knew what the voters wanted to hear, and they rewarded him with a landslide victory in the November election.

Behind the scenes, however, the Johnson administration was maneuvering to obtain a free hand for conducting a more aggressive war in Vietnam. He did not want a formal declaration of war, which might frighten voters. Rather he desired a quietly passed resolution giving him the authority to deploy American forces. Such a resolution would allow him to act without the consent of Congress. Johnson and his advisors were planning to escalate American involvement in the Vietnam War, but they hoped it would go unnoticed.

Johnson used two reported North Vietnamese attacks on the American destroyer *Maddox* as a pretext for going before Congress to ask for the resolution. Actually, he was less than truthful about the circumstances of the attack. The first incident occurred in the Gulf of Tonkin in early August 1964 when the North Vietnamese suspected the *Maddox* of aiding a South Vietnamese commando raid into North Vietnam, a violation of that country's sovereignty. When North Vietnamese patrol boats approached the *Maddox*, the American ship and supporting navy jets opened fire, sinking one of the North Vietnamese ships and crippling two others. Although the North Vietnamese ships had launched several torpedoes, the *Maddox* was not hit and suffered only superficial machine gun damage and a loss of ammunition. The second of the Gulf of Tonkin incidents probably never occurred. Assaulted by high waves, thunderstorms, and freak atmospheric conditions, the *Maddox*'s sonar equipment apparently malfunctioned registering 22 invisible enemy torpedoes. No enemy ships were visually sighted, and none of the electronically sighted torpedoes hit the Maddox or its accompanying ship the

In this photo, a North Vietnamese torpedo boat attacks the American destroyer USS *Maddox*. The attack took place in the Gulf of Tonkin on August 2, 1964, but the incident was not explored fully until publication of the Pentagon Papers in 1971.

C. Turner Joy. Soon after the incident the commander of the *Maddox* reached the conclusion that no attack had ever taken place.

Johnson realized the dubious nature of the second attack. He told an aide, "Hell, those dumb stupid soldiers were just shooting at flying fish." Nevertheless, he went on national television and announced, "Aggression by terror against peaceful villages of South Vietnam has now been joined by open aggression on the high seas against the United States of America." Reassuring the country, he continued, "We know, although others appear to forget, the risks of spreading conflict. We seek no wider war." A few days later he pressed Congress for a resolution. American ships, he emphasized, had been repeatedly attacked, and he wanted authorization to "take all necessary measures" to repel attacks, prevent aggression, and protect American security. It was a broad resolution; Johnson said that it was "like Grandma's nightshirt—it covered everything." Almost without debate, the Senate passed the resolution on August 7 with only two dissenting votes, and the House of Representatives endorsed it unanimously. You "will live to regret it," Wayne Morse, who voted against it in the Senate, told the resolution's supporters. In the years that followed, as Johnson used his new powers to escalate the war, Morse's vote and prediction were vindicated, for the Gulf of Tonkin Resolution allowed Johnson to act in an imperial fashion.

Lyndon's War

Lyndon Johnson liked to personalize things. Once a military aide tried to direct Johnson to the correct helicopter, saying "Mr. President, that's not your helicopter." "Son, they're all my helicopters," Johnson replied. So it was with the Vietnam War. He did not start the war, but once reelected he quickly made it "his war." Over the war he exercised complete control. One authority on the war described Johnson's role:

He made appointments, approved promotions, reviewed troop requests, determined deployments, selected bombing targets, and restricted aircraft sorties. Night after night, wearing a dressing gown and carrying a flashlight, he would descend into the White House basement "situation room" to monitor the conduct of the conflict . . . often, too, he would doze by his bedside telephone, waiting to hear the outcome of a mission to rescue one of "my pilots" shot down over Haiphong or Vinh or Thai Nguyen. It was his war.

When he became president it was still a relatively obscure conflict for most Americans. Public opinion polls showed that 70 percent of the American public paid little attention to U.S. activities in Vietnam. At the end of 1963 only 16,300 U.S. military personnel were in Vietnam; the number rose to 23,300 by the end of 1964. Most of the soldiers there, however, were volunteers. Only a few people strongly opposed America's involvement. All this would change dramatically during the next four years.

With the election behind him, in early 1965 Johnson started to reevaluate the position of the United States. In Saigon crisis followed crisis as one unpopular government gave way to the next. Something had to be done, and Johnson's advisors suggested two courses. The military and most of LBJ's foreign policy experts called for a more aggressive military presence in Vietnam, including bombing raids into North Vietnam and more ground troops. Other advisors, notably Under Secretary of State George Ball, believed the United States was making the same mistakes as the French had made. Ball believed that a land war in Indochina was not in America's best strategic interests and that bombing North Vietnam would only stiffen the resolve of the Communists. Thus escalation of the war could create serious problems. "Once on the tiger's back," Ball noted, "we cannot be sure of picking the place to dismount."

Johnson chose the first course, claiming it would be dishonorable not to come to South Vietnam's aid. In February 1965 Vietcong troops attacked the American base in Pleiku, killing several soldiers. Johnson used the assault as a pretext to commence air raids into the North. Code-named ROLLING THUNDER, the operation was designed to use American technological superiority to defeat North Vietnam. At first, Johnson limited U.S. air strikes to enemy radar and bridges below the 20th parallel. But as the war dragged on, he ordered "his pilots" to hit military targets in metropolitan areas. Between 1965 and 1973, American pilots flew more than 526,000 sorties and dropped 6,162,000 tons of bombs on enemy targets. (As a point of contrast, the total tonnage of explosives dropped in World War II by all the belligerent countries was 2,150,000 tons.) As a result, much of the landscape of South and North Vietnam took on a lunar look.

However, the bombs did not lead to victory. Ironically, as Ball had predicted, the bombing missions actually strengthened the Communist government in North Vietnam. As a U.S. intelligence report noted, the bombing of North Vietnam "had no significantly harmful effects on popular morale. In fact, the regime has apparently been able to increase its control of the populace and perhaps even to break through the political apathy and indifference which have characterized the outlook of the average North Vietnamese in recent years."

The massive use of air power also undermined U.S. counterinsurgency efforts. Colonel John Paul Vann, an American expert on counterinsurgency warfare noted, "The best weapon 'for this type of war' . . . would be a knife. . . . The worst is an airplane. The next worst is artillery. Barring a knife, the best is a rifle—you know who you're killing." By using bombing raids against the enemy in both the North and South, U.S. forces inevitably killed large numbers of civilians, the very people they were there to help. For peasants everywhere in Vietnam, U.S. jets, helicopters, and artillery "meant more bombing, more death, and more suffering."

A larger air war also led to more ground troops. As Johnson informed Ambassador Maxwell Taylor, "I have never felt that this war will be won from the air, and it seems to me what is much more needed and will be more effective is a larger and stronger use of rangers and special forces and marines." Between 1965 and 1968 the escalation of American forces was dramatic. When George Ball warned in 1965 that 500,000 American troops in Vietnam might not be able to win the war, other members of the Johnson administration laughed. By 1968 no one was laughing. Ball's prediction was painfully accurate. Escalation of American troops and deaths went hand in hand. The year-end totals for the United States between 1965 and 1968 were:

1965: 184,300 troops; 636 killed.
1966: 385,300 troops; 6644 killed.
1967: 485,600 troops; 16,021 killed.
1968: 536,000 troops; 30,610 killed.

But still there was no victory.

To Tet and Beyond

Throughout the escalation Johnson was less than candid with the American people. He argued that there had been no real change in American policy and that victory was in sight. Any reporter who said otherwise, he roundly criticized. Increasingly he demanded unquestioning loyalty from his close advisors. Such demands led to an administration "party line." As the war ground on, the "party line" bore less and less similarity to reality.

In late 1967, General William Westmoreland returned to America briefly to assure the public that he could now see the "light at the end of the tunnel." In his annual report Westmoreland commented, "The year ended with the enemy increasingly resorting to desperation tactics; . . . and he has experienced only failure in these attempts." At the time, the American press focused most of its attention on the battle of Khe Sanh, and Westmoreland assured everyone that victory there was certain.

Then with a suddenness that caught all America by surprise, North Vietnam struck into the very heart of South Vietnam. On the morning of January 30, 1968, North Vietnam launched the Tet offensive. "Tet," the Vietnamese holiday that celebrates the lunar new year, traditionally is supposed to determine family fortunes for the rest of the year. Certainly the Tet offensive boded well for North Vietnam. A Vietcong suicide squad broke into the U.S. embassy in Saigon, and Vietnamese Communists mounted offensives against every major target in South Vietnam, including 5 cities, 64 district capitals, 36 provincial capitals, and 50 hamlets.

For what it was worth, the United States repelled the Tet offensive. For a few days the fighting was ferocious and bloody, as the rivals fought in highly populated cities and almost evacuated hamlets. In order to retake Hue, the ancient cultural center close to the border between North and South Vietnam where the fighting lasted for several weeks, allied troops had to destroy part of the city. One observer recorded that the city was left a "shattered, stinking hulk, its streets choked with rubble and rotting bodies." When United States and South Vietnamese troops finally recaptured Hue, they discovered that North Vietnamese and Vietcong soldiers had killed several thousand political leaders, teachers, and other civilians, many of whom had been buried alive in one mass grave. In another village, where victory came at a high price, the liberating American general reported, "We had to destroy the town to save it." Both sides suffered terribly. But after the allies cleared the cities of enemy troops, General Westmoreland judged the episode a great allied victory. In the end, American and South Vietnamese troops recaptured lost areas and South Vietnamese civilians did not rally to the Vietcong cause. Indeed the Vietcong was so decimated by the Tet offensive that it never regained its full fighting strength.

If technically the Tet offensive was a military defeat for North Vietnam, it was also a profound psychological victory. Johnson, his advisors, and his generals had been proclaiming that the enemy was on the run, almost defeated, tired of war, ready to quit. Tet demonstrated that the contrary was true. Upset and confused, CBS anchorman Walter Cronkite, the national voice of reason, expressed the attitude on his nightly newscast: "What the hell is going on? I thought we were winning the war?" The Tet offensive, more than any other single event, turned the media against the war and exposed the widening "credibility gap" between official pronouncements and public beliefs. NBC anchorman Frank McGee reported that the time had come "when we must decide whether it is futile to destroy Vietnam in the effort to save it."

After Tet, Americans stopped thinking about victory and turned toward thoughts of how best to get out of Vietnam. "Lyndon's planes" and "Lyndon's boys" had been unable to achieve Lyndon's objectives. For Johnson this fact was politically disastrous. In the polls his popularity plummeted, and in the New Hampshire primary Democratic peace candidate Eugene McCarthy received surprisingly solid support. On CBS's the *Smothers Brothers Comedy Hour* folk singer Pete Seeger openly criticized Johnson in the song "Waist Deep in the Big Muddy" about a "Big Fool [who] says to push on." Too intelligent a politician not to realize what was happening, on the night of March 31, LBJ went on television and made two important announcements. First, he said that the United States would limit its bombing of North Vietnam and would enter into peace talks any time and at any place. And second, Johnson surprised the nation by saying, "I will not seek, and I will not accept, the nomination of my party for another term as your President." A major turning point had been reached. The gradual escalation of the war was over. The period of deescalation had started. Even in official government circles, peace had replaced victory as America's objective in Vietnam.

The Politics of a Divided Nation

If Johnson's fall seemed remarkably swift, and if it seemed as if he were surrendering power without a fight, it was because he knew that his policies had badly divided the nation. LBJ honestly believed he had pursued the only honorable course in Vietnam, that he had had America's best interests at heart. His problem, however, was *not* that his intentions were dishonorable but that his *modus operandi*—the style of his leadership—involved great duplicity. Instead of fully committing the United States by calling up the reserves and National Guardsmen and by pushing for higher taxes to pay for the war, Johnson gambled that a slow, steady escalation would be enough to force North Vietnam to accept a negotiated peace. All during the buildup, LBJ assured the American people that he was not drastically changing policy and, besides, victory was in sight. But he could not fool all the people all the time, and after the Tet offensive he knew that he could not even fool most of the people any more.

Dissatisfaction with Johnson's policy surfaced first among the young, the very people who were being asked to fight and die for the cause. Most of the young men who were drafted
(Text continues on p. 990)

LOGISTICS IN A GUERRILLA WAR: The Longest War

The Vietnam War was a logistical nightmare for the United States. Fought 9000 miles from America's shores, the United States had to ship hundreds of tons of supplies daily from the United States to bases in the Pacific and finally to fortified positions along the coast of Vietnam. Once the supplies were in Vietnam, they had to be protected from Vietcong guerrillas, who blended into the civilian population and often obtained jobs on U.S. bases. As a result, although American forces established defense perimeters around their bases, the areas were never totally secure. Bombs in U.S. movie theaters or even mess halls were haunting reminders of the unpredictability of guerrilla warfare.

North Vietnam sent much of its supplies south along the Ho Chi Minh Trail. Following a traditional series of trails through mountains and jungles from North Vietnam into Laos and Cambodia and finally emptying into South Vietnam, the Ho Chi Minh Trail was widened into a road capable of handling heavy trucks and thousands of troops. Along the trail, support facilities, often built underground to escape American detection and air strikes, included operating rooms, fuel storage tanks, and supply coaches. Throughout the war, United States forces tried but failed to effectively disrupt the flow of supplies and soldiers south.

The Vietcong tunnel complex created even more problems for American troops. The tunnels allowed Vietcong troops to appear and disappear almost by magic. The most famous tunnel complex was under Cu Chi, approximately 25 miles northeast of Saigon. It contained conference rooms, sleeping chambers, storage halls, and kitchens. U.S. forces bombed, gassed, and defoliated the Cu Chi area, but failed to destroy the tunnels. The "tunnel rats"—South Vietnamese soldiers and short, wiry GI combat engineer SWAT teams—fought heroically in the tunnels, but they too were unable to destroy the complexes. In the end, the unconventional nature of the Vietnam War guaranteed frustration and made it America's longest war.

Map: From *The Tunnels of Cu Chi* by Tom Mangold and John Penycate. Copyright © 1985 by Tom Mangold and John Penycate. Reprinted by permission of Random House, Inc.

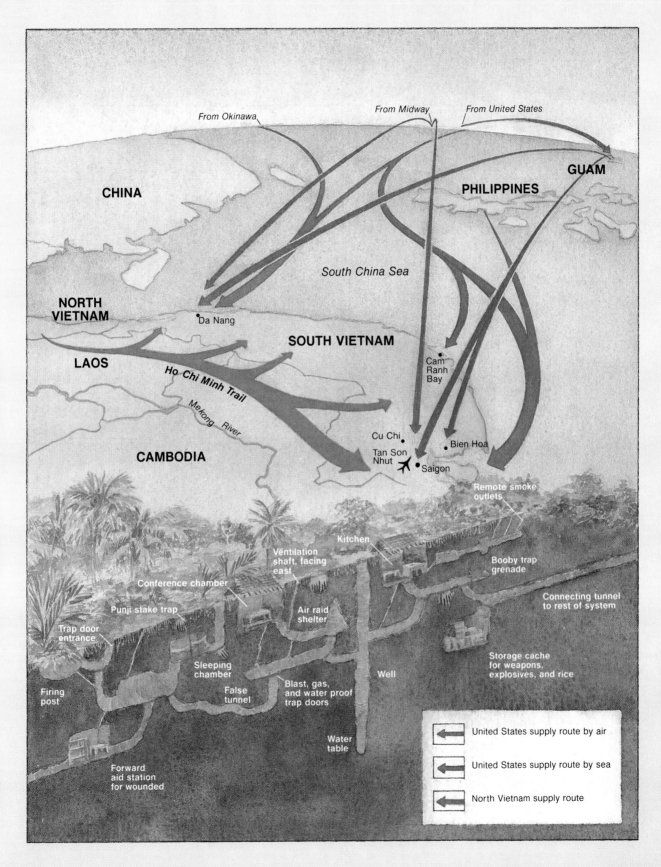

From Okinawa

From Midway

From United States

CHINA

GUAM

PHILIPPINES

South China Sea

NORTH
VIETNAM

Da Nang

SOUTH VIETNAM

LAOS

Ho Chi Minh Trail

Cam
Ranh
Bay

Mekong River

Cu Chi

Bien Hoa

CAMBODIA

Tan Son
Nhut

Saigon

Remote smoke
outlets

Kitchen

Booby trap
grenade

Ventilation
shaft, facing
east

Conference chamber

Connecting tunnel
to rest of system

Punji stake trap

Air raid
shelter

Trap door
entrance

Sleeping
chamber

Well

Storage cache
for weapons,
explosives, and rice

Firing
post

False
tunnel

Blast, gas,
and water proof
trap doors

Water
table

Forward
aid station
for wounded

United States supply route by air

United States supply route by sea

North Vietnam supply route

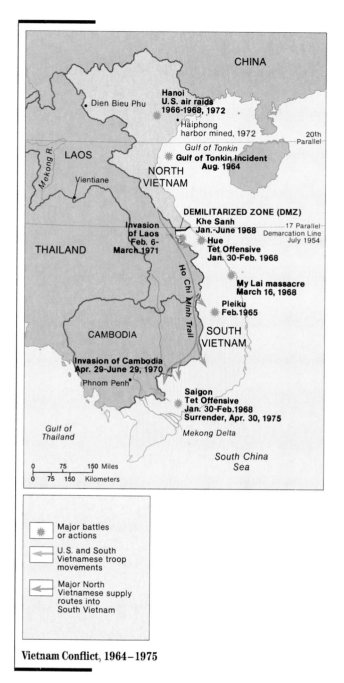

Vietnam Conflict, 1964–1975

provements in South Vietnamese village life. But by his last tour, in 1970, his idealism had died. As he told a friend, "I'm still ready to serve—any time. But as a killing machine, not a humanitarian."

As the war lengthened, an ever growing number of soldiers shared in this disillusionment. The disillusionment took different forms. Some soldiers turned to drugs to relieve the constant stress and fear that the war engendered. Journalist Michael Herr has written eloquently about the horrors of the war: "Satchel charges and grenades blew up jeeps and movie houses, the VC (Vietcong) got work inside all the camps as shoe shine boys and laundresses, . . . they'd starch your fatigues . . . then go home and mortar your area. Saigon and Cholan and Danang held such hostile vibes that you felt that you were being dry sniped every time someone looked at you." Drugs and sex helped some soldiers—many just boys away from home for the first time—to cope with the nature of a guerrilla war. One GI recalled that R&R—the traditional rest and recreation leave—was really I&I—"intoxication and intercourse." A 1969 Pentagon study estimated that nearly two of every three American soldiers in Vietnam were using marijuana and that one of every three or four had tried heroin. In 1970 CBS News televised a "smoke-in," in which GIs smoked marijuana through the barrel of a combat rifle. In such an atmosphere boys became men, fast. "How do you feel," Herr asked, "when a nineteen-year-old kid tells you from the bottom of his heart that he has gotten too old for this kind of shit?"

Other soldiers reacted by viewing all Vietnamese as the enemy. In part the nature of the war against the Vietcong caused this attitude. In a village of "civilians" any man, woman, or child *might* be the enemy. "Vietnam was a dark room full of deadly objects," wrote Herr, "and the VC were everywhere all at once like spider cancer." Tension and anxiety were as ever present as olive drab.

Empty government phrases, however, also contributed to the problem. How could soldiers win the "hearts and minds" of villagers one day and rain napalm on them the next? Reacting to the surface idealism of U.S. policy, one experienced soldier commented, "All that is just a *load* man. We're here to kill gooks, period." The

did serve, and most served bravely. In the early years of "Lyndon's war," many soldiers sincerely believed that they were fighting—and dying—to preserve freedom and nourish democracy in Southeast Asia. One career soldier, who did his first tour in Vietnam in 1966, recalled the idealism of his experience. He talked enthusiastically about American contributions to the im-

My Lai massacre, which saw American soldiers kill more than 100 (the official figure was 122 but it was probably many more) South Vietnamese civilians, was the sad extension of this attitude.

As the war lengthened, morale of American soldiers plummeted. Desertion and absent-without-leave (AWOL) rates skyrocketed. In 1966 the army desertion rate had been 14.9 men per thousand; by 1971 it had risen to 73.5. In 1966 there were 57.2 AWOL incidents per thousand; that figure leaped to 176.9 in 1971. Even worse, "fragging"—the term soldiers used to describe the assassination of overzealous officers and noncommissioned officers (NCOs) by their own troops—increased at an alarming rate. The army claimed that at least 1011 officers and NCOs were killed or wounded by their own men during the Vietnam War.

At home, university students, most of whom had draft exemptions, also reacted to the war and Johnson's policies. They were the earliest and most vocal critics of the Vietnam War. If they lacked a coherent ideology, they were strong in numbers and energy. Between 1946 and 1970 enrollments in institutions of higher education had climbed from 2 million to 8 million. Although not all the students protested against the war, the most politically active ones did. As politicians they formed a curious breed—segregated from society as a whole, freed from adult responsibilities, bound to no real constituency, and encouraged by their teachers to think critically. Most student protesters were from upper middle-class families and could afford the intellectual luxury of being political idealists. (Youth culture as a whole will be discussed in greater detail in Chapter 30.)

Led by such leftist groups as Students for a Democratic Society (SDS), university students called for a more just society in which political life was governed by morality, not greed. During the early 1960s they focused on the civil rights movement, participating in freedom rides and voter registration drives. By the mid-1960s, however, they were increasingly shifting their attention to America's "unjust and immoral" war in Southeast Asia; and with the shift their numbers swelled. In 1962 only ten universities had SDS chapters, and each chapter had only a handful of members. By 1968 the organization boasted more than 100,000 members. By then, too, older voices had joined the student chorus of condemnation.

It was the older voices, energized by the idealism of youth, that led to Johnson's decision not to seek reelection in 1968. For many, it seemed as if the future of American politics belonged to the proponents of peace and morality. Students flocked to presidential candidate Gene McCarthy's peace cause. They cut their long hair, shaved their beards ("be clean for Gene"), put on coats and ties, and worked for McCarthy's campaign. After Johnson pulled his hat out of the ring, Robert Kennedy announced his candidacy. Although McCarthy supporters saw Kennedy as a political opportunist, he spoke eloquently for the cause of humanity and peace. When students at a Catholic university called for more bombings, RFK asked, "Do you understand what that means? It means you are voting to send people, Americans and Vietnamese to die.... Don't you understand that what we are doing to the Vietnamese is not very different than what Hitler did to the Jews." Kennedy, who enjoyed midnight bull sessions on the meaning of existence and looked at ease with his tie loosened and his shirt sleeves rolled above his elbows, spoke a language that radical students understood. He exhibited the passion and commitment that McCarthy lacked. By the conclusion of the campaign, Kennedy had become the foremost peace candidate, and representative of young liberals.

In 1968, Democrat Eugene McCarthy ran for his party's presidential nomination as a peace candidate.

At the celebration party after his narrow victory in the California primary, Kennedy said, "We are a great country, an unselfish country, and a compassionate country. I intend to make that my basis for running." Moments later a fanatic Palestinian shot him in the head. With Kennedy died the dreams of many Americans

Although he was slow to declare his candidacy, Robert Kennedy soon became the darling of the anti-war movement.

for a moral society. Columnist Murray Kempton spoke for many people: "I have liked many public men immensely, but I guess [RFK] is the only one I have ever loved." Although RFK had started in political life as a committed, aggressive anti-Communist and Cold Warrior, by the time of his death he had radically reevaluated his earlier beliefs.

The Democratic party went to the Chicago convention without a candidate. There they battled among themselves—young and old; radical, liberal, and conservative. In the streets, outside the convention hall, police beat protesters in full view of television cameras. An official commission later termed it a "police riot." Inside the convention hall the fighting was largely verbal, but it was just as intense and bitter. Abraham Ribicoff, a senator from Connecticut, accused Chicago's mayor Richard Daley of allowing the police to use "Gestapo tactics" in the street; Daley accused Ribicoff of having unnatural re-

lations with his mother. In the end, the Democratic party chose Hubert Humphrey, Johnson's liberal vice president, as their presidential candidate. Instead of change, the Democratic party chose a representative of the "old politics."

In a more tranquil convention in Miami, the Republican party endorsed Richard M. Nixon, who promised when elected to honorably end the Vietnam War, move against forced busing of black children to white schools, and restore "law and order." More calm and relaxed than ever before, the "new Nixon" claimed to speak for the great majority of Americans who obeyed the nation's laws, paid their taxes, regularly attended church, and loved their country. It was the same message Alabama's Governor George Wallace used as the foundation of his third-party candidacy. Running on the American Independent ticket, Wallace spoke for millions of working-class white Americans, young and old alike, who opposed forced integration of schools and neighborhoods, radical college students, and what they believed was the country's drift toward the left. Although Humphrey finished the campaign strong, Nixon's and Wallace's appeal to traditional values had an undeniable attraction. And on election day, Nixon received 43.4 percent of the popular vote, Humphrey 42.7 percent, and Wallace 13.5 percent. Given the combined votes for Nixon and Wallace—57 percent—it was clear that the country was moving right rather than left.

THE TORTUOUS PATH TOWARD PEACE

During the presidential campaign of 1968, Richard Nixon expected the American voter to accept certain things on faith. First, he asked them to believe that he had a plan to honorably end the war in Vietnam. Second, he hoped that they would "buy" his new public image—the "new Nixon," experienced, statesmanlike, mature, secure, and ever so well adjusted. Most Americans probably did not believe either in the "new Nixon" or his pledge to "bring us to-

gether." On election day only 27 percent of eligible voters cast their ballot for him, but in 1968 that proved enough votes to win the election.

Outsiders on the Inside

If Nixon had developed "new" characteristics, those qualities had not forced out the "old." Richard Nixon still considered himself something of an outsider, a battler against an entrenched political establishment. Reared on the West Coast in humble circumstances, he had to overcome considerable obstacles in his rise to power. In the process certain character traits emerged. He was a hard worker—careful, studious with a tendency toward perfectionism. No detail was too small for his consideration. In addition, he did not shy away from an unpopular task. During his years as Eisenhower's vice president, Nixon had proved particularly adept as a political hatchet man. He was also a loner—shy, introverted, humorless, uncomfortable in social situations. He was essentially a man of action, one who for most of his career carried a list of things to do in the inside pocket of his suit coat. Journalist Tom Wicker noted that the new Nixon was not very different from the old.

At the Democratic convention in Chicago, police attacked thousands of unarmed, middle-class, antiwar college students in what was later termed a "police riot."

Writing of the new Nixon, Wicker observed: "He is, if anything, more reserved and inward, as difficult as ever to know, driven still by deep inner compulsion toward power and personal vindication, painfully conscious of slights and failures, a man who had imposed upon himself a self-control so rigid as to be all but visible."

As a restless outsider, Nixon harbored a heightened suspicion of political insiders. Throughout his career he had been an outspoken critic of State Department officials and other establishment bureaucrats. On taking office he therefore surrounded himself with close advisors who held noncabinet titles. Cabinet appointees, and particularly his secretary of state, William Rogers, had almost no voice in key decisions. Personal aides H. R. Haldeman and John Ehrlichman—called the "Germans" by the White House press corps—advised Nixon on domestic political issues. Vice President Spiro Agnew assumed the role of the administration's hatchet man so well that he became known as "Nixon's Nixon." He attacked the establishment with the ferocity of a professional wrestler verbally abusing an archrival. The "sniveling, hand-wringing power structure," he said, "deserves the violent rebellion it encourages." As for foreign affairs, Nixon relied on his national security advisor, Henry Alfred Kissinger.

Most commentators regarded Kissinger as a strange ally for Nixon. Kissinger, after all, taught at Harvard, was a close associate of Nelson Rockefeller—Nixon's longtime Republican opponent—and had even offered to work for Nixon's Democratic opponent Hubert Humphrey. "Look," Kissinger said in 1968, "I've hated Nixon for years." Yet even while Kissinger was courting Humphrey, he was secretly working for Nixon's election. No matter who won in 1968, Kissinger would be on the victorious side. It was a piece of Machiavellian maneuvering that Nixon might have appreciated.

Beneath Kissinger's sophisticated exterior, he shared with Nixon fundamental characteristics and beliefs. Like Nixon, Kissinger's path to power was not a traditional one. A German Jew, he had lived for five years (between the ages of 10 and 15) in Nazi Germany; he had been verbally and physically abused by his Aryan classmates. With the rest of his family, he fled to the United States during the late 1930s.

After serving as an army translator-interrogator during World War II, he enrolled as a scholarship student at Harvard, from where he was graduated *summa cum laude* in 1950 and was awarded his Ph.D. in 1954. His dissertation, later published as *A World Restored*, examined the ideas and policies of the conservative world leaders and diplomats who reconstructed Europe after the social and political upheavals caused by the Napoleonic Wars. During the late 1950s and 1960s, Kissinger wrote, taught, and emerged as a leading expert on foreign affairs. Kissinger viewed himself as a political realist, and he resisted rigid ideological or moral stands. Successful diplomacy, he believed, demanded flexible and creative leaders.

Vain, irreverent, articulate, and intellectual, Kissinger shared Nixon's desire to alter the very nature of the country's foreign relations and to make history. Neither particularly enjoyed being part of a committee process, and the diplomacy of secrecy and intrigue attracted both. For all their surface differences, the shy politician and the flamboyant scholar were kindred spirits who combined to form an impressive team. As one historian observed, "each filled a vital gap in the other's abilities. Kissinger had no gift for American politics; he needed to serve a president who could manipulate the electorate into supporting his policies. Nixon benefited from Kissinger's good press contacts since his own were disastrous."

Vietnamization: The Idea and the Process

During his campaign Nixon had promised "peace with honor" and suggested that he had a secret plan to achieve those ends. Controversy surrounded just what that plan entailed. Several historians have suggested that Nixon's plan was an updated version of Eisenhower's plan to end the Korean War. In 1953 when Ike took office, he publicly called for peace while secretly sending a message to Chinese and North Korean leaders that if they stalled at the peace talks, he was prepared to use nuclear weapons to end the war. Nixon told his White House aide H. R. Haldeman that his plan was similar to Eisenhower's. He wanted North Vietnam to believe that he was a "madman." "I want the North Vietnamese to believe I've reached the point where I might do anything to stop the war," Nixon told Haldeman. "We'll just slip the word to them that 'for God's sakes, you know Nixon is obsessed about communists. We can't restrain him when he's angry—and he has his hand on the nuclear button'—and Ho Chi Minh himself will be in Paris in two days begging for peace." The "madman theory" helps to explain Nixon's dramatic shifts during his first four years in office as he moved between the poles of peacefully concluding the war and violently expanding the conflict.

One thing was certain, however, Nixon knew that he could not continue Johnson's policy. "I'm not going to end up like LBJ," he remarked, "holed up in the White House afraid to show my face on the street." The country needed something new. Whatever else he did, Nixon realized that to ensure some semblance of domestic tranquility he would have to begin to remove American troops from Vietnam. In May 1969 he announced, "The time is approaching when the South Vietnamese forces will be able to take over some of the fighting fronts now being manned by Americans." That summer he drummed harder on the idea of the South Vietnamese fighting their own war. In what has become known as the "Nixon Doctrine," the president insisted that Asian soldiers must carry more of the combat burden. Certainly the United States would continue to materially aid any anti-Communist struggle, but the aid would not include the wholesale use of American troops.

The Nixon Doctrine formed the foundation of Nixon's Vietnamization policy. Working from the questionable premise that the government of Nguyen Van Thieu was stable and prepared to assume greater responsibility for fighting the war, Nixon announced that he planned to gradually deescalate American military involvement. Increasingly U.S. aid would be limited to war matériel, military advice, and air support. He coupled Vietnamization with a more strenuous effort to move along the peace talks.

Actually, the idea of Vietnamization was hardly new. In 1951 the French had called it *jaunissement,* or "yellowing." Advisors for Eisenhower, Kennedy, and Johnson had suggested one variation or another of the plan as the solution to the war. The major problem was

that the South Vietnamese could not successfully fight the war—not in 1951 or 1961 or 1971. But faced with angry criticism at home, Nixon had no choice but to implement the policy.

At the same time as he extended the olive branch, he expanded the nature of the conflict. Hoping to slow down the flow of North Vietnamese supplies and soldiers into South Vietnam, Nixon ordered American B-52 pilots to bomb the Ho Chi Minh Trail both in Vietnam and in Cambodia. He kept this violation of Cambodian neutrality secret from the American public. It was a bold move, but not very productive. The bombs only reduced the flow of men and supplies by approximately 10 percent.

When both increased bombings of North Vietnam and Kissinger's peace talks with North Vietnamese officials failed to end the war, Nixon resorted to harsher military efforts. After watching *Patton,* his favorite movie, on board the presidential yacht *Sequoia,* he decided to "go for all the marbles" and send American ground forces to Cambodia to destroy Communist supply bases. On the night of April 30, 1970, he went on television and told the American people of his plan. Ignoring previous American violations of Cambodia neutrality, he said that U.S. policy had been "to scrupulously respect the neutrality of the Cambodian people," while North Vietnam had used the border areas for "major base camps, training sites, logistics facilities, weapons and ammunition factories, airstrips and prisoner-of-war compounds," as well as their chief military headquarters. As a result, Nixon announced a joint American and South Vietnamese "incursion" into Cambodia's border regions to be limited to 60 days. In an attempt to rally American support, Nixon emphasized that the country's honor and even manhood were at stake: "We will not be humiliated, we will not be defeated. If when the chips are down the U.S. acts like a pitiful helpless giant, the forces of totalitarianism will threaten free nations and free institutions throughout the world. It is *not our power but our will* that is being tested tonight."

Militarily the "incursion" fell far short of success. Although American forces captured large stockpiles of weapons and supplies, the operation did not force North Vietnam to end the war. But the "incursion" had dangerously enlarged the battlefield. More importantly, the invasion of Cambodia reignited the fires of the peace movement at home. Throughout the country, colleges and universities shut down in protest. Students raged at what they believe was an "immoral, imperialist policy." At Kent State University in Ohio a volley of gunshots fired by Ohio National Guardsmen broke up a peaceful demonstration. The shots killed 4 students and wounded 11 others. Less than two weeks later, policemen shot 2 more innocent students at Jackson State University in Mississippi. Instead of victory or even peace, Nixon's efforts had further divided America.

As an effective policy for ending the war, Vietnamization was a failure. To be sure, the policy allowed Nixon to bring home American combat troops. When Nixon took office 540,000 American troops were in Vietnam; four years later only 70,000 remained. But American reductions were not accompanied by a marked improvement in the South Vietnamese army. This was clearly illustrated by the unsuccessful 1971 South Vietnamese invasion into Laos. If anything, South Vietnam became more dependent on the United States during the years of Vietnamization. By 1972 South Vietnam's only product and export was war, and even this commodity was of inferior quality.

A "Decent Interval"

By 1972 Nixon simply wanted to end the war with as little embarrassment as possible. As a viable country, South Vietnam was hopeless. Without an active U.S. military presence, the country's demise was a forgone conclusion. Negotiations presented the only way out. Nixon and Kissinger hoped to arrange for a peace that would permit the United States and South Vietnam to save face and allow a "decent interval" of time to ensue between the American departure and the collapse of the government in Saigon. In the pursuit of the goal, Nixon changed the character of American foreign policy.

The Soviet Union and the People's Republic of China aided and advised North Vietnam. Yet the two large Communist nations were hardly allies themselves. In fact, the Sino-Soviet split demonstrated to American leaders the fallacy of

In the spring of 1970, Ohio National Guardsmen fired into a group of protesting students at Kent State University, killing four.

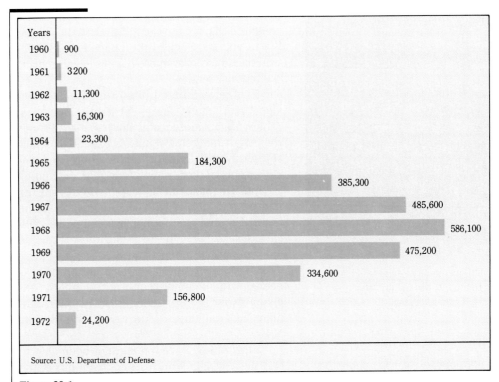

Figure 29.1
U.S. troop levels in Vietnam

Years	
1960	900
1961	3,200
1962	11,300
1963	16,300
1964	23,300
1965	184,300
1966	385,300
1967	485,600
1968	586,100
1969	475,200
1970	334,600
1971	156,800
1972	24,200

Source: U.S. Department of Defense

the old Cold War theme of a monolithic Communist movement. Nixon and Kissinger were astute enough to use the Sino-Soviet rift to improve U.S. relations with both countries. Improved relations, they believed, would move the United States several steps closer to an "honorable" peace in Vietnam. Unfortunately, Nixon and Kissinger greatly overestimated the influence of the Soviet Union and China on North Vietnam.

From his first days in office, Nixon had his eyes on the People's Republic of China, a nation that the United States had refused to recognize. One Nixon aide reported in 1969, "You're not going to believe this, but Nixon wants to recognize China." It seemed remarkable, for Nixon's Cold War record—his opposition to any concession to the Communists—was well known. But Nixon understood that his very record would protect him from public cries of being soft on communism; Nixon knew that unlike Truman, Kennedy, and Johnson, he did not have a Nixon to worry about.

Nixon approached China like a man holding a vase from the Ming dynasty, mixing caution with slow careful movements. In fact, both China and the United States walked on egg shells. Mao Zedung told reporter Edgar Snow that he "would be happy to talk with [Nixon] either as a tourist or as President." And Mao ended China's athletic isolation in 1971 by sending a table tennis team to the world championships in Nagoya, Japan, and then inviting an American team to compete in Beijing. Capitalizing on the success of Ping-Pong diplomacy, in the summer of 1971 Kissinger made a very secret trip to China. Kissinger's mission paved the way for Nixon's own very public trip to China in February 1972. American television cameras recorded Nixon's every move as he toured the Great Wall, the Imperial Palace, and the other sites of historic China. For the White House, one reporter noted, "It was the social event of the year." Constantly smiling and bubbling with excitement, Nixon thoroughly enjoyed the event, going so far as quoting Chairman Mao at an of-

In 1972 Richard Nixon visited China in an attempt to improve relations with that country. It was the first step toward achieving détente with the Soviet Union.

ficial toast and learning to eat with chopsticks. Although full diplomatic relations would not be established until 1979 under Jimmy Carter, Nixon's trip to China was the single most important event in the history of the relations between the United States and the People's Republic of China. It bridged, as Chinese foreign minister Chou En-lai remarked, "the vastest ocean in the world, twenty-five years of no communication."

Concerned about the growing rapprochement between China and America, the Soviet Union sought to move closer to the United States. Once again, Nixon and Kissinger were pleased to oblige. In late May 1972, after many months of preparatory talks, Nixon traveled to Moscow to sign an arms control treaty with Soviet leader Leonid Brezhnev. The Strategic Arms Limitation Treaty of 1972 (SALT I) certainly did not preclude a future nuclear war between the superpowers. Although it froze intercontinental ballistic missile (ICBM) deployment, it did not alter the buildup of the more dangerous multiple independent reentry vehicles (MIRVs), which, according to one historian "was about as meaningful as freezing the cavalry of the European nations in 1938 but not the tanks." As so often has been the case during the Cold War, SALT I provided more a warm

breeze than the real heat wave necessary for a complete thaw of the Cold War. Both the United States and the Soviet Union hoped the SALT I would lead to other, more comprehensive, arms reductions treaties.

In other areas the United States and the Soviet Union made more substantial progress. American businesspeople forged inroads into the Soviet market. Pepsi-Cola executives, metallurgy and ammonia dealers, computer and machine tools traders, and electric gear and mining equipment salespersons all benefited from the improved relations between America and the Soviet Union. Some farmers also reaped significant rewards when disastrous harvests at home led the Soviet Union to purchase several billion dollars worth of American wheat, corn, and soybeans. And, of course, cultural and athletic exchanges and competition provided entertainment for millions of Americans and Soviets alike.

Thus although Nixon had not been able to end the Vietnam War, his 1972 triumphs in the Soviet Union and China gave him more influence with North Vietnam's major allies. His visits to Beijing and Moscow also dazzled American voters. In 1972 Nixon easily defeated Democratic candidate George McGovern, capturing 61 percent of the popular vote and 521 of the 538 votes of the Electoral College. Nixon's success with blue-collar workers, conservative Catholics, and Southerners signified the end of the New Deal coalition.

Once reelected, Nixon again focused on Vietnam. A month before the election, Kissinger had announced, "Peace is at hand," but no sooner was Nixon safely reelected than the peace talks broke down once again. Nixon's response was more and heavier bombing of North Vietnam. Starting on December 18 and continuing for the next ten days, the Christmas bombings—code-named Operation LINEBACKER II—attacked military targets in Hanoi and Haiphong and killed more than 1500 civilians, leveled a hospital, and destroyed large parts of Hanoi. Critics charged that Nixon was attempting to "wage war by tantrum" and that the bombings served no military purpose. Some even suggested that Nixon had become mentally unbalanced. Military authorities, however, maintained that the bombings quickened the pace of the peace process. When the bombings concluded, the warring nations resumed peace talks.

In a week North Vietnam and the United States hammered out a peace, one that was strikingly similar to the October proposal. On January 27, 1973, America ended its active participation in the Vietnam War. The peace treaty provided for the release of all prisoners of war and America's military withdrawal from Vietnam. It also established a monitored cease-fire between North and South Vietnam and set up procedures aimed at solving the differences between the two countries. Nixon quickly claimed that he had won an honorable peace, that his "secret plan" had worked, even if it had taken four years and claimed the lives of 21,000 American, 107,000 South Vietnamese, and more than 500,000 North Vietnamese soldiers. And, of course, the lives of many thousands of Vietnamese civilians. Informing the American people of the peace, Nixon claimed, "South Vietnam has gained the right to determine its own future. . . . Let us be proud that America did not settle for a peace that would have betrayed our ally . . . that would have ended the war for us but continued the war for the fifty million people of Indochina." But as one historian commented, "In all likelihood, the peace accords that were finally signed in January 1973 could have been negotiated four years earlier. In the name of credibility, honor, and patriotism, hundreds of thousands of lives had been lost."

America left the war in 1973, but the war did not end then. All the peace provided for was a "decent interval" between America's withdrawal and North Vietnam's complete victory. When the South Vietnamese leader Nguyen Cao Ky heard Nixon's peace speech, he commented, "I could not stomach [it], so nauseating was its hypocrisy and self-delusion . . . there is no reason why they [the Communists] should stop now. . . . I give them a couple of years before they invade the South." He was right. Almost as soon as the ink on the "peace treaty" was dry, North Vietnam and the Vietcong were once again engaged in a war with the government in South Vietnam. Finally, in the spring of 1975 South Vietnamese forces collapsed. In March North Vietnam forces took Hue and Da Nang; by late April they were close to Saigon. On April

21 President Nguyen Van Thieu publicly lambasted the United States, resigned, and beat a hasty retreat from his country. On April 30 South Vietnam formally announced its unconditional surrender. Vietnam was finally unified. Free elections in 1956 might have accomplished the same results.

The Legacy of the War

Although America's active military participation in the Vietnam War ended in 1973, the controversy engendered by the war raged on long after the firing of the last shot. Much of the controversy centered on the returning veterans. Reports of drug use and fragging frightened many Americans who had come no closer to the war than their television sets. And veterans—most of whom had served their country faithfully and to the best of their abilities—were shocked by the cold, hostile reception they received when they returned to the United States. In *First Blood* (1982), John Rambo, played by Sylvester Stallone, captured the pain of the returning veterans: "Nothing is over. Nothing! You just don't turn it off. It wasn't my war—you asked me, I didn't ask you . . . and I did what I had to do to

The Vietnam War inspired a number of movies dealing with the conflict of veterans on their return home. Some of these movies portrayed the veterans as victims of a tragic war; others like *Rambo: First Blood II* (shown here) made the veteran a hero and transformed the conflict into a noble crusade.

win. . . . Then I came back to the world and I see all those maggots at the airport, protesting me, spitting on me, calling me a baby-killer and all kinds of vile crap. . . . Back there I could fly a gunship, I could drive a tank, I was in charge of million dollar equipment. Back here I can't even hold down a job parking cars. . . . Back here there's nothing!"

During the 1970s and 1980s the returning Vietnam War veteran loomed large in American popular culture. He was first portrayed as a dangerous killer, a deranged ticking time bomb that could explode at any time and in any place. He was Travis Bickle in *Taxi Driver* (1976), a veteran wound so tight that he seemed perpetually on the verge of snapping. Travis Bickle, wrote one film historian, "is the prototypical movie vet: In ways we can only imagine, the horror of the war unhinged him. He's lost contact with other human beings. . . . He's edgy: he can't sleep at night." He waits to explode. Or he was Colonel Kurtz in *Apocalypse Now* (1979), who adjusted to a mad war by going mad himself. Or he was Lieutenant Howard Hunter of the popular "Hill Street Blues" television series. A Vietnam War veteran, Hunter was portrayed as a misfit, a competent policeman but lonely and antisocial.

Not until the late 1970s did popular culture begin to treat the Vietnam War veteran as a victim of the war rather than a madman produced by the war. *Coming Home* (1978) and *The Deer Hunter* (1978) began the popular rehabilitation of the veteran, and such films as *First Blood* (1982), *Rambo: First Blood II* (1985), and *Missing in Action* (1984) transformed the veteran into a hero. On television, "Magnum, P.I.," "The A-Team," and "Air Wolf" also presented the veteran as a misunderstood hero.

The transformation of the veteran that took place in the late 1970s and 1980s indicated a fundamental shift in America's attitude toward the war. Millions of Americans began once again to see the war in terms of a noble crusade that could have been won. As John Rambo said in *Rambo: First Blood II*, "Do we get to win this time?" His former commander replied: "This time it's up to you." This message fit well with the political message of Ronald Reagan's America.

As American filmmakers "Ramboized" the conflict, Vietnam labored to reconstruct a viable nation out of the rubble of war. It was a difficult struggle. Roads and bridges, power plants and factories lay in ruins. Ports suffered from damage and neglect. Raw materials and investment capital were in short supply. If peace brought hope, it also brought the spector of economic ruin.

The recovery of the Socialist Republic of Vietnam has been slow. One of the poorest countries in the world, it has suffered from high inflation and unemployment, food shortages and starvation, and government inefficiency and corruption. In addition, military adventures—such as the 1978 invasion of Kampuchea (formerly Cambodia)—has siphoned off money needed to rebuild the country. Finally, the Soviet Union, Vietnam's closest ally, has not solved Vietnam's economic problems. "Americans without dollars," the Vietnamese have called the Soviets. One Vietnamese joke reflected the new relationship with the Soviet Union. After appealing to the Soviets for loans, Vietnam receives the cable: "Tighten your belts." Vietnam replies: "Send belts."

In 1986 Vietnam committed itself to radical change. A new generation of leaders turned to increased democracy and capitalism to solve their country's problems. They also turned to the West, and particularly the United States, for help. American leaders during the late 1980s and early 1990s, however, rejected Vietnam's pleas for aid. Although Vietnam has weakened its ties to the Soviet Union, withdrawn from Kampuchea, and tried to resolve the prisoners of war–missing in action (POW–MIA) issue, official American policy continues to regard the Socialist Republic of Vietnam as a country untouchable. Vietnam may have won the war, but it has not won peace.

CONCLUSION

The Vietnam War confused and divided the nation. Tim O'Brien captured something of this confusion in his acclaimed novel *Going after Cacciato* (1978). After fighting in the war, his protagonist "didn't know who was right, or what was right; he didn't know if it was a war of self-determination or self-destruction, outright aggression or national liberation; he didn't know which speeches to believe, which books, which

HRONOLOGY
OF KEY EVENTS

1954 The French garrison at Dien Bien Phu falls to Vietnamese nationalists led by Ho Chi Minh; Geneva conference divides Vietnam into two regions with the promise to hold elections to reunify the country in 1956; North Vietnam is led by the Communist government of Ho Chi Minh and South Vietnam by the government of Ngo Dinh Diem

1956 South Vietnam refuses to participate in elections to unify the two Vietnams

1961 John F. Kennedy is inaugurated thirty-fifth president; Alliance for Progress pledges $20 billion in U.S. aid to Latin America over a ten-year period; Cuban exiles stage abortive invasion of Cuba at Bay of Pigs; East Germans erect Berlin Wall; Soviet Union breaks a three-year moratorium on nuclear tests

1962 Cuban missile crisis: In response to Khrushchev's decision to build missile bases in Cuba, President Kennedy imposes a naval blockade of Cuba; Khrushchev orders the bases dismantled; President Kennedy increases the number of American advisors in South Vietnam to approximately 16,000

1963 United States and Soviet Union agree to ban nuclear tests in atmosphere; South Vietnamese army officers arrest and murder President Diem; President Kennedy is assassinated; Lyndon Johnson becomes thirty-sixth president

1964 North Vietnamese torpedo boats attack the U.S. destroyers *Maddox* and *C. Turner Joy* in the Gulf of Tonkin off the North Vietnamese coast; Gulf of Tonkin Resolution gives the president authority to retaliate against North Vietnamese aggression

1965 United States begins regular bombing missions over North Vietnam and sends first American ground combat troops into South Vietnam

1968 Tet offensive: During Tet, the Vietnamese lunar new year, the Viet Cong stage attacks on major South Vietnamese cities; President Johnson suspends the bombing of North Vietnam and announces that he will not run for reelection; Democratic presidential candidate Robert F. Kennedy is assassinated; Richard M. Nixon is elected thirty-seventh president

1969 Nixon announces "Vietnamization" policy; South Vietnam will take increased responsibility for fighting the war

1970 32,000 U.S. troops join the South Vietnamese army in invading Cambodia; in antiwar protests, 4 students are killed and 11 injured at Kent State University in Ohio; and 2 students die and 12 are injured at Jackson State University in Mississippi; Congress repeals Gulf of Tonkin Resolution

1972 Nixon travels to China, ending 25 years of nonrecognition of the People's Republic of China; Strategic Arms Limitation Treaty with the Soviet Union freezes intercontinental ballistic missile deployment

1973 United States ends active participation in the Vietnam War

1975 North Vietnamese forces enter Saigon; North and South Vietnam are reunited; the former South Vietnamese capital is renamed Ho Chi Minh City

politicians; he didn't know if nations would topple like dominos or stand separate like trees; he didn't know who started the war, or why, or when, or with what motives; he didn't know if it mattered."

Richard Nixon promised in 1968 that if he were elected president, he would end the war honorably and bring Americans together again. Instead, he enlarged the scope of the war before ending it and further divided the country. So, too, Johnson had divided the nation. His vision of a better, more just society—the Great Society (see Chapter 30)—was dashed on the rocks of Vietnam. There was in Johnson's position the essence of tragedy. As he later explained to biographer Doris Kearns, "I knew from the start that I was bound to be crucified either way I moved. If I left the woman I really loved—the Great Society—in order to get involved with the bitch of a war on the other side of the world, then I would lose everything at home . . . but if I left that war and let the communists take over South Vietnam, then I would be seen as a coward and my nation would be seen as an appeaser and we would both find it impossible to accomplish anything for anybody anywhere on the entire globe." In Johnson's view he was like a Puritan wrestling with the question of his own salvation:

> Damned if you do,
> Damned if you don't.
> Damned if you will
> Damned if you won't.

Of course, both Nixon and LBJ further injured their cause by using conscious deception in dealing with the American people.

Vietnam, then, destroyed Johnson's presidency, and it helped to undermine Nixon's. It was a war that left scars—on the people who fought in it and on the people who opposed and supported it; on Americans and on Vietnamese; and on U.S. foreign policy and its position in the world. For almost 35 years the United States had been actively involved in Indochina, but its influence in the region effectively ended in 1975. The Vietnam War, like the Communist victory in China in 1949, undercut America's position in Asia.

The most constructive outcome of the war was the lessons it taught. Congress learned that it had to take a more active role in foreign af-

fairs. The War Powers Act (1973), which requires the president to account for his actions within 48 hours of committing troops in a foreign war, demonstrated that the Gulf of Tonkin Resolution had taught Congress a painful lesson. Ho Chi Minh's nationalism taught policymakers that communism was not a monolithic movement and that not all small nations are dominos. Perhaps politicians, policymakers, and citizens alike even learned that national policy should be based on the realities of individual situations and not Cold War stereotypes.

SUGGESTIONS FOR FURTHER READING

OVERVIEWS AND SURVEYS

Stephen E. Ambrose, *Rise to Globalism: American Foreign Policy Since 1938*, 5th ed. (1988); William H. Chafe, *The Unfinished Journey*, 2d ed. (1991), and *The American Woman* (1972); Mario T. García, *Mexican Americans: Leadership, Ideology, Identity, 1930–1960* (1989); Juan Gómez-Quiñones, *Chicano Politics: Reality and Promise, 1940–1990* (1990); Alonzo Hamby, *The Imperial Years* (1976); Godfrey Hodgson, *America in Our Time* (1975); Walter LaFeber, *America, Russia, and the Cold War*, 5th ed. (1985); William Leuchtenburg, *A Troubled Feast*, rev. ed. (1983); Kim McQuaid, *The Anxious Years* (1989); Matt Meier and Feliciano Rivera, *The Chicanos* (1972); James S. Olson and Randy Roberts, *Where the Domino Fell: America in Vietnam, 1945–1990* (1991); Thomas G. Paterson et al., *American Foreign Policy*, 3d ed., 2 vols. (1988); Richard Polenberg, *One Nation Divisible* (1980); Emily and Norman Rosenberg, *In Our Times*, 4th ed. (1991); Julian Samora, *Los Mojados* (1971); Frederick F. Siegel, *A Troubled Journey* (1984); Ronald B. Taylor, *Chavez and the Farm Workers* (1975); Lawrence Wittner, *Cold War America*, rev. ed. (1978).

THE ILLUSION OF GREATNESS

Irving Bernstein, *Promises Kept: John F. Kennedy's New Frontier* (1991); James G. Blight and David A. Welch, *On the Brink: Americans and Soviets Reexamine the Cuban Missile Crisis* (1989); Carl M. Brauer, *John F. Kennedy and the Second Reconstruction* (1977); David Detzer, *The Brink: Cuban Missile Crisis, 1962* (1979); Herbert S. Dinerstein, *The Making of a Missile Crisis: October 1962* (1976); Louise FitzSimons, *The Kennedy Doctrine* (1972); Trumbull Higgins, *The Perfect Failure: Kennedy, Eisenhower, and the C.I.A. at the Bay of Pigs* (1987); Richard D. Mahoney, *JFK: Ordeal in Africa* (1983); Allen Matusow, *The Unraveling of America:*

A History of Liberalism in the 1960s (1984); Bruce Miroff, *Pragmatic Illusions: The Presidential Politics of JFK* (1976); Victor Navasky, *Kennedy Justice* (1971); Jack M. Schick, *The Berlin Crisis, 1958–1962* (1971); Richard Walton, *Cold War and Counterrevolution: The Foreign Policy of John F. Kennedy* (1972); Peter Wyden, *Bay of Pigs* (1979).

VIETNAM: AMERICA'S LONGEST WAR

David L. Anderson, *Trapped by Success: The Eisenhower Administration and Vietnam, 1953–1961* (1991); Larry Berman, *Planning a Tragedy: The Americanization of the War in Vietnam* (1982), and *Lyndon Johnson's War* (1989); Peter Braestrup, *Big Story: How the American Press and Television Reported and Interpreted the Crisis of Tet 1968 in Vietnam and Washington* (1978); Larry E. Cable, *Conflict of Myths: The Development of American Counterinsurgency Doctrine and the Vietnam War* (1986), and *Unholy Grail: The United States and the Wars in Vietnam* (1991); Philip Caputo, *A Rumor of War* (1977); Harry Caudill, *Night Comes to the Cumberlands* (1963); Chester L. Cooper, *The Lost Crusade: America in Vietnam* (1970); Robert A. Divine, ed., *Exploring the Johnson Years* (1981); Bernard Fall, *Street Without Joy: Insurgency in Indochina, 1946–63* (1964), and *The Two Vietnams*, 2d ed. (1967); Frances FitzGerald, *Fire in the Lake* (1972); Todd Gitlin, *The Whole World Is Watching: Mass Media in the Making & Unmaking of the New Left* (1980); Sherry Gershon Gottlieb, *Hell No, We Won't Go: Evading the Draft During Vietnam* (1992); David Halberstam, *The Making of a Quagmire: America and Vietnam During the Kennedy Era*, rev. ed. (1988), and *The Best and the Brightest* (1972); Michael Herr, *Dispatches* (1977); George C. Herring, *America's Longest War: The United States and Vietnam, 1950–1975*, 2d ed. (1986); Seymour Hersh, *My Lai 4: A Report on the Massacre and Its Aftermath* (1970); Stanley Karnow, *Vietnam, A History* (1983); Christopher Lasch, *The Agony of the American Left* (1969); David Levy, *The Debate over Vietnam* (1991); Guenter Lewy, *America in Vietnam* (1978); Abraham Lowenthal, *The Dominican Intervention* (1972); Roger Morris, *Uncertain Greatness: Henry Kissinger and American Foreign Policy* (1977); Don Oberdorfer, *Tet!* (1971); George Reedy, *The Twilight of the Presidency*, rev. ed. (1987); Neil Sheehan, ed., *The Pentagon Papers* (1971); Kathleen J. Turner, *Lyndon Johnson's Dual War: Vietnam and the Press* (1985); Brian VanDeMark, *Into the Quagmire: Lyndon Johnson and the Escalation of the Vietnam War* (1991); Tom Wicker, *JFK and LBJ: The Influence of Personality upon Politics* (1968); Marilyn Young, *The Vietnam Wars: 1945–1990* (1991).

THE TORTUOUS PATH TOWARD PEACE

Carl Bernstein and Robert Woodward, *All the President's Men* (1974); John Dean, *Blind Ambition: The White House Years* (1976); Lloyd C. Gardner, ed., *The Great Nixon Turn-around: America's New Foreign Policy in the Post-Liberal Era* (1973); Stephen Graubard, *Kissinger: Portrait of a Mind* (1973); Robert T. Hartmann, *Palace Politics: An Inside Account of the Ford Years* (1980); Seymour Hersh, *The Price of Power: Kissinger in the Nixon White House* (1983); Leon Jaworski, *The Right and the Power: The Prosecution of Watergate* (1976); J. Anthony Lukas, *Nightmare: The Underside of the Nixon Years* (1976); Richard Nixon, *RN: The Memoirs of Richard Nixon*, 2 vols. (1978); Thomas Powers, *The Man Who Kept the Secrets: Richard Helms & the CIA* (1979); William Safire, *Before the Fall: An Inside View of the Pre-Watergate White House* (1975); Jonathan Schell, *The Time of Illusion* (1975); Arthur M. Schlesinger, Jr., *The Imperial Presidency* (1973); William Shawcross, *Sideshow: Kissinger, Nixon, and the Destruction of Cambodia*, rev. ed. (1987); Edward R. F. Sheehan, *The Arabs, Israelis, and Kissinger* (1976); John Sirica, *To Set the Record Straight: The Break-in, the Tapes, the Conspirators, the Pardon* (1979); Theodore H. White, *Breach of Faith: The Fall of Richard Nixon* (1975).

BIOGRAPHIES

Fawn Brodie, *Richard Nixon* (1981); David Burner, *John F. Kennedy and a New Generation* (1988); Robert Caro, *The Years of Lyndon Johnson: The Path to Power* (1982), and *Means of Ascent* (1990); Warren Cohen, *Dean Rusk* (1980); Paul K. Conkin, *Big Daddy from the Pedernales: Lyndon Baines Johnson* (1986); Ronnie Dugger, *The Politician: The Life and Times of Lyndon Johnson* (1982); Henry Fairlie, *The Kennedy Promise: The Politics of Expectation* (1973); Eric Goldman, *The Tragedy of Lyndon Johnson* (1969); Doris Kearns, *Lyndon Johnson and the American Dream* (1976); Bruce Mazlish, *In Search of Nixon* (1972); Jack Newfield, *Robert Kennedy* (1969); Herbert S. Parmet, *Jack: The Struggles of John F. Kennedy* (1980), and *JFK: The Presidency of John F. Kennedy* (1983); Thomas C. Reeves, *A Question of Character: A Life of John F. Kennedy* (1991); Arthur Schlesinger, Jr., *A Thousand Days: John F. Kennedy in the White House* (1965); Winthrop Yinger, *Cesar Chavez* (1975).

CHAPTER 30

The Struggle for a Just Society

STUDENT POWER

He has been called the nation's nag. He denounced soft drinks for containing excessive amounts of sugar (more than nine teaspoons a can). He warned Americans about the health hazards of red dyes used as food colorings and of nitrates used as preservatives in hot dogs. He even denounced high heels: "It is part of the whole tyranny of fashion, where women will inflict pain on themselves . . . for what, to please men." His name is Ralph Nader and since the mid-1960s he has been the nation's leading consumer advocate.

An extraordinarily frugal and committed crusader on behalf of the nation's consumers, Nader lived for years in an $80-a-month rooming house on about $15,000 a year. He eats in cheap restaurants, has never owned a car, has almost no social life, avoids all junk food, and dresses plainly. In 1983 he was still wearing shoes he had bought while he was in the army in 1959.

His parents came to the United States from Lebanon and settled in Winsted, Connecticut, where they ran a restaurant. Nader credits his parents with instilling the sense of justice and civic duty that has inspired his career.

He was born on February 27, 1934, and speaks at least five foreign languages, including Arabic, Chinese, Portuguese, Spanish, and Russian. He received his bachelor's degree from Princeton (he once wore a bathrobe to class to protest conformity in dress) and earned a law degree at Harvard. At law school, he found his initial cause: automobile safety. After learning that auto accidents were the fourth leading cause of death (behind heart disease, cancer, and strokes), he launched a study of auto injury cases. His research convinced him that the law placed too much emphasis on driver mistakes and not enough on the unsafe design of cars.

In 1963, Nader hitchhiked from Hartford, Connecticut, where he had practiced law, to Washington, D.C., to devote his life to consumer protection. In 1965, he published a best-seller, entitled *Unsafe at Any Speed*, which charged that automakers stressed styling, comfort, speed, power, and a desire to cut costs at the expense of safety. The book sold 60,000 copies in hardcover and 400,000 copies in paperback.

Nader gained public celebrity when the General Motors Corporation hired a detective to investigate his politics, religion, and sex life. General Motors's chairman was forced to apologize for this invasion of privacy before a Senate subcommittee, and eventually paid Nader a $425,000 settlement. Nader used the money to establish more than two dozen public interest groups. The people who work for these groups are known as "Nader's Raiders."

During the 1960s and 1970s, Nader was the driving force behind the passage of more than two dozen landmark consumer protection laws, including the National Traffic and Motor Vehicle Safety Act (which set up a federal agency to establish auto-safety standards and order recalls of cars that failed to meet them), the Occupational Safety and Health Act (which established another agency to set standards for on-the-job safety), the Consumer Products Safety Act, and the Freedom of Information Act (which allows citizens to request and see government records). His efforts have been instrumental in attaining job protection for whistleblowers (employees who expose corrupt or abusive business practices), federal financing of presidential elections, and the creation of the Environmental Protection Agency. Few Americans have ever compiled such a long and impressive list of legislative accomplishment.

But his ultimate goal was not simply to protect consumers from shoddy or dangerous products. It was to reinvigorate the nation's ideal of democracy by encouraging active grass-roots citizen participation in politics. The best answer to society's problems, he believed, was for ordinary citizens to campaign for safer consumer products, better schools, a cleaner environment, and safer workplaces.

During the late 1970s and 1980s, his influence seemed to wane. In 1978, Congress defeated his proposal for a Consumer Protection Agency. Critics dismissed him as a "scold." Said *Newsweek* magazine: "An optimistic society wearies of his endless discontents." In a decade of deregulation, Nader's call for greater regulations seemed out of step with the beat of the times.

As the 1980s ended and the 1990s began, however, it was clear that Nader remained a ma-

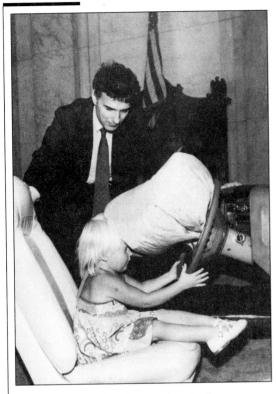

Ralph Nader is the best-known advocate of consumer protection laws in the United States. His group of attorneys, nicknamed "Nader's Raiders," have investigated such wide-ranging problems as automobile safety, the rights of the handicapped, tax reform, the environment, and public health. Here, Nader looks on during a demonstration showing the operation of an automobile air bag safety restraint.

jor force in American politics. He played a central role in passing a California initiative that rolled back the cost of auto insurance. He led a bitter fight against a proposed 51 percent congressional pay raise. And his long campaign for auto safety achieved an important breakthrough when the major automobile manufacturers agreed to install air bags in most of their cars.

Ralph Nader illustrates in vivid terms the difference that one person's life can make. His life also epitomizes the idealism and activism of the 1960s—a decade when hundreds of thousands of ordinary Americans gave new life to the nation's democratic ideals by pressing for racial justice, peace, and improvements in the quality of American life. Black Americans used sit-ins, freedom rides, and protest marches to fight segregation, poverty, and unemployment. Feminists demanded equal employment opportunities and an end to sexual discrimination. Mexican-Americans protested discrimination in voting, education, and employment. Native Americans demanded that the government recognize their land rights and the right of tribes to govern themselves.

Although consumerists, environmentalists, civil rights workers, feminists, and other grass-roots activists seemed to fade from public view during the 1980s, they—like Ralph Nader—never abandoned their causes and today remain a powerful force in American life. Indeed, the success of their very efforts has led to a conservative grass-roots reaction, one in which equally committed Americans have denounced busing, affirmative action, quotas, and abortion.

THE STRUGGLE FOR RACIAL JUSTICE

For black Americans in 1960 the statistics were grim. Their average life span in 1960 was seven years less than white Americans'. Their children had only half the chance of completing high school, only a third the chance of completing college, and a third the chance of entering a profession when they grew up. On average, black Americans earned half as much as white Americans and were twice as likely to be unemployed.

Despite a string of court victories during the late 1950s, many black Americans were still second-class citizens. Six years after the landmark *Brown* v. *Board of Education* decision, just 49 southern school districts had desegregated and less than 1.17 percent of black schoolchildren in the 11 states of the old Confederacy attended public school with white classmates. Less than a quarter of the South's voting age black population could vote, and in certain southern counties blacks could not vote, serve on grand juries and trial juries, or frequent all-white beaches, restaurants, barber shops, hotels, and apartments.

TABLE 30.1

High School Graduates (Percentage of Population Age 25–29)			
	1960	*1966*	*1970*
Blacks			
Male	36	49	54
Female	41	47	58
Whites			
Male	63	73	79
Female	65	79	76

In the North, too, black Americans suffered humiliation, insult, embarrassment, and discrimination. Many neighborhoods, businesses, and unions almost totally excluded blacks. Just as black unemployment had increased in the South with the mechanization of cotton production, so too in northern cities black unemployment soared as labor-saving technology eliminated many semiskilled and unskilled jobs that historically provided many blacks with work. Black families experienced severe strain; the proportion of black families headed by women jumped from 8 percent in 1950 to 21 percent in 1960. "If you're white, you're right," a black folk saying went; "if you're brown stick around; if you're black, stay back."

During the 1960s, however, a growing hunger for full equality arose among black Americans. The Rev. Dr. Martin Luther King, Jr., gave voice to the new mood: "We're through with tokenism and gradualism and see-how-far-you've-comeism. We're through with we've-done-more-for-your-people-than-anyone-else-ism. We can't wait any longer. Now is the time."

TABLE 30.2

Income Distribution 1960, 1969 (Percentage)				
	Blacks and Other Nonwhites		Whites	
	1960	*1969*	*1960*	*1969*
Under $3000	38	20	14	~8
$3000–4999	22	19	14	10
$5000–6999	16	17	19	12
$7000–9999	14	20	26	22
$10,000 and over	~9	24	27	49

Freedom Now

"Now is the time." It became the credo and rallying cry for a generation. On Monday, February 1, 1960, four black freshmen at North Carolina Agricultural and Technical College—Ezell Blair, Jr., Franklin McClain, Joseph McNeill, and David Richmond—walked into the F.W. Woolworth store in Greensboro, North Carolina, and sat down at the lunch counter. They asked for a cup of coffee. A waitress told them that she would only serve them if they stood.

Instead of walking away, the four college freshmen stayed in their seats until the lunch counter closed—giving birth to the "sit-in." The next morning, the 4 college students reappeared at Woolworth's, accompanied by 25 fellow students. On Wednesday, student protests filled 63 of the lunch counter's 66 seats. By the end of the week protesters filled Woolworth's and other lunch counters in town. Now was their time, and they refused to end their nonviolent protest against inequality. Six months later, white city officials granted blacks the right to be served in a restaurant.

Although the student protesters ascribed to King's doctrine of nonviolence, their opponents did not. One black student described a confrontation with white youths at the lunch counter: "Curiously, there were no police inside the store when the white teenagers and others stood in the aisles insulting us, blowing smoke in our faces, grinding out cigarette butts on our backs and finally pulling us off our stools and beating us. Those of us pulled off our seats tried to regain them as soon as possible, but none of us fought back in anger." When the police finally arrived, they arrested black protesters, not the white tormenters.

By the end of February, lunch counter sit-ins had spread through 30 cities in 7 southern states. In Charlotte, North Carolina, a storekeeper unscrewed the seats from his lunch counter. Other stores roped off seats so that every customer had to stand. Alabama, Georgia, Mississippi, and Virginia, hastily passed antitrespassing laws to stem the outbreak of sit-ins. Despite these efforts, the nonviolent student protests spread across the South. Students attacked segregated libraries, lunch counters, and other "public" facilities.

In April, 142 student sit-in leaders from 11 states met in Raleigh, North Carolina, and voted to set up a new group to coordinate the sit-ins, the Student Nonviolent Coordinating Committee (SNCC). The Rev. Dr. Martin Luther King, Jr., told the students that their willingness to go to jail would "be the thing to awaken the dozing conscience of many of our white brothers." The president of Fisk University echoed King's judgment: "This is no student panty raid. It is a dedicated universal effort, and it has cemented the Negro community as it has never been cemented before."

In the summer of 1960, sit-ins gave way to "wade-ins" at segregated public beaches. In Atlanta, Charlotte, Greensboro, and Nashville, black students lined up at white-only box offices of segregated movie theaters. Other students staged pray-ins (at all-white churches), study-ins (at segregated libraries), and apply-ins (at all-white businesses).

By the end of 1960, 70,000 people had taken part in sit-ins in over 100 cities in 20 states. Police arrested and jailed more than 3600 protesters, and authorities expelled 187 students from college because of their activities. Nevertheless, the new tactic worked. On March 21, 1960, lunch counters in San Antonio, Texas, were integrated. By August 1, lunch counters in 15 states had been integrated. By the end of the year, protesters had succeeded in integrating eating establishments in 108 cities.

The Greensboro sit-in initiated a new, activist phase in black America's struggle for equal rights. Fed up with the slow, legalistic approach that characterized the civil rights movement in the past, southern black college students began to attack segregation directly. Instead of relying on court decisions or federal intervention to bring equal rights, students used nonviolent direct action to win civil rights for black Americans.

In the upper South, federal court orders and student sit-ins successfully desegregated lunch counters, theaters, hotels, public parks, churches, libraries, and beaches. But in three states—Alabama, Mississippi, and South Carolina—segregation in restaurants, hotels, and bus, train, and airplane terminals remained intact. In those states, young civil rights activists launched new assaults against segregation.

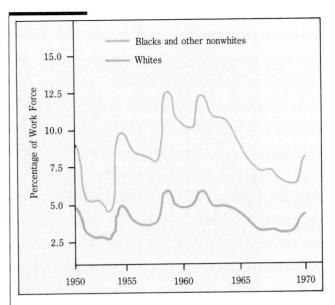

Figure 30.1
Unemployment, 1950–1970

To the Heart of Dixie

In early May 1961 13 men and women, black and white, set out from Washington, D.C., on two buses. They called themselves "freedom riders," and they wanted to demonstrate that despite a federal ban on segregated travel on interstate buses, segregation prevailed throughout much of the South. The freedom riders' trip was sponsored by the Congress of Racial Equality (CORE), a civil rights group dedicated to breaking down racial barriers through nonviolent protest. Inspired by the nonviolent, direct action ideals incorporated in the philosophy of Indian nationalist Mahatma Gandhi, the freedom riders were willing to endure jail and suffer beatings to achieve integration. "We can take anything the white man can dish out," said one black freedom rider, "but we want our rights . . . and we want them now."

In Virginia and North Carolina, the freedom riders met little trouble. Black freedom riders were able to use white restrooms and sit at white lunch counters. But in Winnsboro, South Carolina, police arrested two black freedom riders, and outside Anniston, Alabama, a white hurled a bomb through one of the bus's windows, setting the vehicle on fire. Waiting white

Lunch counter sit-ins in 1960 sparked an advance in the crusade against southern segregation. Such passive resistance tactics proved very effective.

thugs beat the freedom riders as they tried to escape the smoke and flames. Eight other whites boarded the second bus and assaulted the freedom riders before police restrained the attackers.

In Birmingham, Alabama, another mob attacked the second bus with blackjacks and lengths of pipe. In Montgomery, a club-swinging mob of 100 whites attacked the freedom riders; and a group of white youths poured an inflammable liquid on one black man and ignited his clothing. Local police arrived ten minutes later, state police an hour later. Explained Montgomery's police commissioner: "We have no intention of standing police guard for a bunch of troublemakers coming into our city."

In Washington, President Kennedy was appalled by the violence. He hastily deputized 400 federal marshals and Treasury agents and flew them to Alabama to protect the freedom riders' rights. The president publicly called for a "cooling-off period," but conflict continued. When freedom riders arrived in Jackson, Mississippi, 27 were arrested for entering a "white-only" washroom and were sentenced to 60 days on the state prison farm.

The threat of racial violence in the South led the Kennedy administration to pressure the Interstate Commerce Commission to desegregate air, bus, and train terminals. In more than 300 southern terminals, signs saying "white" and "colored" were taken down from waiting room entrances and lavatory doors.

Civil rights activists' next major aim was to open state universities to black students. Many southern states opened their universities to black students without incident. Other states were stiff-backed in their opposition to integration. The depth of hostility to integration was apparent in an incident that took place in February, 1956. A young woman named Autherine Lucy became the first black student ever admitted to the University of Alabama. A mob of 1000 greeted the young woman with chant, "Keep 'Bama White!" Two days later, rioting students threw stones and eggs at the car she was riding to class. Lucy decided to withdraw from school, and for the next seven years no black students attended the University of Alabama.

A major breakthrough occurred in September, 1962, when a federal court ordered the state of Mississippi to admit James Meredith—

sex discrimination had been added by opponents of the civil rights act in an attempt to kill the bill.

Although most white Southerners accepted the new federal law without resistance, many violent incidents occurred. Angry whites vented their rage in shootings and beatings. But despite such incidents, the Civil Rights Act was a success. In the first weeks under the 1964 civil rights law segregated restaurants and hotels from Dallas to Charleston and from Memphis to Tallahassee opened their doors to black patrons. Over the next ten years, the Justice Department would bring legal suits against more than 500 school districts charged with racial discrimination and more than 400 suits against hotels, restaurants, taverns, gas stations, and truck stops.

Voting Rights

The 1964 Civil Rights Act prohibited discrimination in employment and public accommodations. But many blacks were denied an equally fundamental constitutional right, the right to vote. The most effective barriers to black voting were state laws requiring prospective voters to read and interpret sections of the state constitution. In Alabama, voters had to provide written answers to a 20-page test on the Constitution and state and local government. Questions included: Where do presidential electors cast ballots for president? Name the rights a person has after he has been indicted by a grand jury?

In an effort to bring the issue of voting rights to national attention, Martin Luther King, Jr., in early 1965 launched a voter registration drive in Selma, Alabama, a city of 29,500 people—14,400 whites, 15,100 blacks. Despite the fact that the federal government had filed a voting rights suit in 1961, Selma's voting rolls were 99 percent white and 1 percent black.

For seven weeks, King led hundreds of Selma's black residents to the county courthouse to register to vote. In the first attempt to register black voters, more than 400 blacks marched to the county courthouse. They were stopped by County Sheriff James Clark, armed with a billy club and a cattle prod, who herded the marchers into a nearby alleyway. In suc-

On August 28, 1963, over 200,000 African-Americans and whites gathered for a day-long rally at the Lincoln Memorial to demand an end to racial discrimination. The highlight of the event was Martin Luther King, Jr.'s inspiring "I Have a Dream" speech.

ceeding weeks, Clark jailed nearly 2000 black demonstrators for contempt of court, juvenile delinquency, and parading without a permit. When King himself was arrested, he could accurately state that "there are more Negroes in jail with me than there are on the voting rolls." After a federal court ordered Clark not to interfere with orderly registration, the sheriff forced black applicants to stand in line for up to five hours before being permitted to take a "literacy" test. Not a single black voter was added to the registration rolls.

The demonstrations spread to nearby Marion, where 50 state troopers and white toughs attacked 400 black demonstrators. During the attack a young black man named Jimmie Lee Jackson was shot in the stomach; he died eight days later. King responded by calling for a march from Selma to the state capitol of Montgomery, 50 miles away.

On Sunday, March 7, 1965, black voting-rights demonstrators prepared to march. "I can't promise you that it won't get you beaten," King told them, ". . . but we must stand up for what is right!" Led by John Lewis, head of the

After nearly 2000 blacks were arrested for trying to register to vote in Selma, Alabama, demonstrators (including Martin Luther King, Jr.) began a protest march from Selma to Montgomery.

Student Nonviolent Coordinating Committee (SNCC), and Hosea Williams, an official of King's Southern Christian Leadership Conference, the demonstrators, marching double file, headed toward the Edmund Pettus Bridge, across the Alabama River. As they crossed the bridge, 200 state police with tear gas, night sticks, and whips attacked them.

The five day march from Selma to Montgomery finally resumed on March 21, with protection from over 100 federal marshals, 1000 military police, and 1900 federalized Alabama National Guardsmen. The marchers chanted: "Segregation's got to fall . . . you never can jail us all." On March 25, a crowd of 25,000 gathered at the state capitol to celebrate the march's completion. Martin Luther King, Jr., addressed the crowd and called for an end to segregated schools, poverty, and voting discrimination. "I know you are asking today, 'How long will it take?' . . . How long? Not long, because no lie can live forever."

Still, the violence continued. Within hours of the march's end, four Ku Klux Klan members shot and killed a 39-year-old white civil rights volunteer from Detroit named Viola Liuzzo. President Johnson expressed the nation's shock and anger. "Mrs. Liuzzo went to Alabama to serve the struggle for justice," the President said. "She was murdered by the enemies of justice who for decades have used the rope and the gun and the tar and the feather to terrorize their neighbors."

Two measures adopted in 1965 helped safeguard the voting rights of black Americans. On January 23, the states completed ratification of the Twenty-fourth Amendment to the Constitution barring a poll tax in federal elections. At the time, five southern states still had a poll tax. On August 6, President Johnson signed the Voting Rights Act, which prohibited literacy tests and sent federal examiners to seven southern states to register black voters. Within a year, 450,000 southern blacks registered to vote.

Black Nationalism and Black Power

At the same time that such civil rights leaders as the Rev. Dr. Martin Luther King, Jr., fought for racial integration, other black leaders emphasized separatism and identification with Afing, and employment—discrimination that lacked the overt sanction of law. "De facto segregation," wrote James Baldwin, "means that Negroes are segregated but nobody did it." The most obvious example of de facto segregation was the fact that the overwhelming majority of northern black schoolchildren attended predominantly black inner-city schools while most white children attended schools with an overwhelming majority of whites. In 1968—fourteen years after the *Brown* v. *Board of Education* decision—federal courts began to order busing as a way to deal with de facto segregation brought about by housing patterns. In April 1971 in the case of *Swann* v. *Charlotte-Mecklenburg Board of Education*, the Supreme Court upheld "bus transportation as a tool of school desegregation."

Before becoming the first black Supreme Court justice in 1967, Thurgood Marshall presented the legal arguments against school segregation that resulted in the *Brown* v. *Board of Education of Topeka* decision.

The Great Society and the Drive for Black Equality

No American president ever showed a stronger commitment to improving the position of black Americans than Lyndon Baines Johnson, the first Southerner to reside in the White House in half a century. As president he prodded Congress to pass a broad spectrum of civil rights laws, ranging from the Civil Rights Act of 1964 and the Voting Rights Act of 1965 to the 1968 Fair Housing Act barring discrimination in the sale or rental of housing. LBJ also took direct steps to require employers to take "affirmative action" to ensure that black Americans were not discriminated against in employment or promotions. Executive Order 11246, issued in 1965, required government contractors to ensure that job applicants and employees are not discriminated against. It required all contractors to prepare an "affirmative action plan" to achieve these goals.

Johnson broke many other color barriers. In 1966, he named the first black cabinet member, Secretary of Housing and Urban Development Robert Weaver. That same year, he appointed the first black woman, Constance Baker Motley, to the federal bench. In 1967 he appointed Thurgood Marshall to become the first black American to serve on the Supreme Court. But Johnson's most lasting legacy was a battery of domestic antipoverty programs.

LBJ had a vision for America. During the 1964 campaign he often spoke about it. He envisioned an America "where no child will go unfed and no youngster will go unschooled; where every child has a good teacher and every teacher has good pay, and both have good classrooms; where every human being has dignity and every worker has a job; where education is blind to color and employment is unaware of race." Johnson called his vision the Great Society. In a 1964 speech at the University of Michigan, LBJ decisively declared that problems of housing, income, employment, and health were ultimately a federal responsibility. When Johnson left the presidency in 1969, his Great Society program had transformed the federal government. At the end of the Eisenhower presidency in 1961, there were only 45 domestic social programs. By the end of the Johnson administration, the number had climbed to 435. Federal spending on social programs, excluding Social Security, had risen from $9.9 billion in 1960 to $25.6 billion in 1968.

To combat poverty, the federal government raised the minimum wage and enacted programs to train poorer Americans for new and better jobs, including the 1964 Manpower Development and Training Act and the Economic Opportunity Act, which established such programs as the Job Corps and the Neighborhood Youth Corps. To assure adequate housing, in

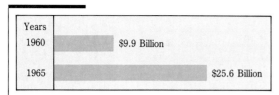

Figure 30.2
Federal spending on social programs, excluding social security

1966 Congress adopted the Model Cities Act to attack urban blight, set up a cabinet-level Department of Housing and Urban Development, and began a program of rent supplements.

To promote education, Congress passed the Higher Education Act in 1965 providing student loans and scholarships, the Elementary and Secondary Schools Act of 1965 to pay for textbooks, and the Educational Opportunity Act of 1968 to help the poor finance college educations. To address the nation's health needs, the Child Health Improvement and Protection Act of 1968 provided for prenatal and postnatal care, the Medicaid Act of 1968 paid for the medical expenses of the poor, and Medicare, established in 1965, extended medical insurance to older Americans under the Social Security system.

When President Johnson announced his Great Society program in 1964, he promised substantial reductions in the number of Americans living in poverty. When he left office, he could legitimately argue that he had delivered on his promise. In 1960, 40 million Americans, 20 percent of the population, were classified as poor. By 1969, their number had fallen to 24 million, 12 percent of the population. Johnson also pledged to qualify the poor for new and better jobs, to extend health insurance to the poor and elderly to cover hospital and doctor costs, and to provide better housing for low-income families. Here too Johnson could say he had delivered. Infant mortality among the poor, which had barely declined between 1950 and 1965, fell by one-third in the decade after 1965 as a result of expanded federal medical and nutritional programs. Before 1965, 20 percent of the poor had never seen a doctor; by 1970 the figure had been cut to 8 percent. The proportion of families living in houses lacking indoor plumbing also declined steeply, from 20 percent in 1960 to 11 percent a decade later.

Despite the widespread view that "in the war on poverty, poverty won," substantial progress had in fact been made. Although critics argued that Johnson took a shotgun approach to reform and pushed poorly thought-out bills through Congress without a coordinated strategy, supporters responded that at least Johnson tried to move toward a more compassionate society. During the 1960s median black family income rose 53 percent; black employment in professional, technical, and clerical occupations doubled; and average black educational attainment increased by four years. The proportion of blacks below the poverty line fell from 55 percent in 1960 to 27 percent in 1968. The black unemployment rate fell 34 percent. The country had taken major strides toward extending equality of opportunity to black Americans. In addition, the number of whites below the poverty line dropped dramatically, and such poverty-plagued regions as Appalachia made significant economic strides.

White Backlash

Ghetto rioting, the rise of black militancy, and resentment over Great Society social legislation combined to produce a backlash among many

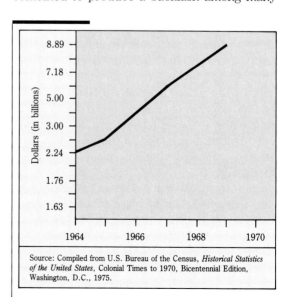

Source: Compiled from U.S. Bureau of the Census, *Historical Statistics of the United States*, Colonial Times to 1970, Bicentennial Edition, Washington, D.C., 1975.

Figure 30.3
Federal aid to education, 1964–1970

whites. In the wake of the riots, many whites fled the nation's cities. The Census Bureau estimated that 900,000 whites moved each year from central cities to the suburbs between 1965 and 1970.

Commitment to bringing black Americans into full equality declined. In 1968 Alabama Governor George Wallace ran for president on the newly formed American Independent party ticket, declaring he would repeal "so-called civil rights laws." Wallace drew nearly 10 million votes in the election, 13.5 percent of the total votes cast, and won sufficient support in such northern states as Illinois and Ohio to swing these states to Republican candidate Richard Nixon.

During his 1968 campaign for the White House, Nixon promised to eliminate "wasteful" federal antipoverty programs and to name "strict constructionists" to the Supreme Court. Once in office, Nixon moved quickly to keep his commitments. In an effort to curb Great Society social programs, Nixon did away with the Model Cities program and the Office of Economic Opportunity. "The time may have come," declared a Nixon aide, "when the issue of race could benefit from a period of benign neglect." The number of investigations to determine whether communities were in compliance with school desegregation fell off sharply, from 16 in 1969, the year Nixon took office, to zero in 1974. The administration urged Congress not to extend the Voting Rights Act of 1965 and to end a fair housing enforcement program.

President Nixon also made a series of Supreme Court appointments that brought to an end the liberal activist era of the Warren Court. During the 1960s, the Supreme Court greatly increased the ability of criminal defendants to defend themselves. In *Mapp* v. *Ohio* (1961), the high court ruled that evidence secured by the police through unreasonable searches must be excluded from trial. In *Gideon* v. *Wainwright* (1963), it declared that indigent defendants have a right to a court-appointed attorney. In *Escobedo* v. *Illinois* (1964), it ruled that suspects being interrogated by police have a right to legal counsel.

As president, Nixon promised to alter the balance between the rights of criminal defendants and society's rights. He selected Warren Burger, a moderate conservative, to replace Earl Warren as chief justice of the Supreme Court and then nominated two convervative white Southerners for a second court vacancy, only to have both nominees rejected (one for financial improprieties, the other for alleged insensitivities to civil rights). He eventually named four justices to the high court: Burger, Harry Blackmun, Lewis Powell, and William Rehnquist.

Under Chief Justice Burger and his successor William Rehnquist, the Supreme Court clarified the remedies that can be used to correct past racial discrimination. In 1974 the Court limited the use of school busing for purposes of racial desegregation by declaring that busing could not take place across school district lines. In 1978 in the landmark *Bakke* case, the Court held that educational institutions could take race into account when screening applicants, but could not use rigid racial quotas. In 1979 in the controversial *Weber* "reverse-discrimination" case, the court ruled that employers and unions could legally establish voluntary programs, including the use of quotas, to aid minorities and women in employment.

The Struggle Continues

Over the past quarter century, black Americans have made impressive social and economic gains, yet full equality remains an unrealized dream. State-sanctioned segregation in restaurants, hotels, courtrooms, libraries, drinking fountains, and public washrooms was eliminated and many barriers to equal opportunity were shattered. In political representation, educational attainment, and representation in white-collar and professional occupations, black Americans have made striking gains. Between 1960 and 1988 the number of black officeholders swelled from just 300 to nearly 6600 and the proportion of blacks in professional positions quadrupled. Black mayors have governed many of the nation's largest cities, including Chicago, Detroit, Los Angeles, Philadelphia, and Washington, D.C. Respect for black culture has also grown. The number of black performers on television and in film has grown, though most still appear in comedies or crime stories. Today, the most popular television performers (Bill Cosby and Oprah), the most popular movie star (Eddie Murphy), and many of the most popular musicians and sports stars are black.

Nevertheless, millions of black Americans still do not share fully in the promise of American life. According to census figures, blacks still suffer twice the unemployment rate of whites and earn only about half as much. The poverty rate among black families is three times that of whites, the same ratio as in the 1950s. Forty percent of black children are raised in fatherless homes and almost half of all black children are born into families earning less than the poverty level.

Separation of the races in housing and schooling remains widespread. Nationally, less than a quarter of all black Americans live in integrated neighborhoods and only about 38 percent of black children attend racially integrated schools. And despite great gains in black political clout, blacks still do not hold political offices in proportion to their share of the population. In 1990 there were only 400 black legislators (state and federal), against 7335 white legislators, and altogether blacks still make up less than two percent of the nation's officeholders.

Although the United States has eliminated many obstacles to black progress, reformers maintain that much remains to be done before the country attains Martin Luther King's dream of a nation where "all of God's children, black man and white man, Jew and Gentile, Protestant and Catholic, will be able to join hands and sing in the words of the old Negro spiritual, 'Free at Last, Free at Last, Thank God Almighty, I'm Free at Last.' "

Tom Bradley, the son of a sharecropper, became the first black mayor of Los Angeles in 1973, winning more than 56 percent of the total vote.

THE YOUTH REVOLT

During the 1960s, one age group of Americans loomed larger than any other: youth. Their skepticism of corporate and bureaucratic authority, their strong emotional identification with the underprivileged, and their intense desire for stimulation and instant gratification shaped the nation's politics, dress, music, and film. Unlike their parents, who had grown up amid the hardships of the depression and the patriotic sacrifices of World War II, young people of the 1960s grew up during a period of rapid economic growth. Feeling a deep sense of economic security, they sought personal fulfillment and tended to dismiss their parents generation's success-oriented lives. "Never trust anyone over 30," went a popular saying.

Never before had young people been so numerous or so well-educated. During the 1960s, there was a sudden explosion in the number of teenagers and young adults. As a result of the depressed birthrates during the 1930s and the postwar baby boom, the number of young people aged 14 to 25 jumped 40 percent in a decade, until they constituted 20 percent of the nation's population. The nation's growing number of young people received far more schooling than their parents. Over 75 percent graduated high school and nearly 40 percent went on to higher education.

At no earlier time in American history had the gulf between the generations seemed so wide. Blue jeans, long hair, psychedelic drugs, casual sex, hippie communes, campus demonstrations, and rock music all became symbols of the distance separating youth from the world of conventional adulthood.

The New Left

Late in the spring of 1962, five dozen college students gathered at a lakeside camp near Port Huron, Michigan, to discuss politics. For four days and nights the members of an obscure student group known as Students for a Democratic Society (SDS) talked passionately about such topics as civil rights, foreign policy, and the quality of American life. At 5 o'clock in the morning of June 16 the gathering ended. The participants had agreed on a political platform that expressed their sentiments. This manifesto, one of the pivotal political documents of the 1960s, became known as the Port Huron Statement.

The goal set forward in the Port Huron Statement was the creation of a radically democratic political movement in the United States that rejected hierarchy and bureaucracy. In its most important paragraphs, the document called for "participatory democracy"—direct individual involvement in the decisions that affected their lives. This notion would become the battle cry of the student movement of the 1960s—a movement that came to be known as the New Left.

The Port Huron Statement's chief author was Tom Hayden. Hayden had been born on December 11, 1939, in Royal Oak, Michigan, a predominantly Catholic working-class suburb of Detroit. From an early age, Hayden had been unusually politically conscious and questioning of established authority. In high school, his idols were critics of conventional society, such as J. D. Salinger's Holden Caulfield and *Mad Magazine's* Alfred E. Neuman. He then attended the University of Michigan, where he edited the university's student newspaper. He read Jack Kerouac's beat novel *On the Road*, hitchhiked across the country, and witnessed student protests at the University of California at Berkeley. He spent much of 1961 in the South, worked with the SNCC, and was once badly beaten by local whites in McComb, Mississippi.

During the 1960s, Tom Hayden became one of the key figures in the New Left. In 1968 he flew to North Vietnam as a protest against the Vietnam War. The next year he gained further notoriety as one of the Chicago Seven defendants who were acquitted of charges of conspiring to disrupt the 1968 Democratic presidential convention. Briefly, Hayden dropped out of politics, moved to Venice, California, and lived under a pseudonym. Later, he married actress Jane Fonda and became a member of the California legislature.

During the 1960s, thousands of young college students, like Tom Hayden, became politically active. The first issue to spark student radicalism was the impersonality of the modern university. Many students criticized the bureaucratic, impersonal nature of the modern "megaversity." Students questioned university requirements, restrictions on student political activities, and dormitory rules that limited the hours that male and female students could socialize with each other. Restrictions on students handing out political pamphlets on university property led to the first campus demonstrations that broke out at the University of California at

Tom Hayden (right) was a key figure in student activism in the 1960s. Here Hayden and fellow activists Abbie Hoffman (left) and Jerry Rubin (center) address a crowd in Chicago on the day conspiracy indictments were handed down to the Chicago Seven.

Berkeley and soon spread to other campuses. Mario Savio, leader of the Berkeley Free Speech Movement, succinctly summarized the feelings of many student radicals:

> The university is well structured, well tooled, to turn out people with all the sharp edges worn off, the well-rounded person. . . . This means that the best among the people who enter must for four years wander aimlessly much of the time questioning why they are on campus at all, doubting whether there is any point in what they are doing, and looking forward toward a very bleak existence afterward in a game in which all of the rules have been made up, which one cannot really amend.

Involvement in the civil rights movement in the South initiated many students into radical politics. In the early 1960s, many white students from northern universities began to participate in voter registration drives, freedom schools, sit-ins, and freedom rides in order to help desegregate the South. For the first time, many witnessed poverty, discrimination, and violence first hand.

Student radicalism also drew inspiration from a literature of social criticism that flourished in the 1950s. During that decade, many of the most popular films, novels, and writings aimed at young people criticized conventional middle class life. Popular films, like *Rebel Without a Cause*, and popular novels, like J. D. Salinger's *Catcher in the Rye*, celebrated sensitive, directionless, alienated youths unable to conform to the conventional adult values of suburban and corporate America. Sophisticated works of social criticism, by such maverick sociologists, psychologists, and economists as Herbert Marcuse, Norman O. Brown, Paul Goodman, Michael Harrington, and C. Wright Mills, documented the growing concentration of power in the hands of social elites, the persistence of poverty in a land of plenty, and the stresses and injustices in America's social order.

Above all, student radicalism owed its support to student opposition to the Vietnam War. SDS held its first antiwar march in 1965, which attracted at least 15,000 protestors to Washington, and commanded wide press attention. Over

In the late summer of 1964 the first major student demonstrations took place at the University of California at Berkeley. Student protests against war, racism, and poverty continued throughout the country into the 1970s.

the next three years, oppposition to the war brought thousands of new members to SDS. The organization grew phenomenally, from fewer than a thousand members in 1962 to at least 50,000 in 1968. In addition to its antiwar activities, members of SDS also tried to organize a democratic "interracial movement of the poor" in northern city neighborhoods.

Many members of SDS quickly grew frustrated by the slow pace of social change and began to embrace violence as a tool to transform society. "I'm a nihilist! I'm proud of it, proud of it!" shouted a delegate at a 1967 SDS meeting in Princeton. "Tactics? It's too late. . . . Let's break what we can. Tear them apart." An underground newspaper, the *Berkeley Barb*, proclaimed that the "university cannot be reformed" and called for guerrilla bands to sweep through "college campuses, busting up classrooms, and freeing our brothers from the prison of the university."

After 1968 SDS rapidly tore itself apart as an effective political force. The Marxist-Leninist Progressive Labor party infiltrated the organization. SDS's final convention in 1969 degenerated into a shouting match, as factions tried to shout each other down with chants of "Ho, Ho, Ho Chi Minh!" and "Mao, Mao, Mao Tse-tung!" In 1969 the Weathermen, a surviving faction of SDS, attempted to launch a guerrilla war in the streets of Chicago—an incident known as the "Days of Rage"—to "tear pig city apart." Finally, in 1970 three members of the Weathermen blew themselves up in a Greenwich Village brownstone trying to make a bomb out of a stick of dynamite and an alarm clock.

Throughout the 1960s the SDS and other radical student organizations claimed to speak for the nation's youth, and in thousands of editorials and magazine articles, journalists accepted this claim. In fact, the SDS represented only a small minority of college students, who themselves composed a minority of the country's youth. Far more young Americans voted for George Wallace in 1968 than joined SDS, and most college students during the decade spent far more time studying and enjoying the college experience than protesting. Nevertheless, radical students did help to draw the nation's attention to the problem of racism in American so-

ciety and the moral issues involved in the Vietnam War. In that sense, their impact far exceeded their numbers.

The Making and Unmaking of a Counterculture

The New Left had a series of heroes—ranging from Marx, Lenin, Ho, and Mao to Fidel, Che, and other revolutionaries. It also had its own uniforms, rituals, and music. Faded blue work shirts and jeans, wire-rimmed glasses, and work shoes were de rigueur even if the dirtiest work the wearer performed was taking notes in a college class. The proponents of the New Left emphasized their sympathy with the working class—an emotion that was seldom reciprocated—and listened to labor songs that once fired the hearts of unionists. The political protest folk music of Greenwich Village—of Phil Ochs, Bob Dylan, and their crowd—inspired the New Left.

But the New Left was only one part of youth protest during the 1960s. While the New Left labored to change the world and remake American society, other youths attempted to alter themselves and reorder consciousness. Variously labeled the counterculture, hippies, or flower children, they had their own heroes, music, dress, and approach to life.

In theory, supporters of the counterculture rejected individualism, competition, and capitalism. Adopting rather unsystematic ideas from oriental religions, they sought to become one with the universe. "The solution to the problem of identity is, get lost," wrote Norman O. Brown, whose books influenced the counterculture. All humanity, Brown believed, was part of a single entity, and man existed not as an individual but as part of the whole. As one interpreter of Brown explained, "Body existed, not as location or flesh, but as a field of energy; ego, character, personality were mere illusion. . . . Indeed, knowledge of the unity could be attained only by breaking the bonds of the ego, by having 'no self.' "

But how could one lose oneself? The process began with the act of rejection—of such liberal values as progress, order, reason, achievement, social responsibility; of competition, materialism, the work ethic, and other bourgeois "hang-ups." Rejection of monogamy and releasing one's sexual energy also aided the process. If the counterculture did not invent sex, it claimed to have improved the patent. As in other aspects of the movement, the emphasis was on sharing. The traditional nuclear family gave way to the tribal or communal ideal, where members renounced individualism and private property and shared food, work, and sex. In such a community, love was a general abstract ideal rather than a focused emotion.

The quest for openness with the universe led many youths to experiment with hallucinogenic drugs. LSD had a particularly powerful allure. Under its influence, poets, musicians, politicians, and thousands of other Americans claimed to have tapped into an all-powerful spiritual force. After taking LSD, Henry Luce, founder and president of Time-Life, Inc., claimed that God told him all was right with America. Timothy Leary, the Harvard professor who became the leading prophet of LSD, asserted that the drug would unlock the universe. Picking up on Kennedy's New Frontier theme, Leary told LSD takers "You are venturing out (like the Portuguese sailors, like the astronauts) on uncharted margins. But be assured—it is an old human custom." Poet Allen Ginsberg agreed that LSD led to new insights—after taking the drug he tried to get Kennedy and Khrushchev on the telephone to "settle all this about the bomb once and for all."

Although LSD was outlawed in 1966, the drug continued to spread. Perhaps some takers discovered profound truths, but by the late 1960s drugs had done more harm than good. The history of the Haight-Ashbury section of San Francisco illustrated the problems caused by drugs. In 1967 Haight was the center of the "counterculture," the home of the "flower children." During that "summer of love" the song "Are You Going to San Francisco?" soared to the top of the pop chart, and in the "city of love" hippies ingested LSD, smoked pot, listened to "acid rock," and proclaimed the dawning of a new age. Even the Hell's Angels, an outlaw motorcycle group, temporarily joined the act, serving as the hippies' private police force. But even as *Time* magazine described Haight as "the vibrant epicenter of the hippie movement," the

area was suffering from severe problems. High levels of racial violence, venereal disease, rape, drug overdoses, and poverty ensured more bad trips than good. "No doubt real love existed somewhere in the Haight," noted one historian. "But the case of the sixteen-year-old girl who was shot full of speed and raffled off in the streets was closer to the dominant reality."

Even music, which along with drugs and sex formed the counterculture trinity, failed to alter human behavior. In 1969 journalists hailed the Woodstock Music Festival as a symbol of love. But a few months later a group of Hell's Angels violently interrupted the Altamont Raceway music festival. As Mick Jagger sang "Sympathy for the Devil" an Angel stabbed to death a black man.

Like the New Left, the counterculture fell victim to its own excesses. Sex, drugs, and rock and roll did not solve the problems facing the United States. And by the end of the 1960s the counterculture had lost its force.

LIBERATION MOVEMENTS

The struggle of black Americans for racial justice inspired a host of other groups to seek full equality. Women, Mexican-Americans, Native Americans, and many other deprived groups protested against discrimination and organized to promote social change.

Women's Liberation

Hosted by Jack Bailey, a gravel-voiced former carnival barker, it was one of the most popular daytime television shows of the 1950s. Five times a week, three women, each with a hard-luck story, recited their tales of woe—diseases, retarded children, poverty—and the studio audience, with the aid of an applause meter, decided which woman was the most miserable. She became "Queen for a Day." Bailey put a crown on her head, wrapped her in a mink coat (which she got to keep for 24 hours), and told her about the new Cadillac she would get to drive (also for the next 24 hours). And then came gifts for the queen; a year's supply of Helena Rubinstein cosmetics; a Clairol permanent and once-over by a Hollywood makeup art-

The popular television show "Queen for a Day" reinforced established female sex roles by providing winners with everything they needed to be better housewives. Here, host Jack Bailey crowns the "Queen for a Day."

ist; and the electric appliances necessary for female happiness—a toaster oven, automatic washer, automatic dryer, and an iron. Altogether, everything a woman needed to be a prettier and better housewife.

One woman in the television audience was Betty Friedan. A 1942 honors graduate of Smith College and former psychology Ph.D. candidate at the University of California at Berkeley, Friedan had quit graduate school, married, moved to the New York suburbs, and bore three children in rapid succession. American culture told her that husband, house, children, and electric appliances were true happiness. But Friedan was not happy. And she was not alone.

In 1957 Friedan sent out a questionnaires to fellow members of her college graduating class. The replies amazed her. Again and again, she found women suffering from "a sense of dissatisfaction." Over the next five years, Friedan

interviewed other women at PTA meetings and suburban cocktail parties, and she repeatedly found an unexplainable sense of melancholy and incompleteness. "Sometimes a woman would say 'I feel empty somehow . . . incomplete.' Or she would say, 'I feel as if I don't exist.'" Friedan was not the only observer to detect a widespread sense of discontent among American women. Doctors identified a new female malady, the housewife's syndrome, characterized by a mixture of frustration and exhaustion. CBS broadcast a television documentary entitled "The Trapped Housewife." *Newsweek* magazine noted that the nation's supposedly happy housewife was "dissatisfied with a lot that women of other lands can only dream of. Her discontent is deep, pervasive, and impervious to the superficial remedies which are offered at every hand." *The New York Times* editorialized, "Many young women . . . feel stifled in their homes." *Redbook* magazine ran an article entitled "Why Young Mothers Feel Trapped" and asked for examples of this problem. It received 24,000 replies.

Why, Friedan asked, were American women so discontented? In 1963 she published her answer in a book entitled *The Feminine Mystique*. This book, one of the most influential books ever written by an American, helped to launch a new movement for women's liberation. The book touched a nerve, but the origins of the movement lay in the role of females in American society.

Sources of Discontent

During the 1950s, many American women reacted against the poverty of the depression and the upheavals of World War II by placing renewed emphasis on family life. Young women married earlier than had their mothers, and had more children and bore them faster. The average marriage age of American women dropped to 20, a record low. The fertility rate rose 50 percent between 1940 and 1950—producing a population growth rate approaching that of India. Growing numbers of women decided to forsake higher education or a full-time career and achieve emotional fulfillment as wives and mothers. A 1952 advertisement for Gimbel's department store expressed the prevailing point of view. "What's college?" the ad asked. "That's where girls who are above cooking and sewing go to meet a man so they can spend their lives cooking and sewing." By "marrying at an earlier age, rearing larger families," and purchasing a house in the suburbs, young women believed, in the words of *McCall's* magazine, that they could find their "deepest satisfaction."

Politicians, educators, psychologists, and the mass media all echoed the view that women would find their highest fulfillment managing a house and caring for children. Adlai Stevenson, the Democratic presidential nominee in 1952 and 1956, told the graduating women at Smith College in 1955 that their role in life was to "influence us, men and boys" and "restore valid, meaningful purpose to life in your home." Many educators agreed with the president of Barnard College, who argued that women could not compete with men in the workplace because they "had less physical strength, a lower fatigue point, and a less stable nervous system." Women's magazines pictured housewives as happy with their tasks and depicted career women as neurotic, unhappy, and dissatisfied.

Already, however, a series of dramatic social changes was underway that would contribute to a rebirth of feminism. A dramatic upsurge took place during the 1950s in women's employment and education. More and more married women entered the labor force, and by 1960 the proportion of married women working outside the home was one in three. The number of women receiving college degrees also rose. The proportion of bachelor's and master's degrees received by women rose from just 24 percent in 1950 to over 35 percent a decade later. Meanwhile, beginning in 1957 the birthrate began to drop as women elected to have fewer children. A growing discrepancy had begun to appear between the popular image of women as full-time housewives and mothers and the actual realities of many women's lives.

Feminism Reborn

Women in 1960 played a limited role in American government. Although women comprised about half of the nation's voters, there were no female Supreme Court justices, federal appeals court justices, governors, cabinet officers, or ambassadors. Only 2 of 100 U.S. senators and 15 of 435 representatives were women. Of 307 federal district judges, 2 were women. Of 7700 members of state legislatures, 234 were women. Nor were these figures atypical. Only 2 American women had ever been elected governor, only 2 had ever served in a president's cabinet, and only 6 had ever served as ambassador.

Economically, women workers were concentrated in low-paying service and factory jobs. The overwhelming majority worked as secretaries, waitresses, beauticians, teachers, nurses, and librarians. Only 3.5 percent of the nation's lawyers were women, 10 percent of the nation's scientists, and less than 2 percent of the nation's leading business executives.

Lower pay for women doing the same work as men was commonplace. One out of every three companies had separate pay scales for

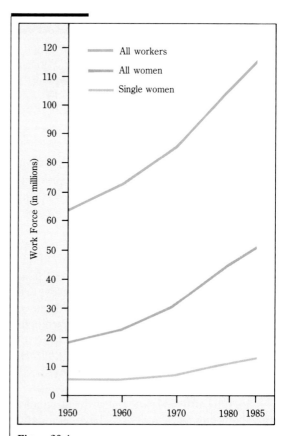

Figure 30.4
Women in the work force, 1950–1985

male and female workers. A female bank teller typically made $15 a week less than a man with the same amount of experience, and a female laundry worker made 49 cents an hour less than her male counterpart. Altogether, the earnings of women working full-time averaged only about 60 percent of those of men.

In many parts of the country, the law discriminated against women. In three states—Alabama, Mississippi, and South Carolina—women could not sit on juries. Many states restricted married women's right to make contracts, sell property, engage in business, control their own earnings, and make wills. Six states gave fathers preference in the custody of young children after a divorce. In practically every state, men had a legal right to have intercourse with their wives and to administer an unspecified amount of physical punishment.

Women were often portrayed in the mass media in an unrealistic and stereotyped way. Popular magazines like *Reader's Digest* and popular television shows like "I Love Lucy" often depicted women as stupid or foolish, jealous of other women, irresponsible about money, and overanxious to marry.

In December 1961 President John F. Kennedy placed the issue of women's rights on the national political agenda. Eager to fulfill a debt to women voters—he had not named a single woman to a policymaking position—Kennedy established a President's Commission on the Status of Women, the first presidential panel ever to examine the status of American women. Chaired by Eleanor Roosevelt, the commission was to recommend ways to combat "the prejudices and outmoded customs [that] act as barriers to the full realization of women's rights."

In 1963, the year that Betty Friedan published *The Feminine Mystique*, the commission issued its report. The report's recommendations included a call for an end to all legal restrictions on married women's right to own property, to enter into business, and to make contracts; equal opportunity in employment; and greater availability of child-care services.

The most important reform to grow out of the commission's investigations was the 1963 Equal Pay Act, which required equal pay for men and women who performed the same jobs under equal conditions. The Equal Pay Act was

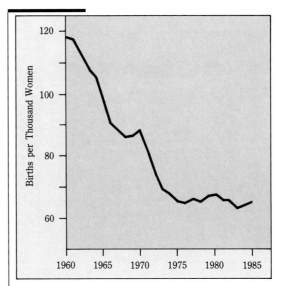

Figure 30.5
American birthrate, 1960–1985

the first federal law to prohibit discrimination on the basis of sex.

The next year, Congress enacted a new weapon in the fight against sex discrimination. Title VII of the 1964 Civil Rights Act prohibited discrimination in hiring or promotion based on race, color, religion, national origin, or sex by private employers and unions. As originally proposed, the bill only outlawed racial discrimination; but in a futile effort to block the measure, Representative Howard Smith of Virginia amended the bill to prohibit discrimination on the basis of sex. Some liberals including Representative Edith Green of Oregon, a co-sponsor of the 1963 Equal Pay Act, opposed the amendment on the grounds that it diverted attention from racial discrimination. But it passed in the House of Representatives 168 to 133. "We made it! God Bless America!" shouted a female voice from the House gallery when the amendment passed.

The Civil Rights Act made it illegal for employers to discriminate against women in hiring and promotion unless the employer could show that sex was a "bona fide occupational qualification" (for example, hiring a man as an attendant for a men's restroom). To investigate complaints of employment discrimination, the

(Text continues on p. 1036)

THE MODERN FAMILY

Does a father have the right to give his children his last name even if his wife objects? Can an expectant mother obtain an abortion without her husband's permission? Should a teenager, unhappy with her parents' restrictions on her smoking, dating, and choice of friends, be allowed to have herself placed in a foster home? Should a childless couple be permitted to hire a "surrogate mother" to be artificially inseminated and carry a child to delivery? These are among the questions that the nation's courts have had to wrestle with as the nature of American family life has, in the course of a generation, been revolutionized.

During the 1950s, the Cleavers on the television show "Leave It to Beaver" epitomized the American family. In 1960, over 70 percent of all American households were like the Cleavers: made up of a bread-winner father, a homemaker mother, and their kids. Today, "traditional" families with a working husband, an unemployed wife, and one or more

children make up less than 15 percent of the nation's households. And as America's families have changed, the image of the family portrayed on television has changed accordingly. Recent television families run the gamut from two-career families like the Huxtables on "The Cosby Show" to two single mothers and their children on "Kate and Allie," and an unmarried couple who cohabit in the same house on "Who's the Boss."

Profound changes have reshaped American family life in recent years. In a decade, divorce rates doubled. The number of divorces today is twice as high as in 1966 and three times higher than in 1950. The rapid upsurge in the divorce rates contributed to a dramatic increase in the number of single-parent households—or what used to be known as broken homes. The number of households consisting of a single woman and her children has tripled since 1960. A sharp increase in female-headed homes has been ac-

companied by a startling increase in the number of couples cohabitating outside of marriage. The number of unmarried couples living together has quadrupled since 1970.

What accounts for these upheavals in family life? One of the most far-reaching forces for change has been a sexual revolution far more radical than the early twentieth century "revolution in morals and manners." Contemporary Americans are much more likely than their predecessors to postpone marriage, to live alone, and to engage in sexual intercourse outside of marriage. Today, over 80 percent of all women say that they were not virgins when they married, compared to less than 20 percent a generation ago. Extra-marital sex has also increased sharply. Back in the 1940s, just 8 percent of married women under the age of 25 had committed adultery. Today the estimated figure is 24 percent. Meanwhile, the proportion of children born to unmarried mothers has climbed from just 5 percent in 1960 to over 20 percent today.

The roots of these developments were planted during the early 1960s, when a new openness about sexuality swept the nation's literature, movies, theater, advertising, and fashion. In 1960, the birth control pill was introduced, offering a highly effective method of contraception. Two years later, Grossinger's resort in New York State's Catskill Mountains introduced the first singles-only weekend, thereby acknowledging couples outside marriage. In 1964, the first "singles bar" opened in New York City; the musical *Hair* introduced nudity to the Broadway stage; California designer Rudi Gernreich created the first topless bathing suit; and bars sprouted featuring topless waitresses and dancers. Sexually oriented magazines began to display pubic hair and filmmakers began to show simulated sexual acts on the screen. A new era of public sexuality was ushered in and as a result it became far easier and more acceptable to have an active social life and sex life outside of marriage.

At the same time, the nation's courts and state legislatures liberalized laws governing sex and contraception. In 1957, the Supreme Court narrowed the legal definition of obscenity, ruling that the portrayal of sex in art, literature, and film was entitled to constitutional protections of free speech, unless the work was utterly without redeeming social value. In 1962, Illinois became the first state to decriminalize all forms of private sexual conduct between consenting adults. In succeeding years, the Supreme Court struck down a series of state statutes that prohibited the prescription or distribution of contraceptives, and in 1973, in the case of *Roe* v. *Wade*, the high court decriminalized abortion. These legal decisions, to a large extent, took government out of the business of regulating private heterosexual behavior and defining the sexual norms according to which citizens were supposed to live.

Another factor reshaping family life has been a massive influx of mothers into the work force. As late as 1940, less than 12 percent of white married women were in the work force; today the figure is nearly 60 percent and over half of all mothers of preschoolers work outside the home. The major forces that have propelled women into the work force include a rising cost of living, which spurred many families to seek a second source of income; increased control over fertility through contraception and abortion, which allows women to work without interruption; and rising educational levels, which lead many women to seek employment for intellectual stimulation and fulfillment.

As wives have assumed a larger role in their family's financial support, they have felt justified in demanding that husbands perform more child care and housework. At the same time, fewer children have a full-time mother and as a result an increasing number of young children are cared for during the day by adults other than their own parent. Today, over two-thirds of all 3- to 5-year-olds take part in a day-care, nursery school, or prekindergarten program, compared to a fifth in 1970.

Feminism has been another major force that has transformed American family life. The women's liberation movement attacked the societal expectation that women defer to the needs of spouses and children as part of their roles as wives and mothers. Militant feminist activists like Ti-Grace Atkinson denounced marriage as "slavery" and "legalized rape." The larger mainstream of the women's movement articulated a powerful critique of the idea that child care and housework were the apex of a woman's accomplishments or her sole means of fulfillment.

The feminist movement awakened American women to what many viewed as one of the worst forms of social and political oppression: sexism. The introduction of this awareness would go far beyond the feminists themselves. Although only a small minority of American women openly declared themselves to be feminists, the arguments of the women's movement drastically altered women's attitudes toward family roles, child care, and housework. As a result of feminism, a substantial majority of women now believe that both husband and wife should have jobs, do housework, and take care of children.

The changes that have taken place in family life have been disruptive and troubling and have transformed the family into a major political battleground. Both liberals and conservatives have offered their own proposals about how the American family can best be strengthened. Conservative activists, fearful that climbing rates of divorce, single parenthood, and working mothers represent a breakdown of family values, launched a politically influential "profamily movement" during the 1970s. They sought to restrict access to abortion, block ratification of the proposed Equal Rights Amendment to the Constitution, restrict eroticism on television, and limit teenagers' access to contraceptive information. Liberals have approached family issues from a different tack. Unlike conservatives, they are more willing to use government social policies to strengthen family life. Some of the proposals they have made to strengthen families include expanded nutritional and health programs for pregnant women, federal subsidies for day-care services for low-income families, uniform national standards for child-care centers, and a requirement that employers give parents unpaid leave to take care of a newborn or seriously ill child. Without a doubt, the family will remain one of the hottest political issues in the years to come.

act set up the Equal Employment Opportunity Commission (EEOC).

At first, the EEOC focused its enforcement efforts on racial discrimination and largely ignored sex discrimination. The commission's director considered the provision prohibiting sex discrimination "a fluke . . . conceived out of wedlock," and the EEOC rejected a proposal that separate want ads for men and women be outlawed.

To pressure the EEOC to enforce the law prohibiting sex discrimination, Betty Friedan and 300 other women formed the National Organization for Women (NOW) in 1966, with Friedan as president. The organization pledged "to take action to bring women into full participation in the mainstream of American society now, exercising all the privileges and responsibilities thereof in truly equal partnership with men." NOW filed suit against the EEOC "to force it to comply with its own government rules." It also sued the country's 1300 largest corporations for sex discrimination, lobbied President Johnson to issue an executive order that would include women within federal affirmative action requirements, and challenged airline policies that required stewardesses to retire after they married or reached the age of 32.

At its second national conference in November 1967, NOW drew up an eight-point bill of rights for women. It called for adoption of an Equal Rights Amendment (ERA) to the Constitution, prohibiting sex discrimination; equal educational, job training, and housing opportunities for women; and repeal of laws limiting access to contraceptive devices and abortion.

Two proposals produced fierce dissension within the new organization. One source of disagreement was the Equal Rights Amendment. The amendment consisted of two dozen words: "Equality of rights under the law shall not be denied or abridged by the United States or by any state on account of sex." It had originally been proposed in 1923 to mark the seventy-fifth anniversary of the Seneca Falls Women's Rights Convention and was submitted to Congress at almost every session. For over 40 years, professional women, who favored the amendment, battled with organized labor and the Women's Bureau of the Labor Department, which opposed the amendment on the ground that it en-

dangered "protective" legislation that set minimum wages and maximum hours for less-skilled women workers. At NOW's convention, women from the United Automobile Workers (UAW) opposed inclusion of the ERA in the Bill of Rights. When they lost, the UAW stopped providing NOW with office space and clerical services.

The other issue that generated controversy was the call for reform of abortion laws. In 1967 only one state—Colorado—had reformed nineteenth-century legal statutes that made abortion a criminal offense. Dissenters believed that NOW should avoid controversial issues that would divert attention away from economic discrimination.

Despite internal disagreements, NOW's membership grew rapidly, reaching 40,000 by 1974 and 175,000 by 1988. The group broadened its attention to include such issues as the plight of poor and nonwhite women, domestic violence, rape, sexual harrassment, the role of women in sport, and the rights of lesbians. At the same time, the organization claimed a number of achievements. Two victories were particularly important. In 1967, NOW persuaded President Lyndon Johnson to issue Executive Order 11375, which prohibited government contractors from discriminating on the basis of sex and required them to take "affirmative action" to ensure that women are properly represented in their work force. The next year, the EEOC ruled that separate want ads for men and women were a violation of Title VII of the 1964 Civil Rights Act.

Radical Feminism

Alongside the National Organization for Women, other more radical feminist groups emerged during the 1960s among college students involved in the civil rights movement and the New Left. Women within these organizations for social change often found themselves treated as "second-class citizens," responsible for kitchen work, typing, and serving "as a sexual supply for their male comrades after hours." "We were the movement secretaries and the shit-workers," one woman recalled; "we were the earth mothers and the sex-objects for the movement's men." In 1964 Ruby Doris Smith

Women have been involved in protest movements throughout the years. Here women march in support of the Equal Rights Amendment. Failure to achieve ratification by the required three-fourths of states sent the amendment to its final defeat in 1982.

Robinson presented an indignant assault on the treatment of women civil rights workers in a paper entitled "The Position of Women in SNCC," to a SNCC staff meeting. Stokely Carmichael reputedly responded, "The only position for women in SNCC is prone."

Women in the New Left also expressed unhappiness. "You are allowed to participate and to speak," noted one woman, "only the men stop listening when you do . . . How many times have you seen men get up and actually walk out of a room while a woman speaks, or begin to whisper to each other as she starts?" When women tried to raise the "woman question" at SDS's 1965 convention, men responded with "catcalls, storms of ridicule and verbal abuse, 'She just needs a good screw,' or . . . 'She's a castrating female.' "

In cities across the country, independent women's groups sprouted up in 1967. In the fall, at the first national gathering of women's groups at the National Conference for New Politics, women demanded 51 percent of all committee seats in the name of minority rights. When men refused to meet their demand, the women walked out—signaling the beginning of a critical split between the New Left and the women's movement. The next year, radical women's groups appeared on the front pages of the nation's newspapers when they staged a protest of the Miss America pageant and provided a "freedom trash can," in which women could throw "old bras, girdles, high heeled shoes, women's magazines, curlers, and other instruments of torture to women." They concluded their rally by crowning a sheep Miss America.

Over the next three years the number of women's liberation groups rapidly multiplied, bearing such names as the Redstockings, WITCH (the Women's International Terrorist Conspiracy from Hell), and the Feminists. By 1970 there were at least 500 women's liberation groups, including 50 in New York, 25 in Boston, 30 in Chicago, and 35 in San Francisco. Women's liberation groups established the first feminist book stores, battered women's shelters, rape crisis centers, and abortion counseling centers. In 1971 Gloria Steinem and others published *Ms.*, the first national feminist magazine. The first 300,000 copies were sold out in eight days.

Radical new ideas began to fill the air. One women's liberation leader, Ti-Grace Atkinson, denounced marriage as "slavery," "legalized rape," and "unpaid labor." Meanwhile, a host of new words and phrases entered the language, such as "consciousness raising," "Ms.," "bra burning," "sexism," "male chauvinist pig."

On August 26, 1970, the fiftieth anniversary of the ratification of the Nineteenth Amendment, the women's liberation movement dramatically demonstrated its growing strength by mounting a massive Strike for Equality. In New York City, 50,000 women marched down Fifth Avenue; in Boston, 2000 marched; in Chicago, 3000. Members of virtually all feminist groups joined together in a display of unity and strength.

The Growth of Feminist Ideology

Feminists subscribe to no single doctrine or set of goals. All are united, however, by a belief that women have historically occupied a subordinate position in politics, education, and the economic system. Modern feminist thought traces its roots to a book published by a famous French philosopher Simone de Beauvoir in 1949. Entitled *The Second Sex*, the book traced the assumptions, customs, educational practices, jokes, laws, and modes of speech that socialize young women to believe that they are inferior beings.

A decade and a half later, Betty Friedan made another important contribution to the development of feminist ideology. In *The Feminine Mystique*, she analyzed and criticized the role of educators, psychologists, sociologists, and the mass media in conditioning women to believe that they could only find fulfillment as housewives and mothers. By requiring women to subordinate their own individual aspirations to the welfare of their husbands and children, the "feminine mystique" prevented women from achieving self-fulfillment and inevitably left women unhappy.

In the years following the publication of *The Feminine Mystique*, feminists developed a large body of literature analyzing the economic, psychological, and social roots of female subordination. It was not until 1970, however, that the more radical feminist writings reached the broader reading public with the publication of Shulamith Firestone's *The Dialectic of Sex*, Germaine Greer's *The Female Eunuch*, and Kate Millett's *Sexual Politics*. These books argued that gender distinctions structure virtually every aspect of individual lives, not only in such areas as law and employment, but also in personal relationships, language, literature, religion, and an individual's internalized self-perceptions. Even more controversially, these works attributed female oppression to men and an ideology of male supremacy. "Women have very little idea how much men hate them," declared Greer. As examples of misogyny these authors cited pornography, grotesque portrayals of women in literature, sexual harrassment, wife abuse, and rape.

Since 1970 feminist theory has exploded into many different directions. Today, there are more than 30 national feminist news and opinion magazines along with an additional 20 academic journals dealing with women's issues. Women's historians, feminist literary and film critics, and physical and social scientists have begun to take insights derived from feminism and ask new questions about women's historical experience, the sex and status differences between women and men, sex role socialization, economic and legal discrimination, and the depiction of women in literature.

The Supreme Court and Sex Discrimination

Despite its conservative image, the Supreme Court under chief justices Warren Burger and William Rehnquist has been active in the area of sex discrimination and women's rights. In contrast to the Warren Court, which ruled on only one major sex discrimination case—upholding a law that excluded women from serving on juries—the Burger and Rehnquist Courts have considered numerous cases involving women's rights.

The Burger Court issued its first important discrimination decision in 1971. In its landmark decision, *Griggs* v. *Duke Power Company*, the Court established the principle that regardless of an employer's intentions, any employment practice is illegal if it has a "disparate" impact on women or minorities and "if it cannot be shown to be related to job performance." In subsequent cases, the Court legitimized the use of statistics in measuring employment discrimination and approved the use of back pay in compensating discrimination victims.

In 1975 the Burger Court reversed the Warren Court by striking down a Louisiana statute calling for all-male juries. In subsequent decisions, the high court ruled against a Utah law setting different ages at which men and women became adults and overturned an Alabama law setting minimum height and weight requirements for prison guards, standards that meant that almost no woman would qualify.

The Court has not yet set an absolute rule that laws and employment practices must treat men and women the same. In 1976 the Court adopted its current standard for sex discrimination. The Court's test is that to be constitutional, a policy that discriminates on the basis of sex must be "substantially related to an important government objective."

The Court's most controversial decision involving women's rights was delivered in 1973 in the case of *Roe* v. *Wade*. A single, pregnant Texas waitress, assigned the pseudonym Jane Roe in order to protect her privacy, brought suit against Dallas district attorney Henry Wade, to prevent him from enforcing a nineteenth-century Texas statute prohibiting abortion. The Court ruled on the woman's behalf and struck down the Texas law and all similar laws in other states. In its ruling, the Court declared that the decision to have an abortion is a private matter of concern only to a woman and her physician, and that only in the last three months of pregnancy could the government limit the right to abortion.

Many Americans—including many Catholic lay and clerical organizations—bitterly opposed the Supreme Court's *Roe* v. *Wade* decision and banded together to form the "right to life" movement, which ran Ellen MacCormack as a presidential candidate in the 1976 presidential primaries. Like feminist and civil rights organizations, the right to life movement drew on a broad base of popular discontent, and it often employed direct, nonviolent protests to demonstrate its belief that the nation's laws were unjust. The major legislative success of the right to life movement was adoption by Congress of the so-called Hyde Amendment, which permitted states to refuse to fund abortions for indigent women.

The Equal Rights Amendment

In March 1972 the Congress passed an Equal Rights Amendment (ERA) to the United States Constitution, prohibiting sex discrimination, with only 8 dissenting votes in the Senate and 24 in the House. Before the year was over, 22 state legislatures ratified the ERA. Ratification by 38 states was required before the amendment would be added to the Constitution. Over the next 5 years, only 13 more states ratified the amendment—and 5 states rescinded their ratification. In 1978, Congress gave proponents of the amendment 39 more months to complete ratification, but no other state gave its approval.

The ERA had been defeated, but why? Initially, opposition came largely from organized labor, which feared that the amendment would eliminate state "protective legislation," that established minimum wages and maximum hours for women workers. Increasingly, however, resistance to the amendment came from women of lower economic and educational status, whose self-esteem and self-image were bound up with being wives and mothers and who wanted to ensure that women who devoted their lives to their families were not accorded lower status than women who worked outside the home.

The leader of the anti-ERA movement was Phyllis Schlafly, a Radcliffe-educated mother of six from Alton, Illinois. A larger than life figure, Schlafly earned a law degree at the age of 54, wrote nine books (including the 1964 best-seller *A Choice Not an Echo*), and created her own

Right-to-life groups, backed by Protestant fundamentalists, conservatives, and the Catholic church, scored a victory with the Hyde amendment. However, prochoice groups helped organize privately funded agencies and clinics to allow women a choice.

lobbying group, the Eagle Forum. Schlafly argued that the ERA was unnecessary because women were already protected by the Equal Pay Act of 1963 and the Civil Rights Act of 1964, which barred sex discrimination, and that the amendment would outlaw separate public restrooms for men and women and deny wives the right to financial support. She also raised the "women in combat" issue by suggesting that the passage of the ERA would mean that woman would have to fight alongside men during war.

Impact of the Women's Liberation Movement

Since 1960 women have made enormous social gains. Gains in employment have been particularly impressive. During the 1970s, the number of working women climbed 42 percent and much of the increase was in what traditionally was considered "men's" work and professional work. The percentage of lawyers who were women increased by 9 percentage points; the percentage of professors by 6 points; of doctors by 3.6 points. By 1986, women made up 15 per-

cent of the nation's lawyers, 40 percent of all computer programmers, and 29 percent of the country's managers and administrators.

Striking gains have been made in undergraduate and graduate education. Today, for the first time in American history, women constitute a majority of the nation's college students and nearly as many women as men receive master's degrees. In addition, the number of women students receiving degrees from professional schools—including dentistry, law, and medicine—has shot upward, from just 1425 in 1966 to over 20,000 by the early 1990s. Women comprise nearly a third of the students attending law school and medical school.

Women have also made impressive political gains. In 1988 over two dozen women served in Congress, over 80 served as mayors of large cities, and over a thousand served in state legislatures. In 1984, for the first time, a major political party nominated a woman, Geraldine Ferraro, for the vice presidency. Ten percent of the top appointed offices during the Reagan administration went to women and Sandra Day

TABLE 30.4

Occupation by Sex, 1972, 1980 and 1989 (Percentage)

Occupation	1972/Female	1980/Female	1989/Female
Professional/technical	39.3	44.3	45.2
Accountants	21.7	36.2	48.6
Computer specialists	16.8	25.7	35.7
Engineers	0.8	4.0	7.6
Lawyers and judges	3.8	12.8	22.3
Life/physical scientists	10.0	20.3	26.9
Physicians/dentists	9.3	12.9	16.5
Professors	28.0	33.9	38.7
Engineering/science technicians	9.1	17.8	19.2
Writers/artists/entertainers	31.7	39.3	46.0
Sales	41.6	45.3	49.3
Real estate agents/brokers	36.7	50.7	51.0
Clerks, retail	68.9	71.1	81.8
Clerical	75.6	80.1	80.0
Bookkeepers	97.9	90.5	91.7
Clerical supervisors	57.8	70.5	58.2
Office machine operators	71.4	72.6	62.6
Secretaries	99.1	99.1	98.3
Crafts workers	3.6	6.0	8.6
Blue-collar supervisors	6.9	10.8	n/a*
Machinists and jobsetters	0.6	4.0	n/a*
Tool and die makers	0.5	2.8	n/a*
Mechanics (except automobile)	1.0	2.6	3.1

*n/a, not available.
U.S. Bureau of the Census, *Statistical Abstract of the United States: 1982–83* (103d edition), *1991* (111th edition), Washington, D.C., 1982, 1991.

O'Connor was named the first woman to sit on the Supreme Court. Three women held cabinet posts and the president appointed a woman ambassador to the United Nations. By 1988 over 15,000 women held elective office.

In spite of all that has been achieved, however, problems remain. Most women today continue to work in a relatively small number of traditional "women's" jobs and a full-time female worker earned only 68 cents for every $1 paid to men. Even more troubling is the fact that large numbers of women live in poverty. The "feminization of poverty" was one of the growing trends of the 1970s and 1980s. Today, nearly half of all marriages end in divorce and many others end in legal separation and desertion—and the economic plight of these women is often grave. Families headed by women are four and a half times as likely to be poor as families headed by males. Although female-headed families constitute only 15 percent of the U.S. population, they account for over 50 percent of the poor population.

Chicano Liberation

On election day, 1963, hundreds of Mexican-Americans in Crystal City, Texas, the "spinach capital of the world," gathered near a statue of Popeye the Sailor to do something that many had never done before: vote. Although Mexican-Americans outnumbered Anglos two to one, Anglos controlled all five seats on the Crystal City council. For three years, organizers struggled to register Mexican-American voters. When the election was over, Mexican-Americans had won

TABLE 30.5

Ratio of Divorces to Marriages, 1890–1987

1890	1–17
1900	1–12
1910	1–11
1920	1–7
1930	1–5
1940	1–6
1950	1–4.3
1960	1–3.8
1970	1–3.5
1980	1–2
1987	1–2.1

control of the city council. "We have done the impossible," declared Albert Fuentes, who led the voter registration campaign. "If we can do it in Crystal City, we can do it all over Texas. We can awaken the sleeping giant."

As the 1960s began, Mexican-Americans shared problems of poverty and discrimination with other minority groups. The median income of a Mexican-American family was just 62 percent of the median income of the general population, and over a third of Mexican-American families lived on less than $3000 a year. Unemployment was twice the rate among non-Hispanic whites and four-fifths of employed Mexican-Americans were concentrated in semi-skilled and unskilled jobs, a third in agriculture.

Educational attainment lagged behind other groups (Mexican-Americans averaged less than nine years of schooling as recently as 1970), and Mexican-American pupils were concentrated in predominantly Mexican-American schools, less well staffed and supplied than non–Mexican-American schools, with few Hispanic or Spanish-speaking teachers. Gerrymandered election districts and restrictive voting legislation resulted in the political underrepresentation of Mexican-Americans. They were underrepresented or excluded from juries by requirements that jurors be able to speak and understand English.

During the 1960s, a new Mexican-American militancy arose. In 1962 César Chávez began to organize California farm workers, and three years later, in Delano, California, he led his first strike. At the same time that Chávez led the struggle for higher wages, enforcement of state labor laws, and recognition of the farm worker union, Reies Lopez Tijerina fought to win compensation for the descendants of families whose lands had been seized illegally. In 1963 Tijerina founded the Alianza Federal de Mercedes (the Federal Alliance of Land Grants) in New Mexico to restore the legal rights of heirs to Spanish and Mexican land grants that had been guaranteed under the treaty ending the Mexican War.

In Denver, Rodolfo ("Corky") Gonzales formed the Crusade for Justice in 1965 to protest school discrimination; provide legal, medical, and financial services and jobs for Chicanos; and foster the Mexican-American cultural heritage. La Raza Unida political parties arose in a number of small towns with large Mexican-American populations. On college campuses across the Southwest, Mexican-Americans formed political organizations.

In 1968 Congress responded to the demand among Mexican-Americans for equal educational opportunity by enacting legislation encouraging school districts to adopt bilingual education programs to instruct non-English speakers in both English and their native language. In a more recent action, Congress moved in 1986 to legalize the status of many immigrants, including many Mexicans, who entered the United States illegally. The Immigration Reform and Control Act of 1986 provided permanent legal residency to undocumented workers who had lived in the United States since before 1982 and prohibits employment of illegal aliens.

Since 1960 Mexican-Americans have made impressive political gains. During the 1960s four Mexican-Americans—Senator Joseph Montoya of New Mexico and representatives Eligio de la Garza and Henry B. Gonzales of Texas and Edward R. Roybal of California— were elected to Congress. In 1974 two Chicanos were elected governors—Jerry Apodaca in New Mexico and Raul Castro in Arizona—becoming the first Mexican-American governors since early in this century. In 1981 Henry Cisneros of San Antonio became the first Mexican-American mayor of a large city.

Today, the 10.5 million Mexican-Americans, the nation's second largest minority group, continue to struggle to expand their political influence, improve their economic position, and preserve their distinctive culture.

The Native American Power Movement

In November 1969, 200 Native Americans seized the abandoned federal penitentiary on Alcatraz Island in San Francisco Bay. For 19 months Indian activists occupied the island in order to draw attention to conditions on the nation's Indian reservations. Alcatraz, the Native Americans said, symbolized conditions on reservations: "It has no running water; it has inadequate sanitation facilities; there is no industry, and so unemployment is very great; there are no health care facilities; the soil is rocky and unproductive." The activists, who called themselves Indians of All Tribes, offered to buy Alcatraz from the federal government for "$24 in glass beads and red cloth."

On Thanksgiving Day, 1970, 350 years after the Pilgrims' arrival, Wampanoag Indians, who had taken part at the first Thanksgiving, held a National Day of Mourning at Plymouth, Massachusetts. A tribal representative declared, "We forfeited our country. Our lands have fallen into the hands of the aggressor. We have allowed the white man to keep us on our knees." Meanwhile, another group of Native Americans established a settlement at Mount Rushmore, to demonstrate Indian claims to the Black Hills.

During the late 1960s and early 1970s, a new spirit of political militancy arose among the first Americans, just as it had among black Americans and women. No other group, however, faced problems more severe than Native Americans. Throughout the 1960s, American Indians were the nation's poorest minority group, worse off than any other group according to virtually every socioeconomic measure. In 1970 the Indian unemployment rate was 10 times the national average, and 40 percent of the Native American population lived below the poverty line. In that year, Native American life expectancy was just 44 years, a third less than that of the average American. In one Apache town of 2500 on the San Carlos reservation in

Henry Cisneros, elected mayor of San Antonio in 1981, was interviewed by Walter Mondale in 1984 as a potential Democratic vice-presidential nominee.

Arizona, there were only 25 telephones and most homes had outdoor toilets and relied on wood-burning stoves for heat.

Conditions on many of the nation's reservations were not unlike those found in underdeveloped areas of Latin America, Africa, and Asia. The death rate among Native Americans exceeded that of the U.S. population as a whole by a third. Deaths caused by pneumonia, hepatitis, dysentery, strep throat, diabetes, tuberculosis, alcoholism, suicide, and homicide were 2 to 60 times higher than the entire U.S. population. Half a million Indian families lived in unsanitary dilapidated dwellings, many in shanties, huts, or even abandoned automobiles.

On the Navajo reservation in Arizona, which is roughly the size of West Virginia, most families lived in the midst of severe poverty. The birthrate was very high; two-and-a-half times the overall U.S. rate and the same as India's. Living standards were low; the average family's purchasing power was about the same as a family in Malaysia. The typical house had just one or two rooms, and 60 percent of the reservation's dwellings had no electricity and 80 percent had no running water or sewers. Educational levels were low. The typical resident had completed just five years of school, and fewer than one adult in six had graduated high school.

During World War II Native Americans began to revolt against such conditions. In 1944 Native Americans formed the National Congress of American Indians (NCAI), the first major intertribal association. Among the group's primary concerns were protection of Indian land rights and improved educational opportunities for Native Americans. When Congress voted in 1953 to allow states to assert legal jurisdiction over Indian reservations without tribal consent and the federal government sought to transfer federal Indian responsibilities for a dozen tribes to the states (a policy known as "termination") and to relocate Indians into urban areas, the NCAI led opposition to these measures. "Self-determination rather than termination!" was the NCAI slogan. Earl Old Person, a Blackfoot leader, commented, "It is important to note that in our Indian language the only translation for termination is to 'wipe out' or 'kill off' . . . how can we plan our future when the Indian Bureau threatens to wipe us out as a race? It's like trying to cook a meal in your tipi when someone is standing outside trying to burn the tipi down."

By the late 1950s a new spirit of Indian nationalism had arisen. In 1959 the Tuscarora tribe, which lived in upstate New York, successfully resisted efforts by the state power authority to convert reservation land into a reservoir. In 1961 a militant new Indian organization appeared, the National Indian Youth Council, which began to use the phrase "Red Power" and sponsored demonstrations, marches, and "fish-ins" to protest state efforts to abolish Indian fishing rights guaranteed by federal treaties. Native Americans in the San Francisco Bay area in 1964 established the Indian Historical Society to present history from the Indian point of view, while the Native American Rights Fund brought legal suits against states that had taken Indian land and abolished Indian hunting, fishing, and water rights in violation of federal treaties. Many tribes also took legal action to prevent strip mining or spraying of pesticides on Indian lands.

The best known of all Indian Power groups was AIM, the American Indian Movement, formed by a group of Chippewas in Minneapolis in 1966 to protest alleged police brutality. In the fall of 1972, AIM led urban Indians, traditionalists, and young Indians along the "Trail of Broken Treaties" to Washington, D.C., seized the offices of the Bureau of Indian Affairs in Washington, D.C., and occupied them for a week in order to dramatize Indian grievances. In the spring of 1973, 200 heavily armed Indians took over the town of Wounded Knee, South Dakota, site of an 1890 massacre of 300 Sioux by the U.S. army cavalry, and occupied the town for 71 days.

Indians are no longer a vanishing group of Americans. The 1980 census recorded an Indian population of 1.38 million in the United States, 72 percent over the figure reported in 1970 and four times the number recorded in 1950. About half of these people live on reservations, which cover 52.4 million acres in 27 states, while most others live in urban areas. The largest Native American populations are located in Alaska, Arizona, California, New Mexico, and Oklahoma. As the Indian population has grown in size, individual Indians have claimed many accomplishments, including receipt of the Pulitzer Prize for fiction by N. Scott Momaday, a Kiowa.

Although Native Americans continue to face severe problems of employment, income, and education, they have demonstrated conclusively that they will not abandon their Indian identity and culture or be treated as dependent wards of the federal government.

Members of the American Indian Movement occupied the town of Wounded Knee, South Dakota, for over two months to focus attention on Native American grievances.

CHRONOLOGY OF KEY EVENTS

1960 Four black freshman at North Carolina Agricultural and Technical College in Greensboro, North Carolina, stage the first sit-in to protest segregation; Student Nonviolent Coordinating Committee (SNCC) is founded

1961 Congress of Racial Equality (CORE) stages freedom rides to expose segregation in transportation; *Mapp* v. *Ohio* holds that evidence obtained by unreasonable searches must be excluded at trial

1962 James Meredith enrolls at the University of Mississippi; Students for a Democratic Society (SDS) issue Port Huron Statement; Cesar Chavez begins to organize California farm workers

1963 George C. Wallace is inaugurated Alabama governor; Martin Luther King, Jr., leads demonstrations against segregation in Birmingham, Alabama; racial violence in the South leaves 10 people dead, 35 black homes and churches firebombed; Betty Friedan publishes *The Feminine Mystique*, helping launch a new feminist movement; Equal Pay Act, first federal law to prohibit sex discrimination, requires equal pay for identical work; *Gideon* v. *Wainright* holds that indigent defendants have a right to a court-appointed attorney; March on Washington, D.C., for civil rights and jobs; John F. Kennedy is assassinated; Lyndon Johnson becomes thirty-sixth president

1964 President Johnson announces War on Poverty; Manpower Development and Training Act and Economic Opportunity Act establish the Job Corps and Neighborhood Youth Corps; in *Escobedo* v. *Illinois*, Supreme Court rules that suspects being interrogated by police have a right to legal counsel; Civil Rights Act prohibits discrimination in employment and public facilities; Twenty-fourth Amendment prohibits poll taxes in federal elections

1965 Malcolm X is assassinated; Martin Luther King, Jr., leads demonstrations in Selma, Alabama, to bring issue of voting rights to national attention; Voting Rights Act prohibits literacy tests and sends federal examiners to seven southern states to register black voters; riot in Watts, predominantly black section of Los Angeles, results in 34 deaths; Medicare extends medical insurance to older Americans; Executive Order 11246 requires government contractors to prepare affirmative action plans; Ralph Nader publishes *Unsafe at Any Speed*

1966 SNCC and CORE embrace black nationalism; Black Panther party is organized; National Organization for Women is formed; Congress passes Model Cities Act to attack urban blight

1967 Riots take place in 127 cities

1968 Medicaid expanded to cover the medical expenses of the poor; assassination of Martin Luther King, Jr., in Memphis, Tennessee, is followed by riots in 168 cities

1971 In *Swann* v. *Charlotte-Mecklenburg Board of Education*, U.S. Supreme Court upholds school busing as a tool of racial integration

1973 *Roe* v. *Wade* decision legalizes abortion

1979 *Weber* "reverse-discrimination" case rules that employers could establish voluntary programs including quotas to aid minorities and women

1986 Immigration Reform and Control Act provides permanent legal residency to undocumented workers who have lived in United States since 1982

CONCLUSION

During the 1960s, many groups, including black Americans, women, Mexican-Americans, and Native Americans, struggled for equal rights. Early in the decade, black college students, impatient with the slow pace of legal change, staged sit-ins, freedom rides, and protest marches to challenge legal segregation in the South. Passionately committed to a philosophy of nonviolent direct action, these students suffered beatings and went to jail to achieve integration. Their efforts led the federal government to pass the Civil Rights Act of 1964, prohibiting discrimination in public facilities and employment, and the Twenty-fourth Amendment to the Constitution and the Voting Rights Act in 1965, guaranteeing black voting rights.

Despite significant legal gains, many black Americans felt a growing sense of frustration and anger. The violence perpetrated by white racists and a growing white backlash against civil rights led black nationalists to downplay the goal of integration and instead emphasize black political power, community control of schools, creation of black businesses, and black pride. Frustration also grew in urban ghettoes, where the black poor faced problems of poverty, unemployment, and de facto segregation that were not addressed by civil rights legislation. In the summer of 1965, black frustration erupted into violence in Watts, a predominantly black district of Los Angeles, and over the next three years, over 150 major riots occurred.

In a farreaching effort to reduce poverty, alleviate hunger and malnutrition, extend medical care, provide adequate housing, and enhance the employability of the poor, black and white, President Johnson launched his Great Society program in 1964. Although critics charged that federal public assistance food subsidies, health programs, and child care programs contributed to welfare dependence, family breakup, and an increase in out-of-wedlock births, the programs did succeed in cutting the proportion of families living in poverty in half.

The example of the civil rights movement inspired other groups to press for equal opportunity. The women's movement fought for passage of antidiscrimination laws, equal educational and employment opportunities, and a transformation of traditional views about women's place in society. Mexican-Americans battled for bilingual education programs in schools, unionization of farm workers, improved job opportunities, and increased political power. Native Americans pressed for control over Indian lands and resources, the preservation of Indian cultures, and tribal self-government.

SUGGESTIONS FOR FURTHER READING

OVERVIEWS AND SURVEYS

Taylor Branch, *Parting the Waters: America in the King Years* (1988); Wiliam H. Chafe, *Unfinished Journey*, 2d ed. (1991); Richard N. Goodwin, *Remembering America: A Voice from the Sixties* (1988); Godfrey Hodgson, *America in Our Time* (1976); Allen Matusow, *The Unraveling of America: A History of Liberalism in the 1960s* (1984); William O'Neill, *Coming Apart* (1971).

THE STRUGGLE FOR RACIAL JUSTICE

Sally Belfrage, *Freedom Summer* (1965); Michel Belknap, *Federal Law and Southern Order: Racial Violence and Constitutional Conflict in the Post-Brown South* (1987); Derrick Bell, *And We Are Not Saved: The Elusive Quest for Racial Justice* (1987); Jack Bloom, *Class, Race, and the Civil Rights Movement* (1987); Carl Brauer, *John F. Kennedy and the Second Reconstruction* (1977); Clayborne Carson, *In Struggle: SNCC and the Black Awakening of the 1960s* (1981); William H. Chafe, *Civilities and Civil Rights* (1980); Ronald P. Formisano, *Boston Against Busing: Race, Class, and Ethnicity in the 1960s and 1970s* (1991); David Garrow, *Bearing the Cross: Martin Luther King, Jr. and the Southern Christian Leadership Conference* (1986), and *The FBI and Martin Luther King* (1981); David R. Goldfield, *Black, White, and Southern: Race Relations and Southern Culture* (1990); Hugh Davis Graham, *The Civil Rights Era: The Origins and Development of National Policy* (1990); Vincent Harding, *There is a River: The Black Struggle for Freedom in America* (1981); Walter A. Jackson, *Gunnar Myrdal and America's Conscience: Social Engineering and Racial Liberalism* (1990); Richard Kluger, *Simple Justice: The History of the Brown v. Board of Education and Black America's Struggle for Equality* (1975); Steven Lawson, *Black Ballots* (1976), and *Running for Freedom: Civil Rights and Black Politics*

(1991): Nicholas Lemann, *The Promised Land: The Great Black Migration and How It Changed America* (1991); Doug McAdam, *Freedom Summer* (1988); August Meier and Elliot Rudwick, *CORE: A Study in the Civil Rights Movement, 1942–1968* (1973); Stephen Oates, *Let the Trumpet Sound: The Life and Times of Martin Luther King, Jr.* (1982); Frank R. Parker, *Black Votes Count: Political Empowerment in Mississippi* (1990); Thomas R. Peake, *Keeping the Dream Alive: A History of the Southern Christian Leadership Conference* (1987); Armstead L. Robinson and Patricia Sullivan, eds., *New Directions in Civil Rights Studies* (1991); Bernard Schwartz, *Inside the Warren Court* (1983); Howard Sitkoff, *The Struggle for Black Equality* (1981); Melvin I. Urofsky, *A Conflict of Rights: The Supreme Court and Affirmative Action* (1991), and *The Continuity of Change: The Supreme Court and Individual Liberties, 1953–1986* (1990); Nancy J. Weiss, *Whitney M. Young, Jr., and the Struggle for Civil Rights* (1989); John White, *Black Leadership in America*, 2d ed. (1990); Juan Williams, *Eyes on the Prize: America's Civil Rights Years* (1987); Eugene Wolfenstein, *The Victims of Democracy: Malcolm X and the Black Revolution* (1980); C. Vann Woodward, *Strange Career of Jim Crow*, 3d ed. (1974).

THE YOUTH REVOLT

Paul Buhle, *History and the New Left* (1990); Morris Dickstein, *Gates of Eden: American Culture in the Sixties* (1977); Todd Gitlin, *The Sixties* (1987), and *The Whole World Is Watching: The Mass Media in the Making & Unmaking of the New Left* (1980); Maurice Isserman, *. . . If I Had a Hammer: The Death of the Old Left and the Birth of the New Left* (1987); W. J. Rorabaugh, *Berkeley at War: The 1960s* (1989); Theodore Roszak, *The Making of a Counter Culture* (1969); Stanley Rothman and S. Robert Lichter, *Roots of Radicalism* (1982); Kirkpatrick Sale, *SDS* (1973); Jon Wiener, *Come Together: John Lennon in His Time* (1984).

LIBERATION MOVEMENTS

Rodolfo Acuña, *Occupied America*, 3d ed. (1988); Mary Jo Bane, *Here to Stay: American Families in the Twentieth Century* (1978); Mario Barrera, *Race and Class in the Southwest* (1979); Judith Barwick, *In Transition: How Feminism, Sexual Liberation, and the Search for Self-Fulfillment Have Altered America* (1979); Mary Frances Berry, *Why ERA Failed* (1986); Albert Camarillo, *Hispanics in a Changing Society* (1979); William H. Chafe, *Women and Equality* (1977); Andrew J. Cherlin, ed., *The Changing American Family and Public Policy* (1988); Sara Evans, *Personal Politics: The Roots of Women's Liberation in the Civil Rights Movement and the New Left* (1979); Victor R. Fuchs, *How We Live* (1983); Mario T. García, *Mexican Americans: Leadership, Ideology and Identity* (1989); Juan Gómez-Quiñones, *Chicano Politics* (1990); Hazel W. Hertzberg, *The Search for an American Identity* (1971); Judith Hole and Ellen Levine, *Rebirth of Feminism* (1971); Peter Iverson, *The Navajo Nation* (1981); Virginia Sánchez Korrol, *From Colonia to Community* (1983); Sar A. Levitan et al., *What's Happening to the American Family? Tensions, Hopes, Realities* (1988); Matt S. Meier and Feliciano Rivera, *The Chicanos* (1972); Steven Mintz and Susan Kellogg, *Domestic Revolutions: A Social History of American Family Life* (1988); Joan Moore and Harry Pachon, *Hispanics in the United States* (1985); Roger Nichols, *The American Indian: Past and Present*, 3d ed. (1985); David Popenoe, *Disturbing the Nest: Family Change and Decline in Modern Societies* (1988); Leila Rupp and Verta Taylor, *Survival in the Doldrums: The American Women's Rights Movement, 1945 to the 1960s* (1987).

CHAPTER 31

America in Our Time

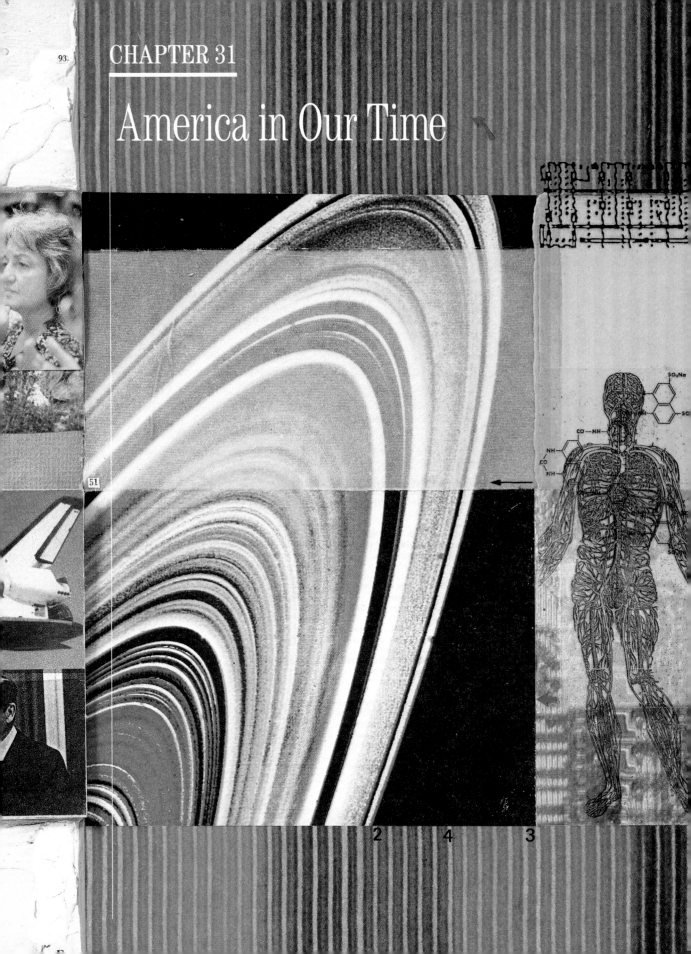

Shortly after 1 A.M. on the morning of June 17, 1972, Frank Wills, a security guard at the Washington, D.C., Watergate office complex, spotted a strip of masking tape covering the lock of a basement door. He removed it. A short while later, he found the door taped open again. He called the police, who found two more taped locks, and a jammed door leading into the offices of the Democratic National Committee. Inside they discovered five men carrying cameras and electronic eavesdropping equipment.

The White House press secretary soon dismissed the incident as a "third-rate burglary attempt," but the identities of the burglars suggested something more serious. One, James McCord, was chief security coordinator and electronics expert of the Committee for the Reelection of the President. Others had links to the CIA. Two of the burglars carried papers bearing the name Howard Hunt, a special White House consultant, and $6500, which was traced to President Nixon's campaign committee.

At first, the Watergate break-in seemed like a minor incident. But it set in motion a chain of events that eventually forced Richard Nixon to resign the presidency. Over the course of the next year, it became clear that the break-in was one of a series of secret operations coordinated by the White House and financed by illegal campaign contributions, operations which posed a threat to America's constitutional system of government.

The Watergate break-in had its roots in Richard Nixon's obsession with secrecy and political intelligence. In July 1970 he approved a plan to use the FBI, CIA, National Security Agency, and Defense Intelligence Agency to gather information on campus demonstrators, antiwar protestors, and other radicals, which involved opening personal mail and breaking and entering into offices and residences. FBI Director J. Edgar Hoover called the Huston plan (named after the plan's originator, Nixon aide Tom Huston) "clearly illegal," and it was rescinded. But the Nixon administration subsequently established a secret unit to carry out similar illegal activities.

To stop leaks of information to the press, in 1971 the Nixon White House assembled a team of "plumbers," consisting of former CIA operatives. This private police force, paid for in part by illegal campaign contributions, engaged in a wide range of criminal acts such as tapping the phones of officials and journalists suspected of handling leaked information; burglarizing the office of a psychiatrist consulted by Daniel Ellsberg, who had leaked the Pentagon Papers, a secret Pentagon history of the Vietnam War, to the press; and fabricating a State Department cable linking the Kennedy administration to the assassination of South Vietnam's President Diem.

In 1972 when President Nixon was running for reelection, his campaign committee authorized another series of illegal activities. It hired Donald Segretti to stage "dirty tricks" against potential Democratic candidates, which included mailing letters that falsely accused Senator Henry Jackson of homosexuality and fathering an illegitimate child. It considered a plan to use call girls to blackmail Democrats at their national convention and to kidnap anti-Nixon radical leaders. The committee also authorized $250,000 for intelligence gathering operations. Four times the committee sent burglars to break into Democratic headquarters.

The Watergate scandal led to the downfall of Richard Nixon. Here the Senate Watergate Committee questions Nixon aide H. R. Haldeman.

he did pardon Nixon. In the realm of economic policy, he began by urging tax increases and budget cuts and then called for a large tax cut. His energy policy was crippled by the same indecision. At first, he tried to raise prices by imposing import fees on imported oil and ending domestic price controls, then he abandoned that position in the face of severe political pressure.

Carter, too, suffered from the charge that he modified his stances in the face of political pressure. He came to office determined to cut military spending, calling for the abolition of nuclear weapons and the withdrawal of American troops from South Korea. By the end of his term, after Soviet forces occupied Afghanistan and Iran took several hundred American hostages, Carter spoke of the need for sustained growth in defense spending, upgrading nuclear forces in Europe, and developing a new strategic bomber.

Critics accused both Ford and Carter of substituting slogans for concrete policies—for Ford, WIN ("Whip Inflation Now"); for Carter, energy conservation as the "moral equivalent of war" ("meow" to the program's critics). Both were described as "passionless presidents," who failed to project a clear vision of where they wanted to lead the country. But in their defense, both faced serious problems, ranging from dealing with rising oil prices to confronting third-world terrorists.

On the domestic front, both lacked the political skills and the base of popular support necessary to get a coherent program through Congress. Both alienated the activist wings of their parties. Ford failed to win the support of Republican right wingers, who supported Ronald Reagan in the 1976 primaries; Carter failed to win over Democratic liberals, who favored Edward Kennedy in the 1980 primaries. Carter ran for the presidency by running against the Washington establishment, but once elected he seemed to lack the political acumen necessary to get his programs enacted, most notably SALT II, a second strategic arms agreement with the Soviet Union.

By the end of their presidencies, a growing number of Americans doubted that Ford and Carter had come to grips with the burdens of their office. Their triumphs did not inspire the nation; their failures provoked scorn. During his two-and-a-half years in office, Ford succeeded in healing the deep political divisions produced by Watergate, but his record in office failed to win the nation's confidence. During his single term, Carter negotiated peace between Israel and Egypt, normalized relations with China, improved American relations with Latin America, and placed a new emphasis on human rights in American foreign policy; but Americans were more concerned about double-digit inflation, interest rates approaching 20 percent, and Carter's failure to secure release of American diplomats held hostage in Iran.

WRENCHING ECONOMIC TRANSFORMATIONS

He is the personification of American business. His autobiography stood on the top of the best-seller list for years. A thick, powerful slab of a man, Lee Iacocca is the picture of a successful, confident American businessman. The irony of the picture is, of course, that Lee Iacocca is also the most visible symbol of the American automobile industry, which is in turn the most prominent example of the failure of American industry to compete in a changing world economy.

At one time, the car makers in Detroit produced automobiles that mirrored America's strength and power. They were big, heavy, powerful cars, with such expensive options as power windows, power brakes, and power steering. When an engineer at Chrysler designed a smaller, low-slung car, K. T. Keller, the

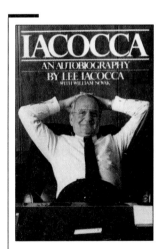

The cover of Lee Iacocca's autobiography portrays him as the consummate successful businessperson. Despite the decline in the American automobile industry, he put the ailing Chrysler company back on its feet.

company's top executive, remarked in disgust, "Chrysler builds cars to sit in, not to piss over." So what if they weren't energy efficient. So what if they only traveled 10 to 13 miles on a gallon of gas. Until 1973, gas was cheap; just 37 cents a gallon that year.

Detroit—the land of big cars, of General Motors, Ford, and Chrysler—was Iacocca's world. From 1946 to 1978 he worked for Ford, climbing the corporate ladder from salesman to zone manager, to district manager, to divisional head, to president of Ford. He was the driving force behind Ford's most popular car—the Mustang.

In 1978, Henry Ford II, the grandson of the company's founder, fired Iacocca. Iacocca lashed back: "Your timing stinks," he told Ford. "We've just made a billion eight for the second year in a row. That's three and a half billion in the past two years. But mark my words, Henry. You may never see a billion eight again. And do you know why? Because you don't know how the _____ we made it in the first place!"

In Iacocca's angry words there was more truth than perhaps he even realized. In the late 1970s, the American automotive industry had crashed into new economic realities. Although Middle Eastern oil had been inexpensive during the period between 1945 and the early 1970s, economic realities dictated that the price *must* eventually rise dramatically. Each year more and more nations entered the industrial ranks; each year the consumption of oil increased; each year the limited supplies of oil decreased. These simple economic facts combined with emerging Arab nationalism and the solidarity of the Organization of Petroleum Exporting Countries (OPEC) were bound to drive up the price of oil. As the price of a gallon of gas charged toward the dollar mark, American drivers purchased smaller, better engineered, fuel-efficient cars from Japan and Europe. By 1982, Japanese cars had captured 30 percent of the U.S. market.

Men like Iacocca looked to the government for help. After being fired from Ford, Iacocca accepted the top position at Chrysler. With the help of a $1.2 billion loan from Washington, he put the ailing company on its feet again.

Since 1973, the American economy has undergone a series of wrenching economic transformations. Economic growth slowed; productivity flagged; inflation rose; and major industries faltered in the face of foreign competition. Despite a massive influx of women into the work force, family wages stagnated. A quarter century of rapid post–World War II economic growth ended.

This economic slowdown was not confined to the United States; all major industrialized nations experienced slower economic growth. Annual growth in America's real national output per employed person averaged 1.8 percent between 1960 and 1973; it dropped to 0.1 percent between 1974 and 1978. Japan's rate fell from 8.9 percent during the first period to 3.2 percent in the second; West Germany's fell from 4.7 to 3 percent.

The causes of worldwide economic decline are hotly contested. It has been attributed to surges in world oil prices during the 1970s; to the growing expense of government policies designed to protect public health, safety, and the environment and to aid the poor; to alleged foreign "dumping" of products at prices below their cost of production; to demands of organized labor for higher wages; to low productivity increases in the expanding service sector; and to excessive government deficits.

If the causes of economic stagnation remain unclear, the social and political consequences have been profound—evident in a sharp influx of wives into the work force, tax revolts and demands for tax reform, and calls for protection of American industry.

The Age of Inflation

In 1967, the average price of a three-bedroom house was $17,000. A brand new Cadillac convertible went for $6700 and a new Volkswagen $1497. A portable typewriter cost $39 and a man's gray flannel suit $60. A Hershey chocolate bar sold for a nickel; a pound of sirloin for 89 cents; and a gallon of regular gasoline cost 39 cents. Two decades later, the prices of these products had quadrupled.

The upsurge in inflation started when Lyndon Johnson decided to fight the Vietnam War without raising taxes enough to pay for it. By 1968 the war was costing the United States $3 billion dollars a month, and the federal budget

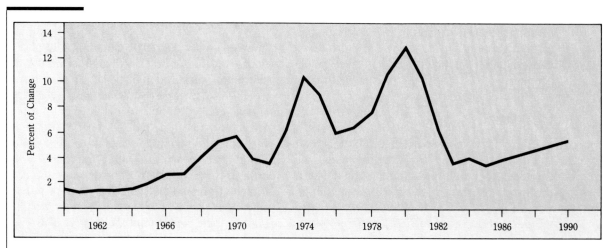

Figure 31.1
Consumer price index, 1960–1990

skyrocketed to $179 billion. With hundreds of thousands of Americans in the military service and even more working in defense-related industries, unemployment fell, wages rose, demand mushroomed, and government deficits increased. Inflation accelerated in the early 1970s as a result of a series of crop failures and sharp rises in commodities, especially oil.

High inflation had many negative effects on the American economy. It wiped out many families' savings. It provoked labor turmoil, as teachers, sanitation workers, auto workers, and others went on strike to try to win wage settlements ahead of inflation. It encouraged speculation in tangible assets—like art, antiques, precious metals, and real estate—rather than productive investment in new factories and technology. Above all, the effects of inflation seemed extremely unfair. Certain organized interest groups were able to keep up with inflation, while other less powerful groups, such as welfare recipients, saw the value of their benefits decline significantly.

This surge of inflation contributed to an abrupt reversal of a 20-year period of steady income growth. Inflation reduced the purchasing power of most Americans and pushed many into higher tax brackets.

Inflation raised the prices of virtually all goods and services, but it had a particularly large impact on two areas of the economy:

health care and housing, which experienced price rises far above the inflation rate. One result was a sharp increase in the number of Americans unable to afford health insurance. Another consequence was a sharp increase in the proportion of income that Americans spent on housing. For most of the post–World War II period, a family expected to spend 25 percent of its total income on housing, but by the 1980s six million American households were paying more than half their income on rent. An increase in homelessness was the most graphic symbol of this mounting housing problem.

For over a decade, family wages remained flat. The hourly wages of American workers peaked in 1973, the year of the first OPEC oil embargo. Wages flattened between 1973 and 1977, then fell sharply in 1978, 1979, and 1980. During the 1980s, real wages rose at a modest rate, but by the end of the decade they had climbed to just $36 over 1973 levels.

One consequence of shrinking paychecks was a rash of tax revolts. Traditionally Americans paid a much lower level of taxes than people in the rest of the industrialized world. After World War II, however, the level of taxation rose steadily. Between 1955 and 1988, taxes grew at twice the rate of household income. In 1955, a median family of four paid an average federal tax rate of 9 percent. By 1988, the rate was 24 percent. With paychecks squeezed by inflation, taxpayers revolted. California voters touched off the national tax revolt in 1978 with the passage of Proposition 13, which cut state taxes, capped public spending, and curtailed public services.

Oil Embargo

Political unrest in the oil-rich Middle East contributed significantly to America's economic troubles. After suffering a humiliating defeat at the hands of Israel in the 1973 "Yom Kippur" war, Arab leaders unsheathed a new political weapon: oil. In order to pressure Israel out of territory conquered in the 1967 and 1973 wars, Arab nations cut oil production 25 percent and embargoed all oil exports to the United States. Leading the struggle was OPEC, which had been founded by Iran, Saudi Arabia, and Venezuela in 1960 to fight a reduction in prices by oil companies.

Because Arab nations controlled 60 percent of the proven oil reserves in the non-Communist world, they had the western nations over a barrel. Production cutbacks produced an immediate global shortage. The United States imported a third of its oil from Arab nations; western Europe imported 72 percent from the Middle East; Japan, 82 percent.

Gas prices rose, and long lines formed at gas pumps. President Nixon asked Americans to forego outdoor Christmas displays and to reduce thermostats to 68 degrees. Some factories shortened the work week and some shopping centers restricted business hours.

The Arab struggle for higher oil prices began in 1970, when the ruler of Libya, Col. Muammar Qaddafi, launched a bitter, ten-month battle for high oil royalties. As a result, he was able to increase Libya's oil royalties by 120 percent within two years—from $1 a barrel to $2.20 a barrel.

The oil crisis brought to an end an era of cheap and ample energy. Americans had to learn to live with smaller cars and less heating and air conditioning. But the crisis did have a positive side effect. It increased public consciousness about the environment and stimulated awareness of the importance of conservation. But for millions of Americans the lessons were painful to learn.

Foreign Competition and Deindustrialization

It was January 17, 1949. Standing idly on the dock, waiting for work to begin, several longshoremen snickered in disbelief. The car looked ridiculously un-American. Tiny and ugly, it resembled half a walnut shell with wheels, or better yet, an insect, a "bug," a "beetle." Ben Pon, the official Volkswagen agent to the United States, was aboard the Dutch freighter *Westerdam* in New York Harbor, holding a press conference to introduce the VW to American consumers. He called the car the "Victory Wagon," but skeptical reporters dubbed it "Hitler's car." It was. A generation of American moviegoers remembered seeing it in 1930s newsreels touting Germany's economic recovery. But how could it ever appeal to Americans? The Volkswagen was slow, dull, small, and fuel efficient, just when Americans were lusting after fins, scoop grilles, and chrome—lots of chrome. In 1949 Americans purchased 6,250,000 new automobiles. Two were VWs. The longshoremen were right, but not for long. They were laughing at the future.

In 1947, the United States was truly the world's factory. Half of all the world's manufacturing took place in the United States. Americans made 57 percent of the world's steel and 80 percent of the world's cars. It was inevitable that other countries would eventually challenge American manufacturers. Still, the experience was painful for millions of Americans. During the early 1960s, foreign manufacturers produced 6 percent of the cars purchased by Americans. That figure climbed to 10.6 percent in the late 1960s, 15 percent in the early 1970s, and 20 percent in the late 1970s. The decline in the American share of the market meant fewer jobs in the American automobile, steel, and rubber industries.

The foreign penetration extended far beyond the market for compact cars. Foreign countries began to dominate the highly profitable, technologically advanced fields, such as consumer electronics, luxury automobiles, and machine tools. Americans discovered that technologies their country had pioneered—such as semiconductors, color televisions, and video cassette recorders—were now produced almost exclusively by foreign manufacturers.

Few economic developments aroused as much public concern during the 1970s as the loss of American jobs in basic industry. Between mid-1975 and early 1981, 24 tire plants shut down in the United States, resulting in 20,000 lost jobs. Since the early 1970s, the steel industry eliminated the jobs of over 120,000 steelworkers. During the 1970s General Electric reduced its U.S. employment by 25,000; RCA cut its U.S. employment by 14,000. According to one estimate, 30 million jobs disappeared during the 1970s as the direct result of plant, store, and office shutdowns.

The decline of basic industry had a high human cost. Displaced workers saw their savings depleted, mortgages foreclosed, and health and pension benefits lost. Even when they found new jobs, they typically had to settle for wages substantially below what they had earned before. Plant shutdowns and closings had profound effects on entire communities, which lost their tax bases at the time that they needed to fund health and welfare services.

American jobs were lost in basic industry principally because the same goods could be produced in foreign countries at a far lower cost. American and even Japanese companies shifted low-skill production work to such places as South Korea, Taiwan, Hong Kong, Singapore, and Indonesia where they paid much lower wages.

The decline of the nation's major industries also had profound political consequences. It has led to demands for protective tariffs, quotas, and voluntary limitations on imported goods, including steel, autos, and shoes. It has also led to proposals to restrict foreign investment by American companies, and to ensure that goods sold domestically contain a certain minimum proportion of American-produced components. The steel industry received protection from foreign competition beginning in 1969. Japanese automakers agreed to voluntarily restrict exports to the United States in 1981.

Whipping Stagflation

During the 1960s, the primary goal of economic policy was to encourage growth and keep unemployment low. Inflationary pressures were successfully tamed through "jawboning" industry leaders and unions to keep prices and wages stable. But by the early 1970s the economy started to suffer from *stagflation*—high unemployment and inflation coupled with stagnant economic growth. This presented economic policymakers with a new and perplexing problem. Stagflation contradicted the last 40 years of Keynesian economic experience. Unemployment and inflation usually did not coexist. When unemployment was high, prices had been stable or even declining. Policymakers could increase government spending, reduce taxes, and expand the money supply—all of which augmented consumer purchasing power and created jobs—without having to worry about creating an inflation problem. When inflation had been the problem, jobs were plentiful. Policymakers could raise taxes, trim government spending, and contract the money supply, reducing consumer demand and the upward pressure on prices without producing a recession. The object was to maintain full employment (defined as 96 percent employment) and keep inflation under 2 percent a year. But how to attack both inflation and unemployment at the same time? This was the question that presidents Nixon, Ford, and Carter had to address.

The problem with stagflation was the pain of its options. To attack inflation by reducing consumer purchasing power only made unemployment worse. The other choice was no better. Stimulating purchasing power and creating jobs also drove prices higher. Not surprisingly, economic policy during the 1970s was a nightmare of confusion and contradiction.

By 1971, pressures produced by the Vietnam War and federal social spending, coupled with increase in foreign competition, pushed the inflation rate to 5 percent and unemployment to 6 percent. President Richard Nixon responded by increasing federal budget deficits and devaluing the dollar. These policies were an attempt to stimulate the economy and to make American goods more competitive overseas. Nixon also imposed a 90-day wage and price freeze to curb inflation. The freeze was followed by a mandatory set of wage-price guidelines, and then by voluntary controls. Inflation stayed at about 4 percent during the freeze, but once controls were lifted, inflation resumed its up-

(Text continues on p. 1062)

AMERICA AND THE WORLD
THE POLITICS OF OIL

This photo of a mass of derricks, typical of early oil drilling operations, in the Spindletop oil fields of Texas was taken during the heyday of oil production in the early twentieth century. When consumption outpaced production, the search for new reserves led to offshore sites. The oil platform pictured here is in the Gulf of Mexico off the coast of Louisiana.

The modern era of oil production began on August 27, 1859, when Edwin L. Drake drilled the first successful oil well—69 feet deep—near Titusville in northwestern Pennsylvania. Just 5 years earlier, the invention of the kerosene lamp had ignited an intense demand for oil. By drilling an oil well, Drake had hoped to meet the growing demand for oil for lighting and lubrication.

Drake's success inspired hundreds of small companies to explore for oil. In 1860, world oil production reached 500,000 barrels; by the 1870s production soared to 20 million barrels annually. In 1879, the first oil well was drilled in California; and in 1887, in Texas. But as production boomed, prices fell and oil industry profits declined.

In 1882, John D. Rockefeller devised a solution to the problem of unbridled competition in the oil fields: the Standard Oil trust, which brought together 40 of the nation's leading refiners. Through its control of refining, Standard Oil was temporarily able to control the price of oil.

During the early twentieth century, oil production continued to climb. By 1920, oil production reached 450 million barrels annually—prompting fear that the nation was about to run out of oil. Government officials predicted that the nation's oil reserves would last just 10 years.

Up until around 1910, the United States produced between 60 and 70 percent of the world's oil supply. As fear grew that American oil reserves were dangerously depleted, the search for oil turned worldwide. Oil was discovered in Mexico at the beginning of the twentieth century, in Iran in 1908, in Venezuela during World War I, and in Iraq in 1927. Many of the new oil discoveries occurred in areas dominated by Britain and the Netherlands: in the Dutch East Indies, Iran, and British mandates in the Middle East. By 1919, Britain controlled 50 percent of the world's proven oil reserves.

After World War I, a bitter struggle for control of world oil reserves erupted. The British, Dutch, and French excluded American companies from purchasing oil fields in territories under their control. Congress retaliated in 1920 by adopting the Mineral Leasing Act, which denied access to American oil reserves to any foreign country that restricted American access to its reserves. The dispute was ultimately resolved during the 1920s, when American oil companies were finally allowed to drill in the British Middle East and the Dutch East Indies.

The fear that American oil reserves were nearly exhausted ended abruptly in 1924, with the discovery of enormous new oil fields in Texas, Oklahoma, and California. These discoveries, along with production from new fields in Mexico, the Soviet Union, and Venezuela, combined to drastically depress oil prices. By 1931, with crude oil selling for 10 cents a barrel, domestic oil producers demanded restrictions on production in order to raise prices. Texas and Oklahoma passed state laws and stationed militia units at oil fields to prevent drillers from exceeding production quotas. Despite these measures, prices continued to fall.

In a final bid to solve the problem of overproduction, the federal government stepped in. Under the National Recovery Administration (NRA), the federal government imposed production restraints, import restrictions, and price regulations. After the Supreme Court declared the NRA unconstitutional, the federal government imposed a tariff on foreign oil.

During World War II, the oil surpluses of the 1930s quickly disappeared. Six billion of the seven billion barrels of petroleum used by the allies during the war came from the United States. Public officials again began to worry that the United States was running out of oil.

It seemed imperative that the United States secure access to foreign oil reserves. Increasingly, policymakers and the oil industry focused their attention on the Middle East, particularly the Persian Gulf, which they believed would become the center of postwar oil production. As early as the 1930s, Britain had gained control over Iran's oil fields and the United States discovered oil reserves in Kuwait and Saudi Arabia. After World War II ended, Middle Eastern oil production surged upward. Gradually, American dependence on Middle Eastern oil increased.

During the 1950s, a combination of cheap fuel and a burgeoning consumer culture led to an orgy of consumption. With only 6 percent of the world's population, the United States accounted for one-third of global oil consumption. Foreign oil was so cheap that coal-burning utilities made the expensive shift to oil and natural gas. World oil prices were so low that Iranian, Venezuelan, and Arabian oil producers banded together in 1960 to form OPEC, the Organization of Petroleum Exporting Countries, a producers' cartel, to negotiate for higher oil prices.

By the early 1970s, the United States depended on the Middle East for one-third of its oil. Foreign oil producers were finally in a position to raise world oil prices. The oil embargo of 1973 and 1974, during which oil prices quadrupled, and the oil crisis of 1978 and 1979, when oil prices doubled, graphically illustrated how vulnerable the nation had become to foreign producers.

The oil crises of the 1970s had an unanticipated side effect. Rising oil prices stimulated conservation and exploration for new oil sources. As a result of increasing supplies and declining demand, oil prices fell from $35 a barrel in 1981 to $9 a barrel in 1986. This sharp slide in world oil prices was one of the factors that led Iraq to invade neighboring Kuwait in 1990, in a bid to gain control over 40 percent of Middle Eastern oil reserves.

In the century-and-a-half since Edwin L. Drake drilled the first oil well, the history of the oil industry has been a story of vast swings between periods of overproduction, when low prices and profits led oil producers to devise ways to restrict output and thereby raise prices, and periods when oil appeared to be on the brink of exhaustion, stimulating a global search for new sources. This cycle may now be approaching an end, as world oil supplies may truly be reaching their natural limits. With proven world oil reserves anticipated to last fewer than 40 years, the era of oil production that began near Titusville may be coming to an end. In the years to come, the search for new sources of oil will be transformed into a quest for entirely new sources of energy.

ward climb, leading Nixon to impose another 60-day wage and price freeze in June 1973.

In 1974 during the first oil embargo, inflation hit 12 percent. Gerald Ford, the new president, initially attacked the problem in a traditional Republican fashion, tightening the money supply by raising interest rates and limiting government spending. He also unveiled in 1975 his WIN ("Whip Inflation Now") program and urged Americans to wear WIN lapel buttons. In the end, WIN proved to be no more than a series of ineffectual wage and price guidelines monitored by the federal government. In the subsequent recession, unemployment reached 9 percent.

When Jimmy Carter took office in January, 1977, 7.4 percent of the work force was unemployed. Carter responded with an ambitious spending program and called for the Federal Reserve (the Fed) to expand the money supply. Within two years, inflation had accelerated to 13.3 percent.

With inflation getting out of hand, Paul Volcker, the chairman of the Federal Reserve Board, announced that the Fed's primary goal would be to fight inflation by restraining the growth of the money supply. Unemployment increased and interest rates moved to their highest levels in the nation's history. Volcker was convinced that wringing inflation out of the economy required a prolonged period of substantial unemployment. In November 1982 the so-called Volcker recession reached a painful climax. Unemployment hit 10.8 percent, the highest since 1940. One out of every five American workers went some time without a job and poverty had increased from 13 percent of the population (or 29.3 million in 1980) to 15 percent in 1982 (34.4 million). But interest rates had fallen, inflation was down, and the stock market was bullish.

Along with high interest rates, the Carter administration adopted another weapon in the battle against stagflation: deregulation. Convinced that rather than protecting consumers, regulators too often protected the industries they were supposed to oversee, the Carter administration deregulated air and surface transportation and the savings and loan industry (the Reagan administration would deregulate telecommunications).

Declines in exports and increases in imports continue to trouble U.S. industry in the 1990s.

The effects of deregulation are hotly contested. Rural towns suffered cutbacks of bus, rail, and air service. Truckers and rail workers lost economic benefits of regulation. Travelers complained about rising air fares and congested airports. Cable TV viewers resented rising rates. Champions of deregulation argued that the policy increased competition, stimulated new investment, and forced inefficient firms either to become more efficient or shut down.

A NEW AMERICAN ROLE IN THE WORLD

In his inaugural address in 1961, John Kennedy made a famous pledge: "Let every nation know, whether it wishes us well or ill, we shall pay any price, bear any burden, meet any hardship, support any friend or oppose any foe to assure the survival and the success of liberty."

By 1973, in the wake of the Vietnam War, American foreign policymakers regarded Kennedy's stirring pledge as unrealistic. The Vietnam War offered a lesson about the limits of American power. It underscored the need to distinguish between vital national interests and peripheral interests, and to balance America's military commitments with its limited resources. Above all, the Vietnam War appeared to illustrate the dangers of obsessive anti-Communism. Such a policy failed to recognize the fact that the world was becoming more complex, that power blocs were shifting, and that the interests of Communist countries and the United States could sometimes overlap. Too often, American policy seemed to have driven nationalists and reformers into Communist hands and to have led the United States to support corrupt, unpopular authoritarian regimes.

The great challenge facing American foreign policy makers was how to preserve the nation's international prestige and influence in the face of declining defense budgets and mounting congressional opposition to direct overseas intervention.

Détente

As president, Richard Nixon radically redefined America's relationship with its two foremost adversaries, China and the Soviet Union. In a remarkable turnabout from his record of staunch anti-Communism, he opened relations with China and began strategic arms limitation talks with the Soviet Union. The goal of this policy, known as *détente* (the easing of tensions between nations), was to continue to resist and deter Soviet adventurism while striving for "more constructive relations" with the Communist world.

Nixon and Henry Kissinger, the German-born former Harvard professor who served as assistant for national security affairs and later secretary of state, believed that it was necessary to curb the arms race, improve great power relationships, and learn to coexist with Communist regimes. In Kissinger's view, American foreign policy of the 1950s and 1960s rested on "an outmoded foreign policy concept": an ideological commitment to contain communism. His goal was to shift the focus of American policy away from a moralistic anti-Communism to issues of national interest. The Nixon administration sought to use the Chinese and Soviet need for western trade and technology as a way to extract foreign policy concessions.

The new direction of American foreign policy was inaugurated in 1971 when the Nixon Administration made the first overtures to China. Since 1949 U.S. policy recognized the Jiang Jieshi regime on Taiwan as the legitimate government of China and refused to recognize the Chinese Communist government. In 1972 Nixon took part in a summit meeting in Beijing, walked the Great Wall, and slowly expanded American trade with China (see Chapter 29 for a fuller discussion of Nixon's foreign policy).

Less dramatic, but no less important, was the beginning of a détente with the Soviet Union, culminating in a massive trade pact and strategic arms limitation talks. In a 1972 summit meeting in Moscow, the United States and Soviet Union vowed not to seek "unilateral advantages" against each other.

Recognizing that one of the legacies of Vietnam was a reluctance on the part of the American public to risk overseas interventions, Nixon and Kissinger also sought to build up regional powers that shared American strategic interests, most notably China, Iran, and Saudi Arabia.

By the late 1970s, an increasing number of Americans regarded the Nixon-Kissinger strategy of détente, strategic arms limitation, and support of regional superpowers as a failure. A growing number of Americans believed that the Soviet hardliners viewed détente as a mere tactic to lull the West into relaxing its vigilance. Soviet Communist party chief Leonid Brezhnev reinforced this view in 1976 when he told the Twenty-fifth Communist Party Congress: "We make no secret of the fact that we see détente as the way to create more favorable conditions for peaceful socialist and Communist construction." He also announced what came to be known as the "Brezhnev Doctrine," that the Soviet Union was prepared to intervene anywhere if "bid by our revolutionary conscience, our Communist convictions" and that it was the Soviet Union's right to support "the struggle of other peoples for freedom and progress." The Soviet leader boasted of gains that his country had made at the United States's expense—in Vietnam, Angola, Cambodia, Ethiopia, and Laos.

An alarming Soviet arms buildup contributed to the sense that détente was not working.

By 1975, the Soviet Union had 50 percent more intercontinental ballistic missiles (ICBMs) than the United States, 30 times as many antiaircraft missile launchers, 3 times as many army personnel, 3 times as many attack submarines, and 4 times as many tanks. The United States continued to have a powerful strategic deterrent, holding a 9000 to 3200 advantage in deliverable nuclear bombs and warheads. But the gap between the countries was narrowing.

Superpower Battlegrounds

By the end of the 1970s détente had been overcome by a revived cold war. During the late 1970s the Middle East, Africa, and the Near East all emerged as arenas for superpower conflict. In southern Africa, a major problem was the unwillingness of whites to yield power to their countries' black majorities. In Rhodesia Henry Kissinger succeeded in persuading 274,000 whites to peacefully transfer majority rule to the nation's 6.1 million blacks. In

Angola, a former Portuguese colony, 13,000 Cuban troops helped install a Communist government.

In the Middle East the United States achieved a tremendous diplomatic success by negotiating peace between Egypt and Israel. Since the founding of Israel in 1948, Egypt's foreign policy had been built around destroying the Jewish state. The two countries seemed to divide their time between fighting wars and planning to fight wars. The fighting resulted in an enlarged Israel and a weakened Egypt. Then in 1977, Anwar el-Sadat, the practical and far-sighted leader of Egypt, decided to seek peace with Israel. To demonstrate that his intentions were sincere, he even traveled to Israel and spoke with the Israeli Knesset. It was an act of rare political courage, for Sadat risked alienating Egypt from the rest of the Arab world without a firm commitment for a peace treaty with Israel.

Although both countries wanted peace, major obstacles had to be overcome. Sadat wanted

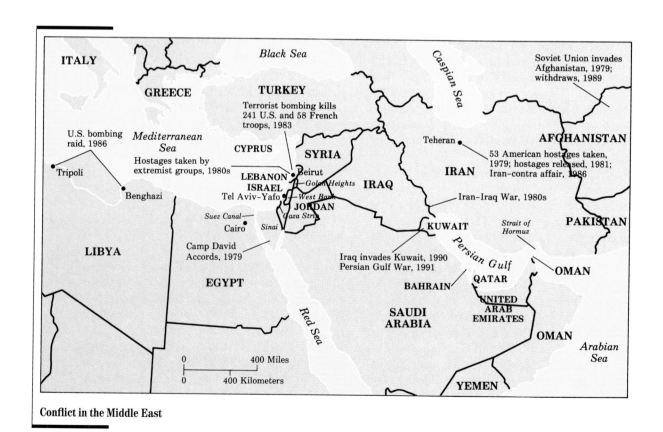

Conflict in the Middle East

Ronald Reagan is a man of many paradoxes. A staunch conservative, he is the only American president to have served as president of a union; he was also a founding member of such liberal organizations as Americans for Democratic Action and United World Federalists. A strong defender of traditional family values, he was the first divorced person to become president. A leading opponent of abortion, he signed one of the nation's first laws legalizing abortion while governor of California.

When he was elected president in 1980, he was already well known to the American people as a movie actor and radio and television announcer. He had risen to celebrity from extremely modest beginnings. His shoe-salesman father drank and gambled, and young Reagan grew up in a succession of small Illinois towns—Tampico, where he was born on February 6, 1911, Galesburg, Monmouth, and Dixon. To help support his family, he worked as a lifeguard, and is credited with rescuing 70 drowning people. In order to attend Eureka College, a 250-student Disciples of Christ school, he washed dishes. As a freshman he led a weeklong student strike that forced college officials to rescind cuts in the educational program.

He graduated in 1932, in the depths of the depression, and eventually became a sportscaster at radio station WHO in Des Moines. His ultimate goal, however, was Hollywood, and in 1937 he received a screen test at Warner Brothers and landed a $200 a week contract. He eventually made 50 movies but never became a major star. "I became the Errol Flynn of the B's," he said. He became identified with one role: George Gipp, the Notre Dame halfback, in *Knute Rockne, All American* (1940), whose dying words were "win one for the gipper." After World War II, with his movie career winding down, he was elected to six terms as president of the Screen Actors Guild. In 1954, he turned to television, hosting "GE Theater" and "Death Valley Days."

In politics, he started out as a self-described "hemophiliac bleeding-heart liberal," who staunchly supported Franklin D. Roosevelt and the New Deal. As head of the Screen Actors Guild, however, he became concerned about Communist infiltration of the labor movement in Hollywood. "Then I discovered at first hand the cynicism, the brutality, the complete lack of morality of their positions and the cold-bloodedness of their attempt, at any cost, to gain control of that industry." In 1948 he supported Harry Truman, but in 1952 and 1956, he voted for Dwight Eisenhower and in 1960 he led Democrats for Nixon.

Reagan was catapulted into the national political spotlight in 1964 when he gave an emotional television speech in support of Republican nominee Barry Goldwater, denouncing big government, foreign aid, welfare, urban renewal, and high taxes. Two years later, he successfully ran for governor of California as a "citizen politician." Declaring that there are simple answers to the state's problems, he took office in 1967 promising to cut state spending by ten percent, reduce welfare costs, and crack down on student protesters. In fact, during his eight years as governor, state spending and taxes nearly doubled and state aid to schools and local services rose substantially. But he did slow the growth of state employment, required able-bodied welfare recipients to take job training courses or perform public service work, and left his successor a $500 million budget surplus.

In the 1980 presidential campaign, Reagan drew strong support from white Southerners, suburban Catholics, the nation's 40 million evangelical Christians, and particularly the New Right, a confederation of disparate political and religious groups bound together by their concern over what they considered the erosion of values in America. He truly captured the nation's imagination in March 1981 when an assassin's bullet nearly killed him. Reagan responded to the shooting with remarkable courage. From his hospital bed, he sent a message to his wife Nancy, "Honey, I forgot to duck."

Reaganomics

When President Reagan took office he promised to cut inflation, rebuild the nation's defenses, restore economic growth, and trim the size of the federal government by limiting its role in welfare, education, and housing. He pledged to end exorbitant union contracts to make American goods competitive again, to drastically cut taxes to stimulate investment and purchasing power, and to decontrol businesses strangled by federal regulation in order to restore competition. If in his eight years in office Reagan did not achieve his complete agenda—his policies trimmed little from the size of the federal government, failed to make American goods competitive in the world market, and led to increased consolidation rather than competition—many Americans believed that his ecomonic policies had improved the country's many economic problems.

Reagan blamed the country's economic ills on declining capital investment and a tax structure biased against work and productive investment. To stimulate the economy, he persuaded Congress to slash tax rates. In 1981, he pushed a bill through Congress cutting taxes 5 percent in 1981 and 10 percent in 1982 and 1983. In 1986, the administration pushed through another tax bill, which substantially reduced tax rates on the wealthiest Americans to 28 percent, while closing a variety of tax loopholes.

In a symbolic attack on inflationary wage increases, Reagan, in August 1981, dismissed 15,000 striking air traffic controllers, breaking their union and dealing a devastating blow to organized labor. Union leaders condemned the firings, but in an antiunion atmosphere most Americans backed Reagan. His popularity ratings soared.

To strengthen the nation's defenses, the Reagan administration doubled the defense budget, even with adjustments for the rate of inflation. Between 1981 and 1987, the defense budget jumped from $165 billion a year to more than $330 billion. Reagan believed that a militarily strong America would not have been humiliated by Iran and would have discouraged Soviet adventurism.

To "liberate free enterprise from fifty years of liberal Democratic restraints," Reagan expanded the Carter administration's efforts to decontrol and deregulate the economy. In 1982, Congress deregulated the banking industry and lifted ceilings on interest rates. Federal price controls on airfares were lifted as well. In 1983, Congress deregulated the natural gas industry. The Department of Transportation postponed the application of federally mandated passive restraint systems and fuel efficiency standards for automobiles; the Environmental Protection Agency relaxed its interpretation of the Clean Air Act; and the Department of the Interior opened up large areas of the federal domain, including offshore oil fields, to private development.

The results of deregulation were mixed. Bank interest rates became more competitive, but smaller banks found it difficult to hold their own against larger institutions. Natural gas prices increased once decontrol set in, but so did production, easing some of the country's dependence on foreign fuel. Airfares on high-traffic routes between major cities dropped dramatically in the 1980s when price controls were lifted, but fares for short, low-traffic flights skyrocketed. Most critics agreed, however, that deregulation had restored some short-term competition to the marketplace. Yet in the long term, competition also led to increased business failures and consolidation.

The urge for deregulation carried over to Reagan's social programs. Convinced that federal welfare programs promoted "acceptance of indolence, promiscuity, easy abortion, casual attitudes toward marriage and divorce, and maternal indifference to child-rearing responsibilities," Reagan halted the growth of social welfare programs and limited benefits to those

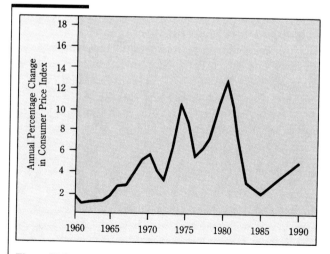

Figure 31.2
Inflation, 1960–1990

he considered the "truly needy." The Reagan administration curtailed spending on a variety of social welfare programs. Between 1981 and 1984, spending on Aid to Families with Dependent Children was reduced 13 percent; food stamps, 13 percent; child nutrition, 28 percent; job training for young people, 53 percent; programs to prevent child abuse, 12 percent; and mental health services, 26 percent. The Reagan administration also eliminated cash welfare assistance for the working poor, reduced federal subsidies for child care services for low-income families, and cut grants used to pay for the regulation of child care programs. A symbol of Reagan social service cuts was an attempt by the Agriculture Department in 1981 to allow ketchup to be counted as a vegetable in school lunches.

Reagan left office with the economy in the midst of its longest post–World War II expansion. The economy was growing faster, with less inflation, than any time since the mid-1960s. Adjusted for inflation, disposable personal income per person rose 20 percent after 1980. Inflation fell to less than 4 percent. Unemployment was down to around 5 percent. These figures compared favorably to January 1981, the month Reagan became president, when inflation was running at 13 percent a year and unemployment stood at 7.4 percent.

Reagan's critics, however, charged that Reagan had only created the illusion of prosperity. They denounced the massive federal budget deficit, which increased $1.5 trillion during the Reagan presidency, three times the debt accumulated by all 39 of Reagan's presidential predecessors. They decried the growing income gap between rich and poor, as well as the expensive consequences of reduced government regulation, such as cleaning up federal nuclear weapons facilities, and, especially, bailing out the nation's savings and loans industry. This last problem, however, would fall to Reagan's successor as president, George Bush.

The Celebration of Wealth

In 1981, the year Ronald Reagan was inaugurated as president, ABC television introduced the smash hit "Dynasty," a show celebrating glamour and greed. It was, in the eyes of many

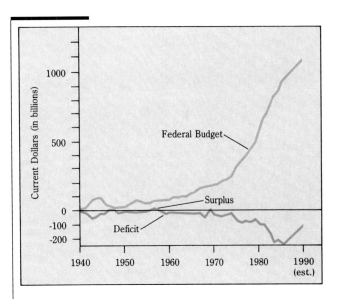

Figure 31.3
U.S. budget deficits, 1940–1990

social commentators, an appropriate beginning for the 1980s—a decade of greed, selfishness, and an anything-goes attitude. It was a decade when financier Ivan Boesky claimed, "Greed is not a bad thing. You shouldn't feel guilty"; when Nancy Reagan spent $25,000 on her inaugural wardrobe and $209,508 on new White House china; when the circulation of *Money* magazine climbed from 800,000 to 1.85 million; when the prime-time soap opera about the super-rich, "Dallas," reached number one in the ratings; and when Madonna had a pop music hit entitled "Material Girl." On television advertisers told consumers, "Yes, you can have it all, you deserve it all, all for you, yes . . ." President Reagan's message was similar. Americans could have it all—low taxes, a strong defense, and middle-class entitlements.

Michael Milken, a financial wizard at the investment banking firm of Drexel Burnham Lambert, personified the "go-go" spirit of the "roaring eighties." After graduating from the Wharton School in 1969, Milken joined Drexel at a salary of $25,000 a year. Milken was convinced that the stock market valued many corporations for far less than the worth of the company's assets. By using low-grade, risky "junk bonds" to finance corporate acquisitions, cor-

(Text continues on p. 1074)

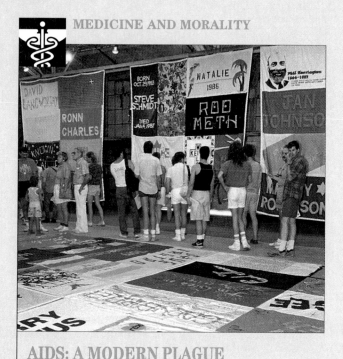

AIDS: A MODERN PLAGUE

Americans have long debated what to do about sexually transmitted disease (STD). Health officials have insisted that STD is a medical problem that should be handled like any other communicable disease: through research, treatment, public education, and the vigorous application of modern techniques of epidemiology. Others have argued that STD is primarily a moral problem.

World War I brought the issue to a head. Army planners debated whether to concentrate on trying to prevent STD through educational propaganda against extramarital sex (accompanied by a crackdown on red-light districts), or whether to sanction the use of condoms and focus on medical treatment to cure infection. In the end, they elected to combine both approaches. Moreover, when the identical problem

reappeared in World War II, the government promptly adopted the same solution: scary propaganda against extramarital sex, followed by condoms and treatment for soldiers who surrendered to temptation. Even the debate over treatment sounded like an echo. The discovery of penicillin precipitated another round of arguments over whether this new "wonder drug" should be given to soldiers who contracted STD, and the dispute was settled exactly as it had been in World War I: Wayward souls received treatment.

Following World War II, public funding for STD work rose and the number of cases fell. The victory over STD, however, proved to be short-lived, for the infection rates tripled between 1950 and 1975. What happened? In part, health officials were victims of their own

success. Given the power of new antibiotics, doctors stopped worrying as much about the social behavior that led to transmission, and they became less vigilant in their efforts to track down the partners of infected patients. Yet the doctors were not solely to blame. The public's apathy was reflected in reduced health budgets for STD work.

The lull ended in the 1980s with the appearance of acquired immune deficiency syndrome (AIDS), the most terrifying disease of modern times. As early as 1980, physicians began reporting a strange medical phenomenon among gay men. Patients from these groups were falling prey to fatigue, a puzzling combination of infections, a rare skin cancer known as Kaposi's sarcoma, and eventual death. No one recovered from the disease.

After prolonged and ill-funded research, AIDS was finally linked to a retrovirus, which scientists named the "human immunodeficiency virus," or HIV. Additional research soon revealed AIDS cases among heterosexuals, Haitians, hemophiliacs, and intravenous drug users, indicating that the disease was not limited to a single group; rather, it threatened everyone. But why did it take so long to mobilize research efforts and public awareness? The explanation lies in long-standing attitudes about STD.

First and foremost, AIDS was widely regarded as a "gay" disease, and homosexuals were a favorite target of the "new right" and the "moral majority," whose political clout had helped put Ronald Reagan in the White House. Patrick Buchanan, White House director of communications, proclaimed that homosexuals had "declared war on nature, and now nature is extracting an awful retribution." By the time the United States finally took notice of AIDS in 1987, more than 21,000 Americans had died from the disease. Part of the reason lay in President Reagan's cutbacks in domestic programs: AIDS became another casualty of Reaganomics, another victim of the administration's hostility to social services. In the end, however, a series of shocking events forced the government to act: These included the discovery of AIDS-contaminated hospital blood supplies; the appearance of AIDS in heterosexuals; and the surprisingly bold anti-AIDS campaign of Surgeon General C. Everett Koop.

Koop recommended AIDS education for school children "at the earliest date possible," and he further advocated the promotion and use of condoms. Conservatives were outraged and charged the government with attempting to promote immorality. But Koop and other public health officials held firm. The government sponsored television and radio commercials warning the public against "unsafe sex" and mailed an explicit brochure on AIDS to every household in America.

As the public's concern rose, various groups demanded that AIDS sufferers be quarantined. Though health authorities repeatedly stressed that casual contacts could not spread the disease, many people feared the worst. The objections of civil libertarians, who opposed quarantine, left them cold, as did the arguments of those who rejected quarantine on practical grounds. (Where were tens of thousands of AIDS sufferers to be kept? Who was to pay for their care during this forced isolation?) While these arguments kept any serious movement for quarantine from developing, the public remained edgy. Some parents withdrew their children from schools where AIDS patients were enrolled, and AIDS sufferers found that many of their co-workers wanted them removed from their jobs.

Yet some of the reactions to AIDS within the gay community were no less extreme. Granted, most gay leaders struggled from the outset to publicize AIDS and to promote safe sex and monogamous relationships. But other gays reacted with denial. Some initially believed (or chose to believe) that AIDS was a heterosexual propaganda tactic designed to crush the nascent gay movement. To many, gay liberation meant not merely toleration of homosexuality but a celebration of sexuality, a reordering of values with greater emphasis on the long-suppressed pleasure principle. Multiple and unprotected contacts were the final necessary step to political freedom. Others proclaimed that AIDS could never hit them. And still others became resigned and carried on as usual. In the gay community they became known as Doris Days, after the actress famous for singing "*Que será, será.*"

The end of the AIDS story cannot be written, for no one can predict the impact this deadly disease will have on American society. To date (1992), more than 60,000 Americans have been diagnosed with the disease, more than 33,000 have died from it, and another 1.5 million are believed to be infected. With a cure nowhere in sight, medical authorities expect to be confronted by literally hundreds of thousands of AIDS patients by the turn of the century. Their care will be both protracted and expensive. Who will pay for it?

Despite these grim realities, sex researchers report few changes in the public's private behavior, especially in those groups that are at high risk for contracting the disease. Though hard data are lacking, the experts agree that "unsafe sex" remains a common practice among adolescents and young adults, and the same holds true for many gays, particularly those who are just becoming sexually active. Thus, even in the midst of this terrifying plague, modern-day health authorities, like their progressive ancestors, have found it difficult to modify behavior in order to prevent venereal infections. And like the progressives, many Americans today will no doubt continue to place their hopes on education and on the search for new medical advances with which to eradicate AIDS, debating all the while whether those who contract the disease should be pitied or condemned.

porate raiders or takeover artists purchased and then dismantled companies for a huge profit. In 1987, Milken earned $550 million by financing acquisitions.

The Reagan years witnessed a corporate merger and takeover boom of unprecedented proportions. In one Milken-backed raid, Texas oilman T. Boone Pickens threatened to acquire Gulf Oil in 1984. To get rid of Pickens, Gulf paid the oilman $400 million. The culmination of the boom occurred when Kohlberg, Kravis, Roberts and Co. purchased RJR Nabisco for $24.9 billion.

During the 1980s, 100,000 Americans became millionaires every year and the average earnings of the top 20 percent of the population rose $9000 a year after inflation. The earnings of the bottom 20 percent, however, fell $576 to $8800. In addition, many of the new jobs created during the Reagan years were in the low-wage service industries.

By the early 1990s, there were signs that the time had come to pay for the financial excesses of the 1980s. Following a 508-point fall in the Dow Jones industrial average on October 19, 1987—a 22.6 percent plunge—many Wall Street stock brokerage firms began to lay off employees, cutbacks which continued despite the market's recovery. In 1989, Milken, his brother Lowell, and a former Drexel employee were indicted on 98 counts of criminal racketeering, securities fraud, and other crimes. The next year, Drexel Burnham Lambert agreed to pay a fine of $650 million and filed for bankruptcy. Wall Street speculator Ivan Boesky was fined $100 million for insider trading and sentenced to jail. Those Americans who had participated in the ambition, greed, vanity, and excess of the eighties seemed to be getting their comeupance. Capturing the popular mood, the 1989 film *Wall Street* follows the downfall of Gordon Gekko, a figure based on men like Milken and Boesky. At his height of power, Gekko asserts, "Greed . . . is good. Greed is right. . . . Greed—mark my words—will save . . . the U.S.A." In the film's end, however, greed landed Gekko in prison.

The Reagan Doctrine

During the early years of the Reagan presidency, Cold War tensions between the Soviet Union and the United States intensified. Reagan entered office deeply suspicious of the Soviet Union. During the 1980 presidential campaign he described communism as "a form of insanity [that] is contrary to human nature" and said that détente "has been a one-way street that the Soviets have used to continue moving toward the Marxist goal of a socialist, one world state."

In September 1983, a few months after President Reagan had described the Soviet Union as "an evil empire" and called for a space-based missile defense system—Star Wars—a Soviet fighter shot down Korean Airlines flight 007 that had strayed into Soviet airspace, killing all 269 passengers on board. This incident intensified superpower conflict and set the stage for other confrontations.

Reagan and his advisors tended to view every regional conflict through a Cold War lens. Nowhere was this more true than in the Caribbean and Central America. He was determined not to allow a Communist government to take power in the Caribbean, Mexico, or Central America. Fidel Castro's successful revolution in Cuba in 1959, and his subsequent alignment

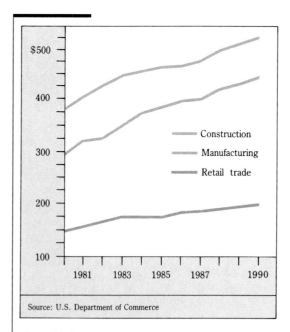

Figure 31.4
Weekly earnings, 1980–1990

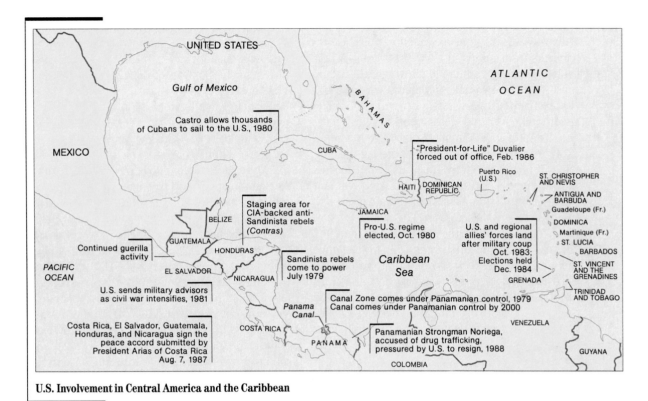

U.S. Involvement in Central America and the Caribbean

with the Soviet Union, had created serious problems for the United States, and Reagan was not about to allow it to happen again.

In October 1983 Prime Minister Maurice Bishop of Grenada, a small island nation in the Caribbean, was assassinated and a more radical Marxist government took power. Soviet money and Cuban troops came to Grenada, and when they began constructing an airfield capable of landing large military aircrafts, the Reagan administration decided to overthrow the Communists and restore a pro-American regime. On October 25 American troops invaded Grenada, killed or captured 750 Cuban soldiers, and established a new government. Although most Latin American nations condemned the invasion as "Yankee imperialism," the Grenadans themselves approved the American humbling of the "Marxist thugs." The invasion, however, sent a clear message throughout the region that the Reagan administration would not tolerate communism in its hemisphere.

In his 1985 state of the union address, President Reagan spelled out the "Reagan Doctrine" in foreign policy: American support for anti-

Communist revolutions. "We must not break faith with those who are risking their lives on every continent from Afghanistan to Nicaragua to defy Soviet-supported aggression."

In Afghanistan, the United States provided aid to anti-Soviet freedom fighters, ultimately helping to force Soviet troops to withdraw. It was in Nicaragua, however, that the Reagan doctrine received its most controversial application.

In 1979 Nicarguans revolted against the corrupt Somoza regime. A new junta took power, dominated by young Marxists known as Sandinistas. The Sandinistas insisted that they favored free elections, nonalignment, and a mixed economy, but once in power they postponed elections, forced opposition leaders into exile, and turned to the Soviet bloc for arms and advisors. For the Reagan administration, Nicaragua looked "like another Cuba," a clearinghouse for the exportation of Marxism and revolution to El Salvador, Guatemala, and Honduras.

In his first months in office, President Reagan approved covert training of anti-Sandinista rebels (called "contras"), some of whom were former members of the Somoza National Guard. While the contras waged war on the Sandinistas from camps in Honduras, the CIA provided assistance, mining Nicaraguan harbors and issuing a manual offering ways of assassinating Sandinistas. In 1984 Congress ordered an end to all covert aid to the contras.

The Reagan administration circumvented Congress by soliciting contributions for the contras from private individuals and from foreign governments seeking U.S. favor. The president also permitted the sale of arms to Iran, with profits diverted to the contras. The arms sale and transfer of funds to the contras were handled surreptitiously through the CIA intellegence network, apparently with the full support of CIA director William Casey. Exposure of the Iran-Contra Affair in late 1986 threatened the Reagan presidency and provoked a major congressional investigation. The ensuing scandal seriously weakened the influence of the president.

The American preoccupation with Nicaragua began to subside in 1987, after President Oscar Arias Sanches of Costa Rica proposed a regional peace plan. In national elections in 1990, the Nicaraguan opposition routed the Sandinistas, bringing an end to ten turbulent years of Sandinista rule.

Controversy and unrest arose in the Reagan administration when no one would accept responsibility for the Iran-contra affair.

A Remarkable Ideological Turnaround

Following the accession of Mikhail Gorbachev to power in the Soviet Union in March 1985, Cold War tensions began to ease. Only five years after denouncing the Soviet Union as "the focus of evil in the modern world," President Reagan began to make peace with the Soviet Union, offering concessions that made it possible to conclude a treaty eliminating intermediate range nuclear weapons and to begin negotiations on a strategic arms reduction treaty.

It was the rise to power of a new Soviet leader that helped ease Reagan's visceral anti-Communism. In 1982, 75-year-old Soviet party leader Leonid Brezhnev died. His regime had been marked by growing stagnation, corruption, and a huge military buildup. His successor, Yuri V. Andropov, former KGB head, died after only 15 months in power and was replaced by Konstantin U. Chernenko, a Brezhnev loyalist, who died just a year later. His successor was Mikhail S. Gorbachev, a 54-year-old agricultural specialist with little formal experience in foreign affairs.

Gorbachev pledged to continue his predecessors' policies, but within weeks he called for sweeping political liberalization—*glasnost*—and economic reform—*perestroika*. Within a year of his election as Communist party general secretary, Gorbachev solidified control over the Soviet state by removing almost half of the directors of ministries and state commissions and top leaders in Central Committee politics.

During the late 1980s, Mikhail Gorbachev reshaped world politics. East-West confrontations were replaced by negotiations. The arms race slowed down and there was a trend toward arms control and disarmament. In 1989, old-style rulers were deposed in Eastern Europe in a wave of revolutions. For his accomplishments, he was awarded the 1990 Nobel Peace Prize.

Within the Soviet Union Gorbachev brought, in George Bush's words, "historically significant change, both political and economic." He allowed wider freedom of press, assembly, travel, and religion, and permitted churches across the country to reopen. He persuaded the Communist party leadership to end its constitutionally guaranteed monopoly on power; created the Soviet Union's first working legislature; allowed the first nationwide competitive elections in 1989; and freed hundreds of political prisoners, largely ending persecution for political views.

In an effort to boost the sagging Soviet economy, he legalized small private business cooperatives, won parliamentary approval for the leasing of lands to individuals with the right of inheritance, and approved foreign investment within the Soviet Union.

In foreign policy, he abandoned the traditional Soviet aim of parity with the United States, the commitment to a protective chain of satellite nations in Eastern Europe, and the Brezhnev doctrine of military intervention in Communist countries. He cut the Soviet defense budget, withdrew 115,000 Soviet troops from Afghanistan, unilaterally pulled 500,000 Soviet troops and 10,000 tanks out of Europe, agreed to let a unified Germany become a member of NATO, and agreed with the United States to destroy short-range and medium-range nuclear weapons.

He stimulated settlement of conflicts in Angola, Namibia, Cambodia, and Nicaragua. Most dramatically, Gorbachev actively promoted the democratization of the countries of Eastern Europe, easing their transformation from satellite states into budding new democracies.

The Reagan Revolution in Perspective

Ronald Reagan was the first president since Andrew Jackson to complete two terms in office and then hand power over to a successor from his own political party. He dampened inflation, restored public confidence in government, and presided over the beginning of the end of the Cold War. He left office more popular than he arrived.

His critics, however, derided him as a "Dr. Feelgood" who reassured Americans with a "narcotic of cheerfulness" while problems accumulated. Reagan's critics were particularly concerned about his economic legacy. While inflation eased, unemployment fell, and the gross national product doubled from $2.7 trillion to $5.3 trillion, the national debt tripled, from $909 billion to almost $2.9 trillion, soaking up savings, causing interest rates to rise, depressing local economies, and forcing the federal government

In order to stimulate the Soviet economy, Mikhail Gorbachev launched his program of *perestroika*, or economic restructuring, which welcomed foreign investment and encouraged joint ventures with foreign businesses. *Perestroika* permitted U.S. businesses, like this American pizzeria, to operate in Moscow.

to shift more and more expensive responsibilities onto the states. During Reagan's years in office, interest on the federal debt doubled to 14 percent of the federal budget—more than the combined budgets of the Agriculture, Commerce, Education, Energy, Interior, Justice, Labor, State, and Transportation departments. Corporate and individual debt also soared. During the 1990s, the American people consumed $1 trillion more goods and services than they produced. The United States also became the world's biggest debtor, as a result of a weak dollar, a low level of exports, and the need to borrow abroad to finance budget deficits. By 1990 foreign holdings in the United States amounted to $1.5 trillion, compared with $1.2 trillion in U.S. assets abroad.

President Reagan's critics also charged that he starved vital social welfare programs for funds and was insensitive on racial issues. On national television, he had disparaged civil rights leaders for "doing very well [by] keeping alive the feeling that they're victims of prejudice." He had also opposed extending the scope of the 1965 Voting Rights Act, and in 1982 he approved tax-exempt status for private schools accused of racial discrimination (a practice overruled by the Supreme Court a year later).

The Last Presidential Campaign of the Cold War

In the presidential election of 1984, Ronald Reagan and Vice President George Bush won in a landslide over Walter Mondale and Geraldine Ferraro, the first woman nominated for vice president on a major party ticket. In 1988, however, the Democrats seemed to have a good shot at winning the White House, with the Soviet threat diminishing and the militant antigovernment, antitax sentiment of the late 1970s subsiding.

The Republican candidate, Vice President George Bush, was said to have the best resume in Washington. The son of a Connecticut banker and senator, Bush attended prep school at Andover and joined the military on his eighteenth birthday, winning the Distinguished Service Cross during World War II. After the war, he made a fortune in the Texas oil business, and then he went to Washington where he served as a representative, ambassador to the United Nations, envoy to China, and director of the CIA. His Democratic opponent, Massachusetts governor Michael Dukakis, was a serious, hardworking son of Greek immigrants.

Mudslinging and personal invective are nothing new in American politics, but the 1988 campaign was unusually vacuous and cynical. There were real differences between the candidates—over health care, housing policy, foreign policy, and defense spending—but these differences were submerged in a battle over character, abortion, prison furloughs, school prayer, and patriotism. The most emotional issue of the campaign involved the Pledge of Allegiance. Seizing on Governor Dukakis's veto of a 1977 Massachusetts bill requiring teachers to lead their classes in the pledge, Vice President Bush suggested that his opponent's liberalism led him to place civil liberties above patriotism. "Should public-school teachers be required to lead our children in the Pledge of Allegiance?" Bush asked his audience at the Republican convention. "My opponent says no—but I say yes."

The 1988 presidential campaign dramatized a development that had been reshaping American politics since the late 1960s: the growing power of media consultants and pollsters, who market candidates much as cigarette manufacturers or soap companies sell their products, by emphasizing imagery and symbolism. Republican handlers portrayed the Democrats as fiscally irresponsible, soft on defense, and purveyors of the notion that America was in decline, while picturing the GOP as the party of patriotism, low taxes, and vigilant anti-Communism. Democrat strategists, in turn, argued that the Republicans reduced taxes for the wealthy while transferring responsibility for national problems like drugs, homelessness, education, pollution, and a decaying infrastructure to the states. At the end of a race that saw both candidates use negative campaigning, Bush was elected the forty-first president of the United States, with 56 percent of the popular vote.

THE BUSH PRESIDENCY

Presidents' inaugural addresses often set the tone for their entire terms in office. At his inauguration, Jimmy Carter stressed the limits of American power in the world: "We have learned that 'more' is not necessarily 'better,' that even our great nation has its recognized limits." Ronald Reagan set an entirely different tone in his inaugural address, in which he voiced his desire to reduce government's social welfare role: "Government is not the solution to our problem; government is the problem."

In his inaugural address, Bush signaled a departure from the avarice and greed of the Reagan era by calling for a "new engagement in the lives of others." He promised to be more of a "hands on" administrator than President Reagan, and he committed his presidency to creating a "kindler, gentler" nation, more sensitive and caring to the poor and disadvantaged.

In his first state of the union address, Bush

repeated his call for new initiatives to address the nation's social problems. His vision for America was a society where "there's a job for everyone who wants one;" where "women working outside the home can be confident their children are in safe and loving care." He called for new legislation to ensure a clean environment, equal opportunity for the disabled, aid to the homeless, and drug-free streets and schools. The challenge he confronted as president was to address many long-ignored problems in the face of a deficit-ridden federal budget and a $3 trillion federal debt.

A Kindler, Gentler Nation

During his first years in office, President Bush and the Democratic-controlled Congress addressed many issues ignored during the Reagan years. For the first time in eight years, the federal government raised the minimum wage from $3.35 to $4.25 an hour. Between 1981, when it was last raised, and 1989, inflation had eroded the value of the minimum wage by 27 percent. For the first time in 13 years, Congress amended federal air pollution laws in order to reduce noxious emissions from smokestacks and tailpipes and reduce acid rain. For the first time since 1971, Congress considered child care legislation, and ultimately voted to provide subsidies to low-income families to defray the costs of child care. In other actions, Congress prohibited job discrimination against the disabled, required nutrition labeling on processed foods, and expanded immigration into the United States.

In two areas critics accused President Bush of reneging on his promise of a "kindler, gentler" nation. He vetoed a new civil rights bill bolstering protections for minorities and women against job discrimination, on the grounds that it would lead to quotas, and he also vetoed a bill that would have provided up to six months of unpaid family leave for workers with newly born or adopted children or emergencies. In November 1991, however, Bush signed a compromise Civil Rights Act, which made it easier for workers to win antidiscrimination lawsuits.

Economic Policy

Many Americans believed that the end of the Cold War would bring a huge peace dividend, which could be used to reduce the federal budget deficit and fund domestic social programs. Soon after Bush took office, however, Americans learned that much of the peace dividend would have to be spent to clean up nuclear wastes produced at federal facilities and to bail out the nation's troubled savings and loan industry—at an estimated cost between $325 billion and $500 billion.

The roots of the savings and loan crisis were planted during the presidency of Jimmy Carter, when high inflation and high interest rates threatened to bankrupt savings institutions. With their resources tied up in long-term home mortgages, the savings institutions could not compete with other financial institutions permitted to pay high interest rates.

A 1980 law lifted limits on the interest rates savings institutions could pay and allowed them to make a limited amount of investments in commercial real estate. In 1982 and 1983, when President Reagan was in the White House, Congress broadened the institutions's capacity to make unsecured commercial loans and investments in commercial real estate. In the mid-1980s, falling oil prices led to a collapse of land values especially in Texas, California, and the Southwest, creating huge losses for savings institutions invested in real estate. By the end of the decade these institutions began to fail in large numbers. The mounting bills for the savings and loan bailout propelled President Bush in 1990 to violate his 1988 "no new taxes" campaign pledge.

Foreign Policy

Every president since John F. Kennedy—with the single exception of Jimmy Carter—has felt it necessary early in his administration to assert American interests with the unilateral use of force. George Bush was no exception. The first important foreign policy act of the Bush administration was an invasion of Panama, which the Pentagon called Operation JUST CAUSE. The origins of the conflict stretched back to 1987 when a high Panamanian military official accused strong-man General Manuel Antonio Noriega of committing fraud in the 1984 presidential election and of drug trafficking. Violent street demonstrations broke out in Panama. Angry Panamanians called for Noriega's overthrow. Noriega responded by declaring a state of emergency. The crisis escalated when two Florida grand juries indicted the general on charges that he protected and assisted the Medellín drug cartel.

U.S.-Panamanian relations deteriorated further when Noriega voided results of the 1989 presidential election and sent paramilitary forces into the streets of Panama City where they beat up opposition candidates. Conflict grew imminent when Noriega declared his country in a "state of war" against the United States. A day later four unarmed American military personnel were fired on at a roadblock by Panamanian troops, and one American was killed. Bush dispatched a force of 10,000 troops to safeguard the lives of Americans and protect the integrity of the Panama Canal treaties. It is estimated that between 300 and 800 Panamanian civilians and military personnel died during the invasion. There were 23 American casualties. In the end, however, Noriega was forced out of power and deported to the United States to stand trial for drug trafficking.

United States troops patrol the streets of Panama City during the U.S. invasion of Panama in December 1989.

Collapse of Communism

The collapse of Communist regimes in Eastern Europe dominated the world scene as the 1990s began. On New Year's Day, 1989, Communist parties held power in Czechoslovakia, East Germany, Hungary, Poland, Bulgaria, and Romania. Czechoslovakia was run by an aging brutal dictatorship that imprisoned noted writers like Vaclav Havel and stripped dissidents of their jobs. Romania was ruled by dictator Nicolae Ceausescu, perhaps the most corrupt and brutal of the Eastern European dictators. For 28 years, the Berlin Wall had stood as the symbol of the division of Europe, a reinforced concrete and barbed-wire scar that separated the East from the West. By the year's end, the Berlin Wall had been smashed and Eastern European Communist parties had collapsed.

Across Eastern Europe, citizens took to the streets and overthrew 40 years of Communist rule. Like a series of falling dominos, from Poland and East Germany in the north to Hungary and Czechoslovakia in the middle to Romania and Bulgaria in the south, Communist parties

fell from power. In Poland, Solidarity, a party and union founded by shipyard workers, won a landslide victory over Communists in parliamentary elections and established Poland's first non-Communist government since World War II. In Hungary, the Communist party disbanded, reconstituting itself as a Socialist party, and rewrote the Hungarian constitution to allow independent parties to contest free elections.

Tens of thousands of East Germans, seeking passage to West Germany, escaped across the Hungarian-Austrian border, while protestors demanded reforms in the largest antigovernment demonstrations in that nation's history. As a result East German Communist party chief Erich Honecker was ousted. Almost exactly a year later, East and West Germany were reunified.

Popular protests in East Germany and Hungary inspired 30,000 Czechoslovakians to demonstrate in Prague. Riot police brutally crushed the peaceful demonstration, clubbing and tear-gassing hundreds of people. This led more than 200,000 people to take to the streets in Prague and other cities, demanding free elections and resignations of hard-line Communist leaders. As a result, Czechoslovakia's top Communist leadership resigned, and on December 29, 1989, Vaclav Havel was elected president.

In Bulgaria, hard-liner Todor Zhivkov, long-time Communist party chief, was ousted and replaced by a moderate, Petar Mladenov. Then, in the largest protest since Bulgaria became a Communist nation, 50,000 people in Sofia demanded free elections, respect for human rights, and an end to 45 years of police repression.

In Timisoara, Romania, thousands of people were killed in protests against the Communist government. Then, in what appears to have been more of a coup than a revolution, Romanian Communist leader Nicolae Ceausescu was executed and a new government took power, promising free elections.

The speed and the success of the Eastern European revolutions surprised Westerners. To be sure, millions of Eastern Europeans had long hoped for fundamental changes. Poles and Hungarians had fought and died for change in 1956, as had Czechs in 1968. Throughout the 1980s Solidarity had pressed for change in Poland. The economic failure of communism was clear to millions of people living in Eastern Europe. They realized that each year they fell further behind the West economically. But the political leaders in Eastern Europe ruled confidently, knowing that the Soviet Union, backed by the Red Army, would always send in the tanks when the forces for change became too great.

Mikhail Gorbechev changed the 40-year pattern. At the same time as he moved toward reform within the Soviet Union and détente with the West, he pushed the conservative regimes of Eastern Europe outside his protective umbrella. No more Red Army, no more tanks to the rescue. Eastern European leaders had long expected the unexpected, but they had never bargained on a liberal Soviet leader. One authority on the region observed, "Eastern European leaders were left on their own with nothing between them and their subjects except the most incriminating thing of all: their own record." And it was a record on which no leader would care to run for office.

Gorbachev, who had wanted to reform communism, had not anticipated the swift swing toward democracy in Eastern Europe. Nor had he fully foreseen the impact that democracy in Eastern Europe would have on the Soviet Union. By 1990 leaders of several Soviet repub-

lics began to demand independence or greater autonomy within the Soviet Union. The Baltic republics of Lithuania, Latvia, and Estonia wanted to leave the Soviet Union. The republic of Russia, led by its president Boris Yeltsin, also demanded greater autonomy, if not outright independence. The republics of the Ukraine and Moldavia, as well as several of the southern republics, similarly voiced discontent with the traditional political arrangement of the Soviet Union.

Gorbachev had to balance the growing demand for radical political change within the Soviet Union with the demand by Soviet hard-liners that he dam the new democratic currents and turn back the clock. It was a near impossible task. Faced with dangerous political opposition

For nearly three decades the Berlin Wall was the most visible symbol of the Cold War and of the division between East and West. The most dramatic incident marking the end of the Cold War was the destruction of the Wall in November 1989.

(Text continues on p. 1084)

AMERICA AND THE WORLD
THE END OF TWO ERAS

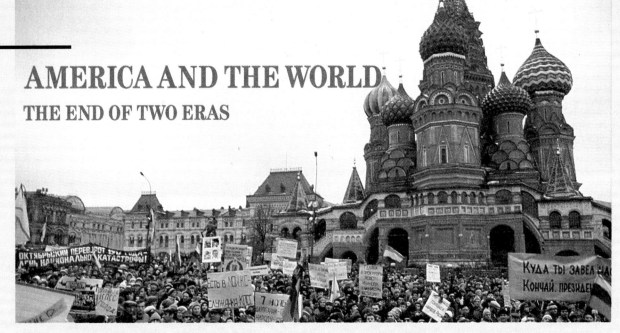

On November 7, 1990, on the anniversary of the 1917 revolution that brought Lenin to power, demonstrators in Moscow gathered to protest Communist rule.

The dates on the obituary read 1922 to 1991. When the death was duly recorded in newspapers and magazines throughout the world only a handfull of bureaucrats mourned the corpse. That body—the Union of Soviet Socialist Republics (USSR)—was the light that failed. Born in the cold and ice of a late Russian December, the USSR promised equality and justice. Driven by the belief in communism, Vladimir Lenin, the leader of the Bolsheviks who came to power in Russia in 1917 and founded the USSR five years later, announced that Russia was only the first step. Eventually, he said, communism would free the entire world and introduce a new epoch of peace, prosperity, and happiness for all people. The epoch never arrived. It remained only in the minds of the true believers. Instead of liberating the world, Soviet leaders suppressed freedom inside the Soviet Union. As one journalist noted in his obituary of the Soviet Union, "There is no reason to mourn the death of a country that killed millions of its own citizens in the collectivization campaign, the purges and the famines that were used as an instrument of government policy."

Born in a brutal Russian winter, the USSR died in an equally severe winter. About the death there was a singular note of irony. The Soviet leader who had done the most to reform and humanize the country caused its death. Mikhail Gorbachev became the leader of the Soviet Union in 1985. He was relatively young—in 1980 he had become the youngest full member of the Politburo, the ruling body in the USSR—and very well educated. He knew that every year his country was falling further and further behind the west in every material sense. Determined to correct the slide, he introduced measures to restructure the Soviet economy (*perestroika*) and to create a new political openness (*glasnost*). His economic measures never worked, but his political initiatives worked all too well. First, Eastern Europe used the new openness to break away from the Soviet orbit. Then, the USSR's Baltic republics of Lithuania, Latvia, and Estonia demanded and received independence. Finally, the remaining 12 republics of the Soviet Union decided that the union was unworkable and undesirable. Gorbachev attempted to hold the republics together but failed. On Christmas Day, 1991, he faced the reality that the Soviet Union no longer existed and resigned from office.

The Soviet newspaper *Tzvestia* commented that Gorbachev "did all he could." Perhaps no leader could have kept the Soviet Union from breaking apart once liberalization had started. Political freedom was singularly out of step with Soviet political traditions. But Gorbachev did fail in several areas. A man who had risen through the Soviet bureaucracy, Gorbachev failed to significantly reform or abolish that bureaucracy even though it became clear that that very bureaucracy was the primary obstacle to *perestroika*. In addition, he never devised a plan to allow enough freedom in the individual republics, and he even tacitly permitted Soviet security forces to use tanks and guns to suppress the Baltic independence movements. But most importantly, Gorbachev's *perestroika* did not work because it did not bring a new era of prosperity to the Soviet Union. Gorbachev admitted that "the old system fell apart even before the new system began to work," but as one authority commented, "there was no new system." Like every Soviet leader since Lenin, Gorbachev promised far more than he delivered.

The death of the Soviet Union posed immense problems both for the newly independent republics and the United States. Even before Gorbachev's resignation, 11 of the 12 remaining republics—only the republic of Georgia was excluded—joined together into a new confederation called the Commonwealth of Independent States. Led by the republics of Russia, Belorussia, and Ukraine, the new entity was more an alliance than a state. The republics agreed to cooperate in economic reforms aimed at moving them toward a free enterprise system and maintain at least temporarily the ruble as the common currency. Further, and without being very specific, they announced that the Commonwealth would coordinate economic, military, and foreign policies of its independent members. Central to the Commonwealth, however, was the idea that each member was and remained a sovereign nation. To underscore this idea, the Commonwealth located its capital in Minsk rather than Moscow, the seat of Soviet power, or St. Petersburg, the capital of czarist Russia.

From the first, the Commonwealth faced a difficult task. Disputes quickly arose over how to divide the military and economic resources of the old Soviet Union. The sovereign republics had to decide how to divide the forces and equipment of the Red Army and the Soviet Navy as well as the Soviet state treasury, central television network, space infrastructure, and the hundreds of other assets once controlled by the Soviet Union. As a symbol of the great change, in February 1992 the Commonwealth Olympic team competed in the Albertville Winter Games under the Olympic flag and their victories were marked by the playing of the Olympic anthem.

Even more pressing than the decision on how to divide Soviet property was the conversion to a limited free-market system. In early 1992 the Commonwealth lifted most price controls and the cost of goods shot upward. The prices of such basic commodities as bread and gasoline, over which some controls still existed, tripled or quadrupled literally overnight. The prices of noncontrolled items increased much more. A kilo of *kolbasa* sausages was 2.20 rubles in January 1991; the price rose to 43.75 rubles (and as high as 200 rubles in particularly hard-pressed St. Petersburg) in January 1992. The ruble itself experienced the shock. The official exchange used to be 1.8 per dollar; in January 1992 the exchange rate rose to well over 100 rubles per dollar. The economic changes created severe hardships for people whose monthly income averaged 400 rubles. Many citizens of the Commonwealth considered the winter of 1992 as the worst in their lives.

The death of the Soviet Union also had a profound effect on the United States. On one level the United States had to redirect its foreign policy. The era of the Cold War was over. The Soviet Union, America's Cold War rival, no longer existed. President George Bush responded to the changes by announcing victory in the Cold War, recognizing the new independent republics, and sending aid to the beleaguered members of the Commonwealth. Although Americans continued to worry about who controlled the Commonwealth's nuclear weapons, there was no longer the fear of war between the Soviet Union and the United States.

On another level, the end of the Cold War undermined one of the organizing principles of American culture. American mass culture in particular revolved around the idea of "us" and "them." Throughout the Cold War era Hollywood made successful movies that played on this theme. From such movies as *I was a Communist for the FBI*, *My Son John*, *Dr. Strangelove*, *Fail Safe*, *Red Alert*, and *On the Beach* to the James Bond action pictures and John Wayne westerns, Cold War issues provided the explicit or implicit basis for the films. Not to be outdone, popular writers capitalized on Cold War themes. John Le Carre, William F. Buckley, Jr., and Tom Clancy wrote best-sellers that centered on Cold War plots. Television also pitted "us" against "them" on numerous programs. During the 1960s "The Man from U.N.C.L.E.," "Mission Impossible," and "I Spy" were popular programs that featured Cold War stories. Even sports were influenced by the Cold War. In particular, the Olympic Games reflected Cold War tension and anxieties. American cheers of "U.S.A., U.S.A." at Olympic events became ritualistic Cold War chants.

American education and science similarly were partial hostages to the Cold War. After the success of the Soviet *Sputnik* in 1957, Congress appropriated funds for the establishment of the National Aeronautics and Space Administration (N.A.S.A.) and passed the National Defense Education Act. In the Cold War the space race and education became highly political issues. President John F. Kennedy's decision to push America's space program toward putting a person on the moon—a decision that many of America's leading scientists opposed—was more a response to the Cold War than the needs of science. And Neil Armstrong's July 21, 1969, moon walk was confirmation of America's victory in the space race.

The death of the Soviet Union, then, ended two eras. How citizens of both the United States and the Commonwealth of Independent States will respond to that death will be one of the most important issues in the 1990s and the twenty-first century.

from the right and the left and with economic failure throughout the Soviet Union, Gorbachev tried to satisfy everyone and in the process satisfied no one.

Gorbachev's unsuccessful balancing act ended on August 18, 1991. On that day elements of the Soviet army and the KGB, attempted a right-wing political coup. They confronted Gorbachev at his vacation retreat on the Black Sea and demanded that he effectively transfer his power to them. After Gorbachev told the coup members to "go to hell," he was placed under house arrest.

From the first, however, the coup faced problems. It did not have the cooperation of all of the important generals and little of the sympathy of the average soldier. In addition, it lacked popular support. Boris Yeltsin, the most popular leader in the Soviet Union, denounced the coup and rallied public support against it. On August 21, the coup fell apart. Several conspirators committed suicide and most of the rest were arrested. Gorbachev returned to power.

The failure of the right to grasp power strengthened the left. The Baltic republics quickly announced their independence, and the Soviet Union formed a new confederation that granted far greater freedom and autonomy to the individual republics. In the end, what the right had hoped to prevent, it accelerated.

The move away from dictatorship was not confined to Eastern Europe and the Soviet Union. It also swept Latin America. In 1983, a year-and-a-half after defeat in a war with Britain over the Falkland Islands, Argentina returned to democratic rule. In 1986, Jean-Claude Duvalier of Haiti fled into exile, ending his family's 28-year dictatorship. At the end of the 1980s, Brazil, Chile, Costa Rica, Honduras, and Nicaragua inaugurated elected presidents committed to a market economy and free elections.

The winds of change blew across countries as disparate as the Philippines and South Africa. In 1973 Philippines President Ferdinand Marcos imposed martial law and made himself a virtual dictator. He jailed 6000 political prisoners. In 1986, Ferdinand Marcos was forced into exile after he tried to steal an election from Corazon C. Aquino. Riding the crest of "people power," she became president of her island nation. In South Africa, there were signs that minority white rule might be coming to an end, as Nelson Mandela was released from a South African prison after 27 years and the government legalized the African National Congress, lifted a 30-year ban on black political demonstrations, and ordered municipalities to integrate their beaches.

The First Crisis of the Post–Cold War Era

At 2 A.M., August 2, 1990, 80,000 Iraqi troops invaded and occupied Kuwait, a small, oil-rich emirate on the Persian Gulf, touching off the first major international crisis of the post–Cold War era. Days later, Iraq annexed Kuwait as the country's nineteenth province. Iraq's leader, Saddam Hussein, justified the invasion on the grounds that Kuwait, which he accused of intentionally depressing world oil prices, was a historic part of Iraq.

Iraq's invasion caught the United States off guard. The Hussein regime was a brutal military dictatorship that ruled by secret police and used poison gas against Iranians, Kurds, and Shiite Moslems. For years the United States and other countries had tried to moderate Iraq's leader Saddam Hussein. During the 1970s and 1980s, the United States—and Britain, France, the Soviet Union, West Germany—sold Iraq an awesome arsenal of weapons, including missiles, tanks, and the equipment needed to produce biological, chemical, and nuclear weapons. During Baghdad's eight-year-long war with Iran, the United States, which opposed the growth of Moslem fundamentalist extremism, tilted toward Iraq.

On August 6, 1990, President Bush dramatically declared, "This aggression will not stand." With Iraqi forces poised near the Saudi Arabian border, the Bush administration dispatched 180,000 troops to protect the Saudi kingdom. In a sharp departure from American foreign policy during the Reagan presidency, Bush also organized an international coalition against Iraq, convincing Turkey and Syria to close Iraqi oil pipelines, winning Soviet support for an arms embargo, and establishing a multinational army to protect Saudi Arabia, with contingents from western and Arab nations, including Britain,

Lacking public and popular support, the attempted right-wing coup in the Soviet Union collapsed within days. Here, protestors cheer the soldiers who have withdrawn their tanks from the coup.

Egypt, France, Italy, and Syria. In the United Nations, the administration succeeded in persuading the Security Council to adopt a series of resolutions condemning the Iraqi invasion, demanding restoration of the Kuwaiti government, and imposing an economic blockade.

Bush's decision to draw "a line in the sand" grew naturally out of his personal experience and his vision of the role of the United States in world affairs. As a 16-year-old high school student, Bush heard Franklin D. Roosevelt's Secretary of War Henry L. Stimson declare that it was the obligation of the United States to protect less-powerful countries against aggression. Inspired by Stimson's words, Bush dropped out of school to enlist as a naval pilot, flying Avenger torpedo and dive bombers. At 19, he was the navy's youngest pilot. On September 2, 1944, Bush's airplane was shot down and two crewmen died. Bush landed in the sea and managed to find a life raft. Later a submarine picked him up.

The decision to resist Iraqi aggression also reflected the president's assessment of vital national interests. Iraq's invasion gave Saddam Hussein direct control over a significant portion of the world's oil supply. It disrupted the Middle East balance of power and placed Saudi Arabia and the Persian Gulf emirates in jeopardy. Iraq's battle-hardened war machine—consisting of 545,000 troops, 5000 tanks, 500 fighter aircraft, and chemical and biological weapons—threatened the security of such valuable U.S. allies as Egypt and Israel.

On November 8, 1990, two days after midterm elections, the crisis took a dramatic turn when President Bush surprised the nation by doubling the 150,000 American troops deployed in the Persian Gulf. Iraqi forces in Kuwait had climbed to 430,000 and coalition forces had to increase if it hoped to eject Iraq from Kuwait by force. The troop increase produced a strong reaction from Congress. Many members demanded that Bush receive prior approval from Congress for any use of force against Iraq. Before going to Congress, the president went to the United Nations for a resolution permitting the use of force against Iraq after January 15, 1991. Then, after a heated debate, Congress gave the president authority to wage war.

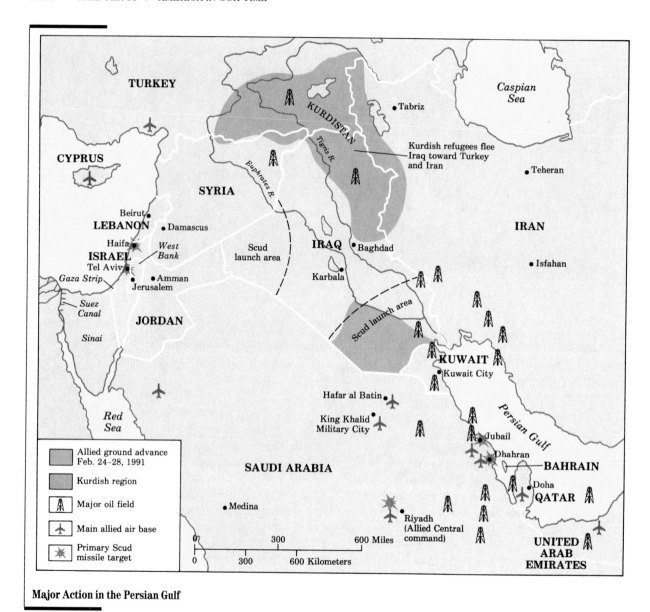

Major Action in the Persian Gulf

In a last-ditch effort to avert war, U.S. Secretary of State James Baker and Iraq's Foreign Minister Tariq Aziz met in Geneva for more than six hours. The talks failed. Aziz told Baker: "Your Arab allies will desert you. They will not kill other Arabs. Your alliance will crumble and you will be left lost in the desert." On January 15, Bush signed a national security directive authorizing the liberation of Kuwait.

President Bush's decision to reverse Iraqi aggression and liberate Kuwait was an enormous political and military gamble. The 545,000-strong Iraqi army, the world's fourth largest, was equipped with antiship Exocet missiles, top-of-the-line Soviet T-72 tanks, and long-range artillery capable of firing nerve gas. The Iraqi leader tried to break up the allied coalition by launching Scud missiles at Israeli cities in order to bring Israel into the war. This strategy was thwarted by Israeli restraint and the American decision to send Patriot antimissile missiles to the Jewish state. Iraq also engaged in what some environmentalists called "eco-terrorism"—setting fire to Kuwaiti oil wells and deliberately spewing oil into the Persian Gulf.

A month of allied bombing gave the coalition forces air supremacy and destroyed thousands of Iraqi tanks and artillery pieces, supply routes and communications lines, command-and-control bunkers, and limited Iraq's ability to produce nuclear, chemical, and biological weapons. Iraqi troop morale suffered so badly under the bombing that an estimated 30 percent of Baghdad's forces deserted before the ground campaign started.

The allied ground campaign relied on deception, mobility, and overwhelming air superiority to defeat a larger Iraqi army. The allied strategy was to mislead the Iraqis into believing that the allied attack would occur along the Kuwaiti coastline and Kuwait's border with Saudi Arabia. Meanwhile, General H. Norman Schwarzkopf, American commander of coalition forces, shifted more than 300,000 American, British, and French troops into western Saudia Arabia, allowing them to strike deep into Iraq and trap Iraqi forces deep in southern Iraq and Kuwait. Only 100 hours after the ground war started, the war ended.

The end of the war did not mean the end of suffering or even hostilities. Saddam Hussein remained in power, and in the war's aftermath he brutally suppressed independence movements by two minority groups—the Shiites and the Kurds—in his own country. Nor did the liberated Kuwait move toward a more liberal nation. But Saddam's power in the region was dramatically limited.

The Significance of the Persian Gulf Conflict

The Persian Gulf conflict was the most popular American war since World War II, restoring American confidence in its position as the world's sole superpower and helping to exorcise the ghost of Vietnam that had haunted American foreign policy debates for more than a decade—a time of doubt, drift, and demoralization that began with the Vietnam War and the Watergate scandal appeared to have ended.

Public debate over the Persian Gulf conflict was also haunted by the specter of Vietnam. Antiwar protesters, some of whom waved banners proclaiming "No Blood for Oil," questioned whether the war would advance U.S. interests in the Arab world and whether it would bring stability and security to the Perisan Gulf. Some critics argued that the Iraqi takeover of Kuwait was a product of a maldistribution of Arab oil wealth between poorly populated, rich oil producers like Kuwait and Saudi Arabia and large, poor Arab states. Others questioned the wisdom of defending countries like Kuwait that deny such basic personal freedoms as the right of women to drive a car.

The Vietnam War exerted a powerful influence on the thinking of American military and political leaders. During the 1970s and 1980s a consensus gradually emerged that the United States should not fight a war that did not involve vital American interests, that lacked clearly defined objectives, and that failed to have broad public and congressional support.

The war with Iraq illustrated many of the lessons that Americans had learned from the nation's unhappy experience in Vietnam—an inconclusive, unpopular war. In stark contrast to the Vietnam War, which was fought without a clear definition of victory, the Persian Gulf War had a clearly designated goal: to force Iraq to leave Kuwait. Even after the United States had routed the Iraqi army and could easily have carried the ground war to the Iraqi capital of Baghdad, Bush made it clear that the United States was eager to withdraw its forces as soon as possible.

Also, unlike Vietnam, which was fought without clear congressional authority or international support, the Persian Gulf War received strong support from Congress, the United Nations, and an international coalition that included some 30 nations. And finally, unlike Vietnam, the Persian Gulf War was fought without half measures. The United States agreed to no cease-fire until its adversary's army was routed.

Years may have to pass before historians will be able to conclusively evaluate the consequences of the Persian Gulf War. Only the future will tell whether America's success against Iraq made future wars less likely by deterring aggression and whether the war brought stability to the Middle East.

In a scene recalling the antiwar protests of the 1960s, demonstrators in San Francisco show their disapproval of U.S. military involvement in the Persian Gulf.

Assessing the Bush Presidency

In January 1991 *Time* magazine placed George Bush on its cover. It pictured him with two faces, because his presidency seemed to have two very different images. "One was a foreign policy profile that was a study in resoluteness," the magazine said, "the other a domestic visage just as strongly marked by wavering and confusion."

In the Persian Gulf War, Bush acted from clear, unequivocal principles. Convinced that it was necessary to humiliate Saddam Hussein and prove that America would resist aggression, Bush demonstrated that a determined and skillful president has the power to move a reluctant nation. Throughout the Persian Gulf crisis, Bush repeatedly convinced the American people that resolute action was necessary. In early August, 1990, a Gallup poll found that 56 percent of the American people opposed sending troops to defend Saudi Arabia; yet Bush succeeded in mobilizing overwhelming public support for his decision to deploy troops in the kingdom. Just ten days before he launched the ground war, a poll

found only 11 percent of American people favored such a step. The day after the ground war began, 75 percent approved.

In domestic affairs, in stark contrast, Bush's leadership was less decisive. On such issues as taxes, abortion, and civil rights, he adopted a flexible, pragmatic approach that led some critics to describe him as a political chameleon. Unlike Ronald Reagan, who brought a series of fixed philosophical principles to domestic issues, Bush appeared less interested in domestic affairs and more willing to flip-flop on his pledge not to raise taxes.

A New Covenant

Bush's failure to alter the downward slide of the American economy played the crucial role in the 1992 presidential election. In a bitter three-way contest, marked by intense assaults on the candidates' records and characters, Arkansas Governor Bill Clinton defeated George Bush and Texas businessman Ross Perot to become the first Democratic president in 12 years. President Bush, whose popularity soared to 90

CHRONOLOGY OF KEY EVENTS

1970 President Nixon approves Huston plan to use the government intelligence agencies to gather information on domestic "radicals"; plan is later rescinded

1971 A secret tape-recording system is installed in the White House; Nixon authorizes establishment of plumbers unit to "stop security leaks and investigate other sensitive matters"

1972 Five burglars arrested breaking into Democratic national headquarters at Washington's Watergate Office Complex; President Nixon takes part in summit in China; President Nixon is reelected with 61 percent of the vote

1973 Televised Senate hearings on Watergate begin; Spiro Agnew pleads no contest to a charge of income tax evasion and resigns as vice president

1974 Federal grand jury indicts Nixon aides for perjury and obstruction of justice and names the president as an unindicted coconspirator; House Judiciary Committee adopts three articles of impeachment against President Nixon; Nixon becomes the first president to resign from office; Ford becomes thirty-eighth president; Federal Campaign Reform Act sets limits on private campaign contributions and provides tax funds to presidential candidates

1975 Cambodia seizes American merchant ship *Mayaguez*

1976 Jimmy Carter is elected thirty-ninth president; Soviet Premier Leonid Brezhnev announces the "Brezhnev Doctrine"

1978 President Carter mediates Egyptian-Israeli peace settlement; Iranian revolution begins

1979 United States formally recognizes China; Iranian militants seize American hostages; Soviet Union invades Afghanistan; Somoza regime in Nicaragua is overthrown; Sandinistas take power

1980 Ronald Reagan is elected fortieth president

1981 American hostages are released from Iran; Reagan is shot in assassination attempt; Reagan approves covert training of anti-Sandinista contras; Reagan tax cuts are approved

1982 Congress deregulates banking industry and lifts controls on air fares

1983 Reagan proposes "Star Wars" missile defense system: United States topples Communist government on the Caribbean island of Grenada; Soviet fighter shoots down Korean Airlines flight 007

1984 Congress orders an end to all covert aid to Nicaraguan contras

1985 United States begins secret arms-for-hostages negotiations with Iran; Mikhail Gorbachev becomes leader of the Soviet Union

1986 Profits from Iranian arms sales are diverted to Nicaraguan contras

1987 Iran-Contra hearings; stock market plunges 508 points in a single session

1988 George Bush is elected forty-first president

1989 Opposition defeats Sandinistas in Nicaraguan elections; Communist regimes collapse in Eastern Europe

1990 Iraqi troops invade and occupy Kuwait

1991 U.S., Western, and Arab forces eject Iraq from Kuwait by force; failed coup in Soviet Union results in a shift in power to the Soviet republics and in independence for Lithuania, Latvia, and Estonia; confirmation hearings for Clarence Thomas to the U.S. Supreme Court focus national attention on the issue of sexual harassment; United States and Soviet Union host peace talks between Israelis, Palestinians, and Arab states

1992 Bill Clinton is elected forty-second president

percent after the Persian Gulf War, received 38 percent of the vote, to Clinton's 43 percent and Perot's 19 percent.

The central issue in the election was the nation's sluggish economy. During the Bush presidency, fewer new jobs were created than in any other presidential term since World War II. Indeed, fewer Americans were on private payrolls at the end of this term than when he took office. Unemployment reached the highest level in eight years; personal incomes stagnated; businesses failed in record numbers; the federal debt surpassed $4 trillion; and medical care absorbed 15 percent of the nation's output, while a quarter of the population lacked health insurance. Poverty rose to the highest rate in over two decades—a fact dramatically underscored by the outbreak of the deadliest riot in America's history, in Los Angeles in April 1992.

President Clinton pledged a "new covenant" for America: a new approach to government between the unfettered free market championed by the Republicans and the welfare state economics that the Democratic party had represented in the past. He called for higher taxes on the wealthiest Americans, reduced defense spending, college aid for all qualified students, and expanded job training programs. A new era in the nation's history, Clinton promised, had begun.

CONCLUSION

As the twentieth century draws to a close, America's ideals of democracy and personal freedom are ascendant across the world. From Tiananmen Square—where Chinese students erected a goddess of liberty modeled on the Statue of Liberty—to the Philippines, popular protests and demonstrations have called for "government of the people, for the people, and by the people." In Eastern Europe, the former Soviet Union, and across Latin America, people demand free speech, freedom of religion, freedom of the press, and free markets.

Yet paradoxically, as American ideals and values flourish abroad, Americans are anxious about their economy and their country's future. Many are angry, expressing cynical contempt toward their government.

The American economy remains the world's most productive. Nevertheless, many fear that American competitiveness and inventiveness are declining. The economic picture is mixed. The American economy today is almost three times as large as Japan's and nearly twice as large as the combined economies of Germany, France, and Britain. The average American worker still produces a third more than the average Japanese worker. The proportion of national income invested in research and development is as large as in Europe and Japan.

Yet at the same time other nations save more and invest more than the United States, and are increasing the productivity of their industries faster than America. Except for a few areas of trade—such as high-tech products, financial services, and aircraft—foreign countries dominate the most technologically advanced fields, such as consumer electronics, luxury automobiles, and machine tools.

Other economic problems also prompt concern. The national debt and federal deficit stand at record levels. Foreign ownership of American factories, real estate, and stocks and bonds is actually greater than American ownership of foreign assets. No longer does the United States possess the world's highest level of per capita income.

Americans also worry about crime, the state of their central cities, and the level of health and education in their society. The level of crime and violence in the United States is the highest in the industrialized world. No one, not even presidents, has been immune from the threat of violence. Four of the last eight presidents have been targets of assassins' bullets. The nation's infant death rate is higher than that of 19 other nations and is twice as high as Japan's. Schooling is a particular source of dismay. Standardized tests indicate that America's schoolchildren lag behind those in other advanced societies in almost every branch of learning—foreign languages, geography, mathematics, natural sciences. America's rates of drug use, juvenile delinquency, teenage pregnancy, and teen suicide are the highest in the industrialized world.

At the end of World War II, many commentators referred to the twentieth century as the "American century." Today, the United States remains the mightiest, most productive nation in the world, a model of freedom and pluralism that people across the globe still strive to emulate. The great question Americans ask as the "American century" comes to an end is whether the people who have reached the moon and routed the Iraqi army have the commitment and will to solve the down-to-earth problems that confront their cities, their schools, and their physical environment.

SUGGESTIONS FOR FURTHER READING

OVERVIEWS AND SURVEYS

Michael Barone, *Our Country: The Shaping of America from Roosevelt to Reagan* (1990); Peter N. Carroll, *It Seemed Like Nothing Happened: The Tragedy and Promise of the 1970s* (1990); William H. Chafe, *The Unfinished Journey: America Since World War II*, 2d ed. (1991); Frederick F. Siegel, *Troubled Journey: From Pearl Harbor to Ronald Reagan* (1984).

CRISIS OF POLITICAL LEADERSHIP

Terry Deibel, *Presidents, Public Opinion, and Power: The Nixon, Carter, and Reagan Years* (1986); Stanley I. Kutler, *The Wars of Watergate: The Last Crisis of Richard Nixon* (1990); J. Anthony Lukas, *Nightmare: The Underside of the Nixon Years* (1976); Kim McQuaid, *The Anxious Years: America in the Vietnam-Watergate Era* (1989); Richard E. Neustadt, *Presidential Power and Modern Presidents*, rev. ed. (1990); James Reichley, *Conservatives in an Age of Change: The Nixon and Ford Administrations* (1981); Edward L. and Frederick H. Schapsmeier, *Gerald R. Ford's Date with Destiny: A Political Biography* (1989); Jonathan Schell, *The Time of Illusion* (1975); Arthur M. Schlesinger, Jr., *The Imperial Presidency* (1973).

WRENCHING ECONOMIC TRANSFORMATIONS

Barry Bluestone and Bennett Harrison, *The Deindustrialization of America* (1982); David Calleo, *The Imperious Economy* (1982); Emmett Dedmon, *Challenge and Response: A Modern History of the Standard Oil Company* (1984); Thomas Edsall, *The New Politics of Inequality* (1984); Michael Goldfield, *The Decline of Organized Labor in the United States* (1987); Frank Levy, *Dollars and Dreams: The Changing American Income Distribution* (1987); Martin V. Melosi, *Coping with Abundance: Energy and Environment in Industrial America* (1985); Norman E. Nordhauser, *The Quest for Sta-*

bility: Domestic Oil Regulation (1979); Bernard Nossiter, *Fat Years and Lean Years: The American Economy Since Roosevelt* (1990); Michael Piore, *The Second Industrial Divide* (1984); Stephen G. Rabe, *The Road to OPEC* (1982); Herbert Stein, *Presidential Economics: The Making of Economic Policy from Roosevelt to Reagan*, 2d ed. (1988); Michael Stoff, *Oil, War, and Security* (1980); Daniel Yergin, *The Prize: The Epic Quest for Oil, Money, and Power* (1990).

A NEW AMERICAN ROLE IN THE WORLD

James A. Bill, *The Eagle and the Lion: The Tragedy of American-Iranian Relations* (1988); Gordon H. Chang, *Friends and Enemies: The United States, China, and the Soviet Union* (1990); Mark Gasiorowski, *U.S. Foreign Policy and the Shah* (1991); J. Michael Hogan, *The Panama Canal in American Politics* (1986); Nikki R. Keddie, *Iran, the United States, and the Soviet Union* (1991); Walter LaFeber, *The Panama Canal*, rev. ed. (1989); Joseph Lepgold, *The Declining Hegemon: The United States and European Defense, 1960–1990* (1990); Richard A. Melanson, *Reconstructing Consensus: American Foreign Policy Since the Vietnam War* (1990); Kuross A. Samii, *Involvement by Invitation: American Strategies of Containment in Iran* (1987); Robert D. Schulzinger, *Henry Kissinger* (1989); Gaddis Smith, *Morality, Reason and Power: American Diplomacy in the Carter Years* (1986); Seth Tillman, *The United States in the Middle East* (1982); Marvin Zonis, *Majestic Failure: The Fall of the Shah* (1991).

THE REAGAN REVOLUTION

Norman C. Amaker, *Civil Rights and the Reagan Administration* (1988); Cynthia J. Arnson, *Crossroads: Congress, the Reagan Administration, and Central America* (1989); Coral Bell, *The Reagan Paradox: American Foreign Policy in the 1980s* (1989); Sidney Blumenthal, *Our Long National Daydream: A Political Pageant of the Reagan Era* (1988); Paul Boyer, ed., *Reagan as President* (1990); Lou Cannon, *President Reagan: The Role of a Lifetime* (1991); Robert Dallek, *Ronald Reagan: The Politics of Symbolism* (1984); Theodore Draper, *A Very Thin Line: The Iran-Contra Affairs* (1991); Thomas Ferguson and Joel Rogers, *Right Turn: The Decline of the Democrats and the Future of American Politics* (1986); Steve Fraser and Gary Gerstle, *The Rise and Fall of the New Deal Order* (1990); Fred Halliday, *From Kabul to Managua: Soviet-American Relations in the 1980s* (1989); J. David Hoeveler, Jr., *Watch on the Right: Conservative Intellectuals in the Reagan Era*

(1991); Haynes Johnson, *Sleepwalking Through History: America in the Reagan Years* (1991); David E. Kyvig, ed., *Reagan and the World* (1990); Jane Mayer and Doyle McManus, *Landslide: The Unmaking of the President, 1984–1988* (1988); John L. Palmer, ed., *Perspectives on the Reagan Years* (1986); Robert Pastor, *Condemned to Repetition: The United States and Nicaragua* (1987); Martin Wattenberg, *The Decline of American Political Parties, 1952–1988* (1990), and *The Rise of Candidate-Centered Politics: Presidential Elections of the 1980s* (1991); Garry Wills, *Reagan's America* (1987).

THE BUSH PRESIDENCY

Sidney Blumenthal, *Pledging Allegiance: The Last Campaign of the Cold War* (1990); Kevin Buckley, *Panama: The Whole Story* (1991); Jill Crystal, *Oil and Politics in the Gulf* (1990); E. J. Dionne, Jr., *Why Americans Hate Politics* (1991); Alan Ehrenhalt, *The United States of Ambition: Politicians, Power, and the Pursuit of Office* (1991); Robert O. Freedman, *Moscow and the Middle East* (1991); Moshe Lewin, *The Gorbachev Phenomenon* (1991); Martin Mayer, *The Greatest Ever Bank Robbery: The Collapse of the Savings and Loan Industry* (1990); Henry R. Nau, *The Myth of America's Decline* (1990); William Pfaff, *Barbarian Sentiments: How the American Century Ends* (1989); Stephen Pizzo, et al., *Inside Job: The Looting of America's Savings and Loans* (1989); Gail Sheehy, *The Man Who Changed the World: The Lives of Mikhail S. Gorbachev* (1990); Lawrence J. White, *The S&L Debacle* (1991); Garry Wills, *Under God: Religion and American Politics* (1990); Bob Woodward, *The Commanders* (1991).

Appendix

The Declaration of Independence

In Congress, July 4, 1776

The Unanimous Declaration of the thirteen United States of America

When, in the course of human events, it becomes necessary for one people to dissolve the political bonds which have connected them with another, and to assume, among the powers of the earth, the separate and equal station to which the laws of nature and of nature's God entitle them, a decent respect to the opinions of mankind requires that they should declare the causes which impel them to the separation.

We hold these truths to be self-evident: That all men are created equal; that they are endowed by their Creator with certain unalienable rights; that among these are life, liberty, and the pursuit of happiness; that, to secure these rights, governments are instituted among men, deriving their just powers from the consent of the governed; that whenever any form of government becomes destructive of these ends, it is the right of the people to alter or to abolish it, and to institute new government, laying its foundation on such principles, and organizing its powers in such form, as to them shall seem most likely to effect their safety and happiness. Prudence, indeed, will dictate that governments long established should not be changed for light and transient causes; and accordingly all experience hath shown that mankind are more disposed to suffer, while evils are sufferable, than to right themselves by abolishing the forms to which they are accustomed. But when a long train of abuses and usurpations, pursuing invariably the same object, evinces a design to reduce them under absolute despotism, it is their right, it is their duty, to throw off such government, and to provide new guards for their future security. Such has been the patient sufferance of these colonies; and such is now the necessity which constrains them to alter their former systems of government. The history of the present King of Great Britain is a history of repeated injuries and usurpations, all having in direct object the establishment of an absolute tyranny over these states. To prove this, let facts be submitted to a candid world.

He has refused his assent to laws, the most wholesome and necessary for the public good.

He has forbidden his governors to pass laws of immediate and pressing importance, unless suspended in their operation till his assent should be obtained; and when so suspended, he has utterly neglected to attend to them.

He has refused to pass other laws for the accommodation of large districts of people, unless those people would relinquish the right of representation in the legislature, a right inestimable to them, and formidable to tyrants only.

He has called together legislature bodies at places unusual, uncomfortable, and distant from the depository of their public records, for the sole purpose of fatiguing them into compliance with his measures.

He has dissolved representative houses repeatedly, for opposing with manly firmness, his invasions on the rights of the people.

He has refused for a long time, after such dissolutions, to cause others to be elected; whereby the legislative powers, incapable of annihilation, have returned to the people at large for their exercise; the state remaining, in the mean time, exposed to all the dangers of invasions from without and convulsions within.

He has endeavored to prevent the population of these states; for that purpose obstructing the laws for naturalization of foreigners; refusing to pass others to encourage their migration hither, and raising the conditions of new appropriations of lands.

He has obstructed the administration of justice, by refusing his assent to laws for establishing judiciary powers.

He has made judges dependent on his will alone, for the tenure of their offices, and the amount and payment of their salaries.

He has erected a multitude of new offices, and sent hither swarms of officers to harass our people and eat out their substance.

He has kept among us, in times of peace, standing armies, without the consent of our legislatures.

He has affected to render the military independent of, and superior to, the civil power.

He has combined with others to subject us to a jurisdiction foreign to our constitution, and unacknowledged by our laws, giving his assent to their acts of pretended legislation:

For quartering large bodies of armed troops among us;

For protecting them, by a mock trial, from punishment for any murders which they should commit on the inhabitants of these states;

For cutting off our trade with all parts of the world;

For imposing taxes on us without our consent;

For depriving us, in many cases, of the benefits of trial by jury;

For transporting us beyond seas, to be tried for pretended offenses;

For abolishing the free system of English laws in a neighboring province, establishing therein an arbitrary government, and enlarging its boundaries, so as to render it at once an example and fit instrument for introducing the same absolute rule into these colonies;

For taking away our charters, abolishing our most valuable laws, and altering fundamentally the forms of our governments;

For suspending our own legislatures, and declaring themselves invested with power to legislate for us in all cases whatsoever.

He has abdicated government here, by declaring us out of his protection and waging war against us.

He has plundered our seas, ravaged our coasts, burned our towns, and destroyed the lives of our people.

He is at this time transporting large armies of foreign mercenaries to complete the works of death, desolation, and tyranny already begun with circumstances of cruelty and perfidy scarcely paralleled in the most barbarous ages, and totally unworthy the head of a civilized nation.

He has constrained our fellow-citizens, taken captive on the high seas, to bear arms against their country, to become the

In all cases affecting ambassadors, other public ministers and consuls, and those in which a State shall be party, the Supreme Court shall have original jurisdiction. In all the other cases before mentioned, the Supreme Court shall have appellate jurisdiction, both as to law and fact, with such exceptions, and under such regulations, as the Congress shall make.

The trial of all crimes, except in cases of impeachment, shall be by jury; and such trial shall be held in the State where said crimes shall have been committed; but when not committed within any State, the trial shall be at place or places as the Congress may by law have directed.

Section 3   Treason against the United States shall consist only in levying war against them, or in adhering to their enemies, giving them aid and comfort. No person shall be convinced of treason unless on the testimony of two witnesses to the same overt act, or on confession in open court.

The Congress shall have power to declare the punishment of treason, but no attainder of treason shall work corruption of blood, or forfeiture except during the life of the person attainted.

ARTICLE IV

Section 1   Full faith and credit shall be given in each State to the public acts, records, and judicial proceedings of every other State. And the Congress may by general laws prescribe the manner in which such acts, records, and proceedings shall be proved, and the effect thereof.

Section 2   The citizens of each State shall be entitled to all privileges and immunities of citizens in the several States.

A person charged in any State with treason, felony, or other crime, who shall flee from justice, and be found in another State, shall on demand of the executive authority of the State from which he fled, be delivered up, to be removed to the State having jurisdiction of the crime.

No person held to service or labor in one State under the laws thereof, escaping into another, shall, in consequence of any law or regulation therein, be discharged from such service or labor, but shall be delivered up on claim of the party to whom such service or labor may be due.

Section 3   New States may be admitted by the Congress into this Union; but no new State shall be formed or erected within the jurisdiction of any other State; nor any State be formed by the junction of two or more States, or parts of States, without the consent of the legislatures of the States concerned as well as of the Congress.

The Congress shall have power to dispose of and make all needful rules and regulations respecting the territory or other property belonging to the United States; and nothing in this Constitution shall be so construed as to prejudice any claims of the United States, or of any particular State.

Section 4   The United States shall guarantee to every State in this Union a republican form of government, and shall protect each of them against invasion; and on application of the legislature, or of the executive (when the legislature cannot be convened), against domestic violence.

ARTICLE V

The Congress, whenever two-thirds of both houses shall deem it necessary, shall propose amendments to this Constitution, or, on the application of the legislatures of two-thirds of the several States, shall call a convention for proposing amendments, which, in either case, shall be valid to all intents and purposes, as part of this Constitution, when ratified by the legislatures of three-fourths of the several States, or by conventions in three-fourths thereof, as the one or the other mode of ratification may be proposed by the Congress; provided *that no amendments which may be made prior to the year one thousand eight hundred and eight shall in any manner affect the first and fourth clauses in the ninth section of the first article*; and that no State, without its consent, shall be deprived of its equal suffrage in the Senate.

ARTICLE VI

All debts contracted and engagements entered into, before the adoption of this Constitution, shall be as valid against the United States under this Constitution, as under the Confederation.

This Constitution, and the laws of the United States which shall be made in pursuance thereof; and all treaties made, or which shall be made, under the authority of the United States, shall be the supreme law of the land; and the judges in every State shall be bound thereby, anything in the Constitution or laws of any State to the contrary notwithstanding.

The Senators and Representatives before mentioned, and the members of the several State legislatures, and all executive and judicial officers, both of the United States and of the several States, shall be bound by oath or affirmation to support this Constitution; but no religious test shall ever be required as a qualification to any office or public trust under the United States.

ARTICLE VII

The ratification of the conventions of nine States shall be sufficient for the establishment of this Constitution between the States so ratifying the same.

Done in Convention by the unanimous consent of the States present, the seventeenth day of September in the year of our Lord one thousand seven hundred and eighty-seven and of the Independence of the United States of America the twelfth. In witness whereof we have hereunto subscribed our names.

GEORGE WASHINGTON,
President and Deputy from Virginia

New Hampshire
JOHN LANGDON
NICHOLAS GILMAN

Massachusetts
NATHANIEL GORHAM
RUFUS KING

Connecticut
WILLIAM S. JOHNSON
ROGER SHERMAN

New York
ALEXANDER HAMILTON

New Jersey
WILLIAM LIVINGSTON
DAVID BREARLEY
WILLIAM PATERSON
JONATHAN DAYTON

Pennsylvania
BENJAMIN FRANKLIN
THOMAS MIFFLIN
ROBERT MORRIS
GEORGE CLYMER
THOMAS FITZSIMONS
JARED INGERSOLL
JAMES WILSON
GOUVERNEUR MORRIS

Delaware
GEORGE READ
GUNNING BEDFORD, JR.
JOHN DICKINSON
RICHARD BASSETT
JACOB BROOM

Maryland
JAMES MCHENRY
DANIEL OF ST. THOMAS JENIFER
DANIEL CARROLL

Virginia
JOHN BLAIR
JAMES MADISON, JR.

North Carolina
WILLIAM BLOUNT
RICHARD DOBBS SPRAIGHT
HU WILLIAMSON

South Carolina
J. RUTLEDGE
CHARLES C. PINCKNEY
PIERCE BUTLER

Georgia
WILLIAM FEW
ABRAHAM BALDWIN

Amendments to the Constitution

*The first ten Amendments (the Bill of Rights) were adopted in 1791.

AMENDMENT I

Congress shall make no law respecting an establishment of religion, or prohibiting the free exercise thereof; or abridging the freedom of speech, or of the press; or the right of the people peaceably to assemble, and to petition the government for a redress of grievances.

AMENDMENT II

A well-regulated militia being necessary to the security of a free State, the right of the people to keep and bear arms shall not be infringed.

AMENDMENT III

No soldier shall, in time of peace, be quartered in any house without the consent of the owner, nor in time of war but in a manner to be prescribed by law.

AMENDMENT IV

The right of the people to be secure in their persons, houses, papers, and effects, against unreasonable searches and seizures, shall not be violated, and no warrants shall issue but upon probable cause, supported by oath or affirmation, and particularly describing the place to be searched, and the persons or things to be seized.

AMENDMENT V

No person shall be held to answer for a capital, or otherwise infamous crime, unless on a presentment or indictment of a grand jury, except in cases arising in the land or naval forces, or in the militia, when in actual service in time of war or public danger; nor shall any person be subject for the same offense to be twice put in jeopardy of life or limb; nor shall be compelled in any criminal case to be a witness against himself, nor be deprived of life, liberty, or property, without due process of law; nor shall private property be taken for public use without just compensation.

AMENDMENT VI

In all criminal prosecutions, the accused shall enjoy the right to a speedy and public trial, by an impartial jury of the State and district shall have been previously ascertained by law, and to be informed of the nature and cause of the accusation; to be confronted with the witnesses against him; to have compulsory process for obtaining witnesses in his favor, and to have the assistance of counsel for his defense.

AMENDMENT VII

In suits at common law, where the value in controversy shall exceed twenty dollars, the right of trial by jury shall be preserved, and no fact tried by a jury shall be otherwise reexamined in any court of the United States, than according to the rules of the common law.

AMENDMENT VIII

Excessive bail shall not be required, nor excessive fines imposed, nor cruel and unusual punishments inflicted.

AMENDMENT IX

The enumeration in the Constitution, of certain rights, shall not be construed to deny or disparage others retained by the people.

AMENDMENT X

The powers not delegated to the United States by the Constitution, nor prohibited by it to the States, are reserved to the States respectively, or to the people.

AMENDMENT XI
[Adopted 1798]
The judicial power of the United States shall not be construed to extend to any suit in law or equity, commenced or prosecuted against one of the United States by citizens of another State, or by citizens or subjects of any foreign state.

AMENDMENT XII
[Adopted 1804]
The electors shall meet in their respective States, and vote by ballot for President and Vice-President, one of whom, at least, shall not be an inhabitant of the same State with themselves; they shall name in their ballots the person voted for as President, and in distinct ballots the person voted for as Vice-President, and they shall make distinct lists of all persons voted for as President, and of all persons voted for as Vice-President, and of the number of votes for each, which lists they shall sign and certify, and transmit sealed to the seat of government of the United States, directed to the President of the Senate;—the President of the Senate shall, in the presence of the Senate and House of Representatives, open all the certificates and the votes shall then be counted;—the person having the greatest number of votes for President shall be the President, if such number be a majority of the whole number of electors appointed; and if no person have such majority, then from the persons having the highest number not ex-

ceeding three on the list of those voted for as President, the House of Representatives shall choose immediately, by ballot, the President. But in choosing the President, the votes shall be taken by States, the representation from each State having one vote; a quorum for this purpose shall consist of a member or members from two-thirds of the States, and a majority of all the States shall be necessary to a choice. And if the House of Representatives shall not choose a President whenever the right of choice shall devolve upon them, before *the fourth day of March* next following, then the Vice-President shall act as President, as in the case of the death or other constitutional disability of the President.

The person having the greatest number of votes as Vice-President shall be the Vice-President, if such number be a majority of the whole number of electors appointed; and if no person have a majority, then from the two highest numbers on the list the Senate shall choose the Vice-President; a quorum for the purpose shall consist of two-thirds of the whole number of Senators, and a majority of the whole number shall be necessary to a choice. But no person constitutionally ineligible to the office of President shall be eligible to that of Vice-President of the United States.

AMENDMENT XIII

[Adopted 1865]

Section 1   Neither slavery nor involuntary servitude, except as a punishment for crime whereof the party shall have been duly convicted, shall exist within the United States, or any place subject to their jurisdiction.

Section 2   Congress shall have power to enforce this article by appropriate legislation.

AMENDMENT XIV

[Adopted 1868]

Section 1   All persons born or naturalized in the United States, and subject to the jurisdiction thereof, are citizens of the United States and of the State wherein they reside. No State shall make or enforce any law which shall abridge the privileges or immunities of citizens of the United States; nor shall any State deprive any person of life, liberty, or property, without due process of law; nor deny to any person within its jurisdiction the equal protection of the laws.

Section 2   Representatives shall be apportioned among the several States according to their respective numbers, counting the whole number of persons in each State, excluding Indians not taxed. But when the right to vote at any election for the choice of Electors for President and Vice-President of the United States, Representatives in Congress, the executive and judicial officers of a State, or the members of the legislature thereof, is denied to any of the male inhabitants of such State, being twenty-one years of age and citizens of the United States, or in any way abridged, except for participation in rebellion, or other crime, the basis of representation therein shall be reduced in the proportion which the number of such male citizens shall bear to the whole number of male citizens twenty-one years of age in such State.

Section 3   No person shall be a Senator or Representative in Congress, or Elector of President and Vice-President, or hold any office, civil or military, under the United States, or under any State, who, having previously taken an oath, as a member of Congress, or as an officer of the United States, or as a member of any State legislature, or as an executive or judicial officer of any State, to support the Constitution of the United States, shall have engaged in insurrection or rebellion against the same, or given aid

or comfort to the enemies thereof. Congress may, by a vote of two-thirds of each house, remove such disability.

Section 4   The validity of the public debt of the United States, authorized by law, including debts incurred for payment of pensions and bounties for services in suppressing insurrection or rebellion, shall not be questioned. But neither the United States nor any State shall assume or pay any debt or obligation incurred in aid of insurrection or rebellion against the United States, or any claim for the loss of emancipation of any slave; but all such debts, obligations, and claims shall be held illegal and void.

Section 5   The Congress shall have power to enforce, by appropriate legislation, the provisions of this article.

AMENDMENT XV

[Adopted 1870]

Section 1   The right of citizens of the United States to vote shall not be denied or abridged by the United States or by any State on account of race, color, or previous condition of servitude.

Section 2   The Congress shall have power to enforce this article by appropriate legislation.

AMENDMENT XVI

[Adopted 1913]

The Congress shall have power to lay and collect taxes on incomes, from whatever source derived, without apportionment among the several States, and without regard to any census or enumeration.

AMENDMENT XVII

[Adopted 1913]

Section 1   The Senate of the United States shall be composed of two Senators from each State, elected by the people thereof, for six years; and each Senator shall have one vote. The electors in each State shall have the qualifications requisite for electors of [voters for] the most numerous branch of the State legislatures.

Section 2   When vacancies happen in the representation of any State in the Senate, the executive authority of such State shall issue writs of election to fill such vacancies: Provided, that the Legislature of any State may empower the executive thereof to make temporary appointments until the people fill the vacancies by election as the Legislature may direct.

Section 3   This amendment shall not be so construed as to affect the election or term of any Senator chosen before it becomes valid as part of the Constitution.

AMENDMENT XVIII

[Adopted 1919; Repealed 1933]

Section 1   After one year from the ratification of this article the manufacture, sale, or transportation of intoxicating liquors within, the importation thereof into, or the exportation thereof from the United States and all territory subject to the jurisdiction thereof, for beverage purposes, is hereby prohibited.

Section 2   The Congress and the several States shall have concurrent power to enforce this article by appropriate legislation.

Section 3   This article shall be inoperative unless it shall have been ratified as an amendment to the Constitution by the legislatures of the several States, as provided by the Constitution, within seven years from the date of the submission thereof to the States by the Congress.

AMENDMENT XIX

[Adopted 1920]

Section 1   The right of citizens of the United States to vote shall not be denied or abridged by the United States or by any State on account of sex.

Section 2   The Congress shall have power to enforce this article by appropriate legislation.

AMENDMENT XX

[Adopted 1933]

Section 1   The terms of the President and Vice-President shall end at noon on the 20th day of January, and the terms of Senators and Representatives at noon on the 3d day of January, of the years in which such terms would have ended if this article had not been ratified; and the terms of their successors shall then begin.

Section 2   The Congress shall assemble at least once in every year, and such meeting shall begin at noon on the 3d day of January, unless they shall by law appoint a different day.

Section 3   If, at the time fixed for the beginning of the term of the President, the President-elect shall have died, the Vice-President-elect shall become President. If a President shall not have been chosen before the time fixed for the beginning of his term, or if the President-elect shall have failed to qualify, then the Vice-President-elect shall act as President until a President shall have qualified; and the Congress may by law provide for the case wherein neither a President-elect nor a Vice-President-elect shall have qualified, declaring who shall then act as President, or the manner in which one who is to act shall be selected, and such persons shall act accordingly until a President or Vice-President shall have qualified.

Section 4   The Congress may by law provide for the case of the death of any of the persons from whom the House of Representatives may choose a President whenever the right of choice shall have devolved upon them, and for the case of the death of any of the persons from whom the Senate may choose a Vice-President whenever the right of choice shall have devolved upon them.

Section 5   Sections 1 and 2 shall take effect on the 15th day of October following the ratification of this article.

Section 6   This article shall be inoperative unless it shall have been ratified as an amendment to the Constitution by the Legislatures of three-fourths of the several States within seven years from the date of its submission.

AMENDMENT XXI

[Adopted 1933]

Section 1   The eighteenth article of amendment to the Constitution of the United States is hereby repealed.

Section 2   The transportation or importation into any State, Territory, or Possession of the United States for delivery or use

therein of intoxicating liquors, in violation of the laws thereof, is hereby prohibited.

Section 3   This article shall be inoperative unless it shall have been ratified as an amendment to the Constitution by conventions in the several States, as provided in the Constitution, within seven years from the date of submission thereof to the States by the Congress.

AMENDMENT XXII

[Adopted 1951]

Section 1   No person shall be elected to the office of President more than twice, and no person who has held the office of President, or acted as President, for more than two years of term to which some other person was elected President shall be elected to the office of President more than once. But this article shall not apply to any person holding the office of President when this article was proposed by the Congress, and shall not prevent any person who may be holding the office of President, or acting as President, during the term within which this article becomes operative from holding office of President or acting as President during the remainder of such term.

Section 2   This article shall be inoperative unless it shall have been ratified as an amendment to the Constitution by the legislatures of three-fourths of the several States within seven years from the date of its submission to the States by the Congress.

AMENDMENT XXIII

[Adopted 1961]

Section 1   The District constituting the seat of Government of the United States shall appoint in such manner as the Congress may direct:

A number of electors of President and Vice-President equal to the whole number of Senators and Representatives in Congress to which the District would be entitled if it were a State, but in no event more than the least populous State; they shall be in addition to those appointed by the States, but they shall be considered for the purposes of the election of President and Vice-President, to be electors appointed by a State; and they shall meet in the District and perform such duties as provided by the twelfth article of amendment.

Section 2   The Congress shall have the power to enforce this article by appropriate legislation.

AMENDMENT XXIV

[Adopted 1964]

Section 1   The right of citizens of the United States to vote in any primary or other election for President or Vice-President, for electors for President or Vice-President, or for Senator or Representative in Congress, shall not be denied or abridged by the United States or any State by reason of failure to pay any poll tax or other tax.

Section 2   The Congress shall have the power to enforce this article by appropriate legislation.

AMENDMENT XXV

[Adopted 1967]

Section 1   In case of the removal of the President from office or of his death or resignation, the Vice-President shall become President.

Section 2   Whenever there is a vacancy in the office of the Vice President, the President shall nominate a Vice President who shall take office upon confirmation by a majority vote of both Houses of Congress.

Section 3   Whenever the President transmits to the President pro tempore of the Senate and the Speaker of the House of Representatives his written declaration that he is unable to discharge the powers and duties of his office, and until he transmits to them a written declaration to the contrary, such powers and duties shall be discharged by the Vice-President as Acting President.

Section 4   Whenever the Vice President and a majority of either the principal officers of the executive departments or of such other body as Congress may by law provide, transmit to the President pro tempore of the Senate and the Speaker of the House of Representatives their written declaration that the President is unable to discharge the powers and duties of his office, the Vice President shall immediately assume the powers and duties of the office as Acting President.

Thereafter, when the President transmits to the President pro tempore of the Senate and the Speaker of the House of Representatives his written declaration that no inability exists, he shall resume the powers and duties of his office unless the Vice President and a majority of either the principal officers of the executive department[s] or of such other body as Congress may by law provide, transmit within four days to the President pro tempore of the Senate and the Speaker of the House of Representatives

their written declaration that the President is unable to discharge the powers and duties of his office. Thereupon Congress shall decide the issue, assembling within forty-eight hours for that purpose if not in session. If the Congress, within twenty-one days after receipt of the latter written declaration, or if Congress is not in session, within twenty-one days after Congress is required to assemble, determines by two-thirds vote of both Houses that the President is unable to discharge the powers and duties of his office, the Vice President shall continue to discharge the same as Acting President; otherwise, the President shall resume the powers and duties of his office.

AMENDMENT XXVI
[Adopted 1971]

Section 1   The right of citizens of the United States, who are eighteen years of age or older, to vote shall not be denied or abridged by the United States or by any State on account of age.

Section 2   The Congress shall have power to enforce this article by appropriate legislation.

AMENDMENT XXVII
[Adopted 1992]

No law varying the compensation for the services of the Senators and Representatives shall take effect, until an election of Representatives shall have intervened.

Presidential Elections

Year	Candidates	Parties	Popular Vote		Electoral Vote	Voter Participation
1789	**GEORGE WASHINGTON**		*		69	
	John Adams				34	
	Others				35	
1792	**GEORGE WASHINGTON**		*		132	
	John Adams				77	
	George Clinton				50	
	Others				5	
1796	**JOHN ADAMS**	Federalist	*		71	
	Thomas Jefferson	Democratic-Republican			68	
	Thomas Pinckney	Federalist			59	
	Aaron Burr	Dem.-Rep.			30	
	Others				48	
1800	**THOMAS JEFFERSON**	Dem.-Rep.	*		73	
	Aaron Burr	Dem.-Rep.			73	
	John Adams	Federalist			65	
	C. C. Pinckney	Federalist			64	
	John Jay	Federalist			1	
1804	**THOMAS JEFFERSON**	Dem.-Rep.	*		162	
	C. C. Pinckney	Federalist			14	
1808	**JAMES MADISON**	Dem.-Rep.	*		122	
	C. C. Pinckney	Federalist			47	
	George Clinton	Dem.-Rep.			6	
1812	**JAMES MADISON**	Dem.-Rep.	*		128	
	De Witt Clinton	Federalist			89	
1816	**JAMES MONROE**	Dem.-Rep.	*		183	
	Rufus King	Federalist			34	
1820	**JAMES MONROE**	Dem.-Rep.	*		231	
	John Quincy Adams	Dem.-Rep.			1	
1824	**JOHN Q. ADAMS**	Dem.-Rep.	108,740	(30.5%)	84	26.9%
	Andrew Jackson	Dem.-Rep.	153,544	(43.1%)	99	
	William H. Crawford	Dem.-Rep.	46,618	(13.1%)	41	
	Henry Clay	Dem.-Rep.	47,136	(13.2%)	37	
1828	**ANDREW JACKSON**	Democratic	647,286	(56.0%)	178	57.6%
	John Quincy Adams	National Republican	508,064	(44.0%)	83	
1832	**ANDREW JACKSON**	Democratic	687,502	(55.0%)	219	55.4%
	Henry Clay	National Republican	530,189	(42.4%)	49	
	John Floyd	Independent			11	
	William Wirt	Anti-Mason	33,108	(2.6%)	7	
1836	**MARTIN VAN BUREN**	Democratic	765,483	(50.9%)	170	57.8%
	W. H. Harrison	Whig			73	
	Hugh L. White	Whig	739,795	(49.1%)	26	
	Daniel Webster	Whig			14	
	W. P. Magnum	Independent			11	
1840	**WILLIAM H. HARRISON**	Whig	1,274,624	(53.1%)	234	80.2%
	Martin Van Buren	Democratic	1,127,781	(46.9%)	60	
	J. G. Birney	Liberty	7069		—	

*Electors selected by state legislatures.

Year	Candidates	Parties	Popular Vote		Electoral Vote	Voter Participation
1844	**JAMES K. POLK**	Democratic	1,338,464	(49.6%)	170	78.9%
	Henry Clay	Whig	1,300,097	(48.1%)	105	
	J. G. Birney	Liberty	62,300	(2.3%)	—	
1848	**ZACHARY TAYLOR**	Whig	1,360,967	(47.4%)	163	72.7%
	Lewis Cass	Democratic	1,222,342	(42.5%)	127	
	Martin Van Buren	Free-Soil	291,263	(10.1%)	—	
1852	**FRANKLIN PIERCE**	Democratic	1,601,117	(50.9%)	254	69.6%
	Winfield Scott	Whig	1,385,453	(44.1%)	42	
	John P. Hale	Free-Soil	155,825	(5.0%)	—	
1856	**JAMES BUCHANAN**	Democratic	1,832,955	(45.3%)	174	78.9%
	John C. Frémont	Republican	1,339,932	(33.1%)	114	
	Millard Fillmore	American	871,731	(21.6%)	8	
1860	**ABRAHAM LINCOLN**	Republican	1,865,593	(39.8%)	180	81.2%
	Stephen A. Douglas	Democratic	1,382,713	(29.5%)	12	
	John C. Breckinridge	Democratic	848,356	(18.1%)	72	
	John Bell	Union	592,906	(12.6%)	39	
1864	**ABRAHAM LINCOLN**	Republican	2,213,655	(55.0%)	212	73.8%
	George B. McClellan	Democratic	1,805,237	(45.0%)	21	
1868	**ULYSSES S. GRANT**	Republican	3,012,833	(52.7%)	214	78.1%
	Horatio Seymour	Democratic	2,703,249	(47.3%)	80	
1872	**ULYSSES S. GRANT**	Republican	3,597,132	(55.6%)	286	71.3%
	Horace Greeley	Democratic; Liberal Republican	2,834,125	(43.9%)	66	
1876	**RUTHERFORD B. HAYES**	Republican	4,036,298	(48.0%)	185	81.8%
	Samuel J. Tilden	Democratic	4,300,590	(51.0%)	184	
1880	**JAMES A. GARFIELD**	Republican	4,454,416	(48.5%)	214	79.4%
	Winfield S. Hancock	Democratic	4,444,952	(48.1%)	155	
1884	**GROVER CLEVELAND**	Democratic	4,874,986	(48.5%)	219	77.5%
	James G. Blaine	Republican	4,851,981	(48.2%)	182	
1888	**BENJAMIN HARRISON**	Republican	5,439,853	(47.9%)	233	79.3%
	Grover Cleveland	Democratic	5,540,309	(48.6%)	168	
1892	**GROVER CLEVELAND**	Democratic	5,556,918	(46.1%)	277	74.7%
	Benjamin Harrison	Republican	5,176,108	(43.0%)	145	
	James B. Weaver	People's	1,041,028	(8.5%)	22	
1896	**WILLIAM McKINLEY**	Republican	7,104,779	(51.1%)	271	79.3%
	William J. Bryan	Democratic People's	6,502,925	(47.7%)	176	
1900	**WILLIAM McKINLEY**	Republican	7,207,923	(51.7%)	292	73.2%
	William J. Bryan	Dem.-Populist	6,358,133	(45.5%)	155	
1904	**THEODORE ROOSEVELT**	Republican	7,623,486	(57.9%)	336	65.2%
	Alton B. Parker	Democratic	5,077,911	(37.6%)	140	
	Eugene V. Debs	Socialist	402,283	(3.0%)	—	
1908	**WILLIAM H. TAFT**	Republican	7,678,908	(51.6%)	321	65.4%
	William J. Bryan	Democratic	6,409,104	(43.1%)	162	
	Eugene V. Debs	Socialist	420,793	(2.8%)	—	
1912	**WOODROW WILSON**	Democratic	6,293,454	(41.9%)	435	58.8%
	Theodore Roosevelt	Progressive	4,119,538	(27.4%)	88	
	William H. Taft	Republican	3,484,980	(23.2%)	8	
	Eugene V. Debs	Socialist	900,672	(6.0%)	—	
1916	**WOODROW WILSON**	Democratic	9,129,606	(49.4%)	277	61.6%
	Charles E. Hughes	Republican	8,538,221	(46.2%)	254	
	A. L. Benson	Socialist	585,113	(3.2%)	—	
1920	**WARREN G. HARDING**	Republican	16,152,200	(60.4%)	404	49.2%
	James M. Cox	Democratic	9,147,353	(34.2%)	127	
	Eugene V. Debs	Socialist	919,799	(3.4%)	—	

Year	Candidates	Parties	Popular Vote		Electoral Vote	Voter Participation
1924	**CALVIN COOLIDGE**	Republican	15,725,016	(54.0%)	382	48.9%
	John W. Davis	Democratic	8,386,503	(28.8%)	136	
	Robert M. La Follette	Progressive	4,822,856	(16.6%)	13	
1928	**HERBERT HOOVER**	Republican	21,391,381	(58.2%)	444	56.9%
	Alfred E. Smith	Democratic	15,016,443	(40.9%)	87	
	Norman Thomas	Socialist	267,835	(0.7%)	—	
1932	**FRANKLIN D. ROOSEVELT**	Democratic	22,821,857	(57.4%)	472	56.9%
	Herbert Hoover	Republican	15,761,841	(39.7%)	59	
	Norman Thomas	Socialist	881,951	(2.2%)	—	
1936	**FRANKLIN D. ROOSEVELT**	Democratic	27,751,597	(60.8%)	523	61.0%
	Alfred M. Landon	Republican	16,679,583	(36.5%)	8	
	William Lemke	Union	882,479	(1.9%)	—	
1940	**FRANKLIN D. ROOSEVELT**	Democratic	27,244,160	(54.8%)	449	62.5%
	Wendell L. Willkie	Republican	22,305,198	(44.8%)	82	
1944	**FRANKLIN D. ROOSEVELT**	Democratic	25,602,504	(53.5%)	432	55.9%
	Thomas E. Dewey	Republican	22,006,285	(46.0%)	99	
1948	**HARRY S TRUMAN**	Democratic	24,105,695	(49.5%)	304	53.0%
	Thomas E. Dewey	Republican	21,969,170	(45.1%)	189	
	J. Strom Thurmond	State-Rights Democratic	1,169,021	(2.4%)	38	
	Henry A. Wallace	Progressive	1,156,103	(2.4%)	—	
1952	**DWIGHT D. EISENHOWER**	Republican	33,936,252	(55.1%)	442	63.3%
	Adlai E. Stevenson	Democratic	27,314,992	(44.4%)	89	
1956	**DWIGHT D. EISENHOWER**	Republican	35,575,420	(57.6%)	457	60.6%
	Adlai E. Stevenson	Democratic	26,033,066	(42.1%)	73	
	Other	—	—		1	
1960	**JOHN F. KENNEDY**	Democratic	34,227,096	(49.9%)	303	62.8%
	Richard M. Nixon	Republican	34,108,546	(49.6%)	219	
	Other	—	—		15	
1964	**LYNDON B. JOHNSON**	Democratic	43,126,506	(61.1%)	486	61.7%
	Barry M. Goldwater	Republican	27,176,799	(38.5%)	52	
1968	**RICHARD M. NIXON**	Republican	31,770,237	(43.4%)	301	60.6%
	Hubert H. Humphrey	Democratic	31,270,533	(42.7%)	191	
	George Wallace	American Indep.	9,906,141	(13.5%)	46	
1972	**RICHARD M. NIXON**	Republican	47,169,911	(60.7%)	520	55.2%
	George S. McGovern	Democratic	29,170,383	(37.5%)	17	
	Other	—	—		1	
1976	**JIMMY CARTER**	Democratic	40,828,587	(50.0%)	297	53.5%
	Gerald R. Ford	Republican	39,147,613	(47.9%)	241	
	Other	—	1,575,459	(2.1%)	—	
1980	**RONALD REAGAN**	Republican	43,901,812	(50.7%)	489	52.6%
	Jimmy Carter	Democratic	35,483,820	(41.0%)	49	
	John B. Anderson	Independent	5,719,722	(6.6%)	—	
	Ed Clark	Libertarian	921,188	(1.1%)	—	
1984	**RONALD REAGAN**	Republican	54,455,075	(59.0%)	525	53.3%
	Walter Mondale	Democratic	37,577,185	(41.0%)	13	
1988	**GEORGE H. W. BUSH**	Republican	48,886,000	(53.4%)	426	57.4%
	Michael S. Dukakis	Democratic	41,809,000	(45.6%)	111	
1992	**BILL CLINTON**	Democratic	43,728,375	(43%)	370	55.0%
	George H. W. Bush	Republican	38,167,416	(38%)	168	
	Ross Perot	—	19,237,247	(19%)	—	

*Electors selected by state legislatures.

Vice Presidents and Cabinet Members by Administration

The Washington Administration (1789–1797)

Vice President	John Adams	1789–1797
Secretary of State	Thomas Jefferson	1789–1793
	Edmund Randolph	1794–1795
	Timothy Pickering	1795–1797
Secretary of Treasury	Alexander Hamilton	1789–1795
	Oliver Wolcott	1795–1797
Secretary of War	Henry Knox	1789–1794
	Timothy Pickering	1795–1796
	James McHenry	1796–1797
Attorney General	Edmund Randolph	1789–1793
	William Bradford	1794–1795
	Charles Lee	1795–1797
Postmaster General	Samuel Osgood	1789–1791
	Timothy Pickering	1791–1794
	Joseph Habersham	1795–1797

The John Adams Administration (1797–1801)

Vice President	Thomas Jefferson	1797–1801
Secretary of State	Timothy Pickering	1797–1800
	John Marshall	1800–1801
Secretary of Treasury	Oliver Wolcott	1797–1800
	Samuel Dexter	1800–1801
Secretary of War	James McHenry	1797–1800
	Samuel Dexter	1800–1801
Attorney General	Charles Lee	1797–1801
Postmaster General	Joseph Habersham	1797–1801
Secretary of Navy	Benjamin Stoddert	1798–1801

The Jefferson Administration (1801–1809)

Vice President	Aaron Burr	1801–1805
	George Clinton	1805–1809
Secretary of State	James Madison	1801–1809
Secretary of Treasury	Samuel Dexter	1801
	Albert Gallatin	1801–1809
Secretary of War	Henry Dearborn	1801–1809
Attorney General	Levi Lincoln	1801–1805
	Robert Smith	1805
	John Breckinridge	1805–1806
	Caesar Rodney	1807–1809
Postmaster General	Joseph Habersham	1801
	Gideon Granger	1801–1809
Secretary of Navy	Robert Smith	1801–1809

The Madison Administration (1809–1817)

Vice President	George Clinton	1809–d. 1812
	Elbridge Gerry	1813–d. 1814
Secretary of State	Robert Smith	1809–1811
	James Monroe	1811–1817
Secretary of Treasury	Albert Gallatin	1809–1813
	George Campbell	1814
	Alexander Dallas	1814–1816
	William Crawford	1816–1817
Secretary of War	William Eustis	1809–1812
	John Armstrong	1813–1814
	James Monroe	1814–1815
	William Crawford	1815–1817
Attorney General	Caesar Rodney	1809–1811
	William Pinkney	1811–1814
	Richard Rush	1814–1817
Postmaster General	Gideon Granger	1809–1814
	Return Meigs	1814–1817
Secretary of Navy	Paul Hamilton	1809–1813
	William Jones	1813–1814
	Benjamin Crowninshield	1814–1817

The Monroe Administration (1817–1825)

Vice President	Daniel Tompkins	1817–1825
Secretary of State	John Quincy Adams	1817–1825
Secretary of Treasury	William Crawford	1817–1825
Secretary of War	George Graham	1817
	John C. Calhoun	1817–1825
Attorney General	Richard Rush	1817
	William Wirt	1817–1825
Postmaster General	Return Meigs	1817–1823
	John McLean	1823–1825
Secretary of Navy	Benjamin Crowninshield	1817–1818
	Smith Thompson	1818–1823
	Samuel Southard	1823–1825

The John Quincy Adams Administration (1825–1829)

Vice President	John C. Calhoun	1825–1829
Secretary of State	Henry Clay	1825–1829
Secretary of Treasury	Richard Rush	1825–1829
Secretary of War	James Barbour	1825–1829
	Peter Porter	1828–1829
Attorney General	William Wirt	1825–1829
Postmaster General	John McLean	1825–1829
Secretary of Navy	Samuel Southard	1825–1829

The Jackson Administration (1829–1837)

Vice President	John C. Calhoun	1829–1832
	Martin Van Buren	1833–1837
Secretary of State	Martin Van Buren	1829–1831
	Edward Livingston	1831–1833
	Louis McLane	1833–1834
	John Forsyth	1834–1837
Secretary of Treasury	Samuel Ingham	1829–1831
	Louis McLane	1831–1833
	William Duane	1833
	Roger B. Taney	1833–1834
	Levi Woodbury	1834–1837
Secretary of War	John H. Eaton	1829–1831
	Lewis Cass	1831–1837
	Benjamin Butler	1837
Attorney General	John M. Berrien	1829–1831
	Roger B. Taney	1831–1833
	Benjamin Butler	1833–1837
Postmaster General	William Barry	1829–1835
	Amos Kendall	1835–1837
Secretary of Navy	John Branch	1829–1831
	Levi Woodbury	1831–1834
	Mahlon Dickerson	1834–1837

The Van Buren Administration (1837–1841)

Vice President	Richard M. Johnson	1837–1841
Secretary of State	John Forsyth	1837–1841
Secretary of Treasury	Levi Woodbury	1837–1841
Secretary of War	Joel Poinsett	1837–1841
Attorney General	Benjamin Butler	1837–1838
	Felix Grundy	1838–1840
	Henry D. Gilpin	1840–1841
Postmaster General	Amos Kendall	1837–1840
	John M. Niles	1840–1841
Secretary of Navy	Mahlon Dickerson	1837–1838
	James Paulding	1838–1841

The William Harrison Administration (1841)

Vice President	John Tyler	1841
Secretary of State	Daniel Webster	1841
Secretary of Treasury	Thomas Ewing	1841
Secretary of War	John Bell	1841
Attorney General	John J. Crittenden	1841
Postmaster General	Francis Granger	1841
Secretary of Navy	George Badger	1841

The Tyler Administration (1841–1845)

Vice President	None	
Secretary of State	Daniel Webster	1841–1843
	Hugh S. Legaré	1843
	Abel P. Upshur	1843–1844
	John C. Calhoun	1844–1845
Secretary of Treasury	Thomas Ewing	1841
	Walter Forward	1841–1843
	John C. Spencer	1843–1844
	George Bibb	1844–1845

Secretary of War	John Bell	1841
	John C. Spencer	1841–1843
	James M. Porter	1843–1844
	William Wilkins	1844–1845
Attorney General	John J. Crittenden	1841
	Hugh S. Legaré	1841–1843
	John Nelson	1843–1845
Postmaster General	Francis Granger	1841
	Charles Wickliffe	1841
Secretary of Navy	George Badger	1841
	Abel P. Upshur	1841
	David Henshaw	1843–1844
	Thomas Gilmer	1844
	John Y. Mason	1844–1845

The Polk Administration (1845–1849)

Vice President	George M. Dallas	1845–1849
Secretary of State	James Buchanan	1845–1849
Secretary of Treasury	Robert J. Walker	1845–1849
Secretary of War	William L. Marcy	1845–1849
Attorney General	John Y. Mason	1845–1846
	Nathan Clifford	1846–1848
	Isaac Toucey	1848–1849
Postmaster General	Cave Johnson	1845–1849
Secretary of Navy	George Bancroft	1845–1846
	John Y. Mason	1846–1849

The Taylor Administration (1849–1850)

Vice President	Millard Fillmore	1849–1850
Secretary of State	John M. Clayton	1849–1850
Secretary of Treasury	William Meredith	1849–1850
Secretary of War	George Crawford	1849–1850
Attorney General	Reverdy Johnson	1849–1850
Postmaster General	Jacob Collamer	1849–1850
Secretary of Navy	William Preston	1849–1850
Secretary of Interior	Thomas Ewing	1849–1850

The Fillmore Administration (1850–1853)

Vice President	None	
Secretary of State	Daniel Webster	1850–1852
	Edward Everett	1852–1853
Secretary of Treasury	Thomas Corwin	1850–1853
Secretary of War	Charles Conrad	1850–1853
Attorney General	John J. Crittenden	1850–1853
Postmaster General	Nathan Hall	1850–1852
	Samuel D. Hubbard	1852–1853
Secretary of Navy	William A. Graham	1850–1852
	John P. Kennedy	1852–1853
Secretary of Interior	Thomas McKennan	1850
	Alexander Stuart	1850–1853

The Pierce Administration (1853–1857)

Vice President	William R. King	1853–d. 1853
Secretary of State	William L. Marcy	1853–1857
Secretary of Treasury	James Guthrie	1853–1857

Secretary of War	Jefferson Davis	1853–1857
Attorney General	Caleb Cushing	1853–1857
Postmaster General	James Campbell	1853–1857
Secretary of Navy	James C. Dobbin	1853–1857
Secretary of Interior	Robert McClelland	1853–1857

The Buchanan Administration (1857–1861)

Vice President	John C. Breckinridge	1857–1861
Secretary of State	Lewis Cass	1857–1860
	Jeremiah S. Black	1860–1861
Secretary of Treasury	Howell Cobb	1857–1860
	Philip Thomas	1860–1861
	John A. Dix	1861
Secretary of War	John B. Floyd	1857–1861
	Joseph Holt	1861
Attorney General	Jeremiah S. Black	1857–1860
	Edwin M. Stanton	1860–1861
Postmaster General	Aaron V. Brown	1857–1859
	Joseph Holt	1859–1861
	Horatio King	1861
Secretary of Navy	Isaac Toucey	1857–1861
Secretary of Interior	Jacob Thompson	1857–1861

The Lincoln Administration (1861–1865)

Vice President	Hannibal Hamlin	1861–1865
	Andrew Johnson	1865
Secretary of State	William H. Seward	1861–1865
Secretary of Treasury	Samuel P. Chase	1861–1864
	William P. Fessenden	1864–1865
	Hugh McCulloch	1865
Secretary of War	Simon Cameron	1861–1862
	Edwin M. Stanton	1862–1865
Attorney General	Edward Bates	1861–1864
	James Speed	1864–1865
Postmaster General	Horatio King	1861
	Montgomery Blair	1861–1864
	William Dennison	1864–1865
Secretary of Navy	Gideon Welles	1861–1865
Secretary of Interior	Caleb B. Smith	1861–1863
	John P. Usher	1863–1865

The Andrew Johnson Administration (1865–1869)

Vice President	None	
Secretary of State	William H. Seward	1865–1869
Secretary of Treasury	Hugh McCulloch	1865–1869
Secretary of War	Edwin M. Stanton	1865–1867
	Ulysses S. Grant	1867–1868
	Lorenzo Thomas	1868
	John M. Schofield	1868–1869
Attorney General	James Speed	1865–1866
	Henry Stanbery	1866–1868
	William M. Evarts	1868–1869
Postmaster General	William Dennison	1865–1866
	Alexander Randall	1866–1869
Secretary of Navy	Gideon Welles	1865–1869

Secretary of Interior	John P. Usher	1865
	James Harlan	1865–1866
	Ovrille H. Browning	1866–1869

The Grant Administration (1869–1877)

Vice President	Schuyler Colfax	1869–1873
	Henry Wilson	1873–d. 1875
Secretary of State	Elihu B. Washburne	1869
	Hamilton Fish	1869–1877
Secretary of Treasury	George S. Boutwell	1869–1873
	William Richardson	1873–1874
	Benjamin Bristow	1874–1876
	Lot M. Morrill	1876–1877
Secretary of War	John A. Rawlins	1869
	William T. Sherman	1869
	William W. Belknap	1869–1876
	Alphonso Taft	1876
	James D. Cameron	1876–1877
Attorney General	Ebenezer Hoar	1869–1870
	Amos T. Ackerman	1870–1871
	G. H. Williams	1871–1875
	Edwards Pierrepont	1875–1876
	Alphonso Taft	1876–1877
Postmaster General	John A. J. Creswell	1869–1874
	James W. Marshall	1874
	Marshall Jewell	1874–1876
	James N. Tyner	1876–1877
Secretary of Navy	Adolph E. Borie	1869
	George M. Robeson	1869–1877
Secretary of Interior	Jacob D. Cox	1869–1870
	Columbus Delano	1870–1875
	Zachariah Chandler	1875–1877

The Hayes Administration (1877–1881)

Vice President	William A. Wheeler	1877–1881
Secretary of State	William M. Evarts	1877–1881
Secretary of Treasury	John Sherman	1877–1881
Secretary of War	George W. McCrary	1877–1879
	Alex Ramsey	1879–1881
Attorney General	Charles Devens	1877–1881
Postmaster General	David M. Key	1877–1880
	Horace Maynard	1880–1881
Secretary of Navy	Richard W. Thompson	1877–1880
	Nathan Goff, Jr.	1881
Secretary of Interior	Carl Schurz	1877–1881

The Garfield Administration (1881)

Vice President	Chester A. Arthur	1881
Secretary of State	James G. Blaine	1881
Secretary of Treasury	William Windom	1881
Secretary of War	Robert T. Lincoln	1881
Attorney General	Wayne MacVeagh	1881
Postmaster General	Thomas L. James	1881
Secretary of Navy	William H. Hunt	1881
Secretary of Interior	Samuel J. Kirkwood	1881

The Arthur Administration (1881–1885)

Vice President	None	
Secretary of State	F. T. Frelinghuysen	1881–1885
Secretary of Treasury	Charles J. Folger	1881–1884
	Walter Q. Gresham	1884
	Hugh McCulloch	1884–1885
Secretary of War	Robert T. Lincoln	1881–1885
Attorney General	Benjamin H. Brewster	1881–1885
Postmaster General	Timothy O. Howe	1881–1883
	Walter Q. Gresham	1883–1884
	Frank Hatton	1884–1885
Secretary of Navy	William H. Hunt	1881–1882
	William E. Chandler	1882–1885
Secretary of Interior	Samuel J. Kirkwood	1881–1882
	Henry M. Teller	1882–1885

The Cleveland Administration (1885–1889)

Vice President	Thomas A. Hendricks	1885–d. 1885
Secretary of State	Thomas F. Bayard	1885–1889
Secretary of Treasury	Daniel Manning	1885–1887
	Charles S. Fairchild	1887–1889
Secretary of War	William C. Endicott	1885–1889
Attorney General	Augustus H. Garland	1885–1889
Postmaster General	William F. Vilas	1885–1888
	Don M. Dickinson	1888–1889
Secretary of Navy	William C. Whitney	1885–1889
Secretary of Interior	Lucius Q. C. Lamar	1885–1888
	William F. Vilas	1888–1889
Secretary of Agriculture	Norman J. Colman	1889

The Benjamin Harrison Administration (1889–1893)

Vice President	Levi P. Morton	1889–1893
Secretary of State	James G. Blaine	1889–1892
	John W. Foster	1892–1893
Secretary of Treasury	William Windom	1889–1891
	Charles Foster	1891–1893
Secretary of War	Redfield Proctor	1889–1891
	Stephen B. Elkins	1891–1893
Attorney General	William H. H. Miller	1889–1891
Postmaster General	John Wanamaker	1889–1893
Secretary of Navy	Benjamin F. Tracy	1889–1893
Secretary of Interior	John W. Noble	1889–1893
Secretary of Agriculture	Jeremiah M. Rusk	1889–1893

The Cleveland Administration (1893–1897)

Vice President	Adlai E. Stevenson	1893–1897
Secretary of State	Walter Q. Gresham	1893–1895
	Richard Olney	1895–1897
Secretary of Treasury	John G. Carlisle	1893–1897
Secretary of War	Daniel S. Lamont	1893–1897
Attorney General	Richard Olney	1893–1895
	James Harmon	1895–1897
Postmaster General	Wilson S. Bissell	1893–1895
	William L. Wilson	1895–1897
Secretary of Navy	Hilary A. Herbert	1893–1897
Secretary of Interior	Hoke Smith	1893–1896
	David R. Francis	1896–1897
Secretary of Agriculture	Julius S. Morton	1893–1897

The McKinley Administration (1897–1901)

Vice President	Garret A. Hobart	1897–d. 1899
	Theodore Roosevelt	1901
Secretary of State	John Sherman	1897–1898
	William R. Day	1898
	John Hay	1898–1901
Secretary of Treasury	Lyman J. Gage	1897–1901
Secretary of War	Russell A. Alger	1897–1899
	Elihu Root	1899–1901
Attorney General	Joseph McKenna	1897–1898
	John W. Griggs	1898–1901
	Philander C. Knox	1901
Postmaster General	James A. Gary	1897–1898
	Charles E. Smith	1898–1901
Secretary of Navy	John D. Long	1897–1901
Secretary of Interior	Cornelius N. Bliss	1897–1899
	Ethan A. Hitchcock	1899–1901
Secretary of Agriculture	James Wilson	1897–1901

The Theodore Roosevelt Administration (1901–1909)

Vice President	Charles Fairbanks	1905–1909
Secretary of State	John Hay	1901–1905
	Elihu Root	1905–1909
	Robert Bacon	1909
Secretary of Treasury	Lyman J. Gage	1901–1902
	Leslie M. Shaw	1902–1907
	George B. Cortelyou	1907–1909
Secretary of War	Elihu Root	1901–1904
	William H. Taft	1904–1908
	Luke E. Wright	1908–1909
Attorney General	Philander C. Knox	1901–1904
	William H. Moody	1904–1906
	Charles J. Bonaparte	1906–1909
Postmaster General	Charles E. Smith	1901–1902
	Henry C. Payne	1902–1904
	Robert J. Wynne	1904–1905
	George B. Cortelyou	1905–1907
	George von L. Meyer	1907–1909
Secretary of Navy	John D. Long	1901–1902
	William H. Moody	1902–1904
	Paul Morton	1904–1905
	Charles J. Bonaparte	1905–1906
	Victor H. Metcalf	1906–1908
	Truman H. Newberry	1908–1909
Secretary of Interior	Ethan A. Hitchcock	1901–1907
	James R. Garfield	1907–1909
Secretary of Agriculture	James Wilson	1901–1909
Secretary of Labor and Commerce	George B. Cortelyou	1903–1904
	Victor H. Metcalf	1904–1906
	Oscar S. Straus	1906–1909
	Charles Nagel	1909

The Taft Administration (1909–1913)

Vice President	James S. Sherman	1909–d. 1912
Secretary of State	Philander C. Knox	1909–1913

Secretary of Treasury	Franklin MacVeagh	1909–1913
Secretary of War	Jacob M. Dickinson	1901–1911
	Henry L. Stimson	1911–1913
Attorney General	George W. Wickersham	1909–1913
Postmaster General	Frank H. Hitchcock	1909–1913
Secretary of Navy	George von L. Meyer	1909–1913
Secretary of Interior	Richard A. Ballinger	1909–1911
	Walter L. Fisher	1911–1913
Secretary of Agriculture	James Wilson	1909–1913
Secretary of Labor and Commerce	Charles Nagel	1909–1913

The Wilson Administration (1913–1921)

Vice President	Thomas R. Marshall	1913–1921
Secretary of State	Williams J. Bryan	1913–1915
	Robert Lansing	1915–1920
	Bainbridge Colby	1920–1921
Secretary of Treasury	William G. McAdoo	1913–1918
	Carter Glass	1918–1920
	David F. Houston	1920–1921
Secretary of War	Lindley M. Garrison	1913–1916
	Newton D. Baker	1916–1921
Attorney General	James C. McReyolds	1913–1914
	Thomas W. Gregory	1914–1919
	A. Mitchell Palmer	1919–1921
Postmaster General	Albert S. Burleson	1913–1921
Secretary of Navy	Josephus Daniels	1913–1921
Secretary of Interior	Franklin K. Lane	1913–1920
	John B. Payne	1920–1921
Secretary of Agriculture	David F. Houston	1913–1920
	Edwin T. Meredith	1920–1921
Secretary of Commerce	William C. Redfield	1913–1919
	Joshua W. Alexander	1919–1921
Secretary of Labor	William B. Wilson	1913–1921

The Harding Administration (1921–1923)

Vice President	Calvin Coolidge	1921–1923
Secretary of State	Charles E. Hughes	1921–1923
Secretary of Treasury	Andrew Mellon	1921–1923
Secretary of War	John W. Weeks	1921–1923
Attorney General	Harry M. Daugherty	1921–1923
Postmaster General	Will H. Hays	1921–1922
	Hubert Work	1922–1923
	Harry S. New	1923
Secretary of Navy	Edwin Denby	1921–1923
Secretary of Interior	Albert B. Fall	1921–1923
	Hubert Work	1923
Secretary of Agriculture	Henry C. Wallace	1921–1923
Secretary of Commerce	Herbert C. Hoover	1921–1923
Secretary of Labor	James J. Davis	1921–1923

The Coolidge Administration (1923–1929)

Vice President	Charles G. Dawes	1925–1929
Secretary of State	Charles E. Hughes	1923–1925
	Frank B. Kellogg	1925–1929

Secretary of Treasury	Andrew Mellon	1923–1929
Secretary of War	John W. Weeks	1923–1925
	Dwight F. Davis	1925–1929
Attorney General	Henry M. Daugherty	1923–1924
	Harlan F. Stone	1924–1925
	John G. Sargent	1925–1929
Postmaster General	Harry S. New	1923–1929
Secretary of Navy	Edwin Derby	1923–1924
	Curtis D. Wilbur	1924–1929
Secretary of Interior	Hubert Work	1923–1928
	Roy O. West	1928–1929
Secretary of Agriculture	Henry C. Wallace	1923–1924
	Howard M. Gore	1924–1925
	William M. Jardine	1925–1929
Secretary of Commerce	Herbert C. Hoover	1923–1928
	William F. Whiting	1928–1929
Secretary of Labor	James J. Davis	1923–1929

The Hoover Administration (1929–1933)

Vice President	Charles Curtis	1929–1933
Secretary of State	Henry L. Stimson	1929–1933
Secretary of Treasury	Andrew Mellon	1929–1932
	Ogden L. Mills	1932–1933
Secretary of War	James W. Good	1929
	Patrick J. Hurley	1929–1933
Attorney General	William D. Mitchell	1929–1933
Postmaster General	Walter F. Brown	1929–1933
Secretary of Navy	Charles F. Adams	1929–1933
Secretary of Interior	Ray L. Wilbur	1929–1933
Secretary of Agriculture	Arthur M. Hyde	1929–1933
Secretary of Commerce	Robert P. Lamont	1929–1932
	Roy D. Chapin	1932–1933
Secretary of Labor	James J. Davis	1929–1930
	William N. Doak	1930–1933

The Franklin D. Roosevelt Administration (1933–1945)

Vice President	John Nance Garner	1933–1941
	Henry A. Wallace	1941–1945
	Harry S Truman	1945
Secretary of State	Cordell Hull	1933–1944
	Edward R. Stettinius, Jr.	1944–1945
Secretary of Treasury	William H. Woodin	1933–1934
	Henry Morgenthau, Jr.	1934–1945
Secretary of War	George H. Dern	1933–1936
	Henry A. Woodring	1936–1940
	Henry L. Stimson	1940–1945
Attorney General	Homer S. Cummings	1933–1939
	Frank Murphy	1939–1940
	Robert H. Jackson	1940–1941
	Francis Biddle	1941–1945
Postmaster General	James A. Farley	1933–1940
	Frank C. Walker	1940–1945
Secretary of Navy	Claude A. Swanson	1933–1940
	Charles Edison	1940
	Frank Knox	1940–1944
	James V. Forrestal	1944–1945
Secretary of Interior	Harold L. Ickes	1933–1945

Secretary of Agriculture	Henry A. Wallace	1933–1940
	Claude R. Wickard	1940–1945
Secretary of Commerce	Daniel C. Roper	1933–1939
	Harry L. Hopkins	1939–1940
	Jesse Jones	1940–1945
	Henry A. Wallace	1945
Secretary of Labor	Frances Perkins	1933–1945

The Truman Administration (1945–1953)

Vice President	Alben W. Barkley	1949–1953
Secretary of State	Edward R. Stettinius, Jr.	1945
	James F. Byrnes	1945–1947
	George C. Marshall	1947–1949
	Dean G. Acheson	1949–1953
Secretary of Treasury	Fred M. Vinson	1945–1946
	John W. Snyder	1946–1953
Secretary of War	Robert P. Patterson	1945–1947
	Kenneth C. Royall	1947
Attorney General	Tom C. Clark	1945–1949
	J. Howard McGrath	1949–1952
	James P. McGranery	1952–1953
Postmaster General	Frank C. Walker	1945
	Robert E. Hannegan	1945–1947
	Jesse M. Donaldson	1947–1953
Secretary of Navy	James V. Forrestal	1945–1947
Secretary of Interior	Harold L. Ickes	1945–1946
	Julius A. Krug	1946–1949
	Oscar L. Chapman	1949–1953
Secretary of Agriculture	Clinton P. Anderson	1945–1948
	Charles F. Brannan	1948–1953
Secretary of Commerce	Henry A. Wallace	1945–1946
	W. Averell Harriman	1946–1948
	Charles W. Sawyer	1948–1953
Secretary of Labor	Lewis B. Schwellenbach	1945–1948
	Maurice J. Tobin	1948–1953
Secretary of Defense	James V. Forrestal	1947–1949
	Louis A. Johnson	1949–1950
	George C. Marshall	1950–1951
	Robert A. Lovett	1951–1953

The Eisenhower Administration (1953–1961)

Vice President	Richard M. Nixon	1953–1961
Secretary of State	John Foster Dulles	1953–1959
	Christian A. Herter	1959–1961
Secretary of Treasury	George M. Humphrey	1953–1957
	Robert B. Anderson	1957–1961
Attorney General	Herbert Brownell, Jr.	1953–1958
	William P. Rogers	1958–1961
Postmaster General	Arthur E. Summerfield	1953–1961
Secretary of Interior	Douglas McKay	1953–1956
	Fred A. Seaton	1956–1961
Secretary of Agriculture	Ezra T. Benson	1953–1961
Secretary of Commerce	Sinclair Weeks	1953–1958
	Lewis L. Strauss	1958–1959
	Frederick H. Mueller	1959–1961
Secretary of Labor	Martin P. Durkin	1953
	James P. Mitchell	1953–1961

Secretary of Defense	Charles E. Wilson	1953–1957
	Neil H. McElroy	1957–1959
	Thomas S. Gates, Jr.	1959–1961
Secretary of Health, Education, and Welfare	Oveta Culp Hobby	1953–1955
	Marion B. Folsom	1955–1958
	Arthur S. Flemming	1958–1961

The Kennedy Administration (1961–1963)

Vice President	Lyndon B. Johnson	1961–1963
Secretary of State	Dean Rusk	1961–1963
Secretary of Treasury	C. Douglas Dillon	1961–1963
Attorney General	Robert F. Kennedy	1961–1963
Postmaster General	J. Edward Day	1961–1963
	John A. Gronouski	1963
Secretary of Interior	Stewart L. Udall	1961–1963
Secretary of Agriculture	Orville L. Freeman	1961–1963
Secretary of Commerce	Luther H. Hodges	1961–1963
Secretary of Labor	Arthur J. Goldberg	1961–1962
	W. Willard Wirtz	1962–1963
Secretary of Defense	Robert S. McNamara	1961–1963
Secretary of Health, Education, and Welfare	Abraham A. Ribicoff	1961–1962
	Anthony J. Celebrezze	1962–1963

The Lyndon Johnson Administration (1963–1969)

Vice President	Hubert H. Humphrey	1965–1969
Secretary of State	Dean Rusk	1963–1969
Secretary of Treasury	C. Douglas Dillon	1963–1965
	Henry H. Fowler	1965–1969
Attorney General	Robert F. Kennedy	1963–1964
	Nicholas Katzenbach	1965–1966
	Ramsey Clark	1967–1969
Postmaster General	John A. Gronouski	1963–1965
	Lawrence F. O'Brien	1965–1968
	Marvin Watson	1968–1969
Secretary of Interior	Stewart L. Udall	1963–1969
Secretary of Agriculture	Orville L. Freeman	1963–1969
Secretary of Commerce	Luther H. Hodges	1963–1964
	John T. Connor	1964–1967
	Alexander B. Trowbridge	1967–1968
	Cyrus R. Smith	1968–1969
Secretary of Labor	W. Willard Wirtz	1963–1969
Secretary of Defense	Robert F. McNamara	1963–1968
	Clark Clifford	1968–1969
Secretary of Health, Education, and Welfare	Anthony J. Celebrezze	1963–1965
	John W. Gardner	1965–1968
	Wilbur J. Cohen	1968–1969
Secretary of Housing and Urban Development	Robert C. Weaver	1966–1969
	Robert C. Wood	1969
Secretary of Transportation	Alan S. Boyd	1967–1969

The Nixon Administration (1969–1974)

| Vice President | Spiro T. Agnew | 1969–1973 |
| | Gerald R. Ford | 1973–1974 |

Secretary of State	William P. Rogers	1969–1973
	Henry A. Kissinger	1973–1974
Secretary of Treasury	David M. Kennedy	1969–1970
	John B. Connally	1971–1972
	George P. Shultz	1972–1974
	William E. Simon	1974
Attorney General	John N. Mitchell	1969–1972
	Richard G. Kleindienst	1972–1973
	Elliot L. Richardson	1973
	William B. Saxbe	1973–1974
Postmaster General	Winton M. Blount	1969–1971
Secretary of Interior	Walter J. Hickel	1969–1970
	Rogers Morton	1971–1974
Secretary of Agriculture	Clifford M. Hardin	1969–1971
	Earl L. Butz	1971–1974
Secretary of Commerce	Maurice H. Stans	1969–1972
	Peter G. Peterson	1972–1973
	Frederick B. Dent	1973–1974
Secretary of Labor	George P. Shultz	1969–1970
	James D. Hodgson	1970–1973
	Peter J. Brennan	1973–1974
Secretary of Defense	Melvin R. Laird	1969–1973
	Elliot L. Richardson	1973
	James R. Schlesinger	1973–1974
Secretary of Health, Education, and Welfare	Robert H. Finch	1969–1970
	Elliot L. Richardson	1970–1973
	Caspar W. Weinberger	1973–1974
Secretary of Housing and Urban Development	George Romney	1969–1973
	James T. Lynn	1973–1974
Secretary of Transportation	John A. Volpe	1969–1973
	Claude S. Brinegar	1973–1974

The Ford Administration (1974–1977)

Vice President	Nelson A. Rockefeller	1974–1977
Secretary of State	Henry A. Kissinger	1974–1977
Secretary of Treasury	William E. Simon	1974–1977
Attorney General	William B. Saxbe	1974–1975
	Edward Levi	1975–1977
Secretary of Interior	Rogers Morton	1974–1975
	Stanley K. Hathaway	1975
	Thomas Kleppe	1975–1977
Secretary of Agriculture	Earl L. Butz	1974–1976
	John A. Knebel	1976–1977
Secretary of Commerce	Frederick B. Dent	1974–1975
	Rogers Morton	1975–1976
	Elliot L. Richardson	1976–1977
Secretary of Labor	Peter J. Brennan	1974–1975
	John T. Dunlop	1975–1976
	W. J. Usery	1976–1977
Secretary of Defense	James R. Schlesinger	1974–1975
	Donald Rumsfeld	1975–1977
Secretary of Health, Education, and Welfare	Caspar W. Weinberger	1974–1975
	Forrest D. Mathews	1975–1977
Secretary of Housing and Urban Development	James T. Lynn	1974–1975
	Carla A. Hills	1975–1977
Secretary of Transportation	Claude S. Brinegar	1974–1975
	William T. Coleman	1975–1977

The Carter Administration (1977–1981)

Vice President	Walter F. Mondale	1977–1981
Secretary of State	Cyrus R. Vance	1977–1980
	Edmund Muskie	1980–1981
Secretary of Treasury	W. Michael Blumenthal	1977–1979
	G. William Miller	1979–1981
Attorney General	Griffin Bell	1977–1979
	Benjamin R. Civiletti	1979–1981
Secretary of Interior	Cecil D. Andrus	1977–1981
Secretary of Agriculture	Robert Bergland	1977–1981
Secretary of Commerce	Juanita M. Kreps	1977–1979
	Philip M. Klutznick	1979–1981
Secretary of Labor	F. Ray Marshall	1977–1981
Secretary of Defense	Harold Brown	1977–1981
Secretary of Health, Education, and Welfare	Joseph A. Califano	1977–1979
	Patricia R. Harris	1979
Secretary of Health and Human Services	Patricia R. Harris	1979–1981
Secretary of Education	Shirley M. Hufstedler	1979–1981
Secretary of Housing and Urban Development	Patricia R. Harris	1977–1979
	Moon Landrieu	1979–1981
Secretary of Transportation	Brock Adams	1977–1979
	Neil E. Goldschmidt	1979–1981
Secretary of Energy	James R. Schlesinger	1979–1979
	Charles W. Duncan	1979–1981

The Reagan Administration (1981–1989)

Vice President	George Bush	1981–1989
Secretary of State	Alexander M. Haig	1981–1982
	George P. Shultz	1982–1989
Secretary of Treasury	Donald Regan	1981–1985
	James A. Baker, III	1985–1988
	Nicholas Brady	1988–1989
Attorney General	William F. Smith	1981–1985
	Edwin A. Meese, III	1985–1988
	Richard Thornburgh	1988–1989
Secretary of Interior	James Watt	1981–1983
	William P. Clark, Jr.	1983–1985
	Donald P. Hodel	1985–1989
Secretary of Agriculture	John Block	1981–1986
	Richard E. Lyng	1986–1989
Secretary of Commerce	Malcolm Baldrige	1981–1987
	C. William Verity, Jr.	1987–1989
Secretary of Labor	Raymond Donovan	1981–1985
	William E. Brock	1985–1988
	Ann Dore McLaughlin	1988–1989
Secretary of Defense	Caspar W. Weinberger	1981–1988
	Frank Carlucci	1988–1989
Secretary of Health and Human Services	Richard Schweiker	1981–1983
	Margaret Heckler	1983–1985
	Otis R. Bowen	1985–1989
Secretary of Education	Terrel H. Bell	1981–1985
	William J. Bennett	1985–1988
	Lauro F. Cavazos	1988–1989
Secretary of Housing and Urban Development	Samuel Pierce	1981–1989

Secretary of Transportation	Drew Lewis	1981–1983
	Elizabeth Dole	1983–1987
	James L. Burnley, IV	1987–1989
Secretary of Energy	James Edwards	1981–1982
	Donald P. Hodel	1982–1985
	John S. Herrington	1985–1989

The Bush Administration (1989–1993)

Vice President	J. Danforth Quayle	1989–
Secretary of State	James A. Baker, III	1989–1992
Secretary of Treasury	Nicholas F. Brady	1988–
Attorney General	Richard Thornburgh	1989–1991
	William Barr	1991–
Secretary of Interior	Manuel Lujan, Jr.	1989–
Secretary of Agriculture	Clayton K. Yeutter	1989–1991
	Edward Madigan	1991–

Secretary of Commerce	Robert A. Mosbacher	1989–1991
	Barbara Hackman Franklin	1992–
Secretary of Labor	Elizabeth H. Dole	1989–1990
	Lynn Morley Martin	1991–
Secretary of Defense	Richard Cheney	1989–
Secretary of Health and Human Services	Louis W. Sullivan	1989–
Secretary of Education	Lauro F. Cavazos	1989–1990
	Lamar Alexander	1991–
Secretary of Housing and Urban Development	Jack F. Kemp	1989–
Secretary of Transportation	Samuel K. Skinner	1989–1991
	Andrew H. Card, Jr.	1992–
Secretary of Energy	James D. Watkins	1989–
Secretary of Veterans Affairs	Edward J. Derwinski	1989–1992

Supreme Court Justices

Name	Terms of Service[1]	Appointed by	Name	Terms of Service[1]	Appointed by
John Jay	1789–1795	Washington	Lucious Q. C. Lamar	1888–1893	Cleveland
James Wilson	1789–1798	Washington	**Melville W. Fuller**	1888–1910	Cleveland
John Rutledge	1790–1791	Washington	David J. Brewer	1890–1910	B. Harrison
William Cushing	1790–1810	Washington	Henry B. Brown	1891–1906	B. Harrison
John Blair	1790–1796	Washington	George Shiras, Jr.	1892–1903	B. Harrison
James Iredell	1790–1799	Washington	Howell E. Jackson	1893–1895	B. Harrison
Thomas Johnson	1792–1793	Washington	Edward D. White	1894–1910	Cleveland
William Paterson	1793–1806	Washington	Rufus W. Peckham	1896–1909	Cleveland
John Rutledge[2]	1795	Washington	Joseph McKenna	1898–1925	McKinley
Samuel Chase	1796–1811	Washington	Oliver W. Holmes	1902–1932	T. Roosevelt
Oliver Ellsworth	1796–1800	Washington	William R. Day	1903–1922	T. Roosevelt
Bushrod Washington	1799–1829	J. Adams	William H. Moody	1906–1910	T. Roosevelt
Alfred Moore	1800–1804	J. Adams	Horace H. Lurton	1910–1914	Taft
John Marshall	1801–1835	J. Adams	Charles E. Hughes	1910–1916	Taft
William Johnson	1804–1834	Jefferson	Willis Van Devanter	1911–1937	Taft
Brockholst Livingston	1807–1823	Jefferson	Joseph R. Lamar	1911–1916	Taft
Thomas Todd	1807–1826	Jefferson	**Edward D. White**	1910–1921	Taft
Gabriel Duvall	1811–1835	Madison	Mahlon Pitney	1912–1922	Taft
Joseph Story	1812–1845	Madison	James C. McReynolds	1914–1941	Wilson
Smith Thompson	1823–1843	Monroe	Louis D. Brandeis	1916–1939	Wilson
Robert Trimble	1826–1828	J. Q. Adams	John H. Clarke	1916–1922	Wilson
John McLean	1830–1861	Jackson	**William H. Taft**	1921–1930	Harding
Henry Baldwin	1830–1844	Jackson	George Sutherland	1922–1938	Harding
James M. Wayne	1835–1867	Jackson	Pierce Butler	1923–1939	Harding
Roger B. Taney	1836–1864	Jackson	Edward T. Sanford	1923–1930	Harding
Philip P. Barbour	1836–1841	Jackson	Harlan F. Stone	1925–1941	Coolidge
John Cartron	1837–1865	Van Buren	**Charles E. Hughes**	1930–1941	Hoover
John McKinley	1838–1852	Van Buren	Owen J. Roberts	1930–1945	Hoover
Peter V. Daniel	1842–1860	Van Buren	Benjamin N. Cardozo	1932–1938	Hoover
Samuel Nelson	1845–1872	Tyler	Hugo L. Black	1937–1971	F. Roosevelt
Levi Woodbury	1845–1851	Polk	Stanley F. Reed	1938–1957	F. Roosevelt
Robert C. Grier	1846–1870	Polk	Felix Frankfurter	1939–1962	F. Roosevelt
Benjamin R. Curtis	1851–1857	Fillmore	William O. Douglas	1939–1975	F. Roosevelt
John A. Campbell	1853–1861	Pierce	Frank Murphy	1940–1949	F. Roosevelt
Nathan Clifford	1858–1881	Buchanan	**Harlan F. Stone**	1941–1946	F. Roosevelt
Noah H. Swayne	1862–1881	Lincoln	James F. Byrnes	1941–1942	F. Roosevelt
Samuel F. Miller	1862–1890	Lincoln	Robert H. Jackson	1941–1954	F. Roosevelt
David Davis	1862–1877	Lincoln	Wiley B. Rutledge	1943–1949	F. Roosevelt
Stephen J. Field	1863–1897	Lincoln	Harold H. Burton	1945–1958	Truman
Salmon P. Chase	1864–1873	Lincoln	**Frederick M. Vinson**	1946–1953	Truman
William Strong	1870–1880	Grant	Tom C. Clark	1949–1967	Truman
Joseph P. Bradley	1870–1892	Grant	Sherman Minton	1949–1956	Truman
Ward Hunt	1873–1882	Grant	**Earl Warren**	1953–1969	Eisenhower
Morrison R. Waite	1874–1888	Grant	John Marshall Harlan	1955–1971	Eisenhower
John M. Harlan	1877–1911	Hayes	William J. Brennan, Jr.	1956–1990	Eisenhower
William B. Woods	1881–1887	Hayes	Charles E. Whittaker	1957–1962	Eisenhower
Stanley Matthews	1881–1889	Garfield	Potter Stewart	1958–1981	Eisenhower
Horace Gray	1882–1902	Arthur	Byron R. White	1962–	Kennedy
Samuel Blatchford	1882–1893	Arthur	Arthur J. Goldberg	1962–1965	Kennedy

Chief Justices in bold type

[1]The date on which the justice took his judicial oath is here used as the date of the beginning of his service, for until that oath is taken he is not vested with the prerogatives of his office. Justices, however, receive their commissions ("letters patent") before taking their oath—in some instances, in the preceding year.
[2]Acting Chief Justice; Senate refused to confirm appointment.

Name	Terms of Service[1]	Appointed by	Name	Terms of Service[1]	Appointed by
Abe Fortas	1965–1970	Johnson	Sandra Day O'Connor	1981–	Reagan
Thurgood Marshall	1967–1991	Johnson	**William H. Rehnquist**	1986–	Reagan
Warren E. Burger	1969–1986	Nixon	Antonin Scalia	1986–	Reagan
Harry A. Blackmun	1970–	Nixon	Anthony Kennedy	1988–	Reagan
Lewis F. Powell, Jr.	1971–1988	Nixon	David H. Souter	1990–	Bush
William H. Rehnquist	1971–1986	Nixon	Clarence Thomas	1991–	Bush
John Paul Stevens	1975–	Ford			

Chief Justices in bold type

[1] The date on which the justice took his judicial oath is here used as the date of the beginning of his service, for until that oath is taken he is not vested with the prerogatives of his office. Justices, however, receive their commissions ("letters patent") before taking their oath—in some instances, in the preceding year.

[2] Acting Chief Justice; Senate refused to confirm appointment.

Admission of States to the Union

State	Date of Admission	State	Date of Admission
1. Delaware	December 7, 1787	26. Michigan	January 26, 1837
2. Pennsylvania	December 12, 1787	27. Florida	March 3, 1845
3. New Jersey	December 18, 1787	28. Texas	December 29, 1845
4. Georgia	January 2, 1788	29. Iowa	December 28, 1846
5. Connecticut	January 9, 1788	30. Wisconsin	May 29, 1848
6. Massachusetts	February 6, 1788	31. California	September 9, 1850
7. Maryland	April 28, 1788	32. Minnesota	May 11, 1858
8. South Carolina	May 23, 1788	33. Oregon	February 14, 1859
9. New Hampshire	June 21, 1788	34. Kansas	January 29, 1861
10. Virginia	June 25, 1788	35. West Virginia	June 20, 1863
11. New York	July 26, 1788	36. Nevada	October 31, 1864
12. North Carolina	November 21, 1789	37. Nebraska	March 1, 1867
13. Rhode Island	May 29, 1790	38. Colorado	August 1, 1876
14. Vermont	March 4, 1791	39. North Dakota	November 2, 1889
15. Kentucky	June 1, 1792	40. South Dakota	November 2, 1889
16. Tennessee	June 1, 1796	41. Montana	November 8, 1889
17. Ohio	March 1, 1803	42. Washington	November 11, 1889
18. Louisiana	April 30, 1812	43. Idaho	July 3, 1890
19. Indiana	December 11, 1816	44. Wyoming	July 10, 1890
20. Mississippi	December 10, 1817	45. Utah	January 4, 1896
21. Illinois	December 3, 1818	46. Oklahoma	November 16, 1907
22. Alabama	December 14, 1819	47. New Mexico	January 6, 1912
23. Maine	March 15, 1820	48. Arizona	February 14, 1912
24. Missouri	August 10, 1821	49. Alaska	January 3, 1959
25. Arkansas	June 15, 1836	50. Hawaii	August 21, 1959

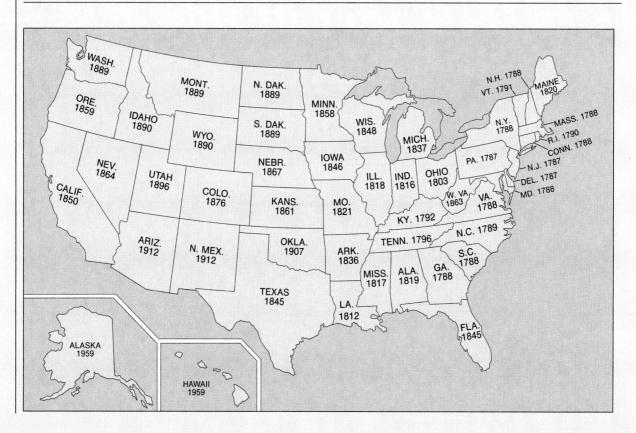

U.S. Population, 1790–1990

Year	Population	Percent Increase	Population Per Square Mile	Sex (rounded to nearest million) Male	Female	Median Age
1790	3,929,214		4.5	NA	NA	NA
1800	5,308,483	35.1	6.1	NA	NA	NA
1810	7,239,881	36.4	4.3	NA	NA	NA
1820	9,638,453	33.1	5.5	5	5	16.7
1830	12,866,020	33.5	7.4	7	6	17.2
1840	17,069,453	32.7	9.8	9	8	17.8
1850	23,191,876	35.9	7.9	12	11	18.9
1860	31,443,321	35.6	10.6	16	15	19.4
1870	39,818,449	26.6	13.4	19	19	20.2
1880	50,155,783	26.0	16.9	26	25	20.9
1890	62,947,714	25.5	21.2	32	31	22.0
1900	75,994,575	20.7	25.6	39	37	22.9
1910	91,972,266	21.0	31.0	47	45	24.1
1920	105,710,620	14.9	35.6	54	52	25.3
1930	122,775,046	16.1	41.2	62	61	26.4
1940	131,669,275	7.2	44.2	66	66	29.0
1950	150,697,361	14.5	50.7	75	76	30.2
1960	179,323,175	18.5	50.6	88	91	29.5
1970	203,302,031	13.4	57.4	99	104	28.0
1980	226,545,805	11.4	64.0	110	116	30.0
1985	237,839,000	5.0	64.0	117	123	31.3
1990	249,975,000	1.1	70.3	121	127	32.6

NA = Not available.

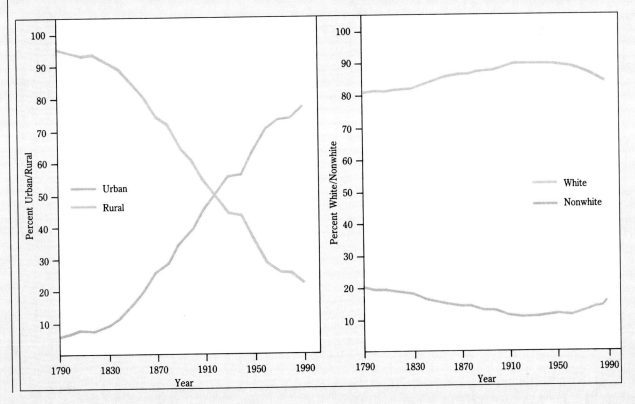

A-27

Employment, 1870–1990

Year	Number of Workers (in Millions)	Male/Female Employment Ratio	Percentage of Workers in Unions
1870	12.5	85/15	—
1880	17.4	85/15	—
1890	23.3	83/17	—
1900	29.1	82/18	3
1910	38.2	79/21	6
1920	41.6	79/21	12
1930	48.8	78/22	7
1940	53.0	76/24	27
1950	59.6	72/28	25
1960	69.9	68/32	26
1970	82.1	63/37	25
1980	108.5	58/42	23
1985	108.9	57/43	19
1990	126.4	55/45	16.4

Unemployment

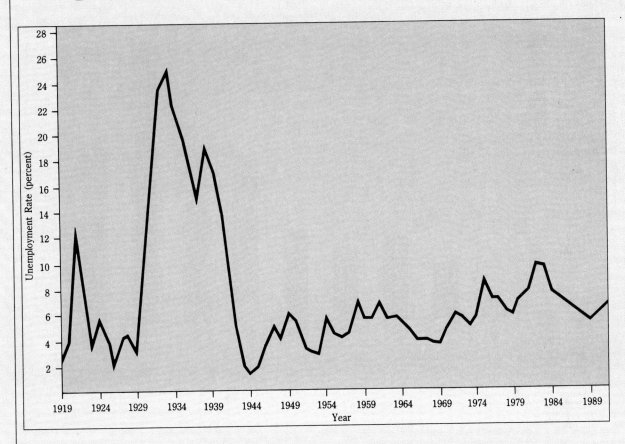

Regional Origins of Immigration

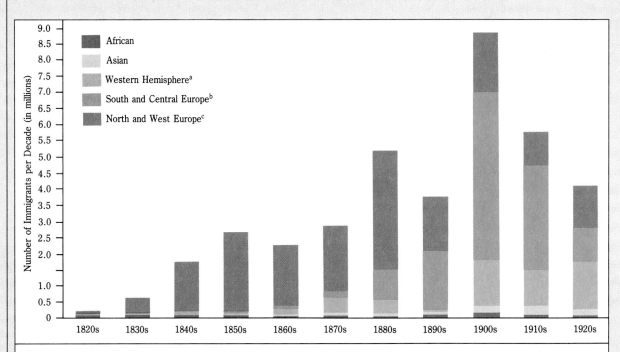

^aCanada and all countries in South America and Central America.
^bItaly, Spain, Portugal, Greece, Germany (Austria included, 1938-1945), Poland, Czechoslovakia (since 1920), Yugoslavia (since 1920), Hungary (since 1861), Austria (since 1861, except 1938-1945), U.S.S.R. (excludes Asian U.S.S.R. between 1931 and 1963), Latvia, Estonia, Lithuania, Finland, Romania, Bulgaria, Turkey (in Europe), and other European countries not classified elsewhere.
^cGreat Britain, Ireland, Norway, Sweden, Denmark, Iceland, Netherlands, Belgium, Luxembourg, Switzerland, France.
SOURCE: Stephan Thernstrom, ed., *Harvard Encyclopedia of American Ethnic Groups* (1980), p. 480; and U.S. Bureau of the Census, *Statistical Abstract of the United States, 1984* (1983), p. 9.

Total Federal Debt

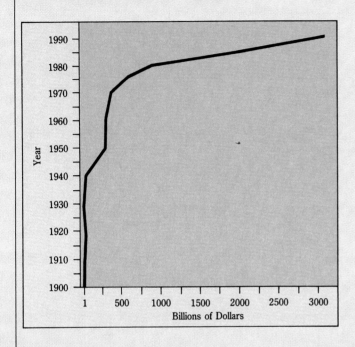

Credits

Contents

Chapter Openers

Chapter 1 Arapaho buffalo skull: Museum of the American Indian, Heye Foundation. Christopher Columbus: The Metropolitan Museum of Art, Gift of J. Pierpont Morgan, 1900. "Falls at Colville": Royal Ontario Museum, Toronto. Corn: Arents Collection/New York Public Library, Astor, Lenox and Tilden Foundations.

Chapters 2–6 "Pilgrims Going to Church": The New-York Historical Society, New York City. Ad for colony of Virginia: Rare Books and Manuscripts Division/New York Public Library, Astor, Lenox and Tilden Foundations. Slave sale broadside: American Antiquarian Society. Section and plan of blockhouse: Thomas Anburey, *Travels Through the Interior Parts of America*, 1789. Plan of Philadelphia. Library of Congress (Map Division). "Mrs. Elizabeth Freake and Baby Mary": Worcester Art Museum, Worcester, Mass. Declaration of Independence: National Archives. Slave ship: Library of Congress.

Chapters 7–13 National Bank of the United States: Stokes Collection, Prints Division/New York Public Library, Astor, Lenox and Tilden Foundations. North wing of the Capitol: Library of Congress. Plan of the City of Washington: Stokes Collection, Prints Division/New York Public Library, Astor, Lenox and Tilden Foundations. American sailor: The New-York Historical Society, New York City. "Fairview Inn": Maryland Historical Society, Baltimore, Hampton, the Seat of General Charles Ridgley, Maryland: Historical Society of Pennsylvania. Cotton plantation: Library of Congress. "Progress of Cotton": Yale University Art Gallery, Mabel Brady Garvan Collection. Pioneers: Denver Public Library, Western Collection. Ad for *Uncle Tom's Cabin*: The New-York Historical Society, New York City.

Chapters 14–16 Captured slave: Musée de l'Homme, Paris. Slave sale broadside: State Historical Society of Wisconsin. Slave nurse: Cook Collection/Valentine Museum, Richmond, Va. Robert E. Lee: Library of Congress. Union soldier: Chicago Historical Society. Pickett's Charge: Gettysburg National Military Park. Battle of the Crater: The Commonwealth Club, Richmond, Virginia. Ulysses S. Grant: Library of Congress. 1st Virginia Regiment: Cook Collection/Valentine Museum, Richmond, Va. Infantry at Fort Lincoln: Library of Congress. Ruins of Richmond, Virginia: Library of Congress. Elizabeth Cady Stanton: Culver Pictures. Susan B. Anthony: The Sophia Smith Collection (Women's History Archive), Smith College, Northampton, Mass.

Chapters 17–22 Chinese fire hose team: Library of Congress. Cowboys: Montana Historical Society, Helena. Cattle brands: From *We Pointed Them North*, copyright 1954, University of Oklahoma Press. Sitting Bull: Library of Congress. George Custer: Library of Congress. Golden spike ceremony: Union Pacific Railroad Museum Collection. Cowboy: © Charles J. Belden, Whitney Gallery of Western Art, Cody, Wyo. Football team: Steve Karchin Collection. Ferris wheel: Chicago Historical Society. Horse: *Treasury of American Design*. Skyscraper: The New-York Historical Society, New York City. Edison's electric light bulbs: Greenfield Village and Henry Ford Museum, Dearborn, Mich. Immigrants: International Museum of Photography/George Eastman House. Schoolroom: Brown Brothers.

Chapters 23–27 Immigrant: International Museum of Photography/George Eastman House. Jack Johnson: Bettmann Archive. Lusitania ad: Culver Pictures. Henry Ford in Model T: UPI/Bettmann. Shell casing factory: National Archives. WW I soldier: Smithsonian Institution. WW I soldiers: Charlotte Iglarsh Collection. FDR and Eleanor: UPI/Bettmann. Charles Lindbergh: Bettmann Archive. Flappers: Schomberg Collection/New York Public Library, Astor, Lenox and Tilden Foundations. Soldiers wearing gas masks: UPI/Bettmann. Wall Street, October 29, 1929: Brown Brothers. Mickey Mouse: © Walt Disney Productions. Hitler and Mussolini: National Archives. Woman kissing WW II soldier: U.S. Army. Blimp and bombers: U.S. Navy Photo. U.S. at War headline: *San Francisco Chronicle*, December 8, 1941. WW II poster: National Archives. Sailors: U.S. Navy Photo. Mushroom cloud over Nagasaki: U.S. Air Force photo.

Chapters 28–31 Dwight Eisenhower: Library of Congress. Woman in kitchen: Bettmann Archive. Suburban homes: FPG. Noguchi table, Eames chair: © Herman Miller, Inc., Zeeland, Mich. Fabric samples: Alexander Girard, © Herman Miller, Inc., Zeeland, Mich. Martin Luther King, Jr.: Costa Manos/Magnum Photos. Kennedy-Nixon debate: Wide World Photos. Missiles: Cornell Capa/Magnum Photos. Helicopter, Vietnam: UPI/Bettmann. March on Washington, 1963: Robert W. Kelley, LIFE Magazine © 1970 Time Inc. Saturn rings photographed from Voyager 2: NASA. Woodstock Festival: Elliot Landy/Magnum Photos. Soldiers, Vietnam: Philip Jones Griffiths/Magnum Photos. Antiwar demonstration: Jean-Claude Lejeune. Astronauts on moon: NASA. Betty Friedan: Michael Ginsburg/Magnum Photos. Sam Ervin, Senate Watergate Investigating Committee: Mark Godfrey/Archive Pictures. Richard Nixon: Hiroji Kubota/Magnum Photos. Student demonstration: Wayne Miller/Magnum Photos. Supreme Court Justice Sandra Day O'Connor: Owen Franken/Sygma. Space shuttle: UPI/Bettmann Newsphotos. Ronald Reagan and Mikhail Gorbachev: Sygma.

Chapter Photos

Unless otherwise acknowledged, all photographs are the property of Scott, Foresman and Company. Page abbreviations are as follows: (T)top, (C)center, (B)bottom, (L)left, (R)right, (Ins)inset.

Chapter 1

5 Courtesy of the Pilgrim Society, Plymouth, Mass. **7L** Photographed by Hillel Burger/The Peabody Museum of Archaeology and Ethnology **7R** Library of Congress **8** Tony Linck **9** National Gallery of Canada, Ottawa **12** Holbein, *The Dance of Death* **13** The British Library **15** Rare Book Room/New York Public Library, Astor, Lenox and Tilden Foundations **17** The Granger Collection, New York **18** Osterreichische Nationalbibliothek, Vienna **21** Johnson Collection, Philadelphia **22TL** Thyssen-Bornemisza Collection **22TC** National Portrait Gallery, London **22BR** Musée Historique de la Reformation, Geneva **25** National Portrait Gallery, London **26** Johann Theodor DeBry, *America*, 1617 **28** Courtesy of the Trustees of the British Museum **31** Courtesy of The Newberry Library, Chicago

Chapter 2

39 Duke University Library, Durham, N.C. **40** The Granger Collection, New York **42** Courtesy of the Trustees of the British Museum **43T** National Maritime Museum, Greenwich, England **43B** National Portrait Gallery, London **45** The Colonial Williamsburg Foundation **47** Courtesy of the Pilgrim Society, Plymouth, Mass. **48B** State Library of Massachusetts **51** Courtesy of the Pilgrim Society, Plymouth, Mass. **52** Courtesy American Antiquarian Society **54** Culver Pictures **56L** Rare Book Room/New York Public Library, Astor, Lenox and Tilden Foundations **56R** The Huntington Library and Art Gallery, San Marino, Calif. **58** The Essex Institute, Salem, Mass. **59** Courtesy of the Trustees of the British Museum **60** National Library of Medicine, Bethesda, Md. **64** Collection of Tazwell Ellett **65** The Granger Collection, New York **67** Abby Aldrich Rockefeller Folk Art Center

Chapter 3

75 Charleston Library Society **76** Picture Collection/New York Public Library, Astor, Lenox and Tilden Foundations **81** Pennsylvania Academy of the Fine Arts **82** Abby Aldrich Rockefeller Folk Art Center **86** Picture Collection/New York Public Library, Astor, Lenox and Tilden Foundations **91** Philadelphia Museum of Art Collection **92** The Granger Collection, New York **95** Mr. and Mrs. Wharton Sinkler Collection/Philadelphia Museum of Art Collection **96** National Portrait Gallery, London **98** Princeton University Libraries **99R** National Portrait Gallery, London **100** Henry E. Huntington Library and Art Gallery, San Marino, Calif. **102** *LaSalle Erecting a Cross and Taking Possession of the Land March 1682*—George Catlin/National Gallery of Art, Washington, D.C. **104** Mabel Garvan Collection/Copyright Yale University Art Gallery

Chapter 4

112 Spencer Collection/New York Public Library, Astor, Lenox and Tilden Foundations **113** The Royal Academy of Arts, London **115** Mount Vernon Ladies Association **116** Rare Book Division/New York Public Library, Astor, Lenox and Tilden Foundations **120B** Massachusetts Historical Society **124** Library of Congress **125** Shelburne Museum, Shelburne, Vt. **127** John Carter Brown Library, Brown University **128** Courtesy The Henry Francis du Pont Winterthur Museum **131** Centennial gift of Watson Grant Cutter/Courtesy, Museum of Fine Arts, Boston **133** The Rhode Island Historical Society **137** Historical Society of Pennsylvania

Chapter 5

145 Courtesy of the Valley Forge Historical Society **146** Courtesy Concord Museum, Concord, Mass. **150** Bequest of Grace Wilkes, 1922/The Metropolitan Museum of Art **152** Copyright Yale University Art Gallery **154L** Independence National Historical Park Collection **154R** Library of Congress **155** Copyright Yale University Art Gallery **158** Library of Congress **160(All)** Anne S. K. Brown Military Collection, Brown University **161L** New York Public Library, Astor, Lenox and Tilden Foundations **161R** Massachusetts Historical Society **163** Courtesy of the Valley Forge Historical Society **164** The National Archives **167** National Gallery of Canada, Ottawa **171** Collection of Mrs. Preston Davie **172** Virginia State Library and Archives

Chapter 6

181L Library of Congress **181R** Historical Society of Pennsylvania **183** The Bettmann Archive **187** Pennsylvania Academy of the Fine Arts **189** The New-York Historical Society, New York City **190** New York Public Library, Astor, Lenox and Tilden Foundations **194** Massachusetts Historical Society **196** The Granger Collection, New York **198** Private Collection **200T** Art Resource, New York **200B** Mother Bethel AME Church, Philadelphia **201** Historical Society of York County, Pennsylvania **203** Virginia Museum of Fine Arts, Richmond, Va.

Chapter 7

213 Smithsonian Institution **214** Historical Society of York County, Pennsylvania **215** Library of Congress **218** Prints Division/New York Public Library, Astor, Lenox and Tilden Foundations **220** The Bettmann Archive **224** Gift of Edgar William and Bernice Chrysler Garbisch, 1963/The Metropolitan Museum of Art **226** From B.J. Lossing, *Our Country* **227** Harvard University Portrait Collection, Bequest of Ward Nicholas Boylston **229** White House Historical Association/Smithsonian Institution **231** Library of Congress **232** Courtesy The White House Collection

Chapter 8

238L Copyright Yale University Art Gallery, Bequest of Oliver Burr Jennings, B.A. 1917, in memory of Miss Anne Burr Jennings **238R** Bequest of Oliver Burr Jennings, B.A., 1917, in memory of Miss Anne Burr Jennings/Copyright Yale University Art Gallery **239** Smithsonian Institution **240** Robert Llewellyn **243** Washington and Lee University, Lexington, Va. **245** Collection of the Louisiana State Museum **248** The New-York Historical Society, New York City **251** Library of Congress **252L** Library of Congress **252R** Field Museum of Natural History, Chicago **255** Anne S. K. Brown Military Collection, Brown University **258** Mariners Museum, Newport News, Va.

Chapter 9

264 Mabel Brady Garvan Collection/Copyright Yale University Art Gallery **265** Stokes Collection, New York Public Library, Astor, Lenox and Tilden Foundations **267L** In the Collection of the Corcoran Gallery of Art **267R** National Portrait Gallery, Smithsonian Institution/Art Resource, New York **269** Shelburne Museum, Shelburne, Vt. **270** In the Collection of the Corcoran Gallery of Art **272** Naval Historical Foundation **274** Rogers Fund/The Metropolitan Museum of Art **275** Stokes Collection/New York Public Library, Astor, Lenox and Tilden Foundations **276** Mark Keys *Lockport on the Erie Canal*, 1832/Munson-Williams-Proctors Institute Museum of Art, Utica, New York **279** *Harper's Weekly* **282** Courtesy Historical Society of Western Pennsylvania **283** Miriam and Ira D. Wallach Division of Art, Prints and Photographs Division/New York Public Library, Astor, Lenox and Tilden Foundations **284** Courtesy South Carolina Historical Society, Charleston

Chapter 10

295 The New-York Historical Society, New York City **299** Rare Book Division/New York Public Library, Astor, Lenox and Tilden Foundations **301** Historical Society of Pennsylvania **304** Library of Congress **305** Brooks Memorial Art Gallery, Memphis **307** Courtesy American Antiquarian Society **310** *Harper's Weekly* **313** City of Boston Art Commission **315** Chicago Historical Society **319** Courtesy The White House Collection

Chapter 11

326 Culver Pictures **328** Courtesy of Spanierman Gallery, New York **330** Courtesy American Antiquarian Society **332** Library of Congress **333** Collection of Mrs. Screven Lorillard **335** Courtesy American Antiquarian Society **336** Courtesy Cornell University Library **339L** Gift of I. N. Phelps Stokes, Edward S. Hawes, Alice Mary Hawes, Marion Augusta Hawes, 1937/The Metropolitan Museum of Art **339R** Sophia Smith Collection, Smith College, Northampton, Mass. **342T** Library of Congress **344** H. Armstrong Roberts **345** The Huntington Library and Art Gallery, San Marino, Calif. **348** New York Public Library, Astor, Lenox and Tilden Foundations **349** UPI/Bettmann **351** Concord Free Public Library **352** The Bettmann Archive **353** Concord Free Public Library **354** Courtesy Lilly Library, Indiana University, Bloomington, Ind. **355** Rare Book Division/New York Public Library, Astor, Lenox and Tilden Foundations **357** Hinman B. Hurlbut Collection/The Cleveland Museum of Art **359L** Culver Pictures **359R** The Granger Collection, New York

Chapter 12

366 Gift of George Hoadley/Copyright Yale University Art Gallery **367** International Museum of Photography/George Eastman House **370** Historical Society of Pennsylvania **373** Library of Congress **374** Picture Collection/New York Public Library **377** Culver Pictures **378** The Granger Collection, New York **388** The New-York Historical Society, New York City **389** *Harper's Weekly* **391** Picture Collection, The New York Public Library **393** Abby Aldrich Rockefeller Folk Art Center **395** Courtesy Jay P. Altmayer

Chapter 13

403 California Dept. of Parks and Recreation **404** Amon Carter Museum of Western Art, Fort Worth, Tex. **405** *Collier's Weekly*, 1906 **407** The Bancroft Library, University of California, Berkeley **408** The Bancroft Library, University of California, Berkeley **409** Smithsonian Institution **412** Bureau of Agricultural Economics/The National Archives **413** The Museum of the City of New York **414** Messina Studios/De Golyer Library, S.M.U. **415** Friends of the Governor's Mansion, Austin, Tex. **416** Courtesy of the Texas State Archive **418** Thomas Gilcrease Institute of American History & Art, Tulsa **423** Brigham Young University Fine Arts Collection **424** Union Pacific Railroad Museum Collection **425** National Academy of Design, New York

Chapter 14

441L Indiana Historical Society **441R** California State Library **446** Library of Congress **448** National Museum of American Art, Smithsonian Institution, Gift of William T. Evans/Art Resource, New York **450T** The New-York Historical Society, New York City **450B** New York Public Li-

Index

The World

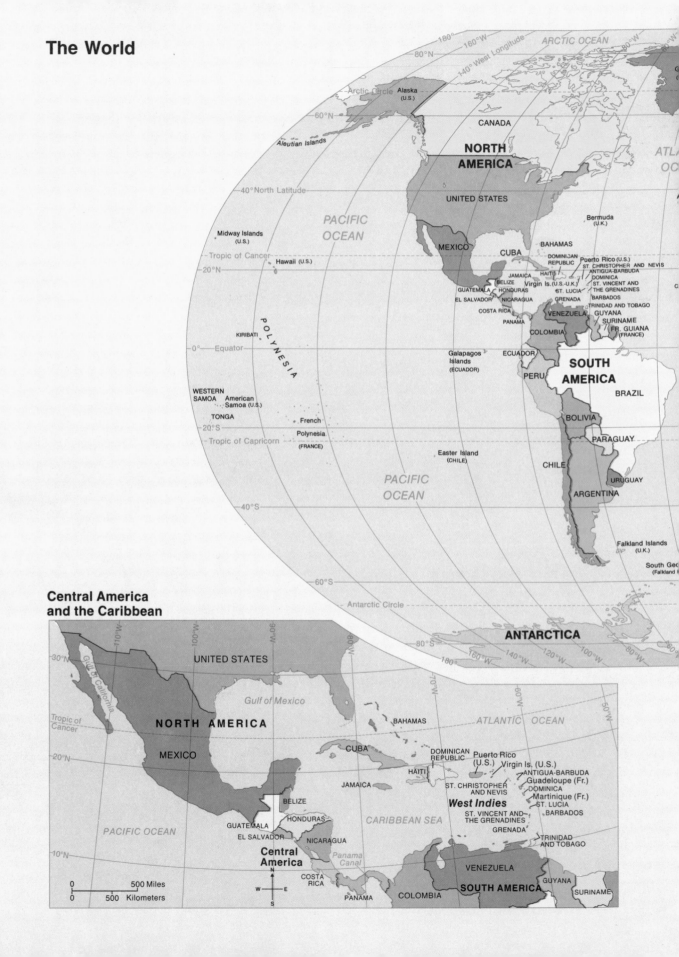

ARCTIC OCEAN

80°N

Arctic Circle

Alaska
(U.S.)

Aleutian Islands

60°N

CANADA

NORTH
AMERICA

ATLANTIC
OCEAN

40°North Latitude

UNITED STATES

PACIFIC
OCEAN

Midway Islands
(U.S.)

Tropic of Cancer

Hawaii (U.S.)

20°N

MEXICO

CUBA

BAHAMAS

Bermuda
(U.K.)

DOMINICAN
REPUBLIC

Puerto Rico (U.S.)
ST. CHRISTOPHER AND NEVIS
ANTIGUA-BARBUDA

HAITI

JAMAICA

BELIZE

Virgin Is. (U.S.-U.K.)

DOMINICA
ST. VINCENT AND
THE GRENADINES

GUATEMALA

HONDURAS

ST. LUCIA

EL SALVADOR

NICARAGUA

GRENADA

BARBADOS

COSTA RICA

TRINIDAD AND TOBAGO

PANAMA

VENEZUELA

GUYANA

KIRIBATI

COLOMBIA

SURINAME
FR. GUIANA
(FRANCE)

POLYNESIA

0° Equator

Galapagos
Islands
(ECUADOR)

ECUADOR

SOUTH
AMERICA

PERU

BRAZIL

WESTERN
SAMOA

American
Samoa (U.S.)

TONGA

French

BOLIVIA

20°S

Polynesia
(FRANCE)

Tropic of Capricorn

Easter Island
(CHILE)

PARAGUAY

CHILE

URUGUAY

PACIFIC
OCEAN

ARGENTINA

40°S

Falkland Islands
(U.K.)

South Geo
(Falkland Is

60°S

Antarctic Circle

80°S

ANTARCTICA

160°W

140°W

120°W

100°W

80°W

Central America
and the Caribbean

30°N

110°W

100°W

90°W

80°W

UNITED STATES

Gulf of California

Gulf of Mexico

Tropic of
Cancer

NORTH AMERICA

BAHAMAS

ATLANTIC OCEAN

60°W

50°W

20°N

MEXICO

CUBA

DOMINICAN
REPUBLIC

Puerto Rico
(U.S.)

Virgin Is. (U.S.)

HAITI

ANTIGUA-BARBUDA

JAMAICA

Guadeloupe (Fr.)

DOMINICA

ST. CHRISTOPHER
AND NEVIS

Martinique (Fr.)
ST. LUCIA

West Indies

BELIZE

CARIBBEAN SEA

ST. VINCENT AND
THE GRENADINES

BARBADOS

GUATEMALA

HONDURAS

GRENADA

EL SALVADOR

NICARAGUA

TRINIDAD
AND TOBAGO

PACIFIC OCEAN

10°N

Central
America

N

Panama
Canal

VENEZUELA

GUYANA

W   E

COSTA
RICA

S

PANAMA

COLOMBIA

SOUTH AMERICA

SURINAME

0   500 Miles

0   500 Kilometers